On Animation
The Director's Perspective
VOLUME 2

On Animation
The Director's Perspective
VOLUME 2

Editor
Ron Diamond

Interviewers
Bill Kroyer and Tom Sito

Associate Editors
James Brusuelas and Tom Knott

CRC Press
Taylor & Francis Group
Boca Raton London New York

CRC Press is an imprint of the
Taylor & Francis Group, an **informa** business

Associate Editors: James Brusuelas and Tom Knott
Cover design by Alan Bodner (bodnerart.com)

CRC Press
Taylor & Francis Group
6000 Broken Sound Parkway NW, Suite 300
Boca Raton, FL 33487-2742

© 2020 by Taylor & Francis Group, LLC
CRC Press is an imprint of Taylor & Francis Group, an Informa business

No claim to original U.S. Government works

Printed on acid-free paper

International Standard Book Number-13: 978-1-138-06656-4 (Paperback)
978-1-138-06709-7 (Hardback)

Visit the Taylor & Francis Web site at
http://www.taylorandfrancis.com

and the CRC Press Web site at
http://www.crcpress.com

For Lisa, Sara, and Anna

CONTENTS

FOREWORD

My love affair with animation started around 1962 not with a movie in a theater, but with an album on a record player. It was a 78 RPM of "Cinderella," with songs and story. I carried it around our house on a small portable turntable and listened to "Bibbidi-Bobbidi-Boo," "A Dream Is a Wish Your Heart Makes," the entire soundtrack really, ad nauseam.

Such is the magic of animated films. The great ones (and there are so many great ones) become so powerfully ingrained in our culture that a little girl can fall hopelessly in love with animation just by listening to the music.

I'm sure that, on more than one occasion, my parents were tempted to break that scratchy record, but instead they let my love affair deepen. I am forever grateful they were so tolerant because, improbably enough, 30 years later animation would become my career … and my passion.

In 1992, I began work as the producer of *Toy Story*. At the time, I had only worked in live action and had just come off of *Dances with Wolves* and *The Addams Family*. Live action and animation are very different expressions of the film art form (I describe it as the difference between a sprint and a marathon), but at the center of both is the director.

And now, as I start development on my eighth animated feature, I think about the creative team that will collaborate on that film, and I am excited to meet the person who will be the director.

The directors featured in this collection of interviews are masters of the art. Each has a different way of working and brings something entirely unique to the mix. Each has a specialty, whether it is traditional animation, computer animation, or stop-motion. Using imagery, words, and music, they have taken audiences on imaginative journeys to amazing worlds inhabited by unforgettable characters, and created some of the most beloved family entertainment of all time. We and our children, and even our children's children, have watched and re-watched these outstanding pieces of storytelling.

I consider myself very fortunate to know them all and have worked with most. We've been through it all together; the hard work, the long hours, the good days and bad days, the redo, the notes, and ultimately the anxiety-inducing opening weekend.

Thanks to this book, you'll get to know them as well. Bill Kroyer and Tom Sito have spent several years asking questions about how these animation directors got started, how their life experiences influenced their work, what is their process, how do they maintain their vision and still collaborate with their team, what are their biggest challenges, and what brings them joy.

I know that after you spend some time with these incredible individuals, you will have a greater appreciation for the role of the animation director in conjuring up the extraordinary magic of an animated film.

Bonnie Arnold
Producer
DreamWorks Animation

ACKNOWLEDGMENTS

Coming up with the idea for this book was the easy part; making it happen took the combined efforts and enthusiasm of many people over many years. For starters, if it weren't for Ed Catmull, former president of Walt Disney Animation Studios and Pixar Animation Studios, this book would have not have been possible. When I reached out to Ed and told him about the idea, he immediately expressed interest and gave the book his blessing. This opened the doors to meet with the directors who were currently working at Disney, and allowed us to license many critical images, since so many of the directors in the book at one time or another worked at what many referred to as "Disney's." From the beginning to the end, the next most essential person was my friend of over 30 years, animation and VR producer, recruiter, and former director of the Ottawa International Animation Festival, Tom Knott. Tom oversaw the lion's share of the image selection, clearances, and communication with the directors and the studios. Without Tom's significant support and diligent work, this book would not exist.

I'd like to thank Bill Kroyer and Tom Sito for their tireless devotion in researching and interviewing the directors, and for welcoming me as I'd chime in with questions of my own during the interviews. And for their participation, candor, and honesty in sharing their experiences and expertise and giving us a glimpse into their inner worlds, the directors themselves (in the order they appear in the book): John Musker, Ron Clements, John Lasseter, Andrew Stanton, Brenda Chapman, Nick Park, Tomm Moore, Chris Wedge, Roger Allers, Chris Buck, Tim Johnson, Bill Plympton, Brad Bird, Henry Selick, Don Bluth, Pete Docter, Chris Sanders, Dean DeBlois, Vicky Jenson, Rob Minkoff, Jennifer Yuh Nelson, Carlos Saldanha, and Kevin Lima.

Special thanks to our tireless editors James Brusuelas, Jon Hofferman, and Carol Frank, to Bonnie Arnold for a fantastic Foreword, and to Alan Bodner for beautiful cover designs.

Early in the process, we were supported greatly by Dan Sarto, co-founder and COO of AWN, Inc., editors Bill Desowitz and Rick DeMott, and interim coordinator Aria Stewart.

Sincere thanks to all of the studio contacts who facilitated the interviews and the clearance of images: Chris Wiggum, Maraget Adamic, Maxine Hof, Gregory Coleman, Wendy Lefkon, Heather Feng-Yanu, Michelle Moretta, Victoria Manley, Marguerite Enright, Leigh Anna MacFadden, Christine Freeman, Debby Coleman, Kiera McAuliffe, Alex Ambrose, Mary Walsh, Fox Carney, Michael Buckoff, Dave Bossert, Victoria Thornbery, Jerry Rees, Jessica Roberts, Katie Smith, Julia Reeves, Shelley Gorelik, Melanie Bartlett, Casie Nguyen, Andy Bandit,

Lucy Manos, Brook Worley, Laura Baltzer, Patrick Skelly, Jerry Schmitz, Richard Hamilton, David Hail, Beverly Moyer, Michael Garcia, Chase Schultz, Daniel Chun, David Hall, Cathleen Girdner, Kim Kline, Lillian Ritchie, Justin Melillo, Waiolo Shannon, Robbin Kelley, Shanna Robalino, Noreen Ong, Robbin Kelley, Gary Goldman, Kip Goldman, Gabrielle Ruffle, Angie Last, Deborah Rouse, Heather Koopmans, Megan Bradford, Rosemary Colliver, Jenniphur Ryan, Mark Shapiro, Yael Gabbay, Owen Miller, Lorne Mitchell, Julie Heath, Jacklyn Pomales, Margarita Diaz, Andy Jeyes, Roni Lubliner, and Desiree Meade.

A massive thanks to the Acme Filmworks studio crew and the interns for their dedication and support: George Khair, Misty Myers, Diane Schlactus, Masha Evans, Kaitlyn Cavanagh, Josephine Moss, Tara Beyhm, Kelsey Peterson, Hae-Joon Lee, Amy Lee, Christian Kemabia, Helen Shi, Kerin Amit, Nolan Nissle, Dhanesh Jameson, and Molly Tomecek.

And, last but not least, thanks to Lisa Frank, Sara Diamond, Anna Diamond, Mark Diamond, Debi Perluss, Isaac Diamond, Dan Sarto, Debbie Sarto, Becky Sarto, and Nikki Sarto for unbridled support, love, and encouragement.

Tom Knott also offers personal thanks to Will Ryan, Shannon Tindle, and Ann Knott.

Ron Diamond
Executive Producer

EDITORS

Ron Diamond founded ACME Filmworks in 1990 to create commercials, shorts, and long-form animated projects with more than 50 notable international animation artist storytellers. In addition to producing over 1600 commercials, Ron produced the TV Series *Drew Carey's Green Screen Show* for the WB Network and *Drawn from Memory* for PBS' American Playhouse. He is a recognized expert on international animation and lectures at schools and animation festivals worldwide. He curates specialty animation programs for festivals. Since 1998, he curates *The Animation Show of Shows*, a feature length movie comprising new notable international animated shorts; presents them at the major animation studios, tech companies, game companies, animation schools, and animation festivals; and releases them for the general public. He co-founded the Animation World Network (AWN.com) in 1996.

Bill Kroyer is an Oscar-nominated director of animation and computer graphics commercials, short films, movie titles, and theatrical films. Trained in classic hand-drawn animation at the Disney studio, Bill was one of the first animators to make the leap to computer animation as computer image choreographer on Disney's ground-breaking 1982 feature *TRON*. He pioneered the technique of combining hand-drawn animation with computer animation on projects such as his theatrical animated feature film *FernGully: The Last Rainforest* and his short film *Technological Threat*. As senior animation director at Rhythm & Hues Studios, he directed animation on scores of commercials and many feature films, including *Cats and Dogs*, *Garfield*, and *Scooby Doo*. Bill served as co-chair of the Science and Technology Council of the Academy of Motion Picture Arts and Sciences and is a governor of the Academy's Short Films and Feature Animation branch. He is a tenured professor and is director of digital arts at the Dodge College of Film and Media Arts at Chapman University in Orange, California. In 2017, Bill and his wife Sue received the prestigious June Foray Award from the International Animation Society (ASIFA) for significant contributions to the art and industry of animation.

 **Tom Sito** is an animator, animation historian, and professor of animation at the University of Southern California, Los Angeles. His movie credits include Walt Disney's *Beauty and the Beast* (1991), *Who Framed Roger Rabbit* (1988), *The Little Mermaid* (1989), *Aladdin* (1992), *The Lion King* (1994), *Pocahontas* (1995), and *DreamWorks' Shrek* (2001), and *Osmosis Jones* (2001). He has worked on television series such as the *Super Friends* (1978) and *He-Man and the Masters of the Universe* (1983). He is president emeritus of the Animation Guild, Local 839 Hollywood and on the Board of Governors of the Motion Picture Academy of Arts & Sciences. He received the June Foray Award in 2011 and the Dusty Outstanding Alumni Award in 2016. He is the author of several books: *Drawing the Line: The Untold Story of the Animation Unions from Bosko to Bart Simpson* (University of Kentucky Press, 2006), *Timing for Animation,* 2nd Edition (CRC Press/A Focal Press Book, 2009) *Moving Innovation: A History of Computer Animation* (MIT Press, 2013), and *Eat, Drink, Animate: An Animators Cookbook* (CRC Press, 2019). In 2014, he was featured in the PBS American Experience documentary *Walt Disney.*

INTRODUCTION

Animation. Not a day goes by that I don't think about it. Animated images dance through my head: memories of favorite films, snippets of past projects, abstract shapes, and evocative faces. While I work in animation, I don't believe I'm alone in this obsession. For vast numbers of people throughout the world, animation is a singularly rich art form, encompassing some of the most profound and pleasurable cinematic moments we have experienced.

As with all forms of artistic expression, each creation is measured by the success of its realization. However, in animation, the road to a finished product is especially daunting, and the challenges facing an animation director must be met with an especially high degree of resourcefulness, insight, and endurance. In feature animation production, a director must collaborate with multiple teams of highly skilled artists, storytellers, engineers, composers, lyricists, musicians, and producers in an immensely labor-intensive undertaking. To carry forward a personal vision in a process that can take 5 to 7 years, sometimes even longer, requires extraordinary persistence, tenacity, and commitment.

The demands on a director, or in some cases a two-director team, frequently include an in-depth knowledge of fine art, literature, theater, animation, and cinema history, as well as highly refined skills in communication, writing, humor, stagecraft, performance, design, painting, draftsmanship, visual effects, music, camera, lighting, and editing. They must also have the ability to helm a nine-figure production employing the skills of dozens—if not hundreds—of experts and to draw out of them the best they have to offer. And, on top of all that, they must tell a great and beautiful story that appeals to a large and diverse audience.

They must be able to defend their ideas and to challenge them as well, to construct a formidable production plan, and also be ready to tear it down and rethink it if the story isn't working or the characters aren't just right. This is what it takes to be an animated feature film director—as well as to be able to retain a sense of humor, to keep working when exhausted, and to meet crazy deadlines imposed by others or, worse yet, by oneself.

This book is about the blood, sweat, and tears of the craft of animation direction at the most complex levels—but it's also about inspiration and faith in oneself. I believe that by learning more about these artists' personal histories—what grabbed them, often at a very early age—and compelled them to follow the path of animation, we can acquire a deeper understanding of their art and find greater enjoyment in their artistic creations.

For this book, we followed a few basic guidelines. The first was that, to be included, a director had to have directed at least two animated feature films. Apart from providing a baseline qualification (since, unfortunately, we couldn't include everyone), the idea was also to explore what it was like to direct a feature for the first time and how that experience differed from successive directing experiences. We were very interested in this learning process, and we hope you'll find it as fascinating as we did.

In addition, we wanted the directors to speak freely, to be unbridled in the telling of their experiences. We then worked with them to edit the work down to convey an honest and revealing story that clearly leads us through their journeys.

Finally, it was decided that fellow feature film directors should conduct the interviews, since who is better suited to ask informed questions and discuss the ins and outs and nuts and bolts of animation? This turned out to be an inspired idea; our two interviewers, Bill Kroyer and Tom Sito, were exemplary in drawing out the directors and in producing remarkably insightful discussions that have the pleasant familiarity of colleagues talking to colleagues.

I have been fortunate to have known several of these directors since their college days and others along the path and have stayed in touch with them throughout their careers. Their unmistakable glimmer of greatness was visible early on, and we are all the beneficiaries of their brilliance as they went on to direct some of the greatest animated features of our time. These interviews reveal commonalities of the collective experiences of some of our finest contemporary minds, and the lessons they learned. This is not just a book about approaches to animation production but also a primer on how to live a life filled with art, passion, giving, friendship, love, and contentment.

I am truly pleased to present this collection of 23 interviews in two volumes for you to enjoy. As for those directors who couldn't be included, we look forward to publishing future volumes in which we can get to know them and their stories as well.

Ron Diamond
Executive Producer

1
Brad Bird Interview

Brad Bird © Disney/Pixar.
Photo: Deborah Coleman.

I recently asked Brad Bird a question: "What do you know now that you didn't know when you started directing?" He said, "I know I'll never spend four years making a film again. I have too many stories and not enough time to tell them."

That doesn't mean he won't direct animation again, but if he does, he'll be searching for a way to do it that won't require the four-year schedule of *The Incredibles*. Brad didn't get a chance to direct his first feature until he had been in the business for almost two decades. Ironic, considering he was animating in his early teens—earlier than any of us.

Why the late start? Brad started at Disney when he was barely in his twenties, but even then he had a passion for animation and knowledge of film that was unsurpassed. That passion, the insistence on excellence and an aversion to compromise, got him in trouble, got him fired, for simply insisting that the studio hold to the very standards of Walt Disney they claimed to be preserving.

While the rest of us young, struggling animators bought furniture, Brad bought laser discs, which he studied incessantly (while sitting on the floor) on the biggest TV screen he could afford. He is the greatest student of—and lover of—films that I have ever known. When his film career stalled he switched to TV and brought innovation and cinematic excitement to *The Simpsons*.

He finally got his shot helming *The Iron Giant* and hasn't looked back. The innovations, Academy Awards, and record revenues of *The Incredibles* and *Ratatouille* have secured his place in animation royalty. His worldwide hit *Mission: Impossible—Ghost Protocol* proved that his directing skills reach beyond animation.

There are some big stars in Hollywood that have huge success, but when you meet them in person you wonder, "Is that really the guy who did all that?" You never have that doubt with Brad. Whether you are student or an industry icon, spend three minutes talking with him and you will come away with a memorable moment, a story, anecdote, or an observation about the art that will get you thinking, get you laughing, get you inspired.

We interviewed Brad at the Pixar Animation Studios in Emeryville, with a follow-up by phone.

Bill Kroyer

Bill: Tell a little about when you first had the inkling that you might be interested in animation.

Brad: If you'd asked me this question fifteen years ago I would have given you a different answer. I would have said I got interested in animation around the time I started my first animated film at age eleven. But I've since realized that the very first drawings I did were sequential. They weren't very good drawings. They weren't animation; they were more like a storyboard or a comic strip. They showed a character entering a scene, doing something, then exiting a scene or something like that. I'd hold the drawing in a stack, and—as I would tell the story—I'd take the front one and put it in the back, revealing the next drawing, and so forth. I was doing that at three.

Bill: You were pitching to your family!

Brad: Well, the drawings were meant to be viewed in a certain order, and I would tell the story verbally while I was showing the pictures. I think in my own way I was trying to make movies right from the very beginning.

I was considered odd at the time because I wanted to see animated features more than once. Nowadays, you buy them on DVD or whatever and kids see them probably a hundred times, but back in the day the only way you could see them was to go to the theater. My friend's parents and my grandparents thought my mom was a little indulgent, letting me see films more than once. I'm talking about like three or four times.

Bill: Did you go by yourself?

Brad: I'd go with my family once, and then I'd go with friends, and then I'd go with a different group of friends, because the same friends wouldn't go back twice with me. Sometimes my parents dropped me off at the theater and picked me up when the show was over. I sort of knew from the encyclopedia how animation was done, that they were drawings that were slightly different, and at a rapid speed they looked like they were moving.

Bill: What happened at eleven that made you want to make an animated film?

Brad: Something clicked in me when I saw Disney's *Jungle Book* at eleven. I remember watching the panther jumping up on a branch and thinking, "That really looks like a panther. It doesn't just move like a cat; it looks and moves like a panther."

And when that same panther began to talk, I thought, "well this is a rather *stuffy* panther, you know?" Someone was making very specific observations. It's not just any animal; it's a cat. Not only is it a cat, it's a panther. Not only is it a panther, it's a stuffy panther.

And then I realized: adults made this. And somebody's job is to figure out how a stuffy panther moves. This is a person who gets a paycheck and is considered a part of society. Up until then I was dreading becoming a grown-up because I'd see them at my parents' parties milling around, talking about stuff I wasn't interested in, and that was the moment where I realized there are really weird, cool, interesting jobs out there. Suddenly, growing up seemed like a really fantastic destination.

Bill: So up until this moment, when you had that revelation, what were you thinking when you were watching a movie more than once?

Brad: Well, I enjoyed it. I was drawn to it, but if you'd asked me why at the time, I probably couldn't explain more than "I like it." But I think that there was something about animation being like the magic trick that could never really be explained.

You could explain that each drawing was different. You could explain that they were put on pieces of celluloid, placed over backgrounds, and photographed. You could explain the process, but you couldn't explain the magic trick. In other words, it was like explaining a joke; you can sit there and dissect it, but the reason it makes you laugh remains wonderfully mysterious.

With animation, it was like: why do I care about these things that are announcing their unreality every moment? They're not real; they've got flat colors and lines around them. And yet you're getting dramatically wrapped up in them, as if they have lives and feelings. You care about them. You're worried about them. When something dangerous happens to them, you're concerned about their well-being. How does that happen?

When I started making animated films, I had to figure out not just how to move characters around, but filmmaking: Is this moment in a close-up? Or is it in a wide shot or is everything eye level? Or do I cut to a new shot? I started noticing filmmaking in live action films, which got me interested in film in general. So animation was my gateway drug to the entire film medium.

Bill: This film you were making when you were eleven, how did you make it?

Brad: I saw *Jungle Book* and I came out of it and asked, "How did they do that?" And my parents said, "Well, you know how they do it. Each drawing's different, etc." And I said, "Yeah but how could *I* do it?" And there was a guy who was with us that one time, and I'll never forget him. He's a family friend named Marty Dowling, that was the *only* time that I was ever in his presence, and he happened to have taken an animation class at UCLA. So he knew how to do it! And he talked me through all the things I'd need: like a movie camera that could shoot one frame at a time, a camera stand, etc. It was the weirdest serendipity that I asked the question at the one moment that there was somebody around me who could answer it. Because I lived in Oregon and nobody knew anything about animation.

Bill: It wasn't long after this that you started to contact the Disney guys, right?

Brad: A friend of my parents went to Oregon State with George Bruns, who was the composer for Disney. So I met him and he said, "Come down to LA and I'll take you through the studio." So I went down to LA and I met everybody.

Bill: How old were you then?

Brad: Eleven. I met Frank and Ollie, Al Dempster, and Ken Anderson, I met the key people who took me through every department. I remember George introducing me to Frank and Ollie, saying, "Brad just started making an animated film," and they kind of gave me this little smile, very much like, "You're gonna lose interest in two weeks, kid." So, they were shocked when I showed up three years later with a finished film that was fifteen minutes long.

Bill: Was it in color?

Brad: Are you crazy? Fifteen minutes of color?

Bill: I'm just asking!

Brad: I was a *kid*! I've gotta go to school! You're making me feel like a slacker because I didn't do color! The film was my version of *The Tortoise and the Hare*. The tortoise is more of a bad guy and the race ends in a five-way tie. The animation and the design get progressively better as the film goes on.

Bill: Here's the thing I was always wondering about: you talk almost immediately in your career about analyzing filmic aspects of animation, but you're a kid who's eleven who had no one personally teaching you.

Brad: Well, my parents were unbelievably supportive; my mom prodded me along, got me focused on entering a Kodak contest, and even helped me physically assemble the film to make the deadline. My dad built and set up my camera stand. In addition to great parents, I had three books, two of which my parents bought at Disneyland. One was *The Art of Animation* by Bob Thomas, and I wore that thing out. Man, if you look at my copy of that book, it just feels like the juice has been sucked out of every page by just eyeball wear. How that book even retained its spine I can't even tell you. Another one was a very simple book on how to do Disney animation. And then there was the Preston Blair book, which was the best book in terms of basic animation technique.

Bill: Everybody's bible.

Brad: Yeah, the Preston Blair book helped a lot. So when I finished I sent that film to Disney and they responded. They were just starting to get the idea that their animators weren't gonna live forever and they realized they didn't have anybody trained to replace them. So they said, "Any time you're in LA, come in and you can work with one of our animators." I turned to my parents immediately: "We have to get to LA!"

Bill: You're a junior in high school!

Brad: I was in seventh grade. So I came down and they didn't have any training program in place, so they had Milt Kahl be my mentor.

Bill: He's the last guy to train a kid!

Brad: Exactly! [laughter] Because he's not verbal, he's not exactly the most patient guy. You'd think he wouldn't want to be bothered, but he was incredibly generous to me. You know, I somehow had the right constitution for him. He was intense, and in my own kid way, so was I!

Bill: How exactly did you work with him?

Brad: Well, they cleared out a room and just put an animation desk in there. Milt was right down the hall; you went through Johnny Bond's room and turned left and there was Milt's office. Milt was in what was, years later, the largest of the two rooms that made up the "Rat's Nest"!*

Bill: What did he give you to do?

Brad: It wasn't an assignment for a film. It was a teaching exercise. Goofy's late for work and he's running, and he grabs his brief-case and is suddenly surprised because it's filled with anvils. There's no reason why Goofy's briefcase would be full of anvils; I mean, we don't go that deep into it. The idea is to show something where he's got an attitude and then suddenly reacts to something unexpected. So, I would animate it, then Milt would flip it and audibly react. Whatever reaction he had on his first flip-through was the only unfiltered reaction I'd get. Then he'd kind of reset his body and flip it again, and then he'd start going into all the things that were not right about it.

_____

* The "Rat's Nest" was two connecting rooms in D-Wing, originally inhabited by Milt Kahl, Frank Thomas, and Ollie Johnston. When they retired, the next occupants (Brad Bird, John Musker, Henry Selick, Bill Kroyer, Jerry Rees, and Dan Haskett) were given the name "The Rat's Nest" by Don Bluth. Meant as a put-down, the term was embraced by the group, who shared an alternative vision for the future of Disney's animation department.

Bill: You were the only kid in the studio, I'd have to guess.

Brad: Yeah. I would get some double takes, too. I would just go down on vacations or during the summer, whenever I could get down to LA and the door was open.

Bill: So even when you were back home, you'd be sending stuff down to him for comments.

Brad: Yeah, and I started a new film, which was even more complicated than *The Tortoise and the Hare*, and it was in color. For you, Bill.

Bill: In ink, I would assume.

Brad: Hand colored with felt pens! I got like forty seconds into it, and I sent the Disney guys that forty seconds and they loved it. And I suddenly realized: this is going to be the only other film I do, for the rest of my time as a kid!

Bill: Because it was taking you so long?

Brad: It was long and more complicated and in color! I basically realized that I would have to miss the rest of my youth! I said, "I don't think that I can finish this!" Because already I was flirting with outcast geekdom. I only wanted to talk about animation, and my friends could feign interest for maybe thirty seconds, and then their eyes would glaze over. I couldn't say, "I went down to Disney and worked with Milt Kahl!" because that name didn't mean anything to anyone in Corvallis, Oregon, except me!

          I was into this world, but no one else was. So I just said to Disney that for my own mental health I have to do something else. They were disappointed, but they understood. So I stopped animating, discovered girls, played football, got into photography, got into theater ….

Bill: Weren't you a pretty good basketball player?

Brad: [dismissive laugh] But I had a childhood. I got serious about theater, and I was going to go into it in college. But then Disney offered me a scholarship to CalArts, and I went. I was the only student in the animation program at CalArts that was getting *back into* animation after a four-year layoff.

Bill: Totally unique.

Brad: And I thought, "Well, okay … I'll go back into animation and learn a trade. And then I can go do theatre." Then, of course, the moment I got back into animation, I got really interested in it again. Which is ultimately why I love film. I love all of the arts, and film is the only medium I know where all the arts come into play: photography, acting, writing, color, design, movement, music—all of it is in film.

Bill:　　How did you advance your ideas and your craft in your two years at CalArts?

Brad:　　The weirdest and greatest thing about CalArts was suddenly I was surrounded by people who were as interested in animation as I was, and I could actually discuss it with others my age for the first time in my life. You had all these thoughts bottled up and suddenly you find yourself with people who could keep up with you, because they had been thinking the same thing in some other remote small town.

　　　　　One of the weirder things about the Disney program was that the weakest class was animation! Every other class was absolutely topflight: the life drawing class, the caricature class. Bill Moore was the greatest design teacher, probably the best single teacher I've ever had in anything.

Bill:　　Everyone says that about him.

Brad:　　Yeah, he was extraordinary, and I learned more from that class than any other single class. But the guy who taught the animation class at the time was really more of a director. He had only animated a tiny bit, so his notion of actually animating a scene was pretty limited. We ended up compensating for that by putting together our own class unofficially at night.

Bill:　　Self-critiquing.

Brad:　　Right! CalArts had sixteen-millimeter prints of Disney features, and of course we wore them out. We would run them at regular speed, and any one of us at any time could say, "stop," and we'd stop. Then whoever called the stop would point out some specific observation about a particular piece of animation. It was really illuminating, because each student was spotting different things. So we all benefited from each other's eyes. And we taught each other.

Bill:　　Why did you leave after two years?

Brad:　　I was offered a job, along with John Musker, Henry [Selick], Jerry [Rees], and Doug Lefler.

Bill:　　So then you go to the Disney studio and start the training thing.

Brad:　　You know the story. You were there. That's where we met. It was not a great period at Disney. All the guys who really were the masters were out the door when we arrived, and the people who were being elevated into the top positions were people who had been there for twenty years and weren't good enough to rise to the top under the masters. They were interested in holding on to their jobs, and they were threatened by anyone who was talented, I think. As far as the future of Disney feature animation, it was up for grabs, and the young people were divided into two camps: Don Bluth's camp … and the rest of us. I was learning, but half of what I was learning was how *not* to make films.

Jerry Rees, Dan Haskett, Bill Kroyer, Henry Selick, John Musker, and Brad Bird.

Bill: You were there how long?

Brad: A couple of years. I got fired.

Bill: Had you thought of being a director?

Brad: You know, my plan was to animate for fifteen years, or something like that, and then move into directing. So yeah, I animated for a while, but I was very unsatisfied with the kinds of films that were being made and the lack of quality. I felt like I got fired at Disney basically for standing up for the very principles that Disney's master animators had taught me to care about and fight for! Surreal.

Bill: So you left Disney, and am I wrong in guessing that maybe the first thing you directed on screen was your ice skating thing in *Animalympics* … ?

Brad: Yes, yes … and that was a wonderful thing to go into. Thank you, Bill Kroyer, for inviting me to join you on that. That was a wonderful thing to go into after Disney, because it was the opposite of Disney in many ways. They encouraged you to do whatever you could. It was about how much work you did, and how good it was, rather than punching a clock at exactly eight o'clock in the morning … and "behaving" … which is what Disney had turned into as the masters were retiring.

Bill: You storyboarded it, you did the layouts, you did all the animation.

Brad: I cut the music ….

Bill: I think you even inbetweened, most of it.

Brad: A lot of it, because it was kind of funkily timed.

Bill: Is that the only sequence that's ever been in a film where you did it all—board, animate, direct?

Brad: Well, it's very basic staging, but yeah. I animated scenes in *Family Dog*, and I had one scene in *Iron Giant*, but yeah, it's the only sustained piece of animation that I did.

Bill: Your next real directing assignment was *Family Dog*, right?

Brad: It was a key moment for me because I was in my early twenties, and I had already been at the best place in the world for feature animation … and it sucked! All the masters had left Disney, and the people running the studio weren't empowering the young animation talent, and every other studio was worse! I was seriously thinking about quitting animation. But then I thought I should take one last shot. Make a film pitching the kinds of things *I* wanted to see animated and see if anyone would go for it. I sunk my own money into a short film called *A Portfolio of Projects*. Two of the projects were shorts (which included *Family Dog*), and one of them was a feature based on Will Eisner's *The Spirit*. Gary Kurtz got interested in *The Spirit*, and then Jerry Rees and I spent years trying to get a studio to back it. And I could not get that sucker backed, even though I had the producer whose last two films at the time were *Star Wars* and *The Empire Strikes Back*.

         We were told repeatedly by the top people in Hollywood that no animated feature would ever make more than fifty million dollars, and Disney would be the only one that would come close to that. So now when I hear some executive gassing off about what will or won't work, I've absorbed way too much nonsense to give it any credence. Don't listen to anything anyone in a suit tells you about "the business," because the only thing true is what William Goldman says, "Nobody knows anything."

Bill: So *The Spirit* doesn't go but *Family Dog* does?

Brad: That's a complicated story. The simple version is: I wrote an *Amazing Stories* script for Matthew Robbins to direct, and Steven really liked it and had me come down. Tim Burton and I had done storyboards for *Family Dog*, and I showed them to Steven. He said, "Can you do a half an hour of this?," and I said, "Sure." And he said, "Let's do it as an *Amazing Stories*," and so that was my first real directing thing. And that was fun.

Bill: Talk a little bit about that production you set up on Traction Avenue.

Brad: *Amazing Stories* was an anthology show like *Twilight Zone* but with a much bigger budget. Steven got an unprecedented commitment from NBC for forty-four episodes. Our episode was the only episode that was a negative pickup, meaning that they gave us the money and we went off and made it, because neither Amblin nor Universal had an infrastructure for animation.

One of the great things about a negative pickup is that you're given a lump sum of money, and how you spend it is up to you. So I didn't spend anything on the surroundings. Every dime went to what was up on the screen. We were part of a floor of a building that was formerly an open parking lot. They decided to just put up walls, so you could still see the parking spaces painted on the floor. I'm not kidding. In spite of the fact that we were full animation, we delivered well under the average budget of an *Amazing Stories* episode.

Model sheet "The Dog", *Family Dog,* 1987 © Universal.

Bill: Where'd you get the furniture?

Brad: Well, the furniture was very cheap stuff. We were all in one room. So we had a very family sort of atmosphere. The bad thing is that we were under a lot of pressure, and if anybody flipped out or got into an argument, everybody else heard it. We had to go up to the roof to have fights.

Bill: Two things on that show that I think have been kind of typical of your experience as a director are, number one, you had a pretty strong vision in the story reel stage of where you were headed, and number two, you had an amazing ability to recognize and cast talent and to be very inspiring to your team. Those are things that have seemed to be a real trademark. Can you talk a little bit about your first experience with those things on *Family Dog*? You really worked hard on that reel, right?

Brad: Right. We gave a lot of top talent their first animation jobs. Several people who couldn't get into Disney got in after they did *Family Dog*. And production-wise, we were very lean. We didn't do any animation we didn't use. I'm fairly proud of the fact that that's been pretty constant in my career, that I've had very little animation on the cutting room floor. I try not to waste people's energy. However, I will go back and I'll fix animation probably more times than some people like me to do. They always like it later, though.

   I think that what people respond to is the fact that I respect talent. I think that people often underestimate their own talent. There were people on *Family Dog* that thought they were gonna get jobs as inbetweeners and I'd say, "Well, I saw your reel, why don't you animate a scene instead?" They all did really great work. I think often people are capable of more than they think they are.

Bill: How did you strike the balance, and *Family Dog* was a good example, of getting a really talented animator inspired to do something that is primarily already in your own mind the way you want?

Brad: I think that I have in mind who the character is and what I want the moment to feel like. You want to get a 100 percent of the entertainment, but there are many ways to get that 100 percent, as long as it's true to the character. But it's directed toward letting the animator be an animator. I mean, that's the joy of it.

Bill: And an innate skill is that casting, right?

Brad: I learned a lot on that film because we were in one room, and you didn't have walls to diffuse the vibe. Here's a good example: Ralph Eggleston, later a top designer at Pixar, had this manic sort of energy. I mean, he would get a scene and three hours later he would have it roughed out completely, done in a ridiculously short amount of time, but it would be sloppy. I'd say, "If you slowed down a little bit, Ralph, you wouldn't have these problems." I'd give him like twenty fixes, he'd be back two hours later, all twenty fixes done, but with ten other problems.

Tony Fucile, even as a young guy fresh out of CalArts, had a kind of sleepy but precise energy. So I saw Ralph over here spinning like a top, with sparks flying everywhere in uncontrolled spasms of energy, and then I had Tony who's practically falling asleep. So I decided, I'll put 'em next to each other. I moved Ralph right next to Tony. Ralph calmed down and Tony woke up. And it was perfect!

Bill: That's more psychology than casting.

Brad: Well, you need that as a director, too.

Bill: So you finished *Family Dog*, it's a fantastic thing, Amblin wanted to do it as a series, but you decided not to do that. And then you ended up spending your next years in television.

Brad: Well, yeah. No one has better commercial instincts than Spielberg, and I think he was seeing that the time was ripe for a primetime animated cartoon. This was before *The Simpsons*, and as usual his instincts were dead-on.

But *Family Dog* scripts are difficult to write, because the dog doesn't talk. The dog's a dog, and crafting situations so that you see it from the dog's point of view, that all has to be done carefully. We also couldn't do the *Garfield* approach, where the cat can look at the camera and you just hear his voice telling you what he's thinking. Our dog was a dog; he only made dog sounds … which meant it was entirely up to animation to tell you what he was thinking. That takes real craftsmanship. Even though the designs were simple, the animation was not. We could do six seven-minute shorts a year theatrically, but we couldn't do twenty-two half-hour episodes and maintain the quality.

I didn't want to fail Steven Spielberg. I didn't want the second thing that I did to be a bad, pale imitation of the first thing that I did. So, we parted ways, and they went off and did the TV show that they had in mind with Tim Burton and I went off onto *The Simpsons*, which was an idea I thought *could* be done well on a TV schedule.

Bill: How did it come about that you went to *The Simpsons*?

Brad: Jim [Brooks], [Sam] Simon, and Matt [Groening] liked the fact that *Family Dog* had unusual filmmaking in it, that the filmmaking was more like a live-action film. So they invited me to come on *The Simpsons*. What was weird for me was going from doing something that was mine to being a team player, and just helping someone else with their vision.

People thought I was crazy not to lead a series with Steven Spielberg, a series I had created, in favor of taking a supporting role on *The Simpsons*, a show that I had had nothing to do with. But for various reasons (I was also going through a rough time with a tragedy involving my sister), it seemed like the right thing to do at the time. It also allowed me freedom to work on all these episodes, make a lot of contributions that got to the heart of what was or wasn't working with a given episode. I could fix it and improve it without having to do the heavy lifting.

Which also allowed me enough time to go out and try to get movies made, which is what I really wanted to do. So all during the time I was on *The Simpsons* I was trying to get films made. I got films that are still to this day stuck in the catacombs of various studios.

I had no trouble selling ideas to Hollywood; the problem was getting them out of development hell, and I've learned a lot about that since then. I think if they can smell that you are willing to wait to get your dream, they will keep you waiting forever.

My attitude toward trying to get projects financed in the film business has changed. I entered the business loving "yes," and liking "maybe," and hating "no". Now I love "yes" and "no," and I *hate* "maybe". Because "maybe" will suck your life away.

Hollywood is basically a fear-based town, and "maybe" allows them to keep a project from slipping away from them, but they don't have the risk of committing to it, either. So they will load up their trays with "maybes." And the coffers of these companies are rich enough for them to support a lot of "maybes."

Bill: So to get to *Iron Giant*, didn't you give them an ultimatum?

Brad: Oh yeah. I was so sick of the usual cowardice, not saying they didn't want to make it but not backing the idea either. And you'd ask, "Can I have it back?" And the answer was, "No. Because you might make it a hit for somebody else, which makes us look bad," you know what I mean? So by the time *Iron Giant* came around, I fought for a bunch of things in my contract and I would not budge on them. They were not money issues. They were all about creative and time issues.

And one of the things that I insisted on was if they didn't greenlight it in six months, I was out.

Sure enough, they went to six months and one day. I was ready to walk and they greenlit the film. You could absolutely feel that they wanted to stay in "maybe," though. They wanted to see how *Quest for Camelot* did before committing to *Iron Giant*. But because they greenlit us and we were too deep into production by the time *Quest* came out, it was cheaper to finish us than to cancel us. So the only reason that *Iron Giant* actually got made was because I had that one requirement in my contract.

Bill: You finally get your opportunity to direct an animated feature, and it's in this very trying situation.

Brad: I finally get the ticket to board a luxury liner, and it turns out it's the *Titanic*.

Bill: And it's already sinking …

Brad: But the way I looked at it was, we can run around first class, we can have all the brandy and cigars we want, as long as we know that we'll all be dead on the bottom of the ocean in two hours. Part of the deal was that we had to be an incredibly tight and efficient production. Warner's had terrible experiences with their feature animation division before we arrived—it wasted a ton of money and had little to show for it. So we had a complicated film and a tight budget. We struggled every week to hit the productivity numbers, which were aggressive, and the way I said it to the crew was, "As long as we hit the numbers, they'll stay away. If they stay away, we have a shot of making a really great movie here. If we don't hit the numbers, they are gonna start to question everything. And, we don't want them to question everything. It'll kill us … we want to make our film."

Bill: Your experiences as a director are so filled with political and economic intrigue and stress. Try to set that aside for one instant and talk a little bit about what were you thinking of doing when you started *Iron Giant* that you felt might be fresh and different, that would be something that you personally had always wanted to see and had never seen.

Brad: I saw an opportunity to do the kind of animated film *I* wanted to see, something smart and dark and touching. Something that was paced confidently, not the sort of hyperactive rushing around that had become the new norm, this desperate busyness that seemed to suggest a fear that the audience would go for popcorn or grab a remote to change channels if you weren't shrieking at them all the time. I have always been kind of interested in animating humans. Milt was interested in humans, but Disney …

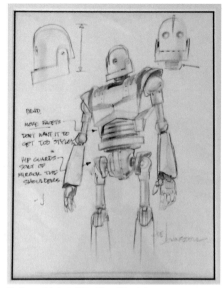

Bill: Lots of talking animals …

Brad: Yeah, I have no problem with talking animals. A lot of my favorite films have talking animals. Remy is a talking animal. It's just that a lot of stories that featured humans weren't being done because the thinking was if it has humans in it, it could be done in live action and therefore shouldn't be done in animation. Well, I even knew when I was starting out that that was idiotic thinking. If the only reason to animate something is because it can't be done in live action, animation would've gone extinct decades ago. Because live action can now do anything. The reason to do something in animation is caricature, and I use that word in a good sense, to get through to the truth of something. The truth can be really unreal-looking.

Visual Development, Mark Whiting, *The Iron Giant*, 1999 © Warner Bros. Licensed by Warner Bros. Entertainment Inc. All Rights Reserved.

I mean, *The Simpsons* in its own weird way gets at a lot of truth that people couldn't face if it were in live action.

I got *Iron Giant* going with this pitch to Warner Brothers: "What if a gun had a soul and didn't want to be a gun?" That's an unusual pitch for an animated film. I mean, you don't hear that sort of idea in the halls of a lot of the animation studios. I think *Giant* had enough of the recognizable "family" elements in it to make Warner's comfortable with making it. But we also were able to squeeze in some darker and headier stuff, which was interesting.

Bill: I think the cinematics of that film are very different from almost any other animated film up to that time, and it had certain live-action style camera moves, cutting and staging, effects, rack focus, that were a very bold cinematic style.

Brad: Thanks.

Bill: Which I think has been sort of a trademark of yours. But the other thing that is, I think, the most remarkable was that as innovative and exciting as they are, they're never what I would call "gratuitous." And I think most agree that people who watch your movies are never conscious of wild camera moves or a wild kind of directing.

Brad: There *are* some wild camera moves …

Bill: But they seem to fit, they seem right for the moment.

Brad: I paid attention to live-action filmmaking when I started making films. I realized that people wouldn't notice flamboyant camerawork if it were psychologically right. The only times that you notice it is when it pulls you out of the movie rather than pulling you into the movie. So, if you can bury the technique in emotion, so that it has an emotional grounding … You're home free.

   Some directors view camera work as almost a chore, and they kind of turn it over to their DP: "You figure out a good place to put the camera, I'm worried about the performance here." To me, where the camera is placed is part of the performance. It's an observer in the room who also has a brain, a take on the scene, and a point of view. The shower scene in *Psycho* is very stylized, very fragmented, but at that point, your own psyche is jagged and you're in a confined space, and you want to get out of there. So, psychologically, it's right to have fragmented, jagged shots.

Bill: I remember going to your house and you had the biggest TV of anybody we knew. And you had scores of laser discs, and you'd just keep popping the laser discs in and saying "watch this move, watch this cut, watch this …" I know you still do this, you watch so many DVDs at your house. If somebody who wanted to be a good director wanted to mimic you, is there a way to watch and learn?

Brad: I think for students there's never been an easier time to study film. In some ways DVDs are making it too easy, because they have the commentaries and all these extra materials at the end explaining everything. I'm almost starting to react against commentaries, because it's breaking down a movie before you've even had a chance to digest it, if you go straight into it.

   The problem with commentaries, and I've done several of them, is that they tend to make people think that the things you're pointing out are the only things worth noticing or the only way to see a particular film. It's probably better to not say anything and let the viewer get their own stuff from it. Because the viewer is gonna make connections that have nothing to do with connections that may have caused the filmmaker to do a moment. And that doesn't mean that they are any less valid.

Bill: So, you finish *Iron Giant*, everyone loved it, but it had a disappointing box office. You've finished your very first big feature film and you've got this kind of odd dichotomy of reactions, but fortunately along comes the Pixar offer.

Brad: It became clear that Warner Brothers was not the best place to do animation. Even after *Iron Giant*, they were kind of asking me to audition again. I pitched *The Incredibles* to Warner, and essentially they said, "Well, we like the idea; if we like the script we'll make it." Well, basically you could say the exact same thing to any cab driver. That's no real commitment, particularly after the hell we had to go through on *IG* … and I felt we had more than proven ourselves.

When I saw *Toy Story*, I had called John Lasseter 'cause I just flipped over it. It was everything that I had been waiting for our generation to do. It honored everything that the old guys taught us that matters, which is: characters, and story, and character, and character, what is your character thinking, what is your character feeling, character, character, character, character, character—that's the reason you do character animation, that's the beginning and end of it.

Toy Story was both absolutely fresh and absolutely classical. It got at the heart of all the things that mattered most, but in a whole new way. The technical stuff was very interesting, but not nearly as interesting as the story that was being told. It was contemporary, it had original characters, but it was far more sincere in how it approached them.

The Incredibles, 2004. © 2004 Disney/Pixar.

There's very clever direction in the opening of *Toy Story*; you begin from the point of view of a kid. Everyone knows what it's like to be a kid and play with a toy. And very subtly, they start to shift to the POV of the still-inanimate toy. As if the film is saying, "You remember how it was to play with a toy? Well, now we're going to show you a toy's point of view." It's subtle, it's sophisticated, it's simple, and clean, and the whole movie is like that.

I had seen John at a Disney premiere party when he was making *Toy Story* and he said, "You know, we should stay in touch." And we did while John was making *Bug's Life* and I was doing *Giant*. So I pitched *The Incredibles* to Pixar and their reaction at the end of the pitch was, "No brainer, let's do it." And I was like … "Really? That's it? Don't I have to walk over coals or give you my first child, or … you know … pay you something?" Pixar was going, "Come on up! Make a film!" The whole mindset was different from Warner's. It couldn't have been more opposite.

I would not say *The Incredibles* was easier than *Iron Giant*. But it was easier in the sense that I had complete support from the studio. It was a really ambitious, really complicated film.

Bill: It was all pretty new to you, because you had not yet worked in 3D.

Brad: It was new to me, and we were pushing them to do something way bigger than they'd ever done before—but with the same amount of resources. A lot of that *Iron Giant/Simpsons/Family Dog* TV training came in handy, because we were trying to do a movie that was three times bigger than anything Pixar had done but didn't cost more or take more time to do. So being very specific about what we were doing from moment to moment became important because we couldn't waste a dime.

The difference was, on *Iron Giant*, I was spending about 30 percent of my energy protecting what the other 70 percent of my energy had produced, flinging my body between the studio and the film, whereas at Pixar, I was spending 100 percent of my energy on the movie itself. And that's the way it should be. I mean movies aren't easy, even if you have support. But if you have real support, you can spend all of your effort on making the movie as good as it can possibly be and not just spend energy keeping your decisions from being undone. That's exhausting.

Bill: Pixar is maybe the best environment for that to happen.

Brad: You can feel it when a filmmaker and a crew are invested in their work and really are excited about the idea of realizing it. You can feel it. These are films that we want to see. If you start defining a filmmaker's job as you would a private sector job—"okay, you're to figure out what would make people of all ages and all different cultures be affected and entertained two years from now"—if you think about it logically like that, you'll go crazy. You'll just go into a fetal ball and curl up in the corner, because it's impossible. You can't know what's gonna entertain a wide spectrum of people all over the world two years from now.

The only way you can even begin to approach it is to say, "What would entertain me? What would I be interested in? What would I find funny? What would I find scary? What would I find dramatically involving?" And then, proceed from there. Because that's something that's possible.

That's one of the things that I object to in a lot of quote unquote "family entertainment." You have a feeling that many of the people making it would not want to sit down and actually watch the film that they're involved with.

I don't think any of the Pixar films feel that way at all. They feel like they assume that people are reasonably intelligent, that they want a story that's well constructed and characters that are engaging. They don't feel focus grouped. Because they aren't.

If you load your slate up with sequels, they suddenly get very happy on Wall Street and say, "This is gonna be a great year for Hollywood because I recognize every single film that's coming out! I know what I'm gonna get!"

Bill: Right, no "old man with a balloon-lifted house" film.

Brad: Right. And no film with cooking rodents. Or silent robots.

Bill: Your films have a lot of live-action influence, like cinematography. Do you think good live-action directors can direct animation?

Brad: A lot of people who don't know animation are directing animation films. That's what you're talking about, really. Gore Verbinsky did one …

Bill: Wes Anderson …

Brad: Wes Anderson made *Fantastic Mr. Fox*. I guess *Tin Tin* is sort of one, right? So it's Spielberg and Peter Jackson and Zemeckis doing mo-cap films. And there are other people, Gary Ross, *Tales of Despereaux*, Zack Snyder, et cetera. It's fashionable now, animation. The technology and the continued success of the animation medium has made it suddenly attractive to the live-action community.

I think, for me, the advantage of an animator directing an animated film is that when you don't get it the way you want you can break it down and get to the absolute pinpoint of what's not right.

We ran into some weird stuff on *The Incredibles*, because we had to convey that Mr. Incredible is strong, but that things he was lifting were really heavy. How do you convey that something is heavy but that somebody is strong enough to lift it?

If you want to see an example of that idea done badly in a live-action film, there's a Jet Li film called *The One*, where he picks up a couple of motorcycles in his hands and smashes 'em together. They look like helium balloons. They do not look at all like he's picking up motorcycles. And rather than being an impressive thing to watch visually, you go "Oh, that's so phony. That's not cool; it's dorky looking." Jet Li should have been lifting real things with some weight, but you can see that that they basically told him, "Okay, you're holding a motorcycle in each hand, now just lift them up and smash them together." But since he was holding no weight, his body reacts as if the motorcycles are like helium balloons.

On films I've directed, because I've animated, I can get in there with the animators and analyze problems on an animation level, you know, "maybe the knee would take a little more of the weight." Now that sounds tedious, and I can understand why a lot of live-action directors wouldn't want to bother with that, and probably you can lean on a good animator, but I feel, if you know the animation, you know how to play to animation's strengths. You're cognizant of what the medium's weaknesses are, so that you can somehow use that to overcome them.

There are certain occupations where people more readily move into directing than others. You see a lot more actors and writers being good directors than you see editors. I view animators on an animated film the way I view actors on a live-action film. In an animated film, the animation is front and center, all the other departments—and they're important, every single one of 'em—are kind of setting the stage for the animator. Animators are kind of center stage. They're the characters, so I think that it helps for a director of animated films to speak that language.

Bill: It's a different way to do a performance than a live-action actor would do. And it will always be different.

Brad: I agree, at its best I think it will always be different. I don't consider mo-cap animation. I'm not against the use of mo-cap; I think that it has a very valuable place in the filmmaking arsenal. I think that Andy Serkis and Weta's work on Gollum and Kong is a testament to that fact that mo-cap can give you a very good basis for performance.

But make no mistake that animators helped make those performances possible as well. It wasn't just wires hooked up to an actor; it was animators finessing it, after the fact. Even on *Avatar*, which had a more sophisticated rig to capture actors' movements, animators took it that last 10 percent. A good animator has the eye to detect what's missing. Even if the mo-cap is really great mo-cap, an animator can really readily discern what's missing, to take it to that full level of life.

Bill: That being the case, do you think it should be called "animation"?

Brad: No, I don't. In mo-cap, animators are not creating a performance from scratch. They're being a performance preserver. You know how energy, like electricity on a grid, diminishes when it's transferred? That's what those animators are doing. They are compensating for nuances of the actor's performance that are lost in transit by boosting the energy back. But just because that's their function on *Avatar* doesn't mean animators can't also turn in beautiful fantastic performances, all by themselves, you know?

Look at the non-Navi creatures in *Avatar*. They're 100 percent animated, and they look absolutely convincing. Then look at a film like *Coraline*. It doesn't look remotely realistic, but it absolutely is engaging. It draws you in. That's the work of animators.

And you care about it. I look at *Wallace and Gromit*, and the dog Gromit doesn't even have a mouth, and yet I know exactly what that dog is thinking, every single second. And I feel for that dog. I feel like I know that dog.

Bill: Gromit is one of the great appealing characters of all time.

Brad: Absolutely. And he doesn't even have a mouth. So I would love it if actors could see animators as brethren, rather than competition. I keep wanting to give a talk to the Screen Actors Guild and tell them to stop viewing animators as the enemy, you know? Put 'em in the Screen Actors Guild!

Muppet puppeteer Frank Oz is an actor. Milt Kahl is an actor. Frank Thomas, Brando, Meryl Streep, they're *all* actors.

Bill: In your story reels, you have a really strong idea of where you're going with story and acting and content. At what point do you start getting an idea of how it should look? How do you collaborate with your designers?

Brad: Although I had a pretty strong visual idea for the way I wanted *The Incredibles* to look, it didn't mean that I was looking for people who would just do my bidding. You go after people who you think can capture something new to expand your vision beyond what you're seeing in your mind. You cast graphic talent the way you cast an actor.

In the case of *Ratatouille*, the film was already going and most of the crew was in place when I took it over. I had admired Harley Jessup and Sharon Calahan's work for years. But the sets were not very well defined because the story kept shifting. And beyond the kitchen and dining room of Gusteau's, they could never figure out what the sets were.

When I got onto it, we had to do a whole new story reel in a very short amount of time, and twenty-two of the film's twenty-five sets. We had to figure out Linguine's apartment, that it had to be both a tiny, borderline-poverty apartment, more like a glorified broom closet, and at the same time be romantic; you had to look out the window and be able to feel that magic of Paris, you know?

It was fun to work with Sharon because we're both ardent fans of cinematographers. She could mention a name and I'd know who she's talking about. "Well we want bounce-light here like Robert Richardson," you know, and she'd say "Okay, got it." That's all I'd need to say. Or she'd pull up some shots from different Conrad Hall movies and say, "A little more like this?" It's like talking about rock 'n' roll with somebody who loves rock 'n' roll. You can just say, "the Byrds," and they know who you're talking about.

Visual development, Dominique Louis, *Ratatouille*, 2007 © Disney/Pixar.

Bill: When you're thinking of a sequence, do you ever think, "Well, the lighting or the art direction's gonna dominate this, as opposed to the acting or the dialogue."

Brad: I don't think about it a lot, except specific scenes. I always knew that the interrogation scene in the barn between Kent and Hogarth was gonna be weird in *Iron Giant*, because I wanted there to be only one too-bright light on Hogarth, with darkness everywhere else. I knew the transition from when the kid gets chloroformed and comes back to reality was gonna be an unbroken transition.

Every once in a while, I'll be shocked because something will so *not* be what I'm imagining that I thought, "Did I not communicate this?" Those times are relatively rare but they happen on every movie. Normally, if you get good people you don't have to manage them a lot; you just have to touch base with them and talk about where you are psychologically.

And you can make little suggestions. In *The Incredibles*, the scene where Bob gets let loose by Mirage and then grabs her throat, that was not lit at all the way I imagined it. I had to get Lou Romano to do a little sketch of the top rim light, so the characters are kind of dark with the hard light, and then, when he lifts her up, he has hard light on him. It's less soft and sleek looking and more hard-ass.

Sometimes I have ideas while I'm writing. I love the whole filmmaking process; I basically could be assigned almost anyone's job filmmaking and be interested in it. I am kind of a geek, and I have fun going from department to department. So sometimes when I'm writing I'm imagining a specific department and where we're gonna be leaning more on it.

On *The Incredibles* I'd noticed that modern action films had lost the tease. I'd always loved sneaking around scenes in the Bond films. And I realized that they didn't have that in the new Bond films anymore. Sneaking around is fun, you know? Now, you just cut, and the character's where he needs to be for the next action scene. So I thought, I'm gonna get some sneaking around in this movie.

Bob starts to penetrate Syndrome's base, and it's cool to show what obstacles he has to overcome. What if a couple of things go wrong? What if you're leaning up against a door, and suddenly it lifts up and you with it? I told everybody involved with those scenes, "Have fun with sneaking around." Even the lighting was all keyed by asking, "What's good sneaking-around lighting?"

It doesn't sound very intellectual, but I trust my people. I don't feel the need to give notes just to give notes. I can't stand that. And I worked for directors that did that. They loved having people taking their notes down and people scurrying after what they want, so they think of meaningless stuff for people to do. I don't enjoy meetings. They're functional, but I don't like drawing them out.

I'm in a meeting to get stuff taken care of and move things out the door. When I first got involved with *Ratatouille*, they were shocked because they'd schedule an hour and a half meeting, and I would deal with it in like twenty minutes and go, "okay, what else?" And they'd go, "Th– … that's it."

Some people want to become directors because they can get people to bring them tea, and they get to point and have people run off in directions that they point to. That's the stuff that they're interested in; they're not that interested in the story or achieving a moment on film. For me, those people aren't really directors. They're people attracted by the *power* of directing and not the filmmaking part, which is the whole point.

I've run into students who talk to me about directing, but they want to talk about making the deal, or what it's like to work with famous people. That's not what's exciting.

Some people will cast famous actors that are wrong just so that they can have the experience of working with that famous person. I would rather have a nonfamous person that's absolutely right for the role … that's more exciting to me. It's more about getting something on film that is … electric, or memorable. The medium is what's exciting, not the other stuff.

Ratatouille, 2007. © 2007 Disney/Pixar.

Bill: I think you convey that sense of energy and excitement to your crews by your ability to not take them down the wrong road.

Brad: Right.

Bill: That's how you kill a spirit in a film. By always changing and fixing it.

Brad: Well, yeah, at least if you're changing stuff and *not* fixing it. And I've said this before, but I really believe it: I learned as much from working on bad films as I did from good experiences like working at Lisberger Studios, where the studio was a fun place to be. But the one line that no one ever puts on a budget, that's absolutely *crucial*, is morale. If morale is bad, you get twenty-five cents out of every dollar you spend. If morale is good you get three dollars out of every dollar you spend.

So whipping people up and getting them excited about what we're doing together is absolutely essential. Films are hard; people work hard. You want creative people. You want people who have their own ideas and who bring them to the table every day. But the challenge is like having an orchestra. You can't say to each player, "Play whatever you want." Individually, each member of an orchestra could play a wonderful thing. But if they all do that at once, it's a mess.

Somehow, without limiting them, you must get them all to weave through each other and support each other, and lift each other up. The film is the goal. The weird thing about directing is that if you do it right, you're only in control maybe a little over 60 percent of the time.

And that's actually good. It's more like a tennis match; you take the first shot, but then the film hits it back to you, and it may push you over into the left side of the court, where you didn't necessarily want to go. But if you go there and hit it back, then it becomes this new thing. And I've tried to force my original thought sometimes, when the film didn't really want to do what I wanted, and it wasn't good.

You can't let the film go out of control, but the best thing is to constantly be asking the film what it wants to be. Or being aware, being open to seeing what the film wants to be, because the film, once you start to create it, starts to have its own momentum.

It's more like martial arts, where you're redirecting energy, rather than blocking energy. You know, if you try to stop it, it'll knock you over. It's about taking the energy that's there and channeling it. Ideas come out of the ether that are better than what you could imagine, and if you're locked on to what you were originally imagining and don't take advantage of gifts that arise, you're limiting what the film could be.

You're doing a dance with a movie. You have to initiate the dance and kind of get the movie up on its feet. But once it's on its feet, you can lead, but you're not the only dancer. The movie's also telling you what it wants to be. And you better be ready to respond to it.

Bill: And by "it" and "the movie," you're also referring to the larger energy of all the people supplying their creative input.

Brad: Absolutely.

Bill: It's a really interesting approach. I think a lot of directors don't do that. They have a rigid idea and I think the films suffer for it.

Brad: And then there are some directors who absolutely have the barest idea of what they want to do and are willing to just trust the storm of the process. Sometimes it yields a good film. It doesn't yield it often enough for me, though.

Bill: The "fix it in post" school?

Brad: Well, it's the "controlled chaos" school, and great films have been made that way, but usually if you look at the filmmaker's entire body of work, it's really inconsistent, you know? I think that my favorite directors are the ones who are strong lead dancers.

Bill: You're a real proponent of people coming with something other than animation to their experience.

Brad: Yeah, particularly when young people ask, "What should I do?" I basically assume that if they're in animation, they're relatively obsessed, because it's not an easy thing to do. You can't do it casually, really. A lot of work yields very little screen time.

The greatest thing for someone trying to learn animation right now is that you can look at the entirety of all the work that's been done; you can buy it or rent it and study it to a degree that we would have died for when I was first learning.

The weakness of having all this work so readily accessible is if you become a library of other people's solutions, it often limits how you solve problems. Don't get me wrong. I think it's valuable to study how other people handled problems. But try to look in your own life for inspiration. Frank and Ollie (and all the great animators from that earlier era) didn't have any animation to look at, so they had to pull from their lives and pull from plays and pull from other areas. The weakness of animators now is their tendency to only look at animation, because that's all they're interested in. And that means all that they're bringing into the medium is what we've already seen.

If they look to their own lives and look to other art forms and other ways of seeing, then they're bringing something into animation that keeps the medium fresh. Nick Park's dad is a tinkerer, an inventor, and that's one of his influences on *Wallace and Gromit*. And those films are incredibly specific to Nick Park. You feel it.

And that's new. If you asked who's the predecessor to Nick Park, I can name some people that did films in clay. I can name people that made films with British humor, but there is no other Nick Park. Nick Park is the only Nick Park. And that's how it should be. Tex Avery was the only Tex Avery. And so if somebody's interested in revitalizing the art form, I think that they have to absolutely look outside of it. And let the larger world feed them, and then they can feed animation.

Bill: You're one of the great students of directors and directing. Having directed three successful animated features, as you started your first job as a director of a live-action picture, did you bring any notions about directing that ended up changing or turned out to be different than what you expected?

Brad: I think the first thing that I did was I kept thinking that I only needed the bit of film that I was shooting. In other words, the shot begins at precisely this point and it ends at precisely this point. I tended to yell "cut" as I imagined a cut, rather than letting the scene play if it was working. We were starting the scene with a few lines to ramp up and ramp out and be a little looser about it. I would call "cut" and everybody would look at me like, "what is he doing?" I started to get the idea that I can shoot extra.

My brain was wired for "the shot begins here and it ends here," which is how somebody thinks in animation. There's no such thing as coverage, although that's changed a little bit with CG. It's not a coverage thing, where you're shooting something from a lot of different angles. You're tailoring. You're blocking for a specific shot, and a shot begins on Frame 47 or whatever and it ends on Frame 134. My first training in all this stuff was all animation, so I was used to having a stopwatch, which is the old-school way of doing animation, where you imagine how long things take and you hit a stopwatch, and you get your basic feeling for timing that way.

While I think that's a good way to do it—and it does give you a good sense of time—it doesn't really have a heck of a lot to do with how you approach things in live action. That was one of the things that I had to wrap my head around, being a little bit looser. Sometimes what happened, too, is if I cut too soon, a piece of film that I really could have used wouldn't be shot because I didn't let the camera roll a little bit more.

When you go into the editing room—which of course, I didn't do until after I finished shooting *Mission*—and you thought that what you wanted in a certain shot, you realize if you had it in another angle, it would be the perfect thing for a certain point. And if you don't shoot it in that other angle because you cut too soon, then you're hosed. A few members of the crew, and even Tom [Cruise],had to remind me, "If you keep rolling, you'll have something you could use. So why not do it?"

I learned pretty quickly to be a little bit looser about all that stuff. It eventually gives you a feeling for how you can orchestrate moments that you will want to have. It's a little looser than animation. You can still be very precise in live action, but there is the luxury of trying things a few different ways and then mixing and matching a bit later.

Bill: Were there other big differences in getting into live action, other things you really enjoyed about it?

Brad: It's not a physical thing. You can't move it as fast as you imagine in animation sometimes, because the camera is not a physical thing in animation. It has no weight. It has no presence in the room. In drawn animation, it's simply another drawing. There is a camera, but it's just moving closer, farther away from flat artwork.

In the case of CG, the camera is like a video game camera, meaning it can be anywhere and move and as fast or as slow as you want it to. While that is a nice thing, I think that it makes a lot of people who direct in CG move the camera incessantly, like a video game camera. It's not anchored to a point of view.

I think that the human eye likes camera stuff that feels a little more physical. ILM, when they first started special effects, started introducing imperfection into camera moves so that it felt more natural with the live action around it. So when an explosion happened, the camera would jar just like it would in real combat footage. Even though the camera in a special effect is not a physical thing and you're dealing with effects that are often not physical as well, if you mimic the physical aspects of that, it makes it feel more real.

When you deal with a real camera in real space, there are limits to how fast you can move. If you want it to move really fast, you have to get up to speed before your shot can start. That is a physical constraint that you don't have in CG.

We were shooting on the Burj Khalifa, which is the tallest building in the world. We were shooting in IMAX, so the camera was huge and heavy, and we needed to control and do these elegant camera moves. It's a lot of trial and error, because you're physically moving a very large, cumbersome camera in space. One part of the shot might be too slow, and in another spot the actor gets ahead of the camera and you don't want him to.

You're trying to choreograph this dance between the camera and the actor and what's happening around the actor. It's performance by camera operators that have to interface with performance by actors. The more complicated your camera moves get, the more ways you have of screwing up. If the actor does this perfect take, but the camera is not in the right spot, that's going to be a problem. Another time, if the camera is perfect but the actor is not so hot, that's equally a problem. You're trying to orchestrate the perfect harmony of all these different aspects.

In animation, you can simply change things until they're all right, whereas in live action you have a schedule that you have to keep. It costs x amount of dollars per minute that you have all these people doing this stuff. You don't get that many times at bat. You get a few, and if you schedule your day right, not all your shots are equally complex. You give yourself more time to do the more difficult shots. It's a little more nerve-wracking because things are a little more out of control. That can be a good thing, as well.

Bill: I would think as an animation director, you would automatically bring a more precise idea of frame composition to each shot than a live-action director might, who often waits to see it, whereas in animation you're always thinking of that. Like you're saying, this idea of coordinating a performance with a precise bit of staging seems very animation-ey.

Brad: That aspect of having to imagine shots and be able to draw them, to convey them to other people in animation was useful. I knew what I wanted. Yeah, it was useful. There are live-action directors, of course, who are very precise about camera and what the camera should be seeing at any given point. I would say that that is an aspect of animation that was helpful when I went into it. There are a lot of animation directors who don't care as much about staging as I think sometimes they should.

Bill: I would guess that before *Mission* you had never done a scene that you had not storyboarded first. Did you storyboard everything in *Mission*?

Brad: Actually, most of *Mission* was not storyboarded. There were only two and a half sequences that were pre-vis'd. One of them was the Burj sequence and the other one was the car park. Then I pre-vis'd about half of the sandstorm car chase. Those were the only ones that were pre-vis'd. We didn't have time to pre-vis the rest.

I was used to storyboarding and I think that I am more involved in the storyboard staging than most animation directors. I try to work that out very early, to a degree that some people think is a little over the top. I was already predisposed to think that way, so when I had to pull stuff out of my pocket, I had something in mind. I think there's a danger in relying too much on that.

When I got into the editing room, I was relieved to find that even if I shot coverage of the same scene on two different days, or even a week apart, I instinctively tended to move the camera the same way at the same point in the scene.

That made things intercut pretty well. The coverage all tended to have the same tone, meaning that if I was shooting a lock-off shot, it would be a series of lock-off shots. Then movement would start at a certain point and it would start for a lot of my coverage, not just one angle. There was a similar quality to the filmmaking that made it easy to intercut. I was very relieved about that, because I was just doing it on the fly. We had a really tough schedule and a very large film that was filmed in a lot of different places on the globe, and stunts. We were shooting a big chunk of it in IMAX. There was a lot of trouble. It was a tall order. Even though the film was bigger than the previous *Mission: Impossible* in terms of the scale of it, we had a shorter schedule and a lower budget. We had to be moving pretty aggressively all the time.

Bill: It sounds like you were storyboarding in your head.

Brad: Yeah. What happened was, we didn't have adequate time to scout some of this stuff. I was arriving at locations and they were saying, "Where do you want to put the camera?", and I was like, "Can I look around first? Jesus!"

They said to me, "We have to have a shot list before you shoot." I was getting back so late and having to get up so early that, after a couple of days, I just said, "Look, I can't go home and do shot lists. It's sleep or shot list. Which one do you think I can do without?"

They said, "You have to get the crew going on something." I just said, "Look, I'll figure out the first shot before I arrive. I'll arrive with a shot. While you guys are working on that shot, I'll figure out the next two. Then I'll just stay ahead of you guys and try to keep my coverage doable in a day." That's how I had to do it. I knew that I had to cover *x* amount of pages of material in a day. I tried to plan out my stuff accordingly.

I had a very good crew. They were a very experienced crew. Very quickly, you start to learn the strategy of shooting one side of the camera facing one side of the room and then facing the other. You try to do all of your coverage on one side before you flip the lights around to do the other.

There's an efficiency, and your AD knows all these tricks on how to move efficiently so that you're not striking stuff and then having to re-put it into place. You start to learn where you can economize and move quickly. I don't shoot a ton of takes on every setup. On some of them, they're simple, so you don't do that many takes. You know you're going to hit something else that's going to take more takes than you want. You want to be able to accommodate that without falling behind schedule.

It was a lot to learn, but I was very lucky in that Tom was not only a very game actor, a wonderful, charismatic presence, but also a producer. Very experienced, and incredibly supportive of what I wanted to do. That makes [things] a lot more accomplishable, when you have somebody of Tom's stature on your side. He was very supportive from day one. That was a huge gift to me on my first live-action film.

Bill: I remember when you were doing *Ratatouille*, I heard you talk about trying to get simulated spontaneity into some of it. It was just hard to do. Now, I guess in a movie like this, spontaneity is there all the time.

Brad: Well, not all the time. *Mission* is a certain genre. There are a lot of action sequences that need to be very well planned out. There are just too many elements going into play. You have to know what you're going to do on set versus what you're going to later in effects, and where the line is drawn.

We built a large part of that car park, but it's supposed to look like a ten- or fifteen-story building and we could afford maybe three or four stories. It was a huge set. It actually worked. It lifted cars up and moved them around. We were designing it so that we could have those three stories be any one of the ten or fifteen stories that's in the movie. But you have to know where you are at any given point. You have to be able to move the cars around so that they look correct for being different stories. Some of them are CG and some of them are real. You have to know what all that stuff is going to be before you can even do a sequence like that.

I say "spontaneous," but it's the actors who are spontaneous within their given scenes. The kind of film that it is, it's not an improv-type film. It's not like a Will Ferrell comedy where they just roll and do 400 different takes of improv and then just pick the best stuff. This is much more tightly controlled than that.

In terms of comparing it to animation, yeah, you can get a running start. You can throw things in there and somebody can come up with a certain line that they say. We were shooting Renner and Paula and Tom was feeding them a line and he improv'd a line just to get a response from Renner. I thought the line was so correct that we went back and filmed

Tom saying it, because it was great. Renner came up with several lines that I liked better than what was in the script, so I just made sure to shoot them. That part was really fun, because it makes it a live thing that everybody can contribute to. You have to keep it so that it's always moving the story forward, but it's fun to let things slide a little bit.

Bill: Now that you had success in both live action and animation, how do you choose what to do next?

Brad: Well, really, you're just trying to be governed by what story interests you and you feel is challenging to you, that you can dedicate a certain amount of energy to, you think you're going to start to understand story really well, but the truth of the matter is, if you're mixing it up and trying different things, you're always a little bit at sea and you don't really totally know what you're doing.

I am far from feeling like I have story licked and all figured out. I feel like every time I start a movie, I'm back in the dark, feeling my way along the walls. Certainly, the film that I'm working on now is no different. I'm learning tremendous amounts. Like I've said before, I think that you have to stay in the attitude of being a student, because if you're doing it right, I think you're always learning something.

Bill: Are you learning something that you wouldn't have learned if you were doing an animated film right now?

Brad: Sure. It's a different way to make films. Some of the lessons are the same. You're still telling a story and still dealing with presenting characters on the screen and trying to do it efficiently and entertainingly.

Absolutely, the skill set is a little bit different than it is in animation. The heat is hotter. You have more pressure. Things are a little more out of control and you have to be okay with that.

Basically, both animation and live action are the medium of cinema. That's really what I'm interested in. I think animation is wonderful. I think the one thing that I would say is that I'm interested in doing animation more quickly. If I can do it quickly and still create the level of quality that I want, I'm going to try to do that.

Bill: If you go back and do another animated film, how might your directing be different based on these live-action experiences?

Brad: I don't know. That's interesting. I did do a couple of sections of *Ratatouille* where I planned them a little differently. It was because I needed them to feel a little more out of control. I didn't tell the voice actor exactly what he was going to say. I prepared a story reel that was elaborate, timed it with animation timing, then played it in the recording booth so the actor had to respond to it in real time. He had to react spontaneously because he was seeing it for the first time.

I did two takes where Linguini moves throughout the kitchen and is grabbing things from people and trying to explain himself—which I told to Lou Romano, who did the voice. I said, "If your character takes something from another character in the kitchen, try to cover for it. Try to make it sound—even though your body is jerking around—your mind is apologizing for what your body is doing." Lou just reacted. I did two takes and then just cherry-picked the best moments.

John Kahrs, the animator, animated a rough pass in 3D, without me telling him where the camera was going to be. When I got the scene back in rough, it had an out-of-control actor on the soundtrack with an animator who didn't know where the camera was going to be, and a camera guy who didn't know which angle I was going to cut to. That meant that I could edit it in a free-flowing manner and let the action determine the cut.

Even though it was still animation and wasn't really totally spontaneous or anything like that, it had a different feeling that it would not have had if it had been planned out from the outset. It had an out-of-control quality that really helped that part of the film.

Bill: It seems to me like you get a feeling as a filmmaker of how a story should be told. It seems like no matter which medium you're in, you're going to find the right way to do it and sometimes they'll resemble each other. I'm guessing that your live-action films have certain animation things about them and your animation films have certain live-action things about them, because you're really just thinking about the story and the filmmaking, making the medium work for you.

Brad: I think that's true. You have a lot of tools in film that you can use. There's the movement. It's not just the movement of people. It's the movement of camera. It's the movement of things in space. The lenses can give you a different feeling, whether it's a long lens or a wide lens.

The Incredibles, 2004. © 2004 Disney/Pixar.

I did a very strange thing in *The Incredibles* for animation. When Bob was in his office, I used the equivalent of really long lenses. Now, even though he was in a claustrophobic office and there was no way you could get those angles in a live-action film without crews putting it on a sound stage and getting way back from it and then zooming in on it. In other words, they were small spaces, but you were covering them with long lenses. It was giving you this very strange feeling of being compressed in a tiny space.

I was virtually building this very claustrophobic set and then moving the camera far away, and then eliminating everything between you and the character. It was continually slicing the set up virtually and getting very close to it. So whenever Bob was at his work, it was compressed and tight and feeling claustrophobic. At the point where he sees the guy getting mugged in the alley, suddenly it goes to wide angle because he's starting to move. He's feeling like his super-hero self—the feeling, suddenly, of space and movement.

Those kinds of qualities, that's like using cinema to get a certain feeling. A lot of my favorite filmmakers are aware of that kind of stuff. I've learned a lot from watching their work.

Bill: I think you're the embodiment of the crossover of animation and live-action, especially now, with CG. There are so many things that can be done; it's really just the cinematic vision that is needed in bringing the same ideas in development.

Brad: We'll see what happens. I'm learning a lot.

Brad Bird © Disney/Pixar. Photo: Deborah Coleman.

2
Henry Selick Interview

Henry Selick © Laika.

What's the toughest thing to do in Hollywood? Win awards? Get rich? Get famous? Be on a first-name basis with superstars? Many people do these things, but in my opinion the toughest thing to do is to be original.

Henry Selick has originality in his DNA. We could see it the first week in the old Disney training program. We were all slugging away on our pencil tests, as was Henry, but he was also working on a film none of us would have dreamed up: *Seepage*. Everything about it was different: the narrative, the design, the mix of mediums. It was hard to imagine Disney ever doing something like it.

And, of course, Disney did not. Henry Selick had to leave to find places to work his magic. Unlike the rest of us, and most of the directors in this book, Henry had an especially challenging path because he literally had to create and invent the entire production process for his films. He didn't walk into studios and take over a crew. He had to build a crew—and a facility—because no one was making films the way Henry Selick wanted to make them.

He has been a true pioneer. I remember visiting his studio in the old Pillsbury Doughboy days and seeing dozens of severed doughboy heads on shelves, because Henry was one of the first to use that innovation of interchangeable expressions. On his masterpiece *Coraline*, he was still mixing it up in ways no one else had dreamed of, using some CG while commissioning other props to be custom-cast in steel!

Henry even moves, talks, and gestures differently from other people! And it's not put on; he's always been that way. He has his own style. He's one of those people that make you feel that the magic of life has no predictable limits.

We interviewed Henry during a press junket on the rooftop of the Belage Hotel in West Hollywood.

Bill Kroyer

Bill: When did you first get interested in animation?

Henry: I was one of those kids who drew all the time, from when I was probably four or five until I was thirteen. Like most kids in the fifties and sixties, I enjoyed the old Disney shorts and Warner Brothers stuff that played on TV. I especially liked the classic *Popeyes* and those wild *Betty Boop* cartoons. Characters like Mickey Mouse, Bugs Bunny, and Popeye are some of the first drawings I ever made. But I was also a big fan of Ray Harryhausen after Mom took me, age five, to see *The Seventh Voyage of Sinbad* down at the Carlton Theater in Red Bank, NJ. I dreamed about his stop-motion Cyclops for years. I also loved the bits of Lotte Reiniger's cutout films that played on a local kids' TV show. The Disney Halloween TV specials that featured "Night on Bald Mountain" and "Legend of Sleepy Hollow" were quite memorable. As far as humor, I thought the *Rocky and Bullwinkle Show* was the funniest thing on TV and the *Peanuts* specials were pretty special. *101 Dalmatians* was the most impactful Disney feature I saw. I don't think I even knew there was a connection between the flipbooks I drew in schoolbooks and the professional cartoons and stop-motion I watched. It would be a lot of years before the light bulb went off and I became an animator.

Bill: Was anybody else in your family artistic?

Henry: My father was, in a way. Restoring old cars was his hobby, and he could make anything out of wood or metal. His shop was awesome and included welding equipment, metal lathes, and a sand blaster. He even knew how to do lost-wax castings. For years, my brother and I were his "helpers" and, while we never had his talent at making stuff, just getting to see how mechanical stuff worked and how to repair or replace it definitely influenced my love of doing stop-motion and all its handmade processes. My father also shot sixteen-millimeter home movies, and sometimes I'd be an actor in one of his gag shots. Despite him being a pretty macho guy, he and my mom encouraged my wanting to be an artist, making sure I didn't trace any images I drew.

In the third grade, I was taken under the wing of a local illustrator, the famous Stanley Meltzoff, and went to his studio once a week for free art lessons. He did paintings for *National Geographic* and *Life* magazine and worked from models, even having a dead horse brought to his studio for a Civil War series. Stanley was a great artist but kind of intimidating so, after a couple of years, I stopped going. Years later, when I told him I was going into animation he told me I was out of my mind, saying, "Animation is factory work!"

I switched from drawing and painting to music when I was around eleven years old—piano and clarinet and guitar, all through high school, along with English and physics because of some great teacher. It wasn't until college that my interest in the visual arts was reignited. I had a lot of catching up to do, but threw myself into life drawing, painting, printmaking, sculpting, and photography. Funny thing, I could never settle on one image in my photos. It was always a series of images that were telling simple stories. I even made a couple of full-size sculptures that had joints because I couldn't settle on a pose. I wanted to keep shifting them. When I was about 20, I saw an experimental animated short on TV. That's when I realized that all my various interests, including music, could come together in one art form. So I signed up for Bruce MacCurdy's course at Syracuse University.

Bill: What was your major at college?

Henry: At the time I was an illustration major. But I was also a musician, playing in bands, so there was a tug-of-war between the art courses and playing music. Honestly, I didn't know what the hell I was going to do.

Bill: Did you make your first film at Syracuse?

Henry: In class I saw a lot of animated shorts from the Canadian Film Board, which used all sorts of techniques like sand painting and pin screen and stop-motion. So I wanted to experiment a bit. My first film used animated cutouts of my artwork set to a pop song called "The Wall Street Shuffle." Then I got to direct other students on an original film of mine using traditional cel animation over backgrounds. It was called *Tube Tales* and, while it was pretty crude, it was nominated for a Student Academy Award. It was in '76 or '77.

Bill: From the Oscars? From the Academy?

Henry: Oh yeah. Got to meet Jack Nicholson and Warren Beatty and Buck Henry, Louise Fletcher and Jacqueline Bisset and Groucho Marx. My short ended up getting beaten by a film from CalArts.

Bill: Is that what brought you to LA?

Henry: The nomination came after I arrived. I'd gotten the animation bug and wanted to learn more from a school that had a full animation department. So, after seeing some excellent student shorts from the California Institute of the Arts, I applied to both the character and experimental animation programs. I got into both programs and ended up taking classes in both departments.

Bill: What was that experience like? You were probably older than most of your fellow students.

Henry: There were a few others who'd done undergraduate work; John Musker and Leslie Margolin come to mind. But most kids in character, like Brad Bird and John Lasseter and Jerry Rees, were right out of high school. The average age was higher in Jules Engel's Experimental Animation Department.

I grew up in New Jersey on Beach Boys and Disneyland promos, so coming to California in '75 was just incredible—it was the promised land. I had a Vespa scooter and I spotted a real roadrunner—the bird—my first week there. CalArts was like no other school I'd ever heard of, a place where you'd find incredibly great graffiti scrawled in the restrooms; world-class dance, music, and design classes and students. As the swimming pool was clothing optional, it'd be the first place to look if you needed a security guard.

Bill: Most of the animators say that they learned more from each other than from the faculty. How long did you stay at CalArts? And how did you develop and change during that time?

Henry: I had some great teachers for the two years I was at CalArts. In experimental, Jules exposed me to international filmmakers like Jan Svankmajer, Jiri Trnka, and Raoul Servais, and his incredibly good taste helped push my work to be better. Disney animator Moe Gollub taught under Jules and really helped me with some tough animal drawings for a film I was making. In character animation, I learned layout and perspective from Disney master Kendall O'Connor; design from Bill Moore; life drawing with Elmer Plummer; and caricature with T. Hee. And I took classes outside the animation programs from the likes of director Sandy McKendrick (*Sweet Smell of Success*) and lighting teacher Kris Malkiewicz. There were lectures by Maurice Noble, Chuck Jones, June Foray, Bill Littlejohn, and Bill Melendez. I got to meet Grim Natwick and John Hubley. And while all art schools have their share of poseurs and frauds, the overall community at CalArts was wonderful. If you needed music for your film, you could hire some of the best musicians in the world—guys that played with Frank Zappa—for a case of beer.

Bill: Did you make films for both the character animation and experimental film programs?

Henry: For character, I mainly did storyboards under Jack Hannah, no finished animation. In experimental, I did a lot of tests and completed one seven-minute film called *Phases* and started a second film, *Seepage*, my first feature stop-motion. I completed that film when I won a grant from the AFI/National Endowment while working at Disney. *Seepage*, using drawings and color, was about an individual whose inner self emerges to battle him as the two transform from one animal to another. In the end, they basically shake hands and merge back together. That was shown at many festivals, won a lot of awards, and was a finalist in the Student Academy Awards.

Seepage, 1992.

Bill: Your CalArts path seems very ironic. You start out with this independent drive, yet you also commit to the more conventional Disney character program.

Henry: I was really clueless about making a living. I never had a master plan; I just wanted to learn all I could. I did have this crazy idea that you could make short films and somehow people would pay you enough to make a living doing that. There was a film that had come out that was hugely successful. Was it Frank Mouris?

Bill: Yeah, Frank Mouris' *Frank Film*.

Henry: Yep, and no one told me how rare that kind of success was or that if you wanted to survive doing animated shorts, you needed to go work at the Canadian Film Board or become a teacher or become a master grant writer. Anyway, after my first year at CalArts, I went looking for a summer job. I failed the inbetweener test at Hanna-Barbera; too slow. Then I went over to Disney and met Eric Larson, one of the nine old men and the guy in charge of trainee animators. Because of the connection between Disney and CalArts, Eric gave me (and John Musker) a job. I spent the summer pretty much doing my own stuff with his amused input.

I returned to CalArts and, after graduating a year later, I went straight back to Disney. But this wasn't like my summer where Mr. Larsen had indulged my personal taste; now I had to deliver Disney-style character animation. And the other people in my group, like Bill Kroyer, John Musker, Brad Bird, and Jerry Rees, were light years ahead of me. Maybe I'd been enjoying *New Yorker* cartoons for too many years, but my sense of humor and character and storytelling just wasn't Disney. My first test was awful and I wasn't sure I'd survive. Good old Eric Larson saved my life, spending extra time with me, convincing me to use a Disney character and not one of my own, saying things like, "That might be humorous in a single frame, but it wouldn't work in one of our films." Under his guidance, I animated Mr. Toad shaving himself in the mirror and came out the other side of the process with a job.

Eric Larson at desk Left: Lorna Pomeroy, Heidi Guedel, Bill Kroyer, Dan Haskett (floor), Emily Jiuliano, Henry Selick, unknown. © Disney.

Bill: I have a really good photo of you and me from that time. It looks like you were really happy. How did you get assigned to *Pete's Dragon*?

Henry: They needed help with inbetweening, so I and some other animator trainees were tested. I could swear Brad Bird and John Musker purposely did poorly, but I passed. Anyway, my animation training was interrupted for a few months while I worked under Dale Oliver, one of the great animation assistants and a glider pilot in World War II.

Bill: How long were you at Disney?

Henry: About four years. The young talent there was phenomenal: Glen Keane, who could draw like Michelangelo, Ron Clements, John Pomeroy, Andy Gaskill. That's where I became friends with Tim Burton and Rick Heinrichs, and Joe Ranft. Frank and Ollie were still working there full-time, as was Woolie Reitherman, and both Marc Davis and Milt Kahl came around. Eric Larson remained my chief mentor; he was someone that I would continually go back to for feedback and suggestions. He taught me how to convey my ideas more clearly in my work and about staging and timing. Glen Keane deserves a lot of credit for my progress as well; it was while training under him that I became a full animator. I loved how he would rough things out with a thick pencil. It was really different from Don Bluth, who wanted us to draw with precision and leave very little room for cleanup.

Bill: What was it like working with Bluth?

Henry: Don was an impressive talent when I first met him, someone with a connection to Disney's past, having worked on *Sleeping Beauty*. And he was the heir-apparent, the guy who was going to lead the new generation at Disney. I never understood why he was working on another film at home, enlisting other Disney talent at night, when it was all going to be his candy store. And I still don't quite understand why he left Disney other than wanting his own name to be featured versus Walt's. Many of my roomies, including Brad Bird, Bill Kroyer, Musker, Jerry Rees, and the super-talented but reluctant Dan Haskett, had serious issues with Don—his directing style, story sense, leadership. I'll admit that when he called us a "Rat's Nest," I did challenge the guy.

"The Rat's Nest" – Henry Selick, Bill Kroyer, Jerry Rees, Brad Bird, and John Musker. ("Rat's Nest" is not a studio term.)

Bill: Was there a specific opportunity that led you away from Disney? Or did you feel it was just time to find something else?

Henry: We came to Disney from CalArts full of excitement and a desire to do great things. But that just wasn't going to happen, even when Don left the studio. The old guard was almost gone and the people now in charge were basically survivors. They might not all be A-list players but it was their studio now. Brad Bird got fired for simply talking like he knew more than one of the directors. Well, he did know more. But they were not going to take that from a twenty-year-old.

In 1981, an opportunity came my way through Jules Engel. A cutout animated feature was being made near San Francisco, with George Lucas as executive producer. It was called *Twice Upon a Time*, had a budget of about two million dollars, and was being directed by John Korty and Chuck Swenson. Compared with Disney at the time, it was a breath of fresh air. There was this Jay Ward kind of humor, with a lot of the dialogue improvised by local comedians. The completed scenes they showed me, featuring the work of Harley Jessup and Carl Willat, were really beautiful. So, I did an animation test for them, passed, and me and my wife Heather, who became a background designer on the film, moved up to the Bay Area. We fell in love with the region and it's been our home base ever since.

Bill: Were you just an animator on *Twice Upon a Time*?

Henry: I started as an animator, then did some background designs, and ended up storyboarding and directing a couple of sequences. My final credit was sequence director.

Bill: Did you do any designs?

Henry: My storyboards were copied pretty exactly, but I was following a style set by John Korty and his art directors. Man, Disney seemed like a country club in comparison to that low-budget show. We were shooting in this converted, three-story house, and if you were on one of the down-shooters pushing cutouts around, you pretty much lived there till your shot was done. It might last two or three days, just bathroom breaks and lots of coffee.

Bill: As a sequence director, were you applying things you learned from Eric Larson, in terms of storyboarding and storytelling? Or did you learn a lot about that during filmmaking?

Henry: I built on what I'd learned from Eric and CalArts and from doing my indie film *Seepage*. When I was being considered for *Twice Upon a Time*, they looked at both my Disney pencil tests and my indie films. It was the indie films that got me the job of sequence director. And I kept on learning during the making of *Twice*.

Bill: Stop motion can be quite different from hand-drawn or CG animation. There isn't the freedom to go back and simply correct scenes. How do you cope with that?

Henry: You have to learn to live with that. Some shots are going to be better than others; all shots are imperfect. You do your best to get good poses and timing in the story reels, shoot a rough rehearsal, and then hope that a great animator performing through one of these puppets in straight-ahead animation delivers something special. We do have the ability to pull frames in post or even create digital inbetweens to slow something down, but it's done very rarely.

Bill: What happened after *Twice Upon a Time*?

Henry: In '83, I got a gig doing storyboards and design for several effects sequences for Walter Murch, the amazing editor and sound designer. He was directing his first feature film, *Return to Oz*, for Disney with producer Gary Kurtz from the first Star Wars features. I got the job through Brad Bird and Jerry Rees, who were trying to get an animated feature, *The Spirit*, based on Will Eisner's comics, going, also with Kurtz. Anyway, I boarded all the Nome King sequences, which were animated in Claymation by Will Vinton's folks in Portland. It was great working with Walter, one of the best editors in the world. He wanted every possible version of a scene.

Bill: Like an editor!

Henry: Yes! He told me it was my job to make perfect "teacups." And it was his job to come in and smash them so that I could make another. I quickly got used to the idea that nothing is precious. And I learned a lot from Walter, still about the smartest guy I know. Afterwards, I worked on a laser disk game for Brad and Jerry as well as some ideas for an anthology show they wanted to do. And I started writing, starting work on a screenplay of my own.

In '86, I was intro'd to director Carroll Ballard (*The Black Stallion*, *Fly Away Home*) via producer Tom Wilhite, former head of production at Disney. Back at Disney, Tom, along with then–head of development Julie Hickson, had given Tim Burton the support to make both *Vincent* and the original *Frankenweenie*. Now, Tom had teamed Carroll with children's author Maurice Sendak to shoot a film of the *Nutcracker Ballet* that Maurice had designed in Seattle. Initially, I was brought in to storyboard the movie but Carroll liked my eye, so he had me shooting some seconds unit as well. I was shooting handheld with this unusual French camera of his, where when you adjusted the eyepiece the entire image would rotate. I remember shooting from the top of a ladder, praying I didn't drop the camera on these poor dancer kids! Additionally, I did some miniatures work. Carroll Ballard is another great filmmaker I learned firsthand from.

Bill: Is there anything specific you learned from Carroll?

Henry: He taught me a huge amount about lighting, about composition, about following and anticipating action with a camera. In my storyboarding work—where I was trying to find shots to capture the dancers at their best—he taught me about focusing on simple patterns of movement and not trying to show everything. Sometimes he'd have me stay up all night reworking a sequence I'd boarded to come up with simpler ways of staging things. The budget of the film was low and Carroll, the guy who wants to shoot a thousand-to-one ratio, was relying on the boards to help narrow his focus.

Bill: But I recall Eric Larson was always staging the shot to convey its emotion. Working as a painter you naturally think about lighting. So you didn't immediately apply that skill while working with Carroll?

Henry: While I'd lit the stop-motion figures in my short film with practical lights, most of the lighting I'd done was created with paint and pencils. Using real lights on real people was very different … Carroll must have thought I was an idiot and I had to learn fast.

Bill: Did you continue working with him, or did you move on to something else?

Henry: Carroll doesn't make a lot of movies. So when *Nutcracker* was finished, I moved on to other things. I worked on a lot of commercials. And I kept writing. My wife, Heather, was more continuously employed than I was.

Bill: Was she at Colossal?

Henry: Yeah, she was at Colossal Pictures in San Francisco, which started out as a very small studio. Then they became the top animation commercial house in the country, maybe the world. They were very innovative and explored a lot of different styles in commercials, special effects, and music videos.

Bill: She eventually became an executive producer, right?

Henry: After it split into two divisions, she ran the animation division. They were doing live action and trying to do a CD magazine at the time. Basically her division paid for everything else.

Bill: Didn't you do Doughboy commercials?

Henry: Yeah, I did. Nine in one season, 1989. I also directed some Ritz Bits stop-motion commercials that played forever on TV.

Bill: Was this your first stop-motion project after working with Caroll Ballard and doing cutout animation on *Twice Upon a Time*?

Henry: Yep. Then, almost simultaneously, I started to do a lot of work for MTV through my own company. I was doing design and direction, boarding things out myself, some of the lighting and animation. There were a lot of young people around who'd come out to work on Art Clokey's new *Gumby* series. I met a lot of great stop-motion animators via that show: Tim Hittle, Trey Thomas, Eric Leighton, Angie Glocka, Owen Klatte. I also started working with Pete Kozachik, who became the Director of Photography on three of the feature films I've directed. From the late eighties to the early nineties there was a burst of stop-motion projects, and the number of people I was working with kept growing and growing. When Tim Burton revived Tim Burton's *The Nightmare Before Christmas*, a lot of them became supervisors. This made the transition from small group to feature movie much easier.

Dollhouse MTV Ident, 1989 © MTV.

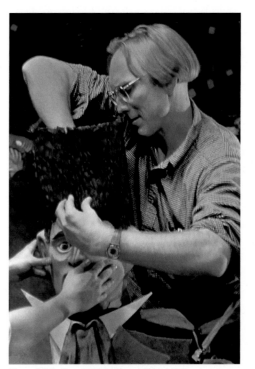

Henry Selick, *Taco M MTV Ident*, 1988 © MTV.

Bill: I visited you during the Doughboy commercials, and you had dozens of Doughboy heads lined up on shelves. I didn't know anything about stop motion; I couldn't imagine you'd use a different head for every frame! How did someone with no experience learn the genre? Who was teaching all these techniques for stop motion?

Henry: You'd study the films and commercials that existed, listen to people like Phil Tippet and Tom St. Amand, who had done stop motion for George Lucas. But there really weren't any teachers at the time.

Bill: What about the head-swapping concept? Was everybody doing that? Or did you just come up with that?

Henry: No, I didn't invent that. George Pal, a director known for his live-action films (the original *Time Machine*), was an animator first (*Jasper*, *Tubby the Tuba*) and is generally given credit for that. Back in the 1940s he came up with the idea of doing full-body replacements for a walk cycle, to give his puppets the same stretch and squash that Disney or Warner's was doing in drawn animation. He was creative director on the Speedy Alka-Seltzer commercials of the 1950s, where each of Speedy's mouth shapes was a new face. When we got the Doughboy spots, we got this kit from the ad agency that was under lock and key. When you opened it, you saw the original Doughboy body with no more than eight separate heads. The body reeked of some toxic substance, not the foam latex we normally used. I'm sure it gave somebody cancer!

Bill: They actually used that model for previous spots?

Henry: Yes, they did. We had to redesign and expand on the Doughboy, however, and completely rebuilt him. I was trying to bring in some stuff I'd learned at Disney, with extendable arms and legs, and we eventually sculpted about twenty-five more expressions. I was always trying to use things I learned at Disney. Funny, I just remembered this art class I used to take in Burbank. It was a night class and a few of us from Disney went there for life drawing. The teacher was this crazy guy …

Bill: The one they called Juicy Harvey?

Henry: His name was Harvey and there was a juice stand in town called *Juicy Harvey's*, so yeah, that was his nickname. He was a good teacher, full of enthusiasm, always saying, "You have to touch the model. Touching, touching, touching, touching, touching." It was a bunch of cool old ladies along with Tim Burton, John Musker, and a few other animators. That's when Tim and I first became friends. He was still going to CalArts. I also became close with Rick Heinrichs at the time, now a famous production designer, who was a CalArts graduate and the first person to take Tim's drawings and sculpt them as 3D beings. Ten years later, Tim had become very successful in live action, and I was doing more and more stop motion up north. That's when he sent Rick up to the Bay Area to ask me if I'd like to direct.

Bill: How did you set it up? Did you simply use your existing crew?

Henry: Yeah, my existing San Francisco crew became the core of the feature crew. As Peter Schneider of Disney explained to me, the film was a low budget gift to Tim from Disney in order to get him back to the studio. They wanted blockbusters, like Tim's *Batman*. So they didn't really care too much about the movie as long as we kept on budget and schedule. With Tim as *Nightmare*'s godfather, there were no studio notes to deal with, no politics; we could put all of our efforts on screen. So, while Tim directed *Batman Returns* and *Ed Wood* in Los Angeles, my crew and I spent three and a half years making *Nightmare* in San Francisco.

Bill: Those were all happening while you're making *Nightmare*?

Henry: Yeah. Tim managed to review all our story reels and animation. I think we only had to reshoot one or two shots in the film.

Bill: What did you get to start the picture? A storyboard? A script?

Henry: There was an original script by Michael McDowell, who had written *Beetlejuice*. And we had Tim's original designs of Jack Skellington, Zero, and Sandy Claws, which Rick had sculpted years earlier. But Tim didn't love Michael's script and so it was rejected. Yet we still had a deadline for delivery!

Bill: Where exactly did you start?

Henry: The one thing about doing musicals (*Nightmare* has ten songs) is that the songs are little stories in and of themselves. And Danny Elfman, meeting with Tim, had come up with two or three songs already. "What's This?" was the first, so we just started boarding it. It was clear Danny, with Tim's input, was going to come up with a song for each big moment in the movie that would pretty much tell the film's story. And we could certainly board those songs and bring them to life in animation. But how to coherently string the songs together? Screenwriter Caroline Thompson was brought in.

Bill: Did she write the story?

Henry: The core of the story was already there, but Caroline did a marvelous job of joining the songs together and expanding the characters. And she was wise enough to keep several of Michael McDowell's original ideas, like when Sally jumps out of a window, breaks apart, and then stitches herself back together.

Bill: When did you get started with the boards?

Henry: Because of our deadline, we jumped right in and started boarding the first few songs, despite there not being an approved script. I had Joe Ranft as head of story and talented board artists like Jorgen Klubien and Mike Cachuela.

camera tilts up

8G

There's color everywhere

8H

whats This?

moving light

9A

There's White Things in The air

9B

Whats This

10A

I cant believe my eyes
I must be dreaming

10B

Wake up Jack
This isnt fair

Storyboards, Joe Ranft,
Tim Burton's *The Nightmare Before Christmas*, 1993 © Touchstone.

Bill: I assume Tim was looking at the reels and giving you notes before you started animating.

Henry: Yeah, luckily he was very positive and had very few notes for us. We had a ton of other work to do at the same time, like making all the puppets, sculpting their different expressions, figuring out at least a couple of sets to build, cast voice actors and record them. And so much designing to do! Art director Dean Taylor and artists Kelly Asbury and Kendall Cronkhite gathered Tim's collection of other characters. We looked at anyone that had influenced him, like Edward Gorey, Charles Adams, and Ronald Searle. New characters often came from the storyboard drawings, like Joe Ranft's sweet little corpse boy and Mike Cachuela's wolfman.

"What's This?," the first song Danny had written, was the first thing we animated. It was set in Christmas Town, so we gave that location a soft, Dr. Seuss feel. And all those shots got finished without a hitch. When we got to the first shot in Halloween Town, however, Tim put on the brakes. It wasn't dark enough. There were too many colors. That's when Rick Heinrichs came in to consult as a production designer. He was brilliant, and we learned a lot from him about textures with a 2D and 3D feel.

And I still remember working on the final battle between Oogie Boogie and Jack. It was just down to me and Mike C. Everyone else had been let go from the story department, and Joe had moved on to *Toy Story*. Tim wouldn't approve anything we drew. But at a certain point I knew we had to go into production or miss our deadline. So I just put the sequence into production.

Bill: Was that the only friction you had with Tim on *Nightmare*?

Henry: I'd come up with a slightly different ending. When I tried to show Tim the story reel, he just put the flatbed machine on high speed. I said, "You don't want to see this?" He got angry and walked out of the room. Then he kicked a hole in the wall. I said, "Tim, you okay?" He pointed to his boots, said, "Yeah, they're steel toes."

Bill: He just didn't like the idea. That's his way of showing you.

Henry: Ninety-nine percent of the time, things were great with Tim and me. There were a few things we'd filmed that he wasn't in love with, like when Santa goes to set things right and gives one of the kids a puppy and takes back Jack's toy from hell. But when he screened it for his friends, they liked it, so it stayed in.

Tim Burton and Henry Selick
Tim Burton's *The Nightmare Before Christmas*, 1993 © Disney.

Bill: When that movie was released, it was a huge success, right?

Henry: *Huge* is a relative term; it came out and made double its cost right away.

Bill: How does that affect your life? What were you doing right after the movie? Were you looking for the next project? Did Tim offer you another job?

Henry: Yeah, my life changed a bit. I met with Steven Spielberg and was offered a live-action film, *Casper the Friendly Ghost*. But when I offered my notes on the script, I was told they weren't interested in my notes, "this is already a green-lit movie." The thing is, I loved stop motion and had already begun thinking of doing *James and the Giant Peach*, one of my and Joe Ranft's favorite Roald Dahl books. We met with Dahl's family, who were in charge of his estate. They came over to visit near the end of *Nightmare Before Christmas* and liked what they saw.

Bill: Did Spielberg's people ever look at your notes?

Henry: Who knows? They might not have been that good. Anyway, there were different opportunities post-*Nightmare* but *James and the Giant Peach* was the choice I made. It was also about keeping the studio we'd set up going.

Bill: Who was financing you?

Henry: Initially it was all Disney, and then the wonderful Jake Ebert came in with co-financing. He'd made remarkable films like *Chariots of Fire*, *Gandhi*, and *Baron Munchausen*.

Bill: Tim was attached to *Peach*?

Henry: Yeah, I asked Tim to produce again along with his business partner, Denise Di Novi. But, because he had no personal interest in *Peach*, he didn't protect the project. There was conflict between Disney live action and Disney animation over the film, and I ended up being stuck with a really angry studio executive who's only about power. He was the kind of guy who throws leftover tuna fish at his assistant. Amazing!

James and the Giant Peach, 1996. © 1996 Disney.

Bill: That says a lot.

Henry: The guy had no respect for our process. Brian Rosen, our line producer, and I'd give him a story reel to review, "We need to hear back on this by this date. After that it starts to cost money." And he always made sure to miss the date, then scream that it couldn't cost any more money.

Bill: And you were essentially in the same facility with the same crew, right?

Henry: Yeah, managed to hold on to most everything and get most everybody back when we finally went into production. Unlike *Nightmare*, where we had to start shooting and figure it out on the way, *James* was developed more tradition-ally, with many writers and many drafts of the script. By the way, Dennis Potter, the brilliant British TV writer, wrote the first draft but the Dahl family rejected it, as it strayed too far from the book. Anyway, we lost a lot of time and money in this process. And our Disney exec, from live action, didn't understand that the shooting script in animation is the story reels. That's where the real writing happens. No matter how good that initial script is, it becomes something else.

Bill: One aspect of directing is studio politics.

Henry: Oh, I'm terrible at it.

Bill: You're an artist. But you have to deal with politics.

Henry: I've watched experts like Tim and my friend David Fincher deal with studio execs. Tim would never answer their questions directly; he'd become a warm, crazy, gesticulating artist and would always make them feel good without ever addressing their concerns. Fincher is more the manipulative, brilliant politician. He knows how to both terrify executives and to match their alarm with the same level so that it cancels out. Me, I'm not good at either approach.

Andrew Birch and Henry Selick, *James and the Giant Peach*, 1996. © Disney.

Bill: When *Peach* was wrapping up, were you offered a multipicture deal?

Henry: [laughs, shaking head] Pixar's *Toy Story* came out between *Nightmare* and *James*, and the world of animation changed forever. Dick Cook (Disney head of production) told me stop motion just wasn't viable anymore. So, no, there was no multipicture deal.

Bill: What did you do?

Henry: I struggled a bit; did a few more commercials. Then a graphic novel, *Dark Town*, showed up, by a Canadian writer, Kaja Blackley. I liked the look and the story, about a puppeteer in a coma whose spirit lives as a puppet with a sidekick in the land between life and death. Eventually I hooked up with this writer, Sam Hamm, who had written *Batman*. He was also a Bay Area guy. We changed the puppeteer into a cartoonist, made his sidekick a cartoon monkey, and renamed the project *Monkeybone*, because *Dark Town* is a racist slang term.

We met with Bay Area–based producer/director Chris Columbus (*Home Alone*, *Harry Potter*), and, with his help, set the project up at 20th Century Fox with Bill Mechanic. The film was intended to be low budget (for a studio picture), with about 75 percent of it done in edgy animation. We were going to do the whole project in the Bay Area, give it an independent feel. But then the live action was moved to Hollywood and things started to transform. I met with Ben Stiller for the lead role, right after *There's Something About Mary*. He wanted to bring in a writer because the script wasn't funny enough. He was right. But my friend, Sam Hamm, was upset because I wasn't supporting him enough. But I can't alienate Ben Stiller either, because if he walks there's no movie. I stupidly chose friendship and we had no movie.

Monkeybone, 2001 © Twentieth Century Fox. All Rights Reserved.

Bill: But you did solve the live-action problem.

Henry: We ended up with Brendan Frasier. He seemed to understand the material and had just been in a great movie, *Gods and Monsters*. Once Brendan was cast, my "indie" movie changed again. They wanted way more live action, less animation. They were paying Brendan his full rate so they wanted him in the whole movie. I couldn't afford to composite him into a lot of animation, so everything that was meant to be miniatures and animation shifted to sets and lots of actors and costumes.

      An animation director is a nobody in live-action Hollywood. They're a tight group and they're going to test you every hour of every day you're shooting. You have to be very macho and ultraconfident in your decisions, many made on the spot, because you'll have to live with them forever. Not like animation, where's there's always more time to think things through. I had a wonderful production designer, Bill Boes, who'd come from animation, and I really liked my DP, Andrew Dunn, and the top camera operator, Mitch Dubin. I mean, if you get through any project and you're still standing, you'll have made some friends.

      Live action finally wrapped and I headed back to the Bay Area to shoot the animation. The Monkeybone character was probably the most complex and interactive stop-motion that had ever been done. Pete Kozachik, the animation DP, was instrumental in figuring out how to make it all work. We built a waist-up blue robot version of Brendan Fraser and matched its moves with the real Brendan's moves so our puppets had something real to interact with. It was fun. I was back in my world. Unfortunately, our champion at Fox, Bill Mechanic, was forced out by Rupert Murdock. The film was recut to pieces, and then it was dumped with no advertising. We got stellar reviews in the *New York Times*, the *LA Times*, and *Entertainment Weekly*, but, with no advertising, *Monkeybone* did terribly at the box office. It's not a great movie, but the stop-motion animation on that film might be the best or among the best that's ever been done.

Bill: Who did the actual animation?

Henry: Folks I'd always worked with: animators included Paul Berry, red-haired genius from England, Trey Thomas, Anthony Scott, Tim Hittle, and a few others. Puppet fabrication by Bonita DeCarlo and puppet sculpt by Damon Bard.

Bill: What happened after *Monkeybone*?

Henry: Well, it'd been an interesting ride so far. Now, it was like I'd gone off a cliff. I was in "director's jail." When your film bombs, you go to an imaginary jail—unless you're Andrew Stanton after *John Carter*—and sometimes you never get out. The best thing that happened near the end of *Monkeybone* was that I met author Neil Gaiman. I knew the *Sandman* comic books he'd written. Neil sent me the pages of his novella, *Coraline*. It wasn't even finished. It was something he had been working on as a side project for years. And he thought it might work as a stop-motion film. I read the pages the day I got them and knew he was right. It was a fantastic story about a girl who discovers another version of her own life where copies of her real mother and father existed, only with buttons for eyes. I took it to Bill Mechanic, who'd set up his own production company after his troubles at Fox over *Fight Club*. I convinced both Bill and Neil to let me write the script. In the end, it took five years to get a studio to back the project.

The Life Aquatic with Steve Zissou, 2004. © 2004 Touchstone Pictures.

Bill: Five years? During that time, were you just writing?

Henry: No, no, no. I probably spent a solid year writing several drafts, but no one would back the movie even if it was done in live action. Then Wes Anderson called and wanted me to do stop-motion sea creatures for his feature *The Life Aquatic with Steve Zissou*. That was a very good gig; in many ways it kept me going. I also got to spend time with Wes and see how he worked. He's got one of the best eyes in the business and I actually learned a lot from him.

Aside from *Life Aquatic,* it was the toughest period of my professional life. I had a great project in *Coraline* but I was coming off of a failed film. I still wanted to do stop-motion features but nobody believed in that anymore. Then there was the tone of *Coraline*—everyone thought it was too scary for kids, yet not scary enough for adults. It took Bill Mechanic announcing we were developing the movie to get a publisher to publish the book.

Bill: I always pointed out the animation in *Life Aquatic.*

Henry: Thanks, I'm proud of that work. One of the great moments of my life was when Ray Harryhausen came to visit our stage. We had just completed the jaguar shark, a huge puppet, seven feet long, that required mechanical model movers for its core swimming motion. The rest of its movements were all hand animated. Ray actually started to cry, he was so happy to see a stop-motion creature being used in live action.

Bill: Were you using motion-control cameras for that as well?

Henry: Oh yeah. We were using basic motion-control equipment as far back as the Pillsbury Doughboy days. Then on *Nightmare*, we went wild. Our DP, Pete Kozachik, with his ILM background, designed several boom cameras. He knew how to build stuff that was cheap and repeatable. On *Life Aquatic*, our DP was Pat Sweeny, and we actually shot everything at the old, predigital ILM. Martin Meunier built all the puppets, and Justin Kohn and Tim Hittle were the main animators. There was even a creature that could turn itself inside out, but that didn't make it into the film.

Bill: During this time were you writing, boarding, and designing *Coraline* all by yourself?

Henry: Yeah. There was no money for anything else. For the first two years I had to pretend it wasn't animation, because Bill had a deal that Disney would distribute his films as long as he didn't make any animated movies. I did meet with Michelle Pfeiffer, potentially the lead actress. But she said, "I don't know about those buttons." And I did meet Dakota Fanning, who was only nine. She was too young at the time, but a connection was made. When things finally got going, she was basically the right age and the right voice.

Bill: How'd this come about then? Suddenly it's on the market?

Henry: My rep, Ellen Goldsmith-Vein, came to me when my career was in the worst place possible. She said, "Henry, I love your work. I think I can make things happen and I'll stick with you." She told me that Phil Knight had been supporting the Vinton Company over the last few years and that he had basically taken over. They wanted to do a CG short film called *Moongirl* and they needed a director. They had a basic premise about a girl who controls the moon. So I grew their premise into a story, pitched it to them, and was invited to direct the short. I said I'd only come up if I could develop a feature: *Coraline*. They agreed, though they weren't actually serious at the time. Regardless, I said yes and commuted for a while from the Bay Area. Eventually my family moved with me to Oregon. The CG on *Moongirl* wasn't easy. While there'd been some CG on *James*, I had a learning curve and the crew I was working with was pretty inexperienced.

Bill: How did you manage?

Henry: We muddled along and the short turned out okay. And in the meantime, I kept pushing *Coraline*. I was also curious as to why Phil Knight was interested in animation. Turned out his son, Travis, is a world-class animator, both CG and stop motion, and the formerly known as Vinton Studio was going to be *his* studio. I basically got Travis' support on *Coraline* and things started coming together. Even then, it was still tough. Laika, as the company was renamed, was developing a more traditional CG feature, *Jack and Ben*, and that was consuming everyone's attention. Finally, Phil told me, "If you can find a distributor for *Coraline,* we'll make the movie." So I went out and found a distributor.

Bill: Just like that? You went out and found a distributor.

Henry: Yes. Although I don't think he expected that I would. *Coraline* was seen as the dark, weird project at Laika, whereas *Jack and Ben* was going to be their sunny Dreamworks-type film.

Bill: How did you find a distributor?

Henry: I was relentless, and I had some luck. I just happened to meet this mid-level exec, Michael Zoumas, on his last day of working for the Weinsteins. He loved *Coraline* and introduced me to Andrew Rona, an exec at Focus Features. Andrew took the project to the top, to James Schamus, and we had our distributor. Phil kept his word and we started the film. The irony is that *Coraline,* Laika's dark-horse project, was the film that got made, whereas the way-more-commercial *Jack and Ben* got shelved.

Coraline, 2009 © Laika.

Bill: *Coraline* was one of the most deluxe stop-motion setups ever. As the underdog film at the studio, how did you manage to create your dream set? Why did they even let you?

Henry: So there had been talk about whether we should use CG, stop motion, or both on *Coraline*. Ultimately, Travis Knight said he wanted to be an animator on this, and he liked stop motion better.

Bill: That's like Spielberg's son saying, "I don't like that movie." So the movie dies.

Henry: Just the CG version died. Since it was going to be stop motion, we needed space for all those sets. We found a huge, industrial building out in Hillsboro, fifteen miles from Portland. Thing is, you don't really *want* a place that's too big because your production will grow to fill it, and it'll cost more. On the one hand, Laika was inexperienced at making movies and we had a lot of growing pains. We worked our butts off but I couldn't say the studio was a well-oiled machine.

On the other hand, I got incredible artistic support from that company. At various times, Focus and Bill Mechanic would freak out about things in the movie. You know how it is. When the latest Harry Potter came out, they'd say, "You have to make it scarier, like that new Harry Potter film." But then a Pixar film would come out and now it was, "*Coraline*'s way too scary. What are you doing?" But Laika never wavered—as long as the ratings board gave us a PG, they were cool with what I was making. Crew-wise, I had an exceptional group of leaders to carry along the inexperienced first-timers. People like lead animators Eric Leighton, Trey Thomas, Brad Schiff, Phil Dale, and Travis; Georgina Haynes and Martin Meunier in puppet fab; Mike Cachuela and Chris Butler in story; Pete Kozachik and company in lighting and camera; Bo Henry and Tom Proust in sets; and on and on.

Bill: I suppose your process at this point amounted to everything you'd ever learned.

Henry: Exactly! And there was also new technology at our fingertips. Martin Meunier and I had seen one of the world's first 3D printers (rapid prototype machines) at Steve Perlman's company in San Francisco. We realized we could use it to print some of the replacement faces for our characters; we didn't have to hand sculpt every single one. So we started sculpting keys and scanning them into the computer.

Bill: Did you inbetween it as well?

Henry: Yeah, we did. Then we'd print them out, paint them, and put them in facial kits. We decided to split the faces horizontally to have separate replacement brows and mouth shapes, giving us thousands of facial expression possibilities. I'd wanted to leave the seam line in the final movie, but it made Phil Knight nervous so we painted it out in post. And we were the first stop-motion feature shot stereoscopically, something I'd wanted to do for years. For what it's worth, *Coraline* actually beat out *Avatar* for best 3D movie of 2009 according to the 3D Film Society.

          Pete Kozachik designed new motion-controlled camera rigs that could do anything. Then, after a falling out with the production designer, I grabbed some set builders and quickly deputized them as art directors. I ended up supervising them, too. It was wild. It was bigger than *Nightmare*. There were a lot more shots, more complexities, and more subtleties in it than we'd ever done before.

Bill: So this was purely a Henry Selick film?

Henry: Yeah, and it's gratifying that people came to see it.

Bill: Working digitally, how did *Coraline* change your process?

Henry: To explain that, let's go back to *Nightmare*. Back then, we were shooting on film and we tried to do everything we could in camera. For example, to put Jack Skellington's ghost dog, Zero, in a shot with Jack, we used a beam splitter—a half-silvered mirror—in front of the lens like in the old *Topper* movies. You'd shoot Jack *through* the semi-transparent mirror while its reflective surface is picking up Zero, who's being animated off to one side. The digital breakthrough on *Nightmare* was simple but significant: we now had video tapes on those old Mitchell 35s and could capture two whole frames of imagery! So if a puppet broke its ankle and fell over in the middle of the shot, you could fix the puppet, line it up with the captured image and not have to start the shot over again. Additionally, the falling snow at the end of the film was CG. On *James and the Giant Peach*, we started using digital cleanup in a big way, and went from hanging an airborne character on boingy spider wire, to attaching them to a precise, controllable rig. Shoot a clean plate and paint out the rig in post. And we created an entire CG ocean for *James*, as well as a giant mechanical shark that attacks the characters on the floating peach. By the time I got to make *Coraline*, my first stop-motion feature in years, it would have been easy to throw all sorts of CG and digital work in the mix. But I asked myself, "Why do stop motion at all, if it's going to buried in CG?" and decided to try and create as much of the imagery as possible with hand animation. That includes a lot of the effects like the other world tearing apart and atmosphere like wind and rain and fog and leaves and stars and fire. Because stop motion's greatest strength is that it's a world of real objects, captured with real light.

Bill: Did you manipulate the character performance in post?

Henry: There was one shot where we experimented with software that could create digital inbetweens. But it killed the look and feeling of stop motion. So, aside from pulling some frames here and there to adjust timing, we did zero manipulation in post. I'd say 98 percent of what you see on screen is the original performance we shot.

Bill: When you developed your characters, were you consolidating the concept first and then casting the voices?

Henry: Well, I lived with the project a long time before it got made. I had been rewriting it and doing sketches and kept a scrapbook with image ideas. There was a newspaper photo I found—an old lady, a former child star I'd never heard of, had just died. And there she was in her heyday, back in the 1920s, holding a little doll that was an exact copy of her. Early merchandise, I guess. That gave me the idea for the Coraline doll the Other Mother makes in the film. Yeah, I went pretty deep during this time, thinking about the characters: who they were, how they would move, how they would sound. I knew we had Dakota Fanning as our lead and her voice was always in my head. Then when we got closer to making the film, I cast the other voices around her.

The Mother—Real Mom and Fun Other Mother and Wicked Other Mother—was the next most important character, and I probably considered eighty or a hundred actresses. I didn't go to them, of course. I just took clips from movies and cut their voices against Dakota's. I ended up with about three finalists, all strong actors with great voices that worked well against Dakota. Terry Hatcher worked best and wanted to do the part. It's funny, Terry didn't resemble the character design when we hired her, but her performance and presence so influenced the animators that the final Mothers and Terry became one and the same.

Bill: In animation you have multiple animators creating one performance with the character. In stop motion, when it comes to creating the character through poses, is it harder to keep the consistency of the character's performance?

Henry: It's not so different than drawn or CG animation; the director works with a supervising animator, building a vocabulary of poses and the all-important walk that help define a character. I try to be specific if I've something in mind. For example, I wanted the Other Father to be fun and silly but move really well. So I told them "He moves just like Danny Kaye." The voice actors really influence this defining stage as well. For the same character, I told John Hodgman to channel Dean Martin. He ended up channeling Bing Crosby, but it was perfect.

Anyway, then the lead animators come on and you try to cast them on what they want to do and what you think they're good at (not always the same thing). You've given them a foundation and they add to that, so that when the full crew comes on there's a lot of material for them to refer to.

Now, I really like the great shapes you get with facial replacements. But an added benefit—which goes a long ways toward keeping consistency between animators—is that

Coraline, 2009 © Laika.

they're all working from the exact same library of faces. It's harder when the character has a mechanical face and every expression has to be hand animated.

Bill: Do stop-motion animators thumbnail all those poses, or do they …

Henry: They're all different. For example, I really discourage shooting live-action reference and then slavishly copying it. Might be because I hated having to use rotoscope on that Christmas special, *Small One*, back at Disney. But on *Coraline*, there was one animator, Ian Whitlock, who was unbelievably good at acting out his scenes. He *became* Coraline. So he'd record himself and match that in his animation and it worked out wonderfully. Other folks would do thumbnails right on their exposure sheets. We always met one on one when a shot was assigned. There'd be puppets to pose. I could do a sketch or act it out, whatever it took, you know? Then all the animators would shoot a rehearsal before going for the take. Some rehearsals were nearly perfect; others were miles away from where they needed to be. But then we'd make adjustments, notes would be taken, and the final take almost always worked out.

Bill: That's quite different from your Disney days.

Henry: Yep, way different.

Bill: The fact that it's manipulated models, real lighting, and real materials gives it a unique kind of energy on the screen. It obviously doesn't have the freedom of a hand drawing. You don't have that ability, as in CG, where you can go back in and find exactly what you want. What is it about the stop-motion medium that appeals to you?

Henry: Two main things. It's all real stuff: the puppets, the lights, the sets and props. There is nothing cooler than moving from one small stage to another, each containing a miniature world where a moment of the film is being created. The second, and equal, thing I like is the direct connection between animator and final on-screen performance. I sense their hands in the shot. I sense them coaxing, struggling, wrestling, as if they're invisible puppeteers. And I love that.

Bill: Is it also about the commitment involved? It's like jumping off a cliff. You summon up the requisite energy and just go with what happens.

Henry: I liken it to crossing a chasm on a tightrope. There's only one way to get to the other side—that's keep moving straight ahead. And we try to do it with style and in character.

Bill: Obviously you have digital options now. You can pretty much fix any kind of scene. But in the beginning, when you're planning something out, how detailed is your vision? You have these surreal sequences of things flying through the air, or a spider falling into its web. They defy gravity and space, and it was all done on a traditional set. Do you know every detail beforehand, or do you just figure it out as you go?

Henry: When I'm writing, I'm not only envisioning how something might look in the movie but even how we'll build it. And, because it took years for *Coraline* to get green-lit, my vision of the film was pretty evolved. Of course, when it comes time to turn your vision into a movie, there are a lot of changes and some things are more challenging than others. That spider web under the Other Mother's floor was monumental. I knew what I wanted, but it took Tom Proust, one of the art directors, to figure out where to get a solid plate of steel cut into an animatable spiral using ultra–high-pressure water. Then they had to rig it sixteen feet up in the air to give it enough travel room.

Bill: You are definitely the most complex hybrid of filmmaking styles. You have all the complexities of live action and animation.

Henry: Here's the deal with me and CG. I'm just not a person who wants to be in the dark. If you make a stop-motion film, you'd understand clearly. You're seeing the shots as you go. You're working with the sum of the parts right away. It's not wire frames, then more steps, and then it all comes together in the end. As in live action, you're seeing the world. I find that more gratifying.

Bill: What do you think will be the next advancement in stop motion?

Henry: There's an animator I've worked with, the talented Phil Beglan, who's come up with a great new way to do facial animation. I'd like to use that. And then there's always the specific challenges of a given film—that's often where innovations come from.

Bill: Do you think you could do a small film in stop motion and achieve the same success as a large feature like *Coraline*?

Henry: Yes, I do. We'd have to get more intimate. And our subject matter will need to be more powerful. Let's not remake the *Hurt Locker*, but, please, something with more weight than is usually allowed in animated features. Of course, there's always the *South Park* route, where super cheap, cute animation is combined with R-rated words and actions. It helps that the writing is brilliant on that show.

Bill: Is there something specific you look for in a story?

Henry: Having great characters, at least one, matters the most. And I suppose there's a fantasy element in everything I do. But I can imagine almost any story as an animated film. Honestly, before we made *Coraline*, most people could only imagine the book as live action. As I was writing the screenplay, it was so easy to see it as a stop-motion film.

One of the new projects I'm developing is an original story of mine about brothers; tonally, you could say it's "from the director of *Coraline*." There's another project based on a book, an epic journey over many years where one character remains constant while the world around him changes. That would be unique, something I have never seen in an animated film.

Bill: You seem to like the limitations inherent to stop motion. It must be a challenge for you.

Henry: I just don't see stop motion as being limited; there are always solutions to every problem we encounter.

Bill: You mentioned earlier that you were a musician in college. Has that experience helped in terms of selecting music and working with musicians?

Henry: Sure. During *Nightmare Before Christmas*, I wanted Danny Elfman to rework a section of the song, *Making Christmas*. He balked. So I wrote some material, recorded it on a keyboard, and cut it into his music. Upon hearing it, Danny said he, of course, could do better. And then he did. On *Coraline*, composer Bruno Coulais was a great collaborator with an easy give and take and lots of discussion. He even liked the song I wrote for the film *Sirens of the Sea* and did a nice orchestration of it.

Bill: People often generalize or even stereotype artists in our business. They say that people who animate in 2D and pencil are crazier because they have to generate so much. On the other hand, people who animate in 3D tend to be a little more reserved because they're more computer oriented. Is there some generalization about the kind of people who go into stop motion?

Henry: Stop-motion animators are more physical than the others. Remember, they're on their feet for days on end, wrestling a performance from a puppet with stiff metal joints. So they'd win in a bar fight. But they also have tender hearts and will give so much of themselves to will their puppet children to life. We're the kids who had the GI Joe clay and would spend hours sculpting and re-sculpting, pretending to bring it to life. That's something I should have mentioned when I talked about why stop motion appeals to me. There's this subconscious element that goes back to childhood. It's that moment when you had that special toy. Whether you could move it or not didn't make a difference. You *imagined* it moving. You gave it life. You connected with it.

Bill: I think that's a perfect place to stop. Thanks Henry. We truly appreciate this.

Henry: As I said in the beginning, I can waste a lot time talking about this stuff.

3
Don Bluth Interview

Don Bluth.

With some filmmakers, everything you need to know ab
is on the screen. That's not the case with Don Bluth. His s
just the films he made, but how he got them made and
feat reveals about him.

While animators may be reclusive, directors must be e
Don could be described as "entrancing." From the very
he had a vocal eloquence and depth of commitment tha
pronouncements on the art and industry of animation
messages from a higher source. Don had a chance to wor
old masters at Disney and had the highest respect for th
With that experience and his matchless work ethic, it is r
that many of the new generation of animators saw hi
mentor—and leader.

When Don left The Walt Disney Studios to start his owr
he did so for a simple reason: he wanted to make a kind o

film that he believed was disappearing from the industry. He succeeded in making not one but ten feature films, a record unmatched by any of his contemporaries.

If there was ever a director who epitomized the glamour gulf between directing live action and animation, it is Don. Although he can work with the biggest stars, he spends more time "on the board" sitting at his animation desk than any director of his era. He really prefers the craft of shaping the movie under his pencil to roaming the departments.

Someone once said that the definition of an artist is one who cannot stop doing what he loves. Don Bluth loves to draw animated movies.

We interviewed Don by Skype from his home in Arizona.

Bill Kroyer

Bill: This book is about animation directors because I don't think people understand what an animation director does. We want to know how you came to be a director and what you eventually brought to this role. That's the essence of the book.

Don: Okay. Ask away.

Bill: When were you first aware of animation? When did you realize that you loved it?

Don: My first experience with animation was of course at a very young age. I think I was four years old when I first saw *Snow White*. So this was way back in the forties. It was frightening and at the same time absolutely gorgeous. I loved the story, the colors, the caricatured dwarves, and even the scary wicked witch. I wanted to see the picture again even after I left the theater. Those images stayed with me, and I remember wondering if I could reproduce the same thing myself at home. I began to draw the characters from memory and collected artwork from the movie. I also quickly learned the name Walt Disney. Anytime a movie came to town that said Walt Disney, I knew immediately that there was something there for me. After *Snow White* came *Pinocchio*, *Bambi*, and *Fantasia*. I became infatuated with this world of animation. I wanted to be part of making it, even as a child. But I knew my drawings didn't look as good as those on screen. I needed to improve. So from that moment up until high school I practiced over and over again. The funny thing is, I learned that you often come to hate a drawing that pleased you so much the previous day. Something happens inside your brain. Your understanding of the process increases. You go back and look at this drawing that was done twenty-four hours ago and say, "Ugh, that doesn't look good." Many artists go through the same thing. No matter how good I thought I was, there was always a way to get better. And that pushed me. I kept pushing to get to that next level.

Bill: You put that great drawing on the fridge at the end of day. The next morning you think, "Oh, my God."

Don: Exactly! Now, animation became an interesting thing because I didn't know how exactly they did it. But around my junior year of high school I met Judge Whitaker in Utah. He was teaching at the University (BYU) and had worked on many Disney films. That was the first time I had met someone from Disney. I learned by just watching him work. He would draw a little bit and then start flipping the paper and animating. At the moment it all came together. I remember thinking, "*Wow*! That's how they do it."

Bill: You never saw anybody flip or even a set of pegs before that?

Don: Nope. They weren't doing many documentaries at Disney at the time. I just saw the pictures. But at that point I knew what I had to do. So I went to various libraries and started collecting books that covered the principles of animation. Growing up on a farm, I think, limited my exposure in the beginning. I just didn't have access to information. Anyway, when I learned that The Walt Disney Studios was in Burbank, I coaxed my parents into sending me to visit my aunt, who just happened to live there. I then pushed her into getting me a tour of the studio. And I naively thought I would meet Walt Disney. As it turned out, my aunt actually knew people that worked at The Walt Disney Studios. She indeed arranged a tour. We had an appointment. I was so excited that I could hardly sleep. But my aunt wasn't good with directions or driving. We got lost. We never found the studio. She lived in Santa Monica and was just horrible with directions. But we did call again and arrange another appointment. This time we got a map and I made sure that we didn't get lost.

It was amazing. They gave me the royal treatment. There was a fellow named Bob Gibeaut (who eventually became VP of operations at the studio) and he personally took me around. I of course kept looking for "the man," but he was nowhere in sight. At the end of the tour, much to my surprise, Bob said, "I'm going to give you some things to take home." They had just finished production on *Peter Pan* and he got a whole stack of cels and put them in my hand. He said, "There you go. Now go back and dream on that." It was such an amazing experience. I couldn't sleep for several nights because it was just so thrilling. After that I only had one goal. I wanted to work there. Eventually my parents decided to sell our farm in

Utah and move to California. But when I graduated from Santa Monica High School in 1955, my parents insisted that I go to college. They sent me back to Utah, to BYU. But after one year I could hardly stand it. Finally I said, "You're wasting your money. I'm not studying and I can't think of anything else. Please, at least let me apply at Disney." This was early summer of 1956. So I called them and they told me to bring in a portfolio. Now, quite ignorantly, I actually asked what they meant by portfolio! They actually had to explain it to me, that I had to bring in a collection of my best artwork. Of course, if I had to ask, I didn't have one. I stayed up most of that night drawing as much as I could.

Bill: You had never attended any art classes?

Don: No. I had never taken any art classes. Even after that I never enrolled in any. I was completely self-taught. So I went out there the next day and …

Bill: Wait. Did you have any idea of what kinds of drawings they wanted to see?

Don: No one gave me any specific instructions. They simply said, "Just bring some of your best drawings." And I did. I remember going out there (to Disney Studios) and sitting in this room with my impromptu portfolio. Unfortunately I can't remember whom I met with that day. Actually, I think it may have been Andy Engman, the animation production manager at that time. He looked at the drawings and there was a lot of, "hmm, hmmmmm," sounds like that. He then left the room with my portfolio. Pretty soon he came back and said "I'm going to show somebody else and I'll be back." Twenty minutes went by and he came back in and said, "Okay, you're hired."

Bill: That was it?

Don: That was it. All I could say was, "When do I start?" On June 19th, 1956, I started working at Disney Studio. They put me in a room with about six other people. They called it the "bullpen." We were inbetweeners.

Ron Diamond: Did you even talk about salary or the terms of your contract?

Don: My gross salary was fifty dollars a week. My take home was thirty-six. That was the starting rate in 1956. At first they gathered clean-up drawings from *Alice in Wonderland*, *Peter Pan*, and several other pictures and told me to inbetween them. Now there was a wonderful guy at Disney Studio at the time named Johnny Bond. He had been at the studio for years. Johnny had the reputation of being able to do the most Donald Duck inbetweens, something like 60 per day. He was the champion. That was the badge he wore on his chest. And he always had a cigar, which he puffed generously in every direction. He was an institution. And he never called you by your name. He gave you a nickname that made you feel like you were part of the gang. I think I was called "Bluther." Anyway, he would come in and tell you what you were doing wrong. After three weeks of working in the bullpen and interacting with Johnny, John Lounsbery then asked if I would work with him. At the time I still lived in Santa Monica and had to carpool to work. Glen Schmidt kindly picked me up every day and drove me to the studio. He was Lounsbery's assistant animator.

Bill: Had you met any other animators? Did you interact with Frank, Ollie, or Eric?

Don: They were in D-Wing on the first floor of the animation building along with Marc Davis and Milt Kahl, and no one ever went to the D-Wing. That was the holy of holies. It was forbidden. But John came to the bullpen and said, "I want you to be my inbetweener." Now, as I said, his current assistant was Glen Schmidt. Within six months, Glen was moved out of the room adjacent to John's and I was moved in. And, that was a problem.

Bill: Carpooling, right?

Don: The carpooling stopped. I was only eighteen and a bit naive. I didn't even realize that I had offended him. About nine months later he came into my room and said, "Don, I've hated you for so long. But I have found the strength to forgive you." I didn't even know there was a problem. So I said, "Forgive me for what?" That's when he explained how he had helped me in the beginning and how I essentially took his job. At that point, I realized that I'd hurt him. I apologized. But my experience with John Lounsbery was great. He was a very emotional actor/animator and very much a great teacher. People at the studio often said, "You have no idea what a blessing it is to work with John Lounsbery." It was true. He was a very supportive teacher. John would push you to do things you thought your skills were incapable of. He wouldn't just give you the answers. Then he would come back into the room, look at your work, and say, "See. You can do it." Instilling that kind of confidence in a young artist was an extremely generous act. I worked hard for him. I remember working on *Sleeping Beauty* and learning the difference between an inbetweener and an animator's assistant. The animator gave you extremes that are very far apart. You have to figure out how to bring that action together. John would put the most amazing timing charts on his drawings. His work was so beautiful. It was never complicated. His lines were natural and free. Drawings that were lightly sketched and on model. You could easily see the figures on the paper. And they were filled with a certain emotion that made them wonderful to look at. You could understand what the character was thinking. It's a shame that so many young people today do not have the chance to see that kind of vision, a drawing on a piece of paper that inspires you. Today, the CG approach is something that reminds me of puppetry more than traditional, hand-drawn animation.

They animate a prebuilt model on a computer. They don't have the thrill of feeling that energy and creativity that emerges in your mind and spirit, which is then expressed with pencil and paper. That is what I learned from John Lounsbery. He was amazing.

Bill: How did your first year go?

Don: In 1956, we were making *Sleeping Beauty*. Walt himself was off building and fretting over Disneyland in Anaheim. It had only been open for a year, and they were fixing a lot of problems at the park. Back then the thought of replacing the nine old men was unheard of. The studio had several good animators. I think the crew was about 600 strong, including all of the animation staff, and we were still in the thrill of just creating animated motion pictures. No one was thinking of replacing them with new people. When we were making *Sleeping Beauty*, we thought we were making the greatest animated movie ever. Everything was going to be perfect: the images, the design, the acting. But the cleanup crew could only accomplish *perfect* cleanup inbetweens of Princess Aurora at an average rate of one drawing per day. So they instituted something called "the drawing count." Basically, they said, "You have to do eight girls a day or we will never get through this picture." By the time we finished making this magnificent masterpiece called *Sleeping Beauty*, the studio had spent in excess of nine million dollars. In those days nine million was a huge sum, let alone the fact that this was an animated feature. The whole process was big. Even the paper on your desk was very wide paper, to accommodate the widescreen Technirama format. And, just flipping this paper to do your drawings became very laborious. It was like flipping pan paper, two and a half fields wide. They assigned a person who came around every day and asked how many birds or squirrels you drew that day. Regardless, I was still in love with everything about the studio. Finally, the feeling that I had when I was four was coming to life. It was real. I was eighteen and in the throes of the animation business. I even began to look around at other animation studios and became very critical of their work. I was bewitched by the beautiful art we were creating at Disney. I wanted to create that feeling of being pulled into a beautiful world. Animation, for me, was like graphic music. It has a rhythm that exists in its line, its timing, colors, and emotions. Walt and his studio understood this.

Now, the downside of this story is that after just one year of this excitement, my church sent me on a mission. I'm a member of the LDS Church and was called to go to Argentina, which means that I would have to learn Spanish and move there. I had never been out of the United States. I didn't know anything about Argentina. When I looked in the encyclopedia I only saw pictures of the naked indigenous people. None of this fit in with my plans. I was really upset. Finally I went to John and said, "I'm leaving the studio because I'm going on a mission to Argentina." John was a very sweet man and would never criticize you with harsh words. Years later I remember him saying, "It was so hard for me not to slap you on the side of the head. I wanted to say that you had the whole thing in your hands. There were people who had been working at the studio for twenty years and had never been promoted. You were only there for a few months and were promoted to assistant animator. Did you know how many people didn't like you because of that? You have to be careful in life. If you go out there and you are really good, that goodness often upsets people." I remember those words because they accurately summed up my whole career. When you try to be the best, jealousy comes into the picture. People get angry with you for doing just that. I think I'm guilty of not reaching out more in the early stages of my career. I didn't help others very much. I'm trying to do that now. But at the time I was too young and too preoccupied about achieving my dream to realize that I was being selfish. Anyway, I went on the mission. I didn't draw for two and half years.

Bill: You didn't draw at all?

Don: Not really. I tried once in a while, but my brain was focused elsewhere. When I came home I decided to go back to BYU for some reason and finish my degree. I didn't even major in art. I majored in English literature.

Ron: Were you drawing at all?

Don: I started drawing again.

Bill: At BYU? And why didn't you study art?

Don: I was at BYU. And I didn't think I was going learn that much. At that point in my life, I knew a lot about music and art. I wanted to study something I knew nothing about. I say this with shame, but at that time I hadn't even read one book cover to cover. I was a farm boy. Literature was an area in which I was truly deficient. And I had a lot of catching up to do. I suddenly found myself in classes surrounded by very intelligent women who seemed to have read everything. So I read and read. In hindsight, this was one of the better decisions I'd ever made. Between my exposure to another country and culture and then studying world literature, I had finally received an education. This experience had an effect on my art. I was ready to draw something that made sense. It wasn't about duplicating other people's drawings anymore. College was great. But in the end, I needed a job. And drawing was the only thing I truly knew how to do.

Bill: Did you immediately think about Disney?

Don: That's a really good question. No, I didn't want to go immediately back to Disney. I don't think I've ever told anyone this before, but I had nightmares while working there. I kept dreaming of being trapped there. Maybe it was because of the way they administrated the artists; I don't know. I was actually somewhat afraid to go back. Instead, my brother Toby and I started a live theater in Santa Monica. We converted an old unoccupied Safeway grocery store into a theater. We produced classic musicals. Our mother made all of the costumes, hundreds of them. I would produce, design, and paint the sets, hunt down props, and play the piano. Toby would direct. We did this for about three and half years.

John and Flo Lounsbery attended a lot of the shows. During these years I met John's daughter, Andy. We started dating. Toby and I cast her as Liesl in *The Sound of Music*. At one point, she wanted to get married. I didn't. We broke up. In the end, the theater's cost outweighed its income and we shut it down. Toby went off to direct live theater with professionals at the Melodyland Theaters. Andy Lounsbery married someone else. It was at that time I decided that I would go back to animation. However, because of the Andy situation, I was too embarrassed to call John for a recommendation to get back into Disney. So, in 1968 I went to work at Filmation Studios.

Bill: Did you apply? Or did you just walk in with a portfolio?

Don: I just walked in with a portfolio. They hired me on the spot and gave me a great salary. In fact, from the start my boss kept giving me raises. Within a year I was making five hundred per week.

Bill: What were you animating? Or were you directing?

Don: At this point I was doing "layout," which, as you know, means you put in key poses of the characters and essentially design the layout. I became so efficient at it that they assigned me to work on their TV specials. My boss, Don Christensen, was giving me raises about every two to three months. He used to come in and stand over my shoulder, smoking. Now, I really don't like the smell of cigarette smoke, and he knew it. But he would come in and blow smoke over my shoulder at my drawings anyway. Clearly he did this on purpose. He would give me the raises but I didn't even know where I stood on the scale between good and not so good, or too good. I thought this might be a case of being good to the point where even Don Christensen didn't like it. He came into my office one day and said, "I cannot give you any more money. You're earning as much money as I do and I will not raise your salary beyond mine." I put my pencil down and replied, "Don, I'm not asking you to do that. I've never asked for a raise. And I don't know why I keep getting them. I don't need the money." He stormed out of the room and said, "Well, just remember … no more raises!" I stuck around for about two more years. Then I began to truly assess what we were doing. We were making commercials and TV stuff, but it just wasn't beautiful. It wasn't satisfying for me as an artist. That's when I thought about giving Disney another shot. So I finally called John Lounsbery and told him that I'd really like to come back. At first, there was this long silence. But then he invited me over for a test. They gave me paper, a room, an animation desk, and told me to animate. At the time, I equated it to like trying to spin straw into gold, with no input from anyone, just make up something. I was there for about two weeks doing these personal animation screen tests. Then one day someone came in, took all my pencil tests, and disappeared for a few hours. Finally he came back in and said, "Okay, you're going to animate. You're going on to animate on *Robin Hood*."

Bill: To be clear, when you were at Filmation you weren't really animating, right? You were just doing layout. Then, without having animated in years, you walked into Disney and you did full animation?

Don: Right. Honestly, I'm always a little bit behind the wagon for some reason. I didn't realize how remarkable it was to have been advanced so quickly. Usually you have to pay some dues, earn your way up, and maybe I was. But all of these doors seem to have just opened. And, I had gone through some unique experiences, which helped me, and by this time I was 33 years old. It's been a very pleasant journey for me. And, no, I had never really animated before this opportunity. My only experience on the board was when I was working on *Sleeping Beauty* as an assistant. I did observe what was going on around me. I learned from watching. And you're right. I wasn't animating at Filmation. My animation experience really amounted to those two weeks of tests. And, to my amazement, they gave me an office in the hallowed D-Wing between veteran key cleanup assistants Dale Oliver and Bud Hester, two doors away from Frank and Ollie, and down the hall from Milt Kahl. When they started to assign me scenes, I closed my door and secluded myself in my office. I would put my pencil down, close my eyes, and visualize what I was trying to put on the paper. That visualization was the guide that took me by the hand and told me what to draw. That was a learning experience for me. That's how I worked on *Robin Hood*. I especially remember the director, Woolie Reitherman. He was a fighter pilot in World War II. And Woolie was a soldier first and foremost. I don't recall ever seeing his soft side at work. When he'd call all the animators upstairs to view their scenes, I remember everyone appearing in the hall with this terrified look on their faces. We'd all go up *en masse* with our tails between our legs. And I got criticized along with the best of them up there. One time he literally said, "This is really quite disappointing. I expected that you would do much better than this." He then pointed out all the possibilities that I had overlooked. I then had to go back and try again.

Bill: It sounds like he was your first animation instructor. Were you mentored by anybody?

Don: Up to that point, no. But I would say that John Lounsbery was my first mentor. Everything I saw him do became very important to me. And every time I was faced with a big challenge, I would recall those moments and ask myself how John would handle things. I wanted to walk in his footsteps. With that in mind I then faced that challenge, and good things always happened. I made corrections and learned what to look for in animation. It's the entertainment, not just the drawings. Because of that early training, Milt and Woolie liked what I was doing. And if Milt Kahl complimented your work, that just gave you a warm feeling inside. On one occasion I even got to go into his office. Now, you have to understand who Milt Kahl was, and most of the young students today, or wannabe animators, haven't a clue who Milt Kahl was. Milt Kahl was the great and dreaded Milt Kahl. It was like going to see the Great Oz. And he kept his door closed all the time. He was good at everything. He was good at chess, fly-fishing. He won awards for that. And he also loved to shoot. He had a pellet gun in his room and you could hear it going off all the time, usually during break times or at lunch. He used phone books for backing the paper targets to protect the wall behind it.

Bill: He was shooting guns in his room?

Don: He had a gun in his room, yeah. Who's going to venture forth and open the door, or even knock? I remember Stan Green, who was his assistant at the time, would just go timidly to the door and lightly knock. You'd hear Milt's loud voice, "COME IN." And poor Stan would tremble, holding Milt's coffee. Milt was the man who could make the best drawings in the whole studio. A true master of his craft, his designs were flawless. And he was a great fan of Picasso. None of us understood the connection between Picasso's drawings and Milt's drawings, but he did. Anyway, one time I had a scene and had to go see Milt to get a drawing. All the veteran animators had this custom. If you couldn't get a drawing to work, go see Milt. One of his drawings would bring everything together beautifully. So I was heading to Milt to get a drawing of Robin Hood. I knocked and Milt opens the door and says, in a very friendly way, "Oh, it's you. Come on in. Come on." He was *actually* nice. But I could see the gun sitting on his table, and there were all these phonebooks that were just shredded to pieces. When I said that I was sent to get his help, he laughed and took my drawing. He said, "First of all, let's put a piece of paper over the top." Then, he began to explain what he was doing as he drew over the top of my drawing. As he made corrections, I noticed something kind of interesting about Milt at that point. You could learn by watching him draw, but it was difficult to learn by listening to him talk. He stuttered a little bit, and he would use the expression, "Well, you sort of do it like this, you know. You know what I mean? You can see it. You just do it like that." That's not a lot of help if you had no idea what he was talking about. Oddly enough, on my website I find people asking me the same question. "Well, tell me how to do it," they say. A lot of times that's not something you can communicate, because it seems to me the muses have to construct that. It's something that comes to you personally. I reflect on that experience a lot, standing behind Milt and getting that drawing. It was amazing.

Bill: At that time, was there a particular technique or point of view that was unique to Milt, something that really helped you?

Don: Yes. What Milt was doing more than anything was emphasizing a particular attitude or approach to directing. He said, "If your scene is not entertaining, then why is it in the picture? You need to think entertainment all the time. I can see a scene that you've got in the reel right now, where the sheriff is running up a stairway. I'm not at all entertained by it. I've watched people my whole life climb stairs, and you've done nothing unusual. You could have him go faster than his legs should carry him. You could have him actually hit the wall and fumble on the way, conveying that he's in a big hurry. But you didn't sit down and think about what would be entertaining." Those words of advice have echoed in my head during my entire career, at Disney and through all of our independent animated films. If it's not entertaining, why do it? A scene can convey a story point or the character's personality, but it can also be entertaining. Woolie [Reitherman] also had this saying, "Some animators, I will give bread and butter scenes. But I will never give the acting scenes to them." *Bread and butter* meant action scenes, somebody running, walking, just getting from point A to point B. But in acting scenes you must show the mind of the character at work. You must show that the character has feelings. You must show that there's a personality there, and it *must* be entertaining! It must tickle people in the audience.

I know that Walt himself, in a famous Disney interoffice memo to art instructor Don Graham back in 1935, author of that in-house Disney animation manual *Analysis of Action*, wrote, "You must caricature what we see in real life, or the audience cannot connect at all with what you're doing. You cannot just draw cartoons. The cartoon characters are symbols. They represent something common to us all, with situations and reactions similar to our own lives. We all go through this." In Cinderella there's a scene where a little mouse wakes up, yawns, and he turns around to find his little tail all in knots. He's been sleeping on it all night. So he picks it up and tries to undo the knots. Why is that so funny? Because every one of us has woken up in the morning in complete disarray, our hair all matted and twisted. So, it's a reflection of the mortal existence. Throughout my entire career the goal has been to make it funny, make it entertaining, make it fresh, and try not to duplicate what another animator has done. That's the hardest part. Because you will subconsciously hold all those images in your head and you'll wind up drawing the same thing someone else has already drawn.

Bill: This sounds like a transitional period for you. What happened after *Robin Hood*?

Don: My next assignment was on *Winnie the Pooh and Tigger Too*. Another door opened and I was promoted to directing animator. Thinking back to when I went back to Disney Studios, it was a very different place. This was in April of 1971. Walt died in 1966, so the new regime was there. Woolie Reitherman was now the producer/director and pretty much in charge of the animation department. And all of the management staff were trying to guess what Walt would have done. That was always the question. What would Walt have done? And in all the cupboards that you opened there was always a picture of Walt. He was ever present, even though he was no longer there physically. And Woolie … Woolie wasn't so much a "What would've Walt done?" kind of guy, because he was trying to be himself. Eventually, because they realized that everyone was growing older, they started thinking about the future of Disney animation and came up with a training program. Eric Larson was in charge of that program. And then Disney extended some financing to help California Institute of the Arts so that they could train new talent in character animation. After they graduated, some would be selected to come into the studio animation training program and get further training, starting with personal screen tests and inbetweening on actual production scenes.

I remember that Dale Baer and I were some of the first to be brought into that program. Over the next two years, Gary Goldman and John Pomeroy would enter the program. It was in 1972 that Gary and I began to question the program. I pointed out that we have a lot more to learn here than just animating. I revealed that I had an editing table and a sixteen-millimeter Moviola and several reels of Warner Bros shorts that I was studying at home. During coffee breaks, we used to talk in my office about how soon it would be when the last of the Nine Old Men would be retiring—actually it would be happening in the next 5 or 6 years; we were reminded of this often by production managers Don Duckwall and Ed Hansen. It seemed daunting to try and learn as much as we would need to know to take on something like directing and supervising other animation staff. And so, a few of the new guys would meet at my house for animation weekends, where we would do marathon viewings of the Disney feature classics, watching four or five films a day. Back in those days, you could get a sixteen-millimeter projector from the studio and check out sixteen-millimeter copies of those classic features and take them home to watch. I suggested that we start collecting more equipment, like a rostrum camera stand and a thirty-five–millimeter stop-motion camera. Then we had some small animation desks built and bought some used 12 Field animation discs. I had to have my Moviola converted to thirty-five millimeter. We even found an old Moviola projector with three attached sound heads. The shutter was mounted out in front of the lens. It looked like it could fly.

As this was going on, Woolie Reitherman called me into his office one day and said, "We've got a lot of animators who are training new animators, but we don't have anybody that's going to be a director. You're going to direct." Once again, a door opened. However, that meant one thing specifically. I had to give up animating. It also meant that you have to hold your cards close to your chest and be careful what you say to people. Woolie said, "'cause you'll either injure them, deflate their morale, or you'll elevate them and inspire them to do better." I think maybe Woolie's directorial advice affected my approach. I may have become less outgoing and even mistrustful of others. Though I did continue to help others with their animation. When I asked when this new journey would begin, he said, "Right now." Then he began to show me how he approached directing.

For instance, he explained how they built animated props. How they would spend hours working over the little model that was going to be Cruella De Vil's car. In those days we didn't have computers to build them. The props were usually constructed with illustration board. We actually built little models, painted them white, outlined them with black acrylic paint, and shot them in stop-motion photography. Then we printed out each frame onto a Photostat with registration peg holes, and the animators animated the characters to those printouts. It was a very different process. At a certain point, he pulled me off *The Rescuers* and dropped *Pete's Dragon* into my lap. He said directly, "You're going to direct the animation and I'm going to step back." That's when I started working with Ken Anderson. *Pete's Dragon* was a combination of live action and animation. Ken explained that I had to go out onto the sound stage where the live-action crew was filming the actors with the director, Don Chaffey, and make sure that when they shoot scenes where the dragon also appeared, there would be room to include the animation of Elliott the dragon in the frame. And we couldn't screw that up. So I went out to the sound stage with Ken and walked around as if I knew what I was doing. Whatever we did, it worked. The budget and the schedule was for just 10 minutes of animation. The plan for Elliott the dragon was that he would be invisible 50 percent of the time. However, when the marketing guys saw the first animated scenes, they

Dave Michener, Ted Berman, Ollie Johnston, Art Stevens, Don Bluth, Frank Thomas, Woolie Reitherman on The Rescuers © Disney.

pushed to have more footage of the dragon. It was doubled to twenty minutes, 1,800 feet. We weren't given additional funds or more time. Then the studio decided to change the date of the premiere of *Pete's Dragon* from Christmastime to Thanksgiving. That reduced our production schedule by a month and gave us only about nine months total to get all of the animation production done. We basically had to work twelve- to fourteen-hour days, seven days a week. And there was no overtime pay for off-the-clock employees, which included me and other key animation staff. This was just the job. We were also developing some green animators. Cliff Nordberg, I think, was the only real veteran animator on the picture. The process was very slow in the beginning. I found myself in a position where people were looking over my shoulder and I was correcting their drawings.

I had so many epiphanies along the way. Years before, I used to stand for hours behind cleanup supervisor Walt Stanchfield at his desk, while he corrected my drawings on *Sleeping Beauty*, and there was a moment on *Pete's Dragon* when Walt came into my room and asked me to help him with a drawing. As he stood behind me, I put his drawing on my registration pegs and placed a blank piece of paper over it—and I froze. I turned to him and said, "Walt, do you realize what's happening here? You should be sitting here, working on my drawing." He laughed, and replied, "Don't be stupid, just draw. This is why I always preach people to treat your fellow-artists nice. You never know when they might end up being your boss."

Bill: As the animation director, how did you bring the dragon to life? How did you give him character and personality? And did you have full control over this, or did you have to consult with the live-action director?

Don: They pretty much expected me to supervise and approve the animation, cleanup, special effects, and color for the dragon scenes, as well as deliver entertaining animation scenes, which would be combined with the live action in a special printing process. Whenever you're making an animated film, at least in my experience, you use the voice talent and the writers to help you develop who the character is. The voice talent will come in and read the words on a page, and through their experience recognize what is expected of the character and say, "Oh, I know who this guy is!" They'll add things to it that you never thought of. For *Pete's Dragon*, casting brought in an actor by the name of Charlie Callas, who was also a stand-up comedian and had been in many live-action pictures. Ken Anderson explained that we didn't want the dragon to talk, just make noises that only the boy could understand. So Charlie Callas began to make these weird sounds, and when he did his face became distorted, strange, and fun. But that wasn't Charlie, that was the dragon. The dragon is every child's friend. He's a big friendly giant who comes into a child's life and helps solve their problems. Every kid in the world is going to love that character. Charlie Callas gave that character, I think, its spirit or its life. The lesson it taught me was simply that you have to know who the character is from the inside-out. And it can also be a very fun process.

There was a moment during this time when I got an opportunity to see Woolie's softer side. He had invited me to his home for dinner. When I arrived and rang the doorbell, he opened the door and he was holding a small fox. It was domesticated and was an indoor pet. I felt like I was intruding in the very personal life of Woolie and his wife, Janie, seeing a side of him that I'd never seen before. It was somewhat disconcerting. The little fox was like a small dog, very comfortable around humans—and definitely Woolie's pet. The experience definitely gave me a different perspective on him.

Bill: What came after *Pete's Dragon*?

Don: After that, there was a short film called *The Small One*, adapted and pitched by Pete Young, one of only a couple of the story trainees. He was being mentored by Eric Larson and Vance Gerry. I think Eric was to produce and he was going to give the directing to Burney Mattinson, his long-time animation assistant. But Woolie stepped in and placed me in charge of the production as the producer/director, as part of his plan to groom me to replace himself. What a dilemma for me. Woolie just ignored Eric's plan and stuck me in the middle. Plus, I was aware that this would be the first religious-based film that Walt Disney Productions would create, and maybe the last. This was Joseph, Mary, and the birth of Christ. So they were trying to figure out how best to animate the story. I was stumped. We still had a very green crew. Worse still, the studio didn't give us much of a budget, nor money for anyone to write songs. We, my assistant director, Rick Rich, and I actually wrote our own. He wrote one, and I wrote two songs that went into that movie! Essentially resources were limited because it was a short. There wasn't going to be an opportunity to recoup the costs. There weren't videos or DVDs back in those days. Regardless, we finished making that picture. I remember going into a projection room with Woolie Reitherman and a lot of the other animators to watch the final product. Now that was judgment day. When the lights came up, he turned around, looked at me, and said, "I just watched Hanna-Barbera inbetweened." That was a slap in the face. It was his way of saying, that's not what we do at the Disney studio. And that was another big lesson for me, or more of a reminder: If it isn't entertaining, if it doesn't reflect real life, then it's nothing. It's just moving drawings. I put that in my cache of things I'd been taught. The next movie I direct wouldn't be like that.

Now something happened, something I think is really important. And this goes back in time a bit. In 1972, all of us in the training program knew we were being trained as animators, and thus we didn't know how to put a movie together. We didn't know how to create "texture" in a film, to place a slow sequence next to a fast one, or how you put a sad sequence next to a happy one. We could only do individual scenes. So Gary Goldman and I decided to learn how. We decided to go out into my garage and make a picture. We would stumble along and learn the process as a result. And if we don't know the answers, we'll go ask the old masters at the studio. I remember asking Frank Thomas how they

from the left, Don Bluth, John Pomeroy with his back to the camera,
1st row: John Musker, Brad Bird and Jerry Reese, 2nd row: Heidi Guedel, Linda Miller and Emily Jiuliano,
3rd: Jeff Vareb, Gary Goldman, Chuck Harvey and Bill Hajee on The Small One © Disney.

made the water in *Fantasia* so clear and real. He rolled his eyes and said, "You know, no one ever wrote that down. I don't remember. I think it had something to do with lacquer we used to make the cell paint transparent." I was just astounded. I assumed that because Disney had been pioneering animation for almost half a century that someone was keeping track. And so there were many other questions that I asked and no one remembered. That really compelled us to go out on our own and experiment. We were going to have to find a lot of answers on our own.

Bill: What was this garage project?

Don: It started with something we called *The Piper*. It was based on a poem that my brother Toby had written. We worked on it as a short for about two and half years. After we had storyboarded about twenty minutes and animated about 400 feet, we invited John and Florence Lounsbery to my house and showed them the film. It was excruciatingly painful, actually embarrassing to watch with one of the Disney animation masters sitting in my living room. It was then that we realized that the story wasn't appropriate for a short; too much information in too short of time to make sense of the story. It was like watching sports highlights. The very next weekend we decided to scrap *The Piper* and chose something simpler. I came up with a story based on a kitten that lived in our woodpile, back on my parents' farm in Payson, Utah. Toby took the first stab at a script. When we got into production, I rewrote it. The picture was a short that lasted twenty-seven minutes. It was called *Banjo the Woodpile Cat*. We thought we might get our money back, if we could just get one showing on television. Of course it took years before that happened. When John Pomeroy came aboard at Disney in February of 1973, we invited him to come see what we were doing in the garage. He was there on *The Piper* and endured the pain of starting over with us. During the next several years, we had spent a lot of money on *Banjo*. I had even taken out a second mortgage on my house to pay the orchestra for the music score. But it was so exciting, learning all these lessons. Every weekend we would get together at my house, and sometimes on weeknights. About four years into this second garage project, we wondered if we would ever recoup our investment of time and money. Then, in late 1978, we thought, what if we took it to Disney, they might agree to buy it and let us finish it there during regular work hours.

I went to the new head of the Disney Studio, Ron Miller. I said, "Ron, we're working on a side project and making numerous discoveries. Would you like to see it?" Unfortunately, he turned us down. This was also the time when the kids from CalArts started grumbling down in the bullpen. They were unhappy with the studio. They were evidently unhappy with me. In the end I went to Ron and said, "This is too hard. I don't think I'm your guy. I'm not going to be your director. I don't even want to be a directing animator. I just want to go to my office and animate." Woolie [Reitherman] was overseeing the development of *The Fox and the Hound* and *The Black Caldron*, and I'm sure I disappointed him by asking to step down and just animate. But I didn't feel like I was letting him down. I had no idea what I was doing. But by that time I knew that I was going to leave the Disney Studio.

Around this time Gary [Goldman] got a call from ex-Disney executive Jim Stewart, suggesting that he knew we were unhappy at the studio, and asked if they could finance us, would we leave Disney? Would we start a studio and produce a feature? And, if we would leave, do we have a story in mind? Strange, but just weeks before this call, Ken Anderson had brought a book to my office called *Mrs. Frisby and the Rats of NIMH*. He told me that he had brought it to Woolie's attention and got shot down. Woolie told him that they "already had a mouse—Mickey Mouse," and that they'd already made a mouse movie, *The Rescuers*. Gary told Jim we already had a company—which we incorporated for the *Banjo* property. We named it *Don Bluth Productions, Inc*. And, yes, there is a book that we would like to produce as a movie. Their company was called *Aurora Productions*, formed by three ex-Disney execs, Jim [Stewart], Rich Irvine, and Jon Lang. They had an investor, a man from Chicago, who was interested. They knew that we had experience but only as cogs in the Disney animation machine. Jim wanted to know if we had anything that we had done on our own, which would show that we could handle directing and producing a film on our own. We did have one example—*Banjo the Woodpile Cat*. It was about 90 percent animated and about 70 percent in color. They asked if they could show it to the investor. When he saw the short film, he liked it and felt that it justified investing in a film with us. He put up $5.7 million dollars. But Gary [Goldman], John [Pomeroy], and I weren't going to leave our garage comrades behind. I called a meeting for everyone who was working on *Banjo* and said, "Guys, we're taking our short and leaving. We're not asking you to leave, but you are welcome if you want to come with us." It was on my birthday, September 13th, 1979, that we went to Ed Hansen, who was the animation production manager at the time, and told him we couldn't make it happen there at the studio, that we were resigning to make our own animated feature films and were going to compete with them, and that we felt it was the only way to wake them up. He sat in his chair and laughed out loud. He said, "You haven't a clue what you're saying. You cannot make a feature film."

Animation Drawing, *Banjo the Woodpile Cat*, 1979 © Don Bluth Productions.

Bill: He actually erupted in laughter?

Don: He did. And that only made us want to succeed more. So we left. The picture we made was based on the book that Ken [Anderson] shared with us, *Mrs. Frisby and the Rats of NIMH*, which was a Newberry Award–winning novel.

Bill: What made you choose that?

Don: As I said earlier, Gary, John, and I had read the book and knew right away that Ken was right. It had potential. The story deals with basic, common issues of morality and making the right choices. It was perfect. We had scheduled it for thirty months. However, late in the production, Aurora and MGM/UA decided to move the release date up by two months, to the Fourth of July weekend. We completed it in two years and five months. It was probably the most wonderful experience of my career, and it's a picture that we never really duplicated. We never made one better, in my opinion. We poured our heart and souls into the movie. It was purely the result of our desire to create something special. We tried our best to bring back some strong story elements and production values missing from those Disney films from the early sixties and all through the mid-seventies.

Bill: Talk a bit about the difficulties of assuming the role of director, producer, and editor. That must have been challenging.

Don: Actually, it was easier than at Disney. We owned the company. My name was on the door. Just that alone gave me authority to lead—very different from being an employee director. Further, directing and running a studio is completely different from the act of animating itself—or even just directing. With artists, you'll discover that many can become very jealous or feel inferior. There's a lot of competition going on in the background. Some artists even feel like they don't count or they don't have any self-importance. You have to monitor that and make sure everyone feels like they're part of the team, that their talent is needed and appreciated. A successful project depends on that. Then you have the issue of finance. How do you keep the money flowing? You have to make sure you're on schedule and that you're spending correctly. You just can't run out of money. That takes a lot of management. There were two guys to help us oversee the finances, one at Aurora and our in-house production manager, Fred Craig. It usually came down to not creating enough inventory, or not making our footage goals, and lots of weekly meetings to discuss problems. There were many meetings that had nothing to do with animating but more about how to monitor the system or work continuity from department to department and the flow of inventory to each. It can be very frustrating.

And if you want to make good movies, you need to keep the crew happy and focused. That was a major part of my job as a director, trying to keep everyone balanced, satisfied, and working. It was tough learning how to guide an artist toward the bigger picture, to take the focus off themselves and transfer it to the project as a whole.

Bill: When you finished *The Secret of NIMH*, how were things financially for your new studio?

Don: When we finished *The Secret of NIMH*, we were already five months into our second film with Aurora; it was called *East of the Sun: West of the Moon*. I thought *NIMH* was going to do it for us. We're going to compete with the Disney Studio. But it was not financially a success. We were only two-thirds financed on *East of the Sun*, and the union contract was to expire on July 31, 1982.

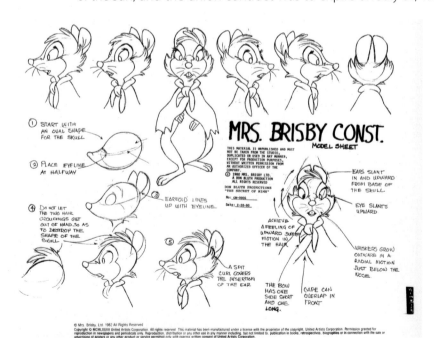

Sketches, Don Bluth, "*THE SECRET OF N.I.M.H.*", © 1982 MGM Television Entertainment Inc. All rights reserved. Courtesy of MGM Media Licensing.

Model sheet, "Ms. Brisby", "*THE SECRET OF N.I.M.H.*", © 1982 MGM Television Entertainment Inc. All rights reserved. Courtesy of MGM Media Licensing.

Negotiations with the big studios got stalled and Local 839 voted to strike. We didn't even consider the effects of this action. We were a union house but not part of the Producer's Association. We were new at this and just waiting for the agreement. But the next week Bud Hester, our union president, arrived on our doorstep in Studio City and told all of the artists that they would have to leave the building. That meant that the editors and the camera operators would leave too, in order to respect their colleagues in 839. That left only Gary [Goldman], John [Pomeroy], our production manager, the receptionist, and me in the building. Then we received a call from Aurora telling us that the investors got cold feet and decided to not continue with the cash flow for *East of the Sun*, for two reasons: *NIMH*'s box office failure and fear of what financial damage the union demands would do to our budget. We sat there in the building for the next two months wondering how we would recover. Then, in early October we received a call from a Rick Dyer, an entrepreneur/inventor and owner of Advanced Micro Systems. He wanted to meet us and talk about a collaboration. Rick came up to our studio with another man, Jim Pierce, the co-owner of an arcade game manufacturer and distribution company. Gary, John, and I met with them in our conference room. Rick introduced Mr. Pierce, and then he said, "I just saw your *Secret of NIMH*. I'm making an arcade game called *Dragon's Lair* and you guys are the ones that should animate it." He explained that he had convinced Jim that it should be a three-way partnership, with each of the companies raising the startup money required to do their part of creating the sample of the game. Jim disclosed that Cinematronics was in Chapter 11, bankruptcy. He believed that Rick's concept would bring success. With his share of profits he could pay his debtors and get out of Chapter 11.

Now I had never even been to an arcade. I didn't know what a video game was. But it was a job, so we agreed. But when they brought in the scripts, they just weren't that good. Going back to my old lessons I could see some entertainment was missing. If you lose your money and don't win, you still want some reward. I said, "Why don't we do several kinds of death scenes that are funny, amusing, and everybody goes, 'Wow!' That way the player at least still gets entertained." The fun of making *Dragon's Lair* was seeing how many ways we could kill the little knight. That was the fun part. And this was to be done using the latest laser disc technology, which would allow us to animate the story like a movie, linear. If someone died, the game could access any death sequence on the disc; otherwise the player simply progressed forward in the story. And since we were putting the crew back to work, and since this wasn't a major feature movie, it was an opportunity to let the animators experiment once again. So they did and had fun doing it. Then, remembering that we had to find the startup money ourselves, we went into a mini-panic. I called my bother Sam, who loaned us about $35,000, which only covered us for about three weeks. So, we had to figure out a budget and schedule, and Jim Pierce needed to have a sample of the game for the upcoming March 1983 Arcade Game convention in Chicago. Gary [Goldman] came up with a budget of $300,000 for the demo. We then borrowed money from one of our attorney's friends, Ott Sorentino, of Sorentino's restaurant. By the time our attorney found a qualified investor, we had borrowed over $100,000 from family, friends, friends of friends, and, our new partners, Rick and Jim. Finally, an investor was brought in and put up the $300,000, for a 10 percent share of our profits. That investment paid back our debt and got us to the March gaming convention. Jim Pierce called from Chicago and notified us that the game was the talk of the show. Within two days it was on national television. Cinematronics had presold about $8 million worth of the game at the show. We were financed. And our part would cost a total of $1.3 million. When Rick's company finally programmed all that animation and put it in the arcade, it was a far bigger success than *NIMH*. It made a lot of money.

Ron: Did you release that?

Don: No. Cinematronics handled the distribution. You have to watch out for distributors. When the money starts rolling in, and we were told it was about $32 million dollars, the money can disappear, especially if they are in bankruptcy and do not satisfy their debt and continue to protect themselves in bankruptcy. Cinematronics used the incoming revenue to cover Rick's costs and finance us for the balance of *Dragon's Lair*, develop and produce *Space Ace*, and *Dragon's Lair II: Time Warp*. The profit

Animation drawing, *Dragon's Lair*, 1993 © Bluth Group.

Model sheet, "Dirk the Daring", *Dragon's Lair*, 1993 © Bluth Group.

money never really came back to us. And actually, in late March of 2004, they owed us production costs of around $350,000 on *Dragon's Lair II* and about $4.5 million in profits from the other two games. We had been informed that they had in excess of $12.5 million in their account. They called and told Gary that the arcade market was crashing again and they were cutting off our cash flow and shutting down the third game. We didn't even have enough money to make payroll. We called our attorney in a panic, who advised that we need to get a good bankruptcy attorney to fight the shutdown. We had an unfinished game and our two companies, Don Bluth Productions and Bluth Group, Ltd., were in bankruptcy court. It was the only way to go after Cinematronics. They had all of the partners' money but refused to distribute the funds. Then they turned over their business management to their bankruptcy attorneys and a trustee. Eventually, four and a half years later we won in court. No money was left in Cinematronics' account, but the court eventually awarded Bluth Group the three games. We were able to finally finish *Dragon's Lair II*. A company by the name of Leland Corporation had purchased Cinematronics from the bankruptcy court and called us in Ireland to inquire about us finishing the game and licensing it to them for distribution. And those games, thirty years later, are still on the shelf today. I still can't figure out how to play them. In 1984 *Dragon's Lair* went into the Smithsonian Institute along with *Pong* and *Pac-Man*. In 2010 it appeared as an app on the Apple iTunes store.

Ron: That sounds like a happy ending.

Don: Well, yes, sort of. We did end up owning the trademarks and copyrights to the three games. Their continued success, I believe, is that the animation is entertaining to watch and I'd have to credit Woolie [Reitherman], Milt [Kahl] and John [Lounsbery]. If it's not entertaining, it shouldn't be there.

Ron: How did you start the next feature film?

Don: That's a story in itself. We didn't start *An American Tail* until January of 1985. Back in the late summer of 1982, Jerry Goldsmith, who composed the music on *NIMH*, was friends with Steven Spielberg and brought the film to his attention. We got a call from Steven's office requesting our studio copy of *The Secret of NIMH* that Steven could watch in the privacy of his home. The next day they asked if they could keep the film for another day to show Kathy Kennedy and Frank Marshall. Then Steven called us up and invited us over to meet with him. We went to his office at Warner Brothers and talked about the film. Steven told us that he was amazed. He had thought the golden age of animation was over when Walt died. When he learned how much the movie cost to make, he was even more astounded. He asked if we wanted to make a movie together. Of course we said yes! We started telling him of our list of titles we'd like to produce, but he said that he would like to select the project. We left his office thrilled with the opportunity. But then the months went by with no news. We continued with the video games and it was about two years later when *An American Tail* actually surfaced. We had been in bankruptcy since the end of March and were staying alive doing small projects and commercials. Then, finally in August of '84, we were contacted by Amblin's marketing exec, Brad Globe, and producer, Kathy Kennedy, to come over to Amblin, their new offices at Universal, for a meeting. They had a script for us to read. We met in Kathy's office. We liked the title but felt the story was weak. Further, there were a few story panels done, which had the mice human-size. It reminded us of *Planet of the Apes*. Steven agreed. Once the deal was done, Amblin hired two writers from *Sesame Street*, Tony Geiss and Judy Freudberg, to come in and rewrite the existing concept. And so in January 1985, we started from scratch. Tony and Judy flew out from New York and worked in-house with us for six months. The story became about the Mousekewitz family; the little boy's name was Mousy Mousekewitz. After the first few pages of new script were delivered to Steven, he changed Mousy's name to Fievel, which was Steven's grandfather's name. It was the story of his family. A lot of things were changed to fit the new storyline. One of the two writers, Tony Geiss, wrote a song, called "Hey Mr. Man in the Moon." But Steven felt it wasn't quite right for the film. Then Steven brought in songwriters Barry Man and Cynthia Weil, who worked with James [Horner]. Finally, the three of them came up with four songs including the hit song, "Somewhere Out There."

Bill: How did directing work, considering that you're working with a big director like Steven?

Don: There's always somebody above you. That's just part of movie making. I remember Steven saying, "I'm going to arrange for Universal to provide you guys the money to do this. I'm going to give you some time and space to do it. I want you to be as creative as you can. I know you guys will make me a beautiful movie. But I'd like to approve the script and want your storyboards sent to me. I'll review and approve them. If there is anything I can add, I'll add it." He was extremely generous. He would send our boards back with little notes here and there. It was a pleasure. It was one of the easiest things I ever did, because they were always such positive suggestions. They made the picture better and it was easy for me to see that. Steven was as interested in creating real entertainment as I was. So once again I was being instructed by one of the best. We didn't hit a problem until we started on *The Land Before Time*.

Bill: You have a reputation for being hands-on during the boarding and layout stage. Going back to *An American Tail*, how involved were you at that stage?

Don: Well, yes, that's always been my flaw. But then, isn't that the director's job. And we were on a limited budget. I had done all of the storyboarding on *NIMH*, and it worked both for efficiency and budget. I believe that the more I can put into the storyboards, the more visual direction I can give. This way the entire crew can see the vision of the story. And it helps reduce the amount of time of explaining what I'm looking for in blocking or choreographing each scene. But some argue that it slights the animators' creativity. In the early years of my career we would explore the Disney animation morgue (archive) and we found the storyboards for the animation in *Song of the South*. Those storyboard panels were done by Bill Peet and Ken Anderson. Every panel reminds you of the scenes in the film. The character drawings were in great poses and on-model, and they had included background information in each story panel, creating a clear plan for the animation continuity. It helped the animators and the layout department. I could board faster and come up with more gags faster. And the faster you can conceptualize the boards, the sooner you have a road map for the entire project. That saves money. Until you have that road map, the studio is simply devouring money. As an independent studio, money was a big issue. Now the last thing I wanted was to send mediocre storyboards over to Steven Spielberg that I would have to correct later. So, yes I did get very hands-on. I did it myself. I couldn't allow us to get in trouble with the budget. And, quite frankly, we couldn't afford the additional staff. This was also easy to do with a small crew. Later, when I was working with a large room full of storyboard people, I knew that great ideas can emerge if you don't rush the process. There's a lot of creative talent to tap into. So it's a better way to work. And I would just go in and play the Steven Spielberg part at that point. I would observe and say, "Have you considered doing this?" Or, "Perhaps you might try it this way." However, it is a more expensive process.

Ron: As you said, Steven left notes on your boards, but did you learn anything from him as a director?

Don: Absolutely. I've always been one who learns by watching other people. I guess I'm eclectic in a way because I can just absorb things from various people and make it my own. When I was on the set and watching Steven shoot live action, I noticed that we were quite similar in our approach. Steven had a vision and he made sure that vision came to life. That's essentially how I've felt my entire career. I wanted to get hands-on because I had a vision, and I wanted that vision to come to life. I believe that's the mark of a good director. When Disney Studios was in its heyday, it was Walt Disney. He was the guy that was making everything happen. Everyone was working to build his vision, even if they couldn't see it. That's why when he was gone everyone kept asking, "What would he have done?" For years, everyone simply followed his lead. I remember one occasion, when we were making *The Land Before Time*, we were invited over to London to show the work print to Steven and George [Lucas]. When the lights came up after the screening, George, said, "Well, that scared the shit out of me!" Steven agreed. It was mainly about the *Tyrannosaurus rex*. They looked at the *T. rex* chasing the three little dinosaurs and said, "That's beautiful, and it's almost all in color. I love it. But we're going to have mothers holding their crying children in the lobbies of the theaters. That means we're going to lose ticket sales. If I cut out about a minute of that scary stuff, which you have so diligently put in there, the mothers and their kids will probably stay in their seats. And they're going to tell their friends to go see the movie. I'm ready to lose a minute." Steven was thinking a few steps ahead of the game. While you're focused entirely on the artwork, he was thinking in terms of *show business*. You're going to sell tickets, and that's going to allow you the freedom and the capability of making another picture. Or you're going to lose tickets, in which case you're going to lose popularity. That's an important issue for Steven.

Bill: So what happened after *An American Tail*?

Don: Let's go back twenty-two months, to December of '84. When Steven and Universal began serious discussions about *American Tail*, Universal felt that because of *NIMH*'s box office failure, a non-Disney animated film was a high risk, so they offered us just $7.5 million to do *American Tail*. This is after we showed them a budget of $11.3 million. At that time, our two companies, Don Bluth Productions and Bluth Group, Ltd., were in bankruptcy court suing our gaming partnership and game distributor for production monies and profits owed to us. We didn't feel that Universal would appreciate doing business with a company in bankruptcy. We had a business consultant working for us. He was a semi-retired mergers and acquisitions expert, Morris Sullivan, who said he would see if he could raise financing for our feature film projects. He ended up guiding Bluth Group, Ltd., through its bankruptcy. Morris offered to incorporate a company to do business with Universal, with Gary [Goldman], John [Pomeroy], and I as contracted producers and director. When we were told the maximum amount they were willing to spend, Morris immediately started inquiring about off-shore options to create an ink and paint facility with that entire operation in Ireland, with plans to move core members of the staff to that location at some time in the future.

            American Tail hadn't gone into the theaters yet, and we still had all of the people on as paid staff. We needed the next project. We were in talks about picture number two—about dinosaurs, which would eventually be called *The Land Before Time*, but nothing was in writing, other than our *American Tail* contract, which gave them the rights to two films from us—the second "to be determined." We needed to keep the money flowing, so we went to Universal and explained that fact. But they clearly stated that they were not going to greenlight the picture until they were sure that *American Tail* was going to make money.

Bill: What did you do for funds?

Don: It was a serious issue; we didn't want to lose momentum nor have to lay off any of the talented crew. And that's the argument we submitted. Amblin came to our side, as did some of the Universal execs, but still no movement on green-lighting *Land*.

            Morris [Sullivan] had closed the deal with the Industrial Development Authority in Ireland by the summer of '85. Gary had gone over and set up testing artists to train as cel painters and inkers. The company had hired 100 trainees there in Dublin, 26 of whom we tested for inbetweening and brought them to the US during *An American Tail* to train in various follow-up duties in the animation processes, from inbetweeners to Xerox and Paint Lab technicians, one even as a camera operator. They were here with us for a year. Morris' plan was working. Universal saw that we were making deadlines and meeting the budget requirements. They agreed to pay for the *Land Before Time* story and script development, character design, storyboarding, recording voice talent and rough animation, and paying the payroll for those working on *Land* with *American Tail* funds—but only on a week-to-week basis, with approval from top brass at Universal. Those funds were to be reimbursed from the approved *Land* budget, but they still did not guarantee to greenlight the film.

Ireland had specifically asked us to come to Dublin to live, work, and train Irish workers how to make animation. If we did that, they would give us money for each person we hired and trained. It was such a good deal that when Morris finally informed us one day that we're moving to Ireland. Immediately I said, "Who's we? Who's going to Ireland?" I had just remodeled my house. I was a happy guy. When it came time to move, we took eighty-seven US and Canadian animation artists and technicians, and even their families and pets, to Ireland to complete *Land Before Time*. In the summer of 1986, Gary [Goldman] and Morris went over to find a suitable building. We had to create a fully operating studio ground up. We had to round up everything that goes into a studio, including the chairs and desks, our two custom-built, multiplane rostrum cameras, the editorial equipment, the video animation tester, then build new animation desks in Ireland, and have additional custom-made 16 Field animation discs manufactured and shipped from Hollywood to Ireland! "I just wanted to draw," that's what I kept saying to everyone. They replied, "Just shut up. We're building a new facility!" So we were going take the risk, move, and start to build out a facility, as we waited for *Land Before Time* to be greenlit. But, finally near the end of August, Universal sent a letter to Morris agreeing to a "pay or play" agreement, basically agreeing to greenlight *The Land Before Time*. By the time we put Gary and the crew on a plane in mid-November 1986, we had about 25 percent of *Land* storyboarded, layouts done for about twelve minutes, and 1,000 feet of the film in rough pencil test. John and I stayed back for the *American Tail* premiere on the weekend of November 18th, and then flew out on the 21st for Dublin.

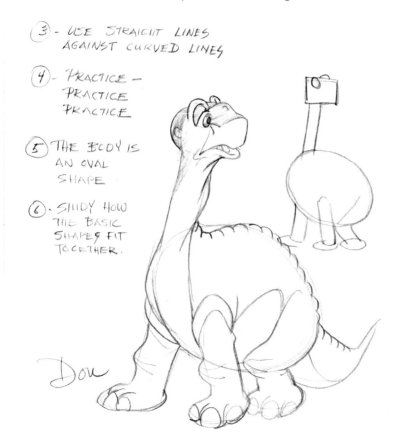

3 - USE STRAIGHT LINES AGAINST CURVED LINES

4 - PRACTICE — PRACTICE PRACTICE

5 THE BODY IS AN OVAL SHAPE

6 - STUDY HOW THE BASIC SHAPES FIT TOGETHER.

Sketch, Don Bluth, *The Land Before Time*, 1988 © Don Bluth Ireland.

Bill: After the facility was built, where did you start?

Don: While we were making the transition to Ireland and getting production up and running again, Steven [Spielberg] was off making *Empire of the Sun*. It became really difficult to get ahold of him due to his schedule, and we needed his approval on our storyboards. Sometimes we had to wait up to three weeks for a response. And during that time we literally had to wait. We couldn't animate further. In the end, we decided to go ahead and animate anyway. It was the only way to keep the picture on schedule. The longer we waited, the more we drove up the budget.

Bill: Did those delays affect the overall production in any way?

Don: Well, Steven was busy. We didn't get as many suggestions. But the delays in getting his storyboard reviews caused a lot of frustration. Sometimes, to stay on schedule we had to move forward without the approvals. Then Steven's late notes would cause us to have to restage and reanimate some scenes. This really upset the animators. No one likes to have to reanimate, especially scenes that I had already approved. But making *Land Before Time* was both enjoyable and an interesting experience. One time I remember late in the production, mid-spring of '88, just a few months before the scheduled release of the film, Steven called and said that he and George thought that the story wasn't quite working. Steven was still buried in *Empire of the Sun*, and George was in London. He said that George could spare a couple of days to go through the script with us. So, John [Pomeroy], Gary [Goldman], and I flew over and met with George at Elstree Studios in Borehamwood, England. He had just released *Willow*. We took over a large conference room in the main building and used George's executive assistant to type up the new material in a copy of the previously approved script. There was restructuring or repositioning of the approved sequences and new descriptive text and dialogue added to the script to smooth out the transitions for the sequence changes. George is a really good story guy. The final product turned out to be a very big success. It did extremely well at the box office. And I think that movie spawned around twelve direct-to-video sequels.

Bill: Did you guys work on the sequel?

Don: No, we didn't. We only made the original movie. They did ask us to do the sequel to *An American Tail*, but at the same budget as the first. We had to decline. We would have had to cut the budget by 40 percent. So, after that we went right into our next movie, which was *All Dogs Go to Heaven*. Originally, I had remembered the title as a book. I had heard of it during the fourth grade. My teacher talked about it. But when I found the book, it had no story at all. It was simply an anthology of dogs. The title, however, I thought was a great title. Like a lot of people, I had many dogs growing up. And as a child you wonder what happens to them after they die. What if they do go to heaven? Maybe you'll meet them again. So we started working up a story about heaven, earth, dogs, and angels. It got horrible fast. Eventually we hired two writers from the states to come in and help us. One actually won an Oscar for his work on *Witness*. We thought he might know something about writing. But when he got off the airplane carrying his Oscar, we wondered if we'd made a mistake.

Bill: Are you kidding? He actually brought his Oscar?

Don: He brought it with him. I immediately turned to Gary and said, "We're in for trouble. Why is he carrying his Oscar?" Sure enough, we got off to a rough start. Then came an old friend from *Chinatown* …

Bill: Robert Towne.

Don: Robert Towne. Yes, very good. He called to let us know that he was in London meeting with the head of Universal Studios and was thinking of taking a trip over to Ireland with his wife and asked if he could drop by the studio. It was perfect timing because we needed his advice. We were having the hardest time with this story, and I asked him for just one hint that might help us get on track. He said, "Tell me your story in four minutes." As I quickly tried to tell the story, he stared at me for the longest time. Then, as I expected wisdom to flow from his mouth, his initial response was, "Where's the bathroom?" Okay, so he comes backs and says, "All right, you need to get rid of about half a dozen of your angels. The less heaven, the better. Just keep it on earth. Here's your story." And he lays it out in just a few sentences. It works perfectly. After we wrote it down, we still needed a writer. Fortunately, a USC film school graduate, who had won first prize for his short live-action film, sent us a script. His name was David N. Weiss. This was long before he became well known for his work on the *Rugrats*, *Shrek*, and *Smurf* movies. David would stand up and pace around the room, screaming the lines that he was writing. He'd act it out while someone wrote it down. He just couldn't sit down and write. David performed the entire movie of *All Dogs Go to Heaven* for us in my office in Ireland. Then we proceeded to make the picture.

Bill: Not all in one session, right?

Don: No, that probably took a couple of months. And afterward, of course, there's a lot of rewriting. You go back and correct your mistakes. And, as storyboarding proceeded, inspiration would come and more changes would have to be made to the script.

Bill: How did the boarding of the story change?

Don: I started out, but then added other artists that I thought were ready to storyboard, Dan Kuenster, who was one of our directing animators, and Larry Leker, the head of the layout department that wanted to show me what he could do storyboarding.

One of our big questions was about what the dog should look like. We needed some kind of connection with this dog. Now, back while making *Space Ace*, our second video game, there was a dog that came running through our parking lot with a pack of about seven dogs. Burt Reynolds had just left the building after a story meeting—strangely enough—about a junk-yard dog (and a private detective), which we were working on as a feature concept to cast Burt in. It wasn't for *All Dogs Go to Heaven*. It was going to be called *Canine Mystery*. As the dogs were running through the parking lot, suddenly this German shepherd split off from the others and came over to us. He was just covered with fleas. The dog had no collar and his ribs were showing. He looked like he'd been out on his own for some time. So we rescued him and brought him into the studio. Gary [Goldman]'s girlfriend, Cathy Carr, took the dog to a vet. She had him sheep-dipped and neutered, all in the same day. Gary brought the dog to work every day for the next 13 years. He became the studio mascot and we called him Burt, after Mr. Reynolds. He would regularly visit every person in the building.

So thinking about our studio mascot Burt, we realized there was no question at all about this dog, who is the central character in the movie. He should be a German shepherd and his name should be Burt. Obviously we changed the name later, but for *All Dogs* we did go after Burt Reynolds for the voice. And that brought in a whole new level of strangeness, fun, and craziness. Burt came in and made up a dog voice, which was not Burt Reynolds. We were expecting Burt's natural voice. He flew in on a helicopter, got off, went straight into the sound booth, and started talking in this strange voice. Now, how am I going to tell Burt Reynolds that that voice isn't what we want? I try, but Burt isn't interested in reading as himself. So then we bring in Dom DeLouise. He's not only Burt's good friend, but he had worked with us on h*NIMH*. Dom tells me flat out, "You're not going to be able to direct Burt. I can tell you that right now. Why don't you put me in the movie too. Let me be another dog, maybe his sidekick. Let me get with Burt and I'll get you the gold." That's how Dom DeLouise became Itchy the dog. When we went into the recording session he said, "Put the tape on and don't turn it off. Just roll it. Let me take care of Burt." Dom goes in, listens to Burt's dog voice, and just cuts into him. He says, "What the hell is that? You're going to look stupid." He then starts talking with Burt about pictures they've made in the past, giving him suggestions and advice. Burt got encouraged to start reading the lines just like the Burt we knew and wanted. And then they started creating their own lines, some of which we used in the final script. The session went on for about two hours. We had reels of tape. It was a gold mine. Even when it came to singing, Dom was a big help. He just told Burt that he was going to sing. It wasn't easy for him, but he did it. And he sounded great.

Bill: That's funny since he actually made a country music album.

Don: I know. Maybe he got inspired after that experience.

Bill: Since you had to create this movie from scratch, did you treat the project differently? As a director, was this movie your baby?

Don: I'd like to say yes. But I can't say that I was more partial to it. Nor was it the only movie we've created "from scratch." *An American Tail*'s story and script had to be rethought and rewritten, while I started storyboarding the pogrom sequence. *The Land Before Time* came with just Steven's brief verbal concept. Neither had a book that we might have adapted. We have brought in writers on all of our films, with the exception of *NIMH*. It had an award-winning book to work from. And *All Dogs* was the second film that we had to overlap from a previous production.

    I did change the process. I would turn over the production to Gary [Goldman] once the storyboarding was done and I was happy with the quality of the animation that was being produced. Then I would start the next film's script and storyboarding process. So I jumped off *The Land Before Time* and onto *All Dogs* while Gary finished *Land*. It was apparent that I had to adjust to accommodate continuity of product. *All Dogs* was the first film that I shared directing credits. It was with Gary and Dan Kuenster. Dan had become a very good storyboard artist and could actually imitate my style of drawing. But to answer the question, I think all directors must feel that the films they direct are their babies. I've always felt very close to any movie that I was directing because it was like raising a child. You have to nurture it and provide the right kind of environment so that it grows into a wonderful movie. You're completely involved. And at the end it's always sad when you say good-bye to these characters. You create them. You truly get to know them because they have a personality and a voice. Then they're gone. It's extremely emotional to walk away. In fact, I'm not sure why, but I never go back and look at any of our pictures. I don't look back and say, "Oh, isn't that wonderful?" Nothing like that ever happens unless someone sits me down to ask technical questions about animating. The thrill of animation, for me, is putting the picture together, solving the dilemma of unifying all these little thousands of pieces so that they entertain in a visually beautiful way. I learned early on that children all over the world would watch these movies on video, over and over, memorizing the dialogue, and actually live in that fantasy world when the real world gets too hard for them. I've always felt very privileged to be able to provide that fantasy world. And if they go in and learn something from it, that just makes me even happier.

Bill: You also had more control than ever before on *All Dogs Go to Heaven*. You were a director with a fully functional studio behind you. Did this change your approach to directing? Did you evolve in any specific way?

Don: Well, it's not so simple, even at that level. As we moved into the next picture, the business side of the industry just seemed to take over the act of filmmaking. We conceptualized this picture called Rock-A-Doodle. In came the financier's marketing guru, "You can't show this! You can't show that!" I kept finding myself in the middle of this mass of marketing and financial people. I believe Frank Thomas used to say, "It's hard to remember when you're up to your ass in alligators that all you want to do is drain the swamp." All I wanted to do was animate. By some miracle we managed to make twelve animated films. And there were times that I really don't know how we did it. We certainly had our share of bumps in the road, outside the realm of creativity. Every time we tried to own a part of what we were creating we were held at bay. It felt like we were the goose that laid golden eggs, and all they wanted was to own us, or destroy us.

Character development, *Thumbelina*, Don Bluth Productions © 1994.

Bill: So what brought you back to the States?

Don: We had sold off parts of the store until there was nothing left to sell [laughs]. Actually, it was a lot more complicated than that. We no longer owned the company. In 1990, about 10 months before the completion of *Rock-A-Doodle*, our company closed a $60 million, three-picture deal with a Belgian investor. It was a great deal. However, a few months into the production of *A Troll in Central Park*, he ran into financial problems and asked if a wealthy associate could come in and take his position in the deal. Suddenly we were in a new negotiation. The negotiation went on and on until the advanced funds that we had for production started diminishing. This put our company in a weak position and with almost 490 employees between Dublin and Burbank. With no bank to bail us out, we agreed to transfer our shares in the company in exchange for the $60 million in funding from another source. Cash flow began again and then in the spring of 1993, with *A Troll in Central Park* and *Thumbelina* complete and in postproduction, and *The Pebble and the Penguin* just a few months from completion, the investor's bank came in and shut down the operation, a move that forced us into the protection of receivership or bankruptcy in Dublin. After about four months in the courts, the company was bought by a subsidiary of Star TV in China. They asked us to stay and complete the dubs of the first two films and complete production of the third film. We agreed. At least it would keep the Dublin crew employed and perhaps give us an opportunity to make more films. However, after agreeing to stay with the new company, which was using our Don Bluth namesake, they eventually reneged on the agreed contract and refused to sign it. However, what really brought us back was when I received a call from Bill Mechanic, the then-president of Walt Disney International Distribution and Worldwide Video divisions. He was being recruited to become chairman at 20th Century Fox.

Bill said he wanted to meet with me and Gary, since he would not move to Fox unless they would allow him to build a feature animation division. He knew our work but didn't know us. He had heard that we were difficult to work with and wanted to meet us in person and get to know us. He wanted us to help him build that animation division. By the end of January of 1994 we signed with Fox. And, oddly enough, we took most of the Americans, Canadians, many of our trained Irish, plus our top internationals from Spain, Brazil, and East Germany with us back home to the USA! Better still, Fox built the new studio in Phoenix, Arizona. It was so nice to be warm again. Ireland was not warm. The people were, but the weather … often misty and cold—cold to the bone. And we were very fortunate to have brought members of our trained crew back with us, 162 of them. Disney was producing animated films as fast as they could. Jeffrey Katzenberg had just left Disney, joining Spielberg and Geffen to start DreamWorks SKG; he was taking as many Disney animation staff with him as he could recruit. Between them, they hired most of the best-trained talent in LA. When it was announced that Fox had struck a deal with us, Fox was inundated with over 10,000 applicants

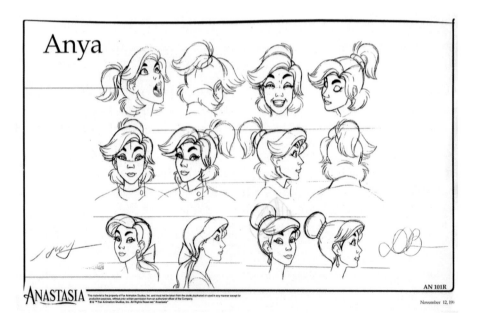

Model sheet, "Anya", *Anastasia*, 1997 © Fox.

Sketch, *Anastasia*, 1997 © Fox.

from around the world in the first month. When we finally started making *Anastasia*, we had hired animation artists from fourteen different countries, many of them from Canada, the Philippines, and local Arizona artists.

Our first film with Fox Animation, *Anastasia*, was a really fun picture to make. I had no idea that making an animated feature in widescreen had become quite so easy. You didn't have to work on wide paper anymore. There was no more Xeroxing images onto cels. In fact, we didn't use cels anymore. We just scanned the drawings in and then added color. We could add multiple levels to the animation. We could quickly do all those beautiful things that I saw Walt do in those classic animated films from the golden age of animation. You were limited only by your imagination. It was a wonderful time. Then, after *Anastasia*, Fox LA didn't have a project ready.

There was a story called *Planet Ice*, something science fiction, that was stalled and going nowhere fast. Bill Mechanic asked Gary and me if we could do anything with it. There was some recorded dialogue and something like three sequences storyboarded, which had been scanned and edited as a digital work-print, but no animation. However, there were piles of preproduction drawings for character designs and location paintings to look at. Since we hadn't been officially assigned our second project yet, money for the Phoenix animation studio was running out. Bill said candidly, "Either take this science fiction film and make it, or we have to lay everybody off." We had no choice. We took it and made what eventually became *Titan A.E.* Well, wait a minute, I almost forgot *Bartok the Magnificent*. This was a movie we came up with after *Anastasia*, in order to keep the studio crew intact, and give time to Chris [Meledandri] and his LA writers time to come up with the next feature film concept.

Bill: That was your spin-off from *Anastasia*?

Don: Yes. It was a prequel. It was never distributed theatrically as a motion picture. It went straight to video; it was planned as a direct-to-video project. However, it did keep the wolf from the door.

Storyboards, *Titan A.E.*, 2000 © Fox.

And as we made *Titan A.E.*, something was brewing again. There was a lot of politics going on at 20th Century Fox. Bill Mechanic had made a picture called *Fight Club*, which according to rumor, Rupert Murdoch did not like. So there was a little bit of friction there. Bill, as it turned out, was being eliminated from the studio. Since we were his baby, they chose not to promote *Titan*. That definitely hurt us. And when Bill was officially removed from Fox, the Arizona Fox Animation Studio went down too. Basically, that was the last door that opened … and slammed shut. There you have it.

Bill: What about new methods like motion capture? Did you find yourself adjusting your style as new technology was introduced?

Don: I believe the human eye is able to look at cartoons and accept them as they are. There's no problem. When you look at an animated movie that is depicting human movement, if the movement is too caricatured or too sloppy, the audience can lose the willing suspension of disbelief. And that pulls them out of the picture. I've always advocated shooting live action anytime you're trying to approach human movement. Otherwise you might miss some of the subtle nuances of the human body's rhythm. Many people don't know this, but the entire movie of *Cinderella* was shot live action, as was our *Anastasia*.

Bill: What about postproduction? How involved are you? Do you find yourself going back and making significant changes?

Don: I'm really not good in postproduction. I just don't have enough patience to sit there and go back and forth, back and forth. Gary Goldman is exceptionally good at it. I just let him have it. My attention is entirely consumed by the storyboard and preproduction. That's where you make critical decisions about characters, close-ups, long shots, lighting, *et cetera*. That's where I believe my editing strength really comes into play.

Bill: Is there anything you would like to say before we wrap up?

Don: If I had to look back on my whole career, on all the people that I had the privilege of working with, like Steven Spielberg, George Lucas, and all the actors who gave us their voices, it's almost too much to take in. It simply amazes me. I've worked with truly amazing and talented people. And that includes individuals that are not famous at all. They just worked diligently to help us put something beautiful on the screen. It's the people. That's been the joy in my career. We created unique worlds that have encouraged, inspired, and simply made people happy, whether they were having a great day or a horrible one. We gave them a sweet place in which to get lost, for just a little bit. I have no regrets. Walking away from the Disney Studio was a good thing. It forced me to cut my own path. And I always knew that

I could do that. So now I'm just trying to make sure I'm giving it all back. There are lessons that need to be passed on. We've made movies with modern technology and with antiquated technology, and I believe, second only to good storytelling (writing), drawing is still the seed and inspiration to good animation filmmaking, be it traditional hand-drawn or CG animation. Anyway, it's been great talking with you guys. Thank you for including me as one of the many animation directors you are interviewing for your book.

Ron: Thanks for taking the time to sit with us. This book wouldn't be complete without your story.

4
Pete Docter Interview

Pete Docter © Pixar.
Photo: Deborah Coleman.

Pete Docter has called his life "blessed." Others might call it lucky, but most would say that it was the audience that got lucky when Pete entered animation.

He had an unlikely start, growing up in Minnesota, never a hotbed of the industry. But strangely (or luckily), Pete stumbled onto the only animation company in the state and got some early training and encouragement. When it came time to go to school he made another fortuitous move, enrolling in the only existing character animation program in the West—CalArts. There he met some of the artists who would change the future of the business. One of them, John Lasseter, offered him a job at the only company he has ever worked for since: Pixar.

You could call Pete a towering presence, since he is (and always has been for his age) extremely tall. He has a remarkably mild, relaxed way of leading a team. His career was an example of the peculiar

Pixar culture, where a "nondirector type" is given trust and support and becomes the ultimate directorial success; a director with not just an unusual personal style but an absolutely original creative vision.

When Pete Docter accepted his Oscar for *Up*, he said, in front of that worldwide TV audience: "Never did I dream that making a flip book out of my third-grade math book would lead to this." Pete still likes flip books; he draws one every year and sends copies out as his family Christmas card. I treasure my collection. It takes talent to do a flip book. To take the time to do one when you're a world-famous director is something else again.

We interviewed Pete at the Four Seasons Hotel in Beverly Hills.

Bill Kroyer

Bill: When did you first become aware of animation and when did you first think that you might be an animator?

Pete: Well, I remember doing flip books in the corners of my math book in second grade. Even before that, I think it started for me with *Charlie Brown*. You know, there's something about those drawings, the expressivity of Schultz's work that made me think, "Wow, I gotta figure this out." But then what really hooked me was movement. Not drawing—though I always admired great drawings. You know how there's always the kid that's in your class who's the master draftsman and who's drawing dragons and horses and stuff? That was not me. My passion was making things move. That's what got me hooked.

Bill: You figured that out by yourself?

Pete: Yeah. I don't remember, maybe I saw some television special on animation or something. But I made tons—and my mom still has them of course—tons of flip books and movies.

Bill: What happened in high school? Did you somehow find a way to improve your skills in animation in high school?

Pete: There was not much going on in terms of animation or film in my high school art classes. We got to make belt buckles and linoleum prints and things, but nobody really knew anything about animation. And of course this was before the

Internet—you really had to search for information. I remember hearing about the Preston Blair animation book, and I looked almost a year for it because I didn't know it would be at the art store. I was looking at bookstores.

Bill: But you knew about it?

Pete: Yeah, I read mention of it somewhere. And then of course *The Illusion of Life* came out and when I saw that I poured over every page, trying to absorb it all. It surprised me though how much of the book's focus was on acting. This just shows you where I was. I was looking for more information on technique, like how do you get things to move nicely, with follow-through and overlap and the squash-and-stretch? Frank [Thomas] and Ollie [Johnston] covered that, but most of their focus was on the inner workings of characters and storytelling. That surprised me.

Bill: It's interesting about timing and culture. That book was so influential. There's a whole generation that found that book and managed to build a career out of it. So by the time you got to high school, had you done anything that was like a legitimate film that was actually shot with a camera?

Pete: I had made a whole bunch of really bad Super 8 silent animated films at home on my own. And then I was lucky enough to be placed in this high school program that took kids that had a passion for something and paired them with companies. Another classmate who was into artificial intelligence went over to Honeywell. I got placed at this commercial animation house called *Bajus-Jones*.

Bill: Where were you doing this?

Pete: Bajus-Jones was in Edina. I grew up in Bloomington, Minnesota.

Bill: Wasn't Bajus-Jones the only animation company in Minnesota?

Pete: So far as I knew, pretty much, yeah. So what they did was fantastic. They told me, "Well, you seem like a kid with a passion for this. Come on in, here's the paper, there's the down-shooter, use anything you want." So I just sat there all day and did my own stuff. And they said, "This will be your mentor, Bill Barder. He's working, so don't bug him too much, but if you have questions, you can go to him." Once in a while I'd go in with a scene and he'd take a look and give me pointers. So I did this film that was a really clunky sort of parody of an advertisement for the *Gifted and Talented Testing Institute*.

Bill: Commercial piece?

Pete: Yeah, it was promoting this made-up gifted and talented school, and this egghead kid comes in and they give him these tests. It barely makes sense, but that's your early stuff.

Bill: Unbelievable break. To actually live near an animation studio, and be allowed to go in while you're still in high school.

Pete: Before that I'd done my own stuff using my dad's Super 8 camera. I'd figured out looking at Super 8 film footage that each one of those little frames is slightly different. And I knew my flip books were the same principle, so I figured, "I wonder if I could film my flip books?" I tried filming as I flipped through one, and then later I tried just triggering the shutter, "Click!" once per image. Then I turned the page and "Click!" did it again, and again … and it worked! The camera took two or three frames per click, but it looked like it was moving. Eventually I wore out my dad's camera, because it was not built for that sort of thing.

Bill: Were there any good animators at Bajus-Jones who you could learn directly from?

Pete: Well, the guy that I mentioned, Bill Barder, was a great draftsman. And he was very patient with me. We stay in contact to this day. The thing, of course, working at a commercial house, you have to have this wide range of styles, because you're going from sort of RO Blechman style to Kurtz & Friends style to who knows what. So Bill was great and I got some good experience there. But it was really CalArts that took me to the next level.

Bill: So in 1986 you entered CalArts with a bit of a head start, I would think?

Pete: I was one of the only people in my class that had actually done animation before starting at school. At that time, it was hard to get access to the kind of equipment you needed to create animated films. All the other guys there had an interest in it and, of course, had drawn a lot, but, yeah, I had a head start.

Bill: How did that change your experience compared to others there? Did you end up being more productive? Do you think you got more out of it?

Pete: Well, it's funny. I remember, as I struggled to animate that first year, after five or six months there was something that just kind of clicked, and after that I could feel movement. That was the first step for me, going from just making a series of still drawings to really feeling movement. It's a difficult concept to really articulate; you just sort of feel it.

Bill: I always called it "going in the zone." You know, you're in the zone. You're not even aware of anything going on.

Pete: Yeah, absolutely. You get lost in the work when you're really going.

Bill: How long were you there? You actually graduated from CalArts, right?

Pete: I graduated after three years. I'd had credits that I transferred over from the University of Minnesota, where I'd gone for one year before attending CalArts.

Bill: How did you see yourself progressing in those three years? Other than getting that initial feeling of movement, how far do you think you came?

Pete: Well, my first-year film was called *Winter*. It was about a little kid who gets dressed up and wants to go outside, and he's all bundled up and he can't even move and he tips over. It's kind of a nothing idea, but I remember it came about as I was talking to Barry Johnson, and I was telling this story about my sister, you know, growing up in Minnesota—it's so frigid cold that you have to bundle kids up in multiple layers—and she could barely walk, and it made us all laugh. And he says, "That would be a good idea for a film." And I thought, "Hey, maybe he's right!" So I boarded it out, and it was clunky, crude drawing compared to some of the other guys. But when all the films screened, mine got big laughs. In fact it made it into *Mike and Spike's Festival of Animation*, and it was one of the biggest laughs in that show. And I realized something about films: it's really all about the idea. I initially thought it was about the quality of your drawings, good design, or how well something moved. But of course it's really all about the idea.

Joe Ranft, who was a story teacher at CalArts, used to say that making animated films is like telling a joke and waiting for three years to see if anyone laughs. It's tough to wait that long for a response, but filmmaking really is a lot like joke telling, or storytelling. And I think it's really important to be in the audience for the reaction, because that's what really teaches you.

Bill: Were there teachers or students that had a particular influence on you when you were there?

Pete: Oh yeah. Everybody! [Laughter] The first thing that shocked me was sitting down in Bob Winquist's class—he was the general director of the program—and he said, "We're going to teach you design." And I thought, "What the heck does design have to do with anything? I wanna draw cartoons!" Just shows you how ignorant I was. Bob's approach grew out of the Chouinard Art Institute, which was to teach the basic principles of abstract design: contrast, shape variation, contour continuation, all those basic concepts. And I'm surprised to this day how often I use that stuff in every single thing I do, from story, to character design, to sound design, to movement. All those basic principles apply to everything.

Winter, 1988.

Next Door, 1990.

Bill: Why is that so important to getting the story or the character across?

Pete: Well these fundamental principles are key to putting ideas across—for getting your ideas to read to the audience. They apply not only to design, but storytelling. When you first learn stuff, it's all very, very intellectual. But once you use them for a while, they become a natural, instinctive part of your work. They're also great tools for making things better. You'll be working on a project and you just know, "Something about this isn't working. How can I make it better?" And you step back and analyze, and it's that time that those concepts are so important.

Bill: After CalArts you went right to Pixar, which in a way was a second job because you'd already been at Bajus-Jones.

Pete: I'd also been an intern at Disney between my second and third year. Oh, and while I was at CalArts, Mike Giaimo—who's another huge influence—was teaching character design, and during the day at that time he was working at Bob Rogers and Company. Mike drafted a couple of us for a couple of weeks to do some story work.

Bill: It's interesting how you were influenced so much by design, and not so much by the animation teachers there.

Pete: Well, design and story were big for me, which I was not expecting. Chris Buck was my animation teacher. He was great, not just in being a very patient teacher, but also in adapting himself to what each student was trying to do, both with drawing and movement. "Oh, I see you're doing sort of a Canadian Film Board style," or a UPA thing or whatever. He'd support what you were doing instead of trying to change it to his style. He's an amazing animator. But even there, much of Chris' emphasis was on acting and story. So he was really great.

Bill: So that meant you were able to kind of flow with your more natural inclination and style. Did you feel like you had a style that was different than others?

Pete: Not really. I just kind of did what appealed to me. I love the work of Bill Watterson, which is pretty obvious in my first student film. I really relied on those "storytelling poses." I'd go from one pose to another and then just hold. And it was the pauses and funny expressions that were getting the laughs. So in a sense that first film wasn't really full animation. I remember it was Russ Edmonds, my second-year animation teacher, who pushed me to go beyond that. He said, "You can do the poppy, pose-to-pose thing. That's great. Now push further and do more full, fluid stuff."

Bill: How did the Pixar hire come about?

Pete: Well, I'd seen Pixar's films in the festivals. And John Lasseter had seen my films in the festivals. But I never even considered applying at Pixar because everybody knew it was just John Lasseter and a bunch of technical guys up there.

Bill: It was a tiny place in those days.

Pete: Yeah. So apparently John went to his friend Joe Ranft—my story teacher—and asked him, "Are there any good up-and-coming students that might be good hires for us?" And Joe thought of me. I remember having lunch at Tiny Naylor's with Joe Ranft and John Lasseter and thinking, "How did I get here?!"

Bill: And that was it? John just asked you to come work with him?

Pete: He said, "Could you come up?" And I didn't even ask what they were paying. I'm telling you, much of this was luck. I was born in the right year. Two years before, the only jobs out there were on *He-Man and the Masters of the Universe* and, you know, crappy stuff like that. And then right as I graduated, *The Simpsons* was starting, Disney was on the upswing, there were all kinds of opportunities. Going into school, my dream was to someday be like Frank Thomas or Ollie Johnston. "I'm gonna work at Disney and draw and animate." But instead I went to this up-and-coming computer company that hadn't really done much except short films.

Bill: So you were the tenth hire and the third animator?

Pete: Within the animation group, yeah.

Bill: Who were the other two?

Pete: John was first. And then, I think three months earlier, Andrew Stanton had been hired. So as I arrived, John said, "Well, I'm busy, so sit down and watch Andrew. Learn by watching him. He's animating his first commercial." I guess Andrew had worked on the story and some design work up until that point, so this was his first animation. I was sitting watching him, expecting to learn. And I did learn some new expletives. He couldn't get the computer to do anything!

Bill: Was it a Lifesavers thing or something?

Pete: Trident chewing gum. There was this singing mint leaf on top of a piano and an ice cube playing the piano [laughter].

Bill: Were you drawing there or did they teach you the computer right away?

Pete: It was just right into the computer. I learned key-framing and the sort of layered approach that computer animation required, which is totally different, of course, than drawing. And I remember thinking, "If I was drawing this, I'd be done in minutes.

From left to right—Pete Docter, Andrew Stanton, John Lasseter, and Joe Ranft at Pixar Animation Studios, © Pixar.
Photo: Deborah Coleman.

Instead this is taking me hours!" It was really frustrating, initially. But, in the end, I learned a new way to think, and it was really valuable. Even if I were to go back to hand-drawn, what I learned from computer animation was great analysis. Plus, with computers you can try something and if you don't like it, you just revert to the last saved version and off you go.

So, first thing I did was a Listerine boxing commercial that John directed. It was funny—I thought for sure the hand of the artist came through in the drawings, and that with CG you wouldn't be able to tell my work from anyone else's. But a guy I went to school with, Donavan Cook, he had seen the commercial, and over the phone he picked out exactly which scenes I animated. Of course there's no drawing at all—computer animation is sort of like animating a puppet. And so the fact that he was able to pick out my scenes ... well, I guess it was kind of bad because my stuff stood out so much. But I took it as a compliment at the time.

Bill: And what was it about your stuff that he was thinking about?

Pete: Well, my stuff was way more extreme and bouncy, and John was much more subtle with his work. But I think we kind of influenced each other. I remember him saying that he really liked how far I was pushing things. And of course his control and subtlety was something that I definitely had to learn.

Bill: So you encountered the thing that people who go from drawing to computers come up against: the need to analyze and break down and reconstruct the pieces in order to find that zone feel. Before you felt it; now all of a sudden you're confronted with this thing where you can't just feel it. And that's something that probably a lot of people end up not being able to do.

Pete: Yeah, it's true. *Toy Story* was educational for me because there were so many different artists from different backgrounds. This was the first computer-animated feature. Of course there were one or two people that had done computer animation for years up to that point, but by and large we had to train these guys. Some—like stop-motion animators—adapted pretty readily. Computer animation is closer to the way stop-motion animators think, it seems to me. Whereas for others—especially the hand-drawn guys with years of experience—the more years they'd had in another medium, the harder it was to shift their way of thinking. The key for me was thumbnailing. You know, if I could thumbnail something out and know it in my head, then I could start to break it down, and know what the torso is doing, and the upper leg, and the knee, and so on.

Bill: How long did you work on commercials and those kinds of things before you moved onto the next project?

Pete: Well, too long for me. I actually talked to John about leaving Pixar at one point. "All of my friends are down at Disney doing acting; they're doing serious feature work, and we're here making bouncy happy products. I just don't know how much longer I can wait." And I remember him saying, "Well, fine, go if you have to, but I think you'd be making a big mistake. We're just on the edge of something." Luckily I didn't leave, thank goodness.

Bill: So he didn't tell you what it was?

Pete: Well, I knew that they were trying to land this television special, because I was working on the story with him and Andrew and eventually Joe Ranft. But to be honest I doubt that John knew of anything specific at that point. He just had a general optimism and confidence in what we were doing. Of course the television special didn't work out, and it was quite a few months after that finally the Disney thing landed. It was late '91 or something in there when we started working on it.

Bill: When that happened, what was your role in it?

Pete: It pretty much just flowed right from the way we always worked. Every commercial we got, John, Andrew, and I would sit down and we would just brainstorm. The great thing we had with the Pixar short films … since they had won Oscars and were so entertaining, it meant that the clients, beyond just the look of computer graphics, wanted our creative input as well. So we would take their ideas and say, "Well all right, the way they planned this spot is really kind of lousy. What are they trying to do here? Let's make our own version." And so the feature developed in the same way, where the three of us would get together and talk. What seemed great yesterday seemed crappy today, so we'd redo it and redo it again. John would rope us both in on everything. He'd say, "What do you guys think?" He's a great collaborator. We had a weird situation on that movie, because apparently John had been sought after by Disney for years, asking him to come back and work there. He'd worked at Disney years earlier but was let go. John kept telling them, "No, let us do a computer film up here for you guys." Prior to that, all animation at Disney was done in house.

Tim Burton broke that mold with *Nightmare Before Christmas*, which was produced in San Francisco with Henry Selick directing, and it worked out well enough for Disney to say, "All right, let's try it again." So John came back to Andrew and me and basically asked, "So what do you guys want to do? What should this film be about?" Of course this was exactly the opposite of everybody else in Hollywood who have their scripts they've been trying desperately to get made for 18 years. So we had this weird backwards situation. We had developed a story for this TV special, which was about a toy. Joe Ranft told John that he'd developed these great characters in the Pixar short films and felt they could be taken further. So the TV special was based around the character in the short film *Tin Toy*. And that's really where *Toy Story* started; it was built from that.

Bill: So the small studio and informal setup allowed you to be kind of a generalist in the production, right? Rather than being pigeonholed, your first experience on a feature was a broad experience.

Pete: Very much so. Scriptwriting, boarding, character design, everything. In fact, when students today ask me about working at Pixar, I always suggest they find a small studio to start out in. Find somewhere that you can contribute all around and really get your feet wet and can have more of an effect on the end result.

Bill: In the production, did you focus primarily on animation?

Pete: Story and design first, then animation. See, we were so naive, we thought: first you do the story, then that's done; and then you go on and build the characters and sets, then that's done; and then you animate and so on. So our plan was we were going to wrap up story, and then Andrew and I would go on and be co-heads of animation. And of course, the story was a lot harder to nail down than we thought, and we struggled on and on. When it got time to shift into production, the thought was that I'd lead the charge, train the animators, test models, and so on. And Andrew would come along when the story was locked. Well, story just kept getting revised, and so Andrew stayed with Joe working on story and I ended up as the sole supervising animator.

Bill: How much animation did you end up doing?

Pete: Quite a bit. I don't remember footage, but I did stuff on almost every character, and quite a bit on Woody. I can still go through that film and point out who did every scene.

Bill: You were also probably involved in software revision and making recommendations for the tools.

Pete: Well, you know the software had developed over the course of the short films and commercials. I don't recall a ton of software changes during production. It was pretty rudimentary, looking back—when we started on *Toy Story*, we didn't even have inverse kinematics. So when Woody would walk, or even stand and shift his weight, we had to work with this tool that we called *IKT*—inverse kinematics tool—which would calculate frame-by-frame what the two joints should do to make his foot lock in this place. The tool would step through and place values for the joints into the spreadsheet

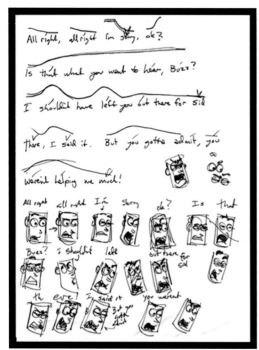

Sketches, Pete Docter, *Toy Story,* © Disney/Pixar.

tool on every frame. And usually you'd hit record, and you would come back and the foot would be wobbling all over the place. You'd have to go back and hand-massage it so it would stop shuddering and just stay still. So we animators spent a lot of time doing stuff like that. I remember thinking, "Shouldn't a computer be able to figure out these calculations better than me?"

Bill: Were there dedicated riggers, or were you kind of doing that as well?

Pete: No, we animators didn't do any rigging. I would work with the riggers—we called them *modelers* at that point—to figure out where we wanted controls and stuff. I had done a little bit on commercials, both modeling and rigging, but there were separate groups of people that did that on *Toy Story*, as well as shading and lighting. We animators focused exclusively on the movement.

Bill: So on *Toy Story* you were the animation supervisor. What's next?

Pete: Well, what happened along the way—and this was a product of being so small and casual—was that Andrew and I would go everywhere with John. We'd go to recording sessions with Tom Hanks and Tim Allen, the orchestra scoring sessions, and I'd sit in on layout—all to help in any way I could. And along the way, I watched how the whole process went. So when John was out of the office, Andrew and I could fill in. We knew what he wanted, and we knew the history of what we'd already tried. But just as importantly, that really trained both of us for directing in the future. I don't think John was really thinking that far ahead—maybe he was, but I think more likely it's just that's the way he likes to work; he thrives on collaboration. I really respected the way John ran animation dailies. It was a completely open forum. Everyone would speak up with opinions on everyone else's work. I always figured he took this from his days at Disney, but apparently he learned it at ILM in the late eighties. It was an environment where everybody was free to throw out ideas. So, you know, shots would be shown and anybody from any part of the room could say, "You know, what if his eyebrow was reversed? That would be better because ... blah blah blah." So you'd shout out suggestions and at the end of course John would synopsize, "All right, Mr. Animator, here are the three things I want you to do: bang bang bang." But out of this open discussion I think we really learned a lot from each other. I had a great education, watching and participating.

Bill: Are those things you continue to use in your own work?

Pete: Oh yeah, absolutely.

Bill: What an amazing thing to be able to do—because you had not really been exposed before to scoring or recording or anything like that.

Pete: No. Well, growing up I was part of a youth symphony in Minnesota, and I'd written and arranged an orchestral score for my third-year film. So I'd had very fundamental, bare bones–level exposure to music scoring, but this was at a whole new level. I learned how to talk to a composer and things like that.

Bill: What did you learn about talking to a composer that became valuable?

Pete: Well, something I learned was not to tell people how to do their job. You tell them what's necessary to inspire them. And usually that means speaking more emotionally about things—as opposed to, "I want a B-flat here," or, "take the cellos out," or whatever. Instead, you want to say, "I'm looking for the feeling of anxiety or tension here," or, "I want that sense of a beautiful spring morning and you can feel the wind in your hair." It's the same when you're communicating with animators. I don't want to tell them, "Have his hand here in frame seven and then, in five frames, move up to this." It's more productive to say, "I want him to burn his hand, and you know what that feels like when you've touched the stove and, aach, it's that searing pain." So you communicate that feeling you're after, and the animator will then kick in all these ideas, much better ideas than I would ever have. Same thing with composers. That way the film is not just the director's ideas; it's a collaboration of artists working together, plussing every stage.

Bill: And how do you direct actors?

Pete: I try to do the same thing. Working with actors is especially dangerous after you've built your reels and you have a scratch track. After you watch them like 8,000 times, those scratch performances get drilled into your head. You have a certain cadence and a read that's stuck in your ear, and there's a great temptation to try to get that from the actor. You want to do a line-read: "Say it like this." But every time you do that, even if the actor asks for it, you end up with

Michael Giacchino and Pete Docter © Pixar. Photo: Deborah Coleman.

a stilted performance. I've learned instead to tune my ear to listen for believability, so that when the actor is performing the line, I just try to sense whether it feels truthful. That's what I listen for. You want to feel that they are actually in that head space, that they're going through this, whatever this scene is. I remember talking to Tom Hanks, because he was just amazing. He would do fifteen, twenty takes, and each one totally felt like he just came up with that dialog right there on the spot. Of course, it's all written on the page. So I asked him, "What's going through your head as you're acting?" and he said, "Ideally, as little as possible." He was trying not to kill the performance by overanalyzing or overthinking. Of course that doesn't really work for us as animators—you do really have to analyze everything. But that was a guide for me as to how to talk to the actors. Just get them there emotionally, and they'll do the job.

Bill: The animator component is so much more complicated because the character is created by an entire team.

Pete: Yeah.

Bill: How do you discover your characters? Is there a point where you feel you're starting to know them in the design stage, or are you waiting until the actor performs?

Pete: Well, I think the key is the word you just used, "discover." You know, I used to imagine that the way stories were created was that Walt Disney would wake up one morning and just say, "*Dumbo!*," and it would be fully formed in his head and they would just make that. And the reality is, of course, that it's this weird, organic, messy process, where you have one thing, and then you add something else, and then you take parts away. For Buzz Lightyear, for example, we had very clear ideas on what he was like when we started. At that point he was sort of a "Dudley Do-Right" type—you know, he even spoke in that sort of announcerly, superhero voice. And that's what we were looking for initially when it came to casting voice talent. But John had listened to some of Tim Allen's comedy and thought he would be great, and so he hired him. I listened to the dialog recorded at the first session and I remember Andrew and I look-ing at each other going, "This is a disaster. He can't do what we're looking for." You know, because we had that "Dudley Do-Right" kind of approach in mind. And he was approaching the role much more casually, or suave, like a cop.

Sketch, Pete Docter, *Toy Story*, © Disney/Pixar.

So out of desperation we started to adjust the writing to this, and in the end, because of Tim Allen's contributions and us writing to that, I think the character of Buzz is much more specific and unique than it would have been if we had just gone with the "Dudley Do-Right" guy. Since then, this process of rewriting to fit the actor is something we do routinely on almost every role.

Bill: How did *Monsters, Inc.* come about?

Pete: Well, I remember I was in the shower. I had been doing a sort of postanalysis of *Toy Story* for myself, and I was surprised how many people had confessed to me that they too believed their toys came to life when they weren't in the room. I thought, "I wonder if there are other commonly held childhood beliefs like this?" Well, I knew there were monsters that hid in my closet at night. The subject matter seemed to hold promise to me, so I put together a short pitch. The story I brought in was totally different, but I came in—there was a small group of us, just Jeff Pidgeon and Harley Jessup working in development at that time—and I pitched it to them. And over the course of weeks, months, we built on the idea, and it totally changed. Jill Culton came on shortly thereafter, and between the four of us, plus John and Andrew, this was the core group that really contributed heavily to creating the story and characters that we ended up with on *Monsters, Inc.*

Bill: So I guess the chemistry of the studio is starting to change now, right? It's growing, getting bigger.

Pete: Right.

Bill: And this is your first time as a lead on a project at Pixar. On *Monsters, Inc.*, you are really the guy.

Pete: Well, yeah, but that was sort of ill defined. Early on I was in charge of the development group. But I don't think it was really definitive that I was going to direct it. I don't remember exactly when that came along. After *Toy Story*, John Lasseter went right on into *A Bug's Life*, and then when *Toy Story 2* sort of blew up he took that on. So he was on three films, one after another, and I think he was ready to take a break. [Laughter]

Sketch, Pete Docter, *Monsters, Inc.*, © Disney/Pixar.

Bill: What was it like to have to take on that amount of work? Did you feel you had to impose a certain way of working or did it organically form around you?

Pete: Well, I remember feeling very nervous because I'm not a take-that-hill, fill-the-room kind of guy. I work well with people one on one, but I'm not the guy to put up in front to charge up the troops and give 'em an inspirational speech. Brad Bird can do that. He's just crazy good. I always feel awkward. I relate to the "shy people" Garrison Keillor talks about. So directing was uncomfortable for me at the beginning. I also had this idea that now everybody works for me, and I have this weight of responsibility. And of course what you realize very quickly is that we all work for the story. They're not working for me— we're all in the service of what's going to best communicate this story to the audience.

Bill: Did you ever feel that your reticence put you in jeopardy at Pixar?

Pete: Oh yeah. I mean, there was a time when Steve Jobs took me on a walk and said, "You know, I don't know if things are working out with you. You need to step it up. When times get hard, people need to know they can count on the leader. And I don't sense that's coming from you."

Bill: At what stage was this?

Pete: This was about halfway through—two or three years in. We were just starting production, and we were still struggling with story.

Bill: How did you react to that discussion?

Pete: Well, of course my stress level went way up. But I was the first director there who was not John, so I had to find my own way. I think in part Steve was reacting to how sort of flippant I seemed to be. My attitude was, "Let's just have fun and enjoy this." And Steve had an intensity and seriousness about him that made him who he was, and that's what everybody respected about him. But that's not who I am. And being insecure, I struggled sometimes to hear my own instincts. That inner voice is kind of quiet sometimes. Everyone has to find their own way of working. Regardless, I think the key to the whole directing thing is understanding story: how to craft a good story. That's the hard part. Because once you crack the story, you have these amazing talented people, and if you feed them the right information and steer them the right way, the film comes into focus.

Bill: Did you take anything away from that encounter with Steve Jobs? Did it affect the way you worked after that?

Pete: This sounds crass—but it made me realize the importance of salesmanship. Early on I had in my head what I wanted, but I wasn't really very good at telling other people and standing up for it. "Here's my vision, here's how it's all going to come together."

That is something that is really important, and John is just instinctively good at it. You know, anytime you sit down with somebody, it's your opportunity to get them excited about what they're working on and show them how beautiful this could be, how it will affect people, and how important what they're doing is to the story. And that goes for the team of artists but also for executives. You have to be able to refocus and see it from their perspective—how they're seeing it and what's important to them about this story.

Bill: OK, so you're in the middle of *Monsters, Inc.* Steve has this conversation with you and the story isn't working. How did you deal with that?

Pete: I took it very personally. You know, I had pitched this concept and everybody went, "Yeah, okay, I'm on board! *Monsters. That sounds great!*" Especially when we came up with the idea that they scare kids for a living, that's their job, they clock in, they clock out. You have all this workplace humor, juxtaposed with these big guys with fangs and slobber and horns, and everybody could see the potential in that. But the next step was finding our main character. You need to fall in love with and care about that main character, so that you as the audience want what he wants. And we just didn't have a good grasp on that until very late in production. There was this sort of vacuum, this hole in the center of the story. People were asking, "What is this guy really about?" And there again, if I could have articulated more fully my thoughts—and I had this in my head from early on—the heart of the film was the relationship between this big hulking monster and this little kid who changes him. He loves his job, but he's torn by his feelings for this kid. And the fearlessness that the kid has, and the fear that the monster has towards the kid, seemed like great potential for humor—and ultimately emotion. If I could have communicated that to people, it would have been easier. I think the thing that really turned that around was when board artist Nate Stanton—he's Andrew Stanton's brother—storyboarded this scene where Sulley is waiting for the little girl to go to the bathroom and they end up in this sort of peek-a-boo game. And people suddenly reacted to that. "Oh yeah, this is funny, this is entertaining. Okay, I see where this is going." But up until then, I wasn't able to communicate where I was placing my chips. You know, what's the audience gonna get when they go to this movie?

Bill: So what was your role at that moment as a director?

Pete: I was trying to find the core of the film. At that point, you do that by building the reels. We learned early on that story reels are the proof that shows whether you have a film or you don't. And so you're trying to discover the film in these little pieces. So you go, "Okay, in this scene we've proven how Mike and Sulley are going to relate to each other and how funny that's going to be. And now people can extrapolate through the rest of the film backwards and forward and see what it's going to be like."

Monsters, Inc., 2001. © 2001 Disney/Pixar.

Then you look for the next building block. Initially you're feeling around in the dark for any little toehold. Joe Ranft had these great analogies. He told me once that working on story is like driving a car with all bald tires, and you're stuck in the mud, and the more you accelerate, the more you just sink. And then you finally discover that you have one tire that has a little bit of tread on it. So you move all the sandbags over so you'll just dig in on that one tire, and it sloooowly starts to pull you out of the mud, and then you get a little more traction, and so on. And finally you're out and running.

Bill: That's fantastic!

Pete: Yeah, I know. Joe sure had a great way of looking at things. We miss him.

Bill: Every director has a different way of working with his team. You have your head of story, you have your production designer, you have your editor, all of whom are massively important. How did you find yourself relating to your team in your first big directorial effort?

Pete: I think my strength and weakness is that I'm a people pleaser—I want everybody to be happy. This instinct comes in very handy when it comes to making the film. I want the audience to be satisfied—that's what drives every decision. But it got me in trouble when I first started directing, when it came to giving feedback. I didn't want to upset anybody, so when someone came to me with an idea, I'd be like, "Yeah, that sounds great." In the back of my head I'm thinking, "That's not going to work." But I don't want to make him mad or shut him down. So this is like a disaster waiting to happen, right? You absolutely have to make decisions and close doors, and be very clear about where things should go, or you'll get nowhere. Of course since then I've discovered ways of being positive, of steering people when they come with ideas or directions that don't work with the direction I'm going. Sometimes you do just have to say flat out, "You know what, that's a great idea for a different movie, but it doesn't work here." And you try to explain clearly, "Here's what I'm trying to put across." So that's been a big lesson for me. The positive side to my trying to make everyone happy is that I do feel like I listen and that ultimately the people I work with contribute creatively to the film in big ways. It's one of the great pleasures, getting all these great new fresh ideas that wouldn't have occurred in one brain. It makes for a much stronger film.

Bill: That's a huge lesson—retaining your personal style of consideration for people without rolling over. Since at the end of the day, the film has to come first. The story and the film come first.

Pete: You have to hold to the things that make the film speak to you, and yet also invite in all the other ideas, people, and talents that you have around you.

Bill: What kind of a personal support staff did you have on *Monsters, Inc.*? Were there director's assistants or people taking notes? Being the first one after John to attempt this at Pixar, you probably had to be blazing a trail and doing something different.

Pete: I inherited the production process that had been developed on *Toy Story* and *A Bug's Life*, and we used the same kind of system on *Monsters, Inc.* The producer, Darla Anderson, had produced *A Bug's Life* with John, so at least one of us knew what was going on! We did make a few changes to the pipeline. I think the key is that you don't ever want to force a system on anybody. You're making a movie, not a process. Everybody's different, everybody responds to different things, and you tailor the system to work with the people you have. Changes were based on people and the technical needs of the show.

For example, *Monsters, Inc.* was the first film to have a simulation department, for Sulley's fur and Boo's shirt. That department didn't exist before *Monsters, Inc.* because we didn't need it until then. Also, there's a whole team of people who don't get mentioned much who are really important in making our films. The production manager is a pivotal position. He or she puts together the daily schedule in a way that allows us to focus on the right things at the right time. They tell us when we need to make certain decisions so that departments downstream have time to do their job. Then there are managers for every group—animation, story, art, lighting, et cetera—and they help us know what's going on in every department, who's available when, and so on. And then in any given meeting there's generally someone keeping track of the schedule and keeping us on time so I don't have to be constantly looking up at the clock and saying, "Oh, I only have fifteen minutes." That way, I can lose myself in the moment until somebody comes and says, "Wrap it up, we need you at the next meeting." In the end, there might be three or four hundred people working on a movie. It's like mobilizing an army, and you really have to have great lieutenants, both creatively and managerially.

Bill: Is there anything you learned on *Monsters, Inc.* that you were able to use when the time came to do *Up*?

Pete: In terms of the creative process, I learned that chaos is an essential part of the production—that you can't go in thinking, "I'm gonna have every *T* crossed and *I* dotted, and it's going to be smooth sailing." It's not going to be smooth. It's going to be a mess. And you can't take that personally. That was the big lesson for me. On *Monsters, Inc.*, I must have aged ten years in three. Because I was carrying this weight of, "I'm a failure as a person because I can't get this to go." And by the second one I realized, no, that's just the process. You don't have to know what every single shot's going to be right out of the gate. You do have to know your basics: "What is this movie about? How am I going to connect to the people watching it? What is the main character and what makes him getable and likeable?" You have to know those kind of things and be able to talk about them with your crew. Then you work your way down to the details. You have to realize that this is a long-distance run, and you have to pace yourself. Don't work weekends and nights from day one or you're gonna die before you even get halfway.

Bill: *Up* was a project that you conceived from the start. Where did the idea come from?

Pete: I spent maybe a year developing a few ideas, and there was one, a really bizarre one that I developed with Bob Peterson. It showed a lot of potential early on, but then it just got weirder. And this is where I started understanding more fully about how you need to have an emotional connection with the audience, that people go to movies to see their own life reflected up there in some way, maybe in a way that they hadn't really thought of before. The characters in this film were sort of these weird, Muppety, made-up creatures that lived on a made-up planet. Not to say you couldn't connect with characters like that, but we had so many bizarre elements to the thing. And so after pitching for a few months and not getting traction we thought, "All right, let's pull back a little bit, let's make it a grouchy human instead of a fuzzy, red, furry creature." And we talked a lot about, "Okay, what's going to make this relatable? What's going to get people emotionally hooked on it?" The bizarre, Muppety guy had lived on a floating city, this city in the sky, and that was initially very appealing to me. I started to analyze: "What is it about that idea I like, and why?" And I realized it was the isolation, the idea of just getting away from the world, which I definitely felt an empathy for. But then I realized, "Well, if he lives in a city, there are other people. So that doesn't really get to that feeling of escape and isolation. Let's make it a house instead." And then, so it's not just a house floating around magically, let's explain it a little more. How is it floating? Maybe it's held up by thousands of balloons! That's where *Up* came from. It was certainly not a "eureka" epiphany moment. It was born out of a feeling, the desire to get away from it all, this man getting away from the world in his floating house.

Sketch, Pete Docter, *Up*, © Disney/Pixar.

Bill: Can you talk a little more about discovering that character? Did he change and evolve from what you originally thought he would be?

Pete: I'd done a bunch of drawings. I had one of a super-grouchy guy holding a big bunch of happy colorful balloons. That kind of started the character. Then Bob Peterson and I talked about him a lot, pulling from our own observations of our grandfathers and other older folks we knew. I did a bunch of exploratory drawings, with different observations and behavior: Carl eats stewed prunes for breakfast, or he has a problem with ear hair, and all these little specific things. Bob wrote a lot of great scenes that we'd throw out for each other. And between all that, the character started developing. I think that these films are really a reflection of the people that work on them, so when you hire someone, especially someone in a key position, you really have to know what you're getting, because that person is going to influence the film in a big way. Bob Peterson has a lot of old man in him, and he is so much of what went into that character. Ronnie del Carmen was our head of story, and he had great insights into old men. He channeled his father, who apparently had some grouchy old man tendencies. A few of the story guys, like Tony Rosenast, really brought Carl to life in their boards, and of course the animators ... they all contribute to the character. And then, when you cast someone like Ed Asner ... We had listened to a bunch of different actors, but Ed really clicked. We recorded him, watched his mannerisms, looked for words he would use in his natural speech patterns, and this all affected the way we would write. We'd try to play to his strengths, you know, using clipped, short sounds and shortened sentences. We often cut out words or sentences, because Carl is a guy who doesn't want to communicate. He wants to be left alone, so he's not using as many words. Plus it was funny. We learned that from Ed.

Sketch, Pete Docter, *Up*, © Disney/Pixar.

Bill: Did you look at any other work for inspiration?

Pete: You know, probably the single biggest influence early on was a film called *The Station Agent*, written and directed by Tom McCarthy. Tom also wrote and directed a film called *The Visitor* about illegal immigrants in New York, which sounds all controversial and political, but he simplifies it down to these great relationships, very simple scenes where he's somehow able to strip out a lot of extraneous blabiddy-blah. Every word, every scene, is just what he needs, and no more. *The Station Agent* was about a man who wants to be left alone and only slowly is drawn into an odd sort of community. Very similar to our character. We learned a lot from it and eventually even hired Tom on to write for a short while.

Bill: Did you use the same kind of production system you used on *Monsters, Inc.*?

Pete: The production was pretty similar in general, but the specifics were different, because of the talents of the people involved. On *Up*, Bob Peterson was the co-writer and co-director, and his strength was story, and humor, and characters. So he was very much involved in building the reels. Once the reels were locked, I directed all other aspects by myself as Bob left the show to develop another project. I was also lucky to have Ronnie Del Carmen, who's strong in staging, and he worked with Patrick Lin, our layout supervisor, who really helped me and bolstered the cinematography. That was slightly different than *Monsters, Inc.*, where co-director Lee Unkrich commandeered editing and layout, based on his strengths.

Bill: Even though you had a solid approach and basically knew where you were going, did you have any kind of crash and burn on *Up*—somewhere in the middle when you felt, "Man, something here is just really not working?"

Pete: Really, our crash and burn was early on, when the project was on the verge of getting killed altogether. We refocused in a pretty major way. I do feel that there were enough other things going on at the studio at that time that we had a freedom that isn't always the case as we were developing the show. When we first started boarding, we were left alone for a stretch of six months, which meant that we could fail a couple of times and fix things to our liking before we had to drop our pants and show everybody else. It's a lot to ask of anybody to get it right the first time. So that gave us a leg up. Then too, thankfully Pixar has come to expect failure. By that I mean, it doesn't surprise everyone anymore when the first screening isn't perfect. Our process is, "Well, we know we're not going to get it right, let's get it wrong so we have something to fix and make it right. And we're all going to be a part of that." Anyway, that allowed us to get some pretty decent reels, so we never really had a screening where people walked away going, "Ohhhh boy," which does seem to happen in many of our films.

Concept artwork, Lou Romano and Don Shank, *Up* © Disney/Pixar.

Bill: *Up* seems like such a personal movie. Do you feel like only you could have made it?

Pete: Thanks. Yeah, I do.

Bill: What would you say most distinguishes it as your work and your style as an artist?

Pete: Well, the subject matter itself is an odd blend of deep emotional truth along with wacky talking dogs and broad physical comedy. That blend is not easy to pull off, but it's something I'm intrigued with. It's what attracted me to *Dumbo*. You have the fun of what animation can do, but hopefully it's built on a bedrock of something truthful that makes the film more than just kooky, wacky characters. Then too, in deciding on the look for the film, I got a lot of feedback from folks saying they thought we needed to go more realistic in the design. Folks felt that we needed that realism for the audience to connect with these characters and this sort of story. I felt the opposite … that if we made things more stylized, and we abstracted things a bit, people would connect more easily. It's hard for me to pinpoint what makes my films distinctly "me," because I don't think about it that way. I just make a film that I want to see. Inevitably, it's lots of little decisions that make any work unique. Other people wouldn't have made the same choices.

Bill: It must have been really satisfying to you, to have everybody be so wrong about …

Pete: [laughs] Well, you never know!

Bill: Let's face it. No studio in Hollywood would have green-lit a movie about an eighty-year-old guy. And I think every-body's reaction was, "Thank god for Pixar because they let an artist run with a vision."

Pete: Some of those articles in the *Times*, or wherever, prior to the film's release, they'd say things like, "Pixar's lost their marbles, nobody's gonna go see this, this is where they go down in flames." And truthfully, we had no idea what would happen. Having seen the audience reaction with the guys here and the folks at Disney, I was pretty sure it wouldn't be an absolute bomb. But I felt like it would be a smaller, niche film for us. So the fact that it's gone out there in the world and it was second only to *Finding Nemo* as our most profitable film … It's still kind of baffling to me.

Bill: Do merchandising considerations ever play a part in your creative decisions?

Pete: No, thank goodness. One of the big things we got lambasted for on *Up* was: "Who's gonna buy a toy of a grouchy old man?" That may have been something of a self-fulfilling prophecy, because they really didn't make much merchandise. I know that toys and tie-ins are a part of what we all do, and you just have to embrace that or figure out some way of dealing with it. Either you care about it deeply and passionately, as John does—you know, he just loves all those toys, and he wants to make them as good as he can, so he can own them too—or you just throw up your hands and say, "You know, somebody else can deal with that. I don't really want to." Thankfully we don't even think about marketing until the project is well into production. And even then, there's a consumer products group that comes in to think about what would make a good toy or whatever. They involve us filmmakers, but our first and primary job is to make as good a movie as we can.

Bill: Speaking of toys, during your time at Pixar, you got married and had a couple of kids. Does having a family affect your creative process or have an influence on the way you work?

Pete: Absolutely. Brad Bird says it well: "You can't create the illusion of life unless you're out there living it. You can't just live alone in a shack sitting at a computer or sketchbook. You have to have life experiences to draw from." Having a family influenced my work in a lot of ways. My son was born right at the beginning of the development of *Monsters, Inc.*, and that film became a personal story. It's a guy who really loves his work, but then this kid comes along, and the kid and his work are at odds with each other. How does he come to terms with those two things? It's a story about becoming a parent. Life not only informs the work, it is essential to the very core of the work. Also, just being a parent, and learning how to be consistent and strong and loving at the same time, this has helped me as a director. One thing that kids really need is consistency. You can't come in one day expecting this, and the next day expecting that, and the next day something else. They're going to be confused. Consistency as a director is key.

Bill: What do you think about the two-director system? Have you ever thought it might be easier on you to do that? Or do you think you're strictly a solo director?

Pete: Well, I'll just say that I don't think it works for the way we work at Pixar. There needs to be one final voice, the person who drives the thing. Pixar is built around the 1970s idea of "auteur" filmmaking in that sense. When it comes to production, it's probably closer to the craftsmanship and long-term investment of the Hollywood "studio system" of the 1920s to 40s. Anyway, back when I started *Monsters, Inc.*, there were certain people at Disney who felt, "Okay Pete, given your inexperience, it's not in our best interest to trust you entirely with this production. Let's give you a partner, because that's worked really well for us at Disney." And they were able to convince John of that. And right away I said, "Look, I'm not a power-hungry guy or anything, but that's not going to work." And sure enough, as we tried it out, progress was very slow because I was always checking with this other guy to make sure he liked where we were going. I'm not someone who needs to be in control. But at the end of the day there has to be one person who's telling the story. One person whose life experiences are on the screen, who makes the decisions and says, "Let's do this," and on we go. Now, having said that, at Pixar we have co-directors, which is confusing to people. But what *co-director* really means is—for example, on *Monsters, Inc.*, as I was flailing around with editing and layout, I was able to get Lee Unkrich, who worked on *Toy Story* and *A Bug's Life* with John. And besides being an amazing editor, he stages things beautifully—he knows exactly where the camera should be. And he is economical and direct, and works to reduce the number of shots, et cetera. So for incredibly complicated things, like building the door-vault sequence at the end, that was all based on storyboards and ideas that I knew I wanted, but Lee figured out how to do that, along with the layout team. So that was his area of expertise. And that's the way co-directors work at Pixar. They are in charge of one or more areas of the process, while at the same time they know that the director has the final say and that it's his vision. It's a very tough gig.

Bill: What would you say is your favorite part and least favorite part of being a director?

Pete: Hmmm. Probably the answer to both of those questions is: the early days of development. It's simultaneously the most stress-inducing, unsure, vague part of the process, and yet it's also the most exciting. The potential is everywhere, you can go any number of directions, and yet you create these worlds from scratch. It's why I personally am not as excited about sequels, because I feel like I already know that world and characters. I'm more interested to do something new, to explore.

Bill: So is directing your life now, or do you see yourself maybe trying something different before moving on to your next project as a director?

Pete: Well, every once in a while I miss animating. And I do still have fantasies of doing a hand-drawn film. Maybe because Brad and Andrew went into live action, I get asked whether I'm interested in that and, once in a while, I come up with a story that feels more like a live-action story. But I can't say it's something I'm hungry to do. I really like the way animation works and what the medium brings to the party. You know that everything on the screen is entirely artificial, and yet you believe in it. It's that illusion of life that fascinates me.

Bill: Do you have any advice or recommendations for beginning animators?

Pete: Years ago I wrote to Frank Thomas and Ollie Johnston and asked them that same question. They were nice enough to write back, and I still have their letters. They're really charming because they obviously typed the letters themselves, with some of the letters crossed out in pen, and with mistakes and things. But Frank went through a whole list of things the aspiring student needs, which was primarily drawing ability—to draw both human and animals in movement—and a deep study of human behavior—basically to be a good actor. But then his last point was: "And luck certainly has a lot to do with it too." He's right. It does help to get good breaks. But when those good breaks come up, you also have to have the talents and ability to take advantage of them. I feel that drawing is never a bad thing, even if you're a computer animator. Watching people and drawing them … I have sketchbooks full of people. Drawing is a great tool to help you communicate when you talk with your collaborators. A lot of the time it's just quickest to whip out some paper and do a sketch. Drawing also helps you see. There's a lot of stuff I've only noticed consciously because I've drawn it.

Bill: Aside from Frank and Ollie, is there anyone, inside or outside the industry, who you would say was an important influence? Someone who changed the way that you think or work or create?

Pete: Frank Oz, who I got to know as a result of *Monsters, Inc.*, and his work on the *Muppets*. What an amazing performer. He does Fozzie Bear and Bert and Grover, and Miss Piggy—some of the strongest characters in history, period—regardless of the medium. I asked him once, "Where do these characters come from?" I was expecting some deep internal process that he'd worked out, or at least some tips or clues into his approach. You know what his answer was? "I have no idea." That tells you what a mystery this whole thing is, creating characters and story. It's just an intuitive thing. It's what we were talking about where you have to trust your gut, just feel these things through. Then, at some point, you step out of the pool and you analyze what you're swimming towards, and then you jump back in. It was fun getting to know Frank and talk shop. Not just because I'm so in awe of his work, but also because he has great, great insights into the process. Joe Grant was a big influence, getting to know him, and looking at his drawings and trying to see how he thinks. He did great drawings, but they were never just great drawings. They always had ideas in there that would inspire beyond the draftsmanship. Joe was a master at the "less is more" thing, where instead of detailing everything out, he alluded to it, or suggested it, in a pose, in a behavior, or just outside the frame somehow. Something Joe talked about a lot … He would say, "What are you giving the audience to take home?" I was confused by that initially, but I learned what he meant: "What is the emotional core of the story? What is the audience going to feel?" Because you can have these great intellectual ideas, but just because something is clever doesn't always mean they stick with you. The emotional connection is the thing that has long-term impact and that the audience is going to keep going back to.

Bill: Are there any film directors, aside from Frank Oz, who have inspired you?

Pete: Charlie Chaplin. His films are really similar to Disney's films. What I love about them is the simplicity of the story structure. He's not trying to overload it with plot. He just presents a series of great situations, where he can have fun along the way. So it's a scene of him trying to eat spaghetti or whatever, and next is a scene where he escapes from a cop, but he puts all the scenes together in a way that builds to this great thing at the end. They have wonderful structure to them, but it's simple structure—which is very hard to do. We're always struggling to do that, to simplify the story so that you can just enjoy the performance and have fun with animation, the way they did in those great films in the twenties, thirties, and forties.

Bill: Are there any more contemporary directors?

Pete: Jacques Tati isn't exactly current, but he pops to mind. He does things similar to Chaplin, where he'll just let scenes play. There's not the same broadly expressed poses and things; it's more like natural behavior. To me, watching Tati films are sort of like sitting in an airport and watching people. They're really fascinating that way. Miyazaki does a similar thing, where he's somehow able to capture these little truths of life. The common wisdom in Hollywood is that films are all about "what happens next," you gotta keep the audience moving and keep the plot moving. And Miyazaki proves that you don't have to have anything happening next. What's happening right now, if it's truthful, and the audience relates to it and identifies … There are great laughs and a great connection when you find those sort of things. In terms of more contemporary filmmakers, I always look forward to Tom McCarthy's work. His stories are brilliantly simple and always have great truth to them. I love all of Carol Ballard's films. And of course there are the undisputed masters like Spielberg … There's always something to learn from in all of his films.

Bill: Aside from the terrifying Steve Jobs encounter, have there been other experiences that were particularly frightening, disappointing, or just very tough to get through?

Pete: There's been a lot of them, mostly having to do with screenings. You know, you're working on these things, and you're so close to them that you can't really even see what you're looking at anymore. And then you show it, and stuff you thought was hilarious just dies, and stuff that you thought was emotionally true rings hollow …

Bill: Do you always approach screenings with trepidation, or are there times where you feel like you've really got it?

Pete: Nowadays I'd say I approach screenings with "excitement," a combination of joy and fear. I usually have things I like, that I feel good about, but I'm fearful other people won't react to it, or that I loused it up somehow. You know, in film school we all complained about audience previews and how wimpy that was, that "real filmmakers" don't change their story because of audience preview cards. I still think to some degree that's correct. But I remember talking to John Lasseter once, and he told me, "I don't think of myself as an artist, I think of myself as an entertainer." He's right. If I stand up there on the stage and tell jokes and nobody laughs, I'm a lousy comedian, regardless of what I personally think of the jokes. Our job is to reach people, to affect them and connect with them. If they don't respond, then I need to change the way I'm putting across my message so that it rings true. It might be that the subject matter isn't resonating, or maybe it's just the way I'm saying it. It may take rephrasing a joke, or twisting the sentence in such a way that the punchline is at the end, or whatever. Your job is to talk to people and say something that makes them feel.

Bill: That's a fantastic thought. I think that really addresses the whole question of why it's not sacrificing your integrity to change the ending or something to better convey the sense of the film.

Pete: Yeah. I had an experience on *Monsters, Inc.* where we did have an audience preview screening and there were a lot of areas where we could tell we had problems: people were bored, people were restless, people were too scared. Right at the beginning of the film, for example, we had this scene where the tension builds, and this monster looms up over a kid, and it's getting more and more scary, and suddenly the lights go on and some monster says, "All right, look, can you tell me what you did wrong?," and the film went on from there. But we had built up a scary mood, and there were no laughs for about fifteen minutes. And we realized, it's like that old story about *A Funny Thing Happened on the Way to the Forum*. Apparently in tryouts the show was not playing well, so they added that song *Comedy Tonight* at the beginning, basically telling you, "This is a musical. It's funny. It's a comedy! Please laugh!" And once you have that song, it sets the tone right away, and then people feel they have permission to laugh. We did the same thing on *Monsters*. We added a title sequence, which set a light-hearted, goofy tone, and we also changed the opening scene to include slapstick. Instead of just turning on the lights, the monster gets scared, reels back, slips, and does all the pratfall stuff. Right away, sitting in the audience, you can feel the relief from the tension. The kids laughed. You could feel them think, "Okay, this is gonna be a comedy." So there's a lot you can learn in watching your films with the audience. After the screening, they have all the comment cards and focus groups, and once in a while you can learn some stuff from those too, like which story points didn't communicate, or where people were confused. But most of the time you learn just by sitting and watching the film with the audience.

Bill: In contrast to the frightening experience of screenings, have you had any single moment of great elation in your career?

Pete: Well, at that same screening, one of the big notes in the discussion afterwards was that people wanted to see the little girl again. I don't know if you remember the film, but the door's been shredded, and Mike has reassembled it. Sulley puts the last piece in. The light goes on, and he goes, "Boo?" and you just hear off-screen, "Kitty!" And people in the audience said, "I want to see them hug, I want to see them get back together." And we talked about it, but there was one thing I was sure of: no matter what I came up with, I would never be able to beat what's in the audience's head. It'd never measure up. So I held firm on that, even against some pretty big pressure. So I got my ending, and at the end of the day a lot of people have told me that that they feel it's a really nice, emotional ending to the film.

Ronnie Del Carmen, Ralph Eggleston, Pete Docter and Albert Lozano, *Inside Out*, © Disney/Pixar.
Photo: Deborah Coleman.

Bill: The greatest ending.

Pete: Thanks! It felt good to be right. It doesn't happen all the time.

Bill: Did inside out present any new challenges you had not faced before?

Pete: The concept itself was rather abstract—we set it inside the mind, not the brain—which was a large part of the attraction for me. It was a chance to make up a world rather than being tied to real life. But, it quickly became apparent that the design of the *Mind World* could not be whatever we wanted—nor was it really based on research. It needed to reflect the girl herself and what she was going through. The events in the human world had to have a direct, physical effect on the mind world, which would then affect Joy's journey. We were essentially telling two stories at once, and they connected through the design. That was tough. I'm sure Production Designer Ralph Eggleston felt like he aged 40 years in the 4 years he was on the film, but he was patient with us and designed some of the most amazing sets I'd ever seen.

Inside Out, 2015. © 2015 Disney/Pixar.

Bill: How does being both the writer and the director affect your process of working with other writers/storyboard artists to solve story problems?

Pete: People often mistake writing with dialog. What characters say can be entertaining, but the real writing—the stuff that makes people stay in their seats—is the ordering of the events themselves, and how characters react. In that sense, I've always been part of the writing process, from Toy Story on.

However, sitting at the keyboard to get scenes started is really one of the most difficult parts of the process. I was lucky to collaborate with several great writers on *Inside Out*. I'm glad I did, because it's always difficult to remain objective. I wouldn't recommend that first time directors try to write and direct, because it's too easy to get stuck with how you *think* it is, instead of how it really is. And really, the primary job of the director is to look at the film as an audience member.

That said, sometimes writing or drawing can bring out ideas inside you that wouldn't have come out otherwise. Then, you show them to your partners who are brave enough to tell you they stink. Then, you rewrite them again.

Bill: Having directed three feature films, what advice you would pass on to budding film directors?

Pete: People think directors are allowed to do whatever they want, as if their ultimate goal is self-satisfaction. A director out for self-satisfaction alone had better be prepared to get into another line of work.

On the other hand, I have no stomach for movies that are just desperate, frenetic grabs for audience attention. If you have a chance to make a movie, it damn well better say something.

One way to look at this is to imagine both of these goals at opposite ends of a see-saw. Too much weight on either side, and the thing tips over. We've all seen self-indulgent personal statements that feel like you're at the therapist's office; or the desperate loud blockbusters that try so hard to please everyone yet feel empty. A successful entertainer says something true meaningful and personal, in a way that hits right at the heart of everyone watching. And, if you're lucky enough to have that opportunity, I believe it's your responsibility to do your darnedest to add something to the human experience.

5
Chris Sanders Interview

Chris Sanders.

I first met Chris Sanders while working on *The Little Mermaid*. During the great Disney 2D musicals of the 1990s, Chris was one of the mainstays of the story department, while I would alternate between storyboarding and animation. We got to know each other well during the development periods of experimentation between big film projects. And of all things, we liked to play in the team paintball games organized by director Gary Trousdale (*Beauty and the Beast, Atlantis*). Memorable games were Disney Animation vs. Warner Bros., and Disney vs. Beverly Hills 90210. For the poster for the last event, Chris did a delightful drawing of Mickey shooting it out with a beautiful 90210 babe in a camouflage bustier.

Chris always had a wonderful personal design style. His whimsical characters look as though they are having as much fun as we are watching them. Chris has an athletic build rare among the denizens of the drawing table. As the years roll on, age and responsibility fail to diminish his youthful exuberance.

Tom Sito

Ron Diamond: Could we maybe talk a little bit about your youth and how you discovered animation?

Chris: Yeah. Absolutely. I can't say that I remember everything. Of course, I loved *The Wonderful World of Disney* and never missed an episode. Disney and Disneyland were bigger than life to me. I grew up in Colorado, and we went to California for the first time on a family vacation when I was seven. We stayed at a little motel not too far from the park. You could see it from the walkway in front of our motel room door. When I got my first glimpse of Disneyland from that walkway, I threw up. [laughs] I was that excited to see Disneyland! I couldn't believe I was there.

I remember in particular *The Three Caballeros*. That bit of animation was such pure energy and joy. That's when animation went from being something I just loved to something I paid a lot more attention to. Oddly enough, the next big turn-ing point for me animation-wise was *The Pink Panther Show* on TV (DePatie-Freleng). One day, instead of a cartoon, they showed a little special about how they made *The Pink Panther* cartoon. As opposed to the Disney specials, where animation was always presented as somewhat magical, like the characters drew themselves, this special explained how the process actually worked. It talked about how an art director, for example, keeps the characters legible in front of the backgrounds. In contrast to that, Disney tended to keep the process of animation a lot more vague. Which is fine, unless you're a kid in Colorado that wanted to know how this whole thing worked. Oh, and Disney shows always passed by the story room and never went in. That was skipping the most important part, as it turned out. So this *Pink Panther Show* really got into the nuts and bolts of animation.

Ron: How old were you at the time?

Chris: I was probably eleven or twelve. A friend of mine also had a Super 8mm projector that could freeze-frame. We bought some Disney animation on *Super 8* and would step through it one frame at a time. My friend was actually the first one who said to me, "It's not one drawing per frame. A lot of the frames are the same drawing twice!" I didn't believe him at first.

He had to walk me through it. Some frames had only one drawing, but most had two. We ran this whole film backwards and forwards, over and over again.

Ron: And when did you first try animation?

Chris: Around the same time, I think. Of course I didn't have any idea how you did inbetweens and extremes. I only knew that animators worked on light tables, so I built one. Well, my grandfather built one for me. But we both had to sit down and figure it out. When it was done, I animated a scene. Then, I shot it on *Super 8*. The timing was terrible. It was atrocious. It looked weird. I was so upset and depressed that I never tried it again. I used the light table for other things. I simply didn't know what a light table was for. It wasn't until I got to CalArts that I learned that important lesson. It would have been nice to get the bit of information earlier. But when I was young I just generally imitated the process.

Fun With Father, 1984.

Ron: Were you telling stories, or trying to do storyboards in terms of figuring out what your concept would be?

Chris: No. I think at that point I was simply trying to make something move around. I wasn't really doing stories.

Ron: No flip books?

Chris: That's the other thing. I think I did just a few rudimentary flip books. Oddly enough, story really eluded me for a very, very long time. It wasn't till college that I took a story writing class. I remember being bold enough to say, "I have a stupid question. What's a story? What makes up a story?" Up to that point I could write little scenes, but they really didn't go anywhere. The teacher looked at me and said, "Story is change." That hit me hard. It was so simple. Why didn't I think of that? Now whenever I talk to kids about story, I explain that it's all about a character changing, or a character changing something around them. Why do you like that movie or television show? Most likely, it's because you are emotionally connected to the character and how he or she changes.

When I was working with Howard Ashman on *Beauty and the Beast*, we were all trying to figure out what exactly the songs were about. At one point, he kept asking, "What's the deal with Belle? Why is the town focused on her? In *The Little Mermaid* when Ariel sings 'Part of Your World', that song was originally titled 'I Want Feet'. That's what's it's really about. She just wants feet." [Laughs] That was the first time I saw someone tear off the glitter and all the fancy trimmings in order to see the bare bones. 'Part of Your World' is really about feet, and everything else is built on top of that. So, we spent a lot of time talking about what's the deal with Belle (*Beauty and the Beast*). And the best thing we came up with was that she was odd to everybody around her. To us, she would seem nor-

Story Sketch, Chris Sanders, *Beauty and the Beast*, 1991 © Disney.

mal because she's just a girl who likes to read and dream, and she's a pretty stable person. Everybody around her, however, is rather small-minded. After that first day with Howard, I asked another potentially stupid question. I said, "How do you know where to put the songs?" Howard replied, "That's easy. I put them at the story turns." Once again, it seemed so clear. [Laughs]. The music guides you through the story. Ariel goes in to see the sea witch and comes out with feet. That's a turning point. I also have to say that it's incredibly tough to write a song that can drive a story through a turn, and Howard could make it look easy. Anyway, it's amazing how important the music is to moving the story along.

So we spent a lot of time talking about what's the deal with Belle (*Beauty and the Beast*). And the best thing we came up with was that she was odd to everybody around her. To us, she would seem normal because she's just a girl who likes to read and dream, and she's a pretty stable person. Everybody around her, however, is rather small-minded. As we then started to talk more about the songs, I asked another potentially stupid question. I said, "How do you know where to put the songs?" Howard replied, "That's easy. I put them where the story turns." Once again, why didn't that occur to me before? [Laughs]. The music guides you through the story. Ariel goes in to see the sea witch and comes out with feet. That's a turning point. Thinking about that moment, I have to say it's a lot easier to write a song about suffering than it is about change. Anyway, it's amazing how important the music is to moving the story along.

Story sketches, Chris Sanders, *Beauty and the Beast*, 1991 © Disney.

Tom: That makes me think of Gilbert and Sullivan musicals, where every song introduces a character.

Chris: That's why Dean and I have a hard time with musicals sometimes. You're sitting there thinking, "Oh no! Here comes the music! It's going to be a while before anything happens."

Ron: Did you have a favorite short film? Something that stands out, and you think everybody should see?

Chris: Well, I don't really know if you would call it a short. When I was a kid I saw Buster Keaton's silent films. Those, I think, had the most influence on me, and they still do. I've collected so many of them on DVD and video. Some of them you can't even get on DVD, so I still hope to find them on VHS tapes. I actually have to keep an old VHS player alive and running so I can watch them.

Ron: Was there a particular film?

Chris: It's actually a feature film. It's a Laurel and Hardy film called *The Air Raid Wardens*. It's a film that has a special place in my heart. It has an unexpected, emotionally resonant core and a scene that is honestly one of the most true and touching things I've ever seen on film. Those early movies are masterworks of timing. The older ones have no sound or color, so everything has to be conveyed through the physical interaction between characters and objects. We often assume silent pictures are low-tech, so they must be easy to make, right? Well, I'm sure if someone tried to make one today, it would present an unexpected challenge. In fact, you would probably learn something about filmmaking by simply focusing on those basics of performance. I'm always watching *Buster Keaton* or *Charlie Chaplain*. I'm just incredibly impressed by them. As a kid I just thought they were the funniest people in the world. Their movies were magic. I couldn't believe that grown men had made these films. I remember a Keystone Cops scene where this huge hook and ladder from a fire truck was out of control and was sweeping people off sidewalks. If you had anything to do during the day, why wouldn't you want to make a film about an out-of-control fire truck?

Tom: Now let's delve a bit into your personal technique. Let's start with where your ideas come from. How do you come up with an idea for a movie?

Chris: The only film I ever made from an original idea was *Lilo & Stitch*. It started out as a children's book that I tried to write. That was in 1981, seventeen years before *Lilo & Stitch* was ever pitched to Disney. It was about this little monstrous, alien creature that lived in a forest. It was a mystery where he had come from. The story was all about him working out his relationship with all the other creatures in the forest.

It was a complex idea, too long for a children's book. I dropped the project, but not before I had designed the character and made a clay model of him. After I shelved the idea, I stored the model in a box. Seventeen years later, in the last days of *Mulan*, Tom Shumacher [Disney Producer] took me out for sushi and asked if I had any ideas for an upcoming feature. At first, I said no. But then, I remembered my little alien monster. It had never occurred to me to think of the story as a movie until that moment. After I pitched the story to Tom, he made one key suggestion. He said, "If this thing is an alien, being in the world of animals might not have enough contrast. However, if you move the creature into the world of humans, then you'll have that contrast." So that's where the alien in the human world idea came from.

Overall, when it comes to any idea for a film, I tend to go more toward the emotional wavelength first and then build around that. I tend to work with scenes that way as well. I follow the emotional tone. And I always think about the turning points, about how relationships would change. In terms of story, there's an emotional destination I want. With those basic concepts, I can then work out the details. I can't just say, "What if an alien landed on Earth," and then work from there in a linear fashion. I need that emotional tone and the general context of character development first. That means I start at the end and work backward toward the very beginning of the story.

Tom: A movie like *The Croods* with a caveman setting is a *tabula rasa* (clean slate) where you could interpret their Stone Age world as anything from very primitive like *Quest for Fire* (1981), to a parody of modern society like *The Flintstones*. Where do you draw your line?

Chris: This was one of the main things we had to do. The sensibilities came from the story. And we were telling a much more subtle story than if they just grunted. It was a story about families, a father and a daughter, about how families relate to new things. The cool thing about cavemen is they are not assigned to any one particular culture or nationality. When you take all this away, a dad is a dad and a daughter is a daughter.

Keeping one eye on the Flintstones, we tried very carefully to not put too many modern phrases in. When Grugg would say, "Let's put on the brakes here," we had to stop and think, no, that's too modern. He wouldn't say that.

Tom: As someone like yourself with a distinct design style, how do take that unique vision and transfer it over to a staff of 500 people? How do you maintain your vision?

Chris: You have to find somebody who knows how it works. We found two people on *Lilo & Stitch*. Sue Nichols (Mazerowski) was given the task of not only taking my style and dissecting it but also explaining it. I didn't even know I had a style until she successfully dissected it and then explained it in this booklet. It was a bit of a revelation to me. I didn't think there was anything that I was doing over and over again that could be considered a style. For example, she pointed out that a lot of my characters look like they're filled with sand, and that sand runs down to the bottom. She noticed that their extremities tend to flare out and feel heavy. She said I never use straight lines. It was amazing. With that information in hand we then found an artist that could replicate my style: Byron Howard. We gave him the task of designing our insular characters, things that I didn't have time to do. I think he did a lot better job that I would have done in that respect. You just have to find the right people.

Tom: And what about designing *The Croods*?

Chris: One of the real treats was designing cave-people. We wanted to create characters people would want to look at, but not make them look too "princessy." Eep (Emma Stone) was a good example. Making her hands and feet small gave her character a certain amount of grace. She was broad shouldered, she had a good silhouette, but not princess-pretty by any means. We tended to think of each person as an animal. Eep was a cat, Grugg her father was a gorilla, Sandy was a terrier. It worked into their mindset. Eep as a cat or panther could climb and leap. Grugg can't climb, so he was against it.

Story sketches, Chris Sanders, *The Croods*, 2013 © DreamWorks Animation LLC.

Tom: I liked the joke of Gran (Cloris Leachman) having a tail.

Chris: Gran was designed with a lizard in mind. One of our designers was fitting her and drew her with a lizard tail, when he decided just to give her a real lizard tail. Pointing out she was further back in the evolutionary scheme of things.

Tom: What's your favorite part about being a director?

Chris: I guess there'd be two things. One of them is just working with amazing artists. It sounds like such a stock answer, but it's true. A few weeks ago, I had the opportunity to talk to James Cameron. We got to sit down and ask him questions, almost one on one. That was amazing. I never would have had that opportunity if I hadn't been directing at DreamWorks. The other is just really getting to know different people at the studio, these amazing designers, background artists, and animators. They come from all over the world. Some came over from France for *Lilo & Stitch*. I guess I just love any aspect of filmmaking. I don't know if there are any other jobs in the world where you can keep trying to improve yourself. You can keep working till the last day of your life and you'll still be pushing it. And the studios want you to do the best work that you can do.

I worked with a guy named Chris Doffend, and I loved what he drew. I was always going into his room and asking, "What are you drawing today? Got anything?" Seeing his stuff and his logs was inspiring. And every year I go to Comic Con and walk away inspired. I need to keep going, do better. On top of that, if I stop and realize that I'm paid to draw, that's even a better feeling. That's the kind of thing you dream about as a kid. I never watched the Oscars when I was young. My parents did, of course. I always went downstairs and did something else. I was drawing. I didn't watch them because I really wanted to make a movie, and that was everyone who actually did. I just thought, "I'll never do that." I think it kind of hurt to watch. It was this amazing thing that I'll never get to do. But I ended up doing it, and that's still an incredible feeling. When I talk to kids about animation and directing, I always tell them it's possible. It may seem like this unapproachable world. But it is possible.

Tom: How about your least favorite thing?

Chris: The least favorite part of directing is the incessant schedule. We occasionally have to fight against it, but I understand the problem. There are a million things we have to do during the day. It's the housekeeping and scheduling that becomes very difficult. And it actually does cut into the movie occasionally. We've had a few episodes where we had to avoid some of our commitments so that we could focus on a few scenes. If it wasn't absolutely essential, it was removed from the schedule. On *How to Train Your Dragon* we were so bogged down with meetings. It was frustrating. We would be on the verge of solving a problem and then someone in production says, "Sorry, you have to move on."

Tom: How is your interaction with upper management? They often require your attention as much as the crew.

Chris: You have to learn how to interact with those above. You have to learn what might trigger a bad reaction and avoid it as long as you can, unless you absolutely have to confront it. On *Dragon* we wanted to do a few sequences with no dialogue. But you don't just pitch it like that. You wait until the sequence moves along. You work the storyboards, put some music in it, and then you present it. If you pitch something they're not necessarily well informed about, or something experimental, of course skepticism might emerge. It just might seem too risky. If you have something more substantive to show them, then you're maintaining control over your vision and what you want for the movie. As a director, you're the only person that's not allowed to panic. You're the only person that's not allowed to panic. And people panic around you. I'm kind of surprised how many times that happens. Even producers panic and get flustered easily. You can't freak out and start saying, "We'll never get this done. This will never work." Confidence and calm is everything. Your crew is depending on you. If I do need to vent, I find someone off the grid to vent my frustrations to. It's better that way, and it's healthier. I try to stay open and give each meeting my all. The last thing you want is to turn into this machine that just goes in and out of the office each day. You have to lighten up and stay personable. Don't be the guy that just walks into the room and says, "Show me your stuff," and then walks out. Making a movie is hard enough as it is. As a director, don't make it harder.

Tom: Some directors have the entire film in their mind before production starts. Others watch it evolve during production. Where do you fall in that context?

Chris: It's a two-part answer. I have always had the end of the story first and then work backwards. As I mentioned before, I have the emotional feel and that important turning point, but I'm usually searching for the beginning, the way into that turning point and end. I have also learned to embrace structure a lot more. The experience of making *Dragon* has especially changed my life as a filmmaker. I had always avoided structure and preferred freeform. But we only had one year to complete *Dragon*.

When we sat down with Jeffrey [Katzenberg], he said, "We usually have about three chances to make a movie like this. You guys get one. You have to get it right the first time." So, we didn't mess around. We got down to the structure right away, and within two weeks we had simplified it and began building up from there. You must have that structure down. You have to know exactly what the characters are doing and why. There will always be difficult variables and problems to solve. But if you know your character and the structure of his journey, you can avoid months, if not years, of struggling to get it right.

Working on *Mulan* was the complete opposite. I'm really surprised at how long we avoided the structure. There were so many variables concerning this Chinese girl trying to break through the limitations of her traditional society. There were so many questions concerning how she would do this. We struggled for over a year without making any progress. Worse still, after so many drafts and changes, we ended up coming full circle and settling on some of our original ideas.

Tom: Some directors will make an animator redo a scene around six times. But then they go back and choose the first one.

Chris: When Dean [DeBlois] and I started directing *Lilo & Stitch*, we felt very uncomfortable directing the animators. Animators are very talented artists. They're experts in their realm. Still, we have to go in and to a certain extent tell them what to do. Neither Dean nor I are animators. We focus on the story and boarding. So when you're talking to an artist that is clearly more talented at painting and drawing than you, there can be a little intimidation there. But you have to look at their animation and make comments. The way that works for us is to talk to them like one would to an actor. We'll talk about what the scene needs to accomplish in terms of story and conveying emotion. We never get into the finite details of timing and movement. I'm not going to suggest how to move a character's ears or shoulders. I'm more likely to say, "I think there is more tension behind this than I'm seeing."

        This is why Dean and I are always in the story. That's what directing is. Ultimately it's all about story, whether you are talking about the lighting of the scene, the animation, or the design of a character. You have to make sure your animators

Visual development, Chris Sanders, *Lilo & Stitch*, 2002 © Disney.

and crew are working and creating to bring out your story. You've created a very specific tone, and the animators need to respond to that.

Tom: Did you have any mentors or people that inspired you when you first got into story?

Chris: Vance Gerry was such a great communicator when it came to storyboarding. His work is the very definition of a story artist. And I don't think I've ever seen anybody do it as well. But Ed Gombert was the one that could truly get into a scene. He had this innate ability to keep it fresh and original. I even recall directors taking advantage of that. Ed would nail a scene, delivering exactly what it needed. But the director would say, "Try it again. What if it was like this?" They knew he would go away and come back with exactly what they asked for. After a few more requests, they would have multiple takes on a scene. I never cared for that approach. I never wanted to do that to anybody. Besides Ed, working on *Beauty and the Beast* was a period of intense learning. I was working with Joe Ranft, Brenda Chapman, and Roger Allers. These guys were not only in tune with one another, but they were also having fun developing the story. They were bringing great characters to life. That was probably my favorite time at Disney. Every Friday we had storyboard pitches, and we were all in one big building in which we could see each other down this long hallway. You could always hear people talking and coming up with ideas. The energy was just perfect. Whenever I do a movie I still reference *Beauty and the Beast* as being the ideal experience.

Ron: What about your crew? Do you to try replicate that same atmosphere?

Chris: Of course, but it really comes down to the people working for you. I need people that are absolutely amazing at what they do. When it comes to finding that story and fixing the problems that arise, I always feel like we're a bunch of firefighters on the scene of an oil well fire. I don't want anybody there that does not know what they're doing. You want them to be very good, so you can put this fire out as soon as possible.

Tom: How has it been working with Dean [DeBlois] on consecutive projects?

Chris: One of the nice things about working together consistently is that you learn the same lessons. We were able to change things as we navigated the learning curve together. On *Lilo & Stitch* we both experienced the same frustration of stepping on a lot of Alan Silvestri's work as he created the music for certain segments of dialogue. We had to learn to let the music do the talking too, because it can do so much for your movie. The music has a very important job. We learned a lot from Alan Silvestri that we were able to put into practice on *How to Train Your Dragon*. You work hard to get the movie about halfway done, and then the music comes in and carries it across the finish line. I remember sitting with Alan and going through sequences in detail. At one point he asked us, "Where did Stitch change?" We didn't have it on screen. That moment was basically between scenes. At that moment it was a tough bit of criticism to swallow. We hadn't avoided this scene. We simply worked around it, because we couldn't figure it out. Finally Alan said, "Put it up on screen. I'll do it." So we did. We figured it out, and Alan gave it a meaningful score that captures that moment of change. I've never forgotten that. It was the music that got us to the end.

Tom: How did you and Dean [DeBlois] collaborate creatively? Do you guys sit together over drinks at someone's house and discuss it? Or do you go off and write separately and then later compare notes?

Chris: Well, we both create in very different ways, which I think is good for our working relationship. I'm always developing ideas using sketchbooks, and Dean goes off and makes music-driven shorts. So we're always creating and coming up with ideas. One thing we do now is meet for dinner once a week and simply talk about stories that we care about. It could be an idea for a book, a TV series, or a movie. It doesn't matter. It's about keeping the ball rolling, and it's always inventive and fun. But when it comes to the actual writing, we tend to do it together or at least in close proximity so that we can push each other. I think there were only a few days on *Dragon* that we actually wrote at different locations.

Dean and I are very different people. He is a cold-weather person and I'm more of hot-weather guy. We would never bump into each other on the street. And on weekends we have our own stuff to do. But when it's time to work, we need to work together in the same room. Even if I'm boarding and he's doing

Story sketches, Chris Sanders, *How To Train Your Dragon*, 2010 © DreamWorks Animation LLC. All Rights Reserved.

Story sketches, Chris Sanders, *How To Train Your Dragon*, 2010 © DreamWorks Animation LLC. All Rights Reserved.

Story sketches, Chris Sanders, *How To Train Your Dragon*, 2010 © DreamWorks Animation LLC. All Rights Reserved.

something else, we work in the same room. There's always moments where one of us removes our earphones and asks an important question. That's how we work together. And when it comes to the film score, we'll often listen to the same music as we write and develop sequences.

Tom: That's fascinating, because a lot of people, regardless of creative tastes, tend to be very different when it comes to music.

Chris: Well, when it comes to film scores, we're on the same page. And this is one of the reasons why we collaborate so well; we are making the same movie tonally. We might approach the details of a scene in different ways, but we are always writing the same movie. That makes exchanging ideas and negotiating much easier.

Ron: Are there any film scores that you find useful in your visualization?

Chris: When we were boarding the climactic battle between the gargantuan dragon and Hiccup, *The Dark Knight* (Hans Zimmer and James Newton Howard) score helped us create that serious energy that the moment required. That was a great one to have playing in the background. Overall, it depends on what you're writing. If it's something light and sweet, Dean often pulls out the *Cider House Rules* or *Chocolat* (Rachel Portman). If we need something exciting and energized, the Hans Zimmer catalogue is always waiting. Of course, if we want something triumphant, there is John Williams.

Tom: Overall, how important is the role of music in your films?

Chris: It plays a significant role. I've never boarded a sequence without music. When I know the tone for a given scene, I'll put on a piece of music that I think could possibly be the temp music for that moment. And I'll just put it on repeat. I'll let it go for hours, even days sometimes, to get this thing going. It's the most important tool I have. I even use music when I pitch the storyboard. And that music will actually stick all the way into the story reel.

Tom: And this is temp stuff?

Chris: It's temp stuff. The funny thing is, there were two temp tracks that I used to board a sequence which were then put in the actual story reel. When the score was written, they were remarkably close to those pieces of music that I had used.

Tom: What sequences were they?

Chris: There was a sequence where the Beast died and is resurrected. The music was nearly identical to this album of piano music that I was listening to when I did the scene. That sweet, tense little beat was perfect for that moment of transformation, thrill, and hope. In fact, I still wonder whether it should have been boarded differently. I originally boarded that scene where everyone stands back during the transformation. After it's over, the beast is on the ground with his back to Belle. He still looks a lot like the beast from her point of view. As he straightens up, the first changed thing you see is his hand. Only then does he turn to look at her, revealing his full transformation.

Tom: Now that you've done a few pictures, do you feel like your personal style, as a director, has evolved?

Chris: I've learned how to get closer with my crew and to understand their jobs better. And the technology has changed so drastically that it's a different experience from when I first started. In the beginning nobody talked about an "animation pipeline." The first time I heard that term I pictured something fairly linear. But then they unfolded this thing that was a model pipeline, and it really looked more like a city sewer system. But it didn't make any sense, because it wasn't a linear process at all. During production you'd move backwards and forwards through this pipeline. They really should rename it. Anyway, I'm trying to stay current with the technology. I want to understand it.

            And that brings me back to the point of getting to know your crew personally. Your crew and this technology go hand in hand. If you know them, if you can truly talk to them, then you'll get what you want. You'll also recognize quickly what certain individuals excel at. Obviously you don't want to pigeonhole anybody. But film after film, you learn who to go to in order to solve specific problems. On *Dragon*, everyone was doing their job so incredibly well that we decided to save time by not spending a lot of time with them. I wish we could have, not because they needed it. They didn't need our input. They knew exactly what they were doing. But it would have been nice just to connect with them and to be inspired by them. I'd say we saw them twice a month, maybe three times. We didn't even have any notes to give them. That's how good they were doing.

Still, the meetings are essential. It's the moment to communicate important information to the crew, to make sure everything is moving in the right direction, and to help them with whatever they need. As directors, you're immersed in story. Any slight shift in the narrative needs to be passed on to the crew. Also, just coming together as a group is a good thing. Everyone can help each other. It's a good way of avoiding potential disasters.

Tom: Do you ever have any happy accidents, like when an artist comes back with something completely unexpected?

Chris: Yeah! Dean and I actually encourage it. We may have a good idea, but that doesn't mean it can't be refined and improved upon. Artists are always capable of bringing a deeper layer to a character. And sometimes you have to indulge a different vision for a given scene. It may not be the way you envisioned it, but it might add something important to the bigger picture. If it does, you go with it. And if you really want that, you have to drop in on your artists when they are in the midst of doing something. That's when you'll find something unexpected. Sure, everyone wants to have something completely finished before they show it to anybody. But that's not necessarily the best thing to do.

We had a terrific accident on *Dragon*. There was a piece of unfinished, temporary animation that was somehow cut into the reel. When we saw it we were stunned. It's when Hiccup finds this wounded dragon in the woods. The dragon had first appeared lifeless. And it isn't until he puts his boot against it that he realizes it's still alive. From Hiccup's point of view we ran the camera down the dragon's body. After you pass the wing the head is there, looking at Hiccup. But in the shot we saw the eyes closed at first. Then as the camera passes the wing the eye is now open. It was a very creepy moment, because you really think the dragon is dead. That bit of animation wasn't supposed to be in the reel, but it was so good. The scene wouldn't have been as good without it. Overall, you just have to be open. Look at your artists' work in progress. You never know what you might see.

Tom: What do you think of drawing on Cintiq digital tablets and the mini-movies you can create on a laptop? When you started storyboarding everyone used pens and corkboards.

Chris: It's an amazing tool, and it makes it easier to sell your ideas. I remember the difficulty of trying to explain why a certain scene was so important and engaging in my storyboard. But the drawing wasn't going to move and help me in that respect. Cintiq allows you to animate that moment. If you're skilled, you can convey subtle things much easier. It definitely helps pitching your concept. On the other hand, once you've seen the presentation, it's hard to talk about. It's over and done. You're not looking at the links in the chain of action. If you have questions concerning timing and the progression of action, you have to click backwards and forwards through it. Basically, you have to search for the issue that's bothering you.

Dean and I prefer a combination of the two methods. That may sound like a misuse of time, but you get the best presentation possible. You show the little movie made with Cintiq, and then haul out the boards. You can see the sequence of action in chunks. It's far easier to analyze it, let alone just talk about it. You can edit on the boards. You can't do that with a reel. It's a lot of work. But it's worth it.

Tom: How have you learned to manage your time after four pictures? A lot of people in animation are more of the couch potato type. You always seem more into sports and physical activity.

Chris: I've learned to focus more on what I'm doing. When I get to work, I work. I get it done. And if I'm truly stuck, I move onto something else. So I'm a lot better at having multiple things going on at once. When I come into the office I actually have a choice of what to work on. That's helped tremendously. Some days you just don't feel clever, and you're not. It's just not happening that day. When you have other things to do, that stops you from wandering the halls and wasting other people's time.

Realizing that has made me more efficient. It also tends to give me time for little things. If I get a board done, then I really can run down the hall and just pop in on somebody for a quick chat. Essentially I've created a flexible schedule that keeps me productive at all times. And this is completely different from the strict schedules you come across at studios. That kind of schedule can actually hinder progress. In my opinion, it's better to run a studio like a hospital. If you've got a patient that needs help, you grab the necessary specialist and get the job done. After you fix him, you move onto the next one. And when an emergency occurs, everybody gets right on it. I did that on *Dragon* and actually got in trouble for it. I was in editorial when a layout issue needed to be resolved. Instead of allowing a note taker to document my response, I got Gil on the phone and we handled it. The studio didn't like that. They wanted me to use the note taker since that was their job. I really hate that. We'll be in a meeting talking about ideas in the most general way possible, and there are three people behind you typing away on their computers. You get these giant printouts that contain everything. But all we really need is what was decided in the end.

Tom: They want to document every change.

Chris: Yeah. I don't think they really believe that you can keep a living version of the film in your head all the time. It's always being updated based on the people you talk to during the day. In a way, an animated film has its own oral history during production. But I'm very unaware of which stuff is actually written down. When we check the notes they're usually written down wrong. Worse still, we talk in film code most of the time. That doesn't help the note takers at all. Not to mention, no one speaks in slow, perfectly grammatical English. Honestly, I just prefer this oral communication aspect of animation's culture. It makes the process feel tribal.

Tom: Do you like working with your editor in post? Some directors really like this part of the job, cutting reels and bringing everything together. And do you and Dean do that together or split it up?

Chris: It's important that we are both in editorial because that's a very influential moment in making a film. I would even like to see editorial have a greater role in that respect. One of the shortcomings of animation is that we're not supplying editorial with a lot of extra footage. Their choices are limited compared to the coverage they get in live action. Regardless, those in that room have the greatest impact on the final product, so Dean and I have never divided that up, along with recording. We only divide up animation. It just wouldn't make much sense. As you're putting everything together, this is the opportunity to discuss, even argue, over what works and what doesn't. We hash it out face to face and walk away with the actual film. It's probably our favorite thing to do. Yeah, it can become grueling as you dissect your entire movie. But this is where we get to see our movie emerge. It's exciting.

Tom: So both of you work with the actors during recording sessions?

Chris: There's no question that Dean is a lot more comfortable with the actors. I don't fear them, but Dean just jumps right in and gets involved with the process. Our amount of interaction with them is pretty equal, but Dean tends to take the lead. There is clearly a certain joy that he takes from it. I tend to get really nervous. In fact, I just had a recording session yesterday with Ryan Reynolds in which I remembered that actors get a little nervous before they start. Tom Schumacher had a simple solution for this. He said, "If you ever have the opportunity, go to dinner with the person that you're going to record the night before. Or at the very least have coffee with them that morning." Taking that one or two hours to talk will have a profound effect on the recording session. Afterwards you won't be this stranger telling them to assume the role of aardvark!

Tom: Have you ever had an idea that you desperately wanted to get to the screen but either couldn't or were prevented from doing so?

Chris: *American Dog.* [laughs]

Tom: That of course was the project you started at Disney that was ultimately completed by others and renamed *Bolt*.

Chris: I'm okay with what happened. There was so much boarded that's not even in the script right now. It's one of those projects that you hope you can return to eventually. I think it's just a waiting game. But it was an interesting experience having things shift suddenly. I actually watched it (*Bolt*) for the first time about two weeks ago. I totally understand why they wanted to change directions. It wasn't their cup of tea. I actually like the changes they made. I think it would have been frustrating if the movie were essentially the same but with only slight changes. And I suppose my scenes and storylines are still sitting there on the shelf. I could actually pull them out and do them again. But it would be completely different.

Sketch, Chris Sanders, *An American Dog* (unproduced), 2007 © Disney.

Tom: Related to that, many directors have a project in mind that they'd like to do someday. For many years John Huston wanted to do *The Man Who Would Be King*. Do you have a project like that?

Chris: I have a few things I want to do. Oddly, there are several movies that frustrate me so much I just want to remake them. *Down Periscope* is a good example, the Kelsey Grammer submarine film. I just want to rewrite and recast it. And I'd love to remake the *Air Raid Wardens*. Dean and I have actually sketched out no less than twenty projects, five of which are high priority. There are even a few live-action projects in that mix, which would be great to do. After all, the industry still likes to put you in a box and say, "This is all you can do." Going from traditional animation to CG animation and then maybe live action would mean that we could just choose the right medium for the story.

Tom: I remember asking Bob Zemeckis at the premiere of *Roger Rabbit*, "Would you do another animated film?" He said, "NO! It's like watching paint dry."

Chris: But for people who love the detail it really is fun. It's very rewarding because there are endless opportunities to fiddle with things. You could start a discussion about the texture of rocks, and it might go on for months. You might even need to have a meeting solely devoted to moss. You might have to bring in a moss expert, if you really want to get into it. Seriously, though, you do have a schedule. It's a game of focusing on the things that really count. And that's why you have to let your people do their job, because they're great with the details. You have a few initial discussions and then send them on their way. It's the bigger discussions that matter. On *Lilo & Stitch* we had a large meeting to inform everyone that we wanted to use watercolor with a 1940s feel.

Tom: What about sequels? Within the last ten years, this almost seems mandatory. People, let alone the studio, want another *Shrek* or another *Ice Age*.

Chris: If it's a straight-to-TV sequel, then I wouldn't be inclined to make it. It's such an immense effort to get the first one done. Even if you are lucky enough to get it right the first time, and people want another one, it's still hard to turn around and think, "Okay, I'm going to do this again." It might be easier, since you have the designs and the style already nailed down. And there have been sequels that were frankly better than the original. But you don't expect it to be better. There is some reservation when you think about doing it all over again. Take the fourth *Shrek* as an example. You immediately think, "Is there anything left?" But I never would have expected a fourth one to be that good. Every time I see clips from another one, I just have to find out now.

So sequels have turned out to be rather cool, especially in the case of what DreamWorks has done. They're bold and have found a very original voice that has kept the studio thriving. I feel so lucky to be there because a lot of other studios have merged. DreamWorks is independent and fosters this healthy environment that embraces all kinds of ideas and voices. I'm all about that. It's like Paramount Studios back in the day. You go to the cafeteria and find gladiators sitting next to cowboys at the lunch table. And then a girl in a sailor's outfit walks by, because they just finished that big dance number. It's just a fun place to be.

Tom: Do you think your films have specific tone or style?

Chris: Yeah, I think they do. However, it's hard to describe it simply. But I think that *Mulan*, *Lilo & Stitch*, and *How to Train Your Dragon* are indicative of that style. They're all stylistically linked together. Although the stories are different, there is a consistent tone. There is always a distinct level of seriousness underwriting the lighthearted and even fun moments. I don't think I could ever do excessive slapstick or a movie with nothing but gags. There has to be something substantial about the story that I'm telling. I think that's ultimately the hook that sinks into the audience.

Tom: *Mulan* and *Lilo* were of course 2D films, but *Dragon* is 3D and very much stereoscopic. Did the change in technology have any effect on your style as a director?

Chris: I don't think it changed. I've always felt that CG films have a hard time conveying deep emotion. I don't know why that is, but I just think there is something about the look of the characters that doesn't innately convey emotion. You have to be careful what you focus on with close-ups. You don't want to start looking at eyelashes, nostrils, and pores, things that might emphasize technological artificiality. But at the same time CG offers an entirely new way for an audience to interact with an animated film.

On *Lilo & Stitch* we had less money and less time to make that movie. We had to embrace the strengths of hand-drawn animation. We chose to use watercolor because you can see the brush strokes. You see the mistakes on the backgrounds. It gave the film a look that was very similar to children's illustration, as opposed to the deep canvas stuff that was being done on movies like *Tarzan*. With CG we can render caricatured shapes, caricatured characters and environments, and bring in very realistic textures that create a suspension of disbelief that is most associated with live-action films. The audience can stop thinking of it as a cartoon and become truly immersed in it.

Tom: What's nice about *Dragon* is that its 3D wasn't overbearing. It wasn't just about shooting something that momentarily reaches out and grabs the audience. The paddleball effect. What exactly did you have in mind when it came to employing 3D technology?

Chris: We knew that every film going forward was going to be in 3D; 3D or not 3D wasn't something we thought about. But we did have creative choices concerning how extreme or invasive it was going to be. We insisted from the very beginning that we never wanted it to be the cart that leads the horse. We didn't want to use it in a way that removes the audience from that storytelling moment. We also didn't want it to look artificial or overly engineered. It had to accentuate the moment and add emotional intensity. When Hiccup is reaching to Toothless in that cove, for example, the CG brings you into to the moment and then backs you out slowly.

Tom: That scene is so crucial to the film. That's when they become friends. I've heard that you didn't rush into making it either. You knew that you needed that scene, but you also wanted to develop these characters first, so that you could really capture how these two would become friends. It reminds me of *The Black Stallion*, when the boy and the horse become friends.

Chris: That's exactly the kind of response we wanted! Hiccup was going to befriend the scariest dragon in the Viking world. And that was a substantial change from the original book, where both are more childlike characters. When we made that change, we actually talked about *The Black Stallion* because it has such wonderful scenes of a boy bonding with this fiercely beautiful animal. As for time, we didn't have complete freedom. There was always some kind of time constraint. That scene just seemed to get all the time it needed to develop. We also wanted to do something that we really hadn't had the luxury of doing in previous films. We wanted to create moments of character silence so we could have the score and the cinematography take you to a deeper place. It also created a bit of a problem.

It was over five minutes, which was something that had never been done before in animation. The studio jumped on that right away. Fortunately Dean and I were able to convince the studio to let it live until the testing phase. And when the movie was tested, people loved that scene. We got great feedback.

Tom: Thank you, Chris.

Chris: Sure. Any time.

6
Dean DeBlois Interview

Dean DeBlois.

I didn't know Dean DeBlois that well at first. I had known his partner Chris Sanders at Walt Disney since we worked together on *The Little Mermaid*. When Dean and Chris teamed up, I had already moved onto other projects. Dean is a big bear of a man, with a rich dark beard and piercing blue eyes, and a soft-spoken civility that is characteristic of his Canadian background. In recent years I've had the opportunity to talk film with him at the Motion Picture Academy and at the USC Film School. We found we had a lot of friends in common, from Disney story man Joe Grant to colleagues back in Canada. I've come to appreciate Dean's sharp mind and quick wit. Ron and I sat down with Dean in a room on the DreamWorks campus (the common nickname for the studio lot).

Tom Sito

Tom: So where did you get your start? What got you interested in animation?

Dean: As a kid in Quebec I was kind of raised on comic books, so I loved animation from an early age. But that was all Hollywood, and Hollywood was a place far, far away. So I learned how to draw through comic books. I would save up my allowance and buy one or two every week. That's where I learned anatomy, staging, and dynamic posing. It all came from comic books. I wanted to be an Ernie Chan. I wanted to draw for *Savage Sword of Conan* when I grew up! After high school I even had a short job at a local comic book company. But it just wasn't what I dreamed it would be. And Marvel just seemed a world away. As I was looking for jobs, I didn't want to just draw. I wanted to be involved in telling of a story. I loved writing short stories every bit as much as I loved drawing. Then I discovered a Classical Animation program at [Sheridan] college. I was selected for the summer program and learned the basic skills of animating. More importantly, I practiced telling a story through animation. This was exactly what I had been looking for. And that's when I decided that I wanted to be a part of the animation industry. After the program ended, I managed to get a job at a local TV animation studio in Canada. I worked on some Canadian TV series like *The Raccoons* for a few years.

Ron Diamond: Was there ever a short film that you found inspiring?

Dean: That would have to be *Sandman*. It came out in the early nineties by an animator named Paul Berry, who afterward was hired to work on Tim Burton's *The Nightmare Before Christmas*. I think his character design and stop motion was very important in the development of that film, which I don't think he was really credited for. It had great character designs and a certain dark-ness to it, like it grew out of a classic Grimm's fairy tale. I've always loved that creepy or ghostly atmosphere, things like "The Legend of Sleepy Hollow." I still don't think too many people have seen it. And I remember meeting Paul Berry on the streets of Soho. He had a *Nightmare Before Christmas* jacket on, one with a big Jack Skellington on the back. I said, "I love your short film and the influence it had on Tim's work." He was really thankful that somebody had noticed.

Dean DeBlois at Bluth.

Tom: So when did you and Chris Sanders team up?

Dean: After Canada I got hired by Don Bluth's studio in Ireland. I was there for four years. The films I worked on weren't all that great, but the experience was amazing. Toward the end I was actually Don's storyboard assistant. I learned a lot from him. I don't think Don had a knack for story, but he was an incredibly passionate filmmaker in most every other way. And he was an incredible draftsman. All he needed was a pencil and a piece of paper. He never needed any underdrawings. But since I was so interested in story, working on the board was where I wanted to be. After doing so much layout work at Don's studio, I managed to get a job at Disney as *Mulan* began production. Since there was no layout work needed, they put me in the story department with Chris Sanders and few other people. That's when Chris and I met. We had such similar sensibilities that we continued to work on stories and short stories both on and off the clock. That working relationship is what eventually brought us together on *Lilo & Stitch*.

Tom: How did you and Chris break down your duties?

Dean: We try to do everything together, because ours was never a forced union. We had come together on our own, and we enjoyed each other's contributions to the same overriding ideas. If I were to describe our relationship, I would say that we always have the same goal in mind, but we approach it from different angles. And when those different angles merge they actually create more texture and depth to a given scene. Consequently, we also go to animation dailies together so that our two perspectives can create a better end result. Sometimes the job demands that we split up. When that happens we tend to focus on our individual strengths. I came from a layout background, so I would spend a lot of time in the layout department. Chris, with his experience in character rotations and prop rotations at Marvel, tends to spend a lot of time with cleanup. Overall, anything that's key to the performance, like animation or art direction, we oversee together.

Tom: You both like to work on the scripts. Is there anything while writing that you have to visualize?

Dean: Writing-wise, the one thing that Chris and I have been pretty consistent in, ever since *Mulan*, is that we don't write with cartoon hats on. We don't write for animation. We write for movies. We want to make it feel real, even if the situation is ridiculous. The caricature comes from the story itself. It doesn't come from the way we write it. We want you to believe in the stakes. We want you to believe in the emotions. It's real peril. People can get hurt. People can die. People can fall in love and out of love. That has to feel real so that the audience is part of it, even though there's this giant suspension of disbelief based on whatever medium we're working in. If we did a stop-motion animated film, or if we did live action, which are things we plan to do one day, we would take the same approach. If we believe in the characters and we write it that way, then hopefully the audience will too.

Tom: Chris also mentioned that you two even work together with the actors during recording sessions.

Dean: Yeah, we don't leave the actor alone inside the booth. We tend to sit in there in order to read with the actor and provide constant feedback. Chris usually does the reading while I listen with earphones. Together we evaluate as we go. But we still provide creative freedom so that the actor can contribute. A lot of experimentation can occur during a recording session. Sometimes we even record multiple actors together in the room, so that they can play off of each other and even step on each other's lines. The traditional animation process avoids this method, but we love the energy of building a scene this way. When you capture actors interacting in an organic fashion, the scene ends up with a more realistic feel.

Chris Sanders and Dean DeBlois at Disney, Disney characters © Disney.

Tom: Do you cast a voice with a character in mind, or do you even create a character with a specific actor in mind?

Dean: That's a tricky question. The cast was in place on *How to Train Your Dragon* when we inherited the movie. On *Lilo & Stitch* we had character types in mind. In the case of Tia Carrere and Ving Rhames, it seemed so clear right away. Their voices just fit. But in the case of Jay Baruchel, for Hiccup, we initially thought he wasn't the right guy. Since the character was so young, he was overdoing it. The voice was very forced, nasally, and cartoony. When we met him and just had a normal conversation, that's when we heard the voice we wanted. We wanted Jay's natural voice. And he was very relieved to hear it. Jay felt like he had been pushed into performing in a range that was foreign to him.

How To Train Your Dragon, 2010 © DreamWorks Animation LLC. All Rights Reserved.

Tom: That's common for live-action actors when they first make the jump to animation. They tend to overdo it.

Dean: Yeah, they almost seem uneasy about the idea of just using their own voices. Some go even further. At the end of *Dragon*, we set up a screening for Gerard Butler and a bunch of his friends. They loved it. But Gerard came over to us and said, "I love the movie. But I want to redo all of my lines." He saw how big and imposing his character is, and he thought he didn't give him a big enough voice. I explained, "We record first and animate later." But he still insisted on trying to match the finished animation. He wanted more mass, more accent.

Ron: Can you talk a little more about how you work with actors?

Dean: Sure. Chris and I essentially take the same approach. Much like the crew, they are professionals at what they do. So you can't micromanage that. You have to let them do their thing. In that sense, when we write dialogue, it's always temporary. We want them to take a look at it and add their own touches. We are very much open to interpretation and ideas—as long as it doesn't lead into a tangent that takes us away from the story. Ever since *Lilo & Stitch*, we also sit down with the actors before recording begins. We like to get to know them and talk about the character and the tone of the film. That way they get a good grasp of the overall story.

　　　　　　When Gerard Butler first came onto the film [*How to Train Your Dragon*], we had a two-hour conversation about his character. He wanted him to have texture and be a man that the audience could relate to. He didn't want to only give speeches like Leonidas in *300*. So we quickly explained the father and son premise of the story. This is a man whose youthful heroic exploits defined him, and he wants the same thing for his son. However, his son is the complete opposite. As a parent, as a human being, he has to learn to accept that. In the beginning the two have a dysfunctional relationship. They don't honestly talk to each other. The blacksmith Gobber is the go-between, the means by which they communicate. Gerard not only quickly understood what we were going for but also began to think about how he could apply his skills as an actor to that role.

Tom: How do you feel about using celebrities as opposed to experienced voice talent?

Dean: You choose the voice that is right for the character, regardless of whether the actor is famous or not. The studios tend to want a name that they can market. But I think we're seeing more and more that it really doesn't reflect much in the box office. *Up* wasn't boasting huge names and it did amazingly well. Some movies that had nothing but celebrity casting did rather poorly at the box office. Still, sometimes those great actors are great for a reason. But the only thing I don't like is stunt casting. It was inappropriate for the movie. Again, it all comes back to casting the right voice for the character. That's it.

Tom: How do you deal with the powers above? Sometimes a director has to be a salesman when it comes to studio politics in order to get your vision approved.

Dean: In our case, Chris is very charismatic and easily interacts with the execs. I envy people like that. They can get people to buy anything, which is a fantastic ability to have when your movie hinges upon a pitch. Although I don't have that big personality in the room, I do have confidence in my ideas and my method. So when I'm pitching, I tend to invite everyone into my process. And I address both the strengths and weaknesses of the idea. I own the project, and I think that instills confidence in people.

In the beginning, my biggest concern about coming to the studio was Jeffrey [Katzenberg]'s reputation. Rumor had it that no one was really a director at DreamWorks. Everything was supposedly under Jeffrey's thumb. But that just wasn't the case. On my first day Jeffrey said, "I want three things. I want a father-and-son story, a Harry Potter tone, and a big David and Goliath ending. Give me those three things and you guys can have free reign." Later, when we invited him to view our progress, he would make a few comments and then leave. He left us to figure it out. Jeffrey wanted a few specific key things, and you had to give it to him. Other than that, you had the creative responsibility of making the movie. And although he always made astute observations, he explained that the process worked better if he wasn't in the room very much. Personalities at the top can vary greatly. Everybody wants the opportunity to color the project with their own sensibilities. As a director you have to listen to those who are paying for the movie. At the same time you still have to maintain a strong creative role. You have to know that you are making a movie that you'll be proud of. In the end, making a movie is a collaborative process that includes the execs. Jeffrey was just a great boss in that respect.

Tom: Have you ever worked with that producer who essentially wants to be another director on the film? Or have you mostly dealt with producers like Jeffrey, who sit back and oversee things from a distance?

Dean: I've been very lucky because I've worked with strong and creatively adept producers, the kind that support your vision and go to bat for you if the situation arises. Any studio has lots of demands, and there are always individuals that want to micromanage. You need a

Lilo & Stitch, 2002. © 2002 Disney.

creative buffer, somebody who can help you solve big problems and keep the studio focused on the movie's creative vision. If not, you can feel like a ping-pong ball being bounced around. We saw that happen on *Mulan*. There were too many people pulling creatively at the project, with no consistency regarding point of view. We had two directors who often didn't see eye to eye, a producer who had her own ideas about the movie, and a very driven editor with his own agenda. On top of that, at one point we had six writers pulling the story in different directions. It was quite chaotic for a while. In many ways *Lilo & Stitch* was a direct response to that. Besides directing, Chris and I took control of writing, storyboarding, and worked closely with our editor. It was the only way to maintain consistency. I really appreciate producers who don't try to be a second or third director. Their job is to balance the responsibility of the budget and the time it takes to make the movie, and to protect it from bureaucratic abuse.

Tom: What is your favorite part of being a director?

Dean: Well, from a selfish standpoint, it's easier to promote ideas that you strongly believe in. Those key, creative decisions are simply placed in your lap, and so you have the freedom to convey the emotions and imagery you want. When you're lower in the ranks, you have to convince a lot of people. I've been in both positions and I definitely prefer directing. From a more selfless point of view, I love being part of an experience that people look back fondly on. Even though *Mulan* was difficult, people were proud of the movie. This goal was so important when we started *Lilo & Stitch*

Dean DeBlois and Chris Sanders © Disney.

that we gathered everyone together in an assembly hall and said, "We have a smaller budget, less time, and a very ambitious movie. But we also want everybody to go home on the weekends and see their families. Let's have a good time." It was all about doing what needed to be done, yet still allowing the crew to have their lives, stay healthy, and see their loved ones.

Ron: How did you do that? Making it possible for your crew, let alone yourself, to go home at a decent time is not always easy.

Dean: It came down to simplifying some of the process. We couldn't afford Deep Canvas and a lot of the technology that the bigger movies had. So we simplified the character designs and did away with shadows. We ditched realism for a hand-painted watercolor look. We removed details. We removed pencil line mileage, like the prints from t-shirts and the pockets from jeans. In the end, no one really noticed. But that helped. Still, we had a tough schedule. Chris and I, as for *Dragon*, we started on the project in October 2008, and the movie had to be finished and out of animation by December 2009. We used a lot of the characters that had been rigged and the environments that had been built, but we started with the story from scratch. And we had to build new characters. It was tough on everyone, but they really believed in what they were doing. When you're running a ship that everyone is just happy to be on, it's a great feeling. It's important to me that people are proud of the movie, regardless of what the critics think.

Tom: What's your least favorite part of being a director?

Dean: Making concessions when you don't believe in them. It's that moment when you have to take on a note that you disagree with. It's a rare thing, actually. I wouldn't say that it happens very often. And this isn't just about disagreeing with the studio head. Chris and I have locked horns a few times, and one of us had to back down. When *Lilo & Stitch* was screened for the ratings board they didn't want to give us a G rating because of a few violent scenes. The powers that be at Disney made us go back and change sequences that worked really well. In the end we still didn't get the G rating. But then we were officially beyond the point of no return. We couldn't put things back to the way they were, the way we wanted them in the first place.

Ron: Do you think you've grown or evolved as director?

Dean: I think I'll be a student of story my entire life. But I've definitely learned some important lessons along the way. Telling a great story means that you have to know its elements, its overall structure and how to weave story lines together, and how to mine a scene for that gold that's just going to resonate with the audience. Embedding universal themes within a fresh, new story is important to me. I'm kind of obsessed with it. Looking back at my first experience in the story department on *Mulan*, I'm amazed that it took about five years to make. Knowing what I do now, I think we could have made it in half that time.

I think *Dragon* was a chance to prove that if you invest a lot in story, the other elements of the filmmaking process will come together quickly and smoothly. I've had a lot of time to observe other people's choices and directing styles. I've found my favorites and I've tried to emulate them. One of the things I do to keep the creative juices flowing is make music documentaries and films. It's rewarding because it has no structure. It's not about narrative. And the creative direction isn't subject to the whims of a collective body. You don't have to please others. It's all you and the band, and you're free to experiment however you wish. I love being able to grab a camera and try different lenses, different lighting effects, and different ways of editing the final product. It's truly gratifying.

Tom: You wrote *How to Train Your Dragon 2* by yourself and directed it yourself.

Dean: In the beginning I was nervous about it, but you are never really truly alone. I have the story team, and all the other creative heads to take suggestions from. A lot of people give a lot of good input, but you can't implement everything. You try to stay objective. Everything about the story needs to filter through you.

How To Train Your Dragon 2, 2014 © DreamWorks Animation LLC. All Rights Reserved.

Ron: What advice would you give someone new to the industry about developing a good story?

Dean: When Chris and I sit down to work on a project together, the first question is, "What would you pay to see? What excites you? What kind of world would grab you and take your breath away?" Once we get the ball rolling, then we talk about who the hero is and the back story that's driving him. You have to figure out what this character wants and needs, even if he can't see it himself. These are the core issues that you have to lay out in the beginning. It's something I learned from John Lasseter. He used to talk about the story minus the exact details. He simply wanted to know who this guy was, what kind of journey he's on, and what does he discover. It didn't make a difference if he was human or an animal, or if he was in the desert or the rainforest. I always tell students to read Blake Snyder's *Save the Cat* books, because they're a treasure trove of great story tools and truths. I also remember some great advice from Zack Schwartz, one of my teachers at Sheridan College. He was a background painter on *Snow White*. He said, "If it reads as a postage stamp, it will read as a billboard." I always remember that. First, see it in its most simple, strongest form. Then it will only get bolder, bigger, and better as you expand upon it.

Tom: When you first got started, were there any artists that inspired you?

Dean: Yeah, I was very lucky. On my very first day at Disney I was given an office that was about six doors down from Joe Grant. I met Joe on my first day, and that's when I realized he'd been there from the start. He was there the day that Walt came in and said, "I got this crazy idea. I want to make a feature length cartoon." He had this incredible wealth of knowledge and lessons to pass down. He was always evolving. Even when he left to pursue pottery and do greeting cards, he just kept developing as an artist. Joe was the guy I could go to for anything. He even took a creative interest in stuff I was doing outside of work. Any story I was developing, I always took it to him first. Any artwork that I finished, I would show him. Joe was also responsible for introducing me to Bill Pete. Bill was very inspiring. I would visit him at his home and just learn from him. One time he wanted to take me upstairs to his studio and show me a collection of his artwork. But his wife wouldn't let him, because she said it was too messy up there.

And I've had other heroes along the way. I got to meet Steven Spielberg. After he watched *Dragon*, he actually talked to us like colleagues. That was an amazing moment. James Cameron, after *Avatar*, also came over to view some of our sequences. He gave us great feedback, lots of compliments. In fact, after the Academy Awards, he grabbed us and said to his wife, "These are the guys I was telling you about." James Cameron actually went home and talked about our movie. Pretty cool.

Tom: Do you ever feel overwhelmed by the number of decisions you have to make on a daily basis? Do you get frustrated?

Dean: Looking back, frustration emerges when you just can't fix the thing that needs fixing. I particularly remember this early on. When I first got into story, I remember seeing well–thought-out storyboards that presented solutions to certain problems. But then they were cut apart, rearranged, and then manipulated by the director or the editors. That was frustrating. When you're the director and writer, it's in your hands. But when they seem tied, when you can't find a solution, or when you can't solve it the way you want to, that's when I feel frustrated. After all, you need to feed the machine. You're the director. It's your responsibility. And that's why you have to depend upon your team and even your producer. It's a creative brain trust, and they cannot only help you solve a problem, they can also prevent you from forcing a bad idea. It may seem great to you. You may strongly believe in it. But there's an audience out there. There are other people involved. And you have to answer to them. It's not just about you and your tastes in the end.

Tom: Would you work again with preexisting material? Or are you only interested in developing your own stories now?

Dean: To a certain extent, *Dragon* was based on a kids' book. We definitely brought our own interpretation to it. And we stuck to the essentials. It was a father-and-son story set in the world of Vikings and dragons. But almost every other detail went away.

How To Train Your Dragon, 2010 © DreamWorks Animation LLC. All Rights Reserved.

We also redesigned the major characters. Toothless, for example, used to be a little iguana-sized dragon. And so, even as an adaptation, it still required a lot of reinvention. Overall, getting involved in a preexisting property isn't that appealing to me. The only way I would do it is if I were allowed to put a creative spin on it, something I could believe in.

Tom: Since you're such a story guy, do you ever miss storyboarding?

Dean: I do. It's such an important stage in the creation of an animated feature. If you're writing the script and directing the picture, storyboarding is this in-between moment where somebody takes that script and does an interpretation of it. It's not always what you had in mind. And you have to be very open-minded about it, because it might be better than what you had in mind. But often that's where you can get frustrated, because the artist missed something that was so important to you and the story. So, sometimes it requires sitting down and drawing it out with the artist and letting them go from there. You can't get bogged down, because that's not your job.

Making an animated feature is a collaborative effort. It's better to have other people putting a spin on it, as long as they know what the bigger picture is. That's what you're there to remind them about. You can't let them engage in open exploration. That's a bad way to direct. Of course, everyone wanted to jump right into *How to Train Your Dragon 2*. But I had to push back. I wanted time to write a story that works before we start exploring it visually. It makes everyone's life much easier. And hopefully we avoid the frustration and wasted time allotted to designing various locations or exploring moments that aren't going to be in the movie.

Tom: Do you like the editing process? Some directors love it, because they sit down and go through sequences.

Dean: I love it! I appreciate what a good editor can bring to the process. I've worked with some really bossy ones and with some really collaborative ones. I particularly like working with Darren Holmes and John Carr. They bring in their own ideas, but they're always in tune with the overall feel and tone of the movie.

Ron: Do you also want the story finished before you bring in a composer?

Dean: Yes. I want to know that the story is locked in place before bringing the composer in. That said, I'd love to get the composer in as early as possible. They are a key part of storytelling. When Chris and I brought Alan Silvestri into the mix, he was able to pick out moments that we had either been avoiding or burying under dialogue. He added a whole new layer to the story as he removed the temporary score and inserted music that enhanced the emotions of a given scene. And when we worked with John Powell he was always experimenting. He would talk with us about music in general. He wanted to know what was on our iPods. Those conversations led to some interesting choices in the beginning. The original music was inspired by a piece of music that came from an Icelandic quartet called *Sigur Ros*. I had made a feature documentary about them. John found it to be really inspiring and rose to outdo it in the end. It captured the emotion of the scene perfectly. John's ideas added a lot to the movie.

Ron: Now you did mention how comic books were an important inspiration early on. But was there a pivotal moment when you just knew that you were going to work in animation?

Dean: Well, I remember being mesmerized when the Queen turned into a witch in *Snow White*, and when she is on the cliff with the lightning flashing in the background. The animation was so fluid. And that's when I started to think about the artist that actually drew that scene. The scene in *Dumbo* when his mother rocks him to sleep through the bars of the cage was also a powerful moment. However, I just didn't see the avenue by which I could pursue animation. That's why I focused on comic books. It wasn't until I stumbled upon the animation program at Sheridan College that I began to learn about the process. It was kind of funny, actually. Until that moment I didn't think you could study animation at school.

Ron: What other movies inspired you?

Dean: The imagery in *Pinocchio* and *Bambi* was so poetic and evocative. And as children's films, they were very bold, considering the powerful themes involved. I remember just wanting to live in those worlds. They were definitely inspirations as I moved into layout, because I wanted to draw worlds like that. In particular the European designs in *Pinocchio* fascinated me. That architecture was very romantic. It got my imagination going.

Ron: You eventually traveled to Europe, right?

Dean: When I went to work for Don Bluth, I found myself in Ireland. So that landscape and architecture was suddenly all around me. You didn't have to go far to find dilapidated ruins and castles. And on weekends I traveled to places like Denmark and Spain. I was always interested in the macabre, so I took the opportunity to visit the catacombs and the famous cemeteries in Paris. I also went to Scotland and visited Loch Ness. I was in my early twenties. It was a great time.

Ron: What about live-action movies?

Dean: I remember loving *Escape to Witch Mountain*; the theme of a younger protagonist in over his or her head in a supernatural world just resonated with me. *E.T.* was also a big influence. And, of course, there was *Star Wars*, the Indiana Jones series, and

The Black Stallion, which was such an emotionally powerful film. I think one of the most influential movies was *Blade Runner*. I actually learned to storyboard by studying Ridley Scott's directing choices. Don Bluth's studio had a conference room where I would eat dinner and watch his movies after work. I'd pause between every cut and draw the before and after frame. I really wanted to understand why certain moments in certain movies elicited such a response. For example, that scene where Rutger Hauer catches Harrison Ford from falling and then gives his death speech, that scene is so beautifully played out. I found it so poetic. People in the theater really responded to that scene. I also did the same thing with James Cameron's *The Abyss*. I drew every frame before and after cuts in key scenes. I didn't have access to anyone's boards, so I used live action to teach myself filmmaking.

Ron: As an animation director, do you think you've evolved differently because you used live action as a reference?

Dean: Maybe. I know that I appreciate live-action sensibilities. And I dislike that wacky, animation cliché where everything is just silly. Animation is a medium, not a genre. Yet people are still quick to categorize it as kids' stuff. It's something you give the babysitter to distract the kids with. It's much more powerful than that. There is a suspension of disbelief. If you do it right, you can transport people to places that they have never dreamed of. What James Cameron did with *Avatar* is basically what great animation does. In the case of *Dragon*, I'm currently working on the sequels, but I'm looking at it as a trilogy. It has the potential to grow and become this epic world like *The Lord of the Rings*. And the tone and themes will become more mature as the storyline grows.

Tom: In *How to Train Your Dragon 2* you have aged Hiccup and the other characters, instead of keeping them perpetually children, like the Charlie Brown characters.

Dean: Yes, I always saw *How to Train Your Dragon* as a trilogy showing Hiccup attaining manhood. In the first film he was fifteen and afraid of what was ahead, afraid of girls, afraid of dragons, afraid of his coming place in life. In *Dragon 2* we move up five years, so the endless playfulness of being fifteen doesn't make sense. At fifteen you already feel like an adult, but it is the last year that you are treated as a child. That is a very confusing time period. In *Dragon 2*, Hiccup is twenty. He is more confident and beginning to recognize his responsibilities. His relationship with his father has also evolved. Also in the first movie we completely played out the theme of dragons and humans mistrusting of one another. It didn't make sense to rehash that theme again.

Tom: So you are a triple threat. A writer, an animator, and a director.

Dean: I was a so-so animator. I'm a better layout guy and storyboard artist.

Ron: Do you play an instrument too?

Dean: No. I'm just fascinated by people who can. I am a serious music fan, both scores and live music. I go to a lot of concerts. Mostly I listen to alternative stuff. Sigur Ros is such an inspiring band that I felt compelled to make a documentary about them. Their music is so cinematic, so full of imagery. When I saw them at the Hollywood Bowl, they had the audience in their hands. Their music reaches out and grabs the audience in a powerful way. Great film scores do the same thing. They transcend dialogue and go right for the heart. It puts you in a unique emotional space. Whether you realize it or not, a good score is one of the reasons why you love that movie so much.

Tom: Can you talk a little bit more about what it's like to co-direct?

Dean: Sure, absolutely. Chris and I met back in 1994 on *Mulan*. He was head of the storyboard department on that film. I had just joined the studio as a layout artist, but then I quickly became part of the story team. And after Chris went off to develop a film as a director, I became head of story. There were just about ten of us then. But Chris and I had the same interests and artistic tendencies, especially for taking a fresh approach to characters and a love of quirky moments. So we were always in sync in terms of developing and writing a scene.

When it came time to do *Lilo & Stitch*, it was just a natural collaboration. Chris and I wrote well together. We direct well together. I think it's because we have different points of view, yet our artistic voice is essentially the same. Our sensibilities overlap, and that's important because we share the same goal. On the other hand, there's enough difference between us that it keeps what we do fresh. When we divide up scenes we usually gravitate towards those that we have a certain vibe for. So we don't often find ourselves wanting to write the same scene. When we're done we then read each other's work. Here, I think, is the most important moment in our process. There's a great deal of trust in each other's sensibilities, tastes, and judgment. If either of us starts pulling stuff out of those scenes, we trust that decision. No one immediately says, "You have to put that stuff back in!" If we do have a difference of opinion, we talk about it. The story is always the most important thing in the room, not our feelings. We make our decisions based on that alone. It's the way we bring together our subtle differences to make the story better that keeps our process, and our material, invigorating and fresh.

We both have that time alone to write a scene. It's a creative moment that's indicative of our individual voices. But I trust Chris to react to the best stuff in that scene. He'll usually say, "I see where you're going and I really like this. This part felt a little long. What if you do this instead?" That's when the dialogue starts. We always give each other a moment to get our ideas out on paper, so that the idea exists before you start tampering with it.

Tom: On *How to Train Your Dragon 2*, you were directing it alone (Chris Sanders moved over to direct *The Croods*). What have you learned about the process since you started?

Dean: [laughs] First, it's a lot more work! Seriously, you have to be the champion of your convictions. Three years later even the best ideas lose their freshness and people start to think they should be changed. I find myself standing up for ideas. You have to believe in what you originally saw in them.

Ron: Well, we really appreciate your taking the time to talk with us. Thanks, Dean.

Dean: It's been my pleasure.

Dean DeBlois and Chris Sanders © Disney.

7
Vicky Jenson Interview

Vicky Jenson © DreamWorks.

Vicky Jenson and I have known each other since she started working at Filmation Studios in the mid-1980s. Vicky is an effervescent woman, bubbling over with ideas and talent. She can design, paint, storyboard, art direct as well as direct, both animation as well as live action. She co-directed *Shrek*, the first animated feature film to win an Academy Award, and she worked with the likes of Robert De Niro and Martin Scorsese. She began in animation at a time when women were not expected to do more than clean up and color characters. But the word "no" had never been part of her vocabulary. Vicky kicked down barriers for women filmmakers with her fashionable suede boots, and did it all with grace and good humor. We sat down with Vicky at DreamWorks Studio to talk about her amazing career.

Tom Sito

Ron Diamond: Now let's start with a little background. When did your interest in animation begin? What was your inspiration?

Vicky: I got into the industry the way a lot of people did: nepotism! [laughs] I started painting cels for my brother-in-law at a very young age. He had a small animation studio that made commercials for things like Breck hair shampoo and Jerseymaid milk.

Ron: Was this here in LA?

Vicky: This was here in LA. I was painting cels while babysitting for him and my sister. I was about thirteen, earning a whopping five bucks per hour! Of course that five bucks also included the babysitting!

Ron: Was there a short film that influenced and inspired you?

Vicky: I remember watching *The Violinist* by Ernie Pintoff as a kid. We didn't have VCRs or DVDs then. We would rent a projector from the library and pick up a few films on 16 mm. My little brother got really good being a projectionist and even set up a little theater in his bedroom. Along with classic features my dad wanted us to see, like *Citizen Kane* and *Potemkin*, we used to watch this one short cartoon every time. It resonated with me for a couple of reasons. I did play a musical instrument when I was a kid, but mostly it was this great combination of poignancy and comedy. This man learns that life is better when it's in balance. I just thought that was a tremendous lesson. We grew up with a lot of expectation in our family to be artistic and to excel at whatever dream we wanted to pursue. That little cartoon just reminded me to keep it in balance.

Ron: Were you already considering animation as a career?

Vicky: No, I didn't think of animation as a possible career at all. I was going to be a painter or dancer. I was taking ballet and cello lessons at the time. Working in animation was just my summer job. Painting backgrounds at Hanna-Barbera was very seasonal work. I was paying my way through college at the Academy of Art in San Francisco by working each summer in LA.

When I first worked at Hanna-Barbera as a background painter on *The Smurfs* and other cartoons, I just didn't think of it as a career. But then I was hired on at Filmation and I started storyboarding and earning lots of money. Things started to change. Shows became syndicated, the work was no longer seasonal; it was much more permanent. I didn't even finish my last semester of college because there was so much work. Everyone at school kept saying, "You're already doing the work that we're trying to get into." Still, it didn't feel like my dream or the plan that I had for myself. I didn't have that feeling until I started directing.

When I started directing, I found that it embraced everything that I was interested in. You get to play with music, movement, the story, and yet you don't have to animate! I was never an animator. I was always a storyboard artist or a background painter, a designer. I just didn't have the patience for actually animating! But I just love conducting the whole thing, working with all the moving parts and telling the bigger picture.

Tom: What was it like working at Hanna-Barbera? That must have felt like a big factory.

Vicky: I worked upstairs in the background department. It was a bit of a boy's club. I was one of only three women painting backgrounds, but the other two, Gloria Wood and Lorraine Andrina, worked at home. I was tough, confident, and somehow I fit in. As a department we were very much our own entity. Sometimes it seemed everybody else in the building couldn't stand us because we were so noisy! We played loud music and held dart competitions, with darts we made from pushpins and tape. Worst of all, we would put a handful of pennies in a Sparkletts bottle and toss it around the concrete floor. To the departments downstairs it must have sounded like thunder and we knew it! Oh, the calls we got from the other departments!

Tom: Who was the head of the department?

Vicky: Al Gmuer. He was great. It was such a fun time. There was a quota system to manage how much we were expected to paint. If you painted anything for "stock," backgrounds that were used throughout the series, your painting counted double. We had to paint at least twenty fields a week, so stock was highly desired because when you reached your quota you got to go home! Another plus was getting assigned a "pan." Pans were the long paintings used for scenes where a character had to run or drive. These were super easy and so super lucrative! One of the guys even had a license plate that only background painters could understand. It said, "Repeat Pan." It's hard to explain. Nobody understands an eighty A to E pan anymore. I feel like a dinosaur.

Tom: Artists who create backgrounds and storyboards, once established, tend to get very settled in their careers. You, on the other hand, seemed to be rather restless. When did you first start thinking about directing? What attracted you to it?

Vicky: It wasn't really about being restless; it was about the challenge. Every time I took a job it was either to try something new or work with somebody I always wanted to work with. It was all about learning more and getting more experience. I tried animating, but like I said, I didn't have the patience for it. I liked storyboarding because it kind of included animation, in that I got to draw the characters acting. But I didn't have to stress any of the technicalities like staying on model or registration. The idea of directing didn't even come up until I was at Universal working on the *Baby Huey* series as an art director and story artist. It was a little show that aired at six in the morning, I think about eight people saw it. It was the first time I got to write an episode, storyboard it, and then direct it. I went nuts. I just put everything into it that had ever influenced me. It was so exciting and so much fun. A few months later DreamWorks formed and they were looking for people. At this point I definitely wanted to direct but I wanted to learn more about it. I put together a portfolio and applied to AFI's directing program for women. Everyone I knew was sending their resumes to DreamWorks but that was my plan B. At the time, the straightest path to directing in animation was as a story artist. I told myself if I didn't get into AFI, I'd apply to DreamWorks. And that is exactly what happened! Years later, after *Shrek*, I kind of rubbed their noses in it when they invited me to give a talk.

Baby Huey, Vicky Jenson, 1994 © DreamWorks Animation LLC.

Tom: That's kind of like when Disney once brought Charles Schulz in to talk to the crew, the first thing he said was, "This is interesting. I remember applying to Disney in 1950 before I sold *Peanuts*. I got a very nice letter back saying, 'Thank you. But we are only looking for good artists.'"

Vicky: Oh no. [laughs]

Tom: Okay, we have to get to the feminist question. Your career overlaps with the older generation, the old boys' club. Did you ever feel like you hit a glass ceiling?

Vicky: If there was, I just didn't see it. I wouldn't see it. I remember getting a comment or two when I was painting backgrounds at Hanna-Barbera, something like, "You don't paint like a girl at all!" And there was also, "You paint great for a girl." What does a girl paint like? I don't know. I just ignored that stuff. And it never intimidated me. I did my job and learned from everybody who was there. I think that attitude came from my family. My mom and dad never raised us to feel limited. We had something to contribute, and we could do that if we wanted to. On the job I just plowed ahead.

Tom: Well, even at Filmation there were always a few guys that were pretty old school about women.

Vicky: I shared a room with a chauvinist. He was afraid of birds. So I just "unknowingly" brought in birds a lot. I think the flapping scared him out of the office eventually. But it didn't make a difference that those guys were around. I didn't care if they were arrogant or felt threatened. They didn't seem to be the ones that could get in the way of me moving forward, if I needed to. This is making me sound ambitious, but it wasn't like that. I just wanted to learn how to do new things, like how to paint clouds for the *Smurfs* or *Flintstones*. And I was always fearless when it came to asking questions. I think they just kept giving me more work because I kept asking.

I was the same in the live-action world. When I was storyboarding a low-budget horror movie I kept talking about how I was in love with production design because I was taking a class at UCLA. When their original production designer decided to leave because the budget became too low, they asked me if I wanted to put my money where my mouth was and take the job. I jumped at the chance and spent nine weeks in Yugoslavia. Our budget was so low I had to wear a lot of hats on that movie. On top of being production designer and story artist, I became the set decorator and even got to be a puppeteer on the creature. None of this would've happened if I kept my mouth shut. Talking about my dreams out loud seemed to make them come true.

Tom: Unlike some of the other directors we've talked to, you came up through the Hollywood factory system. Back when everyone viewed animation as a blue-collar, day-laborer kind of job. How did you motivate yourself and refrain from getting stuck in that mentality? When you have to clock in every morning, it's easy to grow disaffected.

Vicky: I just never looked at it as a paycheck. Anything you're going to spend that much time doing each day of your life should be meaningful. For me, it wasn't a job. It was art in some way or another. It didn't matter what I was working on. I'd always find something about it that represented an artistic experience. I was going to learn something. Anything. Once, when storyboarding, I decided I wanted to learn how to draw with a brush like … oh dear, who did the comic strip *Pogo*?

Tom: Walt Kelly.

Vicky: Yes, Walt Kelly. I LOVE those drawings. So I would make these challenges for myself like: "I'm going to learn how to ink on this show." Even if I didn't care what the show is about. It was never a nine-to-five job. Every day was a lesson. Every season was a school semester. When I first started at DreamWorks, when we were making *El Dorado*, Will Finn and David Silverman would give me a sequence and say, "Just make it 'Vicky,' you know, just make it Vickyfied." I would take that sequence, give it my own personal treatment, and just keep moving forward.

Tom: You never went to film school, right?

Vicky: Right.

Tom: So most of your skills were acquired on the job and through mentoring?

Vicky: It was all on-the-job training. As I mentioned earlier, I grew up around art. I had art books and I drew all the time. But I never formally studied film or took courses in story structure or theory of cinematography. It was all a mystery until I was actually doing it on the job. For example, when I started storyboarding, we had to create a half-hour show in a month. We'd get a script and have to visualize it. Suddenly, while I'm at the movies or watching something on TV, I was aware of cuts, close-ups, and establishing shots. I couldn't look at a movie any other way again. Even when it came to live action I was learning by the seat of my pants.

Color studies, Vicky Jenson, *The Road to El Dorado*, 2000 © DreamWorks Animation LLC.

Tom: You're like Chuck Jones in that way. Chuck didn't go to college or have any formal training. He learned everything as he went along. And at the end of his life he was very much like Mark Twain. He really wanted to get under the skin of the project.

Vicky: Sometimes you can't learn anything until you actually do it. People can give you all the advice in the world, but it's just going to bounce off your forehead until you experience it. That's when you say, "Oh that's what they were talking about. Damn it! Why didn't I listen?" School is great, but I think you have to experience the gymnastics of filmmaking at the same time. I don't regret anything. If I went to film school, perhaps the theory and lessons would have limited me in some way or scared me off.

Tom: Talk a little more about your experiences in live action. How is it different in your experience? Are there any parallels?

Vicky: Yes, certainly, but there are some distinct differences. For instance there is an immediacy to live action. Obviously for both animation and live action you do as much prep as you can but in live action the thing to remember is that you're creating and gathering all the pieces that you think you will need for the editorial process after. In animation I was used to pre-editing. You're planning out what you need because in animation you don't animate coverage. When animation directors come over to live action, they often end up editing in the camera. Ivan Reitman, my producer on my first live-action feature, kept saying that to me during the dailies, "Stop editing in the camera. You're not giving yourself enough coverage. You're not giving yourself enough choices. What if your idea doesn't work?" That's very true. When we're storyboarding for animation we toss the boards away all the time and try again. In live action you don't have the opportunity to cut together a story reel. You have to plan for a lot of different possibilities. You have to give yourself some room to play with later on. That was a hard lesson for me. And that's probably the biggest difference between the two. I still love live action. I would do it again in a heartbeat. I love the interaction with the actors, watching them create that magic. In animation we are so used to hyper-controlling every edit, every audio edit, every blink. My DP kept saying, "Just count to ten before you yell 'cut,' because you don't know what the actor might do." I thought that was really good advice.

Tom: What about working with the crew? Some animation directors said they experienced a kind of passive-aggressive resistance from live-action crews, because they didn't come up through the traditional roles of a live-action set. Did you ever run into any of that?

Vicky: I don't think so. If I did, that old filter must have kicked in. I just ignored the negativity. But I've always been very inclusive. I didn't go into it assuming that everyone was out to get me. There is a really good book on directing live action called

The Working Director. It points out that everyone on set has their own issues to deal with. Your location manager isn't there to help you make a great movie. He is there to make sure he can park the trucks. Your first AD isn't necessarily there to make sure you're making a great movie either. That's YOUR job. He's thinking about airplanes flying overhead or schools nearby, the potential background noise that will make his job difficult. Everybody is fighting their own battle in some way. You're the one leading them through this whole process, and they need to feel included in the bigger picture. If you do that, they'll jump through fire for you. Not every director does this, and the movie still gets made. I wanted to create a more inclusive environment. For example, I tended to tell everybody, no matter what their position was on the movie, what the theme of my movie was all about. I wanted to talk to them about it artistically. I knew if I pulled them in they'd contribute ideas I might never think of on my own. And it worked. Everyone felt more invested. Even the prop designer on my short would come to me with little things he'd found that didn't just work, they illustrated the theme.

Tom: When you started directing, how was the transition from working on a film to managing one?

Vicky: It entailed a lot of personal growth. I came from a very opinionated, loud family. I was never afraid to speak out, and that got me noticed. It made me visible. But like everyone, I had to learn to balance being the boss and having empathy for my crew. As I said, everyone is fighting their own battles on set. Still, you need to make sure that everybody is making the same move. Your ego needs to be in check. I might look at a scene and want to draw it myself. But that's not my job anymore. I've surrounded myself with the best people I can find. I need to convey my vision in order to help my crew do their jobs.

Tom: The difficulty of letting go is quite common amongst directors that used to animate or storyboard. You still want to jump in and do it yourself.

Vicky: Well, when you don't jump in, when you back off and set someone else's mind in motion, one of the greatest benefits is being surprised. Your artist can come back with something wonderful and unexpected. You have all these incredibly talented people working with you. As you let them work, you get to watch some wonderful ideas unfold. Then suddenly you have a wealth of ideas to work with and you too get to be surprised.

Tom: Are there any anecdotes that you'd like to share? Was there anything so unexpectedly cool that you just had to use it?

Vicky: There are dozens. It happens all the time. We tend not to think of animation as spontaneous, but it can be. And it doesn't make a difference when that great moment or idea happens. You can use it. In live action, that can be difficult unless you have money for reshoots. Otherwise, you can't just go back and put it in. One of the cool things about animation is that you don't have to stop until the producer tells you to stop!

Ron: Did directing live action influence or change the way you direct animation?

Vicky: Yes. Live action forced me to be a stronger storyteller. You have your feet to the fire. You're working so fast, and you have to keep the story and its characters clear. The same thing goes for animation. Without a strong story and characters, you just have pretty pictures. That's certainly not a revelation. But it is a hard lesson to learn on a live-action set. In animation you have so many people there to help you. You have so many chances to change things. You get spoiled. You get to attack the story in well-defined pieces. In the storyboard process you can come up with new ideas and make the movie funnier. That was very much my experience on *Shrek*. On *Shark Tale* the story was not so clear. The original script was too violent. And we only knew where the movie started and where it ended. There was an entire process of discovery in between, and that was a great experience. But I like to start with a good story first!

Tom: On both *Shrek* and *Shark Tale* you had a lot of Hollywood stars cast in those key roles. Do you have certain actors in mind when you are creating new characters?

Vicky: No, not always. *Shrek* was simply unique that way. It was definitely a new way of approaching animation. Before that, directors didn't really let actors shape a character the way Mike Myers and Eddie Murphy did, or as Robin Williams did in *Aladdin*.

Tom: Do you like working with actors in recording studios?

Vicky: Definitely! It's really one of my favorite parts of the job. It's actually the reason why I went into live action in the first place. I loved working with actors. In animation the drawing can sometimes consume everyone's attention. Acting often gets lost. I'm just so enamored with watching the performance unfold and finding the different ways that you can work a scene. As the director you get pulled into the actors' process, the way he or she finds that character. I love being a part of that.

Tom: Most big name actors are not familiar with the animation process. How was it, directing someone like Robert De Niro or Will Smith in the recording studio?

Vicky: I made sure that it became familiar to them, so that it didn't seem so mechanical. To me, it's not voice-over. It is acting. So, I would shape a session like a rehearsal and work in ways that were familiar to them from live action. We worked in bigger story beats rather than just taking the scenes line by line and having them say it three different ways. I saw a lot of animation directors doing that at the time. Instead, we would read the whole scene together and get comfortable with it, like in a rehearsal. Then we would work on the different tactics the character might use to accomplish what he or she might be after for the whole scene. It made the performances more personal and authentic. I also never let an actor work in a vacuum during a recording session. I made sure that my actors are also good actors, so that Robert or Will had something real to react to. In fact, a lot of my direction would be to the reader because I knew that would have an effect on the actor's response. There needs to be a connection between the players in that recording studio. I wasn't so worried about making sure the line came out the way I heard it in my head; I just wanted to make sure it was honest and maybe even surprising. In preparation, I would put myself in the actor's shoes and ask a lot of questions of my characters. What do you want out of him in this scene? What do you want him to do? Are you trying to pick a fight with him? Are you trying to win him over to your side? And then I would explore what tactics one might use to do these things. The tactics are the acting choices that make the performance unique. I might pick a fight with someone differently than you do. Those are the kinds of questions going through the actors' minds. And that's how I approached it. I would get my coverage from my actors, from what they brought to the role.

Tom: Did you ever show them storyboards? Some actors like to look at storyboards and some don't.

Vicky: Yes. We did that a lot on *Shrek*. Not always on *Shark Tale*. By that time I was more into the whole actor process. But when we did, it was generally early in the process to get the actor excited about the role. It was a way to give them a handle on the character. But we always wanted the actor to have the freedom to play with the character anyway, no matter what we had boarded.

Tom: Were you able to get two actors in the same room? It's often tough to schedule celebrities.

Vicky: Yes, I did! I got Robert De Niro and Martin Scorsese together. It was also the first time I joined actors inside the recording booth. I just couldn't stay outside in the control room. I needed to be there with them like any director would when running a rehearsal. And that's how I ran the session, like a rehearsal. And it was so much fun. There were no costumes or props, just them. It was a great scene. But that shouldn't be surprising. I think while this was the eleventh movie they'd done together it was the FIRST time they were both actually acting together.

Tom: Did you keep the tape running? You have to capture that spontaneity. In rehearsals you get all this great stuff, but then the actual take is sometimes just okay.

Vicky: Oh yeah, we did. And you want to let them know that they're free to fail. Otherwise they won't take chances. Or I'll say, "I got this great idea. Now it might not work …" Then they really cut loose, because it's not their fault if it doesn't work. It's my fault! It's something I learned from my wonderful directing mentor Judith Weston. I cannot thank her enough for all she's taught me over the years. She was my secret weapon. Bill Damaschke [Chief Creative Officer] had

Storyboards, Vicky Jenson, *Shrek*, 2004 © DreamWorks Animation LLC.

Storyboards, Vicky Jenson, *Shrek,* 2004 © DreamWorks Animation LLC.

asked me what I was doing differently from the other directors. I guess he'd noticed a difference in the performances and I think a couple of the actors had mentioned how great the experience had been. After trying to keep her to myself I finally told him I'd been working with her. She began giving workshops to story artists and directors at DreamWorks soon after that!

Tom: How about music? When you're working on ideas for film, do you simultaneously have music in your mind?

Vicky: I actually do. I get a song that will, in a way, represent the tone of the movie. I'll listen to it over and over and over again. It'll be in my car, my home, even in the background while I'm drawing. That happened when I was first storyboarding on *Shrek*. One of the first sequences was rather tough. I had worked on it. Raman Hui had worked on it. Other people worked on it. But I had John Cale's "Hallelujah," his version of the Leonard Cohen song, in my head. I suggested it to my co-director Andrew Adamson and our editor Sim Evan-Jones, and they agreed they'd always liked that song, too. That song fit the moment. I sat with a junior editor and we cut out all the naughty bits of the song and storyboarded right to it.

  I did the same thing on my short film. I remember listening, over and over again, to this song by Luna, "California (All the Way)." I listened all through preproduction, as I storyboarded, and it eventually became the title song. I even had it arranged as classical music and used it in the key scene at the end of the short.

Tom: What's the difference between directing a short and a feature?

Vicky: Well, a short can be, should be, essentially all you. It may be the closest you'll get to making something completely personal. Although you will work on it with a lot of other people, it doesn't require anyone else's approval. There's no studio involved. There's no note session. But in my case there was a producer telling me, as many producers might tell other directors on any other studio film, "We're hemorrhaging money!" Only this time the producer was also telling me "And it's your money!"

Tom: When you're directing, do you generate artwork personally? Some people don't do any. John Musker told me he hasn't animated in years. But Richard Williams would try to draw a lot.

Vicky: I draw a lot. I draw a lot even on a live-action set. I'm very visual when it comes to explaining myself. I was drawing a lot for my DP and my location manager. On *Shrek* and *Shark Tale*, I definitely drew a lot. I even painted on *Shrek*. I was giving a lot of work and sketches to the animators. It's a way of communicating for me, because I think visually. I'm not trying to do an animator's job. It's just that when I try verbally explaining any of my more visual ideas I can tend to get a bit frustrated with the words. Then I inevitably say, "Get me a Sharpie." That's the only phrase that'll come out. I did this pile of commercials a couple of years ago, Old Navy stuff, which was really fun and goofy. The same thing happened. There's a mannequin that takes five people to move into position. I started saying, "Head to the left. Put the arm up. You have to move … Just give me a Sharpie!" I drew it out for them.

Tom: Do you ever have that moment when an artist takes your sketch and completely reinterprets it?

Vicky: Yes. And if it's not interpreted in a way that works for the film or the scene, then this is where your skills as a director come into play. Some people can be really great at one thing, but not so great at another. They may try their best, but it's not work-

Color studies, Vicky Jenson, *Shrek*, 2004 © DreamWorks Animation LLC.

ing. You have to guide them. You have to direct them without barking orders. It's not so easy to do sometimes. You have to say it in the most constructive way possible, "I need you to express my vision in this case, not yours."

Tom: You have anywhere from 5 to 500 artists, who all have big egos, and they all must act like the film is being drawn by one hand. Management skills are something that no one really teaches you. And in the end, you just can't say, "Do it because I say so."

Vicky: If you can sit down with them and talk it through early on, even sketch out some ideas with them, that can create a connection over the concept. Now the artist has authored the idea with you. They are invested. When you leave and come back a week later, your artist isn't going to feel left out. They feel valued because they are valued.

Tom: What's your favorite part about directing?

Vicky: In animation, I love settling into editorial. I love it!

Tom: A bunch of people say that.

Vicky: I would make my tea and sit down with either Sim Evan-Jones, Nick Fletcher, or John Venzon. I even got to work with the great Sheldon Kahn [*Ghostbusters*, *Out of Africa*]! Then I just wait, like a kid in a theater, to see how they'd pulled it all together. Then we'd work in my thoughts. And I love calling a board artist in and showing them their sequence for the first time. They'll either see how something isn't working, or they'll quickly point out how something should be fixed. They are a part of the process, and you can see it their body language. They run off and start drawing. It's really fun.

Tom: Okay, what's the worst part of the job?

Vicky: Telling somebody something they don't want to hear. But it has to be done. Changes can be rough sometimes. But that's part of the job.

Tom: Story artists in particular feel like they had a better idea. And you rarely meet a screenwriter who says, "That's exactly the way I saw this scene when I wrote it."

Vicky: Well, when it's a success, then they say that. And when it's not, it's quite easy for everyone to come down hard on a director. When I first got the job, Conrad Vernon said, "Tell me what happens to you guys when you go through those big director doors, because you all come out different." I think he knows why now!

Tom: He knows.

Vicky: All the battles you have to fight …

Tom: "A director is part artist, part commander, but also part salesman and diplomat." How do you deal with the inevitable politics?

Vicky: I ran into a lot of problems initially. My nature has always been, "If I have an opinion, I'm right! Of course I'm right! How could you say I'm not? I'm right!" Again, I grew up in an opinionated family. We argued; it was normal. But you don't argue on a film. I just had to get over that. I think I alienated a couple of producers initially, but in time I found a way to understand that people above you are there for a reason, too, just like the artists are there for a reason. They may not be drawing, but that doesn't mean they're not creative. We had a lot of them on *Shark Tale*, probably too many. But that wasn't their fault, and each brought something to the table. It was only after I let their voices and ideas be heard, just like

I did with all the artists, that I really understood and respected that position as well. If you handle it properly, it's not going to be a big speed bump for you. Some producers are actually not used to everyone getting an opinion, especially those coming over from live action. For them, it's like having the electrician or the guy holding the boom say, "I don't think that was a good take." But a great idea can come from anywhere, including your producer! I say that jokingly, but I think it's just a lot easier for artists to respect the jobs they understand. It isn't as easy for a lot of artists to understand what a producer does.

Shark Tale, 2004 © DreamWorks Animation LLC.

Tom: Some producers are very opinionated and wish to influence the creative process directly. While others just don't get involved. When I was at Warner Bros. my instructions were essentially, "Here's fifty million dollars. Go away and in a year come back, and it'd better be really good." Of course, each film presented a different situation. Do you think you have a personal style, as a director?

Vicky: I know I do. People seem to like the way I run a set. It's kind of a happy environment. It's an inclusive environment. And there's always a lot of laughter. I don't think I'm as good at creating a lot of crazy, fun games as Kelly Asbury. When I worked for him, he always came up with stuff that made Friday afternoon so much fun. He was so good at creating camaraderie.

Ron: I want to go back a little bit and talk about your parents. Can you tell us a little more about your early influences? You mentioned that they encouraged you to be artistic.

Vicky: The arts were really important to my parents, so my siblings and I were exposed to lots of things early on. There were always a lot of art books around the house. We went to museums. We took music classes. My dad would also try to expose us to what he thought were the great movies. I started watching François Truffaut films at a very early age. But I ended up with a broader range of influences than just classical art, classical music, and art films. I appreciated popular culture as well. A pop song can move you just as much as a piece of classical music. Just don't tell my mom that!

Tom: Do you have a favorite director?

Vicky: I watched a lot of Woody Allen. His understanding of people and relationships is so keen. I adore *Crimes and Misdemeanors*. That movie is pure genius. The films that move me aren't just funny but actually have a tremendous amount of heart in them. There's a solid exploration of a truth. There's some kind of revelation that reminds us of something we all know is true, something basically human. Look at what Chris and Dean did with *How to Train Your Dragon*. That story is strong and powerful, but at the same time it's charming and gorgeous. That's what storytelling is all about. It's bigger than the laughs.

Tom: When *Shrek* was about to be released into theaters, did anyone have a sense of how successful that movie was going to be?

Vicky: Nobody had a clue. It was weird. It really felt like a movie that we were sort of making in our garage. We were up north, far away from the main hub of DreamWorks. It was just this funny little building. We'd sit there, come up with an idea, and then do it. The project felt very small as a result. I don't mean that it didn't seem like a big story, just that it felt personal and even, dare I say, "indie." Now we knew it was funny. After it started to come together, laughter was an unavoidable consequence of watching some of these scenes. But we really just didn't have a clue that it was going to turn into this blockbuster. On opening weekend I remember getting a phone call from Jeffrey at six in the morning telling me the numbers were outstanding. Then he called me on the second weekend to tell me the numbers had gone up. I said, "Well, good." He then said, "No, you don't understand. That doesn't happen. Movies never go up the second week. They always drop. They don't go up." That's when it hit me. This is something big.

Tom: How do you pace your workload? Some people say that directing is kind of like dancing on a snowball rolling downhill.

Vicky: I remember people telling me to just ride the horse in the direction it's going. You just have to hang on. Honestly, I didn't really go with that approach. I leaned into it. If I have to stay there till nine o'clock at night, I'm there till nine. If somebody has to tell me to go home, then I'll go home. I suppose the only thing I truly pace is picking my battles. Problems tend to work themselves out better that way.

Tom: Don't fall on the grenade over every little thing.

Vicky: Yes. And sometimes you have to pick another day for a battle. You don't have to give up on it. There may be another way to approach it later.

Tom: Crews often respond well to directors that roll up their sleeves and do stuff. Dick Williams was like that. And he never drove you harder than he drove himself.

Vicky: I think I fall into that camp. It's not just a nine-to-five job. It's what's defining me at that moment. It's living, breathing, changing, and growing. And I'll keep going until someone says "stop."

Tom: How do you deal with moments in which you're creatively stuck or blocked? How do you solve that problem?

Vicky: You say, "I don't know." It's always okay to do that because you're going to have problems that you can't solve right away. And some things you don't have to decide right at that second. I'd rather wait than make a really bad decision. Now sometimes you have to make a decision, obviously. But that can also be the exciting part of the job, coming up with a solution on the spot. It can really happen that way on a live-action set. Your location's not available. It's starting to rain. You're going to have to shoot indoors. What do you do? You can't just say, "Let me think about it. We'll come back tomorrow." You have to do something.

Tom: What about your crew and creative partners? How do you choose them?

Vicky: Hmm. You choose them based on how they smell and how you connect over alcohol … [laughs] No, I don't know. I don't have any unique system. You look at resumes and portfolios. In the end it just comes down to talking with them. That moment of communication is key.

Tom: What's the most insane or bizarre moment that you've experienced as a director? Peter Farrelly jokes about the stiff hair scene in *There's Something About Mary*. Evidently, the prop people brought him forty examples of fake semen and said, "Pick one."

Vicky: [laughs] I did have a similar experience. I needed some on-camera cat poop for Michael Keaton to step in. The prop master brought me an entire tray of different kinds and colors of cat poo. It was a little overwhelming. The one that was made from a fudge brownie from the craft service table actually looked the best! Needless to say no one ate the fudge brownies after that. [laughs]

Tom: [laughs] That's when you've earned your money for the day.

Ron: How do you work with composers? How much control over the music do they get?

Vicky: Composers have a tremendous amount of control, but it can initially be very frustrating for them because we use temp music in our cuts and we tend to grow very attached to these clips after working with them for two to three years.

Oh, it's the composer's bane! I've had many composers complain about this, although they completely understand why it happens. And sometimes it's even their own music from another movie. Seriously, Hans Zimmer has probably heard that same little clip that everyone takes from *True Romance* countless times. It's this lovely delicate piece of music, and they'll put it in every lovely little delicate scene on every movie that he works on!

But like I said, they know it's a necessary evil. They know you need to screen the movie with music that works. They can't come in and freely compose at will. The best know how to encourage you to be open and listen to a new idea.

Ron: Do you always bring composers in at the end of the project?

Vicky: It can be difficult to bring them in much earlier for a variety of reasons. First, obviously, they're generally busy on other movies or not available to be part of the development process. But, most importantly, your movie just changes so much early on. The music will be in flux as much as the story is until you start to lock things down. When the themes are clearer and consistent, then it's time to underline the tone and emotions of the movie.

Tom: Is there any job that you miss doing? It's often very difficult for an animator to stop animating once they sit in that director's chair.

Vicky: I love painting color keys and storyboarding. But those are the two things I can still do if there's time. On every project I've done at least one key. Even if it were live action I would do at least one key and a little bit of storyboarding. As for other jobs I've held, I don't miss ink and paint and I don't miss working at McDonald's!

Tom: What's it like working with a co-director?

Vicky: I think in some ways it's great and I understand why it was the convention for so long in feature animation. There's so much to do on an animated film. It really helps having somebody else there. Andrew and I divided the workload. Each of us took a sequence, so we got to do everything that the director should do in leading those sequences. It also allowed us to focus and give a lot more attention to our sequences. Sometimes we'd swap sequences later, or if one of our workloads got too heavy we'd shift things around. That worked far better than dividing it by department, which we did on *Shark Tale*. And I think it was also done on *Prince of Egypt*. It just made it more difficult to keep control of the main vision and idea of the movie. As things move through various departments unexpected changes can occur.

Tom: With co-directors you can also bring together two unique skill sets. You came from a traditional animation background and Andrew excelled in digital animation.

Vicky: We were definitely a good pair in the end. Andrew was also great with story, though I didn't really recognize it when I started as a story artist on the movie. I already knew Kelly Asbury, Andrew's original co-director on the movie, and he is this completely outgoing and funny guy, very charismatic. Andrew didn't come from animation and he was a bit of an unknown to the story crew.

When I was asked by Jeffrey to direct with Andrew it initially felt like an arranged marriage, but I think we ultimately became a good team and balanced each other's strengths. His strong CG and effects background was priceless. I certainly didn't have that. I didn't even know how to work email back then! I learned so much from him. It was a perfect situation. I creatively directed the project and I learned something new in the process.

Andrew Adamson and Vicky Jenson, 2001 © DreamWorks.

Tom: Would you work with a co-director again?

Vicky: Actually no, I don't think so. I've reached a point in my life and work where I feel the value of a single artistic vision at the helm can create more unique stories. And that's what we all want, the audiences, the filmmakers, and the hopefully the studios!

Tom: It seems like in the last few years in Hollywood, and even in animation, directors have started in writing and have their idea ready to go. In the old Hollywood system you'd take a story, put a director on it, and then add a crew.

Vicky: I think that's changing. I'm glad too. You get a clearer vision. You have directors that are passionately connected to the story. It's better for a studio if the director comes in with the passion to lead, because you need that. A film is going to absorb your life for several years so it [had] better come from deep inside you. I'm writing now as well. This is my latest challenge. I think creating stories I will ultimately direct will be the closest I can get to the original thrill of making my first short. It can't get more personal or more original than that.

Tom: Did you ever experience what the industry calls "kill your children"? It's that moment when you have a great idea that's just not working. You have no choice but to let it go.

Vicky: Yes, a few actually. So many fun ideas have to be drowned. But the good ones come back in other forms, even in other movies. But I've learned to not get too attached. I think storyboarding teaches you that. You can't treat your idea as this precious object. It's going to change. That's why I storyboard now with a Sharpie. I can't get too attached. In the end it's all about the story. If it's good, it'll stick.

Tom: How do you deal with criticism and reviews?

Vicky: Every director gets them at some point. It's unavoidable. After my live-action feature I gathered together all my worst reviews and put them together on Facebook. It ends with one I actually like. Three stars by Roger Ebert! Sometimes the movie just doesn't turn out the way you hoped. You learn from that. You work harder next time. You test your ideas more. You push to see if people actually understand what you're trying to say. And in the end it really is subjective anyway. All art is subjective.

Tom: What advice would you give a first-time director?

Vicky: Have a clear idea about the story you're trying to tell. Make your own personal connection to it. See if others can connect to that as well. Test it. Is your theme universal? Do people get the message you are trying to convey? Is this idea worth all the work it is going to take to make this movie? Once you have these questions answered and start to bring artists onboard, don't feel like you have to author every idea in getting that story to the screen. It takes teamwork. And on that note, get to know everybody. Walk around and be connected. Leave your door open. As people are hired, go to all the different offices and try to get to know their names. Try to make a strong connection with them and connect them to the ideas of your story.

Ron: The studios have had huge development departments for years. All the studios have them, especially in terms of live action. That's what keeps the whole industry going. Now, many directors in animation are being asked to come and pitch movie ideas, which kind of circumvents that entire system. A director doesn't have the same support system that a development department has. Where do you find support? Where do you get the necessary training and mentoring for story development, let alone how to pitch a movie? Looking back at your movies at DreamWorks, all of them were developed and pitched by someone else.

Vicky: I haven't had a lot of experience pitching original ideas, yet. Currently I'm writing for the first time, and it's something that I'm really excited about. I'm also writing another script on spec. I think it's important to have people you can show your work to, someone you respect and whom you can bounce ideas off. I'd actually like to form a writer's group because I like creative input.

I like sitting and talking about writing with people that are immersed in the process. And I don't like working in a vacuum. That's kind of alien to me. At the moment I have an amazing creative producer and it makes all the difference in the world.

Ron: What about mentors? Did anybody offer any guidance about developing your own projects?

Vicky: My directing mentor, whom I mentioned before, is Judith Weston. I adore her. I've brought her a lot of scripts in the past as well as my own writing. Taking scenes into her workshop has been absolutely invaluable to me. Her insights and analysis never to surprise and inform me and affect my work.

Tom: You've done just about everything: feature films, live action, animation, shorts, commercials. Do you have a favorite medium?

Vicky: The one I'm in. All of them. Honestly, I've always jumped back and forth between live action and animation. Right now I'm really excited to make an animated feature again. But ultimately the medium just doesn't matter. It's the challenge that excites me. I'm excited about getting back on an animated feature because I feel like I understand how to make it work more concisely now, without as much of the searching. And it's a commitment that I appreciate. You have your vision, and you have to muscle through the day. Even when you think you don't have enough time to get it done, you do. I love that feeling. I can find that experience on any kind of set, regardless of medium.

Tom: Since you were raised in the traditional animation pipeline, is it at all strange how everything is digital now? Even the job classifications are different now, as well as the responsibilities and duties.

Vicky: If somebody designed a log for you in 2D, they wouldn't bring you the cylinder first. They'd actually bring you a drawing of the log. Now you see things in iterations. You receive a log that is the right volume but has no texture. How do you comment on that? That took me a while to understand. But I got to the point where I could recognize that. For instance, I just knew it was going to be too big for *Shrek* to step on. You have to recognize what stage you're at and learn what comments are appropriate. That comes with experience and time.

Tom: Where do you see yourself in ten years?

Vicky: Oh, I hate that question. I never see myself in ten years, so I can't answer that.

Ron: How about in the director's book of directors who've made four feature-length, animated films?

Vicky: Okay. Four by then? Why not. Living in Venice, maybe? Wouldn't that be cool?

Tom: Okay, last question. Did you ever have a chance to work with previsualization?

Vicky: I did. It's actually a funny story. There was this Warner Bros. project right after *Shark Tale*. It was *The Extraordinary Adventures of Alfred Kropp*. I was completely energized and was ready to jump in. I wanted to do exactly what Zack Snyder did to get *300*. So I approached about five different previsualization studios to see who would give me the best deal. I was creating a chase sequence with a Porsche and six motorcycles. Michael Cera and Clive Owen were driving. Those were the two actors I wanted to cast. And Clive Owen is a knight in our modern time. Anyway, it was this big action sequence. So I paid for a previs sequence and brought that into my pitch meeting with the head of Warner Bros. live action to prove a chick could handle action. I also brought in a huge fold-out Photoshop poster board of my thoughts for the script. It looked like a trifold science fair project. It looked like a timeline of the whole movie with clever little Photoshopped sticky notes for where the changes in the script were going to be. It also had samples of what the production design was going to look like. I wanted to convey that I've got this whole movie in my head and, better yet, it's theirs for the taking! I even had a poster designed. The head of Warner Bros. loved the pitch. But … they had already decided not to pick up the book! Nobody told me! This thing cost me around twenty-five thousand dollars. A month later I get the script for *Post Grad*. I put together a CD of some hip music and Photoshopped what an advertisement for the movie might look like on Myspace. That was it. I got the job. Cost—zero.

Tom: It's like when Mike Gabriel showed up to pitch *Pocahontas* with one card. He had made a logo for *Pocahontas* and said, "Let's do *Pocahontas*." Some other guys who pitched had eighteen paintings and other visual props and got nowhere.

Vicky: All it takes is a strong idea. If you can see the movie, even if you're just looking at a poster, and quickly get what this movie is all about, then you're most likely going to see it. Making a movie is not easy and it's very complicated. But the concept should be that simple to grasp.

Ron: I think that's a perfect note on which to end. Thanks Vicky.

Vicky: My pleasure.

Color Study, Vicky Jenson, *Shrek*, 2004 © DreamWorks Animation LLC.

8
Rob Minkoff Interview

Rob Minkoff.

To paraphrase F. Scott Fitzgerald: "Directors are different from you and me." They are artists who seem deceptively normal but have that extra something that is critically not what others have. Take Rob Minkoff, a wonderful guy, funny, considerate, easygoing, but when the chips are down he just seems to know the answer, or know the right person, or comes up with the idea that's needed.

His most famous "save" was arguably *The Lion King*, when he joined a troubled production and in a few intense days of sequestered brainstorming helped set the course for the most successful 2D film of all time. Rob knows how to connect the dots, but he has that essential skill of all great directors: he connects with people.

Rob is another guy with terrific talent as an animator that never did as much animation as we wished he would have. He did a few scenes for me on separate projects and they were always brilliant, funny, and seemingly effortless. Rob wasn't content to sit behind a drawing desk all his life. Every time I ran into him, I was amazed to find out that he had moved on to some completely different opportunity.

Very few directors have hits in 2D animation, 3D animation, and live action, but Rob has done that. He's not afraid of new challenges. I visited him on the set of his first live-action movie, *Stuart Little*, and I was amazed at how nonchalant and frank he was about what he didn't know! He got a kick out of explaining to me all the things that he needed to learn that he didn't experience as a director in animation. I think the crew loved him because they knew he wasn't a fake. In fact, he brought the critical eye of an animator to that film, and that's what made it work.

A student once asked Rob to name a director's most important asset. His answer was unique and revealing: "You have to make people believe you can do it."

We interviewed him at his hilltop home in Los Angeles.

Bill Kroyer

Bill: When did you first discover animation?

Rob: My first experience goes back to early childhood. I watched all kinds of cartoons on television. Like most kids, I would say animation fascinated me because of its magical quality. It's an illusion. Animation creates an alternate reality for the audience. I also remember an old Disney flipbook. It was a sequence of Mickey Mouse drawings. He was wearing a cowboy outfit and wielding a lasso. And my dad, who owned an audiovisual shop in Palo Alto, had a couple of Super 8 films. One was a *Mighty Mouse* cartoon and another was from *Sleeping Beauty*, where the prince fights the dragon. I watched that a lot.

Bill: Is that how you got hooked?

Rob: Pretty much. I became deeply fascinated by it, and then it became an obsession. I was constantly looking for animation everywhere. But I was mostly limited to television.

Bill: When did you start drawing your own stuff?

Rob: My cousin, Michael, actually got me started. During a family visit, my two older brothers and I watched him draw this odd character. It was this little fuzz ball with a long nose and dull eyes. It was amazing to watch this little guy come to life on a blank sheet of paper. I wanted to do that too!

Bill: When was your first experience with actually animating something?

Rob: That was in high school, in the ninth grade. I was in a children's theater production of *Snow White and the Seven Dwarfs*. It was the fortieth anniversary of the original production back in 1937. This was the Children's Theater in Palo Alto. In fact, during that production I met Kirk Wise.

Bill: Really? Kirk was in the same production?

Rob: He was. I played the Huntsman. He played the Queen's bat. And when we discovered we both liked drawing and cartoons, naturally we became friends. He had a copy of the book *Tex Avery: King of Cartoons*, and another by Andrew Loomis called *Fun with a Pencil*, which I borrowed from him for an extended period. We ended up animating a short together in high school, which I used as a portfolio piece for CalArts. The only thing I did before that was a flipbook. And a stop-motion film about an egg.

Bill: I assume you didn't have any film or animation classes in high school.

Rob: I had a film appreciation class, but it wasn't animation.

Bill: So you and Kirk just figured it out all by yourselves?

Rob: We didn't have a choice. It was the only way to do it. We read the Preston Blair animation book for the basics and ordered animation paper from Cartoon Colour.

Bill: You actually got punched paper?

Rob: We got punched paper and discs. We even built a wooden frame for it. Like I said, I was obsessed with animation! In fact, let me tell you this funny story. Around the same time I was asked to babysit these eight and ten-year-old sisters, Jenny and Emily Shapiro.

Their father was famous because he produced the movie *The Groove Tube*. So, as I'm hanging out at their house I notice this book on the coffee table. On the cover was an embossed picture of Mickey Mouse. It was the famous *Art of Walt Disney* by Christopher Finch. I began to look through it. "WHERE DID YOU GET THIS? THIS IS AMAZING!" Jenny and Emily promptly replied, "Our uncle wrote it." It turns out their uncle is Christopher Finch! Sure enough, I open the book and see their names in the dedication. When I got home, I went straight to my parents and said, "I want the *Art of Walt Disney* for my birthday!" Fortunately, on August 11, 1977, I got it. And when I got to CalArts three years later, I realized I wasn't alone. It was basically the animation bible. Everybody had their own story about when they first found that book, and what it took to get a copy.

Bill: How did you find out about CalArts?

Rob: Kirk told me about CalArts in high school. When he said that there was a school that teaches animation, I thought he was joking. But Kirk had the brochure to prove it. In fact, it was the only school that I applied to. My parents were so concerned that they took me to dinner specifically to ask me not to go until I had an undergraduate degree. They thought art school alone was too risky. Of course, they supported my dream. They were just trying to protect me. But the obsession still lingered. So, with a little luck, I left Kirk behind and went to CalArts in 1980. Suddenly I was meeting people like Kelly Asbury, Chris Sanders, and Chris Bailey.

Bill: I'm sure it was refreshing to meet other people interested in animation.

Rob: Exactly! At CalArts there were tons of people like me with similar stories. But I was fortunate to have Kirk as a friend. Back in high school we'd meet regularly after school to watch cartoons and draw. It was at that time that I started to recognize different directors, particularly Chuck Jones at Warner Bros. I would always carefully examine the credits of any cartoon to see who the director was. I liked Chuck Jones' stuff a lot. I didn't just like Bugs Bunny because of the character himself, but because of the style of a Chuck Jones' Bugs Bunny cartoon. I began to truly appreciate how a director can influence tone and style. Seriously, if you pay attention, there are several variations of Bugs Bunny. It depends on the director. I remember being in the same room as Chuck for the first time. There was a tribute to Mel Blanc at the Academy Theater and everybody from CalArts went. Chuck was one of the speakers.

Bill: Did you meet him?

Rob: No, I was too shy. But Jeff DeGrandis, my classmate, was not shy at all. He was wearing rabbit ears and fearlessly took the seat right behind Chuck. Jeff immediately struck up a conversation, and Chuck graciously responded. He was interested in what everyone had to say. Before I knew it, Chuck was drawing in everyone's sketchbook! But I was just too shy to approach him. A couple of weeks later Kelly Asbury grabbed me and said, "Hey, do you want to meet Chuck Jones?" Apparently, Jeff DeGrandis called Linda Jones, Chuck's daughter, who ran Chuck Jones Enterprises. Now if you can't tell, Jeff had a big personality, big enough to get invited to Chuck's house! At eighteen years old, I was just in awe of his courage. He was on the phone with Linda for forty-five minutes! What could they possibly have to talk about for that long? Lucky for us, she told Jeff to bring some friends. Since Kelly knew that Chuck was one of my favorite directors, he immediately came to me. So, on a Sunday afternoon, four of us went to visit Chuck. It was Kelly, Jeff, Chris Bailey, and I.

Bill: The house in Corona del Mar?

Rob: Yes, it was this beautiful house overlooking the ocean. I had never seen how an animation director lived. It was rather spectacular! I think we spent about four hours there, listening to stories about his time at Warner Brothers. Chuck was a very good storyteller. Needless to say, I was awestruck. I was eighteen years old and sitting in the house of my hero, a guy who inspired me to get into animation. Then, much to our surprise, he said, "Next time you guys come over, bring drawings." No one expected a second invite. But we weren't going to say no. About two months later we returned, with drawings. Chuck gathered us around his drawing board and began to critique and even draw for us. Chuck Jones actually gave us private drawing lessons. It was amazing!

Bill: At this time were you thinking about becoming a director, or were you focused only on being an animator?

Rob: I guess I was thinking about both. The thought of becoming an animator was pretty obvious for me. As I mentioned, I did a lot of children's theater. Acting was nothing new. And animating a character is essentially a form of acting. But CalArts, at the time, didn't exactly encourage you to animate. It was a big issue with the people running the program. Jack Hanna and Bob McCray insisted that we not animate too soon. The underlying assumption on their part was, "You're not ready. You can't do it." To me, that didn't make sense. I knew I could animate. I had already done it! So I was forced to animate on the sly!

Bill: Did they ever give you any specific reasons why?

Rob: I think that came from their experience working at Disney. The studio had a particular method for advancement. You had to come up through the ranks. You had to start as an inbetweener, then work your way up as an assistant, and then you could get a scene. And that was a long process. They openly talked about how it took years to become an animator.

At first you say, "I guess that's the system." But then you realize that it doesn't make much sense. When I finally went to Disney, this turned out to be a problem. People were getting positions based solely on their longevity, their senior status. Promotions didn't have much to do with talent or whether they were the right person for the job. This was a completely institutionalized process. Like it or not, the process of artistic assessment is subjective. You can't institutionalize that. So, that was the method at CalArts because the people who were teaching the program were ex-Disney guys. They were still mentally in that process. I think the rule of thumb was that it took ten years to become an animator at Disney!

Bill: How long did you stay at CalArts?

Rob: I was there for three years. At the end of my second year at CalArts something kind of devastating happened. Disney didn't hire anyone. That was a huge blow to the students. In my first year they hired nine people! That got us excited about our future prospects—then, suddenly, nothing. Worse still, rumor had it Disney didn't like our films. Apparently, they were too dark.

Bill: Your sophomore film?

Rob: Yeah. It was kind of a *Hansel and Gretel* story. This devious candymaker invites two kids into his store in order to turn them into candy. He literally is going to pick them up and toss them into the candy-making machine. Well, I suppose it was a little dark. But we can probably thank Tim Burton for that! In our first year they showed Tim's pencil test, and it was amazing. This little film essentially displayed every major concept that Tim is now known for. It was called *Stalk of the Celery Monster*. That film had a profound effect on us.

Bill: Did that influence your third-year film?

Rob: Well, before that, and after Disney chose not to hire anyone, Dan Jeup came in and announced that three people had been selected to do an internship. I was one of them. We got to do a summer internship with Eric Larson in the summer of 1982. This happened to coincide with the animation strike. No one was in the building because they were all out on the street picketing. That made the experience very strange. We actually had to cross a picket line to get inside the building. We weren't scabs because we weren't employed per se. We were just interns. But the nice thing was that we had Eric all to ourselves. He literally had nothing to do but teach us. At this time I also met Don Hahn, Ron Rocha, and Burny Mattinson, who wasn't picketing because he was a director. Mostly the place was empty, and that gave us an opportunity to do something we couldn't have done otherwise. We went into everybody's office and looked at their stuff. We looked at Ed Gombert's boards, Vance Gerry's boards for *The Great Mouse Detective*, which at the time was called *Basil of Baker Street*. We saw boards that Tim Burton had done for *The Black Cauldron*. One day we got very bold. We decided to march upstairs and meet Ron Miller. He had Walt Disney's old office, and we just wanted to step into that room. So we went up to Lucille … Lucille was Ron's assistant, right?

Bill: Right.

Rob: Anyway, we went in and introduced ourselves. Unfortunately, Ron was away in Europe. Hey, we tried, right? As we're leaving, Lucille says she'll tell him we stopped by. Now we didn't think anything would come of this, but sure enough Eric Larson comes in about a week later with a concerned look on his face. He says, "I just got a call from Ron Miller's office. He'd like to see you up there in fifteen minutes." We marched back up those stairs and right into Walt's old office. And it turned out to be a great moment. After all, Ron is a physically intimidating guy. He's about 6' 6" and plain huge! When he shakes your hand, yours disappears into his. But he was so nice. We sat and talked for forty-five minutes about animation and CalArts.

Bill: Was the building that empty during your entire internship?

Rob: It was empty the whole time. Now the next year, my third year, you asked if Disney's decision not to hire influenced my film. It did. I was working on a film that was quite ambitious. It was all in verse, kind of Dr. Seuss-ish. Ultimately, I realized that I couldn't do it. The film was just too much. Finally, in the middle of the year, I went to visit Eric Larson. I remember him saying, "Don't forget the character! That's all we care about. Just don't forget the character." Then it hit me. My film had no character! There was a ton of elaborate storytelling but no character. I had a panic attack. I really wanted to get hired. I really wanted a job! So, I scrapped the film. With about five weeks left before the show I started a new one. It was a short about a kid whose ice cream falls from the cone before he has a chance to enjoy it. He's very sad, but tries to paint a smiley face in the fallen ice cream, which kind of makes him happy again. It was an acting thing, all performance. Now I wanted to hide the fact that I was starting from scratch, but it was impossible. We were recording animation tests on video reels that everyone could look at back then. You couldn't hide it from anyone. People kept saying, "What are you doing? Don't change anything now! Finish the other film." But there was no turning back. Fortunately, I finished it and I got hired. Disney only took two of us that year.

Bill: What was it like stepping into a fully functioning studio? As you said, it was empty during your internship.

Rob: This was July of 1983, and *Black Cauldron* was still in production. First, we had an inbetweening test, which was a difficult skill to learn. It terrified me, actually. I also found it rather tedious.

Bill: They actually gave you an introduction to inbetweening?

Rob: Yes. First we just had to learn it. We had to get the line right. It had to be the right width. Then we had to do an actual test with Eric, which consisted of both inbetweening and a piece of animation. I did this leprechaun who dances around with his hat. I remember getting help from Chris Buck, who was working on *Roger Rabbit* at the time.

Bill: Was this the very early stages of *Roger Rabbit*?

Rob: Yeah, before Steven Spielberg and Robert Zemeckis were involved. Daryl Van Citters, Chris Buck, and Mike Giaimo had been working on it. They even shot a live-action test with Mike Gabriel as the detective. I was basically hanging out with these guys in the beginning. Joe Ranft had introduced me to them. I'd met Joe my first year at CalArts. He'd come back from Disney to give advice and critique the animation tests for some of the students. It was totally informal. Just something Joe wanted to do. We became very close after that. What an amazing talent and all-around human being he was. It was such a tragedy to lose him so young. I still think of him quite often. Anyway, I'd finally gotten a job at Disney and my first assignment was inbetweening on *The Black Cauldron* under Phil Nibbelink. It was a pretty tough job, except that Phil had all the cute girls working as his inbetweeners.

Bill: How long did that go on?

Rob: For about six months. To keep my sanity, I would take drawing breaks. I would stop inbetweening, pull out a fresh piece of paper, and draw something for fun. Then I would go back to inbetweening. After a while, I acquired a large stack of drawings, which sort of helped me later. There was a small group working on *Basil of Baker Street—The Great Mouse Detective*, that is. They were thinking about bringing in a new face for some character design work. Brian McEntee recommended me to John Musker. Eventually, John called and asked me to come to his office. He also told me to bring drawings. I reached into my desk, grabbed the stack, and walked upstairs to his office. About a week later Ed Hansen, who was running the animation department, called and said they wanted me as a character designer on the film.

Bill: So John saved you, huh?

Rob: Yes, he did. But it was only supposed to be for a limited time. Ed made it clear that as soon as I was finished it was back to inbetweening! They didn't want me to get too comfortable! I didn't care. I was just happy to get out for a while. But then the good thing was I never went back to inbetweening. Somehow I managed to stay on the movie.

Bill: What was it like, working on your first big production as a designer?

Rob: *Basil* had quite a history by the time I arrived. John and Ron had been developing the movie. It was edgy, adult, and very smart. Heavily influenced by Monty Python's absurdist humor, which I loved! This was the vision I saw when I peeked at the boards during my internship. When they pitched it to Ron Miller, he basically made them start all over again. Joe Ranft had the funniest drawing of Ron Miller at the time. It didn't look anything like him, but it was Ron as a giant blue man with blood vessels popping out of his head. The caption read, "WHERE IS THE GODDAMN WARMTH?!" So, Burny was brought in as producer, and Dave Michener also came on board as a director. We had three directors. The entire tone and feel of the movie changed. Ron Miller wanted it to be more "Disney." But if you look back at Walt's films, there was some incredibly interesting, dynamic, and scary stuff in those movies. Needless to say, everyone was frustrated. But that didn't stop me from appreciating the opportunity I had. I got to be a character designer. This was my chance to move forward. Eventually, they assigned me to work on some animation, which pushed me into the role of animator. Then someone said, "You should be an animation supervisor." I replied, "Sure. That sounds great!"

Bill: This was all on *The Great Mouse Detective*?

Rob: Yeah, it didn't take the ten years that Bob McCray and Jack Hanna said it would. But any kind of sudden advancement was met with skepticism by the senior staff. That's not an easy position for anyone to be in, but Disney was changing. There was a new generation of people that wanted something else, something better. And the frustration was often visible. I remember hearing a story about Brad Bird kicking a Sparkletts bottle down the hallway. But that's how everybody felt.

Bill: But Brad had already left Disney before you'd got there.

Rob: Yes. But soon after starting, I began hearing that Brad Bird and Jerry Rees were going to make an animated movie, based on Will Eisner's *The Spirit*, in Northern California. Brett Newton came to me and said, "Have you heard about this thing that Jerry and Brad are doing? It's gonna cause a huge revolution in animation! They're gonna hire everybody who's any good out of Disney who wants to leave and go work on a movie that's gonna break all the rules and be the salvation of animation." Of course I thought it sounded fantastic. He put me in touch with Brad and Jerry, and I soon arranged a meeting up in Northern California. Unfortunately, things weren't as bustling as Brett had claimed. It was very quiet there. It was just Brad and Jerry. They showed me the test, which I think John Musker and possibly Glen Keane had worked on. It was amazing stuff. But I didn't get the feeling that production was going to take off anytime soon. And it never did.

Eventually, I did end up working for both of them, Brad on *Family Dog* and Jerry on *The Brave Little Toaster*. I was still technically an animator at Disney, but I indulged in a little creative freelance work for them. I guess it helped with the frustration I felt at the time.

Bill: Didn't you briefly leave Disney to work with Jerry Rees?

Rob: I did. I went to see Don Hahn, who was then kind of managing the animation department at Disney. I said, "I've got this opportunity to do designs on this Jerry Rees project." Don was very gracious and understanding. I was very nervous about leaving. I had wanted to work at Disney for so long, and they took me in. But it wasn't quite the place the literature promised. Don said, "If you want to go, go. It's okay. You can come back anytime." So I took a deep breath and left Disney even though there was no guarantee I would be taken back. The door could have been closed forever.

Bill: Did you go to Taiwan?

Rob: No, I didn't. I spent about five weeks with Jerry up in Hollywood but going to Taiwan just didn't feel right. So I went back to Don, who said, "If you want to come back, it's totally fine." I immediately jumped at my chance to go back.

Bill: Is this when the takeover occurred?

Rob: It was around that time. I remember when I first heard Ron Miller was leaving. I was in John Musker's sweatbox watching some animation tests with him and Ron Clements. Steve Hulett walked in with the press release that Ron Miller had resigned. I remember being somewhat excited about the possibilities, but Ron Clements had a dour expression and said quite gravely, "It can always get worse!" And soon after, I was there when John and Ron had to pitch *The Great Mouse Detective* to the new head of Disney, Michael Eisner. I had no idea what was going to happen. They had the opportunity to kill it, if they wanted. In fact, I'd heard that they'd considered shutting down animation entirely but Roy Disney wouldn't let them.

Bill: Did the takeover affect you in any way?

Rob: Absolutely. The old Disney rules simply vanished. There was a lot of creative freedom, for better or worse. Around that time I co-wrote a song with Ron Rocha, who had been Don Hahn's assistant. Ron was an amateur composer, and Disney needed music for *Oliver & Company*. I boldly agreed, and we wrote a song for Georgette, the villain. It was called "Curiosity Killed the Cat," which we thought was very clever. But Peter Schneider and all the creative people on the movie gave us an ironic, "good effort," and "we'll get back to you." It was a classic moment. Anyway, that didn't stop us. Ron approached me a few months later and said, "Do you want to write another song?" He'd heard they were looking for something new. I said, "OK, let's try again." So we wrote another song. Shockingly, they bought it! They put it in the movie!

Bill: What was the song?

Rob: It was called "Good Company." It was just a short little ditty, a kind of nursery rhyme lullaby. They had set up a makeshift recording studio that Howard Ashman and Alan Menken were using to write the score for *The Little Mermaid*. Other people were using it too, including the Sherman Brothers. Anyway, when we recorded the demo late one night, George Scribner, Mike Gabriel, and Roger Allers overheard us. They thought it was the Sherman Brothers working on a different project. Apparently, as they were listening they said, "Hey, that would really work for us." So, we were ahead of the game when we finally presented the song.

Bill: Didn't you end up working on *Mermaid*?

Rob: Yes, I came on as a character designer, working on Ursula. John and Ron had written her as a kind of a Joan Collins-esque character, skinny with high cheekbones. I did a drawing based on Divine, John Waters's muse. She was a 300-pound diva in blue and pink makeup. Somehow it got on the board of designs, and when Howard Ashman was presented the material, he spotted my drawing and said, "Let's do that!" Of course, Ursula evolved considerably. The octopus tentacles were added, for example. I brought in my CalArts roommate, Max Kirby, who'd been an actor in the theater department, to do live-action reference. And animated the first scenes of Ursula in the movie. For a walk cycle I took footage from an undersea special featuring an octopus and used it as reference. It turned out quite well. John offered me the position of supervising animator, but at that point I really wanted to direct and was looking for opportunities to do that.

Character development, Rob Minkoff, *The Little Mermaid* © Disney.

Bill: You wanted to create and see an entire story up on the screen.

Rob: Yeah, that was the idea. It was also around this time that I helped push the studio to create a visual development department. I went to every artist who was important and said, "It's not right that we don't have a department where people can design and draw to influence the storytelling and creative process." It was only being done on script because that was Jeffrey Katzenberg's approach. "This is the way we do it in live action." But it didn't make sense to me, especially considering Disney's history. So I pushed. I got everybody on board and we made an appeal to Peter Schneider. We were all very happy to learn that Peter had succeeded in getting Jeffrey's approval to set it up. I think Chris Sanders was the first person that was hired for the new department. So that was how I was spending my time … making trouble.

Bill: What about directing?

Rob: Around that time, I started working on the *Roger Rabbit* shorts, which went into development after the feature came out. I got my own team and we put together three different shorts that we had to pitch to Steven Spielberg, Frank Marshall, Kathy Kennedy, Roy Disney, and Jeffrey.

Roller Coaster Rabbit, 1990. © 1990 Touchstone Pictures & Amblin Entertainment, Inc.

Bill: WOW! That's a tough room.

Rob: It sure was. But this led to my first opportunity to direct. It was a successful pitch. Roy, Peter, and Charlie Fink, the head of development, met in Charlie's office to discuss how the pitches went. Then they invited me in and said, "Rob, we want you to direct this *Roger Rabbit* short."

Bill: So you were happy with the finished product?

Rob: It was released with *Honey, I Shrunk the Kids*. Overall people responded pretty well to it. Then Peter Schneider called me and asked if I would go to Florida to direct the second one, *Roller Coaster Rabbit*.

Bill: Were you a hands-on director? Did you draw boards?

Rob: I did whatever needed to be done.

Bill: Well, you can do that on small crews.

Rob: True. But I didn't do it Chuck Jones style. I didn't draw every pose and put it on an exposure sheet.

Bill: … Or like Don Bluth, who pretty much drew all the boards in the beginning. Was there a director that influenced you, somebody guiding your approach? I'm specifically referring to an animation director.

Rob: I guess that would have to be John Musker. I got to observe firsthand how he worked. But I certainly developed my own ideas about directing. And I was good at pitching a sequence. I think that was a result of my theater background. When I put together a board for a pitch, there was plenty of rehearsal involved. And like any rehearsal, it was an interactive and collaborative event. For me, a pitch was a miniproduction. At the same time, I was also influenced by live action. Billy Wilder was a favorite of mine. I'm a huge fan of *Sunset Boulevard*, which deals with a period of Hollywood history that was gone and forgotten. I related to that. Disney was that way, too, by the time I got there. It was gone.

Bill: What brought you to *The Lion King*?

Rob: It was a somewhat circuitous route. While I was in Florida, Peter Schneider called to ask if I would come in to direct *Beauty and the Beast*. They had been working with Dick Purdham but had decided to make a change. Kirk Wise and Gary Trousdale were already on it as heads of story. But Peter explained that Howard Ashman was coming aboard as the supervising creative producer. I was more interested in directing a picture from my own vision and I turned it down. It wasn't an easy decision, and one I would certainly think twice about. But I consoled myself that it was the right thing to do when I got hired to direct the sequel to *Roger Rabbit*.

Bill: How did that happen?

Rob: I had gotten exposed to live action while working with Frank Marshall on the live-action tags to the *Roger Rabbit* shorts. When my contract was up, Jeffrey sat me down and said, "We want to extend your contract. But we want you to sign you under a new deal. What do you want? What do you want to accomplish?" My response, "I'd really like the opportunity to do live action." He said, "Okay, fine. I can't promise at this very moment when that will happen. But it will. Within six years you'll have a shot at live action." I didn't have to wait long. When I got back from Florida, they offered me a five-minute short called *Mickey's Audition* about Mickey coming to Hollywood and becoming Disney's newest star. It was essentially based on the *Roger Rabbit* concept. They're not animated characters. They're toons. They exist. It was filled with cameos. It had Mel Brooks, Jonathan Winters, Angela Lansbury, Ed Begley, Jr., Carol Kane, and Joe Piscopo. Even Michael Eisner was in it. Eventually, I realized that to tell the story properly we needed to have Walt Disney in it. It would be odd to put Michael Eisner in and not have Walt. So I called Roy Disney and said, "Roy, this may sound crazy, but you look a lot like Walt Disney. Would you be willing to play Walt?" Fortunately, he agreed. It was a big success.

Bill: What was this used for?

Rob: It was a preshow for a ride at the MGM Studio tour. They'd bring people out of the audience and say, "Here, audition for a movie." After that, I got asked to read the script for the *Roger Rabbit* sequel. Jeffrey had always said I would direct the animation for it. But this time they wanted me to come in and pitch myself to direct the whole thing. I met with Jeffrey, Kathy Kennedy, and Frank Marshall and they ended up hiring me. But after a year of developing the script the project got shelved. It was a terrible blow. I picked myself up and took on the third *Roger Rabbit* short, *Trail Mix-Up*, but before it was finished I got a call from Tom Schumacher to come in on *The Lion King*, which was still being called *King of the Jungle*.

Bill: Was there another director at that time?

Rob: Yes. Roger Allers had been working with George Scribner, who had directed *Oliver & Company*. But George wasn't happy with the first couple of songs Elton John had written and left the project. I was in New York when Tom called me. It was the same week as the Academy Awards, when *Beauty and the Beast* was nominated for Best Picture. Obviously, I was feeling some regret at having passed up the chance to direct it. My first day on *The Lion King* was April 1st, 1992—I'll never forget that date. The night before, I sat down at home and read through the script. My concern was it was a bit too dry, too much like a true-life adventure. The next day I went into the office to view their ten minutes of story reel.

The Lion King, 1994. © 1994 Disney.

Bill: And?

Rob: Roger and Don came in and I asked a very straightforward question: "How much of this has to stay?" Don said, "None of it." I was happy to hear it.

Bill: Wow! You were willing to start from scratch?

Rob: Nobody loved the movie as it was. Starting over was the only option we had. Initially, Roger, Don, and I sat around and discussed how we could change the story. We had to redevelop a lot of characters. Timon and Pumbaa were originally childhood friends of Simba. And Rafiki was a kind of an advisor to Mufasa, not a shaman witchdoctor. We brought in Kirk Wise, Gary Trousdale, and Brenda Chapman and spent two days together working out a new approach. Those two days were responsible for the movie that we ended up making. When we had all the sequences up, we pitched it to Michael, Jeffrey, Roy Disney, Peter, and Tom.

Bill: Did you make any changes after that pitch?

Rob: Sure, but the structure of the movie never really changed. We maybe added one sequence to the outline. But we essentially had the movie. The big question during those two days was how to make the movie more epic. I had seen an inspiring documentary called *Lions and Hyenas: Eternal Enemies* by Dereck and Beverly Joubert. It was an incredibly powerful *story about their life and death* struggle. I just knew that if we could capture some of its power *Lion King* could be a great film. We didn't have a writer at the time, so any development had to be done on the boards. We were definitely meeting with writers, though, and we met some interesting people. We met Joss Whedon, who had worked on *Toy Story*, and we also met Billy Bob Thornton, before *Sling Blade*.

Bill: As a writer?

Rob: Yeah. He walked in wearing black leather from head to toe with metal studs and rivets. Pretty awesome. But maybe not right for our movie.

Bill: So you've reworked the story of *Lion King* …

Rob: The pitch was well received, but Michael asked if the story was based on anything. They had just made *Beauty and the Beast*, *Aladdin*, and *The Little Mermaid*, all based on famous stories. But it wasn't based on anything. Then Michael said, "Isn't this *King Lear*? Couldn't this be *King Lear*? Maybe we could turn it into *King Lear*."

Bill: Really?

Rob: Then Maureen Donnelly, who was the producer of *The Little Mermaid*, said, "No, it's not *King Lear*. It's *Hamlet*." Everyone then chimes in, "It's *Hamlet*, of course. His father is killed by the uncle." Michael promptly says, "Yes! We're doing *Hamlet*!"

Bill: *Hamlet* in Africa.

Rob: *Hamlet* with lions in Africa.

The Lion King, 1994. © 1994 Disney.

Bill: So that was the reassurance that was needed? Are we following the previously successful model?

Rob: Yeah.

Bill: Classic studio.

Rob: Obviously we knew we weren't making *Hamlet*. The question was, what do we take from *Hamlet*? We took the idea that he is a character in the throes of indecision. "To be or not to be? That is the question." That actually sounded like our pitch. Simba doesn't really stand up to his responsibility. He runs to the jungle, where he meets Timon and Pumbaa. Then Nala comes and wants him to return. But he's not sure until his father's ghost appears. Simba had to reach this point of emotional confusion and then choose to return. But we needed that critical follow-up scene with Rafiki. But conveying that moment was a creative challenge. We tried to board it several different ways but nothing seemed to work. It wasn't mystical or deep enough. Then Irene Mecchi said, as a joke, "Why doesn't Rafiki just hit him over the head with his stick?" We all laughed. But the simplicity of the idea was just so clear. We did it, and it played great.

Bill: Film is a collaborative medium.

Rob: It sure is. But, to pull it off, everyone has to be working under a unified creative vision. They need to be aware of the bigger picture. That's when you get great collaborative moments. We needed our "To be or not to be" scene, so we came together and got one.

Bill: But how did you feel about not being the sole director?

Rob: It turned out okay because Roger and I happened to work very well together. We didn't know each other all that well, but we had enough mutual respect to operate as a team. And we knew that we were working in an institutionalized system and tried to be as smart as we could about it. Also, rather than do everything together, we decided to divide up the movie. We would work together on the storyboard, agree on it, and then divide it up sequence by sequence.

Bill: Could you comment on each other's sequences?

Rob: Yes, we could, and did. But each of us had final say over our own sequences. But this process only worked if we agreed on the storyboard first. That's the stage where you truly go back and forth, show your ideas to everybody, and figure out what this movie is all about. We had to be in sync early on; otherwise it wasn't going to work. And if the pitch wasn't successful, we had to go back to the drawing board and come to an agreement all over again.

Bill: What were your disagreements like?

Rob: Honest. If you didn't like something, you had to explain why. That's part of the process. But when it came to directing the sequences, it was a little different. If Roger expressed doubt about something of mine, I still had final say. And vice versa. Overall, there was a foundation of mutual respect. We were a team, and we were emotionally invested in making a great film.

Bill: What was the hardest thing about directing *The Lion King*?

Rob: *Pocahontas* was put into production at the same time, and the whole studio was very excited about it. I remember Jeffrey saying, "*Pocahontas* is a home run! It's *Romeo and Juliet*. It's *Westside Story*. It's gonna be great! *Lion King*, on the other hand, is an experiment. But it's good to take chances. If it doesn't do well, if it only makes fifty million at the box office, that's okay." After that, all the animators wanted to work on *Pocahontas*.

Bill: What did you do?

Rob: We had to compete, and it wasn't easy. Anybody that was important got to decide which production they wanted to work on. We had some great people; don't get me wrong. But guys like Glen Keane were hard to get. On the other hand, this turned into a big opportunity for new talent at the studio. They were young and green, but super eager. We did have some experienced hands like Andreas Deja, for example, who did Scar, and Mark Henn doing young Simba. But many of the others were first timers. We were the black sheep project but that turned out to be a good thing. I don't think we could have created the same movie under any other circumstances.

Bill: That doesn't sound too bad.

Rob: When you're left alone, you have more freedom. We exploited that. We had a chance to experiment. Sometimes we went too far. For example, Elton John had written the demo for "Can You Feel the Love Tonight?" But when we got our hands on it we decided it might be more interesting if we handled it unconventionally. We decided to lampoon it a bit and have it sung by Timon and Pumbaa. We recoded Nathan Lane and Ernie Sabella and boarded it that way. We cut it together and brought it to Atlanta to show Elton.

Bill: How did that go?

Rob: Terribly. He said, What is this? There has always been a classic love song in a Disney movie. It's always been my dream to write one." Obviously, he was right and we had to take a step back and rethink it. But we ended up having Timon and Pumbaa sing the intro and outro of the song and it worked really well. We might never have done that if we hadn't experimented first.

Bill: What about "Hakuna Matata"?

Rob: Tim Rice and Elton had written a song called "He's Got It All Worked Out." It was Timon singing about Pumbaa. We had to board the whole thing and pitch it. When it finally got to Jeffrey he looked at us like, "You can do better." And we got to take another crack at it. We came up with this concept about eating bugs as a metaphor for Timon and Pumbaa's whole lifestyle. In the eyes of Simba, it's gross, weird, and just plain different. And this was supposed to be a fun song. Well, some liked that concept, others didn't. We ended up having a big meeting to hash it out. Finally, it was Tim who said, "The song needs a trademark slogan. It needs to be like "Supercalifragilisticexpialidocious" or "Bibbidi-Bobbidi-Boo." Roger and Brenda had been to Africa on the scouting trip and had come back with a few African expressions, one of which was *hakuna matata*. Tim said, "That's got some potential. I can work with that."

Bill: I don't think I've heard that story before.

Rob: So, Tim and Elton wrote the song. But at first it was more of slow song with a long introductory verse. The hardest thing to do in a musical is to get the characters singing so that the audience goes along with them. The transition has to be natural and smooth. You don't want the movie to stop so that the singing can begin. Unfortunately, Tim and Elton weren't around, it was just Roger and I. But I did have something of a musical background. At any rate, we had to make the call. We decided to cut the verse and start with the chorus, just jump straight into "Hakuna Matata" and its philosophy. We boarded it and it worked. But when we pitched it to Chris Montan, the music supervisor at Disney, he said, "You can't start with the chorus." I said, "Why not? The Beatles did it," and sang, "Can't Buy Me Love!" I knew Chris was a Beatles fan. He agreed. So that's the way we did it.

Bill: That's a great example of your skills as a director. It's not always easy to convince somebody on the spot that your idea is the better one.

Rob: Like I said before, pitching was something I was good at.

Bill: Okay, *The Lion King* debuts, and suddenly you're the director of the biggest movie ever, right?

Rob: Just before the movie opened I got a call from one of my agents, who asked if I'd be willing to talk to one of his other clients. Turns out it was Francis Coppola. "Are you kidding?," I was thinking. Apparently, he wanted to ask me about how we storyboarded *The Lion King*. He was working on his own version of *Pinocchio*. I got home one day and found a message on my answering machine from Francis asking, "for a little advice." I was so excited, I called my mom and played her the message. Later that summer, I got invited to his winery in Northern California. I had lunch with his long-time production designer Dean Tavoularis, who had done *The Godfather* AND *Star Wars*. I mean, come on! Also, Francis' mother, Italia, joined us. Francis stood in the kitchen wearing shorts and a T-shirt and made pasta. I was in movie heaven.

Bill: So your deal was over? How did *Stuart Little* come to you?

Rob: I spent about two years after leaving Disney trying to get a live-action movie off the ground. I worked with Bob Zemeckis briefly on a movie he was producing for Universal. I also worked on a version of *Mr. Popper's Penguins*, where I met the producers Craig Zadan and Neil Meron. After that I worked with them on a live-action version of *Into the Woods*. Obviously working with Stephen Sondheim was one of the highlights of my career. But getting these films off the ground proved frustrating. I started to lose hope when I got a call from Jason Clark, who I'd met while working on *Into The Woods*. He was brought onto that film to help bring the budget down from around eighty million to somewhere south of sixty. He was very close with the head of production at Columbia Pictures, and they were looking for a director for *Stuart Little*. Jason got me pumped up to meet with them about it. I read the script, which was written by M. Night Shyamalan, who hadn't yet become famous from *The Sixth Sense*. In fact, he had just sold that script and had to leave us to start prepping the picture. We needed other writers and brought on Lowell Ganz and Babaloo Mandel, who I'd met on *Into The Woods*. Jason came on as a producer and we got underway sometime in '97–'98.

Bill: Do you think your skills and experience gave you an advantage on a project like *Stuart Little*?

Rob: Doing that first movie was a trial by fire. I hadn't come up through the live-action process so I wasn't familiar with all the requirements. When we started filming, I wasn't doing any coverage. I was just shooting what I needed to cut the film together as I imagined it. After all, that's what you do in animation. After the second week, the studio stopped me outright and said, "You have to shoot the coverage, too." So it was a learning experience.

Bill: You're directing a movie, but you have an animation director, Henry Anderson, working under you. How did that differ from working with a co-director like Roger?

Rob: In Henry's case I treated him like he was the supervising animator. He would work directly with the animation team and then at various stages I would go over the shots with him and give direction. Then he'd relay that back to the team.

Roger, on the other hand, was a full partner in the creative process. But Henry's contribution developing the character of Stuart for the film was immeasurable. But as far as the live actors' performances or the overall storytelling of the film, that was my responsibility.

Bill: When you were directing the live actors in scenes with Stuart, were you subconsciously visualizing Stuart's performance as an animator would?

Rob: We tried when possible to storyboard. Unfortunately, the script kept changing prior to principle photography and it became impossible to keep up with it. When we got to the stage we had to start from scratch with blocking and staging. Fortunately, I had Guillermo Navarro as my cinematographer.

Rob Minkoff and Jonathan Lipnicki, *Stuart Little 2*, © Sony.

He was an amazing collaborator and gave me confidence to work things out in rehearsal. We would figure it out and then plan the shot list and just start building the sequence. We always had an actor off camera performing Stuart Little's lines. Jim Doughan, who I'd met originally as an actor in the *Groundlings*, was always around and gave us a sense of what Stuart was up to. That way if there was any improvisation going on we could include Stuart. What was tough was playing every scene without seeing the main actor's performance. We had a little Stuart doll that we referred to as the "stuffy" to stand in for Stuart, but it wasn't very emotive. Now, as an animator, I could imagine what Stuart might be doing and that helped me see if the actor's performances were believable.

Bill: So you were steering their performances based on what you sensed was coming in animation?

Rob: Well, I wasn't thinking Stuart's performance was already a fixed thing. Good acting is sometimes reacting and you can't know exactly what's going to happen with the actors until it happens. It's good to know what you want but be open to what happens in the moment. I knew that no matter what the actors were giving, Stuart would be right there with them giving back. I had faith in the animators and knew they'd be able to go toe-to-toe with Geena Davis or Hugh Laurie or any of the other "live" actors. That's one of the challenges of animation, to make it appear spontaneous. Getting that requires a willingness to improvise and go with the flow.

Bill: I remember you saying you had trouble with eye lines and came up with an interesting solution.

Rob: It became apparent very quickly that getting the actors to look in the right place was going to be a challenge, especially if Stuart was moving around at all. If the actors didn't look like they were looking at Stuart, it ruined the whole illusion. We would make marks with tape whenever that was appropriate, but sometimes even when the actors had

Stuart Little, 1999 © Sony.

exactly the same mark it would appear they were looking in different places. So we even resorted to using different marks for different actors in the same scene. What became really challenging was getting the cats to look in the right place. The animal trainers were unbelievable. They managed to get the cats to walk on cue and stop on their marks, but getting them to look at Stuart when he wasn't there was impossible. Someone from the camera crew came up with a brilliant solution. He brought in a laser pointer that he had synchronized with the camera shutter so you'd see the red dot but it wouldn't show up on film. It would turn off when the shutter was open. This turned out to work not only for the cats but for the humans as well.

Bill: That last sequence with all the cats in the tree—was that literally like herding cats?

Rob: There's an old saying in Hollywood, "never work with animals or children." I've made a career doing both. The cats turned out to be amazing performers. But it was the animal trainers that were the true magicians. They could get the animals to do ridiculous things. But they were very particular about how the animals were treated. I remember one situation where we weren't getting the shot. I needed the cat playing Monty to laugh at Stuart. I imagined him throwing his head back in a hearty guffaw. We tried getting the cat to do it with traditional methods but nothing worked. Finally, I asked the trainer if I could pick up the cat. He let me and I very gently picked him up under his arms and used him like a puppet. On cue I rolled him off camera and he surprised me by opening his mouth in what appeared to be a giant laugh. It worked great. When the clock is ticking you do what you have to do.

Bill: Stuart was another big hit for you, and you decided to do the sequel. Easy decision? Easier picture to make?

Rob: Well, at first I really didn't want to do it. I had barely gotten through the first one and was surprised and gratified it became a hit. But when I finally made up my mind to do the sequel, I was determined to make it better than the first one. I thought that would be reason enough to do it. One of the things that frustrated me about the first one was Stuart didn't get to move around as much as I would've liked. That was mostly due to late changing script pages and having to pull it together on the set. We couldn't have elaborate shots because that would take time to plan. And if you don't have the script until right before shooting there's no time. But on the sequel I wanted to move the camera a lot more and we got to do that. So in many ways *Stuart Little 2* is a superior film to the first one. That fact was mentioned in many critics' reviews and that was nice to see.

Bill: How did *The Forbidden Kingdom* come your way? Did your animation background help you with a martial arts picture?

Rob: I think having an animation background is good for any kind of filmmaking. Animation is the ultimate storytelling medium. You have to imagine everything in advance. Being able to visualize things is the key. And what happens on a martial arts film is the ultimate in filmmaking. We had the master marital arts choreographer Yuen Wo Ping handling the action. He was the only guy that both Jackie Chan and Jet Li would listen to. Jackie had made his first hits under Wo Ping's direction. But he hadn't worked with him in almost thirty years. Jet had worked with him a number of times on his recent pictures.

Bill: So what was it that attracted you to it?

Rob: I had read the script, which was called *The Monkey King* at that time. It wasn't a traditional retelling of the Chinese classic. It was a mash-up of all sorts of characters and storylines from Chinese films and mythology. It was very clever and I'd been thinking about doing a film in China since I'd first visited there in 1997. I met with Casey Silver, the producer, many times before he finally chose me to direct the picture. There was a sizable amount of visual effects in the film and I was comfortable with that. But I think it was the fact that I already owned an apartment in Beijing. I'd bought it in 2005 after my future mother-in-law suggested it would make a good investment. Turns out she was right. But it showed my commitment to China and that I understood the culture and knew my way around.

Bill: You're one of the few guys who has had success in both animation and live action. You had the most successful 2D animated film with *The Lion King*, and now you've done a fully CG animated film with *Mr. Peabody & Sherman*. Why did you decide to go back into full CG?

Rob: It's interesting. It wasn't really a decision to go back, because I actually had the first conversation about making this movie in 2002. It was twelve years ago, when I was working on *Stuart Little*. I didn't really imagine at the time that it would take this long to get the movie out, so it wasn't really a decision just to go back. I brought the project to DreamWorks in 2005, and it took them almost six years before they were ready to green-light the movie. Then it took three years to make.

Mr. Peabody & Sherman, 2014 © DreamWorks Animation LLC.

Bill: Wow. That's Hollywood, isn't it?

Rob: Very much so. In fact, it's interesting, because in the interim, between the time that I pitched it and the time that they green-lit it, I think DreamWorks were already committed to making CGI movies, but then the whole idea of making all of them in 3D was something that was more recent, and so that became part of the production as well.

Bill: With so much directing experience behind you now in both mediums, how did you approach this movie? Did you approach it in a way different from other things you've done in the past?

Rob: Well, the truth is that this is the first time I'd actually done a 100-percent CGI movie, so a lot of it was new to me. I found the production process really a cross between an animated movie and a live-action movie, because now, with everything in 3D, you think about it in terms of a live-action movie more so than an animated movie. Because the camera is a virtual camera and it can function like a regular camera, you think about it or set up shots that you might set up in a live-action movie.

Bill: At DreamWorks, don't you block with mocap, so you have almost a live-action step there?

Rob: I think on other productions, they do. We didn't. We went from storyboards to previs. There was a little bit of animation done, a threadbare, bare-bones animation by the previs department. The previs is the equivalent of layout, so it was a layout step. But we never did mocap. What we did do, interestingly, was that the animators actually acted out their own scenes and recorded them, and then we would play them as part of the launch and approval process. We would go through the storyboard phase, edit it into the story reel, then go through the layout process. Then we would launch each shot deliberately, one at a time. The animators would go away, and rather than showing thumbnails, they would actually just act out the shots, and we would look at them and review them and give them notes and suggestions—critiques or whatever. Then they would go away, and either they would begin their animation process—in which case we might see something that amounted to a pose-test—or, if necessary, they would go back and do another physical performance before getting it right.

Bill: Would every animator do that? Was it a policy you tried to put in?

Rob: It was a policy. It was actually not my idea. It was Jason Schleifer's idea—Jason was our head of animation—and I think he'd used that technique before. Jason comes from an acting background. He's been a performer, so he was very comfortable with it and I was comfortable with the idea of it, having a similar background. In fact, we both grew up in the same hometown—many years apart. And both acted at the Palo Alto Children's Theater. Anyway, that was something he suggested. The idea of animators performing or acting out their shots made sense to me as an animator, but it was never something that we would show or be critiqued on by the director in my experience as an animator, but it seemed like a reasonable way of going about it. Even though the animators themselves weren't necessarily trained actors, they were getting across the idea of their shots in a performance, and you could at least work with them on what they were doing—and sometimes the performance was pretty good. Either way, there was going to be another step of animation to approve or not. It wasn't really that we were locking ourselves into the performance, and since it wasn't a mocap performance, they were just using it as a rough guide anyway.

Bill: Interesting. I had never heard of anybody approaching it with the acting like that. Individual animators will go into a room and film themselves on their iPhones or something, but making it a policy where you actually review it is a new thing. Do you think you would want to do that every time?

Rob: I would say it worked very well. Part of the challenge of making the movie was that I was based in Glendale, while most of the studio was actually up in Redwood City at PDI. So for the most part, we would have to do everything via teleconference, which turned out to work surprisingly well. Again, it was an adjustment to get there, but if you had a good system of how you handled approvals and reviews, you could overcome that limitation.

         One of the things Jason would do was isolate the individual animators. There would be a room of animators for any launch or any review, but when it came to a specific animator's shots, that animator would actually go and sit in the middle of the room, sitting next to Jason. They were isolated and you could obviously see them very well and you knew who you were talking to and could focus. Also, I think it made reviews very concentrated. You'd have to boil down what it was you were thinking or wanting to express in a way that could be communicated on the video teleconference (VTC). It became, I would say, pretty efficient.

Bill: After working in live action, was it unusual for you to go back, to not have a cinematographer that would help you block things out? Nothing really like that exists in that system, right?

Rob: It was a guy named Kent Seki. He was really the DP of the movie. Early on in the production, we did hire a consultant, Guillermo Navarro, who I'd already worked with on Stuart Little, and who had done a lot of work at DreamWorks Animation. It was interesting. I was feeling a little bit like that piece of manpower was missing, so we brought Guillermo in.

         He went through a couple of sequences—which, of course, were early on—so they changed pretty dramatically through the course of the production. But it was good to experience it that way, and then Ken was able to step up into that role.

We managed to do most of the film after Guillermo was involved, but it was a good test case for how different it is when you have a DP involved.

Bill: Did you find yourself doing anything different as a director? Having done so many things now, did you feel more at ease? Did you feel that you anticipated things better?

Rob: Because I've had to do a little bit of everything, it was just a matter of getting to better understand the unique process of doing a CGI movie, and then working with the particular individuals. That's another thing that can change from one movie to another, and you never really know until you get there how someone is going to work or think. You have to apply yourself as a director to understand how to communicate best with your team. There's a gradual, getting-to-know-everyone process, which I think also works both ways, because the team, obviously, has worked with a variety of directors, and every director comes at it differently. My tendency is to be very collaborative, pretty much for the simple reason that I can remember my experiences as an animator and the way I would always want the directors to work with me. As an animator, I wanted to make a contribution to the film, so I encourage that from the team.

Bill: Did you ever pick up a pencil and do thumbnails for anybody?

Rob: Yes, but rarely. We had a Cintiq in the VTC room that you could use if you needed to draw a pose to clarify something. Occasionally, I would or could do that, but I found, again, that it was not necessarily the most efficient. When it comes to that kind of thing, I like the animators to take responsibility for their work.

Bill: I know there's a point, when you become a director, that you feel like you're intruding on their turf.

Rob: I want them to bring their best selves to the project, and their commitment, and a sense that they are participating and can have some ownership over what they've done. That's the kind of creative environment that I like, and I think the feedback I got from people is that they really appreciated that and felt more rewarded through the process. It's hard if you're working with a director who basically forces you to do it exactly a certain way. It's pretty limiting in terms of the creative satisfaction. For me, again, it was the idea that my job as a director was to make sure that the ideas were expressed clearly. I look at it like there's an infinite number of ways of approaching any particular idea to communicate it, and it can be very specific to the individual, but there's no one way of doing anything. There certainly is my way of doing it, which is not the same way as your way or any other individual animator. The most important thing is that they were communicating the thing that needed to be communicated and that I, as the director, felt was the important idea, the important thing to communicate.

If they were accomplishing that, if they were expressing the idea as I saw was necessary for the story and for the film, then I was okay with the form. Occasionally, if I didn't like the way the animation was done or anything, I would give them notes and suggestions and criticisms, but I would express it in a way that they understood it and could go and do it. Typically it was like, "The idea is not being expressed clearly enough," or even sometimes, "The animation is not good. This is not good animation." But I would hopefully think of it as a benchmark or a touchstone that they would understand, or at least maybe Jason would understand, that it's mechanically not good; it should be improved, or the idea's not clear and it's not being communicated properly.

Bill: But you want each animator to bring his own unique feel to it.

Rob: Exactly. It's like when you're working with a human actor. You cast your human actor because they're bringing some-thing to the role; it's not because they're a puppet. I want the animators to feel like they're the actors of the movie and that they have a responsibility for the performance. We have a series of supervising animators, so you can rely on them to govern the style. You make sure the best animators are obviously leading the charge and the younger or less-experienced animators have something to work towards, so you get a unified look in everything.

Bill: You don't want to give them visual line readings.

Rob: That's exactly right. You do if you have to. Sometimes you'll resort to that. It's a last resort. You want them to get it themselves, but if they can't get it themselves, then if you have to hold their hand, you do. But I would prefer that they can do it, and generally, you get better work from people, and certainly more enthusiasm.

Bill: You had the original idea for this project years ago and finally got it up. Then when it gets going, of course, the industry—especially different studios—have different ideas of who the audiences are that they're targeting. Did the project morph and change in ways, as you went along with it, different from how you originally conceived it?

Rob: "Yes" is the simple answer. When we first brought it to DreamWorks, we had an entirely different pitch on what the story would be. We then hired a writer, developed the first draft of the screenplay, and the studio didn't like it—not to put too fine of a point on it. They felt it was too dark, too satirical, too edgy. So we took a step back and said, "Okay, how are we going to change the direction of the storytelling?" I understood it, because the movie that I pitched and started was probably not necessarily for their core audience, which is families. I understood who they are as a company and what they're trying to do, and the fact that they feel like they have a brand and a style.

I would say even within that, they were pretty flexible. I think the way the movie turned out wasn't so much a typical DreamWorks movie, so there was certainly some room to make the film unique. But like I said, we were in development for six years, so we went through—I don't even know—a half a dozen approaches before the studio was happy with the one that they green-lit.

Bill: I take it you were happy with the final approach, or is there a previous version that you preferred?

Rob: I was very happy with it. But that doesn't mean I liked it better than some of the earlier versions. The first one, for instance, really appealed to my sense of humor, which can be a little darker and more subversive than what we landed on for the final version. But I'm very pleased with how it turned out. It's still a little highbrow, which I'm proud of.

Bill: I especially enjoyed the historical jokes. Of course, it's a history-based thing, but it was pretty funny how you hit some of those figures in history and how you portrayed them. I really enjoyed that. You've been directing now for twenty years. How is the business different for a director? Have you seen a change?

Rob: There are more animated movies being made, which may be the biggest difference. But how is it different for a director? It doesn't seem different for me particularly. Obviously, the tools and techniques have changed—that's the biggest difference—but as far as working with the studio, it's not that much different.

Bill: It all depends on, I guess, the project and the studio person you're working with, right?

Rob: Right. And I think every director has a different relationship with the studio. Obviously, because I go back with Jeffrey such a long way—I've been through it all, up and down, with him—that familiarity becomes comfortable on both sides, which allows more freedom, which is good.

Bill: But he has that kind of Socratic method, right? He doesn't tell you how to fix it. He just says, "I feel there's something missing here."

Rob: There was a little bit of both, but your job is to go away and figure it out. His notes are generally pretty straightforward—"This isn't funny. The pacing is slow. This idea …" He can get specific. If he doesn't feel like the idea is coming across or if the character is not working or if the emotional moment isn't there, he'll give you his opinion, and then it's your job to go figure out … First of all, it's to agree or not. But because it's a collaborative situation, you've got a producer involved, or in our case two, Jason Clark and Alex Schwartz, there was Bill Damaschke—who was head of creative at DreamWorks—you have an editor, a head of story, a writer. Those are all people that are going to weigh in on how it's going. Before we'd screen for Jeffrey, of course, we're going to screen for ourselves. Hopefully, we'll be able to screen it a week ahead, because we'll look at it and we'll have our own set of notes. Then we'll discuss amongst ourselves what works and what doesn't work and what needs to be improved and how to improve it, and then we'll take a week to do what we can to fix the problems that we see before we go show it to the studio. But then when the studio sees it, they'll have their notes. Sometimes you feel like you've achieved a certain amount and you've missed the mark on a certain amount. It just keeps the process moving forward. I think it's a healthy process to constantly review the work and to get an outside opinion about it.

Certainly, at Disney, that was the way it was done, and I think it's still done that way. It's interesting. You hear a lot about the films at Pixar and Disney, because of Ed Catmull and John [Lasseter], being "director driven." And yet, when you examine what they do, they have a very similar process. They will always review the material. They show the material to their creative brain trust. Certainly John sees it and gives notes and opinions and feedback and says, "This works. This doesn't work. You need to fix this, and go do that." Then the team, led by the director, will go ahead and do that and, again, come back several months later with another screening and review.

Bill: There are obviously differences between directing a live picture and an animated picture. Now you've done every-thing—2D, live, 3D—are there things you prefer about one of those directing experiences or things that you are glad to not have to do in one of those directing experiences?

Rob: It's funny. Directing a movie is a mixture of joy and pain. I haven't found it different on any movie. It's like when things are working, it's great, and when things are not working, it's painful. And you're always having to engage in it. But I have to say that I feel very fortunate to be able to do it, because it's a lot of fun. It's a lot of fun even when it's not fun.

Bill: Since this book is about directors of animated films, you're one who is in a good position to compare the difference in skill sets and challenges between directing live action vs. animation. How do they compare?

Rob: First off, animation is a lot quieter than live action. The pressure can be intense when you're on set shooting a live-action picture, especially if things aren't pulling together. Animation is so much more deliberate. You plan everything out. Hans Zimmer once pointed out there are no mistakes in an animated film. Everything is put there for a reason. "There are no cigarette butts lying about." You storyboard, build your reels, record your voices, design the characters and the world, plan the layouts, and supervise the animators. But it's generally handled one artist at a time. In live action, you've got the entire cast and crew working simultaneously to create something. The whole orchestra is playing at the same time. But when you break it down, animation and live action probably have more similarities than differences. Both are mediums for telling stories. Both require writers, actors, musicians, costume designers, set designers, et cetera, et cetera.

Bill: What do you still find challenging about directing?

Rob: I still feel like I'm learning how to do it. Every movie is different, so there's always a new challenge. And since I've always gravitated towards doing things I haven't done before, my life is an ongoing learning process.

Bill: Is that what keeps you going?

Rob: Probably, since I would never want to do something I've already done. It wouldn't be as challenging.

Bill: Among the films you've directed, is there a favorite?

Rob: *The Lion King* is clearly the most successful, and perhaps the best loved. But if I have to choose a favorite, I hope it's my next film.

Bill: I think that sentiment accurately describes you as a director.

9
Jennifer Yuh Nelson Interview

Jennifer Yuh Nelson.

When I first became an animator in the 1970s, the image I formed of animation directors was of silver-haired lions like Woolie Reitherman and Chuck Jones. Larger-than-life, cigar-chomping, scotch-swilling leaders of men.

What is delightful about Jennifer Yuh Nelson is that her career runs roughshod over all those stereotypes of what an animation director should be. A slim, almost waifish, soft-spoken, Asian-American woman, she just happens to like making kick-ass action movies and comedies and is one of the best storyboard artists the medium has seen in our time.

She perfected her technique doing storyboards on Todd McFarlane's moody noir series *Spawn*. At DreamWorks she excelled at creating storyboards for *Spirit: Stallion of the Cimarron*, *Sinbad: Legend of the Seven Seas*, *Madagascar*, and *Kung Fu Panda*. DreamWorks quickly recognized her ability and made her director of the *Kung Fu Panda* franchise.

Her directorial debut, *Kung Fu Panda 2*, for a time was the highest-grossing film ever made by a woman ($665 million), until surpassed by Jennifer Lee's *Frozen*. In 2016, Jennifer Yuh Nelson was named to the Board of Governors of the Motion Picture Academy of Arts and Sciences for Short Films and Feature Animation. That same year she began developing her first live-action film project.

Her career is a testament to the idea that regardless of gender or background, anybody can do anything if they have the talent and the will to use it. We interviewed Jennifer in her office at DreamWorks Animation.

Tom Sito

Ron: Back in the day, when we first started this whole thing, the idea was to interview leading directors who've had a chance to direct at least two movies. Because there's one thing about making one movie, where you're kind of finding a way, you're beaten up by everybody in the process. The second time you're kind of a little more knowledgeable about what you're doing and hopefully have learned through scar tissue.

Jen: [smiles] "It never gets easier." Each one's just equally as hard, no matter what.

Ron: But you learn in the process, you have experience working with crew, and with all of that.

Jen: Wasn't it like some forms of torture, though? There's the torture like if something bad is going to happen to you when you walk in, but there's the form of torture that tells you exactly what to expect and—

Ron: That's Hitchcock's philosophy of filmmaking.

Jen: [laughs]

Ron: So, Tom's going to lead the questions and I'll maybe pop in occasionally … though I actually would like to start off with one quick question. And that has to do with whether you've seen something early in your career, something before you became an animator. Was there any animated short film, that made you go, "that's it."

Jen: Do *Looney Tunes* qualify?

Ron: Yes. Absolutely!

Jen: I used to watch those all the time, because when I was a little kid, and first came here to the States, I didn't know a lick of English. And my mom would plop me down in front of the TV for a couple hours and I'd watch *Looney Tunes*. That's how I learned English … [smiles] It made me talk really weird.

There's *Looney Tunes*, *Merrie Melodies*, all [that] stuff that's playing in the afternoons. When you're a kid, you just watch these things on rotation all the time … *Tom and Jerry* cartoons ….

Ron: And those had an impact on you?

Jen: Because some of them were just visually amazing and beautiful. There were some that were simpler in appearance, but some of them were, I mean, they were meant for the theater. And they were meant for adults—that was the big difference. They're meant for adults … they didn't censor them back then either. 'Cause after a couple years they said, "Oh! There are all sorts of un-PC things!" And they'd snip them all up, but they left them alone on the first broadcast and, so you see them [in their] unaltered glory, and they were beautiful.

What [was] that … *Peace on Earth* (MGM 1939). That one was so beautiful … I was, like, watching that, like, that's insane, it didn't even have any words in it really … so I could actually get it. It was so beautiful.

Tom: That movie used to run during wartime, like *You're a Sap, Mr. Jap* and *Bugs Bunny Nips the Nips*.

Jen: Yeah, it was all very not PC at all. But then you know, I was Korean, so you know, I was used to seeing all sorts of anti-Japanese propaganda as a kid.

Tom: So let's start with a little bit of your background and how you got into animation. You must have had a very interesting path.

Jen: When I was a kid, I drew a lot. My sisters drew, we all drew together, and all of us were illustration majors in college. We all went to CalState Long Beach. And I had always assumed I'd do book illustration, magazine illustration, editorial art, comic books … that kind of thing. I didn't really like illustration very much, but it was what was available to us. No storyboard classes, no animation classes, nothing like that at the time at our school.

But strangely enough, a lot of the CalArts teachers would also teach at CalState Long Beach's illustration department. And there I learned about what storyboards were because David Lowery, who did a lot of Steven Spielberg movies back then, came in to do one of those guest speaker things. He showed his boards, and I was just amazed at how beautiful they were! I realized that there was something called *storyboarding*. That I was doing storyboarding before I knew what storyboarding was. I would be drawing stories, I would be doing little film reels of what all these scenes could be, and I wanted to do that so badly I actually thought I would go into live-action storyboards. But when I graduated, I saw all the jobs were in animation. Everybody was hiring for animation, everybody thought that it's the big moneymaker, so all these studios were popping up everywhere. So there were a lot of opportunities for kids straight out of school.

Tom: What year was that?

Jen: I graduated in 1994. I was actually in my final semester and, you know, final semesters are always that rattling time, where you kind of have stuff to do, but you kind of don't. I was working on [my] thesis, and my sister called me up and she was working at an animation studio at the time. She said, "We need a PA [production assistant]! So why don't you come be a PA while you're finishing your classes as a part-time job? Now it was in Woodland Hills, so I drove my mom's car. It was a Hyundai Excel, and it was 8 years old and barely making it. So I would drive from Long Beach up to Woodland Hills after class in the worst traffic ever, and the air conditioning didn't exist. And the engine would overheat—it would barely go over the hill.

Illustration by Jennifer Yuh Nelson.

Tom: Those early Hyundais …

Jen: The first Hyundai Excel. It had a putt-putt engine. I'd have to turn on the car's heater just to make it over the overpasses. Otherwise the engine would overheat.

Ron: What was going on at the studio at the time?

Jen: They were doing these little direct-to-video stories.

One of the producers there was walking by, and he saw that I was doing sketches and he saw that I could draw, so he put me to work. It was such a tiny hole-in-the-wall company; everybody had five jobs. I was doing cleanup and character design, in addition to photo copying and making model packs. But I was only there for about four or five months, then I moved to Hanna-Barbera.

Ron: Did you observe anything there that stuck with you?

Jen: It was my first "office job," where you go in and actually park your car in an underground parking garage. To actually see an office building, see the kitchen and how they make coffee. How people work their business and what a producer does, and what a director does, and what everybody's jobs are. What was really useful was, because it was such a small place, you could see everything. It wasn't like the departments were over there and separated; you can't walk in. Everybody had five different jobs. So you'd look and see what everybody's doing, everybody's desks were right next to each other. So just learning what it was to work in a professional environment, showing up in the morning at a certain time of the day, breaking for lunch, that kind of stuff.

Tom: What was Hanna-Barbera like? Because they were really old school. And I can't think of a single storyboard artist who's a woman.

Jen: There were very few.

Tom: Yeah, yeah. So with a lot of those old guys like Bob Goe, Bob Taylor, and Alex Lovy, who had been there for decades.

Jen: Not only was it rare for woman to be doing storyboards, but I was a little kid.

Ron: And you were hired to do storyboards initially?

Jen: I wasn't. I was actually hired to do character cleanup. And there was already a character designer for Johnny Quest. So I was taking those rough sketches, and doing the clean line version, and going blind using a technical pencil, making a perfect line.

Tom: Back then the quality of the line was important.

Jen: Yeah, there was line quality 'cause they had to make cels out of it. So I was doing that, but within just a couple months, they had these one-minute openings that was separate from the Johnny Quest show itself. I had always made a lot of noise about "I wish I could someday do storyboards." So one of the producers said … just on a whim, he says, "Here—here's a one-page cold open. Just try it. Not for production, just to try it. Just to train yourself." And I grabbed it and ran to my office, came back within two hours, and I had done it, two hours … and I said "here!" He sat and looked at it, then he and the other producer looked at it. Then they just took the rest of the script and handed it to me. And that's how I got my first storyboard job.

Tom: Cool.

Jen: Yeah. I wanted it so badly.

Ron: Had you been practicing storyboarding at all? Or did you do comics or anything that would lead you to do story-boards before that?

Jen: I had been doing storyboards since I was five, when I didn't know what it was. I had so many pages and pages of stories in my head. My sisters and I would come up with stories together, and I would literally [story] board entire films without knowing what it was. Because that was the only way I could output the films in my head, 'cause I didn't have a camera. You didn't have access to cameraphones back then. So at that age, I was doing storyboards

Storyboards, Jennifer Yuh Nelson.

and what I had to learn, actually, was interesting. It was not how to think of film; it was how to limit what I was doing so it was animatable. Because I hadn't been trained in animation, I didn't know animation camera, which is actually a very specific thing. Like there's pan, push, fade—that's all you get. You don't get rotation, you don't get like a lot of parallax, you don't get any of that for TV animation. So what I had to learn was what not to do.

Tom: Yeah, Hanna-Barbera was good for that. When I worked on Saturday morning TV stuff, you learned how to economize, but you made the most out of what you had.

Jen: Yeah, you have to really, really economize, and that was a great training ground for that. 'Cause you can't do everything that you can do in live action. And the other thing that was really confusing to me was I was a huge watcher of anime, and anime breaks all the laws of what we can do here. They do rotating camera, they do bi-pack, they do all that stuff on TV shows, and we just couldn't do it here.

Tom: The first time I ever saw your work, I think you were working on *Spawn*. In storyboards there are comedy people, and there are action-adventure people. You always struck me as being more the action-adventure kind. It's like, what attracted you to that more than—I mean without, without stereotyping, it seems a lot of young Korean girls that I know prefer the *Hello Kitty* kind of design.

Jen: I know. I don't understand that. I just don't get it. I've never liked *Hello Kitty*. I've never understood that sort of 2D design sensibility. I mean it's a very specific thing: you either think of design or think of motion and space. Design and space just don't go together. And I'd always thought spatially. I'd always been interested in more action-adventure stuff, because I was raised on anime. And I remember when I was first starting out at Hanna-Barbera, anime was barely getting over here.

Tom: It was just starting to catch on in the US.

Jen: *Akira*, *Ghost in the Shell* was around and people were like, "Oh." And that's what I wanted to do. That's what appealed to me. What I thought was cool.

Tom: One old-timer said that anime was all "nine-year-old kids in SS uniforms blowing up robots." [laughs]

Jen: And that. That's cool. Why not? I remember just, you know, talk about being in an old-school environment, and then you're trying to get this anime sensibility in some of the stuff and it was not necessarily understood. [laughs] But that's what I want to do. I want to do, like, hardcore action anime stuff. And, not just with the design sensibility or storytelling sensibility; they do stuff with camera and cutting, the editing style which they just did not do in American animation. And it was not more labor-intensive—it was just a sensibility. And that's what I was raised on, wanted to do, was interested in just coming in and seeing all that.

Ron: You said—you said that in live action, though, didn't you? In some of the movies you were watching? What kind of movies stood out to you as kind of really important cinematically?

Jen: Of course, things like *Blade Runner* and you know, *Terminator* and all that stuff was happening when I was growing up. And in the 80s they did movies that didn't really dwell on seriousness, and it was just all about how cool something could be. You could tell probably everyone just got high on coke and made something. And had that crazy over-the-top sensibility, and that's what I thought was really fun to watch about them. They didn't take themselves too seriously, and they were just fun to watch.

Tom: I didn't realize until I had seen some very early Japanese anime … how focused they were on graphic frame composition in films. While American 1940s cartoons, like Hanna-Barbera's *Tom & Jerry* and *Bugs Bunny*, were all studying Buster Keaton and focused on performance.

Jen: Central … character in a space.

Tom: Buster Keaton and Chaplin came from the English musical hall and vaudeville, where you stood on stage and did your routine.

Jen: Right. Exactly, it was very theater stage-based. And I remember when I was first learning about the process, because again I wasn't trained in animation, I knew nothing about it. I came in cold and people were trying to tell me, explain to me what "crossing the line" was. And I was sitting there and I could not understand what they meant by "crossing the line." Because in my mind, it's what the camera sees and how you naturally would—I don't think "crossing the line," I just think what feels right. And they're trying to explain to me what "crossing the line" was and I realize that is based on stage terminology. I had no experience in that.

But the thing that's different about anime vs. American animation, is it's all focused on the subject matter, and American animation is about character. And what is a character going to do—it's that sort of stage philosophy, whereas in [the] Asian sensibility, a lot of it was environmental. It was about, "What is the space that the character is in?" *Akira* was about, "What is the feeling of nighttime?" When the motorcycle's going through the streets. And the feeling of the streaks of light behind a character. It has nothing to do with the character. It's an emotion, viscerally what the character is experiencing. So much more emotion-based rather than theatrically based.

Tom: Hollywood animation since the 1930s, you know, the star system, the focus was on the performing actor, the person. And the stuff around him was negligible. While with anime, it's about the complete whole composition.

Storyboards, Jennifer Yuh Nelson, *Madagascar*, 2005 © DreamWorks Animation LLC.

Jen: So, things like the whole composition, the environment, how the motion goes across cuts, no one did that in American animation at the time, TV animation. They [didn't] bother; it wasn't something that was noticed or cared about as much. And multicuts of action, you know, people would not do that because it was expensive to do multicuts, whereas things like that are so common nowadays. People expect to see that action shot, to see perfect hookups of action across a multicut moment.

Tom: Did you ever run into stereotyping? You know, you'd get an old-school producer who would take one look at you and say, "Oh, you probably want to do *Care Bear* stuff, right?"

Jen: Every single day. Every single day.

Tom: Yeah, I was wondering how you dealt with that.

Jen: Well, the fact is I would be terrible on those shows. I think there's a choice where people make assumptions about you and then you can either agree with those assumptions and bend to them, or you can say, "No, the way I can be the most useful to you is like this." I think that it just makes business sense and creative sense—if a producer sees that they can make use of

0400
2695

0400 -
2730

Storyboard panel, Jennifer Yuh Nelson, *Madagascar*, 2005 © DreamWorks Animation LLC.

Storyboard panel, Jennifer Yuh Nelson, *Madagascar*, 2005 © DreamWorks Animation LLC.

Storyboard panel, Jennifer Yuh Nelson, *Madagascar*, 2005 © DreamWorks Animation LLC.

you in a certain way, they're not going to push you out of that. They go, "This widget is useful doing this. Why put it over there when I can see I can use it for this? Didn't expect that to do that but it works." So, that's—that's been my career. Every single time I meet someone new. It's not like something I ever said; it's just very much understood.

Look at me, and you assume something, and I understand that. I didn't spend my life deciding, okay, I'm going to try to make people understand by looking at me that I am a certain way. I could just go out and get a crazy haircut, tattoos all over my face, wear leather all the time, pull up on a motorcycle. You know, I could do that, but honestly, I don't think that would be very good. [laughs] I understand that the natural response will be a certain thing, and then what I usually do is I nod when they say, "Well, how about this project?" I nod, and then I say, "Well, how about this?", and I show them what I do. And then usually the conversation changes pretty quickly.

Tom: People who can do really good action-adventure, really good action cutting, are rare in Hollywood, especially in TV. Many are frustrated comic book artists who think they can do storyboards, but it's not the same. It's not a comic book.

Jen: It's motion. It's time. And print comics are often about composition of beautiful poses in a page layout ... What I love is dealing with the percussive cutting, the speed of action. And I always like approaching action scenes like a deeply emotional scene, because there's nothing as emotional as a life and death action. Characters going through massive dynamic ranges of emotion. That's what makes me excited to do action scenes—because you feel so much more. Everything is hyper-real, and everything's moving quickly, and you experience it that much more.

Tom: What's cool about your stuff is, when some people board action, it's like video game, first-person shooter action. It's bang! bang! ... but your stuff is cerebral. It's more like you can tell what the characters are thinking, while they're going through everything, rather than some avatar mindlessly moving from A to B.

Jen: I think it's the most important thing, really. Because you either have an action [scene] for [action's] sake—that's where you can literally interchange any moment in any [other]—or you can have an action scene that's all about what is the character trying to achieve, and then you know what the stakes are. And then, it's like watching ... a sporting event or something ... you know, "Okay, the team has this—the points are like this, and then if they get this particular goal then it's going to go over overtime, or not, and maybe they'll make the playoffs." I don't know anything about sports, so I'm making all this crap up, so I don't know. But unless you know what it means to the players, the game doesn't mean anything—then it's a technicality. And action scenes, a lot of the time they think the reason why people don't respect action scenes as much as I think they deserve to be respected, is because they don't necessarily address that emotion of that action scene. Because they're really hard to do, but they don't get the respect of, like, you know, [a] touching emotional scene with two people crying in a room, which is also an incredible feat of acting but is not necessarily an incredible feat of filmmaking.

Ron: When did you first become aware [that] you wanted to do action scenes? When did you start thinking about art direction, lighting, and even camera work in regards to your action scenes? Because those are all important components of building a scene.

Jen: Very important and I think that, well, people have asked me that before, and I have a very un-useful answer to that ... unfortunately. In that, I'm one of all those weird fishes where I think of an action scene finished in its entirety in my head before I ever start, so that includes lighting, sound, cutting, acting, everything, every single detail. So, I can't think of an action scene without those things. I don't think of those as separate things. Everything is helpful to progress the narrative of the action scene. So, I've always thought of it that way. Even when I think back on those action scenes I was thinking of when I was five or six years old, they had lighting on them, they had mood in them, they had all that part of the storytelling narrative. So, later on it was just a process of understanding what each department covered, but I didn't think of them as being separate things.

Tom: When we were mentioning mentors before, like David Lowery, did you have any other sort of major people in your [life] who showed you the ropes?

Jen: Yeah, my sisters did that a lot. Because coming from a family of artists was a big advantage. I think that a lot of people are just weird mutations in their family, and they're the only artist and everybody thinks they're weird ... that's kind of what happens. But my family was weird in that all of us were artists. And so growing up 'cause I was the youngest, I could see two and a half years in the future in my middle sister, and two and a half years in the future from her from my older sister—as far as ability, progress, classes she took, you know, what she'd do with her job, all that. I could see five years into the future at all times.

Tom: Mention your sisters' names so we spell them right.

Jen: Oh, Gloria Yuh Jenkins, she's the oldest. And Catherine Yuh Rader, she's the middle sister and she also works at DreamWorks. She's been on all the *Panda* movies too, and she worked on all the *Shrek* movies ... She's the reason I got onto

Spirit: Stallion of the Cimarron, because I was at *Spawn*, HBO and she heard about *Spirit* and she said, "Hey! They need people who can draw horses. It was hard to find people drawing horses.

Tom: People either like to draw horses or they don't. You could draw a rabbit a hundred different ways, and it still looks like a rabbit. If you don't draw a horse perfect, it looks like a dog or …

Jen: … a donkey. It's not a horse. And it's got to be a beautiful horse, like an acting, beautiful, emoting horse. I drew horses all the time, and so my sister said, "Send in your portfolio." And I said, "Okay." So I sent in my book, and I got hired. And I ended up working with you.

Tom: I always remember one of the things that impressed me the most [that] you did back on *Spirit: Stallion of the Cimarron* was you storyboarded a sequence of one of the ways that they used to train wild horses. Horses that refused to be ridden, they would blindfold them. They'd cover their eyes and then you'd get on the horse's back and the horse would be intimidated because he couldn't see. And you actually did a storyboard sequence of Spirit in the first person being blindfolded, sensing the rider was getting on his back, and another man is about to open the corral gate, and Spirit still manages to throw him anyway. But you did it from the point of view of Spirit, while he's blindfolded. I was like, holy shit!

Jen: And it wasn't a black screen. [laughs]

Tom: But it was so damn good, and the directors went, "Meh."

Jen: Yeah, it got thrown out. But you know, it was an interesting experiment, and it was that whole thing of thinking [of] things a different way, finding a different way of telling a story. That particular idea, it was based off those martial arts movies where the character is either blinded and they have to use sound. And you could see the way they turn their head, and you can experientially tell the story of what that character has to do, in order to win the fight. But it's told through the emotion and the experience of that character. That's from watching all those action movies where you go, "Oh my gosh, the guy's been blinded by acid and he's still going to take care of that guy." It's so much more nail biting. But it's solved with the slight tilt of the head, and the showing the sounds of what the character's hearing and putting it together. Seeing the connections made, and stuff like that.

Tom: Wow, cool.

Jen: Yeah, it's fun.

Tom: One thing I always admired about you was your patience, because every picture has a certain amount of … you know, political stuff, directors, and ego flying around. I remember you would storyboard these beautiful sequences that they would just piss down a hole somewhere. And you would just go, "Hmm." And I was thinking, like, "God, I would've walked right out of here. I would have quit three times by now." You had the patience of Job. Amazing.

Jen: I probably went out and punched a wall afterwards. I'm sure I let it out somehow. I also think it's because, why do people do what we do? I'm not goal oriented, I'm process oriented. I had worked on a lot of stuff on TV, that if it ever got made, I'm happy. But while you're working on it, you don't necessarily assume it's going to get made. You have to find joy every day doing the job, doing the actual work of the job, whether or not it, as we say, whether or not the bicycle chain is actually attached to a wheel, you're still going to spin. [laughs] But so I enjoyed doing the work and I knew when I was working on *Spirit*, I didn't know how to do feature boards, I had no idea what I was doing at the time. I walked in cold, [had] never done feature boards ever, right? Worked on TV, different animal, different format, different thought process. And I was learning every day, so I was getting something out of it every day, and, yes, the boards got tossed out on a regular basis. And that was also something I learned, because in TV, you never throw out boards. Done—you have one pass, one round of revisions and you're done, that's all you could afford to do. Whereas a feature is twenty, thirty times maybe? And then the scene is thrown out. [laughs]

Tom: Your stuff on *Spawn* was pretty theatrical already. Because HBO was asking for, like, a more cinematic look to the stuff. Who was in charge at *Spawn*?

Jen: It was Eric Radomski. He was the supervising director on *Spawn*. And basically the supervising director of all the shows, and now he's there overseeing Marvel Animation. But he was a cool guy, and the producer was Catherine Winder, who did *Angry Birds*. Yeah, she was super cool.

Tom: HBO's commitment to animation then seemed like they could take it or leave it. They would do a series and then they'd go, "Meh."

Jen: Everybody and their brother was starting an animation studio that time, "Let's try it and see what happens in a couple years, and do a couple shows and see what happens." But I don't necessarily think they wanted to stay in it for a long time.

Tom: Is that where you met your husband?

Jen: I did. I have a funny story about that. So when I first left Hanna-Barbera and jumped over to HBO, I said, "I really want to do storyboards." I talked to Eric [Radomski], and Eric said, "I'm sorry. I got a guy for doing storyboards already." And I'm like,

"Shit! A guy is already doing storyboards." And then he said, "But I got a character design position …" And I said, "Eh, I'll do it. Because, why not? And I know how to do that. So I'll do that. And maybe, maybe … if I'm here, they'll give me storyboards eventually." So I started the job doing the character designs. Then that storyboard artist came in one day. I was like, "That's the guy that took my job," and he's wearing, like, dark sunglasses, and a trenchcoat indoors when he walked in. And I was like, "Why is he wearing shades indoors? I don't know if he's trustworthy 'cause he's wearing shades indoors and also he took my job. But he also really looks like kind of a sweet guy." And we became such good friends. And we became best friends. We worked together for about two and a half years. And then eventually, after two and a half years, we were both happy to be available. Oh well, I guess we might as well start dating. So we got married. And Catherine Winder said that me and him were the best thing that came out of that place.

Tom: [laughs]

Jen: Well, we got married and we're still married eighteen years later. [laughs] And the best thing is, I respect his art. He was a really great story artist, so I said, "I don't feel so bad you took my job, because I could see why they wanted you."

Kung Fu Panda 2, 2011 © DreamWorks Animation LLC.

Tom: There is a thing with professional couples. The usual type of match would be like me and my wife. My wife's job is in the back end of production and I'm at the beginning. So our responsibilities are unrelated. But, when you have animator and animator, or you two are storyboard and storyboard, do you ever feel like you are in competition with one another?

Jen: Never. And I think it goes back to the fact that me and my sisters growing up were all artists. We never competed—it was never a competition thing; and what's good for one, you just smile and celebrate what's happening. So it's good for everybody. It was never a competition thing. And in his case, it was never a competition thing. 'Cause if good things happen to him, if he got work, I was like, "Yay, you deserve it, it's great!" And also he was really good. And he did things differently than I did. So I would watch what he did, and go, "Oh, so that's how you approach a shot, and that's how you draw a character, and that's a cool pose I never would have thought of." And it actually made me better, looking at what he was doing. And over the years, you know couples, they start resembling each other more. Our stuff never looked the same, but each other's stuff sort of crept into the other's stuff. I would draw a pose, and I would say, "That's one of your poses." [laughs] But it never quite looked like what he would do, though.

Tom: What is your favorite part of being a director?

Jen: My favorite part has to be what people tell me, that they are able to do the best work they've ever done. And I think that a job of a director is to get everyone to do their best work. It's not about throwing your weight around and being in charge all the time. 'Cause if you do that, you're going to be beat up, being proved wrong quite a lot. But when people are in an environment, in a situation, [where they] have the information that they need to feel creatively fulfilled and get that rush of, "I am working on something that I'm really happy to see exist," then that makes me happy.

Tom: That is pretty close to what Richard Williams told me.

Jen: Really?

Tom: Yeah, yeah. He said, he says, "Sometimes what's more satisfying than being able to go further than you think you could, is creating a climate for others to do better than they thought they ever could."

Jen: Yeah. Because that's why we're in this business, right? We want to make something that people look at and go, "Wow." And then look at each other and go, "We made that. That didn't exist. We made something that we can be proud of at the end of all the blood, sweat, and tears."

Tom: So now I have to ask, what's your least favorite part?

Jen: The least favorite … I think the least favorite is the horrific weight of responsibility that each of your decisions could affect the livelihoods of many, many people. The buck stops with you, and you have to make those hard decisions. And you know that there will be casualties involved. You know, there may be people's ideas you can't use, or things that could cause someone to lose a weekend with their family, or maybe entire scenes that people work really hard [on] have to be cut out. Those things are really hard to do and you have to make those decisions and make sure the movie's going to be great, and people will have jobs at the end of the day. But that weight of responsibility, it actually goes against the creative process. Because you have to be okay with not having a stake in order to be creatively free. But it's—it's a very exhausting part of the work.

Ron: So there were a couple of times you made people work through the weekend and it was worth it, and maybe a couple of times where it wasn't worth it?

Jen: Yeah. It's like generals of an army—you look at them and go, "We got to take that bridge; a lot of you are going to die. But we got to do it, or we are going to lose the war." That's the role of the leader. You have to ask someone to do the hard work, and it's terribly sad at times.

Tom: There are people who storyboard and they are happy just to storyboard for the rest of their life. There are people who animate, or who character design, and [are] happy to do that for the rest of their life. But when you start directing, you're yielding a certain amount of creative input, because it's not you drawing. It's more about your ability to motivate and inspire your team.

Jen: Right, it's not you doing the work; it's about getting everyone else to do the work.

Tom: Yes. For someone who storyboards so well, how did you handle giving up that responsibility?

Jen: It was very tough actually. Because I think a lot of people when they first start out directing, they end up just trying to do everything themselves, and that's just not what a director is. That just means you're overworking an artist, meaning you. That's not also the best way to motivate people to do the best work.

So, what I ended up doing is finding the parts that I felt like I really needed to do, which may be very surgical little things I just wanted. I saw a moment so clearly I thought, "There's no point in sending someone off to do this; it'll take me a short period of time to just bang it out." So I would try and surgically figure out what parts that I really had to do, but try to outsource, delegate everything else.

And part of it is understanding that it doesn't have to be exactly the way you saw it being done, as long as the point is made. We were talking about before, that there are different styles of directing. There are the directors that will tell you if it's similar to trying to find a place on a map, the destination. He can either say, "This is the address, figure it out." And then there's the directors that will say, "Turn left, turn right, turn left, go 100 feet, go turn right, turn right, turn right, turn left, and then go another 100 feet, and then stop, and then go another 2 feet, and then make a left, and right, and left, and right, and left." I prefer being the "this is the address, figure it out" [type]. Because that is the point of the shot, of the movie, of the character, or that's the point we have to achieve that the audience has to understand. And there are so many people that will do getting to that destination better than you would. And that's a big thing. I think people respect and understand that there are simply people that will get you there better than you would have. You may know where to go, but let everybody else come up with creative solutions on how to get there.

Kung Fu Panda 3, 2016 © DreamWorks Animation LLC.

Tom: When did you know from the time you were storyboarding, "I could direct"?

Jen: In TV or feature?

Tom: I think the first time you ever thought you could be a director.

Jen: I again [had a] very nontraditional approach to ending up being a director. When I was in TV, my producer was Catherine Winder. I was actually in Australia, working on a live-action movie, 'cause I [had] left HBO, gone to Australia to work on storyboards and illustrations because I wanted to do something different, and I was young and crazy. And then she called me up towards the end of the thing and said, "Hey, how are you doing?" I said, "Oh great. I'm almost done, I don't know what to do and I don't know if I'll stay in live action or come back to animation. Knowing I can't stay here, because I can't live in Australia forever. I miss my family." So she said, "Come back and direct in TV." And I'm like, "Okay … I have no idea how to do that." She said, "Don't worry. You'll do fine." And so, I was pushed. I didn't say, "I want to come back, make me a director and I'll come back." I was told, "Come back and direct and you'll be fine." [laughs] I said, "Okay…" So that's why I directed in TV. And a similar thing happened to me when it was my first time directing in feature animation because on *Kung Fu Panda 1*, Melissa Cobb had set me up to do that two-minute opening sequence, because no one there did 2D animation anymore … Isn't that sad? Like the whole pipeline was gone, they didn't have any of the equipment anymore. They barely had anything to scan anything. So they had to outsource the 2D animation. Melissa said, "Go become essentially a sequence director and just do it because the directors are too busy." So I ran off. What's great training for that was I was a head of story on a film, but as a head of story you don't necessarily go into every department and follow the whole pipeline leading into that. You just kind of stop and peel off. For instance, you're never sitting in lighting dailies as a head of story.

    So it was great training for me. And later on, Melissa told me she did it on purpose. She said she could tell my personality type wasn't the kind of person that walks in and says, "I'm going to be the director and blah, blah, blah." I was more like, "I just want to do some cool work and I'm not sure if I can do that …" I'm not the most crazy, overly self-confident person in the world. I need a big push a lot of the time. And so she told me that she did it in order for me to get confidence in myself. That she knew that I wouldn't do a jump like that until I had a preponderance of evidence to prove to myself that I could do it without destroying people's lives. That's kind of what I was doing 'cause I was thinking first of the responsibilities of the job. And the fact that it's such a scary responsibility.

    So at the end of the first movie, when both directors said, "We don't want to do another one," they had other things they wanted to do. I think John wanted to do live action, Mark wanted to [do] *The Little Prince*, so they left. Melissa Cobb came to me and said, "You're going to direct the second movie." And it wasn't a "You should direct the second movie" or "Will you direct the second movie?" It's like, "You're going to direct the second movie." And I said, "No …" And she said,

"Yes, you are." And I go, "No, I'm not." And then finally she said, "You can do it." And I said, "I can't do it. I don't know how to do it." I'm like, "Are you crazy? I'm not going to do this." And she said, "You've already done it because that's why I put you on that thing (the 2D prologue) so I can train you to do it. And you were in every meeting as a head of story. You were working with the writers, you were working with every aspect of this, and so you have to do it." So I said, "… Okay."

But I was scared to death. I remember going home and saying to my husband, "Oh crap, they asked me to direct a movie …" It wasn't good news. It was traumatic.

Ron: In your early period directing, were you learning from mentors? Or from observation of past experiences?

Jen: Just a bit of everything because as a head of story, and I got to say, I was a very, very included head of story. They brought me into everything, they were very open with everything, so I was able [to] observe everything, down to [the] dynamics of the meeting. I actually think it's easier to learn when they're not staring at you to perform in the meeting. When you're in as an observer in a meeting, you can be very clear on what's going on. You're not clouded by performance anxiety. I would watch meetings where things got done, and it was literally like watching a ping-pong match of colors. You go, that person did that because of this, and that person is saying that because of this. And that person said that, and they're doing this, and they're getting that alliance figured out. I was watching this like a *Game of Thrones* episode—it was so educational.

Ron: So it was studio politics. It wasn't necessarily what was right for the particular scene, or …

Jen: I think that essentially that part of directing, the actual craft, was something I already knew. Because I had done head of story on two productions, I'd been working for years on the actual process of animation, I understood what all the departments did at that point. What I didn't know is the politics angle of being a director. That's the thing I had to learn, because it's a very different job. You walk into a meeting and all of a sudden all the eyeballs look at you, and there's huge baggage that everybody has expectations on what you're supposed to be doing. You never would have had that as a head of story. That's the part I had to learn.

Ron: You were saying some interesting things about being a woman and going to Japan. Maybe you could talk a little bit about that.

Jen: I was at HBO, and it was *Spawn* and it was my first time going overseas to oversee animation there. It was Madhouse and DR Movie. Madhouse was like this really happy new place. A really cool bunch of people. But I had a mortifying experience for my first time in Japan. This amazing studio, founded by amazing people, all this amazing art everywhere, and then I had a penicillin reaction.

Tom: Oh no.

Jen: I had developed a minor infection, I was taking penicillin. I had never had problems with it before. All of a sudden I'm in Japan, and I suddenly, like, go full-on allergic ICU (intensive care unit)!

Tom: Oh, my God!

Jen: Like, my skin went bright red, you know, and I couldn't breathe. It was [the] middle of the night in a foreign country. So they had to rush me to emergency in the Ginza.

        They had to give me all sorts of shots. I was spending my first week in Japan; three of those days were in the ICU in a teaching hospital. But they were all such sweet people, very lovely. Talk about the worst case scenario! That's what happens when you go to meet a bunch of people for the first time.

Tom: Wow.

Jen: But everybody was very supportive and nice about it. But I think that, you know, it was not great. [laughs]

Tom: Did you run into the thing about losing face? When working at an American studio like Hanna-Barbera, which is a lot of old-school animators, when you get tough critique it's no big deal. I had old Disney guys saying, "Idiot! Don't you know how to do this?" And they meant nothing by it. But when you go to Japan or Asia, you have to think about artists losing face. You know you can't say, "this is bad, this is wrong, this stinks," because then they lose face. You have to couch it in a way that's …

Jen: Yeah, you can say, "how about this?" for this suggestion of an idea. And you know, it. Strangely, I think it's cause I'm Asian, but I tend to do that anyway. Even here, I don't walk up to someone and say, "This is crap." I don't tend to do that. I just …

Tom: I remember Iwao Takamoto (1925–2007) at Hanna-Barbera was famous for judging work by saying, "This is good, this is very good, good! Now you … do it again."

All: [laugh]

Jen: Yeah, I mean, even though I was raised here, I did have an Asian family and there was a lot of [influence]. I think part of that is not necessarily being as antagonistic in some situations. I mean you get your point across the same.

Kung Fu Panda 2, 2011 © DreamWorks Animation LLC.

Ron: And with acting, with actors, was it the same?

Jen: It depended on the actor. I directed the second one, so I had a longer-term relationship with most of the leads than Ale had. But then if they were new actors, neither of us had known them. So we would differ to each other. Maybe it was a scene that one of us knew more about than the other because maybe he boarded it. Or maybe I boarded it. And so we would trade off according to who would lead a session. But usually it was the both of us crouched over a little microphone and doing stuff.

Tom: When you're working with an actor, that's usually the protocol. There is only one voice giving instructions to the actor and so—

Jen: Yes, I think it's important … One person would lead a session. Because a recording session is this sort of direct line between the actor and the director.

Tom: Yes.

Jen: Even if you're not in the room, even if you're in the recording booth … the tech area, there is eye contact all between you and the actors all the time. They are constantly thinking, "Am I doing it right?" They do that all the time. So it has to be one person.

Tom: Yes.

Jen: And the whole time, as the director, you're sitting there and you're like a little sheepdog, going to look at the sheep. It's a similar body language as a sheep dog, when they're tap, tap, tap, tap, tap, tap, tap. That's what you're doing the whole time, a little there, a little there, a little there, poke, poke, poke, that—that's it.

Tom: Yes.

Jen: So that's what you're doing, and you can't do that if there's five people involved. You can't. They [the actors] don't know who to look at.

Tom: Do you like working, like, with the actors?

Jen: I do, I love them. And that's something I never got to do as a head of story. When I first started doing it as a director, I was scared to death because these were all massive celebrities and stuff. But I realized it's just like working with an animator. And there [are] a lot of the same processes of how I'm going to have to go through and figure out what the moment is. How to feel what the character is feeling at that moment. So I would communicate to them like an artist and they get it.

Tom: I know a lot of editors who like it that way.

Jen: … 'Cause they can think. And you need different ideas outside of what you expected. Strange, that I actually think it's faster. If you have five people, yelling and screaming in the room, and the poor editor is trying to cut and … and then they're recutting and recutting and recutting, and they never actually get to a point. Soon you're spending the 3 am sessions with nothing to show for it and everyone's tired. Or you do it the other way where you get someone to think. You can get to a solution much more efficiently. That's what I think.

Ron: Did you use the same editor on both pictures?

Jen: Yeah.

Ron: Did it become more intuitive as it went along?

Jen: Very. Me and Clare Knight have a very easy way of working. I think that editors and directors, it's almost like a marriage. You kind of have to find a good match. If you don't have a way of shorthand, it's a lot harder. With me and her, it's always been very, very smooth. We're both relatively quiet people; we're not the kind of people that yell and scream in a room.

And when we work, it's relatively serene. She has, like, an espresso in her office, and she has candles, and always smells nice, and it's clean. Then we sit in there and it's very efficient, the way we work.

Tom: Have you ever had any examples [of] what you call a happy accident? Something you weren't planning, or you know, something somebody said. And you just go, "That's nice, keep it. Put it in."

Jen: There was in the second *Panda* movie. We were cutting the big emotional revelation moment where Po understands the truth of what happened when he was a little baby, and his mom saved his life. Part of it was in 2D, and then when the truth comes out, it becomes 3D. And the transition used to be one shot longer in 2D, so that it becomes 3D [from] his POV (point of view) of the mother. Although, what's interesting is, Clare was cutting that area and we realized that we didn't really have a particular shot quite long enough. We were looking at it, and she suggested that the reveal is exactly the same moment as the change in medium. They negate each other. So, she said, "Let's shift it, so that the reveal happens earlier and the truth and revelation happens one shot later." So we cut out a shot, and all of a sudden it hit you viscerally. That's one of those things you can't quite quantify. Whether something will make you cry, until you actually do it. And she took out this distracting medium shot in that moment where it's supposed to be emotionally engaged, which was a distraction. She took that out, and all of a sudden the moment worked!

Tom: In *Who Framed Roger Rabbit*, when Jessica was singing the torch song "Why Don't You Do Right." At the very end, where she pulls Hoskins close to her lips by his tie and sings, "Why don't you do right, like some other man … Doo"— like that. There was a little pause. The shot had background actors wallah. All these actors going groaning in ecstasy, "OOH! uhhUUHHH." Then right in that pause, where she says, "why don't—like some other man," a guy in the back goes "UH!" I remember we were sitting in editorial, and Bob Zemeckis asked, "Is that funny?" It was a complete accident. "Just leave it in, it's funny, it works!" [laughs] It's great when you can catch those little things once in a while.

Jen: I think that animation is such a overcooked process—everything has to be thought out so much that you kind of have to force the accidents and treasure them when they do happen. Because otherwise it could be such a forgone process; everything is so predictable because we can control everything.

Tom: Do you encourage with the actors a certain amount of improv?

Jen: We depend on improv with the actors. A natural way of speaking is not necessarily a natural way of writing. Especially a character that is as prone to outburst as Po. And Jack [Black], he's very much into input, all the callouts, a lot of them are just stuff he made up. But also it's just that they are grasping the reality of the emotion of the moment. If it doesn't feel right, you throw out the script page and figure it out on the spot with the actor.

Kung Fu Panda 3, 2016 © DreamWorks Animation LLC.

Tom: William Shatner used to make me laugh because he was in a radio experience and—part of his humor was his—he would change tempo and speed, so he'd go "Hahaha—who're you talkin' to?" [laughs] And he did it so well. So, like, he would just—he'd make you laugh. It's just like … That's good. [Laughs]

Jen: That's great.

Tom: I want to touch on music. How much does music factor in what you do?

Jen: To me, music is 30 percent of the emotional experience of the movie. That's why we bother to do a scratch music track even when we're looking at the rough version of the movie. We try to do a rough music pass, because you have to have some emotional framework for what you're watching. In fact, it can sometimes fool you into thinking a crappy scene is a lot better than it is, 'cause the music's great. But the music is so important, so, so important. I don't understand why we leave it as late as we do. Mainly because of the availability of the composer, you can't lock up a composer for three years—they got other stuff to do, other movies. But it's so important, and it's so frightening 'cause sometimes, you've lived with a scratch music track forever, and you think, "I think it works." And then you throw it all out and you start over with the real music, and everything feels different.

Tom: Yeah.

Jen: It's terrifying 'cause you think, "Did we break it? Are we delusional? Is this a piece of crap? I don't know." But the music has to go through its process, too. They have to have their sketch, and then their honing, and then their polish and all that stuff. And once they get to it—it feels quite amazing. You now think, "Why did I ever load that scratch track in the first place? It's crap!" [laughs]

Tom: Now that you've done a couple [of] pictures, do you feel like you've evolved a personal style?

Jen: Personal style? That's interesting, because in some ways I think the second one was more my personal style than the third one, because the third one was a collaboration. And so there are sections of the third one that are more me, and sections that are more of Ale [Alessandro Carloni]. I think he was pointing it out some time before that some parts that are kind of epic and emotional and kind of over-the-top action stuff are mine, and the ones that have that cute little character, sweet and funny stuff [are] actually his. But it's kind of counter intuitive again, if you look at us and think that. But the sort of personal stuff that I have is getting to that emotional, sort of pushed emotional point, where I think a lot of people are afraid to go, because they think it's going to be too much for the kids. I think kids can take a lot. I could take a lot when I was a kid, I was watching all sorts of stuff. But to be able to get to that deep emotional sort of … revelation, where you make grown men cry, that's the thing that I like to do.

Tom: I see. Everybody has a pet project they keep in their back pocket … Like, director John Houston wanted to do Kipling's *The Man Who Would Be King* for many years. Do you have something that you'd like to tackle someday? Like, "I really want to do grand opera." [laughs]

Jen: Well, I've always wanted to do an action, live-action movie. That's why I got into storyboarding in the first place. I've never actually done that, because in animation you can push things only so far before you start having people thinking you're traumatizing the children. The thing is, I think something like Panda, I could find things in it that were action packed, and I could get a lot of jollies out of it. But I would love to go full, hardcore action someday.

Ron: I understand you do some drawing on your own, of your own ideas. Are they sketches for movies, or are they just meanderings

Jen: When I say that I've been doing storyboarding since I was five, I've been working on these types of stories since I was five. And so, I do storyboards, very elaborate storyboards. They're kind of aggressive, very violent, action, sci-fi stories. And their entire arcs and all. Everything I've learned, I've put into this. In some ways I think even though I call that my R&D, work is my R&D. Because that's where I get the joy, and in doing all this, I can learn better how to do that ... strange. So yeah, I do drawings at home all the time. And they're full-on, full-on stories and stuff, but I'll never pitch them.

Ron: Would you ever make them on your own? If you had somebody [who] said, "Oh, here's twenty or fifty million dollars, go ahead and make it." Would you want to make it yourself?

Jen: No. No, isn't that weird?

Ron: Never?

Jen: The reason is that they're already done for me. For the viewing audience of one. They're already done up here [points to her head], so there's really no point in taking the responsibility and pressure of someone giving me fifty million dollars and then they have a say. No one has a say on this stuff; it's already done. So I could do that for other things. But for that, it's to be kept here. I think I showed some of that in the class talks and stuff. The only times I ever show it is when I, like, talk to classes. It's not for pitching to a studio.

Ron: So are they Sam Peckinpah-ish violence? Or is there a moral bent to it? Or a societal statement of some sort?

Jen: They're actually—it's kind of like this epic emotional family drama with sci-fi biotechnology involved. [laughs]

Tom: Oh, one of those. [laughs]

Jen: But the reason why I like it is it frees me from a lot of the narrative constraints, fitting it into a two-hour movie. Or a ten-hour miniseries. Or whether it fits a certain demographic. Or whether it's understandable for moms with kids to see, or anything like that. Of all the several stories, the one I'm mainly working on nowadays is just stepping in and looking at someone's life and understanding what character is built through this particular person's life. And for me that's fascinating, because I take pieces of that all the time and put it into things I'm working on. It just, you know, because you've spent this much brain energy creating a reality—creating entire complex characters and motivations. Informative moments and backstories and weird interactions and completely crazy sorts of scenarios. And all that stuff that on a job, you don't have time to figure out. You've got to come up with stuff like that. And then you go, "Oh, I have that idea." And that's a crazy undercurrent to a character that you don't often see and you can throw that in there. So I do that all the time. I just cull stuff out of there.

Tom: Okay, so now we have to ask the inevitable question. What would be your advice for the people trying to follow you?

Jen: There's a couple things for me; I've been asked that before by students and it's what I would've found useful. 'Cause when you're young and starting out, you don't have as much experience, and everything is scary. I would say just don't take either the success or the failures personally. It's not about you; it's about the context of that job. So, don't walk into it and get devastated if you get turned down. And don't suddenly get completely chuffed if you're hired for something.

Kung Fu Panda 3, 2016 © DreamWorks Animation LLC.

Because often it's not about you. So just try and find the thing that you like to do, that you would do anyway, whether or not someone else told you that you had to do it. And if you can find joy in doing that thing, then eventually you will get a job doing that thing. But don't let other people dictate what you end up doing by their tastes. You know, if someone says, "I love you because you do this! You're fantastic!" then you may veer towards doing that. That may not be what you want to do; that may not even be what you're good at. But someone said you're good at it, you must do that more, right? But that sort of—it's all a mirage. You just got to find the thing that you find joy in doing and get joy doing that. And do not be discouraged, or overly encouraged, by what other people say. 'Cause that's how you maintain your core.

Tom: Did you ever want to do something completely different?

Jen: The thing is, every project that I've ever signed up to do has something in it that makes me very happy. Even things that you'd go, "Why would she have worked on that?" Like *Happy, the Littlest Bunny*, 'cause there were things on that that made me happy because I was learning something. So every project that I've done, I'm doing [it] because it's teaching me something. And I've always done this thing where I try to figure out, what am I going to learn this year? What am I going to learn [on] this project? What's my goal? What am I going to get out of this thing? And maybe it was like I ran off to do a live-action movie because I wanted to learn how to draw gigantic architectural things—I had never learned how to do that. And so within five months, I could learn how to freehand gigantic cities. That's something that I didn't know how to do before, but—or the one year I thought, "I want to learn all about military aircraft. Or this year I'm going to learn exactly how to use a motorcycle. [laughs] All that, stuff like that, that's all research and development. And so all the movies, all the projects I've worked on, even though they may not necessarily be exactly, purely what my personal sensibility is … each one has taught me something significant.

Tom: Well, I think that about does it.

Jen: Cool.

Ron: That okay? Have we not covered anything that you feel that should be included?

Jen: Oh, I don't know. I mean life is complicated, so I don't know what parts are interesting. [laughs]

10
Carlos Saldanha Interview

Carlos Saldanha, photographer Antelmo Villarreal.

Although I knew many at Blue Sky Studios in Connecticut, I had not had the pleasure of meeting Carlos Saldanha until we talked for this book. I had known of his work as a director (and co-director) of hit films like *Rio* (2010), *Rio 2* (2014), *Robots* (2005), and the *Ice Age* films. His film *Ice Age: Dawn of the Dinosaurs* (2009) became an international sensation. It was the highest grossing animated title internationally and the second highest worldwide at the time of release. We met for the interview when he was out at the Twentieth Century Fox studio. A slight, wiry man with a broad smile, I found him a very pleasant fellow and very enthusiastic about the art of animation. Although originally from Brazil, his years living in the New York City area allowed him the opportunity to cultivate a fine Manhattan brogue, so that it awoke in me the lingua franca of my homeland (Brooklyn).

So like, uh … let's do dis …

Tom Sito

Tom: Thank you for doing this. So, to begin, can you please talk a little bit about your own background and how you came into animation? You're originally from Brazil?

Carlos: Yes, I'm originally from Brazil. I was born in Rio. I came from a very average middle-class family. My dad was in the military. My mom was a homemaker. We traveled a lot because being in the service, my dad had to move around the country. But I got to spend most of my teenager years in Rio. I always loved to draw. Usually if I didn't have anything to do, I'd get a pencil and paper and spend my time drawing characters and little comic strips. I also loved watching cartoons and the Disney animation classics on TV. I remember having all the Disney movies in book form or on record, tiny, colorful little vinyls that told the story of *Bambi, Pinocchio*, and all that stuff. I immersed myself into the world of storytelling and animation. So, I grew up with the old classics. I grew up with the *Looney Tunes* also, all those fun cartoons that people here grew up with.

Ron: Did you ever think you could do this for a living?

Carlos: Not until much later in the game. For me drawing was always a hobby. You know, like after a long day in school, I would come back home and I'd draw a little bit. I'd see something I liked and I would draw it or paint it. But I never had training. I never even thought it would be possible to have any training. But when I graduated from high school I thought maybe I'd go to art school. I was very young, I was just sixteen when I finished high school, so my parents looked at me and said, "Art school? Are you crazy? No, don't go to art school. You're too young to go to art school! What are you going to do with art?"

I also loved computers. I took my first computer class in high school. I was excited about the computer's possibilities, especially video gaming and stuff, 'cause you could do graphics on the computer. I was the Commodore 64 kind of generation. So my parents suggested I pursue that instead and maybe do something related to art later. So I went to computer science school and really loved it. But I remember always catching myself doing graphics. To me it was less about the programming and more about designing fun screen layouts, logos, and pop-up menus. I was more interested in the visual aspects of it than actually the programming part of it. Even though I ended up working as a programmer, working with systems and creating software, I was much more driven to the communication and visual aspects of computer science. I was interested in how the message could appear on the screen in the best way possible.

I worked with it (computers) for a couple of years, while at the same time I was always watching movies. I loved sci-fi movies, and my favorite movie was *Blade Runner* (1982). I loved that movie, and kept wanting to be in that world! Creating worlds like that. Not even talking about animation at that stage. I was more into visual effects. But again, being in Brazil was kind of tough, because there was no market for that. And I didn't even know how to get started.

Then I came upon this compilation tape, I think it was a SIGGRAPH tape. I know it was from some kind of big festival that had a bunch of short films. All CG. When looking at that tape I saw *Luxo, Jr.* (1986). I thought, "This is great! Look at this, the guy made it look real. It looks real, but it has a heart, it has a story behind it. I love this stuff. This is what I wanna do!"

For about a year, I started to look around for the possibilities in Brazil. There were some CG companies in Brazil, especially for big TV networks that were starting to tap into computer graphics. But I couldn't find a way in. And then I talked to someone that said, "Well, there are schools in the US that you can attend and you can see if you like it or not." That's when I learned about the School of Visual Arts (SVA) in New York City. I said, "Um, it sounds like a good idea. Maybe I can go to New York and see what happens."

So, I broke my piggy bank. [laughs] I worked hard to try to get together every cent that I could to come to the US and attend school. I was so crazy! I was only twenty, when I suddenly told my girlfriend, "Let's get married and go to the US, and maybe we'll stay there for three months, four months. Who knows? Maybe we will come back." And she said, "Ok, but I have to stop college." "Yeah, stop for a little while and then we'll come back and you can continue," I told her. So it was one of those crazy things you do when you're young, in love, and you don't think too much. We took the leap and drove our parents crazy. Everybody was saying, "Are you out of your mind? You're going to quit your job and go somewhere you don't know?" I explained, "I have to try this. I got a gut feeling that it's what I love."

I came to New York and I started with classes at the School of Visual Arts. I didn't have money to pay for college. I just paid for that semester, just so I could see if I had any kind of potential. And, you know, the minute that I sat at that computer, that's when I found my passion! I think the software was Digital Arts running on a PC. To me it was the fastest, biggest, meanest machine that I could ever imagine! Nowadays I don't think you can even run Google on that one. [laughs] Yet right there, the minute I sat down on the first day of class, I said, "This is what I want to do for the rest of my life," and since then I've never stopped.

No Time for Love, 1993.

Tom: How did you first connect with Blue Sky Studios?

Carlos: Well, when I was at SVA, the continuation class was taught by Bruce Wands. He was the head of the undergraduate program and worked with the graduate program. I remember being very impressed with SVA's facilities. Back home, at college, there were maybe a handful of computers that I had limited access to. There at SVA there were forty computer workstations and I had twenty-four-hour access. A lot of computers and software playing, yet the room was empty. Nobody was using it. I was like a kid in a candy store. I was there from nine in the morning to nine at night every single day of the three months that I planned to stay in the US.

Tom: So you really jumped at the opportunity.

Carlos: I was very diligent and organized in a way, just wanting to learn it all. When the teacher saw that it was the end of the class, he said to me, "You've got to continue this and you've got to take the master's program." I said, "How am I going to do it?" I was supposed to go back to Brazil. And he just said, "Well, see if you can stay." I had to get a visa. I have to get paperwork done. I had to get money. I borrowed money from friends. But in the end everything worked out fine. I was accepted into their master's program. There, one of my teachers was Chris Wedge. And that's when the Blue Sky connection really began. He was my teacher of animation, and he ended up hiring me.

Tom: Okay, let's set aside biography for now, and focus on your technique as a director. You've developed some characters around some pretty well-known actors. When developing a character, do you work with the actors? Are you at the recording sessions?

Carlos: Yeah, I work with them, and I rely a lot on them to help me. Because I have a

Chris Wedge, Carlos Saldanha, and TBD, *Ice Age*, 2002 © Twentieth Century Fox. All Rights Reserved.

pretty good idea what the character is all about. When I design, I create a character thinking about what kind of mannerisms the character has. I would always think of them not speaking, but think of them acting. And that's why I can probably help the actor in saying "so this character is like THIS, and is going to do THIS and THAT." I would give them the broad strokes of the character. Then I would rely on their acting chops to bring it to the next level. You find happy surprises. We have been very fortunate with a lot of our casting.

Tom: Do you have any examples?

Carlos: Take Sid (the sloth) in *Ice Age*, for example. John [Leguizamo] had originally given us about a hundred potential accents for that character. A hundred different ways the character might talk. Until we came upon the lisp. Then that became the trademark of the character. John continued to help us with the comedy of Sid. When an actor contributes so much at that level, it makes the character better. It's the kind of stuff that we look for when we work with actors. "What is [it] that you can bring to the character that would make the character better than I imagine?"—that's the question. It's a matter of discovery. We never get it right off the bat. Usually the first few sessions with the actors is more trying to figure out what it's going to sound like, or how it is going to be. Only after that can we really get into the character. We can take the character to the next level.

Tom: Do you bring storyboards in and take them (the actors) through [them]? Or do you just work directly from script?

Carlos: We do a couple of things. Scripts are good, but there're always revisions and changes so maybe the actor doesn't have time to read everything beforehand. Some actors are very good at doing their homework. They come in with the lines memorized, and that's awesome.

　　　　　If they come in prepared, that helps me quite a bit. But some of them don't come in prepared, and they have to do it on the fly. That takes a little longer, but it's fine too. And I always try to bring the sequences on storyboards (onto the recording stage) so that they can watch it, so they can see what the situation is. I tell them, "Oh, imagine a glacier and then you are at the bottom of the glacier and then you're doing …" Sometimes it's hard. So I show them the sequence and then talk about it. Then they get to know it. Sometimes I would show some animation tests so that they can see how their character performs.

Tom: Sometimes I would run into an actor who didn't like to work with a storyboard. They'd tell you, "I don't want to be influenced by the character's acting on the storyboard."

Carlos: Some of them don't like to; many don't like hearing temp voices. And I try to avoid that too, because I don't want to lead them in the wrong direction. I don't want them to feel obligated to match the temp voice. And some of them don't like hearing their voices. It's interesting. Sometimes when I have the sequences with their voices they get self-conscious. They always say, "Oh, I can do better than that," which is good. [laughs] But I only do it surgically. I only show them stuff when it's really important for them to get the context of what I'm trying to get. Other than that, I try not to show too much.

Tom: How does music play a role in what you do? When you are conceiving of the idea of a picture, do you already have some music in mind?

Carlos: Music is huge. I think it's almost fifty-fifty. With the right music you get the moment to play ten times better. The wrong music can destroy the moment. So I take music very seriously. I cannot play anything, and I'm not musically knowledgeable myself. But I love putting music into projects and finding that perfect song. Some projects require more than others, but I think it's a very crucial part of the work.

Tom: Do you work with a sound designer?

Carlos: I listen to a lot of stuff and I work with the editor. In all my movies I have the same editor, so over time we developed libraries of music. It's tricky because sometimes you go to the same source, and it's like, "Wait, I already heard that music in *Ice Age: The Meltdown*, and that music I used in *Robots*." So you start to get picky. We are always searching for something fresh, so we spend quite a lot of time listening to sound bites and music, cutting them into the reels, trying it out. He [the editor] does the first pass and sees how I react. Sometimes, depending on the project, we ask the [music] supervisor to come in and help us shape it because we don't have a lot of time. Cutting music takes longer than cutting [story] boards. Finding the right music is very difficult.

Tom: Many directors say a very important part of their job is choosing an editor and working with him or her, because they spend so much of their time working in close proximity together. So you and your editor have a good relationship?

Carlos: Yeah, we have a great relationship. Harry [Hitner] is amazing, and it is true, most of my time I spend in editorial. It's quality time because outside of editorial I'm moving around the company, fifteen minutes here, twenty minutes there, an hour here.

It's always jumping from department to department, trying to keep the thing going. When I get to editing, it is a time when I can sit down, look at the movie, and actually make the movie in real time. Like when I need the panels for this, I need a shot here, I need music there. It feels more intimate. You get to see the movie that you are making. I love that part of the process.

Tom: The other thing that you guys [Blue Sky] do really well is the pantomime scenes. There seems to be a musical quality to your sound effects. With a good sound effect, you get a laugh even without any dialogue.

Carlos: Yeah, it's tough, too. I think it's a combination of many things: music, sound effects, animation, visuals. When it all comes together, you get a great moment.

Tom: Who is the voice of Scrat?

Carlos: Scrat is Chris Wedge. That was one of those happy surprises. We didn't have much time to choose. We were thinking about some big names to make those little sounds. We did do a lot of temp tracks. A lot of what we called "The Blue Sky Players." We have our cast of temp voices at Blue Sky that we keep going to for all these sounds and scratch voices, before we get the real actors to come in. Chris was making all the sounds for Scrat, and it was so good. So why change it?

Ice Age: The Meltdown, 2006 © Twentieth Century Fox. All Rights Reserved.

Tom: It's much like when Hanna and Barbera were creating the characters of Tom and Jerry. The famous stock scream of when Tom gets hit, "Agghhhh," is director Bill Hanna himself. Apparently, he [Bill] kept trying actors all day, saying, "No, not like that, like this, 'agghhhh!!'" Joe Barbera finally said, "Bill, why don't we just use your scream?"

Carlos: I think that was exactly what happened with Scrat. We went through a casting but no one sounded as good as Chris.

Tom: Earlier, you mentioned happy accidents. Do you ever get happy accidents, like either the performance of an artist or, or the way the sequence would come together, you'd think, "Wow, we really have something here"?

Carlos: Yeah, there is a lot of that in the process; that's part of what makes working on an animated project so special. There are sequences that you struggle with a lot. For example, one that we all struggled with is where we had that sequence of the dodos in the first [*Ice Age*] movie. We worked so hard in that sequence to find comedy and dialogue. It just was not there, to a point that it almost got cut. We didn't know what to do with it. A happy surprise emerged when animators got their hands on it. We started to discover the fun of the characters. The dodos, the quirkiness of the characters, came to life. It became one of my favorite sequences in the movie, one of those happy accidents. I think they do happen, not often, but they do happen. Scrat is one of them, too. Originally we only had Scrat at the beginning of the movie. We had an idea for him in the end, but we didn't have him in the middle, so we added that. He became such a big star that we had to start to create more for him.

Tom: Now that you've directed several pictures, you know the whole process can be overwhelming. Have you modified the way you schedule your day in terms of pacing yourself? How did you learn to relegate your time?

Carlos: I don't know if I learned yet! [laughs] I find that every movie that I work on is getting harder and harder. I had this assumption that it would all get easier as I went along. At least some aspects of it have gotten easier. My comfort level has gotten easier with the crew, and with the phases of what to expect and how things miraculously get solved.

Tom: You're better at letting things go now?

Carlos: No, not good, no! I might have gotten better at picking my battles. But letting things go is always tough. I know the minute I say, "Approved," it is a point of no return. It's just gone, and I'm like, "ahhhhh, don't go!!" [laughs] So I try to only say that when I really feel it's ready to move on. But sometimes I can't, sometimes the shot is way overdue and maybe there is nothing more I can get out of the actor, or the animator, or myself. Then I feel that I need to let it go. Sleep on it and see. I create a list of what we call CBB, "Could Be Better." Every time a shot moves forward, if I'm not a 100 percent sure, I put a little check mark on it. Eventually at the end of the project I'll have a list of all the shots that I can go back to. We've been very successful at managing that. I need to deal with scheduling and getting things to move forward without sacrificing quality. I'm a quality freak. I'm very "it needs to be perfect." But I did learn that sometimes it's just one shot. It's only two seconds on the screen. Maybe the foot is not a 100 percent in the right position that I thought it should be. Who cares? Nobody is looking specifically at that foot, you know. But again, I understand the importance of the details. I always have a little devil and angel on my shoulder saying, "Let it go! You gotta let go!" "No, no! Work on it!" I'm always role-playing with those two voices in my head.

Tom: Have you ever been the sole director? Or did you always work with a co-director?

Carlos: When I worked on *Ice Age*, I was co-director with Chris [Wedge]. On *Robots*, I was again co-director with Chris. Then I jumped to *Ice Age: The Meltdown* and did it all by myself. Then *Ice Age: Dawn of the Dinosaurs*, I had a co-director, Mike Thurmeier, who was one of my top animators and an amazing guy. I always got along with him. He had the kind of personality and talent that fit the director's role perfectly. He was so brilliant all the way through. Chris had trusted me and brought me in on the first *Ice Age* as his co-director so I could also learn and grow. I felt the same way about Mike coming to *Ice Age: Dawn of the Dinosaurs*. It would be a great project for him to come on as a director, to both learn and help me more.

Tom: Now that you've done a picture both ways, which do you prefer?

Carlos: I like to direct, but, I really value the co-director role. If you have the

Ice Age: Dawn Of The Dinosaurs, 2009 © Twentieth Century Fox. All Rights Reserved.

right person, it's an awesome collaboration. If you have trust and if you share similar sensibilities or similar philosophies on the project, it becomes an amazing collaboration. I was very fortunate to have had Mike on board.

Tom: How did you and Mike divide up your responsibilities? Some teams like to split up sequences of the film. Others split approvals of the various departments.

Carlos: We did a little bit of both. It depends on the need. I have two editors, so we would split it up. Mike would stay with one half. I would stay with the other. We work together on shaping a sequence. He understood what was happening in my head, in which direction I was going to go. And if he had other thoughts, we would just work towards that, too. We would brainstorm on that. But then I would say, "Why don't you take over that sequence and try to shape it a little bit and then show it to me? I'll give you my notes and you can continue to work and vice versa. I'll show you what I'm working on, and if you have some thoughts, I can work on that too." So we tried to divide and conquer. I trust him so much in animation. I'd say, "Mike, just go over there and take care of it." And he would. Finding the sensibilities and what each can best contribute to the project, I think that's the key to working well together, and I think it worked out great for us.

Mike Thurmeier and Carlos Saldanha, *Ice Age: Dawn Of The Dinosaurs*, 2009 © Twentieth Century Fox. All Rights Reserved.

Tom: Let's talk a bit about the film *Rio* (2011), because that project occupies a special place in your work history. Is it true that it was a story that originated from you?

Carlos: Yes. It's interesting because most of the projects at Blue Sky already came with a script, or we were pitched an idea. We were given a base treatment, even though in many instances the movie that ended up being made is not exactly how it came to us. It was the seed of an existing idea. With the exception of maybe *Robots*, which was something that was started at Blue Sky, all the other movies were either based on stories like *Horton Hears a Who!*, from a book, or *Ice Age*, which came as a script from Twentieth Century Fox.

Tom: So where did *Robots* come from?

Carlos: *Robots* was an idea that we had at Blue Sky. We pitched the idea (to Fox), and after the green light it evolved from there. But *Rio*, my next project, was an idea I had since the end of *Ice Age: The Meltdown* (2006). I'm from Brazil and I'm from Rio. I always thought that the city was so photogenic, so great to shoot in. There are so many flavors and the culture is so rich. The music, the colors ... Why not try to figure out a movie about Rio? I had that movie in my head, and I said, "Maybe one day I can make it." So I pitched the story and the studio liked it.

    I had this dream of making a project that could portray Brazil. I can show some aspects of my culture in animation that would be not aimed only at Brazilians, but for the whole world. The idea was there, but I had to finish *Ice Age: Dawn of the Dinosaurs* (2009), so I couldn't spend too much time on it. Halfway through *Ice Age: Dawn of the Dinosaurs*, they came to me and asked, "Carlos, what about that idea that you had about Brazil? What do you think about it?" I said, "Wow, I have it in some shape or form in my head." I pitched it again and they said, "We want to make that movie, but we want that movie to be our next movie." I said "Okay, but I'm still in the middle of *Ice Age: Dawn of the Dinosaurs*." "Well, maybe you can work on it in your spare time," was their response. I was working on both projects at the same time! Lesson learned. Never work on two projects at the same time. Even though I've done it twice, don't do it! [laughs] It kills you! I did that with *Robots*. I was halfway through *Robots* until *Ice Age: The Meltdown* came along and then they said, "We need *Ice Age: The Meltdown* for 2000 …" I don't remember the year anymore. So, I say, "Oh yeah, I can do it." I was young and inexperienced. I did it and it worked out fine. Then I said, I'm never going to do this again. In the middle of *Ice Age: Dawn of the Dinosaurs*, *Rio* came to life, and it's like, "How am I going to do them both?" So that's how it got started. But the story did take a few turns. For instance, originally I had penguins in the story. It was a year before those other films—

Development art, *Rio*, 2011 © Twentieth Century Fox. All Rights Reserved.

Tom: *Happy Feet* (2006) and then *Surf's Up* (2007).

Carlos: Yeah, and then after *Surf's Up* they said to me, "You cannot make a movie about penguins." I said, "Oh God!" There was also the DreamWorks' stuff; they put penguins in *Madagascar* (2005). So the penguin idea was out but luckily I had already created some great bird characters that I loved. I said, "Maybe I can make those characters the stars of the story …?"

Tom: And you don't want to go back to Joe Carioca (the Brazilian parrot that debuted in Walt Disney's *The Three Caballeros* in 1942)?

Carlos: No, you don't. I didn't want to do that at all and not because I didn't like the character. I couldn't do better than that. It is a great character. But I didn't want my characters to be compared with that. So, I had to reshape the story. But still we kept the essence of my original thought. What would be the experience of going through Rio de Janeiro as an outsider? That was the essential premise. When I lived here [America], I would go back to Rio on vacation and get that little bit of a "foreign eye." You see the things that you never noticed before. Things that you took for granted you appreciate more, and the things that you always hated are still there [laughs]. I wanted to find a way to capture that experience, somehow. A fish-out-of-water story, somebody from the outside who comes to Brazil. We did that through the eyes of a bird. Even though he was from Brazil, he never lived in Brazil. It was a bird that went to Brazil and actually found his roots, found his connection to that world.

Development art, *Rio*, 2011 © Twentieth Century Fox. All Rights Reserved.

I always liked that aspect of the story.

To the second part of the question, it's been much harder on this one (*Rio*) than for example *Ice Age*. In *Ice Age* it was a world that we introduced. We created a neat little package: these are the characters, this is the world that we want to come up with, this is the story that we want to tell. So I focused more on the creation of that element without the responsibility of trying to be true to anything, or trying to be true to an existing culture.

In *Rio* I'm dealing with a world and a culture that exists, a culture that I am a part of, and at the same time a culture that I need to be detached from if I want to convey it to the world. So, I couldn't be focused on what my childhood experience was, because that doesn't always apply to a childhood experience of a kid in France or in the United States. I have to find what are the common aspects of this world, of this culture, that would translate well to a global audience. I have to insert a foreigner's eye into the story. I've always tried to find a balance. What is authentic? What is stereotypical? What is good? What can I understand because I'm from there? What can't I understand? So it's been much more difficult than the other pictures.

Tom: While dealing with this concept that you are personally invested in, how do you maintain that single vision of yours when bringing in writers, story artists, people who are coming completely from the outside?

Carlos: The project has been much harder than the other ones because 99 percent of the crew has never been to Rio de Janeiro, or have a very limited notion of what Brazil is all about. It puts a lot more of a burden on me to try to convey what I want to tell, and that has to be reflected in the writing. It's simple things like words. When they try to put foreign words in, they put it in Spanish, but we speak Portuguese. I had to pass my knowledge along without destroying their creative process. It's very hard for them to contribute to the process because I have it all in my head, and I have to find a way to convey even a simple thing like building a sidewalk in *Rio*. I have to explain Brazilians built their sidewalks with mosaics of rocks instead of poured concrete, so it looks different than their idea of a sidewalk, et cetera.

We actually took a small crew to Rio for Carnival (*Carnaval* in Brazilian): the art director, the head of story (storyboards), the writers, the producer, the head of animation. We all went to Rio for a five-day extravaganza. When we arrived we hit the ground running. I tried to take them to the locations that I wanted to shoot, so they could understand the geography. I kept saying, you can't have a sequence here and then all of sudden, two minutes later, be over there. We were talking about completely opposite sides of town, so I drove them to all the locations. Some of the guys went hang gliding. We went to the carnival parade. We managed to do a lot of fun stuff that related to the movie. When we came back, I didn't have to explain the world so much anymore. Now the art director knew the lighting; now they knew the locations. I think it's very important to immerse yourself. To avoid the stereotypes, or if you use the stereotypes, to use them in a proper way so it doesn't become a caricature of what you're trying to say.

Tom: Have you discovered anything new about Rio de Janeiro through the eyes of your creative team?

Carlos: Yes. I did. I wanted them all to be like my main protagonist, Blu, the macaw from the Midwest, because they had never been to Rio. Every little thing for me that is second nature, like sidewalks, or the way people dressed, the way people go to the beach, the way people move around, the way the people talk, little things [like] that. Things that I just don't pay attention to, for them, were new. Flavors that they discovered—you know, habits that for me were natural—were awkward. When we all went to the Carnaval parade, we all had to wear a costume and we had to be basically half-naked. We were used to being in the office together with our jackets and coats. Now suddenly we had feathers on and crazy costumes all around us and we're partying and in the parade! It was weird! [laughs]

We all went to the beach one morning just to observe. We took a camera with us so we were shooting people on the beach. I think that broke stereotypes. One of my guys said to me, "Oh no, we can't go to the beach! Everybody's gonna be beautiful and gorgeous and we're gonna stand out." I reassured them, "Guys, don't worry about it. The beach is as democratic as you can think of. You're gonna see the most beautiful person here, and you're gonna see the ugliest one there, or you're gonna see an old lady in a thong. All the extremes will be there." And when we got down to the beach, they [the crew] were having the best time of their lives spotting the different kinds of people. That was something that was much more fun to discover through their eyes.

Tom: In the process of directing, what was the most bizarre, absurd moment you've had as a director?

Carlos: I've seen myself in embarrassing situations just for the good of the project. Carnival was interesting, because *Rio* is so close to home. It's so close to my heart that I was terrified of the trip. What if they [the crew] don't like it? If they didn't like it, it could make the process of making the movie tough. How am I gonna get them to do something fun, if they themselves didn't think it was fun? How can they create something beautiful if they didn't think it was beautiful?

But in the end the experience was much more satisfying for them than they ever expected, and Carnaval was a big part of it. I showed them videos, but because they had never been there, they never felt the sensation of being in a parade with 60,000 people watching and cheering and celebrating and dancing from nine at night till five in the morning nonstop. They and I were impressed. You know, I grew up with that stuff, but I never actually had been to a parade.

Tom: You never danced in the Carnaval before?

Carlos: No, I never did. My sister did, my friends did, but I never personally did it. So, I was a first-timer the same way that they were. I was terrified that they would not enjoy it. At two in the morning we were standing up, waiting, very hot, waiting for our turn to go parade in these awkward costumes. They're heavy and cumbersome, even a little painful. We were like, "Okay, let's give it a shot!" And then we went in and it was a great moment. It united us. It was towards the end of the trip and at the end we were all celebrating, "We did it! We went through the parade." It was very, very fun. But it was awkward to be next to my story artist, the head of animation, the writers, half-naked, dancing at Carnaval! [laughs]

Tom: It's funny 'cause most animation people probably have their impressions of Rio de Janeiro formed from watching Disney's *Saludos Amigos* or *Three Caballeros*.

Carlos: Yeah, well, it's a completely different place, you know. I tried to make sure that I gave them as much exposure to key elements as possible. You cannot discover Rio in five days, but you can pretty much get a sense of what you are looking for, the vibe that you're looking for, the energy that you're looking for in a movie, colors and everything. It was a great experience.

Tom: How did you approach *Rio 2*?

Carlos: When I started *Rio 2*, I wanted to continue the story. When I created Blu and Jewel, they were the last of their kind. Now I wanted to tell the story of them and their family, their kids, et cetera. I wanted them to find more of their kind. I wanted to evolve their designs and create new characters. I also wanted to get them out of the city.

Tom: How did you approach Blu and Jewel as characters for the sequel?

Carlos: It's what I like about doing a sequel. I know these characters. Now I can evolve them outside their comfort zones. That they don't stay the same. They are growing as well.

Development art, *Rio 2*, 2014 © Twentieth Century Fox. All Rights Reserved.

Tom: In the first *Rio* you showed us your city, Rio de Janeiro. *Rio 2* was more about the Amazon jungle.

Carlos: *Rio 1* was in part the portrayal of a city. The city of Rio itself was a character in the film. Now I wanted the jungle to be a character. When I brought my crew to Rio, they were all like Blu. They were alone and out of their element. For *Rio 2*, I wanted to be Blu. So I went to the jungle myself. I had never been. In fact, for many Brazilians, the Amazon is a very faraway place. I wanted to show it is an amazing place, and worthy of preservation. I wanted to show its complexity of life, its harmony. Trees and animals coexisting. It is precious. When people disrupt it and destroy that harmony, it's gone forever. You cannot simply rebuild it again like rebuilding more buildings in a city.

Tom: *Rio 2* has a lot more music in it. How do you approach directing musical numbers?

Carlos: We started working on it right away. We knew the fun part would be the musical numbers. In the first *Rio* we were locked into a certain amount of physical reality. Being in Rio. Being in Carnaval. Being in the city. But going from Rio to the Amazon allowed us to explore different rhythms. To let our imaginations go. Some places have been stylized, but I wanted people to feel as if they were in the Amazon, as in the first film they were in Rio.

Development art, *Rio 2*, 2014 © Twentieth Century Fox. All Rights Reserved.

Tom: Getting back to the *Ice Age* films, *Ice Age: Dawn of the Dinosaurs*, as well as *Ice Age: Continental Drift*, had such great success around the world. It surprised everybody in the Hollywood film industry. I mean, it's a good film, like the other *Ice Age* films. But this film was record-breaking in box office, with most of that coming from outside North America. There were long lines at theaters in Latin America. Why do you think this *Ice Age* struck such a chord with international audiences?

Carlos: I don't know. It's an interesting take on the market. For the longest time, studios always thought about the domestic market more than the world market. But the box office then started to take a turn. The world box office grew much more than I think the US did. Countries where you didn't have a lot of penetration suddenly became huge markets. And now a lot of the movies perform better at the box office outside the US. The *Ice Age* movies are a good example.

Tom: Why do you think that?

Carlos: I think because the movie carries a very universal language. The language of animation. Scrat has that old-fashioned way of doing pantomime with no dialogue. He reached the world without words. Another key for the success of *Ice Age* was how each country found their own talent to dub the voices into their language. They evolved quite a bit. Before that you would find dub artists that would do the voiceovers, and it would be the same kind of voices for every movie. But they're now doing casting in their own countries for the voices of the characters, and that made the movies take an extra leap. They're native. Like in Germany, the character for Sid, Otto, is a superstar, and known there now as Sid. Even though he was a very famous comedian prior to the role, now he worked into his comedy shows a bit of imitating Sid. It created this feeling of a local production, not so much an American production in Germany or an American production in Brazil. So it exploded around the world.

Tom: Do you ever run into a creative block? If so, how do you deal with it?

Carlos: Uh, I do. I can't afford them. Sometimes you have two days to come up with something or you have to solve a problem in the next day or so. I rely a lot on my crew to help when I find that I have a creative block. I try to bring the top heads of the studio together and say, "Look guys, I can't solve this. Any light at the end of the tunnel from you guys? Can you help me out?" And usually, in the brainstorm session, something comes out. Might not be the final solution, but at least it allows me to break out of my block and just find a different path. And sometimes it's a matter of coming up with something new to replace what we can't solve. But I've been very successful reaching out to my creative crew and asking them for help. But I do reach that point, you know, sometimes you're thinking of so many things or you're so stressed that you're just kind of like, "Argh, I don't know what to do!" [laughs]

Tom: I hear you on that. How often do you look at your individual sequence reels instead of the entire movie?

Carlos: I work on the sequences on a daily basis. I usually look at the whole movie maybe once a month, or when I have to prepare for a screening. My goal is to have as much of the movie up on reels as soon as I can, before production starts. But in reality, we have to start production while still finessing the script and the story. It's not the ideal scenario, but our schedules are so tight we usually don't have another option. What we try to do is fast track in production the sequences that we think will stick, and hope the story won't change too much.

Tom: At Walt Disney feature, we used to call that "feeding the beast." Putting sequences into production early so you don't have a lot of artists sitting around idle.

Carlos: Yeah, we're getting that increasingly. Part of it is, I think, because of the successes of our movies there's an expectation. It's the price you pay for maybe doing something right. Even before you start creating, they already have interest in whatever's coming out of your head. So nowadays, with the explosion of animation in the market, they have to start thinking way earlier. When there were only five animated movies a year you could take your time. There was not a lot of competition. Now it's like sixteen movies a year, you know.

Tom: Twenty-one last year (2012).

Carlos: It's insane. You pretty much have more than one movie a month out there. So the markets are going crazy. We've become [a] huge focus of promotional partners because of *Ice Age*. The minute that I said I was making a movie about Rio, we got our groups together and everybody was eager to start.

Tom: As a director, you're not only an artist but also a commander on a battlefield. You also have to be a bit of a salesman and diplomat to deal with the notes from above. How do you handle the studio creative execs?

Carlos: I understand that even though the idea might come from me or the concepts might come from me, once I put it out there and it gets taken, it becomes ours. Not theirs or mine. It becomes a collective project. So I never go into a project with a false impression that, "Close the door. I am creating!" I have to expose myself even more than I wish I could. But at the same time I'm aware of that. I prepare myself when I go into a project, knowing that there will be notes, there will be presentations, there will be conflict. But that also might be valuable. There might be some good discoveries and someone from upstairs could be my ally. I never treat the process as being Us vs. Them. I try to avoid labels and avoid conflict as much as I can, because it damages more than helps. Sometimes there are moments that I wish I didn't have to go through, and sometimes I can't wait for the moment that I can share. But it's a known process. I don't get surprised—"[gasp] Oh my

God, I have to show the movie? Oh my God, I got notes?" [laughs]. I also share the movie with the crew and I know I will get 300 pages of notes from everybody. Some notes are good, some notes are like, "Okay, are you sure you're watching the same movie I'm watching?" But it is important. It's part of the process.

Tom: Do you ever feel pressured to outdo what you have done before, sort of like Steven Spielberg after *Jurassic Park* (1993)? Every movie of his now has to be more successful than the last.

Carlos: If you go through the history of many film directors, it's not always consistent. You get some great gems, and then you get some that are not so good. I try to battle it every time, but I'm quite aware of that possibility. I'm very realistic about it.

Tom: Let's get back to some of the earlier stuff that got you started. Who were some of the artists that inspired you?

Carlos: I wasn't exposed to art as much as I wish I could have been. I always enjoyed Chuck Jones cartoons and Walt Disney stories. There are animated films that always get stuck in my head. *Bambi* has this whole chunk of my life. The fire in the forest I remember as a kid, when the father comes in and reveals the death of the mother ... I like that kind of moment. A coming-of-age moment for Bambi. It always felt powerful to me. Then there's that emotional moment of *Dumbo* and his mom when they must separate. There's all these great visual moments that get stuck in my head. Scary, emotional, or comedic. *Dumbo*, *Pinocchio*, and *Bambi*, that trio of movies, stay much more vivid in my head than, say, for example, *Snow White* or some of the other classics from Disney, like *Sleeping Beauty*. Those don't stick in my head as much as those three movies do, character-wise.

Tom: Yeah, they kind of reach inside and touch you on an emotional level.

Carlos: I think so. I love movies, I've seen a lot of them. But, again, I keep going back to the most classic, like *Blade Runner* (1982). I think it's the only movie that I watched over thirty times. [laughs] I still like it today. If I'm flipping through the channels and that movie is playing, I have to stop and watch it. I can't help it. One day, I want to make a movie like that. Sci-fi. Oh, I'm crazy about sci-fi, like *Star Wars*, all that kind of stuff. It's got all the elements that I want.

Ron: Any other people whose work you admire?

Carlos: Because I've always been at Blue Sky, I never got too exposed to other studios. I admire a lot of the directors out there. I see what they're doing and try to be inspired by cinematographers and animators. John Lasseter is somebody special. I have a special feeling for him because I remember being inspired by his short *Luxo, Jr.* I remember the first year I was at Blue Sky. I was a newbie and Chris Wedge was very good friends with John. That year there was a big SIGGRAPH convention (annual computer animation society convention). It was my first SIGGRAPH. I was so excited. We came to LA and there was a Disney party. And I was like, "Oh gosh, a Disney party! We can go to a Disney party!" And when we were there, at Disneyland, they had closed down Typhoon Lagoon to the public just for our party. I went with Chris and I remember it was at one of the rides. Suddenly John Lasseter was right there. I was so nervous when I shook his hand. I was thinking, "Wow, this is great! Three years ago when I was in Brazil packing my bags, trying to come to the United States, I never thought I would even pass close to somebody like that!" It was one of those little moments that I still remember, you know, as silly it might be. It was cool. I admire Brad Bird quite a bit, too. I think his projects are brilliant. I remember going to a screening of *Iron Giant* in New York. The movie wasn't fully finished yet, but we got invited because one of our producers had worked on it. Brad was there and I remember going through that experience, "Wow, I wish one day I could have a movie playing …" I admire those guys for the milestones that they set in animation. I can always look at their work and be blown away by what they can do.

Tom: Do you now mentor young people yourself?

Carlos: When I was studying animation at SVA, I started to teach to make my tuition more manageable. I enjoyed it so much I continued it even after I started working at Blue Sky. I always felt it was a great way to interact with the animators and hopefully mentor them in their creative process. Actually, the best part of it was that I was also inspired by their ideas and excitement for the craft. Unfortunately I don't teach anymore, but I feel that at Blue Sky or at the talks I give at festivals I am able to continue to influence or inspire new talent.

Tom: You started as an animator. Do you ever miss animating?

Carlos: I do. Sometimes I catch myself thinking, how would I animate that shot? But now I'm so rusty that I'm terrified of the idea. The animators that I have now are so much better than I was. [laughs] I can remember my thinking process when I went through animation, like the curves and the way to play with the timing. I still have the presets in my head. After a while it just comes to you second nature. You know how to achieve a hand gesture or a head take. I still have those in my head, and I keep thinking, "Will that still work? If I tried to sit down and do it?"

Tom: CG animation today is this kind of technological arms race. Every year, there seems to be new software and programs that are faster and more powerful. How important do you feel it is to be personally on top of the latest gadgetry, or are you at the point now where you can tell the animators what you need?

Carlos: I kind of gave up that quest for knowing everything awhile back, I think maybe on *Ice Age: The Meltdown*, because I couldn't keep up. So I focused on trying to keep the essence of what my knowledge is and not try to work it all out myself. I just let it be up to them, animators and tech support, to discover.

Ron: What you are trying to achieve as a filmmaker is telling good stories. As you mentioned, *Rio* is the first movie of your own creation that really reflects your personal vision. When it comes to story, is there a theme that you are looking to express, some kind of underling concept that you want to show?

Carlos: When I think about a story, I always start thinking about the emotional drive behind it. What is the pathos that you get from the character? How do you relate your life to their lives?

But I always try to take a light-hearted approach to it. I have a hard time conceiving something too dark. Not that I don't enjoy dark stories, I love them, but when I create something in my head, I just don't go there naturally. Tim Burton does it beautifully, and I love his movies. They are a perfect combination of darkness, fun, and emotion. I love his creative take on it. My creative process tends to be much more animated, less dialogue, much more [swashbuckling] fun. A lot of movement, a lot of contraptions, a lot of fun stuff to do. I always look at Charlie Chaplin and Buster Keaton as my reference for animation.

Tom: It's interesting that when we talked about this to Chris Wedge, he talked a lot about giving the audience a good experience. It's something that the audience will enjoy, and then you reiterate that theme in terms of broad audience appeal.

Carlos: I start a project with that in mind. You are making a movie as a collaborative effort with the studio. The end goal for all of us is a successful piece of work that our audience will enjoy. It's important for me to feel like I've made something I can stand behind and believe in. I always feel like the movie is somewhat mine. My creative juices go into it. The movie comes from my head, and from my creative team. But I'm always making the movie for a broad audience, not just America, not just Brazil, but for the world. I'm aware of my responsibilities, both to myself and to the audience.

That's why I'm a super fan of shorts. That's what I tell students when they come to me. I say, "Do a short movie and put your heart and soul into it. That will probably be the only time that you'll make a movie that is 100 percent yours." I still look at my old reels and I think, "Even though it's not perfect, the animation is not great, and the story could be better, it's still my baby. Who cares? It's an ugly baby, but I love my baby!" [laughs] So I have pride in that. I take pride in the struggle. I take pride in being able to do something without a lot of help.

Tom: Is there a short film you've seen in your past that might stand out as a classic?

Carlos: A short movie that I have close to my heart is something that represents a milestone in my creative process and my transition to computers. It was *Luxo, Jr.*, John Lasseter's short. When I saw that movie, in my head all the possibilities opened up. I could create a simple story. I could make inanimate objects come to life and make it look realistic. The fun, the comedy, and the emotion were packed into that little movie. It was short, sweet, and great to look at. Every time I look at that movie I feel a little nostalgia. It's how I got started. This is how I got excited about computer animation. And it gave me enough juice to go after my dream to become a director.

Tom: You have directed several films now. How have you evolved as a filmmaker?

Carlos: Every film you make feels like it's your first. Each time I'm thinking, "Holy shit! How am I gonna do this?" [laughs] It doesn't get easier, because every new movie you want to be better than the previous ones. But I am completely happy with that in myself. I think over the years I have become better at fighting for what I want in a picture. You can't put things in a movie that you do not like, because you are going to have to live with that film for years after. I think I am better at determining what kind of movie I want to make.

Tom: Do you have any closing thoughts on directing?

Carlos: I admire the directors that come from artistic backgrounds, like the guys that came from life drawing, or music, or those kinds of backgrounds. I didn't come from that kind of background. I was never trained on paper. I could never draw too well. To my parents I was Picasso! But for myself, I wasn't like the animators that could draw those beautiful pictures. I could never do it. I was never trained to do it. I always felt a bit embarrassed about it. Originally, I came from a technical background. When I sat down at the computer I could model something or could create something that was in my head without compromises. I just made it. It was easy. I said, "WOW! This is the tool I need to be creative. I don't need to draw.

I need to work on the computer." That is why I was so happy when I discovered computer animation, because I could act on a lot of instinct that was my own. It's a natural ability that might not be as polished or maybe not as perfect technically. But I have a gut feeling, and I made that part of my creative process. I have to trust, even with all the forces that work around all the notes; the crew, and me. I have to make sure my gut instinct remains intact. That's how I became what I am, by simply trusting in what I thought was aesthetically right. And it paid off. All the times that I had to second-guess, everything became mushy and I wasn't as connected to it. So I strive to preserve that first look.

Tom: Well, great, that's wonderful. We are done. *Obrigado.*

Carlos: *De nada.*

Carlos Saldanha, *Rio*, 2011 © Twentieth Century Fox. All Rights Reserved.

11
Kevin Lima Interview

Kevin Lima *Enchanted* © Disney.

When word got out that Kevin Lima was chosen to direct *A Goofy Movie*, a lot of us had the same reaction: "Kevin's a good animator, so he'll make a good director." But Kevin was bringing a lot more to the table than his time behind the drawing disc.

As we all eventually learned, this upbeat, positive guy had a remarkable personal story and a very unusual pathway to success. He not only embodied the essential qualities of the animation journeyman, but touched on a lot of other skills, from character designer to storyboarding to animating. All of these accomplishments added to his quiver of talents, but none of them satisfying his creative goals.

Directing *Goofy* became his revelation. He found that those years spent working his way through the hands-on pipeline of production were the perfect foundation for directing animation. On the relatively low-budget *Goofy* movie, he was given a rare freedom to make most of the decisions, and he loved it.

But Kevin discovered that the talent that would ultimately bring him the most success was not one that he had learned through experience or "pencil mileage," but one that came by pure instinct: his natural empathy with performers.

It's amusing to hear him assert that he had absolutely no training that qualified him to direct a live-action film (*102 Dalmatians*), but in that evaluation he echoes the experience of every director in this book. The qualities of the veteran animation director, from visualizing imagery to expressing a powerful, personal vision, are essential ingredients of success. But no amount of work or practice can supply that elusive ingredient of talent. Kevin has that sensitivity, and sensibility, to create an entrancing performance.

We interviewed Kevin at Pixar Animation Studios.

Bill Kroyer

Bill: When did you first become aware of animation as something that you might see yourself being interested in doing?

Kevin: My interest goes way back. I can't remember a time when I wasn't interested, to be quite honest with you. My mom tells a story about how I went to see *The Jungle Book* with her, and when the movie was over I turned to her and said, "That's what I'm going to do when I grow up!" And she kind of nodded and said, "Yeah, yeah, that's great, Kevin. You just go ahead and do that." I think I was five. And here I am today, having followed that dream. I was one of those rare kids that drew from the time … you know I can't remember not drawing. I can't remember not being creative. I can't remember not wanting to be in animation.

Bill: Where did you grow up?

Kevin: We lived in Pawtucket, Rhode Island, a little mill town just north of Providence. And we were fairly poor. We didn't have much money at all. My mom worked at the toy company Hasbro when I was a kid. I used to ride my bike to the Hasbro factory on a Sunday morning and jump the fence and dig through the trash compactor to see if I could find discarded toys. My grandmother was really influential in that she was the one who was always encouraging me to be an artist. She was the one who spent time with me because my parents were both working. She got me into puppetry pretty early on, so at a very young age—I was about twelve—I became a puppeteer. I made all of my own puppets, I wrote the shows and did all of the voices. So I've always, always had a storytelling streak.

Bill: When did you start figuring out how animation was done?

Kevin: I didn't make films. I didn't have the money to make films. So I went into puppetry pretty heavily. At the age of fourteen I joined a professional puppetry troupe in Rhode Island called *The Puppet Workshop*. I was their intern. I started directing the shows at age sixteen. And then in high school, I had an art teacher, Mr. Venditto, who said, "You know what? You should really follow your love of cartooning and go into animation." He was the one who did the research and found CalArts for me. But my first year of college, I didn't go. My first year out of high school I said, "No. I'm gonna go into theater." I had caught the theater bug. I went to Emerson College in Boston, spent a year attempting to act and said, "This isn't the life for

Kevin Lima at CalArts.

me. I can't do this." And in the second semester of that year applied to CalArts and got in. Basically what I did for my portfolio was design a film. I didn't shoot the film, but I designed the film, designed all the characters, and drew a little storyboard. And it was my only hope. If I didn't get in at CalArts, I didn't know what I was gonna do.

Bill: Was it the only place you applied?

Kevin: It was the only place I applied.

Bill: So you show up for fall semester, you've never been there …

Kevin: I'd never animated! I knew the basic principles from having drawn from the Preston Blair animation book, but I had never animated.

Bill: So how was that year?

Kevin: You know what? It was a phenomenal group of students, I have to say.

Bill: It was that second wave.

Kevin: I was in the class that graduated just as Disney had stopped hiring new talent. I was at the end of the big first Disney push to hire animators. Rob Minkoff was there, Gary Trousdale, Gary Conrad, Chris Bailey, and Kelly Asbury were in the class ahead of me. My classmates were Kirk Wise, Tim Hauser, Dan Jeup, Steve Moore, and Fred Kline. And we were all very determined students. We said to ourselves, "We're gonna be somebody." And it's amazing; you look at that group of people and see how many of them have actually made movies. It's a phenomenal number of successful, talented artists.

Bill: Talk a little bit about your learning experience at CalArts. You'd never animated. Did you pick it up fast?

Kevin: I had some draftsmanship skills, so I could draw, a bit, which made it a little easier. But I'll tell you, we all learned from each other. And that was tough. I was talking about this the other day with someone who went to college at Sheridan. They started learning the basics from the first day they showed up at school. A bouncing ball, animating a potato sack, all that stuff. We didn't learn any of that! When we got to school, they threw a cleaned-up scene at you and said, "Inbetween this scene." And most of us had never done anything like that before. So we'd inbetween the scene, shoot it on the Lion Lamb videotape recorder, and we all thought we were geniuses 'cause we could put a line between two other lines. There was one kid in my class, Dan Jeup, who came in knowing quite a bit. While in high school, Dan had written to and started a relationship with one of the nine old men, Eric Larson. So he knew a bunch, and he taught us a bunch. And the upperclassmen taught us a bunch. We really didn't have an animation teacher, per se, and we just sort of struggled through it, learning from each other.

Bill: And you made films, right?

Kevin: We all made films. I think I made three films in my four years.

Let's Misbehave.

Bill: So the undergraduates felt you were a reasonably decent animator?

Kevin: I didn't think I was any good. But I thought I could handle it. I got lucky. In my fourth year, we all worked freelance at the Disney studio on a project called *Sport Goofy*. I was assigned Chris Buck as a supervising animator, and he basically put me through animation boot camp. The project was giving us scenes and treating us like we were animators, but very few of us had ever animated professionally.

Bill: When you graduated, what did you do?

Kevin: I went to work on *The Brave Little Toaster*. It's the first full-time job I had in animation, with Jerry Rees directing. It was a bunch of kids like me makin' a film. Joe Ranft was there. Randy Cartwright was there. Rebecca Rees and Brian McEntee were there. And I got really lucky because Jerry let me do some character design. After five or six months of designing in LA, I went to Taiwan for six months.

Bill: Were you animating?

Kevin: I had designed the characters so they thought, "Oh, he knows how to put them together, so let's have him animate." So I animated a bunch of it. My first experience and I'm trying to animate thirty feet a week!

Bill: Thirty feet a week!?

Kevin: That was rough! But it was a grand adventure. I got to go to a new country, something I never thought I'd do. I thought I'd be sitting at Disney in one of those cushy little offices, but nope! Out into the world and making it happen.

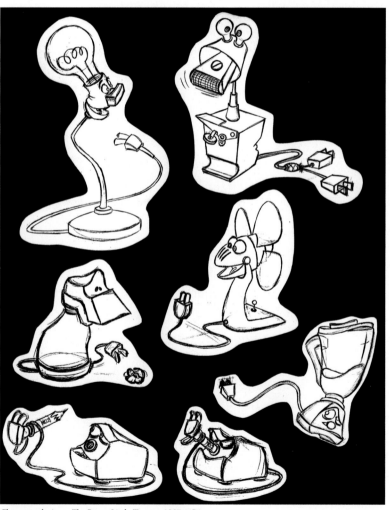

Character designs, *The Brave Little Toaster*, 1987 © Disney.

Bill: So *Toaster* is over, what happens then?

Kevin: *Toaster*'s over, and Jerry Rees is developing future projects at Hyperion, three or four different films, but none of them caught fire. So I went to work on *The Chipmunk Adventure* with the Bagdasarians.

Bill: Oh, that's right, Sue [Kroyer] was there. And …

Kevin: Sue was there, yep. And Glen Keane! And it was a big break for me because I got to animate some Chipette scenes, they're the female Chipmunks, under the tutelage of Glen Keane. It was humbling because I actually thought I knew something at this point. I had been to Taiwan and I had animated thirty feet a week! I'm bringing my scenes to Glen Keane and suddenly you realize, you don't know anything. You're back at square one. I had received such minimal training and I was struggling through, just basically making it up to meet each deadline. Each scene was a brand new experience. I had no chops.

Bill: It's just as valuable to learn what you don't know. To know how far there is left for you to go.

Kevin: To be quite honest with you, I get that lesson every single day. Even what I'm doing right now, directing live action, I realize, "Boy, I just know so little!"

Bill: Did Glen's style, that aspect of entertainment animation, that sophistication, did that start to get through to you at that point?

Kevin: I was overwhelmed working with Glen. His craft, his ability to draw; his ability to act was overwhelming. He could draw anything from any angle and I couldn't do that. The eternal struggle of being an animator is how you take what you see in your mind's eye and have it come through your hand into a pencil onto the paper. How do you communicate it in a way that everyone else understands? I was really lucky having worked with Glen. Not only that every day was a master class in animation, but when he went back to Disney, he said to the management, "You should hire this kid."

Bill: And that's how you went back.

Kevin: Well, I was never there to begin with. I was in that first class at Disney that no one was hired by the studio. So, I just took all the drawings I had done up to that point, put them into a portfolio, and I handed it in, and their reaction was, "Where have you been?" I remember, I was told Ed Hansen, the production administrator at the time, at Disney, asked at a portfolio review, "Where has this kid been all these years? Why don't we know about him?" Well, I was at CalArts and you looked at my portfolio and you rejected me. That's where I've been! So I was hired to work on *Oliver & Company* as an animator.

Bill: And you were paid an assistant salary?

Kevin: I was happy to be paid at all. And it was slow at the beginning on *Oliver*, so I got a lucky break, and got to do a bunch of character designs on *The Little Mermaid* for directors John Musker and Ron Clements, which was great. Once animation on

Oliver got up and running, I went to work full time as an animator and struggled, and struggled. I was one of those guys that, you know, was doing one point five feet of film a week at Disney.

Bill: Not quite thirty feet a week …

Kevin: And sitting behind that desk, day and night, trying to pull it together. Trying to figure out how to make it work at Disney. I was kind of in trouble. Trying to figure out who I was, and is this really what I wanted? Am I doing the thing that I had dreamed about? Is it what I thought it would be? Only getting to work on this one little sliver of something? As opposed to when I was a kid, designing and directing a whole puppet show, a forty-five minute performance!

Bill: So how long did you stay on *Oliver*?

Kevin: I worked on the whole movie. Then I said, "You know, I'm not having a good time. I'm not happy. I'm not fast. You're not happy with me. Can I do something else?" And that's when Mike Gabriel and Hendel Butoy took me on board *The Rescuers Down Under* as character designer.

Bill: Is that where you met Brenda?

Kevin: No, Brenda and I met at school. I was a senior and she was a freshman.

Bill: But you got married on *Rescuers*.

Kevin: We got married while we were both working on *The Rescuers Down Under*. In 1988. Yeah, designing away and having basically the time of my life, to be quite honest with you, having a really good time. I love to develop character, to have it all come together in one drawing, to not be limited by your ability to act with a pencil! Not just to breathe life into something over many drawings, but to look at one drawing and create a personality. That was easier for me.

Brenda Chapman and Kevin Lima.

Bill: Very directorial.

Kevin: It is. You have much more control over the moment. You're not being handed something and being told what to do. You're there at the birth of something extraordinary.

Bill: So *Rescuers* finishes …

Kevin: I went into development for a little while. Worked a little bit on the very beginnings of *The Lion King* and on a couple of different titles in development. And then *Aladdin* came along and I took on a new challenge and became part of the story team. I became a storyboard artist. I think you can sort of sense a theme here of not being able to stay with one thing for very long. So I traveled from one thing to another to another, and I'd last a good year and a half, two years on each endeavor, then totally burn out and be looking for the next thing. So, at this point I became a story artist on *Aladdin*. I really enjoyed it. I had done character design at the beginning of *Aladdin*, and then I took those characters and started to explore them in a story context. I had gotten to know Howard Ashman a little bit while exploring character designs of Ursula on *The Little Mermaid*. I was really into musical theater, so I approached him and got to know him a bit. On *Aladdin* I was lucky enough to get to storyboard a couple of songs that he and Alan Menken had written for the movie, and that was a great thrill. When that was done I said, "Okay, what's next?"

Character design, Ursula, Kevin Lima, *The Little Mermaid*, 1989 © Disney.

Bill: You're going through director boot camp here. You're animating, you're designing, you're storyboarding …

Kevin: I only realized that at the end of the road. I had no idea I was doing that, collecting a full education, as I was doing it. I realized while working on *Aladdin* that I "wanna do it all!" After *Aladdin*, I had started animating on an Epcot film called *Cranium Command*. While struggling to animate again, I met a Production Assistant on the project, Kevin Traxler, who was producing community theatre. He approached me and asked, "Hey, you wanna direct a show?" So I ended up directing a community theatre version of *Into the Woods*, the musical by Stephen Sondheim and James Lapine. And when it was done, I thought, "Boy, this is so much more exciting and immediate!" And the folks at Disney all came out and saw it. And I said to myself, "Ah, this is my moment." And I went to the executive group, the folks that controlled all of our futures at Disney, and proclaimed, "I wanna direct! That's what I wanna do; that's my next step." And they basically said to me, "You know, Kev, there's no room at the inn. There are no movies for you to direct. We don't have a spot." So I said, "Okay. See you later." And I left, went out into the big world trying to find another inn. I approached Tom Wilhite at Hyperion Studios, where I had worked on *The Brave Little Toaster*, and said, "Hey, do you have anything going on?" And he said, "Yeah, come on! Let's develop some stuff." But nothing ever got off the ground. And then I did some freelance storyboard work for Jerry Rees on a project over at Disney Television. And when Jerry decided not to direct it, they asked me.

Bill: And that was …?

Kevin: *A Goofy Movie.*

Bill: Back at Disney. Now you get your chance to direct.

Kevin: I'm directing.

Bill: And what crew were they going to give you on that? Not Disney Feature Animation …

Kevin: No, no. *A Goofy Movie* was a television animation project and I moved to Paris for close to a year to animate that movie.

Bill: That's right, they did it in Paris.

Kevin: We storyboarded the whole thing stateside and then brought it to Paris for production. And I lived there and dealt with the hardships of living in Paris? Come on! You could be in a lot worse places. And I had the privilege of working with a great group of talented people, who I continued to work with on all of the animated projects that I've been on. And we made this little teeny movie for no money and I got my directorial debut.

Bill: You were your own head of story, right?

Kevin: While in the states storyboarding the film, I worked with Brian Pimental, my head of story and between the two of us we tackled a difficult subject. The goal for me was to create a different kind of animated film. I thought: why can't we make a movie that feels like a John Hughes movie? Why can't we do something that's purely character-based with a modern thread, with a modern dynamic between our characters? And it just happens that your lead is Goofy.

Character design, Kevin Lima, *Aladdin*, 1992 © Disney.

Bill: Because it was a lower budget film, did you have a lot of creative freedom?

Kevin: Yeah. I really felt like I was running the show. I was a singular director. It wasn't a team of directors, as there had always seemed to be on the Disney features. And in fact, maybe it made it harder for me later on, when I moved up to play with the big boys. I got to decide everything. I got to choose my cast. I got to pick my songwriters. If I was dissatisfied with where the story was going, then I was the one responsible for standing up for it and saying, "This isn't working yet."

Bill: This is under Jeffrey [Katzenberg], am I right?

Kevin: Yeah. Jeffrey is still at Disney at this point. And I'd show the film to Jeffrey, usually at 7:30 in the morning. You know, [laughs] it wasn't that bad. I didn't have to come in on Sundays. And he had his notes, but because we were so low budget, he knew there was barely anything he could do. I remember at one point he wanted to change the climax of the film because it wasn't exciting enough for him. So we sat together at the Avid, and it ended up staying exactly the way it was. 'Cause he'd take stuff out and try to move stuff around, and because we couldn't afford to add animation, he agreed, "Yeah, your way is better."

Bill: Language problems in Paris?

Kevin: No. I have some acting ability. So when I couldn't speak to somebody with words, I would act it out. And it's typically what I'd always done anyway, you know? I even do it when I'm directing live action. So, I talk to Amy Adams and I'm acting like Giselle, and the guys behind the camera are flipping the camera on to catch footage of me going around with my little pinkies up. But that's what I do. I talk to them as actors, and the easiest way is to "become." I was able to wear the character while directing.

Kevin Lima directing Glen Close, *102 Dalmations*, 2000 © Disney.

Bill: That was your first experience actually directing a crew of animators.

Kevin: That was.

Bill: So your style is more like directing as an actor than directing like an animator.

Kevin: It was. I didn't tell people how many drawings needed to be from "here to here," or "there's not enough cushion." I didn't do any of that. I never tell an actor to put their hand "up here" and then "Let your wrist lead as you slap him across the face!" I would never do that. It's more about the subtext and what's happening inside and how do we take what's happening inside and make it external? How do we communicate ideas? In fact, it's how I became a live-action director. When I was directing Glenn Close in *Tarzan* she said, "You know, you direct more like a live-action director than an animation director. Have you ever thought about doing a live-action film?" I answered immediately, "Sure!" And when *102 Dalmatians* lost its director late in preproduction, and I was out looking for a directing gig, she asked the studio, "What about Kevin?"

Bill: Glenn Close got you the gig?

Kevin: Yep.

Bill: You have no formal training.

Kevin: I have no formal director training. There are days I wish I had a mentor I'll tell ya. There are days I bemoan, "Boy, I wish I had hounded Robert Zemeckis and gotten him to let me sit on the set with him." You hear about all those guys who got their chops directing television and working under some of the best directors in the business and really learned

Tarzan, 1999 © 1999 Burroughs and Disney.
Tarzan® Owned by ERB, Inc and Used by Permission.

some craft. I, unfortunately, had to make it up on the floor. So, I have a different skill set. Part of it comes from being a puppeteer and having acted on stage. Working with actors as I did in community theatre. Directing animators. My skill set is what I've picked up along the way.

Bill: On *A Goofy Movie*, your first experience, how did you deal with art direction and production design?

Kevin: You hire the best people. And have an opinion. [laughs]

Bill: That's a good one-liner.

Kevin: We were at a little bit of a disadvantage with *A Goofy Movie*, because the most seasoned people in the business weren't going to leave their high profile gigs to work on *A Goofy Movie*. We gathered a group of talented young artists who, like me, were in need of an opportunity. As we dove into making the film, we collected all we had learned individually, color theory, camera psychology, how the pace of three scenes put together can mean more than one scene sitting on its own, and put it all to practice.

Bill: So when the movie is over, now you have the director bug?

Kevin: Yeah, I was definitely bitten. At this point, Jeffrey Katzenberg still at Disney before starting DreamWorks Animation, asks me to do *Tarzan*. But he wants me to do it in a new studio that they're going to open in Vancouver, Canada. And I said to him, "Jeffrey, come on. With a new group of folks in Paris we could barely animate *Goofy*. How do you expect me to animate a naked man?"

Tarzan, 1999 © 1999 Burroughs and Disney.
Tarzan ® Owned by ERB, Inc and Used by Permission.

Bill: [laughs]

Kevin: And we were talking about that when Jeffrey left. And Michael Eisner, I think to keep me from following Jeffrey, called me in and said, "We're going to make *Tarzan*. We want you to direct it." So another opportunity comes my way.

Bill: And when did Chris Buck come on the project?

Kevin: From the beginning I said, "I want to direct *Tarzan* alone." And they said, "We don't do that here at Feature Animation. We always have a team. It's too much work for one person to do." And I looked around and thought, "Who can I stand being with for four or five years? Who would be a good match?" In the same way that you choose your wife, this is gonna be your professional wife, and you're gonna live with this person; you're gonna have to share a vision. It's hard enough for one person to have a vision. How do two people share a vision? I knew that I wasn't gonna be able to give up any piece of the process, you know? I knew that I was gonna want to look at every piece of art and be a part of the discussion on everything. So I was thinking, who is that guy? I had worked with Chris twice before and we were friends, so I thought, "he and I could do this." We've always shared a sensibility. We've always had great, honest conversations about so many different topics. So I asked him. And I said, "But this is how it's got to work. We're both going to be involved in everything."

Bill: What was the toughest part of that movie? You went to Africa.

Kevin: That was not the toughest part of making the movie. Yes, we went to Kenya and Uganda and sat with the mountain gorillas in the Bwindi Impenetrable National Park.

Bill: Worth the trip?

Kevin: It awakened my sense of the natural world around me and I realized while I was trudging through the jungle that the world could be a character within the movie in a way that I'd never really thought about before. And while in Uganda, Dan St. Pierre and I started the conversation about Deep Canvas, a process created specifically for *Tarzan*. All those conversations started in Africa. We talked about, How do you put the characters in the world? How do you create a sense that you could step through the picture plane into the world; that you weren't watching it from afar? Maybe that conversation would never have happened if we hadn't gone on that trip. Sure, we could have animated gorillas; we could have looked at footage of gorillas and figured that out. But to actually feel what it was like to be in that place and step on that ground, influenced so much. Jane's entrance in that movie, of being totally out of sorts, comes from our trip. 'Cause we were trudging through the jungle and it was difficult.

Bill: So you're given an assignment to picture it, but it's not an original vision yet. You need to find the vision …

Kevin: The vision started with the book by Edgar Rice Burroughs. But each participant, each collaborator, has to find their own original vision. Getting back to what was the most difficult part of making the film for me. I wanted to direct. But so did everyone else on the picture. Every storyboard artist wants to direct. Every layout artist wants to direct. Every animator wants to direct. Every artist involved wants to direct his piece of the film. He doesn't really want to be directed. I'm gonna be in trouble for saying this, aren't I? [laughs] So, you're fighting ten different people all wanting their imprint on the material, and you're trying to create one vision for a movie. And I got in trouble time and time again, struggling against that. Because I said, "No, no, no. I'm the director. I get to have it my way. I hold the vision for this movie. I can't expand this acting moment because it will throw off the rhythm of the scene. The gorillas can't be purple because it will destroy the sense of realism. I can't let the story go in that direction over there, because it will totally feel like a canker on the side of a movie that's moving in this direction." So I fought to hold onto the directorial vision of the film a lot.

Bill: Was Chris feeling that same struggle that you were feeling?

Kevin: I don't know if he felt it as viscerally as I felt. Looking back at the animation process through the live-action lens, one of the hardest things is pulling together three or four different people to create one character. The designer, the animator, the cleanup artist, the voice talent. Your character is split in four different directions. And I think it's really the job of an animation director to get all of those disciplines synthesized.

Bill: Did you guys ever crash and burn on *Tarzan?*

Kevin: We didn't have a story crash and burn. We had our struggles, but we never threw out half the film and started

Glenn Close, Kevin Lima, *102 Dalmatians*, 2000. © 2000 Disney.

over. I think I got lucky because *The Lion King* stage show was going on at the same time we were producing *Tarzan*. So all those eyes that were typically worrying at your movie were distracted by their new toy. And that new toy is shiny and exciting, and sparkly, you know? And it's more in their wheelhouse. The theater is where they all came from. Most of our leadership came from the theatre, so they were thrilled to be back on the boards. *Tarzan* also happened in the moment when Jeffrey left the studio. Jeffrey is trying desperately to pull away talent. Disney is trying desperately to hold onto talent. So our movie got incredibly expensive. I think we have the honor of being the most expensive 2D animated film ever made.

Bill: *Tarzan*? Really?

Kevin: I'm pretty sure, or at least that's what I was told. Because of the studio's need to not have Jeffrey succeed, artists who were making four thousand dollars a week are now making ten. And that money has gotta come from somewhere, so they added it to *Tarzan*'s budget.

Bill: That's tough.

Kevin: Yeah, I won't take off my shirt and show you the scars. [laughs] The real hardship of that movie was, how do you hold onto a creative vision when the costs are escalating—and escalating in the middle of production?

Bill: Everybody comments how scenes and sequences can be perceived differently as they move through the pipeline. When you finally see it in final color with effects, there's a different vibe to it. Did you have any wonderful surprises or perplexing disappointments in your first big movie?

Kevin: We had an idea to do a song in which the apes took over the human camp, and it turns into this big *Stomp*-esque number. And we thought, "Ah, this will be hugely original. No one's ever done this before in animation!" And we wrote a song with Phil Collins, and we were all really thrilled and happy. And then as it moved through the process, I started to get this pit in my stomach that it wasn't gonna be what I had hoped, that it wasn't gonna be a highlight. We had trouble boarding it. We had this song we loved, we had this idea we thought could be really great, but we had a lot of trouble boarding it. And, tonally, I realized when it was in color, in the final film, that it just didn't speak in the same voice as the rest of the movie.

Bill: But the balance of course is that it was a tremendously successful movie.

Kevin: Yes, the movie did incredibly well.

Bill: So, now you've done a big movie …

Kevin: Yep. And I'm still not satisfied. [laughs]

Bill: You're hoping that Hollywood will call …

Kevin: And it just happens that the stars aligned again for me.

Bill: Glenn Close …

Kevin: That was the Glenn Close recommendation I spoke about earlier. She recommends me to direct *102 Dalmatians* and I thought, "Okay, this is gonna be good because, you know, she'll look out for me. She'll help me." I talked to her about it. I said, "You know, I've never been on a live-action set. I've never done this before. I appreciate you giving me this recommendation, but what I really need is for you to be my teacher."

Bill: You said that to Glenn Close?

Kevin: I did.

Bill: And she said?

Kevin: She said, "I believe in you, let's do it."

Bill: Did she teach you a lot about directing?

Kevin: She taught me a lot about how to interact with actors in the moment on the set. She didn't teach me about cameras or lights or all that other technical stuff, which was also TOTALLY alien to me. In fact, I just sort of said to everyone supporting me, "I need your help." I hired a DP and I said to him, "You know, I've never done this specific process before and need you to educate me." So my first film became my training ground.

Bill: That's a gigantic step from animation director.

Kevin: It was big.

Bill: The whole nomenclature is totally different.

Kevin: Everything about it is different. Everything about it. I mean, what's totally different is that everything leads to this one moment in time, in which you capture something. Whereas in animation, it's not a single moment; it's multiple moments in time that you're hoping will all come together at the end. So it's a completely different sensibility.

Bill: What did Glenn Close tell you about working with actors on the set that was valuable to you?

Kevin: I don't know if there was any specific one thing. What she really taught me was to treat every actor as an individual, understand what that actor needs in that moment. You have to figure out what you need to be for each actor. Do you need to be a therapist and just listen, do you need to be a father and give unconditional love, do you need to be a disciplinarian and, you get it. And what they need may be different on different days. She taught me to look at each actor as an individual and be able to tell when he or she walks on the set, what the dynamic is, what the temperature is for that day, how to change your approach. Don't be totally locked down to only one way of doing something. Treat the process like it's an organic, growing, ever-changing relationship. And I think I already had a little bit of that going on. I think that's what she saw in me during the *Tarzan* voice recording sessions. That I could see when she was struggling with a scene as Kala, and I could make a suggestion that an actor would understand. I could make an acting-based comment as opposed to asking for a result. Which a lot of animation directors do. "It's kind of slow, could you speed it up? Or, "Could you give me another one that's different?" I was asking her for motivations. I was asking her, "Okay, now I want you to come in and I want you to kill the person across from you."

Bill: [chuckle]

Kevin: And she'd come in with a fury. Because that was the subtext of the scene. "I want to KILL you!"

Bill: Do you think those directorial suggestions would be applicable to working with animators as well?

Kevin: For sure. And I was doing it. I didn't know I was doing it. I didn't realize it. I didn't have the formal training to know that actors think in action verbs. And that the scene is made up of a series of action verbs strung together to create conflict and emotion and shape a scene. I didn't know any of that. But I was doing it. So maybe I was lucky in some ways to have picked up some of that. From my year acting at Emerson College and some of it must have come from the years of puppetry I did way back when.

Bill: I imagine you boarded the film, right?

Kevin: We boarded a lot of *102 Dalmatians*. And I found that boarding is one of the tools that I bring over from animation. Being a visual thinker I have to board the film in order to understand the characters and arrive on set prepared to talk to the actors. The boarding is not just about layout for me. It's not just about how the scenes link together, and how the cutting works from scene to scene. It's about, "Who is that character in the moment and how does that character live through the body of the film?" It's hard for me to get that strictly from the written word. I don't know how, honestly, to dissect a script in that way—in the way that an actor would, because I don't have that training. My training is to dissect the film and gain understanding through storyboards. I learned from *102 Dalmatians* … that I have to hold onto the pieces of the animation process that make me successful. I can't let go of those things. They're an important part of who I am as a live-action director. And with *Enchanted*, I storyboarded the entire movie! I storyboarded the movie to understand the characters and their motivations.

Bill: An animation director, when they storyboard, they're automatically thinking of staging, sort of predeciding how that scene is going to be staged and shot in the end. But in live action, how much of that do you find you bring over to the set? Do you actually think, "Oh, I know I'm going to shoot from this angle," or do you shoot the coverage and then decide later?

Kevin: No, I bring all of it to the set and then I'm ready to let it all go. That's one of the big differences between *102 Dalmatians* and *Enchanted*. On *102 Dalmatians* I held onto that blueprint. I think it made that movie somewhat cold and predictable. I let go of it on *Enchanted*. If I saw something happening between my actors, or staging that happened in the moment, I totally just let it go and redirected or reimagined the specifics of that scene in that moment. And having boarded it allowed me that confidence, because I had the storyboarding to fall back on, you know? You're not standing out there empty with nothing. The homework is done; now you can move forward from that place.

Bill: On *102 Dalmatians*, you were brought in after somebody else was taken out. But Enchanted wasn't that way. They came to you in the early stages, right?

Kevin: I begged for it. I had to beg for that movie.

Bill: And how did that come about? How did you find out that it existed out there?

Kevin: My agent Adriana Alberghetti told me about it. She said, "It's the perfect movie for you." And I complained, "Oh, I don't know, it has

Enchanted, 2007. © 2007 Disney.

animated characters in it and I need to be moving away from animation." And I read it, and my first response was, "Well, I'm not sure about it. It seems like, you know, sort of a familiar romantic comedy." And I was full of hesitation.

Bill: Really?!

Kevin: Honestly! And my agent scolded me, "You're a fool! You need to read it again." So I read it again, and I realized that it was the perfect vehicle for me. It was emotional. It was surprising. And what I found in that second read that didn't exist in the script at the time was that it could be a love letter to everything Disney.

Bill: Right.

Kevin: And I said to myself, "This would be the 'in' for me." I love animation. It courses through my blood. I can make a love letter to the one thing I wanted to do since I was five years old.

Bill: And you knew animation.

Kevin: I knew it!

Bill: And it couldn't have been made by a director who didn't know animation.

Kevin: It's true! And they tried to make it with two other directors before me. It always fell apart. And I think it fell apart because there was a level of cynicism about their approaches. When I dove in, I said, "I'm gonna let all that cynicism go." *Shrek* had happened and had succeeded poking fun at Disney, and I said, "Just let go of all that, and let's embrace our love of everything Disney. Let's just say that we love it, and not be embarrassed to say that we love it, and see where it goes." The executives were scared to death. What I had to do is what we would typically do at Disney Animation: I filled a whole floor of a production building with storyboards and artwork. I hung up all the art we had produced, I got photo clippings for the live-action sections, and I pitched the entire story and I sold them the movie. I used the animation process of beat boarding the film, which is to put together the story of the movie before you even make the movie. You make it in static drawings first, then you make it again, with the camera recording.

Bill: But they paid for the art department?

Kevin: I was a little sneaky with this. I used the idea that if we wanted to have the film by a certain release date, I was going to have to put together the animation before we shot the live-action. Animation takes a certain amount of time to produce and if we wanted to complete the animation by a certain date, we needed to start storyboarding now. The studio was still unsure they wanted to make the film, so I used that storyboarding money, not just to put together the animated section, but to sell them the entire movie.

Bill: Where did you do the animation?

Kevin: It was animated by James Baxter's company, James Baxter Animation, in Pasadena.

Bill: What a lucky choice that was.

Kevin: Lucky? I'm not sure luck had anything to do with it. His company was, by far, the best choice for this gig. Couldn't have had a better character animator than James in charge.

Bill: The key to that movie was finding Amy Adams. I think when most people hear that story they think, "Who would believe that any girl could be that sweet …"

Kevin: Right …

Bill: Did you know you needed somebody like that?

Kevin: They wanted me to hire a star. And I said, "No." Just being bull-headed I said, "No, no, no. This is one of those moments, like casting Julie Andrews as Mary Poppins, where you get to hire someone that the world doesn't yet know about. And they believe in the character 100 percent." You're not carrying a tabloid story about your lead actress while creating a character who exudes purity.

Bill: Right.

Kevin: So I said, "I'm gonna go look for an unknown." And they said, "Okay, you go look for someone, but we want this actress over here to do it." And Amy came in for an audition.

Bill: She had already done *Catch Me If You Can*?

Kevin: She had. She came into the room and I think I had a 103-degree temperature, I was really sick that day. And we were doing fifteen-minute auditions, just moving people in and out and getting a taste of each of them. Amy walked into the

Amy Adams, Kevin Lima, *Enchanted*, 2007 © Disney.

room and I suddenly perked up. You just know! You just have this intuition that it's going to happen. And I invested in her in that moment, and we spent forty-five minutes together and I knew I had found Giselle. I knew: there she was. And I took the tape back to the studio and said, "This is the girl we're hiring." They said, "Okay, we'll watch it, but we want that girl over there." And I said, "Wait 'til you see it!" Dick Cook, then Chairman of the Walt Disney Studios finally saw the audition, and he said, "Go ahead, Kev, hire her. I understand what you're trying to do."

Bill: Casting is a big part of directing, right?

Kevin: It's the biggest part of live-action directing. Casting is everything. I think that's true of animation as well. I think the casting, the coming together of the vocal performance and the animator, if you can get that right, if you can get the chemistry of that right, then you've captured something magic.

Bill: Is there a secret?

Kevin: I don't know if there's a key to casting. What I tend to do is never work on the script thinking about an actor. Never, never. I try to keep it as wide open as possible. And I sort of think of it like, and I learned this from Peter Weir, he talks about his concept of the "Wanted" poster. That you create the "Wanted" poster in the writing, and as it progresses you're starting to think visually. I'm a real visual thinker, so I start to see the character. I board some stuff before I even get the actor, so I've already got a little bit of a mental picture of what I'm going for. Then I wait for that person to walk into the room.

Bill: And …

Kevin: And then I arrest them and I make them do the movie!

Bill: I think when an animation director sees a scene like that Central Park extravaganza in *Enchanted* they think, uh … that would be a big thing to keep …

Kevin: [laughs] Under control?

Bill: Yeah. Number one, is it as big and complex as it looks? And number two, in your animation experience, is there an equivalent to that kind of intensity?

Kevin: I think a scene like that has almost direct correlations to animation. And what I've learned in animation is that there's a great number of people who are coming together to make a moment in time, across many, many different disciplines, happen. And the only way to control it is to have done your prep. It's about being prepared for when each person comes to you and asks a question. It's easy to walk into a scene with three or four people and control the dynamic of those people without extensive prep. It's harder when you've got 400. So you have to really have planned out the scene. Because it was a song, it follows a process very much like animation, in that you record the song beforehand, you storyboard the song, you decide how many characters are in each scene, you know? You've gone through the boards with your choreographer, you've gone on location, you've figured out how many brides and grooms for this section, how many construction workers for that.

Bill: You worked with Phil Collins on *Tarzan* …

Kevin: I did.

Bill: And then you had this big musical live-action picture. Is there a difference in working with composers in live action or animation?

Kevin: I don't treat it any differently. One of the things I do is treat everything like it's possible. I treat everything like it's an animated film, to be quite honest with you, and then I figure out how to do it in live action. The storytelling is the same; the planning is the same. It's just when you get in front of the camera it takes a different set of tools to capture it.

Bill: Are there types of films or types of stories you want to tell from now on?

Kevin: I feel pretty open. I love this idea of creating worlds that don't exist. I love this idea of creating characters that don't exist. You know, that's really where most of my focus goes. Whenever something comes out of me, it's all about bringing together those worlds and things that seem impossible. It doesn't mean it's the only thing I'll ever do. I'm actually looking forward to the challenge of just two actors in a room. 'Cause in some ways you can't hide behind any of the flash. The truth has to be there in the moment, and you either capture it or you don't.

Bill: Two actors in a room will still have a visual effects supervisor.

Kevin: [laughs] It probably will. The thing that is the hardest between the two mediums for me is the fact that you don't ever get to go back if you fail. You don't ever get to go back and do it again. In animation, I always felt like there was a safety net. If we didn't get it this time with the actor in the booth, we'll go back and rewrite it and come and get it again. That doesn't happen very often in live action. So, you gotta make sure it's there on the day and the dynamic is happening. That's the big, big difference: that you don't really have that ability to keep returning to the same scene. So you've gotta be sure, when you walk into the room, that you can make it happen.

Bill: *Enchanted*'s a movie that definitely reflected the balance of your specialties.

Kevin: *Enchanted* was a big example of that for me, in that I was embracing what I loved. And not trying to be someone I'm not. Letting the inspiration come from somewhere deep inside of me is when I've been the most successful. It's such a strange thing to think that somehow it all comes from outside forces, from life's experiences. When I finished *Tarzan*, I hadn't seen my dad in twenty-five years. My parents were divorced when I was nine; my dad disappeared when I was twelve. And I have so many father issues that have worked their way through my films. Goofy and Max in *A Goofy Movie*. Tarzan and Kerchak, the alpha gorilla. And these things just kept coming back. And I thought, "Boy, if I meet my father, if I heal that relationship, I might lose all of that." And what I realize is that the damage was done and you could never heal it. It still follows you, and it still exists within what makes you who you are. But I was so worried, and in that moment I realized I don't need to worry about that stuff anymore.

Bill: Did you meet him again?

Kevin: He actually contacted me.

Bill: Was this after the movie?

Kevin: I think someone had told him I was working on *Tarzan*. And he started trying to figure out where I was and what I was doing, what I had done. And then he wrote me a letter. And here I am, having a baby and releasing a movie at the same time. Actually both of those things happened on the same exact night. I had my daughter on the night that *Tarzan* premiered in theatres. I'm not kidding. So my dad wrote me a letter. And my first instinct was, "What does this guy want?" 'Cause I only knew him as this father who had abandoned his family. It took us a couple months to figure out how we were gonna meet. He was living in Florida. We met in Orlando. I was staying on the Disney property promoting *Tarzan*, and he came down and we had a meeting. We had a meeting; that sounds so official, doesn't it? We came together. It was fine. And I realized how tough he had had it. I had no idea, you know? He was at one point homeless, and he had been sober at that point for about five years.

Bill: He was not working?

Kevin: He held down a job. He was trying to pull his life together. Two years later he died of a brain tumor. So it got me wondering whether or not people know these things are happening and somehow they're trying to pull their life together and make amends.

Bill: So you didn't continue to see him?

Kevin: We kept a relationship going for those two years. I think that relationship sort of formed me in many, many ways. Because as a kid, I escaped into the world of the arts, a world I could control, a world I could build. Here I am as a director, building worlds, creating a sandbox that I invite others to play in. That was very instrumental in making me the artist I am today.

Bill: That is pretty important.

Kevin: Yep. When my mom—we're getting so personal here—When my dad left, my mom sort of fell apart, and we became a welfare family. The whole thing with forcing my way through the front door of the Puppet Workshop is about earning money for my family. Yet finding a place where I could be fulfilled, because I wasn't getting any of it at home. At school, I was the kid who was called the faggot, because I played with puppets and because I drew. So, I just kept building these worlds, you know? It taught me that I had to take care of myself, that I had to go after everything I wanted. Each step in the process, moving from student to professional, growing as an artist, was all about me going after what I wanted. It was about me saying, "I'm going to direct a feature animated film." And going to the right people and saying, "This is what I'm going to do next." And the only way that's going to happen is to ask for it. It's about putting yourself out in the world and saying, "I want it."

Bill: That's the distinctive thing about you. Every director we meet has a different path. With some people, it just seems like they were in the right place at the right time. Other people have a lot of trouble. A lot of knock down, get up. You just kept asking.

Kevin: And when they said, "No," I said, "Okay, I'm gonna go find it somewhere else." With enough headstrong chutzpah to say, "It's gonna happen somewhere." And the whole thing is getting back up on the horse. It's about when you fail, saying, "Okay, how do I learn from this? How do I not let it hold me down?"

INDEX

FOURTH EDITION

GAUGE THEORIES
IN
PARTICLE PHYSICS
A PRACTICAL INTRODUCTION

VOLUME 2
Non-Abelian Gauge Theories
QCD and The Electroweak Theory

GAUGE THEORIES
IN
PARTICLE PHYSICS
A PRACTICAL INTRODUCTION

VOLUME 2
Non-Abelian Gauge Theories
QCD and The Electroweak Theory

Ian J.R. Aitchison • **Anthony J.G. Hey**

CRC Press
Taylor & Francis Group
Boca Raton   London   New York

CRC Press is an imprint of the
Taylor & Francis Group, an **informa** business

CRC Press
Taylor & Francis Group
6000 Broken Sound Parkway NW, Suite 300
Boca Raton, FL 33487-2742

Printed in the United States of America on acid-free paper
Version Date: 2012912

International Standard Book Number: 978-1-4665-1307-5 (Hardback)

Library of Congress Cataloging-in-Publication Data

Aitchison, Ian Johnston Rhind, 1936-
　　Gauge theories in particle physics : a practical introduction / Ian J R Aitchison, Anthony J.G. Hey. -- 4th ed.
　　　v. cm.
　　Includes bibliographical references and index.
　　Contents: v. 1. From relativistic quantum mechanics to QED -- v. 2. Non-Abelian gauge theories : QCD and the electroweak theory.
　　ISBN 978-1-4665-1299-3 (v. 1 : hardback) -- ISBN 978-1-4665-1307-5 (v. 2 : hardback)
　　1. Gauge fields (Physics) 2. Particles (Nuclear physics) 3. Weak interactions (Nuclear physics) 4. Quantum electrodynamics. 5. Feynman diagrams. I. Hey, Anthony J. G. II. Title.

QC793.3.F5A34 2012
539.7'21--dc23
　　　　　　　　　　　　　　　　　　　　　　　　　　　　　　　　　　　　　　2012031181

Visit the Taylor & Francis Web site at
http://www.taylorandfrancis.com

and the CRC Press Web site at
http://www.crcpress.com

To Jessie
and to
Jean, Katherine and Elizabeth

Contents

VII Spontaneously Broken Symmetry 193

Preface to Volume 2 of the Fourth Edition

The main focus of the second volume of this fourth edition, as in the third, is on the two non-Abelian quantum gauge field theories of the Standard Model – that is, QCD and the electroweak theory of Glashow, Salam and Weinberg. We preserve the same division into four parts: non-Abelian symmetries, both global and local; QCD and the renormalization group; spontaneously broken symmetry; and weak interaction phenomenology and the electroweak theory.

However, the book has always combined theoretical development with discussion of relevant experimental results. And it is on the experimental side that most progress has been made in the ten years since the third edition appeared – first of all, in the study of CP violation in B-meson physics, and in neutrino oscillations. The inclusion of these results, and the increasing importance of the topics, have required some reorganization, and a new chapter (21) devoted wholly to them. We concentrate mainly on CP-violation in B-meson decays, particularly on the determination of the angles of the unitarity triangle from B-meson oscillations. CP-violation in K-meson systems is also discussed. In the neutrino sector, we describe some of the principal experiments which have led to our current knowledge of the mass-squared differences and the mixing angles. In discussing weak interaction phenomenology, we keep in view the possibility that neutrinos may turn out to be Majorana particles, an outcome for which we have prepared the reader in (new) chapters 4 and 7 of volume 1.

More recently, on July 4, 2012, the ATLAS and CMS collaborations at the CERN LHC announced the discovery of a boson of mass between 125 and 126 GeV, with production and decay characteristics which are consistent (at the 1σ level) with those of the Standard Model Higgs boson. We can now conclude our treatment of the electroweak theory, and this volume, with a discussion of this historic discovery, which opens a new era in particle physics – one in which the electroweak symmetry-breaking (Higgs) sector of the SM will be rigorously tested.

Our treatment of a number of topics has been updated and, we hope, improved. In QCD, the definition of 2-jet cross sections in e^+e^- annihilation is explained, and used in a short discussion of jet algorithms (sections 14.5 and 14.6). Progress in lattice QCD is recognized with the inclusion of some of the recent impressive results using dynamical fermions (section 16.5). In the chapter on chiral symmetry breaking, a new section (18.3) introduces the

important technique of effective Lagrangians, including the extension to the three-flavour case and the associated mass relations. A much fuller account is given of three-generation quark mixing and the CKM matrix (section 20.7.3), as preparation for chapter 21. The essential points in chapter 21 of the previous edition, relating to problems with the current–current and IVB models, now provide the introductory motivation for the GSW theory in chapter 22.

One item has been banished to an appendix: geometrical aspects of gauge theories, which did after all seem to interrupt the flow of chapter 13 too much (but we hope readers will not ignore it). And another has been brought in from the cold: as already mentioned, Majorana fermions now find themselves appearing for the first time in volume 1.

Acknowledgements

We are very grateful to Paolo Strolin for providing a list of misprints and a very thorough catalogue of excellent comments for volume 2 of the third edition, which has resulted in a large number of improvements in the present text. The CP-violation sections in chapters 20 and 21 were much improved following detailed comments by Abi Soffer, and the neutrino sections in chapter 21 likewise benefited greatly from careful readings by Francesco Tramontano and Tim Cohen; we thank all three for their generous help. The eps files for figures 16.11 and 16.12 were kindly supplied by Christine Davies and Stephan Dürr, respectively. IJRA thanks Michael Peskin and Stan Brodsky for welcoming him as a visitor to the SLAC National Accelerator Laboratory Particle Theory group (supported by the Department of Energy under contract DE-AC02-76SF00515), and Bill Dunwoodie and BaBar colleagues for very kindly arranging for him to be a BaBar Associate; these connections have been invaluable. On a more technical note, IJRA thanks Xing-Gang Wu for some crucial help with JaxoDraw.

Ian J R Aitchison and Anthony J G Hey
October 2012

Part V

Non-Abelian Symmetries

12

Global Non-Abelian Symmetries

12.1 The Standard Model

In the preceding volume, a very successful dynamical theory – QED – has been introduced, based on the remarkably simple *gauge principle*: namely, that the theory should be invariant under local phase transformations on the wave-functions (chapter 2) or field operators (chapter 7) of charged particles. Such transformations were characterized as *Abelian* in section 2.6, since the phase factors commuted. The second volume of this book will be largely concerned with the formulation and elementary application of the remaining two dynamical theories within the Standard Model – that is, QCD and the electroweak theory. They are built on a generalization of the gauge principle, in which the transformations involve more than one state, or field, at a time. In that case, the 'phase factors' become matrices, which generally do not commute with each other, and the associated symmetry is called a '*non-Abelian*' one. When the phase factors are independent of the space-time coordinate x, the symmetry is a 'global non-Abelian' one; when they are allowed to depend on x, one is led to a non-Abelian gauge theory. Both QCD and the electroweak theory are of the latter type, providing generalizations of the Abelian U(1) gauge theory which is QED. It is a striking fact that all three dynamical theories in the Standard Model are based on a gauge principle of local phase invariance.

In this chapter we shall be mainly concerned with two global non-Abelian symmetries, which lead to useful conservation laws but not to any specific dynamical theory. We begin in section 12.1 with the first non-Abelian symmetry to be used in particle physics, the *hadronic isospin* 'SU(2) symmetry' proposed by Heisenberg (1932) in the context of nuclear physics, and now understood as following from QCD and the smallness of the u and d quark masses as compared with the QCD scale parameter $\Lambda_{\overline{\text{MS}}}$ (see section 18.3.3). In section 12.2 we extend this to $\text{SU}(3)_f$ flavour symmetry, as was first done by Gell-Mann (1961) and Ne'eman (1961) – an extension seen, in its turn, as reflecting the smallness of the u, d and s quark masses as compared with $\Lambda_{\overline{\text{MS}}}$. The 'wavefunction' approach of sections 12.1 and 12.2 is then reformulated in field-theoretic language in section 12.3.

In the last section of this chapter, we shall introduce the idea of a global *chiral* symmetry, which is a symmetry of theories with massless fermions. This may be expected to be a good approximate symmetry for the u and d quarks.

But the anticipated observable consequences of this symmetry (for example, nucleon parity doublets) appear to be absent. This puzzle will be resolved in Part VII, via the profoundly important concept of 'spontaneous symmetry breaking'.

The formalism introduced in this chapter for SU(2) and SU(3) will be required again in the following one, when we consider the local versions of these non-Abelian symmetries and the associated dynamical gauge theories. The whole modern development of non-Abelian gauge theories began with the attempt by Yang and Mills (1954) (see also Shaw 1955) to make hadronic isospin into a local symmetry. However, the beautiful formalism developed by these authors turned out *not* to describe interactions between hadrons. Instead, it describes the interactions between the *constituents* of the hadrons, namely quarks – and this in two respects. First, a local SU(3) symmetry (called $SU(3)_c$) governs the strong interactions of quarks, binding them into hadrons (see Part VI). Secondly, a local SU(2) symmetry (called *weak isospin*) governs the weak interactions of quarks (and leptons); together with QED, this constitutes the electroweak theory (see Part VIII). It is important to realize that, despite the fact that each of these two local symmetries is based on the same group as one of the earlier global (flavour) symmetries, the physics involved is completely different. In the case of the strong quark interactions, the $SU(3)_c$ group refers to a new degree of freedom ('colour') which is quite distinct from flavour u, d, s (see chapter 14). In the weak interaction case, since the group is an SU(2), it is natural to use 'isospin language' in talking about it, particularly since flavour degrees of freedom are involved. But we must always remember that it is *weak* isospin, which (as we shall see in chapter 20) is an attribute of leptons as well as of quarks, and hence physically quite distinct from hadronic isospin. Furthermore, it is a parity-violating chiral gauge theory.

Despite the attractive conceptual unity associated with the gauge principle, the way in which each of QCD and the electroweak theory 'works' is actually quite different from QED, and from each other. Indeed it is worth emphasizing very strongly that it is, *a priori*, far from obvious why either the strong interactions between quarks, or the weak interactions, should have anything to do with gauge theories at all. Just as in the U(1) (electromagnetic) case, gauge invariance forbids a mass term in the Lagrangian for non-Abelian gauge fields, as we shall see in chapter 13. Thus it would seem that gauge field quanta are necessarily massless. But this, in turn, would imply that the associated forces must have a long-range (Coulombic) part, due to exchange of these massless quanta – and of course in neither the strong nor the weak inter-action case is that what is observed.[1] As regards the former, the gluon quanta are indeed massless, but the contradiction is resolved by *non-perturbative* effects which lead to *confinement*, as we indicated in chapter 1. We shall discuss

---

[1]Pauli had independently developed the theory of non-Abelian gauge fields during 1953, but did not publish any of this work because of the seeming physical irrelevancy associated with the masslessness problem (Enz 2002, pages 474-82; Pais 2000, pages 242-5).

this further in chapter 16. In weak interactions, a third realization appears: the gauge quanta acquire mass via (it is believed) a second instance of *spontaneous symmetry breaking*, as will be explained in Part VII. In fact a further application of this idea is required in the electroweak theory, because of the chiral nature of the gauge symmetry in this case: the quark and lepton masses also must be 'spontaneously generated'.

12.2   The flavour symmetry SU(2)$_f$

12.2.1   The nucleon isospin doublet and the group SU(2)

The transformations initially considered in connection with the gauge principle in section 2.5 were just global phase transformations on a single wavefunction

$$\psi' = e^{i\alpha}\psi. \tag{12.1}$$

The generalization to non-Abelian invariances comes when we take the simple step – but one with many ramifications – of considering more than one wavefunction, or state, at a time. Quite generally in quantum mechanics, we know that whenever we have a set of states which are *degenerate* in energy (or mass) there is no unique way of specifying the states: any linear combination of some initially chosen set of states will do just as well, provided the normalization conditions on the states are still satisfied. Consider, for example, the simplest case of just two such states – to be specific, the neutron and proton (figure 12.1). This single near coincidence of the masses was enough to suggest to Heisenberg (1932) that, as far as the strong nuclear forces were concerned (electromagnetism being negligible by comparison), the two states could be regarded as truly degenerate, so that any arbitrary linear combination of neutron and proton wavefunctions would be entirely equivalent, as far as this force was concerned, for a single 'neutron' or single 'proton' wavefunction. This hypothesis became known as 'charge independence of nuclear forces'. Thus redefinitions of neutron and proton wavefunctions could be allowed, of the form

$$\psi_p \to \psi'_p = \alpha\psi_p + \beta\psi_n \tag{12.2}$$

$$\psi_n \to \psi'_n = \gamma\psi_p + \delta\psi_n \tag{12.3}$$

for complex coefficients α, β, γ, and δ. In particular, since ψ_p and ψ_n are degenerate, we have

$$H\psi_p = E\psi_p, \qquad\qquad H\psi_n = E\psi_n \tag{12.4}$$

from which it follows that

$$
\begin{aligned}
H\psi'_p &= H(\alpha\psi_p + \beta\psi_n) = \alpha H\psi_p + \beta H\psi_n \tag{12.5}\\
&= E(\alpha\psi_p + \beta\psi_n) = E\psi'_p \tag{12.6}
\end{aligned}
$$

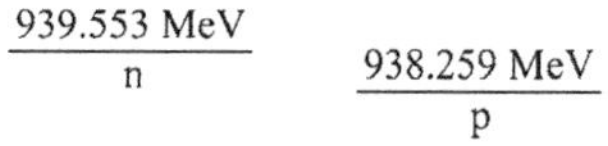

$$\frac{939.553 \text{ MeV}}{\text{n}} \qquad \frac{938.259 \text{ MeV}}{\text{p}}$$

FIGURE 12.1
Early evidence for isospin symmetry.

and similarly

$$H\psi'_{\text{n}} = E\psi'_{\text{n}} \tag{12.7}$$

showing that the redefined wavefunctions still describe two states with the same energy degeneracy.

The two-fold degeneracy seen in figure 12.1 is suggestive of that found in spin-$\frac{1}{2}$ systems in the absence of any magnetic field; the $s_z = \pm\frac{1}{2}$ components are degenerate. The analogy can be brought out by introducing the *two-component nucleon isospinor*

$$\psi^{(1/2)} \equiv \left(\begin{array}{c} \psi_{\text{p}} \\ \psi_{\text{n}} \end{array} \right) \equiv \psi_{\text{p}}\chi_{\text{p}} + \psi_{\text{n}}\chi_{\text{n}} \tag{12.8}$$

where

$$\chi_{\text{p}} = \left(\begin{array}{c} 1 \\ 0 \end{array} \right), \qquad \chi_{\text{n}} = \left(\begin{array}{c} 0 \\ 1 \end{array} \right). \tag{12.9}$$

In $\psi^{(1/2)}$, ψ_{p} is the amplitude for the nucleon to have 'isospin up', and ψ_{n} is that for it to have 'isospin down'.

As far as the states are concerned, this terminology arises, of course, from the formal identity between the 'isospinors' of (12.9) and the two-component eigenvectors (3.60) corresponding to eigenvalues $\pm\frac{1}{2}\hbar$ of (true) spin: compare also (3.61) and (12.8). It is important to be clear, however, that the degrees of freedom involved in the two cases are quite distinct; in particular, even though both the proton and the neutron have (true) spin$-\frac{1}{2}$, the transformations (12.2) and (12.3) leave the (true) spin part of their wavefunctions completely untouched. Indeed, we are suppressing the spinor part of both wavefunctions altogether (they are of course 4-component Dirac spinors). As we proceed, the precise mathematical nature of this 'spin-1/2' analogy will become clear.

Equations (12.2) and (12.3) can be compactly written in terms of $\psi^{(1/2)}$ as

$$\psi^{(1/2)} \rightarrow \psi^{(1/2)'} = \mathbf{V}\psi^{(1/2)}, \qquad \mathbf{V} = \left(\begin{array}{cc} \alpha & \beta \\ \gamma & \delta \end{array} \right) \tag{12.10}$$

where $\mathbf{V}$ is the indicated complex 2×2 matrix. Heisenberg's proposal, then, was that the physics of strong interactions between nucleons remained the same under the transformation (12.10): in other words, a symmetry was involved. We must emphasise that such a symmetry can *only* be exact in the *absence* of electromagnetic interactions: it is therefore an intrinsically approximate symmetry, though presumably quite a useful one in view of the relative weakness of electromagnetic interactions as compared to hadronic ones.

We now consider the general form of the matrix $\mathbf{V}$, as constrained by various relevant restrictions: quite remarkably, we shall discover that (after extracting an overall phase) $\mathbf{V}$ has essentially the same mathematical form as the matrix $\mathbf{U}$ of (4.33), which we encountered in the discussion of the transformation of (real) spin wavefunctions under rotations of the (real) space axes. It will be instructive to see how the present discussion leads to the same form (4.33).

We first note that $\mathbf{V}$ of (12.10) depends on four arbitrary complex numbers, or alternatively on eight real parameters. By contrast, the matrix $\mathbf{U}$ of (4.33) depends on only three real parameters, which we may think of in terms of two to describe the direction of the axis of rotation, and a third for the angle of rotation. However, $\mathbf{V}$ is subject to certain restrictions, and these reduce the number of free parameters in $\mathbf{V}$ to three, as we now discuss. First, in order to preserve the normalization of $\psi^{(1/2)}$ we require

$$\psi^{(1/2)'\dagger}\psi^{(1/2)'} = \psi^{(1/2)\dagger}\mathbf{V}^\dagger\mathbf{V}\psi^{(1/2)} = \psi^{(1/2)\dagger}\psi^{(1/2)} \tag{12.11}$$

which implies that $\mathbf{V}$ has to be *unitary*:

$$\mathbf{V}^\dagger\mathbf{V} = \mathbf{1}_2, \tag{12.12}$$

where $\mathbf{1}_2$ is the unit 2×2 matrix. Clearly this unitarity property is in no way restricted to the case of two states: the transformation coefficients for n degenerate states will form the entries of an $n \times n$ unitary matrix. A trivialization is the case $n = 1$, for which, as we noted in section 2.6, $\mathbf{V}$ reduces to a single phase factor as in (12.1), indicating how all the previous work is going to be contained as a special case of these more general transformations. Indeed, from elementary properties of determinants we have

$$\det\mathbf{V}^\dagger\mathbf{V} = \det\mathbf{V}^\dagger \cdot \det\mathbf{V} = \det\mathbf{V}^* \cdot \det\mathbf{V} =\mid \det\mathbf{V}\mid^2 = 1 \tag{12.13}$$

so that

$$\det\mathbf{V} = \exp(i\theta) \tag{12.14}$$

where θ is a real number. We can separate off such an overall phase factor from the transformations mixing 'p' and 'n', because it corresponds to a rotation of the phase of both p and n wavefunctions by the *same* amount:

$$\psi'_p = e^{i\alpha}\psi_p, \quad \psi'_n = e^{i\alpha}\psi_n. \tag{12.15}$$

The $\mathbf{V}$ corresponding to (12.15) is $\mathbf{V} = e^{i\alpha}\mathbf{1}_2$, which has determinant $\exp(2i\alpha)$ and is therefore of the form (12.1) with $\theta = 2\alpha$. In the field-theoretic formalism of section 7.2, such a symmetry can be shown to lead to the conservation of baryon number $N_u + N_d - N_{\bar{u}} - N_{\bar{d}}$, where bar denotes the antiparticle.

The new physics will lie in the remaining transformations which satisfy

$$\det\mathbf{V} = +1. \tag{12.16}$$

Such a matrix is said to be a *special* unitary matrix, which simply means it has unit determinant. Thus, finally, the **V**'s we are dealing with are *special, unitary, 2×2 matrices*. The set of all such matrices form a *group*. The general defining properties of a group are given in appendix M. In the present case, the elements of the group are all such 2×2 matrices, and the 'law of combination' is just ordinary matrix multiplication. It is straightforward to verify (problem 12.1) that all the defining properties are satisfied here; the group is called 'SU(2)', the 'S' standing for 'special', the 'U' for 'unitary', and the '2' for '2×2'.

SU(2) is actually an example of a *Lie group* (see appendix M). Such groups have the important property that their physical consequences may be found by considering 'infinitesimal' transformations, that is – in this case – matrices **V** which differ only slightly from the 'no-change' situation corresponding to $\mathbf{V} = \mathbf{1}_2$. For such an infinitesimal SU(2) matrix $\mathbf{V}_{\text{infl}}$ we may therefore write

$$\mathbf{V}_{\text{infl}} = \mathbf{1}_2 + i\boldsymbol{\xi} \tag{12.17}$$

where $\boldsymbol{\xi}$ is a 2×2 matrix whose entries are all first-order small quantities. The condition $\det \mathbf{V}_{\text{infl}} = 1$ now reduces, on neglect of second-order terms $0(\boldsymbol{\xi}^2)$, to the condition (see problem 12.2)

$$\text{Tr}\boldsymbol{\xi} = 0. \tag{12.18}$$

The condition that $\mathbf{V}_{\text{infl}}$ be unitary, i.e.

$$(\mathbf{1}_2 + i\boldsymbol{\xi})(\mathbf{1}_2 - i\boldsymbol{\xi}^\dagger) = \mathbf{1}_2 \tag{12.19}$$

similarly reduces (in first order) to the condition

$$\boldsymbol{\xi} = \boldsymbol{\xi}^\dagger. \tag{12.20}$$

Thus $\boldsymbol{\xi}$ is a 2×2 traceless Hermitian matrix, which means it must have the form

$$\boldsymbol{\xi} = \begin{pmatrix} a & b - ic \\ b + ic & -a \end{pmatrix}, \tag{12.21}$$

where a, b, c are infinitesimal real parameters. Writing

$$a = \epsilon_3/2, \quad b = \epsilon_1/2, \quad c = \epsilon_2/2, \tag{12.22}$$

(12.21) can be put in the more suggestive form

$$\boldsymbol{\xi} = \boldsymbol{\epsilon} \cdot \boldsymbol{\tau}/2 \tag{12.23}$$

where $\boldsymbol{\epsilon}$ stands for the three real quantities

$$\boldsymbol{\epsilon} = (\epsilon_1, \epsilon_2, \epsilon_3) \tag{12.24}$$

which are all first-order small. The three matrices $\boldsymbol{\tau}$ are just the familiar Hermitian Pauli matrices

$$\tau_1 = \begin{pmatrix} 0 & 1 \\ 1 & 0 \end{pmatrix}, \tau_2 = \begin{pmatrix} 0 & -i \\ i & 0 \end{pmatrix}, \tau_3 = \begin{pmatrix} 1 & 0 \\ 0 & -1 \end{pmatrix}, \tag{12.25}$$

here called 'tau' precisely in order to distinguish them from the mathematically identical 'sigma' matrices which are associated with the real spin degree of freedom. Hence a general infinitesimal SU(2) matrix takes the form

$$\mathbf{V}_{\mathrm{infl}} = (\mathbf{1}_2 + i\boldsymbol{\epsilon} \cdot \boldsymbol{\tau}/2), \tag{12.26}$$

and an infinitesimal SU(2) transformation of the p-n doublet is specified by

$$\begin{pmatrix} \psi'_{\mathrm{p}} \\ \psi'_{\mathrm{n}} \end{pmatrix} = (\mathbf{1}_2 + i\boldsymbol{\epsilon} \cdot \boldsymbol{\tau}/2) \begin{pmatrix} \psi_{\mathrm{p}} \\ \psi_{\mathrm{n}} \end{pmatrix}. \tag{12.27}$$

The $\boldsymbol{\tau}$-matrices clearly play an important role, since they determine the forms of the three independent infinitesimal SU(2) transformations. They are called the *generators* of infinitesimal SU(2) transformations; more precisely, the matrices $\boldsymbol{\tau}/2$ provide a particular *matrix representation* of the generators, namely the two-dimensional, or 'fundamental' one (see appendix M). We note that they do not commute amongst themselves: rather, introducing $\mathbf{T}^{(\frac{1}{2})} \equiv \boldsymbol{\tau}/2$, we find (see problem 12.3)

$$[T_i^{(\frac{1}{2})}, T_j^{(\frac{1}{2})}] = i\epsilon_{ijk}T_k^{(\frac{1}{2})}, \tag{12.28}$$

where i, j and k run from 1 to 3, and a sum on the repeated index k is understood as usual. The reader will recognize the commutation relations (12.28) as being precisely the same as those of angular momentum operators in quantum mechanics:

$$[J_i, J_j] = i\epsilon_{ijk}J_k. \tag{12.29}$$

In that case, the choice $J_i = \sigma_i/2 \equiv J_i^{(\frac{1}{2})}$ would correspond to a (real) spin-1/2 system. Here the identity between the tau's and the sigma's gives us a good reason to regard our 'p-n' system as formally analogous to a 'spin-1/2' one. Of course, the 'analogy' was made into a mathematical identity by the judicious way in which $\boldsymbol{\xi}$ was parametrised in (12.23).

The form for a *finite* SU(2) transformation $\mathbf{V}$ may then be obtained from the infinitesimal form using the result

$$e^A = \lim_{n \to \infty} (1 + A/n)^n \tag{12.30}$$

generalized to matrices. Let $\boldsymbol{\epsilon} = \boldsymbol{\alpha}/n$, where $\boldsymbol{\alpha} = (\alpha_1, \alpha_2, \alpha_3)$ are three real finite (not infinitesimal) parameters, apply the infinitesimal transformation n times, and let n tend to infinity. We obtain

$$\mathbf{V} = \exp(i\boldsymbol{\alpha} \cdot \boldsymbol{\tau}/2) \tag{12.31}$$

so that

$$\psi^{(1/2)\prime} \equiv \begin{pmatrix} \psi'_p \\ \psi'_n \end{pmatrix} = \exp(i\boldsymbol{\alpha} \cdot \boldsymbol{\tau}/2) \begin{pmatrix} \psi_p \\ \psi_n \end{pmatrix} = \exp(i\boldsymbol{\alpha} \cdot \boldsymbol{\tau}/2)\psi^{(1/2)}. \quad (12.32)$$

Note that in the finite transformation, the generators appear in the exponent. Indeed, (12.31) has the form

$$\mathbf{V} = \exp(iG) \qquad (12.33)$$

where $G = \boldsymbol{\alpha} \cdot \boldsymbol{\tau}/2$, from which the unitary property of $\mathbf{V}$ easily follows:

$$\mathbf{V}^{\dagger} = \exp(-iG^{\dagger}) = \exp(-iG) = \mathbf{V}^{-1} \qquad (12.34)$$

where we used the Hermiticity of the tau's. Equation (12.33) has the general form

$$\text{unitary matrix} = \exp(i \text{ Hermitian matrix}) \qquad (12.35)$$

where the 'Hermitian matrix' is composed of the generators and the transformation parameters. We shall meet generalizations of this structure in the following sub-section for SU(2), again in section 12.2 for SU(3), and a field theoretic version of it in section 12.3.

As promised, (12.32) has essentially the same mathematical form as (4.33). In each case, three real parameters appear. In (4.33) they describe the axis and angle of a physical rotation in real three-dimensional space: we can always write $\boldsymbol{\alpha} = |\boldsymbol{\alpha}|\hat{\boldsymbol{\alpha}}$ and identify $|\boldsymbol{\alpha}|$ with the angle θ and $\hat{\boldsymbol{\alpha}}$ with the axis $\hat{\boldsymbol{n}}$ of the rotation. In (12.32) there are just the three parameters in $\boldsymbol{\alpha}$.[2]

In the form (12.32), it is clear that our 2×2 isospin transformation is a generalization of the global phase transformation of (12.1), except that:

(i) there are now *three* 'phase angles' $\boldsymbol{\alpha}$;

(ii) there are non-commuting matrix operators (the $\boldsymbol{\tau}$'s) appearing in the exponent.

The last fact is the reason for the description 'non-Abelian' phase invariance. As the commutation relations for the $\boldsymbol{\tau}$ matrices show, SU(2) is a non-Abelian group in that two SU(2) transformations do not in general commute. By contrast, in the case of electric charge or particle number, successive transformations clearly commute: this corresponds to an Abelian phase invariance and, as noted in section 2.6, to an Abelian U(1) group.

We may now put our initial 'spin-1/2' analogy on a more precise mathematical footing. In quantum mechanics, states within a degenerate multiplet may conveniently be characterized by the eigenvalues of a complete set of Hermitian operators which commute with the Hamiltonian and with each other.

_____

[2]It is not obvious that the general SU(2) matrix can be parametrized by an angle θ with $0 \le \theta \le 2\pi$, and $\hat{\boldsymbol{n}}$: for further discussion of the relation between SU(2) and the three-dimensional rotation group, see appendix M, section M.7.

In the case of the p-n doublet, it is easy to see what these operators are. We may write (12.4), (12.6) and (12.7) as

$$H_2 \psi^{(1/2)} = E \psi^{(1/2)} \tag{12.36}$$

and

$$H_2 \psi^{(1/2)'} = E \psi^{(1/2)'}, \tag{12.37}$$

where H_2 is the 2×2 matrix

$$H_2 = \begin{pmatrix} H & 0 \\ 0 & H \end{pmatrix}. \tag{12.38}$$

Hence H_2 is proportional to the unit matrix in this two-dimensional space, and it therefore commutes with the tau's:

$$[H_2, \boldsymbol{\tau}] = 0. \tag{12.39}$$

It then also follows that H_2 commutes with $\mathbf{V}$, or equivalently

$$\mathbf{V} H_2 \mathbf{V}^{-1} = H_2 \tag{12.40}$$

which is the statement that H_2 is invariant under the transformation (12.32). Now the tau's are Hermitian, and hence correspond to possible observables. Equation (12.39) implies that their eigenvalues are constants of the motion (i.e. conserved quantities), associated with the invariance (12.40). But the tau's do not commute amongst themselves and so according to the general principles of quantum mechanics we cannot give definite values to more than one of them at a time. The problem of finding a classification of the states which makes the maximum use of (12.39), given the commutation relations (12.28), is easily solved by making use of the formal identity between the operators $\tau_i/2$ and angular momentum operators J_i (cf (12.29)). The answer is[3] that the total squared 'spin'

$$(\mathbf{T}^{(1/2)})^2 = \left(\frac{1}{2}\boldsymbol{\tau}\right)^2 = \frac{1}{4}(\tau_1^2 + \tau_2^2 + \tau_3^2) = \frac{3}{4}\mathbf{1}_2 \tag{12.41}$$

and one component of spin, say $T_3^{(1/2)} = \frac{1}{2}\tau_3$, can be given definite values simultaneously. The corresponding eigenfunctions are just the χ_p's and χ_n's of (12.9), which satisfy

$$\frac{1}{4}\boldsymbol{\tau}^2 \chi_p = \frac{3}{4}\chi_p, \qquad \frac{1}{2}\tau_3 \chi_p = \frac{1}{2}\chi_p \tag{12.42}$$

$$\frac{1}{4}\boldsymbol{\tau}^2 \chi_n = \frac{3}{4}\chi_n, \qquad \frac{1}{2}\tau_3 \chi_n = -\frac{1}{2}\chi_n. \tag{12.43}$$

The reason for the 'spin' part of the name 'isospin' should by now be clear; the term is actually a shortened version of the historical one 'isotopic spin'.

---

[3] See for example Mandl (1992).

In concluding this section we remark that, in this two-dimensional n-p space, the electromagnetic charge operator is represented by the matrix

$$\mathbf{Q}_{\mathrm{em}} = \begin{pmatrix} 1 & 0 \\ 0 & 0 \end{pmatrix} = \frac{1}{2}(\mathbf{1}_2 + \tau_3). \tag{12.44}$$

It is clear that although $\mathbf{Q}_{\mathrm{em}}$ commutes with τ_3, it does not commute with either τ_1 or τ_2. Thus, as we would expect, electromagnetic corrections to the strong interaction Hamiltonian will violate SU(2) symmetry.

12.2.2   Larger (higher-dimensional) multiplets of SU(2) in nuclear physics

For the single nucleon states considered so far, the foregoing is really nothing more than the general quantum mechanics of a two-state system, phrased in 'spin-1/2' language. The real power of the isospin (SU(2)) symmetry concept becomes more apparent when we consider states of *several* nucleons. For A nucleons in the nucleus, we introduce three 'total isospin operators' $\mathbf{T} = (T_1, T_2, T_3)$ via

$$\mathbf{T} = \frac{1}{2}\boldsymbol{\tau}_{(1)} + \frac{1}{2}\boldsymbol{\tau}_{(2)} + \ldots + \frac{1}{2}\boldsymbol{\tau}_{(A)}, \tag{12.45}$$

which are Hermitian. Here $\boldsymbol{\tau}_{(n)}$ is the $\boldsymbol{\tau}$-matrix for the nth nucleon. The Hamiltonian H describing the strong interactions of this system is presumed to be invariant under the transformation (12.40) for all the nucleons independently. It then follows that

$$[H, \mathbf{T}] = 0. \tag{12.46}$$

Thus the eigenvalues of the $\mathbf{T}$ operators are constants of the motion. Further, since the isospin operators for different nucleons commute with each other (they are quite independent), the commutation relations (12.28) for each of the individual $\boldsymbol{\tau}$'s imply (see problem 12.4) that the components of $\mathbf{T}$ defined by (12.45) satisfy the commutation relations

$$[T_i, T_j] = \mathrm{i}\epsilon_{ijk}T_k \tag{12.47}$$

for $i, j, k = 1, 2, 3$, which are simply the standard angular momentum commutation relations, once more. Thus the energy levels of nuclei ought to be characterized – after allowance for electromagnetic effects, and correcting for the slight neutron-proton mass difference – by the eigenvalues of $\mathbf{T}^2$ and T_3, say, which can be simultaneously diagonalized along with H. These eigenvalues should then be, to a good approximation, 'good quantum numbers' for nuclei, if the assumed isospin invariance is true.

What are the possible eigenvalues? We know that the $\mathbf{T}$'s are Hermitian and satisfy exactly the same commutation relations (12.47) as the angular momentum operators. These conditions are all that are needed to show that the eigenvalues of $\mathbf{T}^2$ are of the form $T(T+1)$, where $T = 0, \frac{1}{2}, 1, \ldots$, and that

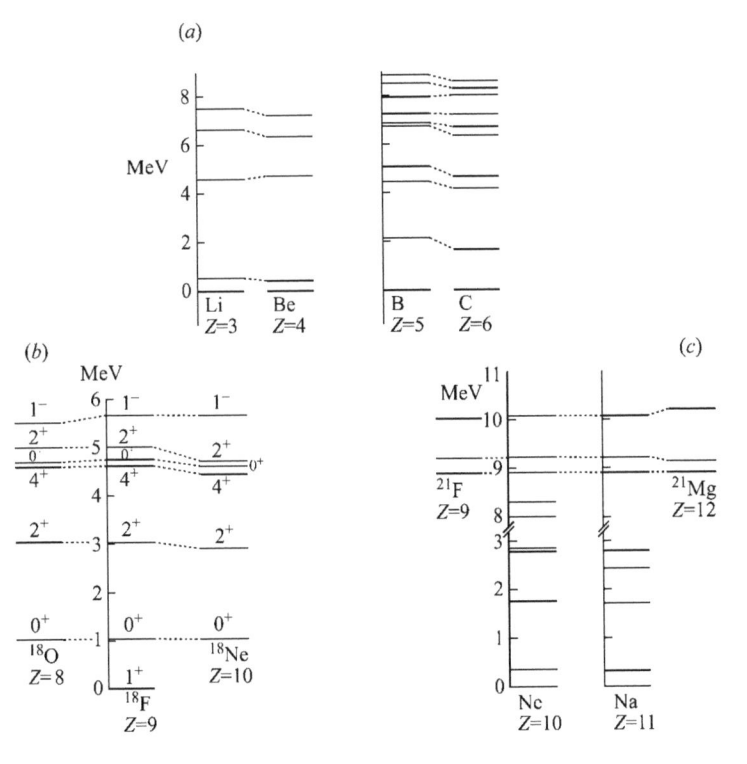

FIGURE 12.2

Energy levels (adjusted for Coulomb energy and neutron-proton mass differences) of nuclei of the same mass number but different charge, showing (a) 'mirror' doublets, (b) triplets and (c) doublets and quartets.

for a given T the eigenvalues of T_3 are $-T, -T+1, \ldots, T-1, T$; that is, there are $2T + 1$ *degenerate states* for a given T. These states all have the same A value, and since T_3 counts $+\frac{1}{2}$ for every proton and $-\frac{1}{2}$ for every neutron, it is clear that successive values of T_3 correspond physically to changing one neutron into a proton or vice versa. Thus we expect to see 'charge multiplets' of levels in neighbouring nuclear isobars. These are indeed observed; figure 12.2 shows some examples. These level schemes (which have been adjusted for Coulomb energy differences, and for the neutron-proton mass difference), provide clear evidence of $T = \frac{1}{2}$ (doublet), $T = 1$ (triplet) and $T = \frac{3}{2}$ (quartet) multiplets. It is important to note that states in the same T-multiplet must have the same J^P quantum numbers (these are indicated on the levels for ^{18}F); obviously the nuclear forces will depend on the space and spin degrees of freedom of the nucleons, and will only be the same between different nucleons if the space-spin part of the wavefunction is the same.

Thus the assumed invariance of the nucleon-nucleon force produces a richer nuclear multiplet structure, going beyond the original n-p doublet. These higher-dimensional multiplets ($T = 1, \frac{3}{2}, \ldots$) are called 'irreducible representations' of SU(2). The commutation relations (12.47) are called the *Lie algebra* of SU(2)[4] (see appendix M), and the general group theoretical problem of understanding all *possible* multiplets for SU(2) is equivalent to the problem of finding matrices which satisfy these commutation relations. These are, in fact, precisely the angular momentum matrices of dimension $(2T + 1) \times (2T + 1)$ which are generalizations of the $\boldsymbol{\tau}/2$'s, which themselves correspond to $T = \frac{1}{2}$, as indicated in the notation $\mathbf{T}^{(\frac{1}{2})}$. For example, the $T = 1$ matrices are 3×3 and can be compactly summarised by (problem 12.5)

$$(T_i^{(1)})_{jk} = -\mathrm{i}\epsilon_{ijk} \tag{12.48}$$

where the numbers $-\mathrm{i}\epsilon_{ijk}$ are deliberately chosen to be the *same* numbers (with a minus sign) that specify the algebra in (12.47); the latter are called the *structure constants* of the SU(2) group (see appendix M, sections M.3–M.5). In general there will be matrices $\mathbf{T}^{(T)}$ of dimensionality $(2T+1) \times (2T+1)$ which satisfy (12.47), and correspondingly $(2T+1)$-dimensional wavefunctions $\psi^{(T)}$ analogous to the two-dimensional ($T = \frac{1}{2}$) case of (12.8). The generalization of (12.32) to these higher-dimensional multiplets is then

$$\psi^{(T)\prime} = \exp(\mathrm{i}\boldsymbol{\alpha} \cdot \mathbf{T}^{(T)})\psi^{(T)}, \tag{12.49}$$

which has the general form of (12.35). In this case, the matrices $\mathbf{T}^{(T)}$ provide a $(2T + 1)$-dimensional matrix representation of the generators of SU(2). We shall meet field-theoretic representations of the generators in section 12.3.

We now proceed to consider isospin in our primary area of interest, which is particle physics.

12.2.3   Isospin in particle physics: flavour SU(2)$_f$

The neutron and proton states themselves are actually only the ground states of a whole series of corresponding $B = 1$ levels with isospin $\frac{1}{2}$ (i.e. doublets). Another series of baryonic levels comes in *four* charge states, corresponding to $T = \frac{3}{2}$; and in the meson sector, the π's appear as the lowest states of a sequence of mesonic triplets ($T = 1$). Many other examples also exist, but with one remarkable difference as compared to the nuclear physics case: no baryon states are known with $T > \frac{3}{2}$, nor any meson states with $T > 1$.

The most natural interpretation of these facts is that the observed states are composites of more basic entities which carry different charges but are nearly degenerate in mass, while the forces between these entities are charge-independent, just as in the nuclear (p,n) case. These entities are, of course,

---

[4]Likewise, the angular momentum commutation relations (12.29) are the Lie algebra of the rotation group SO(3). The Lie algebras of the two groups are therefore the same. For an indication of how, nevertheless, the groups do differ, see appendix M, section M.7.

the quarks: the n contains (udd), the p is (uud), and the Δ-quartet is (uuu, uud, udd, ddd). The u-d isospin doublet plays the role of the p-n doublet in the nuclear case, and this degree of freedom is what we now call SU(2) isospin flavour symmetry at the quark level, denoted by SU(2)$_f$. We shall denote the u-d quark doublet wavefunction by

$$q = \begin{pmatrix} u \\ d \end{pmatrix} \tag{12.50}$$

omitting now the explicit representation label '$(\frac{1}{2})$', and shortening 'ψ_u' to just 'u', and similarly for 'd'. Then, under an SU(2)$_f$ transformation,

$$q \to q' = \mathbf{V}q = \exp(i\boldsymbol{\alpha} \cdot \boldsymbol{\tau}/2)\, q. \tag{12.51}$$

The limitation $T \leq \frac{3}{2}$ for baryonic states can be understood in terms of their being composed of three $T = \frac{1}{2}$ constituents (two of them pair to $T = 1$ or $T = 0$, and the third adds to $T = 1$ to make $T = \frac{3}{2}$ or $T = \frac{1}{2}$, and to $T = 0$ to make $T = \frac{1}{2}$, by the usual angular momentum addition rules). It is, however, a challenge for QCD to explain why, for example, states with four or five quarks should not exist (nor states of one or two quarks!), and why a state of six quarks, for example, appears as the deuteron, which is a loosely bound state of n and p, rather than as a compact $B = 2$ analogue of the n and p themselves.

Meson states such as the pion are formed from a quark and an antiquark, and it is therefore appropriate at this point to explain how *antiparticles* are described in isospin terms. An antiparticle is characterized by having the signs of all its additively conserved quantum numbers reversed, relative to those of the corresponding particle. Thus if a u-quark has $B = \frac{1}{3}, T = \frac{1}{2}, T_3 = \frac{1}{2}$, a ū-quark has $B = -\frac{1}{3}, T = \frac{1}{2}, T_3 = -\frac{1}{2}$. Similarly, the d̄ has $B = -\frac{1}{3}, T = \frac{1}{2}$ and $T_3 = \frac{1}{2}$. Note that, while T_3 is an additively conserved quantum number, the magnitude of the isospin is not additively conserved: rather, it is 'vectorially' conserved according to the rules of combining angular-momentum-like quantum numbers, as we have seen. Thus the antiquarks d̄ and ū form the $T_3 = +\frac{1}{2}$ and $T_3 = -\frac{1}{2}$ members of an SU(2)$_f$ doublet, just as u and d themselves do, and the question arises: given that the (u, d) doublet transforms as in (12.51), how does the $(\bar{u}, \bar{d})$ doublet transform?

The answer is that antiparticles are assigned to the *complex conjugate* of the representation to which the corresponding particles belong. Thus identifying $\bar{u} \equiv u^*$ and $\bar{d} \equiv d^*$ we have[5]

$$q^{*\prime} = \mathbf{V}^* q^*, \quad \text{or} \quad \begin{pmatrix} \bar{u} \\ \bar{d} \end{pmatrix}' = \exp(-i\boldsymbol{\alpha} \cdot \boldsymbol{\tau}^*/2) \begin{pmatrix} \bar{u} \\ \bar{d} \end{pmatrix} \tag{12.52}$$

for the SU(2)$_f$ transformation law of the antiquark doublet. In mathematical terms, this means (compare (12.32)) that the three matrices $-\frac{1}{2}\boldsymbol{\tau}^*$ must

---

[5]The overbar (ū etc.) here stands only for 'antiparticle', and has nothing to do with the Dirac conjugate $\bar{\psi}$ introduced in section 4.4.

represent the generators of SU(2)$_f$ in the **2*** representation (i.e. the complex conjugate of the original two-dimensional representation, which we will now call **2**). Referring to (12.25), we see that $\tau_1^* = \tau_1, \tau_2^* = -\tau_2$ and $\tau_3^* = \tau_3$. It is then easy to check that the three matrices $-\tau_1/2, +\tau_2/2$ and $-\tau_3/2$ do indeed satisfy the required commutation relations (12.28), and thus provide a valid matrix representation of the SU(2) generators. Also, since the third component of isospin is here represented by $-\tau_3^*/2 = -\tau_3/2$, the desired reversal in sign of the additively conserved eigenvalue does occur.

Although the quark doublet (u, d) and antiquark doublet $(\bar{u}, \bar{d})$ do transform differently under SU(2)$_f$ transformations, there is nevertheless a sense in which the **2*** and **2** representations are somehow the 'same': after all, the quantum numbers $T = \frac{1}{2}, T_3 = \pm\frac{1}{2}$ describe them both. In fact, the two representations are 'unitarily equivalent', in that we can find a unitary matrix U_C such that

$$U_C \exp(-i\boldsymbol{\alpha} \cdot \boldsymbol{\tau}^*/2)U_C^{-1} = \exp(i\boldsymbol{\alpha} \cdot \boldsymbol{\tau}/2). \tag{12.53}$$

This requirement is easier to disentangle if we consider infinitesimal transformations, for which (12.53) becomes

$$U_C(-\boldsymbol{\tau}^*)U_C^{-1} = \boldsymbol{\tau}, \tag{12.54}$$

or

$$U_C\tau_1 U_C^{-1} = -\tau_1, \quad U_C\tau_2 U_C^{-1} = \tau_2, \quad U_C\tau_3 U_C^{-1} = -\tau_3. \tag{12.55}$$

Bearing the commutation relations (12.28) in mind, and the fact that $\tau_i^{-1} = \tau_i$, it is clear that we can choose U_C proportional to τ_2, and set

$$U_C = i\tau_2 = \begin{pmatrix} 0 & 1 \\ -1 & 0 \end{pmatrix} \tag{12.56}$$

to obtain a convenient unitary form. From (12.52) and (12.53) we obtain $(U_C q^{*\prime}) = \mathbf{V}(U_C q^*)$, which implies that the doublet

$$U_C \begin{pmatrix} \bar{u} \\ \bar{d} \end{pmatrix} = \begin{pmatrix} \bar{d} \\ -\bar{u} \end{pmatrix} \tag{12.57}$$

transforms in exactly the same way as (u, d). This result is useful, because it means that we can use the familiar tables of (Clebsch-Gordan) angular momentum coupling coefficients for combining quark and antiquark states together, *provided* we include the relative minus sign between the $\bar{d}$ and $\bar{u}$ components which has appeared in (12.57). Note that, as expected, the $\bar{d}$ is in the $T_3 = +\frac{1}{2}$ position, and the $\bar{u}$ is in the $T_3 = -\frac{1}{2}$ position.

As an application of these results, let us compare the $T = 0$ combination of the p and n states to form the (isoscalar) deuteron, and the combination of (u, d) and $(\bar{u}, \bar{d})$ states to form the isoscalar ω-meson. In the first, the isospin part of the wavefunction is $\frac{1}{\sqrt{2}}(\psi_p\psi_n - \psi_n\psi_p)$, corresponding to the $S = 0$ combination of two spin-$\frac{1}{2}$ particles in quantum mechanics given by

$\frac{1}{\sqrt{2}}(|\uparrow\rangle\,|\downarrow\rangle - |\downarrow\rangle\,|\uparrow\rangle)$. But in the second case the corresponding wavefunction is $\frac{1}{\sqrt{2}}(\bar{d}d - (-\bar{u})u) = \frac{1}{\sqrt{2}}(\bar{d}d + \bar{u}u)$. Similarly, the $T = 1$ $T_3 = 0$ state describing the π^0 is $\frac{1}{\sqrt{2}}(\bar{d}d + (-\bar{u})u) = \frac{1}{\sqrt{2}}(\bar{d}d - \bar{u}u)$.

There is a very convenient alternative way of obtaining these wavefunctions, which we include here because it generalizes straightforwardly to $SU(3)$; its advantage is that it avoids the use of the explicit C-G coupling coefficients, and of their (more complicated) analogues in $SU(3)$.

Bearing in mind the identifications $\bar{u} \equiv u^*$, $\bar{d} \equiv d^*$, we see that the $T = 0$ $\bar{q}q$ combination $\bar{u}u + \bar{d}d$ can be written as $u^*u + d^*d$ which is just $q^\dagger q$, (recall that † means transpose and complex conjugate). Under an $SU(2)_f$ transformation, $q \to q' = \mathbf{V}q$, so $q^\dagger \to q'^\dagger = q^\dagger\mathbf{V}^\dagger$ and

$$q^\dagger q \to q'^\dagger q' = q^\dagger\mathbf{V}^\dagger\mathbf{V}q = q^\dagger q \tag{12.58}$$

using $\mathbf{V}^\dagger\mathbf{V} = \mathbf{1}_2$; thus $q^\dagger q$ is indeed an $SU(2)_f$ invariant, which means it has $T = 0$ (no multiplet partners).

We may also construct the $T = 1$ $q - \bar{q}$ states in a similar way. Consider the three quantities v_i defined by

$$v_i = q^\dagger\tau_i q \quad i = 1, 2, 3. \tag{12.59}$$

Under an infinitesimal $SU(2)_f$ transformation

$$q' = (\mathbf{1}_2 + \mathrm{i}\boldsymbol{\epsilon}\cdot\boldsymbol{\tau}/2)q, \tag{12.60}$$

the three quantities v_i transform to

$$v_i' = q^\dagger(\mathbf{1}_2 - \mathrm{i}\boldsymbol{\epsilon}\cdot\boldsymbol{\tau}/2)\tau_i(\mathbf{1}_2 + \mathrm{i}\boldsymbol{\epsilon}\cdot\boldsymbol{\tau}/2)q, \tag{12.61}$$

where we have used $q'^\dagger = q^\dagger(\mathbf{1}_2 + \mathrm{i}\boldsymbol{\epsilon}\cdot\boldsymbol{\tau}/2)^\dagger$ and then $\boldsymbol{\tau}^\dagger = \boldsymbol{\tau}$. Retaining only the first-order terms in $\boldsymbol{\epsilon}$ gives (problem 12.6)

$$v_i' = v_i + \mathrm{i}\frac{\epsilon_j}{2}q^\dagger(\tau_i\tau_j - \tau_j\tau_i)q \tag{12.62}$$

where the sum on $j = 1, 2, 3$ is understood. But from (12.28) we know the commutator of two τ's, so that (12.62) becomes

$$
\begin{aligned}
v_i' &= v_i + \mathrm{i}\frac{\epsilon_j}{2}q^\dagger.2\mathrm{i}\epsilon_{ijk}\tau_k q \quad \text{(sum on } k = 1, 2, 3) \\
&= v_i - \epsilon_{ijk}\epsilon_j q^\dagger\tau_k q \\
&= v_i - \epsilon_{ijk}\epsilon_j v_k,
\end{aligned} \tag{12.63}
$$

which may also be written in 'vector' notation as

$$\boldsymbol{v}' = \boldsymbol{v} - \boldsymbol{\epsilon}\times\boldsymbol{v}. \tag{12.64}$$

Equation (12.63) states that, under an (infinitesimal) $SU(2)_f$ transformation, the three quantities v_i $(i = 1, 2, 3)$ transform into *specific linear combinations* of themselves, as determined by the coefficients ϵ_{ijk} (the ϵ's are just

the parameters of the infinitesimal transformation). This is precisely what is needed for a set of quantities to *form the basis for a representation*. In this case, it is the $T = 1$ representation as we can guess from the multiplicity of three, but we can also directly verify it, as follows. Equation (12.49) with $T = 1$, together with (12.48), tell us how a $T = 1$ triplet should transform: namely, under an infinitesimal transformation (with $\mathbf{1}_3$ the unit 3×3 matrix),

$$
\begin{aligned}
\psi_i^{(1)\prime} &= (\mathbf{1}_3 + \mathrm{i}\boldsymbol{\epsilon} \cdot \mathbf{T}^{(1)})_{ik} \psi_k^{(1)} \quad (\text{sum on } k = 1, 2, 3) \\
&= (\mathbf{1}_3 + \mathrm{i}\epsilon_j T_j^{(1)})_{ik} \psi_k^{(1)} \quad (\text{sum on } j = 1, 2, 3) \\
&= (\delta_{ik} + \mathrm{i}\epsilon_j (T_j^{(1)})_{ik}) \psi_k^{(1)} \\
&= (\delta_{ik} + \mathrm{i}\epsilon_j. - \mathrm{i}\epsilon_{jik}) \psi_k^{(1)} \quad \text{using (12.48)} \\
&= \psi_i^{(1)} - \epsilon_{ijk} \epsilon_j \psi_k^{(1)} \quad \text{using the antisymmetry of } \epsilon_{ijk} \quad (12.65)
\end{aligned}
$$

which is exactly the same as (12.63).

The reader who has worked through problem 4.2(a) will recognize the exact analogy between the $T = 1$ transformation law (12.64) for the isospin bilinear $q^\dagger \boldsymbol{\tau} q$, and the 3-vector transformation law (cf (4.9)) for the Pauli spinor bilinear $\phi^\dagger \boldsymbol{\sigma} \phi$.

Returning to the physics of v_i, inserting (12.50) into (12.59) we find explicitly

$$
v_1 = \bar{u}d + \bar{d}u, \quad v_2 = -\mathrm{i}\,\bar{u}d + \mathrm{i}\,\bar{d}u, \quad v_3 = \bar{u}u - \bar{d}d. \tag{12.66}
$$

Apart from the normalization factor of $\frac{1}{\sqrt{2}}$, v_3 may therefore be identified with the $T_3 = 0$ member of the $T = 1$ triplet, having the quantum numbers of the π^0. Neither v_1 nor v_2 has a definite value of T_3, however: rather, we need to consider the linear combinations

$$
\frac{1}{2}(v_1 + \mathrm{i}v_2) = \bar{u}d \quad T_3 = -1 \tag{12.67}
$$

and

$$
\frac{1}{2}(v_1 - \mathrm{i}v_2) = \bar{d}u \quad T_3 = +1 \tag{12.68}
$$

which have the quantum numbers of the π^- and π^+. The use of $v_1 \pm \mathrm{i}v_2$ here is precisely analogous to the use of the 'spherical basis' wavefunctions $x \pm \mathrm{i}y = r\sin\theta e^{\pm \mathrm{i}\phi}$ for $\ell = 1$ states in quantum mechanics, rather than the 'Cartesian' ones x and y.

We are now ready to proceed to SU(3).

12.3   Flavour SU(3)$_\mathrm{f}$

Larger hadronic multiplets also exist, in which strange particles are grouped with non-strange ones. Gell-Mann (1961) and Ne'eman (1961) (see also Gell-Mann and Ne'eman 1964) were the first to propose SU(3)$_\mathrm{f}$ as the correct

generalization of isospin SU(2)$_f$ to include strangeness. Like SU(2), SU(3) is a group whose elements are matrices – in this case, unitary 3×3 ones, of unit determinant. The general group-theoretic analysis of SU(3) is quite complicated, but is fortunately not necessary for the physical applications we require. We can, in fact, develop all the results needed by mimicking the steps followed for SU(2).

We start by finding the general form of an SU(3) matrix. Such matrices obviously act on 3-component column vectors, the generalization of the 2-component isospinors of SU(2). In more physical terms, we regard the three quark wavefunctions u, d and s as being approximately degenerate, and we consider unitary 3×3 transformations among them via

$$q' = \mathbf{W}q \tag{12.69}$$

where q now stands for the 3-component column vector

$$q = \begin{pmatrix} u \\ d \\ s \end{pmatrix} \tag{12.70}$$

and $\mathbf{W}$ is a 3×3 unitary matrix of determinant 1 (again, an overall phase has been extracted). The representation provided by this triplet of states is called the 'fundamental' representation of SU(3)$_f$ (just as the isospinor representation is the fundamental one of SU(2)$_f$).

To determine the general form of an SU(3) matrix $\mathbf{W}$, we follow exactly the same steps as in the SU(2) case. An infinitesimal SU(3) matrix has the form

$$\mathbf{W}_{\text{infl}} = 1_3 + i\chi \tag{12.71}$$

where χ is a 3×3 traceless Hermitian matrix. Such a matrix involves *eight* independent parameters (problem (12.7)) and can be written as

$$\chi = \boldsymbol{\eta} \cdot \boldsymbol{\lambda}/2 \tag{12.72}$$

where $\boldsymbol{\eta} = (\eta_1, \ldots, \eta_8)$ and the $\boldsymbol{\lambda}$'s are eight matrices generalizing the $\boldsymbol{\tau}$ matrices of (12.25). They are the generators of SU(3) in the three-dimensional fundamental representation, and their commutation relations define the *algebra of SU(3)* (compare (12.28) for SU(2)):

$$[\lambda_a/2, \lambda_b/2] = i f_{abc} \lambda_c/2, \tag{12.73}$$

where a, b and c run from 1 to 8.

The λ-matrices (often called the *Gell-Mann matrices*), are given in appendix M, along with the *SU(3) structure constants* $i f_{abc}$; the constants f_{abc} are all real.

A finite SU(3) transformation on the quark triplet is then (cf (12.32))

$$q' = \exp(i\boldsymbol{\alpha} \cdot \boldsymbol{\lambda}/2)q, \tag{12.74}$$

which also has the 'generalized phase transformation' character of (12.35), now with *eight* 'phase angles'. Thus $\mathbf{W}$ is parametrized as $\mathbf{W} = \exp(i\boldsymbol{\alpha} \cdot \boldsymbol{\lambda}/2)$.

As in the case of SU(2)$_f$, exact symmetry under SU(3)$_f$ would imply that the three states u, d and s were degenerate in mass. Actually, of course, this is not the case: in particular, while the u and d quark masses are of order 1-5 MeV, the s quark mass is greater, of order 100 MeV. Nevertheless it is still possible to regard this as relatively small on a typical hadronic mass scale, so we may proceed to explore the physical consequences of this (approximate) SU(3)$_f$ flavour symmetry.

Such a symmetry implies that the eigenvalues of the $\boldsymbol{\lambda}$'s are constants of the motion, but because of the commutation relations (12.73) not all of these operators have simultaneous eigenstates. This happened for SU(2) too, but there the very close analogy with SO(3) told us how the states were to be correctly classified, by the eigenvalues of the relevant complete set of mutually commuting operators. Here it is more involved – for a start, there are 8 matrices λ_a. A glance at appendix M, section M.4.5, shows that *two* of the λ's are diagonal (in the chosen representation), namely λ_3 and λ_8. This means physically that for SU(3) there are *two* additively conserved quantum numbers, which in this case are of course the third component of hadronic isospin (since λ_3 is simply τ_3 bordered by zeros), and a quantity related to strangeness. Defining the hadronic hypercharge Y by $Y = B + S$, where B is the baryon number ($\frac{1}{3}$ for each quark) and the strangeness values are $S(u) = S(d) = 0$, $S(s) = -1$, we find that the physically required eigenvalues imply that the matrix representing the hypercharge operator is $Y^{(\mathbf{3})} = \frac{1}{\sqrt{3}}\lambda_8$, in this fundamental (three-dimensional) representation, denoted by the symbol $\mathbf{3}$. Identifying $T_3^{(\mathbf{3})} = \frac{1}{2}\lambda_3$ then gives the Gell-Mann–Nishijima relation $Q = T_3 + Y/2$ for the quark charges in units of $|\,e\,|$.

So λ_3 and λ_8 are analogous to τ_3; what about the analogue of $\boldsymbol{\tau}^2$, which is diagonalizable simultaneously with τ_3 in the case of SU(2)? Indeed, (cf (12.41)) $\boldsymbol{\tau}^2$ is a multiple of the 2×2 unit matrix. In just the same way one finds that $\boldsymbol{\lambda}^2$ is also proportional to the unit matrix:

$$(\boldsymbol{\lambda}/2)^2 = \sum_{a=1}^{8}(\lambda_a/2)^2 = \frac{4}{3}\mathbf{1}_3, \qquad (12.75)$$

as can be verified from the explicit forms of the λ-matrices given in appendix M, section M.4.5. Thus we may characterize the 'fundamental triplet' (12.70) by the eigenvalues of $(\boldsymbol{\lambda}/2)^2$, λ_3 and λ_8. The conventional way of representing this pictorially is to plot the states in a $Y - T_3$ diagram, as shown in figure 12.3.

We may now consider other representations of SU(3)$_f$. The first important one is that to which the *antiquarks* belong. If we denote the fundamental three-dimensional representation accommodating the quarks by $\mathbf{3}$, then the antiquarks have quantum numbers appropriate to the 'complex conjugate' of

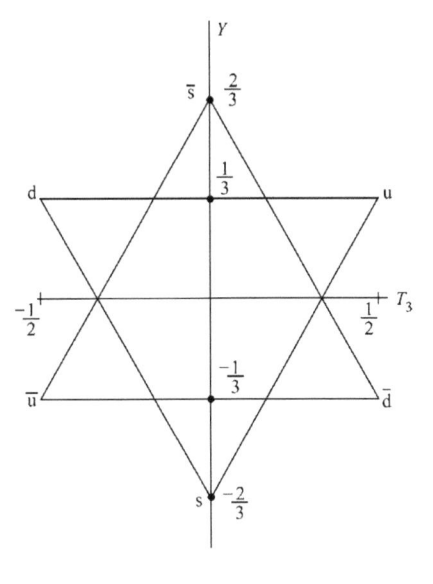

FIGURE 12.3
The $Y - T_3$ quantum numbers of the fundamental triplet **3** of quarks, and of the antitriplet **3*** of antiquarks.

this representation, denoted by **3*** just as in the SU(2) case. The $\bar{q}$ wavefunctions identified as $\bar{u} \equiv u^*, \bar{d} \equiv d^*$ and $\bar{s} \equiv s^*$, then transform by

$$\bar{q}' = \begin{pmatrix} \bar{u} \\ \bar{d} \\ \bar{s} \end{pmatrix}' = \mathbf{W}^* \bar{q} = \exp(-i\boldsymbol{\alpha} \cdot \boldsymbol{\lambda}^*/2)\bar{q} \qquad (12.76)$$

instead of by (12.74). As for the **2*** representation of SU(2), (12.76) means that the eight quantities $-\boldsymbol{\lambda}^*/2$ represent the SU(3) generators in this **3*** representation. Referring to appendix M, section M.4.5, one quickly sees that λ_3 and λ_8 are real, so that the eigenvalues of the physical observables $T_3^{(\mathbf{3}^*)} = -\lambda_3/2$ and $Y^{(\mathbf{3}^*)} = -\frac{1}{\sqrt{3}}\lambda_8/2$ (in this representation) are reversed relative to those in the **3**, as expected for antiparticles. The $\bar{u}, \bar{d}$ and $\bar{s}$ states may also be plotted on the $Y - T_3$ diagram, figure 12.3, as shown.

Here is already one important difference between SU(3) and SU(2): the fundamental SU(3) representation **3** and its complex conjugate **3*** are *not* equivalent. This follows immediately from figure 12.3, where it is clear that the extra quantum number Y distinguishes the two representations.

Larger SU(3)$_f$ representations can be created by combining quarks and antiquarks, as in SU(2)$_f$. For our present purposes, an important one is the eight-dimensional ('octet') representation which appears when one combines the **3*** and **3** representations, in a way which is very analogous to the three-

dimensional ('triplet') representation obtained by combining the $\mathbf{2^*}$ and $\mathbf{2}$ representations of SU(2).

Consider first the quantity $\bar{u}u + \bar{d}d + \bar{s}s$. As in the SU(2) case, this can be written equivalently as $q^\dagger q$, which is invariant under $q \to q' = \mathbf{W}q$ since $\mathbf{W^\dagger W} = \mathbf{1}_3$. So this combination is an SU(3) *singlet*. The *octet* coupling is formed by a straightforward generalization of the SU(2) triplet coupling $q^\dagger \boldsymbol{\tau} q$ of (12.59),

$$w_a = q^\dagger \lambda_a q \qquad a = 1, 2, \ldots 8. \tag{12.77}$$

Under an infinitesimal SU(3)$_\text{f}$ transformation (compare (12.61) and (12.62)),

$$\begin{aligned} w_a \to w_a' &= q^\dagger (\mathbf{1}_3 - \mathrm{i}\boldsymbol{\eta} \cdot \boldsymbol{\lambda}/2)\lambda_a(\mathbf{1}_3 + \mathrm{i}\boldsymbol{\eta} \cdot \boldsymbol{\lambda}/2)q \\ &\approx q^\dagger \lambda_a q + \mathrm{i}\frac{\eta_b}{2}q^\dagger(\lambda_a\lambda_b - \lambda_b\lambda_a)q \end{aligned} \tag{12.78}$$

where the sum on $b = 1$ to 8 is understood. Using (12.73) for the commutator of two λ's we find

$$w_a' = w_a + \mathrm{i}\frac{\eta_b}{2}q^\dagger.2\mathrm{i}f_{abc}\lambda_c q \tag{12.79}$$

or

$$w_a' = w_a - f_{abc}\eta_b w_c \tag{12.80}$$

which may usefully be compared with (12.63). Just as in the SU(2)$_\text{f}$ triplet case, equation (12.80) shows that, under an SU(3)$_\text{f}$ transformation, the eight quantities $w_a(a = 1, 2, \ldots 8)$ transform into specific linear combinations of themselves, as determined by the coefficients f_{abc} (the η's are just the parameters of the infinitesimal transformation).

This is, again, precisely what is needed for a set of quantities to form the basis for a representation – in this case, an eight-dimensional representation of SU(3)$_\text{f}$. For a finite SU(3)$_\text{f}$ transformation, we can 'exponentiate' (12.80) to obtain

$$\boldsymbol{w}' = \exp(\mathrm{i}\boldsymbol{\alpha} \cdot \mathbf{G}^{(8)})\boldsymbol{w} \tag{12.81}$$

where $\boldsymbol{w}$ is an 8-component column vector

$$\boldsymbol{w} = \begin{pmatrix} w_1 \\ w_2 \\ \vdots \\ w_8 \end{pmatrix} \tag{12.82}$$

such that $w_a = q^\dagger \lambda_a q$, and where (cf (12.49) for SU(2))$_\text{f}$) the quantities $\mathbf{G}^{(8)} = (G_1^{(8)}, G_2^{(8)}, \ldots G_8^{(8)})$ are 8×8 matrices, acting on the 8-component vector $\boldsymbol{w}$, and forming an 8-dimensional representation of the algebra of SU(3): that is to say, the $\mathbf{G}^{(8)}$'s satisfy (cf (12.73))

$$\left[G_a^{(8)}, G_b^{(8)}\right] = \mathrm{i}f_{abc}G_c^{(8)}. \tag{12.83}$$

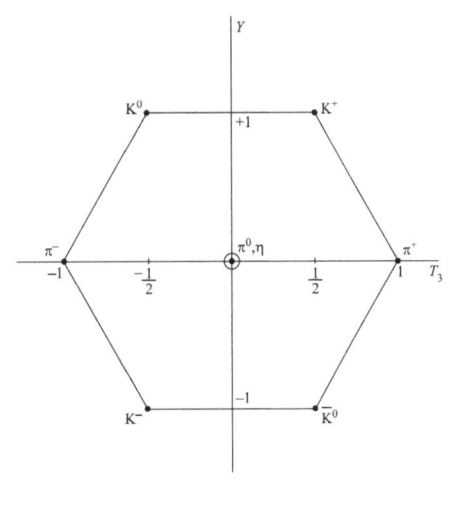

FIGURE 12.4

The $Y - T_3$ quantum numbers of the pseudoscalar meson octet.

The actual form of the $G_a^{(8)}$ matrices is given by comparing the infinitesimal version of (12.81) with (12.80)

$$\left(G_a^{(8)}\right)_{bc} = -\mathrm{i}f_{abc}, \tag{12.84}$$

as may be checked in problem 12.8, where it is also verified that the matrices specified by (12.84) do obey the commutation relations (12.83).

As in the SU(2)$_f$ case, the 8 states generated by the combinations $q^\dagger \lambda_a q$ are not necessarily the ones with the physically desired quantum numbers. To get the $\pi^\pm$, for example, we again need to form $(w_1 \pm \mathrm{i}w_2)/2$. Similarly, w_4 produces $\bar{u}s + \bar{s}u$ and w_5 the combination $-\mathrm{i}\,\bar{u}s + \mathrm{i}\,\bar{s}u$, so the K$^\pm$ states are $w_4 \mp \mathrm{i}w_5$. Similarly the K^0, $\bar{\text{K}}^0$ states are $w_6 - \mathrm{i}w_7$, and $w_6 + \mathrm{i}w_7$, while the η (in this simple model) would be $w_8 \sim (\bar{u}u + \bar{d}d - 2\bar{s}s)$, which is orthogonal to both the π^0 state and the SU(3)$_f$ singlet. In this way all the pseudoscalar octet of π-partners has been identified, as shown on the $Y - T$ diagram of figure 12.4. We say 'octet of π-partners', but a reader knowing the masses of these particles might well query why we should feel justified in regarding them as (even approximately) degenerate. By contrast, a similar octet of vector ($J^P 1^-$) mesons (the ω, ρ, K^* and $\bar{\text{K}}^*$) are all much closer in mass, averaging around 800 MeV; in these states the $\bar{q}q$ spins add to $S = 1$, while the orbital angular momentum is still zero. The pion, and to a much lesser extent the kaons, seem to be 'anomalously light' for some reason: we shall learn the likely explanation for this in chapter 15.

There is a deep similarity between (12.84) and (12.48). In both cases, a representation has been found in which the matrix element of a generator is

minus the corresponding structure constant. Such a representation is always possible for a Lie group, and is called the *adjoint*, or *regular*, representation (see appendix M, section M.5). These representations are of particular importance in gauge theories, as we will see, since gauge quanta always belong to the adjoint representation of the gauged group (for example, the 8 gluons in $SU(3)_c$).

Further flavours c, b and t of course exist, but the mass differences are now so large that it is generally not useful to think about higher flavour groups such as $SU(4)_f$ etc. Instead, we now move on to consider the field-theoretic formulation of global $SU(2)_f$ and $SU(3)_f$.

12.4   Non-Abelian global symmetries in Lagrangian quantum field theory

12.4.1 $SU(2)_f$ and $SU(3)_f$

As may already have begun to be apparent in chapter 7, Lagrangian quantum field theory is a formalism which is especially well adapted for the description of symmetries. Without going into any elaborate general theory, we shall now give a few examples showing how global flavour symmetry is very easily built into a Lagrangian, generalizing in a simple way the global U(1) symmetries considered in section 7.1 and section 7.2. This will also prepare the way for the (local) gauge case, to be considered in the following chapter.

Consider, for example, the Lagrangian

$$\hat{\mathcal{L}} = \bar{\hat{u}}(i\,\not{\partial} - m)\hat{u} + \bar{\hat{d}}(i\,\not{\partial} - m)\hat{d} \tag{12.85}$$

describing two free fermions 'u' and 'd' of equal mass m, with the overbar now meaning the Dirac conjugate for the four-component spinor fields. Note carefully that we are suppressing the space-time arguments of the quantum fields $\hat{u}(x), \hat{d}(x)$. As in (12.50), we are using the convenient shorthand $\hat{\psi}_u = \hat{u}$ and $\hat{\psi}_d = \hat{d}$. Let us introduce

$$\hat{q} = \begin{pmatrix} \hat{u} \\ \hat{d} \end{pmatrix} \tag{12.86}$$

so that $\hat{\mathcal{L}}$ can be compactly written as

$$\hat{\mathcal{L}} = \bar{\hat{q}}(i\,\not{\partial} - m)\hat{q}. \tag{12.87}$$

In this form it is obvious that $\hat{\mathcal{L}}$ – and hence the associated Hamiltonian $\hat{\mathcal{H}}$ – is invariant under the global U(1) transformation

$$\hat{q}' = e^{i\alpha}\hat{q} \tag{12.88}$$

(cf (12.1)) which is associated with baryon number conservation. It is also invariant under global SU(2)$_f$ transformations acting in the flavour u-d space (cf (12.32)):

$$\hat{q}' = \exp(-i\boldsymbol{\alpha} \cdot \boldsymbol{\tau}/2)\hat{q} \tag{12.89}$$

(for the change in sign with respect to (12.51), compare section 7.1 and section 7.2 in the U(1) case). In (12.89), the three parameters $\boldsymbol{\alpha}$ are independent of x.

What are the conserved quantities associated with the invariance of $\hat{\mathcal{L}}$ under (12.89) ? Let us recall the discussion of the simpler U(1) cases studied in sections 7.1 and 7.2. Considering the complex scalar field of section 7.1, the analogue of (12.89) was just $\hat{\phi} \to \hat{\phi}' = e^{-i\alpha}\hat{\phi}$, and the conserved quantity was the Hermitian operator $\hat{N}_\phi$ which appeared in the exponent of the unitary operator $\hat{U}$ that effected the transformation $\hat{\phi} \to \hat{\phi}'$ via

$$\hat{\phi}' = \hat{U}\hat{\phi}\hat{U}^\dagger, \tag{12.90}$$

with

$$\hat{U} = \exp(i\alpha\hat{N}_\phi). \tag{12.91}$$

For an infinitesimal α, we have

$$\hat{\phi}' \approx (1 - i\epsilon)\hat{\phi}, \quad \hat{U} \approx 1 + i\epsilon\hat{N}_\phi, \tag{12.92}$$

so that (12.90) becomes

$$(1 - i\epsilon)\hat{\phi} = (1 + i\epsilon\hat{N}_\phi)\hat{\phi}(1 - i\epsilon\hat{N}_\phi) \approx \hat{\phi} + i\epsilon[\hat{N}_\phi, \hat{\phi}]; \tag{12.93}$$

hence we require

$$[\hat{N}_\phi, \hat{\phi}] = -\hat{\phi} \tag{12.94}$$

for consistency. Insofar as $\hat{N}_\phi$ determines the form of an infinitesimal version of the unitary transformation operator $\hat{U}$, it seems reasonable to call it the *generator* of these global U(1) transformations (compare the discussion after (12.27) and (12.35), but note that here $\hat{N}_\phi$ is a quantum field operator, not a matrix).

Consider now the SU(2)$_f$ transformation (12.89), in the infinitesimal case:

$$\hat{q}' = (1 - i\boldsymbol{\epsilon} \cdot \boldsymbol{\tau}/2)\hat{q}. \tag{12.95}$$

Since the single U(1) parameter ϵ is now replaced by the three parameters $\boldsymbol{\epsilon} = (\epsilon_1, \epsilon_2, \epsilon_3)$, we shall need three analogues of $\hat{N}_\phi$, which we call

$$\hat{\boldsymbol{T}}^{(\frac{1}{2})} = (\hat{T}_1^{(\frac{1}{2})}, \hat{T}_2^{(\frac{1}{2})}, \hat{T}_3^{(\frac{1}{2})}), \tag{12.96}$$

corresponding to the three independent infinitesimal SU(2) transformations. The generalizations of (12.90) and (12.91) are then

$$\hat{q}' = \hat{U}^{(\frac{1}{2})}\hat{q}\hat{U}^{(\frac{1}{2})\dagger} \tag{12.97}$$

and

$$\hat{U}^{(\frac{1}{2})} = \exp(\mathrm{i}\boldsymbol{\alpha} \cdot \hat{\boldsymbol{T}}^{(\frac{1}{2})}) \tag{12.98}$$

where the $\hat{\boldsymbol{T}}^{(\frac{1}{2})}$'s are Hermitian, so that $\hat{U}^{(\frac{1}{2})}$ is unitary (cf (12.35)). It would seem reasonable in this case too to regard the $\hat{\boldsymbol{T}}^{(\frac{1}{2})}$'s as providing a *field theoretic representation* of the generators of SU(2)$_f$, an interpretation we shall shortly confirm. In the infinitesimal case, (12.97) and (12.98) become

$$(1 - \mathrm{i}\boldsymbol{\epsilon} \cdot \boldsymbol{\tau}/2)\hat{q} = (1 + \mathrm{i}\boldsymbol{\epsilon} \cdot \hat{\boldsymbol{T}}^{(\frac{1}{2})})\hat{q}(1 - \mathrm{i}\boldsymbol{\epsilon} \cdot \hat{\boldsymbol{T}}^{(\frac{1}{2})}), \tag{12.99}$$

using the Hermiticity of the $\hat{\boldsymbol{T}}^{(\frac{1}{2})}$'s. Expanding the right-hand side of (12.99) to first order in $\boldsymbol{\epsilon}$, and equating coefficients of $\boldsymbol{\epsilon}$ on both sides, (12.99) reduces to (problem 12.9)

$$[\hat{\boldsymbol{T}}^{(\frac{1}{2})}, \hat{q}] = -(\boldsymbol{\tau}/2)\hat{q}, \tag{12.100}$$

which is the analogue of (12.94). Equation (12.100) expresses a very specific *commutation* property of the operators $\hat{\boldsymbol{T}}^{(\frac{1}{2})}$, which turns out to be satisfied by the expression

$$\hat{\boldsymbol{T}}^{(\frac{1}{2})} = \int \hat{q}^\dagger(\boldsymbol{\tau}/2)\hat{q}\mathrm{d}^3\boldsymbol{x} \tag{12.101}$$

as can be checked (problem 12.10) from the anticommutation relations of the fermionic fields in $\hat{q}$. We shall derive (12.101) from Noether's theorem (Noether 1918) in a little while. Note that if '$\boldsymbol{\tau}/2$' is replaced by 1, (12.101) reduces to the sum of the u and d number operators, as required for the one-parameter U(1) case. The '$\hat{q}^\dagger\boldsymbol{\tau}\hat{q}$' combination is precisely the field-theoretic version of the $q^\dagger\boldsymbol{\tau}q$ coupling we discussed in section 12.1.3. It means that the three operators $\hat{\boldsymbol{T}}^{(\frac{1}{2})}$ themselves belong to a $T = 1$ triplet of SU(2)$_f$.

It is possible to verify that these $\hat{\boldsymbol{T}}^{(\frac{1}{2})}$'s do indeed commute with the Hamiltonian $\hat{H}$:

$$\mathrm{d}\hat{\boldsymbol{T}}^{(\frac{1}{2})}/\mathrm{d}t = -\mathrm{i}[\hat{\boldsymbol{T}}^{(\frac{1}{2})}, \hat{H}] = 0 \tag{12.102}$$

so that their eigenvalues are conserved. That the $\hat{\boldsymbol{T}}^{(\frac{1}{2})}$ are, as already suggested, a field theoretic representation of the generators of SU(2), appropriate to the case $T = \frac{1}{2}$, follows from the fact that they obey the SU(2) algebra (problem 12.11):

$$[\hat{T}_i^{(\frac{1}{2})}, \hat{T}_j^{(\frac{1}{2})}] = \mathrm{i}\epsilon_{ijk}\hat{T}_k^{(\frac{1}{2})}. \tag{12.103}$$

For many purposes it is more useful to consider the raising and lowering operators

$$\hat{T}_\pm^{(\frac{1}{2})} = (\hat{T}_1^{(\frac{1}{2})} \pm \mathrm{i}\hat{T}_2^{(\frac{1}{2})}). \tag{12.104}$$

For example, we easily find

$$\hat{T}_+^{(\frac{1}{2})} = \int \hat{u}^\dagger\hat{d}\,\mathrm{d}^3\boldsymbol{x}, \tag{12.105}$$

which destroys a d quark and creates a u, or destroys a ū and creates a d̄, in either case raising the $\hat{T}_3^{(\frac{1}{2})}$ eigenvalue by $+1$, since

$$\hat{T}_3^{(\frac{1}{2})} = \frac{1}{2} \int (\hat{u}^\dagger \hat{u} - \hat{d}^\dagger \hat{d}) \mathrm{d}^3 \boldsymbol{x} \tag{12.106}$$

which counts $+\frac{1}{2}$ for each u (or d̄) and $-\frac{1}{2}$ for each d (or ū). Thus these operators certainly 'do the job' expected of field theoretic isospin operators, in this isospin-1/2 case.

In the U(1) case, considering now the fermionic example of section 7.2 for variety, we could go further and associate the conserved operator $\hat{N}_\psi$ with a *conserved current* $\hat{N}_\psi^\mu$:

$$\hat{N}_\psi = \int \hat{N}_\psi^0 \mathrm{d}^3 \boldsymbol{x}, \qquad \hat{N}_\psi^\mu = \bar{\hat{\psi}} \gamma^\mu \hat{\psi} \tag{12.107}$$

where

$$\partial_\mu \hat{N}_\psi^\mu = 0. \tag{12.108}$$

The obvious generalization appropriate to (12.101) is

$$\hat{\boldsymbol{T}}^{(\frac{1}{2})} = \int \hat{\boldsymbol{T}}^{(\frac{1}{2})0} \mathrm{d}^3 \boldsymbol{x}, \qquad \hat{\boldsymbol{T}}^{(\frac{1}{2})\mu} = \bar{\hat{q}} \gamma^\mu \frac{\boldsymbol{\tau}}{2} \hat{q}. \tag{12.109}$$

Note that both $\hat{N}_\psi^\mu$ and $\hat{\boldsymbol{T}}^{(\frac{1}{2})\mu}$ are of course functions of the space-time coordinate x, via the (suppressed) dependence of the $\hat{q}$-fields on x. Indeed one can verify from the equations of motion that

$$\partial_\mu \hat{\boldsymbol{T}}^{(\frac{1}{2})\mu} = 0. \tag{12.110}$$

Thus $\hat{\boldsymbol{T}}^{(\frac{1}{2})\mu}$ is a *conserved isospin current operator* appropriate to the $T = \frac{1}{2}$ (u, d) system; it transforms as a 4-vector under Lorentz transformations, and as a $T = 1$ triplet under SU(2)$_f$ transformations.

Clearly there should be some general formalism for dealing with all this more efficiently, and it is provided by a generalization of the steps followed, in the U(1) case, in equations (7.6)–(7.8). Suppose the Lagrangian involves a set of fields $\hat{\psi}_r$ (they could be bosons or fermions) and suppose that it is *invariant* under the infinitesimal transformation

$$\delta \hat{\psi}_r = -\mathrm{i}\epsilon T_{rs} \hat{\psi}_s \tag{12.111}$$

for some set of numerical coefficients T_{rs}. Equation (12.111) generalizes (7.5). Then since $\hat{\mathcal{L}}$ is invariant under this change,

$$0 = \delta \hat{\mathcal{L}} = \frac{\partial \hat{\mathcal{L}}}{\partial \hat{\psi}_r} \delta \hat{\psi}_r + \frac{\partial \hat{\mathcal{L}}}{\partial (\partial^\mu \hat{\psi}_r)} \partial^\mu (\delta \hat{\psi}_r). \tag{12.112}$$

But

$$\frac{\partial \hat{\mathcal{L}}}{\partial \hat{\psi}_r} = \partial^\mu \left(\frac{\partial \hat{\mathcal{L}}}{\partial (\partial^\mu \hat{\psi}_r)} \right) \tag{12.113}$$

from the equations of motion. Hence

$$\partial^\mu \left(\frac{\partial \hat{\mathcal{L}}}{\partial (\partial^\mu \hat{\psi}_r)} \delta \hat{\psi}_r \right) = 0 \tag{12.114}$$

which is precisely a current conservation law of the form

$$\partial^\mu \hat{j}_\mu = 0. \tag{12.115}$$

Indeed, disregarding the irrelevant constant small parameter ϵ, the conserved current is

$$\hat{j}_\mu = -i \frac{\partial \hat{\mathcal{L}}}{\partial (\partial^\mu \hat{\psi}_r)} T_{rs} \hat{\psi}_s. \tag{12.116}$$

Let us try this out on (12.87) with

$$\delta \hat{q} = (-i\boldsymbol{\epsilon} \cdot \boldsymbol{\tau}/2)\hat{q}. \tag{12.117}$$

As we know already, there are now three ϵ's, and so three T_{rs}'s, namely $\frac{1}{2}(\tau_1)_{rs}, \frac{1}{2}(\tau_2)_{rs}, \frac{1}{2}(\tau_3)_{rs}$. For each one we have a current, for example

$$\hat{T}_{1\mu}^{(\frac{1}{2})} = -i \frac{\partial \hat{\mathcal{L}}}{\partial (\partial^\mu \hat{q})} \frac{\tau_1}{2} \hat{q} = \bar{\hat{q}} \gamma_\mu \frac{\tau_1}{2} \hat{q} \tag{12.118}$$

and similarly for the other τ's, and so we recover (12.109). From the invariance of the Lagrangian under the transformation (12.117) there follows the conservation of an associated symmetry current. This is the quantum field theory version of Noether's theorem.

This theorem is of fundamental significance as it tells us how to relate symmetries (under transformations of the general form (12.111)) to 'current' conservation laws (of the form (12.115), and it constructs the actual currents for us. In gauge theories, the *dynamics* is generated from a symmetry, in the sense that (as we have seen in the local U(1) of electromagnetism) the symmetry currents are the dynamical currents that drive the equations for the force field. Thus the symmetries of the Lagrangian are basic to gauge field theories.

Let us look at another example, this time involving spin-0 fields. Suppose we have three spin-0 fields all with the same mass, and take

$$\hat{\mathcal{L}} = \frac{1}{2} \partial_\mu \hat{\phi}_1 \partial^\mu \hat{\phi}_1 + \frac{1}{2} \partial_\mu \hat{\phi}_2 \partial^\mu \hat{\phi}_2 + \frac{1}{2} \partial_\mu \hat{\phi}_3 \partial^\mu \hat{\phi}_3 - \frac{1}{2} m^2 (\hat{\phi}_1^2 + \hat{\phi}_2^2 + \hat{\phi}_3^2). \tag{12.119}$$

It is obvious that $\hat{\mathcal{L}}$ is invariant under an arbitrary rotation of the three $\hat{\phi}$'s among themselves, generalizing the 'rotation about the 3-axis' considered for

the $\hat{\phi}_1 - \hat{\phi}_2$ system of section 7.1. An infinitesimal such rotation is (cf (12.64), and noting the sign change in the field theory case)

$$\hat{\phi}' = \hat{\phi} + \epsilon \times \hat{\phi} \tag{12.120}$$

which implies

$$\delta\hat{\phi}_r = -i\epsilon_a T^{(1)}_{ars}\hat{\phi}_s, \tag{12.121}$$

with

$$T^{(1)}_{ars} = -i\epsilon_{ars} \tag{12.122}$$

as in (12.48). There are of course three conserved $\hat{T}$ operators again, and three $\hat{T}^\mu$'s, which we call $\hat{T}^{(1)}$ and $\hat{T}^{(1)\mu}$ respectively, since we are now dealing with a $T = 1$ isospin case. The $a = 1$ component of the conserved current in this case is, from (12.116),

$$\hat{T}^{(1)\mu}_1 = \hat{\phi}_2\partial^\mu\hat{\phi}_3 - \hat{\phi}_3\partial^\mu\hat{\phi}_2. \tag{12.123}$$

Cyclic permutations give us the other components which can be summarised as

$$\hat{T}^{(1)\mu} = i(\hat{\phi}^{(1)\text{tr}}\,\mathbf{T}^{(1)}\partial^\mu\hat{\phi}^{(1)} - (\partial^\mu\hat{\phi}^{(1)})^{\text{tr}}\,\mathbf{T}^{(1)}\hat{\phi}^{(1)}) \tag{12.124}$$

where we have written

$$\hat{\phi}^{(1)} = \begin{pmatrix} \hat{\phi}_1 \\ \hat{\phi}_2 \\ \hat{\phi}_3 \end{pmatrix} \tag{12.125}$$

and ^{tr} denotes transpose. Equation (12.124) has the form expected of a bosonic spin-0 current, but with the matrices $\mathbf{T}^{(1)}$ appearing, appropriate to the $T = 1$ (triplet) representation of SU(2)$_\text{f}$.

The general form of such SU(2) currents should now be clear. For an isospin T-multiplet of bosons we shall have the form

$$i(\hat{\phi}^{(T)\dagger}\mathbf{T}^{(T)}\partial^\mu\hat{\phi}^{(T)}) - (\partial^\mu\hat{\phi}^{(T)})^\dagger\mathbf{T}^{(T)}\hat{\phi}^{(T)}) \tag{12.126}$$

where we have put the $\dagger$ to allow for possibly complex fields; and for an isospin T-multiplet of fermions we shall have

$$\bar{\hat{\psi}}^{(T)}\gamma^\mu\mathbf{T}^{(T)}\hat{\psi}^{(T)} \tag{12.127}$$

where in each case the $(2T + 1)$ components of $\hat{\phi}$ or $\hat{\psi}$ transforms as a T-multiplet under SU(2), i.e.

$$\hat{\psi}^{(T)\prime} = \exp(-i\boldsymbol{\alpha} \cdot \mathbf{T}^{(T)})\hat{\psi}^{(T)} \tag{12.128}$$

and similarly for $\hat{\phi}^{(T)}$, where $\mathbf{T}^{(T)}$ are the $2T+1 \times 2T+1$ matrices representing the generators of SU(2)$_\text{f}$ in this representation. In all cases, the integral over

all space of the $\mu = 0$ component of these currents results in a triplet of isospin operators obeying the SU(2) algebra (12.47), as in (12.103).

The cases considered so far have all been *free* field theories, but SU(2)-invariant interactions can be easily formed. For example, the interaction $g_1 \bar{\hat{\psi}} \boldsymbol{\tau} \hat{\psi} \cdot \hat{\boldsymbol{\phi}}$ describes SU(2)-invariant interactions between a $T = \frac{1}{2}$ isospinor (spin-$\frac{1}{2}$) field $\hat{\psi}$, and a $T = 1$ isotriplet (Lorentz scalar) $\hat{\boldsymbol{\phi}}$. An effective interaction between pions and nucleons could take the form $g_\pi \bar{\hat{\psi}} \boldsymbol{\tau} \gamma_5 \hat{\psi} \cdot \hat{\boldsymbol{\phi}}$, allowing for the pseudoscalar nature of the pions (we shall see in the following section that $\bar{\hat{\psi}} \gamma_5 \hat{\psi}$ is a pseudoscalar, so the product is a true scalar as is required for a parity-conserving strong interaction). In these examples the 'vector' analogy for the $T = 1$ states allows us to see that the 'dot product' will be invariant. A similar dot product occurs in the interaction between the isospinor $\hat{\psi}^{(\frac{1}{2})}$ and the weak SU(2) gauge field $\hat{\boldsymbol{W}}_\mu$, which has the form

$$g \bar{\hat{q}} \gamma^\mu \frac{\boldsymbol{\tau}}{2} \hat{q} \cdot \hat{\boldsymbol{W}}_\mu \qquad (12.129)$$

as will be discussed in the following chapter. This is just the SU(2) dot product of the symmetry current (12.109) and the gauge field triplet, both of which are in the adjoint ($T = 1$) representation of SU(2).

All of the foregoing can be generalized straightforwardly to SU(3)$_f$. For example, the Lagrangian

$$\hat{\mathcal{L}} = \bar{\hat{q}}(\mathrm{i}\,\slashed{\partial} - m)\hat{q} \qquad (12.130)$$

with $\hat{q}$ now extended to

$$\hat{q} = \begin{pmatrix} \hat{u} \\ \hat{d} \\ \hat{s} \end{pmatrix} \qquad (12.131)$$

describes free u, d and s quarks of equal mass m. $\hat{\mathcal{L}}$ is clearly invariant under global SU(3)$_f$ transformations

$$\hat{q}' = \exp(-\mathrm{i}\boldsymbol{\alpha} \cdot \boldsymbol{\lambda}/2)\hat{q}, \qquad (12.132)$$

as well as the usual global U(1) transformation associated with quark number conservation. The associated Noether currents are (in somewhat informal notation)

$$\hat{G}_a^{(\mathrm{q})\mu} = \bar{\hat{q}} \gamma^\mu \frac{\lambda_a}{2} \hat{q} \qquad a = 1, 2, \ldots 8 \qquad (12.133)$$

(note that there are eight of them), and the associated conserved 'charge operators' are

$$\hat{G}_a^{(\mathrm{q})} = \int \hat{G}_a^{(\mathrm{q})0} \mathrm{d}^3\boldsymbol{x} = \int \hat{q}^\dagger \frac{\lambda_a}{2} \hat{q} \quad a = 1, 2, \ldots 8, \qquad (12.134)$$

which obey the SU(3) commutation relations

$$[\hat{G}_a^{(\mathrm{q})}, \hat{G}_b^{(\mathrm{q})}] = \mathrm{i} f_{abc} \hat{G}_c^{(\mathrm{q})}. \qquad (12.135)$$

SU(3)-invariant interactions can also be formed. A particularly important one is the 'SU(3) dot-product' of two octets (the analogues of the SU(2) triplets), which arises in the quark-gluon vertex of QCD (see chapters 13 and 14):

$$-ig_s \sum_f \bar{\hat{q}}_f \gamma^\mu \frac{\lambda_a}{2} \hat{q}_f \hat{A}^a_\mu. \tag{12.136}$$

In (12.136), $\hat{q}_f$ stands for the $SU(3)_c$ *colour* triplet

$$\hat{q}_f = \begin{pmatrix} \hat{f}_r \\ \hat{f}_b \\ \hat{f}_g \end{pmatrix} \tag{12.137}$$

where '$\hat{f}$' is any of the six quark flavour fields $\hat{u}, \hat{d}, \hat{c}, \hat{s}, \hat{t}, \hat{b}$, and $\hat{A}^a_\mu$ are the 8 ($a = 1, 2, \ldots 8$) gluon fields. Once again, (12.136) has the form 'symmetry current · gauge field' characteristic of all gauge interactions.

12.4.2   Chiral symmetry

As our final example of a global non-Abelian symmetry, we shall introduce the idea of *chiral symmetry*, which is an exact symmetry for fermions in the limit in which their masses may be neglected. We have seen that the u and d quarks have indeed very small masses (≤ 5 MeV) on hadronic scales, and even the s quark mass (~ 100 MeV) is relatively small. Thus we may certainly expect some physical signs of the symmetry associated with $m_u \approx m_d \approx 0$, and possibly also of the larger symmetry holding when $m_u \approx m_d \approx m_s \approx 0$. As we shall see, however, this expectation leads to a puzzle, the resolution of which will have to be postponed until the concept of 'spontaneous symmetry breaking' has been developed in Part VII.

We begin with the simplest case of just one fermion. Since we are interested in the 'small mass' regime, it is sensible to use the representation (3.40) of the Dirac matrices, in which the momentum part of the Dirac Hamiltonian is 'diagonal' and the mass appears as an 'off-diagonal' coupling:

$$\boldsymbol{\alpha} = \begin{pmatrix} \boldsymbol{\sigma} & 0 \\ 0 & -\boldsymbol{\sigma} \end{pmatrix}, \quad \beta = \begin{pmatrix} 0 & 1 \\ 1 & 0 \end{pmatrix}. \tag{12.138}$$

Writing the general Dirac spinor ω as

$$\omega = \begin{pmatrix} \phi \\ \chi \end{pmatrix}, \tag{12.139}$$

we have (as in (4.14), (4.15))

$$E\phi = \boldsymbol{\sigma} \cdot \boldsymbol{p}\phi + m\chi \tag{12.140}$$

$$E\chi = -\boldsymbol{\sigma} \cdot \boldsymbol{p}\chi + m\phi. \tag{12.141}$$

We now recall the matrix γ_5 introduced in section 4.2.1

$$\gamma_5 = i\gamma^0\gamma^1\gamma^2\gamma^3, \tag{12.142}$$

which takes the form

$$\gamma_5 = \begin{pmatrix} 1 & 0 \\ 0 & -1 \end{pmatrix} \tag{12.143}$$

in this representation. The matrix γ_5 plays a prominent role in chiral symmetry, as we shall see. Its defining property is that it anticommutes with the γ^μ matrices:

$$\{\gamma_5, \gamma^\mu\} = 0. \tag{12.144}$$

'Chirality' means 'handedness', from the Greek word for hand, $\chi\epsilon\iota\rho$. Its use here stems from the fact that, in the limit $m \to 0$ the 2-component spinors ϕ, χ become helicity eigenstates (cf problem 9.4), having definite 'handedness'. As $m \to 0$ we have $E \to |\boldsymbol{p}|$, and (12.140) and (12.141) reduce to

$$(\boldsymbol{\sigma} \cdot \boldsymbol{p}/|\boldsymbol{p}|)\tilde{\phi} = \tilde{\phi} \tag{12.145}$$
$$(\boldsymbol{\sigma} \cdot \boldsymbol{p}/|\boldsymbol{p}|)\tilde{\chi} = -\tilde{\chi}, \tag{12.146}$$

so that the limiting spinor $\tilde{\phi}$ has positive helicity, and $\tilde{\chi}$ negative helicity (cf (3.68) and (3.69)). In this $m \to 0$ limit, the two helicity spinors are *decoupled*, reflecting the fact that no Lorentz transformation can reverse the helicity of a massless particle. Also in this limit, the Dirac energy operator is

$$\boldsymbol{\alpha} \cdot \boldsymbol{p} = \begin{pmatrix} \boldsymbol{\sigma} \cdot \boldsymbol{p} & 0 \\ 0 & -\boldsymbol{\sigma} \cdot \boldsymbol{p} \end{pmatrix} \tag{12.147}$$

which is easily seen to commute with γ_5. Thus the massless states may equivalently be classified by the eigenvalues of γ_5, which are clearly ± 1 since $\gamma_5^2 = I$.

Consider then a massless fermion with positive helicity. It is described by the 'u'-spinor $\begin{pmatrix} \tilde{\phi} \\ 0 \end{pmatrix}$ which is an eigenstate of γ_5 with eigenvalue $+1$. Similarly, a fermion with negative helicity is described by $\begin{pmatrix} 0 \\ \tilde{\chi} \end{pmatrix}$ which has $\gamma_5 = -1$. Thus for these states chirality equals helicity. We have to be more careful for antifermions, however. A physical antifermion of energy E and momentum $\boldsymbol{p}$ is described by a 'v'- spinor corresponding to $-E$ and $-\boldsymbol{p}$; but with $m = 0$ in (12.140) and (12.141) the equations for ϕ and χ remain the same for $-E, -\boldsymbol{p}$ as for $E, \boldsymbol{p}$. Consider the spin, however. If the physical antiparticle has positive helicity, with $\boldsymbol{p}$ along the z-axis say, then $s_z = +\frac{1}{2}$. The corresponding v-spinor must then have $s_z = -\frac{1}{2}$ (see section 3.4.3) and must therefore be of $\tilde{\chi}$ type (12.146). So the v-spinor for this antifermion of positive helicity is $\begin{pmatrix} 0 \\ \tilde{\chi} \end{pmatrix}$ which has $\gamma_5 = -1$. In summary, for fermions the γ_5 eigenvalue is equal to the helicity, and for antifermions it is equal to minus the helicity. It is the γ_5 eigenvalue that is called the 'chirality'.

In the massless limit, the chirality of $\tilde{\phi}$ and $\tilde{\chi}$ is a good quantum number (γ_5 commuting with the energy operator), and we may say that 'chirality is conserved' in this massless limit. On the other hand, the massive spinor ω is clearly *not* an eigenstate of chirality:

$$\gamma_5 \omega = \begin{pmatrix} \phi \\ -\chi \end{pmatrix} \neq \lambda \begin{pmatrix} \phi \\ \chi \end{pmatrix}. \tag{12.148}$$

Referring to (12.140) and (12.141), we may therefore regard the mass terms as 'coupling the states of different chirality'.

It is usual to introduce operators $P_{R,L} = \left(\frac{1 \pm \gamma_5}{2}\right)$ which 'project' out states of definite chirality from ω:

$$\omega = \left(\frac{1 + \gamma_5}{2}\right)\omega + \left(\frac{1 - \gamma_5}{2}\right)\omega \equiv P_R\omega + P_L\omega \equiv \omega_R + \omega_L, \tag{12.149}$$

so that

$$\omega_R = \begin{pmatrix} 1 & 0 \\ 0 & 0 \end{pmatrix}\begin{pmatrix} \phi \\ \chi \end{pmatrix} = \begin{pmatrix} \phi \\ 0 \end{pmatrix}, \quad \omega_L = \begin{pmatrix} 0 \\ \chi \end{pmatrix}. \tag{12.150}$$

Then clearly $\gamma_5 \omega_R = \omega_R$ and $\gamma_5 \omega_L = -\omega_L$; slightly confusingly, the notation 'R', 'L' is used for the *chirality* eigenvalue.

We now reformulate the above in field-theoretic terms. The Dirac Lagrangian for a single massless fermion is

$$\hat{\mathcal{L}}_0 = \hat{\bar{\psi}} \mathrm{i} \, \slashed{\partial} \hat{\psi}. \tag{12.151}$$

This is invariant not only under the now familiar global U(1) transformation $\hat{\psi} \to \hat{\psi}' = \mathrm{e}^{-\mathrm{i}\alpha}\hat{\psi}$, but also under the 'global *chiral* U(1)' transformation

$$\hat{\psi} \to \hat{\psi}' = \mathrm{e}^{-\mathrm{i}\theta\gamma_5}\hat{\psi} \tag{12.152}$$

where θ is an arbitrary (x-independent) real parameter. The invariance is easily verified: using $\{\gamma^0, \gamma_5\} = 0$ we have

$$\hat{\bar{\psi}}' = \hat{\psi}'^\dagger \gamma^0 = \hat{\psi}^\dagger \mathrm{e}^{\mathrm{i}\theta\gamma_5}\gamma^0 = \hat{\psi}^\dagger \gamma^0 \mathrm{e}^{-\mathrm{i}\theta\gamma_5} = \hat{\bar{\psi}}\mathrm{e}^{-\mathrm{i}\theta\gamma_5}, \tag{12.153}$$

and then using $\{\gamma^\mu, \gamma_5\} = 0$,

$$\begin{aligned} \hat{\bar{\psi}}'\gamma^\mu\partial_\mu\hat{\psi}' &= \hat{\bar{\psi}}\mathrm{e}^{-\mathrm{i}\theta\gamma_5}\gamma^\mu\partial_\mu\mathrm{e}^{-\mathrm{i}\theta\gamma_5}\hat{\psi} \\ &= \hat{\bar{\psi}}\gamma^\mu\mathrm{e}^{\mathrm{i}\theta\gamma_5}\partial_\mu\mathrm{e}^{-\mathrm{i}\theta\gamma_5}\hat{\psi} \\ &= \hat{\bar{\psi}}\gamma^\mu\partial_\mu\hat{\psi} \end{aligned} \tag{12.154}$$

as required. The corresponding Noether current is

$$\hat{j}_5^\mu = \hat{\bar{\psi}}\gamma^\mu\gamma_5\hat{\psi}, \tag{12.155}$$

and the spatial integral of its $\mu = 0$ component is the (conserved) chirality operator

$$\hat{Q}_5 = \int \hat{\psi}^\dagger \gamma_5 \hat{\psi} \mathrm{d}^3\boldsymbol{x} = \int \left(\hat{\phi}^\dagger \hat{\phi} - \hat{\chi}^\dagger \hat{\chi} \right) \mathrm{d}^3\boldsymbol{x}. \qquad (12.156)$$

We denote this chiral U(1) by U(1)$_5$.

It is interesting to compare the form of $\hat{Q}_5$ with that of the corresponding operator $\int \hat{\psi}^\dagger \hat{\psi} \mathrm{d}^3\boldsymbol{x}$ in the non-chiral case (cf (7.51)). The difference has to do with their behaviour under a transformation already discussed in section 4.2.1, namely *parity*. Under the parity transformation $\boldsymbol{p} \to -\boldsymbol{p}$ and thus, for (12.140) and (12.141) to be covariant under parity, we require $\phi \to \chi$, $\chi \to \phi$; this will ensure (as we saw in section 4.2.1) that the Dirac equation in the parity-transformed frame will be consistent with the one in the original frame. In the representation (12.138), this is equivalent to saying that the spinor $\omega_{\mathbf{P}}$ in the parity-transformed frame is given by

$$\omega_{\mathbf{P}} = \gamma^0 \omega. \qquad (12.157)$$

which implies $\phi_{\mathbf{P}} = \chi$, $\chi_{\mathbf{P}} = \phi$.

All this carries over to the field theory case, with $\hat{\psi}_{\mathbf{P}}(\boldsymbol{x}, t) = \gamma^0 \hat{\psi}(-\boldsymbol{x}, t)$, as we saw in section 7.5.1. Consider then the operator $\hat{Q}_5$ in the parity-transformed frame:

$$
\begin{aligned}
(\hat{Q}_5)_{\mathbf{P}} &= \int \hat{\psi}_{\mathbf{P}}^\dagger(\boldsymbol{x}, t) \gamma_5 \psi_{\mathbf{P}}(\boldsymbol{x}, t) \mathrm{d}^3\boldsymbol{x} = \int \hat{\psi}^\dagger(-\boldsymbol{x}, t) \gamma^0 \gamma_5 \gamma^0 \hat{\psi}(-\boldsymbol{x}, t) \mathrm{d}^3\boldsymbol{x} \\
&= -\int \hat{\psi}^\dagger(\boldsymbol{y}, t) \gamma_5 \hat{\psi}(\boldsymbol{y}, t) \mathrm{d}^3\boldsymbol{y} = -\hat{Q}_5 \qquad (12.158)
\end{aligned}
$$

where we used $\{\gamma^0, \gamma_5\} = 0$ and $\left(\gamma^0\right)^2 = 1$, and changed the integration variable to $\boldsymbol{y} = -\boldsymbol{x}$. Hence $\hat{Q}_5$ is a 'pseudoscalar' operator, meaning that it changes sign in the parity-transformed frame. We can also see this directly from (12.156), making the interchange $\hat{\phi} \leftrightarrow \hat{\chi}$. In contrast, the non-chiral operator $\int \hat{\psi}^\dagger \hat{\psi} \mathrm{d}^3\boldsymbol{x}$ is a (true) scalar, remaining the same in the parity-transformed frame.

In a similar way, the appearance of the γ_5 in the current operator $\hat{j}_5^\mu = \hat{\bar{\psi}} \gamma^\mu \gamma_5 \hat{\psi}$ affects its parity properties: for example, the $\mu = 0$ component $\hat{\psi}^\dagger \gamma_5 \hat{\psi}$ is a pseudoscalar, as we have seen. Problem 4.4(b) showed that the spatial parts $\hat{\bar{\psi}} \boldsymbol{\gamma} \gamma_5 \hat{\psi}$ behave as an *axial vector* rather than a normal (*polar*) vector under parity: that is, they behave like $\boldsymbol{r} \times \boldsymbol{p}$ for example, rather than like $\boldsymbol{r}$, in that they do *not* reverse sign under parity. Such a current is referred to generally as an 'axial vector current', as opposed to the ordinary vector currents with no γ_5.

As a consequence of (12.158), the operator $\hat{Q}_5$ changes the parity of any state on which it acts. We can see this formally by introducing the (unitary) parity operator $\hat{\mathbf{P}}$ in field theory, such that states of definite parity $|+\rangle, |-\rangle$ satisfy

$$\hat{\mathbf{P}}|+\rangle = |+\rangle, \quad \hat{\mathbf{P}}|-\rangle = -|-\rangle. \qquad (12.159)$$

Equation (12.158) then implies that $\hat{\mathbf{P}}\hat{Q}_5\hat{\mathbf{P}}^{-1} = -\hat{Q}_5$, following the normal rule for operator transformations in quantum mechanics. Consider now the state $\hat{Q}_5|+\rangle$. We have

$$\hat{\mathbf{P}}\hat{Q}_5|+\rangle = \left(\hat{\mathbf{P}}\hat{Q}_5\hat{\mathbf{P}}^{-1}\right)\hat{\mathbf{P}}|+\rangle$$
$$= -\hat{Q}_5|+\rangle \tag{12.160}$$

showing that $\hat{Q}_5|+\rangle$ is an eigenstate of $\hat{\mathbf{P}}$ with the opposite eigenvalue, -1.

A very important physical consequence now follows from the fact that (in this simple $m = 0$ model) $\hat{Q}_5$ is a symmetry operator commuting with the Hamiltonian $\hat{H}$. We have

$$\hat{H}\hat{Q}_5|\psi\rangle = \hat{Q}_5\hat{H}|\psi\rangle = E\hat{Q}_5|\psi\rangle. \tag{12.161}$$

Hence for every state $|\psi\rangle$ with energy eigenvalue E, there should exist a state $\hat{Q}_5|\psi\rangle$ with the same eigenvalue E and the opposite parity: that is, chiral symmetry apparently implies the existence of 'parity doublets'.

Of course, it may reasonably be objected that all of the above refers not only to the massless, but also the *non-interacting* case. However, this is just where the analysis begins to get interesting. Suppose we allow the fermion field $\hat{\psi}$ to interact with a U(1)-gauge field $\hat{A}^\mu$ via the standard electromagnetic coupling

$$\hat{\mathcal{L}}_{\text{int}} = q\bar{\hat{\psi}}\gamma^\mu\hat{\psi}\hat{A}_\mu. \tag{12.162}$$

Remarkably enough, $\hat{\mathcal{L}}_{\text{int}}$ is *also* invariant under the chiral transformation (12.152), for the simple reason that the 'Dirac' structure of (12.162) is exactly the same as that of the free kinetic term $\bar{\hat{\psi}}\,\partial\!\!\!/\hat{\psi}$: the 'covariant derivative' prescription $\partial^\mu \to D^\mu = \partial^\mu + iq\hat{A}^\mu$ automatically means that any 'Dirac' (e.g. γ_5) symmetry of the kinetic part will be preserved when the gauge interaction is included. Thus chirality remains a 'good symmetry' in the presence of a U(1) gauge interaction.

The generalization of this to the more physical $m_{\text{u}} \approx m_{\text{d}} \approx 0$ case is quite straightforward. The Lagrangian (12.87) becomes

$$\hat{\mathcal{L}} = \bar{\hat{q}}\,\mathrm{i}\,\partial\!\!\!/\hat{q} \tag{12.163}$$

as $m \to 0$, which is invariant under the γ_5-version of (12.89),[6] namely

$$\hat{q}' = \exp(-\mathrm{i}\boldsymbol{\beta}\cdot\boldsymbol{\tau}/2\gamma_5)\hat{q}. \tag{12.164}$$

There are three associated Noether currents (compare (12.109))

$$\hat{T}_5^{(\frac{1}{2})\,\mu} = \bar{\hat{q}}\gamma^\mu\gamma_5\frac{\boldsymbol{\tau}}{2}\hat{q} \tag{12.165}$$

---

[6]$\hat{\mathcal{L}}_0$ is also invariant under $\hat{q}' = \mathrm{e}^{-\mathrm{i}\theta\gamma_5}\hat{q}$ which is an 'axial' version of the global U(1) associated with quark number conservation. We shall discuss this additional U(1)-symmetry in section 18.1.1.

which are axial vectors, and three associated 'charge' operators

$$\hat{\boldsymbol{T}}_5^{(\frac{1}{2})} = \int \hat{q}^\dagger \gamma_5 \frac{\boldsymbol{\tau}}{2} \hat{q} \mathrm{d}^3 \boldsymbol{x} \qquad (12.166)$$

which are pseudoscalars, belonging to the T=1 representation of SU(2). We have a new non-Abelian global symmetry, called chiral SU(2)$_\mathrm{f}$, which we shall denote by SU(2)$_\mathrm{f\,5}$. As far as their action in the isospinor u-d space is concerned, these chiral charges have exactly the same effect as the ordinary flavour isospin operators of (12.109). But they are pseudoscalars rather than scalars, and hence they flip the parity of a state on which they act. Thus, whereas the isospin raising operator $\hat{T}_+^{(\frac{1}{2})}$ is such that

$$\hat{T}_+^{(\frac{1}{2})}|d\rangle = |u\rangle, \qquad (12.167)$$

$\hat{T}_{+\,5}^{(\frac{1}{2})}$ will also produce a u-type state from a d-type one via

$$\hat{T}_{+\,5}^{(\frac{1}{2})}|d\rangle = |\tilde{u}\rangle, \qquad (12.168)$$

but the $|\tilde{u}\rangle$ state will have opposite parity from $|u\rangle$. Further, since $[\hat{T}_{+\,5}^{(\frac{1}{2})}, \hat{H}] = 0$, this state $|\tilde{u}\rangle$ will be degenerate with $|d\rangle$. Similarly, the state $|\tilde{d}\rangle$ produced via $\hat{T}_{-\,5}^{(\frac{1}{2})}|u\rangle$ will have opposite parity from $|d\rangle$, and will be degenerate with $|u\rangle$. The upshot is that we have two massless states $|u\rangle$, $|d\rangle$ of (say) positive parity, and a further two massless states $|\tilde{u}\rangle$, $|\tilde{d}\rangle$ of negative parity, in this simple model.

Suppose we now let the quarks interact, for example by an interaction of the QCD type, already indicated in (12.136). In that case, the interaction terms have the form

$$\bar{\hat{u}}\gamma^\mu \frac{\lambda_a}{2} \hat{u} \hat{A}_\mu^a + \bar{\hat{d}}\gamma^\mu \frac{\lambda_a}{2} \hat{d} \hat{A}_\mu^a \qquad (12.169)$$

where

$$\hat{u} = \begin{pmatrix} \hat{u}_\mathrm{r} \\ \hat{u}_\mathrm{b} \\ \hat{u}_\mathrm{g} \end{pmatrix}, \hat{d} = \begin{pmatrix} \hat{d}_\mathrm{r} \\ \hat{d}_\mathrm{b} \\ \hat{d}_\mathrm{g} \end{pmatrix} \qquad (12.170)$$

and the 3 × 3 λ's act in the r-b-g space. Just as in the previous U(1) case, the interaction (12.169) is invariant under the global SU(2)$_\mathrm{f\,5}$ chiral symmetry (12.164), acting in the u-d space. Note that, somewhat confusingly, (12.169) is *not* a simple 'gauging' of (12.163): a covariant derivative is being introduced, but in the space of a new (colour) degree of freedom, not in flavour space. In fact, the flavour degrees of freedom are 'inert' in (12.169), so that it is invariant under SU(2)$_\mathrm{f}$ transformations, while the Dirac structure implies that it is also invariant under chiral SU(2)$_\mathrm{f\,5}$ transformations (12.164). All the foregoing can be extended unchanged to chiral SU(3)$_\mathrm{f\,5}$, given that QCD is 'flavour blind', and supposing that $m_\mathrm{s} \approx 0$.

The effect of the QCD interactions must be to bind the quark into nucleons, such as the proton (uud) and neutron (udd). But what about the equally possible states $(\tilde{u}\tilde{u}\tilde{d})$ and $(\tilde{u}\tilde{d}\tilde{d})$, for example? These would have to be degenerate in mass with (uud) and (udd), and of opposite parity. Yet such 'parity doublet' partners of the physical p and n are not observed, and so we have a puzzle.

One might feel that this whole discussion is unrealistic, based as it is on massless quarks. Are the baryons then supposed to be massless too? If so, perhaps the discussion is idle, as they are evidently by no means massless. But it is not necessary to suppose that the mass of a relativistic bound state has any very simple relation to the masses of its constituents: its mass may derive, in part at least, from the interaction energy in the fields. Alternatively, one might suppose that somehow the finite mass of the u and d quarks, which of course breaks the chiral symmetry, splits the degeneracy of the nucleon parity doublets, promoting the negative parity 'nucleon' state to an acceptably high mass. But this seems very implausible, in view of the actual magnitudes of m_u and m_d, compared to the nucleon masses.

In short, we have here a situation in which a *symmetry of the Lagrangian* (to an apparently good approximation) does *not* seem to result in the expected *multiplet structure of the states*. The resolution of this puzzle will have to await our discussion of 'spontaneous symmetry breaking', in Part VII.

In conclusion, we note an important feature of the flavour symmetry currents $\hat{\boldsymbol{T}}^{(\frac{1}{2})\mu}$ and $\hat{\boldsymbol{T}}_5^{(\frac{1}{2})\mu}$ discussed in this and the preceding section. Although these currents have been introduced entirely within the context of *strong* interaction symmetries, it is a remarkable fact that exactly these currents also appear in strangeness-conserving semileptonic *weak* interactions such as β-decay, as we shall see in chapter 20. (The fact that *both* appear is precisely a manifestation of *parity violation* in weak interactions, as we noted in section 4.2.1). Thus some of the physical consequences of 'spontaneously broken chiral symmetry' will involve weak interaction quantities.

Problems

12.1 Verify that the set of all unitary 2×2 matrices with determinant equal to $+1$ form a group, the law of combination being matrix multiplication.

12.2 Derive (12.18).

12.3 Check the commutation relations (12.28).

12.4 Show that the T_i's defined by (12.45) satisfy (12.47).

12.5 Write out each of the 3×3 matrices $T_i^{(1)}(i = 1, 2, 3)$ whose matrix

elements are given by (12.48), and verify that they satisfy the SU(2) commutation relations (12.47).

12.6 Verify (12.62).

12.7 Show that a general Hermitian traceless 3×3 matrix is parametrized by 8 real numbers.

12.8 Check that (12.84) is consistent with (12.80) and the infinitesimal form of (12.81), and verify that the matrices $G_a^{(8)}$ defined by (12.84) satisfy the commutation relations (12.83).

12.9 Verify, by comparing the coefficients of ϵ_1, ϵ_2 and ϵ_3 on both sides of (12.99), that (12.100) follows from (12.99).

12.10 Verify that the operators $\hat{\boldsymbol{T}}^{(\frac{1}{2})}$ defined by (12.101) satisfy (12.100). (Note: use the anticommutation relations of the fermionic operators.)

12.11 Verify that the operators $\hat{\boldsymbol{T}}^{(\frac{1}{2})}$ given by (12.101) satisfy the commutation relations (12.103).

13

Local Non-Abelian (Gauge) Symmetries

...The difference between a neutron and a proton is then a purely arbitrary process. As usually conceived, however, this arbitrariness is subject to the following limitations: once one chooses what to call a proton, what a neutron, at one space time point, one is then not free to make any choices at other space time points.

It seems that this is not consistent with the localized field concept that underlies the usual physical theories. In the present paper we wish to explore the possibility of requiring all interactions to be invariant under *independent* rotations of the isotopic spin at all space time points ....

—Yang and Mills (1954)

Consider the global SU(2) isospinor transformation (12.32), written here again,

$$\psi^{(\frac{1}{2})\prime}(x) = \exp(i\boldsymbol{\alpha} \cdot \boldsymbol{\tau}/2)\psi^{(\frac{1}{2})}(x) \tag{13.1}$$

for an isospin doublet wavefunction $\psi^{(\frac{1}{2})}(x)$. The dependence of $\psi^{(\frac{1}{2})}(x)$ on the space-time coordinate x has now been included explicitly, but the parameters $\boldsymbol{\alpha}$ are independent of x, which is why the transformation is called a 'global' one. As we have seen in the previous chapter, invariance under this transformation amounts to the assertion that the choice of *which* two base states – $(n, p), (u, d), \ldots$ – to use is a matter of convention; any such non-Abelian phase transformation on a chosen pair produces another equally good pair. However, the choice cannot be made independently at all space-time points, only *globally*. To Yang and Mills (1954) (cf the quotation above) this seemed somehow an unaesthetic limitation of symmetry: 'Once one chooses what to call a proton, what a neutron, at one space-time point, one is then not free to make any choices at other space-time points.' They even suggested that this could be viewed as 'inconsistent with the localised field concept', and they therefore 'explored the possibility' of replacing this global (space-time independent) phase transformation by the local (space-time dependent) one

$$\psi^{(\frac{1}{2})\prime}(x) = \exp[ig\boldsymbol{\tau} \cdot \boldsymbol{\alpha}(x)/2]\psi^{(\frac{1}{2})}(x) \tag{13.2}$$

in which the phase parameters $\boldsymbol{\alpha}(x)$ are also now functions of $x = (t, \boldsymbol{x})$ as

39

indicated. Notice that we have inserted a parameter g in the exponent to make the analogy with the electromagnetic U(1) case

$$\psi'(x) = \exp[iq\chi(x)]\psi(x) \tag{13.3}$$

even stronger: g will be a coupling strength, analogous to the electromagnetic charge q. The consideration of theories based on (13.2) was the fundamental step taken by Yang and Mills (1954); see also Shaw (1955).

Global symmetries and their associated (possibly approximate) conservation laws are certainly important, but they do not have the *dynamical* significance of local symmetries. We saw in section 7.4 how the 'requirement' of local U(1) phase invariance led almost automatically to the local gauge theory of QED, in which the conserved current $\bar{\psi}\gamma^\mu\hat{\psi}$ of the global U(1) symmetry is 'promoted' to the role of dynamical current which, when dotted into the gauge field $\hat{A}^\mu$, gave the interaction term in $\hat{\mathcal{L}}_{\text{QED}}$. A similar link between symmetry and dynamics appears if, following Yang and Mills, we generalize the non-Abelian global symmetries of the preceding chapter to local non-Abelian symmetries, which are the subject of the present one.

However, as mentioned in the introduction to chapter 12, the original Yang-Mills attempt to get a theory of hadronic interactions by 'localizing' the flavour symmetry group SU(2) turned out not to be phenomenologically viable (although a remarkable attempt was made to push the idea further by Sakurai (1960)). In the event, the successful application of a local SU(2) symmetry was to the *weak* interactions. But this is complicated by the fact that the symmetry is 'spontaneously broken', and consequently we shall delay the discussion of this application until after QCD – which *is* the theory of strong interactions, but at the quark, rather than the composite (hadronic) level. QCD is based on the local form of an SU(3) symmetry; once again, however, it is *not* the flavour SU(3) of section 12.2, but a symmetry with respect to a totally new degree of freedom, colour. This will be introduced in the following chapter.

Although the application of local SU(2) symmetry to the weak interactions will follow that of local SU(3) to the strong, we shall begin our discussion of local non-Abelian symmetries with the local SU(2) case, since the group theory is more familiar. We shall also start with the 'wavefunction' formalism, deferring the field theory treatment until section 13.3.

13.1   Local SU(2) symmetry

13.1.1   The covariant derivative and interactions with matter

In this section we shall introduce the main ideas of the non-Abelian SU(2) gauge theory which results from the demand of invariance, or covariance,

under transformations such as (13.2). We shall generally use the language of isospin when referring to the physical states and operators, bearing in mind that this will eventually mean *weak* isospin.

We shall mimic as literally as possible the discussion of electromagnetic gauge covariance in sections 2.4 and 2.5 of volume 1. As in that case, no free particle wave equation can be covariant under the transformation (13.2) (taking the isospinor example for definiteness), since the gradient terms in the equation will act on the phase factor $\alpha(x)$. However, wave equations with a suitably defined *covariant derivative* can be covariant under (13.2); physically this means that, just as for electromagnetism, covariance under local non-Abelian phase transformations requires the introduction of a definite force field.

In the electromagnetic case the covariant derivative is

$$D^\mu = \partial^\mu + \mathrm{i}qA^\mu(x). \tag{13.4}$$

For convenience we recall here the crucial property of D^μ. Under a local U(1) phase transformation, a wavefunction transforms as (cf (13.3))

$$\psi(x) \to \psi'(x) = \exp(\mathrm{i}q\chi(x))\psi(x), \tag{13.5}$$

from which it easily follows that the derivative (gradient) of ψ transforms as

$$\partial^\mu\psi(x) \to \partial^\mu\psi'(x) = \exp(\mathrm{i}q\chi(x))\partial^\mu\psi(x) + \mathrm{i}q\partial^\mu\chi(x)\exp(\mathrm{i}q\chi(x))\psi(x). \tag{13.6}$$

Comparing (13.6) with (13.5), we see that, in addition to the expected first term on the right-hand side of (13.6), which has the same form as the right-hand side of (13.5), there is an *extra* term in (13.6). By contrast, the covariant derivative of ψ transforms as (see section 2.4 of volume 1)

$$D^\mu\psi(x) \to D'^\mu\psi'(x) = \exp(\mathrm{i}q\chi(x))D^\mu\psi(x) \tag{13.7}$$

exactly as in (13.5), with no additional term on the right-hand side. Note that D^μ has to carry a prime also, since it contains A^μ which transforms to $A'^\mu = A^\mu - \partial^\mu\chi(x)$ when ψ transforms by (13.5). The property (13.7) ensured the gauge covariance of wave equations in the U(1) case; the similar property in the quantum field case meant that a globally U(1)-invariant Lagrangian could be converted immediately to a locally U(1)-invariant one by replacing ∂^μ by $\hat{D}^\mu$ (section 7.4).

In appendix D of volume 1 we introduced the idea of 'covariance' in the context of coordinate transformations of 3- and 4-vectors. The essential notion was of something 'maintaining the same form', or 'transforming the same way'. The transformations being considered here are gauge transformations rather than coordinate ones; nevertheless it is true that, under them, $D^\mu\psi$ transforms in the same way as ψ, while $\partial^\mu\psi$ does not. Thus the term covariant derivative seems appropriate. In fact, there is a much closer analogy between the 'coordinate' and the 'gauge' cases, which we did not present in volume 1, but give now in appendix N, for the interested reader.

We need the local SU(2) generalization of (13.4), appropriate to the local SU(2) transformation (13.2). Just as in the U(1) case (13.6), the ordinary gradient acting on $\psi^{(\frac{1}{2})}(x)$ does not transform in the same way as $\psi^{(\frac{1}{2})}(x)$: taking ∂^μ of (13.2) leads to

$$
\begin{aligned}
\partial^\mu \psi^{(\frac{1}{2})\prime}(x) \;=\;&\; \exp[ig\boldsymbol{\tau}\cdot\boldsymbol{\alpha}(x)/2]\partial^\mu\psi^{(\frac{1}{2})}(x) \\
&+ ig\boldsymbol{\tau}\cdot\partial^\mu\boldsymbol{\alpha}(x)/2\exp[ig\boldsymbol{\tau}\cdot\boldsymbol{\alpha}(x)/2]\psi^{(\frac{1}{2})}(x) \quad (13.8)
\end{aligned}
$$

as can be checked by writing the matrix exponential $\exp[\mathrm{A}]$ as the series

$$
\exp[\mathrm{A}] = \sum_{n=0}^{\infty} \mathrm{A}^n/n!
$$

and differentiating term by term. By analogy with (13.7), the key property we demand for our *SU(2) covariant derivative* $D^\mu\psi^{(\frac{1}{2})}$ is that this quantity should transform like $\psi^{(\frac{1}{2})}$ – i.e. without the second term in (13.8). So we require

$$
(D'^\mu\psi^{(\frac{1}{2})\prime}(x)) = \exp[ig\boldsymbol{\tau}\cdot\boldsymbol{\alpha}(x)/2](D^\mu\psi^{(\frac{1}{2})}(x)). \quad (13.9)
$$

The definition of D^μ which generalizes (13.4) so as to fulfil this requirement is

$$
D^\mu(\text{acting on an isospinor}) \;=\; \partial^\mu + ig\boldsymbol{\tau}\cdot\boldsymbol{W}^\mu(x)/2. \quad (13.10)
$$

The definition (13.10), as indicated on the left-hand side, is only appropriate for isospinors $\psi^{(\frac{1}{2})}$; it has to be suitably generalized for other $\psi^{(t)}$'s (see (13.44)).

We now discuss (13.9) and (13.10) in detail. The ∂^μ is multiplied implicitly by the unit 2 matrix, and the $\boldsymbol{\tau}$'s act on the two-component space of $\psi^{(\frac{1}{2})}$. The $\boldsymbol{W}^\mu(x)$ are *three* independent gauge fields

$$
\boldsymbol{W}^\mu = (W_1^\mu, W_2^\mu, W_3^\mu), \quad (13.11)
$$

generalizing the single electromagnetic gauge field A^μ. They are called SU(2) gauge fields, or more generally *Yang-Mills fields*. The term $\boldsymbol{\tau}\cdot\boldsymbol{W}^\mu$ is then the 2×2 matrix

$$
\boldsymbol{\tau}\cdot\boldsymbol{W}^\mu = \begin{pmatrix} W_3^\mu & W_1^\mu - iW_2^\mu \\ W_1^\mu + iW_2^\mu & -W_3^\mu \end{pmatrix} \quad (13.12)
$$

using the $\boldsymbol{\tau}$'s of (12.25); the x-dependence of the W^μ's is understood. Let us 'decode' the desired property (13.9), for the algebraically simpler case of an infinitesimal local SU(2) transformation with parameters $\boldsymbol{\epsilon}(x)$, which are of course functions of x since the transformation is local. In this case, $\psi^{(\frac{1}{2})}$ transforms by

$$
\psi^{(\frac{1}{2})\prime} = (1 + ig\boldsymbol{\tau}\cdot\boldsymbol{\epsilon}(x)/2)\psi^{(\frac{1}{2})} \quad (13.13)
$$

and the 'uncovariant' derivative $\partial^\mu\psi^{(\frac{1}{2})}$ transforms by

$$
\partial^\mu\psi^{(\frac{1}{2})\prime} = (1 + ig\boldsymbol{\tau}\cdot\boldsymbol{\epsilon}(x)/2)\partial^\mu\psi^{(\frac{1}{2})} + ig\boldsymbol{\tau}\cdot\partial^\mu\boldsymbol{\epsilon}(x)/2\,\psi^{(\frac{1}{2})}, \quad (13.14)
$$

where we have retained only the terms linear in ϵ from an expansion of (13.8) with $\boldsymbol{\alpha} \to \boldsymbol{\epsilon}$. We have now dropped the x-dependence of the $\psi^{(\frac{1}{2})}$'s, but kept that of $\boldsymbol{\epsilon}(x)$, and we have used the simple '1' for the unit matrix in the two-dimensional isospace. Equation (13.14) exhibits again an 'extra piece' on the right-hand side, as compared to (13.13). On the other hand, inserting (13.10) and (13.13) into our covariant derivative requirement (13.9) yields, for the left-hand side in the infinitesimal case,

$$D'^{\mu}\psi^{(\frac{1}{2})\prime} = (\partial^{\mu} + ig\boldsymbol{\tau} \cdot \boldsymbol{W}'^{\mu}/2)[1 + ig\boldsymbol{\tau} \cdot \boldsymbol{\epsilon}(x)/2]\psi^{(\frac{1}{2})} \tag{13.15}$$

while the right-hand side is

$$[1 + ig\boldsymbol{\tau} \cdot \boldsymbol{\epsilon}(x)/2](\partial^{\mu} + ig\boldsymbol{\tau} \cdot \boldsymbol{W}^{\mu}/2)\psi^{(\frac{1}{2})}. \tag{13.16}$$

In order to verify that these are the same, however, we would need to know $\boldsymbol{W}'^{\mu}$ – that is, the transformation law for the three $\boldsymbol{W}^{\mu}$ fields. Instead, we shall proceed 'in reverse', and use the *imposed* equality between (13.15) and (13.16) to determine the transformation law of $\boldsymbol{W}^{\mu}$.

Suppose that, under this infinitesimal transformation,

$$\boldsymbol{W}^{\mu} \to \boldsymbol{W}'^{\mu} = \boldsymbol{W}^{\mu} + \delta\boldsymbol{W}^{\mu}. \tag{13.17}$$

Then the condition of equality is

$$[\partial^{\mu} + ig\boldsymbol{\tau}/2 \cdot (\boldsymbol{W}^{\mu} + \delta\boldsymbol{W}^{\mu})][1 + ig\boldsymbol{\tau} \cdot \boldsymbol{\epsilon}(x)/2]\psi^{(\frac{1}{2})}$$
$$= [1 + ig\boldsymbol{\tau} \cdot \boldsymbol{\epsilon}(x)/2](\partial^{\mu} + ig\boldsymbol{\tau} \cdot \boldsymbol{W}^{\mu}/2)\psi^{(\frac{1}{2})}. \tag{13.18}$$

Multiplying out the terms, neglecting the term of second order involving the product of $\delta\boldsymbol{W}^{\mu}$ and ϵ and noting that

$$\partial^{\mu}(\epsilon\psi) = (\partial^{\mu}\epsilon)\psi + \epsilon(\partial^{\mu}\psi) \tag{13.19}$$

we see that many terms cancel and we are left with

$$ig\frac{\boldsymbol{\tau} \cdot \delta\boldsymbol{W}^{\mu}}{2} = -ig\frac{\boldsymbol{\tau} \cdot \partial^{\mu}\boldsymbol{\epsilon}(x)}{2}$$
$$+ (ig)^2\left[\left(\frac{\boldsymbol{\tau} \cdot \boldsymbol{\epsilon}(x)}{2}\right)\left(\frac{\boldsymbol{\tau} \cdot \boldsymbol{W}^{\mu}}{2}\right) - \left(\frac{\boldsymbol{\tau} \cdot \boldsymbol{W}^{\mu}}{2}\right)\left(\frac{\boldsymbol{\tau} \cdot \boldsymbol{\epsilon}(x)}{2}\right)\right]. \tag{13.20}$$

Using the identity for Pauli matrices (see problem 3.4(b))

$$\boldsymbol{\sigma} \cdot \boldsymbol{a}\,\boldsymbol{\sigma} \cdot \boldsymbol{b} = \boldsymbol{a} \cdot \boldsymbol{b} + i\boldsymbol{\sigma} \cdot \boldsymbol{a} \times \boldsymbol{b} \tag{13.21}$$

this yields

$$\boldsymbol{\tau} \cdot \delta\boldsymbol{W}^{\mu} = -\boldsymbol{\tau} \cdot \partial^{\mu}\boldsymbol{\epsilon}(x) - g\boldsymbol{\tau} \cdot (\boldsymbol{\epsilon}(x) \times \boldsymbol{W}^{\mu}). \tag{13.22}$$

Equating components of $\boldsymbol{\tau}$ on both sides, we deduce

$$\boxed{\delta \boldsymbol{W}^\mu = -\partial^\mu \boldsymbol{\epsilon}(x) - g[\boldsymbol{\epsilon}(x) \times \boldsymbol{W}^\mu].} \tag{13.23}$$

The reader may note the close similarity between these manipulations and those encountered in section 12.1.3.

Equation (13.23) defines the way in which the SU(2) gauge fields $\boldsymbol{W}^\mu$ transform under an infinitesimal SU(2) gauge transformation. If it were not for the presence of the first term $\partial^\mu \boldsymbol{\epsilon}(x)$ on the right-hand side, (13.23) would be simply the (infinitesimal) transformation law for the $T = 1$ triplet representation of SU(2) – see (12.64) and (12.65) in section 12.1.3. As mentioned at the end of section 12.2, the $T = 1$ representation is the 'adjoint', or 'regular', representation of SU(2), and this is the one to which gauge fields belong, in general. But there is the extra term $-\partial^\mu \boldsymbol{\epsilon}(x)$. Clearly this is directly analogous to the $-\partial^\mu \chi(x)$ term in the transformation of the U(1) gauge field A^μ; here, an independent infinitesimal function $\epsilon_i(x)$ is required for each component $W_i^\mu(x)$. If the ϵ's were independent of x, then $\partial^\mu \boldsymbol{\epsilon}(x)$ would of course vanish and the transformation law (13.23) would indeed be just that of an SU(2) triplet. Thus we can say that under global SU(2) transformations, the $\boldsymbol{W}^\mu$ behave as a normal triplet. But under *local* SU(2) transformations they acquire the additional $-\partial^\mu \boldsymbol{\epsilon}(x)$ piece, and thus no longer transform 'properly', as an SU(2) triplet. In exactly the same way, $\partial^\mu \psi^{(\frac{1}{2})}$ did not transform 'properly' as an SU(2) doublet, under a local SU(2) transformation, because of the second term in (13.14), which also involves $\partial^\mu \boldsymbol{\epsilon}(x)$. The remarkable result behind the fact that $D^\mu \psi^{(\frac{1}{2})}$ *does* transform 'properly' under local SU(2) transformations, is that the extra term in (13.23) precisely cancels that in (13.14)!

To summarize progress so far: we have shown that, for infinitesimal transformations, the relation

$$(D'^\mu \psi^{(\frac{1}{2})\prime}) = [1 + ig\boldsymbol{\tau} \cdot \boldsymbol{\epsilon}(x)/2](D^\mu \psi^{(\frac{1}{2})}) \tag{13.24}$$

(where D^μ is given by (13.10)) holds true if in addition to the infinitesimal local SU(2) phase transformation on $\psi^{(\frac{1}{2})}$

$$\psi^{(\frac{1}{2})\prime} = [1 + ig\boldsymbol{\tau} \cdot \boldsymbol{\epsilon}(x)/2]\psi^{(\frac{1}{2})} \tag{13.25}$$

the gauge fields transform according to

$$\boldsymbol{W}'^\mu = \boldsymbol{W}^\mu - \partial^\mu \boldsymbol{\epsilon}(x) - g[\boldsymbol{\epsilon}(x) \times \boldsymbol{W}^\mu]. \tag{13.26}$$

In obtaining these results, the form (13.10) for the covariant derivative has been assumed, and only the infinitesimal version of (13.2) has been treated explicitly. It turns out that (13.10) is still appropriate for the finite (non-infinitesimal) transformation (13.2), but the associated transformation law for the gauge fields is then slightly more complicated than (13.26). Let us write

$$\mathbf{U}(\boldsymbol{\alpha}(x)) \equiv \exp[ig\boldsymbol{\tau} \cdot \boldsymbol{\alpha}(x)/2] \tag{13.27}$$

so that $\psi^{(\frac{1}{2})}$ transforms by

$$\psi^{(\frac{1}{2})\prime} = \mathbf{U}(\boldsymbol{\alpha}(x))\psi^{(\frac{1}{2})}. \tag{13.28}$$

Then we require

$$D'^{\mu}\psi^{(\frac{1}{2})\prime} = \mathbf{U}(\boldsymbol{\alpha}(x))D^{\mu}\psi^{(\frac{1}{2})}. \tag{13.29}$$

The left-hand side is

$$
\begin{aligned}
& (\partial^{\mu} + ig\boldsymbol{\tau} \cdot \boldsymbol{W}'^{\mu}/2)\mathbf{U}(\boldsymbol{\alpha}(x))\psi^{(\frac{1}{2})} \\
= \; & (\partial^{\mu}\mathbf{U})\psi^{(\frac{1}{2})} + \mathbf{U}\partial^{\mu}\psi^{(\frac{1}{2})} + ig\boldsymbol{\tau} \cdot \boldsymbol{W}'^{\mu}/2\,\mathbf{U}\psi^{(\frac{1}{2})},
\end{aligned}
\tag{13.30}
$$

while the right-hand side is

$$\mathbf{U}(\partial^{\mu} + ig\boldsymbol{\tau} \cdot \boldsymbol{W}^{\mu}/2)\psi^{(\frac{1}{2})}. \tag{13.31}$$

The $\mathbf{U}\partial^{\mu}\psi^{(\frac{1}{2})}$ terms cancel leaving

$$(\partial^{\mu}\mathbf{U})\psi^{(\frac{1}{2})} + ig\boldsymbol{\tau} \cdot \boldsymbol{W}'^{\mu}/2\,\mathbf{U}\psi^{(\frac{1}{2})} = \mathbf{U}ig\boldsymbol{\tau} \cdot \boldsymbol{W}^{\mu}/2\,\psi^{(\frac{1}{2})}. \tag{13.32}$$

Since this has to be true for all (two-component) $\psi^{(\frac{1}{2})}$'s, we can treat it as an operator equation acting in the space of $\psi^{(\frac{1}{2})}$'s to give

$$\partial^{\mu}\mathbf{U} + ig\boldsymbol{\tau} \cdot \boldsymbol{W}'^{\mu}/2\,\mathbf{U} = \mathbf{U}ig\boldsymbol{\tau} \cdot \boldsymbol{W}^{\mu}/2, \tag{13.33}$$

or equivalently

$$\frac{1}{2}\boldsymbol{\tau} \cdot \boldsymbol{W}'^{\mu} = \frac{i}{g}(\partial^{\mu}\mathbf{U})\mathbf{U}^{-1} + \mathbf{U}\frac{1}{2}\boldsymbol{\tau} \cdot \boldsymbol{W}^{\mu}\mathbf{U}^{-1}, \tag{13.34}$$

which defines the (finite) transformation law for SU(2) gauge fields. Problem 13.1 verifies that (13.34) reduces to (13.26) in the infinitesimal case $\boldsymbol{\alpha}(x) \to \boldsymbol{\epsilon}(x)$.

Suppose now that we consider a Dirac equation for $\psi^{(\frac{1}{2})}$:

$$(i\gamma_{\mu}\partial^{\mu} - m)\psi^{(\frac{1}{2})} = 0 \tag{13.35}$$

where both the 'isospinor' components of $\psi^{(\frac{1}{2})}$ are four-component Dirac spinors. We assert that we can ensure *local SU(2) gauge covariance* by replacing ∂^{μ} in this equation by the covariant derivative of (13.10). Indeed, we have

$$
\begin{aligned}
\mathbf{U}(\boldsymbol{\alpha}(x))[i\gamma_{\mu}D^{\mu} - m]\psi^{(\frac{1}{2})} &= i\gamma_{\mu}\mathbf{U}(\boldsymbol{\alpha}(x))[D^{\mu}\psi^{(\frac{1}{2})}] - m\mathbf{U}(\boldsymbol{\alpha}(x)]\psi^{(\frac{1}{2})} \\
&= i\gamma_{\mu}D'^{\mu}\psi^{(\frac{1}{2})\prime} - m\psi^{(\frac{1}{2})\prime}
\end{aligned}
\tag{13.36}
$$

using equations (13.9) and (13.28). Thus if

$$(i\gamma_{\mu}D^{\mu} - m)\psi^{(\frac{1}{2})} = 0 \tag{13.37}$$

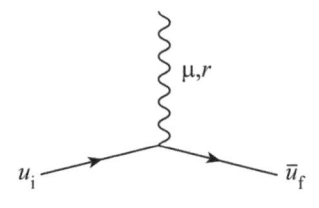

FIGURE 13.1
Vertex for isospinor-W interaction.

then

$$(i\gamma_\mu D'^\mu - m)\psi^{(\frac{1}{2})\prime} = 0, \tag{13.38}$$

proving the asserted covariance. In the same way, any free particle wave equation satisfied by an 'isospinor' $\psi^{(\frac{1}{2})}$ – the relevant equation is determined by the Lorentz spin of the particles involved – can be made locally covariant by the use of the covariant derivative D^μ, just as in the U(1) case.

The essential point here, of course, is that the locally covariant form includes *interactions* between the $\psi^{(\frac{1}{2})}$'s and the gauge fields W^μ, which are determined by the local phase invariance requirement (the 'gauge principle'). Indeed, we can already begin to find some of the Feynman rules appropriate to tree graphs for SU(2) gauge theories. Consider again the case of an SU(2) isospinor fermion, $\psi^{(\frac{1}{2})}$, obeying equation (13.38). This can be written as

$$(i\,\slashed{\partial} - m)\psi^{(\frac{1}{2})} = g(\boldsymbol{\tau}/2)\cdot\boldsymbol{W}\,\psi^{(\frac{1}{2})}. \tag{13.39}$$

In lowest-order perturbation theory the one-W emission/absorption process is given by the amplitude (cf (8.39)) for the electromagnetic case)

$$-ig\int \bar{\psi}_{\rm f}^{(\frac{1}{2})}(\boldsymbol{\tau}/2)\gamma_\mu\psi_{\rm i}^{(\frac{1}{2})}\cdot\boldsymbol{W}^\mu{\rm d}^4x \tag{13.40}$$

exactly as advertized (for the field-theoretic vertex) in (12.129). The matrix degree of freedom in the τ's is sandwiched between the two-component isospinors $\psi^{(\frac{1}{2})}$; the γ matrix acts on the four-component (Dirac) parts of $\psi^{(\frac{1}{2})}$. The external W^μ field is now specified by a spin-1 polarization vector ϵ^μ, like a photon, and by an 'SU(2) polarization vector' a^r ($r = 1, 2, 3$) which tells us which of the three SU(2) W-states is participating. The Feynman rule for figure 13.1 is therefore

$$-ig(\tau^r/2)\gamma_\mu \tag{13.41}$$

which is to be sandwiched between spinors/isospinors $u_{\rm i}, \bar{u}_{\rm f}$ and dotted into ϵ^μ and a^r. (13.41) is a very economical generalization of rule (ii) in Comment (3) of section 8.3.1.

The foregoing is easily generalized to SU(2) multiplets other than doublets. We shall change the notation slightly to use t instead of T for the 'isospin'

quantum number, so as to emphasize that it is *not* the hadronic isospin, for which we retain T; t will be the symbol used for the *weak isospin* to be introduced in chapter 20. The general local SU(2) transformation for a t-multiplet is then

$$\psi^{(t)} \rightarrow \psi^{(t)\prime} = \exp[ig\boldsymbol{\alpha}(x) \cdot \mathbf{T}^{(t)}]\psi^{(t)} \tag{13.42}$$

where the $(2t + 1) \times (2t + 1)$ matrices $T_i^{(t)}$ $(i = 1, 2, 3)$ satisfy (cf (12.47))

$$[T_i^{(t)}, T_j^{(t)}] = i\epsilon_{ijk}T_k^{(t)}. \tag{13.43}$$

The appropriate covariant derivative is

$$D^\mu = \partial^\mu + ig\mathbf{T}^{(t)} \cdot \boldsymbol{W}^\mu \tag{13.44}$$

which is a $(2t + 1) \times (2t + 1)$ matrix acting on the $(2t + 1)$ components of $\psi^{(t)}$. The gauge fields interact with such 'isomultiplets' in a *universal* way – only one g, the same for all the particles – which is prescribed by the local covariance requirement to be simply that interaction which is generated by the covariant derivatives. The fermion vertex corresponding to (13.44) is obtained by replacing $\boldsymbol{\tau}/2$ in (13.40) by $\boldsymbol{T}^{(t)}$.

We end this section with some comments:

(i) It is a remarkable fact that only one constant g is needed. This is *not* the same as in electromagnetism. There, each charged field interacts with the gauge field A^μ via a coupling whose strength is its charge $(e, -e, 2e, -5e \ldots)$. The crucial point is the appearance of the quadratic g^2 multiplying the *commutator* of the $\boldsymbol{\tau}$'s, $[\boldsymbol{\tau} \cdot \boldsymbol{\epsilon}, \boldsymbol{\tau} \cdot \boldsymbol{W}]$, in the $\boldsymbol{W}^\mu$ transformation (equation (13.20)). In the electromagnetic case, there is no such commutator – the associated U(1) phase group is Abelian. As signalled by the presence of g^2, a commutator is a non-linear quantity, and the scale of quantities appearing in such commutation relations is not arbitrary. It is an instructive exercise to check that, once $\delta\boldsymbol{W}^\mu$ is given by equation (13.23) – in the SU(2) case – then the g's appearing in $\psi^{(\frac{1}{2})\prime}$ (equation (13.13)) and $\psi^{(t)\prime}$ (via the infinitesimal version of equation (13.42)) must be the *same* as the one appearing in $\delta\boldsymbol{W}^\mu$.

(ii) According to the foregoing argument, it is actually a mystery why electric charge should be quantized. Since it is the coupling constant of an Abelian group, each charged field could have an arbitrary charge from this point of view: there are no commutators to fix the scale. This is one of the motivations of attempts to 'embed' the electromagnetic gauge transformations inside a larger non-Abelian group structure. Such is the case, for example, in 'grand unified theories' of strong, weak and electromagnetic interactions.

(iii) Finally we draw attention to the extremely important physical significance of the second term $\delta\boldsymbol{W}^\mu$ (equation (13.23)). The gauge fields themselves are not 'inert' as far as the gauge group is concerned: in the SU(2) case they have 'isospin' 1, while for a general group they belong to the regular representation of the group. This is profoundly different from the electromagnetic case, where the gauge field A^μ for the photon is of course uncharged: quite simply, $e = 0$ for a photon, and the second term in (13.23) is absent for A^μ. The fact that non-Abelian (Yang-Mills) gauge fields carry non-Abelian 'charge' degrees of freedom means that, since they are also the quanta of the force field, *they will necessarily interact with themselves*. Thus a non-Abelian gauge theory of gauge fields alone, with no 'matter' fields, has non-trivial interactions and is not a free theory.

We shall examine the form of these 'self-interactions' in section 13.3.2. First, we need to find the equivalent, for the Yang-Mills field, of the Maxwell field strength tensor $F^{\mu\nu}$, which gave us the gauge-invariant formulation of Maxwell's equations, and in terms of which the Maxwell Lagrangian can be immediately written down.

13.1.2   The non-Abelian field strength tensor

A simple way of arriving at the desired quantity is to consider the commutator of two covariant derivatives, as we can see by calculating it for the U(1) case. We find

$$[D^\mu, D^\nu]\,\psi \equiv (D^\mu D^\nu - D^\nu D^\mu)\psi = \mathrm{i}eF^{\mu\nu}\psi \tag{13.45}$$

as is verified in problem 13.2. Equation (13.45) suggests that we will find the SU(2) analogue of $F^{\mu\nu}$ by evaluating

$$[D^\mu, D^\nu]\,\psi^{(\frac{1}{2})} \tag{13.46}$$

where as usual

$$D^\mu(\text{on } \psi^{(\frac{1}{2})}) = \partial^\mu + \mathrm{i}g\boldsymbol{\tau} \cdot \boldsymbol{W}^\mu/2. \tag{13.47}$$

Problem 13.3 confirms that the result is

$$[D^\mu, D^\nu]\,\psi^{(\frac{1}{2})} = \mathrm{i}g\boldsymbol{\tau}/2 \cdot (\partial^\mu\boldsymbol{W}^\nu - \partial^\nu\boldsymbol{W}^\mu - g\boldsymbol{W}^\mu \times \boldsymbol{W}^\nu)\,\psi^{(\frac{1}{2})}; \tag{13.48}$$

the manipulations are very similar to those in (13.20)–(13.23). Noting the analogy between the right-hand side of (13.48) and (13.45), we accordingly expect the SU(2) 'curvature' or field strength tensor, to be given by

$$\boldsymbol{F}^{\mu\nu} = \partial^\mu\boldsymbol{W}^\nu - \partial^\nu\boldsymbol{W}^\mu - g\boldsymbol{W}^\mu \times \boldsymbol{W}^\nu \tag{13.49}$$

or, in component notation,

$$F_i^{\mu\nu} = \partial^\mu W_i^\nu - \partial^\nu W_i^\mu - g\epsilon_{ijk}W_j^\mu W_k^\nu. \tag{13.50}$$

This tensor is of fundamental importance in a (non-Abelian) gauge theory. Since it arises from the commutator of two gauge-covariant derivatives, we are guaranteed that it itself is gauge covariant – that is to say, 'it transforms under local SU(2) transformations in the way its SU(2) structure would indicate'. Now $\boldsymbol{F}^{\mu\nu}$ has clearly three SU(2) components and must be an SU(2) triplet: indeed, it is true that under an infinitesimal local SU(2) transformation

$$\boldsymbol{F}'^{\mu\nu} = \boldsymbol{F}^{\mu\nu} - g\boldsymbol{\epsilon}(x) \times \boldsymbol{F}^{\mu\nu} \qquad (13.51)$$

which is the expected law (cf (12.64)) for an SU(2) triplet. Problem 13.4 verifies that (13.51) follows from (13.49) and the transformation law (13.23) for the $\boldsymbol{W}^{\mu}$ fields. Note particularly that $\boldsymbol{F}^{\mu\nu}$ transforms 'properly', as an SU(2) triplet should, *without* the ∂^{μ} part which appears in $\delta\boldsymbol{W}^{\mu}$.

This non-Abelian $\boldsymbol{F}^{\mu\nu}$ is a much more interesting object than the Abelian $F^{\mu\nu}$ (which is actually U(1)-gauge *invariant*, of course: $F'^{\mu\nu} = F^{\mu\nu}$). $\boldsymbol{F}^{\mu\nu}$ contains the gauge coupling constant g, confirming (cf comment(c) in section 13.1.1) that the gauge fields themselves carry SU(2) 'charge', and act as sources for the field strength. Appendix N shows how these field strength tensors may be regarded as analogous to geometrical curvatures.

It is now straightforward to move to the quantum field case and construct the SU(2) Yang-Mills analogue of the Maxwell Lagrangian $-\frac{1}{4}\hat{F}_{\mu\nu}\hat{F}^{\mu\nu}$. It is simply $-\frac{1}{4}\hat{\boldsymbol{F}}_{\mu\nu} \cdot \hat{\boldsymbol{F}}^{\mu\nu}$, the SU(2) 'dot product' ensuring SU(2) invariance (see problem 13.5), even under *local* transformation, in view of the transformation law (13.51). But before proceeding in this way we first need to introduce local SU(3) symmetry.

13.2 Local SU(3) Symmetry

Using what has been done for global SU(3) symmetry in section 12.2, and the preceding discussion of how to make a global SU(2) into a local one, it is straightforward to develop the corresponding theory of local SU(3). This is the gauge group of QCD, the three degrees of freedom of the fundamental quark triplet now referring to 'colour', as will be further discussed in chapter 14. We denote the basic triplet by ψ, which transforms under a local SU(3) transformation according to

$$\psi' = \exp[i g_s \boldsymbol{\lambda} \cdot \boldsymbol{\alpha}(x)/2]\psi, \qquad (13.52)$$

which is the same as the global transformation (12.74) but with the 8 constant parameters $\boldsymbol{\alpha}$ replaced by x-dependent ones, and with a coupling strength g_s inserted. The SU(3)-covariant derivative, when acting on an SU(3) triplet ψ, is given by the indicated generalization of (13.10), namely

$$D^{\mu}(\text{acting on SU(3) triplet}) = \partial^{\mu} + i g_s \boldsymbol{\lambda}/2 \cdot \boldsymbol{A}^{\mu} \qquad (13.53)$$

where $A_1^\mu, A_2^\mu, \ldots A_8^\mu$ are eight gauge fields which are called *gluons*. The coupling is denoted by 'g_s' in anticipation of the application to strong interactions via QCD.

The infinitesimal version of (13.52) is (cf (13.13))

$$\psi' = (1 + \mathrm{i} g_s \boldsymbol{\lambda} \cdot \boldsymbol{\eta}(x)/2)\psi \tag{13.54}$$

where '1' stands for the unit matrix in the three-dimensional space of components of the triplet ψ. As in (13.14), it is clear that $\partial^\mu \psi'$ will involve an 'unwanted' term $\partial^\mu \boldsymbol{\eta}(x)$. By contrast, the desired covariant derivative $D^\mu \psi$ should transform according to

$$D'^\mu \psi' = (1 + \mathrm{i} g_s \boldsymbol{\lambda} \cdot \boldsymbol{\eta}(x)/2)D^\mu \psi \tag{13.55}$$

without the $\partial^\mu \boldsymbol{\eta}(x)$ term. Problem 13.6 verifies that this is fulfilled by having the gauge fields transform by

$$A_a'^\mu = A_a^\mu - \partial^\mu \eta_a(x) - g_s f_{abc} \eta_b(x) A_c^\mu. \tag{13.56}$$

Comparing (13.56) with (12.80) we can identify the term in f_{abc} as telling us that the 8 fields A_a^μ transform as an SU(3) octet, the η's now depending on x, of course. This is the adjoint, or regular representation of SU(3), as we have now come to expect for gauge fields. However, the $\partial^\mu \eta_a(x)$ piece spoils this simple transformation property under local transformations. But it *is* just what is needed to cancel the corresponding $\partial^\mu \boldsymbol{\eta}(x)$ term in $\partial^\mu \psi'$, leaving $D^\mu \psi$ transforming as a proper triplet via (13.55). The finite version of (13.56) can be derived as in section 13.1 for SU(2), but we shall not need the result here.

As in the SU(2) case, the free Dirac equation for an SU(3)-triplet ψ,

$$(\mathrm{i}\gamma_\mu \partial^\mu - m)\psi = 0, \tag{13.57}$$

can be 'promoted' into one which is covariant under local SU(3) transformations by replacing ∂^μ by D^μ of (13.53), leading to

$$(\mathrm{i}\, \slashed{\partial} - m)\psi = g_s \boldsymbol{\lambda}/2 \cdot \boldsymbol{A}\psi \tag{13.58}$$

(compare (13.39)). This leads immediately to the one gluon emission amplitude (see figure 13.2)

$$-\mathrm{i}g_s \int \bar{\psi}_f \boldsymbol{\lambda}/2 \gamma^\mu \psi_i \cdot \boldsymbol{A}_\mu \mathrm{d}^4 x \tag{13.59}$$

as already suggested in section 12.3.1: the SU(3) current of (12.133) – but this time in *colour* space – is 'dotted' with the gauge field. The Feynman rule for figure 13.2 is therefore

$$-\mathrm{i}g_s \lambda_a/2\, \gamma^\mu. \tag{13.60}$$

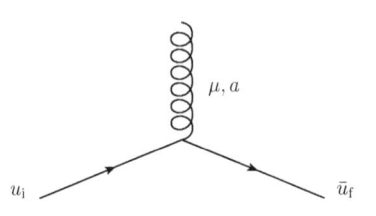

FIGURE 13.2
Quark-gluon vertex.

The SU(3) field strength tensor can be calculated by evaluating the commutator of two D's of the form (13.53); the result (problem 13.7) is

$$F_a^{\mu\nu} = \partial^\mu A_a^\nu - \partial^\nu A_a^\mu - g_s f_{abc} A_b^\mu A_c^\nu \tag{13.61}$$

which is closely analogous to the SU(2) case (13.50) (the structure constants of SU(2) are given by $i\epsilon_{ijk}$, and of SU(3) by if_{abc}). Once again, the crucial property of $F_a^{\mu\nu}$ is that, under *local* SU(3) transformations it develops no '$\partial^\mu \eta_a$' part, but transforms as a 'proper' octet:

$$F_a^{\mu\nu\prime} = F_a^{\mu\nu} - g_s f_{abc} \eta_b(x) F_c^{\mu\nu}. \tag{13.62}$$

This allows us to write down a locally SU(3)-invariant analogue of the Maxwell Lagrangian

$$-\frac{1}{4} F_a^{\mu\nu} F_{a\mu\nu} \tag{13.63}$$

by dotting the two octets together.

It is now time to consider locally SU(2)- and SU(3)-invariant quantum field Lagrangians and, in particular, the resulting self-interactions among the gauge quanta.

13.3 Local non-Abelian symmetries in Lagrangian quantum field theory

13.3.1 Local SU(2) and SU(3) Lagrangians

We consider here only the particular examples relevant to the strong and electroweak interactions of quarks: namely, a (weak) SU(2) doublet of fermions interacting with SU(2) gauge fields W_i^μ, and a (strong) SU(3) triplet of fermions interacting with the gauge fields A_a^μ. We follow the same steps as in the U(1) case of chapter 7, noting again that for quantum fields the sign of the exponents in (13.2) and (13.52) is reversed, by convention; thus (12.89) is replaced

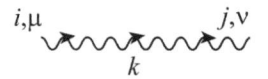

FIGURE 13.3
SU(2) gauge-boson propagator.

by its local version

$$\hat{q}' = \exp(-ig\hat{\boldsymbol{\alpha}}(x) \cdot \boldsymbol{\tau}/2)\hat{q} \qquad (13.64)$$

and (12.132) by

$$\hat{q}' = \exp(-ig_s\hat{\boldsymbol{\alpha}}(x) \cdot \boldsymbol{\lambda}/2)\hat{q}. \qquad (13.65)$$

Correspondingly, the ϵ in (13.23) and the η's in (13.56) become field operators, with a reversal of sign.

The globally SU(2)-invariant Lagrangian (12.87) becomes locally SU(2)-invariant if we replaced ∂^μ by D^μ of (13.10), with $\hat{W}^\mu$ now a quantum field:

$$\begin{aligned} \hat{\mathcal{L}}_{\text{D,local SU(2)}} &= \bar{\hat{q}}(i\,\hat{\slashed{D}} - m)\hat{q} \\ &= \bar{\hat{q}}(i\,\slashed{\partial} - m)\hat{q} - g\bar{\hat{q}}\gamma^\mu\boldsymbol{\tau}/2\hat{q} \cdot \hat{\boldsymbol{W}}_\mu \qquad (13.66) \end{aligned}$$

with an interaction of the form 'symmetry current (12.109) dotted into the gauge field'. To this we must add the SU(2) Yang-Mills term

$$\mathcal{L}_{\text{Y−M,SU(2)}} = -\frac{1}{4}\hat{\boldsymbol{F}}_{\mu\nu} \cdot \hat{\boldsymbol{F}}^{\mu\nu} \qquad (13.67)$$

to get the local SU(2) analogue of $\mathcal{L}_{\text{QED}}$. It is *not* possible to add a mass term for the gauge fields of the form $\frac{1}{2}\hat{\boldsymbol{W}}^\mu \cdot \hat{\boldsymbol{W}}_\mu$, since such a term would not be invariant under the gauge transformations (13.26) or (13.34) of the W-fields. Thus, just as in the U(1) (electromagnetic) case, the W-quanta of this theory are *massless*. We presumably also need a gauge-fixing term for the gauge fields, as in section 7.3.2, which we can take to be[1]

$$\mathcal{L}_{\text{gf}} = -\frac{1}{2\xi}\left(\partial_\mu\hat{\boldsymbol{W}}^\mu \cdot \partial_\nu\hat{\boldsymbol{W}}^\nu\right). \qquad (13.68)$$

The Feynman rule for the fermion-W vertex is then the same as already given in (13.41), while the W-propagator is (figure 13.3)

$$\frac{i\left[-g^{\mu\nu} + (1 - \xi)k^\mu k^\nu/k^2\right]}{k^2 + i\epsilon}\,\delta^{ij}. \qquad (13.69)$$

Before proceeding to the SU(3) case, we must now emphasize three respects

---

[1]We shall see in section 13.5.3 that in the non-Abelian case this gauge-fixing term does *not* completely solve the problem of quantizing such gauge fields; however, it is adequate for tree graphs.

in which our local SU(2) Lagrangian is not suitable (yet) for describing weak interactions. First, weak interactions violate parity, in fact 'maximally', by which is meant that only the 'left-handed' part $\hat{\psi}_L$ of the fermion field enters the interactions with the $\boldsymbol{W}^\mu$ fields, where $\hat{\psi}_L \equiv \left(\frac{1-\gamma_5}{2}\right)\hat{\psi}$; for this reason the weak isospin group is called SU(2)$_L$. Secondly, the physical W$^\pm$ are of course not massless, and therefore cannot be described by propagators of the form (13.69). And thirdly, the *fermion* mass term violates the 'left-handed' SU(2) gauge symmetry, as the discussion in section 12.3.2 shows. In this case, however, the chiral symmetry which is broken by fermion masses in the Lagrangian is a local, or gauge, symmetry (in section 12.3.2 the chiral flavour symmetry was a global symmetry). If we want to preserve the chiral gauge symmetry SU(2)$_L$ – and it is necessary for renormalizability – then we shall have to replace the simple fermion mass term in (13.66) by something else, as will be explained in chapter 22.

The locally SU(3)$_c$-invariant Lagrangian for one quark triplet (cf (12.137))

$$\hat{q}_f = \begin{pmatrix} \hat{f}_r \\ \hat{f}_b \\ \hat{f}_g \end{pmatrix}, \tag{13.70}$$

where 'f' stands for 'flavour', and 'r, b, and g' for 'red, blue, and green', is

$$\bar{\hat{q}}_f(i\hat{\slashed{D}} - m_f)\hat{q}_f - \frac{1}{4}\hat{F}_{a\mu\nu}\hat{F}_a^{\mu\nu} - \frac{1}{2\xi}(\partial_\mu \hat{A}_a^\mu)(\partial_\nu \hat{A}_a^\nu) \tag{13.71}$$

where $\hat{D}^\mu$ is given by (13.53) with $\boldsymbol{A}^\mu$ replaced by $\hat{\boldsymbol{A}}^\mu$, and the footnote before equation (13.68) also applies here. This leads to the interaction term (cf (13.59))

$$-g_s\bar{\hat{q}}_f\gamma^\mu\boldsymbol{\lambda}/2\hat{q}_f \cdot \hat{\boldsymbol{A}}_\mu \tag{13.72}$$

and the Feynman rule (13.60) for figure 13.2. Once again, the gluon quanta must be *massless*, and their propagator is the same as (13.69), with $\delta_{ij} \to \delta_{ab}$ ($a, b = 1, 2, \dots 8$). The different quark flavours are included by simply repeating the first term of (13.71) for all flavours:

$$\sum_f \bar{\hat{q}}_f(i\hat{\slashed{D}} - m_f)\hat{q}_f, \tag{13.73}$$

which incorporates the hypothesis that the SU(3)$_c$-gauge interaction is 'flavour-blind', i.e. exactly the same for each flavour. Note that although the flavour masses are different, the masses of different 'coloured' quarks of the same flavour are the same ($m_u \neq m_d, m_{u,r} = m_{u,b} = m_{u,g}$).

The Lagrangians (13.66)–(13.68), and (13.71), though easily written down after all this preparation, are unfortunately not adequate for anything but tree graphs. We shall indicate why this is so in section 13.3.3. Before that, we want to discuss in more detail the nature of the gauge-field self-interactions contained in the Yang-Mills pieces.

13.3.2   Gauge field self-interactions

We start by pointing out an interesting ambiguity in the prescription for 'covariantizing' wave equations which we have followed, namely 'replace ∂^μ by D^μ'. Suppose we wished to consider the electromagnetic interactions of charged massless spin-1 particles, call them X's, carrying charge e. The standard wave equation for such free massless vector particles would be the same as for A^μ, namely

$$\Box X^\mu - \partial^\mu \partial^\nu X_\nu = 0. \tag{13.74}$$

To 'covariantize' this (i.e. introduce the electromagnetic coupling) we would replace ∂^μ by $D^\mu = \partial^\mu + ieA^\mu$ so as to obtain

$$D^2 X^\mu - D^\mu D^\nu X_\nu = 0. \tag{13.75}$$

But this procedure is not unique: if we had started from the perfectly equivalent wave equation

$$\Box X^\mu - \partial^\nu \partial^\mu X_\nu = 0 \tag{13.76}$$

we would have arrived at

$$D^2 X^\mu - D^\nu D^\mu X_\nu = 0 \tag{13.77}$$

which is not the same as (13.75), since (cf (13.45))

$$[D^\mu, D^\nu] = ieF^{\mu\nu}. \tag{13.78}$$

The simple prescription $\partial^\mu \to D^\mu$ has, in this case, failed to produce a unique wave equation. We can allow for this ambiguity by introducing an arbitrary parameter δ in the wave equation, which we write as

$$D^2 X^\mu - D^\nu D^\mu X_\nu + ie\delta F^{\mu\nu} X_\nu = 0. \tag{13.79}$$

The δ term in (13.79) contributes to the magnetic moment coupling of the X-particle to the electromagnetic field, and is called the 'ambiguous magnetic moment'. Just such an ambiguity would seem to arise in the case of the charged weak interaction quanta $W^\pm$ (their masses do not affect this argument). For the photon itself, of course, $e = 0$ and there is no such ambiguity.

It is important to be clear that (13.79) is fully U(1) gauge-covariant, so that δ cannot be fixed by further appeal to the local U(1) symmetry. Moreover, it turns out that the theory for arbitrary δ is *not renormalizable* (though we shall not show this here): thus the quantum electrodynamics of charged massless vector bosons is in general non-renormalizable.

However, the theory *is* renormalizable if – to continue with the present terminology – the photon, the X-particle, and its antiparticle the $\bar{\text{X}}$ are the members of an SU(2) gauge triplet (like the W's), with gauge coupling constant e. This is, indeed, very much how the photon and the $W^\pm$ are 'unified', but there is a complication (as always!) in that case, having to do with the

necessity for finding room in the scheme for the neutral weak boson Z^0 as well. We shall see how this works in chapter 19; meanwhile we continue with this $X - \gamma$ model. We shall show that when the $X - \gamma$ interaction contained in (13.79) is regarded as a $3 - X$ vertex in a local SU(2) gauge theory, the value of δ has to equal 1; for this value the theory is renormalizable. In this interpretation, the X^μ wave function is identified with '$\frac{1}{\sqrt{2}}(X_1^\mu + iX_2^\mu)$' and $\bar{X}^\mu$ with '$\frac{1}{\sqrt{2}}(X_1^\mu - iX_2^\mu)$' in terms of components of the SU(2) triplet X_i^μ, while A^μ is identified with X_3^μ.

Consider then equation (13.79) written in the form[2]

$$\Box X^\mu - \partial^\nu \partial^\mu X_\nu = \hat{V} X^\mu \tag{13.80}$$

where

$$\begin{aligned} \hat{V} X^\mu &= -ie\left\{[\partial^\nu(A_\nu X^\mu) + A^\nu \partial_\nu X^\mu]\right. \\ &\quad - (1+\delta)[\partial^\nu(A^\mu X_\nu) + A^\nu \partial^\mu X_\nu] \\ &\quad \left. + \delta[\partial^\mu(A^\nu X_\nu) + A^\mu \partial^\nu X_\nu]\right\}, \end{aligned} \tag{13.81}$$

and we have dropped terms of $O(e^2)$ which appear in the 'D^2' term; we shall come back to them later. The terms inside the { } brackets have been written in such a way that each [ ] bracket has the structure

$$\partial(AX) + A(\partial X) \tag{13.82}$$

which will be convenient for the following evaluation.

The lowest-order ($O(e)$) perturbation theory amplitude for '$X \rightarrow X$' under the potential $\hat{V}$ is then

$$-i \int X_\mu^*(f) \hat{V} X^\mu(i) d^4x. \tag{13.83}$$

Inserting (13.81) into (13.83) clearly gives something involving two 'X'-wavefunctions and one 'A' one, i.e. a triple-X vertex (with $A^\mu \equiv X_3^\mu$), shown in figure 13.4. To obtain the rule for this vertex from (13.83), consider the first [ ] bracket in (13.81). It contributes

$$-i(-ie) \int X_\mu^*(2)\{\partial^\nu(X_{3\nu}(3)X^\mu(1)) + X_3^\nu(3)\partial_\nu X^\mu(1)\}d^4x \tag{13.84}$$

where the (1), (2), (3) refer to the momenta as shown in figure 13.4, and for reasons of symmetry are all taken to be ingoing; thus

$$X_3^\mu(3) = \epsilon_3^\mu \exp(-ik_3 \cdot x) \tag{13.85}$$

---

[2]The sign chosen for $\hat{V}$ here apparently *differs* from that in the KG case (3.101), but it does agree when allowance is made, in the amplitude (13.83), for the fact that the dot product of the polarization vectors is negative (cf (7.87)).

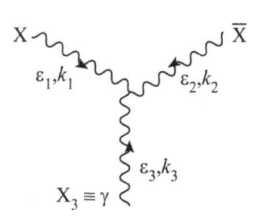

FIGURE 13.4
Triple-X vertex.

for example. The first term in (13.84) can be easily evaluated by a partial integration to turn the ∂^ν onto the $X^*_\mu(2)$, while in the second term ∂_ν acts straightforwardly on $X^\mu(1)$. Omitting the usual $(2\pi)^4\,\delta^4$ energy-momentum conserving factor, we find (problem 13.8) that (13.84) leads to the amplitude

$$i e \epsilon_1 \cdot \epsilon_2\,(k_1 - k_2) \cdot \epsilon_3. \tag{13.86}$$

In a similar way, the other terms in (13.83) give

$$-i e \delta(\epsilon_1 \cdot \epsilon_3\,\epsilon_2 \cdot k_2 - \epsilon_2 \cdot \epsilon_3\,\epsilon_1 \cdot k_1) \tag{13.87}$$

and

$$+i e (1 + \delta)(\epsilon_2 \cdot \epsilon_3\,\epsilon_1 \cdot k_2 - \epsilon_1 \cdot \epsilon_3\,\epsilon_2 \cdot k_1). \tag{13.88}$$

Adding all the terms up and using the 4-momentum conservation condition

$$k_1 + k_2 + k_3 = 0 \tag{13.89}$$

we obtain the vertex

$$+i e \{\epsilon_1 \cdot \epsilon_2\,(k_1 - k_2) \cdot \epsilon_3 + \epsilon_2 \cdot \epsilon_3\,(\delta k_2 - k_3) \cdot \epsilon_1 + \epsilon_3 \cdot \epsilon_1\,(k_3 - \delta k_1) \cdot \epsilon_2\}. \tag{13.90}$$

It is quite evident from (13.90) that the value $\delta = 1$ has a privileged role, and we strongly suspect that this will be the value selected by the proposed SU(2) gauge symmetry of this model. We shall check this in two ways: in the first, we consider a 'physical' process involving the vertex (13.90), and show how requiring it to be SU(2)-gauge invariant fixes δ to be 1; in the second, we 'unpack' the relevant vertex from the compact Yang-Mills Lagrangian $-\frac{1}{4}\hat{X}_{\mu\nu}\cdot\hat{X}^{\mu\nu}$.

The process we shall choose is $X + d \to X + d$ where d is a fermion (which we call a quark) transforming as the $T_3 = -\frac{1}{2}$ component of a doublet under the SU(2) gauge group, its $T_3 = +\frac{1}{2}$ partner being the u. There are two contributing Feynman graphs, shown in figure 13.5(a) and (b). Consider first the amplitude for figure 13.5(a). We use the rule of figure 13.1, with the τ-matrix combination $\tau_+ = (\tau_1 + i\tau_2)/\sqrt{2}$ corresponding to the absorption of

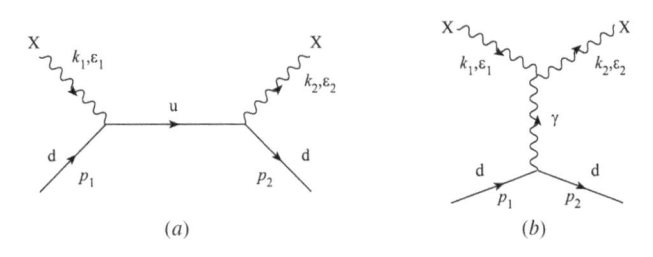

FIGURE 13.5
Tree graphs contributing to $X + d \rightarrow X + d$.

the positively charged X, and $\tau_- = (\tau_1 - i\tau_2)/\sqrt{2}$ for the emission of the X. Then figure 13.5(a) is

$$(-ie)^2 \bar{\psi}^{(\frac{1}{2})}(p_2) \frac{\tau_-}{2} \not{\epsilon}_2 \frac{i}{\not{p}_1 + \not{k}_1 - m} \frac{\tau_+}{2} \not{\epsilon}_1 \psi^{(\frac{1}{2})}(p_1) \tag{13.91}$$

where

$$\psi^{(\frac{1}{2})} = \begin{pmatrix} u \\ d \end{pmatrix}, \tag{13.92}$$

and we have chosen real polarization vectors. Using the explicit forms (12.25) for the τ-matrices, (13.91) becomes

$$(-ie)^2 \bar{d}(p_2) \frac{1}{\sqrt{2}} \not{\epsilon}_2 \frac{i}{\not{p}_1 + \not{k}_1 - m} \frac{1}{\sqrt{2}} \not{\epsilon}_1 d(p_1). \tag{13.93}$$

We must now discuss how to implement gauge invariance. In the QED case of electron Compton scattering (section 8.6.2), the test of gauge invariance was that the amplitude should vanish if any photon polarization vector $\epsilon^\mu(k)$ was replaced by k^μ – see (8.165). This requirement was derived from the fact that a gauge transformation on the photon A^μ took the form $A^\mu \rightarrow A'^\mu = A^\mu - \partial^\mu \chi$, so that, consistently with the Lorentz condition, ϵ^μ could be replaced by $\epsilon'^\mu = \epsilon^\mu + \beta k^\mu$ (cf 8.163) without changing the physics. But the SU(2) analogue of the U(1) gauge transformation is given by (13.26), for infinitesimal ϵ's, and although there is indeed an analogous '$-\partial^\mu \epsilon$' part, there is also an additional part (with $g \rightarrow e$ in our case) expressing the fact that the X's carry SU(2) charge. However this extra part does involve the coupling e. Hence, if we were to make the *full* change corresponding to (13.26) in a tree graph of order e^2, the extra part would produce a term of order e^3. We shall take the view that gauge invariance should hold at each order of perturbation theory separately; thus we shall demand that the tree graphs for X-d scattering, for example, should be invariant under $\epsilon^\mu \rightarrow k^\mu$ for any ϵ.

The replacement $\epsilon_1 \rightarrow k_1$ in (13.93) produces the result (problem 13.9)

$$(-ie)^2 \frac{i}{2} \bar{d}(p_2) \not{\epsilon}_2 d(p_1) \tag{13.94}$$

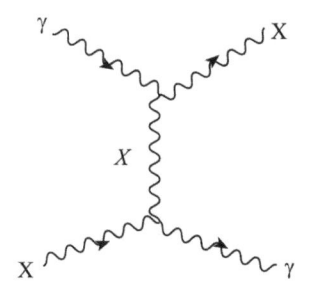
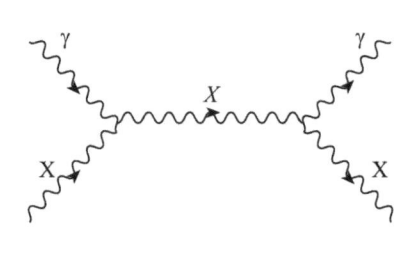

FIGURE 13.6
Tree graphs contributing to $\gamma + X \rightarrow \gamma + X$.

where we have used the Dirac equation for the quark spinors of mass m. The term (13.94) is certainly not zero, but we must of course also include the amplitude for figure 13.5(b). Using the vertex of (13.90) with suitable sign changes of momenta, and the photon propagator of (7.119), and remembering that d has $\tau_3 = -1$, the amplitude for figure 13.5(b) is

$$ie[\epsilon_1 \cdot \epsilon_2 \, (k_1 + k_2)_\mu \quad + \quad \epsilon_{2\mu}\epsilon_1 \cdot (-\delta k_2 - k_2 + k_1) + \epsilon_{1\mu}\epsilon_2 \cdot (k_2 - k_1 - \delta k_1)]$$

$$\times \quad \frac{-ig^{\mu\nu}}{q^2} \times [-ie\bar{d}(p_2)\left(-\frac{1}{2}\right)\gamma_\nu d(p_1)], \qquad (13.95)$$

where $q^2 = (k_1 - k_2)^2 = -2k_1 \cdot k_2$ using $k_1^2 = k_2^2 = 0$, and where the ξ-dependent part of the γ-propagator vanishes since $\bar{d}(p_2) \, \not{q} d(p_1) = 0$. We now leave it as an exercise (problem 13.10) to verify that, when $\epsilon_1 \rightarrow k_1$ in (13.95), the resulting amplitude does exactly cancel the contribution (13.94), *provided that $\delta = 1$*. Thus the $X - \bar{X} - \gamma$ vertex is, assuming the SU(2) gauge symmetry,

$$ie[\epsilon_1 \cdot \epsilon_2 \, (k_1 - k_2) \cdot \epsilon_3 + \epsilon_2 \cdot \epsilon_3 \, (k_2 - k_3) \cdot \epsilon_1 + \epsilon_3 \cdot \epsilon_1 \, (k_3 - k_1) \cdot \epsilon_2]. \quad (13.96)$$

The verification of this non-Abelian gauge invariance to order e^2 is, of course, not a proof that the entire theory of massless X quanta, γ's and quark isospinors will be gauge invariant if $\delta = 1$. Indeed, having obtained the $X - X - \gamma$ vertex, we immediately have something new to check: we can see if the lowest-order $\gamma - X$ scattering amplitude is gauge invariant. The $X - X - \gamma$ vertex will generate the $O(e^2)$ graphs shown in figure 13.6, and the dedicated reader may check that the sum of these amplitudes is *not* gauge invariant, again in the (tree-graph) sense of not vanishing when any ϵ is replaced by the corresponding k. But this is actually correct. In obtaining the $X - X - \gamma$ vertex we dropped an $O(e^2)$ term involving the three fields A, A and X, in going from (13.81) to (13.90): this will generate an $O(e^2)$ $\gamma - \gamma - X - X$ interaction, figure 13.7, when used in lowest-order perturbation theory. One can find the amplitude for figure 13.7 by the gauge invariance requirement

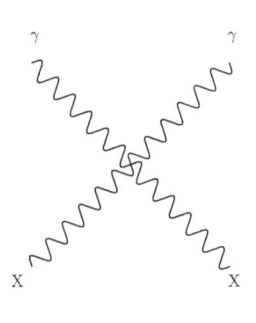

FIGURE 13.7

$\gamma - \gamma - X - X$ vertex.

applied to figures 13.6 and 13.7, but it has to be admitted that this approach is becoming laborious. It is, of course, far more efficient to deduce the vertices from the compact Yang-Mills Lagrangian $-\frac{1}{4}\hat{\boldsymbol{X}}_{\mu\nu} \cdot \hat{\boldsymbol{X}}^{\mu\nu}$, which we shall now do; nevertheless, some of the physical implications of those couplings, such as we have discussed above, are worth exposing.

The SU(2) Yang-Mills Lagrangian for the SU(2) triplet of gauge fields $\hat{\boldsymbol{X}}^{\mu}$ is

$$\hat{\mathcal{L}}_{2,\mathrm{YM}} = -\frac{1}{4}\hat{\boldsymbol{X}}_{\mu\nu} \cdot \hat{\boldsymbol{X}}^{\mu\nu}, \tag{13.97}$$

where

$$\hat{\boldsymbol{X}}^{\mu\nu} = \partial^{\mu}\hat{\boldsymbol{X}}^{\nu} - \partial^{\nu}\hat{\boldsymbol{X}}^{\mu} - e\hat{\boldsymbol{X}}^{\mu} \times \hat{\boldsymbol{X}}^{\nu}. \tag{13.98}$$

$\hat{\mathcal{L}}_{2,\mathrm{YM}}$ can be unpacked a bit into

$$\begin{aligned} & -\quad \frac{1}{2}(\partial_{\mu}\hat{\boldsymbol{X}}_{\nu} - \partial_{\nu}\hat{\boldsymbol{X}}_{\mu}) \cdot (\partial^{\mu}\hat{\boldsymbol{X}}^{\nu}) \\ & +\quad e(\hat{\boldsymbol{X}}_{\mu} \times \hat{\boldsymbol{X}}_{\nu}) \cdot \partial^{\mu}\hat{\boldsymbol{X}}^{\nu} \\ & -\quad \frac{1}{4}e^2\left[(\hat{\boldsymbol{X}}^{\mu} \cdot \hat{\boldsymbol{X}}_{\mu})^2 - (\hat{\boldsymbol{X}}^{\mu} \cdot \hat{\boldsymbol{X}}^{\nu})(\hat{\boldsymbol{X}}_{\mu} \cdot \hat{\boldsymbol{X}}_{\nu})\right]. \end{aligned} \tag{13.99}$$

The $X - X - \gamma$ vertex is in the 'e' term, the $X - X - \gamma - \gamma$ one in the 'e^2' term. We give the form of the latter using SU(2) 'i, j, k' labels, as shown in figure 13.8:

$$\begin{aligned} -\mathrm{i}e^2[&\epsilon_{ijl}\epsilon_{mnl}(\epsilon_1 \cdot \epsilon_3\,\epsilon_2 \cdot \epsilon_4 - \epsilon_1 \cdot \epsilon_4\,\epsilon_2 \cdot \epsilon_3) \\ & + \epsilon_{inl}\epsilon_{jml}(\epsilon_1 \cdot \epsilon_2\,\epsilon_3 \cdot \epsilon_4 - \epsilon_1 \cdot \epsilon_3\,\epsilon_2 \cdot \epsilon_4) \\ & + \epsilon_{iml}\epsilon_{njl}(\epsilon_1 \cdot \epsilon_4\,\epsilon_2 \cdot \epsilon_3 - \epsilon_1 \cdot \epsilon_2\,\epsilon_3 \cdot \epsilon_4)] \end{aligned} \tag{13.100}$$

The reason for the collection of terms seen in (13.96) and (13.100) can be understood as follows. Consider the $3 - X$ vertex

$$\langle k_2, \epsilon_2, j; k_3, \epsilon_3, k \,|\, e(\hat{\boldsymbol{X}}_{\mu} \times \hat{\boldsymbol{X}}_{\nu}) \cdot \partial^{\mu}\hat{\boldsymbol{X}}^{\nu} \,|\, k_1, \epsilon_1, i\rangle \tag{13.101}$$

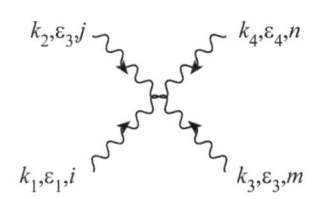

FIGURE 13.8
4 − X vertex.

for example. When each $\hat{X}$ is expressed as a mode expansion, and the initial and final states are also written in terms of appropriate $\hat{a}$'s and $\hat{a}^\dagger$'s, the amplitude will be a vacuum expectation value (vev) of six $\hat{a}$'s and $\hat{a}^\dagger$'s; the different terms in (13.96) arise from the different ways of getting a non-zero value for this vev, by manipulations similar to those in section 6.3.

We end this chapter by presenting an introduction to the problem of quantizing non-Abelian gauge field theories. Our aim will be, first, to indicate where the approach followed for the Abelian gauge field $\hat{A}^\mu$ in section 7.3.2 fails; and then to show how the assumption (nevertheless) that the Feynman rules we have established for tree graphs work for loops as well, leads to violations of unitarity. This calculation will indicate a very curious way of remedying the situation 'by hand', through the introduction of *ghost particles*, only present in loops.

13.3.3   Quantizing non-Abelian gauge fields

We consider for definiteness the SU(2) gauge theory with massless gauge fields $\hat{W}^\mu(x)$, which we shall call gluons, by a slight abuse of language. We try to carry through for the Yang-Mills Lagrangian

$$\hat{\mathcal{L}}_2 = -\frac{1}{4}\hat{F}_{\mu\nu}\cdot\hat{F}^{\mu\nu}, \tag{13.102}$$

where

$$\hat{F}_{\mu\nu} = \partial_\mu\hat{W}_\nu - \partial_\nu\hat{W}_\mu - g\hat{W}_\mu\times\hat{W}_\nu, \tag{13.103}$$

the same steps we followed for the Maxwell one in section 7.3.2.

We begin by re-formulating the prescription arrived at in (7.119), which we reproduce again here for convenience:

$$\hat{\mathcal{L}}_\xi = -\frac{1}{4}\hat{F}_{\mu\nu}\hat{F}^{\mu\nu} - \frac{1}{2\xi}(\partial_\mu\hat{A}^\mu)^2. \tag{13.104}$$

$\hat{\mathcal{L}}_\xi$ leads to the equation of motion

$$\Box\hat{A}^\mu - \partial^\mu\partial_\nu\hat{A}^\nu + \frac{1}{\xi}\partial^\mu\partial_\nu\hat{A}^\nu = 0. \tag{13.105}$$

This has the drawback that the limit $\xi \to 0$ appears to be singular (though the propagator (7.122) is well-behaved as $\xi \to 0$). To avoid this unpleasantness, consider the Lagrangian (Lautrup 1967)

$$\hat{\mathcal{L}}_{\xi B} = -\frac{1}{4}\hat{F}_{\mu\nu}\hat{F}^{\mu\nu} + \hat{B}\partial_\mu \hat{A}^\mu + \frac{1}{2}\xi\hat{B}^2 \qquad (13.106)$$

where $\hat{B}$ is a scalar field. We may think of the '$\hat{B}\partial \cdot \hat{A}$' term as a field theory analogue of the procedure followed in classical Lagrangian mechanics, whereby a constraint (in this case the gauge-fixing one $\partial \cdot \hat{A} = 0$) is brought into the Lagrangian with a 'Lagrange multiplier' (here the *auxiliary* field $\hat{B}$). The momentum conjugate to $\hat{A}^0$ is now

$$\hat{\pi}^0 = \hat{B} \qquad (13.107)$$

while the Euler-Lagrange equations for $\hat{A}^{\mu\nu}$ read

$$\Box\hat{A}^\mu - \partial^\mu\partial_\nu\hat{A}^\nu = \partial^\mu\hat{B}, \qquad (13.108)$$

and for $\hat{B}$ yield

$$\partial_\mu\hat{A}^\mu + \xi\hat{B} = 0. \qquad (13.109)$$

Eliminating $\hat{B}$ from (13.106) by means of (13.109) we recover (13.104). Taking ∂_μ of (13.108) we learn that $\Box\hat{B} = 0$, so that $\hat{B}$ is a free massless field. Applying $\Box$ to (13.109) then shows that $\Box\partial_\mu\hat{A}^\mu = 0$, so that $\partial_\mu\hat{A}^\mu$ is also a free massless field.

In this formulation, the appropriate subsidiary condition for getting rid of the unphysical (non-transverse) degrees of freedom is (cf (7.111))

$$\hat{B}^{(+)}(x) \, | \, \Psi\rangle = 0. \qquad (13.110)$$

Kugo and Ojima (1979) have shown that (13.110) provides a satisfactory definition of the Hilbert space of states. In addition to this it is also essential to prove that all physical results are independent of the gauge parameter ξ.

We now try to generalize the foregoing in a straightforward way to (13.102). The obvious analogue of (13.106) would be to consider

$$\hat{\mathcal{L}}_{2,\xi\,B} = -\frac{1}{4}\hat{\boldsymbol{F}}_{\mu\nu} \cdot \hat{\boldsymbol{F}}^{\mu\nu} + \hat{\boldsymbol{B}} \cdot (\partial_\mu\hat{\boldsymbol{W}}^\mu) + \frac{1}{2}\xi\hat{\boldsymbol{B}} \cdot \hat{\boldsymbol{B}} \qquad (13.111)$$

where $\hat{\boldsymbol{B}}$ is an SU(2) triplet of scalar fields. Equation (13.111) gives (cf (13.108))

$$(\hat{D}^\nu)_{ij}\hat{F}_{j\mu\nu} + \partial_\mu\hat{B}_i = 0 \qquad (13.112)$$

where the covariant derivative is now the one appropriate to the SU(2) triplet $\boldsymbol{F}_{\mu\nu}$ (see (13.44) with $t = 1$, and (12.48)), and i, j are the SU(2) labels. Similarly, (13.109) becomes

$$\partial_\mu\hat{\boldsymbol{W}}^\mu + \xi\hat{\boldsymbol{B}} = \boldsymbol{0}. \qquad (13.113)$$

It is possible to verify that

$$(\hat{D}^\mu)_{ki}(\hat{D}^\nu)_{ij}\hat{F}_{j\mu\nu} = 0 \qquad (13.114)$$

where i, j, k are the SU(2) matrix indices, which implies that

$$(\hat{D}^\mu)_{ki}\partial_\mu\hat{B}_i = 0. \qquad (13.115)$$

This is the crucial result: it implies that the auxiliary field $\hat{B}$ is *not* a free field in this non-Abelian case, and so neither (from (13.113)) is $\partial_\mu\hat{W}^\mu$. In consequence, the obvious generalizations of (7.108) or (13.110) cannot be used to define the physical (transverse) states. The reason is that a condition like (13.110) must hold for all times, and only if the field is free is its time variation known (and essentially trivial).

Let us press ahead nevertheless, and assume that the rules we have derived so far are the correct Feynman rules for this gauge theory. We will see that this leads to physically unacceptable consequences, namely to the *violation of unitarity*.

In fact, this is a problem which threatens all gauge theories if the gauge field is treated covariantly, i.e. as a 4-vector. As we saw in section 7.3.2, this introduces *unphysical degrees of freedom* which must somehow be eliminated from the theory, or at least prevented from affecting physical processes. In QED we do this by imposing the condition (7.111), or (13.110), but as we have seen the analogous conditions will not work in the non-Abelian case, and so unphysical states may make their presence felt, for example in the 'sum over intermediate states' which arises in the unitarity relation. This relation determines the imaginary part of an amplitude via an equation of the form (cf (11.65))

$$2\,\mathrm{Im}\,\langle\mathrm{f}\mid\mathcal{M}\mid\mathrm{i}\rangle = \int\sum_n\langle\mathrm{f}\mid\mathcal{M}\mid\mathrm{n}\rangle\langle\mathrm{n}\mid\mathcal{M}^\dagger\mid\mathrm{i}\rangle\mathrm{d}\rho_n \qquad (13.116)$$

where $\langle\mathrm{f}\mid\mathcal{M}\mid\mathrm{i}\rangle$ is the (Feynman) amplitude for the process i → f, and the sum is over a complete set of physical intermediate states $\mid\mathrm{n}\rangle$, which can enter at the given energy; $\mathrm{d}\rho_n$ represents the phase space element for the general intermediate state $\mid\mathrm{n}\rangle$. Consider now the possibility of gauge quanta appearing in the states $\mid\mathrm{n}\rangle$. Since unitarity deals only with physical states, such quanta can have only the two degrees of freedom (polarizations) allowed for a physical massless gauge field (cf section 7.3.1). Now part of the power of the 'Feynman rules' approach to perturbation theory is that it is manifestly covariant. But there is no completely covariant way of selecting out just the two physical components of a massless polarization vector ϵ_μ, from the four originally introduced precisely for reasons of covariance. In fact, when gauge quanta appear as virtual particles in *intermediate* states in Feynman graphs, they will not be restricted to having only two polarization states (as we shall see explicitly in a moment). Hence there is a real chance

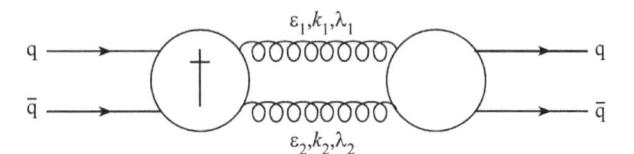

FIGURE 13.9
Two-gluon intermediate state in the unitarity relation for the amplitude for $q\bar{q} \to q\bar{q}$.

that when the imaginary part of such graphs is calculated, a contribution from the unphysical polarization states will be found, which has no counterpart at all in the physical unitarity relation, so that unitarity will not be satisfied. Since unitarity is an expression of conservation of probability, its violation is a serious disease indeed.

Consider, for example, the process $q\bar{q} \to q\bar{q}$ (where the 'quarks' are an SU(2) doublet), whose imaginary part has a contribution from a state containing two gluons (figure 13.9):

$$2 \, \text{Im} \, \langle q\bar{q} \mid \mathcal{M} \mid q\bar{q} \rangle = \int \sum \langle q\bar{q} \mid \mathcal{M} \mid gg \rangle \langle gg \mid \mathcal{M}^\dagger \mid q\bar{q} \rangle d\rho_2 \qquad (13.117)$$

where $d\rho_2$ is the 2-body phase space for the g-g state. The 2-gluon amplitudes in (13.117) must have the form

$$\mathcal{M}_{\mu_1\nu_1} \epsilon_1^{\mu_1}(k_1, \lambda_1) \epsilon_2^{\nu_1}(k_2, \lambda_2) \qquad (13.118)$$

where $\epsilon^\mu(k, \lambda)$ is the polarization vector for the gluon with polarization λ and 4-momentum k. The sum in (13.117) is then to be performed over $\lambda_1 = 1, 2$ and $\lambda_2 = 1, 2$ which are the physical polarization states (cf section 7.3.1). Thus (13.117) becomes

$$2 \, \text{Im} \, \mathcal{M}_{q\bar{q} \to q\bar{q}} = \int \sum_{\lambda_1 = 1, 2; \lambda_2 = 1, 2} \mathcal{M}_{\mu_1\nu_1} \epsilon_1^{\mu_1}(k_1, \lambda_1) \epsilon_2^{\nu_1}(k_2, \lambda_2)$$
$$\times \mathcal{M}^*_{\mu_2\nu_2} \epsilon_1^{\mu_2}(k_1, \lambda_1) \epsilon_2^{\nu_2}(k_2, \lambda_2) d\rho_2. \qquad (13.119)$$

For later convenience we are using real polarization vectors as in (7.81) and (7.82): $\epsilon(k_i, \lambda_i = +1) = (0, 1, 0, 0)$, $\epsilon(k_i, \lambda_i = -1) = (0, 0, 1, 0)$; and of course $k_1^2 = k_2^2 = 0$.

We now wish to find out whether or not a result of the form (13.119) will hold when the $\mathcal{M}$'s represent some suitable Feynman graphs. We first note that we want the unitarity relation (13.119) to be satisfied order by order in perturbation theory: that is to say, when the $\mathcal{M}$'s on both sides are expanded in powers of the coupling strengths (as in the usual Feynman graph expansion), the coefficients of corresponding powers on each side should be

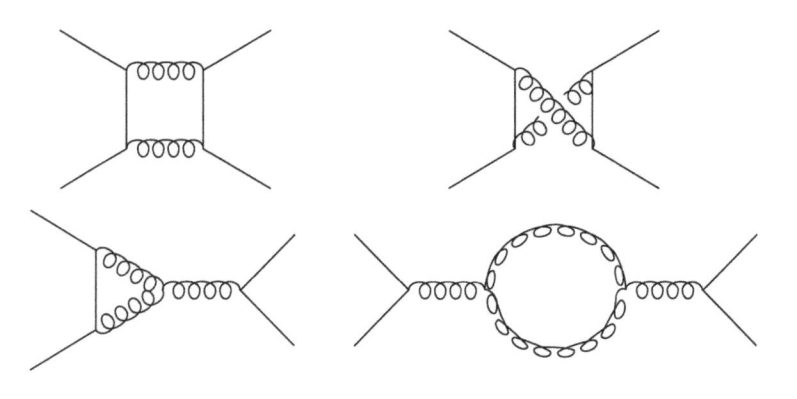

FIGURE 13.10
Some $O(g^4)$ contributions to $q\bar{q} \to q\bar{q}$.

equal. Since each emission or absorption of a gluon produces one power of the SU(2) coupling g, the right-hand side of (13.119) involves at least the power g^4. Thus the lowest-order process in which (13.119) may be tested is for the fourth-order amplitude $\mathcal{M}^{(4)}_{q\bar{q} \to q\bar{q}}$. There are quite a number of contributions to $\mathcal{M}^{(4)}_{q\bar{q} \to q\bar{q}}$, some of which are shown in Figure 13.10; all contain a loop. On the right-hand side of (13.119), each $\mathcal{M}$ involves two polarization vectors, and so each must represent the $0(g^2)$ contribution to $q\bar{q} \to gg$, which we call $\mathcal{M}^{(2)}_{\mu\nu}$; thus both sides are consistently of order g^4. There are three contributions to $\mathcal{M}^{(2)}_{\mu\nu}$ shown in figure 13.11; when these are placed in (13.119), contributions to the imaginary part of $\mathcal{M}^{(4)}_{q\bar{q} \to q\bar{q}}$ are generated, which should agree with the imaginary part of the total $0(g^4)$ loop-graph contribution. Let us see if this works out. We choose to work in the gauge $\xi = 1$, so that the gluon propagator takes the familiar form $-ig^{\mu\nu}\delta_{ij}/k^2$. According to the rules for propagators and vertices already given, each of the loop amplitudes $\mathcal{M}^{(4)}_{q\bar{q} \to q\bar{q}}$ (e.g. those of figure 13.10) will be proportional to the product of the propagators for the quarks and the gluons, together with appropriate 'γ' and 'τ' vertex factors, the whole being integrated over the loop momentum. The extraction of the imaginary part of a Feynman diagram is a technical matter, having to do with careful consideration of the '$i\epsilon$' in the propagators. Rules for doing this exist (Eden *et al.* 1966, section 2.9), and in the present case the result is that, to compute the imaginary part of the amplitudes of figure 13.10, one replaces each gluon propagator of momentum k by

$$\pi(-g^{\mu\nu})\delta(k^2)\theta(k_0)\delta_{ij}. \tag{13.120}$$

That is, the propagator is replaced by a condition stating that, in evaluating the imaginary part of the diagram, the gluon's mass is constrained to have

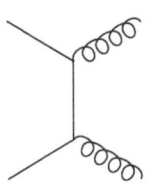
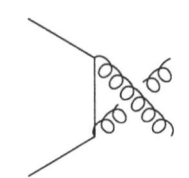
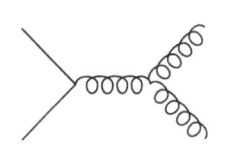

FIGURE 13.11
$O(g^2)$ contributions to $q\bar{q} \rightarrow gg$.

the physical (free-field) value of zero, instead of varying freely as the loop momentum varies, and its energy is positive. These conditions (one for each gluon) have the effect of converting the loop integral with a standard two-body phase space integral for the gg intermediate state, so that eventually

$$2\mathrm{Im}\ \mathcal{M}^{(4)}_{q\bar{q}\rightarrow q\bar{q}} = \int \mathcal{M}^{(2)}_{\mu_1\nu_1}(-g^{\mu_1\mu_2})\mathcal{M}^{(2)}_{\mu_2\nu_2}(-g^{\nu_1\nu_2})\mathrm{d}\rho_2 \qquad (13.121)$$

where $\mathcal{M}^{(2)}_{\mu_1\nu_1}$ is the sum of the three $O(g^2)$ tree graphs shown in figure 13.11, with all external legs satisfying the 'mass-shell' conditions.

So, the imaginary part of the loop contribution to $\mathcal{M}^{(4)}_{q\bar{q}\rightarrow q\bar{q}}$ does seem to have the form (13.116) as required by unitarity, with $|n\rangle$ the gg intermediate state as in (13.119). But there is one essential difference between (13.121) and (13.119): the place of the factor $-g^{\mu\nu}$ in (13.121) is taken in (13.119) by the gluon polarization sum

$$P^{\mu\nu}(k) \equiv \sum_{\lambda=1,2} \epsilon^\mu(k,\lambda)\epsilon^\nu(k,\lambda) \qquad (13.122)$$

for $k = k_1, k_2$ and $\lambda = \lambda_1, \lambda_2$ respectively. Thus we have to investigate whether this difference matters.

To proceed further, it is helpful to have an explicit expression for $P^{\mu\nu}$. We might think of calculating the necessary sum over λ by brute force, using two ϵ's specified by the conditions (cf (7.87))

$$\epsilon^\mu(k,\lambda)\epsilon_\mu(k,\lambda') = -\delta_{\lambda\lambda'}, \quad \epsilon \cdot k = 0. \qquad (13.123)$$

The trouble is that conditions (13.123) *do not fix the ϵ's uniquely if $k^2 = 0$*. (Note the $\delta(k^2)$ in (13.120)). Indeed, it is precisely the fact that any given ϵ_μ satisfying (13.123) can be replaced by $\epsilon_\mu + \lambda k_\mu$ that both reduces the degrees of freedom to two (as we saw in section 7.3.1), and evinces the essential arbitrariness in the ϵ_μ specified only by (13.123). In order to calculate (13.122), we need to put another condition on ϵ_μ, so as to fix it uniquely. A standard choice (see e.g. Taylor 1976, pp 14–15) is to supplement (13.123) with the further condition

$$t \cdot \epsilon = 0 \qquad (13.124)$$

where t is some 4-vector. This certainly fixes ϵ_μ, and enables us to calculate (13.122), but of course now two further difficulties have appeared: namely, the physical results seem to depend on t_μ; and have we not lost Lorentz covariance, because the theory involves a special 4-vector t_μ?

Setting these questions aside for the moment, we can calculate (13.122) using the conditions (13.123) and (13.124), finding (problem 13.11)

$$P_{\mu\nu} = -g_{\mu\nu} - [t^2 k_\mu k_\nu - k \cdot t(k_\mu t_\nu + k_\nu t_\mu)]/(k \cdot t)^2. \qquad (13.125)$$

But only the *first* term on the right-hand side of (13.125) is to be seen in (13.121). A crucial quantity is clearly

$$
\begin{aligned}
U_{\mu\nu}(k,t) &\equiv -g_{\mu\nu} - P_{\mu\nu} \\
&= [t^2 k_\mu k_\nu - k \cdot t(k_\mu t_\nu + k_\nu t_\mu)]/(k \cdot t)^2. \qquad (13.126)
\end{aligned}
$$

We note that whereas

$$k^\mu P_{\mu\nu} = k^\nu P_{\mu\nu} = 0 \qquad (13.127)$$

(from the condition $k \cdot \epsilon = 0$), the same is *not* true of $k^\mu U_{\mu\nu}$ – in fact,

$$k^\mu U_{\mu\nu} = -k_\nu \qquad (13.128)$$

where we have used $k^2 = 0$. It follows that $U_{\mu\nu}$ may be regarded as including polarization states for which $\epsilon \cdot k \neq 0$. In physical terms, therefore, a gluon appearing internally in a Feynman graph has to be regarded as existing in more than just the two polarization states available to an external gluon (cf section 7.3.1). $U_{\mu\nu}$ characterizes the contribution of these unphysical polarization states.

The discrepancy between (13.121) and (13.119) is then

$$2\text{Im}\,\mathcal{M}^{(4)}_{q\bar{q}\to q\bar{q}} = \int \mathcal{M}^{(2)}_{\mu_1\nu_1}[U^{\mu_1\mu_2}(k_1,t_1)]\mathcal{M}^{(2)}_{\mu_2\nu_2}[U^{\nu_1\nu_2}(k_2,t_2)]\mathrm{d}\rho_2, \quad (13.129)$$

together with similar terms involving one P and one U. It follows that these unwanted contributions will, in fact, vanish if

$$k_1^{\mu_1}\mathcal{M}^{(2)}_{\mu_1\nu_1} = 0, \qquad (13.130)$$

and similarly for k_2. This will also ensure that amplitudes are independent of t_μ.

Condition (13.130) is apparently the same as the U(1) gauge invariance requirement of (8.165), already recalled in the previous section. As discussed there, it can be interpreted here also as expressing gauge invariance in the non-Abelian case, working to this given order in perturbation theory. Indeed, the diagrams of figure 13.11 are essentially 'crossed' versions of those in figure 13.5. However, there is one crucial difference here. In figure 13.5, both the X's were physical, their polarizations satisfying the condition $\epsilon \cdot k = 0$. In figure 13.11, by contrast, neither of the gluons, in the discrepant contribution

(13.129), satisfies $\epsilon \cdot k = 0$ – see the sentence following (13.128). Thus the crucial point is that (13.130) must be true for each gluon, *even when the other gluon has* $\epsilon \cdot k \neq 0$. And, in fact, we shall now see that whereas the (crossed) version of (13.130) did hold for our dX $\rightarrow$ dX amplitudes of section 13.3.2, (13.130) *fails* for states with $\epsilon \cdot k \neq 0$.

The three graphs of figure 13.11 together yield

$$\mathcal{M}^{(2)}_{\mu_1\nu_1} \epsilon_1^\mu(k_1,\lambda_1)\epsilon_2^{\nu_1}(k_2,\lambda_2) = g^2\bar{v}(p_2)\frac{\tau_j}{2}\,\not{\epsilon}_2 a_{2j}\frac{1}{\not{p}_1-\not{k}_1-m}\frac{\tau_i}{2}a_{1i}\,\not{\epsilon}_1 u(p_1)$$

$$+ \quad g^2\bar{v}(p_2)\frac{\tau_i}{2}a_{1i}\,\not{\epsilon}_1\frac{1}{\not{p}_1-\not{k}_2-m}\frac{\tau_j}{2}a_{2j}\,\not{\epsilon}_2 u(p_1)$$

$$+ \quad (-\mathrm{i})g^2\epsilon_{kij}[(p_1+p_2+k_1)^{\nu_1}g^{\mu_1\rho} + (-k_2-p_1-p_2)^{\mu_1}g^{\rho\nu_1}$$

$$+ \quad (-k_1+k_2)^\rho g^{\mu_1\nu_1}]\epsilon_{1\mu_1}a_{1i}a_{2j}\epsilon_{2\nu_1}\frac{-1}{(p_1+p_2)^2}\bar{v}(p_2)\frac{\tau_k}{2}\gamma_\rho u(p_1) \quad (13.131)$$

where we have written the gluon polarization vectors as a product of a Lorentz 4-vector ϵ_μ and an 'SU(2) polarization vector' a_i to specify the triplet state label. Now replace ϵ_1, say, by k_1. Using the Dirac equation for $u(p_1)$ and $\bar{v}(p_2)$ the first two terms reduce to (cf (13.94))

$$g^2\bar{v}(p_2)\,\not{\epsilon}_2[\tau_i/2, \tau_j/2]u(p_1)a_{1i}a_{2j}$$

$$= \quad \mathrm{i}g^2\bar{v}(p_2)\,\not{\epsilon}_2\epsilon_{ijk}(\tau_k/2)u(p_1)a_{1i}a_{2j} \quad (13.132)$$

using the SU(2) algebra of the τ's. The third term in (13.131) gives

$$-\mathrm{i}g^2\epsilon_{ijk}\bar{v}(p_2)\,\not{\epsilon}_2(\tau_k/2)u(p_1)a_{1i}a_{2j} \quad (13.133)$$

$$+\mathrm{i}g^2\frac{\epsilon_{ijk}}{2k_1\cdot k_2}\bar{v}(p_2)\,\not{k}_1(\tau_k/2)u(p_1)k_2\cdot\epsilon_2 a_{1i}a_{2j}. \quad (13.134)$$

We see that the first part (13.133) certainly does cancel (13.132), but there remains the second piece (13.134), *which only vanishes if* $k_2 \cdot \epsilon_2 = 0$. This is not sufficient to guarantee the absence of all unphysical contributions to the imaginary part of the 2-gluon graphs, as the preceding discussion shows. *We conclude that loop diagrams involving two (or, in fact, more) gluons, if constructed according to the simple rules for tree diagrams, will violate unitarity.*

The correct rule for such loops must be as to satisfy unitarity. Since there seems no other way in which the offending piece in (13.134) can be removed, we must infer that the rule for loops will have to involve some extra term, or terms, over and above the simple tree-type constructions, which will cancel the contributions of unphysical polarization states. To get an intuitive idea of what such extra terms might be, we return to expression (13.126) for the sum over unphysical polarization states $U_{\mu\nu}$, and make a specific choice for t. We take $t_\mu = \bar{k}_\mu$, where the 4-vector $\bar{k}$ is defined by $\bar{k} = (-\mid \boldsymbol{k} \mid, \boldsymbol{k})$, and $\boldsymbol{k} = (0,0,\mid \boldsymbol{k} \mid)$. This choice obviously satisfies (13.124). Then

$$U_{\mu\nu}(k,\bar{k}) = (k_\mu\bar{k}_\nu + k_\nu\bar{k}_\mu)/(2\mid \boldsymbol{k} \mid^2) \quad (13.135)$$

and unitarity (cf (13.129)) requires

$$\int \mathcal{M}^{(2)}_{\mu_1\nu_1} \mathcal{M}^{(2)}_{\mu_2\nu_2} \frac{(k_1^{\mu_1}\bar{k}_1^{\mu_2} + k_1^{\mu_2}\bar{k}_1^{\mu_1})}{2\mid k_1 \mid^2} \frac{(k_2^{\nu_1}\bar{k}_2^{\nu_2} + k_2^{\nu_2}\bar{k}_2^{\nu_1})}{2\mid k_2 \mid^2} \mathrm{d}\rho_2 \qquad (13.136)$$

to vanish, but it does not. Let us work in the centre of momentum (CM) frame of the two gluons, with $k_1 = (\mid \boldsymbol{k} \mid, 0, 0, \mid \boldsymbol{k} \mid), k_2 = (\mid \boldsymbol{k} \mid, 0, 0, -\mid \boldsymbol{k} \mid), \bar{k}_1 = (-\mid \boldsymbol{k} \mid, 0, 0, \mid \boldsymbol{k} \mid), \bar{k}_2 = (-\mid \boldsymbol{k} \mid, 0, 0, -\mid \boldsymbol{k} \mid)$, and consider for definiteness the contractions with the $\mathcal{M}^{(2)}_{\mu_1\nu_1}$ term. These are $\mathcal{M}^{(2)}_{\mu_1\nu_1} k_1^{\mu_1} k_2^{\nu_1}, \mathcal{M}^{(2)}_{\mu_1\nu_1} k_1^{\mu_1} \bar{k}_2^{\nu_1}$ etc. Such quantities can be calculated from expression (13.131) by setting $\epsilon_1 = k_1, \epsilon_2 = k_2$ for the first, $\epsilon_1 = k_1, \epsilon_2 = \bar{k}_2$ for the second, and so on. We have already obtained the result of putting $\epsilon_1 = k_1$. From (13.134) it is clear that a term in which ϵ_2 is replaced by k_2 as well as ϵ_1 by k_1 will vanish, since $k_2^2 = 0$. A typical non-vanishing term is of the form $\mathcal{M}^{(2)}_{\mu_1\nu_1} k_1^{\mu_1} \bar{k}_2^{\nu_1}/2 \mid \boldsymbol{k} \mid^2$. From (13.134) this reduces to

$$-\mathrm{i}g^2 \frac{\epsilon_{ijk}}{2k_1 \cdot k_2} \bar{v}(p_2) \, \slashed{k}_1(\tau_k/2)u(p_1)a_{1i}a_{2j} \qquad (13.137)$$

using $k_2 \cdot \bar{k}_2/2 \mid \boldsymbol{k} \mid^2 = -1$. We may rewrite (13.137) as

$$j_{\mu k} \frac{-g^{\mu\nu}\delta_{k\ell}}{(k_1 + k_2)^2} \mathrm{i}g\epsilon_{ij\ell}a_{1i}a_{2j}k_{1\nu} \qquad (13.138)$$

where

$$j_{\mu k} = g\bar{v}(p_2)\gamma_\mu(\tau_k/2)u(p_1) \qquad (13.139)$$

is the SU(2) current associated with the q$\bar{\text{q}}$ pair.

The unwanted terms of the form (13.138) can be eliminated if we adopt the following rule (on the grounds of 'forcing the theory to make sense'). In addition to the fourth-order diagrams of the type shown in figure 13.10, constructed according to the simple 'tree' prescriptions, there must exist a previously unknown fourth-order contribution, *only present in loops*, such that it has an imaginary part which is non-zero in the same physical region as the two-gluon intermediate state, and moreover is of just the right magnitude to cancel all the contributions to (13.136) from terms like (13.138). Now (13.138) has the appearance of a one-gluon intermediate state amplitude. The q$\bar{\text{q}} \to$ g vertex is represented by the current (13.139), the gluon propagator appears in Feynman gauge $\xi = 1$, and the rest of the expression would have the interpretation of a coupling between the intermediate gluon and two scalar particles with SU(2) polarizations a_{1i}, a_{2j}. Thus (13.138) can be interpreted as the amplitude for the tree graph shown in figure 13.12, where the dotted lines represent the scalar particles. It seems plausible, therefore, that the fourth-order graph we are looking for has the form shown in figure 13.13. The new scalar particles must be massless, so that this new amplitude has an imaginary part in the same physical region as the gg state. When the imaginary part of figure 13.13 is calculated in the usual way, it will involve

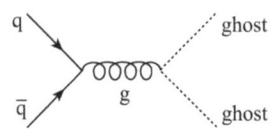

FIGURE 13.12
Tree graph interpretation of the expression (13.138).

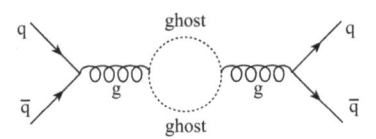

FIGURE 13.13
Ghost loop diagram contributing in fourth order to $q\bar{q} \to q\bar{q}$.

contributions from the tree graph of figure 13.12, and these can be arranged to cancel the unphysical polarization pieces like (13.138).

For this cancellation to work, the scalar particle loop graph of figure 13.13 must enter with the opposite sign from the three-gluon loop graph of figure 13.10, which in retrospect was the cause of all the trouble. Such a relative minus sign between single closed loop graphs would be expected if the scalar particles in figure 13.13 were in fact fermions! (Recall the rule given in section 11.3 and problem 11.2). Thus we appear to need *scalar* particles obeying *Fermi* statistics. Such particles are called 'ghosts'. We must emphasize that although we have introduced the tree graph of figure 13.12, which apparently involves ghosts as external lines, in reality the ghosts are always confined to loops, their function being to cancel unphysical contributions from intermediate gluons.

The preceding discussion has, of course, been entirely heuristic. It can be followed through so as to yield the correct prescription for eliminating unphysical contributions from a single closed gluon loop. But, as Feynman recognized (1963, 1977), unitarity alone is not a sufficient constraint to provide the prescription for more than one closed gluon loop. Clearly what is required is some additional term in the Lagrangian, which will do the job in general. Such a term indeed exists, and was first derived using the path integral form of quantum field theory (see chapter 16) by Faddeev and Popov (1967). The result is that the covariant gauge-fixing term (13.68) must be supplemented by the 'ghost Lagrangian'

$$\hat{\mathcal{L}}_g = \partial_\mu \hat{\eta}_i^\dagger \hat{D}_{ij}^\mu \hat{\eta}_j \qquad (13.140)$$

where the η field is an SU(2) triplet, and spinless, but obeying *anti*commutation relations; the covariant derivative is the one appropriate for an SU(2) triplet,

namely (from (13.44) and (12.48))

$$\hat{D}_{ij}^{\mu} = \partial^{\mu}\delta_{ij} + g\epsilon_{kij}\hat{W}_{k}^{\mu}, \tag{13.141}$$

in this case. The result (13.140) is derived in standard books of quantum field theory, for example Cheng and Li (1984), Peskin and Schroeder (1995) or Ryder (1996). We should add the caution that the form of the ghost Lagrangian depends on the choice of the gauge-fixing term; there are gauges in which the ghosts are absent. Feynman rules for non-Abelian gauge field theories are given in Cheng and Li (1984), for example. We give the rules for tree diagrams, for which there are no problems with ghosts, in appendix Q.

Problems

13.1 Verify that (13.34) reduces to (13.26) in the infinitesimal case.

13.2 Verify equation (13.45).

13.3 Using the expression for D^{μ} in (13.47), verify (13.48).

13.4 Verify the transformation law (13.51) of $F^{\mu\nu}$ under local SU(2) transformations.

13.5 Verify that $F_{\mu\nu} \cdot F^{\mu\nu}$ is invariant under local SU(2) transformations.

13.6 Verify that the (infinitesimal) transformation law (13.56) for the SU(3) gauge field A_a^{μ} is consistent with (13.55).

13.7 By considering the commutator of two D^{μ}'s of the form (13.53), verify (13.61).

13.8 Verify that (13.84) reduces to (13.86) (omitting the $(2\pi)^4\delta^4$ factors).

13.9 Verify that the replacement of ϵ_1 by k_1 in (13.93) leads to (13.94).

13.10 Verify that when ϵ_1 is replaced by k_1 in (13.95), the resulting amplitude cancels the contribution (13.94), provided that $\delta = 1$.

13.11 Show that $P^{\mu\nu}$ of (13.122), with the ϵ's specified by the conditions (13.123) and (13.124), is given by (13.125).

Part VI

QCD and the Renormalization Group

14

QCD I: Introduction, Tree Graph Predictions, and Jets

In the previous chapter we have introduced the elementary concepts and formalism associated with non-Abelian quantum gauge field theories. It is now well established that the strong interactions between quarks are described by a theory of this type, in which the gauge group is an $SU(3)_c$, acting on a degree of freedom called 'colour' (indicated by the subscript c). This theory is called Quantum Chromodynamics, or QCD for short. QCD will be our first application of the theory developed in chapter 13, and we shall devote the next two chapters, and much of chapter 16, to it.

In the present chapter we introduce QCD and discuss some of its simpler experimental consequences. We briefly recall the evidence for the 'colour' degree of freedom in section 14.1, and then proceed to the dynamics of colour, and the QCD Lagrangian, in section 14.2. Perhaps the most remarkable thing about the dynamics of QCD is that, despite its being a theory of the *strong* interactions, there are certain kinematic regimes – roughly speaking, short distances or high energies – in which it is effectively a quite *weakly* interacting theory. This is a consequence of a fundamental property, possessed only by non-Abelian gauge theories, whereby the effective interaction strength becomes progressively smaller in such regimes. This property is called 'asymptotic freedom', and was already mentioned in section 11.5.3 of volume 1. In appropriate cases, therefore, the lowest-order perturbation theory amplitudes (tree graphs) provide a very convincing qualitative, or even 'semi-quantitative', orientation to the data. In sections 14.3 and 14.4 we shall see how the tree graph techniques acquired for QED in volume 1 produce more useful physics when applied to QCD.

However, most of the quantitative experimental support for QCD has come from comparison with predictions which include higher-order QCD corrections; indeed, the asymptotic freedom property itself emerges from summing a whole class of higher-order contributions, as we shall indicate at the beginning of chapter 15. This immediately involves all the apparatus of *renormalization*. The necessary calculations quite rapidly become too technical for the intended scope of this book, but in chapter 15 we shall try to provide an elementary introduction to the issues involved, and to the necessary techniques, by building on the discussion of renormalization given in chapters 10 and 11 of volume 1. The main new concept will be the *renormalization group* (and related ideas),

which is an essential tool in the modern confrontation of perturbative QCD with data. Some of the simpler predictions of the renormalization group technique will be compared with experimental data in the last part of chapter 15.

In chapter 16 we work towards understanding some non-perturbative aspects of QCD. As a natural concomitant of asymptotic freedom, it is to be expected that the effective coupling strength becomes progressively larger at longer distances or lower energies, ultimately being strong enough to lead (presumably) to the confinement of quarks and gluons; this is sometimes referred to as 'infrared slavery'. In this regime perturbation theory clearly fails. An alternative, purely numerical, approach is available however, namely the method of 'lattice' QCD, which involves replacing the space-time continuum by a *discrete lattice* of points. At first sight, this may seem a topic rather disconnected from everything that has preceded it. But we shall see that in fact it provides some powerful new insights into several aspects of quantum field theory in general, and in particular of renormalization, by revisiting it in coordinate (rather than momentum) space. Quite apart from this, however, results from lattice QCD now provide independent confirmation of the theory, in the non-perturbative regime.

14.1   The colour degree of freedom

The first intimation of a new, unrevealed degree of freedom of matter came from baryon spectroscopy (Greenberg 1964; see also Han and Nambu 1965, and Tavkhelidze 1965). For a baryon made of three spin-$\frac{1}{2}$ quarks, the original non-relativistic quark model wave-function took the form

$$\psi_{3\mathrm{q}} = \psi_{3\mathrm{q,space}}\psi_{3\mathrm{q,spin}}\psi_{3\mathrm{q,flavour}}. \tag{14.1}$$

It was soon realized (e.g. Dalitz 1965) that the product of these space, spin and flavour wavefunctions for the ground state baryons was *symmetric* under interchange of any two quarks. For example, the Δ^{++} state mentioned in section 12.2.3 is made of three u quarks (flavour symmetric) in the $J^P = \frac{3}{2}^+$ state, which has zero orbital angular momentum and is hence spatially symmetric, and a symmetric $S = \frac{3}{2}$ spin wavefunction. But we saw in section 7.2 that quantum field theory requires fermions to obey the exclusion principle – i.e. the wavefunction $\psi_{3\mathrm{q}}$ should be *anti*symmetric with respect to quark interchange. A simple way of implementing this requirement is to suppose that the quarks carry a further degree of freedom, called colour, with respect to which the 3q wavefunction can be antisymmetrized, as follows (Fritzsch and Gell-Mann 1972, Bardeen, Fritzsch and Gell-Mann 1973). We introduce a *colour wavefunction* with colour index α:

$$\psi_\alpha \quad (\alpha = 1, 2, 3).$$

We are here writing the three labels as '1, 2, 3', but they are often referred to by colour names such as 'red, blue, green'; it should be understood that this is merely a picturesque way of referring to the three basic states of this degree of freedom, and has nothing to do with real colour! With the addition of this degree of freedom we can certainly form a three-quark wavefunction which is antisymmetric in colour by using the antisymmetric symbol $\epsilon_{\alpha\beta\gamma}$, namely[1]

$$\psi_{3q, \text{ colour}} = \epsilon_{\alpha\beta\gamma}\psi_\alpha\psi_\beta\psi_\gamma \tag{14.2}$$

and this must then be multiplied into (14.1) to give the full 3q wavefunction. To date, *all* known baryon states can be described this way, i.e. the symmetry of the 'traditional' space-spin-flavour wavefunction (14.1) is symmetric overall, while the required antisymmetry is restored by the additional factor (14.2). As far as meson ($\bar{q}q$) states are concerned, what was previously a π^+ wavefunction d^*u is now

$$\frac{1}{\sqrt{3}}(d_1^*u_1 + d_2^*u_2 + d_3^*u_3) \tag{14.3}$$

which we write in general as $(1/\sqrt{3})d_\alpha^\dagger u_\alpha$. We shall shortly see the group theoretical significance of this 'neutral superposition', and of (14.2). Meanwhile, we note that (14.2) is actually the *only* way of making an antisymmetric combination of the three ψ's; it is therefore called a (colour) *singlet*. It is reassuring that there is only one way of doing this – otherwise, we would have obtained more baryon states than are physically observed. As we shall see in section 14.2.1, (14.3) is also a colour singlet combination.

The above would seem a somewhat artificial device unless there were some physical consequences of this increase in the number of quark types – and there are. In any process which we can describe in terms of creation or annihilation of quarks, the *multiplicity* of quark types will enter into the relevant observable cross section or decay rate. For example, at high energies the ratio

$$R = \frac{\sigma(e^+e^- \to \text{hadrons})}{\sigma(e^+e^- \to \mu^+\mu^-)} \tag{14.4}$$

will, in the quark parton model (see section 9.5), reflect the magnitudes of the individual quark couplings to the photon:

$$R = \sum_a e_a^2 \tag{14.5}$$

where a runs over all quark types. For five quarks u, d, s, c, b with respective charges $\frac{2}{3}, -\frac{1}{3}, -\frac{1}{3}, \frac{2}{3}, -\frac{1}{3}$, this yields

$$R_{\text{no colour}} = \frac{11}{9} \tag{14.6}$$

---

[1] In (14.2) each ψ refers to a different quark, but we have not indicated the quark labels explicitly.

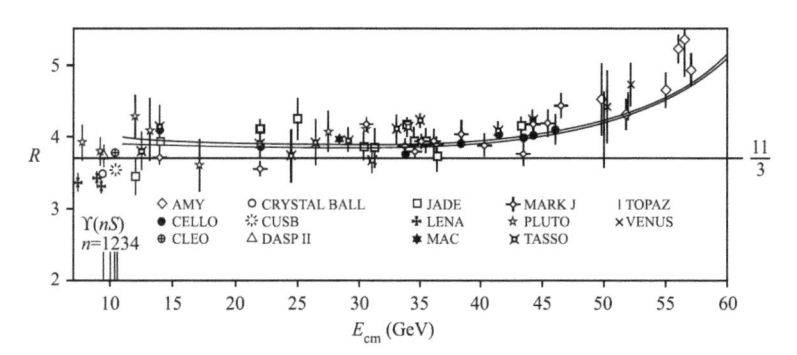

FIGURE 14.1

The ratio R (see (14.4)). Figure reprinted with permission from L. Montanet *et al.* *Physical Review* D **50** 1173 (1994). Copyright 1994 by the American Physical Society.

and

$$R_{\text{colour}} = \frac{11}{3} \tag{14.7}$$

for the two cases, as we saw in section 9.5. (The values $R = 2$ below the charm threshold, and $R = 10/3$ below the b threshold, were predicted by Bardeen *et al.* 1973). The data (figure 14.1) rule out (14.6), and are in good agreement with (14.7) at energies well above the b threshold, and well below the Z^0 resonance peak. There is an indication that the data tend to lie *above* the parton model prediction; this is actually predicted by QCD via higher-order corrections, as will be discussed in section 15.1.

A number of branching fractions also provide simple ways of measuring the number of colours N_c. For example, consider the branching fraction for $\tau^- \to e^- \bar{\nu}_e \nu_\tau$ (i.e. the ratio of the rate for $\tau^- \to e^- \bar{\nu}_e \nu_\tau$ to that for all other decays). τ^- decays proceed via the weak process shown in figure 14.2, where the final fermions can be $e^- \bar{\nu}_e, \mu^- \bar{\nu}_\mu$, or $\bar{u}d$, the last with multiplicity N_c. Thus

$$B(\tau^- \to e^- \bar{\nu}_e \nu_\tau) \approx \frac{1}{2 + N_c}. \tag{14.8}$$

Experiments give $B \approx 18\ \%$ and hence $N_c \approx 3$.

Similarly, the branching fraction $B(W^- \to e^- \bar{\nu}_e)$ is $\sim \frac{1}{3 + 2N_c}$ (from $f = e, \mu, \tau, u$ and c). Experiment gives a value of 10.7 %, so again $N_c \approx 3$.

In chapter 9 we also discussed the Drell–Yan process in the quark parton model; it involves the subprocess $q\bar{q} \to l\bar{l}$ which is the inverse of the one in (14.4). We mentioned that a factor of $\frac{1}{3}$ appears in this case: it arises because we must average over the nine possible initial $q\bar{q}$ combinations (factor $\frac{1}{9}$) and then sum over the number of such states that lead to the colour neutral photon, which is 3 ($\bar{q}_1 q_1, \bar{q}_2 q_2$ and $\bar{q}_3 q_3$). With this factor, and using quark

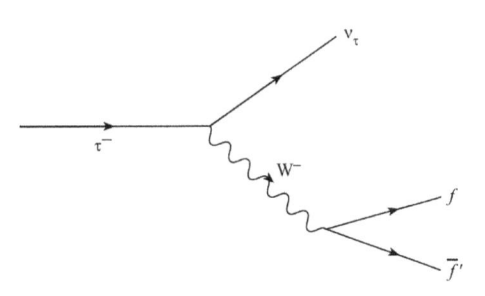

FIGURE 14.2
τ decay.

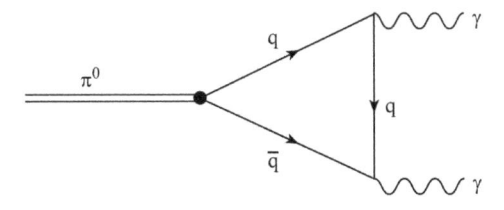

FIGURE 14.3
Triangle graph for π^0 decay.

distribution functions consistent with deep inelastic scattering, the parton model gives a good first approximation to the data.

Finally, we mention the rate for $\pi^0 \to \gamma\gamma$. As will be discussed in section 18.4, this process is entirely calculable from the graph shown in figure 14.3 (and the one with the γ's 'crossed'), where 'q' is u or d. The amplitude is proportional to the square of the quark charges, but because the π^0 is an isovector, the contributions from the $u\bar{u}$ and $d\bar{d}$ states have opposite signs (see section 12.1.3). Thus the rate contains a factor

$$((2/3)^2 - (1/3)^2)^2 = \frac{1}{9}. \tag{14.9}$$

However, the original calculation of this rate by Steinberger (1949) used a model in which the proton and neutron replaced the u and d in the loop, in which case the factor corresponding to (14.9) is just 1 (since the n has zero charge). Experimentally the rate agrees well with Steinberger's calculation, indicating that (14.9) needs to be multiplied by 9, which corresponds to $N_c = 3$ identical amplitudes of the form shown in figure 14.3, as was noted by Bardeen, Fritzsch and Gell-Mann (1973).

14.2   The dynamics of colour

14.2.1   Colour as an SU(3) group

We now want to consider the possible dynamical role of colour – in other words, the way in which the forces between quarks depend on their colours. We have seen that we seem to need three different quark types for each given flavour. They must all have the same mass, or else we would observe some 'fine structure' in the hadronic levels. Furthermore, and for the same reason, 'colour' must be an exact symmetry of the Hamiltonian governing the quark dynamics. What symmetry group is involved? We shall consider how some empirical facts suggest that the answer is $SU(3)_c$.

To begin with, it is certainly clear that the interquark force must depend on colour, since we do *not* observe 'colour multiplicity' of hadronic states: for example we do not see eight other coloured π^+'s $(d_1^* u_2, d_3^* u_1, \dots)$ degenerate with the one 'colourless' physical π^+ whose wavefunction was given previously. The observed hadronic states are all *colour singlets*, and the force must somehow be responsible for this. More particularly, the force has to produce only those very restricted *types* of quark configuration which are observed in the hadron spectrum. Consider again the isospin multiplets in nuclear physics discussed in section 12.1.2. There is one very striking difference in the particle physics case: for mesons *only* $T = 0, \frac{1}{2}$ and 1 occur, and for baryons *only* $T = 0, \frac{1}{2}$, 1 and $\frac{3}{2}$, while in nuclei there is nothing in principle to stop us finding $T = \frac{5}{2}, 3, \dots$ states. (In fact such nuclear states are hard to identify experimentally, because they occur at high excitation energy for some of the isobars – cf figure 1.8(c) – where the levels are very dense). The same restriction holds for $SU(3)_f$ also – only **1**'s and **8**'s occur for mesons; and only **1**'s, **8**'s and **10**'s for baryons. In quark terms, of course, this is what is translated into the recipe: 'mesons are $\bar{q}q$, baryons are qqq'. It is as if we said, in nuclear physics, that only $A = 2$ and $A = 3$ nuclei exist! Thus the quark forces must have a dramatic saturation property: apparently no $\bar{q}qq$, no qqqq, qqqqq, ... states exist. Furthermore, no qq or $\bar{q}\bar{q}$ states exist either – nor, for that matter, do single q's or $\bar{q}$'s. All this can be summarized by saying that the quark colour degree of freedom must be *confined*, a property we shall now assume and return to in chapter 16.

If we assume that only colour singlet states exist (Fritzsch and Gell-Mann 1972, Bardeen, Fritzsch and Gell-Mann 1973), and that the strong interquark force depends only on colour, the fact that $\bar{q}q$ states are seen but qq and $\bar{q}\bar{q}$ are not gives us an important clue as to what group to associate with colour. One simple possibility might be that the three colours correspond to the components of an $SU(2)_c$ triplet 'ψ'. The antisymmetric, colour singlet, three-quark baryon wavefunction of (14.2) is then just the triple scalar product $\psi_1 \cdot \psi_2 \times \psi_3$, which seems satisfactory. But what about the meson wavefunction? Mesons are formed of quarks and antiquarks, and we recall from sections 12.1.3 and

12.2 that antiquarks belong to the complex conjugate of the representation (or multiplet) to which quarks belong. Thus if a quark colour triplet wavefunction ψ_α transforms under a colour transformation as

$$\psi_\alpha \to \psi'_\alpha = V^{(1)}_{\alpha\beta} \psi_\beta \tag{14.10}$$

where $\mathbf{V}^{(1)}$ is a 3×3 unitary matrix appropriate to the $T = 1$ representation of SU(2) (cf (12.48) and (12.49)), then the wavefunction for the 'anti'-triplet is ψ^*_α, which transforms as

$$\psi^*_\alpha \to \psi^{*\prime}_\alpha = V^{(1)*}_{\alpha\beta} \psi^*_\beta. \tag{14.11}$$

Given this information, we can now construct colour singlet wavefunctions for mesons, built from $\bar{q}q$. Consider the quantity (cf (14.3)) $\sum_\alpha \psi^*_\alpha \psi_\alpha$ where ψ^* represents the antiquark and ψ the quark. This may be written in matrix notation as $\psi^\dagger \psi$ where the $\psi^\dagger$ as usual denotes the transpose of the complex conjugate of the column vector ψ. Then, taking the transpose of (14.11), we find that $\psi^\dagger$ transforms by

$$\psi^\dagger \to \psi^{\dagger\prime} = \psi^\dagger \mathbf{V}^{(1)\dagger} \tag{14.12}$$

so that the combination $\psi^\dagger \psi$ transforms as

$$\psi^\dagger \psi \to \psi^{\dagger\prime} \psi' = \psi^\dagger \mathbf{V}^{(1)\dagger} \mathbf{V}^{(1)} \psi = \psi^\dagger \psi \tag{14.13}$$

where the last step follows since $\mathbf{V}^{(1)}$ is unitary (compare (12.58)). Thus the product is *invariant* under (14.10) and (14.11) – that is, it is a colour singlet, as required. This is the meaning of the superposition (14.3).

All this may seem fine, but there is a problem. The three-dimensional representation of SU(2)$_c$ which we are using here has a very special nature: the matrix $\mathbf{V}^{(1)}$ can be chosen to be *real*. This can be understood 'physically' if we make use of the great similarity between SU(2) and the group of rotations in three dimensions (which is the reason for the geometrical language of isospin 'rotations', and so on). We know very well how real three-dimensional vectors transform, namely by an orthogonal 3×3 matrix. It is the same in SU(2). It is always possible to choose the wavefunctions ψ to be real, and the transformation matrix $\mathbf{V}^{(1)}$ to be real also. Since $\mathbf{V}^{(1)}$ is, in general, unitary, this means that it must be orthogonal. But now the basic difficulty appears: there is no distinction between ψ and ψ^*! They both transform by the real matrix $\mathbf{V}^{(1)}$. This means that we can make SU(2) invariant (colour singlet) combinations for $\bar{q}q$ states, and for qq states, just as well as for $\bar{q}q$ states – indeed they are formally identical. But such 'diquark' (or 'antidiquark') states are not found, and hence – by assumption – should *not* be colour singlets.

The next simplest possibility seems to be that the three colours correspond to the components of an SU(3)$_c$ triplet. In this case the quark colour wavefunction ψ_α transforms as (cf (12.74))

$$\psi \to \psi' = \mathbf{W}\psi \tag{14.14}$$

where $\mathbf{W}$ is a special unitary 3×3 matrix parametrized as

$$\mathbf{W} = \exp(\mathrm{i}\boldsymbol{\alpha} \cdot \boldsymbol{\lambda}/2), \tag{14.15}$$

and $\psi^\dagger$ transforms as

$$\psi^\dagger \rightarrow \psi^{\dagger\prime} = \psi^\dagger \mathbf{W}^\dagger. \tag{14.16}$$

The proof of the invariance of $\psi^\dagger\psi$ goes through as in (14.13), and it can be shown (problem 14.1(a)) that the antisymmetric 3q combination (14.2) is also an SU(3)$_\mathrm{c}$ invariant. Thus both the proposed meson and baryon states are colour singlets. It is *not* possible to choose the $\boldsymbol{\lambda}$'s to be pure imaginary in (14.15), and thus the 3×3 $\mathbf{W}$ matrices of SU(3)$_\mathrm{c}$ cannot be real, so that there is a distinction between ψ and ψ^*, as we learned in section 12.2. Indeed, it can be shown (see Carruthers 1966, chapter 3, Jones 1990, chapter 8, and also problem 14.1(b)) that, unlike the case of SU(2)$_\mathrm{c}$ triplets, it is not possible to form an SU(3)$_\mathrm{c}$ colour singlet combination out of two colour triplets qq or anti-triplets $\bar{\mathrm{q}}\bar{\mathrm{q}}$. Thus SU(3)$_\mathrm{c}$ seems to be a possible and economical choice for the colour group.

14.2.2   Global SU(3)$_\mathrm{c}$ invariance, and 'scalar gluons'

As stated above, we are assuming, on empirical grounds, that the only physically observed hadronic states are colour singlets – and this now means singlets under SU(3)$_\mathrm{c}$. What sort of interquark force could produce this dramatic result? Consider an SU(2) analogy again, the interaction of two nucleons belonging to the lowest (doublet) representation of SU(2). Labelling the states by an isospin T, the possible T values for two nucleons are $T = 1$ (triplet) and $T = 0$ (singlet). We know of an isospin-dependent force which can produce a splitting between these states, namely $V\boldsymbol{\tau}_1 \cdot \boldsymbol{\tau}_2$, where the '1' and '2' refer to the two nucleons. The total isospin is $\boldsymbol{T} = \frac{1}{2}(\boldsymbol{\tau}_1 + \boldsymbol{\tau}_2)$, and we have

$$\boldsymbol{T}^2 = \frac{1}{4}(\boldsymbol{\tau}_1^2 + 2\boldsymbol{\tau}_1 \cdot \boldsymbol{\tau}_2 + \boldsymbol{\tau}_2^2) = \frac{1}{4}(3 + 2\boldsymbol{\tau}_1 \cdot \boldsymbol{\tau}_2 + 3) \tag{14.17}$$

whence

$$\boldsymbol{\tau}_1 \cdot \boldsymbol{\tau}_2 = 2\boldsymbol{T}^2 - 3. \tag{14.18}$$

In the triplet state $\boldsymbol{T}^2 = 2$, and in the singlet state $\boldsymbol{T}^2 = 0$. Thus

$$(\boldsymbol{\tau}_1 \cdot \boldsymbol{\tau}_2)_{T=1} = 1 \tag{14.19}$$

$$(\boldsymbol{\tau}_1 \cdot \boldsymbol{\tau}_2)_{T=0} = -3 \tag{14.20}$$

and if V is positive the $T = 0$ state is pulled down. A similar thing happens in SU(3)$_\mathrm{c}$. Suppose this interquark force depended on the quark colours via a term proportional to

$$\boldsymbol{\lambda}_1 \cdot \boldsymbol{\lambda}_2. \tag{14.21}$$

Then, in just the same way, we can introduce the total colour operator

$$\boldsymbol{F} = \frac{1}{2}(\boldsymbol{\lambda}_1 + \boldsymbol{\lambda}_2), \tag{14.22}$$

so that

$$\boldsymbol{F}^2 = \frac{1}{4}(\boldsymbol{\lambda}_1^2 + 2\boldsymbol{\lambda}_1 \cdot \boldsymbol{\lambda}_2 + \boldsymbol{\lambda}_2^2) \tag{14.23}$$

and

$$\boldsymbol{\lambda}_1 \cdot \boldsymbol{\lambda}_2 = 2\boldsymbol{F}^2 - \boldsymbol{\lambda}^2, \tag{14.24}$$

where $\boldsymbol{\lambda}_1^2 = \boldsymbol{\lambda}_2^2 = \boldsymbol{\lambda}^2$, say. Here $\boldsymbol{\lambda}^2 \equiv \sum_{a=1}^{8}(\lambda_a)^2$ is found (see (12.75)) to have the value $16/3$ (the unit matrix being understood). The operator $\boldsymbol{F}^2$ commutes with all components of $\boldsymbol{\lambda}_1$ and $\boldsymbol{\lambda}_2$ (as $\boldsymbol{T}^2$ does with $\boldsymbol{\tau}_1$ and $\boldsymbol{\tau}_2$) and represents the quadratic Casimir operator $\hat{C}_2$ of SU(3)$_c$ (see section M.5 of appendix M), in the colour space of the two quarks considered here. The eigenvalues of $\hat{C}_2$ play a very important role in SU(3)$_c$, analogous to that of the total spin/angular momentum in SU(2). They depend on the SU(3)$_c$ representation: indeed, they are one of the defining labels of SU(3) representations in general (see section M.5). Two quarks, each in the representation $\mathbf{3}_c$, combine to give a $\mathbf{6}_c$-dimensional representation and a $\mathbf{3}_c^*$ (see problem 14.1(b), and Jones (1990) chapter 8). The value of $\hat{C}_2$ for the singlet $\mathbf{6}_c$ representation is $10/3$, and for the $\mathbf{3}_c^*$ representation is $4/3$. Thus the '$\boldsymbol{\lambda}_1 \cdot \boldsymbol{\lambda}_2$' interaction will produce a negative (attractive) eigenvalue $-8/3$ in the $\mathbf{3}_c^*$ states, but a repulsive eigenvalue $+4/3$ in the $\mathbf{6}_c$ states, for two quarks.

The maximum attraction will clearly be for states in which $\boldsymbol{F}^2$ is zero. This is the singlet representation $\mathbf{1}_c$. Two quarks cannot combine to give a colour singlet state, but we have seen in section 12.2 that a quark and an antiquark can: they combine to give $\mathbf{1}_c$ and $\mathbf{8}_c$. In this case (14.24) is replaced by

$$\boldsymbol{\lambda}_1 \cdot \boldsymbol{\lambda}_2 = 2\boldsymbol{F}^2 - \frac{1}{2}(\boldsymbol{\lambda}_1^2 + \boldsymbol{\lambda}_2^2), \tag{14.25}$$

where '1' refers to the quark and '2' to the antiquark. Thus the '$\boldsymbol{\lambda}_1 \cdot \boldsymbol{\lambda}_2$' interaction will give a repulsive eigenvalue $+2/3$ in the $\mathbf{8}_c$ channel, for which $\hat{C}_2 = 3$, and a 'maximally attractive' eigenvalue $-16/3$ in the $\mathbf{1}_c$ channel, for a quark and an antiquark.

In the case of baryons, built from three quarks, we have seen that when two of them are coupled to the $\mathbf{3}_c^*$ state, the eigenvalue of $\boldsymbol{\lambda}_1 \cdot \boldsymbol{\lambda}_2$ is $-8/3$, one half of the attraction in the $\bar{q}q$ colour singlet state, but still strongly attractive. The (qq) pair in the $\mathbf{3}_c^*$ state can then couple to the remaining third quark to make the overall colour singlet state (14.2), with maximum binding.

Of course, such a simple potential model does not imply that the energy difference between the $\mathbf{1}_c$ states and all coloured states is *infinite*, as our strict 'colour singlets only' hypothesis would demand, and which would be one (rather crude) way of interpreting confinement. Nevertheless, we can ask: what single particle exchange process between quark (or antiquark) colour triplets produces a $\boldsymbol{\lambda}_1 \cdot \boldsymbol{\lambda}_2$ type of term? The answer is the exchange of

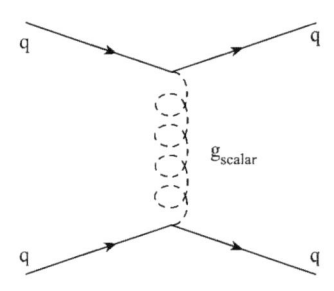

FIGURE 14.4
Scalar gluon exchange between two quarks.

an $SU(3)_c$ octet (8_c) of particles, which (anticipating somewhat) we shall call gluons. Since colour is an exact symmetry, the quark wave equation describing the colour interactions must be $SU(3)_c$ covariant. A simple such equation is

$$(\mathrm{i}\,\partial\!\!\!/ - m)\psi = g_s\frac{\lambda_a}{2}A_a\psi \qquad (14.26)$$

where g_s is a 'strong charge' and A_a ($a = 1, 2, \ldots, 8$) is an octet of *scalar* 'gluon potentials'. Equation (14.26) may be compared with (13.58): in the latter, A_a appears on the right-hand side, because the gauge field quanta are vectors rather than scalars. In (14.26), we are dealing at this stage only with a *global* $SU(3)$ symmetry, not a local $SU(3)$ gauge symmetry, and so the potentials may be taken to be scalars, for simplicity. As in (13.60), the vertex corresponding to (14.26) is

$$-\mathrm{i}g_s\lambda_a/2. \qquad (14.27)$$

(14.27) differs from (13.60) simply in the absence of the γ^μ factor, due to the assumed scalar, rather than vector, nature of the 'gluon' here. When we put two such vertices together and join them with a gluon propagator (figure 14.4), the $SU(3)_c$ structure of the amplitude will be

$$\frac{\lambda_{1a}}{2}\delta_{ab}\frac{\lambda_{2b}}{2} = \frac{\boldsymbol{\lambda_1}}{2}\cdot\frac{\boldsymbol{\lambda_2}}{2} \qquad (14.28)$$

the δ_{ab} arising from the fact that the freely propagating gluon does not change its colour. This interaction has exactly the required '$\boldsymbol{\lambda_1}\cdot\boldsymbol{\lambda_2}$' character in the colour space.

14.2.3 Local $SU(3)_c$ invariance: the QCD Lagrangian

It is tempting to suppose (Fritzsch and Gell-Mann 1972, Fritzsch, Gell-Mann and Leutwyler 1973) that the 'scalar gluons' introduced in (14.26) are, in fact, vector particles, like the photons of QED. Equation (14.26) then becomes

$$(\mathrm{i}\,\partial\!\!\!/ - m)\psi = g_s\frac{\lambda_a}{2}A\!\!\!/_a\psi \qquad (14.29)$$

as in (13.58), and the vertex (14.27) becomes

$$-ig_s\frac{\lambda_a}{2}\gamma^\mu \tag{14.30}$$

as in (13.60). One motivation for this is the desire to make the colour dynamics as much as possible like the highly successful theory of QED, and to derive the dynamics from a gauge principle. As we have seen in the last chapter, this involves the simple but deep step of supposing that the quark wave equation is covariant under *local* $SU(3)_c$ transformations of the form

$$\psi \to \psi' = \exp(ig_s\boldsymbol{\alpha}(x) \cdot \boldsymbol{\lambda}/2)\psi. \tag{14.31}$$

This is implemented by the replacement

$$\partial_\mu \to \partial_\mu + ig_s\frac{\lambda_a}{2}A_{a\mu}(x) \tag{14.32}$$

in the Dirac equation for the quarks, which leads immediately to (14.29) and the vertex (14.30).

Of course, the assumption of local $SU(3)_c$ covariance leads to a great deal more: for example, it implies that the gluons are *massless vector* (spin 1) particles, and that they interact with themselves via *three-gluon* and *four-gluon* vertices, which are the $SU(3)_c$ analogues of the $SU(2)$ vertices discussed in section 13.3.2. The most compact way of summarizing all this structure is via the Lagrangian, most of which we have already introduced in chapter 13. Gathering together (13.71) and (13.140) (adapted to $SU(3)_c$), we write it out here for convenience:

$$\mathcal{L}_{QCD} = \sum_{\text{flavours f}} \bar{\hat{q}}_{f,\alpha}(i\hat{\slashed{D}} - m_f)_{\alpha\beta}\hat{q}_{f,\beta} - \frac{1}{4}\hat{F}_{a\mu\nu}\hat{F}_a^{\mu\nu}$$
$$- \frac{1}{2\xi}(\partial_\mu\hat{A}_a^\mu)(\partial_\nu\hat{A}_a^\nu) + \partial_\mu\hat{\eta}_a^\dagger\hat{D}_{ab}^\mu\hat{\eta}_b. \tag{14.33}$$

In (14.33), repeated indices are as usual summed over: α and β are $SU(3)_c$-triplet indices running from 1 to 3, and a, b are $SU(3)_c$-octet indices running from 1 to 8. The covariant derivatives are defined by

$$(\hat{D}_\mu)_{\alpha\beta} = \partial_\mu\delta_{\alpha\beta} + ig_s\frac{1}{2}(\lambda_a)_{\alpha\beta}\hat{A}_{a\mu} \tag{14.34}$$

when acting on the quark $SU(3)_c$ triplet, as in (13.53), and by

$$(\hat{D}_\mu)_{ab} = \partial_\mu\delta_{ab} + g_sf_{cab}\hat{A}_{c\mu} \tag{14.35}$$

when acting on the octet of ghost fields. For the second of these, note that the matrices representing the $SU(3)$ generators in the octet representation are as given in (12.84), and these take the place of the '$\lambda/2$' in (14.34) (compare (13.141) in the $SU(2)$ case). We remind the reader that the last two terms

in (14.33) are the gauge-fixing and ghost terms, respectively, appropriate to a gauge field propagator of the form (13.69) (with δ_{ij} replaced by δ_{ab} here). The Feynman rules following from (14.33) are given in appendix Q.

As remarked in section 12.3.2, the fact that the QCD interactions (14.33) are 'flavour-blind' implies that the global flavour symmetries discussed in chapter 12 are all preserved by QCD. These include the conservation of each quark flavour (for example, the number of strange quarks minus the number of strange antiquarks is conserved); and the symmetries $SU(2)_f$ and $SU(3)_f$, and the chiral symmetries $SU(2)_{5f}$ and $SU(3)_{5f}$, to the extent that these latter are good symmetries. Further, (14.33) conserves the discrete symmetries **P**, **C** and **T**, in a manner quite analogous to QED, already covered in section 7.5. In the case of **P** and **T**, the gluon fields $\hat{A}_{a\mu}$ have the same transformation properties as the photon field $\hat{A}_\mu$, and the (normally ordered) $SU(3)_c$ currents $\hat{j}^\mu_{fa} = \bar{\hat{q}}_f \gamma^\mu \frac{1}{2}\lambda_a \hat{q}_f$ transform in the same way as the electromagnetic current $\bar{\hat{q}}\gamma^\mu\hat{q}$, ensuring **P** and **T** invariance. Under **C**, the quark fields transform as usual according to (7.151). Charge conjugation for the gluon field needs a little more care. The required rule is

$$\hat{\mathbf{C}}\lambda_a\hat{A}_{a\mu}\hat{\mathbf{C}}^{-1} = -\lambda_a^*\hat{A}_{a\mu}. \tag{14.36}$$

The overall minus sign in (14.36) is analogous to that for the photon field (cf (7.152)). To understand the complex conjugate on the right-hand side of (14.36), recall from (7.153) that the complex scalar field $\hat{\phi} = \frac{1}{\sqrt{2}}(\hat{\phi}_1 - i\hat{\phi}_2)$ transforms according to

$$\hat{\mathbf{C}}(\hat{\phi}_1 - i\hat{\phi}_2)\hat{\mathbf{C}}^{-1} = \hat{\phi}_1 + i\hat{\phi}_2. \tag{14.37}$$

Problem 14.2(a) verifies that the (normally ordered) interaction $\hat{j}^\mu_{fa}\hat{A}_{a\mu}$ is then **C**-invariant. As regards the term $\hat{F}_{a\mu\nu}\hat{F}_a^{\mu\nu}$, we can write it as

$$\frac{1}{2}\text{Tr}(\lambda_a\hat{F}_{a\mu\nu}\lambda_b\hat{F}_b^{\mu\nu}) \tag{14.38}$$

using the relation

$$\text{Tr}(\lambda_a\lambda_b) = 2\delta_{ab}. \tag{14.39}$$

A short calculation (problem 14.2(b)) shows that $\lambda_a\hat{F}_{a\mu\nu}$ transforms under **C** the same way as $\lambda_a\hat{A}_{a\mu}$ (i.e. according to (14.36)). Using the complex conjugate of (14.39), it then follows that (14.38) is invariant under **C**.

14.2.4   The θ-term

In arriving at (14.33) we have relied essentially on the 'gauge principle' (invariance under a local symmetry) and the requirement of renormalizability (to forbid the presence of terms with mass dimension higher than 4). The renormalizability of such a theory was proved by 't Hooft (1971a, b). However,

there is in fact one more gauge invariant term of mass dimension 4 which can be written down, namely

$$\hat{\mathcal{L}}_\theta = \frac{\theta g_{\mathrm{s}}^2}{64\pi^2} \epsilon_{\mu\nu\rho\sigma} \hat{F}_a^{\mu\nu} \hat{F}_a^{\rho\sigma}; \tag{14.40}$$

this is the 'θ-term' of QCD. A full discussion of this term (see for example Weinberg 1996, section 23.6) is beyond our scope, but we shall give a brief introduction to the main ideas.

The reader may wonder, first of all, whether the θ-term should give rise to a new Feynman rule. The answer to this begins by noting that (14.40) can actually be written as a total divergence:

$$\epsilon_{\mu\nu\rho\sigma} \hat{F}_a^{\mu\nu} \hat{F}_a^{\rho\sigma} = \partial_\mu \hat{K}^\mu. \tag{14.41}$$

This is more easily seen in the analogous term for QED, namely $\epsilon_{\mu\nu\rho\sigma} \hat{F}^{\mu\nu} \hat{F}^{\rho\sigma}$. We have

$$\epsilon_{\mu\nu\rho\sigma} \hat{F}^{\mu\nu} \hat{F}^{\rho\sigma} = \epsilon_{\mu\nu\rho\sigma} (\partial^\mu \hat{A}^\nu - \partial^\nu \hat{A}^\mu)(\partial^\rho \hat{A}^\sigma - \partial^\sigma \hat{A}^\rho) \tag{14.42}$$

$$= 4\epsilon_{\mu\nu\rho\sigma} \partial^\mu \hat{A}^\nu \partial^\rho \hat{A}^\sigma \tag{14.43}$$

$$= \partial^\mu (4\epsilon_{\mu\nu\rho\sigma} \hat{A}^\nu \partial^\rho \hat{A}^\sigma), \tag{14.44}$$

where we have used the antisymmetry of the ϵ symbol in (14.43), and also in (14.44) since the contraction of ϵ with the symmetric tensor $\partial^\mu \partial^\rho$ vanishes. We shall not need the explicit form of $\hat{K}^\mu$.

Any total divergence in a Lagrangian can be integrated to give only a 'surface' term in the action, which can usually be discarded, making conventional assumptions about the vanishing of the fields at spatial infinity. There are, however, field configurations ('instantons') which do contribute to the θ-term. Such configurations are not reachable in perturbation theory, and so no perturbative Feynman rules are associated with (14.40). They approach a pure gauge form at spatial infinity, and are therefore associated with the QCD vacuum state; their effect is equivalent to including the term (14.40) in the QCD Lagrangian (see for example Rajaraman 1982).

The term (14.40) has potentially important phenomenological implications, since it conserves $\mathbf{C}$ but violates both $\mathbf{P}$ and $\mathbf{T}$ (and hence also $\mathbf{CP}$). Again, this is easy to see in the QED analogue term (14.42), which equals $8\hat{\boldsymbol{E}} \cdot \hat{\boldsymbol{B}}$ (problem 14.3): we recall that under $\mathbf{P}$, $\hat{\boldsymbol{E}} \to -\hat{\boldsymbol{E}}$ and $\hat{\boldsymbol{B}} \to \hat{\boldsymbol{B}}$, while under $\mathbf{T}$, $\hat{\boldsymbol{E}} \to \hat{\boldsymbol{E}}$ and $\hat{\boldsymbol{B}} \to -\hat{\boldsymbol{B}}$. But we know (section 4.2) that strong interactions conserve both $\mathbf{P}$ and $\mathbf{T}$ to a high degree of accuracy. In particular, the neutron electric dipole moment d_{n}, which would violate both $\mathbf{P}$ and $\mathbf{T}$, is extremely small (see (4.133)). A very crude estimate of the size of d_{n}, induced by the θ-term, is given by dimensional analysis as

$$d_{\mathrm{n}} \sim \frac{e}{M_{\mathrm{n}}} \theta, \tag{14.45}$$

where M_n is the neutron mass. This would imply $\theta < 10^{-12}$. In fact, this estimate is too restrictive, since it turns out (Weinberg 1996, section 23.6) that if any quark has zero mass, θ can be reduced to zero by a global chiral U(1) transformation on that quark field. Although neither of the u and d quark masses are zero, they are small on a hadronic scale, and a suppression of (14.45) is expected, increasing the bound on theta. Estimates suggest $\theta < 10^{-9} - 10^{-10}$.

This may seem an unsatisfactorily special value to force on a dimensionless Lagrangian parameter, when there is nothing in the theory, *a priori*, to prevent something of order unity. This perceived difficulty is referred to as the 'strong **CP** problem'. A possible solution to the problem, in which a very small value of θ could arise naturally was suggested by Peccei and Quinn (1977a, 1977b). Their idea goes beyond the Standard Model, and involves the existence of a new very light pseudoscalar particle, the *axion* (Wilczek 1978, Winberg 1978).

We proceed now with the main topic of this chapter, which is the application of perturbative QCD.

14.3 Hard scattering processes, QCD tree graphs, and jets

14.3.1 Introduction

The fundamental distinctive feature of non-Abelian gauge theories is that they are 'asymptotically free', meaning that the effective coupling strength becomes progressively smaller at short distances, or high energies (Gross and Wilczek 1973, Politzer 1973). This property is the most compelling theoretical motivation for choosing a non-Abelian gauge theory for the strong interactions, and it enables a quantitative perturbative approach to be followed (in appropriate circumstances) even in strong interaction physics. This programme has indeed been phenomenally successful, firmly establishing QCD as the theory of strong interactions, and now – in the era of the LHC – serving as a precision tool to guide searches for new physics.

A proper understanding of how this works necessitates a considerable detour, however, into the physics of renormalization. In particular, we need to understand the important cluster of ideas going under the general heading of the 'renormalization group', and this will be the topic of chapter 15. For the moment we proceed with a discussion of some simple tree-level applications of QCD, which provided early confrontation of QCD with experiment.

Let us begin by recapitulating, from a QCD-informed viewpoint, how the parton model successfully interpreted deep inelastic and large-Q^2 data in terms of almost free point-like partons – now to be identified with the QCD quanta: quarks, antiquarks, and gluons.

In section 9.5 we briefly introduced the idea of *jets* in e^+e^- physics: two well collimated sprays of hadrons, apparently created as a quark–antiquark pair separate from each other at high speed. The angular distribution of the two jets followed closely the distribution expected from the parton-level process $e^+e^- \to \bar{q}q$. The dynamics at the parton level was governed by QED, but QCD is responsible for the way the emerging q and $\bar{q}$ turn themselves into hadrons, a process called parton fragmentation (it occurs for gluons too). We may think of it as proceeding in two stages. First, as the rapidly moving q and $\bar{q}$ begin to separate, they develop perturbative showers of narrowly collimated gluons and quark–antiquark pairs. Then, as the partons separate further, the strength of the forces between them increases, becoming strongly non-perturbative at a separation of about 1 fm, and ensuring that the coloured quanta are all confined into hadrons. As yet we do not have a completely quantitative dynamical understanding of the second, hadronization, stage: it is implemented by means of a model. Nevertheless, we can argue that for the forces to be strong enough to produce the observed hadrons, the dominant processes in hadronization must involve small momentum transfers – that is, the exchange of 'soft' quanta. Thus the emerging hadrons are also well collimated into two jets, whose energy and angular distributions reflect the short-distance physics at the parton level. This simple 2-jet picture will be extended in section 14.4, where we consider $e^+e^- \to 3$ jets.

A somewhat different aspect of parton physics arose in sections 9.2–9.3, where we considered deep inelastic electron scattering from nucleons. There the initial state contained one hadron. Correspondingly, one parton appeared in the *initial* state of the parton-level interaction, and the analysis required new functions measuring the probabilities of finding a particular parton in the parent hadron – the parton distribution functions. These too are beyond the reach of perturbation theory.

We may also consider, finally, hadron-hadron collisions. In this case, we need all three of the features we have been discussing: the parton distribution functions, to provide the intial parton-parton state from the two-hadron state; the perturbative short-distance parton-parton interaction; and the parton fragmentation process in the final state. These three parts to the process are pictured in figure 14.5. The identification and analysis of short distance parton-parton interactions provide direct tests of the tree-graph structure of QCD, and perturbative corrections to it.

This three-part schematization of certain features of hadronic interactions is useful, because although we cannot yet calculate from first principles either the parton distribution functions or the fragmentation process, both are *universal*. The quark and gluon composition of hadrons is the same for all processes, and so measurements in one experiment can be used to predict the results of others. We saw an example of this in the Drell–Yan process of section 9.4. As regards the fragmentation stage, this too will be universal, provided one is interested in sufficiently inclusive aspects of the final state. The

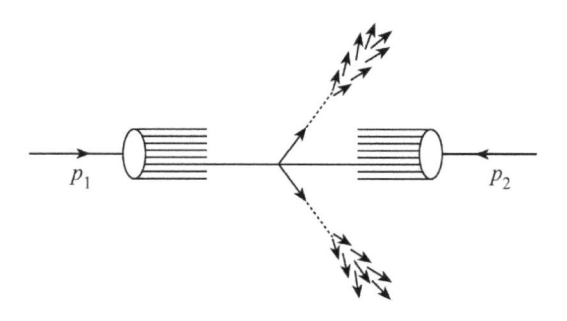

FIGURE 14.5
Hadron-hadron collision involving parton-parton interaction followed by parton fragmentation.

three-part scheme is called *factorization*, and it has been rigorously proved for some cases. We shall return to factorization in section 15.7.

Let us turn now to some of the early data on parton-parton interactions in hadron-hadron collisions.

14.3.2   Two-jet events in p̄p collisions

How are short-distance parton-parton interactions to be identified experimentally? The answer is: in just the same way as Rutherford distinguished the presence of a small heavy scattering centre (the nucleus) in the atom: by looking at secondary particles emerging at large angles with respect to the beam direction. For each secondary particle we can define a transverse momentum $p_T = p \sin \theta$ where p is the particle momentum and θ is the emission angle with respect to the beam axis. If hadronic matter were smooth and uniform (cf the Thomson atom), the distribution of events in p_T would be expected to fall off very rapidly at large p_T values – perhaps exponentially. This is just what is observed in the vast majority of events: the average value of p_T measured for charged particles is very low ($\langle p_T \rangle \sim 0.4$ GeV), but in a small fraction of collisions the emission of high-p_T secondaries is observed. They were first seen (Büsser *et al.* 1972, 1973, Alper *et al.* 1973, Banner *et al.* 1982) at the CERN ISR (CMS energies 30-62 GeV), and were interpreted in parton terms as previously indicated. Referring to figure 14.5, a parton from one hadron undergoes a short-distance 'hard scattering' interaction with a parton from the other, leading in lowest-order perturbation theory to two wide-angle partons, which then fragment into two jets.

We now face the experimental problem of picking out, from the enormous multiplicity of total events, just these hard scattering ones, in order to analyse them further. Early experiments used a trigger based on the detection of a single high-p_T particle. But it turns out that such triggering really reduces

the probability of observing jets, since the probability that a single hadron in a jet will actually carry most of the jet's total transverse momentum is quite small (Jacob and Landshoff 1978; Collins and Martin 1984, Chapter 5). It is much better to surround the collision volume with an array of calorimeters which measure the total energy deposited. *Wide-angle jets* can then be identified by the occurrence of a large amount of total transverse energy deposited in a number of adjacent calorimeter cells: this is then a 'jet trigger'. The importance of calorimetric triggers was first emphasized by Bjorken (1973), following earlier work by Berman, Bjorken and Kogut (1971). The application of this method to the detection and analysis of wide-angle jets was first reported by the UA2 collaboration at the CERN $\bar{\text{p}}$p collider (Banner *et al.* 1982). An impressive body of quite remarkably clean jet data was subsequently accumulated by both the UA1 and UA2 collaborations (at $\sqrt{s} = 546$ GeV and 630 GeV), and by the CDF and D0 collaborations at the FNAL Tevatron collider ($\sqrt{s} = 1.8$ TeV).

For each event the total transverse energy $\sum E_{\text{T}}$ is measured where

$$\sum E_{\text{T}} = \sum_i E_i \sin \theta_i. \tag{14.46}$$

E_i is the energy deposited in the ith calorimeter cell and θ_i is the polar angle of the cell centre; the sum extends over all cells. Figure 14.6 shows the $\sum E_{\text{T}}$ distribution observed by UA2: it follows the 'soft' exponential form for $\sum E_{\text{T}} \leq 60$ GeV, but thereafter departs from it, showing clear evidence of the wide-angle collisions characteristic of hard processes.

As we shall see shortly, the majority of 'hard' events are of two-jet type, with the jets sharing the $\sum E_{\text{T}}$ approximately equally. Thus a 'local' trigger set to select events with localized transverse energy ≥ 30 GeV and/or a 'global' trigger set at ≥ 60 GeV can be used. At $\sqrt{s} \geq 500$–600 GeV there is plenty of energy available to produce such events.

The total $\sqrt{s}$ value is important for another reason. Consider the kinematics of the two-parton collision (figure 14.5) in the $\bar{\text{p}}$p CMS. As in the Drell–Yan process of section 9.4, the right-moving parton has 4-momentum

$$x_1 p_1 = x_1 (P, 0, 0, P) \tag{14.47}$$

and the left-moving one

$$x_2 p_2 = x_2 (P, 0, 0, -P) \tag{14.48}$$

where $P = \sqrt{s}/2$ and we are neglecting parton transverse momenta, which are approximately limited by the observed $\langle p_{\text{T}} \rangle$ value (~ 0.4 GeV, and thus negligible on this energy scale). Consider the simple case of 90^0 scattering, which requires (for massless partons) $x_1 = x_2$, equal to x say. The total outgoing transverse energy is then $2xP = x\sqrt{s}$. If this is to be greater than 50 GeV, then partons with $x \geq 0.1$ will contribute to the process. The parton distribution functions are large at these relatively small x values, due to sea

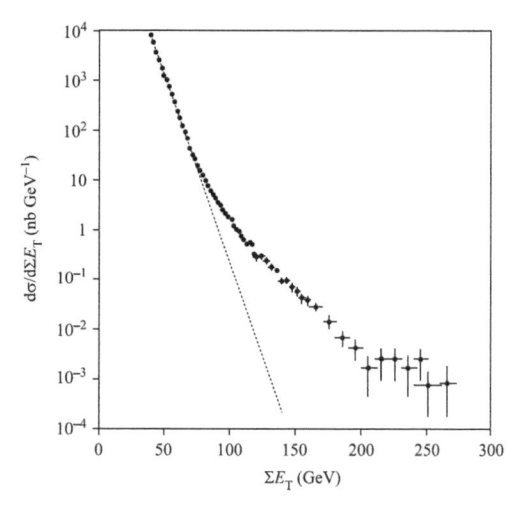

FIGURE 14.6
Distribution of the total transverse energy $\sum E_T$ observed in the UA2 central calorimeter (DiLella 1985).

quarks (section 9.3) and gluons (figure 9.9), and thus we expect to obtain a reasonable cross section.

What are the characteristics of jet events? When $\sum E_T$ is large enough (≥ 150 GeV), it is found that essentially all of the transverse energy is indeed split roughly equally between two approximately back-to-back jets. A typical such event is shown in figure 14.7. Returning to the kinematics of (14.47) and (14.48), x_1 will not in general be equal to x_2, so that – as is apparent in figure 14.7 – the jets will not be collinear. However, to the extent that the transverse parton momenta can be neglected, the jets will be coplanar with the beam direction, i.e. their relative azimuthal angle will be 180^0. Figure 14.8 shows a number of examples in which the distribution of the transverse energy over the calorimeter cells is analyzed as a function of the jet opening angle θ and the azimuthal angle ϕ. It is strikingly evident that we are seeing precisely a kind of 'Rutherford' process, or – to vary the analogy – we might say that hadronic jets are acting as the modern counterpart of Faraday's iron filings, in rendering visible the underlying field dynamics!

We may now consider more detailed features of these two-jet events – in particular, the expectations based on QCD tree graphs. The initial hadrons provide wide-band beams of quarks, antiquarks and gluons[2]; thus we shall have many parton subprocesses, such as $qq \to qq$, $q\bar{q} \to q\bar{q}$, $q\bar{q} \to gg$, $gg \to gg$, etc. The most important, numerically, for a $p\bar{p}$ collider are $q\bar{q} \to q\bar{q}$, $gq \to gq$

---

[2]In the sense that the partons in hadrons have momentum or energy distributions, which are characteristic of their localization to hadronic dimensions.

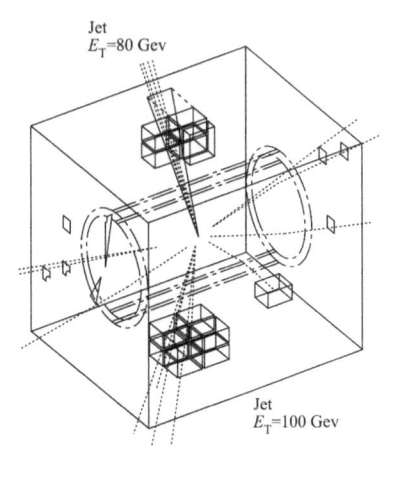

FIGURE 14.7

Two-jet event. Two tightly collimated groups of reconstructed charged tracks can be seen in the cylindrical central detector of UA1, associated with two large clusters of calorimeter energy depositions. Figure reprinted with permission from S Geer in *High Energy Physics 1985, Proc. Yale Advanced Study Institute* eds M J Bowick and F Gursey; copyright 1986 World Scientific Publishing Company.

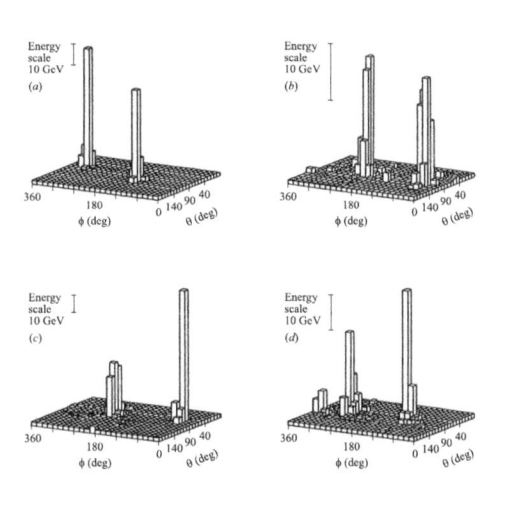

FIGURE 14.8

Four transverse energy distributions for events with $\sum E_T > 100$ GeV, in the θ, ϕ plane (UA2, DiLella 1985). Each bin represents a cell of the UA2 calorimeter. Note that the sum of the ϕ's equals 180^0 (mod 360^0).

TABLE 14.1
Spin-averaged squared matrix elements for one-gluon exchange ($\hat{t}$-channel) processes.

Subprocess	$\lvert\mathcal{M}\rvert^2$
$\left.\begin{array}{l} qq \to qq \\ q\bar{q} \to q\bar{q} \end{array}\right\}$	$\frac{4}{9}\left(\frac{\hat{s}^2+\hat{u}^2}{\hat{t}^2}\right)$
$qg \to qg$	$\frac{\hat{s}^2+\hat{u}^2}{\hat{t}^2} + \dots$
$gg \to gg$	$\frac{9}{4}\left(\frac{\hat{s}^2+\hat{u}^2}{\hat{t}^2}\right) + \dots$

and $gg \to gg$. The cross section will be given, in the parton model, by a formula of the Drell–Yan type, except that the electromagnetic annihilation cross section

$$\sigma(q\bar{q} \to \mu^+\mu^-) = 4\pi\alpha^2/3q^2 \tag{14.49}$$

is replaced by the various QCD subprocess cross sections, each one being weighted by the appropriate distribution functions. At first sight this seems to be a very complicated story, with so many contributing parton processes. But a significant simplification comes from the fact that in the CMS of the parton collision, all processes involving one gluon exchange will lead to essentially the same dominant angular distribution of Rutherford-type, $\sim \sin^{-4}\theta/2$, where θ is the parton CMS scattering angle (recall section 1.3.6). This is illustrated in table 14.1 (taken from Combridge *et al.* 1977), which lists the different relevant spin averaged, squared, one-gluon-exchange matrix elements $\lvert\mathcal{M}\rvert^2$, where the parton differential cross section is given by (cf (6.129))

$$\frac{d\sigma}{d\cos\theta} = \frac{\pi\alpha_s^2}{2\hat{s}} \lvert\mathcal{M}\rvert^2 . \tag{14.50}$$

Here $\alpha_s = g_s^2/4\pi$, and $\hat{s}$, $\hat{t}$ and $\hat{u}$ are the subprocess invariants, so that

$$\hat{s} = (x_1p_1 + x_2p_2)^2 = x_1x_2s \quad \text{(cf (9.84))}. \tag{14.51}$$

Continuing to neglect the parton transverse momenta, the initial parton configuration shown in figure 14.5 can be brought to the parton CMS by a Lorentz transformation along the beam direction, the outgoing partons then emerging back-to-back at an angle θ to the beam axis, so $\hat{t} \propto (1-\cos\theta) \propto \sin^2\theta/2$. Only the terms in $(\hat{t})^{-2} \sim \sin^{-4}\theta/2$ are given in table 14.1. We note that the $\hat{s}, \hat{t}, \hat{u}$ dependence of these terms is the same for the three types of process (and is in fact the same as that found for the 1γ exchange process $e^-\mu^- \to e^-\mu^-$: see problem 8.17, converting $d\sigma/dt$ into $d\sigma/d\cos\theta$). Figure 14.9 shows the two jet angular distribution measured by UA1 (Arnison *et al.* 1985). The broken

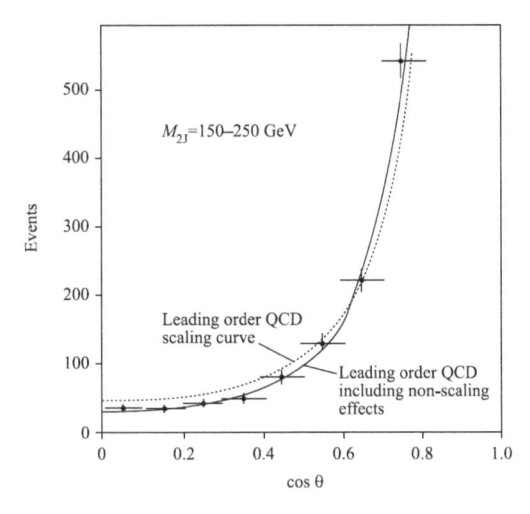

FIGURE 14.9
Two-jet angular distribution plotted against $\cos\theta$ (Arnison *et al.* 1985).

curve is the exact angular distribution predicted by all the QCD tree graphs
– it actually follows the $\sin^{-4}\theta/2$ shape quite closely.

It is interesting to compare this angular distribution with the one predicted
on the assumption that the exchanged gluon is a spinless particle, so that the
vertices have the form '$\bar{u}u$' rather than '$\bar{u}\gamma_\mu u$'. Problem 14.4 shows that in
this case the $1/\hat{t}^2$ factor in the cross section is completely cancelled, thus ruling
out such a model.

This analysis provides compelling evidence for elementary hard scattering events proceeding via the exchange of a massless vector quantum. It is
possible to go much further. Anticipating our later discussion, the small discrepancy between 'tree graph' theory (which is labelled 'leading order QCD
scaling curve' in figure 14.9) and experiment can be accounted for by including corrections which are of higher order in α_s. The solid curve in figure 14.9
includes QCD corrections beyond the tree level, involving the 'running' of the
coupling constant α_s and 'scaling violation' in the effective parton distribution functions, both of which effects will be discussed in the following chapter.
The corrections lead to good agreement with experiment.

The fact that the angular distributions of all the subprocesses are so similar
allows further information to be extracted from these two-jet data. In general,
the parton model cross section will have the form (cf (9.91))

$$\frac{\mathrm{d}^3\sigma}{\mathrm{d}x_1\mathrm{d}x_2\mathrm{d}\cos\theta} = \sum_{a,b} \frac{F_a(x_1)}{x_1} \frac{F_b(x_2)}{x_2} \sum_{c,d} \frac{\mathrm{d}\sigma_{ab\to cd}}{\mathrm{d}\cos\theta} \tag{14.52}$$

where $F_a(x_1)/x_1$ is the distribution function for partons of type 'a' (q, $\bar{q}$ or g),
and similarly for $F_b(x_2)/x_2$. Using the near identity of all $\mathrm{d}\sigma/\mathrm{d}\cos\theta$'s, and

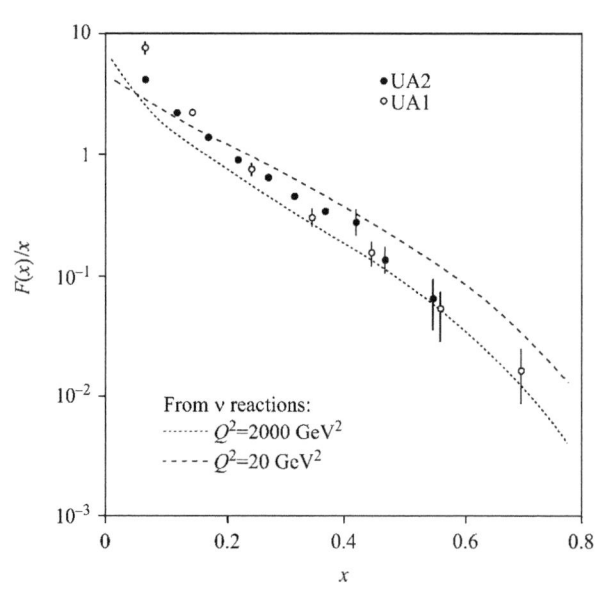

FIGURE 14.10
Effective distribution function measured from two-jet events (Arnison *et al.*
1984 and Bagnaia *et al.* 1984). The broken and chain curves are obtained
from deep inelastic neutrino scattering. Taken from DiLella (1985).

noting the numerical factors in table 14.1, the sums over parton types reduce
to

$$\frac{9}{4}\{g(x_1) + \frac{4}{9}[q(x_1) + \bar{q}(x_1)]\}\{g(x_2) + \frac{4}{9}[q(x_2) + \bar{q}(x_2)]\} \tag{14.53}$$

where $g(x)$, $q(x)$ and $\bar{q}(x)$ are the gluon, quark and antiquark distribution
functions. Thus effectively the weighted distribution function[3]

$$\frac{F(x)}{x} = g(x) + \frac{4}{9}[q(x) + \bar{q}(x)] \tag{14.54}$$

is measured (Combridge and Maxwell, 1984); in fact, with the weights as in
(14.53),

$$\frac{\mathrm{d}^3\sigma}{\mathrm{d}x_1\mathrm{d}x_2\mathrm{d}\cos\theta} = \frac{F(x_1)}{x_1} \cdot \frac{F(x_2)}{x_2} \cdot \frac{\mathrm{d}\sigma_{gg \to gg}}{\mathrm{d}\cos\theta}. \tag{14.55}$$

x_1 and x_2 are kinematically determined from the measured jet variables: from
(14.51),

$$x_1 x_2 = \hat{s}/s \tag{14.56}$$

where $\hat{s}$ is the invariant [mass]^2 of the two-jet system and

$$x_1 - x_2 = 2P_{\mathrm{L}}/\sqrt{s} \quad \text{(cf (9.82))} \tag{14.57}$$

---

[3]The $\frac{4}{9}$ reflects the relative strengths of the quark-gluon and gluon-gluon couplings in
QCD; see problem 14.5.

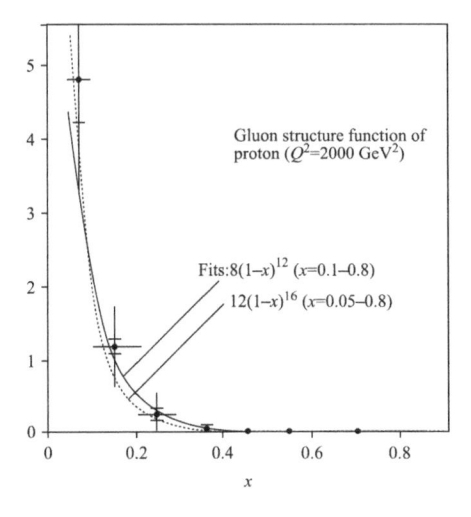

Gluon structure function of proton (Q^2=2000 GeV^2)

Fits:8$(1-x)^{12}$ (x=0.1–0.8)

12$(1-x)^{16}$ (x=0.05–0.8)

FIGURE 14.11
The gluon distribution function $g(x)$ extracted from the effective distribution function $F(x)$ by subtracting the expected contribution from the quarks and antiquarks. Figure reprinted with permission from S Geer in *High Energy Physics 1985, Proc. Yale Theoretical Advanced Study Institute*, eds M J Bowick and F Gursey; copyright 1986 World Scientific Publishing Company.

with P_L the total two-jet longitudinal momentum. Figure 14.10 shows $F(x)/x$ obtained in the UA1 (Arnison *et al.* 1984) and UA(2) (Bagnaia *et al.* 1984) experiments. Also shown in this figure is the expected $F(x)/x$ based on contemporary fits to the deep inelastic neutrino scattering data at $Q^2 = 20$ GeV^2 and 2000 GeV^2 (Abramovicz *et al.* 1982a,b, 1983); the reason for the change with Q^2 will be discussed in section 15.6. The agreement is qualitatively very satisfactory. Subtracting the distributions for quarks and antiquarks as found in deep inelastic lepton scattering, UA1 were able to deduce the gluon structure function $g(x)$ shown in figure 14.11. It is clear that gluon processes will dominate at small x – and even at larger x will be important because of the colour factors in table 14.1.

14.3.3 Three-jet events in $\bar{\text{p}}$p collisions

Although most of the high-$\sum E_T$ events at hadron colliders are two-jet events, in some 10–30% of the cases the energy is shared between three jets. An example is included as (d) in the collection of figure 14.8; a clearer one is shown in figure 14.12. In QCD such events are interpreted as arising from a 2 parton → 2 parton + 1 gluon process of the type gg → ggg, gq → ggq, etc. Once again, one can calculate (Kunszt and Piétarinen 1980, Gottschalk

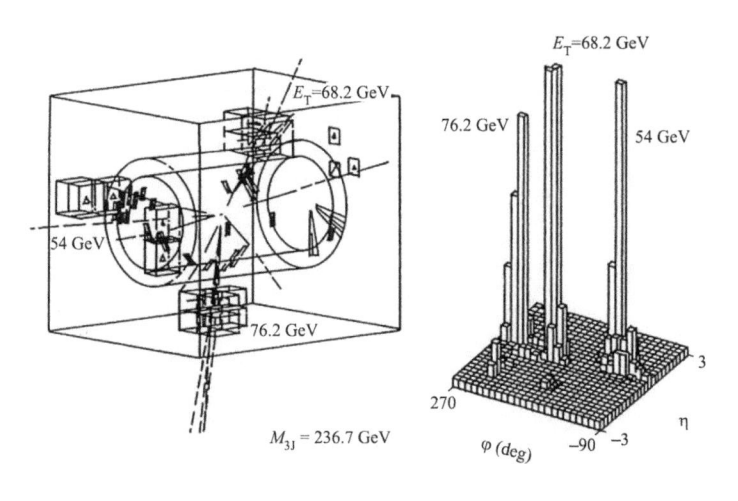

FIGURE 14.12
Three-jet event in the UA1 detector, and the associated transverse energy flow plot. Figure reprinted with permission from S Geer in *High Energy Physics 1985, Proc. Yale Theoretical Advanced Study Institute*, eds M J Bowick and F Gursey; copyright 1986 World Scientific Publishing Company.

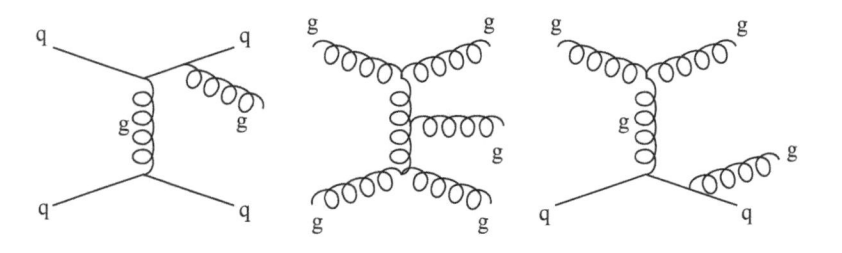

FIGURE 14.13
Some tree graphs associated with three-jet events.

and Sivers 1980, Berends *et al.* 1981) all possible contributing tree graphs, of the kind shown in figure 14.13, which should dominate at small α_s. They are collectively known as QCD single-bremsstrahlung diagrams. Analysis of triple jets which are well separated both from each other and from the beam directions shows that the data are in good agreement with these lowest-order QCD predictions. For example, figure 14.14 shows the production angular distribution of UA2 (Appel *et al.* 1986) as a function of $\cos\theta^*$, where θ^* is the angle between the leading (most energetic) jet momentum and the beam axis, in the three-jet CMS. It follows just the same $\sin^{-4}\theta^*/2$ curve as in the two-jet case (the data for which are also shown in the figure), as expected

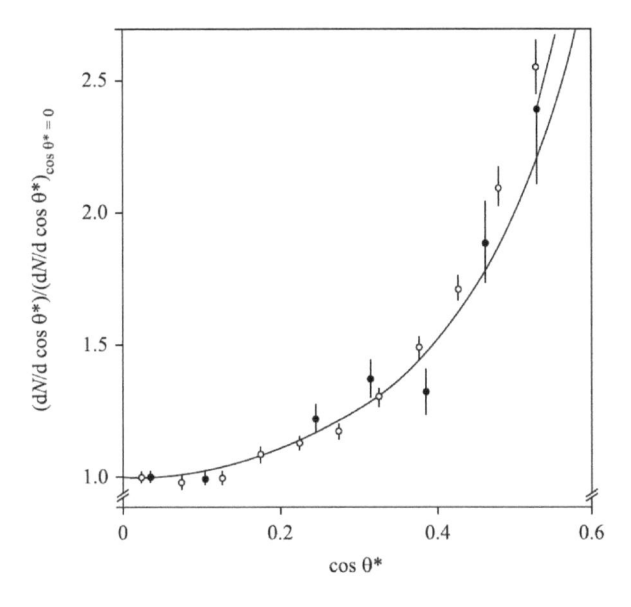

FIGURE 14.14
The distribution of $\cos\theta^*$ ($\bullet$), the angle of the leading jet with respect to the beam line (normalized to unity at $\cos\theta^* = 0$), for three-jet events in $\bar{\text{p}}$p collisions (Appel *et al.* 1986). The distribution for two-jet events is also shown ($\circ$). The full curve is a parton model calculation using the tree graph amplitudes for gg $\to$ ggg, and cut-offs in transverse momentum and angular separation to eliminate divergences (see remarks following equation (14.73)).

for massless quantum exchange; the particular curve is for the representative process gg $\to$ ggg.

Another qualitative feature is that the ratio of three-jet to two-jet events is controlled, roughly, by α_s (compare figure 14.13 with the graphs in table 14.1). Thus an estimate of α_s can be obtained by comparing the rates of 3-jet to 2-jet events in $\bar{\text{p}}$p collisions. Other interesting predictions concern the characteristics of the 3-jet final state (for example, the distributions in the jet energy variables). At this point, however, it is convenient to leave $\bar{\text{p}}$p collisions and consider instead 3-jet events in e$^+$e$^-$ collisions, for which the complications associated with the initial state hadrons are absent.

14.4   3-jet events in e$^+$e$^-$ annihilation

Three-jet events in e$^+$e$^-$ collisions originate, according to QCD, from gluon bremsstrahlung corrections to the two-jet parton level process e$^+$e$^-$ $\to$ γ^* $\to$

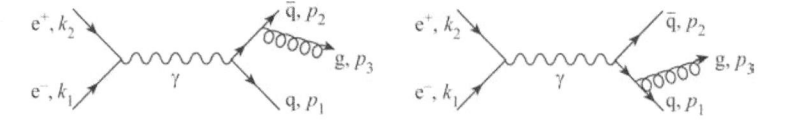

FIGURE 14.15
Gluon brehmsstrahlung corrections to two-jet parton level process.

$q\bar{q}$, as shown in figure 14.15.[4] This phenomenon was predicted by Ellis *et al.*
(1976) and subsequently observed by Brandelik *et al.* (1979) with the TASSO
detector at PETRA, and Barber *et al.* (1979) with MARK-J at PETRA,
thus providing early encouragement for QCD. The situation here is in many
ways simpler and cleaner than in the $\bar{p}p$ case; the initial state 'partons' are
perfectly physical QED quanta, and their total 4-momentum is zero, so that
the three jets have to be coplanar; further, there is only one type of diagram
compared to the large number in the $\bar{p}p$ case, and much of that diagram
involves the easier vertices of QED. Since the calculation of the cross section
predicted from figure 14.15 is relevant not only to three-jet production in e^+e^-
collisions, but also to a satisfactory definition of the two-jet production cross
section, to QCD corrections to the *total* e^+e^- annihilation cross section, and
to scaling violations in deep inelastic scattering as well, we shall now consider
it in some detail. It is important to emphasize at the outset that *quark masses
will be neglected* in this calculation.

14.4.1 Calculation of the parton-level cross section

The quark, antiquark and gluon 4-momenta are p_1, p_2 and p_3 respectively, as
shown in figure 14.15; the e^- and e^+ 4-momenta are k_1 and k_2. The cross
section is then (cf (6.110) and (6.112))

$$d\sigma = \frac{1}{(2\pi)^5}\delta^4(k_1 + k_2 - p_1 - p_2 - p_3)\frac{|\mathcal{M}_{q\bar{q}g}|^2}{2Q^2}\frac{d^3p_1}{2E_1}\frac{d^3p_2}{2E_2}\frac{d^3p_3}{2E_3} \quad (14.58)$$

where (neglecting all masses)

$$\mathcal{M}_{q\bar{q}g} = \frac{e_a e^2 g_s}{Q^2}\bar{v}(k_2)\gamma^\mu u(k_1)\left(\bar{u}(p_1)\gamma_\nu\frac{\lambda_c}{2}\cdot\frac{(\not{p_1}+\not{p_3})}{2p_1\cdot p_3}\cdot\gamma_\mu v(p_2)\right.$$
$$\left. -\bar{u}(p_1)\gamma_\mu\frac{\lambda_c}{2}\cdot\frac{(\not{p_2}+\not{p_3})}{2p_2\cdot p_3}\cdot\gamma_\nu v(p_2)\right)\epsilon^{*\nu}(\lambda)a_c \quad (14.59)$$

and $Q^2 = 4E^2$ is the square of the total e^+e^- energy, and also the square of
the virtual photon's 4-momentum Q, and e_a (in units of e) is the charge of a

---

[4]This is assuming that the total e^+e^- energy is far from the Z^0 mass; if not, the contribution from the intermediate Z^0 must be added to that from the photon.

quark of type 'a'. Note the minus sign in (14.59): the antiquark coupling is $-g_s$. In (14.59), $\epsilon^{*\nu}(\lambda)$ is the polarization vector of the outgoing gluon with polarization λ; a_c is the colour wavefunction of the gluon ($c = 1 \ldots \ldots 8$), and λ_c is the corresponding Gell-Mann matrix introduced in section 12.2; the colour parts of the q and $\bar{q}$ wavefunctions are understood to be included in the u and v factors; and $(\not{p}_1 + \not{p}_3)/2p_1 \cdot p_3$ is the virtual quark propagator (cf (L.6) in appendix L of volume 1) before gluon radiation, and similarly for the antiquark. Since the colour parts separate from the Dirac trace parts, we shall ignore them to begin with, and reinstate the result of the colour sum (via problem (14.5)) in the final answer (14.73).

Averaging over e$^\pm$ spins and summing over final state quark spins and gluon polarization λ (using (8.171), and noting the discussion after (13.93)), we obtain (problem 14.6)

$$\frac{1}{4} \sum_{\text{spins},\lambda} |\mathcal{M}_{\text{q}\bar{\text{q}}\text{g}}|^2 = \frac{e^4 e_a^2 g_s^2}{Q^4} L^{\mu\nu}(k_1, k_2) H_{\mu\nu}(p_1, p_2, p_3) \tag{14.60}$$

where the lepton tensor is, as usual (equation (8.119)),

$$L^{\mu\nu}(k_1, k_2) = 2(k_1^\mu k_2^\nu + k_1^\nu k_2^\mu - k_1 \cdot k_2 g^{\mu\nu}) \tag{14.61}$$

and the hadron tensor is

$$\begin{aligned}
H_{\mu\nu}(p_1, p_2, p_3) &= \frac{1}{p_1 \cdot p_3}[L_{\mu\nu}(p_2, p_3) - L_{\mu\nu}(p_1, p_1) + L_{\mu\nu}(p_1, p_2)] \\
&+ \frac{1}{p_2 \cdot p_3}[L_{\mu\nu}(p_1, p_3) - L_{\mu\nu}(p_2, p_2) \\
&\qquad\qquad + L_{\mu\nu}(p_1, p_2)] \\
&+ \frac{p_1 \cdot p_2}{(p_1 \cdot p_3)(p_2 \cdot p_3)}[2L_{\mu\nu}(p_1, p_2) + L_{\mu\nu}(p_1, p_3) \\
&\qquad\qquad + L_{\mu\nu}(p_2, p_3)] \tag{14.62}
\end{aligned}$$

Combining (14.61) and (14.62) allows complete expressions for the five-fold differential cross section to be obtained (Ellis *et al.* 1976).

For the subsequent discussion it will be useful to integrate over the three angles describing the orientation (relative to the beam axis) of the production plane containing the three partons. After this integration, the (doubly differential) cross section is a function of two independent Lorentz invariant variables, which are conveniently taken to be two of the three s_{ij} defined by

$$s_{ij} = (p_i + p_j)^2. \tag{14.63}$$

Since we are considering the massless case $p_i^2 = 0$ throughout, we may also write

$$s_{ij} = 2p_i \cdot p_j. \tag{14.64}$$

These variables are linearly related by

$$2(p_1 \cdot p_2 + p_2 \cdot p_3 + p_3 \cdot p_1) = Q^2 \tag{14.65}$$

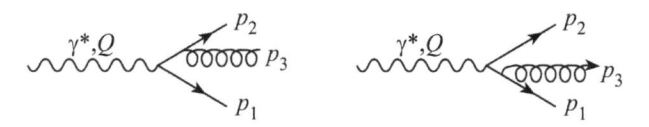

FIGURE 14.16
Virtual photon decaying to q̄qg.

as follows from

$$(p_1 + p_2 + p_3)^2 = Q^2 \tag{14.66}$$

and $p_i^2 = 0$. The integration yields (Ellis *et al.* 1976, 1977)

$$\frac{d^2\sigma}{ds_{13}ds_{23}} = \frac{2}{3}\alpha^2 e_a^2 \alpha_s \frac{1}{(Q^2)^3} \left(\frac{s_{13}}{s_{23}} + \frac{s_{23}}{s_{13}} + \frac{2Q^2 s_{12}}{s_{13}s_{23}} \right) \tag{14.67}$$

where $\alpha_s = g_s^2/4\pi$.

We may understand the form of this result in a simple way, as follows. It seems plausible that after integrating over the production angles, the lepton tensor will be proportional to $Q^2 g^{\mu\nu}$, all directional knowledge of the k_i having been lost. Indeed, if we use $-g^{\mu\nu}L_{\mu\nu}(p,p) = 4p \cdot p'$ together with (14.62) we easily find that

$$-\frac{1}{4}g^{\mu\nu}H_{\mu\nu} = \frac{p_1 \cdot p_3}{p_2 \cdot p_3} + \frac{p_2 \cdot p_3}{p_1 \cdot p_3} + \frac{p_1 \cdot p_2 Q^2}{(p_1 \cdot p_3)(p_2 \cdot p_3)} = \frac{s_{13}}{s_{23}} + \frac{s_{23}}{s_{13}} + \frac{2Q^2 s_{12}}{s_{13}s_{23}}, \tag{14.68}$$

exactly the factor appearing in (14.67). In turn, the result may be given a simple physical interpretation. From (7.118) we note that we can replace $-g^{\mu\nu}$ by $\sum_{\lambda'} \epsilon^\mu(\lambda')\epsilon^{\nu*}(\lambda')$ for a virtual photon of polarization λ', the $\lambda' = 0$ state contributing negatively. Thus effectively the result of doing the angular integration is (up to constants and Q^2 factors) to replace the lepton factor $\bar{v}(k_2)\gamma^\mu u(k_1)$ by $-i\epsilon^\mu(\lambda')$, so that $\mathcal{M}_{q\bar{q}g}$ is proportional to the $\gamma* \to q\bar{q}g$ processes shown in figure 14.16. But these are basically the same amplitudes as the ones we already met in Compton scattering (section 8.6). To compare with section 8.6.3, we convert the initial state fermion (electron/quark) into a final state antifermion (positron/antiquark) by $p \to -p$, and then identify the variables of figure 14.16 with those of figure 8.14 (a) by

$$p' \to p_1 \quad k' \to p_3 \quad -p \to p_2 \quad s \to 2p_1 \cdot p_3 = s_{13}$$
$$t \to 2p_1 \cdot p_2 = s_{12} \quad u \to 2p_2 \cdot p_3 = s_{23}. \tag{14.69}$$

Remembering that in (8.181) the virtual γ had squared 4-momentum $-Q^2$, we see that the Compton '$\sum |\mathcal{M}|^2$' of (8.181) indeed becomes proportional to the factor (14.68), as expected.

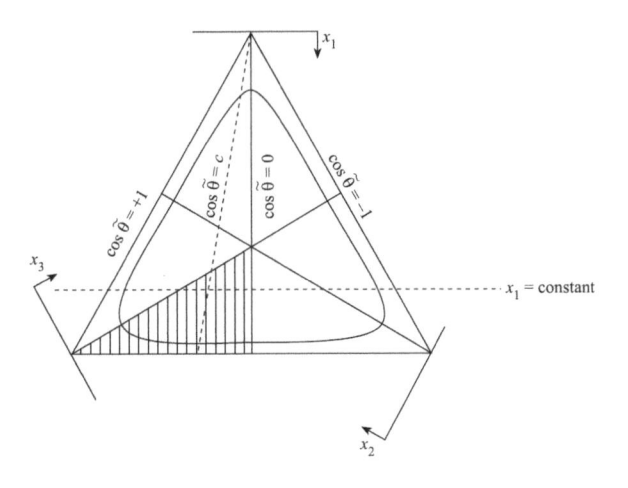

FIGURE 14.17
The kinematically allowed region in (x_i) is the interior of the equilateral triangle.

14.4.2 Soft and collinear divergences

In three-body final states of the type under discussion here it is often convenient to preserve the symmetry between the s_{ij}'s and use *three* (dimensionless) variables x_i defined by

$$s_{23} = Q^2(1 - x_1) \text{ and cyclic permutations.} \tag{14.70}$$

These are related by (14.65), which becomes

$$x_1 + x_2 + x_3 = 2. \tag{14.71}$$

An event with a given value of the set x_i can then be plotted as a point in an equilateral triangle of height 1, as shown in figure 14.17. In order to find the limits of the allowed physical region in this x_i space, we now transform from the overall three-body CMS to the CMS of 2 and 3 (figure 14.18). If $\tilde{\theta}$ is the angle between 1 and 3 in this system, then (problem 14.7)

$$
\begin{aligned}
x_2 &= (1 - x_1/2) + (x_1/2)\cos\tilde{\theta} \\
x_3 &= (1 - x_1/2) - (x_1/2)\cos\tilde{\theta}.
\end{aligned}
\tag{14.72}
$$

The limits of the physical region are then clearly $\cos\tilde{\theta} = \pm 1$, which correspond to $x_2 = 1$ and $x_3 = 1$. By symmetry, we see that the entire perimeter of the triangle in figure 14.17 is the required boundary: physical events fall anywhere inside the triangle. (This is the massless limit of the classic Dalitz plot, first introduced by Dalitz (1953) for the analysis of $K \to 3\pi$.) Lines of constant $\tilde{\theta}$ are shown in figure 14.17.

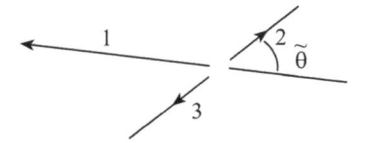

FIGURE 14.18
Definition of $\tilde{\theta}$.

Now consider the distribution provided by the QCD bremsstrahlung process, equation (14.67), which can be written equivalently as

$$\frac{d^2\sigma}{dx_1 dx_2} = \sigma_{\mathrm{pt}} \frac{2\alpha_{\mathrm{s}}}{3\pi} \left(\frac{x_1^2 + x_2^2}{(1 - x_1)(1 - x_2)} \right) \tag{14.73}$$

where σ_{pt} is the pointlike $e^+e^- \to$ hadrons total cross section of (9.99), and a factor of 4 has been introduced from the colour sum (problem 14.5). The factor in large parentheses is (14.68) written in terms of the x_i (problem 14.8). The most striking feature of (14.73) is that it is *infinite* as x_1 or x_2, or both, tend to 1 – and in such a way that the cross section integrated over x_1 and x_2 diverges logarithmically.

This is a quite different infinity from the ones encountered in the loop integrals of chapters 10 and 11. No integral over an arbitrarily large internal momentum is involved here – the tree amplitude itself is becoming singular on the phase space boundary. We can trace the origin of the singularity back to the denominator factors $(p_1 \cdot p_3)^{-1} \sim (1 - x_2)^{-1}$ and $(p_2 \cdot p_3)^{-1} \sim (1 - x_1)^{-1}$ in (14.59). These become zero in two distinct configurations of the gluon momentum:

$$\text{(i)} \quad p_3 \propto p_1 \ \text{ or } \ p_3 \propto p_2 \ \ (\text{using } p_i^2 = 0) \tag{14.74}$$

$$\text{(ii)} \quad p_3 \to 0 \tag{14.75}$$

which are easily interpreted physically. Condition (i) corresponds to a situation in which the 4-momentum of the gluon is parallel to that of either the quark or the antiquark; this is called a 'collinear divergence' and the configuration is pictured in figure 14.19(a). If we restore the quark masses, $p_1^2 = m_1^2 \neq 0$ and $p_2^2 = m_2^2 \neq 0$, then the factor $(2p_1 \cdot p_3)^{-1}$, for example, becomes $((p_1 + p_3)^2 - m_1^2)^{-1}$ which only vanishes as $p_3 \to 0$, which is condition (ii). The divergence of type (i) is therefore also termed a 'mass singularity', as it would be absent if the quarks had mass. Condition (ii) corresponds to the emission of a very 'soft' gluon (figure 14.19(b)) and is called a 'soft, or infrared, divergence'. In contrast to this, the gluon momentum p_3 in type (i) does *not* have to be vanishingly small.

(a) $\qquad\qquad\qquad\qquad\qquad\qquad\qquad$ (b)

FIGURE 14.19
Gluon configurations leading to divergences of equation (14.73): (a) gluon
emitted approximately collinear with quark (or antiquark): (b) soft gluon
emission. The events are viewed in the overall CMS.

It is apparent from these figures that in either of these two cases the
observed final state hadrons, after the fragmentation process, will in fact resemble a *two*-jet configuration. Such events will be found in the regions $x_1 \approx 1$
and/or $x_2 \approx 1$ of the kinematical plot shown in figure 14.17, which correspond
to strips adjacent to two of the boundaries of the triangle. Events outside these
strips should be essentially three-jet events, corresponding to the emission of
a hard, non-collinear gluon. To isolate such events, we must keep away from
the boundaries of the triangle (the strip along the third boundary $x_3 = 1$ will
not contain a divergence, but will be included in a physical jet measure – see
the following section). Thus to order $\alpha^2\alpha_s$ the total annihilation cross section
to three jets is given by the integral of (14.73) over a suitably defined inner
triangular region in figure 14.17.

Assuming such a separation of three- and two-jet events can be done satisfactorily (see the next section), their ratio carries important information –
namely, it should be proportional to α_s. This follows simply from the extra
factor of g_s associated with the gluon emissions in figure 14.15. Glossing over
a number of technicalities (for which the reader is referred to Ellis, Stirling
and Webber 1996, section 3.3), we show in figure 14.20 a compilation of data
on the fraction of three-jet events at different e$^+$e$^-$ annihilation energies. The
most remarkable feature of this figure is, of course, that this fraction – and
hence α_s – *changes with energy, decreasing as the energy increases*. This is, in
fact, direct evidence for asymptotic freedom. A more recent comparison between theory and experiment (the agreement is remarkable) will be presented
in the following chapter, section 15.3, after we have introduced the theoretical
framework for calculating the energy dependence of α_s.

14.5 Definition of the two-jet cross section in e$^+$e$^-$ annihilation

As just noted, the integral of (14.73) over the remaining regions of figure 14.17,
near the phase-space boundaries, will contribute to the two-jet annihilation
cross section – and it is divergent. Clearly this is not a physically acceptable

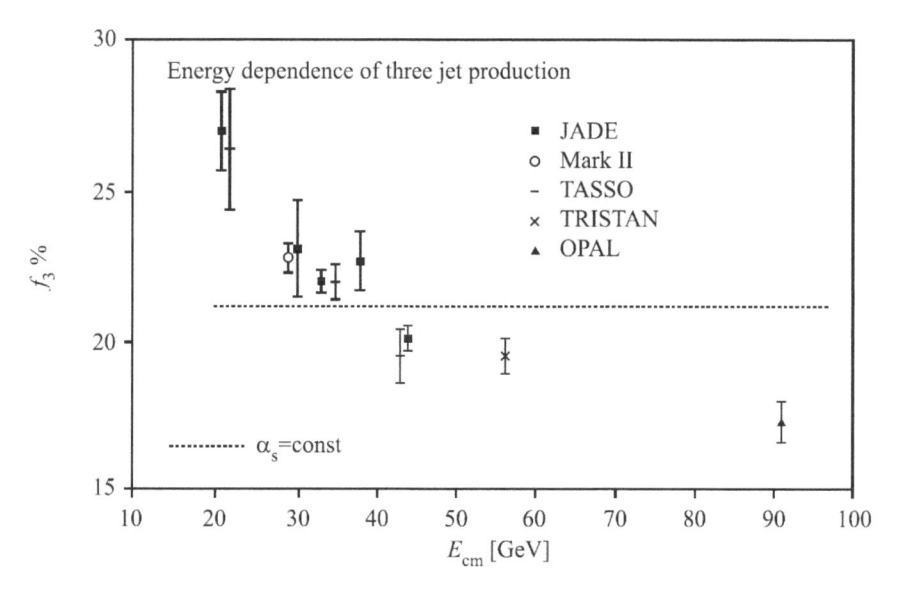

FIGURE 14.20

A compilation of three-jet fractions at different e^+e^- annihilation energies. Adapted from Akrawy *et al.* (OPAL) (1990); figure from R K Ellis, W J Stirling and B R Webber (1996) *QCD and Collider Physics*, courtesy Cambridge University Press.

result: we want a finite two-jet cross section. The cure lies in recognizing that at the order to which we are working, namely $\alpha^2\alpha_s$, other parton-level graphs can contribute. These are the one-gluon loop graphs shown in figure 14.21, which are of order $\alpha\alpha_s$. They turn out to contain exactly the same soft and collinear divergences, this time associated with configurations of virtual momenta inside the loops. In a carefully defined two-jet cross section, these two classes of divergences (one from real gluon emission, the other from virtual gluons) actually cancel.

Let us call the amplitude for the sum of these three graphs F_{vg}, where 'vg' stands for virtual gluon. F_{vg} is the order α_s correction to the original order α parton-level graph of figure 9.17, shown here again in figure 14.22, with amplitude F_γ. The cross section from these contributions is proportional to $|F_\gamma + F_{vg}|^2$. There are three terms in this expression: one of order α^2, from $|F_\gamma|^2$; another of order $\alpha^2\alpha_s^2$, from $|F_{vg}|^2$, which we drop since it is of higher order in α_s; and an *interference* term of order $\alpha^2\alpha_s$, the same as (14.73). Thus the interference term must be included in calculating the two-jet cross section to this order. When it is, the soft and collinear divergences cancel[5]: the resulting two-jet cross section is IRC (infrared and collinear) 'safe'.

---

[5] The usual ultraviolet divergences in the loop graphs are removed by conventional renormalization.

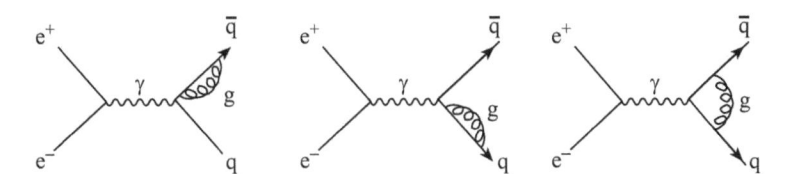

FIGURE 14.21
Virtual gluon corrections to figure 14.20.

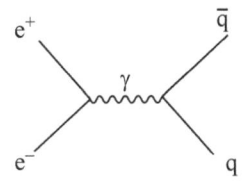

FIGURE 14.22
One-photon annihilation amplitude in $e^+e^- \to \bar{q}q$.

This result was first shown by Sterman and Weinberg (1977), in a paper which initiated the modern treatment of jets within the framework of QCD. They defined the two-jet differential cross section to include those events in which all but a fraction ϵ of the total e^+e^- energy E ($= \sqrt{Q^2}$) is emitted within some pair of oppositely directed cones of half-angle $\delta \ll 1$, lying at an angle θ to the e^+e^- beam line. Including the contributions of real and virtual gluons up to order $\alpha\alpha_s$, the result is (Muta 2010, section 5.4.1)

$$\left(\frac{d\sigma}{d\Omega}\right)_{2-\text{jet}} = \left(\frac{d\sigma}{d\Omega}\right)_{\text{pt}} \left[1 - \frac{4}{3}\frac{\alpha_s}{\pi}\left(3\ln\delta + 4\ln\delta\ln 2\epsilon + \frac{\pi^2}{3} - \frac{5}{2}\right)\right], \quad (14.76)$$

where $(\frac{d\sigma}{d\Omega})_{\text{pt}}$ is the contribution of the lowest-order graph, figure 14.22, which is given by equation (9.102) summed over quark colours and charges; terms of order δ and ϵ, and higher powers, are neglected. It is evident from (14.76) that the jet parameters ϵ and δ serve to control the soft and collinear divergences, which reappear as ϵ and δ tend to zero; they are 'resolution parameters'.

The remarkable cancellation of the soft and collinear divergences between the real and virtual emission processes is actually a general result in QED (recall that in chapter 11 we declined to pursue the problem of such infrared divergences). The Bloch–Nordsieck (1937) theorem states that 'soft' singularities cancel between real and virtual processes when one adds up all final states which are indistinguishable by virtue of the energy resolution of the apparatus. The Kinoshita (1962) Lee and Nauenberg (1964) theorem states, roughly speaking, that mass singularities are absent if one adds up all indis-

tinguishable mass-degenerate states. This is the reason for the finiteness of the Sterman-Weinberg 2-jet cross section, in an analogous QCD case.

Returning to (14.76), it is important to note that the angular distribution of this well-defined two-jet process is given precisely by the lowest-order expression (9.102), just as was hoped in the simple parton model of section 9.5. Of course, the cross section depends on the jet parameters δ and ϵ. The formula (14.76) can be used, for example, to estimate the angular radius of the jets, as a function of E.

Although the Sterman-Weinberg jet definition was historically the first, it is not the only possible one. Another, in some ways simpler, definition (Kramer and Lampe 1987) is directly phrased in terms of the offending denominators s_{13}^{-1} and s_{23}^{-1} in (14.67). Let us introduce the dimensionless jet mass variables

$$y_{ij} = s_{ij}/Q^2 = 2E_iE_j(1 - \cos\theta_{ij})/Q^2 \tag{14.77}$$

for any two partons i and j; s_{12} will be included, though no singularity is involved. Here E_i and E_j are the (massless) parton energies, and θ_{ij} is the angle between their 3-momenta, in the overall CMS. Then i and j are defined to be in one jet if y_{ij} is less than some given number y. Note that for small θ_{ij}, $s_{ij} \approx E_iE_j\theta_{ij}^2/Q^2$, so the single parameter y provides effectively both an energy and an angle cut. Clearly this definition is equivalent to a formulation in terms of strips $1 \le x_k < 1 - y$ on figure 14.7, as discussed earlier. Including contributions, as before, from figures 14.22, 14.21, and 14.16, the resulting 2-jet cross section is found to be (Kramer and Lampe 1987)

$$\sigma_{2-\text{jet}} = \sigma_{\text{pt}}[1 - \frac{2}{3}\frac{\alpha_s}{\pi}(2\ln^2 y + 3\ln y - 4y\ln y + 1 - \pi^2/3)]. \tag{14.78}$$

Terms of order y were calculated numerically. These include the contribution from the (non-singular) region $y_{12} < y$, where the two quarks are in one jet and the other jet is a pure gluon jet. Plainly the IRC singularities have been eliminated from (14.78), at the cost of the jet mass resolution parameter y. Kramer and Lampe also calculated the order α_s^2 corrections to (14.78).

These two ways of regulating the IRC divergences in the 2-jet partonic cross section have each been extensively developed into *jet algorithms*, as we shall briefly discuss in section 14.6.2.

14.6   Further developments

14.6.1   Test of non-Abelian nature of QCD in $e^+e^- \to$ 4 jets

We have seen in section 14.3.1 how the colour factors associated with different QCD vertices (problem 14.5) play an important part in determining the relative weights of different parton-level processes. The quark-gluon colour factor

C_F enters into the parton-level three-jet amplitude (14.67), but the triple-gluon vertex is not involved at order α_s. This vertex is an essential feature of non-Abelian gauge theories, being absent in Abelian theories such as QED. A direct measurement of the triple-gluon vertex colour factor, C_A, can be made in the process $e^+e^- \to 4$ jets.

4-jet events originate from the parton-level process $e^+e^- \to q\bar{q}g$ via three mechanisms: the emission of a second bremsstrahlung gluon, splitting of the first gluon into two gluons, and splitting of the first gluon into n_f quark pairs. As problem 14.5 shows, these three types of splitting vertices are characterized in cross sections by the colour factors C_F, C_A and $n_f T_R$, so that the cross section can be written as (Ali and Kramer 2011)

$$\sigma_{4-\text{jet}} = \left(\frac{\alpha_s}{\pi}\right) C_F[C_F \sigma_{bb} + C_A \sigma_{gg} + n_f T_R \sigma_{q\bar{q}}]. \tag{14.79}$$

Measurements yield (Abbiendi *et al.* 2001)

$$
\begin{aligned}
C_A/C_F &= 2.29 \pm 0.06[\text{stat.}] \pm 0.14[\text{syst.}] \\
T_R/C_F &= 0.38 \pm 0.03[\text{stat.}] \pm 0.06[\text{syst.}],
\end{aligned}
\tag{14.80}
$$

in good agreement with the theoretical predictions $C_A/C_F = 9/4$ and $T_R/C_F = 3/8$ in QCD.

14.6.2   Jet algorithms

From the examples already discussed in this chapter, it is clear that jets are an essential element in making comparisons between experimental measurements involving final state particles in detectors, and theoretical calculations at the parton level using perturbative QCD. Conceptually, jets provide a common representation for these two classes of event – those at the detector level, and those at the parton level. For precision comparisons, it is necessary to have a rigorous definition of a jet – a *jet algorithm* – which should be equally applicable at the detector, and at the parton, level. In the more than thirty years that have passed since Sterman and Weinberg's 1977 paper, many jet definitions have been developed and applied. All involve the basic notion of clustering together objects that are in some sense 'near' to each other. Two main classes of jet algorithm may be distinguished: cone algorithms based on proximity in coordinate space, as in the Sterman-Weinberg approach, and used extensively, until recently, at hadron colliders; and sequential recombination algorithms based on proximity in momentum space, as in the jet-mass criterion of Kramer and Lampe (1987), and widely used at e^+e^- and e p colliders. Recent general reviews of jet algorithms are provided by Salam (2010) and by Ali and Kramer (2011); see also Ellis *et al.* (2008), Campbell *et al.* (2007), and Kluth (2006). Here we shall give only a brief introduction to sequential recombination algorithms – all of which are IRC safe – since it seems likely that they will dominate future jet analyses.

The JADE algorithm (Bartel *et al.* 1986, Bethke *et al.* 1988) is a prominent early example of sequential recombination algorithms applied in e^+e^- annihilation reactions. Particles are clustered in a jet iteratively as long as the quantity y_{ij} of (14.77) is less than some prescribed value y_c. If for some pair (i, j), $y_{ij} < y_c$, particles i and j are combined into a compound object (with the resultant 4-momentum, typically), and the process continues by pairing the compound with a new particle k. The procedure stops when all y_{ij} distances are greater than y_c, and the compounds that remain at this stage are the jets, by definition.

One drawback with this scheme is that in higher orders of perturbation theory one meets terms of the form $\alpha_s^2 \ln^{2n} y$ (generalizations of the $\alpha_s \ln^2 y$ term in (14.78)). Such terms can be large enough to invalidate a perturbative approach. Also, it is possible for two soft particles moving in opposite directions to get combined in the early stages of clustering, which runs counter to the intuitive notion of a jet being restricted in angular radius. The k_t-algorithm (Catani *et al.* 1991) avoids these problems by replacing the y_{ij} of (14.77) by

$$y_{ij} = 2\min.[E_i^2, E_j^2](1 - \cos\theta_{ij})/Q^2. \tag{14.81}$$

This amounts to defining 'distance' by the minimum transverse momentum k_t of the particles in nearby collinear pairs. The use of the minimum energy ensures that the distance between two soft, back-to-back particles is larger than that between a soft particle and a hard one that is close to it in angle. The k_t algorithm was widely used at LEP.

The basic idea of the k_t algorithm was extended to hadron colliders (Ellis and Soper 1993, Catani *et al.* 1993), where the total energy of the hard scattering particles is not well defined experimentally. The distance measure y_{ij} is replaced by

$$d_{ij} = \min.[p_{ti}^{2p}, p_{tj}^{2p}][(y_i - y_j)^2 + (\phi_i - \phi_j)^2]/R^2 \tag{14.82}$$

where, for particle i, p_{ti} is the transverse momentum with respect to the (beam) z-axis, y_i is the rapidity along the beam axis (defined by $y_i = \frac{1}{2}\ln[(E_i + p_{zi})/(E_i - p_{zi})]$), ϕ_i is the azimuthal angle in the plane transverse to the beam, and R is a jet parameter. The variables y_i, ϕ_i have the property that they are invariant under boosts along the beam direction. In addition, recombination with the beam jets is controlled by the quantity $d_{ij} = k_{ti}^{2p}$, which is included along with the d_{ij}'s when recombining all the particles into (i) jets with non-zero transverse momentum, and (ii) beam jets. The power parameter p takes the value 1 in the (extended) k_t algorithm, and -1 in the 'anti-k_t' algorithm (Cacciari *et al.* 2008). Whereas the former (and $p = 0$) leads to irregularly shaped jet boundaries, the latter leads to cone-like boundaries. The choice $p = -1$ was made in early LHC analyses.

Problems

14.1

(a) Show that the antisymmetric 3q combination of equation (14.2) is (i) a determinant, and (ii) invariant under the transformation (14.14) for each colour wavefunction.

(b) Suppose that p_α and q_α stand for two $SU(3)_c$ colour wavefunctions, transforming under an infinitesimal $SU(3)_c$ transformation via

$$p' = (1 + i\boldsymbol{\eta} \cdot \boldsymbol{\lambda}/2)p,$$

and similarly for q. Consider the antisymmetric combination of their components, given by

$$\begin{pmatrix} p_2 q_3 - p_3 q_2 \\ p_3 q_1 - p_1 q_3 \\ p_1 q_2 - p_2 q_1 \end{pmatrix} \equiv \begin{pmatrix} Q_1 \\ Q_2 \\ Q_3 \end{pmatrix};$$

that is, $Q_\alpha = \epsilon_{\alpha\beta\gamma} p_\beta q_\gamma$. Check that the three components Q_α transform as a $\mathbf{3}_c^*$, in the particular case for which only the parameters η_1, η_2, η_3 and η_8 are non-zero. [Note: you will need the explicit forms of the $\boldsymbol{\lambda}$ matrices (appendix M); you need to verify the transformation law

$$Q' = (1 - i\boldsymbol{\eta} \cdot \boldsymbol{\lambda}^*/2)Q.]$$

14.2

(a) Verify that the normally ordered QCD interaction $\bar{\hat{q}}_f \gamma^\mu \frac{1}{2} \lambda_a \hat{q}_f \hat{A}_{a\mu}$ is C-invariant.

(b) Show that $\lambda_a \hat{F}_{a\mu\nu}$ transforms under $\mathbf{C}$ according to (14.36).

14.3 Verify that the Lorentz-invariant 'contraction' $\epsilon_{\mu\nu\rho\sigma} \hat{F}^{\mu\nu} \hat{F}^{\rho\sigma}$ of two $U(1)$ (Maxwell) field strength tensors is equal to $8\boldsymbol{E} \cdot \boldsymbol{B}$.

14.4 Verify that the cross section for the exchange of a single massless scalar gluon between two quarks (or between a quark and an antiquark) contains no '$1/\hat{t}^2$' factor.

14.5 This problem is concerned with the evaluation of various '*colour factors*'.

(a) Consider first the colour factor needed for equation (14.73). The 'colour wavefunction' part of the amplitude (14.59) is

$$\sum_c a_c(c_3) \chi^\dagger(c_1) \frac{\lambda_c}{2} \chi(c_2) \tag{14.83}$$

where c_1, c_2 and c_3 label the colour degree of freedom of the quark, antiquark and gluon respectively, and the sum on the index c has been indicated explicitly. The χ's are the colour wavefunctions of the quark and antiquark, and are represented by three-component column vectors; a convenient choice is

$$\chi(r) = \begin{pmatrix} 1 \\ 0 \\ 0 \end{pmatrix}, \quad \chi(b) = \begin{pmatrix} 0 \\ 1 \\ 0 \end{pmatrix}, \quad \chi(g) = \begin{pmatrix} 0 \\ 0 \\ 1 \end{pmatrix} \quad (14.84)$$

by analogy with the spin wavefunctions of SU(2). The cross section is obtained by forming the modulus squared of (14.83) and summing over the colour labels c_i:

$$\sum_{c,c_1,c_2,c_3} a_c(c_3)\chi_r^*(c_1)\frac{(\lambda_c)_{rs}}{2}\chi_s(c_2)\chi_l^*(c_2)\frac{(\lambda_d)_{lm}}{2}\chi_m(c_1)a_d^*(c_3)$$

$$(14.85)$$

where summation is understood on the matrix indices on the χ's and λ's, which have been indicated explicitly. In this form the expression is very similar to the *spin* summations considered in chapter 8 (cf equation (8.62)). We proceed to evaluate it as follows:

(i) Show that

$$\sum_{c_2}\chi_s(c_2)\chi_l^*(c_2) = \delta_{sl}.$$

(ii) Assuming the analogous result

$$\sum_{c_3} a_c(c_3)a_d^*(c_3) = \delta_{cd}$$

show that (14.85) becomes

$$\sum_{c=1}^{8}\left(\frac{\lambda_c}{2}\frac{\lambda_c}{2}\right)_{rr},$$

where the (implied) sum on r runs from 1 to 3.

(iii) The expression $\sum_c \frac{\lambda_c}{2}\frac{\lambda_c}{2}$ is just the Casimir operator $\hat{C}_2$ (see section M.5 in appendix M) for SU(3) in the fundamental representation **3**, which from (M.67) has the value $C_F\mathbf{1}_3$, where $\mathbf{1}_3$ is the unit 3×3 matrix, and $C_F = 4/3$. Hence show that the colour factor for (14.73) is 4.

Note that if we averaged over the colours of the initial quark, or considered one particular colour, the colour factor would be C_F.

(b) The colour part for the triple gluon vertex $g_1 \to g_2 + g_3$ is

$$\sum_{c,d,e} a_d^*(c_2) a_e^*(c_3) f_{dec} a_c(c_1).$$

Show that the modulus squared of this, averaged over the initial gluon colours and summed over the final gluon colours, is

$$\frac{1}{8} \sum_{c,d,e} f_{dec} f_{dec},$$

where each of c, d, e runs from 1 to 8. Deduce using (12.84) that this expression can be written as

$$\frac{1}{8} \sum_e \left(\sum_d G_d^{(8)} G_d^{(8)} \right)_{ee} ,$$

where $G_d^{(8)}$, $(d = 1 \ldots 8)$ are the 8×8 matrices representing the generators of SU(3) in the **8**-dimensional (adjoint) representation (see section 12.2). The expression $(\sum_d G_d^{(8)} G_d^{(8)})$ is the SU(3) Casimir operator $\hat{C}_2$ in the adjoint representation, which from (M.67) has the value $C_A 1_8$, where 1_8 is the 8×8 unit matrix, and $C_A = 3$. Hence show that the (averaged, summed) triple gluon vertex colour factor is $C_A = 3$.

(c) The colour part of the $g \to q + \bar{q}$ vertex is

$$\chi_r^*(c_3) \left(\frac{\lambda_c}{2} \right)_{rs} \chi_s(c_2) a_c(c_1).$$

Show that the modulus squared of this, averaged over the initial gluon colours and summed over the final quark colours is

$$\frac{1}{8} \sum_c \left(\frac{\lambda_c}{2} \frac{\lambda_c}{2} \right)_{rr} = \frac{1}{2}.$$

This number is usually denoted by T_R.

14.6 Verify equation (14.60).

14.7 Verify equation (14.72).

14.8 Verify that expression (14.68) becomes the factor in large parentheses in equation (14.73), when expressed in terms of the x_i's.

15

QCD II: Asymptotic Freedom, the Renormalization Group, and Scaling Violations

In the previous chapter we learned that QCD amplitudes contributing to $e^+e^- \to$ jets generally have IRC singularities, but that finite physical cross sections can be obtained by including together kinematically indistinguishable final states. The partial cross sections (for example $\sigma(e^+e^- \to 2$ jets$)$) will depend on the IRC cut-off parameter(s). What about the *fully inclusive* process $e^+e^- \to$ hadrons, where all final states are summed over? At order $\alpha\alpha_s$, the parton-level diagrams contributing to this process are the same ones we considered in section 14.5, namely figures 14.16, 14.21 and 14.22. If we denote the amplitudes for these contributions by F_{rg} (for real gluon emission), F_{vg} (for virtual gluon emission) and F_γ for the Born graph, then the partial cross section $\sigma(e^+e^- \to 2$ jets$)$ includes $|F_\gamma|^2$, the interference term $2\mathrm{Re}(F_\gamma F_{vg}^*)$, and the integral of $|F_{rg}|^2$ over strips near the boundaries of figure 14.17. At this order, the partial cross section $\sigma(e^+e^- \to 3$ jets$)$ is given by the integral of $|F_{rg}|^2$ over the remaining (interior) region of figure 14.17. The corresponding total cross section is thus simply the sum of $|F_\gamma|^2$, $2\mathrm{Re}(F_\gamma F_{vg}^*)$, and the integral of $|F_{rg}|^2$ over the whole of the $x_1 - x_2$ phase space. Clearly the IRC singularities will cancel, as in the 2-jet cross section, and the result will not depend on any IRC cut-off parameter. Indeed, the result is (see for example Muta 2010, section 5.1.2)

$$\sigma(e^+e^- \to \text{hadrons}) = \sigma_{pt}(Q^2)(1 + \alpha_s/\pi). \tag{15.1}$$

This fully inclusive cross section is finite and free of IRC cut-offs.

At first sight, this result might appear satisfactory. It predicts a cross section somewhat greater than σ_{pt}, as is observed in figure 14.1 – from which we might infer that $\alpha_s \sim 0.5$ or less. Assuming the expansion parameter is α_s/π, the implied perturbation series in powers of α_s would seem to be rapidly convergent. However, this is an illusion, which is dispelled as soon as we go to the next order in α_s (i.e. to the order $\alpha^2\alpha_s^2$ in the cross section).

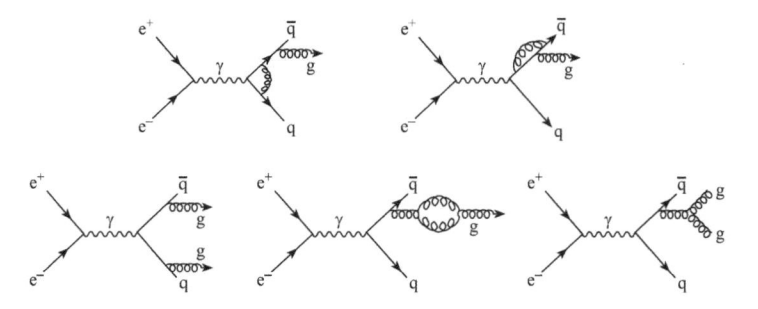

FIGURE 15.1
Some higher-order processes contributing to $e^+e^- \to$ hadrons at the parton level.

15.1   Higher-order QCD corrections to $\sigma(e^+e^- \to$ hadrons): large logarithms

Some typical graphs contributing to this order of the cross section are shown in figure 15.1 (note that, as with the $O(\alpha^2\alpha_s)$ terms, some graphs will contribute via their modulus squared and some via interference terms). The result was obtained numerically by Dine and Saperstein (1979), and analytically by Chetyrkin *et al.* (1979) and by Celmaster and Gonsalves (1980). For our present purposes, the crucial feature of the answer is the appearance of a term

$$\sigma_{\mathrm{pt}}\left[-\beta_0 \frac{\alpha_s^2}{\pi} \ln(Q^2/\mu^2)\right] \tag{15.2}$$

where μ is a mass scale (about which we shall shortly have a lot more to say, but which for the moment may be thought of as related in some way to an average quark mass), and the coefficient β_0 is given by

$$\beta_0 = \left(\frac{33 - 2N_f}{12\pi}\right) \tag{15.3}$$

where N_f is the number of 'active' flavours (e.g. $N_f = 5$ above the $b\bar{b}$ threshold). The term (15.2) raises the following problem. The ratio between it and the $O(\alpha\alpha_s)$ term is clearly

$$-\beta_0\alpha_s \ln(Q^2/\mu^2). \tag{15.4}$$

If we take $N_f = 5, \alpha_s \approx 0.4, \mu \sim 1$ GeV and $Q^2 \sim (10 \text{ GeV})^2$, (15.4) is of order 1, and can in no sense be regarded as a small perturbation. Furthermore, the correction (15.4), by itself, would predict large *scaling violations* in this cross

section – that is, large Q^2-dependent departures from the point-like Born cross section, $\sigma_{\mathrm{pt}}(Q^2)$. But the data actually follow the point-like prediction very well.

Suppose that, nevertheless, we consider the sum of (15.1) and (15.2), which is

$$\sigma_{\mathrm{pt}}[1 + \frac{\alpha_{\mathrm{s}}}{\pi}\{1 - \beta_0\alpha_{\mathrm{s}}\ln(Q^2/\mu^2)\}]. \tag{15.5}$$

This suggests that one effect, at least, of these higher-order corrections is to convert α_{s} to a Q^2-dependent quantity, namely $\alpha_{\mathrm{s}}\{1 - \beta_0\alpha_{\mathrm{s}}\ln(Q^2/\mu^2)\}$. We have seen something very like this before, in equation (11.56), for the case of QED. There is, however, one remarkable difference: here the coefficient of the ln is *negative*, whereas that in (11.56) is positive. Apart from this (vital!) difference, however, we can reasonably begin to think in terms of an effective 'Q^2-dependent strong coupling constant $\alpha_{\mathrm{s}}(Q^2)$'.

Pressing on with the next order $(\alpha^2\alpha_{\mathrm{s}}^3)$ terms, we encounter a term (Samuel and Surguladze 1991, Gorishnii *et al.* 1991)

$$\sigma_{\mathrm{pt}}\left[\alpha_{\mathrm{s}}\beta_0\ln(Q^2/\mu^2)\right]^2\frac{\alpha_{\mathrm{s}}}{\pi}, \tag{15.6}$$

and the ratio between this and (15.2) is precisely (15.4) once again! We are now strongly inclined to suspect that we are seeing, in this class of terms, an expansion of the form $(1+x)^{-1} = 1 - x + x^2 - x^3 \ldots$. If true, this would imply that all terms of the form (15.2) and (15.6), and higher, *sum up* to give (cf (11.63))

$$\sigma_{\mathrm{pt}}\left[1 + \frac{\alpha_{\mathrm{s}}/\pi}{1 + \alpha_{\mathrm{s}}\beta_0\ln(Q^2/\mu^2)}\right]. \tag{15.7}$$

The 're-summation' effected by (15.7) has a remarkable effect: the 'dangerous' large logarithms in (15.2) and (15.6) are now effectively in the *denominator* (cf (11.56)), and their effect is such as to *reduce* the effective value of α_{s} as Q^2 increases – exactly the property of *asymptotic freedom*.

We hasten to say that of course this is not how the property was discovered – which was, rather, through the calculations of Politzer (1973) and Gross and Wilczek (1973). Prior to their work, it was widely believed that any quantum field theory would have a running coupling which behaved like that of QED which, as we saw in section 11.5.3, increases for large Q^2 (short distances). Such behaviour would make the scaling violations due to a term like (15.7) even worse. It was therefore a mystery how quantum field theory could account for the small scaling violations seen in the data. The discovery that the running couplings of non-Abelian gauge theories became weaker at large Q^2 opened the way for a quantitative understanding of parton-model scaling, and perturbative QCD corrections to it.

To place the asymptotic freedom calculation in its proper context requires a considerable detour. Referring to our previous discussion, we may ask: are we guaranteed that still-higher-order terms will indeed continue to contain pieces corresponding to the expression of (15.7)? And what exactly is the

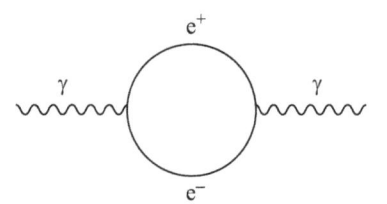

FIGURE 15.2
One-loop vacuum polarization contribution to Z_3.

mass parameter μ? Answering these questions will lead to the important body of ideas going under the name of the 'renormalization group'.

15.2   The renormalization group and related ideas in QED

15.2.1   Where do the large logs come from?

We have taken the title of this section from that of Section 18.1 in Weinberg (1996), which we have found very illuminating, and to which we refer for a more detailed discussion.

As we have just mentioned, the phenomenon of 'large logarithms' arises also in the simpler case of QED. There, however, the factor corresponding to $\alpha_s \beta_0 \sim \frac{1}{4}$ is $\alpha/3\pi \sim 10^{-3}$, so that it is only at quite unrealistically enormous $|q^2|$ values that the corresponding factor $(\alpha/3\pi)\ln(|q^2|/m_e^2)$ (where m_e is the electron mass) becomes of order unity. Nevertheless, the origin of the logarithmic term is essentially the same in both cases, and the technicalities are much simpler for QED (no photon self-interactions, no ghosts). We shall therefore forget about QCD for a while, and concentrate on QED. Indeed, the discussion of renormalization of QED given in chapter 11 will be sufficient to answer the question in the title of this subsection.

For the answer does, in fact, fundamentally have to do with renormalization. Let us go back to the renormalization of the charge in QED. We learned in chapter 11 that the renormalized charge e was given in terms of the 'bare' charge e_0 by the relation $e = e_0(Z_2/Z_1)Z_3^{\frac{1}{2}}$ (see (11.6)), where in fact due to the Ward identity Z_1 and Z_2 are equal (section 11.6), so that only $Z_3^{\frac{1}{2}}$ is needed. To order e^2 in renormalized perturbation theory, including only the e^+e^- loop of figure 15.2, Z_3 is given by (cf (11.31))

$$Z_3^{[2]} = 1 + \Pi_\gamma^{[2]}(0) \tag{15.8}$$

where, from (11.23) and (11.24),

$$\Pi_\gamma^{[2]}(q^2) = 8e^2 i \int_0^1 dx \int \frac{d^4 k'}{(2\pi)^4} \frac{x(1-x)}{(k'^2 - \Delta_\gamma + i\epsilon)^2} \tag{15.9}$$

and $\Delta_\gamma = m_e^2 - x(1-x)q^2$ with $q^2 < 0$. We regularize the k' integral by a cut-off Λ as explained in sections 10.3.1 and 10.3.2, obtaining (problem 15.1)

$$\Pi_\gamma^{[2]}(q^2) = -\frac{e^2}{\pi^2} \int_0^1 dx\, x(1-x) \left\{ \ln\left(\frac{\Lambda + \sqrt{\Lambda^2 + \Delta_\gamma}}{\Delta_\gamma^{\frac{1}{2}}} \right) - \frac{\Lambda}{(\Lambda^2 + \Delta_\gamma)^{1/2}} \right\}. \tag{15.10}$$

Setting $q^2 = 0$ and retaining the dominant $\ln\Lambda$ term, we find that

$$\left(Z_3^{[2]} \right)^{\frac{1}{2}} = 1 - \left(\frac{\alpha}{3\pi} \right) \ln(\Lambda/m_e). \tag{15.11}$$

It is not a coincidence that the coefficient $\alpha/3\pi$ of the ultraviolet divergence is also the coefficient of the $\ln(|q^2|/m_e^2)$ term in (11.55)–(11.57); we need to understand why.

We first recall how (11.55) was arrived at. It refers to the *renormalized* self-energy part, which is defined by the 'subtracted' form

$$\bar{\Pi}_\gamma^{[2]}(q^2) = \Pi_\gamma^{[2]}(q^2) - \Pi_\gamma^{[2]}(0). \tag{15.12}$$

In the process of subtraction, the dependence on the cut-off Λ disappears and we are left with

$$\bar{\Pi}_\gamma^{[2]}(q^2) = -\frac{2\alpha}{\pi} \int_0^1 dx\, x(1-x) \ln\left[\frac{m_e^2}{m_e^2 - q^2 x(1-x)} \right] \tag{15.13}$$

as in equation (11.34). For large values of $|q^2|$ this leads to the 'large log' term $(\alpha/3\pi)\ln(|q^2|/m_e^2)$. Now, in order to form such a term, it is obviously not possible to have just '$\ln|q^2|$' appearing: the argument of the logarithm must be dimensionless, so that some mass scale must be present, to which $|q^2|$ can be compared. In the present case, that mass scale is evidently m_e, which entered via the quantity $\Pi_\gamma^{[2]}(0)$, or equivalently via the renormalization constant $Z_3^{[2]}$ (cf (15.11)). This is the beginning of the answer to our questions.

Why is it m_e that enters into $\Pi_\gamma^{[2]}(0)$ or Z_3? Part of the answer – once again – is of course that a '$\ln\Lambda$' cannot appear in that form, but must be '$\ln(\Lambda/\text{some mass})$'. So we must enquire: what determines the 'some mass'? With this question we have reached the heart of the problem (for the moment). The answer is, in fact, not immediately obvious: it lies in the *prescription used to define the renormalized coupling constant*; this prescription, whatever it is, determines Z_3.

The value (15.8) (or (11.31)) was determined from the requirement that the $O(e^2)$ corrected photon propagator (in $\xi = 1$ gauge) had the simple form

$-ig_{\mu\nu}/q^2$ as $q^2 \to 0$; that is, as the photon goes on-shell. Now, this is a perfectly 'natural' definition of the renormalized charge – but it is by no means forced upon us. In fact the appearance of a singularity in $Z_3^{[2]}$ as $m_e \to 0$ suggests that it is inappropriate to the case in which fermion masses are neglected. We could in principle choose a different value of q^2, say $q^2 = -\mu^2$, at which to 'subtract'. Certainly the difference between $\Pi_\gamma^{[2]}(q^2 = 0)$ and $\Pi_\gamma^{[2]}(q^2 = -\mu^2)$ is finite as $\Lambda \to \infty$, so such a redefinition of 'the' renormalized charge would only amount to a finite shift. Nevertheless, even a finite shift is alarming, to those accustomed to a certain 'sanctity' in the value $\alpha = \frac{1}{137}$! We have to concede, however, that if the point of renormalization is to render amplitudes finite by taking certain constants from experiment, then any choice of such constants should be as good as any other – for example, the 'charge' defined at $q^2 = -\mu^2$ rather than at $q^2 = 0$.

Thus there is, actually, a considerable *arbitrariness* in the way renormalization can be done – a fact to which we did not draw attention in our earlier discussions in chapters 10 and 11. Nevertheless, it must somehow be the case that, despite this arbitrariness, *physical results remain the same*. We shall come back to this important point shortly.

15.2.2   Changing the renormalization scale

The recognition that the *renormalization scale* ($-\mu^2$ in this case) is arbitrary suggests a way in which we might exploit the situation, so as to avoid large '$\ln(|q^2|/m_e^2)$' terms: we renormalize at a *large* value of μ^2! Consider what happens if we define a new $Z_3^{[2]}$ by

$$Z_3^{[2]}(\mu) = 1 + \Pi_\gamma^{[2]}(q^2 = -\mu^2). \tag{15.14}$$

Then for $\mu^2 \gg m_e^2$, but $\mu^2 \ll \Lambda^2$, we have

$$\left(Z_3^{[2]}(\mu)\right)^{\frac{1}{2}} = 1 - \left(\frac{\alpha}{3\pi}\right)\ln\left(\Lambda/\mu\right), \tag{15.15}$$

and a new renormalized self-energy

$$\bar{\Pi}_\gamma^{[2]}(q^2, \mu) = \Pi_\gamma^{[2]}(q^2) - \Pi_\gamma^{[2]}(q^2 = -\mu^2)$$
$$= -\frac{e^2}{2\pi^2}\int_0^1 dx\, x(1-x)\ln\left[\frac{m_e^2 + \mu^2 x(1-x)}{m_e^2 - q^2 x(1-x)}\right]. \tag{15.16}$$

For μ^2 and $-q^2$ both $\gg m_e^2$, the logarithm is now $\ln(|q^2|/\mu^2)$ which is small when $|q^2|$ is of order μ^2. It seems, therefore, that with this different renormalization prescription we have 'tamed' the large logarithms.

However, we have forgotten that, for consistency, the 'e' we should now be using is the one defined, in terms of e_0, via

$$e_\mu = \left(Z_3^{[2]}(\mu)\right)^{\frac{1}{2}} e_0 = \left(1 - \frac{\alpha}{3\pi}\ln(\Lambda/\mu)\right)e_0 \tag{15.17}$$

rather than

$$e = \left(Z_3^{[2]}\right)^{\frac{1}{2}} e_0 = \left(1 - \frac{\alpha}{3\pi}\ln(\Lambda/m_e)\right) e_0, \tag{15.18}$$

working always to one-loop order with an e^+e^- loop. The relation between e_μ and e is then

$$e_\mu = \frac{\left(1 - \frac{\alpha}{3\pi}\ln(\Lambda/\mu)\right)}{\left(1 - \frac{\alpha}{3\pi}\ln(\Lambda/m_e)\right)} e \approx \left(1 + \frac{\alpha}{3\pi}\ln(\mu/m_e)\right) e \tag{15.19}$$

to leading order in α. Equation (15.19) indeed represents, as anticipated, a finite shift from 'e' to 'e_μ', but the problem with it is that a 'large log' has resurfaced in the form of $\ln(\mu/m_e)$ (remember that our idea was to take $\mu^2 \gg m_e^2$). Although the numerical coefficient of the log in (15.19) is certainly small, a similar procedure applied to QCD will involve the larger coefficient $\beta_0\alpha_s$ as in (15.5), and the correction analogous to (15.19) will be of order 1, invalidating the approach.

We have to be more subtle. Instead of making one jump from m_e^2 to a large value μ^2, we need to proceed in stages. We can calculate e_μ from e as long as μ is not too different from m_e. Then we can proceed to $e_{\mu'}$ for μ' not too different from μ, and so on. Rather than thinking of such a process in discrete stages $m_e \to \mu \to \mu' \to \ldots$, it is more convenient to consider infinitesimal steps – that is, we regard $e_{\mu'}$ at the scale μ' as being a continuous function of e_μ at scale μ, and of whatever other dimensionless variables exist in the problem (since the e's are themselves dimensionless). In the present case, these other variables are μ'/μ and m_e/μ, so that $e_{\mu'}$ must have the form

$$e_{\mu'} = E(e_\mu, \mu'/\mu, m_e/\mu). \tag{15.20}$$

Differentiating (15.20) with respect to μ' and letting $\mu' = \mu$ we obtain

$$\mu \frac{de_\mu}{d\mu} = \beta_{em}(e_\mu, m_e/\mu) \tag{15.21}$$

where

$$\beta_{em}(e_\mu, m_e/\mu) = \left[\frac{\partial}{\partial z} E(e_\mu, z, m_e/\mu)\right]_{z=1}. \tag{15.22}$$

For $\mu \gg m_e$ equation (15.21) reduces to

$$\mu \frac{de_\mu}{d\mu} = \beta_{em}(e_\mu, 0) \equiv \beta_{em}(e_\mu), \tag{15.23}$$

which is a form of *Callan–Symanzik equation* (Callan 1970, Symanzik 1970); it governs the change of the coupling constant e_μ as the renormalization scale μ changes.

To this one-loop order, it is easy to calculate the crucial quantity $\beta_{\text{em}}(e_\mu)$. Returning to (15.17), we may write the bare coupling e_0 as

$$
\begin{aligned}
e_0 &= e_\mu \left(1 - \frac{\alpha}{3\pi} \ln(\Lambda/\mu)\right)^{-1} \\
&\approx e_\mu \left(1 + \frac{\alpha}{3\pi} \ln(\Lambda/\mu)\right) \\
&\approx e_\mu \left(1 + \frac{\alpha_\mu}{3\pi} \ln(\Lambda/\mu)\right)
\end{aligned}
\tag{15.24}
$$

where the last step follows from the fact that e and e_μ differ by $O(e^3)$, which would be a higher-order correction to (15.24). Now the unrenormalized coupling is certainly independent of μ. Hence, differentiating (15.24) with respect to μ at fixed e_0, we find

$$
\left.\frac{de_\mu}{d\mu}\right|_{e_0} - \frac{e_\mu \alpha_\mu}{3\pi\mu} - \ln(\Lambda/\mu) \cdot \frac{e_\mu^2}{4\pi^2} \left.\frac{de_\mu}{d\mu}\right|_{e_0} = 0.
\tag{15.25}
$$

Working to order e_μ^3 we can drop the last term in (15.25), obtaining finally (to one-loop order)

$$
\left.\mu\frac{de_\mu}{d\mu}\right|_{e_0} = \frac{e_\mu^3}{12\pi^2} \quad \left(\equiv \beta_{\text{em}}^{[2]}(e_\mu)\right).
\tag{15.26}
$$

We can now integrate equation (15.26) to obtain e_μ at an arbitrary scale μ, in terms of its value at some scale $\mu = M$, chosen in practice large enough so that for variable scales μ greater than M we can neglect m_e compared with μ, but small enough so that $\ln(M/m_e)$ terms do not invalidate the perturbation theory calculation of e_M from e. The solution of (15.26) is then (problem 15.2)

$$
\ln(\mu/M) = 6\pi^2 \left(\frac{1}{e_M^2} - \frac{1}{e_\mu^2}\right)
\tag{15.27}
$$

or equivalently

$$
e_\mu^2 = \frac{e_M^2}{1 - \frac{e_M^2}{12\pi^2} \ln(\mu^2/M^2)},
\tag{15.28}
$$

which is

$$
\alpha_\mu = \frac{\alpha_M}{1 - \frac{\alpha_M}{3\pi} \ln(\mu^2/M^2)}
\tag{15.29}
$$

where $\alpha = e^2/4\pi$. The crucial point is that the 'large log' is now in the *denominator* (and has coefficient $\alpha_M/3\pi$!). We note that the general solution of (15.23) may be written as

$$
\ln(\mu/M) = \int_{e_M}^{e_\mu} \frac{de}{\beta_{\text{em}}(e)}.
\tag{15.30}
$$

We have made progress in understanding how the coupling changes as the renormalization scale changes, and how 'large logarithmic' change as in (15.19) can be brought under control via (15.29). The final piece in the puzzle

is to understand how this can help us with the large $-q^2$ behaviour of our cross section, the problem we originally started from.

15.2.3 The RGE and large $-q^2$ behaviour in QED

To see the connection we need to implement the fundamental requirement, stated at the end of section 15.2.2, that predictions for physically measurable quantities must *not* depend on the renormalization scale μ. Consider, for example, our annihilation cross section σ for $e^+e^- \to$ hadrons, pretending that the one-loop corrections we are interested in are those due to QED rather than QCD. We need to work in the spacelike region, so as to be consistent with all the foregoing discussion. To make this clear, we shall now denote the 4-momentum of the virtual photon by q rather than Q, and take $q^2 < 0$ as in sections 15.2.1 and 15.2.2. Bearing in mind the way we used the 'dimensionless-ness' of the e's in (15.20), let us focus on the dimensionless ratio $\sigma/\sigma_{\rm pt} \equiv S$. Neglecting all masses, S can only be a function of the dimensionless ratio $|q^2|/\mu^2$ and of e_μ:

$$S = S(|q^2|/\mu^2, e_\mu). \tag{15.31}$$

But S must ultimately have no μ dependence. It follows that *the μ^2 dependence arising via the $|q^2|/\mu^2$ argument must cancel that associated with e_μ.* This is why the μ^2-dependence of e_μ controls the $|q^2|$ dependence of S, and hence of σ. In symbols, this condition is represented by the equation

$$\left(\left.\frac{\partial}{\partial\mu}\right|_{e_\mu} + \left.\frac{de_\mu}{d\mu}\right|_{e_0} \frac{\partial}{\partial e_\mu} \right) S\left(|q^2|/\mu^2, e_\mu\right) = 0, \tag{15.32}$$

or

$$\left(\left.\mu\frac{\partial}{\partial\mu}\right|_{e_\mu} + \beta_{\rm em}(e_\mu)\frac{\partial}{\partial e_\mu} \right) S\left(|q|^2/\mu^2, e_\mu\right) = 0. \tag{15.33}$$

Equation (15.33) is referred to as 'the renormalization group equation (RGE) for S'. The terminology goes back to Stueckelberg and Peterman (1953), who were the first to discuss the freedom associated with the choice of renormalization scale. The 'group' connotation is a trifle obscure – but all it really amounts to is the idea that if we do one infinitesimal shift in μ^2, and then another, the result will be a third such shift; in other words, it is a kind of 'translation group'. It was, however, Gell-Mann and Low (1954) who realized how equation (15.33) could be used to calculate the large $|q^2|$ behaviour of S, as we now explain.

It is convenient to work in terms of μ^2 and α rather than μ and e. Equation (15.33) is then

$$\left(\left.\mu^2\frac{\partial}{\partial\mu^2}\right|_{\alpha_\mu} + \beta_{\rm em}(\alpha_\mu)\frac{\partial}{\partial\alpha_\mu} \right) S\left(|q^2|/\mu^2, \alpha_\mu\right) = 0, \tag{15.34}$$

where $\beta_{\text{em}}(\alpha_\mu)$ is defined by

$$\beta_{\text{em}}(\alpha_\mu) \equiv \mu^2 \frac{\partial \alpha_\mu}{\partial \mu^2}\bigg|_{e_0}. \tag{15.35}$$

From (15.35) and (15.26) we deduce that, to the one-loop order to which we are working,

$$\beta_{\text{em}}^{[2]}(\alpha_\mu) = \frac{e_\mu}{4\pi} \beta_{\text{em}}^{[2]}(e_\mu) = \frac{\alpha_\mu^2}{3\pi}. \tag{15.36}$$

Now introduce the important variable

$$t = \ln(|q^2|/\mu^2). \tag{15.37}$$

Equation (15.34) then becomes

$$\left[-\frac{\partial}{\partial t} + \beta_{\text{em}}(\alpha_\mu) \frac{\partial}{\partial \alpha_\mu} \right] S\left(e^t, \alpha_\mu\right) = 0. \tag{15.38}$$

This is a first-order differential equation which can be solved by implicitly defining a new function – the *running coupling* $\alpha(|q^2|)$ – as follows (compare (15.30)):

$$t = \int_{\alpha_\mu}^{\alpha(|q^2|)} \frac{d\alpha}{\beta_{\text{em}}(\alpha)}. \tag{15.39}$$

To see how this helps, we have to recall how to differentiate an integral with respect to one of its limits – or, more generally, the formulae

$$\frac{\partial}{\partial a} \int^{f(a)} g(x) dx = g\left(f(a)\right) \frac{\partial f}{\partial a}. \tag{15.40}$$

First, let us differentiate (15.39) with respect to t at fixed α_μ; we obtain

$$1 = \frac{1}{\beta_{\text{em}}(\alpha(|q^2|))} \frac{\partial \alpha(|q^2|)}{\partial t}. \tag{15.41}$$

Next, differentiate (15.39) with respect to α_μ at fixed t (note that $\alpha(|q^2|)$ will depend on μ and hence on α_μ); we obtain

$$0 = \frac{\partial \alpha(|q^2|)}{\partial \alpha_\mu} \frac{1}{\beta_{\text{em}}(\alpha(|q^2|))} - \frac{1}{\beta_{\text{em}}(\alpha_\mu)} \tag{15.42}$$

the minus sign coming from the fact that α_μ is the lower limit in (15.39). From (15.41) and (15.42) we find

$$\left[-\frac{\partial}{\partial t} + \beta_{\text{em}}(\alpha_\mu) \frac{\partial}{\partial \alpha_\mu} \right] \alpha(|q^2|) = 0. \tag{15.43}$$

It follows that $S(1, \alpha(|q^2|))$ is a solution of (15.38).

This is a remarkable result. It shows that all the dependence of S on the (momentum)^2 variable $|q^2|$ enters through that of the running coupling $\alpha(|q^2|)$. Of course, this result is only valid in a regime of $-q^2$ which is much greater than all quantities with dimension (mass)^2 – for example the squares of all particle masses, which do not appear in (15.31). This is why the technique applies only at 'high' $-q^2$. The result implies that if we can calculate $S(1, \alpha_\mu)$ (i.e. S at the point $q^2 = -\mu^2$) at some definite order in perturbation theory, then replacing α_μ by $\alpha(|q^2|)$ will allow us to predict the q^2-dependence (at large $-q^2$). All we need to do is solve (15.39). Indeed, for QED with one e^+e^- loop we have seen that $\beta_{em}^{[2]}(\alpha) = \alpha^2/3\pi$. Hence integrating (15.39) we obtain

$$\alpha(|q^2|) = \frac{\alpha_\mu}{1 - \frac{\alpha_\mu}{3\pi}t} = \frac{\alpha_\mu}{1 - \frac{\alpha_\mu}{3\pi}\ln(|q^2|/\mu^2)}. \tag{15.44}$$

This is almost exactly the formula we proposed in (11.57), on plausibility grounds.[1]

Suppose now that the leading QED perturbative contribution to $S(1, \alpha_\mu)$ is $S_1\alpha_\mu$. Then the terms contained in $S(1, \alpha(|q^2|))$ in this approximation can be found by expanding in powers of α_μ:

$$\begin{aligned} S(1, \alpha(|q^2|)) &\approx 1 + S_1\alpha(|q^2|) = 1 + S_1\alpha_\mu \left[1 - \frac{\alpha_\mu}{3\pi}t\right]^{-1} \\ &= 1 + S_1\alpha_\mu \left[1 + \frac{\alpha_\mu t}{3\pi} + \left(\frac{\alpha_\mu t}{3\pi}\right)^2 + \dots\right], \end{aligned} \tag{15.45}$$

where $t = \ln(|q^2|/\mu^2)$. The next-higher-order calculation of $S(1, \alpha_\mu)$ would be $S_2\alpha_\mu^2$, say, which generates the terms

$$S_2\alpha^2(|q^2|) = S_2\alpha_\mu^2 \left[1 + \frac{2\alpha_\mu t}{3\pi} + \dots\right]. \tag{15.46}$$

Comparing (15.45) and (15.46) we see that each power of the large log factor appearing in (15.46) comes with one more power of α_μ than in (15.45). Provided α_μ is small, then, the *leading* terms in $t, t^2, \dots$ are contained in (15.45). It is in this sense that replacing $S(1, \alpha_\mu)$ by $S(1, \alpha(|q^2|))$ sums all 'leading log terms'.

In fact, of course, the one-loop (and higher) corrections to S in which we are really interested are those due to QCD, rather than QED, corrections. But the logic is exactly the same. The leading ($O(\alpha_s)$) perturbative contribution to $S = \sigma/\sigma_{pt}$ at $q^2 = -\mu^2$ is given in (15.1) as $\alpha_s(\mu^2)/\pi$. It follows that the 'leading log corrections' at high $-q^2$ are summed up by replacing this expression by $\alpha_s(|q^2|)/\pi$, where the running $\alpha_s(|q^2|)$ is determined by solving (15.39) with the QCD analogue of (15.36) – to which we now turn.

---

[1] The difference has to do, of course, with the different renormalization prescriptions. Eq (11.57) is written in terms of an 'α' defined at $q^2 = 0$, and without neglect of m_e.

15.3   Back to QCD: asymptotic freedom

15.3.1   One loop calculation

The reader will of course have realized, some time back, that the quantity β_0 introduced in (15.3) must be precisely the coefficient of α_s^2 in the one-loop contribution to the β-function of QCD defined by

$$\beta_s = \mu^2 \frac{\partial \alpha_s}{\partial \mu^2}\bigg|_{\text{fixed bare } \alpha_s} \quad ; \tag{15.47}$$

that is to say,

$$\beta_s(\text{one loop}) = -\beta_0 \alpha_s^2 \tag{15.48}$$

with

$$\beta_0 = \frac{33 - 2N_f}{12\pi}. \tag{15.49}$$

For $N_f \leq 16$ the quantity β_0 is *positive*, so that the sign of (15.48)) is opposite to that of the QED analogue, equation (15.36). Correspondingly, (15.44) is replaced by

$$\alpha_s(|q^2|) = \frac{\alpha_s(\mu^2)}{[1 + \alpha_s(\mu^2)\beta_0 \ln(Q^2/\mu^2)]}, \tag{15.50}$$

where $Q^2 = |q^2|$.[2] Then replacing α_s in (15.1) by (15.50) leads to (15.7).

Thus in QCD the strong coupling runs in the opposite way to QED, becoming smaller at large values of Q^2 (or small distances) – the property of asymptotic freedom. The justly famous result (15.49) was first obtained by Politzer (1973), Gross and Wilczek (1973), and 't Hooft. 't Hooft's result, announced at a conference in Marseilles in 1972, was not published. The published calculation of Politzer and of Gross and Wilczek quickly attracted enormous interest, because it immediately offered a way to understand how the successful parton model could be reconciled with the undoubtedly very strong binding forces between quarks. The resolution, we now understand, lies in quite subtle properties of renormalized quantum field theory, involving first the exposure of 'large logarithms', then their re-summation in terms of the running coupling, and of course the crucial sign of the β-function. Not only did the result (15.49) explain the success of the parton model: it also, we repeat, opened the prospect of performing reliable perturbative calculations in a *strongly* interacting theory, at least at high Q^2. For example, at sufficiently high Q^2, we can reliably compute the β function in perturbation theory. The result of Politzer and of Gross and Wilczek, when combined with

---

[2]Except that in (15.50) α_s is evaluated at large *spacelike* values of q^2, whereas in (15.7) it is wanted at large *timelike* values. Readers troubled by this may consult Peskin and Schroeder (1995) section 18.5. The difficulty is evaded in the approach of section 15.6 below.

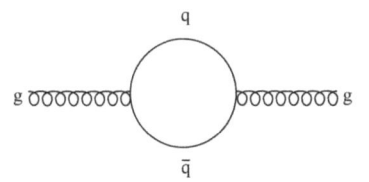

FIGURE 15.3

qq̄ vacuum polarization correction to the gluon propagator.

the motivations for a colour $SU(3)$ group discussed in the previous chapter, led rapidly to the general acceptance of QCD as the theory of strong interactions, a conclusion reinforced by the demonstration by Coleman and Gross (1973) that no theory without Yang-Mills fields possessed the property of asymptotic freedom.

In section 11.5.3 we gave the conventional physical interpretation of the way in which the running of the QED coupling tends to *increase* its value at distances short enough to probe inside the screening provided by e^+e^- pairs ($|q|^{-1} \ll m_e^{-1}$). This vacuum polarization screening effect is also present in (15.49) via the term $-\frac{2N_f}{12\pi}$, the value of which can be quite easily understood. It arises from the '$q\bar{q}$' vacuum polarization diagram of figure 15.3, which is precisely analogous to the e^+e^- diagram used to calculate $\bar{\Pi}_\gamma^{[2]}(q^2)$ in QED. The only new feature in figure 15.3 is the presence of the $\frac{\lambda}{2}$-matrices at each vertex. If 'a' and 'b' are the colour labels of the ingoing and outgoing gluons, the $\frac{\lambda}{2}$-matrix factors must be

$$\sum_{\alpha,\beta=1}^{3} \left(\frac{\lambda_a}{2}\right)_{\alpha\beta} \left(\frac{\lambda_b}{2}\right)_{\beta\alpha} \tag{15.51}$$

since there are no free quark indices (of type α, β) on the external legs of the diagram. It is simple to check that (15.51) has the value $\frac{1}{2}\delta_{ab}$ (this is, in fact, the way the λ's are conventionally normalized). Hence for one quark flavour we expect '$\alpha/3\pi$' to be replaced by '$\alpha_s/6\pi$', in agreement with the second term in (15.49).

The all-important, positive, first term must therefore be due to the gluons. The one-loop graphs contributing to the calculation of β_0 are shown in figure 15.4. They include figure 15.3, of course, but there are also, characteristically, graphs involving the gluon self-coupling which is absent in QED, and also (in covariant gauges) ghost loops. We do not want to enter into the details of the calculation of $\beta(\alpha_s)$ here (they are given in Peskin and Schroeder 1995, chapter 16, for example), but it would be nice to have a simple intuitive picture of the 'antiscreening' result in terms of the gluon interactions, say. Unfortunately no fully satisfactory simple explanation exists, though the reader may be inter-

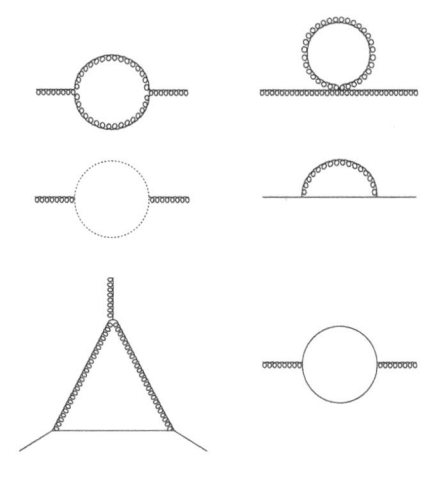

FIGURE 15.4
Graphs contributing to the one-loop β function in QCD. The curly line represents a gluon, a dotted line a ghost (see section 13.3.3) and a straight line a quark.

ested to consult Hughes (1980, 1981) and Nielsen (1981) for a 'paramagnetic' type of explanation, rather than a 'dielectric' one.

Returning to (15.50), we note that the equation effectively provides a prediction of α_s at any scale Q^2, given its value at a particular scale $Q^2 = \mu^2$, which must be taken from experiment. The reference scale is now normally taken to be the Z^0 mass; the value $\alpha_s(m_Z^2)$ then plays the role in QCD that $\alpha \sim 1/137$ does in QED.

Despite appearances, equation (15.50) does not really involve two parameters – after all, (15.47) is only a first-order differential equation. By introducing

$$\ln \Lambda_{\text{QCD}}^2 = \ln \mu^2 - 1/(\beta_0 \alpha_s(\mu^2)), \qquad (15.52)$$

equation (15.50) can be rewritten (problem 15.3) as

$$\alpha_s(Q^2) = \frac{1}{\beta_0 \ln(Q^2/\Lambda_{\text{QCD}}^2)}. \qquad (15.53)$$

Equation (15.53) is equivalent to (cf (15.30))

$$\ln \left(Q^2/\Lambda_{\text{QCD}}^2 \right) = \int_{\alpha_s(Q^2)}^{\infty} \frac{d\alpha_s}{\beta_s(\text{one loop})} \qquad (15.54)$$

with $\beta_s(\text{one loop}) = -\beta_0 \alpha_s^2$. Λ_{QCD} is therefore an integration constant, representing the scale at which α_s would diverge to infinity (if we extended our calculation beyond its perturbative domain of validity). More usefully, Λ_{QCD}

is a measure of the scale at which α_s really does become 'strong'. The extraction of a value of Λ_{QCD} is a somewhat complicated matter, as we shall briefly indicate in the following section, but a typical value is in the region of 200 MeV. Note that this is a distance scale of order $(200 \text{ MeV})^{-1} \sim 1$ fm, just about the size of a hadron – a satisfactory connection.

15.3.2 Higher-order calculations, and experimental comparison

So far we have discussed only the 'one-loop' calculation of $\beta(\alpha_s)$. The general perturbative expansion for β_s can be written as

$$\beta_s(\alpha_s) = -\beta_0 \alpha_s^2 - \beta_1 \alpha_s^3 - \beta_2 \alpha_s^4 + \ldots \qquad (15.55)$$

where β_0 is the one-loop coefficient given in (15.49), β_1 is the two-loop coefficient, and so on. β_1 was calculated by Caswell (1974) and Jones (1974), and has the value

$$\beta_1 = \frac{153 - 19 N_f}{24 \pi^2}. \qquad (15.56)$$

The three-loop coefficient β_2, obtained by Tarasov *et al.* (1980) and by Larin and Vermaseren (1993), is

$$\beta_2 = \frac{77139 - 15099 N_f + 325 N_f^2}{3456 \pi^2}. \qquad (15.57)$$

The four-loop coefficient β_3 was calculated by van Ritbergen *et al.* (1997) and by Czakon (2005); we shall not give it here. A technical point to note is that while β_0 and β_1 are independent of the scheme adopted for renormalization (see appendix O), the higher-order coefficients do depend on it; the value (15.57) is in the widely used $\overline{\text{MS}}$ scheme. Likewise, Λ_{QCD} will be scheme-dependent (see appendix O), and the value $\Lambda_{\overline{\text{MS}}}$ will be used here (the 'QCD' now being understood).

Only in the one-loop approximation for β_s can an analytic solution of (15.47) be obtained. However, a useful approximate solution can be found iteratively, as follows. Consider the two-loop version of (15.54), namely

$$\ln(Q^2/\Lambda_{\overline{\text{MS}}}^2) = -\int \frac{d\alpha_s}{\beta_0 \alpha_s^2 + \beta_1 \alpha_s^3}. \qquad (15.58)$$

Expanding the denominator and integrating gives

$$\ln(Q^2/\Lambda_{\overline{\text{MS}}}^2) = \frac{1}{\beta_0 \alpha_s} + \frac{b_1}{\beta_0} \ln \alpha_s + C, \qquad (15.59)$$

where $b_1 = \beta_1/\beta_0$ and C is a constant. In the $\overline{\text{MS}}$ scheme, C is given by $C = (b_1/\beta_0) \ln \beta_0$. Then the equation for α_s is

$$L = \frac{1}{\beta_0 \alpha_s} + \frac{b_1}{\beta_0} \ln \beta_0 \alpha_s, \qquad (15.60)$$

where we have defined $L = \ln(Q^2/\Lambda_{\overline{MS}}^2)$. In first approximation, one sets b_1 to zero and finds $\alpha_s = (1/\beta_0 L)$ as before. To obtain the next approximation, we set $\alpha_s = (1/\beta_0 L)$ in the b_1 term of (15.60), and solve for α_s to first order in b_1. This gives (problem 15.4 (a))

$$\alpha_s = \frac{1}{\beta_0 L} - \frac{1}{\beta_0^3 L^2} \beta_1 \ln L. \tag{15.61}$$

Problem 15.4 (b) carries the calculation to the three-loop stage.

The current world average value of $\alpha_s(m_Z^2)$ is (Bethke 2009)

$$\alpha_s(m_Z^2) = 0.1184 \pm 0.0007. \tag{15.62}$$

The remarkable precision of this number represents extraordinary consistency among the many methods used to determine it[3], which include deep inelastic scattering, electroweak fits, $e^+e^- \to$ jets, and lattice calculations (see chapter 16). If (15.62) is used to determine $\Lambda_{\overline{MS}}$ from (15.61), one finds $\Lambda_{\overline{MS}} = 231$ MeV; using the 3-loop formula of problem 15.4 (b) gives $\Lambda_{\overline{MS}} = 213$ MeV (Bethke 2009).

These values of $\Lambda_{\overline{MS}}$ are for $N_f = 5$, appropriate for the Z^0 mass region, well above the b threshold. As Q^2 runs to smaller values, and a quark mass threshold is crossed, N_f changes by one unit, and so correspondingly do the coefficients $\beta_0, \beta_1, \dots$. Physical quantities must however be continuous across a quark threshold. This requires that the values of α_s above and below that threshold satisfy certain matching conditions (Rodrigo and Santamaria 1993, Bernreuther and Wetzel 1982, Chetyrkin *et al.* 1997). These are satisfied by allowing $\Lambda_{\overline{MS}}$ to depend on N_f. At one and two loop order, the matching condition is simply $\alpha_s^{(N_f-1)} = \alpha_s^{(N_f)}$, which can be straightforwardly implemented in terms of $\Lambda_{\overline{MS}}^{(N_f-1)}$ and $\Lambda_{\overline{MS}}^{(N_f-1)}$. In higher orders the matching conditions contain additional terms, which are required at $(n-1)$-loop order for an n-loop calculation of α_s.

Figure 15.5 shows a summary (Bethke 2009) of measurements of α_s as a function of the energy scale Q, compared with the QCD prediction. The latter is evaluated in 4-loop approximation, using 3-loop threshold matching conditions at the masses $m_c = 1.5$ GeV and $m_b = 4.7$ GeV. The agreement is perfect, a triumph for both experiment and theory.

15.4 $\sigma(e^+e^- \to$ hadrons) revisited

We may now return to the physical process which originally motivated this extensive detour. The perturbative corrections to $\sigma_{pt}(Q^2)$ are expressed as a

---

[3]With the exception of a long-standing systematic difference: results from structure functions prefer a smaller value of $\alpha_s(m_Z^2)$ than most of the others.

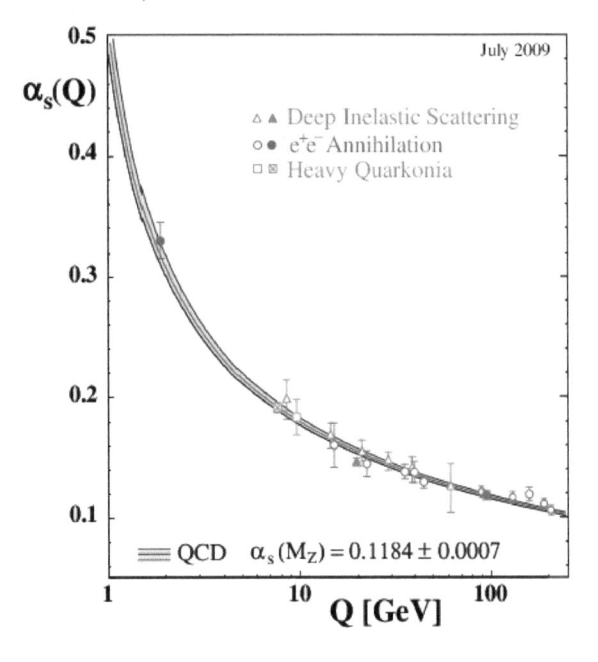

FIGURE 15.5
Comparison between measurements of α_s and the theoretical prediction, as a function of the energy scale Q (Bethke 2009). (See color plate I.)

power series in α_s,

$$\sigma(e^+e^- \to hadrons) = \sigma_{pt}(Q^2)\left[1 + \sum_{n=1}^{\infty} c_n(Q^2/\mu^2)\left(\frac{\alpha_s(\mu^2)}{\pi}\right)^n\right], \quad (15.63)$$

where μ is the renormalization scale. (A similar expansion can be written for many other physical quantities too.) The coefficients from c_2 onwards depend on the renormalization scheme (see appendix O), and are usually quoted in the $\overline{MS}$ scheme. c_1 is the leading order (LO) coefficient, and we already know that $c_1 = 1$ from (15.1). c_2 is the next-to-leading (NLO) coefficient; $c_2(1)$ was calculated by Dine and Sapirstein (1979), Chetyrkin *et al.* (1979) and by Celmaster and Gonsalves (1980), and has the value $1.9857 - 0.1152N_f$. The next-to-next-to-leading (NNLO) coefficient $c_3(1)$ was calculated by Samuel and Surguladze (1991) and by Gorishnii *et al.* (1991), and is equal to -12.8 for five flavours. The N3LO coefficient $c_4(1)$ (which requires the evaluation of some twenty thousand diagrams) may be found in Baikov *et al.* (2008) and Baikov *et al.* (2009).

The physical cross section $\sigma(e^+e^- \to hadrons)$ must be independent of the renormalization scale μ^2, and this would also be true of the series in (15.63) if an infinite number of terms were kept: the μ^2-dependence of the coefficients

$c_n(Q^2/\mu^2)$ would cancel that of $\alpha_s(\mu^2)$. This requirement can be imposed order by order in α_s to fix the μ^2-dependence of the coefficients, and is a direct way of applying the RGE idea. Consider, for example, truncating the series at the $n = 2$ stage:

$$\sigma(e^+e^- \to \text{hadrons}) \approx \sigma_{pt}(Q^2) \left(1 + \frac{\alpha_s(\mu^2)}{\pi} + c_2(Q^2/\mu^2)(\alpha_s(\mu^2)/\pi)^2\right).$$
$$(15.64)$$

Differentiating with respect to μ^2 and setting the result to zero we obtain

$$\mu^2 \frac{dc_2}{d\mu^2} = -\frac{\pi\beta(\alpha_s(\mu^2))}{(\alpha_s(\mu^2))^2} \qquad (15.65)$$

where an $O(\alpha_s^3)$ term has been dropped. Substituting the one-loop result (15.48) – as is consistent to this order – we find

$$c_2(Q^2/\mu^2) = c_2(1) - \pi\beta_0 \ln(Q^2/\mu^2). \qquad (15.66)$$

The second term on the right-hand side of (15.66) gives the contribution identified in (15.2).

In practice only a finite number of terms $n = N$ will be available, and a μ^2-dependence will remain, which implies an uncertainty in the prediction of the cross section (and similar physical observables), due to the arbitrariness of the scale choice. This uncertainty will be of the same order as the neglected terms, i.e. of order α_s^{N+1}. Thus the scale dependence of a QCD prediction gives a measure of the uncertainties due to neglected terms. For $\sigma(e^+e^- \to \text{hadrons})$ the choice of scale $\mu^2 = Q^2$ is usually made, so as to avoid large logarithms in relations such as (15.66).

Before proceeding to our second main application of the RGE, scaling violations in deep inelastic scattering, it is necessary to take another detour, to enlarge our understanding of the scope of the RGE.

15.5   A more general form of the RGE: anomalous dimensions and running masses

The reader may have wondered why, for QCD, all the graphs of figure 15.6 are needed, whereas for QED we got away with only figure 11.3. The reason for the simplification in QED was the equality between the renormalization constants Z_1 and Z_2, which therefore cancelled out in the relation between the renormalized and bare charges e and e_0, as briefly stated before equation (15.8) (this equality was discussed in section 11.6). We recall that Z_1 is the field strength renormalization factor for the charged fermion in QED, and Z_1 is the vertex part renormalization constant; their relation to the counter terms

was given in equation (11.7). For QCD, although gauge invariance does imply generalizations of the Ward identity used to prove $Z_1 = Z_2$ (Taylor 1971, Slavnov 1972), the consequence is no longer the simple relation '$Z_1 = Z_2$' in this case, due essentially to the ghost contributions. In order to see what change $Z_1 \neq Z_2$ would make, let us return to the one-loop calculation of β for QED, pretending that $Z_1 \neq Z_2$. We have

$$e_0 = \frac{Z_1}{Z_2} Z_3^{-\frac{1}{2}} e_\mu \qquad (15.67)$$

where, because we are renormalizing at scale μ, all the Z_i's depend on μ (as in (15.15)), but we shall now not indicate this explicitly. Taking logs and differentiating with respect to μ at constant e_0, we obtain

$$\mu \frac{\mathrm{d}}{\mathrm{d}\mu}\Big|_{e_0} \ln Z_1 - \mu \frac{\mathrm{d}}{\mathrm{d}\mu}\Big|_{e_0} \ln Z_2 - \frac{1}{2}\mu \frac{\mathrm{d}}{\mathrm{d}\mu}\Big|_{e_0} \ln Z_3 + \frac{\mu}{e_\mu} \frac{\mathrm{d}e_\mu}{\mathrm{d}\mu}\Big|_{e_0} = 0. \qquad (15.68)$$

Hence

$$\beta(e_\mu) \equiv \mu \frac{\mathrm{d}e_\mu}{\mathrm{d}\mu}\Big|_{e_0} = e_\mu \gamma_3 + 2e_\mu \gamma_2 - e_\mu \mu \frac{\mathrm{d}}{\mathrm{d}\mu} \ln Z_1, \qquad (15.69)$$

where

$$\gamma_2 \equiv \frac{1}{2}\mu \frac{\mathrm{d}}{\mathrm{d}\mu}\Big|_{e_0} \ln Z_2, \qquad \gamma_3 = \frac{1}{2}\mu \frac{\mathrm{d}}{\mathrm{d}\mu}\Big|_{e_0} \ln Z_3. \qquad (15.70)$$

To leading order in e_μ, the γ_3 term in (15.70) reproduces (15.26) when (15.15) is used for Z_3, the other two terms in (15.68) cancelling via $Z_1 = Z_2$. So if, as in the case of QCD, Z_1 is not equal to Z_2, we need to introduce the contributions from loops determining the fermion field strength renormalization factor, as well as those related to the vertex parts (together with appropriate ghost loops), in addition to the vacuum polarization loop associated in the Z_3.

Quantities such as γ_2 and γ_3 have an interesting and important significance, which we shall illustrate in the case of γ_2 for QED. Z_2 enters into the relation between the propagator of the bare fermion $\langle \Omega | T(\hat{\psi}_0(x)\hat{\bar{\psi}}_0(0)) | \Omega \rangle$ and the renormalized one, via (cf (11.2))

$$\langle \Omega | T(\hat{\bar{\psi}}(x)\hat{\psi}(0)) | \Omega \rangle = \frac{1}{Z_2} \langle \Omega | T(\hat{\bar{\psi}}_0(x)\hat{\psi}_0(0)) | \Omega \rangle, \qquad (15.71)$$

where (cf section 10.1.3) $|\Omega\rangle$ is the vacuum of the interacting theory. The Fourier transform of (15.71) is, of course, the Feynman propagator:

$$\tilde{S}'_F(q^2) = \int \mathrm{d}^4 x\, e^{iq \cdot x} \langle \Omega | T(\hat{\bar{\psi}}(x)\hat{\psi}(0)) | \Omega \rangle. \qquad (15.72)$$

Suppose we now ask: what is the large $-q^2$ behaviour of (15.72) for space-like q^2, with $-q^2 \gg m^2$ where m is the fermion mass? This sounds very similar to the question answered in 15.2.3 for the quantity $S(|q^2|/\mu^2, e_\mu)$. However,

the latter was dimensionless whereas (recalling that $\hat{\psi}$ has mass dimension $\frac{3}{2}$) $\tilde{S}'_F(q^2)$ has dimension M^{-1}. This dimensionality is, of course, just what a propagator of the free-field form $i/(\not{q} - m)$ would provide.

Accordingly, we extract this $(\not{q})^{-1}$ factor (compare $\sigma/\sigma_{\rm pt}$) and consider the dimensionless ratio $\tilde{R}'_F(|q^2|/\mu^2, \alpha_\mu) = \not{q}\tilde{S}'_F(q^2)$. We might guess that, just as for $S(|q^2|/\mu^2, \alpha_\mu)$, to get the leading large $|q^2|$ behaviour we will need to calculate $\tilde{R}'_F$ to some order in α_μ, and then replace α_μ by $\alpha(|q^2|/\mu^2)$. But this is not quite all. The factor Z_2 in (15.71) will – as noted above – depend on the renormalization scale μ, just as Z_3 of (15.15) did. Thus when we change μ, the normalization of the $\hat{\psi}$'s will change via the $Z_2^{\frac{1}{2}}$ factors – of course by a finite amount here – and we must include this change when writing down the analogue of (15.33) for this case (i.e. the condition that the 'total change, on changing μ, is zero'). The required equation is

$$\left[\mu^2 \frac{\partial}{\partial \mu^2}\bigg|_{\alpha_\mu} + \beta(\alpha_\mu)\frac{\partial}{\partial \alpha_\mu} + \gamma_2(\alpha_\mu) \right] \tilde{R}'_F(|q^2|/\mu^2, \alpha_\mu) = 0. \qquad (15.73)$$

The solution of (15.73) is somewhat more complicated than that of (15.33). We can gain insight into the essential difference caused by the presence of γ_2 by considering the special case $\beta(\alpha_\mu) = 0$. In this case, we easily find

$$\tilde{R}'_F(|q^2|/\mu^2, \alpha_\mu) \propto (\mu^2)^{-\gamma_2(\alpha_\mu)}. \qquad (15.74)$$

But since $\tilde{R}'_F$ can only depend on μ via $|q^2|/\mu^2$, we learn that if $\beta = 0$ then the large $|q^2|$ behaviour of $\tilde{R}'_F$ is given by $(|q^2|/\mu^2)^{\gamma_2}$ – or, in other words, that at large $|q^2|$

$$\tilde{S}'_F(|q^2|/\mu^2, \alpha_\mu) \propto \frac{1}{\not{q}} \left(\frac{|q^2|}{\mu^2} \right)^{\gamma_2(\alpha_\mu)}. \qquad (15.75)$$

Thus, *at a zero of the β-function*, $\tilde{S}'_F$ has an 'anomalous' power law dependence on $|q^2|$ (i.e. in addition to the obvious $\not{q}^{-1}$ factor), which is controlled by the parameter γ_2. The latter is called the 'anomalous dimension' of the fermion field, since its presence effectively means that the $|q^2|$ behaviour of $\tilde{S}'_F$ is not determined by its 'normal' dimensionality M^{-1}. The behaviour (15.75) is often referred to as 'scaling with anomalous dimension', meaning that if we multiply $|q^2|$ by a scale factor λ, then $\tilde{S}'_F$ is multiplied by $\lambda^{\gamma_2(\alpha_\mu)-1}$ rather than just λ^{-1}. Anomalous dimensions turn out to play a vital role in the theory of critical phenomena – they are, in fact, closely related to 'critical exponents' (see section 16.4.3, and Peskin and Schroeder 1995, chapter 13). Scaling with anomalous dimensions is also exactly what occurs in deep inelastic scattering of leptons from nucleons, as we shall see in section 15.6.

The full solution of (15.73) for $\beta \neq 0$ is elegantly discussed in Coleman (1985), chapter 3; see also Peskin and Schroeder (1995) section 12.3. We quote

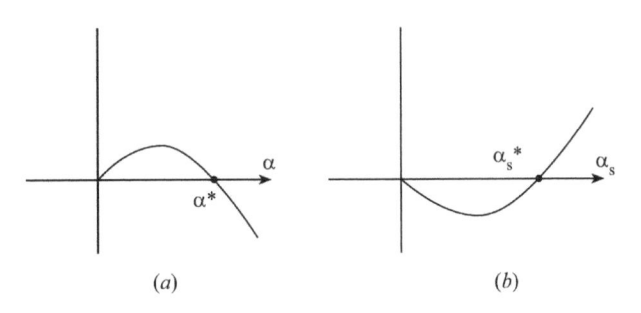

FIGURE 15.6
Possible behaviour of β functions. (a) The slope is positive near the origin (as in QED), and negative near $\alpha = \alpha^*$. (b) The slope is negative at the origin (as in QCD), and positive near $\alpha_s = \alpha_s^*$.

it here:

$$\tilde{R}_F'(|q^2|/\mu^2), \alpha_\mu), = \tilde{R}_F'(1, \alpha(|q^2|/\mu^2)) \exp\left\{ \int_0^t dt' \gamma_2(\alpha(t')) \right\}. \qquad (15.76)$$

The first factor is the expected one from section 15.2.3; the second results from the addition of the γ_2 term in (15.73). Suppose now that $\beta(\alpha)$ has a zero at some point α^*, in the vicinity of which $\beta(\alpha) \approx -B(\alpha - \alpha^*)$ with $B > 0$. Then, near this point the evolution of α is given by (cf (15.39))

$$\ln(|q^2|/\mu^2) = \int_{\alpha_\mu}^{\alpha(|q^2|)} = \frac{d\alpha}{-B(\alpha - \alpha^*)}, \qquad (15.77)$$

which implies

$$\alpha(|q^2|) = \alpha^* + \text{constant} \times (\mu^2/|q^2|)^B. \qquad (15.78)$$

Thus asymptotically for large $|q^2|$, the coupling will evolve to the '*fixed point*' α^*. In this case, at sufficiently large $-q^2$, the integral in (15.76) can be evaluated by setting $\alpha(t') = \alpha^*$, and $\tilde{R}_F'$ will scale with an anomalous dimension $\gamma_2(\alpha^*)$ determined by the fixed point value of α. The behaviour of such an α is shown in figure 15.6(a). We emphasize that there is no reason to believe that the QED β function actually does behave like this.

The point α^* in figure 15.6(a) is called an ultraviolet-stable fixed point: α 'flows' towards it at large $|q^2|$. In the case of QCD, the β function starts out negative, so that the corresponding behaviour (with a zero at a $\alpha_s^* \neq 0$) would look like that shown in figure 15.6(b). In this case, the reader can check (problem 15.5) that α_s^* is reached in the infrared limit $q^2 \to 0$, and so α_s^* is called an infrared-stable fixed point. Clearly it is the slope of β near the fixed point that determines whether it is u-v or i-r stable. This applies equally to a fixed point at the origin, so that QED is i-r stable at $\alpha = 0$ while QCD is u-v stable at $\alpha_s = 0$.

We must now point out to the reader an error in the foregoing analysis, in the case of a gauge theory. The quantity Z_2 is not gauge invariant in QED (or QCD), and hence γ_2 depends on the choice of gauge. This is really no surprise, because the full fermion propagator itself is not gauge invariant (the free-field propagator is gauge invariant, of course). What ultimately matters is that the complete physical amplitude for any process, at a given order of α, be gauge invariant. Thus the analysis given above really only applies – in this simple form – to non-gauge theories, such as the ABC model of chapter 6, or to gauge-invariant quantities.

This is an appropriate point at which to consider the treatment of quark masses in the RGE-based approach. Up to now we have simply assumed that the relevant $|q^2|$ is very much greater than all quark masses, the latter therefore being neglected. While this may be adequate for the light quarks u, d, s, it seems surely a progressively worse assumption for c, b and t. However, in thinking about how to re-introduce the quark masses into our formalism, we are at once faced with a difficulty: how are they to be defined? For an unconfined particle, such as a lepton, it seems natural to define 'the' mass as the position of the pole of the propagator (i.e. the 'on-shell' value $p^2 = m^2$), a definition we followed in chapters 10 and 11. Significantly, renormalization is required (in the shape of a mass counter-term) to achieve a pole at the 'right' physical mass m, in this sense. But this prescription is inherently perturbative, and cannot be used for a confined particle, which never 'escapes' beyond the range of the non-perturbative confining forces, and whose propagator can therefore never approach the form $\sim (\not{p} - m)^{-1}$ of a free particle.

Our present perspective on renormalization suggests an obvious way forward. Just as there was, in principle, no *necessity* to define the QED coupling parameter e via an on-shell prescription, so here a mass parameter in the Lagrangian can be defined in any way we find convenient; all that is necessary is that it should be possible to determine its value from some measurable quantity (for example, quark masses from lattice QCD predictions of hadron masses). Effectively, we are regarding the 'm' in a term such as $-m\bar{\hat{\psi}}(x)\hat{\psi}(x)$ as a 'coupling constant' having mass dimension 1 (and, after all, the ABC coupling itself had mass dimension 1). Incidentally, the operator $\bar{\hat{\psi}}(x)\hat{\psi}(x)$ *is* gauge invariant, as is any such *local* operator. Taking this point of view, it is clear that a renormalization scale will be involved in such a general definition of mass, and we must expect to see our mass parameters 'evolve' with this scale, just as the gauge (or other) couplings do. In turn, this will get translated into a $|q^2|$-dependence of the mass parameters, just as for $\alpha(|q^2|)$ and $\alpha_{\mathrm{s}}(|q^2|)$.

The RGE in such a scheme now takes the form

$$\left[\mu^2 \frac{\partial}{\partial \mu^2} + \beta(\alpha_{\mathrm{s}})\frac{\partial}{\partial \alpha_{\mathrm{s}}} + \sum_i \gamma_i(\alpha_{\mathrm{s}}) + \gamma_m(\alpha_{\mathrm{s}})m\frac{\partial}{\partial m}\right] R(|q^2|/\mu^2, \alpha_{\mathrm{s}}, m/|q|) = 0$$

$$(15.79)$$

where the partial derivatives are taken at fixed values of the other two vari-

ables. Here the γ_i are the anomalous dimensions relevant to the quantity R, and γ_m is an analogous 'anomalous mass dimension', arising from finite shifts in the mass parameter when the scale μ^2 is changed. Just as with the solution (15.76) of (15.73), the solution of (15.79) is given in terms of a 'running mass' $m(|q^2|)$. Formally, we can think of γ_m in (15.79) as analogous to $\beta(\alpha_s)$ and $\ln m$ as analogous to α_s. Then equation (15.41) for the running α_s,

$$\frac{\partial \alpha_s(|q^2|)}{\partial t} = \beta(\alpha_s(|q^2|)) \tag{15.80}$$

where $t = \ln(|q^2|/\mu^2)$, becomes

$$\frac{\partial (\ln m(|q^2|))}{\partial t} = \gamma_m(\alpha_s(|q|^2)). \tag{15.81}$$

Equation (15.81) has the solution

$$m(|q^2|) = m(\mu^2) \exp \int_{\ln \mu^2}^{\ln |q^2|} d \ln |q'^2| \, \gamma_m(\alpha_s(|q'^2|)). \tag{15.82}$$

To one-loop order in QCD, $\gamma_m(\alpha_s)$ turns out to be $-\frac{1}{\pi}\alpha_s$ (Peskin and Schroeder 1995, section 18.1). Inserting the one-loop solution for α_s in the form (15.53), we find

$$m(|q^2|) = m(\mu^2) \left[\frac{\ln(\mu^2/\Lambda^2)}{\ln(|q^2|/\Lambda^2)} \right]^{\frac{1}{\pi\beta_0}}, \tag{15.83}$$

where $(\pi\beta_0)^{-1} = 12/(33 - 2N_f)$. Thus the quark masses decrease logarithmically as $|q^2|$ increases, rather like $\alpha_s(|q^2|)$. It follows that, in general, quark mass effects are suppressed both by explicit $m^2/|q^2|$ factors, and by the logarithmic decrease given by (15.83). Further discussion of the treatment of quark masses is contained in Ellis, Stirling and Webber (1996), section 2.4; see also the review by Manohar and Sachrajda in Nakamura *et al.* 2010.

15.6 QCD corrections to the parton model predictions for deep inelastic scattering: scaling violations

As we saw in section 9.2, the parton model provides a simple intuitive explanation for the experimental observation that the nucleon structure functions in deep inelastic scattering depend, to a good first approximation, only on the dimensionless ratio $x = Q^2/2M\nu$, rather than on Q^2 and ν separately; this behaviour is referred to as 'scaling'. Here M is the nucleon mass, and Q^2 and ν are defined in (9.7) and (9.8). In this section we shall show how QCD

corrections to the simple parton model, calculated using RGE techniques, predict observable violations of scaling in deep inelastic scattering. As we shall see, comparison between the theoretical predictions and experimental measurements provides strong evidence for the correctness of QCD as the theory of nucleonic constituents.

15.6.1   Uncancelled mass singularities at order α_s.

The free parton model amplitudes we considered in chapter 9 for deep inelastic lepton-nucleon scattering were of the form shown in figure 15.7 (cf figure 9.4). The obvious first QCD corrections will be due to real gluon emission by either the initial or final quark, as shown in figure 15.8, but to these we must add the one-loop virtual gluon processes of figure 15.9 in order (see below) to get rid of infrared divergences similar to those encountered in section 14.4.2, and also the diagram of figure 15.10, corresponding to the presence of gluons in the nucleon. To simplify matters, we shall consider what is called a 'non-singlet structure function' F_2^{NS}, such as $F_2^{\mathrm{ep}} - F_2^{\mathrm{en}}$ in which the (flavour) singlet gluon contribution cancels out, leaving only the diagrams of figures 15.8 and 15.9.

We now want to perform, for these diagrams, calculations analogous to those of section 9.2, which enabled us to find the e-N structure functions νW_2 and MW_1 from the simple parton process of figure 15.7. There are two problems here: one is to find the parton level W's corresponding to figure 15.8 (leaving aside figure 15.9 for the moment) – cf equations (9.29) and (9.30) in the case of the free parton diagram figure 15.7; the other is to relate these parton W's to observed nucleon W's via an integration over momentum fractions. In section 9.2 we solved the first problem by explicitly calculating the parton level $\mathrm{d}^2\sigma^i/\mathrm{d}Q^2\mathrm{d}\nu$ and picking off the associated νW_2^i, W_1^i. In principle, the same can be done here, starting from the five-fold differential cross section for our $e^- + q \rightarrow e^- + q + g$ process. However, a simpler – if somewhat heuristic – way is available. We note from (9.46) that in general $F_1 = MW_1$ is given by the transverse virtual photon cross section

$$W_1 = \sigma_T/(4\pi^2\alpha/K) = \frac{1}{2}\sum_{\lambda=\pm 1}\epsilon_\mu^*(\lambda)\epsilon_\nu(\lambda)W^{\mu\nu} \qquad (15.84)$$

where $W^{\mu\nu}$ was defined in (9.3). Further, the Callan–Gross relation is still true (the photon only interacts with the charged partons, which are quarks with spin $\frac{1}{2}$ and charge e_i), and so

$$F_2/x = 2F_1 = 2MW_1 = \sigma_T/(4\pi^2\alpha/2MK). \qquad (15.85)$$

These formulae are valid for both parton and proton W_1's and $W^{\mu\nu}$'s, with appropriate changes for parton masses $\hat{M}$. Hence the parton level $2\hat{F}_1$ for figure 15.8 is just the transverse photon cross section as calculated from the graphs of figure 15.11, divided by the factor $4\pi^2\alpha/2\hat{M}\hat{K}$, where as usual '$\hat{\ }$' denotes kinematic quantities in the corresponding parton process. This cross section,

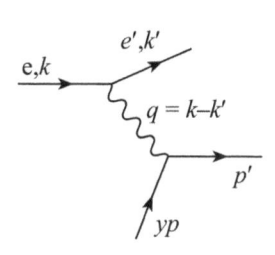

FIGURE 15.7
Electron-quark scattering via one-photon exchange.

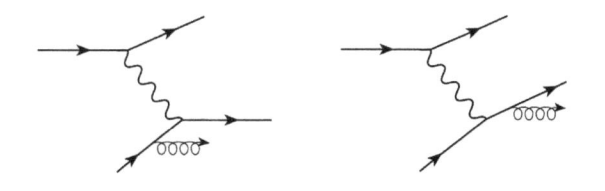

FIGURE 15.8
Electron-quark scattering with single-gluon emission

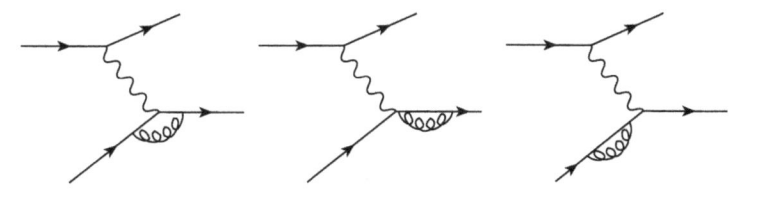

FIGURE 15.9
Virtual single-gluon corrections to figure 15.7.

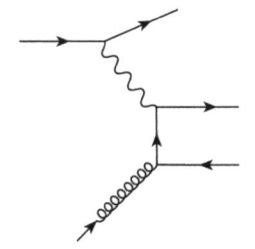

FIGURE 15.10
Electron-gluon scattering with $\bar{q}q$ production.

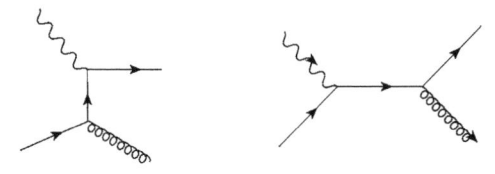

FIGURE 15.11
Virtual photon processes entering into figure 15.8.

however, is – apart from a colour factor – just the virtual Compton cross section calculated in section 8.6. Also, taking the same (Hand) convention for the individual photon flux factors,

$$2\hat{M}\hat{K} = \hat{s}. \tag{15.86}$$

Thus for the parton processes of figure 15.9,

$$
\begin{aligned}
2\hat{F}_1 &= \hat{\sigma}_T/(4\pi^2\alpha/2\hat{M}\hat{K}) \\
&= \frac{\hat{s}}{4\pi^2\alpha}\int_{-1}^{1} d\cos\theta \cdot \frac{4}{3}\cdot\frac{\pi e_i^2\alpha\alpha_s(\mu^2)}{\hat{s}}\left(-\frac{\hat{t}}{\hat{s}}-\frac{\hat{s}}{\hat{t}}+\frac{2\hat{u}Q^2}{\hat{s}\hat{t}}\right) \tag{15.87}
\end{aligned}
$$

where, in going from (8.181) to (15.87), we have inserted a colour factor $\frac{4}{3}$ (problem 14.5 (a)), renamed the variables $\hat{t}\to\hat{u},\hat{u}\to\hat{t}$ in accordance with figure 15.11, and replaced α^2 by $e_i^2\alpha\alpha_s(\mu^2)$.

Before proceeding with (15.87), it is helpful to consider the other part of the calculation – namely the relation between the nucleon F_1 and the parton $\hat{F}_1$. We mimic the discussion of section 9.2, but with one significant difference: the quark 'taken' from the proton still has momentum fraction y (momentum yp), but now its longitudinal momentum must be degraded in the final state due to the gluon bremsstrahlung process we are calculating. Let us call the quark momentum after gluon emission zyp (figure 15.12). Then, assuming as in section 9.2 that it stays on-shell, we have

$$q^2 + 2zyq\cdot p = 0 \tag{15.88}$$

or

$$x = yz, \qquad x = Q^2/2q\cdot p, \qquad q^2 = -Q^2 \tag{15.89}$$

and we can write (cf (9.31))

$$\frac{F_2}{x} = 2F_1 = \sum_i \int_0^1 dy f_i(y)\int_0^1 dz\, 2\hat{F}_1^i\delta(x-yz) \tag{15.90}$$

where the $f_i(y)$ are the parton distribution functions introduced in section 9.2 (we often call them $q(x)$ or $g(x)$ as the case may be) for parton type i, and

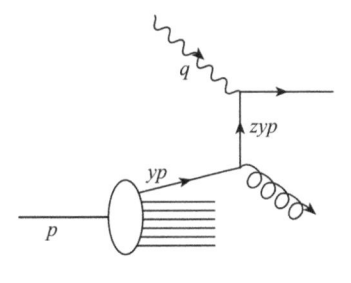

FIGURE 15.12
The first process of figure 15.11, viewed as a contribution to e^--nucleon scattering.

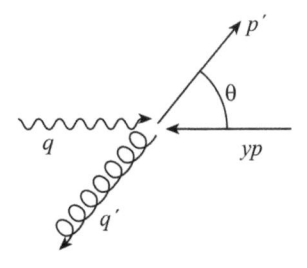

FIGURE 15.13
Kinematics for the parton process of figure 15.12.

the sum is over contributing partons. The reader may enjoy checking that (15.90) does reduce to (9.34) for free partons by showing that in that case $2\hat{F}_1^i = e_i^2 \delta(1-z)$ (see Halzen and Martin 1984, section 10.3, for help), so that $2F_1^{\text{free}} = \sum_i e_i^2 f_i(x)$.

To proceed further with the calculation (i.e. of (15.87) inserted into (15.90)), we need to look at the kinematics of the $\gamma q \to qg$ process, in the CMS. Referring to figure 15.13, we let k, k' be the magnitudes of the CMS momenta $\mathbf{k}, \mathbf{k'}$. Then

$$
\begin{aligned}
\hat{s} &= 4k'^2 = (yp+q)^2 = Q^2(1-z)/z, \quad z = Q^2/(\hat{s}+Q^2) \\
\hat{t} &= (q-p')^2 = -2kk'(1-\cos\theta) = -Q^2(1-c)/2z, \quad c = \cos\theta \\
\hat{u} &= (q-q')^2 = -2kk'(1+\cos\theta) = -Q^2(1+c)/2z.
\end{aligned} \tag{15.91}
$$

We now note that in the integral (15.87) for $\hat{F}_1$, when we integrate over $c = \cos\theta$, we shall obtain an infinite result

$$
\sim \int^1 \frac{dc}{1-c} \tag{15.92}
$$

associated with the vanishing of $\hat{t}$ in the 'forward' direction (i.e. when q and p'

are parallel). This is a divergence of the 'collinear' type, in the terminology of section 14.4.2 – or, as there, a 'mass singularity', occurring in the zero quark mass limit. If we simply replace the propagator factor $\hat{t}^{-1} = [(q - p')^2]^{-1}$ by $[(q - p')^2 - m^2]^{-1}$, where m is a quark mass, then (15.92) becomes

$$\sim \int^1 \frac{dc}{(1 + 2m^2 z/Q^2) - c} \tag{15.93}$$

which will produce a factor of the form $\ln(Q^2/m^2)$ as $m^2 \to 0$. Thus m regulates the divergence. We have here an uncancelled mass singularity, and it *violates scaling*. This crucial physical result is present in the lowest-order QCD correction to the parton model, in this case. As we are learning, such logarithmic violations of scaling are a characteristic feature of all QCD corrections to the free (scaling) parton model.

We may calculate the coefficient of the $\ln Q^2$ term by retaining in (15.87) only the terms proportional to $\hat{t}^{-1}$:

$$2\hat{F}_1^i \approx e_i^2 \int_{-1}^1 \frac{dc}{1-c} \left(\frac{\alpha_s(\mu^2)}{2\pi} \cdot \frac{4}{3} \cdot \frac{1+z^2}{1-z} \right) \tag{15.94}$$

and so, for just one quark species, this QCD correction contributes (from (15.90)) a term

$$\frac{e_i^2 \alpha_s(\mu^2)}{2\pi} \int_x^1 \frac{dy}{y} q(y) \left\{ \hat{P}_{qq}(x/y) \ln(Q^2/m^2) + C(x/y) \right\} \tag{15.95}$$

to $2F_1$, where

$$\hat{P}_{qq}(z) = \frac{4}{3} \left(\frac{1+z^2}{1-z} \right), \tag{15.96}$$

and $C(x/y)$ has no mass singularity.

Our result so far is therefore that the 'free' quark distribution function $q(x)$, which depended only on the scaling variable x, becomes modified to

$$q(x) + \frac{\alpha_s(\mu^2)}{2\pi} \int_x^1 \frac{dy}{y} q(y) \left\{ \hat{P}_{qq}(x/y) \ln \left(Q^2/m^2 \right) + C(x/y) \right\} \tag{15.97}$$

$$= q(x) + \frac{\alpha_s(\mu^2)}{2\pi} \int_0^1 dy \int_0^1 dz \delta(zy - x) q(y) \{ \hat{P}_{qq}(z) \ln(Q^2/m^2)$$
$$+ C(z) \} \tag{15.98}$$

due to lowest-order gluon radiation. Clearly, this corrected distribution function violates scaling because of the $\ln Q^2$ term. But the result as it stands cannot represent a well-controlled approximation, since it contains divergences as $z \to 1$ and as $m^2 \to 0$.

We postpone discussion of the mass divergence until the next section. The divergence as $z \to 1$ is a standard infrared divergence (the quark momentum

yzp after gluon emission becomes equal to the quark momentum yp before emission), and we expect that it can be cured by including the virtual gluon diagrams of figure 15.9, as indicated at the start of the section (and as was done analogously in the case of e^+e^- annihilation). This has been verified explicitly by Kim and Schilcher (1978) and by Altarelli *et al.* (1978 a, b; 1979). Alternatively, we follow the procedure of Altarelli and Parisi (1977). First we regulate the divergence as $z \to 1$ by defining a regulated function $1/(1-z)_+$ such that

$$\int_0^1 \frac{f(z)}{(1-z)_+} \mathrm{d}z = \int_0^1 \frac{f(z)-f(1)}{(1-z)} \mathrm{d}z = \int_0^1 \ln(1-z) \frac{\mathrm{d}f(z)}{\mathrm{d}z} \mathrm{d}z, \qquad (15.99)$$

where $f(z)$ is any test function sufficiently regular at the end points. Now the gluon loops which will cancel the i-r divergence only contribute at $z \to 1$, in leading log approximation. Thus the i-r finite version of $\hat{P}_{qq}$ has the form

$$P_{qq}(z) = \frac{4}{3} \frac{1+z^2}{(1-z)_+} + A\delta(1-z). \qquad (15.100)$$

The coefficient A is determined by the physical requirement that the net number of quarks (i.e. the number of quarks minus the number of antiquarks) does not vary with Q^2. From (15.98) this implies

$$\int_0^1 P_{qq}(z)\mathrm{d}z = 0. \qquad (15.101)$$

Inserting (15.100) into (15.101), and using (15.99), we find (problem 15.6)

$$A = 2, \qquad (15.102)$$

so that

$$P_{qq}(z) = \frac{4}{3} \frac{(1+z^2)}{(1-z)_+} + 2\delta(1-z). \qquad (15.103)$$

The function P_{qq} is called a 'splitting function', and it has an important physical interpretation. The quantity $\alpha_s(\mu^2)/(2\pi)\, P_{qq}(z)$ is, for $z < 1$, the probability that, to first order in α_s, a quark having radiated a gluon is left with a fraction z of its original momentum. Similar functions arise in QED in connection with what is called the 'equivalent photon approximation' (Weizsäcker 1934, Williams 1934, Chen and Zerwas 1975). The application of these techniques to QCD corrections to the free parton model is due to Altarelli and Parisi (1977), who thereby opened the way to this simpler and more physical way of understanding scaling violations, which had previously been discussed mainly within the rather technical operator product formalism (Wilson 1969).

We must now find some way of making sense, physically, of the uncancelled mass divergence in (15.97).

15.6.2   Factorization, and the order α_s DGLAP equation

The key is to realize that when two partons are in the collinear configuration their relative momentum is very small, and hence the interaction between them is very strong, beyond the reach of a perturbative calculation. This suggests that we should absorb such uncalculable effects into a modified distribution function $q(x, \mu_F^2)$ given by

$$q(x, \mu_F^2) = q(x) + \frac{\alpha_s(\mu^2)}{2\pi} \int_x^1 \frac{dy}{y} q(y) P_{qq}(x/y) \left\{ \ln(\mu_F^2/m^2) + C(x/y) \right\}$$
(15.104)

which we have to take from experiment. Note that we have also absorbed the non-singular term $C(x/y)$ into $q(x, \mu_F^2)$. In terms of this quantity, then, we have

$$
\begin{aligned}
F_2(x, Q^2) &\equiv e_i^2 x q(x, Q^2) \\
&= x e_i^2 \int_x^1 \frac{dy}{y} q(y, \mu_F^2) \left\{ \delta(1 - x/y) + \frac{\alpha_s(\mu^2)}{2\pi} P_{qq}(x/y) \ln(Q^2/\mu_F^2) \right\}
\end{aligned}
$$
(15.105)

(15.106)

to this order in α_s, and for one quark type.

This procedure is, of course, very reminiscent of ultraviolet renormalization, in which u-v divergences are controlled by similarly importing some quantities from experiment. In this example, we have essentially made use of the simple fact that

$$\ln(Q^2/m^2) = \ln(Q^2/\mu_F^2) + \ln(\mu_F^2/m^2).$$
(15.107)

The arbitrary scale μ_F is analogous to renormalization scale μ (which we have retained in $\alpha_s(\mu^2)$), and is here referred to as a 'factorization scale'. It is the scale entering into the separation in (15.107), between one (uncalculable) factor which depends on the i-r parameter m but not on Q^2, and the other (calculable) factor which depends on Q^2. The scale μ_F can be thought of as one which separates the perturbative short-distance physics from the non-perturbative long-distance physics. Thus partons emitted at small transverse momenta $< \mu_F$ (i.e. approximately collinear processes) should be considered as part of the hadron structure, and are absorbed into $q(x, \mu_F^2)$. Partons emitted at large transverse momenta contribute to the short-distance (calculable) part of the cross section. Just as for the renormalization scale, the more terms that can be included in the perturbative contributions to the mass-singular terms, the weaker the dependence on μ_F will be. We have demonstrated the possibility of factorization only to $O(\alpha_s)$, but proofs to all orders in perturbation theory exist; reviews are provided by Collins and Soper (1987, 1988).

Returning now to (15.106), the reader can guess what is coming next: we shall impose the condition that the physical quantity $F_2(x, Q^2)$ must be independent of the choice of factorization scale μ_F^2. Differentiating (15.106)

partially with respect to $\mu_{\rm F}^2$, and setting the result to zero, we obtain (to order $\alpha_{\rm s}$ on the right-hand side)

$$\mu_{\rm F}^2 \frac{\partial q(x, \mu_{\rm F}^2)}{\partial \mu_{\rm F}^2} = \frac{\alpha_{\rm s}(\mu^2)}{2\pi} \int_x^1 \frac{dy}{y} P_{\rm qq}(x/y) q(y, \mu_{\rm F}^2). \tag{15.108}$$

This equation is the analogue of equation (15.35) describing the running of the coupling $\alpha_{\rm s}$ with μ^2, and is a fundamental equation in the theory of perturbative applications of QCD. It is called the DGLAP equation, after Dokshitzer (1977), Gribov and Lipatov (1972), and Altarelli and Parisi (1977). The above derivation is not rigorous: a more sophisticated treatment (Georgi and Politzer 1974, Gross and Wilczek 1974) confirms the result and extends it to higher orders.

Equation (15.108) shows that, although perturbation theory cannot be used to calculate the distribution function $q(x, \mu_{\rm F}^2)$ at any particular value $\mu_{\rm F}^2 = \mu_0^2$, it can be used to predict how the distribution *changes* (or 'evolves') as $\mu_{\rm F}^2$ varies. (We recall from (15.105) that $q(x, \mu_0^2)$ can be found experimentally via $xq(x, \mu_0^2) = 2F_2(x, Q^2 = \mu_0^2)/e_i^2$.) As in the case of $\sigma(e^+e^- \to$ hadrons) and the scale μ^2, the choice of factorization scale is arbitrary, and would cancel from physical quantities if all powers in the perturbation series were included. Truncating at N terms results in an ambiguity of order $\alpha_{\rm s}^{(N+1)}$. In deep inelastic predictions, the standard choice for scales is $\mu^2 = \mu_{\rm F}^2 = Q^2$.

The way the non-singlet distribution changes can be understood qualitatively as follows. The change in the distribution for a quark with momentum fraction x, which absorbs the virtual photon, is given by the integral over y of the corresponding distribution for a quark with momentum fraction y, which radiated away (via a gluon) a fraction x/y of its momentum with probability $(\alpha_{\rm s}/2\pi)P_{\rm qq}(x/y)$. This probability is high for large momentum fractions: high-momentum quarks lose momentum by radiating gluons. Thus there is a predicted tendency for the distribution function $q(x, \mu^2)$ to get smaller at large x as μ^2 increases, and larger at small x (due to the build-up of slower partons), while maintaining the integral of the distribution over x as a constant. The effect is illustrated qualitatively in figure 15.14. In addition, the radiated gluons produce more $q\bar{q}$ pairs at small x. Thus the nucleon may be pictured as having more and more constituents, all contributing to its total momentum, as its structure is probed on ever smaller distance (larger μ^2) scales.

In general, the right-hand side of (15.108) will have to be supplemented by terms (calculable from figure 15.10) in which quarks are generated from the gluon distribution; the equations must then be closed by a corresponding one describing the evolution of the gluon distributions (Altarelli 1982). In the now commonly used notation, this generalization of (15.108) reads

$$\mu_{\rm F}^2 \frac{\partial f_{i/{\rm p}}(x, \mu_{\rm F}^2)}{\partial \mu_{\rm F}^2} = \sum_{j={\rm q,g}} \frac{\alpha_{\rm s}(\mu_{\rm F}^2)}{2\pi} \int_x^1 \frac{dy}{y} P_{i \leftarrow j}^{(1)}(x/y) f_{j/{\rm p}}(y, \mu_{\rm F}^2), \tag{15.109}$$

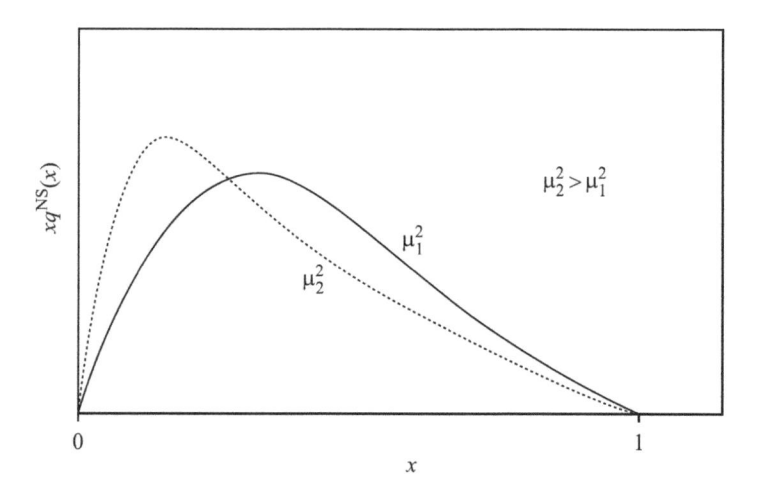

FIGURE 15.14
Evolution of the distribution function with μ^2.

where the sum is over quark types q and gluons g, $P^{(1)}_{i\leftarrow j}$ is the $j \rightarrow i$ splitting function to this order, and $f_{i/p}$ is the parton distribution function for partons of type i in the proton. In our previous notation, $P^{(1)}_{q\leftarrow q}(x/y) = P_{qq}(x/y)$, and $f_{q/p}(x, \mu^2_F) = q(x, \mu^2_F)$. The other splitting functions may be found in Altarelli (1982).

Both the splitting functions and expression (15.106) for $F_2(x, Q^2)$ can be extended to higher orders in α_s. Thus the perturbative expansion (15.106) becomes

$$F_2(x, Q^2) = x \sum_{n=0}^{\infty} \frac{\alpha_s^n(\mu^2_F)}{(2\pi)^n} \sum_{i=q,g} \int_x^1 \frac{dz}{z} C^{(n)}_{2,i}(z, Q^2, \mu^2_F) f_{i/p}(x/z, \mu^2_F), \quad (15.110)$$

where we have chosen $\mu = \mu_F$. The expansion (15.110) is analogous to (15.63), and as in that case the coefficient functions will depend on μ^2_F in such a way that, order by order, the μ^2_F dependence will cancel. At zeroth order the coefficients are the μ^2_F-independent free parton ones, $C^{(0)}_{2,q} = e^2_q \delta(1 - z)$ and $C^{(0)}_{2,g} = 0$. In most cases the coefficients have been calculated up to order α^2_s (Nakamura *et al.* 2010).

We ought also to mention that there are in principle non-perturbative corrections to both (15.63) and (15.110), which are of order $(\Lambda^2_{\overline{MS}}/Q^2)^2$ and $(\Lambda^2_{\overline{MS}}/Q^2)$ respectively.

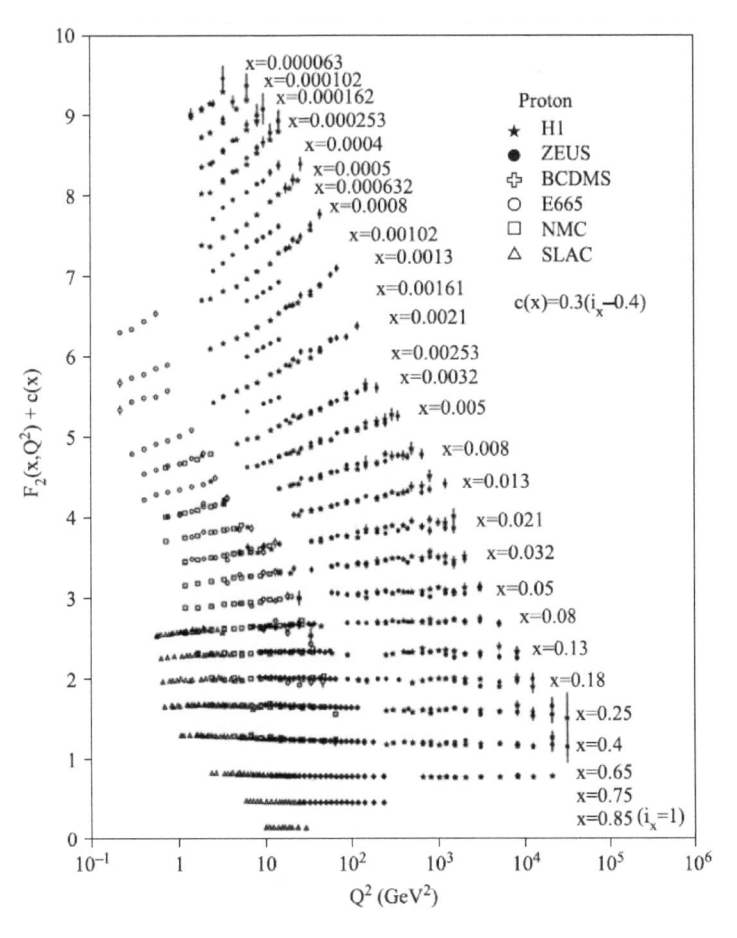

FIGURE 15.15

Q^2-dependence of the proton structure function F_2^{p} for various fixed x values (Hagiwara *et al.* 2002). i_x is a number depending on the x-bin, ranging from $i_x = 1$ ($x = 0.85$) to $i_x = 28$ ($x = 0.000063$). Figure reprinted with permission from K Hagiwara *et al.* *Phys.Rev.* D **66** 010001 (2002). Copyright 2002 by the American Physical Society.

15.6.3 Comparison with experiment

Data on nucleon structure functions do indeed show the trend described in the previous section. Figure 15.15 shows the Q^2-dependence of the proton structure function $F_2^{\mathrm{p}}(x, Q^2) = \sum e_i^2 x f_{i/\mathrm{p}}(x, Q^2)$ for various fixed x values, as compiled by B. Foster, A.D. Martin and M.G. Vincter for the 2002 Particle Data Group review (Hagiwara *et al.* 2002). Clearly at larger x ($x \geq 0.13$) the function gets smaller as Q^2 increases, while at smaller x it increases.

Fits to the data have been made in various ways. One (theoretically convenient) way is to consider 'moments' (Mellin transforms) of the structure functions, defined by

$$M_q^n(t) = \int_0^1 dx\, x^{n-1} q(x,t), \qquad (15.111)$$

where we have taken $\mu^2 = \mu_F^2$ and introduced the variable $t = \ln \mu^2$. Taking moments of both sides of (15.108) and interchanging the order of the x and y integrations, we find

$$\frac{dM_q^n(t)}{dt} = \frac{\alpha_s(t)}{2\pi} \int_0^1 dy\, y^{n-1} q(y,t) \int_0^y \frac{dx}{y} (x/y)^{n-1} P_{qq}(x/y). \qquad (15.112)$$

Changing the variable to $z = x/y$ in the second integral, and defining[4]

$$\gamma_{qq}^n = 4 \int_0^1 dz\, z^{n-1} P_{qq}(z), \qquad (15.113)$$

we obtain

$$\frac{dM_q^n(t)}{dt} = \frac{\alpha_s(t)}{8\pi} \gamma_{qq}^n M_q^n(t). \qquad (15.114)$$

Thus the integral in (15.108) – which is of convolution type – has been reduced to product form by this transformation. Now we also know from (15.47) and (15.48) that

$$\frac{d\alpha_s}{dt} = -\beta_0 \alpha_s^2 \qquad (15.115)$$

with $\beta_0 = (33 - 2N_f)/12\pi$ as usual, to this (one-loop) order. Thus (15.114) becomes

$$\frac{d\ln M_q^n}{d\ln \alpha_s} = -\frac{\gamma_{qq}^n}{8\pi\beta_0} = -d_{qq}^n, \text{ say.} \qquad (15.116)$$

The solution to (15.116) is easily found to be

$$M_q^n(t) = M_q^n(t_0) \left(\frac{\alpha_s(t_0)}{\alpha_s(t)} \right)^{d_{qq}^n}. \qquad (15.117)$$

Applying the prescription (15.99) to γ_n, we find (problem 15.9)

$$\gamma_{qq}^n = -\frac{8}{3} \left[1 - \frac{2}{n(n+1)} + 4 \sum_{j=2}^n \frac{1}{j} \right] \qquad (15.118)$$

---

[4]The notation is not chosen accidentally: the γ's are indeed anomalous dimensions of certain operators which appear in Wilson's operator product approach to scaling violations (Wilson 1969); interested readers may pursue this with Peskin and Schroeder 1995, chapter 18.

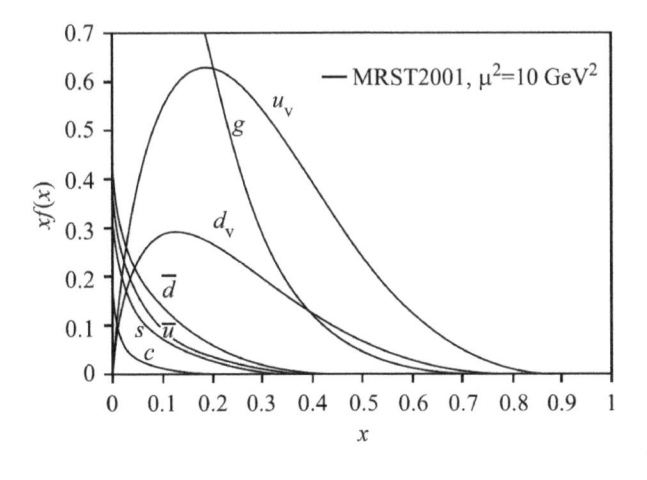

FIGURE 15.16
Distributions of x times the unpolarized parton distributions $f(x, \mu^2)$ (where $f = u_v, d_v, \bar{u}, \bar{d}, s, c, g$) using the MRST2001 parametrization (Martin *et al.* 2002) at a scale $\mu^2 = 10\,\text{GeV}^2$. Figure reprinted with permission from K Hagiwara *et al.* *Phys. Rev.* D **66** 010001 (2002). Copyright 2002 by the American Physical Society.

and then

$$d^n_{qq} = \frac{4}{33 - 2N_f} \left[1 - \frac{2}{n(n+1)} + 4 \sum_{j=2}^{n} \frac{1}{j} \right]. \tag{15.119}$$

We emphasize again that all the foregoing analysis is directly relevant only to distributions in which the flavour singlet gluon distributions do not contribute to the evolution equations. In the more general case, analogous splitting functions P_{qg}, P_{gq} and P_{gg} will enter, folded appropriately with the gluon distribution function $g(x, t)$, together with the related quantities $\gamma^n_{qg}, \gamma^n_{gq}$ and γ^n_{gg}. Equation (15.108) is then replaced by a 2×2 matrix equation for the evolution of the quark and gluon moments M^n_q and M^n_g.

Returning to (15.117), one way of testing it is to plot the logarithm of one moment, $\ln M^n_q$, versus the logarithm of another, $\ln M^m_q$, for different n, m values. A more direct procedure, applicable to the non-singlet case too of course, is to choose a reference point μ^2_0 and parametrize the parton distribution functions $f_i(x, t_0)$ in some way. These may then be evolved numerically, via the DGLAP equations, to the desired scale. Figure 15.16 shows a typical set of distributions at $\mu^2 = 10\,\text{GeV}^2$ (Martin *et al.* 2002). A global numerical fit is then performed to determine the best values of the parameters, including the parameter $\Lambda_{\overline{MS}}$ which enters into $\alpha_s(t)$. An example of such a fit, due to Martin *et al.* (1994), is shown in figure 15.17.

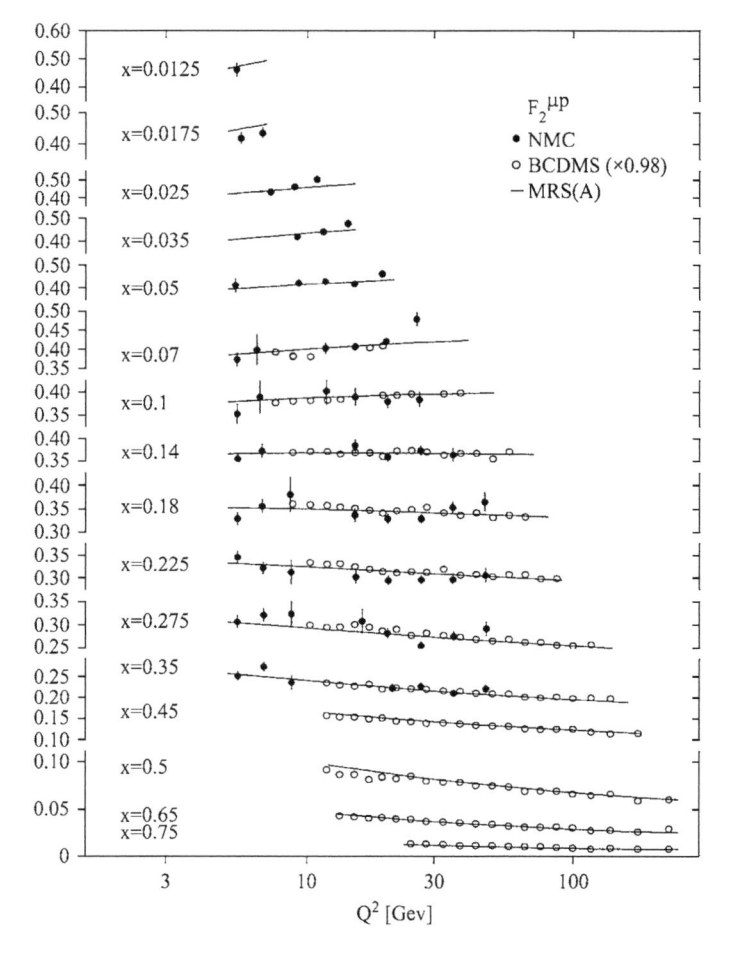

FIGURE 15.17
Data on the structure function F_2 in muon-proton deep inelastic scattering, from BCDMS (Benvenuti *et al.* 1989) and NMC (Amaudruz *et al.* 1992). The curves are QCD fits (Martin *et al.* 1994) as described in the text. Figure reprinted with permission from A D Martin *et al.* *Phys. Rev.* D **50** 6734 (1994). Copyright 1994 by the American Physical Society.

It may be worth pausing to reflect on how far our understanding of *structure* has developed, via quantum field theory, from the simple 'fixed number of constituents' models which are useful in atomic and nuclear physics. When nucleons are probed on finer and finer scales, more and more partons (gluons, q q̄ pairs) appear, in a way quantitatively predicted by QCD. The precise experimental confirmation of these predictions (and many others, as discussed by Ellis, Stirling and Webber 1996, for example) constitutes a remarkable vote of confidence, by Nature, in relativistic quantum field theory.

Problems

15.1 Verify equation (15.10).

15.2 Verify equation (15.27).

15.3 Check that (15.50) can be rewritten as (15.53).

15.4 (a) Verify (15.61). (b) Show that the next term in the expansion (15.60) is

$$\frac{(b_2 - b_1^2)}{\beta_0} \alpha_s$$

where $b_2 = \beta_2/\beta_0$. By iteratively solving the resulting modified equation (15.60), show that the corresponding correction to (15.61) is

$$+ \frac{1}{\beta_0^3 L^3} [b_1^2 (\ln^2 L^2 - \ln L - 1) + b_2].$$

15.5 Verify that for the type of behaviour of the β function shown in figure 15.7(b), α_s^* is reached as $q^2 \to 0$.

15.6 Verify equation (15.102).

15.7 Check that the electromagnetic charge e has dimension $(\text{mass})^{\epsilon/2}$ in $d = 4 - \epsilon$ dimensions.

15.8 Verify equation (O.20) in appendix O.

15.9 Verify equation (15.118).

16

Lattice Field Theory, and the Renormalization Group Revisited

16.1 Introduction

Throughout this book, thus far, we have relied on perturbation theory as the calculational tool, justifying its use in the case of QCD by the smallness of the coupling constant at short distances; note, however, that this result itself required the summation of an infinite series of perturbative terms. As remarked in section 15.3, the concomitant of asymptotic freedom is that α_s really does become strong at small Q^2, or at long distances of order $\Lambda_{\overline{\mathrm{MS}}}^{-1} \sim 1$ fm. Here we have no prospect of getting useful results from perturbation theory: it is the *non-perturbative regime*. But this is precisely the regime in which quarks bind together to form hadrons. If QCD is indeed the true theory of the interaction between quarks, then it should be able to explain, ultimately, the vast amount of data that exists in low energy hadronic physics. For example: what are the masses of mesons and baryons? Are there novel colourless states such as glueballs? Is $SU(2)_f$ or $SU(3)_f$ chiral symmetry spontaneously broken? What is the form of the effective interquark potential? What are the hadronic form factors, in electromagnetic (chapter 9) or weak (chapter 20) processes?

After more than 30 years of theoretical development, and machine advances, numerical simulations of *lattice QCD* are now yielding precise answers to many of these questions, thereby helping to establish QCD as the correct theory of the strong interactions of quarks, and also providing reliable input needed for the discovery of new physics. Lattice QCD is a highly mature field, and many technical details are beyond our scope. Rather, in this chapter we aim to give an elementary introduction to lattice field theory in general, including some important insights that it generates concerning the renormalization group. We return to QCD in the final section, with some illustrative results.

In thinking about how to formulate a non-perturbative approach to quantum field theory, several questions immediately arise. First of all, how can we regulate the ultraviolet divergences, and thus define the theory, if we cannot get to grips with them via the specific divergent integrals supplied by perturbation theory? We need to be able to regulate the divergences in a way which does not rely on their appearance in the Feynman graphs of pertur-

bation theory. As Wilson (1974, 1975) was the first to propose, one quite natural non-perturbative way of regulating ultraviolet divergences is to approximate continuous space-time by a discrete lattice of points. Such a lattice will introduce a minimum distance – namely the lattice spacing 'a' between neighbouring points. Since no two points can ever be closer than a, there is now a corresponding maximum momentum $\Lambda = \pi/a$ (see following equation (16.6)) in the lattice version of the theory. Thus the theory is automatically ultraviolet finite from the start, without presupposing the existence of any perturbative expansion; renormalization questions will, however, enter when we consider the a dependence of our parameters. As long as the lattice spacing is much smaller than the physical size of the hadrons one is studying, the lattice version of the theory should be a good approximation. Of course, Lorentz invariance is sacrificed in such an approach, and replaced by some form of hypercubic symmetry; we must hope that for small enough a this will not matter. We shall discuss how simple field theories are 'discretized' in the next section; scalar fields, fermion fields, and gauge fields each require their own prescriptions.

Next, we must ask how a discretized quantum field theory can be formulated in a way suitable for numerical computation. Any formalism based on non-commuting *operators* seems to be ruled out, since it is hard to see how they could be numerically simulated. Indeed, the same would be true of ordinary quantum mechanics. Fortunately a formulation does exist which avoids operators: Feynman's *sum over paths* approach, which was briefly mentioned in section 5.2.2. This method is the essential starting point for the lattice approach to quantum field theory, and it will be introduced in section 16.3. The sum over paths approach does not involve quantum operators, but fermions still have to be accommodated somehow. The way this is done is briefly described in section 16.3: see also appendix P.

It turns out that this formulation enables direct contact to be made between quantum field theory and *statistical mechanics*, as we shall discuss in section 16.3.3. This relationship has proved to be extremely fruitful, allowing physical insights and numerical techniques to pass from one subject to the other, in a way that has been very beneficial to both. In section 16.4 we make a worthwhile detour to explore the physics of renormalization and of the RGE from a lattice/statistical mechanics perspective, before returning to QCD in section 16.5.

16.2   Discretization

16.2.1   Scalar fields

We start by considering a simple field theory involving a scalar field ϕ. Postponing until section 16.3 the question of exactly how we shall use it, we assume

that we shall still want to formulate the theory in terms of an action of the form

$$S = \int d^4x \; \mathcal{L}(\phi, \boldsymbol{\nabla}\phi, \dot{\phi}). \tag{16.1}$$

It seems plausible that it might be advantageous to treat space and time as symmetrically as possible, from the start, by formulating the theory in 'Euclidean' space, instead of Minkowskian, by introducing $t = -i\tau$; further motivation for doing this will be provided in section 16.3. In that case, the action (16.1) becomes

$$S \;\rightarrow\; -i \int d^3x d\tau \; \mathcal{L}(\phi, \boldsymbol{\nabla}\phi, i\frac{\partial\phi}{\partial\tau}) \tag{16.2}$$

$$\equiv \; i \int d^3x d\tau \; \mathcal{L}_{\mathrm{E}} \equiv iS_{\mathrm{E}}. \tag{16.3}$$

A typical free scalar action is then

$$S_{\mathrm{E}}(\phi) = \frac{1}{2} \int d^3x d\tau \; \left[(\partial_\tau \phi)^2 + (\boldsymbol{\nabla}\phi)^2 + m^2\phi^2 \right]. \tag{16.4}$$

We now represent all of space-time by a finite-volume 'hypercube'. For example, we may have N_1 lattice points along the x-axis, so that a field $\phi(x)$ is replaced by the N_1 numbers $\phi(n_1 a)$ with $n_1 = 0, 1, \ldots N_1 - 1$. We write $L = N_1 a$ for the length of the cube side. In this notation, integrals and differentials are replaced by the finite sums and difference expressions

$$\int dx \rightarrow a \sum_{n_1}, \qquad \frac{\partial\phi}{\partial x} \rightarrow \frac{1}{a}[\phi(n_1 + 1) - \phi(n_1)], \tag{16.5}$$

so that a typical integral (in one dimension) becomes

$$\int dx \left(\frac{\partial\phi}{\partial x} \right)^2 \rightarrow a \sum_{n_1} \frac{1}{a^2} [\phi(n_1 + 1) - \phi(n_1)]^2. \tag{16.6}$$

As in all our previous work, we can alternatively consider a formulation in momentum space, which will also be discretized. It is convenient to impose periodic boundary conditions such that $\phi(x) = \phi(x + L)$. Then the allowed k-values may be taken to be $k_{\nu_1} = 2\pi\nu_1/L$ with $\nu_1 = -N_1/2+1, \ldots 0, \ldots N_1/2$ (we take N_1 to be even). It follows that the maximum allowed magnitude of the momentum is then π/a, indicating that a^{-1} is (as anticipated) playing the role of our earlier momentum cut-off Λ. We then write

$$\phi(n_1) = \sum_{\nu_1} \frac{1}{(N_1 a)^{\frac{1}{2}}} e^{i2\pi\nu_1 n_1/N_1} \tilde{\phi}(\nu_1), \tag{16.7}$$

which has the inverse

$$\tilde{\phi}(\nu_1) = \left(\frac{a}{N_1} \right)^{\frac{1}{2}} \sum_{n_1} e^{-i2\pi\nu_1 n_1/N_1} \phi(n_1), \tag{16.8}$$

since (problem 16.1)

$$\frac{1}{N_1} \sum_{n_1=0}^{N_1-1} e^{i2\pi n_1(\nu_1-\nu_2)/N_1} = \delta_{\nu_1,\nu_2}. \tag{16.9}$$

Equation (16.9) is a discrete version of the δ-function relation given in (E.25) of volume 1. A one-dimensional version of the mass term in (16.4) then becomes (problem 16.2)

$$\frac{1}{2} \int \mathrm{d}x \; m^2 \phi(x)^2 \to \frac{1}{2} m^2 \sum_{\nu_1} \tilde{\phi}(\nu_1)\tilde{\phi}(-\nu_1), \tag{16.10}$$

while

$$\frac{1}{2} \int \mathrm{d}x \left(\frac{\partial \phi}{\mathrm{d}x}\right)^2 \to \frac{2}{a^2} \sum_{\nu_1} \tilde{\phi}(\nu_1) \sin^2\left(\frac{\pi \nu_1}{N_1}\right) \tilde{\phi}(-\nu_1) \tag{16.11}$$

$$= \frac{1}{2a^2} \sum_{k_{\nu_1}} \tilde{\phi}(k_{\nu_1}) 4 \sin^2\left(\frac{k_{\nu_1} a}{2}\right) \tilde{\phi}(-k_{\nu_1}). \tag{16.12}$$

Thus a one-dimensional version of the free action (16.4) is

$$\frac{1}{2} \sum_{k_{\nu_1}} \tilde{\phi}(k_{\nu_1}) \left[\frac{4\sin^2(k_{\nu_1} a/2)}{a^2} + m^2\right] \tilde{\phi}(-k_{\nu_1}). \tag{16.13}$$

In the continuum case, (16.13) would be replaced by

$$\frac{1}{2} \int \frac{\mathrm{d}k}{2\pi} \tilde{\phi}(k) \left[k^2 + m^2\right] \tilde{\phi}(-k) \tag{16.14}$$

as usual, which implies that the propagator in the discrete case is proportional to

$$\left[\frac{4\sin^2(k_{\nu_1} a/2)}{a^2} + m^2\right]^{-1} \tag{16.15}$$

rather than to $\left[k^2 + m^2\right]^{-1}$ (remember we are in one-dimensional Euclidean space). The two expressions do coincide in the continuum limit $a \to 0$. The manipulations we have been going through will be easily recognized by readers familiar with the theory of lattice vibrations and phonons, and lead to a satisfactory discretization of scalar fields. For Dirac fields the matter is not so straightforward.

16.2.2   Dirac fields

The first obvious problem has already been mentioned: how are we to represent such entirely non-classical objects, which obey anticommutation relations? This is part of the wider problem of representing field operators in

a form suitable for numerical simulation, which we defer until section 16.3. There is, however, a quite separate problem which arises when we try to repeat for the Dirac field the discretization used for the scalar field.

First note that the Euclidean Dirac matrices γ_μ^{E} are related to the usual Minkowski ones γ_μ^{M} by $\gamma_{1,2,3}^{\mathrm{E}} \equiv -i\gamma_{1,2,3}^{\mathrm{M}}, \gamma_4^{\mathrm{E}} \equiv -i\gamma_4^{\mathrm{M}} \equiv \gamma_0^{\mathrm{M}}$. They satisfy $\{\gamma_\mu^{\mathrm{E}}, \gamma_\nu^{\mathrm{E}}\} = 2\delta_{\mu\nu}$ for $\mu = 1, 2, 3, 4$. The Euclidean Dirac Lagrangian is then $\bar\psi(x) \left[\gamma_\mu^{\mathrm{E}} \partial_\mu + m\right] \psi(x)$, which should be written now in Hermitean form

$$m\bar\psi(x)\psi(x) + \frac{1}{2}\left\{\bar\psi(x)\gamma_\mu^{\mathrm{E}}\partial_\mu\psi(x) - (\partial_\mu\bar\psi(x))\gamma_\mu^{\mathrm{E}}\psi(x)\right\}. \tag{16.16}$$

The corresponding 'one-dimensional' discretized action is then

$$a\sum_{n_1} m\bar\psi(n_1)\psi(n_1) \quad + \quad \frac{a}{2}\left\{\sum_{n_1}\bar\psi(n_1)\gamma_1^{\mathrm{E}}\left[\frac{\psi(n_1+1) - \psi(n_1)}{a}\right]\right.$$
$$\left. - \sum_{n_1}\left(\frac{\bar\psi(n_1+1) - \bar\psi(n_1)}{a}\right)\gamma_1^{\mathrm{E}}\psi(n_1)\right\} \tag{16.17}$$

$$= a\sum_{n_1}\left\{m\bar\psi(n_1)\psi(n_1) + \frac{1}{2a}\left[\bar\psi(n_1)\gamma_1^{\mathrm{E}}\psi(n_1+1) - \bar\psi(n_1+1)\gamma_1^{\mathrm{E}}\psi(n_1)\right]\right\}. \tag{16.18}$$

In momentum space this becomes (problem 16.3)

$$\sum_{k_{\nu_1}}\bar{\tilde\psi}(k_{\nu_1})\left[i\gamma_1^{\mathrm{E}}\frac{\sin(k_{\nu_1}a)}{a} + m\right]\tilde\psi(k_{\nu_1}), \tag{16.19}$$

and the inverse propagator is $\left[i\gamma_1^{\mathrm{E}}\frac{\sin(k_{\nu_1}a)}{a} + m\right]$. Thus the propagator itself is

$$\left[m - i\gamma_1^{\mathrm{E}}\frac{\sin(k_{\nu_1}a)}{a}\right] / \left[m^2 + \frac{\sin^2(k_{\nu_1}a)}{a^2}\right]. \tag{16.20}$$

But here there is a problem: in addition to the correct continuum limit $(a \to 0)$ found at $k_{\nu_1} \to 0$, an alternative finite $a \to 0$ limit is found at $k_{\nu_1} \to \pi/a$ (consider expanding $a^{-1}\sin\left[(\pi/a - \delta)a\right]$ for small δ). Thus two modes survive as $a \to 0$, a phenomenon known as the 'fermion doubling problem'. Actually in four dimensions there are *sixteen* such corners of the hypercube, so we have far too many degenerate lattice copies (which are called different 'tastes', to distinguish them from the real quark flavours).

Various solutions to this problem have been proposed. Wilson (1975), for example, suggested adding the extra term

$$-\frac{1}{2a}r\sum_{n_1}\bar\psi(n_1)[\psi(n_1+1) + \psi(n_1-1) - 2\psi(n_1)] \tag{16.21}$$

to the fermion action in this one-dimensional case, where r is dimensionless. Evidently this is a *second* difference, and it would correspond to the term

$$-\frac{1}{2}ra \int \mathrm{d}^3x \mathrm{d}\tau \ \bar{\psi}(x)(\partial_\tau^2 + \boldsymbol{\nabla}^2)\psi(x) \qquad (16.22)$$

in the four-dimensional continuum action. Note the presence of the lattice spacing 'a' in (16.22), which ensures its disappearance as $a \to 0$. The higher-derivative term $\bar{\psi}(\partial_\tau^2 + \boldsymbol{\nabla}^2)\psi$ has mass dimension 5, and therefore requires a coupling constant with mass dimension -1, i.e. a length in units $\hbar = c = 1$; it is, in fact, a non-renormalizable term. However, if we recall the discussion of section 11.8 in volume 1, we would expect it to be suppressed at low momenta much less than the cut-off π/a. Hence it is natural to see a coupling proportional to a appearing in (16.22). (We shall see in section 16.5.3 how renormalization group ideas provide a different perspective on such non-renormalizable interactions, classifying them as 'irrelevant').

How does the extra term (16.21) help the doubling problem? One easily finds that it changes the (one-dimensional) inverse propagator to

$$\left[i\gamma_1^{\mathrm{E}} \ \frac{\sin(k_{\nu_1}a)}{a} + m\right] + \frac{r}{a}(1 - \cos(k_{\nu_1}a)). \qquad (16.23)$$

By considering the expansion of the cosine near $k_{\nu_1} \approx 0$ it can be seen that the second term disappears in the continuum limit, as expected. However, for $k_{\nu_1} \approx \pi/a$ it gives a large term of order $\frac{1}{a}$ which adds to the mass m, effectively banishing the 'doubled' state to a very high mass, far from the physical spectrum.

Unfortunately there is a price to pay. The problem is that, as we learned in section 12.3.2, the QCD lagrangian has an exact chiral symmetry for massless quarks. To the extent that m_u and m_d (and m_s, but less so) are small on a hadronic scale such as $\Lambda_{\overline{\mathrm{MS}}}$, we expect chiral symmetry to have important physical consequences. These will indeed be explored in chapter 18. For the moment, we note merely that it is important for lattice-based QCD calculations to be able to deal correctly with the light quarks. Now we cannot simply choose the bare Lagrangian mass parameters to be small, and leave it at that. In any interacting theory, renormalization effects will cause shifts in these masses. In a chirally symmetric theory, or one which is chirally symmetric as a fermion mass goes to zero, such a mass shift is proportional to the fermion mass itself; in particular it does not simply add to the mass. We drew attention to this fact in the case of the electron mass renormalization in QED, in section 11.2. So in chirally symmetric theories, mass renormalizations are 'protected', in this sense. But the modification (16.21), while avoiding physical fermion doublers, breaks chiral symmetry badly. This can easily be seen by noting (see (12.154) for example) that the crucial property required for chiral symmetry to hold is

$$\gamma_5 \ \slashed{D} + \slashed{D}\gamma_5 = 0, \qquad (16.24)$$

where $\not{D}$ is the $SU(3)_c$-covariant Dirac derivative. Any addition to $\not{D}$ which is proportional to the unit 4×4 matrix will violate (16.24), and hence break chiral symmetry. The Lagrangian mass m itself is of this form, and it breaks chiral symmetry, but 'softly' – i.e. in a way that disappears as m goes to zero (thereby preserving the symmetry in this limit). The Wilson addition (16.21) also breaks chiral symmetry, but it remains there even as $m \to 0$: it is a 'hard' breaking.

This means that in the theory with the Wilson modification (i.e. with 'Wilson fermions') fermion mass renormalization will not be protected by the chiral symmetry, so that large additive renormalizations are possible. This will require repeated fine-tunings of the bare mass parameters, to bring them down to the desired small values. And it turns out that this seriously lengthens the computing time.

Another approach ('staggered fermions') was suggested by Kogut and Susskind (1975), Banks *et al.* (1976), and Susskind (1977). This essentially involves distributing the 4 spin degrees of freedom of the Dirac field across different lattice sites (we shall not need the details). At each site there is now a *one*-component fermion, with the colour degrees of freedom, which speeds the calculations. The 16-fold 'doubling' degeneracy can be re-arranged as four different tastes of 4-component fermions, while retaining enough chiral symmetry to forbid additive mass renormalizations.

Since the different components of the staggered Dirac field now live on different sites, they will experience slightly different gauge field interactions. (These are of course local in the continuum limit, but the point remains true after discretization, as we shall see in the following section.) These interactions will mix fields of different tastes, causing new problems, but they can be suppressed by adding further terms to the action. There is still the 4-fold degeneracy to get rid of, but a trick is available for that, as we shall explain in section 16.3.

One might wonder if a lattice theory with fermions could be formulated such that it both avoids doublers and preserves chiral symmetry. For quite a long time it was believed that this was not possible – a conclusion which was essentially the content of the Nielsen–Ninomaya theorem (Nielsen and Ninomaya 1981a, b, c). But more recently a way was found to formulate chiral gauge theories with fermions satisfactorily on the lattice at finite spacing a. The key is to replace the condition (16.24) by the Ginsparg–Wilson (1982) relation

$$\gamma_5 \not{D} + \not{D} \gamma_5 = a \not{D} \gamma_5 \not{D} . \tag{16.25}$$

This relation implies (Lüscher 1998) that the associated action has an exact symmetry, with infinitesimal variations proportional to

$$\delta\psi = \gamma_5 \left(1 - \frac{1}{2} a \not{D} \right) \psi \tag{16.26}$$

$$\delta\overline{\psi} = \overline{\psi} \left(1 - \frac{1}{2} a \not{D} \right) \gamma_5 . \tag{16.27}$$

The symmetry under (16.26)–(16.27), which is proportional to the infinitesimal version of (12.152) as $a \to 0$, provides a lattice theory with all the fundamental symmetry properties of continuum chiral gauge theories (Hasenfratz *et al.* 1998). Finding an operator which satisfies (16.25) is, however, not so easy – but that problem has now been solved, indeed in three different ways: Kaplan's 'domain wall' fermions (Kaplan 1992); 'classically perfect fermions' (Hasenfratz and Niedermayer 1994); and overlap fermions (Narayanan and Neuberger 1993a, b, 1994, 1995). Unfortunately all these proposals are computationally more expensive than the Wilson or staggered fermion alternatives.

16.2.3   Gauge fields

Having explored the discretization of actions for free scalars and Dirac fermions, we must now think about how to implement gauge invariance on the lattice. In the usual (continuum) case, we saw in chapter 13 how this was implemented by replacing ordinary derivatives by *covariant derivatives*, the geometrical significance of which (in terms of parallel transport) is discussed in appendix N. It is very instructive to see how the same ideas arise naturally in the lattice case.

We illustrate the idea in the simple case of the Abelian $U(1)$ theory, QED. Consider, for example, a charged scalar field $\phi(x)$, with charge e. To construct a gauge-invariant current, for example, we replaced $\phi^\dagger \partial_\mu \phi$ by $\phi^\dagger (\partial_\mu + ieA_\mu)\phi$, so we ask: what is the discrete analogue of this? The term $\phi^\dagger(x)\frac{\partial}{\partial x}\phi(x)$ becomes, as we have seen,

$$\phi^\dagger(n_1)\frac{1}{a}[\phi(n_1 + 1) - \phi(n_1)a] \tag{16.28}$$

in one dimension. We do *not* expect (16.28) by itself to be gauge invariant, and it is easy to check that it is not. Under a gauge transformation for the continuous case, we have

$$\phi(x) \to e^{ie\theta(x)}\phi(x), A(x) \to A(x) + \frac{d\theta(x)}{dx}; \tag{16.29}$$

then $\phi^\dagger(x)\phi(y)$ transforms by

$$\phi^\dagger(x)\phi(y) \to e^{-ie[\theta(x)-\theta(y)]}\phi^\dagger(x)\phi(y), \tag{16.30}$$

and is clearly not invariant. The essential reason is that this operator involves the fields at two *different* points, and so the term $\phi^\dagger(n_1)\phi(n_1 + 1)$ in (16.28) will not be gauge invariant either. The discussion in appendix N prepares us for this: we are trying to compare two 'vectors' (here, fields) at two different points, when the 'coordinate axes' are changing as we move about. We need to parallel transport one field to the same point as the other, before they can be properly compared. The solution (N.18) shows us how to do this. Consider the quantity

$$\mathcal{O}(x, y) = \phi^\dagger(x)\exp[ie\int_y^x A dx']\phi(y). \tag{16.31}$$

Under the gauge transformation (16.29), $\mathcal{O}(x, y)$ transforms by

$$\mathcal{O}(x, y) \to \phi^\dagger(x)e^{-ie\theta(x)}e^{\{ie\int_y^x A dx' + ie[\theta(x) - \theta(y)]\}}e^{ie\theta(y)}\phi(y) = \mathcal{O}(x, y), \tag{16.32}$$

and it is therefore gauge invariant. The familiar 'covariant derivative' rule can be recovered by letting $y = x + dx$ for infinitesimal dx, and by considering the gauge-invariant quantity

$$\lim_{dx \to 0} \left[\frac{\mathcal{O}(x, x + dx) - \mathcal{O}(x, x)}{dx}\right]. \tag{16.33}$$

Evaluating (16.33) one finds (problem 16.4) the result

$$\phi^\dagger(x)\left(\frac{d}{dx} - ieA\right)\phi(x) \tag{16.34}$$

$$\equiv \phi^\dagger(x)D_x\phi(x) \tag{16.35}$$

with the usual definition of the covariant derivative. In the discrete case, we merely keep the finite version of (16.31), and replace $\phi^\dagger(n_1)\phi(n_1+1)$ in (16.28) by the gauge invariant quantity

$$\phi^\dagger(n_1)U(n_1, n_1 + 1)\phi(n_1 + 1), \tag{16.36}$$

where the *link variable* U is defined by

$$U(n_1, n_1 + 1) = \exp\left[ie\int_{(n_1+1)a}^{n_1 a} A dx'\right]. \tag{16.37}$$

Note that

$$U(n_1, n_1 + 1) \to \exp[-ieA(n_1)a] \tag{16.38}$$

in the small a limit.

Similarly, the free Dirac term $\bar{\psi}(n_1)\gamma_1^E\psi(n_1 + 1) - \bar{\psi}(n_1 + 1)\gamma_1^E\psi(n_1)$ in (16.18) is replaced by the gauge-invariant term

$$\bar{\psi}(n_1)\gamma_1^E U(n_1, n_1 + 1)\psi(n_1 + 1) - \bar{\psi}(n_1 + 1)\gamma_1^E U(n_1 + 1, n_1)\psi(n_1). \tag{16.39}$$

The generalization to more dimensions is straightforward. In the non-Abelian $SU(2)$ or $SU(3)$ case, 'eA' in (16.38) is replaced by $gt^a A^a(n_1)$ where the t's are the appropriate matrices, as in the continuum form of the covariant derivative. A link variable $U(n_2, n_1)$ may be drawn as in figure 16.1. Note that the order of the arguments is significant: $U(n_2, n_1) = U^{-1}(n_1, n_2) = U^\dagger(n_1, n_2)$ from (16.38), which is why the link carries an arrow.

Thus gauge invariant discretized derivatives of charged fields can be constructed. What about the Maxwell action for the U(1) gauge field? This does not exist in only one dimension ($\partial_\mu A_\nu - \partial_\nu A_\mu$ cannot be formed), so let us move into two. Again, our discussion of the geometrical significance of $F_{\mu\nu}$ as

FIGURE 16.1
Link variable $U(n_2; n_1)$ in one dimension.

a curvature guides us to the answer. Consider the product $U_\square$ of link variables around a square path (figure 16.2) of side a (reading from the right):

$$
\begin{aligned}
U_\square \;=\;& U(n_x, n_y; n_x, n_{y+1})U(n_x, n_{y+1}; n_{x+1}, n_{y+1}) \\
& \times\, U(n_{x+1}, n_{y+1}; n_{x+1}, n_y)U(n_{x+1}, n_y; n_x, n_y). \quad (16.40)
\end{aligned}
$$

It is straightforward to verify, first, that $U_\square$ is gauge invariant. Under a gauge transformation, the link $U(n_{x+1}, n_y; n_x, n_y)$, for example, transforms by a factor (cf equation (16.32))

$$
\exp\{ie[\theta(n_{x+1}, n_y) - \theta(n_x, n_y)]\}, \quad (16.41)
$$

and similarly for the three other links in $U_\square$. In this Abelian case the exponentials contain no matrices, and the accumulated phase factors cancel out, verifying the gauge invariance. Next, let us see how to recover the Maxwell action. Adding the exponentials again, we can write

$$
\begin{aligned}
U_\square \;\equiv\;& \exp\{-iea A_y(n_x, n_y) - iea A_x(n_x, n_y + 1) \\
& + iea A_y(n_x + 1, n_y) + iea A_x(n_x, n_y)\} \quad (16.42) \\
=\;& \exp\left\{-iea^2 \left[\frac{A_x(n_x, n_y + 1) - A_x(n_x, n_y)}{a}\right]\right. \\
& \left. + iea^2 \left[\frac{A_y(n_x + 1, n_y) - A_y(n_x, n_y)}{a}\right]\right\} \quad (16.43) \\
=\;& \exp\left\{+iea^2 \left(\frac{\partial A_y}{\partial x} - \frac{\partial A_x}{\partial y}\right)\right\}, \quad (16.44)
\end{aligned}
$$

using the derivative definition of (16.5). For small 'a' we may expand the exponential in (16.44). We also take the real part to remove the imaginary terms, leading to

$$
\sum_\square (1 - \operatorname{Re} U_\square) \to \frac{1}{2} \sum_\square e^2 a^4 (F_{xy})^2, \quad (16.45)
$$

where $F_{xy} = \frac{\partial A_y}{\partial x} - \frac{\partial A_x}{\partial y}$ as usual. To relate this to the continuum limit we must note that we sum over each such *plaquette* with only one definite orientation, so that the sum over plaquettes is equivalent to half of the entire

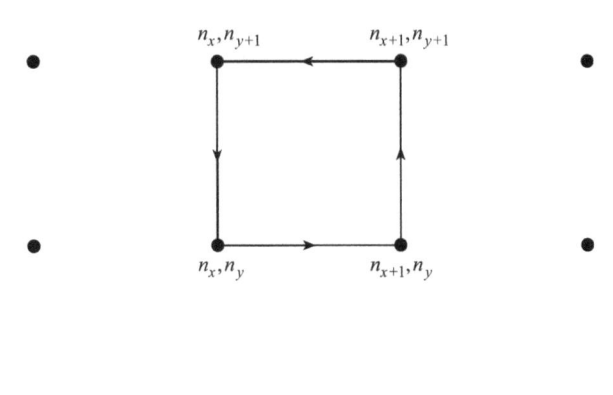

FIGURE 16.2

A simple plaquette in two dimensions.

sum. Thus

$$\sum_{\square}(1 - \mathrm{Re}\, U_{\square}) \;\rightarrow\; \frac{1}{4}\sum_{n_1,n_2} e^2 a^4 F_{xy}^2$$

$$\rightarrow\; e^2 a^2 \int\int \frac{1}{4} F_{xy}^2 \,\mathrm{d}x\mathrm{d}y. \tag{16.46}$$

(Note that in two dimensions 'e' has dimensions of mass.) In four dimensions similar manipulations lead to the form

$$S_{\mathrm{E}} = \frac{1}{e^2}\sum_{\square}(1 - \mathrm{Re}\, U_{\square}) \rightarrow \frac{1}{4}\int \mathrm{d}^3x\mathrm{d}\tau F_{\mu\nu}^2 \tag{16.47}$$

for the lattice action, as required. In the non-Abelian case, as noted above, 'eA' is replaced by 'gt · A'; for SU(3), the analogue of (16.47) is

$$S_g = \frac{2}{g^2}\sum_{\square}\mathrm{Tr}(1 - \mathrm{Re}\, U_{\square}), \tag{16.48}$$

where the trace is over the SU(3) matrices.

16.3   Representation of quantum amplitudes

So (with some suitable fermionic action) we have a gauge-invariant 'classical' field theory defined on a lattice, with a suitable continuum limit. (Actually,

the $a \to 0$ limit of the quantum theory is, as we shall see in section 16.5, more subtle than the naive replacements (16.5) because of renormalization issues, as should be no surprise to the reader by now). However, we have not yet considered how we are going to turn this classical lattice theory into a quantum one. The fact that the calculations are mostly going to have to be done numerically seems at once to require a formulation that avoids non-commuting operators. This is precisely what is provided by Feynman's *sum over paths* formulation of quantum mechanics and of quantum field theory, and it is therefore an essential element in the lattice approach to quantum field theory. In this section we give a brief introduction to this formalism, starting with quantum mechanics.

16.3.1   Quantum mechanics

In section 5.2.2 we stated that in this approach the amplitude for a quantum system, described by a Lagrangian L depending on one degree of freedom $q(t)$, to pass from a state in which $q = q^i$ at $t = t_i$ to a state in which $q = q^f$ at time $t = t_f$, is proportional to (with $\hbar = 1$)

$$\sum_{\text{all paths } q(t)} \exp\left(i \int_{t_i}^{t_f} L(q(t), \dot{q}(t)) dt\right), \tag{16.49}$$

where $q(t_i) = q^i$, and $q(t_f) = q^f$. We shall now provide some justification for this assertion.

We begin by recalling how, in ordinary quantum mechanics, state vectors and observables are related in the Schrödinger and Heisenberg pictures (see appendix I of volume 1). Let $\hat{q}$ be the canonical coordinate operator in the Schrödinger picture, with an associated complete set of eigenvectors $|q\rangle$ such that

$$\hat{q}|q\rangle = q|q\rangle . \tag{16.50}$$

The corresponding Heisenberg operator $\hat{q}_{\text{H}}(t)$ is defined by

$$\hat{q}_{\text{H}}(t) = e^{i\hat{H}(t-t_0)}\hat{q}e^{-i\hat{H}(t-t_0)} \tag{16.51}$$

where $\hat{H}$ is the Hamiltonian, and t_0 is the (arbitrary) time at which the two pictures coincide. Now define the Heisenberg picture state $|q_t\rangle_{\text{H}}$ by

$$|q_t\rangle_{\text{H}} = e^{i\hat{H}(t-t_0)}|q\rangle . \tag{16.52}$$

We then easily obtain from (16.50)–(16.52) the result

$$\hat{q}_{\text{H}}(t)|q_t\rangle_{\text{H}} = q|q_t\rangle_{\text{H}} , \tag{16.53}$$

which shows that $|q_t\rangle_{\text{H}}$ is the (Heisenberg picture) state which at time t is an eigenstate of $\hat{q}_{\text{H}}(t)$ with eigenvalue q. Consider now the quantity

$$_{\text{H}}\langle q_{t_f}^f | q_{t_i}^i \rangle_{\text{H}} \tag{16.54}$$

which is, indeed, the amplitude for the system described by $\hat{H}$ to go from q^i at t_i to q^f at t_f. Using (16.52) we can write

$$_H\langle q^f_{t_f}|q^i_{t_i}\rangle_H = \langle q^f|e^{-i\hat{H}(t_f-t_i)}|q^i\rangle ; \tag{16.55}$$

we want to understand how (16.55) can be represented as (16.49).

We shall demonstrate the connection explicitly for the special case of a free particle, for which

$$\hat{H} = \frac{\hat{p}^2}{2m} . \tag{16.56}$$

For this case, we can evaluate (16.55) directly as follows. Inserting a complete set of momentum eigenstates, we obtain[1]

$$
\begin{aligned}
\langle q^f|e^{-i\hat{H}(t_f-t_i)}|q^i\rangle &= \int_{-\infty}^{\infty} \langle q^f|p\rangle\langle p|e^{-i\hat{H}(t_f-t_i)}|q^i\rangle \, dp \\
&= \frac{1}{2\pi}\int_{-\infty}^{\infty} e^{ipq^f}e^{-ip^2(t_f-t_i)/2m}e^{-ipq^i} \, dp \\
&= \frac{1}{2\pi}\int_{-\infty}^{\infty} \exp\left\{-i\left[\frac{p^2(t_f-t_i)}{2m} - p(q^f-q^i)\right]\right\} dp .
\end{aligned}
\tag{16.57}
$$

To evaluate the integral, we complete the square via the steps

$$
\begin{aligned}
\frac{p^2(t_f-t_i)}{2m} - p(q^f-q^i) &= \left(\frac{t_f-t_i}{2m}\right)\left[p^2 - \frac{2mp(q^f-q^i)}{t_f-t_i}\right] \\
&= \left(\frac{t_f-t_i}{2m}\right)\left\{\left[p - \frac{m(q^f-q^i)}{t_f-t_i}\right]^2 - \frac{m^2(q^f-q^i)^2}{(t_f-t_i)^2}\right\} \\
&= \left(\frac{t_f-t_i}{2m}\right)p'^2 - \frac{m(q^f-q^i)^2}{2(t_f-t_i)} ,
\end{aligned}
\tag{16.58}
$$

where

$$p' = p - \frac{m(q^f-q^i)}{t_f-t_i} . \tag{16.59}$$

We then shift the integration variable in (16.57) to p', and obtain

$$\langle q^f|e^{-i\hat{H}(t_f-t_i)}|q^i\rangle = \frac{1}{2\pi}\exp\left[i\frac{m(q^f-q^i)^2}{2(t_f-t_i)}\right]\int_{-\infty}^{\infty} dp' \exp\left[-\frac{i(t_f-t_i)p'^2}{2m}\right] . \tag{16.60}$$

As it stands, the integral in (16.60) is not well-defined, being rapidly oscillatory for large p'. However, it is at this point that the motivation for passing to

---

[1] Remember that $\langle q|p\rangle$ is the q-space wavefunction of a state with definite momentum p, and is therefore a plane wave; we are using the normalization of equation (E.26) in volume 1.

'Euclidean' space-time arises. If we make the replacement $t \to -i\tau$, (16.60) becomes

$$\langle q^{\mathrm{f}}|e^{-\hat{H}(\tau_{\mathrm{f}}-\tau_{\mathrm{i}})}|q^{\mathrm{i}}\rangle = \frac{1}{2\pi}\exp\left[-\frac{m(q^{\mathrm{f}}-q^{\mathrm{i}})^2}{2(\tau_{\mathrm{f}}-\tau_{\mathrm{i}})}\right]\int_{-\infty}^{\infty}\mathrm{d}p'\exp\left[-\frac{(\tau_{\mathrm{f}}-\tau_{\mathrm{i}})p'^2}{2m}\right]$$

(16.61)

and the integral is a simple convergent Gaussian. Using the result

$$\int_{-\infty}^{\infty}\mathrm{d}\xi e^{-b\xi^2} = \sqrt{\frac{\pi}{b}}$$

(16.62)

we finally obtain

$$\langle q^{\mathrm{f}}|e^{-\hat{H}(\tau_{\mathrm{f}}-\tau_{\mathrm{i}})}|q^{\mathrm{i}}\rangle = \left[\frac{m}{2\pi(\tau_{\mathrm{f}}-\tau_{\mathrm{i}})}\right]^{\frac{1}{2}}\exp\left[-\frac{m(q^{\mathrm{f}}-q^{\mathrm{i}})^2}{2(\tau_{\mathrm{f}}-\tau_{\mathrm{i}})}\right].$$

(16.63)

We must now understand how the result (16.63) can be represented in the form (16.49). In Euclidean space, (16.49) is

$$\sum_{\mathrm{paths}}\exp\left(-\int_{\tau_{\mathrm{i}}}^{\tau_{\mathrm{f}}}\frac{1}{2}m\left(\frac{\mathrm{d}q}{\mathrm{d}\tau}\right)^2\mathrm{d}\tau\right)$$

(16.64)

in the free-particle case. We interpret the τ integral in terms of a discretization procedure, similar to that introduced in section 16.2. We split the interval $\tau_{\mathrm{f}} - \tau_{\mathrm{i}}$ into N segments each of size ϵ, as shown in figure 16.3. The τ-integral in (16.64) becomes the sum

$$m\sum_{j=1}^{N}\frac{(q^j - q^{j-1})^2}{2\epsilon},$$

(16.65)

and the 'sum over paths', in going from $q^0 \equiv q^{\mathrm{i}}$ at τ_{i} to $q^N \equiv q^{\mathrm{f}}$ at τ_{f}, is now interpreted as a multiple integral over all the intermediate positions $q^1, q^2, \ldots, q^{N-1}$ which paths can pass through at 'times' $\tau_1, \tau_2, \ldots, \tau_{N-1}$:

$$\frac{1}{A(\epsilon)}\int\int\cdots\int\exp\left[-m\sum_{j=1}^{N}\frac{(q^j - q^{j-1})^2}{2\epsilon}\right]\frac{\mathrm{d}q^1}{A(\epsilon)}\frac{\mathrm{d}q^2}{A(\epsilon)}\cdots\frac{\mathrm{d}q^{N-1}}{A(\epsilon)},$$

(16.66)

where $A(\epsilon)$ is a normalizing factor, depending on ϵ, which is to be determined.

The integrals in (16.66) are all of Gaussian form, and since the integral of a Gaussian is again a Gaussian (cf the manipulations leading from (16.57) to (16.60), but without the 'i' in the exponents), we may perform all the integrations analytically. We follow the method of Feynman and Hibbs (1965), section 3.1. Consider the integral over q^1:

$$I^1 \equiv \int\exp\left\{-\frac{m}{2\epsilon}\left[(q^2 - q^1)^2 + (q^1 - q^{\mathrm{i}})^2\right]\right\}\mathrm{d}q^1.$$

(16.67)

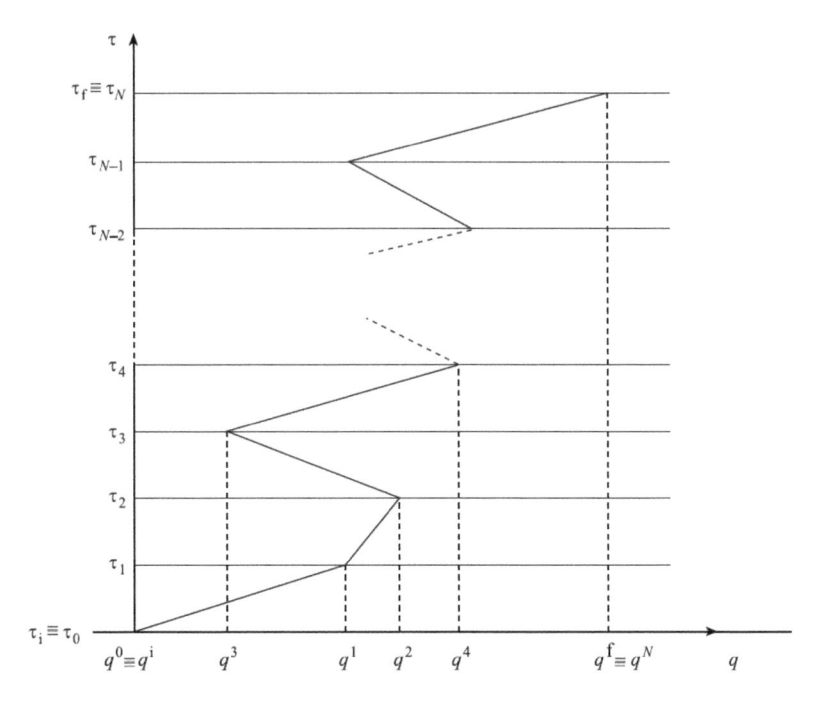

FIGURE 16.3
A 'path' from $q^0 \equiv q^i$ at τ_i to $q^N \equiv q^f$ at τ_f, via the intermediate positions $q^1, q^2, \ldots, q^{N-1}$ at $\tau_1, \tau_2, \ldots, \tau_{N-1}$.

This can be evaluated by completing the square, shifting the integration variable, and using (16.62), to obtain (problem 16.5)

$$I^1 = \left(\frac{\pi\epsilon}{m}\right)^{\frac{1}{2}} \exp\left[\frac{-m}{4\epsilon}(q^2 - q^i)^2\right] . \tag{16.68}$$

Now the procedure may be repeated for the q^2 integral

$$I^2 \equiv \int \exp\left\{-\frac{m}{4\epsilon}(q^2 - q^i)^2 - \frac{m}{2\epsilon}(q^3 - q^2)^2\right\} dq^2 , \tag{16.69}$$

which yields (problem 16.5)

$$I^2 = \left(\frac{4\pi\epsilon}{3m}\right)^{\frac{1}{2}} \exp\left[\frac{-m}{6\epsilon}(q^3 - q^i)^2\right] . \tag{16.70}$$

As far as the exponential factors in (16.63) in (16.64) are concerned, the pattern is now clear: after $n - 1$ steps we shall have an exponential factor

$$\exp\left[-m(q^n - q^i)^2/(2n\epsilon)\right] . \tag{16.71}$$

Hence, after $N - 1$ steps we shall have a factor

$$\exp\left[-m(q^f - q^i)^2/2(\tau_f - \tau_i)\right] , \tag{16.72}$$

remembering that $q^N \equiv q^f$ and that $\tau_f - \tau_i = N\epsilon$. So we have recovered the correct exponential factor of (16.63), and all that remains is to choose $A(\epsilon)$ in (16.66) so as to produce the same normalization as (16.63).

The required $A(\epsilon)$ is

$$A(\epsilon) = \sqrt{\frac{2\pi\epsilon}{m}} , \tag{16.73}$$

as we now verify. For the first (q^1) integration, the formula (16.66) contains two factors of $A^{-1}(\epsilon)$, so that the result (16.68) becomes

$$
\begin{aligned}
\frac{1}{[A(\epsilon)]^2} I^1 &= \frac{m}{2\pi\epsilon} \left(\frac{\pi\epsilon}{m}\right)^{\frac{1}{2}} \exp\left[-\frac{m}{4\epsilon}(q^2 - q^i)^2\right] \\
&= \left(\frac{m}{2\pi 2\epsilon}\right)^{\frac{1}{2}} \exp\left[-\frac{m}{4\epsilon}(q^2 - q^i)^2\right] .
\end{aligned}
\tag{16.74}
$$

For the second (q^2) integration, the accumulated constant factor is

$$\frac{1}{A(\epsilon)} \left(\frac{m}{2\pi 2\epsilon}\right)^{\frac{1}{2}} \left(\frac{4\pi\epsilon}{3m}\right)^{\frac{1}{2}} = \left(\frac{m}{2\pi 3\epsilon}\right)^{\frac{1}{2}} . \tag{16.75}$$

Proceeding in this way, one can convince oneself that after $N - 1$ steps, the accumulated constant is

$$\left(\frac{m}{2\pi N\epsilon}\right)^{\frac{1}{2}} = \left[\frac{m}{2\pi(\tau_f - \tau_i)}\right]^{\frac{1}{2}} , \tag{16.76}$$

as in (16.63).

The equivalence of (16.63) and (16.64) (in the sense $\epsilon \to 0$) is therefore established for the free-particle case. More general cases are discussed in Feynman and Hibbs (1965) chapter 5, and in Peskin and Schroeder (1995) chapter 9. The conventional notation for the path-integral amplitude is

$$\langle q^f | e^{-\hat{H}(\tau_f - \tau_i)} | q^i \rangle = \int \mathcal{D}q(\tau) e^{-\int_{\tau_i}^{\tau_f} L\, d\tau} , \tag{16.77}$$

where the right-hand side of (16.77) is interpreted in the sense of (16.66).

We now proceed to discuss further aspects of the path-integral formulation. Consider the (Euclideanized) amplitude $\langle q^f | e^{-\hat{H}(\tau_f - \tau_i)} | q^i \rangle$, and insert a complete set of energy eigenstates $|n\rangle$ such that $\hat{H}|n\rangle = E_n|n\rangle$:

$$\langle q^f | e^{-\hat{H}(\tau_f - \tau_i)} | q^i \rangle = \sum_n \langle q^f | n \rangle \langle n | q^i \rangle e^{-E_n(\tau_f - \tau_i)} . \tag{16.78}$$

Equation (16.78) shows that if we take the limits $\tau_i \to -\infty$, $\tau_f \to \infty$, then the

state of lowest energy E_0 (the ground state) provides the dominant contribution. Thus, in this limit, our amplitude will represent the process in which the system begins in its ground state $|\Omega\rangle$ at $\tau_i \to -\infty$, with $q = q^i$, and ends in $|\Omega\rangle$ at $\tau_f \to \infty$, with $q = q^f$.

How do we represent propagators in this formalism? Consider the expression (somewhat analogous to a field theory propagator)

$$G_{fi}(t_a, t_b) \equiv \langle q^f_{t_f} | T \{\hat{q}_H(t_a)\hat{q}_H(t_b)\} | q^i_{t_i}\rangle \,, \tag{16.79}$$

where T is the usual time-ordering operator. Using (16.51) and (16.52), (16.79) can be written, for $t_b > t_a$, as

$$G_{fi}(t_a, t_b) = \langle q^f | e^{-i\hat{H}(t_f - t_b)} \hat{q} e^{-i\hat{H}(t_b - t_a)} \hat{q} e^{-i\hat{H}(t_a - t_i)} | q^i\rangle \,. \tag{16.80}$$

Inserting a complete set of states and Euclideanizing, (16.80) becomes

$$\begin{aligned} G_{fi}(t_a, t_b) &= \int dq^a dq^b \ q^a q^b \langle q^f | e^{-\hat{H}(\tau_f - \tau_b)} | q^b\rangle \\ &\quad \times \langle q^b | e^{-\hat{H}(\tau_b - \tau_a)} | q^a\rangle \langle q^a | e^{-\hat{H}(\tau_a - \tau_i)} | q^i\rangle \,. \end{aligned} \tag{16.81}$$

Now, each of the three matrix elements has a discretized representation of the form (16.63), with say $N_1 - 1$ variables in the interval (τ_a, τ_i), $N_2 - 1$ in (τ_b, τ_a) and $N_3 - 1$ in (τ_f, τ_b). Each such representation carries one 'surplus' factor of $[A(\epsilon)]^{-1}$, making an overall factor of $[A(\epsilon)]^{-3}$. Two of these factors can be associated with the $dq^a dq^b$ integration in (16.81), so that we have a total of $N_1 + N_2 + N_3 - 1$ properly normalized integrations, and one 'surplus' factor $[A(\epsilon)]^{-1}$ as in (16.66). If we now identify $q(\tau_a) \equiv q^a$, $q(\tau_n) \equiv q^b$, it follows that (16.81) is simply

$$\int \mathcal{D}q(\tau) q(\tau_a) q(\tau_b) e^{-\int_{\tau_i}^{\tau_f} L\, d\tau} \,. \tag{16.82}$$

In obtaining (16.82), we took the case $\tau_b > \tau_a$. Suppose alternatively that $\tau_a > \tau_b$. Then the order of τ_a and τ_b inside the interval (τ_i, τ_f) is simply reversed, but since q^a and q^b in (16.81), or $q(\tau_a)$ and $q(\tau_b)$ in (16.82), are ordinary (commuting) numbers, the formula (16.82) is unaltered, and actually does represent the matrix element (16.79) of the time-ordered product.

16.3.2 Quantum field theory

The generalizations of these results to the field theory case are intuitively clear. For example, in the case of a single scalar field $\phi(\mathbf{x})$, we expect the analogue of (16.82) to be (cf (16.4))

$$\int \mathcal{D}\phi(x) \, \phi(x_a)\phi(x_b) \exp\left[-\int_{\tau_i}^{\tau_f} \mathcal{L}_E(\phi, \nabla\phi, \partial_\tau \phi)\, d^4 x_E\right] \,, \tag{16.83}$$

where
$$d^4 x_E = d^3 \mathbf{x} d\tau, \tag{16.84}$$

and the boundary conditions are given by $\phi(\mathbf{x}, \tau_i) = \phi^i(x)$, $\phi(\mathbf{x}, \tau_f) = \phi^f(x)$, $\phi(\mathbf{x}, \tau_a) = \phi^a(x)$ and $\phi(\mathbf{x}, \tau_b) = \phi^b(x)$, say. In (16.83), we have to understand that a *four*-dimensional discretization of Euclidean space-time is implied, the fields being Fourier-analyzed by four-dimensional generalizations of expressions such as (16.7). Just as in (16.79)–(16.82), (16.83) is equal to

$$\langle \phi^f(x) | e^{-\hat{H}\tau_f} T \left\{ \hat{\phi}_H(x_a) \hat{\phi}_H(x_b) \right\} e^{-\hat{H}\tau_i} | \phi^i(x) \rangle . \tag{16.85}$$

Taking the limits $\tau_i \to -\infty$, $\tau_f \to \infty$ will project out the configuration of lowest energy, as discussed after (16.78), which in this case is the (interacting) vacuum state $|\Omega\rangle$. Thus in this limit the surviving part of (16.85) is

$$\langle \phi^f(x) | \Omega \rangle e^{-E_\Omega \tau} \langle \Omega | T \left\{ \hat{\phi}_H(x_a) \hat{\phi}_H(x_b) \right\} | \Omega \rangle e^{-E_\Omega \tau} \langle \Omega | \phi^i(x) \rangle \tag{16.86}$$

with $\tau \to \infty$. The exponential and overlap factors can be removed by dividing by the same quantity as (16.85) but without the additional fields $\phi(x_a)$ and $\phi(x_b)$. In this way, we obtain the formula for the *field theory propagator* in four-dimensional Euclidean space:

$$\langle \Omega | T \left\{ \hat{\phi}_H(x_a) \hat{\phi}_H(x_b) \right\} | \Omega \rangle = \lim_{\tau \to \infty} \frac{\int \mathcal{D}\phi \, \phi(x_a) \phi(x_b) \exp[-\int_{-\tau}^{\tau} \mathcal{L}_E d^4 x_E]}{\int \mathcal{D}\phi \exp[-\int_{-\tau}^{\tau} \mathcal{L}_E d^4 x_E]} . \tag{16.87}$$

Vacuum expectation values of time-ordered products of more fields will simply have more factors of ϕ on both sides.

Perturbation theory can be developed in this formalism also. Suppose $\mathcal{L}_E = \mathcal{L}_E^0 + \mathcal{L}_E^{\text{int}}$, where $\mathcal{L}_E^0$ describes a free scalar field and $\mathcal{L}_E^{\text{int}}$ is an interaction, for example $\lambda \phi^4$. Then, assuming λ is small, the exponential in (16.87) can be expressed as

$$\exp\left[-\int d^4 x_E \left(\mathcal{L}_E^0 + \mathcal{L}_E^{\text{int}} \right) \right] = \left(\exp - \int d^4 x_E \, \mathcal{L}_E^0 \right) \left(1 - \lambda \int d^4 x_E \phi^4 + \dots \right) \tag{16.88}$$

and both numerator and denominator of (16.87) may be expressed as vevs of products of free fields. Compact techniques exist for analyzing this formulation of perturbation theory (Ryder 1985, chapter 6, Peskin & Schroeder 1995, chapter 9), and one finds exactly the same 'Feynman rules' as in the canonical (operator) approach.

In the case of gauge theories, we can easily imagine a formula similar to (16.87) for the gauge field propagator, in which the integral is carried out over all gauge fields $A_\mu(x)$ (in the $U(1)$ case, for example). But we already know from chapter 7 (or from chapter 13 in the non-Abelian case) that we shall not be able to construct a well-defined perturbation theory in this way, since the gauge field propagator will not exist unless we 'fix the gauge' by imposing

some constraint, such as the Lorentz gauge condition. Such constraints can be imposed on the corresponding path integral, and indeed this was the route followed by Faddeev and Popov (1967) in first obtaining the Feynman rules for non-Abelian gauge theories, as mentioned in section 13.5.3.

In the discrete case, the appropriate integration variables are the link variables $U(l_i)$ where l_i is the ith link. They are elements of the relevant gauge group – for example $U(n_1, n_1 + 1)$ of (16.3.1) is an element of $U(1)$. In the case of the unitary groups, such elements typically have the form (cf (12.35)) $\sim \exp(\text{i Hermitean matrix})$, where the 'Hermitean matrix' can be parametrized in some convenient way – for example, as in (12.31) for $SU(2)$. In all these cases, the variables in the parametrization of U vary over some bounded domain (they are essentially 'angle-type' variables, as in the simple $U(1)$ case), and so, with a finite number of lattice points, the integral over the link variables is well-defined without gauge-fixing. The integration measure for the link variables can be chosen so as to be gauge invariant, and hence provided the action is gauge invariant, the formalism provides well-defined expressions, independently of perturbation theory, for vevs of gauge invariant quantities.

There remains one more conceptual problem to be addressed in this approach: namely, how are we to deal with fermions? It seems that we must introduce new variables which, though not quantum field operators, must nevertheless *anti*commute with each other. Such 'classical' anticommuting variables are called *Grassmann variables*, and are briefly described in appendix P. Further details are contained in Ryder (1985) and in Peskin and Schroeder (1995) section 9.5. For our purposes, the important point is that the fermion Lagrangian is *bilinear* in the (Grassmann) fermion fields ψ, the fermionic action for one flavour having the form

$$S_{\psi_{\text{f}}} = \int \mathrm{d}^4 x_{\text{E}} \, \bar{\psi}_{\text{f}} M_{\text{f}}(U) \psi_{\text{f}}, \qquad (16.89)$$

where M_{f} is a matrix representing the Dirac operator $\mathrm{i}\,\slashed{D} - m_{\text{f}}$ in its discretized and Euclideanized form. This means that in a typical fermionic amplitude of the form (cf the denominator of (16.87))

$$Z_{\psi_{\text{f}}} = \int \mathcal{D}\bar{\psi}_{\text{f}} \mathcal{D}\psi_{\text{f}} \exp[-S_{\psi_{\text{f}}}], \qquad (16.90)$$

one has essentially an integral of Gaussian type (albeit with Grassmann variables), which can actually be performed analytically[2]. The result is simply $\det [M_{\text{f}}(U)]$, the determinant of the Dirac operator matrix. For N_{f} flavours, this easily generalizes to

$$\prod_{\text{f}=1}^{N_{\text{f}}} \det M_{\text{f}}(U). \qquad (16.91)$$

---

[2]See appendix P.

Now we may write

$$\prod_{f=1}^{N_f} \det M_f(U) = \exp\left[\sum_f \ln \det M_f(U)\right], \qquad (16.92)$$

so that the effect of N_f fermions is to contribute an additional term

$$S_{\text{eff}}(U) = -\sum_f \ln \det[M_f(U)] \qquad (16.93)$$

to the gluonic action. But although formally correct, this fermionic contribution is computationally very time-consuming to include. Until the mid-1990s it could not be done, and instead calculations were made using the *quenched approximation*, in which the determinant is set equal to a constant independent of the link variables U. This is equivalent to the neglect of closed fermion loops in a Feynman graph approach, i.e. no vacuum polarization insertions on virtual gluon lines. Vacuum polarization amplitudes typically behave as q^2/m_f^2 for $q^2 \ll m_f^2$, where q is the momentum flowing into the loop (see equation (11.39), for example, in the case of QED). The quenched approximation is therefore poorer for the light quarks u, d and s.

By the later 1990s it was possible to include the determinant provided the quark masses were not too small: the computation slowed down seriously for light quark masses. So calculations were done for unphysically large values of m_u, m_d and m_s, and the results extrapolated towards the physical values.

Beginning in the early 2000s, however, more precise calculations with substantially lighter quark masses became possible, using the staggered fermion formulation discussed in section 16.2.2. It will be recalled that this saves a factor of four in the number of degrees of freedom. But there is still the remaining problem of the four unwanted additional 'tastes'. If these tastes are degenerate, as they would be in the continuum limit, then we can use the simple trick of replacing $S_{\text{eff}}(U)$ by $\frac{1}{4}S_{\text{eff}}(U)$, which means that we take the fourth root of the staggered fermion determinant. The true physical (non-degenerate) quark flavour multiplicity still remains, of course, and we arrive at

$$S_{\text{eff,stag.}} = -\ln \det\{M_{\text{stag. u}}(U)M_{\text{stag. d}}(U)M_{\text{stag. s}}(U)\}^{1/4}. \qquad (16.94)$$

Unfortunately, things are not so simple away from the continuum limit, at finite lattice spacing a. Bernard, Golterman and Shamir (2006) pointed out that the quantity

$$\{\det M_{\text{stag.}}(U)\}^{1/4} \qquad (16.95)$$

cannot be represented by a local single-taste theory except in the continuum limit: at finite a, it represents a non-local single-taste action. Locality is a very fundamental property of all successful quantum field theories, and its recovery from (16.95) in the limit $a \to 0$ is not obvious. We refer to Sharpe (2006) for a full discussion, and further references. Meanwhile, as we shall see in section 16.6, some of the currently (in 2011) most accurate published results in lattice QCD are using staggered fermions with the 'rooting' procedure.

16.3.3 Connection with statistical mechanics

Not the least advantage of the path integral formulation of quantum field theory (especially in its lattice form) is that it enables a highly suggestive connection to be set up between quantum field theory and statistical mechanics. We introduce this connection now, by way of a preliminary to the discussion of renormalization in the following section.

The connection is made via the fundamental quantity of equilibrium statistical mechanics, the *partition function* Z defined by

$$Z = \sum_{\text{configurations}} \exp\left(-\frac{H}{k_{\mathrm{B}}T}\right), \tag{16.96}$$

which is simply the 'sum over states' (or configurations) of the relevant degrees of freedom, with the Boltzmann weighting factor. H is the classical Hamiltonian evaluated for each configuration. Consider, for comparison, the denominator in (16.87), namely

$$Z_\phi = \int \mathcal{D}\phi \, \exp(-S_{\mathrm{E}}), \tag{16.97}$$

where

$$S_{\mathrm{E}} = \int \mathrm{d}^4 x_{\mathrm{E}} \mathcal{L}_{\mathrm{E}} = \int \mathrm{d}^4 x_{\mathrm{E}} \left\{ \frac{1}{2}(\partial_\tau \phi)^2 + \frac{1}{2}(\boldsymbol{\nabla}\phi)^2 + \frac{1}{2}m^2\phi^2 + \lambda\phi^4 \right\} \tag{16.98}$$

in the case of a single scalar field with mass m and self-interaction $\lambda\phi^4$. The Euclideanized Lagrangian density $\mathcal{L}_{\mathrm{E}}$ is like an energy density: it is bounded from below, and increases when the field has large magnitude or has large gradients in τ or $\boldsymbol{x}$. The factor $\exp(-S_{\mathrm{E}})$ is then a sensible statistical weight for the fluctuations in ϕ, and Z_ϕ may be interpreted as the partition function for a system described by the field degree of freedom ϕ, but of course in *four* 'spatial' dimensions.

The parallel becomes perhaps even stronger when we discretize space-time. In an Ising model (see the following section), the Hamiltonian has the form

$$H = -J \sum_n s_n s_{n+1}, \tag{16.99}$$

where J is a constant, and the sum is over lattice sites n, the system variables taking the values ± 1. When (16.99) is inserted into (16.96), we arrive at something very reminiscent of the $\phi(n_1)\phi(n_1 + 1)$ term in (16.6). Naturally, the effective 'Hamiltonian' is not quite the same – though we may note that Wilson (1971b) argued that in the case of a ϕ^4 interaction the parameters can be chosen so as to make the values $\phi = \pm 1$ the most heavily weighted in S_{E}. Statistical mechanics does, of course, deal in three spatial dimensions, not the four of our Euclideanized space-time. Nevertheless, it is remarkable that

quantum field theory in three spatial dimensions appears to have such a close relationship to equilibrium statistical mechanics in four spatial dimensions.

One insight we may draw from this connection is that, in the case of pure gauge actions (16.47) or (16.48), the gauge coupling is seen to be analogous to an inverse temperature, by comparison with (16.96). One is led to wonder whether something like *transitions between different 'phases'* exist, as coupling constants (or other parameters) vary – and, indeed, such changes of 'phase' can occur.

A second point is somewhat related to this. In statistical mechanics, an important quantity is the *correlation length* ξ, which for a spin system may be defined via the *spin-spin correlation function*

$$G(\boldsymbol{x}) = \langle s(\boldsymbol{x})s(\boldsymbol{0}) \rangle = \sum_{\text{all } s(\boldsymbol{x})} s(\boldsymbol{x})s(\boldsymbol{0})\mathrm{e}^{-H/k_\mathrm{B}T} \ , \tag{16.100}$$

where we are once more reverting to a continuous $\boldsymbol{x}$ variable. For large $|\boldsymbol{x}|$, this takes the form

$$G(\boldsymbol{x}) \propto \frac{1}{|\boldsymbol{x}|} \exp\left(\frac{-|\boldsymbol{x}|}{\xi(T)}\right) \ . \tag{16.101}$$

The Fourier transform of this (in the continuum limit) is

$$\tilde{G}(\boldsymbol{k}^2) \propto \left(\boldsymbol{k}^2 + \xi^{-2}(T)\right)^{-1} \ , \tag{16.102}$$

as we learned in section 1.3.3. Comparing (16.100) with (16.87), it is clear that (16.100) is proportional to the propagator (or Green function) for the field $s(\boldsymbol{x})$; (16.102) then shows that $\xi^{-1}(T)$ is playing the role of a mass term m. Now, near a critical point for a statistical system, correlations exist over very large scales ξ compared to the inter-atomic spacing a; in fact, at the critical point $\xi(T_\mathrm{c}) \sim L$, where L is the size of the system. In the quantum field theory, as indicated earlier, we may regard a^{-1} as playing a role analogous to a momentum cut-off Λ, so the regime $\xi \gg a$ is equivalent to $m \ll \Lambda$, as was indeed always our assumption. Thus studying a quantum field theory this way is analogous to studying a four-dimensional statistical system near a critical point. This shows rather clearly why it is not going to be easy: correlations over all scales will have to be included. At this point, we are naturally led to the consideration of *renormalization* in the lattice formulation.

16.4   Renormalization, and the renormalization group, on the lattice

16.4.1   Introduction

In the continuum formulation which we have used elsewhere in this book, fluctuations over short distances of order Λ^{-1} generally lead to divergences

in the limit $\Lambda \to \infty$, which are controlled (in a renormalizable theory) by the procedure of renormalization. Such divergent fluctuations turn out, in fact, to affect a renormalizable theory only through the values of some of its parameters and, if these parameters are taken from experiment, all other quantities become finite, even as $\Lambda \to \infty$. This latter assertion is not easy to prove, and indeed is quite surprising. However, this is by no means all there is to renormalization theory: we have seen the power of 'renormalization group' ideas in making testable predictions for QCD. Nevertheless, the methods of chapter 15 were rather formal, and the reader may well feel the need of a more physical picture of what is going on. Such a picture was provided by Wilson (1971a) (see also Wilson and Kogut 1974), using the 'lattice + path integral' approach. Another important advantage of this formalism is, therefore, precisely the way in which, thanks to Wilson's work, it provides access to a more intuitive way of understanding renormalization theory. The aim of this section is to give a brief introduction to Wilson's ideas, so as to illuminate the formal treatment of the previous chapter.

In the 'lattice + path integral' approach to quantum field theory, the degrees of freedom involved are the values of the field(s) at each lattice site, as we have seen. Quantum amplitudes are formed by integrating suitable quantities over all values of these degrees of freedom, as in (16.87) for example. From this point of view, it should be possible to examine specifically how the 'short distance' or 'high momentum' degrees of freedom affect the result. In fact, the idea suggests itself that we might be able to perform explicitly the integration (or summation) over those degrees of freedom located near the cutoff Λ in momentum space, or separated by only a lattice site or two in co-ordinate space. If we can do this, the result may be compared with the theory as originally formulated, to see how this 'integration over short-distance degrees of freedom' affects the physical predictions of the theory. Having done this once, we can imagine doing it again – and indeed *iterating* the process, until eventually we arrive at some kind of 'effective theory' describing physics in terms of 'long-distance' degrees of freedom.

There are several aspects of such a programme which invite comment. First, the process of 'integrating out' short-distance degrees of freedom will obviously *reduce* the number of effective degrees of freedom, which is necessarily very large in the case $\xi \gg a$, as envisaged above. Thus it must be a step in the right direction. Secondly, the above sketch of the 'integrating out' procedure suggests that, at any given stage of the integration, we shall be considering the system as described by parameters (including masses and couplings) *appropriate to that scale*, which is of course strongly reminiscent of RGE ideas. And thirdly, we may perhaps anticipate that the result of this 'integrating out' will be not only to render the parameters of the theory scale-dependent, but also, in general, to introduce new kinds of *effective interactions* into the theory. We now consider some simple examples which we hope will illustrate these points.

FIGURE 16.4
A portion of the one-dimensional lattice of spins in the Ising model.

16.4.2   Two one-dimensional examples

Consider first a simple one-dimensional Ising model with Hamiltonian (16.99) and partition function

$$Z = \sum_{\{s_n\}} \exp\left[K \sum_{n=0}^{N-1} s_n s_{n+1}\right], \tag{16.103}$$

where $K = J/(k_\mathrm{B}T) > 0$. In (16.103) all the s_n variables take the values ± 1 and the 'sum over $\{s_n\}$' means that all possible configurations of the N variables $s_0, s_1, s_2, \ldots, s_{N-1}$ are to be included. The spin s_n is located at the lattice site na, and we shall (implicitly) be assuming the periodic boundary condition $s_n = s_{N+n}$. Figure 16.4 shows a portion of the one-dimensional lattice with the spins on the sites, each site being separated by the lattice constant a. Thus, for the portion $\{s_{N-1}, s_0, \ldots s_4\}$ we are evaluating

$$\sum_{s_{N-1}, s_0, s_1, s_2, s_3, s_4} \exp[K(s_{N-1}s_0 + s_0 s_1 + s_1 s_2 + s_2 s_3 + s_3 s_4)]. \tag{16.104}$$

Now suppose we want to describe the system in terms of a 'coarser' lattice, with lattice spacing $2a$, and corresponding new spin variables s'_n. There are many ways we could choose to describe the s'_n, but here we shall only consider a very simple one (Kadanoff 1977) in which each s'_n is simply identified with the s_n at the corresponding site (see figure 16.5). For the portion of the lattice under consideration, then, (16.104) becomes

$$\sum_{s_{N-1}, s'_0, s_1, s'_1, s_3, s'_2} \exp\left[K\left(s_{N-1}s'_0 + s'_0 s_1 + s_1 s'_1 + s'_1 s_3 + s_3 s'_2\right)\right]. \tag{16.105}$$

If we can now perform the sums over s_1 and s_3 in (16.105), we shall end up (for this portion) with an expression involving the 'effective' spin variables s'_0, s'_1 and s'_2, situated twice as far apart as the original ones, and therefore providing a more 'coarse grained' description of the system. Summing over s_1 and s_3 corresponds to 'integrating out' two short-distance degrees of freedom as discussed earlier.

In fact, these sums are easy to do. Consider the quantity $\exp(Ks'_0 s_1)$, expanded as a power series:

$$\exp(Ks'_0 s_1) = 1 + Ks'_0 s_1 + \frac{K^2}{2!} + \frac{K^3}{3!}(s'_0 s_1) + \ldots \tag{16.106}$$

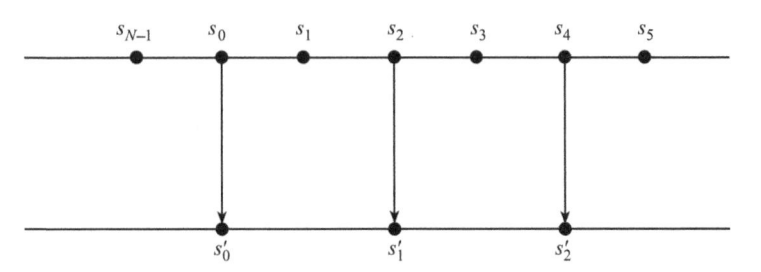

FIGURE 16.5
A 'coarsening' transformation applied to the lattice portion shown in figure 16.4. The new (primed) spin variables are situated twice as far apart as the original (unprimed) ones.

where we have used $(s'_0 s_1)^2 = 1$. It follows that

$$\exp(K s'_0 s_1) = \cosh K \left(1 + s'_0 s_1 \tanh K\right), \qquad (16.107)$$

and similarly

$$\exp(K s_1 s'_1) = \cosh K \left(1 + s_1 s'_1 \tanh K\right). \qquad (16.108)$$

Thus the sum over s_1 is

$$\sum_{s_1=\pm 1} \cosh^2 K \left(1 + s'_0 s_1 \tanh K + s_1 s'_1 \tanh K + s'_0 s'_1 \tanh^2 K\right). \qquad (16.109)$$

Clearly, the terms linear in s_1 vanish after summing, and the s_1 sum becomes just

$$2 \cosh^2 K \left(1 + s'_0 s'_1 \tanh^2 K\right). \qquad (16.110)$$

Remarkably, (16.110) contains a new 'nearest-neighbour' interaction, $s'_0 s'_1$, just like the original one in (16.103), but with an *altered coupling* (and a different spin-independent piece). In fact, we can write (16.110) in the standard form

$$\exp\left[g_1(K) + K' s'_0 s'_1\right] \qquad (16.111)$$

and then use (16.107) to set

$$\tanh K' = \tanh^2 K \qquad (16.112)$$

and identify

$$g_1(K) = \ln\left(\frac{2 \cosh^2 K}{\cosh K'}\right). \qquad (16.113)$$

Exactly the same steps can be followed through for the sum on s_3 in (16.105), and indeed for *all* the sums over the 'integrated out' spins. The upshot is that, apart from the accumulated spin-independent part, the new partition

function, defined on a lattice of size $2a$, has the same form as the old one, but with a new coupling K' related to the old one K by (16.112).

Equation (16.112) is an example of a *renormalization transformation*: the number of degrees of freedom has been halved, the lattice spacing has doubled, and the coupling K has been renormalized to K'.

It is clear that we could apply the same procedure to the new Hamiltonian, introducing a coupling K'' which is related to K' , and thence to K by

$$\tanh K'' = (\tanh K')^2 = (\tanh K)^4. \tag{16.114}$$

This is equivalent to *iterating* the renormalization transformation; after n iterations, the effective lattice constant is $2^n a$, and the effective coupling is given by

$$\tanh K^{(n)} = (\tanh K)^n. \tag{16.115}$$

The successive values $K', K'', \ldots$ of the coupling under these iterations can be regarded as a '*flow*' in the (one-dimensional) space of K-values: a *renormalization flow*.

Of particular interest is a point (or points) K^* such that

$$\tanh K^* = \tanh^2 K^*. \tag{16.116}$$

This is called a *fixed point* of the renormalization tranformation. At such a point in K-space, changing the scale by a factor of 2 (or 2^n for that matter) will make no difference, which means that the system must be in some sense ordered. Remembering that $K = J/(k_\mathrm{B}T)$, we see that $K = K^*$ when the temperature is 'tuned' to the value $T = T^* = J/(k_\mathrm{B}K^*)$. Such a T^* would be the temperature of a *critical point* for the thermodynamics of the system, corresponding to the onset of ordering. In the present case, the only fixed points are $K^* = \infty$ and $K^* = 0$. Thus there is no critical point at a non-zero T^*, and hence no transition to an ordered phase. However, we may describe the behaviour as $T \to 0$ as 'quasi-critical'. For large K, we may use

$$\tanh K \simeq 1 - 2\mathrm{e}^{-2K} \tag{16.117}$$

to write (16.115) as

$$K^{(n)} = K - \frac{1}{2}\ln n, \tag{16.118}$$

which shows that K^n changes only very slowly (logarithmically) under iterations when in the vicinity of a very large value of K, so that this is 'almost' a fixed point.

We may represent the flow of K, under the renormalization transformation (16.115), as in figure 16.6. Note that the flow is away from the quasi-fixed point at $K^* = \infty$ ($T = 0$) and towards the (non-interacting) fixed point at $K^* = 0$.

A renormalization transformation which has a fixed point at a finite (neither zero nor infinite) value of the coupling is clearly of greater interest, since

FIGURE 16.6
'Renormalization flow': the arrows show the direction of flow of the coupling K as the lattice constant is increased. The starred values are fixed points.

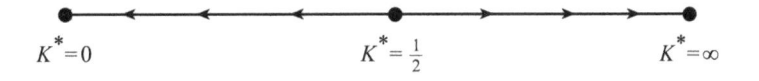

FIGURE 16.7
The renormalization flow for the transformation (16.120).

this will correspond to a critical point at a finite temperature. A simple such example given by Kadanoff (1977) is the transformation

$$K' = \frac{1}{2}(2K)^2 \tag{16.119}$$

for a doubling of the effective lattice size, or

$$K^{(n)} = \frac{1}{2}(2K)^n \tag{16.120}$$

for n such iterations. The model leading to (16.120) involves fermions in one dimension, but the details are irrelevant to our purpose here. The renormalization transformation (16.120) has three fixed points: $K^* = 0$, $K^* = \infty$ and the finite point $K^* = \frac{1}{2}$. The renormalization flow is shown in figure 16.7.

The striking feature of this flow is that the motion is always away from the finite fixed point, under successive iterations. This may be understood by recalling that at the fixed point (which is a critical point for the statistical system) the correlation length ξ must be infinite (as $L \to \infty$). As we iterate away from this point, ξ decreases and we leave the fixed (or critical) point. For this model, ξ is given by Kadanoff (1977) as

$$\xi = \frac{a}{|\ln 2K|} \tag{16.121}$$

which indeed goes to infinity at $K = \frac{1}{2}$.

16.4.3 Connections with particle physics

Let us now begin to think about how all this may relate to the treatment of the renormalization group in particle physics, as given in the previous chapter.

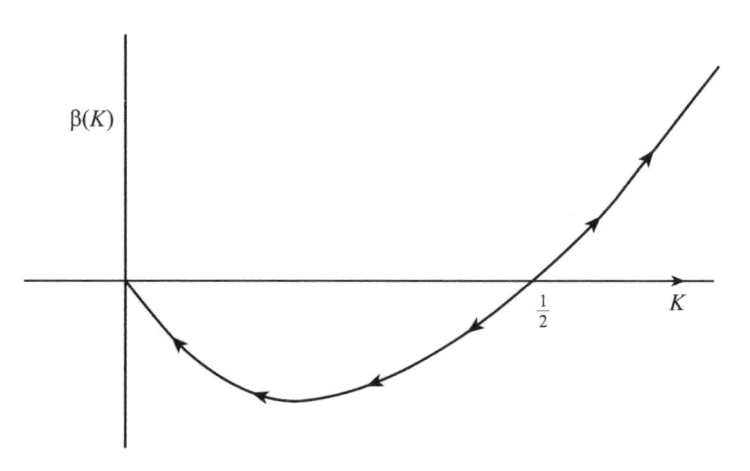

FIGURE 16.8
The β-function of (16.124); the arrows indicate increasing f.

First, we need to consider a continuous change of scale, say by a factor of f. In the present model, the transformation (16.120) then becomes

$$K(fa) = \frac{1}{2}(2K(a))^f. \tag{16.122}$$

Differentiating (16.122) with respect to f, we find

$$f\frac{dK(fa)}{df} = K(fa)\ln[2K(fa)]. \tag{16.123}$$

We may reasonably call (16.123) a renormalization group equation, describing the 'running' of $K(fa)$ with the scale f, analogous to the RGE's for α and α_s considered in chapter 15. In this case, the β-function is

$$\beta(K) = K\ln(2K), \tag{16.124}$$

which is sketched in figure 16.8. The zero of β is indeed at the fixed (critical) point $K = \frac{1}{2}$, and this is an infrared unstable fixed point, the flow being away from it as f increases.

The foregoing is exactly analogous to the discussion in section 15.5: see in particular figure 15.6 and the related discussion. Note, however, that in the present case we are considering rescalings in *position* space, not momentum space. Since momenta are measured in units of a^{-1}, it is clear that scaling a by f is the same as scaling k by $f^{-1} = t$, say. This will produce a change in sign in dK/dt relative to dK/df, and accounts for the fact that $K = \frac{1}{2}$ is an infrared unstable fixed point in figure 16.8, while α_s^* is an infrared stable fixed point in figure 15.6(b). Allowing for the change in sign, figure 16.8 is quite analogous to figure 15.6(a).

We have emphasized that, at a critical point, and in the continuum limit, the correlation length $\xi \to \infty$, or equivalently the mass parameter (cf (16.102)) $m = \xi^{-1} \to 0$. In this case, the Fourier transform of the spin-spin correlation function should behave as

$$\tilde{G}(\mathbf{k}^2) \propto \frac{1}{\mathbf{k}^2}. \qquad (16.125)$$

This is indeed the $\mathbf{k}^2$-dependence of the propagator of a free, massless scalar particle, but – as we learned for the fermion propagator in section 15.5 – it is no longer true in an interacting theory. In the interacting case, (16.125) generally becomes modified to

$$\tilde{G}(\mathbf{k}^2) \propto \frac{1}{(\mathbf{k}^2)^{1-\frac{\eta}{2}}}, \qquad (16.126)$$

or equivalently

$$G(\mathbf{x}) \propto \frac{1}{|\mathbf{x}|^{1+\eta}} \qquad (16.127)$$

in three spatial dimensions, and in the continuum limit. Thus, at a critical point, the spin-spin correlation function exhibits scaling under the transformation $\mathbf{x}' = f\mathbf{x}$, but it is not free-field scaling. Comparing (16.126) with (15.75), we see that $\eta/2$ is precisely the *anomalous dimension* of the field $s(\mathbf{x})$, so – just as in section 15.5 – we have an example of scaling with anomalous dimension. In the statistical mechanics case, η is a *critical exponent*, one of a number of such quantities characterizing the critical behaviour of a system. In general, η will depend on the coupling constant $\eta(K)$: at a non-trivial fixed point, η will be evaluated at the fixed point value K^*, $\eta(K^*)$. Enormous progress was made in the theory of critical phenomena when the powerful methods of quantum field theory were applied to calculate critical exponents (see for example Peskin & Schroeder 1995, chapter 13, and Binney *et al.* 1992).

In our discussion so far, we have only considered simple models with just one 'coupling constant', so that diagrams of renormalization flow were one-dimensional. Generally, of course, Hamiltonians will consist of several terms, and the behaviour of all their coefficents will need to be considered under a renormalization transformation. The general analysis of renormalization flow in multi-dimensional coupling space was given by Wegner (1972). In simple terms, the coefficients show one of three types of behaviour under renormalization transformations such that $a \to fa$, characterized by their behaviour in the vicinity of a fixed point: (i) the difference from the fixed point value grows as f increases, so that the system moves away from the fixed point (as in the single-coupling examples considered earlier); (ii) the difference decreases as f increases, so the system moves towards the fixed point; (iii) there is no change in the value of the coupling as f changes. The corresponding coefficients are called, respectively, (i) *relevant*, (ii) *irrelevant* and (iii) *marginal* couplings; the terminology is also frequently applied to the operators in the Hamiltonians

themselves. The intuitive meaning of 'irrelevant' is clear enough: the system will head towards a fixed point as $f \to \infty$ whatever the initial values of the irrelevant couplings. The critical behaviour of the system will therefore be independent of the number and type of all irrelevant couplings, and will be determined by the relatively few (in general) marginal and relevant couplings. Thus *all* systems which flow close to the fixed point will display the same critical exponents determined by the dynamics of these few couplings. This explains the property of *universality* observed in the physics of phase transitions, whereby many apparently quite different physical systems are described (in the vicinity of their critical points) by the same critical exponents.

Additional terms in the Hamiltonian are, in fact, generally introduced following a renormalization transformation. In the quantum field case, we may expect that renormalization transformations associated with $a \to fa$, and iterations thereof, will in general lead to an effective theory involving all possible couplings allowed by whatever symmetries are assumed to be relevant. Thus, if we start with a typical 'ϕ^4' scalar theory as given by (16.98), we shall expect to generate all possible couplings involving ϕ and its derivatives. At first sight, this may seem disturbing: after all, the original theory (in four dimensions) is a renormalizable one, but an interaction such as $A\phi^6$ is *not* renormalizable according to the criterion given in section 11.8 (in four dimensions ϕ has mass dimension unity, so that A must have mass dimension -2). It is, however, essential to remember that in this 'Wilsonian' approach to renormalization, summations over momenta appearing in loops do not, after one iteration $a \to fa$, run up to the original cut-off value π/a, but only up to the lower cut-off π/fa. The additional interactions compensate for this change.

In fact, we shall now see how the coefficients of non-renormalizable interactions correspond precisely to *irrelevant* couplings in Wilson's approach, so that their effect becomes negligible as we iterate to scales much larger than a. We consider continuous changes of scale characterized by a factor f, and we discuss a theory with only a single scalar field ϕ for simplicity. Imagine, therefore, that we have integrated out, in (16.97), those components of $\phi(\mathbf{x})$ with $a < |\mathbf{x}| < fa$. We will be left with a functional integral of the form (16.97), but with $\phi(\mathbf{x})$ restricted to $|\mathbf{x}| > fa$, and with additional interaction terms in the action. In order to interpret the result in Wilson's terms, we must rewrite it so that it has the same general form as the original Z_ϕ of (16.97). A simple way to do this is to rescale distances by

$$\mathbf{x}' = \frac{\mathbf{x}}{f} \qquad (16.128)$$

so that the functional integral is now over $\phi(\mathbf{x}')$ with $|\mathbf{x}'| > a$, as in (16.97). We now *define* the fixed point of the renormalization transformation to be that in which all the terms in the action are *zero*, except the 'kinetic' piece; this is the 'free-field' fixed point. Thus, we require the kinetic action to be

unchanged:

$$\int d^4 x_E \, (\partial_\mu \phi)^2 \; = \; \int d^4 x_E' (\partial_\mu' \phi')^2$$

$$= \; \int \frac{1}{f^2} d^4 x_E (\partial_\mu \phi')^2 \,, \qquad (16.129)$$

from which it follows that $\phi' = f\phi$. Consider now a term of the form $A\phi^6$:

$$A \int d^4 x_E \, \phi^6 = \frac{A}{f^2} \int d^4 x_E' \, \phi'^6 \,. \qquad (16.130)$$

(16.130) shows that the 'new' A' is related to the old one by $A' = \frac{A}{f^2}$, and in particular that, as f increases, A' decreases and is therefore an *irrelevant* coupling, tending to zero as we reach large scales. But such an interaction is precisely a non-renormalizable one (in four dimensions), according to the criterion of section 11.8. The mass dimension of ϕ is unity, and hence that of A must be -2 so that the action is dimensionless; couplings with negative mass dimensions correspond to non-renormalizable interactions. The reader may verify the generality of this result for any interaction with p powers of ϕ, and q derivatives of ϕ.

However, the mass term $m^2 \phi^2$ behaves differently:

$$m^2 \int d^4 x_E \, \phi^2 = m^2 f^2 \int d^4 x_E' \, \phi'^2 \qquad (16.131)$$

showing that $m'^2 = m^2 f^2$ and the 'coupling' m^2 is *relevant*, since it grows with f^2. Such a term has positive mass dimension, and corresponds to a 'super-renormalizable' interaction. Finally, the $\lambda \phi^4$ interaction transforms as

$$\lambda \int d^4 x_E \, \phi^4 = \lambda \int d^4 x_E' \, \phi'^4 \qquad (16.132)$$

and so $\lambda' = \lambda$. The coupling is *marginal*, which may correspond (though not necessarily) to a renormalizable interaction. To find out if such couplings increase or decrease with f, we have to include higher-order loop corrections. The foregoing analysis in terms of the suppression of non-renormalizable interactions by powers of f^{-1} parallels precisely the similar one in section 11.8. We saw that such terms were suppressed at low energies by factors of E/Λ, where Λ is the cut-off scale beyond which the theory is supposed to fail on physical grounds (e.g. Λ might be the Planck mass). The result is that as we renormalize, in Wilson's sense, down to much lower energy scales, the non-renormalizable terms disappear and we are left with an effective renormalizable theory. This is the field theory analogue of 'universality'.

These ideas have an important application in lattice QCD. One of the reasons for systematic inaccuracies in lattice computations is that the continuum is being simulated by a lattice of finite spacing. Symanzik (1983) showed

that corrections to continuum theory results stemming from finite lattice spacing could be diminished systematically by the use of lattice actions that also include suitable irrelevant terms. This procedure is routinely adopted in accurate lattice calculations with 'Symanzik-improved' actions.

One further word should be said about terms such as '$m^2\phi^2$' (which arise in the Higgs sector of the Standard Model, for instance). As we have seen, m^2 scales by $m'^2 = m^2 f^2$, which is a rapid growth with f. If we imagine starting at a very high scale, such as 10^{15} TeV and flowing down to 1 TeV, then the 'initial' value of m will have to be very finely 'tuned' in order to end up with a mass of order 1 TeV. Thus, in this picture, it seems unnatural to have scalar particles with masses much less than the physical cut-off scale, unless some symmetry principle 'protects' their light masses. We shall return to this problem in section 22.8.1.

We now return to lattice QCD, with a brief survey of some of the impressive results now being obtained numerically.

16.5   Lattice QCD

16.5.1   Introduction, and the continuum limit

Let us begin by considering some numbers. The lattice must be large enough so that the spatial dimension R of the object we wish to describe – say the size of a hadron – fits comfortably inside it, otherwise the result will be subject to 'finite size effects' as the hypercube side length L is varied. We also need $R \gg a$, or else the granularity of the lattice resolution will become apparent. Further, as indicated earlier, we expect the mass m (which is of order R^{-1}) to be very much less than a^{-1}. Thus ideally we need

$$a \ll R \sim 1/m \ll L = Na \qquad (16.133)$$

so that N must be large. For example, if $N = 64$ and $a \sim 0.1$fm the condition (16.133) would be reasonably satisfied by a light hadron mass. But remember that each field at each lattice point is an independent degree of freedom: dealing with integrals such as (16.87) presents a formidable numerical challenge.

Ignoring any statistical inaccuracy, the results will depend on the parameters g_L and N, where g_L is the bare lattice gauge coupling (we assume for simplicity that the quarks are massless). Despite the fact that g_L is dimensionless, we shall now see that its value actually controls the physical size of the lattice spacing a, as a result of renormalization effects. The computed mass of a hadron M, say, must be related to the only quantity with mass dimension, a^{-1}, by a relation of the form

$$M = \frac{1}{a}f(g_L). \qquad (16.134)$$

Thus in approaching the continuum limit $a \to 0$, we shall also have to change

g_L suitably, so as to ensure that M remains finite. This is, of course, quite analogous to saying that, in a renormalizable theory, the bare parameters of the theory depend on the momentum cut-off Λ in such a way that, as $\Lambda \to \infty$, finite values are obtained for the corresponding physical parameters (see the last paragraph of section 10.1.2, for example). In practice, of course, the extent to which the lattice 'a' can really be taken to be very small is severely limited by the computational resources available – that is, essentially, by the number of mesh points N.

Equation (16.134) should therefore really read

$$M = \frac{1}{a} f\left(g_L(a)\right) . \tag{16.135}$$

As $a \to 0$, M should be finite and independent of a. However, we know that the behaviour of $g_L(a)$ at small scales is in fact calculable in perturbation theory, thanks to the asymptotic freedom of QCD. This will allow us to determine the form of $f(g_L)$, up to a constant, and lead to an interesting prediction for M (equations (16.141)–(16.142)).

Differentiating (16.135) we find

$$0 = \frac{dM}{da} = -\frac{1}{a^2} f\left(g_L(a)\right) + \frac{1}{a} \frac{df}{dg_L} \frac{dg_L(a)}{da} , \tag{16.136}$$

so that

$$\left(a \frac{dg_L(a)}{da}\right) \frac{df}{dg_L} = f\left(g_L(a)\right) . \tag{16.137}$$

Meanwhile, the scale dependence of g_L is given (to one loop order) by

$$a \frac{dg_L(a)}{da} = \frac{\beta_0}{4\pi} g_L^3(a) , \tag{16.138}$$

where the sign is the opposite of (15.47) since $a \sim \mu^{-1}$ is the relevant scale parameter here (compare the comments after equation (16.124)). The integration of (16.138) requires, as usual, a dimensionful constant of integration (cf (15.53)):

$$\frac{g_L^2(a)}{4\pi} = \frac{1}{\beta_0 \ln(1/a^2\Lambda_L^2)} . \tag{16.139}$$

Equation (16.139) shows that $g_L(a)$ tends logarithmically to zero as $a \to 0$, as we expect from asymptotic freedom. Λ_L can be regarded as a lattice equivalent of the continuum $\Lambda_{\overline{MS}}$, and it is defined (at one loop order) by

$$\Lambda_L \equiv \lim_{g_L \to 0} \frac{1}{a} \exp\left(-\frac{2\pi}{\beta_0 g_L^2}\right) . \tag{16.140}$$

Equation (16.140) may also be read as showing that the lattice spacing a must go exponentially to zero as g_L tends to zero. Higher-order corrections can of course be included.

In a similar way, integrating (16.137) using (16.138) gives, in (16.134),

$$M = \text{constant} \times \left[\frac{1}{a} \exp \left(-\frac{2\pi}{\beta_0 g_L^2} \right) \right] \tag{16.141}$$

$$= \text{constant} \times \Lambda_L . \tag{16.142}$$

Equation (16.141) is known as *asymptotic scaling*: it predicts how any physical mass, expressed in lattice units a^{-1}, should vary as a function of g_L. The form (16.142) is remarkable, as it implies that all calculated masses must be proportional, in the continuum limit $a \to 0$, to the same universal scale factor Λ_L.

How are masses calculated on the lattice? The principle is very similar to the way in which the ground state was selected out as $\tau_i \to -\infty$, $\tau_f \to +\infty$ in (16.78). Consider a correlation function for a scalar field, for simplicity:

$$\begin{aligned}
C(\tau) &= \langle \Omega | \phi(\mathbf{x} = 0, \tau) \phi(0) | \Omega \rangle \\
&= \sum_n |\langle \Omega | \phi(0) | n \rangle|^2 \, e^{-E_n \tau} .
\end{aligned} \tag{16.143}$$

As $\tau \to \infty$, the term with the minimum value of E_n, namely $E_n = M_\phi$, will survive; M_ϕ can be measured from a fit to the exponential fall-off as a function of τ.

The behaviour predicted by (16.141) and (16.142) can be tested in actual calculations. A quantity such as the ρ meson mass is calculated via a correlation function of the form (16.143), the result being expressed in terms of a certain number of lattice units a^{-1} at a certain value of g_L. By comparison with the known ρ mass, a^{-1} can be converted to GeV. Then the calculation is repeated for a different g_L value and the new a^{-1} (GeV) extracted. A plot of $\ln[a^{-1}(\text{GeV})]$ versus $1/g_L^2$ should then give a straight line with slope $2\pi/\beta_0$ and intercept $\ln \Lambda_L$. Figure 16.9 shows such a plot, taken from Ellis *et al.* (1996), from which it appears that the calculations are indeed being performed close to the continuum limit. The value of Λ_L has been adjusted to fit the numerical data, and has the value $\Lambda_L = 1.74$ MeV in this case. This may seem alarmingly far from the kind of value expected for Λ_{QCD}, but we must remember that the renormalization schemes involved in the two cases are quite different. In fact, we may expect $\Lambda_{\text{QCD}} \approx 50\Lambda_L$ (Montvay and Munster (1994), section 5.1.6).

16.5.2   The static q$\bar{\text{q}}$ potential

The calculations of m_ρ represented in figure 16.9 were done in the quenched approximation. As a first example of a calculation with dynamical (unquenched) fermions we show in figure 16.10 a lattice calculation of the static q$\bar{\text{q}}$ potential (Allton *et al.* 2002, UKQCD Collaboration), using two degenerate flavours of

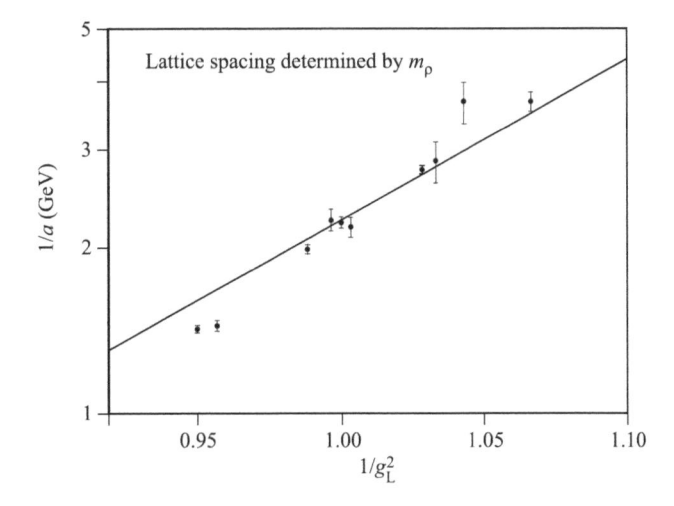

FIGURE 16.9
$\ln(a^{-1}$ in GeV) plotted against $1/g_{\rm L}^2$; figure from R K Ellis, W J Stirling and B R Webber (1996) *QCD and Collider Physics*, courtesy Cambridge University Press, as adapted from Allton (1995).

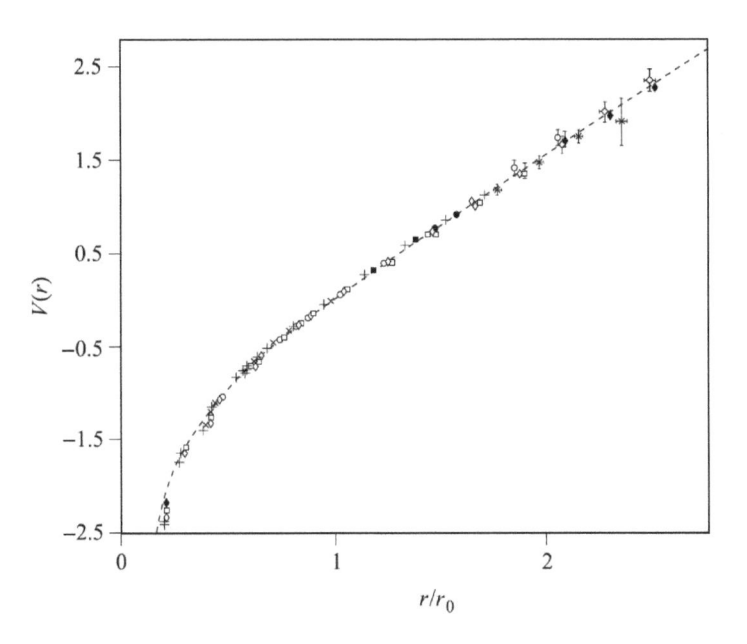

FIGURE 16.10
The static QCD potential, expressed in units of r_0. The broken curve is the functional form (16.147). Figure reprinted with permission from C R Allton *et al.* (UKQCD Collaboration) *Phys. Rev.* D **65** 054502 (2002). Copyright 2002 by the American Physical Society.

dynamical quarks[3] on a $16^3 \times 32$ lattice. As usual, one dimensionful quantity has to be fixed in order to set the scale. In the present case this has been done via the scale parameter r_0 of Sommer (1994), defined by

$$r_0^2 \left.\frac{dV}{dr}\right|_{r=r_0} = 1.65 . \tag{16.144}$$

Applying (16.144) to the Cornell (Eichten *et al.* 1980) or Richardson (1979) phenomenological potentials gives $r_0 \simeq 0.49$ fm, conveniently in the range which is well-determined by $c\bar{c}$ and $b\bar{b}$ data. The data are well described by the expression

$$V(r) = V_0 + \sigma r - \frac{A}{r} , \tag{16.145}$$

where in accordance with (16.144)

$$\sigma = \frac{(1.65 - A)}{r_0^2} , \tag{16.146}$$

and where V_0 has been chosen such that $V(r_0) = 0$. Thus (16.145) becomes

$$r_0 V(r) = (1.65 - A) \left(\frac{r}{r_0} - 1\right) - A \left(\frac{r_0}{r} - 1\right) . \tag{16.147}$$

This is – up to a constant – exactly the functional form mentioned in chapter 1, equation (1.33). The quantity $\sqrt{\sigma}$ (there called b) is referred to as the 'string tension', and has a value of about 465 MeV in the present calculations. Phenomenological models suggest a value of around 440 MeV (Eichten *et al.* 1980). The parameter A is found to have a value of about 0.3. In lowest-order perturbation theory, and in the continuum limit, A would be given by one-gluon exchange as

$$A = \frac{4}{3}\alpha_{\rm s}(\mu) \tag{16.148}$$

where μ is some energy scale. This would give $\alpha_{\rm s} \simeq 0.22$, a reasonable value for $\mu \simeq 3$ GeV. Interestingly, the form (16.147) is predicted by the 'universal bosonic string model' (Lüscher *et al.* 1980, Lüscher 1981), in which A has the 'universal' value $\frac{\pi}{12} \simeq 0.26$.

The existence of the linearly rising term with $\sigma > 0$ is a signal for confinement, since – if the potential maintained this form – it would cost an infinite amount of energy to separate a quark and an antiquark. But at some point, enough energy will be stored in the 'string' to create a $q\bar{q}$ pair from the vacuum: the string then breaks, and the two $q\bar{q}$ pairs form mesons. There is no evidence for string breaking in figure 16.10, but we must note that the largest distance probed is only about 1.3 fm.

---

[3]Comparison with matched data in the quenched approximation revealed very little difference, in this case.

16.5.3 Calculation of $\alpha(M_Z^2)$

Our second example of a precision lattice calculation with dynamical quarks is the determination of $\alpha_s(M_Z^2)$ by Davies *et al.* (2008) (HPQCD Collaboration). The reported value is

$$\alpha_s(M_Z^2) = 0.1183(8). \tag{16.149}$$

The accuracy of this result is extremely impressive, and it implies that this determination is an important ingredient in the world average value quoted in (15.62). It is worth sketching some of the elements that went into this landmark calculation.

The work used 12 gluon configurations from the MILC collaboration (Aubin *et al.* 2004), and built on a joint effort by several groups (see Davies *et al.* (HPQCD, UKQCD, MILC, and Fermilab collaborations) 2004). Vacuum polarization effects from all three light quarks u, d and s were included, using a Symanzik-improved staggered-quark discretization, with rooting. The effects of c and b quarks were incorporated using perturbation theory. The strange quark mass was physical, while the u and d quark mass (set to be the same) was three times too large, but small enough for chiral perturbation theory (see chapter 18) to be reliable for extrapolating to the physical mass.

There were 5 parameters: $m_u = m_d, m_s, m_c, m_b$ and the bare QCD coupling g_L (or equivalently the lattice spacing a). The mass parameters were tuned to reproduce experimentally measured values of $m_\pi^2, 2m_K^2 - m_\pi^2, m_D$ and m_Υ respectively. The lattice spacing was adjusted to make the $\Upsilon - \Upsilon'$ mass difference agree with experiment (Gray *et al.* 2005). With the free parameters all determined, the simulation accurately reproduced QCD, and predictions for physical quantities could proceed. *En passant*, we show in figure 16.11 results obtained (Davies *et al.* 2004), divided by experimental results, for nine different quantities, with and without quark vacuum polarization (left and right panels respectively). The values on the left deviate from experiment by as much as $10\% - 15\%$; those on the right agree with experiment to within systematic and statistical errors of 3% or less.

To extract a value of the coupling constant, the general strategy is to calculate (with the tuned simulation) a non-perturbative numerical value for a short-distance quantity, for which perturbation theory should be reliable. Then, by comparing the numerically computed value to the known perturbative expansion, a value of the coupling constant can be found.

In this case, the quantities calculated were vacuum expectation values of small Wilson loop operators W_{mn} (and related quantities) where

$$W_{mn} \equiv \frac{1}{3}\langle 0|\text{Re Tr P} \exp[-ig_L \int_{nm} A \cdot dx]|0\rangle, \tag{16.150}$$

where P denotes path ordering, $A_\mu = \boldsymbol{\lambda}/2 \cdot \boldsymbol{A}_\mu$ is the QCD (matrix-valued) vector potential, and the integral is over a closed $ma \times na$ rectangular path, not necessarily planar. The 1×1 Wilson loop is just the vev of the simple plaquette operator $U_\square$ of section 16.2.3.

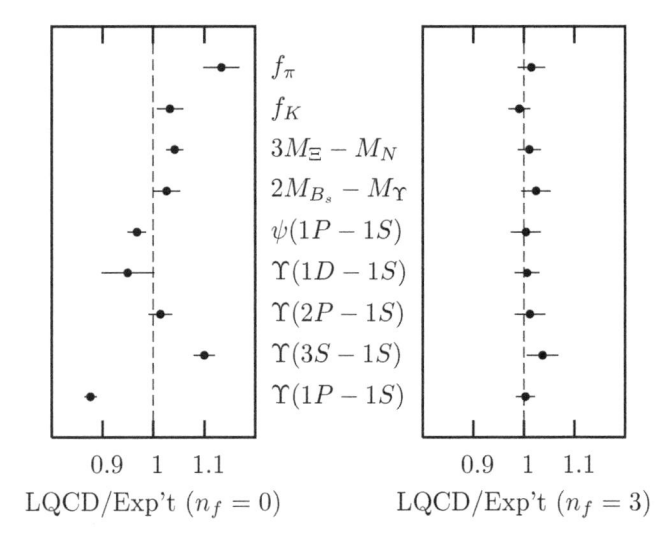

FIGURE 16.11
Lattice QCD results divided by experimental results for nine different quantities, with and without quark vacuum polarization (left and right panels, respectively). Figure reprinted with permission from C T H Davies *et al.* (HPQCD Collaboration) *Phys. Rev. Lett.* **92** 022001 (2004). Copyright 2004 by the American Physical Society.

In order to compare the numerical evaluation of (16.150) with perturbation theory, one has to decide what is a suitable expansion parameter. It was shown by Lepage and Mackenzie (1993) that the obvious first choice, the bare lattice coupling constant, is generally a poor one due to renormalization effects, even for short distance quantities. Instead, a renormalized coupling should be used – but this raises the questions of what renormalization *scheme* to adopt, and what *scale* at which to evaluate the (now running) coupling. In the present case, the scheme proposed by Brodsky, Lepage and Mackenzie (1983) was followed. It is defined in terms of the heavy quark potential $V(q)$, and is called the 'V-scheme'. The strong coupling in the V-scheme is defined by

$$V(q) = -\frac{4}{3}\frac{4\pi\alpha_{\rm V}(q)}{q^2} \tag{16.151}$$

with no higher-order corrections.

The numerically calculated short-distance quantities $Y^{(r)}$ are therefore to be expanded as the series

$$Y^{(r)} = \sum_{n=1}^{\infty} c_n^{(r)}\alpha_{\rm V}^n(d^{(r)}/a), \tag{16.152}$$

where $c_n^{(r)}$ and $d^{(r)}$ are dimensionless constants independent of the lattice spacing a, but dependent on the particular $Y^{(r)}$, and $\alpha_V(d^{(r)}/a)$ is the running QCD coupling in the V-scheme, with $N_f = 3$ light quark flavours. The perturbative coefficients $c_n^{(r)}$ for the various Y's were computed using Feynman diagrams, for $n \leq 3$, for the same quark and gluon actions which were used to create the sets of gluon field configurations employed in the numerical evaluation of the Y's. The renormalization scale $d^{(r)}/a$ varies for each short-distance quantity, being chosen according to the Lepage-Mackenzie (1993) prescription (or in some cases a more robust procedure due to Hornbostel, Lepage and Morningstar (2003)).

There were 22 $Y^{(r)}$'s, each of which was analyzed separately, fitting the expansion (16.152) to the 12 values of that Y calculated using the 12 gluon configurations. In the simplest terms, the result of each such fit would be the value of α_V at a particular scale, which was chosen to be $\alpha_V(7.5\ \text{GeV})$. The values required at the scales $\alpha_V(d^{(r)}/a_i)$ were found by numerically integrating the evolution equation (at four-loop order) for α_V; here a_i is the lattice spacing for each configuration (there were 6 different spacings). In fact, the fitting was more sophisticated, including further parameters related to various corrections; the interested reader can consult Davies *et al.* (2008) for the details. Having obtained $\alpha_V(7.5\ \text{GeV})$, this was then converted to the $\overline{\text{MS}}$ scheme, using the relation (Brodsky, Lepage and Mackenzie 1983)

$$\alpha_V(\mu) = \alpha_{\overline{\text{MS}}}(e^{-5/6}\mu). \tag{16.153}$$

Finally, the resultant $\alpha_{\overline{\text{MS}}}$ was evolved to M_Z^2. The value (16.149) is the final result after performing a weighted average over the 22 separate determinations. A full discussion of the error estimate, which includes finite lattice spacing, finite lattice volume, and chiral extrapolation uncertainties, is given in Davies *et al.* (2008).

16.5.4 Hadron masses

For our last example of a precise lattice QCD calculation, it is appropriate to consider the mass spectrum of light hadrons. After all, protons and neutrons account for nearly all the mass of ordinary matter, and 95% of their mass is the result of QCD interactions. It has long been a fundamental challenge to predict hadron masses accurately from QCD.

As one example of such calculations, we show in figure 16.12 the light hadron spectrum of QCD as reported by Dürr *et al.* (2008). Horizontal lines and bands are the experimental values (which have been isospin-averaged) with their decay widths. The solid circles are the predicted values. Vertical error bars represent combined statistical and systematic error estimates. The masses of the π, K and Ξ have no error bars, because they have been used to set the values of $m_u = m_d$, m_s and the overall scale, respectively. Once again, the agreement with experiment is very impressive.

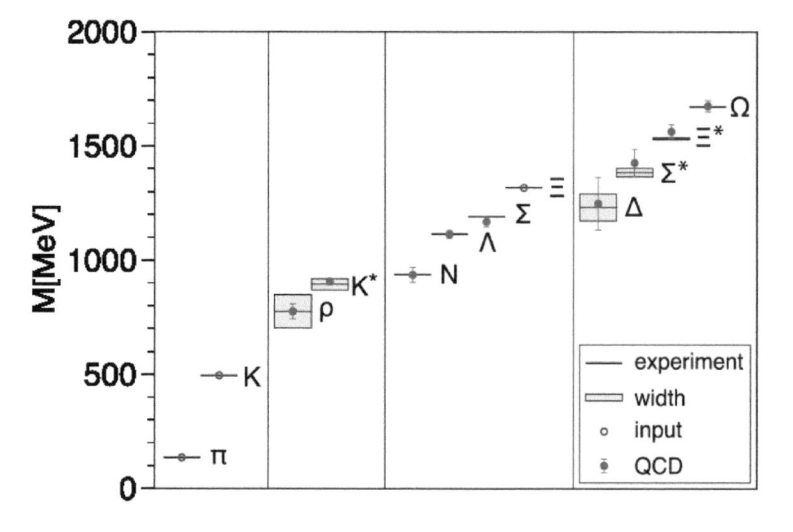

FIGURE 16.12
The light hadron spectrum of QCD, from Dürr *et al.* (2008). (See color plate II.)

These calculations used a Symanzik-improved gauge action (Lüscher and Weisz 1985), and 2+1 flavours of light dynamical Wilson fermions, with various improvements (Morningstar and Peardon 2004). The physical scale was set either by fitting to the mass of the Ξ, or to the mass of the Ω; the two ways gave consistent results. Pion masses in the range (approximately) 800 MeV to 190 MeV were used to extrapolate to the physical value, with lattice sizes approximately four times the inverse pion mass. A particular type of finite-volume effect arises in the case of strongly decaying resonant states: a procedure for reconstructing the infinite-volume resonance mass, given by Lüscher (1986, 1991a, 1991b), was followed here. This was satisfactory, except for the ρ and Δ at the lightest pion mass point, which was omitted from the extrapolation for these two channels. For further details, and additional references, we refer the reader to the supplementary material to Dürr *et al.* (2008) provided online.

We have been able to give only a brief introduction into what is now, almost forty years after its initial inception by Wilson (1974), the highly mature field of lattice QCD. A great deal of effort has gone into ingenious and subtle improvements to the lattice action, to the numerical algorithms, and to the treatment of fermions – to name a few of the issues. Lattice QCD is now a major part of particle physics. From the perspective of this chapter and the previous one, we can confidently say that, both in the short-distance (perturbative) regime, and in the long-distance (non-perturbative) regime, QCD is established as the correct theory of the strong interactions of quarks, beyond reasonable doubt.

Problems

16.1 Verify equation (16.9).

16.2 Verify equation (16.10).

16.3 Show that the momentum space version of (16.18) is (16.19).

16.4 Use (16.31) in (16.33) to verify (16.34).

16.5 Verify (16.68) and (16.70).

16.6 In a modified one-dimensional Ising model, spin variables s_n at sites labelled by $n = 1, 2, 3, \ldots N$ take the values $s_n = \pm 1$, and the energy of each spin configuration is

$$E = -\sum_{n=1}^{N-1} J_n s_n s_{n+1} \, ,$$

where all the constants J_n are positive. Show that the partition function Z_N is given by

$$Z_N = 2 \prod_{n=1}^{N-1} (2 \cosh K_n) \, ,$$

where $K_n = J_n/k_B T$. Hence calculate the entropy for the particular case in which all the J_n's are equal to J and $N \gg 1$, and discuss the behaviour of the entropy in the limits $T \to \infty$ and $T \to 0$.

Let 'p' denote a particular site such that $1 \ll p \ll N$. Show that the average value $\langle s_p s_{p+1} \rangle$ of the product $s_p s_{p+1}$ is given by

$$\langle s_p s_{p+1} \rangle = \frac{1}{Z_N} \frac{\partial Z_N}{\partial K_p}.$$

Show further that

$$\langle s_p s_{p+j} \rangle = \frac{1}{Z_N} \frac{\partial^j Z_N}{\partial K_p \partial K_{p+1} \ldots \partial K_{p+j-1}}.$$

Hence show that in the case $J_1 = J_2 = \ldots = J_N = J$,

$$\langle s_p s_{p+j} \rangle = e^{-ja/\xi} \, ,$$

where

$$\xi = -a/[\ln(\tanh K)] \, ,$$

and $K = J/k_B T$. Discuss the physical meaning of ξ, considering the $T \to \infty$ and $T \to 0$ limits explicitly.

Part VII

Spontaneously Broken Symmetry

17

Spontaneously Broken Global Symmetry

Previous chapters have introduced the non-Abelian symmetries SU(2) and SU(3) in both global and local forms, and we have seen how they may be applied to describe such typical physical phenomena as particle multiplets, and massless gauge fields. Remarkably enough, however, these symmetries are also applied, in the Standard Model, in two cases where the physical phenomena appear to be very different. Consider the following two questions: (i) Why are there no signs in the baryonic spectrum, such as parity doublets in particular, of the global chiral symmetry introduced in section 12.3.2? (ii) How can weak interactions be described by a local non-Abelian gauge theory when we know the mediating gauge field quanta are not massless? The answers to these questions each involve the same fundamental idea, which is a crucial component of the Standard Model, and perhaps also of theories which go beyond it. This is the idea that a symmetry can be 'spontaneously broken', or 'hidden'. By contrast, the symmetries considered hitherto may be termed 'manifest symmetries'.

The physical consequences of spontaneous symmetry breaking turn out to be rather different in the global and local cases. However, the essentials for a theoretical understanding of the phenomenon are contained in the simpler global case, which we consider in this chapter. The application to spontaneously broken chiral symmetry will be treated in chapter 18, and spontaneously broken local symmetry will be discussed in chapter 19, and applied in chapter 22.

17.1 Introduction

We begin by considering, in response to question (i) above, what could go wrong with the argument for symmetry multiplets that we gave in chapter 12. To understand this, we must use the field theory formulation of section 12.3, in which the generators of the symmetry are Hermitian field operators, and the states are created by operators acting on the vacuum. Thus consider two states $|A\rangle$, $|B\rangle$[1] :

$$|A\rangle = \hat{\phi}_A^\dagger |0\rangle, \qquad |B\rangle = \hat{\phi}_B^\dagger |0\rangle \qquad (17.1)$$

_____

[1]We now revert to the ordinary notation $|0\rangle$ for the vacuum state, rather than $|\Omega\rangle$, but it must be borne in mind that $|0\rangle$ is the full (interacting) vacuum.

where $\hat{\phi}_A^\dagger$ and $\hat{\phi}_B^\dagger$ are related to each other by (cf (12.100))

$$[\hat{Q}, \hat{\phi}_A^\dagger] = \hat{\phi}_B^\dagger \tag{17.2}$$

for some generator $\hat{Q}$ of a symmetry group, such that

$$[\hat{Q}, \hat{H}] = 0. \tag{17.3}$$

(17.2) is equivalent to

$$\hat{U}\hat{\phi}_A^\dagger\hat{U}^{-1} \approx \hat{\phi}_A^\dagger + i\epsilon\hat{\phi}_B^\dagger \tag{17.4}$$

for an infinitesimal transformation $\hat{U} \approx 1 + i\epsilon\hat{Q}$. Thus $\hat{\phi}_A^\dagger$ is 'rotated' into $\hat{\phi}_B^\dagger$ by $\hat{U}$, and the operators will create states related by the symmetry transformation. We want to see what are the assumptions necessary to prove that

$$E_A = E_B, \quad \text{where} \quad \hat{H}|A\rangle = E_A|A\rangle \quad \text{and} \quad \hat{H}|B\rangle = E_B|B\rangle. \tag{17.5}$$

We have

$$E_B|B\rangle = \hat{H}|B\rangle = \hat{H}\hat{\phi}_B^\dagger|0\rangle = \hat{H}(\hat{Q}\hat{\phi}_A^\dagger - \hat{\phi}_A^\dagger\hat{Q})|0\rangle. \tag{17.6}$$

Now if

$$\hat{Q}|0\rangle = 0 \tag{17.7}$$

we can rewrite the right-hand side of (17.6) as

$$\begin{aligned}
\hat{H}\hat{Q}\hat{\phi}_A^\dagger|0\rangle &= \hat{Q}\hat{H}\hat{\phi}_A^\dagger|0\rangle \quad \text{using (17.3)} \quad = \hat{Q}\hat{H}|A\rangle = E_A\hat{Q}|A\rangle \\
&= E_A\hat{Q}\hat{\phi}_A^\dagger|0\rangle = E_A(\hat{\phi}_B^\dagger + \hat{\phi}_A^\dagger\hat{Q})|0\rangle \quad \text{using (17.2)} \\
&= E_A|B\rangle \quad \text{if (17.7) holds;}
\end{aligned} \tag{17.8}$$

whence, comparing (17.8) with (17.6), we see that

$$E_A = E_B \quad \text{if (17.7) holds.} \tag{17.9}$$

Remembering that $\hat{U} = \exp(i\alpha\hat{Q})$, we see that (17.7) is equivalent to

$$|0\rangle' \equiv \hat{U}|0\rangle = |0\rangle. \tag{17.10}$$

Thus a multiplet structure will emerge provided that the vacuum is left invariant under the symmetry transformation. *The 'spontaneously broken symmetry' situation arises in the contrary case – that is, when the vacuum is not invariant under the symmetry,* which is to say when

$$\hat{Q}|0\rangle \neq 0. \tag{17.11}$$

In this case, the argument for the existence of symmetry multiplets breaks down, and although the Hamiltonian or Lagrangian may exhibit a non-Abelian

symmetry, this will not be manifested in the form of multiplets of mass-degenerate particles.

The preceding italicized sentence does correctly define what is meant by a spontaneously broken symmetry in field theory, but there is another way of thinking about it which is somewhat less abstract though also less rigorous. The basic condition is $\hat{Q}|0\rangle \neq 0$, and it seems tempting to infer that, in this case, the application of $\hat{Q}$ to the vacuum gives, not zero, but *another possible vacuum*, $|0\rangle'$. Thus we have the physically suggestive idea of 'degenerate vacua' (they must be degenerate since $[\hat{Q}, H] = 0$). We shall see in a moment why this notion, though intuitively helpful, is not rigorous.

It would seem, in any case, that the properties of the *vacuum* are all-important, so we begin our discussion with a somewhat formal, but nonetheless fundamental, theorem about the quantum field vacuum.

17.2 The Fabri–Picasso theorem

Suppose that a given Lagrangian $\hat{\mathcal{L}}$ is invariant under some one-parameter continuous global internal symmetry with a conserved Noether current $\hat{j}^\mu$, such that $\partial_\mu \hat{j}^\mu = 0$. The associated 'charge' is the Hermitian operator $\hat{Q} = \int \hat{j}^0 \mathrm{d}^3\boldsymbol{x}$, and $\dot{\hat{Q}} = 0$. We have hitherto assumed that the transformations of such a U(1) group are representable in the space of physical states by unitary operations $\hat{U}(\lambda) = \exp \mathrm{i}\lambda\hat{Q}$ for arbitrary λ, with the vacuum invariant under $\hat{U}$, so that $\hat{Q}|0\rangle = 0$. Fabri and Picasso (1966) showed that there are actually *two* possibilities:

(i) $\hat{Q}|0\rangle = 0$, and $|0\rangle$ is an eigenstate of $\hat{Q}$ with eigenvalue 0, so that $|0\rangle$ is invariant under $\hat{U}$(i.e. $\hat{U}|0\rangle = |0\rangle$));
or

(ii) $\hat{Q}|0\rangle$ does not exist in the space (its norm is infinite).

The statement (ii) is technically more correct than the more intuitive statements '$\hat{Q}|0\rangle \neq 0$' or '$\hat{U}|0\rangle = |0\rangle$'', suggested above.

To prove this result, consider the vacuum matrix element $\langle 0|\hat{j}^0(x)\hat{Q}|0\rangle$. From translation invariance, implemented by the unitary operator[2] $\hat{U}(x) = \exp \mathrm{i}\hat{P} \cdot x$ (where $\hat{P}^\mu$ is the 4-momentum operator) we obtain

$$\begin{aligned} \langle 0|\hat{j}^0(x)\hat{Q}|0\rangle &= \langle 0|e^{\mathrm{i}\hat{P}\cdot x}\hat{j}^0(0)e^{-\mathrm{i}\hat{P}\cdot x}\hat{Q}|0\rangle \\ &= \langle 0|e^{\mathrm{i}\hat{P}\cdot x}\hat{j}^0(0)\hat{Q}e^{-\mathrm{i}\hat{P}\cdot x}|0\rangle \end{aligned}$$

---

[2]If this seems unfamiliar, it may be regarded as the 4-dimensional generalization of the transformation (I.7) in appendix I of volume 1, from Schrödinger picture operators at $t = 0$ to Heisenberg operators at $t \neq 0$.

where the second line follows from

$$[\hat{P}^{\mu}, \hat{Q}] = 0 \tag{17.12}$$

since $\hat{Q}$ is an *internal* symmetry. But the vacuum is an eigenstate of $\hat{P}^{\mu}$ with eigenvalue zero, and so

$$\langle 0|\hat{j}^{0}(x)\hat{Q}|0\rangle = \langle 0|\hat{j}^{0}(0)\hat{Q}|0\rangle \tag{17.13}$$

which states that the matrix element we started from is in fact independent of x. Now consider the norm of $\hat{Q}|0\rangle$:

$$\langle 0|\hat{Q}\hat{Q}|0\rangle = \int \mathrm{d}^{3}\boldsymbol{x}\langle 0|\hat{j}^{0}(x)\hat{Q}|0\rangle \tag{17.14}$$

$$= \int \mathrm{d}^{3}\boldsymbol{x}\langle 0|\hat{j}^{0}(0)\hat{Q}|0\rangle, \tag{17.15}$$

which must diverge in the infinite volume limit, unless $\hat{Q}|0\rangle = 0$. Thus either $\hat{Q}|0\rangle = 0$ or $\hat{Q}|0\rangle$ has infinite norm. The foregoing can be easily generalized to non-Abelian symmetry operators $\hat{T}_{i}$.

Remarkably enough, the argument can also, in a sense, be reversed. Coleman (1966) proved that if an operator

$$\hat{Q}(t) = \int \mathrm{d}^{3}\boldsymbol{x}\hat{j}^{0}(x) \tag{17.16}$$

is the spatial integral of the $\mu = 0$ component of a 4-vector (but *not assumed* to be conserved), and if it annihilates the vacuum

$$\hat{Q}(t)|0\rangle = 0, \tag{17.17}$$

then in fact $\partial_{\mu}\hat{j}^{\mu} = 0$, $\hat{Q}$ is independent of t, and the symmetry is unitarily implementable by operators $\hat{U} = \exp(\mathrm{i}\lambda\hat{Q})$.

We might now simply proceed to the chiral symmetry application. We believe, however, that the concept of spontaneous symmetry breaking is so important to particle physics that a more extended discussion is amply justified. In particular, there are crucial insights to be gained by considering the analogous phenomenon in condensed matter physics. After a brief look at the ferromagnet, we shall describe the Bogoliubov model for the ground state of a superfluid, which provides an important physical example of a spontaneously broken global Abelian U(1) symmetry. We shall see that the excitations away from the ground state are *massless modes* and we shall learn, via Goldstone's theorem, that such modes are an inevitable result of spontaneously breaking a global symmetry. Next, we shall introduce the 'Goldstone model' which is the simplest example of a spontaneously broken global U(1) symmetry, involving just one complex scalar field. The generalization of this to the non-Abelian case will draw us in the direction of the Higgs sector of the Standard Model.

Returning to condensed matter systems, we introduce the BCS ground state for a superconductor, in a way which builds on the Bogoliubov model of a superfluid. We are then prepared for the application, in chapter 18, to spontaneous chiral symmetry breaking (question (i) above), following Nambu's profound analogy with one aspect of superconductivity. In chapter 19 we shall see how a different aspect of superconductivity provides a model for the answer to question (ii) above.

17.3 Spontaneously broken symmetry in condensed matter physics

17.3.1 The ferromagnet

We have seen that everything depends on the properties of the vacuum state. An essential aid to understanding hidden symmetry in quantum field theory is provided by Nambu's (1960) remarkable insight that the *vacuum* state of a quantum field theory is analogous to the ground state of an interacting many-body system. It is the state of lowest energy – the equilibrium state, given the kinetic and potential energies as specified in the Hamiltonian. Now the ground state of a complicated system (for example, one involving interacting fields) may well have unsuspected properties – which may, indeed, be very hard to predict from the Hamiltonian. But we can postulate (even if we cannot yet prove) properties of the quantum field theory vacuum $|0\rangle$ which are analogous to those of the ground states of many physically interesting many-body systems – such as superfluids and superconductors, to name two with which we shall be principally concerned.

Now it is generally the case, in quantum mechanics, that the ground state of any system described by a Hamiltonian is non-degenerate. Sometimes we may meet systems in which apparently more than one state has the same lowest energy eigenvalue. Yet in fact none of these states will be the true ground state: tunnelling will take place between the various degenerate states, and the true ground state will turn out to be a unique linear superposition of them. This is, in fact, the only possibility for systems of finite spatial extent, though in practice a state which is not the true ground state may have an extremely long lifetime. However, in the case of fields (extending presumably throughout all space), the Fabri–Picasso theorem shows that there is an alternative possibility, which is often described as involving a 'degenerate ground state' – a term we shall now elucidate. In case (a) of the theorem, the ground state is unique. For, suppose that several ground states $|0, a\rangle, |0, b\rangle, \ldots$ existed, with the symmetry unitarily implemented. Then one ground state will be related to another by

$$|0, a\rangle = \mathrm{e}^{\mathrm{i}\lambda\hat{Q}}|0, b\rangle \tag{17.18}$$

for some λ. However, in case (a) the charge annihilates a ground state, and so all of them are really identical. In case (b), on the other hand, we cannot write (17.18) – since $\hat{Q}|0\rangle$ does not exist – and we do have the possibility of many degenerate ground states. In simple models one can verify that these alternative ground states are all orthogonal to each other, in the infinite volume limit – or perhaps more physically, the limit in which the number of degrees of freedom becomes infinite. And each member of every 'tower' of excited states, built on these alternative ground states, is also orthogonal to all the members of other towers. But any single tower must constitute a complete space of states. It follows that states in different towers belong to *different* complete spaces of states, that is to different – and inequivalent – 'worlds', each one built on one of the possible orthogonal ground states.

At first sight, a familiar example of these ideas seems to be that of a ferromagnet, below its Curie temperature T_C. Consider an 'ideal Heisenberg ferromagnet' with N atoms each of spin $1/2$, described by a Hamiltonian of Heisenberg exchange form $H_S = -J \sum \hat{S}_i \cdot \hat{S}_j$, where i and j label the atomic sites. This Hamiltonian is invariant under spatial rotations, since it only depends on the dot product of the spin operators. Such rotations are implemented by unitary operators $\exp(i\hat{S} \cdot \boldsymbol{\alpha})$ where $\hat{S} = \sum_i \hat{S}_i$, and spins at different sites are assumed to commute. As usual with angular momentum in quantum mechanics, the eigenstates of H_S are labelled by the eigenvalues of total squared spin, and of one component of spin, say of $\hat{S}_z = \sum_i \hat{S}_{iz}$. The quantum mechanical ground state of H_S is an eigenstate with total spin quantum number $S = N/2$, and this state is $(2 \cdot N/2 + 1) = (N+1)-$ fold degenerate, allowing for all the possible eigenvalues $(N/2, N/2 - 1, \ldots - N/2)$ of $\hat{S}_z$ for this value of S. We are free to choose any one of these degenerate states as 'the' ground state, say the state with eigenvalue $S_z = N/2$.

It is clear that the ground state is not invariant under the spin-rotation symmetry of H_S, which would require the eigenvalues $S = S_z = 0$. Furthermore, this ground state is degenerate. So two important features of what we have so far learned to expect of a spontaneously broken symmetry are present – namely, 'the ground state is not invariant under the symmetry of the Hamiltonian', and 'the ground state is degenerate'. However, it has to be emphasized that this ferromagnetic ground state does, in fact, respect the symmetry of H_S, in the sense that it belongs to an irreducible representation of the symmetry group: the unusual feature is that it is not the 'trivial' (singlet) representation, as would be the case for an invariant ground state. The spontaneous symmetry breaking which is the true model for particle physics is that in which a many body ground state is *not* an eigenstate (trivial or otherwise) of the symmetry operators of the Hamiltonian: rather it is a superposition of such eigenstates. We shall explore this for the superfluid and the superconductor in due course.

Nevertheless, there are some useful insights to be gained from the ferromagnet. First, consider two ground states differing by a spin rotation. In the first, the spins are all aligned along the 3-axis, say, and in the second along

the axis $\hat{\boldsymbol{n}} = (0, \sin\alpha, \cos\alpha)$. Thus the first ground state is

$$\chi_0 = \begin{pmatrix} 1 \\ 0 \end{pmatrix}_1 \begin{pmatrix} 1 \\ 0 \end{pmatrix}_2 \cdots \begin{pmatrix} 1 \\ 0 \end{pmatrix}_N \qquad \text{(N products)} \qquad (17.19)$$

while the second is (cf (4.31), (4.32))

$$\chi_0^{(\alpha)} = \begin{pmatrix} \cos\alpha/2 \\ i\sin\alpha/2 \end{pmatrix}_1 \cdots \begin{pmatrix} \cos\alpha/2 \\ i\sin\alpha/2 \end{pmatrix}_N . \qquad (17.20)$$

The scalar product of (17.19) and (17.20) is $(\cos\alpha/2)^N$, which goes to zero as $N \to \infty$. Thus any two such 'rotated ground states' are indeed orthogonal in the infinite volume (or infinite number of degrees of freedom) limit.

We may also enquire about the excited states built on one such ground state, say the one with $\hat{S}_z$ eigenvalue $N/2$. Suppose for simplicity that the magnet is one-dimensional (but the spins have all three components). Consider the state $\chi_n = \hat{S}_{n-}\chi_0$ where $\hat{S}_{n-}$ is the spin lowering operator $\hat{S}_{n-} = (\hat{S}_{nx} - i\hat{S}_{ny})$ at site n, such that

$$\hat{S}_{n-} \begin{pmatrix} 1 \\ 0 \end{pmatrix}_n = \begin{pmatrix} 0 \\ 1 \end{pmatrix}_n ; \qquad (17.21)$$

so $\hat{S}_{n-}\chi_0$ differs from the ground state χ_0 by having the spin at site n flipped. The action of $\hat{H}_S$ on χ_n can be found by writing

$$\sum_{i\neq j} \hat{\boldsymbol{S}}_i \cdot \hat{\boldsymbol{S}}_j = \sum_{i\neq j} \frac{1}{2}(\hat{S}_{i-}\hat{S}_{j+} + \hat{S}_{j-}\hat{S}_{i+}) + \hat{S}_{iz}\hat{S}_{jz} \qquad (17.22)$$

(remembering that spins on different sites commute), where $\hat{S}_{i+} = \hat{S}_{ix} + i\hat{S}_{iy}$. Since all $\hat{S}_{i+}$ operators give zero on a spin 'up' state, the only non-zero contributions from the first (bracketed) term in (17.22) come from terms in which either $\hat{S}_{i+}$ or $\hat{S}_{j+}$ act on the 'down' spin at n, so as to restore it to 'up'. The 'partner' operator $\hat{S}_{i-}$ (or $\hat{S}_{j-}$) then simply lowers the spin at i (or j), leading to the result

$$\sum_{i\neq j} \frac{1}{2}(\hat{S}_{i-}\hat{S}_{j+} + \hat{S}_{j-}\hat{S}_{i+})\chi_n = \sum_{i\neq n} \chi_i. \qquad (17.23)$$

Thus the state χ_n is not an eigenstate of $\hat{H}_S$. However, a little more work shows that the superpostitions

$$\tilde{\chi}_q = \frac{1}{\sqrt{N}} \sum_n e^{iqna} \chi_n \qquad (17.24)$$

are eigenstates; here q is one of the discretized wavenumbers produced by appropriate boundary conditions, as is usual in one-dimensional 'chain' problems. The states (17.24) represent *spin waves*, and they have the important

feature that for low q (long wavelength) their frequency ω tends to zero with q (actually $\omega \propto q^2$). In this respect, therefore, they behave like massless particles when quantized – and this is another feature we should expect when a symmetry is spontaneously broken.

The ferromagnet gives us one more useful insight. We have been assuming that one particular ground state (e.g. the one with $S_z = N/2$) has been somehow 'chosen'. But what does the choosing? The answer to this is clear enough in the (perfectly realistic) case in which the Hamiltonian $\hat{H}_S$ is supplemented by a term $-g\mu B \sum_i \hat{S}_{iz}$, representing the effect of an applied field B directed along the z-axis. This term will indeed ensure that the ground state is unique, and has $S_z = N/2$. Consider now the two limits $B \to 0$ and $N \to \infty$, both at finite temperature. When $B \to 0$ at finite N, the $N+1$ different S_z eigenstates become degenerate, and we have an ensemble in which each enters with an equal weight; there is therefore no loss of symmetry, even as $N \to \infty$ (but only *after* $B \to 0$). On the other hand, if $N \to \infty$ at finite $B \neq 0$, the single state with $S_z = N/2$ will be selected out as the unique ground state and this asymmetric situation will persist even in the limit $B \to 0$. In a (classical) mean field theory approximation we suppose that an 'internal field' is 'spontaneously generated', which is aligned with the external B and survives even as $B \to 0$, thus 'spontaneously' breaking the symmetry.

The ferromagnet therefore provides an easily pictured system exhibiting many of the features associated with spontaneous symmetry breaking; most importantly, it strongly suggests that what is really characteristic about the phenonenon is that it entails 'spontaneous ordering'.[3] Generally such ordering occurs below some characteristic 'critical temperature', T_C. The field which develops a non-zero equilibrium value below T_C is called an 'order parameter'. This concept forms the basis of Landau's theory of second-order phase transitions (see for example chapter XIV of Landau and Lifshitz 1980).

We now turn to an example much more closely analogous to the particle physics applications: the superfluid.

17.3.2   The Bogoliubov superfluid

Consider the non-relativistic Hamiltonian (in the Schrödinger picture)

$$\hat{H} = \frac{1}{2m} \int d^3x \, \boldsymbol{\nabla}\hat{\phi}^\dagger \cdot \boldsymbol{\nabla}\hat{\phi}$$
$$+ \frac{1}{2} \int \int d^3x \, d^3y \, v(|\boldsymbol{x} - \boldsymbol{y}|)\hat{\phi}^\dagger(\boldsymbol{x})\hat{\phi}^\dagger(\boldsymbol{y})\hat{\phi}(\boldsymbol{y})\hat{\phi}(\boldsymbol{x}) \quad (17.25)$$

where $\hat{\phi}^\dagger(\boldsymbol{x})$ creates a boson of mass m at position $\boldsymbol{x}$. This $\hat{H}$ describes identical bosons interacting via a potential v, which is assumed to be weak (see, for example, Schiff 1968 section 55, or Parry 1973 chapter 1). We note

---

[3]It is worth pausing to reflect on the idea that *ordering* is associated with *symmetry breaking*.

at once that $\hat{H}$ is invariant under the global U(1) symmetry

$$\hat{\phi}(\boldsymbol{x}) \rightarrow \hat{\phi}'(\boldsymbol{x}) = \mathrm{e}^{-\mathrm{i}\alpha}\hat{\phi}(\boldsymbol{x}), \tag{17.26}$$

the generator being the conserved number operator

$$\hat{N} = \int \hat{\phi}^\dagger \hat{\phi} \, \mathrm{d}^3\boldsymbol{x} \tag{17.27}$$

which obeys $[\hat{N}, \hat{H}] = 0$. Our ultimate concern will be with the way this symmetry is 'spontaneously broken' in the superfluid ground state. Naturally, since this is an Abelian, rather than a non-Abelian, symmetry the physics will not involve any (hidden) multiplet structure. But the nature of the 'symmetry breaking ground state' in this U(1) case (and in the BCS model of section 17.7) will serve as a physical model for non-Abelian cases also.

We begin by re-writing $\hat{H}$ in terms of mode creation and annihilation operators in the usual way. We expand $\hat{\phi}(\boldsymbol{x})$ as a superposition of solutions of the $v = 0$ problem, which are plane waves quantized in a large cube of volume Ω:

$$\hat{\phi}(\boldsymbol{x}) = \frac{1}{\Omega^{\frac{1}{2}}} \sum_{\boldsymbol{k}} \hat{a}_{\boldsymbol{k}} \mathrm{e}^{\mathrm{i}\boldsymbol{k}\cdot\boldsymbol{x}} \tag{17.28}$$

where $\hat{a}_{\boldsymbol{k}}|0\rangle = 0$, $\hat{a}_{\boldsymbol{k}}^\dagger|0\rangle$ is a one-particle state, and $[\hat{a}_{\boldsymbol{k}}, \hat{a}_{\boldsymbol{k}'}^\dagger] = \delta_{\boldsymbol{k},\boldsymbol{k}'}$, with all other commutators vanishing. We impose periodic boundary conditions at the cube faces, and the free particle energies are $\epsilon_k = \boldsymbol{k}^2/2m$. Inserting (17.28) into (17.25) leads (problem 17.1) to

$$\hat{H} = \sum_{\boldsymbol{k}} \epsilon_k \hat{a}_{\boldsymbol{k}}^\dagger \hat{a}_{\boldsymbol{k}} + \frac{1}{2\Omega} \sum_\Delta \bar{v}(|\boldsymbol{k}_1 - \boldsymbol{k}_1'|)\hat{a}_{\boldsymbol{k}_1}^\dagger \hat{a}_{\boldsymbol{k}_2}^\dagger \hat{a}_{\boldsymbol{k}_2'} \hat{a}_{\boldsymbol{k}_1'} \Delta(\boldsymbol{k}_1 + \boldsymbol{k}_2 - \boldsymbol{k}_1' - \boldsymbol{k}_2')$$
$$\tag{17.29}$$

where the sum is over all momenta $\boldsymbol{k}_1, \boldsymbol{k}_2, \boldsymbol{k}_1', \boldsymbol{k}_2'$ subject to the conservation law imposed by the Δ function:

$$\Delta(\boldsymbol{k}) \;=\; 1 \qquad \text{if } \boldsymbol{k} = 0 \tag{17.30}$$
$$\;=\; 0 \qquad \text{if } \boldsymbol{k} \neq 0. \tag{17.31}$$

The interaction term in (17.29) is easily visualized as in figure 17.1. A pair of particles in states $\boldsymbol{k}_1', \boldsymbol{k}_2'$ is scattered (conserving momentum) to a pair in states $\boldsymbol{k}_1, \boldsymbol{k}_2$ via the Fourier transform of v:

$$\bar{v}(|\boldsymbol{k}|) = \int v(r)\mathrm{e}^{-\mathrm{i}\boldsymbol{k}\cdot\boldsymbol{r}}\mathrm{d}^3\boldsymbol{r}. \tag{17.32}$$

Now, below the superfluid transition temperature T_S, we know that in the limit as $v \rightarrow 0$ the ground state has all the particles 'condensed' into the lowest energy state, which has $\boldsymbol{k} = \boldsymbol{0}$. Thus the ground state will be proportional to

$$|N, 0\rangle = (\hat{a}_0^\dagger)^N|0\rangle. \tag{17.33}$$

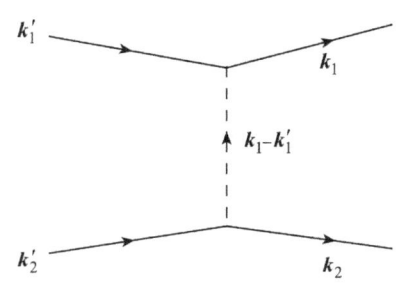

FIGURE 17.1
The interaction term in (17.29).

When a weak repulsive v is included, it is reasonable to hope that most of the particles remain in the condensate, only relatively few being excited to states with $\mathbf{k} \neq \mathbf{0}$. Let N_0 be the number of particles with $\mathbf{k} = \mathbf{0}$, where by assumption $N_0 \approx N$. We now consider the limit N (and N_0) $\to \infty$ and $\Omega \to \infty$ such that the density $\rho = N/\Omega$ (and $\rho_0 = N_0/\Omega$) stays constant. Bogoliubov (1947) argued that in this limit we may effectively replace both $\hat{a}_0$ and $\hat{a}_0^\dagger$ in the second term in (17.29) by the number $N_0^{1/2}$. This amounts to saying that in the commutator

$$\frac{\hat{a}_0}{\Omega^{1/2}} \frac{\hat{a}_0^\dagger}{\Omega^{1/2}} - \frac{\hat{a}^\dagger}{\Omega^{1/2}} \frac{\hat{a}_0}{\Omega^{1/2}} = \frac{1}{\Omega} \tag{17.34}$$

the two terms on the left-hand side are each of order N_0/Ω and hence finite, while their difference may be neglected as $\Omega \to \infty$. Replacing $\hat{a}_0$ and $\hat{a}_0^\dagger$ by $N_0^{1/2}$ leads (problem 17.2) to the following approximate form for $\hat{H}$:

$$\hat{H} \approx \hat{H}_{\mathrm{B}} \equiv \sum_{\mathbf{k}}{}' \hat{a}_{\mathbf{k}}^\dagger \hat{a}_{\mathbf{k}} E_k + \frac{1}{2} \frac{N^2}{\Omega} \bar{v}(0)$$

$$+ \frac{1}{2} \sum_{\mathbf{k}}{}' \frac{N}{\Omega} \bar{v}(|\mathbf{k}|)[\hat{a}_{\mathbf{k}}^\dagger \hat{a}_{-\mathbf{k}}^\dagger + \hat{a}_{\mathbf{k}} \hat{a}_{-\mathbf{k}}], \tag{17.35}$$

where

$$E_k = \epsilon_k + \frac{N}{\Omega} \bar{v}(|\mathbf{k}|), \tag{17.36}$$

primed summations do not include $\mathbf{k} = \mathbf{0}$, and terms which tend to zero as $\Omega \to \infty$ have been dropped (thus, N_0 has been replaced by N).

The most immediately striking feature of (17.35), as compared with $\hat{H}$ of (17.29), is that $\hat{H}_{\mathrm{B}}$ does not conserve the U(1) (number) symmetry (17.26) while $\hat{H}$ does: it is easy to see that for (17.26) to be a good symmetry, the number of $\hat{a}$'s must equal the number of $\hat{a}^\dagger$'s in every term. Thus the ground state of $\hat{H}_{\mathrm{B}}$, $|\mathrm{ground}\rangle_{\mathrm{B}}$, cannot be expected to be an eigenstate of the number

operator. However, it is important to be clear that the number non-conserving aspect of (17.35) is of a completely different kind, conceptually, from that which would be associated with a (hypothetical) '*explicit*' number violating term in the original Hamiltonian – for example, the addition of a term of the form '$\hat{a}^\dagger \hat{a}\hat{a}$'. In arriving at (17.35), we effectively replaced (17.28) by

$$\hat{\phi}_B(\boldsymbol{x}) = \rho_0^{1/2} + \frac{1}{\Omega^{1/2}} \sum_{\boldsymbol{k} \neq 0} \hat{a}_{\boldsymbol{k}} e^{i\boldsymbol{k}\cdot\boldsymbol{x}} \tag{17.37}$$

where $\rho_0 = N_0/\Omega$, $N_0 \approx N$, and N_0/Ω remains finite as $\Omega \to \infty$. The limit is crucial here: it enables us to picture the condensate N_0 as providing an infinite reservoir of particles, with which excitations away from the ground state can exchange particle number. From this point of view, a number non-conserving ground state may appear more reasonable. The ultimate test, of course, is whether such a state is a good approximation to the true ground state, for a large but finite system.

What is $|\text{ground}\rangle_B$? Remarkably, $\hat{H}_B$ can be exactly diagonalized by means of the *Bogoliubov quasiparticle operators* (for $\boldsymbol{k} \neq 0$)

$$\hat{\alpha}_{\boldsymbol{k}} = f_k \hat{a}_{\boldsymbol{k}} + g_k \hat{a}^\dagger_{-\boldsymbol{k}}, \quad \hat{\alpha}^\dagger_{\boldsymbol{k}} = f_k \hat{a}^\dagger_{\boldsymbol{k}} + g_k \hat{a}_{-\boldsymbol{k}} \tag{17.38}$$

where f_k and g_k are real functions of $k = |\boldsymbol{k}|$. We must again at once draw attention to the fact that this transformation does not respect the symmetry (17.26) either, since $\hat{a}_{\boldsymbol{k}} \to e^{-i\alpha}\hat{a}_{\boldsymbol{k}}$ while $\hat{a}^\dagger_{-\boldsymbol{k}} \to e^{+i\alpha}\hat{a}^\dagger_{-\boldsymbol{k}}$. In fact, the operators $\hat{\alpha}^\dagger_{\boldsymbol{k}}$ will turn out to be precisely *creation operators for quasiparticles* which exchange particle number with the ground state.

The commutator of $\hat{\alpha}_{\boldsymbol{k}}$ and $\hat{\alpha}^\dagger_{\boldsymbol{k}}$ is easily evaluated:

$$[\hat{\alpha}_{\boldsymbol{k}}, \hat{\alpha}^\dagger_{\boldsymbol{k}}] = f_k^2 - g_k^2, \tag{17.39}$$

while two $\hat{a}$'s or two $\hat{a}^\dagger$'s commute. We choose f_k and g_k such that $f_k^2 - g_k^2 = 1$, so that the $\hat{a}$'s and the $\hat{\alpha}$'s have the same (bosonic) commutation relations, and the transformation (17.38) is 'canonical'. A convenient choice is $f_k = \cosh\theta_k$, $g_k = \sinh\theta_k$. We now assert that $\hat{H}_B$ can be written in the form

$$\hat{H}_B = {\sum_{\boldsymbol{k}}}' \omega_k \hat{\alpha}^\dagger_{\boldsymbol{k}} \hat{\alpha}_{\boldsymbol{k}} + \beta \tag{17.40}$$

for certain ω_k and β. Equation (17.40) implies, of course, that the eigenvalues of $\hat{H}_B$ are $\beta + \sum_{\boldsymbol{k}}(n + 1/2)\omega_k$, and that $\hat{\alpha}^\dagger_{\boldsymbol{k}}$ acts as the creation operator for the quasiparticle of energy ω_k, as just anticipated.

We verify (17.40) slightly indirectly. We note first that it implies that

$$[\hat{H}_B, \hat{\alpha}^\dagger_{\boldsymbol{l}}] = \omega_l \hat{\alpha}^\dagger_{\boldsymbol{l}}. \tag{17.41}$$

Substituting for $\hat{a}_{l}^{\dagger}$ from (17.38), we require

$$[\hat{H}_{\mathrm{B}}, \cosh\theta_{l}\,\hat{a}_{l}^{\dagger} + \sinh\theta_{l}\,\hat{a}_{-l}] = \omega_{l}(\cosh\theta_{l}\,\hat{a}_{l}^{\dagger} + \sinh\theta_{l}\,\hat{a}_{-l}), \qquad (17.42)$$

which must hold as an identity in the $\hat{a}$'s and $\hat{a}^{\dagger}$'s. Using the expression (17.35) for $\hat{H}_{\mathrm{B}}$, and some patient work with the commutation relations (problem 17.3), one finds

$$(\omega_{l} - E_{l})\cosh\theta_{l} \;+\; \frac{N}{\Omega}\bar{v}(|l|)\sinh\theta_{l} = 0 \qquad (17.43)$$

$$\frac{N}{\Omega}\bar{v}(|l|)\cosh\theta_{l} \;-\; (\omega_{l} + E_{l})\sinh\theta_{l} = 0. \qquad (17.44)$$

For consistency, therefore, we require

$$E_{l}^{2} - \omega_{l}^{2} - \left(\frac{N}{\Omega^{2}}\right)^{2}(\bar{v}(|l|))^{2} = 0, \qquad (17.45)$$

or (recalling the definitions of E_{l} and ϵ_{l})

$$\omega_{l} = \left[\frac{l^{2}}{2m}\left(\frac{l^{2}}{2m} + 2\rho\bar{v}(|l|)\right)\right]^{1/2} \qquad (17.46)$$

where $\rho = N/\Omega$. The value of $\tanh\theta_{l}$ is then determined via either of (17.43), (17.44).

Equation (17.46) is an important result, giving the frequency as a function of the momentum (or wavenumber); it is an example of a 'dispersion relation'. At the risk of stating the obvious, let us emphasize that equation (17.40) tells us that the original system of interacting bosons is equivalent (under the approximations made) to a system of non-interacting quasiparticles, whose frequency ω_{l} is related to wavenumber by (17.46). These are the true modes of the system. Let us consider this dispersion relation.

First of all, in the non-interacting case $\bar{v} = 0$, we recover the usual frequency-wavenumber relation for a massive non-relativistic particle, $\omega_{l} = l^{2}/2m$. But if $\bar{v}(0) \neq 0$, the behaviour at small l is very different: $\omega_{l} \approx c_{\mathrm{s}}|l|$, where $c_{\mathrm{s}} = (\rho\bar{v}(0)/m)^{1/2}$. This dispersion relation is characteristic of a massless mode, but in this case it is sound rather than light, with speed of sound c_{s}. The spectrum is therefore phonon-like, not (non-relativistic) particle-like. The two behaviours can be easily distinguished experimentally, by measuring the low-temperature specific heat: in three dimensions, for $\omega_{l} \sim l^{2}$ it goes to zero as $T^{3/2}$, whereas for $\omega_{l} \sim |l|$ it goes as T^{3}. The latter behaviour is observed in superfluids. At large values of $|l|$, however, ω_{l} behaves essentially like $l^{2}/2m$ and the spectrum returns to the 'particle-like' one of massive bosons. Thus (17.46) interpolates between phonon-like behaviour at small $|l|$ and particle-like behaviour at large $|l|$.

There is still more to be learned from (17.46). If, in fact, $\bar{v}(|\boldsymbol{l}|) \sim 1/l^2$, then $\omega_l \to$ constant as $|\boldsymbol{l}| \to 0$, and the spectrum would *not* be phonon-like. Indeed, if $\bar{v}(|\boldsymbol{l}|) \sim e^2/l^2$, then $\omega_l \sim |e|(\rho/m)^{1/2}$ for small $|\boldsymbol{l}|$, which is just the 'plasma frequency' ω_p. In particle physics terms, this would be analogous to a dispersion relation of the form $\omega_l \sim (\omega_p^2 + l^2)^{1/2}$, which describes a particle with mass ω_p. Such a $\bar{v}$ is, of course, Colombic (the Fourier transform of $e^2/|\boldsymbol{x}|$), indicating that *in the case of such a long-range force the frequency spectrum acquires a mass-gap*. This will be the topic of chapter 19.

Having discussed the spectrum of quasiparticle excitations, let us now concentrate on the ground state in this model. From (17.40), it is clear that it is defined as the state $|\text{ground}\rangle_B$ such that

$$\hat{\alpha}_{\boldsymbol{k}}|\text{ground}\rangle_B = 0 \qquad \text{for all } \boldsymbol{k} \neq \boldsymbol{0}; \qquad (17.47)$$

i.e. as the state with no non-zero-momentum quasiparticles in it. This is a complicated state in terms of the original $\hat{a}_{\boldsymbol{k}}$ and $\hat{a}_{\boldsymbol{k}}^\dagger$ operators, but we can give a formal expression for it, as follows. Since the $\hat{\alpha}$'s and $\hat{a}$'s are related by a canonical transformation, there must exist a unitary operator $\hat{U}_B$ such that

$$\hat{\alpha}_{\boldsymbol{k}} = \hat{U}_B \hat{a}_{\boldsymbol{k}} \hat{U}_B^{-1}, \qquad \hat{a}_{\boldsymbol{k}} = \hat{U}_B^{-1} \hat{\alpha}_{\boldsymbol{k}} \hat{U}_B. \qquad (17.48)$$

Now we know that $\hat{a}_{\boldsymbol{k}}|0\rangle = 0$. Hence it follows that

$$\hat{\alpha}_{\boldsymbol{k}} \hat{U}_B |0\rangle = 0, \qquad (17.49)$$

and we can identify $|\text{ground}\rangle_B$ with $\hat{U}_B|0\rangle$. In problem 17.4, $\hat{U}_B$ is evaluated for an $\hat{H}_B$ consisting of a single $\boldsymbol{k}$-mode only, in which case the operator effecting the transformation analogous to (17.48) is $\hat{U}_1 = \exp[\theta(\hat{a}\hat{a} - \hat{a}^\dagger \hat{a}^\dagger)/2]$ where θ replaces θ_k in this case. This generalizes (in the form of products of such operators) to the full $\hat{H}_B$ case, but we shall not need the detailed result; an analogous result for the BCS ground state is discussed more fully in section 17.7. The important point is the following. It is clear from expanding the exponentials that $\hat{U}_B$ creates a state in which the number of a-quanta (i.e. the original bosons) *is not fixed*. Thus unlike the simple non-interacting ground state $|N,0\rangle$ of (17.33), $|\text{ground}\rangle_B = \hat{U}_B|0\rangle$ does not have a fixed number of particles in it: that is to say, it is *not* an eigenstate of the symmetry operator $\hat{N}$, as anticipated in the comment following (17.36). This is just the situation alluded to in the paragraph before equation (17.19), in our discussion of the ferromagnet.

Consider now the expectation value of $\hat{\phi}(\boldsymbol{x})$ in any state of definite particle number – that is, in an eigenstate of the symmetry operator $\hat{N}$. It is easy to see that this must vanish (remember that $\hat{\phi}$ destroys a boson, and so $\hat{\phi}|N\rangle$ is proportional to $|N-1\rangle$, which is orthogonal to $|N\rangle$). On the other hand, this is *not* true of $\hat{\phi}_B(\boldsymbol{x})$: for example, in the non-interacting ground state (17.33), we have

$$\langle N, 0|\hat{\phi}_B(\boldsymbol{x})|N, 0\rangle = \rho_0^{1/2}. \qquad (17.50)$$

Furthermore, using the inverse of (17.38)

$$\hat{a}_{\boldsymbol{k}} = \cosh\theta_k \hat{\alpha}_{\boldsymbol{k}} - \sinh\theta_k \hat{\alpha}^\dagger_{-\boldsymbol{k}} \tag{17.51}$$

together with (17.47), we find the similar result:

$$_{\mathrm{B}}\langle \mathrm{ground}|\hat{\phi}_{\mathrm{B}}(\boldsymbol{x})|\mathrm{ground}\rangle_{\mathrm{B}} = \rho_0^{1/2}. \tag{17.52}$$

The question is now how to generalize (17.50) or (17.52) to the complete $\hat{\phi}(\boldsymbol{x})$ and the true ground state $|\mathrm{ground}\rangle$, in the limit $N, \Omega \to \infty$ with fixed N/Ω. We make the *assumption* that

$$\langle \mathrm{ground}|\hat{\phi}(\boldsymbol{x})|\mathrm{ground}\rangle \neq 0; \tag{17.53}$$

that is, we abstract from the Bogoliubov model the crucial feature that *the field acquires a non-zero expectation value in the ground state*, in the infinite volume limit.

We are now at the heart of spontaneous symmetry breaking in field theory. Condition (17.53) has the form of an 'ordering' condition: it is analogous to the non-zero value of the total spin in the ferromagnetic case, but in (17.53) – we must again emphasize – $|\mathrm{ground}\rangle$ is *not* an eigenstate of the symmetry operator $\hat{N}$; if it were, (17.53) would vanish, as we have just seen. Recalling the association 'quantum vacuum ↔ many body ground state' we expect that the occurrence of a non-zero vacuum expectation value (vev) for an operator transforming non-trivially under a symmetry operator will be the key requirement for spontaneous symmetry breaking in field theory. Such operators are generically called *order parameters*. In the next section we show how this requirement necessitates one (or more) massless modes, via Goldstone's theorem (1961).

Before leaving the superfluid, we examine (17.37) and (17.52) in another way, which is only rigorous for a finite system but is nevertheless very suggestive. Since the original $\hat{H}$ has a U(1) symmetry under which $\hat{\phi}$ transforms to $\hat{\phi}' = \exp(-\mathrm{i}\alpha)\hat{\phi}$, we should be at liberty to replace (17.37) by

$$\hat{\phi}'_{\mathrm{B}} = \mathrm{e}^{-\mathrm{i}\alpha}\rho_0^{1/2} + \frac{1}{\Omega^{1/2}}\sum_{\boldsymbol{k}\neq \boldsymbol{0}} \hat{a}_{\boldsymbol{k}}\mathrm{e}^{-\mathrm{i}\alpha}\mathrm{e}^{\mathrm{i}\boldsymbol{k}\cdot\boldsymbol{x}}. \tag{17.54}$$

But in that case our condition (17.52) becomes

$$_{\mathrm{B}}\langle \mathrm{ground}|\hat{\phi}'_{\mathrm{B}}|\mathrm{ground}\rangle_{\mathrm{B}} = \mathrm{e}^{-\mathrm{i}\alpha}{}_{\mathrm{B}}\langle \mathrm{ground}|\hat{\phi}_{\mathrm{B}}|\mathrm{ground}\rangle_{\mathrm{B}}. \tag{17.55}$$

Now $\hat{\phi}' = \hat{U}_\alpha \hat{\phi} \hat{U}_\alpha^{-1}$ where $\hat{U}_\alpha = \exp(\mathrm{i}\alpha\hat{N})$. Hence (17.55) may be written as

$$_{\mathrm{B}}\langle \mathrm{ground}|\hat{U}_\alpha \hat{\phi} \hat{U}_\alpha^{-1}|\mathrm{ground}\rangle_{\mathrm{B}} = \mathrm{e}^{-\mathrm{i}\alpha}{}_{\mathrm{B}}\langle \mathrm{ground}|\hat{\phi}_{\mathrm{B}}|\mathrm{ground}\rangle_{\mathrm{B}}. \tag{17.56}$$

If $|\mathrm{ground}\rangle_{\mathrm{B}}$ were an eigenstate of $\hat{N}$ with eigenvalue N, say, then the $\hat{U}_\alpha$ factors in (17.56) would become just $\mathrm{e}^{\mathrm{i}\alpha N} \cdot \mathrm{e}^{-\mathrm{i}\alpha N}$ and would cancel out, leaving a

contradiction. Instead, however, knowing that $|\text{ground}\rangle_\text{B}$ is not an eigenstate of $\hat{N}$, we can regard $\hat{U}_\alpha^{-1}|\text{ground}\rangle_\text{B}$ as an 'alternative ground state' $|\text{ground}, \alpha\rangle_\text{B}$ such that

$$_\text{B}\langle\text{ground}, \alpha|\hat{\phi}|\text{ground}, \alpha\rangle_\text{B} = e^{-i\alpha}{}_\text{B}\langle\text{ground}|\hat{\phi}_\text{B}|\text{ground}\rangle_\text{B}, \qquad (17.57)$$

the original choice (17.52) corresponding to $\alpha = 0$. There are infinitely many such ground states since α is a continuous parameter. No physical consequence follows from choosing one rather than another, but we do have to choose one, thus 'spontaneously' breaking the symmetry. In choosing say $\alpha = 0$, we are deciding (arbitrarily) to pick the ground state such that $_\text{B}\langle\text{ground}|\hat{\phi}|\text{ground}\rangle_\text{B}$ is aligned in the 'real' direction. By hypothesis, a similar situation obtains for the true ground state. None of the states $|\text{ground}, \alpha\rangle$ is an eigenstate for $\hat{N}$: instead, they are certain coherent superpositions of states with different eigenvalues N, such that the expectation value of $\hat{\phi}$ has a definite phase.

17.4 Goldstone's theorem

We return to quantum field theory proper, and show following Goldstone (1961) (see also Goldstone, Salam and Weinberg 1962) how in case (b) of the Fabri–Picasso theorem massless particles will necessarily be present. Whether these particles will actually be observable depends, however, on whether the theory also contains gauge fields. In this chapter we are concerned solely with global symmetries, and gauge fields are absent; the local symmetry case is treated in chapter 19.

Suppose, then, that we have a Lagrangian $\hat{\mathcal{L}}$ with a continuous symmetry generated by a charge $\hat{Q}$, which is independent of time, and is the space integral of the $\mu = 0$ component of a conserved Noether current:

$$\hat{Q} = \int \hat{j}_0(x) \, \mathrm{d}^3\boldsymbol{x}. \qquad (17.58)$$

We consider the case in which the vacuum of this theory is not invariant, i.e. is not annihilated by $\hat{Q}$.

Suppose $\hat{\phi}(y)$ is some field operator which is not invariant under the continuous symmetry in question, and consider the vacuum expectation value

$$\langle 0|[\hat{Q}, \hat{\phi}(y)]|0\rangle. \qquad (17.59)$$

Just as in equation (17.13), translation invariance implies that this vev is, in fact, independent of y, and we may set $y = 0$. If $\hat{Q}$ were to annihilate $|0\rangle$, the expression (17.18) would clearly vanish: we investigate the consequences of it *not* vanishing. Since $\hat{\phi}$ is not invariant under $\hat{Q}$, the commutator in (17.59) will give some other field, call it $\hat{\phi}'(y)$; thus the hallmark of the hidden symmetry

situation is the existence of some field (here $\hat{\phi}'(y)$) with *non-vanishing vacuum expectation value*, just as in (17.53).

From (17.58), we can write (17.59) as

$$0 \; \neq \; \langle 0|\hat{\phi}'(y)|0\rangle \tag{17.60}$$

$$= \; \langle 0|[\int \mathrm{d}^3\boldsymbol{x}\hat{j}_0(x), \hat{\phi}(y)]|0\rangle. \tag{17.61}$$

Since, by assumption, $\partial_\mu \hat{j}^\mu = 0$, we have as usual

$$\frac{\partial}{\partial x^0} \int \mathrm{d}^3\boldsymbol{x}\hat{j}_0(x) + \int \mathrm{d}^3\boldsymbol{x}\,\mathrm{div}\hat{\boldsymbol{j}}(\mathbf{x}) = 0, \tag{17.62}$$

whence

$$\frac{\partial}{\partial x^0} \int \mathrm{d}^3\boldsymbol{x}\langle 0|[\hat{j}_0(x), \hat{\phi}(y)]|0\rangle \;\; = \;\; -\int \mathrm{d}^3\boldsymbol{x}\langle 0|[\mathrm{div}\hat{\boldsymbol{j}}(x), \hat{\phi}(y)]|0\rangle \tag{17.63}$$

$$= \;\; -\int \mathrm{d}\boldsymbol{S} \cdot \langle 0|[\hat{\boldsymbol{j}}(x), \hat{\phi}(y)]|0\rangle. \tag{17.64}$$

If the surface integral vanishes in (17.64), (17.61) will be independent of x_0. The commutator in (17.64) involves local operators separated by a very large space-like interval, and therefore the vanishing of (17.64) would seem to be unproblematic. Indeed so it is – with the exception of the case in which the symmetry is local and gauge fields are present. A detailed analysis of exactly how this changes the argument being presented here will take us too far afield at this point, and the reader is referred to Guralnik *et al.* (1968) and Bernstein (1974). We shall treat the 'spontaneously broken' gauge theory case in chapter 19, but in less formal terms.

Let us now see how the independence of (17.61) on x_0 leads to the necessity for a massless particle in the spectrum. Inserting a complete set of states in (17.61), we obtain

$$0 \; \neq \; \int \mathrm{d}^3\boldsymbol{x} \sum_n \{\langle 0|\hat{j}_0(x)|n\rangle\langle n|\hat{\phi}(y)|0\rangle - \langle 0|\hat{\phi}(y)|n\rangle\langle n|\hat{j}_0(x)|0\rangle\} \tag{17.65}$$

$$= \; \int \mathrm{d}^3\boldsymbol{x} \sum_n \{\langle 0|\hat{j}_0(0)|n\rangle\langle n|\hat{\phi}(y)|0\rangle\mathrm{e}^{-\mathrm{i}p_n\cdot x} - \langle 0|\hat{\phi}(y)|n\rangle\langle n|\hat{j}_0(0)|0\rangle\mathrm{e}^{\mathrm{i}p_n\cdot x}\}$$

$$\tag{17.66}$$

using translation invariance, with p_n the 4-momentum eigenvalue of the state $|n\rangle$. Performing the spatial integral on the right-hand side we find (omitting the irrelevant $(2\pi)^3$)

$$0 \; \neq \; \sum_n \delta^3(\boldsymbol{p}_n)[\langle 0|\hat{j}_0(0)|n\rangle\langle n|\hat{\phi}(y)|0\rangle\mathrm{e}^{\mathrm{i}p_{n0}x_0} - \langle 0|\hat{\phi}(y)|n\rangle\langle n|\hat{j}_0(0)|0\rangle\mathrm{e}^{-\mathrm{i}p_{n0}x_0}].$$

$$\tag{17.67}$$

But this expression is independent of x_0. *Massive* states $|n\rangle$ will produce explicit x_0-dependent factors $\mathrm{e}^{\pm \mathrm{i} M_n x_0}$ ($p_{n0} \to M_n$ as the δ-function constrains $\boldsymbol{p}_n = \boldsymbol{0}$), hence the matrix elements of $\hat{j}_0$ between $|0\rangle$ and such a massive state must *vanish*, and such states contribute zero to (17.67). Equally, if we take $|n\rangle = |0\rangle$, (17.67) vanishes identically. But it has been assumed to be not zero. Hence *some* state or states must exist among $|n\rangle$ such that $\langle 0|\hat{j}_0|n\rangle \neq 0$ and yet (17.67) is independent of x_0. The only possibility is states whose energy p_{n0} goes to zero as their 3-momentum does (from $\delta^3(\boldsymbol{p}_n)$). Such states are, of course, massless; they are called generically *Goldstone modes*. Thus the existence of a non-vanishing vacuum expectation value for a field, in a theory with a continuous symmetry, appears to lead inevitably to the necessity of having a massless particle, or particles, in the theory. This is the Goldstone result.

The superfluid provided us with an explicit model exhibiting the crucial non-zero expectation value $\langle \text{ground}|\hat{\phi}|\text{ground}\rangle \neq 0$, in which the now expected massless mode emerged dynamically. We now discuss a simpler, relativistic model, in which the symmetry breaking is brought about more 'by hand' – that is, by choosing a parameter in the Lagrangian appropriately. Although in a sense less 'dynamical' than the Bogoliubov superfluid (or the BCS superconductor, to be discussed shortly) this *Goldstone model* does provide a very simple example of the phenomenon of spontaneous symmetry breaking in field theory.

17.5 Spontaneously broken global U(1) symmetry: the Goldstone model

We consider, following Goldstone (1961), a complex scalar field $\hat{\phi}$ as in section 7.1, with

$$\hat{\phi} = \frac{1}{\sqrt{2}}(\hat{\phi}_1 - \mathrm{i}\hat{\phi}_2), \qquad \hat{\phi}^\dagger = \frac{1}{\sqrt{2}}(\hat{\phi}_1 + \mathrm{i}\hat{\phi}_2), \qquad (17.68)$$

described by the Lagrangian

$$\hat{\mathcal{L}}_\mathrm{G} = (\partial_\mu \hat{\phi}^\dagger)(\partial^\mu \hat{\phi}) - \hat{V}(\hat{\phi}). \qquad (17.69)$$

We begin by considering the 'normal' case in which the potential has the form

$$\hat{V} = \hat{V}_\mathrm{S} \equiv \frac{1}{4}\lambda(\hat{\phi}^\dagger \hat{\phi})^2 + \mu^2 \hat{\phi}^\dagger \hat{\phi} \qquad (17.70)$$

with $\mu^2, \lambda > 0$. The Hamiltonian density is then

$$\hat{\mathcal{H}}_\mathrm{G} = \dot{\hat{\phi}}^\dagger \dot{\hat{\phi}} + \boldsymbol{\nabla}\hat{\phi}^\dagger \cdot \boldsymbol{\nabla}\hat{\phi} + \hat{V}(\hat{\phi}). \qquad (17.71)$$

Clearly $\hat{\mathcal{L}}_G$ is invariant under the global U(1) symmetry

$$\hat{\phi} \to \hat{\phi}' = e^{-i\alpha}\hat{\phi}, \tag{17.72}$$

the generator being $\hat{N}_\phi$ of (7.23). We shall see how this symmetry may be 'spontaneously broken'.

We know that everything depends on the nature of the ground state of this field system – that is, the vacuum of the quantum field theory. In general, it is a difficult, non-perturbative, problem to find the ground state (or a good approximation to it – witness the superfluid). But we can make some progress by first considering the theory *classically*. It is clear that the absolute minimum of the classical Hamiltonian $\mathcal{H}_G$ is reached for

(i) $\phi = $ constant, which reduces the $\dot{\phi}$ and $\boldsymbol{\nabla}\phi$ terms to zero;

(ii) $\phi = \phi_0$ where ϕ_0 is the minimum of the classical version of the potential, V.

For $V = V_S$ as in (17.70) but without the hats, and with λ and μ^2 both positive, the minimum of V_S is clearly at $\phi = 0$, and is unique. In the quantum theory, we expect to treat small oscillations of the field about this minimum as approximately harmonic, leading to the usual quantized modes. To implement this, we expand $\hat{\phi}$ about the classical minimum at $\phi = 0$, writing as usual

$$\hat{\phi} = \int \frac{d^3k}{(2\pi)^3\sqrt{2\omega}}[\hat{a}(k)e^{-ik\cdot x} + \hat{b}^\dagger(k)e^{ik\cdot x}] \tag{17.73}$$

where the plane waves are solutions of the 'free' ($\lambda = 0$) problem. For $\lambda = 0$ the Lagrangian is simply

$$\hat{\mathcal{L}}_{\text{free}} = \partial_\mu\hat{\phi}^\dagger\partial^\mu\hat{\phi} - \mu^2\hat{\phi}^\dagger\hat{\phi}, \tag{17.74}$$

which represents a complex scalar field, consisting of two degrees of freedom, each with the same mass μ (see section 7.1). Thus in (17.73) $\omega = (\boldsymbol{k}^2 + \mu^2)^{1/2}$, and the vacuum is defined by

$$\hat{a}(k)|0\rangle = \hat{b}(k)|0\rangle = 0, \tag{17.75}$$

and so clearly

$$\langle 0|\hat{\phi}|0\rangle = 0. \tag{17.76}$$

It seems reasonable to interpret quantum field average values as corresponding to classical field values, and on this interpretation (17.76) is consistent with the fact that the classical minimum energy configuration has $\phi = 0$.

Consider now the case in which the classical minimum is *not* at $\phi = 0$. This can be achieved by altering the sign of μ^2 in (17.70) 'by hand', so that the classical potential is now the 'symmetry breaking' one

$$V = V_{\text{SB}} \equiv \frac{1}{4}\lambda(\phi^\dagger\phi)^2 - \mu^2\phi^\dagger\phi. \tag{17.77}$$

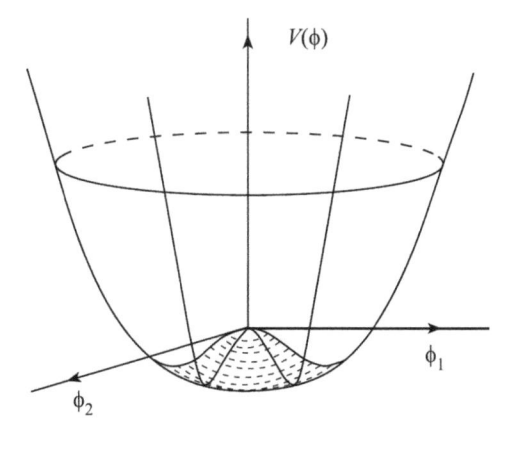

FIGURE 17.2
The classical potential V_{SB} of (17.77).

This is sketched versus ϕ_1 and ϕ_2 in figure 17.2. This time, although the origin $\phi_1 = \phi_2 = 0$ is a stationary point, it is an (unstable) maximum rather than a minimum. The minimum of V_{SB} occurs when

$$(\phi^\dagger \phi) = \frac{2\mu^2}{\lambda}, \tag{17.78}$$

or alternatively when

$$\phi_1^2 + \phi_2^2 = \frac{4\mu^2}{\lambda} \equiv v^2 \tag{17.79}$$

where

$$v = \frac{2|\mu|}{\lambda^{1/2}}. \tag{17.80}$$

The condition (17.79) can also be written as

$$|\phi| = v/\sqrt{2}. \tag{17.81}$$

To have a clearer picture, it is helpful to introduce the 'polar' variables $\rho(x)$ and $\theta(x)$ via

$$\phi(x) = (\rho(x)/\sqrt{2}) \exp(i\theta(x)/v) \tag{17.82}$$

where for convenience the v is inserted so that θ has the same dimension (mass) as ρ and ϕ. The minimum condition (17.81) therefore represents the circle $\rho = v$; any point on this circle, at any value of θ, represents a possible classical ground state – and it is clear that they are (infinitely) degenerate.

Before proceeding further, we briefly outline a condensed matter analogue of (17.77) and (17.81) which may help in understanding the change in sign of the parameter μ^2. Consider the free energy F of a ferromagnet as a function

of the magnetization $\boldsymbol{M}$ at temperature T, and make an expansion of the form

$$F \approx F_0(T) + \mu^2(T)\boldsymbol{M}^2 + \frac{\lambda}{4}\boldsymbol{M}^4 + \cdots \qquad (17.83)$$

valid for weak and slowly varying magnetization. If the parameter μ^2 is positive, it is clear that F has a simple 'bowl' shape as a function of $|\boldsymbol{M}|$, with a minimum at $|\boldsymbol{M}| = 0$. This is the case for T greater than the ferromagnetic transition temperature $T_{\rm C}$. However, if one assumes that $\mu^2(T)$ changes sign at $T_{\rm C}$, becoming negative for $T < T_{\rm C}$, then F will now resemble a vertical section of figure 17.2, the minimum being at $|\boldsymbol{M}| \neq 0$. Any direction of $\boldsymbol{M}$ is possible (only $|\boldsymbol{M}|$ is specified); but the system must choose one particular direction (e.g. via the influence of a very weak external field, as discussed in section 17.3.1), and when it does so the rotational invariance exhibited by F of (17.83) is lost. This symmetry has been broken 'spontaneously' – though this is still only a classical analogue. Nevertheless, the model is essentially the Landau mean field theory of ferromagnetism, and suggests that we should think of the 'symmetric' and 'broken symmetry' situations as different phases of the same system. It may also be the case in particle physics, that parameters such as μ^2 change sign as a function of T, or some other variable, thereby effectively precipitating a phase change.

If we maintain the idea that the vacuum expectation value of the quantum field should equal the ground state value of the classical field, the vacuum in this $\mu^2 < 0$ case must therefore be $|0\rangle_{\rm B}$ such that $_{\rm B}\langle 0|\hat{\phi}|0\rangle_{\rm B}$ does not vanish, in contrast to (17.76). It is clear that this is exactly the situation met in the superfluid (but 'B' here will stand for 'broken symmetry'), and is moreover the condition for the existence of massless (Goldstone) modes. Let us see how they emerge in this model.

In quantum field theory, particles are thought of as excitations from a ground state, which is the vacuum. Figure 17.2 strongly suggests that if we want a sensible quantum interpretation of a theory with the potential (17.77), we had better expand the fields about a point on the circle of minima, about which stable oscillations are likely, rather than about the obviously unstable point $\hat{\phi} = 0$. Let us pick the point $\rho = v$, $\theta = 0$ in the classical case. We might well guess that 'radial' oscillations in $\hat{\rho}$ would correspond to a conventional massive field (having a parabolic restoring potential), while 'angle' oscillations in $\hat{\theta}$ – which pass through all the degenerate vacuua – have no restoring force and are massless. Accordingly, we set

$$\hat{\phi}(x) = \frac{1}{\sqrt{2}}(v + \hat{h}(x))\exp(-\mathrm{i}\hat{\theta}(x)/v) \qquad (17.84)$$

and find (problem 17.5) that $\hat{\mathcal{L}}_{\rm G}$ (with $\hat{V} = \hat{V}_{\rm SB}$ of (17.77) with hats on) becomes

$$\hat{\mathcal{L}}_{\rm G} = \frac{1}{2}\partial_\mu\hat{h}\partial^\mu\hat{h} - \mu^2\hat{h}^2 + \frac{1}{2}\partial_\mu\hat{\theta}\partial^\mu\hat{\theta} + \mu^4/\lambda$$

$$+ \frac{\hat{h}}{v} \partial_\mu \hat{\theta} \partial^\mu \hat{\theta} + \frac{1}{2} \frac{\hat{h}^2}{v^2} \partial_\mu \hat{\theta} \partial^\mu \hat{\theta} - \frac{\lambda}{16} v \hat{h}^3 - \frac{\lambda}{16} \hat{h}^4, \qquad (17.85)$$

Equation (17.85) is very important. First of all, the first line shows that the particle spectrum in the 'spontaneously broken' case is dramatically different from that in the normal case: instead of two degrees of freedom with the same mass μ, one (the θ-mode) is massless, and the other (the h-mode) has a mass of $\sqrt{2}\mu$. We expect the vacuum $|0\rangle_B$ to be annihilated by the mode operators $\hat{a}_h$ and $\hat{a}_\theta$ for these fields. This implies, however, that

$$_B\langle 0 | \hat{\phi} | 0 \rangle_B = v/\sqrt{2} \qquad (17.86)$$

which is consistent with our interpretation of the vacuum expectation value (vev) as the classical minimum, and with the occurrence of massless modes. (The constant term in (17.85), which does not affect equations of motion, merely reflects the fact that the minimum value of V_{SB} is $-\mu^4/\lambda$.) The ansatz (17.84) and the non-zero vev (17.86) may be compared with (17.37) and (17.52), respectively, in the superfluid case.

Secondly, the second line of equation (17.85) shows that only the *derivative* of the $\hat{\theta}$ field appears in the interaction terms, whereas this is not true of the $\hat{h}$ field. Indeed, the Lagrangian for the θ-mode cannot have any dependence on a *constant* value of $\hat{\theta}$, since this could be transformed away by a global U(1) transformation (17.72), which is a symmetry of the theory, and under which $\hat{\theta} \to \hat{\theta} + v\alpha$. This will be an important point to remember when we consider effective Lagrangians for Goldstone modes in section 18.3.

Goldstone's model, then, contains much of the essence of spontaneous symmetry breaking in field theory: a non-zero vacuum value of a field which is not an invariant under the symmetry group, zero mass bosons, and massive excitations in a direction in field space which is 'orthogonal' to the degenerate ground states. However, it has to be noted that the triggering mechanism for the symmetry breaking ($\mu^2 \to -\mu^2$) has to be put in by hand, in contrast to the – admittedly approximate, but more 'dynamical' – Bogoliubov approach. The Goldstone model, in short, is essentially phenomenological.

As in the case of the superfluid, we may perfectly well choose a vacuum corresponding to a classical ground state with non-zero θ, say $\theta = -v\alpha$. Then

$$_B\langle 0, \alpha | \hat{\phi} | 0, \alpha \rangle_B \;=\; e^{-i\alpha} \frac{v}{\sqrt{2}} \qquad (17.87)$$

$$=\; e^{-i\alpha} {}_B\langle 0 | \hat{\phi} | 0 \rangle_B, \qquad (17.88)$$

as in (17.57). But we know (see (7.27) and (7.28)) that

$$e^{-i\alpha} \hat{\phi} = \hat{\phi}' = \hat{U}_\alpha \hat{\phi} \hat{U}_\alpha^{-1} \qquad (17.89)$$

where

$$\hat{U}_\alpha = e^{i\alpha \hat{N}_\phi}. \qquad (17.90)$$

So (17.88) becomes

$$_{\mathrm{B}}\langle 0, \alpha | \hat{\phi} | 0, \alpha \rangle_{\mathrm{B}} = {}_{\mathrm{B}}\langle 0 | \hat{U}_\alpha \hat{\phi} \hat{U}_\alpha^{-1} | 0 \rangle_{\mathrm{B}} \tag{17.91}$$

and we may interpret $\hat{U}_\alpha^{-1} | 0 \rangle_{\mathrm{B}}$ as the 'alternative vacuum' $| 0, \alpha \rangle_{\mathrm{B}}$ (this argument is, as usual, not valid in the infinite volume limit where $\hat{N}_\phi$ fails to exist).

It is interesting to find out what happens to the symmetry current corresponding to the invariance (17.72), in the 'broken symmetry' case. This current is given in (7.23) which we write again here in slightly different notation:

$$\hat{j}_\phi^\mu = \mathrm{i}(\hat{\phi}^\dagger \partial^\mu \hat{\phi} - (\partial^\mu \hat{\phi})^\dagger \hat{\phi}), \tag{17.92}$$

normal ordering being understood. Written in terms of the $\hat{h}$ and $\hat{\theta}$ of (17.84), $\hat{j}_\phi^\mu$ becomes

$$\hat{j}_\phi^\mu = v \partial^\mu \hat{\theta} + 2\hat{h} \partial^\mu \hat{\theta} + \hat{h}^2 \partial^\mu \hat{\theta} / v. \tag{17.93}$$

The term involving just the *single* field $\hat{\theta}$ is very remarkable: it tells us that there is a non-zero matrix element of the form

$$_{\mathrm{B}}\langle 0 | \hat{j}_\phi^\mu(x) | \theta, p \rangle = -\mathrm{i} p^\mu v \mathrm{e}^{-\mathrm{i} p \cdot x} \tag{17.94}$$

where $| \theta, p \rangle$ stands for the state with one θ-quantum (Goldstone boson), with momentum p^μ. This is easily seen by writing the usual normal mode expansion for $\hat{\theta}$, and using the standard bosonic commutation relations for $\hat{a}_\theta(k), \hat{a}_\theta^\dagger(k')$. In words, (17.94) asserts that, *when the symmetry is spontaneously broken, the symmetry current connects the vacuum to a state with one Goldstone quantum, with an amplitude which is proportional to the symmetry breaking vacuum expectation value v, and which vanishes as the 4-momentum goes to zero.* The matrix element (17.94), with $x = 0$, is precisely of the type that was shown to be non-zero in the proof of the Goldstone theorem, after (17.67). Note also that (17.94) is consistent with $\partial_\mu \hat{j}_\phi^\mu = 0$ only if $p^2 = 0$, as is required for the massless θ.

We are now ready to generalize the Abelian U(1) model to the (global) non-Abelian case.

17.6 Spontaneously broken global non-Abelian symmetry

We can illustrate the essential features by considering a particular example, which in fact forms part of the Higgs sector of the Standard Model. We consider an SU(2) doublet, but this time not of fermions as in section 12.3,

but of bosons:

$$\hat{\phi} = \begin{pmatrix} \hat{\phi}^+ \\ \hat{\phi}^0 \end{pmatrix} \equiv \begin{pmatrix} \frac{1}{\sqrt{2}}(\phi_1 + i\phi_2) \\ \frac{1}{\sqrt{2}}(\phi_3 + i\phi_4) \end{pmatrix} \tag{17.95}$$

where the complex scalar field $\hat{\phi}^+$ destroys positively charged particles and creates negatively charged ones, and the complex scalar field $\hat{\phi}^0$ destroys neutral particles and creates neutral antiparticles. As we shall see in a moment, the Lagrangian we shall use has an additional U(1) symmetry, so that the full symmetry is SU(2) × U(1). This U(1) symmetry leads to a conserved quantum number which we call y. We associate the physical charge Q with the eigenvalue t_3 of the SU(2) generator $\hat{t}_3$, and with y, via

$$Q = e(t_3 + y/2) \tag{17.96}$$

so that $y(\phi^+) = 1 = y(\phi^0)$. Thus ϕ^+ and ϕ^0 can be thought of as analogous to the hadronic iso-doublet (K^+, K^0).

The Lagrangian we choose is a simple generalization of (17.69) and (17.77):

$$\hat{\mathcal{L}}_\Phi = (\partial_\mu \hat{\phi}^\dagger)(\partial^\mu \hat{\phi}) + \mu^2 \hat{\phi}^\dagger \hat{\phi} - \frac{\lambda}{4}(\hat{\phi}^\dagger \hat{\phi})^2 \tag{17.97}$$

which has the 'spontaneous symmetry breaking' choice of sign for the parameter μ^2. Plainly, for the 'normal' sign of μ^2, in which '$+\mu^2\hat{\phi}^\dagger\hat{\phi}$' is replaced by '$-\mu^2\hat{\phi}^\dagger\hat{\phi}$', with μ^2 positive in both cases, the free ($\lambda = 0$) part would describe a complex doublet, with four degrees of freedom, each with the same mass μ. Let us see what happens in the broken symmetry case.

For the Lagrangian (17.97) with $\mu^2 > 0$, the minimum of the classical potential is at the point

$$(\phi^\dagger \phi)_{\text{min}} = 2\mu^2/\lambda \equiv v^2/2. \tag{17.98}$$

As in the U(1) case, we interpret (17.98) as a condition on the vev of $\hat{\phi}^\dagger\hat{\phi}$,

$$\langle 0|\hat{\phi}^\dagger\hat{\phi}|0\rangle = v^2/2. \tag{17.99}$$

Before proceeding we note that (17.97) is invariant under global SU(2) transformations

$$\hat{\phi} \to \hat{\phi}' = \exp(-i\boldsymbol{\alpha} \cdot \boldsymbol{\tau}/2)\hat{\phi} \tag{17.100}$$

but also under a separate global U(1) transformation

$$\hat{\phi} \to \hat{\phi}' = \exp(-i\alpha)\hat{\phi} \tag{17.101}$$

where α is to be distinguished from $\boldsymbol{\alpha} \equiv (\alpha_1, \alpha_2, \alpha_3)$. The symmetry is then referred to as SU(2) × U(1), which is the symmetry of the electroweak sector of the Standard Model, except that in that case it is a *local* symmetry.

As before, in order to get a sensible particle spectrum we must expand the fields $\hat{\phi}$ not about $\hat{\phi} = 0$ but about a point satisfying the stable ground state

(vacuum) condition (17.98). That is, we need to define '$\langle 0|\hat{\phi}|0\rangle$' and expand about it, as in (17.84). In the present case, however, the situation is more complicated than (17.84) since the complex doublet (17.95) contains four real fields as indicated in (17.95), and (17.98) becomes

$$\langle 0|\hat{\phi}_1^2 + \hat{\phi}_2^2 + \hat{\phi}_3^2 + \hat{\phi}_4^2|0\rangle = v^2. \tag{17.102}$$

It is evident that we have a lot of freedom in choosing the $\langle 0|\hat{\phi}_i|0\rangle$ so that (17.102) holds, and it is not at first obvious what an appropriate generalization of (17.84) and (17.85) might be.

Furthermore, in this more complicated (non-Abelian) situation a qualitatively new feature can arise: it may happen that the chosen condition $\langle 0|\hat{\phi}_i|0\rangle \neq 0$ is *invariant* under some subset of the allowed symmetry transformations. This would effectively mean that this particular choice of the vacuum state respected that subset of symmetries, which would therefore not be 'spontaneously broken' after all. Since each broken symmetry is associated with a massless Goldstone boson, we would then get fewer of these bosons than expected. Just this happens (by design) in the present case.

Suppose, then, that we could choose the $\langle 0|\hat{\phi}_i|0\rangle$ so as to break this SU(2) × U(1) symmetry completely: we would then expect four massless fields. Actually, however, it is not possible to make such a choice. An analogy may make this point clearer. Suppose we were considering just SU(2), and the field '$\hat{\phi}$' was an SU(2)-triplet, $\hat{\phi}$. Then we could always write $\langle 0|\hat{\phi}|0\rangle = v\mathbf{n}$ where $\mathbf{n}$ is a unit vector; but this form is invariant under rotations about the $\mathbf{n}$-axis, irrespective of where that points. In the present case, by using the freedom of global SU(2) × U(1) phase changes, an arbitrary $\langle 0|\hat{\phi}|0\rangle$ can be brought to the form

$$\langle 0|\hat{\phi}|0\rangle = \begin{pmatrix} 0 \\ v/\sqrt{2} \end{pmatrix}. \tag{17.103}$$

In considering what symmetries are respected or broken by (17.103), it is easiest to look at infinitesimal transformations. It is then clear that the particular transformation

$$\delta\hat{\phi} = -i\epsilon(1 + \tau_3)\hat{\phi} \tag{17.104}$$

(which is a combination of (17.101) and the 'third component' of (17.100)) is still a symmetry of (17.103) since

$$(1 + \tau_3) \begin{pmatrix} 0 \\ v/\sqrt{2} \end{pmatrix} = \begin{pmatrix} 0 \\ 0 \end{pmatrix}, \tag{17.105}$$

so that

$$\langle 0|\phi|0\rangle = \langle 0|\phi + \delta\phi|0\rangle; \tag{17.106}$$

we say that 'the vacuum is invariant under (17.104)', and when we look at the spectrum of oscillations about that vacuum we expect to find only three massless bosons, not four.

Oscillations about (17.103) are conveniently parametrized by

$$\hat{\phi} = \exp(-i\hat{\boldsymbol{\theta}}(x) \cdot \boldsymbol{\tau}/2v) \begin{pmatrix} 0 \\ \frac{1}{\sqrt{2}}(v + \hat{H}(x)) \end{pmatrix}, \qquad (17.107)$$

which is to be compared with (17.84). Inserting (17.107) into (17.97) (see problem 17.6) we easily find that no mass term is generated for the θ fields, while the H field piece is

$$\hat{\mathcal{L}}_H = \frac{1}{2}\partial_\mu \hat{H}\partial^\mu \hat{H} - \mu^2 \hat{H}^2 + \text{interactions} \qquad (17.108)$$

just as in (17.85), showing that $m_H = \sqrt{2}\mu$.

Let us now note carefully that whereas in the 'normal symmetry' case with the opposite sign for the μ^2 term in (17.97), the free-particle spectrum consisted of a degenerate doublet of four degrees of freedom all with the same mass μ, in the 'spontaneously broken' case no such doublet structure is seen: instead, there is one massive scalar field, and three massless scalar fields. The number of degrees of freedom is the same in each case, but the physical spectrum is completely different.

In the application of this to the electroweak sector of the Standard Model, the SU(2) × U(1) symmetry will be 'gauged' (i.e. made local), which is easily done by replacing the ordinary derivatives in (17.97) by suitable covariant ones. We shall see in chapter 19 that the result, with the choice (17.107), will be to end up with three *massive* gauge fields (those mediating the weak interactions) and one *massless* gauge field (the photon). We may summarize this (anticipated) result by saying, then, that when a spontaneously broken non-Abelian symmetry is gauged, those gauge fields corresponding to symmetries that are broken by the choice of $\langle 0|\hat{\phi}|0\rangle$ acquire a mass, while those that correspond to symmetries that are respected by $\langle 0|\hat{\phi}|0\rangle$ do not. Exactly how this happens will be the subject of chapter 19.

We end this chapter by considering a second important example of spontaneous symmetry breaking in condensed matter physics, as a preliminary to our discussion of chiral symmetry breaking in the following chapter.

17.7 The BCS superconducting ground state

We shall not attempt to provide a self-contained treatment of the Bardeen–Cooper–Schrieffer (1957) – or BCS – theory; rather, we wish simply to focus on one aspect of the theory, namely the occurrence of an *energy gap* separating the ground state from the lowest excited levels of the fermionic energy spectrum. The existence of such a gap is a fundamental ingredient of the theory of superconductivity; in the following chapter we shall see how Nambu (1960)

interpreted a chiral symmetry breaking fermionic mass term as an analogous 'gap'. We emphasize at the outset that we shall here not treat electromagnetic interactions in the superconducting state, leaving that topic for chapter 19.

Our discussion will deliberately have some similarity to that of section 17.3.2. In the present case, of course, we shall be dealing with fermions – namely electrons – rather than the bosons of a superfluid. Nevertheless, we shall see that a similar kind of 'condensation' occurs in the superconductor too. Naturally, such a phenomenon can only occur for bosons. Thus an essential element in the BCS theory is the identification of a mechanism whereby pairs of electrons become correlated, the behaviour of which may have some similarity to that of bosons. Now, direct Coulomb interaction between a pair of electrons is repulsive, and it remains so despite the screening that occurs in a solid. But the positively charged ions do provide sources of attraction for the electrons, and may be used as intermediaries (via 'electron-phonon interactions') to promote an effective attraction between electrons in certain circumstances. At this point we recall the characteristic feature of a weakly interacting gas of electrons at zero temperature: thanks to the Exclusion Principle, the electrons populate single particle energy levels up to some maximum energy E_F (the Fermi energy), whose value is fixed by the electron density. It turns out (see for example Kittel 1987, chapter 8) that electron–electron scattering, mediated by phonon exchange, leads to an effective attraction between two electrons whose energies ϵ_k lie in a thin band $E_F - \omega_D < \epsilon_k < E_F + \omega_D$ around E_F, where ω_D is the Debye frequency associated with lattice vibrations. Cooper (1956) was the first to observe that the Fermi 'sea' was unstable with respect to the formation of bound pairs, in the presence of an attractive interaction. What this means is that the energy of the system can be lowered by exciting a pair of electrons above E_F, which then become bound to a state with a total energy less than $2E_F$. This instability modifies the Fermi sea in a fundamental way: a sort of 'condensate' of pairs is created around the Fermi energy, and we need a many-body formalism to handle the situation.

For simplicity we shall consider pairs of equal and opposite momentum $\boldsymbol{k}$, so their total momentum is zero. It can also be argued that the effective attraction will be greater when the spins are antiparallel, but the spin will not be indicated explicitly in what follows: '$\boldsymbol{k}$' will stand for '$\boldsymbol{k}$ with spin up', and '$-\boldsymbol{k}$' for '$-\boldsymbol{k}$ with spin down'. With this by way of motivation, we thus arrive at the *BCS reduced Hamiltonian*

$$\hat{H}_{BCS} = \sum_{\boldsymbol{k}} \epsilon_k \hat{c}^\dagger_{\boldsymbol{k}} \hat{c}_{\boldsymbol{k}} - V \sum_{\boldsymbol{k},\boldsymbol{k}'} \hat{c}^\dagger_{\boldsymbol{k}'} \hat{c}^\dagger_{-\boldsymbol{k}'} \hat{c}_{-\boldsymbol{k}} \hat{c}_{\boldsymbol{k}} \tag{17.109}$$

which is the starting point of our discussion. In (17.109), the $\hat{c}$'s are fermionic operators obeying the usual anticommutation relations, and the ground state is such that $\hat{c}_{\boldsymbol{k}}|0\rangle = 0$. The sum is over states lying near E_F, as above, and the single particle energies ϵ_k are measured relative to E_F. The constant V (with the minus sign in front) represents a simplified form of the effective electron–electron attraction. Note that, in the non-interacting ($V = 0$) part,

$\hat{c}_{\boldsymbol{k}}^{\dagger}\hat{c}_{\boldsymbol{k}}$ is the number operator for the electrons, which because of the Pauli Principle has eigenvalues 0 or 1; this term is of course completely analogous to (7.55), and sums the single particle energies ϵ_k for each occupied level.

We immediately note that $\hat{H}_{\mathrm{BCS}}$ is invariant under the global U(1) transformation

$$\hat{c}_{\boldsymbol{k}} \to \hat{c}_{\boldsymbol{k}}' = e^{-i\alpha}\hat{c}_{\boldsymbol{k}} \tag{17.110}$$

for all $\boldsymbol{k}$, which is equivalent to $\hat{\psi}'(\boldsymbol{x}) = e^{-i\alpha}\hat{\psi}(\boldsymbol{x})$ for the electron field operator at $\boldsymbol{x}$. Thus fermion number is conserved by $\hat{H}_{\mathrm{BCS}}$. However, just as for the superfluid, we shall see that the BCS ground state does not respect the symmetry.

We follow Bogoliubov (1958) and Bogoliubov *et al.* (1959) (see also Valatin 1958), and make a canonical transformation on the operators $\hat{c}_{\boldsymbol{k}}$, $\hat{c}_{-\boldsymbol{k}}^{\dagger}$ similar to the one employed for the superfluid problem in (17.38), as motivated by the 'pair condensate' picture. We set

$$\begin{aligned}
\hat{\beta}_{\boldsymbol{k}} &= u_k\hat{c}_{\boldsymbol{k}} - v_k\hat{c}_{-\boldsymbol{k}}^{\dagger}, & \hat{\beta}_{\boldsymbol{k}}^{\dagger} &= u_k\hat{c}_{\boldsymbol{k}}^{\dagger} - v_k\hat{c}_{-\boldsymbol{k}} \\
\hat{\beta}_{-\boldsymbol{k}} &= u_k\hat{c}_{-\boldsymbol{k}} + v_k\hat{c}_{\boldsymbol{k}}^{\dagger}, & \hat{\beta}_{-\boldsymbol{k}}^{\dagger} &= u_k\hat{c}_{-\boldsymbol{k}}^{\dagger} + v_k\hat{c}_{\boldsymbol{k}}
\end{aligned} \tag{17.111}$$

where u_k and v_k are real, depend only on $k = |\boldsymbol{k}|$, and are chosen so as to preserve *anti*commutation relations for the β's. This last condition implies (problem 17.7)

$$u_k^2 + v_k^2 = 1 \tag{17.112}$$

so that we may conveniently set

$$u_k = \cos\theta_k, v_k = \sin\theta_k. \tag{17.113}$$

Just as in the superfluid case, the transformations (17.111) only make sense in the context of a number non-conserving ground state, since they do not respect the symmetry (17.110). Although $\hat{H}_{\mathrm{BCS}}$ of (17.109) is number conserving, we shall shortly make a crucial number non-conserving approximation.

We seek a diagonalization of (17.109), analogous to (17.40), in terms of the mode operators $\hat{\beta}$ and $\hat{\beta}^{\dagger}$:

$$\hat{H}_{\mathrm{BCS}} = \sum_{\boldsymbol{k}} \omega_k(\hat{\beta}_{\boldsymbol{k}}^{\dagger}\hat{\beta}_{\boldsymbol{k}} + \hat{\beta}_{-\boldsymbol{k}}^{\dagger}\hat{\beta}_{-\boldsymbol{k}}) + \gamma. \tag{17.114}$$

It is easy to check (problem 17.8) that the form (17.114) implies

$$[\hat{H}_{\mathrm{BCS}}, \hat{\beta}_{\boldsymbol{l}}^{\dagger}] = \omega_l\hat{\beta}_{\boldsymbol{l}}^{\dagger} \tag{17.115}$$

as in (17.41), despite the fact that the operators obey *anti*commutation relations. Equation (17.115) then implies that the ω_k are the energies of states created by the *quasiparticle operators* $\hat{\beta}_{\boldsymbol{k}}^{\dagger}$ and $\hat{\beta}_{-\boldsymbol{k}}^{\dagger}$, the ground state being defined by

$$\hat{\beta}_{\boldsymbol{k}}|\mathrm{ground}\rangle_{\mathrm{BCS}} = \hat{\beta}_{-\boldsymbol{k}}|\mathrm{ground}\rangle_{\mathrm{BCS}} = 0. \tag{17.116}$$

Substituting for $\hat{\beta}_l^\dagger$ in (17.115) from (17.111) we therefore require

$$[\hat{H}_{\rm BCS}, \cos\theta_l \,\hat{c}_l^\dagger - \sin\theta_l \,\hat{c}_{-l}] = \omega_l(\cos\theta_l \,\hat{c}_l^\dagger - \sin\theta_l \,\hat{c}_{-l}), \qquad (17.117)$$

which must hold as an identity in the $\hat{c}_l$'s and $\hat{c}_l^\dagger$'s. Evaluating (17.117) one obtains (problem 17.9)

$$(\omega_l - \epsilon_l)\cos\theta_l - V \sin\theta_l \sum_k \hat{c}_{-k}\hat{c}_k = 0 \qquad (17.118)$$

$$-V\cos\theta_l \sum_k \hat{c}_k^\dagger \hat{c}_{-k}^\dagger + (\omega_l + \epsilon_l)\sin\theta_l = 0. \qquad (17.119)$$

It is at this point that we make the crucial 'condensate' assumption: we replace the *operator* expressions $\sum_k \hat{c}_{-k}\hat{c}_k$ and $\sum_k \hat{c}_k^\dagger \hat{c}_{-k}^\dagger$ by their average values, which are *assumed to be non-zero in the ground state*. Since these operators carry fermion number ± 2, it is clear that this assumption is only valid if the ground state does not, in fact, have a definitive number of particles – just as in the superfluid case. We accordingly make the replacements

$$V\sum_k \hat{c}_{-k}\hat{c}_k \to V\,_{\rm BCS}\langle \text{ground}| \sum_k \hat{c}_{-k}\hat{c}_k |\text{ground}\rangle_{\rm BCS} \equiv \Delta \quad (17.120)$$

$$V\sum_k \hat{c}_k^\dagger \hat{c}_{-k}^\dagger \to V\,_{\rm BCS}\langle \text{ground}| \sum_k \hat{c}_k^\dagger \hat{c}_{-k}^\dagger |\text{ground}\rangle_{\rm BCS} \equiv \Delta^* (17.121)$$

In that case, equations (17.118) and (17.119) become

$$\omega_l \cos\theta_l = \epsilon_l \cos\theta_l + \Delta\sin\theta_l \qquad (17.122)$$

$$\omega_l \sin\theta_l = -\epsilon_l \sin\theta_l + \Delta^*\cos\theta_l \qquad (17.123)$$

which are consistent if

$$\omega_l = \pm[\epsilon_l^2 + |\Delta|^2]^{1/2}. \qquad (17.124)$$

Equation (17.124) is the fundamental result at this stage. Recalling that ϵ_l is measured relative to $E_{\rm F}$, we see that it implies that all excited states are separated from $E_{\rm F}$ by a finite amount, namely $|\Delta|$.

In interpreting (17.124) we must however be careful to reckon energies for an excited state as relative to a BCS state having the same number of pairs, if we consider experimental probes which do not inject or remove electrons. Thus relative to a component of $|\text{ground}\rangle_{\rm BCS}$ with N pairs, we may consider the excitation of two particles above a BCS state with $N-1$ pairs. The minimum energy for this to be possible is $2|\Delta|$. It is this quantity which is usually called the *energy gap*. Such an excited state is represented by $\beta_k^\dagger \beta_{-k}^\dagger |\text{ground}\rangle_{\rm BCS}$.

We shall need the expressions for $\cos\theta_l$ and $\sin\theta_l$ which may be obtained as follows. Squaring (17.122), and taking Δ now to be real and equal to $|\Delta|$, we obtain

$$|\Delta|^2(\cos^2\theta_l - \sin^2\theta_l) = 2\epsilon_l|\Delta| \cos\theta_l \sin\theta_l, \qquad (17.125)$$

which leads to

$$\tan 2\theta_l = |\Delta|/\epsilon_l \qquad (17.126)$$

and then

$$\cos\theta_l = \left[\frac{1}{2}\left(1 + \frac{\epsilon_l}{\omega_l}\right)\right]^{1/2}, \qquad \sin\theta_l = \left[\frac{1}{2}\left(1 - \frac{\epsilon_l}{\omega_l}\right)\right]^{1/2}. \qquad (17.127)$$

All our experience to date indicates that the choice 'Δ = real' amounts to a choice of phase for the ground state value:

$$V_{\text{BCS}}\langle\text{ground}| \sum_{\boldsymbol{k}} \hat{c}_{-\boldsymbol{k}} c_{\boldsymbol{k}} |\text{ground}\rangle_{\text{BCS}} = |\Delta|. \qquad (17.128)$$

By making use of the U(1) symmetry (17.110), other phases for Δ are equally possible.

The condition (17.128) has, of course, the by now anticipated form for a spontaneously broken U(1) symmetry, and we must therefore expect the occurrence of a massless mode (which we do not demonstrate here). However, we may now recall that the electrons are charged, so that when electromagnetic interactions are included in the superconducting state, we have to allow the α in (17.110) to become a local function of $\boldsymbol{x}$. At the same time, the massless photon field will enter. Remarkably, we shall learn in chapter 19 that the expected massless (Goldstone) mode is, in this case, not observed: instead, that degree of freedom is incorporated into the gauge field, rendering it massive. As we shall see, this is the physics of the Meissner effect in a superconductor, and that of the 'Higgs mechanism' in the Standard Model. Thus in the (charged) BCS model, both a fermion mass and a gauge boson mass are dynamically generated.

An explicit formula for Δ can be found by using the definition (17.120), together with the expression for $\hat{c}_{\boldsymbol{k}}$ found by inverting (17.111):

$$\hat{c}_{\boldsymbol{k}} = \cos\theta_k \hat{\beta}_{\boldsymbol{k}} + \sin\theta_k \hat{\beta}^\dagger_{-\boldsymbol{k}}. \qquad (17.129)$$

This gives, using (17.120) and (17.129),

$$\begin{aligned}
|\Delta| &= V_{\text{BCS}}\langle\text{ground}| \sum_{\boldsymbol{k}} (\cos\theta_k \hat{\beta}_{-\boldsymbol{k}} + \sin\theta_k \hat{\beta}^\dagger_{\boldsymbol{k}}) \\
&\quad \times (\cos\theta_k \hat{\beta}_{\boldsymbol{k}} + \sin\theta_k \hat{\beta}^\dagger_{-\boldsymbol{k}}) |\text{ground}\rangle_{\text{BCS}} \\
&= V_{\text{BCS}}\langle\text{ground}| \sum_{\boldsymbol{k}} \cos\theta_k \sin\theta_k \hat{\beta}_{-\boldsymbol{k}} \hat{\beta}^\dagger_{-\boldsymbol{k}} |\text{ground}\rangle_{\text{BCS}}, \\
&= V \sum_{\boldsymbol{k}} \frac{|\Delta|}{2[\epsilon_k^2 + |\Delta|^2]^{1/2}}. \qquad (17.130)
\end{aligned}$$

The sum in (17.130) is only over the small band $E_{\text{F}} - \omega_{\text{D}} < \epsilon_k < E_{\text{F}} + \omega_{\text{D}}$ over which the effective electron–electron attraction operates. Replacing the

sum by an integral, we obtain the *gap equation*

$$
\begin{aligned}
1 &= \frac{1}{2} V \cdot N_{\mathrm{F}} \int_{-\omega_{\mathrm{D}}}^{\omega_{\mathrm{D}}} \frac{\mathrm{d}\epsilon}{[\epsilon^2 + |\Delta|^2]^{\frac{1}{2}}} \\
&= V N_{\mathrm{F}} \sinh^{-1}(\omega_{\mathrm{D}}/|\Delta|)
\end{aligned} \tag{17.131}
$$

where N_{F} is the density of states at the Fermi level. Equation (17.131) yields

$$
|\Delta| = \frac{\omega_{\mathrm{D}}}{\sinh(1/VN_{\mathrm{F}})} \approx 2\omega_{\mathrm{D}}\mathrm{e}^{-1/VN_{\mathrm{F}}} \tag{17.132}
$$

for $VN_{\mathrm{F}} \ll 1$. This is the celebrated BCS solution for the gap parameter $|\Delta|$. Perhaps the most significant thing to note about it, for our purpose, is that the expression for $|\Delta|$ is not an analytic function of the dimensionless interaction parameter VN_{F} (it cannot be expanded as a power series in this quantity), and so no perturbative treatment starting from a normal ground state could reach this result. The estimate (17.132) is in reasonably good agreement with experiment, and may be refined.

The explicit form of the ground state in this model can be found by a method similar to the one indicated in section 17.3.2 for the superfluid. Since the transformation from the $\hat{c}$'s to the $\hat{\beta}$'s is canonical, there must exist a unitary operator which effects it via (compare (17.48))

$$
\hat{U}_{\mathrm{BCS}}\,\hat{c}_{\boldsymbol{k}}\,\hat{U}_{\mathrm{BCS}}^{\dagger} = \hat{\beta}_{\boldsymbol{k}}, \quad \hat{U}_{\mathrm{BCS}}\,\hat{c}_{-\boldsymbol{k}}^{\dagger}\,\hat{U}_{\mathrm{BCS}}^{\dagger} = \hat{\beta}_{-\boldsymbol{k}}^{\dagger}. \tag{17.133}
$$

The operator $\hat{U}_{\mathrm{BCS}}$ is (Blatt 1964 section V.4, Yosida 1958, and compare problem 17.4)

$$
\hat{U}_{\mathrm{BCS}} = \prod_{\boldsymbol{k}} \exp[\theta_k(\hat{c}_{\boldsymbol{k}}^{\dagger}\hat{c}_{-\boldsymbol{k}}^{\dagger} - \hat{c}_{\boldsymbol{k}}\hat{c}_{-\boldsymbol{k}})]. \tag{17.134}
$$

Then, since $\hat{c}_{\boldsymbol{k}}|0\rangle = 0$, we have

$$
\hat{U}_{\mathrm{BCS}}^{\dagger}\hat{\beta}_{\boldsymbol{k}}\hat{U}_{\mathrm{BCS}}|0\rangle = 0 \tag{17.135}
$$

showing that we may identify

$$
|\mathrm{ground}\rangle_{\mathrm{BCS}} = \hat{U}_{\mathrm{BCS}}|0\rangle \tag{17.136}
$$

via the condition (17.116). When the exponential in $\hat{U}_{\mathrm{BCS}}$ is expanded out, and applied to the vacuum state $|0\rangle$, great simplifications occur. Consider the operator

$$
\hat{s}_{\boldsymbol{k}} = \hat{c}_{\boldsymbol{k}}^{\dagger}\hat{c}_{-\boldsymbol{k}}^{\dagger} - \hat{c}_{\boldsymbol{k}}\hat{c}_{-\boldsymbol{k}}. \tag{17.137}
$$

We have

$$
\hat{s}_{\boldsymbol{k}}^2 = -\hat{c}_{\boldsymbol{k}}^{\dagger}\hat{c}_{-\boldsymbol{k}}^{\dagger}\hat{c}_{\boldsymbol{k}}\hat{c}_{-\boldsymbol{k}} - \hat{c}_{\boldsymbol{k}}\hat{c}_{-\boldsymbol{k}}\hat{c}_{\boldsymbol{k}}^{\dagger}\hat{c}_{-\boldsymbol{k}}^{\dagger} \tag{17.138}
$$

so that $\hat{s}_{\boldsymbol{k}}^2|0\rangle = -|0\rangle$. It follows that

$$
\begin{aligned}
\exp(\theta_k \hat{s}_{\boldsymbol{k}})|0\rangle &= (1 + \theta_k \hat{s}_{\boldsymbol{k}} - \frac{\theta_k^2}{2} - \frac{\theta_k^3}{3}\hat{s}_{\boldsymbol{k}} \cdots)|0\rangle \\
&= (\cos\theta_k + \sin\theta_k\,\hat{s}_{\boldsymbol{k}})|0\rangle \\
&= (\cos\theta_k + \sin\theta_k\,\hat{c}_{\boldsymbol{k}}^\dagger \hat{c}_{-\boldsymbol{k}}^\dagger)|0\rangle
\end{aligned}
\tag{17.139}
$$

and hence

$$
|\text{ground}\rangle_{\text{BCS}} = \prod_{\boldsymbol{k}}(\cos\theta_k + \sin\theta_k\,\hat{c}_{\boldsymbol{k}}^\dagger \hat{c}_{-\boldsymbol{k}}^\dagger)|0\rangle.
\tag{17.140}
$$

As for the superfluid, (17.140) represents a coherent superposition of correlated pairs, with no restraint on the particle number.

We should emphasize that the above is only the barest outline of a simple version of BCS theory, with no electromagnetic interactions, from which many subtleties have been omitted. Consider, for example, the binding energy E_b of a pair, to calculate which one needs to evaluate the constant γ in (17.114). To a good approximation one finds (see for example Enz 1992) $E_b \approx 3\Delta^2/E_F$. One can also calculate the approximate spatial extension of a pair, which is denoted by the *coherence length* ξ and is of order $v_F/\pi\Delta$ where $k_F = mv_F$ is the Fermi momentum. If we compare E_b to the Coulomb repulsion at a distance ξ we find

$$
E_b/(\alpha/\xi) \sim a_0/\xi
\tag{17.141}
$$

where a_0 is the Bohr radius. Numerical values show that the right-hand side of (17.141), in conventional superconductors, is of order 10^{-3}. Hence the pairs are not really bound, only correlated, and as many as 10^6 pairs may have their centres of mass within one coherence length of each other. Nevertheless, the simple theory presented here contains the essential features which underlie all attempts to understand the dynamical occurrence of spontaneous symmetry breaking in fermionic systems.

We now proceed to an important application in particle physics.

Problems

17.1 Verify (17.29).

17.2 Verify (17.35).

17.3 Derive (17.43) and (17.44).

17.4 Let

$$
\hat{U}_\lambda = \exp[\frac{1}{2}\lambda\theta(\hat{a}^2 - \hat{a}^{\dagger 2})]
$$

where $[\hat{a}, \hat{a}^\dagger] = 1$ and λ, θ are real parameters.

(a) Show that $\hat{U}_\lambda$ is unitary.

(b) Let

$$\hat{I}_\lambda = \hat{U}_\lambda \hat{a} \hat{U}_\lambda^{-1}, \quad \text{and} \quad \hat{J}_\lambda = \hat{U}_\lambda \hat{a}^\dagger \hat{U}_\lambda^{-1}.$$

Show that

$$\frac{\mathrm{d}\hat{I}_\lambda}{\mathrm{d}\lambda} = \theta \hat{J}_\lambda$$

and that

$$\frac{\mathrm{d}^2 \hat{I}_\lambda}{\mathrm{d}\lambda^2} = \theta^2 \hat{I}_\lambda.$$

(c) Hence show that

$$\hat{I}_\lambda = \cosh(\lambda\theta)\,\hat{a} + \sinh(\lambda\theta)\,\hat{a}^\dagger,$$

and thus finally (compare (17.38) and (17.48)) that

$$\hat{U}_1 \hat{a} \hat{U}_1^{-1} = \cosh\theta\,\hat{a} + \sinh\theta\,\hat{a}^\dagger \equiv \hat{\alpha}$$

and

$$\hat{U}_1 \hat{a}^\dagger \hat{U}_1^{-1} = \sinh\theta\,\hat{a} + \cosh\theta\,\hat{a}^\dagger \equiv \hat{\alpha}^\dagger,$$

where

$$\hat{U}_1 \equiv \hat{U}_{\lambda=1} = \exp[\tfrac{1}{2}\theta(\hat{a}^2 - \hat{a}^{\dagger 2})].$$

17.5 Insert the ansatz (17.84) for $\hat{\phi}$ into $\hat{\mathcal{L}}_\mathrm{G}$ of (17.69), with $\hat{V} = \hat{V}_\mathrm{SB}$ of (17.77), and show that the result for the constant term, and the quadratic terms in $\hat{h}$ and $\hat{\theta}$, is as given in (17.85).

17.6 Verify that when (17.107) is inserted in (17.97), the terms quadratic in the fields $\hat{H}$ and $\hat{\theta}$ reveal that $\hat{\theta}$ is a massless field, while the quanta of the $\hat{H}$ field have mass $\sqrt{2}\mu$.

17.7 Verify that the $\hat{\beta}$'s of (17.111) satisfy the required anticommutation relations if (17.112) holds.

17.8 Verify (17.115).

17.9 Derive (17.118) and (17.119).

18

Chiral Symmetry Breaking

In section 12.4.2 we arrived at a puzzle: there seemed good reason to think that a world consisting of u and d quarks and their antiparticles, interacting via the colour gauge fields of QCD, should exhibit signs of the non-Abelian *chiral symmetry* $SU(2)_{f5}$, which was exact in the massless limit $m_u, m_d \to 0$. But, as we showed, one of the simplest consequences of such a symmetry should be the existence of nucleon parity doublets, which are not observed. We can now resolve this puzzle by making the hypothesis (section 18.1) first articulated by Nambu (1960) and Nambu and Jona-Lasinio (1961a), that this chiral symmetry is *spontaneously broken* as a dynamical effect – presumably, from today's perspective, as a property of the QCD interactions, as discussed in section 18.1.1. If this is so, an immediate physical consequence should be the appearance of massless (Goldstone) bosons, one for every symmetry not respected by the vacuum. Indeed, returning to (12.168) which we repeat here for convenience,

$$\hat{T}_{+5}^{(\frac{1}{2})}|d\rangle = |\tilde{u}\rangle, \tag{18.1}$$

we now interpret the state $|\tilde{u}\rangle$ (which is degenerate with $|d\rangle$) as $|d + \text{`}\pi^+\text{'}\rangle$ where 'π^+' is a massless particle of positive charge, but a *pseudo*scalar (0^-) rather than a scalar (0^+) since, as we saw, $|\tilde{u}\rangle$ has opposite parity to $|u\rangle$. In the same way, 'π^-' and 'π^0' will be associated with $\hat{T}_{-5}^{(\frac{1}{2})}$ and $\hat{T}_{35}^{(\frac{1}{2})}$. Of course, no such *massless* pseudoscalar particles are observed: but it is natural to hope that when the small up and down quark masses are included, the real pions (π^+, π^-, π^0) will emerge as 'anomalously light', rather than strictly massless. This is indeed how they do appear, particularly with respect to the octet of mesons, which differ only in q$\bar{\text{q}}$ spin alignment from the 0^- octet. As Nambu and Jona-Lasinio (1961a) said, 'it is perhaps not a coincidence that there exists such an entity [i.e. the Goldstone state(s)] in the form of the pion'.

If this was the only observable consequence of spontaneously breaking chiral symmetry, it would perhaps hardly be sufficient grounds for accepting the hypothesis. But there are two circumstances which greatly increase the phenomenological implications of the idea. First, the vector and axial vector symmetry currents $\hat{\boldsymbol{T}}^{(\frac{1}{2})\mu}$ and $\hat{\boldsymbol{T}}_5^{(\frac{1}{2})\mu}$ of the u-d strong interaction $SU(2)$ symmetries (see (12.109) and (12.165)) happen to be the very same currents which enter into strangeness-conserving semileptonic weak interactions (such as n $\to$ pe$^-\bar{\nu}_e$ and $\pi^- \to \mu^-\bar{\nu}_\mu$), as we shall see in chapter 20. Thus some remarkable connections between weak- and strong-interaction parameters can be

established, such as the Goldberger–Treiman (1958) relation (see section 18.2) and the Adler–Weisberger (Adler 1965, Weisberger 1965) relation. Second, it turns out that the dynamics of the Goldstone modes, and their interactions with other hadrons such as nucleons, are strongly constrained by the underlying chiral symmetry of QCD; indeed, surprisingly detailed *effective theories* (see section 18.3) have been developed, which provide a very successful description of the low energy dynamics of the Goldstone degrees of freedom. Finally we shall introduce the subject of chiral anomalies in section 18.4.

It would take us too far from our main focus on gauge theories to pursue these interesting avenues in any detail. But we hope to convince the reader, in this chapter, that chiral symmetry breaking is an integral part of the Standard Model, being a fundamental property of QCD.

18.1 The Nambu analogy

We recall from section 12.4.2 that for 'almost massless' fermions it is natural to use the representation (3.40) for the Dirac matrices, in terms of which the Dirac equation reads

$$E\phi = \boldsymbol{\sigma}\cdot\boldsymbol{p}\phi + m\chi \tag{18.2}$$

$$E\chi = -\boldsymbol{\sigma}\cdot\boldsymbol{p}\chi + m\phi. \tag{18.3}$$

Nambu (1960) and Nambu and Jona-Lasinio (1961a) pointed out a remarkable analogy between (18.2) and (18.3) and equations (17.122) and (17.123) which describe the elementary excitations in a superconductor (in the case Δ is real), and which we repeat here for convenience:

$$\omega_l \cos\theta_l = \epsilon_l \cos\theta_l + \Delta\sin\theta_l \tag{18.4}$$

$$\omega_l \sin\theta_l = -\epsilon_l \sin\theta_l + \Delta\cos\theta_l. \tag{18.5}$$

In (18.4) and (18.5), $\cos\theta_l$ and $\sin\theta_l$ are respectively the components of the electron destruction operator $\hat{c}_l$ and the electron creation operator $\hat{c}^\dagger_{-l}$ in the quasiparticle operator $\hat{\beta}_l$ (see (17.111)):

$$\hat{\beta}_l = \cos\theta_l\,\hat{c}_l - \sin\theta_l\,\hat{c}^\dagger_{-l}. \tag{18.6}$$

The superposition in $\hat{\beta}_l$ combines operators which transform differently under the U(1) (number) symmetry. The result of this spontaneous breaking of the U(1) symmetry is the creation of the gap Δ (or 2Δ for a number-conserving excitation), and the appearance of a massless mode. If Δ vanishes, (17.126) implies that $\theta_l = 0$, and we revert to the symmetry-respecting operators $\hat{c}_l, \hat{c}^\dagger_{-l}$. Consider now (18.2) and (18.3). Here ϕ and χ are the components of

FIGURE 18.1
The type of fermion–antifermion in the 'Nambu chiral condensate'.

definite chirality in the Dirac spinor ω (compare (12.149)), which is itself not a chirality eigenstate when $m \neq 0$. When m vanishes, the Dirac equation for ω decouples into two separate ones for the chirality eigenstates $\phi_{\mathrm{R}} \equiv \begin{pmatrix} \phi \\ 0 \end{pmatrix}$ and $\phi_{\mathrm{L}} \equiv \begin{pmatrix} 0 \\ \chi \end{pmatrix}$. Nambu therefore made the following analogy:

Superconducting gap parameter Δ	$\leftrightarrow$	Dirac mass m
quasiparticle excitation	$\leftrightarrow$	massive Dirac particle
U(1) number symmetry	$\leftrightarrow$	U(1)$_5$ chirality symmetry
Goldstone mode	$\leftrightarrow$	massless boson.

In short, the mass of a Dirac particle arises from the (presumed) spontaneous breaking of a chiral (or γ_5) symmetry, and this will be accompanied by a massless boson.

Before proceeding we should note that there are features of the analogy, on both sides, which need qualification. First, the particle symmetry we want to interpret this way is SU(2)$_{\mathrm{f}5}$ not U(1)$_5$, so the appropriate generalization (Nambu and Jona-Lasinio 1961b) has to be understood. Second, we must again note that the BCS electrons are charged, so that in the real superconducting case we are dealing with a spontaneously broken *local* U(1) symmetry, not a global one. By contrast, the SU(2)$_{\mathrm{f}5}$ chiral symmetry is not gauged.

As usual, the quantum field theory vacuum is analogous to the manybody ground state. According to Nambu's analogy, therefore, the vacuum for a massive Dirac particle is to be pictured as a condensate of correlated pairs of massive fermions. Since the vacuum carries neither linear nor angular momentum, the members of a pair must have equal and opposite spin: they therefore have the same helicity. However, since the vacuum does *not* violate fermion number conservation, one has to be a fermion and the other an antifermion. This means (recalling the discussion after (12.147)) that they have opposite chirality. Thus a typical pair in the Nambu vacuum is as shown in figure 18.1. We may easily write down an expression for the Nambu vacuum, analogous to (17.140) for the BCS ground state. Consider solutions ϕ_+ and χ_+ of positive helicity in (18.2) and (18.3); then

$$E\phi_+ \;=\; |\boldsymbol{p}|\phi_+ + m\chi_+ \tag{18.7}$$

$$E\chi_+ = -|\boldsymbol{p}|\chi_+ + m\phi_+. \tag{18.8}$$

Comparing (18.7) and (18.8) with (18.4) and (18.5), we can read off the mixing coefficients $\cos\theta_p$ and $\sin\theta_p$ as (cf (17.127))

$$\cos\theta_p = \left[\frac{1}{2}\left(1+\frac{|\boldsymbol{p}|}{E}\right)\right]^{1/2} \tag{18.9}$$

$$\sin\theta_p = \left[\frac{1}{2}\left(1-\frac{|\boldsymbol{p}|}{E}\right)\right]^{1/2} \tag{18.10}$$

where $E=(m^2+\boldsymbol{p}^2)^{1/2}$. The Nambu vacuum is then given by[1]

$$|0\rangle_{\rm N} = \prod_{\boldsymbol{p},s}(\cos\theta_p - \sin\theta_p\hat{c}_s^\dagger(\boldsymbol{p})\hat{d}_s^\dagger(-\boldsymbol{p}))|0\rangle_{m=0}, \tag{18.11}$$

where $\hat{c}_s^\dagger$'s and $\hat{d}_s^\dagger$'s are the operators in *massless* Dirac fields. Depending on the sign of the helicity s, each pair in (18.11) carries ± 2 units of chirality. We may check this by noting that in the mode expansion of the Dirac field $\hat{\psi}$, $\hat{c}_s(\boldsymbol{p})$ operators go with u-spinors for which the γ_5 eigenvalue equals the helicity, while $\hat{d}_s^\dagger(-\boldsymbol{p})$ operators accompany v-spinors for which the γ_5 eigenvalue equals minus the helicity. Thus under a chiral transformation $\hat{\psi}' = {\rm e}^{-{\rm i}\beta\gamma_5}\hat{\psi}$, $\hat{c}_s \to {\rm e}^{-{\rm i}\beta s}\hat{c}_s$ and $\hat{d}_s^\dagger \to {\rm e}^{{\rm i}\beta s}\hat{d}_s^\dagger$, for a given s. Hence $\hat{c}_s^\dagger\hat{d}_s^\dagger$ acquires a factor ${\rm e}^{2{\rm i}\beta s}$. Thus the Nambu vacuum does not have a definite chirality, and operators carrying non-zero chirality can have non-vanishing vacuum expectation values. A mass term $\bar{\hat{\psi}}\hat{\psi}$ is of just this kind, since under $\hat{\psi} = {\rm e}^{-{\rm i}\beta\gamma_5}\hat{\psi}$ we find $\hat{\psi}^\dagger\gamma^0\hat{\psi} \to \hat{\psi}^\dagger{\rm e}^{{\rm i}\beta\gamma_5}\gamma^0{\rm e}^{-{\rm i}\beta\gamma_5}\hat{\psi} = \bar{\hat{\psi}}{\rm e}^{-2{\rm i}\beta\gamma_5}\hat{\psi}$. Thus, in analogy with (17.120), a Dirac mass is associated with a non-zero value for ${}_{\rm N}\langle 0|\bar{\hat{\psi}}\hat{\psi}|0\rangle_{\rm N}$.

In the original conception by Nambu and co-workers, the fermion under discussion was taken to be the nucleon, with 'm' the (spontaneously generated) nucleon mass. The fermion–fermion interaction – necessarily invariant under chiral transformations – was taken to be of the four-fermion type. As we have seen in volume 1, this is actually a non-renormalizable theory, but a physical cut-off was employed, somewhat analogous to the Fermi energy $E_{\rm F}$. Thus the nucleon mass could not be dynamically predicted, unlike the analogous gap parameter Δ in BCS theory. Nevertheless, a gap equation similar to (17.131) could be formulated, and it was possible to show that when it had a non-trivial solution, a massless bound state automatically appeared in the $\bar{\rm f}{\rm f}$ channel (Nambu and Jona-Lasinio 1961a). This work was generalized to the SU(2)$_{\rm f\,5}$ case by Nambu and Jona-Lasinio (1961b), who showed that if the chiral symmetry was broken explicitly by the introduction of a small nucleon mass (~ 5 MeV), then the Goldstone pions would have their observed non-zero (but small) mass. In addition, the Goldberger–Treiman (1958) relation was derived, and a number of other applications were suggested. Subsequently, Nambu with other collaborators (Nambu and Lurie 1962, Nambu

---

[1] A different phase convention is used for $\hat{d}_s^\dagger(-\boldsymbol{p})$ as compared to that for $\hat{c}_{-\boldsymbol{k}}^\dagger$ in (17.111).

and Schrauner 1962) showed how the amplitudes for the emission of a single 'soft' (nearly massless, low momentum) pion could be calculated, for various processes. These developments culminated in the Adler-Weisberger relation (Adler 1965, Weisberger 1965) which involves *two* soft pions.

This work was all done in the absence of an agreed theory of the strong interactions (the NJ-L theory was an illustrative working model of dynamically generated spontaneous symmetry breaking, but not a complete theory of strong interactions). QCD became widely accepted as that theory around 1973. In this case, of course, the 'fermions in question' are quarks, and the interactions between them are gluon exchanges, which conserve chirality as noted in section 12.4.2. The bulk of the masses of the qqq bound states which form baryons is then interpreted as being spontaneously generated, while a small explicit quark mass term in the Lagrangian is responsible for the non-zero pion mass. Let us therefore now turn to two-flavour QCD.

18.1.1 Two flavour QCD and $\mathbf{SU(2)_{fL} \times SU(2)_{fR}}$

Let us begin with the massless case, for which the fermionic part of the Lagrangian is

$$\hat{\mathcal{L}}_q = \bar{\hat{u}} \, \mathrm{i} \hat{\slashed{D}} \hat{u} + \bar{\hat{d}} \, \mathrm{i} \hat{\slashed{D}} \hat{d} \tag{18.12}$$

where $\hat{u}$ and $\hat{d}$ now stand for the field operators,

$$\hat{D}^\mu = \partial^\mu + \mathrm{i} g_\mathrm{s} \boldsymbol{\lambda}/2 \cdot \hat{\boldsymbol{A}}^\mu, \tag{18.13}$$

and the $\boldsymbol{\lambda}$ matrices act on the colour (r,b,g) degree of freedom of the u and d quarks. This Lagrangian is invariant under

(i) $U(1)_f$ 'quark number' transformations

$$\hat{q} \to \mathrm{e}^{-\mathrm{i}\alpha} \hat{q}; \tag{18.14}$$

(ii) $SU(2)_f$ 'flavour isospin' transformations

$$\hat{q} \to \exp(-\mathrm{i}\boldsymbol{\alpha} \cdot \boldsymbol{\tau}/2) \, \hat{q}; \tag{18.15}$$

(iii) $U(1)_{f5}$ 'axial quark number' transformations

$$\hat{q} \to \mathrm{e}^{-\mathrm{i}\beta\gamma_5} \hat{q}; \tag{18.16}$$

(iv) $SU(2)_{f5}$ 'axial flavour isospin' transformations

$$\hat{q} \to \exp(-\mathrm{i}\boldsymbol{\beta} \cdot \boldsymbol{\tau}/2\gamma_5) \, \hat{q}, \tag{18.17}$$

where

$$\hat{q} = \begin{pmatrix} \hat{u} \\ \hat{d} \end{pmatrix}. \tag{18.18}$$

Symmetry (i) is unbroken, and its associated 'charge' operator (the quark number operator) commutes with all other symmetry operators, so it need not concern us further. Symmetry (ii) is the standard isospin symmetry of chapter 12, explicitly broken by the electromagnetic interactions (and by the difference in the masses m_u and m_d, when included). Symmetry (iii) does not correspond to any known conservation law; on the other hand, there are not any near-massless isoscalar 0^- mesons, either, such as must be present if the symmetry is spontaneously broken. The η meson is an isoscalar 0^- meson, but with a mass of 547 MeV it is considerably heavier than the pion. In fact, it can be understood as one of the Goldstone bosons associated with the spontaneous breaking of the larger group $SU(3)_{f5}$, which includes the s quark (see section 18.3.3). In that case, the symmetry (iii) becomes extended to

$$\hat{u} \rightarrow e^{-i\beta\gamma_5}\hat{u}, \quad \hat{d} \rightarrow e^{-i\beta\gamma_5}\hat{d}, \quad \hat{s} \rightarrow e^{-i\beta\gamma_5}\hat{s}, \tag{18.19}$$

but there is still a missing light isoscalar 0^- meson. It can be shown that its mass must be less than or equal to $\sqrt{3}\, m_\pi$ (Weinberg 1975), but no such particle exists. This is the famous 'U(1) problem': it was resolved by 't Hooft (1976a, 1986), by showing that the inclusion of instanton configurations (Belavin et al. 1975) in path integrals leads to violations of symmetry (iii) – see, for example, Weinberg (1996) section 23.5. Finally, symmetry (iv) is the one with which we are presently concerned.

The symmetry currents associated with (iv) are those already given in (12.165), but we give them again here in a slightly different notation which will be similar to the one used for weak interactions:

$$\hat{j}_{i,5}^\mu = \bar{\hat{q}}\gamma^\mu\gamma_5\frac{\tau_i}{2}\hat{q} \qquad i = 1, 2, 3. \tag{18.20}$$

Similarly the currents associated with (ii) are

$$\hat{j}_i^\mu = \bar{\hat{q}}\gamma^\mu\frac{\tau_i}{2}\hat{q} \qquad i = 1, 2, 3. \tag{18.21}$$

The corresponding 'charges' are (compare (12.166))

$$\hat{Q}_{i,5} \equiv \int \hat{j}_{i,5}^0 \, d^3\boldsymbol{x} = \int \hat{q}^\dagger\gamma_5\frac{\tau_i}{2}\hat{q} \, d^3\boldsymbol{x}, \tag{18.22}$$

previously denoted by $\hat{T}_{i,5}^{(\frac{1}{2})}$, and (compare (12.101)),

$$\hat{Q}_i = \int \hat{q}^\dagger\frac{\tau_i}{2}\hat{q} \, d^3\boldsymbol{x}, \tag{18.23}$$

previously denoted by $\hat{\boldsymbol{T}}_5^{(\frac{1}{2})}$. As with all symmetries, it is interesting to discover the *algebra* of the generators, which are the six charges $\hat{Q}_i, \hat{Q}_{i,5}$ in this case. Patient work with the anticommutation relations for the operators in

$\hat{q}(x)$ and $\hat{q}^\dagger(x)$ gives the results (problem 18.1)

$$[\hat{Q}_i, \hat{Q}_j] = i\epsilon_{ijk}\hat{Q}_k \tag{18.24}$$

$$[\hat{Q}_i, \hat{Q}_{j,5}] = i\epsilon_{ijk}\hat{Q}_{k,5} \tag{18.25}$$

$$[\hat{Q}_{i,5}, \hat{Q}_{j,5}] = i\epsilon_{ijk}\hat{Q}_k. \tag{18.26}$$

Relation (18.24) has been seen before in (12.101), and simply says that the $\hat{Q}_i$'s obey a SU(2) algebra. A simple trick reduces the rather complicated algebra of (18.24)–(18.26) to something much simpler. Defining

$$\hat{Q}_{i,R} = \frac{1}{2}(\hat{Q}_i + \hat{Q}_{i,5}) \qquad \hat{Q}_{i,L} = \frac{1}{2}(\hat{Q}_i - \hat{Q}_{i,5}) \tag{18.27}$$

we find (problem 18.2)

$$[\hat{Q}_{i,R}, \hat{Q}_{j,R}] = i\epsilon_{ijk}\hat{Q}_{k,R} \tag{18.28}$$

$$[\hat{Q}_{i,L}, \hat{Q}_{j,L}] = i\epsilon_{ijk}\hat{Q}_{k,L} \tag{18.29}$$

$$[\hat{Q}_{i,R}, \hat{Q}_{j,L}] = 0. \tag{18.30}$$

The operators $\hat{Q}_{i,R}, \hat{Q}_{i,L}$ therefore behave like *two commuting (independent) angular momentum operators*, each obeying the algebra of SU(2). For this reason, the symmetry group of the combined symmetries (ii) and (iv) is called $SU(2)_{fL} \times SU(2)_{fR}$.

The decoupling effected by (18.27) has a simple interpretation. Referring to (18.22) and (18.23), we see that

$$\hat{Q}_{i,R} = \int \hat{q}^\dagger \left(\frac{1+\gamma_5}{2}\right) \frac{\tau_i}{2} \hat{q} \, d^3x \tag{18.31}$$

and similarly for $\hat{Q}_{i,L}$. But $((1\pm\gamma_5)/2)$ are just the projection operators $P_{R,L}$ introduced in section 12.3.2, which project out the chiral parts of any fermion field. Furthermore, it is easy to see that $P_R^2 = P_R$ and $P_L^2 = P_L$, so that $\hat{Q}_{i,R}$ and $\hat{Q}_{i,L}$ can also be written as

$$\hat{Q}_{i,R} = \int \hat{q}_R^\dagger \frac{\tau_i}{2} \hat{q}_R \, d^3x \qquad \hat{Q}_{i,L} = \int \hat{q}_L^\dagger \frac{\tau_i}{2} \hat{q}_L \, d^3x, \tag{18.32}$$

where $\hat{q}_R = ((1+\gamma_5)/2)\hat{q}, \hat{q}_L = ((1-\gamma_5)/2)\hat{q}$. In a similar way, the currents (18.20) and (18.21) can be written as

$$\hat{j}_i^\mu = \hat{j}_{i,R}^\mu + \hat{j}_{i,L}^\mu \qquad \hat{j}_{i,5}^\mu = \hat{j}_{i,R}^\mu - \hat{j}_{i,L}^\mu, \tag{18.33}$$

where

$$\hat{j}_{i,R}^\mu = \bar{\hat{q}}_R \gamma^\mu \frac{\tau_i}{2} \hat{q}_R \qquad \hat{j}_{i,L}^\mu = \bar{\hat{q}}_L \gamma^\mu \frac{\tau_i}{2} \hat{q}_L. \tag{18.34}$$

Thus the $SU(2)_L$ and $SU(2)_R$ refer to the two chiral components of the fermion fields, which is why it is called *chiral symmetry*.

Under infinitesimal SU(2) isospin and axial isospin transformations, $\hat{q}$ transforms by

$$\hat{q} \rightarrow \hat{q}' = (1 - \mathrm{i}\boldsymbol{\epsilon} \cdot \boldsymbol{\tau}/2 - \mathrm{i}\boldsymbol{\eta} \cdot \boldsymbol{\tau}/2\,\gamma_5)\hat{q}. \tag{18.35}$$

This can be rewritten in terms of $\hat{q}_\mathrm{R}$ and $\hat{q}_\mathrm{R}$, using

$$\hat{q} = \hat{q}_\mathrm{R} + \hat{q}_\mathrm{L}, \quad \gamma_5\hat{q}_\mathrm{R} = \hat{q}_\mathrm{R}, \quad \gamma_5\hat{q}_\mathrm{L} = -\hat{q}_\mathrm{L}. \tag{18.36}$$

We find that

$$\hat{q}_\mathrm{R}' = (1 - \mathrm{i}(\boldsymbol{\epsilon} + \boldsymbol{\eta}) \cdot \boldsymbol{\tau}/2)\hat{q}_\mathrm{R} \tag{18.37}$$

and similarly

$$\hat{q}_\mathrm{L}' = (1 - \mathrm{i}(\boldsymbol{\epsilon} - \boldsymbol{\eta}) \cdot \boldsymbol{\tau}/2)\hat{q}_\mathrm{L}. \tag{18.38}$$

Hence $\hat{q}_\mathrm{R}$ and $\hat{q}_\mathrm{L}$ transform quite independently[2], which is why $[\hat{Q}_{i,\mathrm{R}}, \hat{Q}_{j,\mathrm{L}}] = 0$.

This formalism allows us to see immediately why (18.12) is chirally invariant: problem 18.3 verifies that $\hat{\mathcal{L}}_q$ can be written as

$$\hat{\mathcal{L}}_q = \bar{\hat{q}}_\mathrm{R}\,\mathrm{i}\,\slashed{D}q_\mathrm{R} + \bar{\hat{q}}_\mathrm{L}\,\mathrm{i}\,\slashed{D}\hat{q}_\mathrm{L} \tag{18.39}$$

which is plainly invariant under (18.37) and (18.38), since $\hat{D}$ is flavour-blind.

There is as yet no formal proof that this $\mathrm{SU}(2)_\mathrm{L} \times \mathrm{SU}(2)_\mathrm{R}$ chiral symmetry is spontaneously broken in QCD, though it can be argued that the larger symmetry $\mathrm{SU}(3)_\mathrm{L} \times \mathrm{SU}(3)_\mathrm{R}$ – appropriate to three massless flavours – must be spontaneously broken (see Weinberg 1996, section 22.5). This is, of course, an issue that cannot be settled within perturbation theory (compare the comments after (17.132)). Numerical solutions of QCD on a lattice (see chapter 16) do provide strong evidence that baryons acquire large dynamical $(\mathrm{SU}(2)_{\mathrm{f}\,5}$-breaking) mass.

Even granted that chiral symmetry is spontaneously broken in massless two-flavour QCD, how do we know that it breaks in such a way as to leave the isospin ('R + L') symmetry unbroken? A plausible answer can be given if we restore the quark mass terms via

$$\hat{\mathcal{L}}_m = -m_\mathrm{u}\bar{\hat{u}}\hat{u} - m_\mathrm{d}\bar{\hat{d}}\hat{d} = -\frac{1}{2}(m_\mathrm{u} + m_\mathrm{d})\bar{\hat{q}}\hat{q} - \frac{1}{2}(m_\mathrm{u} - m_\mathrm{d})\bar{\hat{q}}\tau_3\hat{q}. \tag{18.40}$$

Now

$$\bar{\hat{q}}\hat{q} = \bar{\hat{q}}_\mathrm{L}\hat{q}_\mathrm{R} + \bar{\hat{q}}_\mathrm{R}\hat{q}_\mathrm{L} \tag{18.41}$$

and

$$\bar{\hat{q}}\tau_3\hat{q} = \bar{\hat{q}}_\mathrm{L}\tau_3 q_\mathrm{R} + \bar{\hat{q}}_\mathrm{R}\tau_3\hat{q}_\mathrm{L}. \tag{18.42}$$

Including these extra terms is somewhat analogous to switching on an external field in the ferromagnetic problem, which determines a preferred direction for the symmetry breaking. It is clear that neither of (18.41) and (18.42) preserves

---

[2]We may set $\boldsymbol{\gamma} = \boldsymbol{\epsilon} + \boldsymbol{\eta}$, and $\boldsymbol{\delta} = \boldsymbol{\epsilon} - \boldsymbol{\eta}$.

$\mathrm{SU(2)_L \times SU(2)_R}$ since they treat the L and R parts differently. Indeed from (18.37) and (18.38) we find

$$
\begin{aligned}
\bar{\hat{q}}_{\mathrm{L}}\hat{q}_{\mathrm{R}} \to \bar{\hat{q}}'_{\mathrm{L}}\hat{q}'_{\mathrm{R}} &= \bar{\hat{q}}_{\mathrm{L}}(1 + \mathrm{i}(\boldsymbol{\epsilon} - \boldsymbol{\eta}) \cdot \boldsymbol{\tau}/2)(1 - \mathrm{i}(\boldsymbol{\epsilon} + \boldsymbol{\eta}) \cdot \boldsymbol{\tau}/2)\hat{q}_{\mathrm{R}} \quad (18.43)\\
&= \bar{\hat{q}}_{\mathrm{L}}\hat{q}_{\mathrm{R}} - \mathrm{i}\boldsymbol{\eta} \cdot \bar{\hat{q}}_{\mathrm{L}}\boldsymbol{\tau}\hat{q}_{\mathrm{R}} \quad (18.44)
\end{aligned}
$$

and

$$
\bar{\hat{q}}_{\mathrm{R}}\hat{q}_{\mathrm{L}} \to \bar{\hat{q}}_{\mathrm{R}}\hat{q}_{\mathrm{L}} + \mathrm{i}\boldsymbol{\eta} \cdot \bar{\hat{q}}_{\mathrm{R}}\boldsymbol{\tau}\hat{q}_{\mathrm{L}}. \quad (18.45)
$$

Equations (18.44) and (18.45) confirm that the term $\bar{\hat{q}}\hat{q}$ in (18.40) is invariant under the isospin part of $\mathrm{SU(2)_L \times SU(2)_R}$ (since $\boldsymbol{\epsilon}$ is not involved), but not invariant under the axial isospin transformations parametrized by $\boldsymbol{\eta}$. The $\bar{\hat{q}}\tau_3\hat{q}$ term explicitly breaks the third component of isospin (resembling an electromagnetic effect), but its magnitude may be expected to be smaller than that of the $\bar{\hat{q}}\hat{q}$ term, being proportional to the difference of the masses, rather than their sum. This suggests that the vacuum will 'align' in such a way as to preserve isospin, but break axial isospin.

18.2 Pion decay and the Goldberger–Treiman relation

We now discuss some of the rather surprising phenomenological implications of spontaneously broken chiral symmetry – specifically, the spontaneous breaking of the axial isospin symmetry. We start by ignoring any 'explicit' quark masses, so that the axial isospin current is conserved, $\partial_\mu\hat{j}^\mu_{i,5} = 0$. From sections 17.4 and 17.5 (suitably generalized) we know that this current has non-zero matrix elements between the vacuum and a 'Goldstone' state, which in our case is the pion. We therefore set (cf (17.94))

$$
\langle 0|\hat{j}^\mu_{i,5}(x)|\pi_j, p\rangle = -\mathrm{i}p^\mu f_\pi \mathrm{e}^{-\mathrm{i}p\cdot x}\delta_{ij} \quad (18.46)
$$

where f_π is a constant with dimensions of mass, and which we expect to be related to a symmetry breaking vev. This is just what we shall find in section 18.3.1. Note that (18.46) is consistent with $\partial_\mu\hat{j}^\mu_{i,5} = 0$ if $p^2 = 0$, i.e. if the pion is massless.

We treat f_π as a phenomenological parameter. Its value can be determined from the rate for the decay $\pi^+ \to \mu^+\nu_\mu$ by the following reasoning. In chapter 20 we shall learn that the effective weak Hamiltonian density for this low energy *strangeness non-changing semileptonic transition* is

$$
\begin{aligned}
\hat{\mathcal{H}}_{\mathrm{W}}(x) = {} & \frac{G_{\mathrm{F}}}{\sqrt{2}}V_{\mathrm{ud}}\bar{\hat{\psi}}_{\mathrm{d}}(x)\gamma^\mu(1 - \gamma_5)\hat{\psi}_{\mathrm{u}}(x)\\
& \times [\hat{\psi}_{\nu_\mathrm{e}}(x)\gamma_\mu(1 - \gamma_5)\hat{\psi}_{\mathrm{e}}(x) + \bar{\hat{\psi}}_{\nu_\mu}(x)\gamma_\mu(1 - \gamma_5)\hat{\psi}_\mu(x)] \quad (18.47)
\end{aligned}
$$

where G_F is Fermi constant and V_{ud} is an element of the Cabibbo–Kobayashi–Maskawa (CKM) matrix (see section 20.7.3). Thus the lowest-order contribution to the S-matrix is

$$-i\langle\mu^+, p_1; \nu_\mu, p_2| \int d^4x \hat{\mathcal{H}}_W(x)|\pi^+, p\rangle$$

$$= -i\frac{G_F}{\sqrt{2}}V_{ud} \int d^4x \langle\mu^+, p_1; \nu_\mu, p_2|\hat{\bar{\psi}}_{\nu_\mu}(x)\gamma_\mu(1-\gamma_5)\hat{\psi}_\mu(x)|0\rangle$$

$$\times \langle 0|\hat{\bar{\psi}}_d(x)\gamma^\mu(1-\gamma_5)\hat{\psi}_u(x)|\pi^+, p\rangle. \tag{18.48}$$

The leptonic matrix element gives $\bar{u}_\nu(p_2)\gamma_\mu(1-\gamma_5)v_\mu(p_1)e^{i(p_1+p_2)\cdot x}$. For the pionic one, we note that

$$\hat{\bar{\psi}}_d(x)\gamma^\mu(1-\gamma_5)\hat{\psi}_u(x) = \hat{j}_1^\mu(x) - i\hat{j}_2^\mu(x) - \hat{j}_{1,5}^\mu(x) + i\hat{j}_{2,5}^\mu(x) \tag{18.49}$$

from (18.20) and (18.21). Further, the currents $\hat{j}_i^\mu$ can have no matrix elements between the vacuum (which is a 0^+ state) and the π (which is 0^-), by the following argument. From Lorentz invariance such a matrix element has to be a 4-vector. But since the initial and final parities are different, it would have to be an axial 4-vector[3]. However, the only 4-vector available is the pion's momentum p^μ which is an ordinary (not an axial) 4-vector. On the other hand, precisely for this reason the axial currents $\hat{j}_{i,5}^\mu$ do have a non-zero matrix element, as in (18.46). Noting that $|\pi^+\rangle = \frac{1}{\sqrt{2}}|\pi_1 + i\pi_2\rangle$, we find that

$$\langle 0|\hat{\bar{\psi}}_d(x)\gamma^\mu(1-\gamma_5)\hat{\psi}_u(x)|\pi^+, p\rangle = -\frac{i}{\sqrt{2}}\langle 0|\hat{j}_{1,5}^\mu - i\hat{j}_{2,5}^\mu|\pi_1 + i\pi_2\rangle \tag{18.50}$$

$$= -\sqrt{2}p^\mu f_\pi e^{-ip\cdot x} \tag{18.51}$$

so that (18.48) becomes

$$i(2\pi)^4\delta^4(p_1 + p_2 - p)[G_F V_{ud}\bar{u}_\nu(p_2)\gamma_\mu(1-\gamma_5)v(p_1)p^\mu f_\pi]. \tag{18.52}$$

The quantity in brackets is, therefore, the invariant amplitude for the process, $\mathcal{M}$. Using $p = p_1 + p_2$, we may replace $\not{p}$ in (18.52) by m_μ, neglecting the neutrino mass.

Before proceeding, we comment on the physics of (18.52). The $(1-\gamma_5)$ factor acting on a v spinor selects out the $\gamma_5 = -1$ eigenvalue which, *if the muon was massless*, would correspond to positive helicity for the μ^+ (compare the discussion in section 12.4.2). Likewise, taking the $(1-\gamma_5)$ through the $\gamma^0\gamma^\mu$ factor to act on $u_\nu^\dagger$, it selects the negative helicity neutrino state. Hence the configuration is as shown in figure 18.2, so that the leptons carry off a net spin angular momentum. But this is forbidden, since the pion spin is zero. Hence the amplitude vanishes for massless muons and neutrinos. Now the muon, at least, is not massless, and some 'wrong' helicity is present in

---

[3] See chapter 4 of volume 1.

FIGURE 18.2
Helicities of *massless* leptons in $\pi^+ \to \mu^+ \nu_\mu$ due to the 'V-A' interaction.

its wavefunction, in an amount proportional to m_μ. This is why, as we have just remarked after (18.52), the amplitude is proportional to m_μ. The rate is therefore proportional to m_μ^2. This is a very important conclusion, because it implies that the rate to muons is $\sim (m_\mu/m_e)^2 \sim (400)^2$ times greater than the rate to electrons – a result which agrees with experiment, while grossly contradicting the naive expectation that the rate with the larger energy release should dominate. This, in fact, is one of the main indications for the 'vector-axial vector', or 'V-A', structure of (18.47), as we shall see in more detail in section 20.2.

Problem 18.4 shows that the rate computed from (18.52) is

$$\Gamma_{\pi \to \mu\nu} = \frac{G_F^2 m_\mu^2 f_\pi^2 (m_\pi^2 - m_\mu^2)^2}{4\pi m_\pi^3}|V_{ud}|^2. \tag{18.53}$$

Including radiative corrections, the value

$$f_\pi \simeq 92 \text{ MeV} \tag{18.54}$$

can be extracted.

Consider now another matrix element of $\hat{j}_{i,5}^\mu$, this time between nucleon states. Following an analysis similar to that in section 8.8 for the matrix elements of the electromagnetic current operator between nucleon states, we write

$$\langle N, p' | \hat{j}_{i,5}^\mu(0) | N, p \rangle$$
$$= \bar{u}(p') \left[\gamma^\mu \gamma_5 F_1^5(q^2) + \frac{i\sigma^{\mu\nu}}{2M} q_\nu \gamma_5 F_2^5(q^2) + q^\mu \gamma_5 F_3^5(q^2) \right] \frac{\tau_i}{2} u(p), \tag{18.55}$$

where the F_i^5's are certain form factors, M is the nucleon mass, and $q = p - p'$. The spinors in (18.55) are understood to be written in flavour and Dirac space. Since (with massless quarks) $\hat{j}_{i,5}^\mu$ is conserved – that is $q_\mu \hat{j}_{i,5}^\mu(0) = 0$ – we find

$$\begin{aligned}
0 &= \bar{u}(p')[\slashed{q}\gamma_5 F_1^5(q^2) + q^2 \gamma_5 F_3^5(q^2)]\frac{\tau_i}{2} u(p) \\
&= \bar{u}(p')[(\slashed{p} - \slashed{p}')\gamma_5 F_1^5(q^2) + q^2 \gamma_5 F_3^5(q^2)]\frac{\tau_i}{2} u(p) \\
&= \bar{u}(p')[-2M\gamma_5 F_1^5(q^2) + q^2 \gamma_5 F_3^5(q^2)]\frac{\tau_i}{2} u(p), \tag{18.56}
\end{aligned}$$

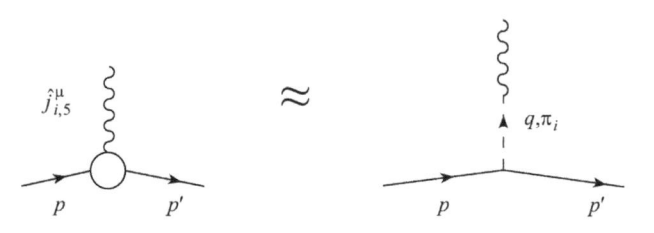

FIGURE 18.3
One pion intermediate state contribution to F_3^5.

using $\not{p}\gamma_5 = -\gamma_5 \not{p}$ and the Dirac equations for $u(p), \bar{u}(p')$. Hence the form factors F_1^5 and F_3^5 must satisfy

$$2MF_1^5(q^2) = q^2 F_3^5(q^2). \tag{18.57}$$

Now the matrix element (18.55) enters into neutron β-decay (as does the matrix element of $\hat{j}_i^\mu(0)$). Here, $q^2 \simeq 0$ and (18.57) appears to predict, therefore, that either $M = 0$ (which is certainly not so) or $F_1^5(0) = 0$. But $F_1^5(0)$ can be measured in β decay, and is found to be approximately equal to 1.26; it is conventionally called g_A. The only possible conclusion is that F_3^5 *must contain a part proportional to* $1/q^2$. Such a contribution can only arise from the propagator of a massless particle – which, of course, is the pion. This elegant physical argument, first given by Nambu (1960), sheds a revealing new light on the phenomenon of spontaneous symmetry breaking: the existence of the massless particle coupled to the symmetry current $\hat{j}_{i,5}^\mu$ 'saves' the conservation of the current.

We calculate the pion contribution to F_3^5 as follows. The process is pictured in figure 18.3. The pion-current matrix element is given by (18.46), and the (massless) propagator is i/q^2. For the $\pi - N$ vertex, the conventional Lagrangian is

$$ig_{\pi NN}\hat{\pi}_i \bar{\hat{N}}\gamma_5\tau_i\hat{N}, \tag{18.58}$$

which is $SU(2)_f$-invariant and parity conserving since the pion field is a pseudoscalar, and so is $\bar{N}\gamma_5 N$. Putting these pieces together, the contribution of figure 18.3 to the current matrix element is

$$2g_{\pi NN}\bar{u}(p')\gamma_5\frac{\tau_i}{2}u(p)\frac{i}{q^2}(-iq^\mu f_\pi), \tag{18.59}$$

and so

$$F_3^5(q^2) = \frac{1}{q^2}2g_{\pi NN}f_\pi \tag{18.60}$$

from this contribution. Combining (18.57) with (18.60) we deduce

$$g_A \equiv \lim_{q^2 \to 0} F_1^5(q^2) = \frac{g_{\pi NN}f_\pi}{M}, \tag{18.61}$$

the Goldberger–Treiman (1958) relation. Taking $M = 939$ MeV, $g_A = 1.26$ and $f_\pi = 92$ MeV one obtains $g_{\pi NN} \approx 12.9$, which is only 5% below the experimental value of this effective pion-nucleon coupling constant.

We can repeat the argument leading to the G-T relation but retaining $m_\pi^2 \neq 0$. Equation (18.46) tells us that $\partial_\mu \hat{j}_{i,5}^\mu / (m_\pi^2 f_\pi)$ behaves like a properly normalized pion field, at least when operating on a near mass-shell pion state. This means that the one-nucleon matrix element of $\partial_\mu \hat{j}_{i,5}^\mu$ is (cf (18.59))

$$2g_{\pi NN} \bar{u}(p') \gamma_5 \frac{\tau_i}{2} u(p) \frac{\mathrm{i}}{q^2 - m_\pi^2} m_\pi^2 f_\pi, \tag{18.62}$$

while from (18.55) it is given by

$$\mathrm{i}\bar{u}(p')[-2M\gamma_5 F_1^5(q^2) + q^2 \gamma_5 F_3^5(q^2)] \frac{\tau_i}{2} u(p). \tag{18.63}$$

Hence

$$-2M F_1^5(q^2) + q^2 F_3^5(q^2) = \frac{2g_{\pi NN} m_\pi^2 f_\pi}{q^2 - m_\pi^2}. \tag{18.64}$$

Also, in place of (18.60) we now have

$$F_3^5(q^2) = \frac{1}{q^2 - m_\pi^2} 2g_{\pi NN} f_\pi. \tag{18.65}$$

Equations (18.64) and (18.65) are consistent for $q^2 = m_\pi^2$ if

$$F_1^5(q^2 = m_\pi^2) = g_{\pi NN} f_\pi / M. \tag{18.66}$$

$F_1^5(q^2)$ varies only slowly from $q^2 = 0$ to $q^2 = m_\pi^2$, since it contains no rapidly varying pion pole contribution, and so we recover the G-T relation again.

Amplitudes involving *two* Goldstone pions can be calculated by an extension of these techniques. However, a much more efficient method is available, through the use of *effective Lagrangians*, which capture the low energy dynamics of the Goldstone modes.

18.3 Effective Lagrangians

18.3.1 The linear and non-linear σ-models

We begin by considering the linear σ-model, which has the same Lagrangian as the one considered in section 17.6,

$$\hat{\mathcal{L}}_\Phi = (\partial_\mu \hat{\phi}^\dagger)(\partial^\mu \hat{\phi}) + \mu^2 \hat{\phi}^\dagger \hat{\phi} - \frac{\lambda}{4}(\hat{\phi}^\dagger \hat{\phi})^4, \tag{18.67}$$

but we shall interpret it differently here. The sign of the μ^2 term has been chosen to induce spontaneous symmetry breaking. In section 17.6, $\hat{\phi}$ was the SU(2) doublet

$$\hat{\phi} = \begin{pmatrix} \frac{1}{\sqrt{2}}(\hat{\phi}_1 + i\hat{\phi}_2) \\ \frac{1}{\sqrt{2}}(\hat{\phi}_3 + i\hat{\phi}_4) \end{pmatrix}, \tag{18.68}$$

in terms of which (18.67) becomes

$$\hat{\mathcal{L}}_\Phi = \frac{1}{2}\partial_\mu\hat{\phi}_a\partial^\mu\hat{\phi}_a + \frac{1}{2}\mu^2\hat{\phi}_a\hat{\phi}_a - \frac{\lambda}{16}(\hat{\phi}_a\hat{\phi}_a)^2, \tag{18.69}$$

where the sum on $a = 1$ to 4 is understood. Evidently (18.69) is invariant under transformations which preserve the 'dot product' $\hat{\phi}_a\hat{\phi}_a$, namely the transformations of SO(4). This group is discussed in appendix M, section M.4.3. We note there that the algebra of the generators of SO(4) is the same as that of SU(2) × SU(2), which is the algebra of the chiral charges in (18.28)–(18.30). This suggests that we should rewrite (18.69) in such a way as to reveal its SU(2)$_L$×SU(2)$_R$ symmetry, rather than its O(4) symmetry. Three of the four fields will then be identified with the Goldstone bosons associated with the spontaneous breaking of the 'R – L' part; they will in turn be identified with the (massless) pions.

One way to bring out the chiral symmetry of (18.69) is to write

$$\hat{\phi} = \begin{pmatrix} (\hat{\pi}_2 + i\hat{\pi}_1)/\sqrt{2} \\ (\hat{\sigma} - i\hat{\pi}_3)/\sqrt{2} \end{pmatrix} = \frac{1}{\sqrt{2}}\hat{\Sigma}\begin{pmatrix} 0 \\ 1 \end{pmatrix}, \tag{18.70}$$

where

$$\hat{\Sigma} = \hat{\sigma} + i\boldsymbol{\tau}\cdot\hat{\boldsymbol{\pi}}. \tag{18.71}$$

Then

$$\hat{\phi}^\dagger\hat{\phi} = \frac{1}{4}\text{Tr}(\hat{\Sigma}^\dagger\hat{\Sigma}), \tag{18.72}$$

and (18.69) becomes

$$\hat{\mathcal{L}}_\Sigma = \frac{1}{4}\text{Tr}(\partial_\mu\hat{\Sigma}^\dagger\partial^\mu\hat{\Sigma}) + \frac{\mu^2}{4}\text{Tr}(\hat{\Sigma}^\dagger\hat{\Sigma}) - \frac{\lambda}{64}\text{Tr}(\hat{\Sigma}^\dagger\hat{\Sigma})^2. \tag{18.73}$$

This Lagrangian is invariant under the SU(2)$_L$× SU(2)$_R$ transformation

$$\hat{\Sigma} \to U_L\hat{\Sigma}U_R^\dagger \tag{18.74}$$

where

$$U_L = \exp(-i\boldsymbol{\alpha}_L\cdot\boldsymbol{\tau}/2), \quad U_R = \exp(-i\boldsymbol{\alpha}_R\cdot\boldsymbol{\tau}/2) \tag{18.75}$$

are two independent SU(2) transformations (remember that $\text{Tr}AB = \text{Tr}BA$). For the case of infinitesimal transformations, we find (problem 18.5)

$$\hat{\sigma} \to \hat{\sigma} - \boldsymbol{\eta}\cdot\hat{\boldsymbol{\pi}} \tag{18.76}$$

$$\hat{\boldsymbol{\pi}} \to \hat{\boldsymbol{\pi}} + \boldsymbol{\eta}\hat{\sigma} + \boldsymbol{\epsilon}\times\hat{\boldsymbol{\pi}}, \tag{18.77}$$

where

$$\eta = (\epsilon_R - \epsilon_L)/2, \quad \epsilon = (\epsilon_R + \epsilon_L)/2. \tag{18.78}$$

Evidently $\epsilon_R = \eta + \epsilon$ and $\epsilon_L = \epsilon - \eta$, which we may compare with the L and R transformation of the quark fields in (18.37), (18.38).

With the sign of μ^2 as in (18.73), the classical potential has a minimum at

$$\hat{\sigma}^2 + \hat{\boldsymbol{\pi}}^2 = 4\mu^2/\lambda \equiv v^2, \tag{18.79}$$

which we interpret as the symmetry breaking condition

$$\langle 0|\hat{\sigma}^2 + \hat{\boldsymbol{\pi}}^2|0\rangle = v^2. \tag{18.80}$$

Let us choose the particular ground state

$$\langle 0|\hat{\sigma}|0\rangle = v, \quad \langle 0|\hat{\boldsymbol{\pi}}|0\rangle = 0, \tag{18.81}$$

which is actually the same as (17.103). Referring back to (18.76) and (18.77) we see that this vacuum is invariant under 'L + R' transformations with parameters ϵ, but not under 'L − R' transformations with parameters η. These correspond respectively to the $SU(2)_f$ flavour isospin, and $SU(2)_{f5}$ axial flavour isospin, transformations on the quark fields. So this vacuum spontaneously breaks the axial isospin symmetry. Fluctuations away from this minimum are described by fields $\hat{\boldsymbol{\pi}}$ and $\hat{s} = \hat{\sigma} - v$. Placing this shift into (18.73) we find that $\hat{\mathcal{L}}_\Sigma$ becomes $\hat{\mathcal{L}}_s$ where

$$\hat{\mathcal{L}}_s = \frac{1}{2}\partial_\mu \hat{s}\partial^\mu \hat{s} - \mu^2 \hat{s}^2 + \frac{1}{2}\partial_\mu \hat{\boldsymbol{\pi}} \cdot \partial^\mu \hat{\boldsymbol{\pi}} - \frac{\lambda}{4}v\hat{s}(\hat{s}^2 + \hat{\boldsymbol{\pi}}^2) - \frac{\lambda}{16}(\hat{s}^2 + \hat{\boldsymbol{\pi}}^2)^2, \tag{18.82}$$

discarding an irrelevant constant. As expected, the field $\hat{s}$ is massive (with mass $\sqrt{2}\mu$), while the fields $\hat{\boldsymbol{\pi}}$ are massless, and may be identified with the Goldstone modes associated with the spontaneous breaking of the axial isospin symmetry.

The Lagrangian $\hat{\mathcal{L}}_s$ incorporates the correct symmetries, and can be used to calculate $\pi - \pi$ scattering, for example (in the massless limit). But it is not the most efficient Lagrangian to use, as we can see from the following considerations. Consider the amplitude for $\pi^+ - \pi^0$ scattering, in tree approximation (Donoghue *et al.* 1992). The contributing terms in $\hat{\mathcal{L}}_s$ are

$$\hat{\mathcal{L}}_{\pi-\pi} = -\frac{\lambda}{16}(\hat{\boldsymbol{\pi}}^2)^2 - \frac{\lambda}{4}v\hat{s}\hat{\boldsymbol{\pi}}^2, \tag{18.83}$$

which we can rewrite in terms of the charged and neutral fields as

$$\hat{\mathcal{L}}_{\pi-\pi} = -\frac{\lambda}{16}(2\hat{\pi}_+^\dagger \hat{\pi}_+ + \hat{\pi}^{0\,2})^2 - \frac{\lambda}{4}v\hat{s}(2\hat{\pi}_+^\dagger \hat{\pi}_+ + \hat{\pi}^{0\,2}). \tag{18.84}$$

Then the terms responsible for $\pi^+ - \pi^0$ scattering at tree level are

$$-\frac{\lambda}{4}\hat{\pi}_+^\dagger \hat{\pi}_+ \hat{\pi}^{0\,2} - \frac{\lambda}{2}v\hat{s}\left(\hat{\pi}_+^\dagger \hat{\pi}_+ + \frac{1}{2}\hat{\pi}^{0\,2}\right). \tag{18.85}$$

The first of these represents a four-pion contact interaction with amplitude

$$-i\lambda/2, \tag{18.86}$$

while the second contributes an s-exchange graph in the t-channel with amplitude

$$(-i\lambda v/2)^2 \frac{i}{q^2 - 2\mu^2}, \tag{18.87}$$

where q is the 4-momentum transfer $q = p'_+ - p_+ = p_0 - p'_0$. The sum of these is

$$-i\lambda/2 \frac{q^2}{q^2 - 2\mu^2}, \tag{18.88}$$

which reduces to iq^2/v^2 for $q \approx 0$. Thus, despite the apparent constant 4-boson piece (18.86), the total amplitude in fact *vanishes* as $q^2 \to 0$, due to a cancellation.

This cancellation is not an accident. It is generally true that Goldstone fields enter only via their derivatives, which bring factors of momenta into the amplitudes. We drew attention to this following equation (17.85), and the same is true of the $\hat{\boldsymbol{\theta}}$ fields in (17.107). This suggests that it is both possible, and more efficient, to recast $\hat{\mathcal{L}}_s$ into a form in which only the derivatives of the Goldstone fields enter. Equation (17.107) indicates how to do this: we define new pion fields (but call them the same) by

$$\hat{\Sigma} = (v + \hat{S})\hat{U}, \quad \hat{U} = \exp(i\boldsymbol{\tau} \cdot \hat{\boldsymbol{\pi}}/v), \tag{18.89}$$

where $\hat{S}$ is invariant under $\mathrm{SU}(2)_\mathrm{L} \times \mathrm{SU}(2)_\mathrm{R}$, and where $\hat{U}$ transforms by

$$\hat{U} \to U_\mathrm{L}\hat{U}U_\mathrm{R}^\dagger. \tag{18.90}$$

Now $\hat{\Sigma}^\dagger\hat{\Sigma} = (v + \hat{S})^2$, and the Goldstone modes have been transformed away from the potential terms in $\hat{\mathcal{L}}_\Sigma$, reappearing in the derivative terms instead. We write the transformed Lagrangian as $\hat{\mathcal{L}}_S$ where

$$\hat{\mathcal{L}}_S = \frac{1}{2}\partial_\mu \hat{S}\partial^\mu \hat{S} - \mu^2\hat{S}^2 + \frac{1}{4}(v + \hat{S})^2\mathrm{Tr}(\partial_\mu\hat{U}\partial^\mu\hat{U}^\dagger) - \frac{1}{4}\lambda v\hat{S}^3 - \frac{\lambda}{16}\hat{S}^4, \tag{18.91}$$

where we have used

$$\hat{U}^\dagger\partial^\mu\hat{u} + \partial^\mu\hat{U}^\dagger\hat{U} = 0, \tag{18.92}$$

which follows from the unitary condition $\hat{U}^\dagger\hat{U} = 1$.

When $\partial_\mu\hat{U}$ is expanded in powers of $\hat{\boldsymbol{\pi}}$, we recover a kinetic energy piece

$$\frac{1}{2}\partial_\mu\hat{\boldsymbol{\pi}} \cdot \partial^\mu\hat{\boldsymbol{\pi}}, \tag{18.93}$$

and all other terms involve derivatives of $\hat{\boldsymbol{\pi}}$. In particular, the term with

the lowest number of derivatives which contributes to the $\pi - \pi$ scattering amplitude is

$$\frac{1}{6v^2}[(\hat{\boldsymbol{\pi}} \cdot \partial_\mu \hat{\boldsymbol{\pi}})(\hat{\boldsymbol{\pi}} \cdot \partial^\mu \hat{\boldsymbol{\pi}}) - \hat{\boldsymbol{\pi}}^2 \partial_\mu \hat{\boldsymbol{\pi}} \cdot \partial^\mu \hat{\boldsymbol{\pi}}], \tag{18.94}$$

since the $\hat{S} - \hat{\boldsymbol{\pi}} - \hat{\boldsymbol{\pi}}$ vertex already has two derivatives. The reader may check that the amplitude for $\pi^+\pi^0 \to \pi^+\pi^0$ calculated from (18.94) is iq^2/v^2, exactly as before, but this time without having to go through the cancellation argument.

The fields in $\hat{\Sigma}$ on the one hand, and in $\hat{S}$ and $\hat{U}$ on the other, are related non-linearly, but a physical amplitude calculated with either representation has turned out to be the same, in this simple case. It is in fact generally true that such non-linear field redefinitions lead to the same physics (Haag 1958, Coleman, Wess and Zumino 1969, Callan, Coleman, Wess and Zumino 1969). It is clearly advantageous to work with $\hat{\mathcal{L}}_S$, which builds in the desired derivatives of the Goldstone modes.

Indeed, we can simplify matters even further. Since $\hat{S}$ is invariant under $SU(2)_L \times SU(2)_R$, the full symmetry of the Lagrangian is maintained with only the field $\hat{U}$, transforming by (18.90), and we may as well discard $\hat{S}$ altogether. The dynamics of the Goldstone sector are then described by the *non-linear* σ-*model*, with Lagrangian

$$\hat{\mathcal{L}}_2 = \frac{v^2}{4}\mathrm{Tr}(\partial_\mu \hat{U} \partial^\mu \hat{U}^\dagger). \tag{18.95}$$

This is the most general Lagrangian that involves the Goldstone fields, exhibits the desired symmetry, and contains only two derivatives.

Since $\hat{\mathcal{L}}_2$ is invariant under the $SU(2)_L \times SU(2)_R$ transformations (18.75), we can calculate the associated Noether currents (problem 18.6), obtaining

$$\hat{j}_{i,L}^\mu(\hat{U}) = \frac{-iv^2}{8}\mathrm{Tr}[\tau_i \hat{U} \partial^\mu \hat{U}^\dagger - \tau_i (\partial^\mu \hat{U})\hat{U}^\dagger] = \frac{-iv^2}{4}\mathrm{Tr}(\tau_i \hat{U} \partial^\mu \hat{U}^\dagger), \tag{18.96}$$

and

$$\hat{j}_{i,R}^\mu(\hat{U}) = \frac{iv^2}{8}\mathrm{Tr}[\tau_i (\partial^\mu \hat{U}^\dagger)\hat{U} - \tau_i \hat{U}^\dagger \partial^\mu \hat{U}] = \frac{-iv^2}{4}\mathrm{Tr}(\tau_i \hat{U}^\dagger \partial^\mu \hat{U}). \tag{18.97}$$

The axial 'R − L' current is then

$$\hat{j}_{i5}^\mu(\hat{U}) = \frac{iv^2}{4}\mathrm{Tr}[\tau_i(\hat{U}\partial^\mu \hat{U}^\dagger - \hat{U}^\dagger \partial^\mu \hat{U})], \tag{18.98}$$

and the vector 'R + L' current is

$$\hat{j}_i^\mu(\hat{U}) = \frac{iv^2}{4}\mathrm{Tr}[\tau_i(\hat{U}\partial^\mu \hat{U}^\dagger + \hat{U}^\dagger \partial^\mu \hat{U})]. \tag{18.99}$$

Expanding (18.98) in powers of the pion field, we find

$$\hat{j}_{i,5}^\mu(\hat{U}) = v\partial^\mu \hat{\pi}_i + \dots, \tag{18.100}$$

which we may compare with (17.93). Just as in equation (17.94), (18.100) implies that this axial current has a matrix element between the vacuum and the one-Goldstone state:

$$\langle 0|\hat{j}^{\mu}_{i,5}(\hat{U})|\pi_j, p\rangle = -\mathrm{i}p^{\mu}v e^{-\mathrm{i}p\cdot x}\delta_{ij}. \tag{18.101}$$

Now comes the pay-off: this is the *same* symmetry current which enters into weak interactions, for which we already defined the vacuum-to-one-particle matrix element in terms of the pion decay constant f_π, via equation (18.46). Comparing (18.101) with (18.46) we identify

$$v = f_\pi. \tag{18.102}$$

Thus, finally, the dynamics of our massless pions, to lowest order in an expansion in powers of momenta, is given by the Lagrangian

$$\hat{\mathcal{L}}_2 = \frac{1}{4}f_\pi^2 \mathrm{Tr}(\partial_\mu \hat{U}\partial^\mu \hat{U}^\dagger). \tag{18.103}$$

It is quite remarkable that the low energy dynamics of the (massless) Goldstone modes is completely determined in terms of one constant, measurable in π decay.

The Lagrangian of (18.103) is an example of an *effective Lagrangian*. By this is meant, broadly, any Lagrangian which involves the presumed relevant degrees of freedom (here the Goldstone modes), and respects desired symmetries of the theory. Evidently it is implied that there is some 'underlying theory', couched in terms of different degrees of freedom (here quarks and gluons), from which the symmetries have been abstracted. It is important to realize that an effective Lagrangian may or may not be renormalizable. Whereas our starting Lagrangian $\hat{\mathcal{L}}_\sigma$ is renormalizable, $\hat{\mathcal{L}}_2$ is not: clearly the latter contains terms with arbitrarily many pion fields, which are operators of arbitrarily high dimension, compensated by negative powers of f_π^2. As it stands, $\hat{\mathcal{L}}_2$ can only be used at tree level – as, for example, in the calculation of $\pi - \pi$ scattering using the interaction (18.94), for which the amplitude has an energy dependence of the form E^2/f_π^2, where E is the order of magnitude of the particles' energy or momentum. This interaction has mass dimension 6, and its coupling $1/f_\pi^2$ has dimension $(\mathrm{mass})^{-2}$, like the 4-fermion interaction considered in section 11.8. It is therefore not renormalizable. However, the argument of section 11.8 suggests that a loop-by-loop renormalization programme is possible, and this was shown to be the case by Weinberg (1979a). Each loop built from the interaction (18.94) will carry an extra two powers of energy, to compensate the $1/f_\pi^2$ in the coupling. Thus f_π (or perhaps this multiplied by factors like 4 and π, if we are lucky) provides the energy scale characteristic of a non-renormalizable theory: as we go up in energy, we need more loops. But, at each loop order new divergences appear, which require additional counter terms for renormalization. Thus at any given order in

E^2/f_π^2, we must ensure that our effective Lagrangian contains all the appropriate counter terms which are allowed by the symmetry. For example, at one-loop order for $\hat{\mathcal{L}}_2$, we need to include the 4-derivative terms

$$\hat{\mathcal{L}}_4 = c_1 \text{Tr}(\partial_\mu \hat{U} \partial^\mu \hat{U}^\dagger \partial_\nu \hat{U} \partial^\nu \hat{U}^\dagger) + c_2 \text{Tr}(\partial_\mu \hat{U} \partial_\nu \hat{U}^\dagger \partial^\mu \hat{U} \partial^\nu \hat{U}^\dagger). \qquad (18.104)$$

To perform a one-loop calculation, one uses $\hat{\mathcal{L}}_2$ at tree-level and in one-loop diagrams, and $\hat{\mathcal{L}}_4$ at tree-level only.

Real pions, however, are not massless, nor are real quarks. We need to extend our effective Lagrangian to include *explicit* chiral symmetry breaking mass terms.

18.3.2 Inclusion of explicit symmetry breaking: masses for pions and quarks

Consider the term

$$\hat{\mathcal{L}}_{m_\pi} = \frac{m_\pi^2}{4} \text{Tr}(\hat{U} + \hat{U}^\dagger). \qquad (18.105)$$

This is invariant only under the restricted set of transformations with $\alpha_L = \alpha_R$, that is transformations such that $U_R = U_L$, for then $\text{Tr}\hat{U} \to \text{Tr}(U_R \hat{U} U_R^\dagger) = \text{Tr}\hat{U}$. Such transformations form the SU(2) flavour isospin group. The term (18.105) breaks the axial isospin group explicitly, which would correspond to transformations with $\alpha_L = -\alpha_R$, or equivalently $U_L = U_R^\dagger$, under which $\hat{U} \to U_L \hat{U} U_L$. Expanding (18.105) to second order in the pion fields, we find the term

$$\hat{\mathcal{L}}_{\text{quad},m_\pi} = -\frac{1}{2} m_\pi^2 \boldsymbol{\pi}^2 \qquad (18.106)$$

which, together with (18.93), shows that the pion field now has mass m_π. Higher-order terms can be added, m_π^2 counting as equivalent to two derivatives. The low energy expansion is now an expansion in both the energy E and the pion mass m_π. This is called *chiral perturbation theory*, or ChPT for short.

For example, to calculate $\pi - \pi$ scattering to order E^2, we use $\hat{\mathcal{L}}_2 + \hat{\mathcal{L}}_{m_\pi}$ at tree-level, expanded up to fourth power in the pion fields. The result is to change the amplitude for $\pi^+\pi^0 \to \pi^+\pi^0$ from $i(p'_+ - p_+)^2/f_\pi^2$ to $i[(p'_+ - p_+)^2 - m_\pi^2]/f_\pi^2$. By considering the general $\pi - \pi$ amplitude, predictions for the scattering lengths can be made for low energy observables, for example the s-wave scattering lengths a_0 and a_2 in the isospin 0 and 2 channels. The results (first calculated by Weinberg 1966 using current algebra techniques) are

$$a_0 = \frac{7m_\pi^2}{32\pi f_\pi^2} = 0.16\, m_\pi^{-1}, \quad a_2 = -\frac{m_\pi^2}{16\pi f_\pi^2} = -0.045\, m_\pi^{-1} \qquad (18.107)$$

The experimental values are $a_0 = 0.26 \pm 0.05\, m_\pi^{-1}$ and $a_2 = -0.028 \pm 0.012\, m_\pi^{-1}$, as given by Donoghue *et al.* (1992). The next order in ChPT improves upon these results.

A systematic exposition of ChPT at the one-loop level was given by Gasser and Leutwyler (1984). Bijnens *et al.* (1996) carried the $\pi - \pi$ calculation to two-loop order; see also Colangelo *et al.* (2001).

It is clear that there must be some relation between the masses of the u and d quarks (in the SU(2) flavour case) and the pion mass, since the latter must vanish in the limit $m_{\mathrm{u}} = m_{\mathrm{d}} = 0$. To see this connection, we consider the quark mass term in the 2-flavour QCD Lagrangian, which is

$$-\bar{\hat{q}} \, \boldsymbol{m}_2 \hat{q}, \quad \boldsymbol{m}_2 = \begin{pmatrix} m_{\mathrm{u}} & 0 \\ 0 & m_{\mathrm{d}} \end{pmatrix}. \tag{18.108}$$

Let us now redefine the quark fields (compare (17.107) and (18.17)) by

$$\hat{q} = \exp[-\mathrm{i}\boldsymbol{\tau} \cdot \hat{\boldsymbol{\pi}} \gamma_5 / (2 f_\pi)] \, \hat{f}. \tag{18.109}$$

This transformation is a perfectly good parametrization of the Goldstone fields associated with the axial symmetry (18.17), and effectively removes them from the new fermion fields $\hat{f}$. The quark mass term now becomes

$$-\bar{\hat{f}} \exp[-\mathrm{i}\boldsymbol{\tau} \cdot \hat{\boldsymbol{\pi}} \gamma_5 / (2 f_\pi)] \, \boldsymbol{m}_2 \exp[-\mathrm{i}\boldsymbol{\tau} \cdot \hat{\boldsymbol{\pi}} / (2 f_\pi)] \hat{f}. \tag{18.110}$$

We now make the assumption that the axial SU(2) is spontaneously broken in QCD, by imposing a non-zero vev on the symmetry-breaking operator $\bar{\hat{f}} \hat{f}$:

$$\langle 0 | \bar{\hat{f}}_i \hat{f}_j | 0 \rangle = -f_\pi^2 B \delta_{ij} \quad (i, j = 1, 2). \tag{18.111}$$

Expanding (18.110) up to second order in the pion fields, retaining just the expectation value of the fermion bilinear[4], we find a mass term

$$-\frac{1}{2} B (m_{\mathrm{u}} + m_{\mathrm{d}}) \hat{\boldsymbol{\pi}}^2, \tag{18.112}$$

from which the relation (Gasser and Leutwyler 1982)

$$m_\pi^2 = -\frac{(m_{\mathrm{u}} + m_{\mathrm{d}})}{f_\pi^2} \langle 0 | \bar{\hat{f}} \hat{f} | 0 \rangle \tag{18.113}$$

follows, where $\bar{\hat{f}} \hat{f}$ represents either $\bar{\hat{f}}_{\mathrm{u}} \hat{f}_{\mathrm{u}}$ or $\bar{\hat{f}}_{\mathrm{d}} \hat{f}_{\mathrm{d}}$. From (18.113) we can see that the *square* of the pion mass is proportional to the average u-d quark mass (provided of course that B does not accidentally vanish), and goes to zero as they do; $\langle 0 | \bar{\hat{f}} \hat{f} | 0 \rangle$ is the 'chiral condensate' (cf figure 18.1).

Lattice QCD (see chapter 16) can be used to test equation (18.113), since simulations can be done for a range of quark masses, and the relation between m_π^2 and $m_{\mathrm{u,d}}$ can be checked. Conversely, ChPT can assist lattice QCD calculations by guiding the extrapolation of the calculated results to quark

---

[4] A formal justification of this step is provided by Weinberg (1996), section 19.6.

mass values lighter than can presently be simulated. For example, Noaki *et al.* (2008) have reported the results of such a calculation, using 2 light dynamical quark flavours, in the overlap fermion formalism (Neuberger 1998a, 1998b), which preserves chiral symmetry at finite lattice spacing. Their pion masses ranged from 290 MeV to 750 MeV, and they compared their results with the predictions of ChPT at one-loop (Gasser and Leutwyler 1984) and two-loop (Colangelo *et al.* 2001). They found good fits to the ChPT formulae, and extracted quark masses (in the $\overline{\text{MS}}$ scheme at the scale 2 GeV) of about 4.5 MeV; they also found $|\langle 0|\bar{\hat{f}}\hat{f}|0\rangle| \sim (235\,\text{GeV})^3$, in the $\overline{\text{MS}}$ scheme at 2 GeV scale. Studies by this and other groups are continuing, with 3 light flavours, lighter pion masses, and other lattice fermion formalisms.

18.3.3 Extension to SU(3)$_{\text{f L}}$×SU(3)$_{\text{f R}}$

To the extent that the strange quark is also 'light' on hadronic scales, the QCD Lagrangian has the larger symmetry of SU(3)$_{\text{f L}}$×SU(3)$_{\text{f R}}$, which breaks spontaneously so as to preserve the flavour symmetry SU(3)$_\text{f}$, and produce an SU(3) octet of pseudoscalar Goldstone bosons: $\pi^\pm, \pi^0, \text{K}^\pm, \text{K}^0, \bar{\text{K}}^0$ and η_8 (see figure 12.4). The effective Lagrangian approach to the dynamics of the Goldstone fields can be easily extended to chiral SU(3). One simply replaces $\hat{U} = \exp(\text{i}\boldsymbol{\tau} \cdot \hat{\boldsymbol{\pi}}/f_\pi)$ by $\hat{V} = \exp(\text{i}\boldsymbol{\lambda} \cdot \hat{\boldsymbol{\phi}}/f_\pi)$ where

$$\frac{1}{\sqrt{2}}\sum_{a=1}^{8}\lambda_a\hat{\phi}_a = \begin{pmatrix} \frac{1}{\sqrt{2}}\hat{\pi}^0 + \frac{1}{\sqrt{6}}\hat{\eta}_8 & \hat{\pi}^+ & \hat{K}^+ \\ \hat{\pi}^- & -\frac{1}{\sqrt{2}}\hat{\pi}^0 + \frac{1}{\sqrt{6}}\hat{\eta}_8 & \hat{K}^0 \\ \hat{K}^- & \bar{\hat{K}}^0 & -\frac{2}{\sqrt{6}}\hat{\eta}_8 \end{pmatrix}. \quad (18.114)$$

One easily verifies that the kinetic terms in

$$\hat{\mathcal{L}}_2 = \frac{f_\pi^2}{4}\text{Tr}\partial_\mu\hat{V}\partial^\mu\hat{V} \quad (18.115)$$

have the correct normalization, using $\text{Tr}\lambda_a\lambda_b = 2\delta_{ab}$. The 3-flavour quark mass term is now

$$-\bar{\hat{f}}\exp[-\text{i}\boldsymbol{\lambda} \cdot \hat{\boldsymbol{\phi}}\gamma_5/(2f_\pi)]\,\boldsymbol{m}_3\exp[-\text{i}\boldsymbol{\lambda} \cdot \hat{\boldsymbol{\phi}}\gamma_5/(2f_\pi)]\,\hat{f} \quad (18.116)$$

where

$$\boldsymbol{m}_3 = \begin{pmatrix} m_\text{u} & 0 & 0 \\ 0 & m_\text{d} & 0 \\ 0 & 0 & m_\text{s} \end{pmatrix}. \quad (18.117)$$

The axial SU(3) symmetry breaking vev is

$$\langle 0|\bar{\hat{f}}_i\hat{f}_j|0\rangle = -f_\pi^2 B\delta_{ij} \quad (i,j=1,2,3) \quad (18.118)$$

and the meson mass term is

$$-\frac{B}{2}\text{Tr}\{(\boldsymbol{\lambda} \cdot \hat{\boldsymbol{\phi}})^2\boldsymbol{m}_3\}. \quad (18.119)$$

This yields (problem 18.7)

$$m_{\pi+}^2 = m_{\pi^0}^2 = B(m_u + m_d), \tag{18.120}$$

$$m_{K+}^2 = B(m_u + m_s), \tag{18.121}$$

$$m_{K^0}^2 = B(m_d + m_s,) \tag{18.122}$$

$$m_{\eta_8}^2 = \frac{1}{3}B(m_u + m_d + 4m_s), \tag{18.123}$$

and there is also a term which mixes π^0 and η_8:

$$m_{\pi\eta}^2 = \frac{B}{\sqrt{3}}(m_u - m_d). \tag{18.124}$$

It is interesting that the charged and neutral pions have the same mass, even though we have made no assumption about the ratio of m_u to m_d. The observed pion mass differences arise from electromagnetism.

If we ignore for the moment electromagnetic mass differences, we can deduce from (18.120)–(18.122) the relation

$$\frac{m_\pi^2}{2m_K^2 - m_\pi^2} = \frac{m_u + m_d}{m_s}. \tag{18.125}$$

The left-hand side is approximately equal to 0.04, so we learn that the non-strange quarks are about 1/25 times as heavy as the strange quark. We also obtain

$$m_{\eta_8}^2 = \frac{1}{3}(4m_K^2 - m_\pi^2), \tag{18.126}$$

which is the Gell-Mann–Okubo formula for the (squared) masses of the pseudoscalar meson octet (Gell-Mann 1961, Okubo 1962). Using average values for the K and π masses, the relation (18.126) predicts $m_{\eta_8}^2 = 566$ MeV, quite close to the η (548 MeV).

Further progress requires the inclusion of electromagnetic effects, since m_u and m_d are themselves comparable to the electromagnetic mass differences. Including these effects, Weinberg (1996) estimates

$$\frac{m_d}{m_s} \approx 0.050, \quad \frac{m_u}{m_s} \approx 0.027; \tag{18.127}$$

see also Leutwyler (1996). Note that the d quark is almost twice as heavy as the u quark: according to QCD, the origin of SU(2) isospin symmetry is not that $m_u \approx m_d$, but that both are very small compared with, say, $\Lambda_{\overline{MS}}$.

All the results we have given are subject to correction by the inclusion of higher-order effects in the ChPT expansion. In the case of chiral SU(3), the fourth-order Lagrangian $\hat{\mathcal{L}}_4$ contains 8 terms (Gasser and Leutwyler 1984, 1985). Donoghue *et al.* (1992) give a clear exposition of ChPT to one-loop order.

18.4 Chiral anomalies

In all our discussions of symmetries so far – unbroken, approximate, and spontaneously broken – there is one result on which we have relied, and never queried. We refer to Noether's theorem, as discussed in section 12.3.1. This states that for every continuous symmetry of a Lagrangian, there is a corresponding conserved current. We demonstrated this result in some special cases, but we have now to point out that while it is undoubtedly valid at the level of the *classical* Lagrangian and field equations, we did not investigate whether quantum corrections might violate the classical conservation law. This can, in fact, happen and when it does the afflicted current (or its divergence) is said to be 'anomalous', or to contain an 'anomaly'. General analysis shows that anomalies occur in renormalizable theories of fermions coupled to both vector and axial vector currents. We may therefore expect to find anomalies among the vector and axial vector flavour currents which we have been discussing.

One way of understanding how anomalies arise is through consideration of the renormalization process, which is in general necessary once we get beyond the classical ('tree level') approximation. As we saw in volume 1, this will invariably entail some *regularization* of divergent integrals. But the specific example of the $O(e^2)$ photon self-energy studied in section 11.3 showed that a simple cut-off form of regularization already violated the current conservation (or gauge invariance) condition (11.21). In that case, it was possible to find alternative regularizations which respected electromagnetic current conservation, and were satisfactory. Anomalies arise when *both* axial and vector symmetry currents are present, since it is not possible to find a regularization scheme which preserves both vector and axial vector current conservation (Adler 1970, Jackiw 1972, Adler and Bardeen 1969).

We shall not attempt an extended discussion of this technical subject. But we do want to alert the reader to the existence of these anomalies; to indicate how they arise in one simple model; and to explain why, in some cases, they are to be welcomed, while in others they must be eliminated.

We consider the classic case of $\pi^0 \to \gamma\gamma$, in the context of spontaneously broken chiral flavour symmetry, with massless quarks and pions. The axial isospin current $\hat{j}^\mu_{i,5}(x)$ should then be conserved, but we shall see that this implies that the amplitude for $\pi^0 \to \gamma\gamma$ must vanish, as first pointed out by Veltman (1967) and Sutherland (1967). We begin by writing the matrix element of $\hat{j}^\mu_{3,5}(x)$ between the vacuum and a 2γ state, in momentum space, as

$$\int d^4x e^{-iq\cdot x} \langle \gamma, k_1, \epsilon_1; \gamma, k_2, \epsilon_2 | \hat{j}^\mu_{3,5}(x) | 0 \rangle$$
$$= (2\pi)^4 \delta^4(k_1 + k_2 - q)\epsilon^*_{1\nu}(k_1)\epsilon^*_{2\lambda}(k_2)\mathcal{M}^{\mu\nu\lambda}(k_1, k_2). \quad (18.128)$$

FIGURE 18.4
The amplitude considered in (18.128), and the one pion intermediate state
contribution to it.

As in figure 18.3, one contribution to $\mathcal{M}^{\mu\nu\lambda}$ has the form $(\text{constant}/q^2)$ due to
the massless π^0 propagator, shown in figure 18.4. This is, once again, because
when chiral symmetry is spontaneously broken, the axial current connects the
pion state to the vacuum, as described by the matrix element (18.46). The
contribution of the process shown in figure 18.4 to $\mathcal{M}^{\mu\nu\lambda}$ is then

$$iq^\mu f_\pi \frac{i}{q^2}\, iA\epsilon^{\nu\lambda\alpha\beta} k_{1\alpha} k_{2\beta} \tag{18.129}$$

where the $\pi^0 \to \gamma\gamma$ amplitude is $A\epsilon^{\nu\lambda\alpha\beta}\epsilon^*_{1\nu}(k_1)\epsilon^*_{2\lambda}(k_2)k_{1\alpha}k_{2\beta}$. Note that this
automatically incorporates electromagnetic gauge invariance (the amplitude
vanishes when the polarization vector of either photon is replaced by its 4-
momentum, due to the antisymmetry of the ϵ symbol), and it is symmetrical
under interchange of the photon labels. Now consider replacing $\hat{j}^\mu_{3,5}(x)$ in
(18.128) by $\partial_\mu \hat{j}^\mu_{3,5}(x)$, which should be zero. A partial integration then shows
that this implies that

$$q_\mu \mathcal{M}^{\mu\nu\lambda} = 0 \tag{18.130}$$

which with (18.129) implies that $A = 0$, and hence that $\pi^0 \to \gamma\gamma$ is forbidden.
It is important to realize that all other contributions to $\mathcal{M}^{\mu\nu\lambda}$, apart from
the π^0 one shown in figure 18.4, will *not* have the $1/q^2$ factor in (18.129), and
will therefore give a vanishing contribution to $q_\mu \mathcal{M}^{\mu\nu\lambda}$ at $q^2 = 0$ which is the
on-shell point for the (massless) pion.

It is of course true that $m_\pi^2 \neq 0$. But estimates (Adler 1969) of the conse-
quent corrections suggest that the predicted rate of $\pi^0 \to \gamma\gamma$ for real π^0's is
far too small. Consequently, there is a problem for the hypothesis of spontaneously broken (approximate) chiral symmetry.

In such a situation it is helpful to consider a detailed calculation performed
within a specific model. This is supplied by Itzykson and Zuber (1980), section 11.5.2; in essentials it is the same as the one originally considered by
Steinberger (1949) in the first calculation of the $\pi^0 \to \gamma\gamma$ rate, and subsequently by Bell and Jackiw (1969) and by Adler (1969). It employs (scalar)
σ and (pseudoscalar) π^0 meson fields, augmented by a fermion of mass m

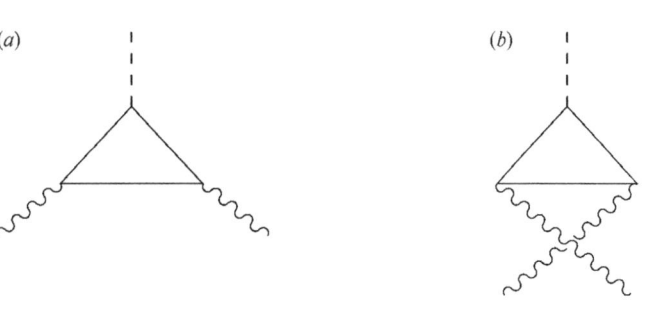

FIGURE 18.5
The two $O(\alpha)$ graphs contributing to $\pi^0 \rightarrow \gamma\gamma$ decay.

and charge $+e$, representing the proton. To order α, there are two graphs to consider, shown in figure 18.5(a) and (b). It turns out that the fermion loop integral is actually convergent. In the limit $q^2 \rightarrow 0$ the result is

$$A = \frac{e^2}{4\pi^2 f_\pi} \tag{18.131}$$

where A is the $\pi^0 \rightarrow \gamma\gamma$ amplitude introduced above. Problem 18.8 evaluates the $\pi^0 \rightarrow \gamma\gamma$ rate using (18.131), to give

$$\Gamma(\pi^0 \rightarrow 2\gamma) = \frac{\alpha^2}{64\pi^3} \frac{m_\pi^3}{f_\pi^2}. \tag{18.132}$$

(18.132) is in very good agreement with experiment.

In principle, various possibilities now exist. But a careful analysis of the 'triangle' graph contributions to the matrix element $\mathcal{M}^{\mu\nu\lambda}$ of (18.128), shown in figure 18.6, reveals that the fault lies in assuming that a regularization exists such that for these amplitudes the conservation equation $q_\mu \langle \gamma\gamma | \hat{j}_{3,5}^\mu(0) | 0 \rangle = 0$ can be maintained, at the same time as electromagnetic gauge variance. In fact, no such regularization can be found. When the amplitudes of figure 18.6 are calculated using an (electromagnetic) gauge invariant procedure, one finds a non-zero result for $q_\mu \langle \gamma\gamma | \hat{j}_{3,5}^\mu(0) | 0 \rangle$ (again the details are given in Itzykson and Zuber (1980)). This implies that $\partial_\mu \hat{j}_{3,5}^\mu(x)$ is not zero after all, the calculation producing the specific value

$$\partial_\mu \hat{j}_{3,5}^\mu(x) = -\frac{e^2}{32\pi^2} \epsilon^{\alpha\nu\beta\lambda} \hat{F}_{\alpha\nu} \hat{F}_{\beta\lambda} \tag{18.133}$$

where the F's are the usual electromagnetic field strengths.

Equation (18.133) means that (18.130) is no longer valid, so that A need no longer vanish: indeed, (18.133) predicts a definite value for A, so we need to see if it is consistent with (18.131). Taking the vacuum $\rightarrow 2\gamma$ matrix element

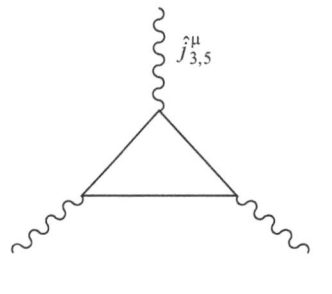

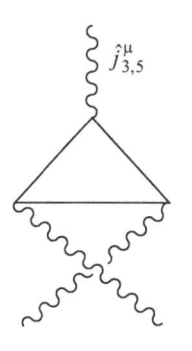

FIGURE 18.6

$O(\alpha)$ contributions to the matrix element in (18.128).

of (18.133) produces (problem 18.9)

$$iq_\mu \mathcal{M}^{\mu\nu\lambda} = \frac{e^2}{4\pi^2} \epsilon^{\alpha\nu\beta\lambda} k_{1\alpha} k_{2\beta} \qquad (18.134)$$

which is indeed consistent with (18.128) and (18.131), after suitably interchanging the labels on the ϵ symbol.

Equation (18.133) is therefore a typical example of 'an anomaly' – the
violation, at the quantum level, of a symmetry of the classical Lagrangian. It
might be thought that the result (18.133) is only valid to order α (though the
$O(\alpha^2)$ correction would presumably be very small). But Adler and Bardeen
(1969) showed that such 'triangle' loops give the *only* anomalous contributions
to the $\hat{\jmath}^\mu_{i,5} - \gamma - \gamma$ vertex, so that (18.133) is true to all orders in α.

The triangles considered above actually used a fermion with integer charge
(the proton). We clearly should use quarks, which carry fractional charge.
In this case, the previous numerical value for A is multiplied by the factor
$\tau_3 Q^2$ for each contributing quark. For the u and d quarks of chiral SU(2) $\times$
SU(2), this gives 1/3. Consequently agreement with experiment is lost unless
there exist three replicas of each quark, identical in their electromagnetic and
SU(2) $\times$ SU(2) properties. Colour supplies just this degeneracy, and thus the
$\pi^0 \to \gamma\gamma$ rate is important evidence for such a degree of freedom, as we noted
in chapter 14.

In the foregoing discussion, the axial isospin current was associated with a
global symmetry; only the electromagnetic currents (in the case of $\pi^0 \to \gamma\gamma$)
were associated with a local (gauged) symmetry, and they remained conserved
(anomaly free). If, however, we have an anomaly in a current associated with
a local symmetry, we will have a serious problem. The whole rather elaborate
construction of a quantum gauge field theory relies on current conservation
equations such as (11.21) or (13.130) to eliminate unwanted gauge degrees
of freedom, and ensure unitarity of the S-matrix. So anomalies in currents

coupled to gauge fields cannot be tolerated. As we shall see in chapter 20, and is already evident from (18.48), axial currents are indeed present in weak interactions and they are coupled to the $W^\pm, Z^0$ gauge fields. Hence, if this theory is to be satisfactory at the quantum level, all anomalies must somehow cancel away. That this is possible rests essentially on the observation that the anomaly (18.133) is independent of the mass of the circulating fermion. Thus cancellations are in principle possible between quark and lepton 'triangles' in the weak interaction case. Bouchiat *et al.* (1972) were the first to point out that, for each generation of quarks and leptons, the anomalies will cancel between quarks and leptons if the fractionally charged quarks come in three colours. The condition that anomalies cancel in the gauged currents of the Standard Model is the remarkably simple one (Ryder 1996, p384):

$$N_c(Q_u + Q_d) + Q_e = 0 \tag{18.135}$$

where N_c is the number of colours and Q_u, Q_d and Q_e are the charges (in units of e) of the 'u', 'd', and 'e' type fields in each generation. Clearly (18.135) is true for each generation of the Standard Model; the condition indicates a remarkable connection, at some deep level, between the facts that quarks come in three colours and have charges which are $1/3$ fractions. The Standard Model provides no explanation for this connection. Anomaly cancellation is a powerful constraint on possible theories ('t Hooft 1980, Weinberg 1996 section 22.4).

Problems

18.1 Verify (18.24)–(18.26).

18.2 Verify (18.28)–(18.30).

18.3 Show that $\mathcal{L}_q$ of (18.12) can be written as (18.39).

18.4 Show that the rate for $\pi^+ \to \mu^+\nu_\mu$, calculated from the lowest-order matrix element (18.52), is given by (18.53).

18.5 Verify the transformation equations (18.76) and (18.77).

18.6

(a) Consider a Lagrangian $\hat{\mathcal{L}}(\hat{\phi}_r, \partial_\mu\hat{\phi}_r)$ where the $\hat{\phi}_r$ could be either bosonic or fermionic fields. Let the fields transform by an infinitesimal local (x-dependent) transformation

$$\hat{\phi}_r \to \hat{\phi}_r - i\epsilon_\alpha(x)T^\alpha_{rs}\hat{\phi}_s \quad \text{(sum on } s\text{)}.$$

Show that the change in $\hat{\mathcal{L}}$ may be written as

$$\delta\hat{\mathcal{L}} = \hat{j}^{\alpha\mu}(x)\partial_\mu\epsilon_\alpha(x) + \epsilon_\alpha(x)\partial_\mu\hat{j}^{\alpha\mu}(x)$$

where

$$\hat{j}^{\alpha\mu}(x) = -\mathrm{i}T^\alpha_{rs}\hat{\phi}_s \frac{\partial\hat{\mathcal{L}}}{\partial(\partial_\mu\hat{\phi}_r)} = \frac{\partial(\delta\hat{\mathcal{L}})}{\partial(\partial_\mu\epsilon_\alpha(x)))}$$

and

$$\partial_\mu\hat{j}^{\alpha\mu}(x) = \frac{\partial(\delta\hat{\mathcal{L}})}{\partial\epsilon_\alpha(x)}. \qquad (1)$$

Deduce that if $\hat{\mathcal{L}}$ is invariant under the global form of this transformation (i.e. constant ϵ_α), then the current defined by (1) is conserved. [This procedure for finding conserved currents for global symmetries is due to Gell-Mann and Levy (1960).]

(b)   Apply the method of part (a) to verify the form of the currents (18.96) and (18.97).

18.7 Verify equations (18.120)–(18.124).

18.8 Verify (18.132), and calculate the π^0 lifetime in seconds.

18.9 Verify (18.134).

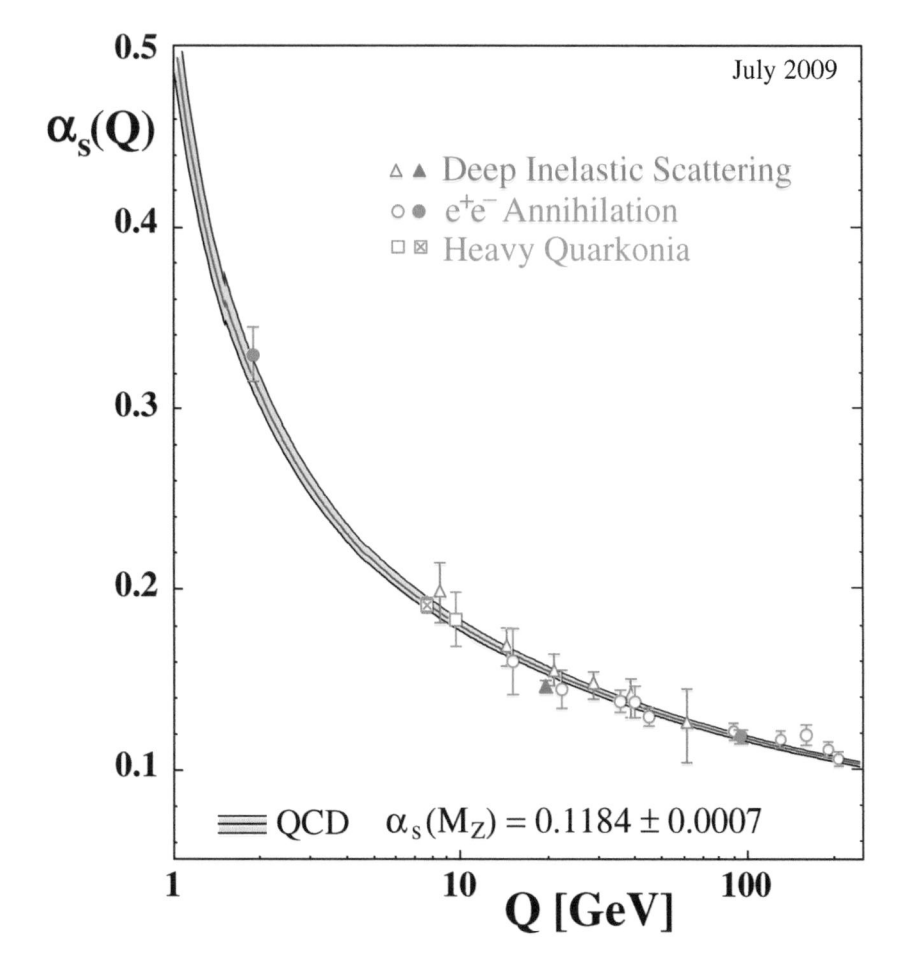

Plate I
Comparison between measurements of α_s and the theoretical prediction, as a function of the energy scale Q (Bethke 2009). (See figure 15.5 on page 129.)

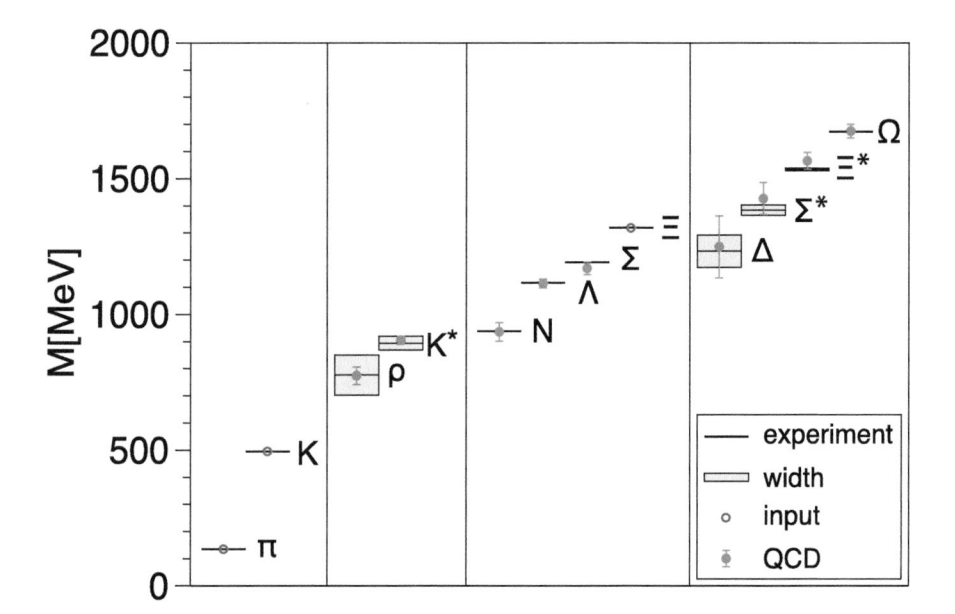

Plate II
The light hadron spectrum of QCD, from Dürr *et al.* (2008). (See figure 16.12 on page 190.)

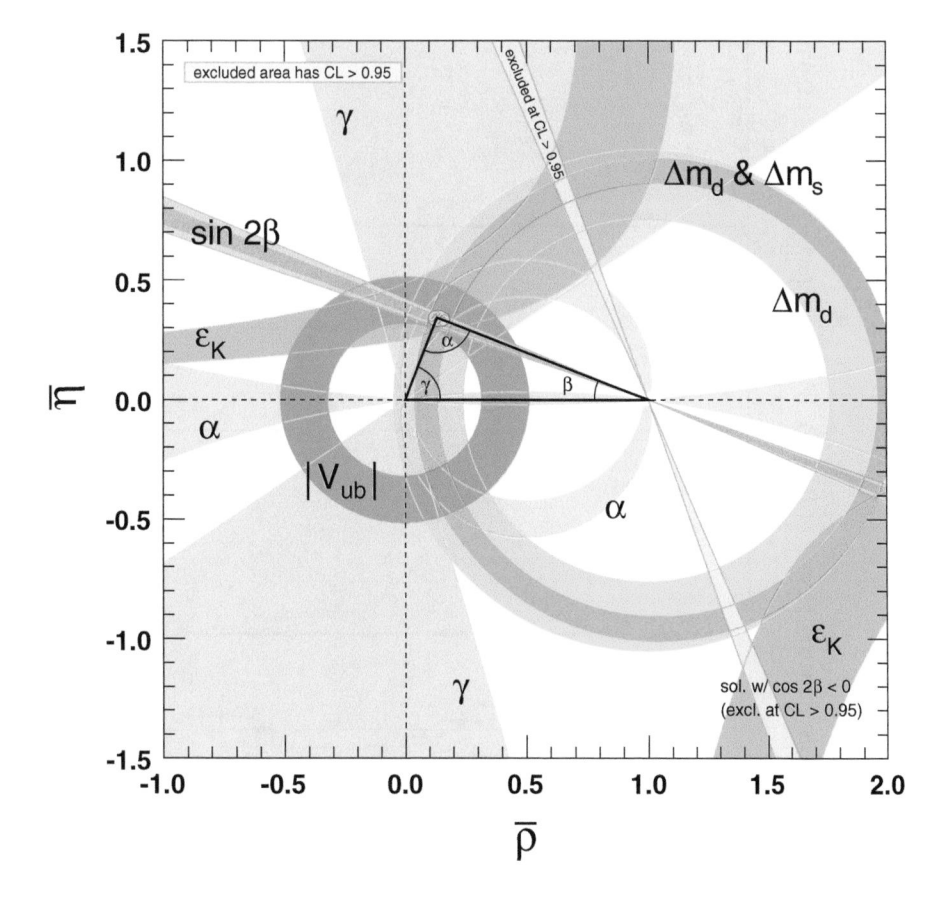

Plate III
Constraints in the $\bar{\rho}, \bar{\eta}$ plane. The shaded areas have 95% CL. [Figure reproduced, courtesy Michael Barnett for the Particle Data Group, from the review of the CKM Quark-Mixing Matrix by A Ceccucci, Z Ligeti and Y Sakai, section 11 in the *Review of Particle Physics*, K Nakamura *et al.* (Partcle Data Group) *Journal of Physics* G **37** (2010) 075021, IOP Publishing Limited.] (See figure 20.11 on page 323.)

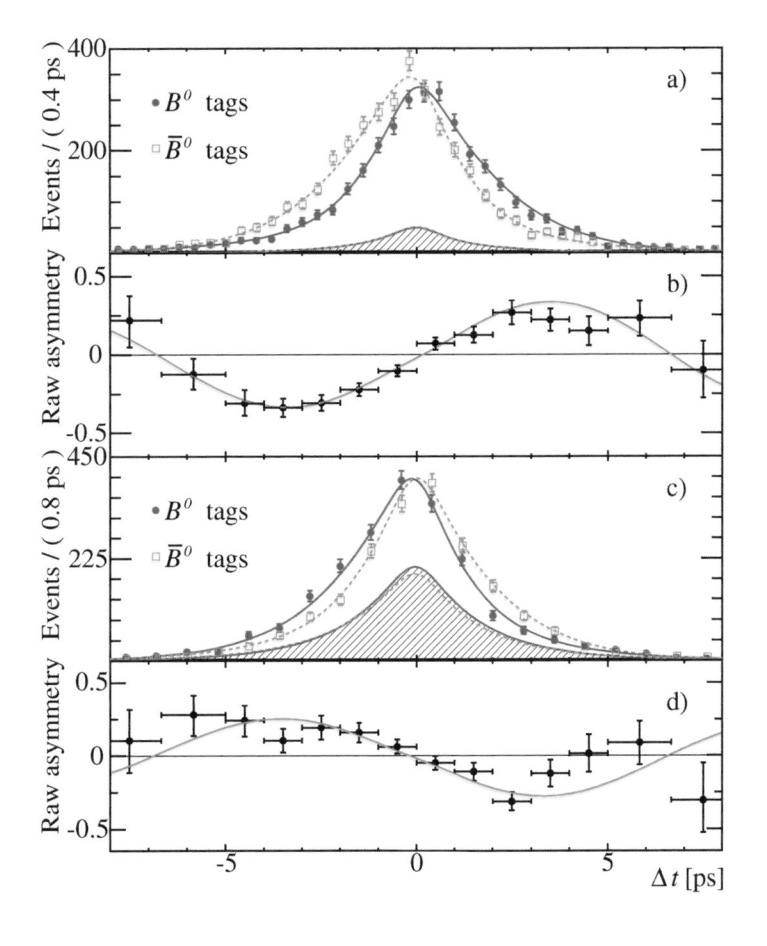

Plate IV
(a) Number of $\eta_f = -1$ candidates in the signal region with a B^0 tag (N_{B^0}) and with a $\bar{B}^0$ tag ($N_{\bar{B}^0}$), and (b) the measured asymmetry $(N_{B^0} - N_{\bar{B}^0})/(N_{B^0} + N_{\bar{B}^0})$, as functions of t; (c) and (d) are the corresponding distributions for the $\eta_f = +1$ candidates. Figure reprinted with permission from Aubert *et al.* (BaBar Collaboration) *Phys. Rev. Lett.* **99** 171803 (2007). Copyright 2007 by the American Physical Society. (See figure 21.7 on page 341.)

19

Spontaneously Broken Local Symmetry

In earlier parts of this book we have briefly indicated why we might want to search for a *gauge* theory of the weak interactions. The reasons include: (i) the goal of unification (e.g. with the U(1) gauge theory QED), as mentioned in section 1.3.5; and (ii) certain 'universality' phenomena (to be discussed more fully in chapter 20), which are reminiscent of a similar situation in QED (see comment (ii) in section 2.6, and also section 11.6), and which are particularly characteristic of a non-Abelian gauge theory, as pointed out in section 13.1 after equation (13.44). However, we also know from section 1.3.5 that weak interactions are short-ranged, so that their mediating quanta must be massive. At first sight, this seems to rule out the possibility of a gauge theory of weak interactions, since a simple gauge boson mass violates gauge invariance, as we pointed out for the photon in section 11.3 and for non-Abelian gauge quanta in section 13.3.1, and will review again in the following section. Nevertheless, there is a way of giving gauge field quanta a mass, which is by '*spontaneously breaking*' the gauge (i.e. local) symmetry. This is the topic of the present chapter. The detailed application to the electroweak theory will be made in chapter 21.

19.1 Massive and massless vector particles

Let us begin by noting an elementary (classical) argument for why a gauge field quantum cannot have mass. The electromagnetic potential satisfies the Maxwell equation (cf (2.22))

$$\Box A^\nu - \partial^\nu(\partial_\mu A^\mu) = j^\nu_{\text{em}} \tag{19.1}$$

which, as discussed in section 2.3, is invariant under the gauge transformation

$$A^\mu \to A'^\mu = A^\mu - \partial^\mu \chi. \tag{19.2}$$

However, if A^μ were to represent a *massive* field, the relevant wave equation would be

$$(\Box + M^2)A^\nu - \partial^\nu(\partial_\mu A^\mu) = j^\nu_{\text{em}}. \tag{19.3}$$

To get this, we have simply replaced the massless 'Klein–Gordon' operator $\Box$ by the corresponding massive one, $\Box + M^2$ (compare sections 3.1 and 5.3).

255

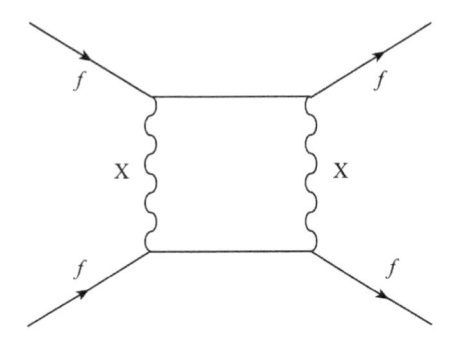

FIGURE 19.1
Fermion–fermion scattering via exchange of two X bosons.

Equation (19.3) is manifestly *not* invariant under (19.2), and it is precisely the mass term $M^2 A^\nu$ that breaks the gauge invariance. The same conclusion follows in a Lagrangian treatment; to obtain (19.3) as the corresponding Euler-Lagrange equation, one adds a mass term $+\frac{1}{2} M^2 A_\mu A^\mu$ to the Lagrangian of (7.66) (see also sections 11.4 and 13.3.1), and this clearly violates invariance under (19.2). Similar reasoning holds for the non-Abelian case too. Perhaps, then, we must settle for a theory involving massive charged vector bosons, $W^\pm$ for example, without it being a gauge theory.

Such a theory is certainly possible, but it will not be *renormalizable*, as we now discuss. Consider figure 19.1, which shows some kind of fermion–fermion scattering (we need not be more specific), proceeding in fourth order of perturbation theory via the exchange of two massive vector bosons, which we will call X-particles. To calculate this amplitude, we need the propagator for the X-particle, which can be found by following the 'heuristic' route outlined in section 7.3.2 for photons. We consider the momentum-space version of (19.3) for the corresponding X^ν field, but without the current on the right-hand side (so as to describe a free field):

$$[(-k^2 + M^2)g^{\nu\mu} + k^\nu k^\mu]\tilde{X}_\mu(k) = 0, \tag{19.4}$$

which should be compared with (7.90). Apart from the '$i\epsilon$', the propagator should be proportional to the inverse of the quantity in the square brackets in (19.4). Problem 19.1 shows that *unlike* the (massless) photon case, this inverse does exist, and is given by

$$\frac{-g^{\mu\nu} + k^\mu k^\nu / M^2}{k^2 - M^2}. \tag{19.5}$$

A proper field-theoretic derivation would yield this result multiplied by an overall factor 'i' as usual, and would also include the '$i\epsilon$' via $k^2 - M^2 \to k^2 - M^2 + i\epsilon$. We remark immediately that (19.5) gives nonsense in the limit

$M \to 0$, thus indicating already that a massless vector particle seems to be a very different kind of thing from a massive one (we can't just take the massless limit of the latter).

Now consider the loop integral in figure 19.1. At each vertex we will have a coupling constant g, associated with an interaction Lagrangian having the general form $g\bar{\psi}\gamma_\mu\hat{\psi}\hat{X}^\mu$ (a $\gamma_\mu\gamma_5$ coupling could also be present but will not affect the argument). Just as in QED, this 'g' is dimensionless but, as we warned the reader in section 11.8, this may not guarantee renormalizability, and indeed this is a case where it does not. To get an idea of why this might be so, consider the leading divergent behaviour of figure 19.1. This will be associated with the $k^\mu k^\nu$ terms in the numerator of (19.5), so that the leading divergence is effectively

$$\sim \int \mathrm{d}^4 k \left(\frac{k^\mu k^\nu}{k^2}\right)\left(\frac{k^\rho k^\sigma}{k^2}\right)\frac{1}{\not{k}}\frac{1}{\not{k}} \tag{19.6}$$

for high k-values (we are not troubling to get all the indices right, we are omitting the spinors altogether, and we are looking only at the large k part of the propagators). Now the first two bracketed terms in (19.6) behave like a constant at large k, so that the divergence is effectively

$$\sim \int \mathrm{d}^4 k \frac{1}{\not{k}}\frac{1}{\not{k}} \tag{19.7}$$

which is quadratically divergent, and indeed exactly what we would get in a 'four-fermion' theory – see (11.98) for example. This strongly suggests that the theory is non-renormalizable.

Where have these dangerous powers of k in the numerator of (19.6) come from? The answer is simple and important. They come from the *longitudinal* polarization state of the massive X-particle, as we shall now explain. The free-particle wave equation is

$$(\Box + M^2)X^\nu - \partial^\nu(\partial_\mu X^\mu) = 0 \tag{19.8}$$

and plane wave solutions have the form

$$X^\nu = \epsilon^\nu e^{-ik\cdot x}. \tag{19.9}$$

Hence the polarization vectors ϵ^ν satisfy the condition

$$(-k^2 + M^2)\epsilon^\nu + k^\nu k_\mu \epsilon^\mu = 0. \tag{19.10}$$

Taking the 'dot' product of (19.10) with k_ν leads to

$$M^2 k \cdot \epsilon = 0, \tag{19.11}$$

which implies (for $M^2 \neq 0$!)

$$k \cdot \epsilon = 0. \tag{19.12}$$

Equation (19.12) is a covariant condition, which has the effect of ensuring that there are just three independent polarization vectors, as we expect for a spin-1 particle. Let us take $k^\mu = (k^0, 0, 0, |\boldsymbol{k}|)$; then the x- and y-directions are 'transverse' while the z-direction is 'longitudinal'. Now, in the rest frame of the X, such that $k_{\text{rest}} = (M, 0, 0, 0)$, (19.12) reduces to $\epsilon^0 = 0$, and we may choose three independent ϵ's as

$$\epsilon^\mu(k_{\text{rest}}, \lambda) = (0, \boldsymbol{\epsilon}(\lambda)) \tag{19.13}$$

with

$$\begin{align}
\boldsymbol{\epsilon}(\lambda = \pm 1) &= \mp 2^{-1/2}(1, \pm i, 0) \tag{19.14} \\
\boldsymbol{\epsilon}(\lambda = 0) &= (0, 0, 1). \tag{19.15}
\end{align}$$

The ϵ's are 'orthonormalized' so that (cf (7.86))

$$\boldsymbol{\epsilon}(\lambda)^* \cdot \boldsymbol{\epsilon}(\lambda') = \delta_{\lambda\lambda'}. \tag{19.16}$$

These states have definite spin projection ($\lambda = \pm 1, 0$) along the z-axis. For the result in a general frame, we can Lorentz transform $\epsilon^\mu(k_{\text{rest}}, \lambda)$ as required. For example, in a frame such that $k^\mu = (k^0, 0, 0, |\boldsymbol{k}|)$, we find

$$\epsilon^\mu(k, \lambda = \pm 1) = \epsilon^\mu(k_{\text{rest}}, \lambda = \pm 1) \tag{19.17}$$

as before, but the longitudinal polarization vector becomes (problem 19.2)

$$\epsilon^\mu(k, \lambda = 0) = M^{-1}(|\boldsymbol{k}|, 0, 0, k^0). \tag{19.18}$$

Note that $k \cdot \epsilon^\mu(k, \lambda = 0) = 0$ as required.

From (19.17) and (19.18) it is straightforward to verify the result (problem 19.3)

$$\sum_{\lambda = 0, \pm 1} \epsilon^\mu(k, \lambda) \epsilon^{\nu *}(k, \lambda) = -g^{\mu\nu} + k^\mu k^\nu / M^2. \tag{19.19}$$

Consider now the propagator for a spin-1/2 particle, given in (7.63):

$$\frac{i(\not k + m)}{k^2 - m^2 + i\epsilon}. \tag{19.20}$$

Equation (7.64) shows that the factor in the numerator of (19.20) arises from the spin sum

$$\sum_s u_\alpha(k, s) \bar{u}_\beta(k, s) = (\not k + m)_{\alpha\beta}. \tag{19.21}$$

In just the same way, the massive spin-1 propagator is given by

$$\frac{i[-g^{\mu\nu} + k^\mu k^\nu / M^2]}{k^2 - M^2 + i\epsilon}, \tag{19.22}$$

the numerator in (19.22) arising from the spin sum (19.19). Thus the dangerous factor $k^\mu k^\nu / M^2$ can be traced to the spin sum (19.19): in particular, at large values of k the longitudinal state $\epsilon^\mu(k, \lambda = 0)$ is proportional to k^μ, and this is the origin of the numerator factors $k^\mu k^\nu / M^2$ in (19.22).

We shall not give further details here (see also section 22.1.2), but merely state that theories with massive charged vector bosons are indeed non-renormalizable. Does this matter? In section 11.8 we explained why it is thought that the relevant theories at presently accessible energy scales should be renormalizable theories. And, apart from anything else, they are much more predictive. Is there, then, any way of getting rid of the offending '$k^\mu k^\nu$' terms in the X-propagator, so as (perhaps) to render the theory renormalizable? Consider the photon propagator of chapter 7 repeated here:

$$\frac{i[-g^{\mu\nu} + (1 - \xi)k^\mu k^\nu / k^2]}{k^2 + i\epsilon}. \tag{19.23}$$

This contains somewhat similar factors of $k^\mu k^\nu$ (admittedly divided by k^2 rather than M^2), but they are gauge-dependent, and can in fact be 'gauged away' entirely, by choice of the gauge parameter ξ (namely by taking $\xi = 1$). But, as we have seen, such 'gauging' – essentially the freedom to make gauge transformations – seems to be possible only in a massless vector theory.

A closely related point is that, as section 7.3.1 showed, free photons exist in only two polarization states (electromagnetic waves are purely transverse), instead of the three we might have expected for a vector (spin-1) particle – and as do indeed exist for massive vector particles. This gives another way of seeing in what way a massless vector particle is really very different from a massive one: the former has only two (spin) degrees of freedom, while the latter has three, and it is not at all clear how to 'lose' the offending longitudinal state smoothly (certainly not, as we have seen, by letting $M \to 0$ in (19.5)).

These considerations therefore suggest the following line of thought: is it possible somehow to create a theory involving massive vector bosons, in such a way that the dangerous $k^\mu k^\nu$ term can be 'gauged away', making the theory renormalizable? The answer is yes, via the idea of *spontaneous breaking* of gauge symmetry. This is the natural generalization of the spontaneous global symmetry breaking considered in chapter 17. By way of advance notice, the crucial formula is (19.74) for the propagator in such a theory, which is to be compared with (19.22).

The first serious challenge to the then widely held view that electromagnetic gauge invariance requires the photon to be massless was made by Schwinger (1962), as we pointed out in section 11.4. Soon afterwards, Anderson (1963) argued that several situations in solid state physics could be interpreted in terms of an effectively massive electromagnetic field. He outlined a general framework for treating the phenomenon of the acquisition of mass by a gauge boson, and discussed its possible relevance to contemporary attempts (Sakurai 1960) to interpret the recently discovered vector mesons ($\rho, \omega, \phi \ldots$) as the gauge quanta associated with a local extension of hadronic flavour sym-

metry. From his discussion, it is clear that Anderson had his doubts about the hadronic application, precisely because, as he remarked, gauge bosons can only acquire a mass if the symmetry is spontaneously broken. This has the consequence, as we saw in chapter 17, that the multiplet structure ordinarily associated with a non-Abelian symmetry would be lost. But we know that flavour symmetry, even if admittedly not exact, certainly leads to identifiable multiplets, which are at least approximately degenerate in mass. It was Weinberg (1967) and Salam (1968) who made the correct application of these ideas, to the generation of mass for the gauge quanta associated with the weak force. There is, however, nothing specifically relativistic about the basic mechanism involved, nor need we start with the non-Abelian case. In fact, the physics is well illustrated by the non-relativistic Abelian (i.e. electromagnetic) case – which is nothing but the physics of superconductivity. Our presentation is influenced by that of Anderson (1963).

19.2 The generation of 'photon mass' in a superconductor: Ginzburg–Landau theory and the Meissner effect

In chapter 17, section 17.7, we gave a brief introduction to some aspects of the BCS theory of superconductivity. We were concerned mainly with the nature of the BCS ground state, and with the non-perturbative origin of the energy gap for elementary excitations. In particular, as noted after (17.128), we omitted completely all electromagnetic couplings of the electrons in the 'microscopic' Hamiltonian. It is certainly possible to complete the BCS theory in this way, so as to include within the same formalism a treatment of electromagnetic effects (e.g. the Meissner effect) in a superconductor. We refer interested readers to the book by Schrieffer (1964), chapter 8. Instead, we shall follow a less 'microscopic' and somewhat more 'phenomenological' approach, which has a long history in theoretical studies of superconductivity, and is in some ways actually closer (at least formally) to our eventual application in particle physics.

In section 17.3.1 we introduced the concept of an 'order parameter', a quantity which was a measure of the 'degree of ordering' of a system below some transition temperature. In the case of superconductivity, the order parameter (in this sense) is taken to be a complex scalar field ψ, as originally proposed by Ginzburg and Landau (1950), well before the appearance of BCS theory. Subsequently, Gorkov (1959) and others showed how the Ginzburg–Landau description could be derived from BCS theory, in certain domains of temperature and magnetic field. This work all relates to static phenomena. More recently, an analogous 'effective theory' for time-dependent phenomena

(at zero temperature) has been derived from a BCS-type model (Aitchison *et al.* 1995). For the moment, we shall follow a more qualitative approach.

The Ginzburg–Landau field ψ is commonly referred to as the 'macroscopic wave function'. This terminology originates from the recognition that in the BCS ground state a macroscopic number of Cooper pairs have 'condensed' into the state of lowest energy, a situation similar to that in the Bogoliubov superfluid. Further, this state is highly *coherent*, all pairs having the same total momentum (namely zero, in the case of (17.140)). These considerations suggest that a successful phenomenology can be built by invoking the idea of a macroscopic wavefunction ψ, describing the condensate. Note that ψ is a 'bosonic' quantity, referring essentially to *paired* electrons. Perhaps the single most important property of ψ is that it is assumed to be normalized to the total density of Cooper pairs n_c via the relation

$$|\psi|^2 = n_c = n_s/2 \tag{19.24}$$

where n_s is the density of superconducting electrons. The quantities n_c and n_s will depend on temperature T, tending to zero as T approaches the superconducting transition temperature T_c from below. The precise connection between ψ and the microscopic theory is indirect; in particular, ψ has no knowledge of the coordinates of individual electron pairs. Nevertheless, as an 'empirical' order parameter, it may be thought of as in some way related to the ground state 'pair' expectation value introduced in (17.121): in particular, the charge associated with ψ is taken to be $-2e$, and the mass is $2m_e$.

The Ginzburg–Landau description proceeds by considering the quantum-mechanical electromagnetic current associated with ψ, in the presence of a static external electromagnetic field described by a vector potential $\boldsymbol{A}$. This current was considered in section 2.4, and is given by the gauge-invariant form of (A.7), namely

$$\boldsymbol{j}_{\text{em}} = \frac{-2e}{4m_e \mathrm{i}} [\psi^*(\boldsymbol{\nabla} + 2\mathrm{i}e\boldsymbol{A})\psi - \{(\boldsymbol{\nabla} + 2\mathrm{i}e\boldsymbol{A})\psi\}^*\psi]. \tag{19.25}$$

Note that we have supplied an overall factor of $-2e$ to turn the Schrödinger 'number density' current into the appropriate electromagnetic current. Assuming now that, consistently with (19.24), ψ is varying primarily through its *phase* degree of freedom ϕ, rather than its modulus $|\psi|$, we can rewrite (19.25) as

$$\boldsymbol{j}_{\text{em}} = -\frac{2e^2}{m_e}\left(\boldsymbol{A} + \frac{1}{2e}\boldsymbol{\nabla}\phi\right)|\psi|^2 \tag{19.26}$$

where $\psi = \mathrm{e}^{\mathrm{i}\phi}|\psi|$. We easily verify that (19.26) is invariant under the gauge transformation (2.41), which can be written in this case as

$$\boldsymbol{A} \;\to\; \boldsymbol{A} + \boldsymbol{\nabla}\chi \tag{19.27}$$
$$\phi \;\to\; \phi - 2e\chi. \tag{19.28}$$

We now replace $|\psi|^2$ in (19.26) by $n_s/2$ in accordance with (19.24), and take the curl of the resulting equation to obtain

$$\boldsymbol{\nabla} \times \boldsymbol{j}_{\mathrm{em}} = -\left(\frac{e^2 n_s}{m_e}\right)\boldsymbol{B}. \qquad (19.29)$$

Equation (19.29) is known as the London equation (London 1950), and is one of the fundamental phenomenological relations in superconductivity.

The significance of (19.29) emerges when we combine it with the (static) Maxwell equation

$$\boldsymbol{\nabla} \times \boldsymbol{B} = \boldsymbol{j}_{\mathrm{em}}. \qquad (19.30)$$

Taking the curl of (19.30), and using $\boldsymbol{\nabla} \times (\boldsymbol{\nabla} \times \boldsymbol{B}) = \boldsymbol{\nabla}(\boldsymbol{\nabla} \cdot \boldsymbol{B}) - \boldsymbol{\nabla}^2 \boldsymbol{B}$ and $\boldsymbol{\nabla} \cdot \boldsymbol{B} = 0$, we find

$$\boldsymbol{\nabla}^2 \boldsymbol{B} = \left(\frac{e^2 n_s}{m_e}\right)\boldsymbol{B}. \qquad (19.31)$$

The variation of magnetic field described by (19.31) is a very characteristic one encountered in a number of contexts in condensed matter physics. First, we note that the quantity $(e^2 n_s/m_e)$ must – in our units – have the dimensions of (length)$^{-2}$, by comparison with the left-hand side of (19.31). Let us write

$$\left(\frac{e^2 n_s}{m_e}\right) = \frac{1}{\lambda^2}. \qquad (19.32)$$

Next, consider for simplicity one-dimensional variation

$$\frac{\mathrm{d}^2 \boldsymbol{B}}{\mathrm{d}x^2} = \frac{1}{\lambda^2}\boldsymbol{B} \qquad (19.33)$$

in the half-plane $x \geq 0$, say. Then the solutions of (19.33) have the form

$$\boldsymbol{B}(x) = \boldsymbol{B}_0 \exp -(x/\lambda); \qquad (19.34)$$

the exponentially growing solution is rejected as unphysical. The field therefore penetrates only a distance of order λ into the region $x \geq 0$. The range parameter λ is called the *screening length*. This expresses the fact that, in a medium such that (19.29) holds, the magnetic field will be 'screened out' from penetrating further into the medium.

The physical origin of the screening is provided by Lenz's law: when a magnetic field is applied to a system of charged particles, induced EMFs are set up which accelerate the particles, and the magnetic effect of the resulting currents tends to cancel (or screen) the applied field. On the atomic scale this is the cause of atomic diamagnetism. Here the effect is occurring on a macroscopic scale (as mediated by the 'macroscopic wavefunction' ψ), and leads to the Meissner effect – the exclusion of flux from the interior of a superconductor. In this case, screening currents are set up within the superconductor, over distances of order λ from the exterior boundary of the material. These

exactly cancel – perfectly screen – the applied flux density in the interior. With $n_{\rm s} \sim 4 \times 10^{28}$ m^{-3} (roughly one conduction electron per atom) we find

$$\lambda = \left(\frac{m_{\rm e}}{n_{\rm s}e^2}\right)^{1/2} \approx 10^{-8} \text{ m}, \tag{19.35}$$

which is the correct order of magnitude for the thickness of the surface layer within which screening currents flow, and over which the applied field falls to zero. As $T \to T_{\rm c}$, $n_{\rm s} \to 0$ and λ becomes arbitrarily large, so that flux is no longer screened.

It is quite simple to interpret equation (19.31) in terms of an 'effective non-zero photon mass'. Consider the equation (19.8) for a free massive vector field. Taking the divergence via ∂_ν leads to

$$M^2 \partial_\nu X^\nu = 0 \tag{19.36}$$

(cf (19.11)), and so (19.8) can be written as

$$(\Box + M^2)X^\nu = 0, \tag{19.37}$$

which simply expresses the fact that each component of X^ν has mass M. Now consider the static version of (19.37), in the rest frame of the X-particle in which (see equation (19.13)) the $\nu = 0$ component vanishes. Equation (19.37) reduces to

$$\boldsymbol{\nabla}^2 \boldsymbol{X} = M^2 \boldsymbol{X} \tag{19.38}$$

which is exactly the same in form as (19.31) (if $\boldsymbol{X}$ were the electromagnetic field $\boldsymbol{A}$, we could take the curl of (19.38) to obtain (19.31) via $\boldsymbol{B} = \boldsymbol{\nabla} \times \boldsymbol{A}$). The connection is made precise by making the association

$$M^2 = \left(\frac{e^2 n_{\rm s}}{m_{\rm e}}\right) = \frac{1}{\lambda^2}. \tag{19.39}$$

Equation (19.39) shows very directly another way of understanding the 'screening length $\leftrightarrow$ photon mass' connection: in our units $\hbar = c = 1$, a mass has the dimension of an inverse length, and so we naturally expect to be able to interpret λ^{-1} as an equivalent mass (for the photon, in this case).

The above treatment conveys much of the essential physics behind the phenomenon of 'photon mass generation' in a superconductor. In particular, it suggests rather strongly that a *second* field, in addition to the electromagnetic one, is an essential element in the story (here, it is the ψ field). This provides a partial answer to the puzzle about the discontinuous change in the number of spin degrees of freedom in going from a massless to a massive gauge field: actually, some other field has to be supplied. Nevertheless, many questions remain unanswered so far. For example, how is all the foregoing related to what we learned in chapter 17 about spontaneous symmetry breaking? Where is the Goldstone mode? Is it really all gauge invariant? And

what about Lorentz invariance? Can we provide a Lagrangian description of the phenomenon? The answers to these questions are mostly contained in the model to which we now turn, which is due to Higgs (1964) and is essentially the *local* version of the U(1) Goldstone model of section 17.5.

19.3   Spontaneously broken local U(1) symmetry: the Abelian Higgs model

This model is just $\hat{\mathcal{L}}_G$ of (17.69) and (17.77), extended so as to be locally, rather than merely globally, U(1) invariant. Due originally to Higgs (1964), it provides a deservedly famous and beautifully simple model for investigating what happens when a *gauge* symmetry is spontaneously broken.

To make (17.69) locally U(1) invariant, we need only replace the ∂'s by $\hat{D}$'s according to the rule (7.123), and add the Maxwell piece. This produces

$$\hat{\mathcal{L}}_H = [(\partial^\mu + iq\hat{A}^\mu)\hat{\phi}]^\dagger [(\partial_\mu + iq\hat{A}_\mu)\hat{\phi}] - \frac{1}{4}\hat{F}_{\mu\nu}\hat{F}^{\mu\nu} - \frac{1}{4}\lambda(\hat{\phi}^\dagger\hat{\phi})^2 + \mu^2(\hat{\phi}^\dagger\hat{\phi}). \quad (19.40)$$

(19.40) is invariant under the local version of (17.72), namely

$$\hat{\phi}(x) \to \hat{\phi}'(x) = e^{-i\hat{\alpha}(x)}\hat{\phi}(x) \quad (19.41)$$

when accompanied by the gauge transformation on the potentials

$$\hat{A}^\mu(x) \to \hat{A}'^\mu(x) = \hat{A}^\mu(x) + \frac{1}{q}\partial^\mu\hat{\alpha}(x). \quad (19.42)$$

Before proceeding any further, we note at once that this model contains four field degrees of freedom – two in the complex scalar Higgs field $\hat{\phi}$, and two in the massless gauge field $\hat{A}^\mu$.

We learned in section 17.5 that the form of the potential terms in (19.40) (specifically the μ^2 one) does not lend itself to a natural particle interpretation, which only appears after making a 'shift to the classical minimum', as in (17.84). But there is a remarkable difference between the global and local cases. In the present (local) case, the phase of $\hat{\phi}$ is completely arbitrary, since any change in $\hat{\alpha}$ of (19.41) can be compensated by an appropriate transformation (19.42) on $\hat{A}^\mu$, leaving $\hat{\mathcal{L}}_H$ the same as before. Thus the field $\hat{\theta}$ in (17.84) can be 'gauged away' altogether, if we choose! But $\hat{\theta}$ was precisely the Goldstone field, in the global case. This must mean that there is somehow no longer any physical manifestation of the massless mode. This is the first unexpected result in the local case. We may also be reminded of our desire to 'gauge away' the longitudinal polarization states for a 'massive gauge' boson: we shall return to this later.

However, a degree of freedom (the Goldstone mode) cannot simply disappear. Somehow the system must keep track of the fact that we started with four degrees of freedom. To see what is going on, let us study the field equation for $\hat{A}^\nu$, namely

$$\Box \hat{A}^\nu - \partial^\nu(\partial_\mu \hat{A}^\mu) = \hat{j}^\nu_{em}, \tag{19.43}$$

where $\hat{j}^\nu_{em}$ is the electromagnetic current contained in (19.40). This current can be obtained just as in (7.141), and is given by

$$\hat{j}^\nu_{em} = iq(\hat{\phi}^\dagger \partial^\nu \hat{\phi} - (\partial^\nu \hat{\phi}^\dagger)\hat{\phi}) - 2q^2 \hat{A}^\nu \hat{\phi}^\dagger \hat{\phi}. \tag{19.44}$$

We now insert the field parametrization (cf (17.84))

$$\hat{\phi}(x) = \frac{1}{\sqrt{2}}(v + \hat{h}(x)) \exp(-i\hat{\theta}(x)/v) \tag{19.45}$$

into (19.44) where $v/\sqrt{2} = 2^{1/2}|\mu|/\lambda^{\frac{1}{2}}$ is the position of the minimum of the classical potential as a function of $|\phi|$, as in (17.81). We obtain (problem 19.4)

$$\hat{j}^\nu_{em} = -v^2 q^2 \left(\hat{A}^\nu - \frac{\partial^\nu \hat{\theta}}{vq} \right) + \text{terms quadratic and cubic in the fields.} \tag{19.46}$$

The linear part of the right-hand side of (19.46) is directly analogous to the non-relativistic current (19.26), interpreting $\hat{\theta}$ as essentially playing the role of ϕ, and $|\psi|^2$ the role of v^2. Retaining just the linear terms in (19.46) (the others would appear on the right-hand side of equation (19.47) following, where they would represent interactions), and placing this $\hat{j}^\nu_{em}$ in (19.43), we obtain

$$\Box \hat{A}^\nu - \partial^\nu \partial_\mu \hat{A}^\mu = -v^2 q^2 \left(\hat{A}^\nu - \frac{\partial^\nu \hat{\theta}}{vq} \right). \tag{19.47}$$

Now a gauge transformation on $\hat{A}^\nu$ has the form shown in (19.42), for arbitrary $\hat{\alpha}$. So we can certainly regard the whole expression $(\hat{A}^\nu - \partial^\nu \hat{\theta}/vq)$ as a perfectly acceptable gauge field. Let us define

$$\hat{A}'^\nu = \hat{A}^\nu - \frac{\partial^\nu \hat{\theta}}{vq}. \tag{19.48}$$

Then, since we know that the left-hand side of (19.47) is invariant under (19.42), the resulting equation for $\hat{A}'^\nu$ is

$$\Box \hat{A}'^\nu - \partial^\nu \partial_\mu \hat{A}'^\mu = -v^2 q^2 \hat{A}'^\nu, \tag{19.49}$$

or

$$(\Box + v^2 q^2)\hat{A}'^\nu - \partial^\nu \partial_\mu \hat{A}'^\mu = 0. \tag{19.50}$$

But (19.50) is nothing but the equation (19.8) for a free massive vector field, with mass $M = vq$! This fundamental observation was first made, in the relativistic context, by Englert and Brout (1964), Higgs (1964), and Guralnik *et al.* (1964); for a full account, see Higgs (1966).

The foregoing analysis shows us two things. First, the current (19.46) is indeed a relativistic analogue of (19.26), in that it provides a 'screening' (mass generation) effect on the gauge field. Second, equation (19.48) shows how the *phase* degree of freedom of the Higgs field $\hat{\phi}$ has been incorporated into a new gauge field $\hat{A}'^{\nu}$, which is massive, and therefore has '*three*' spin degrees of freedom. In fact, we can go further. If we imagine plane wave solutions for $\hat{A}'^{\nu}, \hat{A}^{\nu}$ and $\hat{\theta}$, we see that the $\partial^{\nu}\hat{\theta}/vq$ part of (19.48) will contribute something proportional to k^{ν}/M to the polarization vector of $\hat{A}'^{\nu}$ (recall $M = vq$). But this is exactly the (large k) behaviour of the longitudinal polarization vector of a massive vector particle. We may therefore say that the massless gauge field $\hat{A}^{\nu}$ has 'swallowed' the Goldstone field $\hat{\theta}$ via (19.48) to make the massive vector field $\hat{A}'^{\nu}$. The Goldstone field disappears as a massless degree of freedom, and reappears, via its gradient, as the longitudinal part of the massive vector field. In this way the four degrees of freedom are all now safely accounted for: three are in the massive vector field $\hat{A}'^{\nu}$, and one is in the real scalar field $\hat{h}$ (to which we shall return shortly).

In this (relativistic) case, we know from Lorentz covariance that all the components (transverse and longitudinal) of the vector field must have the same mass, and this has of course emerged automatically from our covariant treatment. But the transverse and longitudinal degrees of freedom respond differently in the non-relativistic (superconductor) case. There, the longitudinal part of $\boldsymbol{A}$ couples strongly to longitudinal excitations of the electrons: primarily, as Bardeen (1957) first recognized, to the collective density fluctuation mode of the electron system – that is, to plasma oscillations. This is a high frequency mode, and is essentially the one discussed in section 17.3.2, after equation (17.46). When this aspect of the dynamics of the electrons is included, a fully gauge invariant description of the electromagnetic properties of superconductors, within the BCS theory, is obtained (Schreiffer 1964, chapter 8).

We return to equations (19.48)–(19.50). Taking the divergence of (19.50) leads, as we have seen, to the condition

$$\partial_{\mu}\hat{A}'^{\mu} = 0 \qquad (19.51)$$

on $\hat{A}'^{\mu}$. It follows that in order to interpret the relation (19.48) as a gauge transformation on $\hat{A}^{\nu}$ we must, to be consistent with (19.51), regard $\hat{A}^{\mu}$ as being in a gauge specified by

$$\partial_{\mu}\hat{A}^{\mu} = \frac{1}{vq}\Box\hat{\theta} = \frac{1}{M}\Box\hat{\theta}. \qquad (19.52)$$

In going from the situation described by $\hat{A}^{\mu}$ and $\hat{\theta}$ to one described by $\hat{A}'^{\mu}$

alone via (19.48), we have evidently chosen a gauge function (cf (19.42))

$$\hat{\alpha}(x) = -\hat{\theta}(x)/v. \tag{19.53}$$

Recalling then the form of the associated local phase change on $\hat{\phi}(x)$

$$\hat{\phi}(x) \to \hat{\phi}'(x) = \mathrm{e}^{-\mathrm{i}\hat{\alpha}(x)}\hat{\phi}(x) \tag{19.54}$$

we see that the phase of $\hat{\phi}$ in (19.45) has been reduced to zero, in this choice of gauge. Thus it is indeed possible to 'gauge $\hat{\theta}$ away' in (19.45), but then the vector field we must use is $\hat{A}'^{\mu}$, satisfying the massive equation (19.50) (ignoring other interactions). In superconductivity, the choice of gauge which takes the macroscopic wavefunction to be real (i.e. $\phi = 0$ in (19.26)) is called the 'London gauge'. In the next section we shall discuss a subtlety in the argument which applies in the case of real superconductors, and which leads to the phenomenon of flux quantization.

The fact that this 'Higgs mechanism' leads to a massive vector field can be seen very economically by working in the particular gauge for which $\hat{\phi}$ is real, and inserting the parametrization (cf (19.45))

$$\hat{\phi} = \frac{1}{\sqrt{2}}(v + \hat{h}) \tag{19.55}$$

into the Lagrangian $\hat{\mathcal{L}}_{\mathrm{H}}$. Retaining only the terms quadratic in the fields one finds (problem 19.5)

$$
\begin{aligned}
\hat{\mathcal{L}}_{\mathrm{H}}^{\mathrm{quad}} &= -\frac{1}{4}(\partial_{\mu}\hat{A}_{\nu} - \partial_{\nu}\hat{A}_{\mu})(\partial^{\mu}\hat{A}^{\nu} - \partial^{\nu}\hat{A}^{\mu}) + \frac{1}{2}q^2 v^2 \hat{A}_{\mu}\hat{A}^{\mu} \\
&\quad + \frac{1}{2}\partial_{\mu}\hat{h}\partial^{\mu}\hat{h} - \mu^2\hat{h}^2.
\end{aligned}
\tag{19.56}
$$

The first line of (19.56) is exactly the Lagrangian for a spin-1 field of mass vq – i.e. the Maxwell part with the addition of a mass term (note that the sign of the mass term is correct for the spatial (physical) degrees of freedom); the second line is the Lagrangian of a scalar particle of mass $\sqrt{2}\mu$. The latter is the mass of excitations of the Higgs field $\hat{h}$ away from its vacuum value (compare the global U(1) case discussed in section 17.5). The necessity for the existence of one or more massive *scalar* particles ('Higgs bosons'), when a gauge symmetry is spontaneously broken in this way, was pointed out by Higgs (1964).

We may now ask: what happens if we start with a certain phase $\hat{\theta}$ for $\hat{\phi}$ but do *not* make use of the gauge freedom in $\hat{A}^{\nu}$ to reduce $\hat{\theta}$ to zero? We shall see in section 19.5 that the equation of motion, and hence the propagator, for the vector particle *depends on the choice of gauge*; furthermore, Feynman graphs involving quanta corresponding to the degree of freedom associated with the phase field $\hat{\theta}$ will have to be included for a consistent theory, even though this must be an unphysical degree of freedom, as follows from the fact

that a gauge can be chosen in which this field vanishes. That the propagator is gauge dependent should, on reflection, come as a relief. After all, if the massive vector boson generated in this way were *simply* described by the wave equation (19.50), all the troubles with massive vector particles outlined in section 19.1 would be completely unresolved. As we shall see, a different choice of gauge from that which renders $\hat{\phi}$ real has precisely the effect of ameliorating the bad high-energy behaviour associated with (19.50). This is ultimately the reason for the following wonderful fact: *massive vector theories, in which the vector particles acquire mass through the spontaneous symmetry breaking mechanism, are renormalizable* ('t Hooft 1971b).

However, before discussing other gauges than the one in which $\hat{\phi}$ is given by (19.55), we first explore another interesting aspect of superconductivity.

19.4   Flux quantization in a superconductor

Though a slight diversion, it is convenient to include a discussion of flux quantization at this point, while we have a number of relevant results assembled. Apart from its intrinsic interest, the phenomenon may also provide a useful physical model for the 'confining' property of QCD, as already discussed in sections 1.3.6 and 16.5.3.

Our discussion of superconductivity so far has dealt, in fact, with only one class of superconductors, called type I; these remain superconducting throughout the bulk of the material (exhibiting a complete Meissner effect), when an external magnetic field of less than a certain critical value is applied. There is a quite separate class – type II superconductors – which allow partial entry of the external field, in the form of thin filaments of flux. Within each filament the field is high, and the material is not superconducting. Outside the core of the filaments, the material is superconducting and the field dies off over the characteristic penetration length λ. Around each filament of magnetic flux there circulates a vortex of screening current; the filaments are often called vortex lines. It is as if numerous thin cylinders, each enclosing flux, had been drilled in a block of type I material, thereby producing a non-simply connected geometry.

In real superconductors, screening currents are associated with the macroscopic pair wavefunction (field) ψ. For type II behaviour to be possible, $|\psi|$ must vanish at the centre of a flux filament, and rise to the constant value appropriate to the superconducting state over a distance $\xi < \lambda$, where ξ is the 'coherence length' of section 17.7. According to the Ginzburg–Landau (GL) theory, a more precise criterion is that type II behaviour holds if $\xi < 2^{1/2}\lambda$; both ξ and λ are, of course, temperature-dependent. The behaviour of $|\psi|$ and B in the vicinity of a flux filament is shown in figure 19.2. Thus, whereas for simple type I superconductivity, $|\psi|$ is simply set equal to a constant, in the

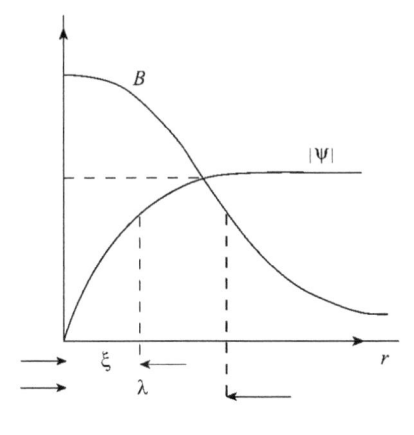

FIGURE 19.2
Magnetic field B and modulus of the macroscopic (pair) wavefunction $|\psi|$ in the neighbourhood of a flux filament.

type II case $|\psi|$ has the variation shown in this figure. Solutions of the coupled GL equations for A and ψ can be obtained which exhibit this behaviour.

An important result is that the flux through a vortex line is quantized. To see this, we write

$$\psi = e^{i\phi}|\psi| \tag{19.57}$$

as before. The expression for the electromagnetic current is

$$\boldsymbol{j}_{\mathrm{em}} = -\frac{q^2}{m}\left(\boldsymbol{A} - \frac{\boldsymbol{\nabla}\phi}{q}\right)|\psi|^2 \tag{19.58}$$

as in (19.26), but in (19.58) we are leaving the charge parameter q undetermined for the moment; the mass parameter m will be unimportant. Rearranging, we have

$$\boldsymbol{A} = -\frac{m}{q^2|\psi|^2}\boldsymbol{j}_{\mathrm{em}} + \frac{\boldsymbol{\nabla}\phi}{q}. \tag{19.59}$$

Let us integrate equation (19.59) around any closed loop $\mathcal{C}$ in the type II superconductor, which encloses a flux (or vortex) line. Far enough away from the vortex, the screening currents $\boldsymbol{j}_{\mathrm{em}}$ will have dropped to zero, and hence

$$\oint_{\mathcal{C}} \boldsymbol{A} \cdot \mathrm{d}\boldsymbol{s} = \frac{1}{q}\oint_{\mathcal{C}} \boldsymbol{\nabla}\phi \cdot \mathrm{d}\boldsymbol{s} = \frac{1}{q}[\phi]_{\mathcal{C}} \tag{19.60}$$

where $[\phi]_{\mathcal{C}}$ is the change in phase around $\mathcal{C}$. If the wavefunction ψ is single-valued, the change in phase $[\phi]_{\mathcal{C}}$ for any closed path can only be zero or an integer multiple of 2π. Transforming the left-hand side of (19.60) by Stokes' Theorem, we obtain the result that the flux Φ through any surface spanning

$\mathcal{C}$ is quantized:

$$\Phi = \int \boldsymbol{B} \cdot \mathrm{d}\boldsymbol{S} = \frac{2\pi n}{q} = n\Phi_0 \qquad (19.61)$$

where $\Phi_0 = 2\pi/q$ is the flux equation (or $2\pi\hbar/q$ in ordinary units). It is not entirely self-evident why ψ should be single-valued, but experiments do indeed demonstrate the phenomenon of flux quantization, in units of Φ_0 with $|q| = 2e$ (which may be interpreted as the charge on a Cooper pair, as usual). The phenomenon is seen in non-simply connected specimens of type I superconductors (i.e. ones with holes in them, such as a ring), and in the flux filaments of type II materials; in the latter case each filament carries a single flux quantum Φ_0.

It is interesting to consider now a situation – so far entirely hypothetical – in which a magnetic monopole is placed in a superconductor. Dirac showed (1931) that for consistency with quantum mechanics the monopole strength g_m had to satisfy the 'Dirac quantization conduction'

$$qg_\mathrm{m} = n/2 \qquad (19.62)$$

where q is any electronic charge, and n is an integer. It follows from (19.62) that the flux $4\pi g_\mathrm{m}$ out of any closed surface surrounding the monopole is quantized in units of Φ_0. Hence a flux filament in a superconductor can originate from, or be terminated by, a Dirac monopole (with the appropriate sign of g_m), as was first pointed out by Nambu (1974).

This is the basic model which, in one way or another, underlies many theoretical attempts to understand confinement. The monopole–antimonopole pair in a type II superconducting vacuum, joined by a quantized magnetic flux filament, provides a model of a meson. As the distance between the pair – the length of the filament – increases, so does the energy of the filament, at a rate proportional to its length, since the flux cannot spread out in directions transverse to the filament. This is exactly the kind of linearly rising potential energy required by hadron spectroscopy (see equations (1.33) and (16.145)). The configuration is stable, because there is no way for the flux to leak away; it is a conserved quantized quantity.

For the eventual application to QCD, one will want (presumably) particles carrying non-zero values of the colour quantum numbers to be confined. These quantum numbers are the analogues of electric charge in the $U(1)$ case, rather than of magnetic charge. We imagine, therefore, interchanging the roles of magnetism and electricity in all of the foregoing. Indeed, the Maxwell equations have such a symmetry when monopoles are present, as well as charges. The essential feature of the superconducting ground state was that it involved the coherent state formed by condensation of electrically charged bosonic fermion pairs. A vacuum which confined filaments of $\boldsymbol{E}$ rather than $\boldsymbol{B}$ may be formed as a coherent state of condensed magnetic monopoles (Mandelstam 1976, 't Hooft 1976). These $\boldsymbol{E}$ filaments would then terminate on electric charges. Now magnetic monopoles do not occur naturally as solutions of QED: they would have to be introduced by hand. Remarkably enough,

however, solutions of the magnetic monopole type do occur in the case of non-Abelian gauge field theories, whose symmetry is spontaneously broken to an electromagnetic $U(1)_{em}$ gauge group. Just this circumstance can arise in a grand unified theory which contains $SU(3)_c$ and a residual $U(1)_{em}$. Incidentally, these monopole solutions provide an illuminating way of thinking about charge quantization: as Dirac (1931) pointed out, the existence of just one monopole implies, from his quantization condition (19.62), that charge is quantized.

When these ideas are applied to QCD, $\boldsymbol{E}$ and $\boldsymbol{B}$ must be understood as the appropriate colour fields (i.e. they carry an $SU(3)_c$ index). The group structure of $SU(3)$ is also quite different from that of $U(1)$ models, and we do not want to be restricted just to static solutions (as in the GL theory, here used as an analogue). Whether in fact the real QCD vacuum (ground state) is formed as some such coherent plasma of monopoles, with confinement of electric charges and flux, is a subject of continuing research; other schemes are also possible. As so often stressed, the difficulty lies in the non-perturbative nature of the confinement problem.

19.5   't Hooft's gauges

We must now at last grasp the nettle and consider what happens if, in the parametrization

$$\hat{\phi} = |\hat{\phi}| \exp(i\hat{\theta}(x)/v) \tag{19.63}$$

we do not choose the gauge (cf (19.52))

$$\partial_\mu \hat{A}^\mu = \Box \hat{\theta}/M. \tag{19.64}$$

This was the gauge that enabled us to transform away the phase degree of freedom and reduce the equation of motion for the electromagnetic field to that of a massive vector boson. Instead of using the modulus and phase as the two independent degrees of freedom for the complex Higgs field $\hat{\phi}$, we now choose to parametrize $\hat{\phi}$, quite generally, by the decomposition

$$\hat{\phi} = 2^{-1/2}[v + \hat{\chi}_1(x) + i\hat{\chi}_2(x)], \tag{19.65}$$

where the vacuum values of $\hat{\chi}_1$ and $\hat{\chi}_2$ are zero. Substituting this form for $\hat{\phi}$ into the master equation for $\hat{A}^\nu$ (obtained from (19.43) and (19.44))

$$\Box \hat{A}^\nu - \partial^\nu(\partial_\mu \hat{A}^\mu) = iq[\hat{\phi}^\dagger \partial^\nu \hat{\phi} - (\partial^\nu \hat{\phi})^\dagger \hat{\phi}] - 2q^2 \hat{A}^\nu \hat{\phi}^\dagger \hat{\phi}, \tag{19.66}$$

leads to the equation of motion

$$\begin{aligned}
(\Box + M^2)\hat{A}^\nu - \partial^\nu(\partial_\mu \hat{A}^\mu) &= -M\partial^\nu \hat{\chi}_2 + q(\hat{\chi}_2 \partial^\nu \hat{\chi}_1 - \hat{\chi}_1 \partial^\nu \hat{\chi}_2) \\
&\quad - q^2 \hat{A}^\nu(\hat{\chi}_1^2 + 2v\hat{\chi}_1 + \hat{\chi}_2^2)
\end{aligned} \tag{19.67}$$

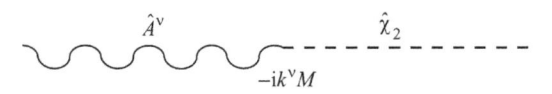

FIGURE 19.3

$\hat{A}^\nu - \hat{\chi}_2$ coupling.

with $M = qv$. At first sight this just looks like the equation of motion of an ordinary massive vector field $\hat{A}^\nu$ coupled to a rather complicated current. However, this certainly cannot be right, as we can see by a count of the degrees of freedom. In the previous gauge we had four degrees of freedom, counted either as two for the original massless $\hat{A}^\nu$ plus one each for $\hat{\theta}$ and $\hat{h}$, or as three for the massive $\hat{A}'^\nu$ and one for $\hat{h}$. If we take this new equation at face value, there seem to be three degrees of freedom for the massive field $\hat{A}^\nu$, and one for each of $\hat{\chi}_1$ and $\hat{\chi}_2$, making *five* in all. Actually, we know perfectly well that we can make use of the freedom gauge choice to set $\hat{\chi}_2$ to zero, say, reducing $\hat{\phi}$ to a real quantity and eliminating a spurious degree of freedom: we have then returned to the form (19.55). In terms of (19.67), the consequence of the unwanted degree of freedom is quite subtle, but it is basic to all gauge theories and already appeared in the photon case, in section 7.3.2. The difficulty arises when we try to calculate the propagator for $\hat{A}^\nu$ from equation (19.67).

The operator on the left-hand side can be simply inverted, as was done in section 19.1, to yield (apparently) the standard massive vector boson propagator

$$\mathrm{i}(-g^{\mu\nu} + k^\mu k^\nu/M^2)/(k^2 - M^2). \tag{19.68}$$

However, the current on the right-hand side of (19.67) is rather peculiar: instead of having only terms corresponding to $\hat{A}^\nu$ coupling to two or three particles, there is also a term involving only one field. This is the term $-M\partial^\nu\hat{\chi}_2$, which tells us that $\hat{A}^\nu$ actually couples directly to the scalar field χ_2 via the gradient coupling $(-M\partial^\nu)$. In momentum space this corresponds to a coupling strength $-ik^\nu M$ and an associated vertex as shown in figure 19.3. Clearly, for a scalar particle, the momentum 4-vector is the only quantity that can couple to the vector index of the vector boson. The existence of this coupling shows that the propagators of $\hat{A}^\nu$ and $\hat{\chi}_2$ are necessarily mixed: the complete vector propagator must be calculated by summing the infinite series shown diagrammatically in figure 19.4. This complication is, of course, completely eliminated by the gauge choice $\hat{\chi}_2 = 0$. However, we are interested in pursuing the case $\hat{\chi}_2 \neq 0$.

In figure 19.4 the only unknown factor is the propagator for $\hat{\chi}_2$. This can be easily found by substituting (19.65) into $\hat{\mathcal{L}}_\mathrm{H}$ and examining the part which is quadratic in the $\hat{\chi}$'s; we find (problem 19.6)

$$\hat{\mathcal{L}}_\mathrm{H} = \frac{1}{2}\partial_\mu\hat{\chi}_1\partial^\mu\hat{\chi}_1 + \frac{1}{2}\partial_\mu\hat{\chi}_2\partial^\mu\hat{\chi} - \mu^2\hat{\chi}_1^2 + \text{ cubic and quartic terms.} \tag{19.69}$$

FIGURE 19.4
Series for the full $\hat{A}^\nu$ propagator.

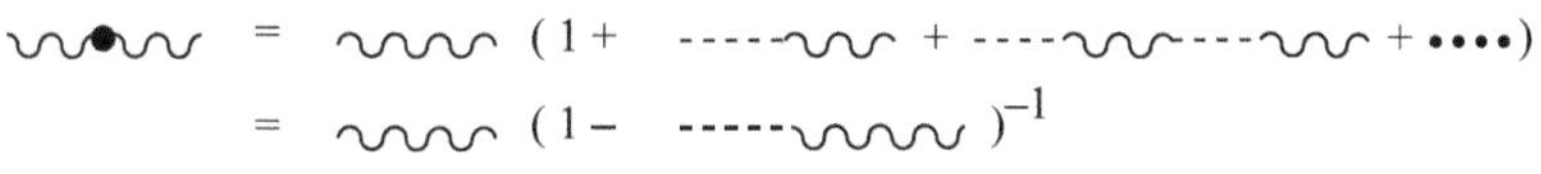

FIGURE 19.5
Formal summation of the series in figure 19.4.

Equation (19.69) confirms that $\hat{\chi}_1$ is a massive field with mass $\sqrt{2}\mu$ (like the $\hat{h}$ in (19.56)), while $\hat{\chi}_2$ is massless. The $\hat{\chi}_2$ propagator is therefore i/k^2. Now that all the elements of the diagrams are known, we can formally sum the series by generalizing the well known result ((cf 10.12)and (11.27))

$$(1 - x)^{-1} = 1 + x + x^2 + x^3 + \dots \tag{19.70}$$

Diagrammatically, we rewrite the propagator of figure 19.4 as in figure 19.5 and perform the sum. Inserting the expressions for the propagators and vector-scalar coupling, and keeping track of the indices, we finally arrive at the result (problem 19.7)

$$i\left(\frac{-g^{\mu\lambda} + k^\mu k^\lambda/M^2}{k^2 - M^2}\right)(g^\nu_\lambda - k^\nu k_\lambda/k^2)^{-1} \tag{19.71}$$

for the full propagator. But the inverse required in (19.71) is precisely (with a lowered index) the one we needed for the photon propagator in (7.91) – and, as we saw there, it does not exist. At last the fact that we are dealing with a gauge theory has caught up with us!

As we saw in section 7.3.2, to obtain a well-defined gauge field propagator we need to *fix the gauge*. A clever way to do this in the present (spontaneously broken) case was suggested by 't Hooft (1971b). His proposal was to set

$$\partial_\mu \hat{A}^\mu = M\xi\hat{\chi}_2 \tag{19.72}$$

where ξ is an arbitrary gauge parameter[1] (not to be confused with the superconducting coherence length). This condition is manifestly covariant, and moreover it effectively reduces the degrees of freedom by one. Inserting (19.72)

---

[1] We shall not enter here into the full details of quantization in such a gauge: we shall effectively treat (19.72) as a classical field relation.

into (19.67) we obtain

$$(\Box + M^2)\hat{A}^\nu - \partial^\nu(\partial_\mu \hat{A}^\mu)(1 - 1/\xi) = q(\hat{\chi}_2 \partial^\nu \hat{\chi}_1 - \hat{\chi}_1 \partial^\nu \hat{\chi}_2)$$
$$- q^2 \hat{A}^\nu(\hat{\chi}_1^2 + 2v\hat{\chi}_1 + \hat{\chi}_2^2). \quad (19.73)$$

The operator appearing on the left-hand side now *does* have an inverse (see problem 19.8) and yields the general form for the gauge boson propagator

$$i\left[-g^{\mu\nu} + \frac{(1 - \xi)k^\mu k^\nu}{k^2 - \xi M^2}\right](k^2 - M^2)^{-1}. \quad (19.74)$$

This propagator is very remarkable[2]. The standard massive vector boson propagator

$$i(-g^{\mu\nu} + k^\mu k^\nu/M^2)(k^2 - M^2)^{-1} \quad (19.75)$$

is seen to correspond to the limit $\xi \to \infty$, and in this gauge the high-energy disease outlined in section 19.1 appears to threaten renormalizability (in fact, it can be shown that there is a consistent set of Feynman rules for this gauge, and the theory is renormalizable thanks to many cancellations of divergences). For any finite ξ, however, the high-energy behaviour of the gauge boson propagator is actually $\sim 1/k^2$, which is as good as the *renormalizable* theory of QED (in Lorentz gauge). Note, however, that there seems to be another pole in the propagator (19.74) at $k^2 = \xi M^2$: this is surely unphysical since it depends on the arbitrary parameter ξ. A full treatment ('t Hooft 1971b) shows that this pole is always cancelled by an exactly similar pole in the propagator for the $\hat{\chi}_2$ field itself. These finite-ξ gauges are called *R gauges* (since they are 'manifestly renormalizable') and typically involve unphysical Higgs fields such as $\hat{\chi}_2$. The infinite-ξ gauge is known as the *U gauge* (U for unitary) since only physical particles appear in this gauge. For tree diagram calculations, of course, it is easiest to use the U gauge Feynman rules: the technical difficulties with this gauge choice only enter in loop calculations, for which the R gauge choice is easier.

Notice that in our master formula (19.74) for the gauge boson propagator the limit $M \to 0$ may be safely taken (compare the remarks about this limit for the 'naive' massive vector boson propagator in section 19.1). This yields the massless vector boson (photon) propagator in a general ξ-gauge, exactly as in equation (7.122) or (19.23).

We now proceed with the generalization of these ideas to the non-Abelian SU(2) case, which is the one relevant to the electroweak theory. The general non-Abelian case was treated by Kibble (1967).

---

[2]A vector boson propagator of similar form was first introduced by Lee and Yang (1962), but their discussion was not within the framework of a spontaneously broken theory, so that Higgs particles were not present, and the physical limit was obtained *only* as $\xi \to 0$.

19.6 Spontaneously broken local SU(2)×U(1) symmetry

We shall limit our discussion of the spontaneous breaking of a local non-Abelian symmetry to the particular case needed for the electroweak part of the Standard Model. This is, in fact, just the local version of the model studied in section 17.6. As noted there, the Lagrangian $\hat{\mathcal{L}}_\Phi$ of (17.97) is invariant under global SU(2) transformations of the form (17.100), and also global U(1) transformations (17.101). Thus in the local version we shall have to introduce three SU(2) gauge fields (as in section 13.1), which we call $\hat{W}_i^\mu(x)(i = 1, 2, 3)$, and one U(1) gauge field $\hat{B}^\mu(x)$. We recall that the scalar field $\hat{\phi}$ is an SU(2)-doublet

$$\hat{\phi} = \begin{pmatrix} \hat{\phi}^+ \\ \hat{\phi}^0 \end{pmatrix}, \tag{19.76}$$

so that the SU(2) covariant derivative acting on $\hat{\phi}$ is as given in (13.10), namely

$$\hat{D}^\mu = \partial^\mu + ig\boldsymbol{\tau} \cdot \hat{\boldsymbol{W}}^\mu/2. \tag{19.77}$$

To this must be added the U(1) piece, which we write as $ig'\hat{B}^\mu/2$, the $\frac{1}{2}$ being for later convenience. The Lagrangian (without gauge-fixing and ghost terms) is therefore

$$\hat{\mathcal{L}}_{G\Phi} = (\hat{D}_\mu\hat{\phi})^\dagger(\hat{D}^\mu\hat{\phi}) + \mu^2\hat{\phi}^\dagger\hat{\phi} - \frac{\lambda}{4}(\hat{\phi}^\dagger\hat{\phi})^2 - \frac{1}{4}\hat{\boldsymbol{F}}_{\mu\nu}\cdot\hat{\boldsymbol{F}}^{\mu\nu} - \frac{1}{4}\hat{G}_{\mu\nu}\hat{G}^{\mu\nu} \tag{19.78}$$

where

$$\hat{D}^\mu\hat{\phi} = (\partial^\mu + ig\boldsymbol{\tau}\cdot\hat{\boldsymbol{W}}^\mu/2 + ig'\hat{B}^\mu/2)\hat{\phi}, \tag{19.79}$$

$$\hat{\boldsymbol{F}}^{\mu\nu} = \partial^\mu\hat{\boldsymbol{W}}^\nu - \partial^\nu\hat{\boldsymbol{W}}^\mu - g\hat{\boldsymbol{W}}^\mu \times \hat{\boldsymbol{W}}^\nu, \tag{19.80}$$

and

$$\hat{G}^{\mu\nu} = \partial^\mu\hat{B}^\nu - \partial^\nu\hat{B}^\mu. \tag{19.81}$$

We must now decide how to choose the non-zero vacuum expectation value that breaks this symmetry. The essential point for the electroweak application is that, after symmetry breaking, we should be left with three massive boson gauge bosons (which will be the $W^\pm$ and Z^0) and one massless gauge boson, the photon. We may reasonably guess that the massless boson will be associated with a symmetry that is *un*broken by the vacuum expectation value. Put differently, we certainly do not want a 'superconducting' massive photon to emerge from the theory in this case, as the physical vacuum is not an electromagnetic superconductor. This means that we do not want to give a vacuum value to a charged field (as is done in the BCS ground state). On the other hand, we do want it to behave as a 'weak' superconductor, generating mass for $W^\pm$ and Z^0. The choice suggested by Weinberg (1967) was

$$\langle 0|\hat{\phi}|0\rangle = \begin{pmatrix} 0 \\ v/\sqrt{2} \end{pmatrix} \tag{19.82}$$

where $v/\sqrt{2} = \sqrt{2}\mu/\lambda^{1/2}$, which we already considered in the global case in section 17.6. As pointed out there, (19.82) implies that the vacuum remains invariant under the combined transformation of 'U(1) + third component of SU(2) isospin' – that is, (19.82) implies

$$\left(\frac{1}{2} + t_3^{(\frac{1}{2})}\right)\langle 0|\hat{\phi}|0\rangle = 0 \tag{19.83}$$

and hence

$$\langle 0|\hat{\phi}|0\rangle \rightarrow (\langle 0|\hat{\phi}|0\rangle)' = \exp\left[i\alpha\left(\frac{1}{2} + t_3^{(1/2)}\right)\right]\langle 0|\hat{\phi}|0\rangle = \langle 0|\hat{\phi}|0\rangle, \tag{19.84}$$

where as usual $t_3^{(1/2)} = \tau_3/2$ (we are using lowercase t for isospin now, anticipating that it is the *weak*, rather than hadronic, isospin – see chapter 21).

We now need to consider oscillations about (19.82) in order to see the physical particle spectrum. As in (17.107) we parametrize these conveniently as

$$\hat{\phi} = \exp(-i\hat{\boldsymbol{\theta}}(x) \cdot \boldsymbol{\tau}/2v) \left(\begin{array}{c} 0 \\ \frac{1}{\sqrt{2}}(v + \hat{H}(x)) \end{array}\right) \tag{19.85}$$

(compare (19.45)). However this time, in contrast to (17.107) but just as in (19.55), we can reduce the phase fields $\hat{\boldsymbol{\theta}}$ to zero by an appropriate gauge transformation, and it is simplest to examine the particle spectrum in this (*unitary*) gauge. Substituting

$$\hat{\phi} = \left(\begin{array}{c} 0 \\ \frac{1}{\sqrt{2}}(v + \hat{H}(x)) \end{array}\right) \tag{19.86}$$

into (19.78) and retaining only terms which are second order in the fields (i.e. kinetic energies or mass terms) we find (problem 19.9)

$$\begin{aligned}
\hat{\mathcal{L}}_{G\Phi}^{\text{free}} &= \frac{1}{2}\partial_\mu\hat{H}\partial^\mu\hat{H} - \mu^2\hat{H}^2 \\
&\quad - \frac{1}{4}(\partial_\mu\hat{W}_{1\nu} - \partial_\nu\hat{W}_{1\mu})(\partial^\mu\hat{W}_1^\nu - \partial^\nu\hat{W}_1^\mu) + \frac{1}{8}g^2v^2\hat{W}_{1\mu}\hat{W}_1^\mu \\
&\quad - \frac{1}{4}(\partial_\mu\hat{W}_{2\nu} - \partial_\nu\hat{W}_{2\mu})(\partial^\mu\hat{W}_2^\nu - \partial^\nu\hat{W}_1^\mu) + \frac{1}{8}g^2v^2\hat{W}_{2\mu}\hat{W}_2^\mu \\
&\quad - \frac{1}{4}(\partial_\mu\hat{W}_{3\nu} - \partial_\nu\hat{W}_{3\mu})(\partial^\mu\hat{W}_3^\nu - \partial^\nu\hat{W}_3^\mu) - \frac{1}{4}\hat{G}_{\mu\nu}\hat{G}^{\mu\nu} \\
&\quad + \frac{1}{8}v^2(g\hat{W}_{3\mu} - g'\hat{B}_\mu)(g\hat{W}_3^\mu - g'\hat{B}^\mu).
\end{aligned} \tag{19.87}$$

The first line of (19.87) tells us that we have a scalar field of mass $\sqrt{2}\mu$ (the Higgs boson, again). The next two lines tell us that the components $\hat{W}_1$ and $\hat{W}_2$ of the triplet $(\hat{W}_1, \hat{W}_2, \hat{W}_3)$ acquire a mass (cf (19.56) in the U(1) case)

$$M_1 = M_2 = gv/2 \equiv M_W. \tag{19.88}$$

The last two lines show us that the fields $\hat{W}_3$ and $\hat{B}$ are mixed. But they can easily be unmixed by noting that the last term in (19.87) involves only the combination $g\hat{W}_3^\mu - g'\hat{B}^\mu$, which evidently acquires a mass. This suggests introducing the normalized linear combination

$$\hat{Z}^\mu = \cos\theta_\mathrm{W}\hat{W}_3^\mu - \sin\theta_\mathrm{W}\hat{B}^\mu \qquad (19.89)$$

where

$$\cos\theta_\mathrm{W} = g/(g^2 + g'^2)^{1/2} \qquad \sin\theta_\mathrm{W} = g'/(g^2 + g'^2)^{1/2}, \qquad (19.90)$$

together with the orthogonal combination

$$\hat{A}^\mu = \sin\theta_\mathrm{W}\hat{W}_3^\mu + \cos\theta_\mathrm{W}\hat{B}^\mu. \qquad (19.91)$$

We then find that the last two lines of (19.87) become

$$-\frac{1}{4}(\partial_\mu\hat{Z}_\nu - \partial_\nu\hat{Z}_\mu)(\partial_\mu\hat{Z}^\nu - \partial^\nu\hat{Z}^\mu) + \frac{1}{8}v^2(g^2 + g'^2)\hat{Z}_\mu\hat{Z}^\mu - \frac{1}{4}\hat{F}_{\mu\nu}\hat{F}^{\mu\nu}, \qquad (19.92)$$

where

$$\hat{F}_{\mu\nu} = \partial_\mu\hat{A}_\nu - \partial_\nu\hat{A}_\mu. \qquad (19.93)$$

Thus

$$M_\mathrm{Z} = \frac{1}{2}v(g^2 + g'^2)^{1/2} = M_\mathrm{W}/\cos\theta_\mathrm{W} \qquad (19.94)$$

and

$$M_\mathrm{A} = 0. \qquad (19.95)$$

Counting degrees of freedom as in the local $\mathrm{U}(1)$ case, we originally had 12 in (19.78) – three massless $\hat{W}$'s and one massless $\hat{B}$, which is 8 degrees of freedom in all, together with 4 $\hat{\phi}$-fields, all with the same mass. After symmetry breaking, we have three massive vector fields $\hat{W}_1$, $\hat{W}_2$ and $\hat{Z}$ with 9 degrees of freedom, one massless vector field $\hat{A}$ with 2, and one massive scalar $\hat{H}$. Of course, the physical application will be to identify the $\hat{W}$ and $\hat{Z}$ fields with those physical particles, the $\hat{A}$ field with the massless photon, and the $\hat{H}$ field with the Higgs boson. In the gauge (19.86), the W and Z particles have propagators of the form (19.22).

The identification of $\hat{A}^\mu$ with the photon field is made clearer if we look at the form of $D_\mu\hat{\phi}$ written in terms of $\hat{A}_\mu$ and $\hat{Z}_\mu$, discarding the $\hat{W}_1$, $\hat{W}_2$ pieces:

$$\begin{aligned}
D_\mu\hat{\phi} = \ & \left\{ \partial_\mu + ig\sin\theta_\mathrm{W}\left(\frac{1+\tau_3}{2}\right)\hat{A}_\mu \right. \\
& \left. + \frac{ig}{\cos\theta_\mathrm{W}}\left[\frac{\tau_3}{2} - \sin^2\theta_\mathrm{W}\left(\frac{1+\tau_3}{2}\right)\right]\hat{Z}_\mu \right\}\hat{\phi}. \qquad (19.96)
\end{aligned}$$

Now the operator $(1+\tau_3)$ acting on $\langle 0|\hat{\phi}|0\rangle$ gives zero, as observed in (19.83),

and this is why $\hat{A}_\mu$ does not acquire a mass when $\langle 0|\hat{\phi}|0\rangle \neq 0$ (gauge fields coupled to *unbroken* symmetries of $\langle 0|\hat{\phi}|0\rangle$ do *not* become massive). Although certainly not unique, this choice of $\hat{\phi}$ and $\langle 0|\hat{\phi}|0\rangle$ is undoubtedly very economical and natural. We are interpreting the zero eigenvalue of $(1 + \tau_3)$ as the electromagnetic charge of the vacuum, which we do not wish to be non-zero. We then make the identification

$$e = g \sin\theta_W \tag{19.97}$$

in order to get the right 'electromagnetic D_μ' in (19.96).

We emphasize once more that the particular form of (19.87) corresponds to a *choice of gauge*, namely the unitary one (cf the discussions in sections 19.3 and 19.5). There is always the possibility of using other gauges, as in the Abelian case, and this will in general be advantageous when doing loop calculations involving renormalization. We would then return to a general parametrization such as (cf (19.65) and (17.95))

$$\hat{\phi} = \begin{pmatrix} 0 \\ v/\sqrt{2} \end{pmatrix} + \frac{1}{\sqrt{2}} \begin{pmatrix} \hat{\phi}_2 - i\hat{\phi}_1 \\ \hat{\sigma} - i\hat{\phi}_3 \end{pmatrix}, \tag{19.98}$$

and add 't Hooft gauge-fixing terms

$$-\frac{1}{2\xi} \left\{ \sum_{i=1,2} (\partial_\mu \hat{W}_i^\mu + \xi M_W \hat{\phi}_i)^2 + (\partial_\mu \hat{Z}^\mu + \xi M_Z \hat{\phi}_3)^2 + (\partial_\mu \hat{A}^\mu)^2 \right\}. \tag{19.99}$$

In this case the gauge boson propagators are all of the form (19.74), and ξ-dependent. In such gauges, the Feynman rules will have to involve graphs corresponding to exchange of quanta of the 'unphysical' fields $\hat{\phi}_i$, as well as those of the physical Higgs scalar $\hat{\sigma}$. These will also have to be suitable ghost interactions in the non-Abelian sector as discussed in section 13.3.3. The complete Feynman rules of the electroweak theory are given in Appendix B of Cheng and Li (1984), for example.

The model introduced here is actually the 'Higgs sector' of the Standard Model, but without any couplings to fermions. We have seen how, by supposing that the potential in (19.78) has the symmetry-breaking sign of the parameter μ^2, the $W^\pm$ and Z^0 gauge bosons can be given masses. This seems to be an ingenious and even elegant 'mechanism' for arriving at a renormalizable theory of massive vector bosons. One may of course wonder whether this 'mechanism' is after all purely phenomenological, somewhat akin to the GL theory of a superconductor. In the latter case, we know that it can be derived from 'microscopic' BCS theory, and this naturally leads to the question whether there could be a similar underlying 'dynamical' theory, behind the Higgs sector. It is, in fact, quite simple to construct a theory in which the Higgs fields $\hat{\phi}$ appear as bound, or composite, states of heavy fermions.

But generating masses for the gauge bosons is not the only job that the Higgs sector does, in the Standard Model: it also generates masses for all

the fermions. As we will see in chapter 22, the gauge symmetry of the weak interactions is a *chiral* one, which requires that there should be no explicit fermion masses in the Lagrangian. We saw in chapter 18 how there is good evidence that the strong QCD interactions break chiral symmetry spontaneously, but that there is also a need for small Lagrangian masses for the quarks, which break chiral symmetry explicitly (so as to give mass to the pions, for example). The leptons are of course not coupled to QCD, and we have to assume Lagrangian masses for them too. Thus for both quarks and leptons chiral-symmetry-breaking mass terms seem to be required. The only way to preserve the weak chiral gauge symmetry is to assume that these fermion masses must, in their turn, be interpreted as arising 'spontaneously' also; that is, *not* via an explicit mass term in the Lagrangian. The dynamical generation of quark and lepton masses would, in fact, be closely analogous to the generation of the energy gap in the BCS theory, as we saw in section 18.1. So we may ask: is it possible to find a dynamical theory which generates masses for *both* the vector bosons, *and* the fermions? Such theories are generically known as 'technicolour models' (Weinberg 1979b, Susskind 1979), and they have been intensively studied (see, for example, Peskin 1997). One problem is that such theories are already tightly constrained by the precision electroweak experiments (see chapter 22), and meeting these constraints seems to require rather elaborate kinds of models. However, technicolour theories do offer the prospect of a new strongly interacting sector, which could possibly be probed at the LHC. But such ideas take us beyond the scope of the present volume. Within the Standard Model, one proceeds along what seems a more phenomenological route, attributing the masses of fermions to their couplings with the Higgs field, in a way that will be explained in chapter 22: briefly, the couplings have the Yukawa form $g_f \bar{\hat{f}} \hat{f} \hat{\phi}$, so that when $\hat{\phi}$ develops a vev v, the fermions gain a mass $m_f = g_f v$.

We now turn, in the last part of the book, to weak interactions and the electroweak theory.

Problems

19.1 Show that

$$[(-k^2 + M^2) g^{\nu\mu} + k^\nu k^\mu] \left(\frac{-g_{\mu\rho} + k_\mu k_\rho/M^2}{k^2 - M^2} \right) = g^\nu_\rho.$$

19.2 Verify (19.18).

19.3 Verify (19.19).

19.4 Verify (19.46).

19.5 Insert (19.55) into $\hat{\mathcal{L}}_{\mathrm{H}}$ of (19.40) and derive (19.56) for the quadratic terms.

19.6 Insert (19.65) into $\hat{\mathcal{L}}_{\mathrm{H}}$ of (19.40) and derive the quadratic terms of (19.69).

19.7 Derive (19.71).

19.8 Write the left-hand side of (19.73) in momentum space (as in (19.4)), and show that the inverse of the factor multiplying $\tilde{\hat{A}}^{\mu}$ is (19.74) without the 'i' (cf problem 19.1).

19.9 Verify (19.87).

Part VIII

Weak Interactions and the Electroweak Theory

20

Introduction to the Phenomenology of Weak Interactions

Public letter to the group of the Radioactives at the district society meeting in Tübingen:

Physikalisches Institut
der Eidg. Technischen Hochschule
Gloriastr.
Zürich

Zürich, 4. Dec. 1930

Dear Radioactive Ladies and Gentlemen,

As the bearer of these lines, to whom I graciously ask you to listen, will explain to you in more detail, how because of the 'wrong' statistics of the N and ^{6}Li nuclei and the continuous β-spectrum, I have hit upon a desperate remedy to save the 'exchange theorem' of statistics and the law of conservation of energy. Namely, the possiblity that there could exist in the nuclei electrically neutral particles, that I wish to call neutrons, which have the spin $\frac{1}{2}$ and obey the exclusion principle and which further differ from light quanta in that they do not travel with the velocity of light. The mass of the neutrons should be of the same order of magnitude as the electron mass and in any event not larger than 0.01 proton masses. – The continuous β-spectrum would then become understandable by the assumption that in β-decay, a neutron is emitted in addition to the electron such that the sum of the energies of the neutron and electron is constant.
. . .

I admit that on a first look my way out might seem to be quite unlikely, since one would certainly have seen the neutrons by now if they existed. But nothing ventured nothing gained, and the seriousness of the matter with the continuous β-spectrum is illustrated by a quotation of my honoured predecessor in office, Mr. Debye, who recently told me in Brussels: 'Oh, it is best not to think about it, like the new taxes.' Therefore one should earnestly discuss each way of salvation. – So, dear Radioactives, examine and judge it. – Unfortunately I cannot appear in Tübingen personally, since I am indispensable here in Zürich because of a ball on the

night of 6/7 December. – With my best regards to you, and also Mr. Back, your humble servant,

W. Pauli

Quoted from Winter (2000), pages 4–5.

At the end of the previous chapter we arrived at an important part of the Lagrangian of the Standard Model, namely the terms involving just the gauge and Higgs fields. The full electroweak Lagrangian also includes, of course, the couplings of these fields to the quarks and leptons. We could at this point simply write these couplings down, with little motivation, and proceed at once to discuss the empirical consequences. But such an approach, though economical, would assume considerable knowledge of weak interaction phenomenology on the reader's part. We prefer to keep this book as self-contained as possible, and so in the present chapter we shall provide an introduction to this phenomenology, following a 'semi-historical' route (for fuller historical treatments we refer the reader to Marshak *et al.* 1969, or to Winter 2000, for example).

Much of what we shall discuss is still, for many purposes, a very useful approximation to the full theory at energies well below the masses of the $W^{\pm}$ (~80 GeV) and Z^0 (~90 GeV). The reason for this is that in the electroweak theory (chapter 22), tree-level amplitudes have a structure very similar to that in the purely electromagnetic case, namely (see equation (8.101))

$$j_{\mathrm{wk}}^{\mu} \frac{(-g_{\mu\nu} + q_{\mu}q_{\nu}/M_{\mathrm{W,Z}}^2)}{q^2 - M_{\mathrm{W,Z}}^2} j_{\mathrm{wk}}^{\nu} \tag{20.1}$$

where j_{wk}^{μ} is a weak current, and we are using (19.75) for the propagator of the exchanged W or Z bosons. For $q^2 \ll M_{\mathrm{W,Z}}^2$, (20.1) becomes proportional to the product of two currents; this 'current–current' form was for many years the basis of weak interaction phenomenology, as we now describe.

20.1　Fermi's 'current–current' theory of nuclear β-decay, and its generalizations

The first quantum field theory of a weak interaction process was proposed by Fermi (1934a,b) for nuclear β-decay, building on the 'neutrino hypothesis' of Pauli. In 1930, Pauli (in his 'Dear Radioactive Ladies and Gentlemen' letter) had suggested that the continuous e$^-$ spectrum in β-decay could be

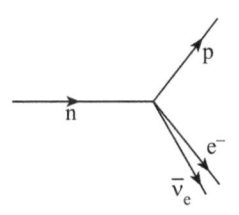

FIGURE 20.1
Four-fermion interaction for neutron β-decay.

understood by supposing that, in addition to the e⁻, the decaying nucleus also emitted a light, spin-$\frac{1}{2}$, electrically neutral particle, which he called the 'neutron'. In this first version of the proposal, Pauli regarded his hypothetical particle as a constituent of the nucleus. This had the attraction of solving not only the problem with the continuous e⁻ spectrum, but a second problem as well – what he called the 'wrong' statistics of the ^{14}N and ^{6}Li nuclei. Taking ^{14}N for definiteness, the problem was as follows. Assuming that the nucleus was somehow composed of the only particles (other than the photon) known in 1930, namely electrons and protons, one requires 14 protons and 7 electrons for the known charge of 7. This implies a half-odd integer value for the total nuclear spin. But data from molecular spectra indicated that the nitrogen nuclei obeyed Bose–Einstein, not Fermi–Dirac statistics, so that – if the usual 'spin-statistics' connection were to hold – the spin of the nitrogen nucleus should be an integer, not a half-odd integer. This second part of Pauli's hypothesis was quite soon overtaken by the discovery of the (real) neutron by Chadwick (1932), after which it was rapidly accepted that nuclei consisted of protons and (Chadwick's) neutrons.

However, the β-spectrum problem remained, and at the Solvay Conference in 1933 Pauli restated his hypothesis (Pauli 1934), using now the name 'neutrino' which had meanwhile been suggested by Fermi. Stimulated by the discussions at the Solvay meeting, Fermi then developed his theory of β-decay. In the new picture of the nucleus, neither the electron nor the neutrino were to be thought of as nuclear constituents. Instead, the electron-neutrino pair had somehow to be created and emitted in the transition process of the nuclear decay, much as a photon is created and emitted in nuclear γ-decay. Indeed, Fermi relied heavily on the analogy with electromagnetism. The basic process was assumed to be the transition neutron→proton, with the emission of an e⁻ν pair, as shown in figure 20.1. The n and p were then regarded as 'elementary' and without structure (point-like); the whole process took place at a single space-time point, like the emission of a photon in QED. Further, Fermi conjectured that the nucleons participated via a weak interaction analogue of the electromagnetic transition *currents* frequently encountered in volume 1 for QED. In this case, however, rather than having the 'charge conserving' form

of $\bar{u}_p \gamma^\mu u_p$ for instance, the 'weak current' had the form $\bar{u}_p \gamma^\mu u_n$, in which the charge of the nucleon changed. The lepton pair was also charged, obviously. The whole interaction then had to be Lorentz invariant, implying that the $e^- \nu$ pair had also to appear in a similar (4-vector) 'current' form. Thus a 'current–current' amplitude was proposed, of the form

$$A \bar{u}_p \gamma^\mu u_n \bar{u}_{e^-} \gamma_\mu u_\nu, \tag{20.2}$$

where A was a constant. Correspondingly, the process was described field theoretically in terms of the local interaction density

$$A \bar{\hat{\psi}}_p(x) \gamma^\mu \hat{\psi}_n(x) \bar{\hat{\psi}}_e(x) \gamma_\mu \hat{\psi}_\nu(x). \tag{20.3}$$

The discovery of positron β-decay soon followed, and then of electron capture; these processes were easily accommodated by adding to (20.3) its Hermitian conjugate

$$A \bar{\hat{\psi}}_n(x) \gamma^\mu \hat{\psi}_p(x) \bar{\hat{\psi}}_\nu(x) \gamma_\mu \hat{\psi}_e(x), \tag{20.4}$$

taking A to be real. The sum of (20.3) and (20.4) gave a good account of many observed characteristics of β-decay, when used to calculate transition probabilities in first-order perturbation theory.

Soon after Fermi's theory was presented, however, it became clear that the observed selection rules in some nuclear transitions could not be accounted for by the forms (20.3) and (20.4). Specifically, in 'allowed' transitions (where the orbital angular momentum carried by the leptons is zero) it was found that, while for many transitions the nuclear spin did not change ($\Delta J = 0$), for others – of comparable strength – a change of nuclear spin by one unit ($\Delta J = 1$) occurred. Now, in nuclear decays the energy release is very small ($\sim$ few MeV) compared to the mass of a nucleon, and so the non-relativistic limit is an excellent approximation for the nucleon spinors. It is then easy to see (problem 20.1) that, in this limit, the interactions (20.3) and (20.4) imply that the nucleon spins cannot 'flip'. Hence some other interaction(s) must be present. Gamow and Teller (1936) introduced the general four-fermion interaction, constructed from bilinear combinations of the nucleon pair and of the lepton pair, but not their derivatives. For example, the combination

$$\bar{\hat{\psi}}_p(x) \hat{\psi}_n(x) \bar{\hat{\psi}}_e(x) \hat{\psi}_\nu(x) \tag{20.5}$$

could occur, and also

$$\bar{\hat{\psi}}_p(x) \sigma_{\mu\nu} \hat{\psi}_n(x) \bar{\hat{\psi}}_e \sigma^{\mu\nu} \hat{\psi}_\nu(x) \tag{20.6}$$

where

$$\sigma_{\mu\nu} = \frac{\mathrm{i}}{2}(\gamma_\mu \gamma_\nu - \gamma_\nu \gamma_\mu). \tag{20.7}$$

The non-relativistic limit of (20.5) gives $\Delta J = 0$, but (20.6) allows $\Delta J = 1$.

Other combinations are also possible, as we shall discuss shortly. Note that the interaction must always be Lorentz invariant.

Thus began a long period of difficult experimentation to establish the correct form of the β-decay interaction. With the discovery of the muon (in 1937) and the pion (ten years later) more weak decays became experimentally accessible, for example μ decay

$$\mu^- \to e^- + \nu + \nu \tag{20.8}$$

and π decay

$$\pi^- \to e^- + \nu. \tag{20.9}$$

Note that we have deliberately called all the neutrinos just 'ν', without any particle/antiparticle indication, or lepton flavour label; we shall have more to say on these matters in section 20.3. There were hopes that the couplings of the pairs (p,n), (ν, e^-) and (ν, μ^-) might have the same form ('universality') but the data was incomplete, and in part apparently contradictory.

The breakthrough came in 1956, when Lee and Yang (1956) suggested that parity was not conserved in all weak decays. Hitherto, it had always been assumed that any physical interaction had to be such that parity was conserved, and this assumption had been built into the structure of the proposed β-decay interactions, such as (20.3), (20.5) or (20.6). Once it was looked for properly, following the analysis of Lee and Yang, parity violation was indeed found to be a strikingly evident feature of weak interactions.

20.2 Parity violation in weak interactions, and V-A theory

20.2.1 Parity violation

In 1957, the experiment of Wu *et al.* (1957) established for the first time that parity was violated in a weak interaction, specifically nuclear β-decay. The experiment involved a sample of ^{60}Co ($J = 5$) cooled to 0.01 K in a solenoid. At this temperature most of the nuclear spins are aligned by the magnetic field, and so there is a net polarization $\langle \boldsymbol{J} \rangle$, which is in the direction opposite to the applied magnetic field. ^{60}Co decays to ^{60}Ni ($J = 4$), a $\Delta J = 1$ transition. The degree of ^{60}Co alignment was measured from observations of the angular distribution of γ-rays from ^{60}Ni. The relative intensities of electrons emitted along and against the magnetic field direction were measured, and the results were consistent with a distribution of the form

$$
\begin{aligned}
I(\theta) &= 1 - \langle \boldsymbol{J} \rangle \cdot \boldsymbol{p}/E & (20.10) \\
&= 1 - Pv \cos \theta & (20.11)
\end{aligned}
$$

where $v, \boldsymbol{p}$ and E are respectively the electron speed, momentum and energy, P is the magnitude of the polarization, and θ is the angle of emission of the electron with respect to $\langle \boldsymbol{J} \rangle$.

Why does this indicate parity violation? To see this, we recall from the discussion of the parity operation $\mathbf{P}$ in section 4.2.1 that the angular momentum $\boldsymbol{J}$ is an axial vector such that $\langle \boldsymbol{J} \rangle \to \langle \boldsymbol{J} \rangle$ under $\mathbf{P}$, while $\boldsymbol{p}$ is a polar vector transforming by $\boldsymbol{p} \to -\boldsymbol{p}$. Hence, in the parity-transformed system, the distribution (20.11) would have the form

$$I_{\mathbf{P}}(\theta) = 1 + Pv \cos \theta \qquad (20.12)$$

The difference between (20.12) and (20.11) implies that, by performing the measurement, we can *determine* which of the two coordinate systems we must in fact be using. The two are inequivalent, in contrast to all the other coordinate system equivalences which we have previously studied (e.g. under three-dimensional rotations, and Lorentz transformations). This is an operational consequence of 'parity violation'. The crucial point in this example, evidently, is the appearance of the *pseudoscalar* quantity $\langle \boldsymbol{J} \rangle \cdot \boldsymbol{p}$ in (20.10), alongside the obviously scalar quantity '1'.

The Fermi theory, employing only vector currents, needs a modification to accommodate this result. We saw in section 4.2.1 that a combination of vector ('V') and axial vector ('A') currents would be parity-violating. Indeed, after many years of careful experiments, and many false trails, it was eventually established (always, of course, to within some experimental error) that the currents participating in Fermi's current–current interaction are, in fact, certain combinations of V-type and A-type currents, for both nucleons and leptons.

20.2.2   V-A theory: chirality and helicity

Quite soon after the discovery of parity violation, Sudarshan and Marshak (1958), and then Feynman and Gell-Mann (1958) and Sakurai (1958), proposed a specific form for the current–current interaction, namely the V-A ('V minus A') structure. For example, in place of the leptonic combination $\bar{u}_{e^-} \gamma_\mu u_\nu$, these authors proposed the form $\bar{u}_{e^-} \gamma_\mu (1 - \gamma_5) u_\nu$, being the difference (with equal weight) of a V-type and an A-type current. For the part involving the nucleons the proposal was slightly more complicated, having the form $\bar{u}_p \gamma_\mu (1 - r\gamma_5) u_n$ where r had the empirical value $r \approx 1.2$. From our present perspective, of course, the hadronic transition is actually occurring at the quark level, so that rather than a transition n $\to$ p we now think in terms of a d $\to$ u one. In this case, the remarkable fact is that the appropriate current to use is, once again, essentially the simple 'V-A' one, $\bar{u}_u \gamma_\mu (1 - \gamma_5) u_d$[1]. *This V-A structure for quarks and leptons is fundamental to the Standard Model.*

---

[1] We shall see in section 20.7 that a slight modification is necessary.

We must now at once draw the reader's attention to a rather remarkable feature of this V-A structure, which is that the $(1 - \gamma_5)$ factor can be thought of as acting either on the u spinor or on the $\bar{u}$ spinor. Consider, for example, a term $\bar{u}_{e^-}\gamma_\mu(1 - \gamma_5)u_\nu$. We have

$$
\begin{aligned}
\bar{u}_{e^-}\gamma_\mu(1 - \gamma_5)u_\nu &= u_{e^-}^\dagger \beta\gamma_\mu(1 - \gamma_5)u_\nu \\
&= u_{e^-}^\dagger (1 - \gamma_5)\beta\gamma_\mu u_\nu \\
&= [(1 - \gamma_5)u_{e^-}]^\dagger \beta\gamma_\mu u_\nu \\
&= \overline{[(1 - \gamma_5)u_{e^-}]}\gamma_\mu u_\nu.
\end{aligned} \tag{20.13}
$$

To understand the significance of this, it is advantageous to work in the representation (3.40) of the Dirac matrices, in which γ_5 is diagonal, namely

$$
\gamma_5 = \begin{pmatrix} 1 & 0 \\ 0 & -1 \end{pmatrix} \quad \alpha = \begin{pmatrix} \sigma & 0 \\ 0 & -\sigma \end{pmatrix} \quad \beta = \begin{pmatrix} 0 & 1 \\ 1 & 0 \end{pmatrix} \quad \gamma = \begin{pmatrix} 0 & -\sigma \\ \sigma & 0 \end{pmatrix}. \tag{20.14}
$$

Readers who have not worked through problem 9.4 might like to do so now; we may also suggest a backward glance at section 12.4.2 and chapter 17.

First of all it is clear that any combination '$(1 - \gamma_5)u$' is an eigenstate of γ_5 with eigenvalue -1:

$$
\gamma_5(1 - \gamma_5)u = (\gamma_5 - 1)u = -(1 - \gamma_5)u \tag{20.15}
$$

using $\gamma_5^2 = 1$. In the terminology of section 12.4.2, '$(1 - \gamma_5)u$' has definite *chirality*, namely L ('left-handed'), meaning that it belongs to the eigenvalue -1 of γ_5. We may introduce the projection operators P_R, P_L of section 12.4.2,

$$
P_L \equiv \left(\frac{1 - \gamma_5}{2}\right) \qquad P_R \equiv \left(\frac{1 + \gamma_5}{2}\right) \tag{20.16}
$$

satisfying

$$
P_R^2 = P_R \qquad P_L^2 = P_L \qquad P_R P_L = P_L P_R = 0 \qquad P_R + P_L = 1, \tag{20.17}
$$

and define

$$
u_L \equiv P_L u, \qquad u_R \equiv P_R u \tag{20.18}
$$

for any u. Then

$$
\begin{aligned}
\bar{u}_1\gamma_\mu\left(\frac{1 - \gamma_5}{2}\right)u_2 &= \bar{u}_1\gamma_\mu P_L u_2 = \bar{u}_1\gamma_\mu P_L^2 u_2 \\
&= \bar{u}_1\gamma_\mu P_L u_{2L} = \bar{u}_1 P_R \gamma_\mu u_{2L} \\
&= u_1^\dagger P_L \beta\gamma_\mu u_{2L} = \bar{u}_{1L}\gamma_\mu u_{2L}
\end{aligned} \tag{20.19}
$$

which formalizes (20.13) and emphasizes the fact that *only the chiral L components of the u spinors enter into weak interactions*, a remarkably simple statement.

To see the physical consequences of this, we need the forms of the Dirac spinors in this new representation, which we shall now derive explicitly, for convenience. As usual, positive energy spinors are defined as solutions of $(\not{p} - m)u = 0$, so that writing

$$u = \begin{pmatrix} \phi \\ \chi \end{pmatrix} \tag{20.20}$$

we obtain

$$\begin{aligned} (E - \boldsymbol{\sigma} \cdot \boldsymbol{p})\phi &= m\chi \\ (E + \boldsymbol{\sigma} \cdot \boldsymbol{p})\chi &= m\phi. \end{aligned} \tag{20.21}$$

A convenient choice of 2-component spinors ϕ, χ is to take them to be *helicity eigenstates* (see section 3.3). For example, the eigenstate ϕ_+ with positive helicity $\lambda = +1$ satisfies

$$\boldsymbol{\sigma} \cdot \boldsymbol{p}\phi_+ = |\boldsymbol{p}|\phi_+ \tag{20.22}$$

while the eigenstate ϕ_- with $\lambda = -1$ satisfies (20.22) with a minus on the right-hand side. Thus the spinor $u(p, \lambda = +1)$ can be written as

$$u(p, \lambda = +1) = N \begin{pmatrix} \phi_+ \\ \frac{(E - |\boldsymbol{p}|)}{m}\phi_+ \end{pmatrix}. \tag{20.23}$$

The normalization N is fixed as usual by requiring $\bar{u}u = 2m$, from which it follows (problem 20.2) that $N = (E + |\boldsymbol{p}|)^{1/2}$. Thus finally we have

$$u(p, \lambda = +1) = \begin{pmatrix} \sqrt{E + |\boldsymbol{p}|}\phi_+ \\ \sqrt{E - |\boldsymbol{p}|}\phi_+ \end{pmatrix}. \tag{20.24}$$

Similarly

$$u(p, \lambda = -1) = \begin{pmatrix} \sqrt{E - |\boldsymbol{p}|}\phi_- \\ \sqrt{E + |\boldsymbol{p}|}\phi_- \end{pmatrix}. \tag{20.25}$$

Now we have agreed that only the chiral 'L' components of all u-spinors enter into weak interactions, in the Standard Model. But from the explicit form of γ_5 given in (20.14), we see that when acting on any spinor u, the projector P_L 'kills' the top two components:

$$P_L \begin{pmatrix} \phi \\ \chi \end{pmatrix} = \begin{pmatrix} 0 \\ \chi \end{pmatrix}. \tag{20.26}$$

In particular

$$P_L u(p, \lambda = +1) = \begin{pmatrix} 0 \\ \sqrt{E - |\boldsymbol{p}|}\phi_+ \end{pmatrix} \tag{20.27}$$

and

$$P_L u(p, \lambda = -1) = \begin{pmatrix} 0 \\ \sqrt{E + |\boldsymbol{p}|}\phi_- \end{pmatrix}. \tag{20.28}$$

Equations (20.27) and (20.28) are very important. In particular, equation (20.27) implies that in the limit of zero mass m (and hence $E \to |\boldsymbol{p}|$), only the *negative helicity* u-spinor will enter. More quantitatively, using

$$\frac{\sqrt{E - |\boldsymbol{p}|}}{\sqrt{E + |\boldsymbol{p}|}} = \frac{\sqrt{E^2 - \boldsymbol{p}^2}}{(E + |\boldsymbol{p}|)} \approx \frac{m}{2E} \qquad \text{for } m \ll E, \qquad (20.29)$$

we can say that *positive helicity components of all fermions are suppressed in V-A matrix elements, relative to the negative helicity components, by factors of order* (m/E). Bearing in mind that the helicity operator $\boldsymbol{\sigma} \cdot \boldsymbol{p}/|\boldsymbol{p}|$ is a pseudoscalar, this 'unequal' treatment for $\lambda = +1$ and $\lambda = -1$ components is, of course, precisely related to the parity violation built in to the V-A structure.

A similar analysis may be done for the v-spinors. They satisfy $(\not{p} + m)v = 0$ and the normalization $\bar{v}v = -2m$. We must however remember the 'small subtlety' to do with the labelling of v-spinors, discussed in section 3.4.3: the 2-component spinors χ_- in $v(p, \lambda = +1)$ actually satisfy $\boldsymbol{\sigma} \cdot \boldsymbol{p}\chi_- = -|\boldsymbol{p}|\chi_-$, and similarly the χ_+'s in $v(p, \lambda = -1)$ satisfy $\boldsymbol{\sigma} \cdot \boldsymbol{p}\chi_+ = |\boldsymbol{p}|\chi_+$. We then find (problem 20.3) the results

$$v(p, \lambda = +1) = \left(\begin{array}{c} -\sqrt{E - |\boldsymbol{p}|}\chi_- \\ \sqrt{E + |\boldsymbol{p}|}\chi_- \end{array} \right) \qquad (20.30)$$

and

$$v(\lambda = -1) = \left(\begin{array}{c} \sqrt{E + |\boldsymbol{p}|}\chi_+ \\ -\sqrt{E - |\boldsymbol{p}|}\chi_+ \end{array} \right). \qquad (20.31)$$

Once again, the action of P_{L} removes the top two components, leaving the result that, in the massless limit, only the $\lambda = +1$ state survives. Recalling the 'hole theory' interpretation of section 3.4.3, this would mean that *the positive helicity components of all antifermions dominate in V-A interactions*, negative helicity components being suppressed by factors of order m/E. The proportionality of the negative helicity amplitude to the mass of the antifermion is of course exactly as noted for $\pi^+ \to \mu^+ \nu_\mu$ decay in section 18.2.

We should emphasize that although the above results, stated in italics, were derived in the convenient representation (20.14) for the Dirac matrices, they actually hold independently of any choice of representation. This can be shown by using general helicity projection operators.

In Pauli's original letter, he suggested that the mass of the neutrino might be of the same order as the electron mass. Immediately after the discovery of parity violation, it was realized that the result could be elegantly explained by the assumption that the neutrinos were strictly massless particles (Landau 1957, Lee and Yang 1957 and Salam 1957). In this case, u and v spinors satisfy the same equation $\not{p}(u \text{ or } v) = 0$, which reduces via (20.21) (in the

$m = 0$ limit) to the two independent two-component 'Weyl' equations.

$$E\phi_0 = \boldsymbol{\sigma} \cdot \boldsymbol{p}\,\phi_0 \qquad E\chi_0 = -\boldsymbol{\sigma} \cdot \boldsymbol{p}\,\chi_0. \qquad (20.32)$$

Remembering that $E = |\boldsymbol{p}|$ for a massless particle, we see that ϕ_0 has positive helicity and χ_0 negative helicity. In this strictly massless case, helicity is Lorentz invariant, since the direction of $\boldsymbol{p}$ cannot be reversed by a velocity transformation with $v < c$. Furthermore, each of the equations in (20.32) violates parity, since E is clearly a scalar while $\boldsymbol{\sigma} \cdot \boldsymbol{p}$ is a pseudoscalar (note that when $m \neq 0$ we can infer from (20.21) that, in this representation, $\phi \leftrightarrow \chi$ under $\mathbf{P}$, which is consistent with (20.32) and with the form of β in (20.14)). Thus the (massless) neutrino could be 'blamed' for the parity violation. In this model, neutrinos have one definite helicity, either positive or negative. As we have seen, the massless limit of the (four-component) V-A theory leads to the same conclusion.

Which helicity is actually chosen by Nature was determined in a classic experiment by Goldhaber *et al.* (1958), involving the K-capture reaction

$$e^- +{}^{152}\,\mathrm{Eu} \to \nu +{}^{152}\,\mathrm{Sm}^*, \qquad (20.33)$$

as described by Bettini (2008), for example. They found that the helicity of the emitted neutrino was (within errors) 100% *negative*, a result taken as confirming the '2-component' neutrino theory, and the V-A theory.

We now know that neutrinos are not massless. This information does not come from studies of nuclear decays, but rather from a completely different phenomenon – that of *neutrino oscillations*, which we shall mention again in the following section, and treat more fully in section 21.4. Neutrino masses are so small that the existence of the 'wrong helicity' component cannot be detected experimentally in processes such as (20.33), or indeed in any of the reactions we shall discuss, apart from neutrino oscillations.

In section 4.2.2 we introduced the charge conjugation operation $\mathbf{C}$ (see also section 7.5.2). As we noted there, $\mathbf{C}$ is not a good symmetry in weak interactions. The V-A interaction treats a negative helicity fermion very differently from a negative helicity antifermion, while one is precisely transformed into the other under $\mathbf{C}$. However, it is clear that the helicity operator itself is odd under $\mathbf{P}$. Thus the $\mathbf{CP}$ conjugate of a negative helicity fermion is positive helicity antifermion, which is what the V-A interaction selects. It may easily be verified (problem 20.4) that the '2-component' theory of (20.32) automatically incorporates $\mathbf{CP}$ invariance. Elegance notwithstanding, however, there are $\mathbf{CP}$-violating weak interactions, as mentioned in section 4.2.3. How this is accommodated within the Standard Model we shall discuss in section 20.7.3.

For charged fermions the distinction between particle and antiparticle is clear; but is there a conserved quantum number which we can use instead of charge to distinguish a neutrino from an antineutrino? That is the question to which we now turn.

20.3 Lepton number and lepton flavours

In section 1.2.1 of volume 1 we gave a brief discussion of leptonic quantum numbers ('lepton flavours'), adopting a traditional approach in which the data is interpreted in terms of conserved quantum numbers carried by neutrinos, which serve to distinguish neutrinos from antineutrinos. We must now examine the matter more closely, in the light of what we have learned about the helicity properties of the V-A interaction.

In 1995, Davis (1955) – following a suggestion made by Pontecorvo (1946) – argued as follows. Consider the e^- capture reaction $e^- + p \rightarrow \nu + n$, which was of course well established. Then in principle the inverse reaction $\nu + n \rightarrow e^- + p$ should also exist. Of course, the cross section is extremely small, but by using a large enough target volume this might perhaps be compensated. Specifically, the reaction $\nu + {}^{37}_{17}\text{Cl} \rightarrow e^- + {}^{37}_{18}\text{Ar}$ was proposed, the argon being detected through its radioactive decay. Suppose, however, that the 'neutrinos' actually used are those which accompany electrons in β^--decay. If (as was supposed in section 1.2.1) these are to be regarded as antineutrinos, '$\bar{\nu}$', carrying a conserved lepton number, then the reaction

$$'\bar{\nu}' + {}^{37}_{17}\text{Cl} \rightarrow e^- + {}^{37}_{18}\text{Ar} \tag{20.34}$$

should *not* be observed. If, on the other hand, the 'ν' in the capture process and the '$\bar{\nu}$' in β-decay are not distinguished by the weak interaction, the reaction (20.34) should be observed. Davis found no evidence for reaction (20.34), at the expected level of cross section, a result which could clearly be interpreted as confirming the 'conserved electron number hypothesis'.

However, another interpretation is possible. The e^- in β-decay has predominately negative helicity, and its accompanying '$\bar{\nu}$' has predominately positive helicity. The fraction of the other helicity present is of the order m/E, where $E \sim$ few Mev, and the neutrino mass is less than 1eV; this is, therefore, an almost undetectable 'contamination' of negative helicity component in the '$\bar{\nu}$'. Now the property of the V-A interaction is that it conserves helicity in the zero mass limit (in which chirality is the same as helicity). Hence the positive helicity '$\bar{\nu}$' from β^--decay will (predominately) produce a positive helicity lepton, which must be the e^+ not the e^-. Thus the property of the V-A interaction, together with the very small value of the neutrino mass, conspire effectively to forbid (20.34), independently of any considerations about 'lepton number'.

Indeed, the 'helicity-allowed' reaction

$$'\bar{\nu}' + p \rightarrow e^+ + n \tag{20.35}$$

was observed by Reines and Cowan (1956) (see also Cowan *et al.* 1956). Reaction (20.35) too, of course, can be interpreted in terms of '$\bar{\nu}$' carrying a lepton number of -1, equal to that of the e^+. It was also established that only 'ν'

produced e⁻ via (20.34), where 'ν' is the helicity -1 state (or, on the other interpretation, the carrier of lepton number $+1$).

The situation may therefore be summarized as follows. In the case of e⁻ and e⁺, all four 'modes' – e⁻$(\lambda = +1)$, e⁻$(\lambda = -1)$, e⁺$(\lambda = +1)$, e⁺$(\lambda = -1)$ – are experimentally accessible via electromagnetic interactions, even though only two generally dominate in weak interactions (e⁻$(\lambda = -1)$ and e⁺$(\lambda = +1)$). Neutrinos, on the other hand, seem to interact only weakly. In their case, we may if we wish say that the participating states are (in association with e⁻ or e⁺) $\bar{\nu}_e$ $(\lambda = +1)$ and $\nu_e(\lambda = -1)$, to a very good approximation. But we may also regard these two states as simply two different helicity states of one particle, rather than of a particle and its antiparticle. As we have seen, the helicity rules do the job required just as well as the lepton number rules. In short, the question is: are these 'neutrinos' distinguished only by their helicity, or is there an additional distinguishing characteristic ('electron number')? In the latter case we should expect the 'other' two states $\bar{\nu}_e(\lambda = -1)$ and $\nu_e(\lambda = +1)$ to exist as well as the ones known from weak interactions.

If, in fact, no quantum number – other than the helicity – exists which distinguishes the neutrino states, then we would have to say that the **C**-conjugate of a neutrino state is a neutrino, not an antineutrino – that is, 'neutrinos are their own antiparticles'. A neutrino would be a fermionic state somewhat like a photon, which is of course also its own antiparticle. Such '**C**-self-conjugate' fermions are called *Majorana fermions* (Majorana 1937), in contrast to the *Dirac* variety, which have all four possible modes present (2 helicities, 2 particle/antiparticle). We discussed Majorana fermions in sections 4.2.2 and 7.5.2.

The distinction between the 'Dirac' and 'Majorana' neutrino possibilities becomes an essentially 'metaphysical' one in the limit of strictly massless neutrinos, since then (as we have seen) a given helicity state cannot be flipped by going to a suitably moving Lorentz frame, nor by any weak (or electromagnetic) interaction, since they both conserve chirality which is the same as helicity in the massless limit. We would have just the two states $\nu_e(\lambda = -1)$ and $\bar{\nu}_e(\lambda = +1)$, and no way of creating $\nu_e(\lambda = +1)$ or $\bar{\nu}_e(\lambda = -1)$. The '−' label then becomes superfluous. Unfortunately, the massless limit is approached smoothly, and neutrino masses are, in fact, so small that the 'wrong helicity' supression factors will make it very difficult to see the presence of the possible states $\nu_e(\lambda = +1)$, $\bar{\nu}_e(\lambda = -1)$.

One much-discussed experimental test case (see, for example, the review by Vogel and Piepke in Nakamura *et al.* 2010) concerns 'neutrinoless double β-decay', which is the process A $\rightarrow$ A$'$ + e⁻ + e⁻, where A, A$'$ are nuclei. If the neutrino emitted in the first β-decay carries no electron-type conserved quantum number, then in principle it can initiate a second weak interaction, exactly as in Davis' original argument, via the diagram shown in figure 20.2. Note that this is a second-order weak process, so that the amplitude contains the very small factor G_F^2. Furthermore, the ν emitted along with the e⁻ at the first vertex will be predominantly $\lambda = +1$, but in the second vertex

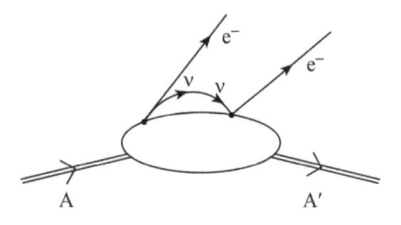

FIGURE 20.2
Double β-decay without emission of a neutrino, a test for Majorana-type neutrinos.

the V-A interaction will 'want' it to have $\lambda = -1$, like the outgoing e^-. Thus there is bound to be one 'm/E' suppression factor, whichever vertex we choose to make 'easy'. (In the case of 3-state neutrino mixing – see section 21.4 – the quantity 'm' will be an appropriately averaged mass.) There is also a complicated nuclear physics overlap factor. The expected half-lives of neutrinoless double β decays depend on the decaying nucleus, but are typically longer than $10^{24} - 10^{25}$ years. Evidently, the observation of this rare process is a formidable experimental challenge; as yet, no confirmed observation exists (see also section 21.4.5).

In the same way, '$\bar{\nu}''$' particles accompanying the μ^-'s in π^- decay

$$\pi^- \to \mu^- + `\bar{\nu}'' \tag{20.36}$$

are observed to produce only μ^+'s when they interact with matter, not μ^-'s. Again this can be interpreted either in terms of helicity conservation or in terms of conservation of a leptonic quantum number L_μ. We shall assume the analogous properties are true for the '$\bar{\nu}'''$'s accompanying τ leptons.

On the other hand, helicity arguments alone would allow the reaction

$$`\bar{\nu}'' + p \to e^+ + n \tag{20.37}$$

to proceed, but as we saw in section 1.2.1 the experiment of Danby *et al.* (1962) found no evidence for it. Thus there is evidence, in this type reaction, for a flavour quantum number distinguishing neutrinos which interact in association with one kind of charged lepton from those which interact in association with a different charged lepton. The electroweak sector of the Standard Model was originally formulated on the assumption that the three lepton flavours L_e, L_μ and L_τ are conserved, and that the neutrinos are massless. It turns out that these two assumptions are related, in the sense that if neutrinos have mass, then (barring degeneracies) 'neutrino oscillations' can occur, in which a state of one lepton flavour can acquire a component of another, as it propagates. Compelling evidence accumulated during the 2000s for oscillations of neutrinos caused by non-zero masses and neutrino mixing.

Strictly speaking, neutrino masses and oscillations lie outside the framework of the original Standard Model, and they are sometimes so regarded. Apart from anything else, the phenomenology of massive neutrinos has to allow for the possibility that they are Majorana, rather than Dirac, fermions. For the moment, we shall continue with a semi-historical path, and proceed with weak interaction phenomenology on the basis of the original Standard Model, with massless neutrinos. We return to the question of neutrino mass when we discuss neutrino oscillations (along with analogous oscillations in meson systems) in chapter 21.

20.4   The universal current × current theory for weak interactions of leptons

After the breakthroughs of parity violation and V-A theory, the earlier hopes (Pontecorvo 1947, Klein 1948, Puppi 1948, Lee, Rosenbluth and Yang 1949, Tiomno and Wheeler 1949) were revived of a universal weak interaction among the pairs of particles (p,n), $(\nu_e, e^-), (\nu_\mu, \mu^-)$, using the V-A modification to Fermi's theory. From our modern standpoint, this list has to be changed by the replacement of (p,n) by the corresponding quarks (u,d), and by the inclusion of the third lepton pair (ν_τ, τ^-) as well as two other quark pairs (c,s) and (t,b). It is to these pairs that the 'V-A' structure applies, as already indicated in section 20.2.2, and a certain form of 'universality' does hold, as we now describe.

Because of certain complications which arise, we shall postpone the discussion of the quark currents until section 20.7, concentrating here on the leptonic currents[2]. In this case, Fermi's original vector-like current $\hat{\bar{\psi}}_e \gamma^\mu \hat{\psi}_\nu$ becomes modified to a *total leptonic charged current*

$$\hat{j}^\mu_{CC}(\text{leptons}) = \hat{j}^\mu_{wk}(e) + \hat{j}^\mu_{wk}(\mu) + \hat{j}^\mu_{wk}(\tau) \qquad (20.38)$$

where, for example,

$$\hat{j}^\mu_{wk}(e) = \hat{\bar{\nu}}_e \gamma^\mu (1 - \gamma_5)\hat{e}. \qquad (20.39)$$

In (20.39) we are now adopting, for the first time, a useful shorthand whereby the field operator for the electron field, say, is denoted by $\hat{e}(x)$ rather than $\hat{\psi}_e(x)$, and the 'x' argument is suppressed. The 'charged' current terminology refers to the fact that these weak current operators $\hat{j}^\mu_{wk}$ carry net charge, in contrast to an electromagnetic current operator such as $\hat{\bar{e}}\gamma^\mu \hat{e}$ which is electrically neutral. We shall see in section 20.6 that there are also electrically neutral weak currents.

---

[2]Very much the same complications arise for the leptonic currents too, in the case of massive neutrinos, as we shall see in section 21.4.

The interaction Hamiltonian density accounting for all leptonic weak interactions is then taken to be

$$\hat{\mathcal{H}}_{CC}^{lep} = \frac{G_F}{\sqrt{2}} \hat{j}_{CC}^{\mu}(leptons) \hat{j}_{CC\mu}^{\dagger}(leptons). \tag{20.40}$$

Note that

$$(\bar{\hat{\nu}}_e \gamma^\mu (1 - \gamma_5) \hat{e})^\dagger = \bar{\hat{e}} \gamma^\mu (1 - \gamma_5) \hat{\nu}_e \tag{20.41}$$

and similarly for the other bilinears. The currents can also be written in terms of the chiral components of the fields (recall section 20.2.2) using

$$2 \bar{\hat{\nu}}_{eL} \gamma^\mu \hat{e}_L = \bar{\hat{\nu}}_e \gamma^\mu (1 - \gamma_5) \hat{e}, \tag{20.42}$$

for example. 'Universality' is manifest in the fact that all the lepton pairs have the same form of the V-A coupling, and the same 'strength parameter' $G_F/\sqrt{2}$ multiplies all of the products in (20.40).

The terms in (20.40), when it is multiplied out, describe many physical processes. For example, the term

$$\frac{G_F}{\sqrt{2}} \bar{\hat{\nu}}_\mu \gamma^\mu (1 - \gamma_5) \hat{\mu} \, \bar{\hat{e}} \gamma_\mu (1 - \gamma_5) \hat{\nu}_e \tag{20.43}$$

describes μ^- decay:

$$\mu^- \to \nu_\mu + e^- + \bar{\nu}_e, \tag{20.44}$$

as well as all the reactions related by 'crossing' particles from one side to the other, for example

$$\nu_\mu + e^- \to \mu^- + \nu_e. \tag{20.45}$$

The value of G_F can be determined from the rate for process (20.44) (see for example Renton 1990, section 6.1.2), and it is found to be

$$G_F \simeq 1.166 \times 10^{-5} \text{GeV}^{-2}. \tag{20.46}$$

This is a convenient moment to notice that the theory is *not renormalizable* according to the criteria discussed in section 11.8 at the end of the previous volume: G_F has dimensions $(\text{mass})^{-2}$. We shall return to this aspect of Fermi-type V-A theory in section 22.1.

There are also what we might call 'diagonal' terms in which the same lepton pair is taken from $\hat{j}_{wk}^\mu$ and $\hat{j}_{wk\mu}^\dagger$, for example

$$\frac{G_F}{\sqrt{2}} \bar{\hat{\nu}}_e \gamma^\mu (1 - \gamma_5) \hat{e} \, \bar{\hat{e}} \gamma_\mu (1 - \gamma_5) \hat{\nu}_e \tag{20.47}$$

which describes reactions such as

$$\bar{\nu}_e + e^- \to \bar{\nu}_e + e^-. \tag{20.48}$$

The cross section for (20.48) was measured by Reines, Gurr and Sobel (1976)

after many years of effort; the value obtained was consistent with the Glashow–Salam–Weinberg theory (see section 22.3), with the parameter $\sin^2 \theta_{\rm W} = 0.29 \pm 0.05$.

It is interesting that some seemingly rather similar processes are forbidden to occur, to first order in $\hat{\mathcal{H}}_{\rm wk}^{\rm lep}$, for example

$$\bar{\nu}_\mu + {\rm e}^- \to \bar{\nu}_\mu + {\rm e}^-. \tag{20.49}$$

For reasons which will become clearer in section 20.6, (20.49) is called a 'neutral current' process, in contrast to all the others (such as β-decay or μ-decay) we have discussed so far, which are called 'charged current' processes. If the lepton pairs are arranged so as to have no net lepton number (for example ${\rm e}^- \bar{\nu}_{\rm e}, \mu^+ \nu_\mu, \nu_\mu \bar{\nu}_\mu$ etc.) then pairs with non-zero charge occur in charged current processes, while those with zero charge participate in neutral current processes. In the case of (20.48), the leptons can be grouped either as $(\bar{\nu}_{\rm e}{\rm e}^-)$ which is charged, or as $(\bar{\nu}_{\rm e}\nu_{\rm e})$ or $({\rm e}^+{\rm e}^-)$ which are neutral. On the other hand, there is no way of pairing the leptons in (20.49) so as to cancel the lepton number and have non-zero charge. So (20.49) is a *purely* 'neutral current' process, while *some* 'neutral current' contribution could be present in (20.48), in principle. In 1973 such neutral current processes were discovered (Hasert *et al.* 1973), generating a whole new wave of experimental activity. Their existence had, in fact, been *predicted* in the first version of the Standard Model, due to Glashow (1961). Today we know that charged current processes are mediated by the $W^\pm$ bosons, and the neutral current ones by the Z^0. We shall discuss the neutral current couplings in section 20.6.

20.5   Calculation of the cross section for $\nu_\mu + {\rm e}^- \to \mu^- + \nu_{\rm e}$

After so much qualitative discussion it is time to calculate something. We choose the process (20.45), sometimes called inverse muon decay, which is a pure 'charged current' process. The amplitude, in the Fermi-like V-A current theory, is

$$\mathcal{M} = -{\rm i}(G_{\rm F}/\sqrt{2})\bar{u}(\mu, k')\gamma_\mu(1 - \gamma_5)u(\nu_\mu, k)\bar{u}(\nu_{\rm e}, p')\gamma^\mu(1 - \gamma_5)u({\rm e}, p). \tag{20.50}$$

We shall be interested in energies much greater than any of the leptons, and so we shall work in the *massless limit*; this is mainly for ease of calculation – the full expressions for non-zero masses can be obtained with more effort.

From the general formula (6.129) for $2 \to 2$ scattering in the CM system, we have, neglecting all masses,

$$\frac{{\rm d}\sigma}{{\rm d}\Omega} = \frac{1}{64\pi^2 s}|\overline{\mathcal{M}}|^2 \tag{20.51}$$

where $|\overline{\mathcal{M}}|^2$ is the appropriate spin-averaged matrix element squared, as in

(8.183) for example. In the case of neutrino-electron scattering, we must average over initial electron states for unpolarized electrons and sum over the final muon polarization states. For the neutrinos there is no averaging over initial neutrino helicities, since only left-handed (massless) neutrinos participate in the weak interaction. Similarly, there is no sum over final neutrino helicities. However, for convenience of calculation, we can in fact sum over both helicity states of both neutrinos since the $(1 - \gamma_5)$ factors guarantee that right-handed neutrinos contribute nothing to the cross section. As for the $e\mu$ scattering example in section 8.7, the calculation then reduces to a product of traces:

$$|\mathcal{M}|^2 = \left(\frac{G_F^2}{2}\right) \text{Tr}[\not{k}'\gamma_\mu(1 - \gamma_5)\,\not{k}\gamma_\nu(1 - \gamma_5)]\frac{1}{2}\text{Tr}[\not{p}'\gamma^\mu(1 - \gamma_5)\,\not{p}\gamma^\nu(1 - \gamma_5)], \tag{20.52}$$

all lepton masses being neglected. We define

$$|\overline{\mathcal{M}}|^2 = \left(\frac{G_F^2}{2}\right) N_{\mu\nu}E^{\mu\nu} \tag{20.53}$$

where the $\nu_\mu \to \mu^-$ tensor $N_{\mu\nu}$ is given by

$$N_{\mu\nu} = \text{Tr}[\not{k}'\gamma_\mu(1 - \gamma_5)\,\not{k}\gamma_\nu(1 - \gamma_5)] \tag{20.54}$$

without a $1/(2s + 1)$ factor, and the $e^- \to \nu_e$ tensor is

$$E^{\mu\nu} = \frac{1}{2}\text{Tr}[\not{p}'\gamma^\mu(1 - \gamma_5)\,\not{p}\gamma^\nu(1 - \gamma_5)] \tag{20.55}$$

including a factor of $\frac{1}{2}$ for spin averaging.

Since this calculation involves a couple of new features, let us look at it in some detail. By commuting the $(1 - \gamma_5)$ factor through two γ matrices ($\not{p}\gamma^\nu$) and using the result that

$$(1 - \gamma_5)^2 = 2(1 - \gamma_5) \tag{20.56}$$

the tensor $N_{\mu\nu}$ may be written as

$$\begin{aligned} N_{\mu\nu} &= 2\text{Tr}[\not{k}'\gamma_\mu(1 - \gamma_5)\,\not{k}\gamma_\nu] \\ &= 2\text{Tr}(\not{k}'\gamma_\mu\,\not{k}\gamma_\nu) - 2\text{Tr}(\gamma_5\,\not{k}\gamma_\nu\,\not{k}'\gamma_\mu). \end{aligned} \tag{20.57}$$

The first trace is the same as in our calculation of $e\mu$ scattering (cf (8.186)):

$$\text{Tr}(\not{k}'\gamma_\mu\,\not{k}\gamma_\nu) = 4[k'_\mu k_\nu + k'_\nu k_\mu + (q^2/2)g_{\mu\nu}]. \tag{20.58}$$

The second trace must be evaluated using the result

$$\text{Tr}(\gamma_5\,\not{a}\,\not{b}\,\not{c}\,\not{d}) = 4i\epsilon_{\alpha\beta\gamma\delta}a^\alpha b^\beta c^\gamma d^\delta \tag{20.59}$$

(see equation (J.37) in appendix J of volume 1). The totally antisymmetric

tensor $\epsilon_{\alpha\beta\gamma\delta}$ is just the generalization of ϵ_{ijk} to four dimensions, and is defined by

$$\epsilon_{\alpha\beta\gamma\delta} = \begin{cases} +1 & \text{for } \epsilon_{0123} \text{ and all even permutations of } 0,1,2,3 \\ -1 & \text{for } \epsilon_{1023} \text{ and all odd permutations of } 0,1,2,3 \\ 0 & \text{otherwise.} \end{cases}$$

(20.60)

Its appearance here is a direct consequence of parity violation. Notice that this definition has the consequence that

$$\epsilon_{0123} = +1 \tag{20.61}$$

but

$$\epsilon^{0123} = -1. \tag{20.62}$$

We will also need to contract two ϵ tensors. By looking at the possible combinations, it should be easy to convince yourself of the result

$$\epsilon_{ijk}\epsilon_{ilm} = \begin{vmatrix} \delta_{jl} & \delta_{jm} \\ \delta_{kl} & \delta_{km} \end{vmatrix} \tag{20.63}$$

i.e.

$$\epsilon_{ijk}\epsilon_{ilm} = \delta_{jl}\delta_{km} - \delta_{kl}\delta_{jm}. \tag{20.64}$$

For the four-dimensional ϵ tensor one can show (see problem 20.6)

$$\epsilon_{\mu\nu\alpha\beta}\epsilon^{\mu\nu\gamma\delta} = -2! \begin{vmatrix} \delta_\alpha^\gamma & \delta_\beta^\gamma \\ \delta_\alpha^\delta & \delta_\beta^\delta \end{vmatrix} \tag{20.65}$$

where the minus sign arises from (20.62) and the 2! from the fact that the two indices are contracted.

We can now evaluate $N_{\mu\nu}$. We obtain, after some rearrangement of indices, the result for the $\nu_\mu \to \mu^-$ tensor:

$$N_{\mu\nu} = 8[(k'_\mu k_\nu + k'_\nu k_\mu + (q^2/2)g_{\mu\nu}) - i\epsilon_{\mu\nu\alpha\beta}k^\alpha k'^\beta]. \tag{20.66}$$

For the electron tensor $E^{\mu\nu}$ we have a similar result (divided by 2):

$$E^{\mu\nu} = 4[(p'^\mu p^\nu + p'^\nu p^\mu + (q^2/2)g^{\mu\nu}) - i\epsilon^{\mu\nu\gamma\delta}p_\gamma p'_\delta]. \tag{20.67}$$

Next, we have to perform the contraction $N_{\mu\nu}E^{\mu\nu}$ in (20.53). In the case of elastic $e^-\mu^-$ scattering considered in section 8.7, the analogous contraction between the tensors $L_{\mu\nu}$ and $M^{\mu\nu}$ was simplified by using the conditions $q^\mu L_{\mu\nu} = q^\nu L_{\mu\nu} = 0$ (see (8.189)), which followed from electromagnetic current conservation at the electron vertex (see (8.188)): $q^\mu \bar{u}(k')\gamma_\mu u(k) = 0$. Here, the analogous vertex is $\bar{u}(\mu, k')\gamma_\mu(1 - \gamma_5)u(\nu_\mu, k)$. In this case, when we contract this with $q^\mu = (k - k')^\mu$ we find a non-zero result:

$$(m_{\nu_\mu} - m_\mu)\bar{u}(\mu, k')u(\nu_\mu, k) + (m_\mu + m_{\nu_\mu})\bar{u}(\mu, k')\gamma_5 u(\nu_\mu, k), \tag{20.68}$$

using the on-shell conditions for the spinors. (In the electromagnetic case, there was no γ_5 term, and the intial and final masses were the same.) The quantity (20.68) vanishes only when the lepton masses vanish, and that is the approximation we shall make: i.e. we shall neglect all lepton masses. Then

$$q^\mu N_{\mu\nu} = q^\nu N_{\mu\nu} = 0, \tag{20.69}$$

and we may write

$$p' = p + q \tag{20.70}$$

and drop all terms involving q in the contraction with $N_{\mu\nu}$. In the antisymmetric term, however, we have

$$\epsilon^{\mu\nu\gamma\delta} p_\gamma (p_\delta + q_\delta) = \epsilon^{\mu\nu\gamma\delta} p_\gamma q_\delta \tag{20.71}$$

since the term with p_δ vanishes because of the antisymmetry of $\epsilon_{\mu\nu\gamma\delta}$. Thus we arrive at

$$E_{\text{eff}}^{\mu\nu} = 8p^\mu p^\nu + 2q^2 g^{\mu\nu} - 4i\epsilon^{\mu\nu\gamma\delta} p_\gamma q_\delta. \tag{20.72}$$

We must now evaluate the '$N \cdot E$' contraction in (20.53). Since we are neglecting all masses, it is easiest to perform the calculation in invariant form before specializing to the 'laboratory' frame. The usual Mandelstam variables are (neglecting all masses)

$$s = 2k \cdot p \tag{20.73}$$
$$u = -2k' \cdot p \tag{20.74}$$
$$t = -2k \cdot k' = q^2 \tag{20.75}$$

satisfying

$$s + t + u = 0. \tag{20.76}$$

The result of performing the contraction

$$N_{\mu\nu} E^{\mu\nu} = N_{\mu\nu} E_{\text{eff}}^{\mu\nu} \tag{20.77}$$

may be found using the result (20.65) for the contraction of two ϵ tensors (see problem 20.6): the answer for $\nu_\mu e^- \rightarrow \mu^- \nu_e$ is

$$N_{\mu\nu} E^{\mu\nu} = 16(s^2 + u^2) + 16(s^2 - u^2) \tag{20.78}$$

where the first term arises from the symmetric part of $N_{\mu\nu}$ similar to $L_{\mu\nu}$, and the second term from the antisymmetric part involving $\epsilon_{\mu\nu\alpha\beta}$. We have also used

$$t = q^2 = -(s + u) \tag{20.79}$$

valid in the approximation in which we are working. Thus for $\nu_\mu e^- \rightarrow \mu^- \nu_e$ we have

$$N_{\mu\nu} E^{\mu\nu} = +32s^2 \tag{20.80}$$

and with

$$\frac{d\sigma}{d\Omega} = \frac{1}{64\pi^2 s}\left(\frac{G_F^2}{2}\right)N_{\mu\nu}E^{\mu\nu} \tag{20.81}$$

we finally obtain the result

$$\frac{d\sigma}{d\Omega} = \frac{G_F^2 s}{4\pi^2}. \tag{20.82}$$

The total cross section is then

$$\sigma = \frac{G_F^2 s}{\pi}. \tag{20.83}$$

Since $t = -2p^2(1 - \cos\theta)$, where p is the CM momentum and θ the CM scattering angle, (20.82) can alternatively be written in invariant form as (problem 20.7)

$$\frac{d\sigma}{dt} = \frac{G_F^2}{\pi}. \tag{20.84}$$

All other purely leptonic processes may be calculated in an analogous fashion (see Bailin 1982 and Renton 1990 for further examples).

When we discuss deep inelastic neutrino scattering in section 20.7.2, we shall be interested in neutrino 'laboratory' cross sections, as in the electron scattering case of chapter 9. A simple calculation gives $s \simeq 2m_e E$ (neglecting squares of lepton masses by comparison with $m_e E$), where E is the 'laboratory' energy of a neutrino incident, in this example, on a stationary electron. It follows that *the total 'laboratory' cross section in this Fermi-like current–current model rises linearly with E*. We shall return to the implications of this in section 20.7.2.

The process (20.45) was measured by Bergsma *et al.* (1983) using the CERN wide band beam ($E_\nu \sim 20$ GeV). The ratio of the observed number of events to that expected for pure V–A was quoted as 0.98 ± 0.12.

20.6 Leptonic weak neutral currents

The first observations of the weak neutral current process $\bar{\nu}_\mu e^- \to \bar{\nu}_\mu e^-$ were reported by Hasert *et al.* (1973), in a pioneer experiment using the heavy-liquid bubble chamber Gargamelle at CERN, irradiated with a $\bar{\nu}_\mu$ beam. As in the case of the charged currents, much detailed experimental work was necessary to determine the precise form of the neutral current couplings. They are, of course, *predicted* by the Glashow–Salam–Weinberg theory, as we shall explain in chapter 22. For the moment, we continue with the current–current approach, parametrizing the currents in a convenient way.

There are two types of 'neutral current' couplings, those involving neutrinos of the form $\bar{\hat{\nu}}_l \dots \hat{\nu}_l$, and those involving the charged leptons of the form

$\bar{\hat{l}}\dots\hat{l}$. We shall assume the following form for these currents (with one eye on the GSW theory to come):

(1) neutrino neutral current

$$g_N c^{\nu_l} \bar{\hat{\nu}}_l \gamma^\mu \left(\frac{1-\gamma_5}{2}\right)\hat{\nu}_l \qquad l = e, \mu, \tau; \tag{20.85}$$

(2) charged lepton neutral current

$$g_N \bar{\hat{l}}\gamma^\mu \left[c_L^l \frac{(1-\gamma_5)}{2} + c_R^l \frac{(1+\gamma_5)}{2}\right]\hat{l} \qquad l = e, \mu, \tau. \tag{20.86}$$

This is, of course, by no means the most general possible parametrization. The neutrino coupling is retained as pure 'V-A', while the coupling in the charged lepton sector is now a combination of 'V-A' and 'V+A' with certain coefficients c_L^l and c_R^l. We may also write the coupling in terms of 'V' and 'A' coefficients defined by $c_V^l = c_L^l + c_R^l, c_A^l = c_L^l - c_R^l$. An overall factor g_N determines the strength of the neutral currents as compared to the charged ones; the c's determine the relative amplitudes of the various neutral current processes.

As we shall see, an essential feature of the GSW theory is its prediction of weak neutral current processes, with couplings determined in terms of one parameter of the theory called 'θ_W', the 'weak mixing angle' (Glashow 1961, Weinberg 1967). The GSW predictions for the parameter g_N and the c's are (see equations (22.59)–(22.62))

$$g_N = g/\cos\theta_W, \quad c^{\nu_l} = \frac{1}{2}, \quad c_L^l = -\frac{1}{2} + a, \quad c_R^l = a \tag{20.87}$$

for $l = e, \mu, \tau$, where $a = \sin^2\theta_W$ and g is the SU(2) gauge coupling. Note that a strong form of 'universality' is involved here too: the coefficients are independent of the 'flavour' e, μ or τ, for both neutrinos and charged leptons.

The following reactions are available for experimental measurement (in addition to the charged current process (20.45) already discussed):

$$\nu_\mu e^- \ \rightarrow \ \nu_\mu e^-, \ \ \bar{\nu}_\mu e^- \rightarrow \bar{\nu}_\mu e^- \ \ (NC) \tag{20.88}$$
$$\nu_e e^- \ \rightarrow \ \nu_e e^-, \ \ \bar{\nu}_e e^- \rightarrow \bar{\nu}_e e^- \ \ (NC + CC) \tag{20.89}$$

where 'NC' means neutral current and 'CC' charged current. Formulae for these cross sections are given in section 22.3. The experiments are discussed and reviewed in Commins and Bucksbaum (1983), Renton (1990), and by Winter (2000). All observations are in excellent agreement with the GSW predictions, with θ_W determined as $\sin^2\theta_W \simeq 0.23$. The reader must note, however, that modern precision measurements are sensitive to higher-order (loop) corrections, which must be included in comparing the full GSW theory

with experiment (see section 22.6). The simultaneous fit of data from all four reactions in terms of the single parameter θ_W provides already strong confirmation of the theory – and indeed such confirmation was already emerging in the late 1970's and early 1980's, before the actual discovery of the $W^{\pm}$ and Z^0 bosons. It is also interesting to note that the presence of vector (V) interactions in the neutral current processes may suggest the possibility of some kind of link with electromagnetic interactions, which are of course also 'neutral' (in this sense) and vector-like. In the GSW theory, this linkage is provided essentially through the parameter θ_W, as we shall see.

20.7   Quark weak currents

We now turn our attention to the weak interactions of quarks. We shall begin by considering an earlier world, when only two generations (four flavours) were known.

20.7.1   Two generations

The original version of V-A theory was framed in terms of a nucleonic current of the form $\bar{\hat{\psi}}_p \gamma^\mu (1 - r\gamma_5) \hat{\psi}_n$. With the acceptance of quark substructure it was natural to re-interpret such a hadronic transition by a charged current of the form $\bar{\hat{u}}\gamma^\mu(1-\gamma_5)\hat{d}$, very similar to the charged lepton currents; indeed, here was a further example of 'universality', this time between quarks and leptons. Detailed comparison with experiment showed, however, that such d $\rightarrow$ u transitions were very slightly weaker than the analogous leptonic ones; this could be established by comparing the rates for n $\rightarrow$ pe$^-\bar{\nu}_e$ and $\bar{\mu} \rightarrow \nu_\mu e^- \bar{\nu}_e$.

But for quarks (or their hadronic composites) there is a further complication, which is the very familiar phenomenon of flavour change in weak hadronic processes (recall the discussion in section 1.2.2). The first step towards the modern theory of quark currents was taken by Cabibbo (1963); in a sense, it restored universality. Cabibbo postulated that the strength of the hadronic weak interaction was *shared* between the $\Delta S = 0$ and $\Delta S = 1$ transitions (where S is the strangeness quantum number), the latter being relatively suppressed as compared to the former. According to Cabibbo's hypothesis, phrased in terms of quarks, the total weak charged current for u, d and s quarks is

$$\hat{j}^\mu_{\text{Cab}}(\text{u}, \text{d}, \text{s}) = \cos\theta_C \bar{\hat{u}}\gamma^\mu \frac{(1 - \gamma_5)}{2} \hat{d} + \sin\theta_C \bar{\hat{u}}\gamma^\mu \frac{(1 - \gamma_5)}{2} \hat{s}, \qquad (20.90)$$

where θ_C is the 'Cabibbo angle' (not to be confused with θ_W). We can now postulate a total weak charged current

$$\hat{j}^\mu_{\text{CC}}(\text{total}) = \hat{j}^\mu_{\text{CC}}(\text{leptons}) + \hat{j}^\mu_{\text{Cab}}(\text{u}, \text{d}, \text{s}), \qquad (20.91)$$

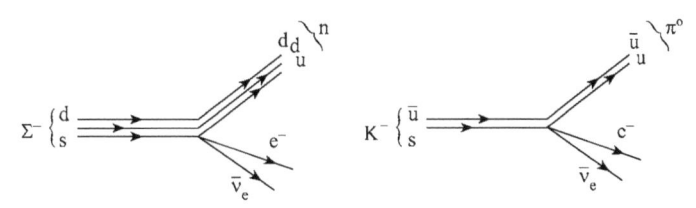

FIGURE 20.3
Strangeness-changing semi-leptonic weak decays.

where $\hat{j}^{\mu}_{CC}$(leptons) is given by (20.38), and then generalize (20.40) to

$$\hat{\mathcal{H}}^{tot}_{CC} = \frac{G_F}{\sqrt{2}} \hat{j}^{\mu}_{CC}(\text{total})\hat{j}^{\dagger}_{CC\mu}(\text{total}). \tag{20.92}$$

The effective interaction (20.92) describes a great many processes. The purely leptonic ones discussed previously are, of course, present in the term $\hat{j}^{\mu}_{CC}$(leptons)$\hat{j}^{\dagger}_{CC\mu}$(leptons). But there are also now all the *semi-leptonic* processes such as the $\Delta S = 0$ (strangeness conserving) one

$$d \rightarrow u + e^- + \bar{\nu}_e, \tag{20.93}$$

and the $\Delta S = 1$ (strangeness changing) one

$$s \rightarrow u + e^- + \bar{\nu}_e. \tag{20.94}$$

The notion that the 'total current' should be the sum of a hadronic and a leptonic part is already familiar from electromagnetism – see, for example, equation (8.91).

The transition (20.94), for example, is the underlying process in semi-leptonic decays such as

$$\Sigma^- \rightarrow n + e^- + \bar{\nu}_e \tag{20.95}$$

and

$$K^- \rightarrow \pi^0 + e^- + \bar{\nu}_e \tag{20.96}$$

as indicated in figure 20.3.

The 's' quark is assigned $S = -1$ and charge $-\frac{1}{3}e$. The s $\rightarrow$ u transition is then referred to as one with '$\Delta S = \Delta Q$', meaning that the change in the quark (or hadronic) strangeness is equal to the change in the quark (or hadronic) charge: both the strangeness and the charge increase by 1 unit. Prior to the advent of the quark model, and the Cabibbo hypothesis, it had been established empirically that all known strangeness-changing semileptonic decays satisfied the rules $|\Delta S| = 1$ and $\Delta S = \Delta Q$. The u-s current in (20.90) satisfies these rules automatically. Note, for example, that the process apparently similar to (20.95), $\Sigma^+ \rightarrow n + e^+ + \nu_e$, is forbidden in the lowest order (it

requires a double quark transition from suu to udd). All known data on such decays can be fit with a value $\sin \theta_C \simeq 0.22$ for the Cabibbo angle θ_C. This relatively small angle is therefore a measure of the suppression of $|\Delta S| = 1$ processes relative to $\Delta S = 0$ ones.

The Cabibbo current can be written in a more compact form by introducing the 'mixed' field

$$\hat{d}' \equiv \cos \theta_C \hat{d} + \sin \theta_C \hat{s}. \qquad (20.97)$$

Then

$$\hat{j}^{\mu}_{\text{Cab}}(u, d, s) = \bar{\hat{u}} \gamma^{\mu} \frac{(1 - \gamma_5)}{2} \hat{d}'. \qquad (20.98)$$

In 1970 Glashow, Iliopuolos and Maiani (GIM) (1970) drew attention to a theoretical problem with the interaction (20.92) if used in *second* order. Now it is, of course, the case that this interaction is not renormalizable, as noted previously for the purely leptonic one (20.40), since G_F has dimensions of an inverse mass squared. As we saw in section 11.7, this means that one-loop diagrams will typically diverge quadratically, so that the contribution of such a second-order process will be of order $(G_F.G_F\Lambda^2)$ where Λ is a cut-off, compared to the first-order amplitude G_F. Recalling from (20.46) that $G_F \sim 10^{-5}$ GeV^{-2}, we see that for $\Lambda \sim 10$ GeV such a correction could be significant if accurate enough data exists. GIM pointed out, in particular, that some second-order processes could be found which violated the (hitherto) well-established phenomenological selection rules, such as the $|\Delta S| = 1$ and $\Delta S = \Delta Q$ rules already discussed. For example, there could be $\Delta S = 2$ amplitudes contributing to the $K_L - K_S$ mass difference (see Renton 1990, section 9.1.6, for example), as well as contributions to unobserved decay modes such as

$$K^+ \to \pi^+ + \nu + \bar{\nu} \qquad (20.99)$$

which has a *neutral* lepton pair in association with a *strangeness change* for the hadron. In fact, experiment placed very tight limits on the rate for (20.99) – and still does: the branching fraction is $(1.7 \pm 1.1) \times 10^{-10}$ (Nakamura *et al.* 2010). This seemed to imply a surprisingly low value of the cut-off, say ~ 3 GeV (Mohapatra *et al.* 1968).

Partly in order to address this problem, and partly as a revival of an earlier lepton-quark symmetry proposal (Bjorken and Glashow 1964), GIM introduced a fourth quark, now called c (the charm quark) with charge $\frac{2}{3}e$. Note that in 1970 the τ-lepton had not been discovered, so only two lepton family pairs (ν_e, e), (ν_μ, μ) were known; this fourth quark therefore did restore the balance, via the two quark family pairs (u,d), (c,s). In particular, a second quark current could now be hypothesized, involving the (c,s) pair. GIM postulated that the c-quark was coupled to the 'orthogonal' d-s combination (cf (20.97))

$$\hat{s}' = -\sin \theta_C \hat{d} + \cos \theta_C \hat{s}. \qquad (20.100)$$

The complete four-quark charged current is then

$$\hat{j}^{\mu}_{\text{GIM}}(u,d,c,s) = \bar{\hat{u}}\gamma^{\mu}\frac{(1-\gamma_5)}{2}\hat{d}' + \bar{\hat{c}}\gamma^{\mu}\frac{(1-\gamma_5)}{2}\hat{s}'. \tag{20.101}$$

The form (20.101) had already been suggested by Bjorken and Glashow (1964). The new feature of GIM was the observation that, assuming an exact $SU(4)_f$ symmetry for the four quarks (in particular, equal masses), all second-order contributions which could have violated the $|\Delta S| = 1, \Delta S = \Delta Q$ selection rules now vanished. Further, to the extent that the (unknown) mass of the charm quark functioned as an effective cut-off Λ, due to breaking of the $SU(4)_f$ symmetry, they estimated m_c to lie in the range 3-4 GeV, from the observed $K_L - K_S$ mass difference.

GIM went on to speculate that the non-renormalizability could be overcome if the weak interactions were described by an $SU(2)$ Yang-Mills gauge theory, involving a triplet (W^+, W^-, W^0) of gauge bosons. In this case, it is natural to introduce the idea of (weak) 'isospin', in terms of which the pairs (ν_e, e), (ν_μ, μ), (u,d'), (c, s') are all $t = \frac{1}{2}$ doublets with $t_3 = \pm\frac{1}{2}$. Charge-changing currents then involve the 'raising' matrix

$$\tau_+ \equiv \frac{1}{2}(\tau_1 + i\tau_2) = \begin{pmatrix} 0 & 1 \\ 0 & 0 \end{pmatrix} \tag{20.102}$$

and charge-lowering ones the matrix $\tau_- = (\tau_1 - i\tau_2)/2$. The full symmetry must also involve the matrix τ_3, given by the commutator $[\tau_+, \tau_-] = \tau_3$. Whereas τ_+ and τ_- would (in this model) be associated with transitions mediated by $W^{\pm}$, transitions involving τ_3 would be mediated by W^0, and would correspond to 'neutral current' transitions for quarks. We now know that things are slightly more complicated than this: the correct symmetry is the $SU(2) \times U(1)$ of Glashow (1961), also invoked by GIM. Skipping therefore some historical steps, we parametrize the *weak quark neutral current* as (cf (20.86) for the leptonic analogue)

$$g_N \sum_{q=u,c,d',s'} \bar{\hat{q}}\gamma^{\mu}[c^q_L\frac{(1-\gamma_5)}{2} + c^q_R\frac{(1+\gamma_5)}{2}]\hat{q} \tag{20.103}$$

for the four flavours so far in play. In the GSW theory, the c^q_L's are predicted to be

$$c^{u,c}_L = \frac{1}{2} - \frac{2}{3}a \qquad c^{u,c}_R = -\frac{2}{3}a \tag{20.104}$$

$$c^{d,s}_L = -\frac{1}{2} + \frac{1}{3}a \qquad c^{d,s}_R = \frac{1}{3}a \tag{20.105}$$

where $a = \sin^2\theta_W$ as before, and $g_N = g/\cos\theta_W$.

One feature of (20.103) is very important. Consider the terms

$$\bar{\hat{d}}'\{\ldots\}\hat{d}' + \bar{\hat{s}}'\{\ldots\}\hat{s}'. \tag{20.106}$$

It is simple to verify that, whereas either part of (20.106) alone contains a *strangeness changing neutral* combination such as $\hat{\bar{d}}\{\ldots\}\hat{s}$ or $\hat{\bar{s}}\{\ldots\}\hat{d}$, such combinations vanish in the sum, leaving the result *diagonal in quark flavour*. Thus there are no first-order neutral flavour-changing currents in this model, a result which will be extended to three flavours in section 20.7.3.

In 1974, Gaillard and Lee (1974) performed a full one-loop calculation of the $K_L - K_S$ mass difference in the GSW model as extended by GIM to quarks and using the renormalization techniques recently developed by 't Hooft (1971b). They were able to predict $m_c \sim 1.5$ GeV for the charm quark mass, a result spectacularly confirmed by the subsequent discovery of the $c\bar{c}$ states in charmonium, and of charmed mesons and baryons of the appropriate mass.

In summary, then, the essential feature of the quark weak currents in the two-generation model is that they have the universal V-A form, but the participating fields are $(\hat{u}, \hat{d}')$, $(\hat{c}, \hat{s}')$ where $\hat{d}'$ and $\hat{s}'$ are not the fields $\hat{d}, \hat{s}$ with definite mass, but rather are related to them by an orthogonal transformation:

$$\left(\begin{array}{c} \hat{d}' \\ \hat{s}' \end{array} \right) = \left(\begin{array}{cc} \cos\theta_C & \sin\theta_C \\ -\sin\theta_C & \cos\theta_C \end{array} \right) \left(\begin{array}{c} \hat{d} \\ \hat{s} \end{array} \right). \tag{20.107}$$

In section 20.8 we shall enlarge this picture to three generations, where significant new features occur, specifically **CP** violation. In chapter 22 we shall see how this transformation from the 'mass' basis to the 'weak interaction' basis arises via the gauge-invariant interactions of the Standard Model.

20.7.2 Deep inelastic neutrino scattering

We now have enough theory to present another illustrative calculation within the framework of the 'current–current' model, this time involving neutrinos and quarks. We shall calculate cross sections for deep inelastic neutrino scattering from nucleons, using the parton model introduced (for electromagnetic interactions) in chapter 9. In particular, we shall consider the processes

$$\nu_\mu + N \quad \rightarrow \quad \mu^- + X \tag{20.108}$$

$$\bar{\nu}_\mu + N \quad \rightarrow \quad \mu^+ + X \tag{20.109}$$

which of course involve the charged currents, for both leptons and quarks. Studies of these reactions at Fermilab and CERN in the 1970s and 1980s played a crucial part in establishing the quark structure of the nucleon, in particular the quark distribution functions.

The general process is illustrated in figure 20.4. By now we are becoming accustomed to the idea that such processes are in fact mediated by the W^+, but we shall assume that the momentum transfers are such that the W-propagator is effectively constant. The effective lepton-quark interaction will then take the form

$$\hat{\mathcal{H}}_{\nu q}^{\text{eff}} = \frac{G_F}{\sqrt{2}} \bar{\hat{\mu}}\gamma_\mu(1-\gamma_5)\hat{\nu}_\mu[\bar{\hat{u}}\gamma^\mu(1-\gamma_5)\hat{d} + \bar{\hat{c}}\gamma^\mu(1-\gamma_5)\hat{s}], \tag{20.110}$$

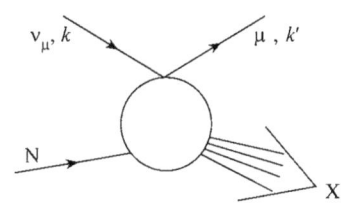

FIGURE 20.4
Inelastic neutrino scattering from a nucleon.

leading to expressions for the parton-level subprocess amplitudes which are exactly similar to that in (20.50) for $\nu_\mu + e^- \to \mu^- + \nu_e$. Note that we are considering only the four flavours u, d, c, s to be 'active', and we have set $\theta_C \approx 0$.

As in (20.53), the ν_μ cross section will have the general form

$$d\sigma^{(\nu)} \propto N_{\mu\nu} W^{\mu\nu}_{(\nu)}(q,p) \tag{20.111}$$

where $N_{\mu\nu}$ is the neutrino tensor of (20.67). The form of the weak hadron tensor $W^{\mu\nu}_{(\nu)}$ is deduced from Lorentz invariance. In the approximation of neglecting lepton masses, we can ignore any dependence on the 4-vector q since

$$q^\mu N_{\mu\nu} = q^\nu N_{\mu\nu} = 0. \tag{20.112}$$

Just as $N_{\mu\nu}$ contains the pseudotensor $\epsilon_{\mu\nu\alpha\beta}$ so too will $W^{\mu\nu}_{(\nu)}$ since parity is not conserved. In a manner similar to equation (9.10) for the case of electron scattering, and following the steps that led from (20.67) to (20.72), we define effective neutrino structure functions by

$$W^{\mu\nu}_{(\nu)} = (-g^{\mu\nu})W_1^{(\nu)} + \frac{1}{M^2}p^\mu p^\nu W_2^{(\nu)} - \frac{i}{2M^2}\epsilon^{\mu\nu\gamma\delta}p_\gamma q_\delta W_3^{(\nu)}. \tag{20.113}$$

In general, the structure functions depend on two variables, say Q^2 and ν, where $Q^2 = -(k - k')^2$ and $\nu = p \cdot q/M$; but in the Bjorken limit approximate scaling is observed, as in the electron case:

$$\left.\begin{array}{c} Q^2 \to \infty \\ \nu \to \infty \end{array}\right\} \quad x = Q^2/2M\nu \text{ fixed} \tag{20.114}$$

$$\nu W_2^{(\nu)}(Q^2, \nu) \quad \to \quad F_2^{(\nu)}(x) \tag{20.115}$$
$$M W_1^{(\nu)}(Q^2, \nu) \quad \to \quad F_1^{(\nu)}(x) \tag{20.116}$$
$$\nu W_3^{(\nu)}(Q^2, \nu) \quad \to \quad F_3^{(\nu)}(x) \tag{20.117}$$

where, as with (9.21) and (9.22), the physics lies in the assertion that the F's

are finite. This scaling can again be interpreted in terms of pointlike scattering from partons – which we shall take to have quark quantum numbers.

In the 'laboratory' frame (in which the nucleon is at rest) the cross section in terms of W_1, W_2 and W_3 may be derived in the usual way from (cf equation (9.11))

$$d\sigma^{(\nu)} = \left(\frac{G_F}{\sqrt{2}}\right)^2 \frac{1}{4k \cdot p} 4\pi M N_{\mu\nu} W^{\mu\nu}_{(\nu)} \frac{d^3 \mathbf{k}'}{2k'(2\pi)^3}. \tag{20.118}$$

In terms of 'laboratory' variables, one obtains (problem 20.9)

$$\frac{d^2\sigma^{(\nu)}}{dQ^2 d\nu} = \frac{G_F^2}{2\pi} \frac{k'}{k} \left(W_2^{(\nu)} \cos^2(\theta/2) + W_1^{(\nu)} 2\sin^2(\theta/2) + \frac{k+k'}{M} \sin^2(\theta/2) W_3^{(\nu)} \right). \tag{20.119}$$

For an incoming antineutrino beam, the W_3 term changes sign.

In neutrino scattering it is common to use the variables x, ν and the 'inelasticity' y where

$$y = p \cdot q / p \cdot k. \tag{20.120}$$

In the 'laboratory' frame, $\nu = E - E'$ (the energy transfer to the nucleon) and $y = \nu/E$. The cross section can be written in the form (see problem 20.9)

$$\frac{d^2\sigma^{(\nu)}}{dx\,dy} = \frac{G_F^2}{2\pi} s \left(F_2^{(\nu)} \frac{1 + (1-y)^2}{2} + x F_3^{(\nu)} \frac{1 - (1-y)^2}{2} \right) \tag{20.121}$$

in terms of the Bjorken scaling functions, and we have assumed the relation

$$2x F_1^{(\nu)} = F_2^{(\nu)} \tag{20.122}$$

appropriate for spin$-\frac{1}{2}$ constituents.

We now turn to the parton-level subprocesses. Their cross sections can be straightforwardly calculated in the same way as for $\nu_\mu e^-$ scattering in section 20.5. We obtain (problem 20.10)

$$\nu q, \bar{\nu}\bar{q}: \quad \frac{d^2\sigma}{dx\,dy} = \frac{G_F^2}{\pi} sx\delta\left(x - \frac{Q^2}{2M\nu}\right) \tag{20.123}$$

$$\nu\bar{q}, \bar{\nu}q: \quad \frac{d^2\sigma}{dx\,dy} = \frac{G_F^2}{\pi} sx(1-y)^2\delta\left(x - \frac{Q^2}{2M\nu}\right). \tag{20.124}$$

The factor $(1-y)^2$ in the $\nu\bar{q}, \bar{\nu}q$ cases means that the reaction is forbidden at $y = 1$ (backwards in the CM frame). This follows from the V-A nature of the current, and angular momentum conservation, as a simple helicity argument shows. Consider for example the case $\nu\bar{q}$ shown in figure 20.5, with the helicities marked as shown. In our current–current interaction there are no gradient coupling terms and therefore no momenta in the momentum-space matrix element. This means that no orbital angular momentum is available to account for the reversal of net helicity in the initial and final states in figure 20.5. The lack of orbital angular momentum can also be inferred physically

FIGURE 20.5
Suppression of $\nu_\mu \bar{q} \to \mu^- \bar{q}$ for $y = 1$: (a) initial state helicities; (b) final state helicities at $y = 1$.

from the 'pointlike' nature of the current–current coupling. For the νq or $\bar{\nu}\bar{q}$ cases, the initial and final helicities add to zero, and backward scattering is allowed.

The contributing processes are

$$\nu d \to l^- u, \qquad \bar{\nu}\bar{d} \to l^+ \bar{u} \tag{20.125}$$
$$\nu \bar{u} \to l^- \bar{d}, \qquad \bar{\nu} u \to l^+ d, \tag{20.126}$$

the first pair having the cross section (20.123), the second (20.124). Following the same steps as in the electron scattering case (sections 9.2 and 9.3) we obtain

$$F_2^{\nu p} = F_2^{\bar{\nu}n} = 2x[d(x) + \bar{u}(x)] \tag{20.127}$$
$$F_3^{\nu p} = F_3^{\bar{\nu}n} = 2[d(x) - \bar{u}(x)] \tag{20.128}$$
$$F_2^{\nu n} = F_2^{\bar{\nu}p} = 2x[u(x) + \bar{d}(x)] \tag{20.129}$$
$$F_3^{\nu n} = F_3^{\bar{\nu}p} = 2[u(x) - \bar{d}(x)]. \tag{20.130}$$

Inserting (20.127) and (20.128) into (20.121), for example, we find

$$\frac{d^2\sigma^{(\nu p)}}{dxdy} = 2\sigma_0 x[d(x) + (1-y)^2\bar{u}(x)] \tag{20.131}$$

where

$$\sigma_0 = \frac{G_F^2 s}{2\pi} = \frac{G_F^2 ME}{\pi} \simeq 1.5 \times 10^{-42}(E/\text{GeV})\text{m}^2 \tag{20.132}$$

is the basic 'pointlike' total cross section (compare (20.83)). Note the small magnitude of this cross section, as compared with the electromagnetic one of equation (B.18) in volume 1, which was $\sigma \approx \frac{86.8}{(s/\text{GeV}^2)} \times 10^{-37}\text{m}^2$. Similarly, one finds

$$\frac{d^2\sigma^{(\bar{\nu}p)}}{dxdy} = 2\sigma_0 x[(1-y)^2 u(x) + \bar{d}(x)]. \tag{20.133}$$

The corresponding results for νn and $\bar{\nu}n$ are given by interchanging $u(x)$ and $d(x)$, and $\bar{u}(x)$ and $\bar{d}(x)$.

The target nuclei usually have high mass number (in order to increase the cross section), with approximately equal numbers of protons and neutrons; it

is then appropriate to average the 'n' and 'p' results to obtain an 'isoscalar' cross section $\sigma^{(\nu N)}$ or $\sigma^{(\bar{\nu} N)}$:

$$\frac{d^2\sigma^{(\nu N)}}{dxdy} = \sigma_0 x[q(x) + (1-y)^2 \bar{q}(x)] \qquad (20.134)$$

$$\frac{d^2\sigma^{(\bar{\nu} N)}}{dxdy} = \sigma_0 x[(1-y)^2 q(x) + \bar{q}(x)] \qquad (20.135)$$

where $q(x) = u(x) + d(x)$ and $\bar{q}(x) = \bar{u}(x) + \bar{d}(x)$.

Many simple and striking predictions now follow from these quark parton results. For example, by integrating (20.134) and (20.135) over x we can write

$$\frac{d\sigma^{(\nu N)}}{dy} = \sigma_0[Q + (1-y)^2 \bar{Q}] \qquad (20.136)$$

$$\frac{d\sigma^{(\bar{\nu} N)}}{dy} = \sigma_0[(1-y)^2 Q + \bar{Q}] \qquad (20.137)$$

where $Q = \int xq(x)dx$ is the fraction of the nucleon's momentum carried by quarks, and similarly for $\bar{Q}$. These two distributions in y ('inelasticity distributions') therefore give a direct measure of the quark and antiquark composition of the nucleon. Figure 20.6 shows the inelasticity distributions as reported by the CDHS collaboration (de Groot *et al.* 1979), from which the authors extracted the ratio

$$\bar{Q}/(Q+\bar{Q}) = 0.15 \pm 0.03 \qquad (20.138)$$

after applying radiative corrections. An even more precise value can be obtained by looking at the region near $y = 1$ for $\bar{\nu} N$ which is dominated by $\bar{Q}$, the small Q contribution ($\propto (1-y)^2$) being subtracted out using νN data at the same y. This method yields

$$\bar{Q}/(Q+\bar{Q}) = 0.15 \pm 0.01. \qquad (20.139)$$

Integrating (20.136) and (20.137) over y gives

$$\sigma^{(\nu N)} = \sigma_0(Q + \frac{1}{3}\bar{Q}) \qquad (20.140)$$

$$\sigma^{(\bar{\nu} N)} = \sigma_0(\frac{1}{3}Q + \bar{Q}) \qquad (20.141)$$

and hence

$$Q + \bar{Q} = 3(\sigma^{(\nu N)} + \sigma^{(\bar{\nu} N)})/4\sigma_0 \qquad (20.142)$$

while

$$\bar{Q}/(Q+\bar{Q}) = \frac{1}{2}\left(\frac{3r-1}{1+r}\right) \qquad (20.143)$$

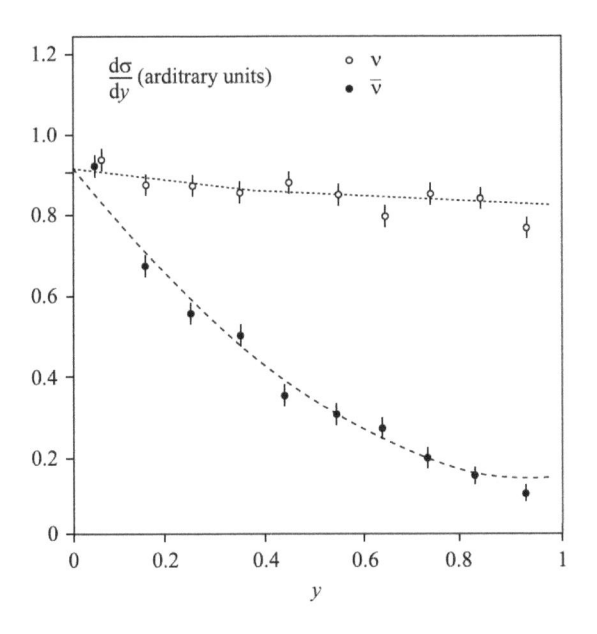

FIGURE 20.6
Charged-current inelasticity (y) distribution as measured by CDHS; figure from K Winter (2000) *Neutrino Physics* 2nd edn, courtesy Cambridge University Press.

where $r = \sigma^{(\nu N)}/\sigma^{(\bar{\nu} N)}$. From total cross section measurements, and including c and s contributions, the CHARM collaboration (Allaby *et al.* 1988) reported

$$Q + \bar{Q} \;=\; 0.492 \pm 0.006(\text{stat}) \pm 0.019(\text{syst}) \qquad (20.144)$$
$$\bar{Q}/Q + \bar{Q} \;=\; 0.154 \pm 0.005(\text{stat}) \pm 0.011(\text{syst}). \qquad (20.145)$$

The second figure is in good agreement with (20.139), and the first shows that only about 50% of the nucleon momentum is carried by charged partons, the rest being carried by the gluons, which do not have weak or electromagnetic interactions.

Equations (20.140) and (20.141), together with (20.132), predict that the total cross sections $\sigma^{\nu N}$ and $\sigma^{\bar{\nu} N}$ rise linearly with energy E. This (parton model) prediction was confirmed as early as 1975 (Perkins 1975), soon after the model's success in deep inelastic electron scattering; later data is included in figure 20.7. In fact, both $\sigma^{\nu N}/E$ and $\sigma^{\bar{\nu} N}/E$ are found to be independent of E up to $E \sim 350$ GeV (Nakamura *et al.* 2010).

Detailed comparison between the data at high energies and the earlier data of figure 20.7 at E_ν up to 15 GeV reveals that the $\bar{Q}$ fraction is increasing with energy. This is in accordance with the expectation of QCD corrections to the parton model (section 15.6): the $\bar{Q}$ distribution is large at small x,

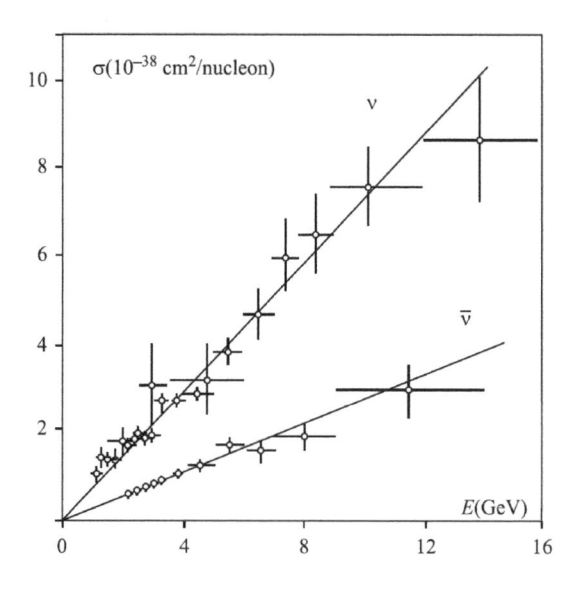

FIGURE 20.7

Low-energy ν and $\bar{\nu}$ cross-sections; figure from K Winter (2000) *Neutrino Physics* 2nd edn, courtesy Cambridge University Press.

and scaling violations embodied in the evolution of the parton distributions predict a rise at small x as the energy scale increases.

Returning now to (20.127)–(20.130), the two sum rules of (9.65) and (9.66) can be combined to give

$$3 = \int_0^1 \mathrm{d}x[u(x) + d(x) - \bar{u}(x) - \bar{d}(x)] \tag{20.146}$$

$$= \frac{1}{2}\int_0^1 \mathrm{d}x(F_3^{\nu\mathrm{p}} + F_3^{\nu\mathrm{n}}) \tag{20.147}$$

$$\equiv \int_0^1 \mathrm{d}x F_3^{\nu\mathrm{N}} \tag{20.148}$$

which is the Gross–Llewellyn Smith sum rule (1969), expressing the fact that the number of valence quarks per nucleon is three. The CDHS collaboration (de Groot *et al.* 1979), quoted

$$I_{\mathrm{GLLS}} \equiv \int_0^1 \mathrm{d}x F_3^{\nu\mathrm{N}} = 3.2 \pm 0.5. \tag{20.149}$$

In perturbative QCD there are corrections expressible as a power series in α_{s}, so that the parton model result is only reached as $Q^2 \to \infty$:

$$I_{\mathrm{GLLS}}(Q^2) = 3[1 + d_1\alpha_{\mathrm{s}}/\pi + d_2\alpha_{\mathrm{s}}^2/\pi^2 + \ldots] \tag{20.150}$$

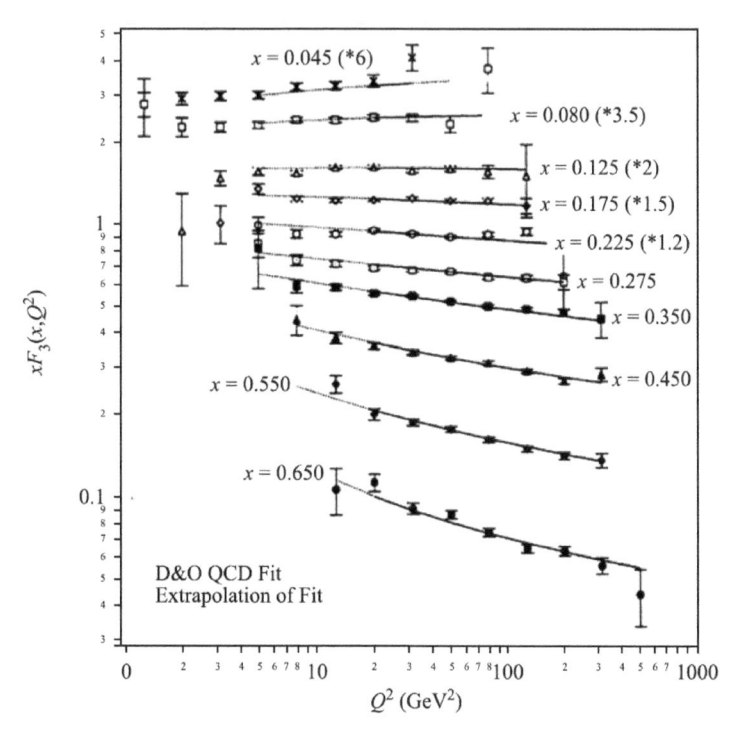

FIGURE 20.8
CCFR neutrino-iron structure functions $xF_3^{(\nu)}$ (Shaevitz *et al.* 1995). The solid line is the next-to-leading order (one-loop) QCD prediction, and the dotted line is an extrapolation to regions outside the kinematic cuts for the fit.

where $d_1 = -1$ (Altarelli *et al.* 1978a, 1978b), $d_2 = -55/12 + N_f/3$ (Gorishnii and Larin 1986) where N_f is the number of active flavours. The CCFR collaboration (Shaevitz *et al.* 1995) measured I_{GLLS} in antineutrino-nucleon scattering at $\langle Q^2 \rangle \sim 3 \text{GeV}^2$. They obtained

$$I_{\text{GLLS}}(\langle Q^2 \rangle = 3 \text{ GeV}^2) = 2.50 \pm 0.02 \pm 0.08 \qquad (20.151)$$

in agreement with the $O(\alpha_s^3)$ calculation of Larin and Vermaseren (1991) using $\Lambda_{\overline{MS}} = 250 \pm 50 \text{MeV}$.

The predicted Q^2 evolution of xF_3 is particularly simple since it is not coupled to the gluon distribution. To leading order, the xF_3 evolution is given by (cf (15.109))

$$\frac{d}{d \ln Q^2}(xF_3(x, Q^2)) = \frac{\alpha_s(Q^2)}{2\pi} \int_x^1 P_{qq}(z) x F_3\left(\frac{x}{z}, Q^2\right) \frac{dz}{z}. \qquad (20.152)$$

Figure 20.8, taken from Shaevitz *et al.* (1995) shows a comparison of the

CCFR data with the next-to-leading order calculation of Duke and Owens (1984). This fit yields a value of α_s at $Q^2 = M_Z^2$ given by

$$\alpha_s(M_Z^2) = 0.111 \pm 0.002 \pm 0.003. \tag{20.153}$$

The Adler sum rule (Adler 1963) involves the functions $F_2^{\bar{\nu}p}$ and $F_2^{\nu p}$:

$$I_A = \int_0^1 \frac{dx}{x}(F_2^{\bar{\nu}p} - F_2^{\nu p}). \tag{20.154}$$

In the simple model of (20.127)–(20.130), the right-hand side of I_A is just

$$2\int_0^1 dx(u(x) + \bar{d}(x) - d(x) - \bar{u}(x)) \tag{20.155}$$

which represents four times the average of I_3 (isospin) of the target, which is $\frac{1}{2}$ for the proton. This sum rule follows from the conservation of the charged weak current (as will be true in the Standard Model, since this is a gauge symmetry current, as we shall see in the following chapter). Its measurement, however, depends precisely on separating the non-isoscalar contribution (I_A vanishes for the isoscalar average 'N'). The BEBC collaboration (Allasia *et al.* 1984, 1985) reported:

$$I_A = 2.02 \pm 0.40; \tag{20.156}$$

in agreement with the expected value 2.

Relations (20.127)–(20.130) allow the F_2 functions for electron (muon) and neutrino scattering to be simply related. From (9.58) and (9.61) we have

$$F_2^{eN} = \frac{1}{2}(F_2^{ep} + F_2^{en}) = \frac{5}{18}x(u + \bar{u} + d + \bar{d}) + \frac{1}{9}x(s + \bar{s}) + \cdots \tag{20.157}$$

while (20.127) and (20.129) give

$$F_2^{\nu N} \equiv \frac{1}{2}(F_2^{\nu p} + F_2^{\nu n}) = x(u + d + \bar{u} + \bar{d}). \tag{20.158}$$

Assuming that the non-strange contributions dominate, the neutrino and charged lepton structure functions should be approximately in the ratio 18/5, which is the reciprocal of the mean squared charged of the u and d quarks in the nucleon. Figure 20.9 shows the neutrino results on F_2 and xF_3 together with those from several μN experiments scaled by the factor 18/5. The agreement is satisfactory for a tree-level parton model calculation.

From (20.127)–(20.130) we see that $F_2^{\nu N} - xF_3^{\nu N} = 2x(\bar{u} + \bar{d})$, which is just the sea distribution; figure 20.9 shows that this is concentrated at small x, as we already inferred in section 9.3.

We have mentioned QCD corrections to the simple parton model at several points. Clearly the full machinery introduced in chapter 16, in the context of deep inelastic charged lepton scattering, can be employed for the case of neutrino scattering also. For further access to this area we refer to Ellis *et al.* (1996), chapter 4, and Winter (2000) chapter 5.

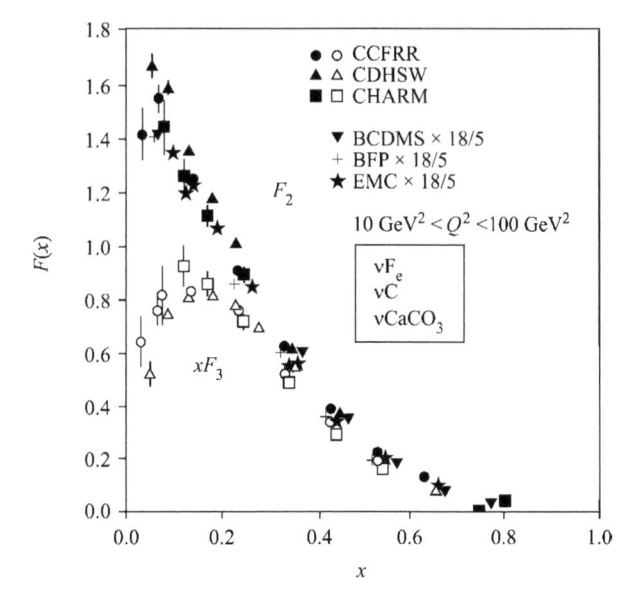

FIGURE 20.9
Comparison of neutrino results (experiments CCFRR, CDHSW and CHARM)
on $F_2(x)$ and $xF_3(x)$ with those from muon production (experiments BCDMS,
BFP and EMC) properly rescaled by the factor 18/5, for a Q^2 ranging between
10 and 1000 GeV^2; figure from K Winter (2000) *Neutrino Physics* 2nd edn,
courtesy Cambridge University Press.

20.7.3 Three generations

We have seen in section 20.2.2 that the V-A interaction violates both **P** and
C, and that it conserves **CP** in interactions with massless neutrinos. But
we know (section 4.2.3) that **CP**-violating transitions occur, among states
formed from quarks in the first two generations, albeit at a very slow rate. Is
it possible, in fact, to incorporate **CP**-violation with only two generations of
quarks?

To answer this question, we need to go back and examine the **CP**-transfor-
mation properties of the interactions in more detail. Rather than work with
the current–current form, which is after all only an approximation valid for
energies much less than $M_{W,Z}$, we shall look at the actual gauge interactions
of the electroweak theory. Given the form of those interactions, we want to
know the condition for **CP**-violation to be present.

Consider then the particular interaction involved in u $\leftrightarrow$ d transitions:

$$V_{\mathrm{ud}}\bar{u}\gamma^\mu \hat{d}\,\hat{W}_\mu + V_{\mathrm{ud}}^*\bar{\hat{d}}\gamma^\mu \hat{u}\,\hat{W}_\mu^\dagger - V_{\mathrm{ud}}\bar{u}\gamma^\mu\gamma_5\hat{d}\,\hat{W}_\mu - V_{\mathrm{ud}}^*\bar{\hat{d}}\gamma^\mu\gamma_5\hat{u}\,\hat{W}_\mu^\dagger, \quad (20.159)$$

where $\hat{W}_\mu = (\hat{W}_\mu^1 - i\hat{W}_\mu^2)/\sqrt{2}$ destroys the W$^+$ or creates the W$^-$. We have

written out the Hermitian conjugate terms explicitly, keeping the coupling V_{ud} complex for the sake of generality, and separating the vector from the axial vector parts. Problem 20.11 shows that the different parts of (20.159) transform under **C** as follows (normal ordering being understood in all cases):

$$\mathbf{C} : \bar{\hat{u}}\gamma^\mu \hat{d} \to -\bar{\hat{d}}\gamma^\mu \hat{u}, \quad \bar{\hat{u}}\gamma^\mu \gamma_5 \hat{d} \to +\bar{\hat{d}}\gamma^\mu \gamma_5 \hat{u}, \tag{20.160}$$

and we also know that under **C**, $\hat{W}_\mu \to -\hat{W}_\mu^\dagger$ (the dagger is as in the charged scalar field case, and the minus sign is as in the photon $\hat{A}_\mu$ case). Hence under **C**, (20.159) transforms into

$$V_{ud}\bar{\hat{d}}\gamma^\mu \hat{u} \, \hat{W}_\mu^\dagger + V_{ud}^* \bar{\hat{u}}\gamma^\mu \hat{d} \, \hat{W}_\mu + V_{ud}\bar{\hat{d}}\gamma^\mu \gamma_5 \hat{u} \, \hat{W}_\mu^\dagger + V_{ud}^* \bar{\hat{u}}\gamma^\mu \gamma_5 \hat{d} \, \hat{W}_\mu. \tag{20.161}$$

Under **P**, $\hat{W}_\mu$ behaves like an ordinary four-vector, so the 'vector·vector' products in (20.161) are even under **P**, while the 'axial vector·vector' products are odd under **P**. Thus finally, under the combined **CP** transformation (20.159) becomes

$$V_{ud}\bar{\hat{d}}\gamma^\mu \hat{u} \, \hat{W}_\mu^\dagger + V_{ud}^* \bar{\hat{u}}\gamma^\mu \hat{d} \, \hat{W}_\mu - V_{ud}\bar{\hat{d}}\gamma^\mu \gamma_5 \hat{u} \, \hat{W}_\mu^\dagger - V_{ud}^* \bar{\hat{u}}\gamma^\mu \gamma_5 \hat{d} \, \hat{W}_\mu. \tag{20.162}$$

Comparing (20.159) with (20.162) we deduce the essential result that this interaction conserves **CP** if and only if

$$V_{ud} = V_{ud}^*, \tag{20.163}$$

that is, if the coupling is real. The same is true for all the other couplings V_{ij}.

The couplings we have introduced in this chapter so far only involve the real Fermi constant G_F, and the elements of the Cabibbo-GIM matrix which enters into the relation between the weakly interacting fields $(\hat{d}', \hat{s}')$ and the fields with definite mass $(\hat{d}, \hat{s})$:

$$\begin{pmatrix} \hat{d}' \\ \hat{s}' \end{pmatrix} = \begin{pmatrix} \cos\theta_C & \sin\theta_C \\ -\sin\theta_C & \cos\theta_C \end{pmatrix} \begin{pmatrix} \hat{d} \\ \hat{s} \end{pmatrix} \equiv \mathbf{V}_{CGIM} \begin{pmatrix} \hat{d} \\ \hat{s} \end{pmatrix}. \tag{20.164}$$

All these couplings are plainly real. But could we perhaps parametrize the $(\hat{d}', \hat{s}') \leftrightarrow (\hat{d}, \hat{s})$ differently, so as to smuggle in a complex, **CP**-violating, coupling?

This is the question that Kobayashi and Maskawa asked themselves in 1972 (Kobayashi 2009, Maskawa 2009). To answer it is not completely straightforward, because we can always change the phases of the quark fields by independent constant amounts. A rephasing of the quark fields in the transition i $\leftrightarrow$ j with coupling V_{ij} changes V_{ij} by the phase factor $\exp i(\alpha_i - \alpha_j)$. We need to know whether, after allowing for this rephasing of the quark fields, an 'irreducible' complex coupling can remain.

First of all, note that the matrix $\mathbf{V}_{CGIM}$ appearing in (20.164) is orthogonal, and this property guaranteed the vanishing of tree-level neutral

strangeness-changing transitions, as we saw after (20.106). But this could just as well be achieved if the matrix was unitary. Now a general 2×2 matrix has 8 real parameters; unitarity gives 2 real conditions from the diagonal elements of $\mathbf{V}_{\text{CGIM}} \mathbf{V}_{\text{CGIM}}^\dagger = \mathbf{I}$, and one complex condition from the off-diagonal elements, leaving four real parameters. If all the elements are taken to be real from the beginning, the matrix becomes orthogonal, as in (20.164), and depends on only one real parameter, the 'rotation' in the 2-dimensional $\hat{d} - \hat{s}$ space. So in the general, unitary case, the matrix will have one real angle parameter, and three phase parameters. But we have four quark fields whose phases we can adjust. In fact, since only phase differences enter, we really only have three free phases at our disposal, but that is just enough to transform away the three phases in the unitary version of $\mathbf{V}_{\text{CGIM}}$, leaving it in the real orthogonal form (20.164). Kobayashi and Maskawa therefore concluded that the 2-generation GIM-type theory could not accommodate **CP**-violation.

In a step which may seem natural now but was very bold in 1972, they decided to see if there was room for **CP**-violation in a 3-generation model. (Remember that there was no sign of any third generation particles at that time.) The matrix transforming from the mass basis to the weak basis is now a 3×3 unitary matrix $\mathbf{V}$, with 18 real parameters. There are three real diagonal conditions from unitarity, and three complex off-diagonal conditions, leaving 9 real parameters. If the elements of $\mathbf{V}$ are taken to be real, one has an orthogonal (rotation) matrix, which can be parametrized by three real Euler angles. That leaves 6 phase parameters in the general unitary $\mathbf{V}$. We also have 6 quark fields, with 5 phase differences which can be adjusted. Thus just one irreducible phase degree of freedom can remain in $\mathbf{V}$, after quark rephasing. Consequently, the three-generation model naturally accommodates **CP**-violation in the quark sector: this was the great discovery of Kobayashi and Maskawa (1973). It was another four years before the existence of the b quark was established, and more than twenty before the t quark was produced.

The 3-generation matrix $\mathbf{V}$, written out in full, is

$$\mathbf{V} = \begin{pmatrix} V_{\text{ud}} & V_{\text{us}} & V_{\text{ub}} \\ V_{\text{cd}} & V_{\text{cs}} & V_{\text{cb}} \\ V_{\text{td}} & V_{\text{ts}} & V_{\text{tb}} \end{pmatrix}, \tag{20.165}$$

and is called the CKM matrix, after Cabibbo, Kobayashi, and Maskawa. Clearly, there is no unique parametrization of $\mathbf{V}$. One that has now become standard (Nakamura *et al.* 2010) is (Chau and Keung 1984)

$$\mathbf{V} = \begin{pmatrix} c_{12}c_{13} & s_{12}c_{13} & s_{13}e^{-i\delta} \\ -s_{12}c_{23} - c_{12}s_{23}s_{13}e^{i\delta} & c_{12}c_{23} - s_{12}s_{23}s_{13}e^{i\delta} & s_{23}c_{13} \\ s_{12}s_{23} - c_{12}c_{23}s_{13}e^{i\delta} & -c_{12}s_{23} - s_{12}c_{23}s_{13}e^{i\delta} & c_{23}c_{13} \end{pmatrix} \tag{20.166}$$

where $c_{ij} = \cos\theta_{ij}$, $s_{ij} = \sin\theta_{ij}$ with $i, j = 1, 2, 3$; the θ_{ij} may be thought of as the three Euler angles in an orthogonal $\mathbf{V}$, and δ is the remaining irreducible **CP**-violating phase. In the limit $\theta_{13} = \theta_{23} = 0$, this CKM matrix reduces to the Cabibbo-GIM matrix with $\theta_{12} \equiv \theta_{\text{C}}$.

However, it would also be desirable to have a measure of **CP**-violation that was independent of quark rephasing. Consider one of the off-diagonal unitarity conditions,

$$V_{ud}V_{ub}^* + V_{cd}V_{cb}^* + V_{td}V_{tb}^* = 0. \tag{20.167}$$

(Note that the complex conjugate of this equation gives another, independent, condition.) The best-measured of these products is $V_{cd}V_{cb}^*$; dividing by this quantity, (20.167) can be written as

$$1 + z_1 + z_2 = 0, \tag{20.168}$$

where

$$z_1 = \frac{V_{td}V_{tb}^*}{V_{cd}V_{cb}^*}, \quad z_2 = \frac{V_{ud}V_{ub}^*}{V_{cd}V_{cb}^*}. \tag{20.169}$$

When viewed in the complex plane, relation (20.168) is the statement that the vectors $(1,0)$, z_1 and z_2 close to form a triangle as shown in figure 20.10, one of 6 such *unitarity triangles* that can be formed. The area Δ of this triangle is

$$\Delta = \frac{1}{2}\mathrm{Im}(z_2 z_1^*) = \frac{1}{2}\mathrm{Im}\left(\frac{V_{ud}V_{ub}^*V_{td}^*V_{tb}}{|V_{cd}|^2|V_{cb}|^2}\right). \tag{20.170}$$

Recalling that a rephasing multiplies V_{ij} by $\exp i(\alpha_i - \alpha_j)$, we see that Δ is rephasing invariant; in particular, so is the numerator J where

$$J \equiv \mathrm{Im}(V_{ud}V_{tb}V_{ub}^*V_{td}^*) \tag{20.171}$$

is a *Jarlskog invariant* (Jarlskog 1985). J may be thought of as follows: (i) strike out the 'c' row and 's' column of **V**; (ii) take the complex conjugate of the off-diagonal elements in the 2×2 matrix that remains; (iii) multiply the four elements and take the imaginary part. There is nothing special about this particular row and column: there are nine different ways of choosing to pair one row with one column, but all such Js are equal up to a sign, because of the unitarity of **V**. In the parametrization (20.166), J takes the form

$$J = c_{12}s_{12}c_{23}s_{23}c_{13}^2 s_{13} \sin \delta, \tag{20.172}$$

which vanishes if any $\theta_{ij} = 0$, or $\pi/2$, or if $\delta = 0$ or π.

The CKM matrix is an integral part of the Standard Model, and testing its validity is an important experimental goal. Various tests are possible. Consider first the magnitudes of the CKM elements. These must satisfy six relations following from the unitarity of **V**: namely, the sum of the squares of the absolute values of the elements of each row, and of each column, must add up to unity.

The magnitudes of the six elements of the first two rows have been determined from measurements of semileptonic decay rates: for example, the amplitude for the tree-level process $d \to u + e^- + \bar{\nu}_e$ is proportional to V_{ud}.

But non-perturbative strong interaction effects enter into the amplitudes for corresponding measured hadronic transitions, such as $n \to p + e^- + \bar{\nu}_e$ or $\pi^- \to \pi^0 + e^- + \bar{\nu}_e$. In many cases these hadronic factors in the matrix elements can now be calculated by unquenched lattice QCD.

The status of the experimental determination of the moduli $|V_{ij}|$ is regularly reviewed by the Particle Data Group. The current results for the unitarity checks are (Ceccucci *et al.* 2010)

$$|V_{ud}|^2 + |V_{us}|^2 + |V_{ub}|^2 = 0.9999 \pm 0.0006 \tag{20.173}$$
$$|V_{cd}|^2 + |V_{cs}|^2 + |V_{cb}|^2 = 1.101 \pm 0.074 \tag{20.174}$$
$$|V_{ud}|^2 + |V_{cd}|^2 + |V_{td}|^2 = 1.002 \pm 0.005 \tag{20.175}$$
$$|V_{us}|^2 + |V_{cs}|^2 + |V_{ts}|^2 = 1.098 \pm 0.074. \tag{20.176}$$

Evidently these results are fully consistent with the CKM prediction of unitarity.

The most accurate values of the nine magnitudes are obtained by a global fit to all the available measurements, imposing the constraints of 3-generation unitarity. The current result for the magnitudes, imposing these constraints, is (Ceccucci *et al.* 2010)

$$\mathbf{V} = \begin{pmatrix} 0.9428 \pm 0.00015 & 0.2253 \pm 0.0007 & 0.00347^{+0.00016}_{-0.00012} \\ 0.2252 \pm 0.0007 & 0.97345^{+0.00015}_{-0.00016} & 0.0410^{+0.0011}_{-0.0007} \\ 0.00862^{+0.00026}_{-0.00020} & 0.0403^{+0.0011}_{-0.0007} & 0.999152^{+0.000030}_{-0.000045} \end{pmatrix}, \tag{20.177}$$

and the Jarlskog invariant is $J = (2.91^{+0.19}_{-0.11}) \times 10^{-5}$.

From (20.177) it follows that the mixing angles are small, and moreover satisfy a definite hierarchy

$$1 \gg \theta_{12} \gg \theta_{23} \gg \theta_{13}. \tag{20.178}$$

In more physical terms, hadrons evidently prefer to decay semileptonically to the nearest generation. Also, because the elements V_{ub}, V_{cb}, V_{td} and V_{ts}, which connect the third generation to the first two, are all quite small, the physics of the first two generations is hardly influenced by the presence of the third. This reflects, in quantitative terms, the success of the Cabibbo-GIM description, and the fact that the **CP**-violation seen in the K-meson sector is so weak. **CP**-violation is much more visible in B physics, as Carter and Sanda (1980, 1981) were the first to suggest, and as we shall discuss in the following chapter.

Consider now the complex-valued off-diagonal unitarity conditions, in particular the condition (20.168). Following Wolfenstein (1983), we identify s_{12} as the small parameter λ, and write $V_{cb} \simeq s_{23} = A\lambda^2$ and $V_{ub} = s_{13}\exp(-i\delta) = A\lambda^3(\rho - i\eta)$ with $A \simeq 1$ and $|\rho - i\eta| < 1$. This gives

$$\mathbf{V} = \begin{pmatrix} 1 - \lambda^2/2 & \lambda & A\lambda^3(\rho - i\eta) \\ -\lambda & 1 - \lambda^2/2 & A\lambda^2 \\ A\lambda^3(1 - \rho - i\eta) & -A\lambda^2 & 1 \end{pmatrix}, \tag{20.179}$$

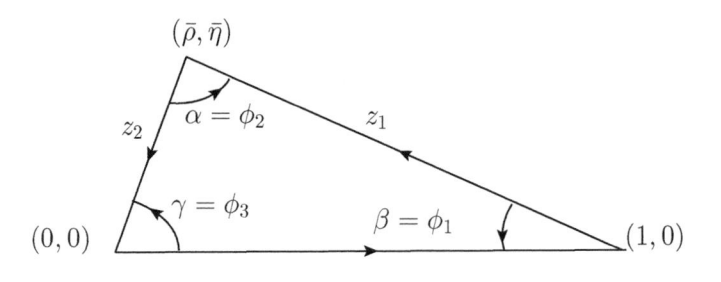

FIGURE 20.10
The unitarity triangle represented by (20.168).

neglecting terms of order λ^4 and higher. Then

$$z_1 = \frac{V_{td}V_{tb}^*}{V_{cd}V_{cb}^*} \simeq \rho + i\eta - 1, \quad z_2 = \frac{V_{ud}V_{ub}^*}{V_{cd}V_{cb}^*} \simeq -(\rho + i\eta), \quad J \simeq A^2\lambda^6\eta. \quad (20.180)$$

The unitarity triangle represented by the condition (20.168), or alternatively $-z_1 - z_2 = 1$, is therefore a triangle on the base (1,0), with sides $\rho + i\eta$ and $1 - (\rho + i\eta)$. Buras *et al.* (1994) showed that including terms up to order λ^5 changes (ρ, η) to $(\bar{\rho}, \bar{\eta})$ where $\bar{\rho} = (1 - \lambda^2/2)\rho$, $\bar{\eta} = (1 - \lambda^2/2)\eta$. The top vertex of the triangle in figure 20.10 is therefore at the point $(\bar{\rho}, \bar{\eta})$. The angles α, β and γ (also called ϕ_2, ϕ_1 and ϕ_3) are defined by

$$\alpha \equiv \phi_2 \equiv \arg\left(-\frac{V_{td}V_{tb}^*}{V_{ud}V_{ub}^*}\right) \approx \arg - \left(\frac{1 - \bar{\rho} - i\bar{\eta}}{\bar{\rho} + i\bar{\eta}}\right) \quad (20.181)$$

$$\beta \equiv \phi_1 \equiv \arg\left(-\frac{V_{cd}V_{cb}^*}{V_{td}V_{tb}^*}\right) \approx \arg\left(\frac{1}{1 - \bar{\rho} - i\bar{\eta}}\right) \quad (20.182)$$

$$\gamma \equiv \phi_3 \equiv \arg\left(-\frac{V_{ud}V_{ub}^*}{V_{cd}V_{cb}^*}\right) \approx \arg(\bar{\rho} + i\bar{\eta}) \quad (20.183)$$

The sides of this triangle are determined by the magnitudes of the CKM elements, and so another check is provided by the condition that the three sides should close to form a triangle. Further independent constraints are provided by measurements of the angles α, β, and γ which are directly related to **CP**-violation effects, as we shall discuss in the following chapter. Figure 20.11 shows a plot of all the constraints in the $\bar{\rho}, \bar{\eta}$ plane from many different measurements (combined following the approach of Charles *et al.* 2005 and Höcker *et al.* 2001), and the global fit, as presented by Ceccucci *et al.* (2010). The annular region labelled by $|V_{ub}|$ represents, for example, the uncertainty in the determination of $|z_2| = |V_{ud}V_{ub}^*/V_{cd}V_{cb}^*|$, which is principally due to the uncertainty in $|V_{ub}|$. The region labelled by Δm_d represents the constraint on

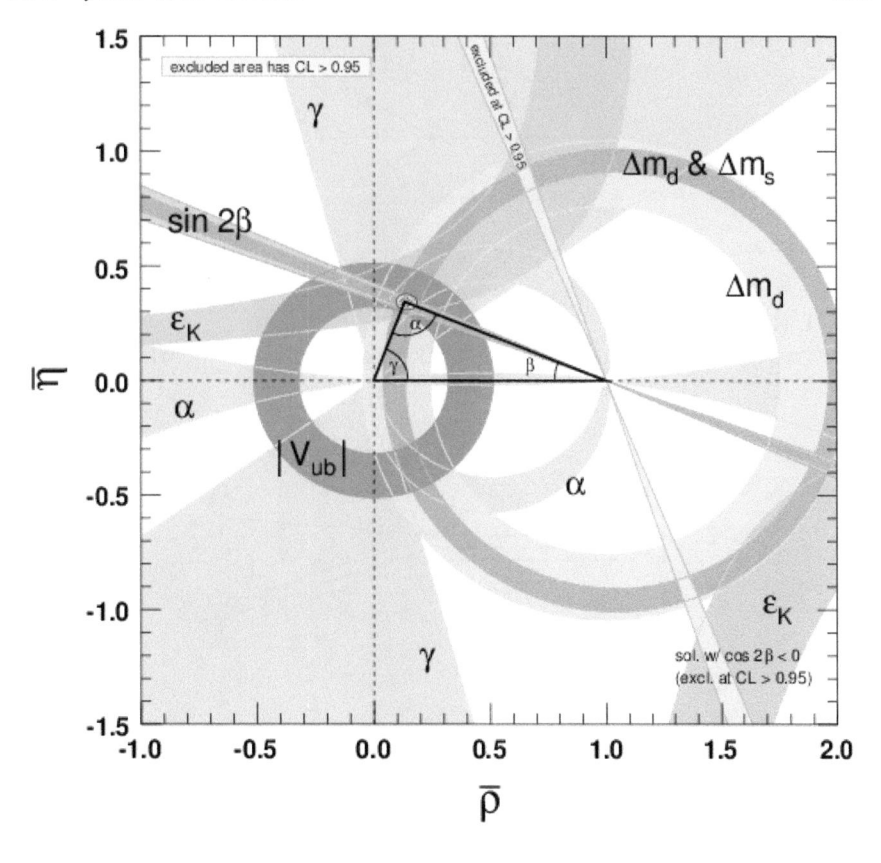

FIGURE 20.11

Constraints in the $\bar{\rho}, \bar{\eta}$ plane. The shaded areas have 95% CL. [Figure reproduced, courtesy Michael Barnett for the Particle Data Group, from the review of the CKM Quark-Mixing Matrix by A Ceccucci, Z Ligeti and Y Sakai, section 11 in the *Review of Particle Physics*, K Nakamura *et al.* (Partcle Data Group) *Journal of Physics* G **37** (2010) 075021, IOP Publishing Limited.] (See color plate III.)

$|z_1| = |V_{td}V_{tb}^*/V_{cd}V_{cb}^*|$, where $|V_{td}|$ is deduced from the value of the $B^0 - \bar{B}^0$ mass difference Δm_d measured in $B^0 - \bar{B}^0$ oscillations mediated by top-quark dominated box diagrams (see section 21.2.1 in the following chapter); here the uncertainties are dominated by lattice QCD. Figure 20.11 represents an enormous experimental effort, especially in the decade 2000-2010. The 95% CL regions all overlap consistently. It is quite remarkable how the single **CP**- violating parameter, three-generation scheme of Kobayashi and Maskawa (1973) has withstood this searching test.

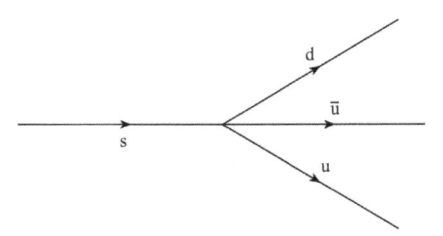

FIGURE 20.12
Effective four-fermion non-leptonic weak transition at the quark level.

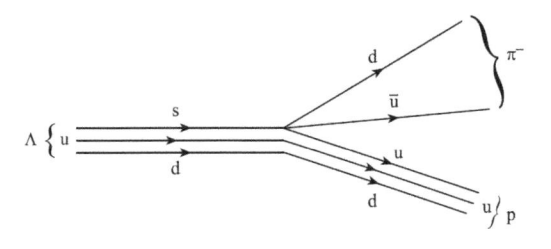

FIGURE 20.13
Non-leptonic weak decay of Λ^0 using the process of figure 20.12, with the addition of two 'spectator' quarks.

20.8 Non-leptonic weak interactions

The CKM 6-quark charged weak current, which replaces the GIM current (20.101), is

$$\hat{j}^\mu_{\rm CKM}({\rm u,d,s,c,t,b}) = \bar{\hat{u}}\gamma^\mu \frac{(1-\gamma_5)}{2}\hat{d}' + \bar{\hat{c}}\gamma^\mu \frac{(1-\gamma_5)}{2}\hat{s}' + \bar{\hat{t}}\gamma^\mu \frac{(1-\gamma_5)}{2}\hat{b}',$$

(20.184)

and the effective weak Hamiltonian of (20.92) (as modified by CKM) clearly contains the term

$$\hat{\mathcal{H}}^q_{\rm CC}(x) = \frac{G_{\rm F}}{\sqrt{2}}\hat{j}^\mu_{\rm CKM}(x)\hat{j}^\dagger_{\mu\rm CKM}(x)$$

(20.185)

in which no lepton fields are present (just as there are no quarks in (20.40)). This interaction is responsible, at the quark level, for transitions involving four quark (or antiquark) fields at a point. For example, the process shown in figure 20.12 can occur. By 'adding on' another two quark lines u and d, which undergo no weak interaction, we arrive at figure 20.13, which represents the non-leptonic decay $\Lambda^0 \to {\rm p}\pi^-$.

This figure is, of course, rather symbolic since there are strong QCD interactions (not shown) which are responsible for binding the three-quark systems into baryons, and the qq̄ system into a meson. Unlike the case of deep inelastic lepton scattering, these QCD interactions can not be treated perturbatively, since the distance scales involved are typically those of the hadron sizes ($\sim$ 1 fm), where perturbation theory fails. This means that non-leptonic weak interactions among hadrons are difficult to analyze quantitatively, though progress can be made via lattice QCD. Similar difficulties also arise, evidently, in the case of semi-leptonic decays. In general, one has to begin in a phenomenological way, parametrizing the decay amplitudes in terms of appropriate form factors (which are analogous to the electromagnetic form factors introduced in chapter 8). In the case of transitions involving at least one heavy quark Q, Isgur and Wise (1989, 1990) noticed that a considerable simplification occurs in the limit $m_Q \to \infty$. For example, one universal function (the 'Isgur–Wise form factor') is sufficient to describe a large number of hadronic form factors introduced for semi-leptonic transitions between two heavy pseudoscalar (0^-) or vector (1^-) mesons. For an introduction to the Isgur–Wise theory we refer to Donoghue *et al.* (1992).

The non-leptonic sector is, however, the scene of some very interesting physics, such as $K^0 - \bar{K}^0$ and $B^0 - \bar{B}^0$ oscillations, and **CP** violation in the $K^0 - \bar{K}^0, D^0 - \bar{D}^0$ and $B^0 - \bar{B}^0$ systems. We shall discuss these phenomena in the following chapter.

Problems

20.1 Show that in the non-relativistic limit ($|\boldsymbol{p}| \ll M$) the matrix element $\bar{u}_{\mathrm{p}} \gamma^\mu u_{\mathrm{n}}$ of (20.2) vanishes if p and n have different spin states.

20.2 Verify the normalization $N = (E + |\boldsymbol{p}|)^{1/2}$ in (20.23).

20.3 Verify (20.30) and (20.31).

20.4 Verify that equations (20.32) are invariant under **CP**.

20.5 The matrix γ_5 is defined by $\gamma_5 = i\gamma^0\gamma^1\gamma^2\gamma^3$. Prove the following properties:

(a) $\gamma_5^2 = 1$ and hence that

$$(1 + \gamma_5)(1 - \gamma_5) = 0;$$

(b) from the anticommutation relations of the other γ matrices, show that

$$\{\gamma_5, \gamma_\mu\} = 0$$

and hence that

$$(1 + \gamma_5)\gamma_0 = \gamma_0(1 - \gamma_5)$$

and

$$(1 + \gamma_5)\gamma_0\gamma_\mu = \gamma_0\gamma_\mu(1 + \gamma_5).$$

20.6

(a) Consider the two-dimensional antisymmetric tensor ϵ_{ij} defined by

$$\epsilon_{12} = +1, \epsilon_{21} = -1, \qquad \epsilon_{11} = \epsilon_{22} = 0.$$

By explicitly enumerating all the possibilities (if necessary), convince yourself of the result

$$\epsilon_{ij}\epsilon_{kl} = +1(\delta_{ik}\delta_{jl} - \delta_{il}\delta_{jk}).$$

Hence prove that

$$\epsilon_{ij}\epsilon_{il} = \delta_{jl} \qquad \text{and} \qquad \epsilon_{ij}\epsilon_{ij} = 2$$

(remember, in two dimensions, $\sum_i \delta_{ii} = 2$).

(b) By similar reasoning to that in part (a) of this question, it can be shown that the product of two three-dimensional antisymmetric tensors has the form

$$\epsilon_{ijk}\epsilon_{lmn} = \begin{vmatrix} \delta_{il} & \delta_{im} & \delta_{in} \\ \delta_{jl} & \delta_{jm} & \delta_{jn} \\ \delta_{kl} & \delta_{km} & \delta_{kn} \end{vmatrix}.$$

Prove the results

$$\epsilon_{ijk}\epsilon_{imn} = \begin{vmatrix} \delta_{jm} & \delta_{jn} \\ \delta_{km} & \delta_{kn} \end{vmatrix} \qquad \epsilon_{ijk}\epsilon_{ijn} = 2\delta_{kn} \qquad \epsilon_{ijk}\epsilon_{ijk} = 3!$$

(c) Extend these results to the case of the four-dimensional (Lorentz) tensor $\epsilon_{\mu\nu\alpha\beta}$ (remember that a minus sign will appear as a result of $\epsilon_{0123} = +1$ but $\epsilon^{0123} = -1$).

20.7 Starting from the amplitude for the process

$$\nu_\mu + e^- \rightarrow \mu^- + \nu_e$$

given by the current–current theory of weak interactions,

$$\mathcal{M} = -i(G_F/\sqrt{2})\bar{u}(\mu)\gamma_\mu(1 - \gamma_5)u(\nu_\mu)g^{\mu\nu}\bar{u}(\nu_e)\gamma_\nu(1 - \gamma_5)u(e),$$

verify the intermediate results given in section 20.5 leading to the result

$$d\sigma/dt = G_F^2/\pi$$

(neglecting all lepton masses). Hence show that the local total cross section for this process rises linearly with s:

$$\sigma = G_F^2 s/\pi.$$

20.8 The invariant amplitude for $\pi^+ \to e^+\nu$ decay may be written as (see (18.52))

$$\mathcal{M} = (G_F V_{ud}) f_\pi p^\mu \bar{u}(\nu) \gamma_\mu (1 - \gamma_5) v(e)$$

where p^μ is the 4-momentum of the pion, and the neutrino is taken to be massless. Evaluate the decay rate in the rest frame of the pion using the decay rate formula

$$\Gamma = (1/2m_\pi)|\mathcal{M}|^2 \text{dLips}(m_\pi^2; k_e, k_\nu).$$

Show that the ratio of $\pi^+ \to e^+\nu$ and $\pi^+ \to \mu^+\nu$ rates is given by

$$\frac{\Gamma(\pi^+ \to e^+\nu)}{\Gamma(\pi^+ \to \mu^+\nu)} = \left(\frac{m_e}{m_\mu}\right)^2 \left(\frac{m_\pi^2 - m_e^2}{m_\pi^2 - m_\mu^2}\right)^2.$$

Repeat the calculation using the amplitude

$$\mathcal{M}' = (G_F V_{ud}) f_\pi p^\mu \bar{u}(\nu) \gamma_\mu (g_V + g_A \gamma_5) v(e)$$

and retaining a finite neutrino mass. Discuss the e^+/μ^+ ratio in the light of your result.

20.9

(a) Verify that the inclusive inelastic neutrino-proton scattering differential cross section has the form

$$\frac{d^2\sigma^{(\nu)}}{dQ^2 d\nu} = \frac{G_F^2 k'}{2\pi k} \left(W_2^{(\nu)} \cos^2(\theta/2) + W_1^{(\nu)} 2\sin^2(\theta/2) \right.$$
$$\left. + \frac{(k+k')}{M} \sin^2(\theta/2) W_3^{(\nu)} \right)$$

in the notation of section 20.7.2.

(b) Using the Bjorken scaling behaviour

$$\nu W_2^{(\nu)} \to F_2^{(\nu)} \qquad M W_1^{(\nu)} \to F_1^{(\nu)} \qquad \nu W_3^{(\nu)} \to F_3^{(\nu)}$$

rewrite this expression in terms of the scaling functions. In terms of the variables x and y, neglect all masses and show that

$$\frac{d^2\sigma^{(\nu)}}{dx dy} = \frac{G_F^2}{2\pi} s[F_2^{(\nu)}(1-y) + F_1^{(\nu)} xy^2 + F_3^{(\nu)}(1-y/2)yx].$$

Remember that

$$\frac{k' \sin^2(\theta/2)}{M} = \frac{xy}{2}.$$

(c) Insert the Callan–Gross relation

$$2xF_1^{(\nu)} = F_2^{(\nu)}$$

to derive the result quoted in section 20.7.2:

$$\frac{d^2\sigma^{(\nu)}}{dxdy} = \frac{G_F^2}{2\pi} sF_2^{(\nu)} \left(\frac{1 + (1-y)^2}{2} + \frac{xF_3^{(\nu)}}{F_2^{(\nu)}} \frac{1 - (1-y)^2}{2} \right).$$

20.10 The differential cross section for $\nu_\mu q$ scattering by charged currents has the same form (neglecting masses) as the $\nu_\mu e^- \to \mu^- \nu_e$ result of problem 20.7, namely

$$\frac{d\sigma}{dt}(\nu q) = \frac{G_F^2}{\pi}.$$

(a) Show that the cross section for scattering by antiquarks $\nu_\mu \bar{q}$ has the form

$$\frac{d\sigma}{dt}(\nu \bar{q}) = \frac{G_F^2}{\pi}(1-y)^2.$$

(b) Hence prove the results quoted in section 20.7.2:

$$\frac{d^2\sigma}{dxdy}(\nu q) = \frac{G_F^2}{\pi} sx\delta(x - Q^2/2M\nu)$$

and

$$\frac{d^2\sigma}{dxdy}(\nu \bar{q}) = \frac{G_F^2}{\pi} sx(1 - y^2)\delta(x - Q^2/2M\nu)$$

(where M is the nucleon mass).

(c) Use the parton model prediction

$$\frac{d^2\sigma^{(\nu)}}{dxdy} = \frac{G_F^2}{\pi} sx[q(x) + \bar{q}(x)(1-y)^2]$$

to show that

$$F_2^{(\nu)} = 2x[q(x) + \bar{q}(x)]$$

and

$$\frac{xF_3^{(\nu)}(x)}{F_2^{(\nu)}(x)} = \frac{q(x) - \bar{q}(x)}{q(x) + \bar{q}(x)}.$$

20.11 Verify the transformation laws (20.160).

21

CP Violation and Oscillation Phenomena

In this chapter we shall continue with the phenomenology of weak interactions, introducing two topics which have been the focus of intense experimental effort in the recent decade: **CP** violation in B meson decays, and oscillations in both neutral meson and neutrino systems. In the following chapter we take up again the gauge theory theme, with the Glasow-Salam-Weinberg electroweak theory.

CP violation was first discovered in the decays of neutral K mesons (Christenson *et al.* 1964), but we shall not follow a historical approach to this subject. Instead we shall concentrate on B-meson decays, where the effects are far larger, and much clearer to interpret theoretically than in the K-meson case. **CP** violation is reviewed in Branco *et al.* (1999), Bigi and Sanda (2000) and Harrison and Quinn (1998). We aim simply to illustrate the principles with some particular examples. In particular, we shall generally not discuss theoretical predictions; our main emphasis will be on describing selected experiments which have allowed determinations of the angles α, β and γ of the unitarity triangle, figure 20.10.

We saw in section 20.7.3 that, in the Standard Model, **CP** violation is attributable solely to one irreducible phase degree of freedom, δ, in the CKM matrix **V**. Clearly, to measure this phase, it is necessary (as usual in quantum mechanics) to create situations where it enters into the *interference* between two complex amplitudes. Two situations may be distinguished (Carter and Sanda 1980):

(i) interference between two decay amplitudes $B^0 \to X$ and $\bar{B}^0 \to X$, where the B^0 and $\bar{B}^0$ have been produced in a coherent state by mixing, and decay to a common hadronic final state X;

(ii) interference between two different amplitudes for a single B-meson to decay to a final state X.

Method (ii) ('direct **CP** violation') can be applied to charged as well as neutral mesons.

The mixing in method (i) is formally similar to that involved in neutrino oscillations, which we treat after the meson case. We shall therefore start in section 21.1 with an example illustrating method (ii). We set up the mixing formalism and apply it to **CP** violation in B decays in section 21.2; we discuss K decays in section 21.3. Neutrino oscillations are treated in section 21.4.

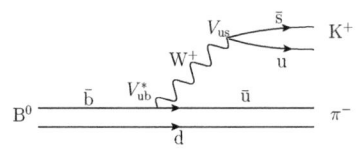

FIGURE 21.1
Tree diagram contribution to $B^0 \to K^+\pi^-$ via the quark transition $\bar{b} \to \bar{s}u\bar{u}$.

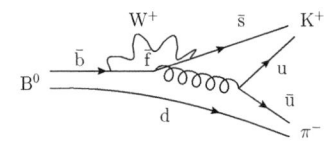

FIGURE 21.2
Penguin diagrams ($\bar{f} = \bar{u}, \bar{c}, \bar{t}$) contributing to $B^0 \to K^+\pi^-$ via the quark transition $\bar{b} \to \bar{s}\,u\,\bar{u}$.

21.1   Direct CP violation in B decays

Consider the decays

$$B^0 \to K^+\pi^- \quad \text{and} \quad \bar{B}^0 \to K^-\pi^-. \tag{21.1}$$

The first of these can proceed via the quark transitions shown in figure 21.1, which (in parton-like language) is a 'tree-diagram'. Of course, long-distance strong interaction effects will come into play in forming the hadronic states B^0, K^+ and π^-, and in final state interactions between the K^+ and π^-; we do not represent these strong interactions in figure 21.1, or in subsequent similar diagrams. We are specifically interested in the *weak phase* of figure 21.1, since it is this quantity which changes sign under the **CP** transformation ($V_{ij} \to V_{ij}^*$), and this phase change will lead to observable **CP** violation effects. By contrast, the strong interaction phases – which will play an important role – will be **CP** invariant, but we do not need to display them yet. So we write the amplitude for figure 21.1 as

$$A_{\mathrm{T}}(B^0 \to K^-\pi^-) = V_{ub}^* V_{us}\, t_{\bar{u}}, \tag{21.2}$$

where the CKM couplings have been displayed.

There are, however, three order-α_s loop corrections to figure 21.1, shown in figure 21.2, where $\bar{f} = \bar{u}, \bar{c}$ and $\bar{t}$. We write the amplitude for the sum of

these three 'penguin' diagrams as

$$A_P(B^0 \to K^+\pi^-) = V_{us}V_{ub}^* \, p_{\bar{u}} + V_{cs}V_{cb}^* \, p_{\bar{c}} + V_{ts}V_{tb}^* \, p_{\bar{t}}, \tag{21.3}$$

where $p_{\bar{f}}$ is the penguin amplitude with $\bar{f}$ in the loop. It is convenient to use a unitarity relation to rewrite $V_{ts}V_{tb}^*$ in terms of the other two related CKM products:

$$V_{ts}V_{tb}^* = -V_{us}V_{ub}^* - V_{cs}V_{cb}^*, \tag{21.4}$$

so that the total amplitude becomes

$$A(B^0 \to K^+\pi^-) = V_{ub}^*V_{us}T_{K\pi} + V_{cs}V_{cb}^*P_{K\pi}, \tag{21.5}$$

where

$$T_{K\pi} = t_{\bar{u}} + p_{\bar{u}} - p_{\bar{t}}, \qquad P_{K\pi} = p_{\bar{c}} - p_{\bar{t}}. \tag{21.6}$$

In terms of the parametrization (20.179), (21.5) becomes

$$A(B^0 \to K^+\pi^-) = A\lambda^4(\rho + i\eta)T_{K\pi} + A\lambda^2(1 - \lambda^2/2)P_{K\pi}. \tag{21.7}$$

Similarly, the amplitude for the charge-conjugate reaction is

$$A(\bar{B}^0 \to K^-\pi^+) = A\lambda^4(\rho - i\eta)T_{K\pi} + A\lambda^2(1 - \lambda^2/2)P_{K\pi}. \tag{21.8}$$

We can now calculate the decay-rate asymmetry

$$\mathcal{A}_{K\pi} = \frac{|A(\bar{B}^0 \to K^-\pi^+)|^2 - |A(B^0 \to K^+\pi^-)|^2}{|A(\bar{B}^0 \to K^-\pi^+)|^2 + |A(B^0 \to K^+\pi^-)|^2}. \tag{21.9}$$

To simplify things, let us take a common complex factor K out of the expressions (21.7) and (21.8) and write them as

$$A(B^0 \to K^+\pi^-) = K(e^{i\gamma} + Re^{i(\delta_P - \delta_T)}) \tag{21.10}$$
$$A(\bar{B}^0 \to K^-\pi^+) = K(e^{-i\gamma} + Re^{i(\delta_P - \delta_T)}), \tag{21.11}$$

where (see equation (20.183)) γ is the phase of $\rho + i\eta$, R is real, and $\delta_P - \delta_T$ is the difference in (strong) phases between $P_{K\pi}$ and $T_{K\pi}$. Then we easily find

$$\mathcal{A}_{K\pi} = \frac{2R\sin\gamma \, \sin(\delta_T - \delta_P)}{1 + R^2 + 2R\cos\gamma \, \cos(\delta_T - \delta_P)}. \tag{21.12}$$

Thus we see that, for a **CP**-violating signal, there must be two interfering amplitudes leading to a common final state, and the amplitudes must have both different weak phases and different strong phases. An order of magnitude estimate of the effect can be made as follows. First, note that $P_{K\pi}$ is not ultraviolet divergent, since it is the difference of two penguin contributions; its magnitude is expected to be of order $\alpha_s/\pi \sim 0.05$. The tree contribution in (21.7) carries an extra factor of $\lambda^2 \sim 0.05$ as compared with the penguin contribution, so that R is of order 1. This indicates that the asymmetry should be significant.

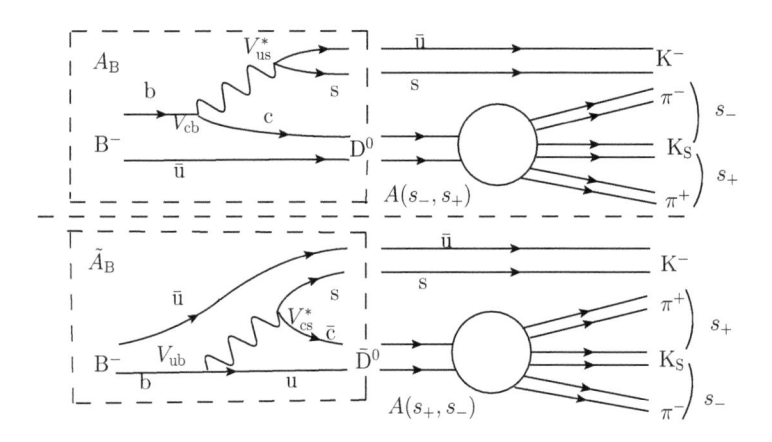

FIGURE 21.3

Left-hand part: tree diagram contributions to $B^- \to D^0 K^-$ (upper diagram, via quark transition b → cūs), and to $B^- \to \bar{D}^0 K^-$ (lower diagram, via quark transition b → uc̄s). Right-hand part: decays of D^0 and $\bar{D}^0$ to the common $\pi^+ \pi^- \pi^0$ state.

Indeed non-zero values of $\mathcal{A}_{K\pi}$ have been reported by both the BaBar and Belle collaborations:

$$\text{BaBar (Aubert } \textit{et al.} \text{ 2004)} : \mathcal{A}_{K\pi} = -0.133 \pm 0.030 \pm 0.009 \qquad (21.13)$$

$$\text{Belle (Chao } \textit{et al.} \text{ 2005)} : \mathcal{A}_{K\pi} = -0.113 \pm 0.022 \pm 0.008 \qquad (21.14)$$

where the first error is statistical and the second is systematic.

Altough $\mathcal{A}_{K\pi}$ is sensitive to the **CP**-violating angle γ, it is not easy to extract γ cleanly from these measurements. Both the tree and the penguin amplitudes involve non-perturbative factors for producing a particular meson state from the corresponding qq̄ state; the strong phases are also not calculable.

A decay with no penguin contributions, but still with two interfering channels, would have fewer uncertainties. (It is also less likely to be affected by new physics, which could provide short-distance corrections to penguin loops.) One such example is provided by the decays (i) $B^- \to D^0 K^-$ and (ii) $B^- \to \bar{D}^0 K^-$, which can interfere when the $(D^0 K^-)$ and $(\bar{D}^0 K^-)$ states decay to a common final state. Here the quark transition in (i) is b → cūs, and in (ii) is b → uc̄s; in neither case is a penguin contribution possible.

The tree-level diagrams which contribute are shown in the left-hand parts of figure 21.3 (we shall discuss the right-hand parts in a moment). We denote the amplitude for $B^- \to D^0 K^-$ by A_B, and note that $A_B \sim A\lambda^3$. The amplitude for $B^- \to \bar{D}^0 K^-$, $\tilde{A}_B$, differs in three ways from A_B: (i) it is colour-suppressed by a factor $1/3$ since the c̄ and u have to be colour matched; (ii)

it contains the factor $V_{ub}V_{cs}^* \sim A\lambda^3(\rho - i\eta)$; (iii) it will have a different strong interaction phase. With these factors in mind, we write

$$\tilde{A}_B = r_B A_B e^{i(\delta_B - \gamma)} \qquad (21.15)$$

where δ_B is the difference in strong phases between $\tilde{A}_B$ and A_B, and r_B is the magnitude ratio of the amplitudes. Since $|\rho - i\eta| \sim 0.38$, r_B is of order 0.1–0.2, allowing for the colour suppression.

Once again, the asymmetry is proportional to

$$|1 + r_B \exp[i(\delta_B - \gamma)]|^2 - |1 + r_B \exp[i(\delta_B + \gamma)]|^2 \approx 4r_B \sin \delta_B \sin \gamma. \qquad (21.16)$$

This involves γ, but the relative smallness of r_B tends to reduce the sensitivity to γ. An alternative determination of γ can be made (Attwood *et al.* 2001, Giri *et al.* 2003) by making use of three-body decays (to a common channel) of D^0 and $\bar{D}^0$, such as D^0, $\bar{D}^0 \to K_S \pi^+ \pi^-$. If we denote the amplitude for $D^0 \to K_S \pi^+ \pi^-$ by $A(s_-, s_+)$ (see figure 21.3), where $s_- = (p_K + p_{\pi^-})^2$ and $s_+ = (p_K + p_{\pi^+})^2$ are the indicated invariant masses, then the amplitude for the B^- to decay to $K^- K_S \pi^+ \pi^-$ via the D^0 path is[1]

$$A_- = A_B D[A(s_-, s_+) + r_B e^{i(\delta_B - \gamma)} A(s_+, s_-)], \qquad (21.17)$$

and the amplitude for the charge conjugate reaction $B^+ \to K_S \pi^- \pi^+$ is

$$A_+ = A_B D[A(s_+, s_-) + r_B e^{i(\delta_B + \gamma)} A(s_+ - s_+)], \qquad (21.18)$$

where D is the D meson propagator. The event rate for the B^- decay is then $\Gamma_-(s_-, s_+)$ where (Aubert *et al.* 2008)

$$\Gamma_-(s_-, s_+) \propto |A(s_-, s_+)|^2 + r_B^2 |A(s_+, s_-)|^2 +$$
$$2\left[x_- \text{Re}\{A(s_-, s_+)A^*(s_+, s_-)\} + y_- \text{Im}\{A(s_-, s_+)A^*(s_+, s_-)\}\right] \qquad (21.19)$$

and the rate for B^+ decay is $\Gamma_+(s_-, s_+)$ where

$$\Gamma_+(s_-, s_+) \propto |A(s_+, s_-)|^2 + r_B^2 |A(s_-, s_+)|^2 +$$
$$2\left[x_+ \text{Re}\{A(s_+, s_-)A^*(s_-, s_+)\} + y_+ \text{Im}\{A(s_+, s_-)A^*(s_-, s_+)\}\right]. \qquad (21.20)$$

Here

$$x_- = r_B \cos(\delta_B - \gamma), \quad y_- = r_B \sin(\delta_B - \gamma) \qquad (21.21)$$
$$x_+ = r_B \cos(\delta_B + \gamma), \quad y_+ = r_B \sin(\delta_B + \gamma). \qquad (21.22)$$

The geometry of the **CP**-violating parameters is shown in figure 21.4. Note that the separation of the B^- and B^+ positions in the (x, y) plane is equal to

---

[1]We are neglecting D^0-$\bar{D}^0$ mixing and **CP** asymmetries in D decays, which are at the 1% or less level (Grossman *et al.* 2005).

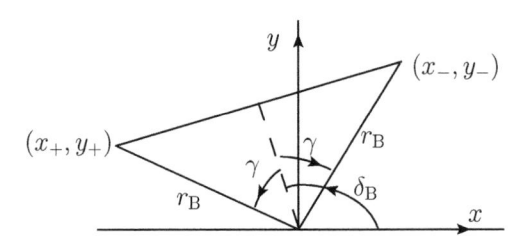

FIGURE 21.4

Geometry of the **CP**-violating parameters $x_\pm, y_\pm$.

$2r_B|\sin\gamma|$, and is a measure of direct **CP** violation. The angle between the lines connecting the B^- and B^+ centres to the origin (0,0) is equal to 2γ.

If the functional dependence of both the modulus and the phase of $A(s_-, s_+)$ were known, then the rates would depend on only three variables, r_B, δ_B, and γ (or equivalently on $x_\pm, y_\pm$). In fact, $A(s_-, s_+)$ can be determined from a Dalitz plot analysis of the decays of D^0 mesons coming from $D^{*+} \to D^0\pi^+$ decays produced in $e^+e^- \to c\bar{c}$ events; the charge of the low-momentum π^+ identifies the flavour of the D^0. Such an analysis is a well-established tool in the study of three-hadron final states, originating in the pioneer work of Dalitz (1953), in connection with the decay $K \to 3\pi$. The partial rate for $D^0(\bar{D}^0) \to K_S\pi^+\pi^-$ is (see the kinematics section of Nakamura *et al.* 2010)

$$d\Gamma \propto |A(s_-, s_+)|^2 ds_- ds_+. \tag{21.23}$$

The physical region in the s_-, s_+ plane is a bounded oval-like region, which would be uniformly populated if $A(s_-, s_+)$ were a constant. In reality, the decay is dominated by quasi two-body states, in particular

$$
\begin{aligned}
D^- &\to K^{*-}(s_-)\,\pi^+ &\text{(CA)} \\
&\to K^{*+}(s_+)\,\pi^- &\text{(DCS)} \\
&\to K_S\,\rho^0(s_0), &\text{(CP)}
\end{aligned}
\tag{21.24}
$$

where (CA) means CKM-favoured, (DCS) means doubly CKM-suppressed, and (CP) means that it is a **CP** eigenstate. The Dalitz plot shows a dense band of events at $s_- = m^2_{K^{*-}}$ corresponding to the K^{*-} resonance, a band at $s_+ = m^2_{K^{*+}}$, and a band at $s_0 = m^2_\rho$, where $s_0 = (p_{\pi^+} + p_{\pi^-})^2$ and $s_+ + s_- + s_0 = m^2_D + m^2_K + 2m^2_\pi$.

The Dalitz-plot analysis proceeds by writing (Aubert *et al.* 2008) $A(s_-, s_+)$ as a coherent sum of terms representing the quasi two-body modes, together with a non-resonant background. Once $A(s_-, s_+)$ is known, it is inserted into $\Gamma_\mp(s_-, s_+)$ to obtain $(x_\pm, y_\pm)$ from the Dalitz plot distributions of the signal modes of the $B^\mp$ decays. From these, the quantities r_B, δ_B and finally δ can be inferred.

This method has been applied by both BaBar and Belle to determine γ. Their most recently published results are

$$\text{BaBar (Aubert } et\ al.\ 2010): \quad \gamma \ = \ 68 \pm 14 \pm 4 \pm 3° \quad (21.25)$$

$$\text{Belle (Poluektov } et\ al.\ 2010): \quad \gamma \ = \ 78.4^{+10.8}_{-11.6} \pm 3 \pm 8.9° \quad (21.26)$$

where the last uncertainty is due to the D-decay modelling (which ignores, for example, rescattering among the three final state particles). Both these experiments use decays $B^\pm \to DK^\pm, B^\pm \to D^*K^\pm$ with $D^* \to D\pi^0$ and $D^* \to D\gamma$; BaBar in addition uses the decays $D^0 \to K_S K^+ K^-$.

We now turn to the other main method of detecting **CP** violation, through the interference between decays of (for example) B^0 and $\bar{B}^0$ mesons that have been produced in a coherent state by mixing. For this we need to set up the formalism describing time-dependent mixing.

21.2 CP violation in B meson oscillations

B^0-$\bar{B}^0$ oscillations have been studied by the BaBar and Belle collaborations at the PEP2 and KEKB asymmetric $e^+ e^-$ colliders. These machines operate at a centre of mass energy equal to the mass of the $\Upsilon(4S)$ resonance state, which is some 20 MeV above the threshold for $B^0\,\bar{B}^0$ production. If produced in a symmetric $e^+ e^-$ collider (with equal and opposite momenta for the e^+ and e^-), the produced B mesons would move very slowly, $v/c \sim 0.06$, covering a distance of only some 30 μm before decaying ($c\tau$ for B mesons is about 460 μm). This would make it impossible to resolve the decay vertices of the two Bs, as is required in order to observe B^0-$\bar{B}^0$ oscillations, since the accuracy of the decay vertex reconstruction is roughly 100 μm. Oddone (1989) suggested making $e^+\,e^-$ collisions with asymmetric energy colliding beams, so that the B mesons now move with the motion of the centre of mass, which can be considerable. For example, at PEP2 (e^- 9 GeV, e^+ 3.1 GeV) $\beta_{\mathrm{cm}} \sim 0.5$ and $\gamma_{\mathrm{cm}} \sim 1.15$, so that the distance travelled in the (asymmetric) lab frame during the lifetime of an average B meson is ~ 250 μm, which is measurable. At KEKB (e^- 8 GeV, e^- 3.5 GeV), $\beta_{\mathrm{cm}}\gamma_{\mathrm{cm}} \sim 0.425$.

Since the $\Upsilon(4S)$ state has $J = 1$, the decay $\Upsilon \to BB$ leaves the B mesons in a p wave state, which is forbidden for two identical spinless bosons; therefore one must be a B^0 and the other a $\bar{B}^0$, but we do not know which is which until one has been identified ('tagged') in some way. The flavour of the tagged B may be determined, for example, by the charge of the lepton emitted in the semi-leptonic decays $B^0 \to D^-\ell^+\nu_e, \bar{B}^0 \to D^+\ell^-\bar{\nu}_e$. We shall not describe the evolution of the BB coherent state following production; interested readers may consult Cohen *et al.* (2009) for an instructive discussion, which also covers neutrino oscillations. We shall be interested in the time dependence of the state of the meson which partners the tagged meson, once the correlated

state has been collapsed by the tagging at time $t = 0$ say; the partner meson will be reconstructed by its decay products. Note that the partner meson can decay earlier or later than the tagged one; its state vector has that time dependence which ensures that it becomes the correlate of the tagged particle at $t = 0$.

21.2.1   Time-dependent mixing formalism

We denote the neutral meson by B (which will usually be B^0, but could also be K^0 or D^0), and its **CP**-conjugate by $\bar{B}$. According to the theory of Weisskopf and Wigner (1930a, 1930b) (see also appendix A of Kabir 1968) a state that is initially in some superposition of $|B\rangle$ and $|\bar{B}\rangle$, say

$$|\psi(0)\rangle = a(0)|B\rangle + b(0)|\bar{B}\rangle, \tag{21.27}$$

will evolve in time to a general superposition

$$|\psi(t)\rangle = a(t)|B\rangle + b(t)|\bar{B}\rangle \tag{21.28}$$

governed by an effective Hamiltonian **H** with matrix elements, in the 2-state subspace,

$$\mathbf{H} = \mathbf{M} - \mathrm{i}\frac{\mathbf{\Gamma}}{2} = \begin{pmatrix} A & p^2 \\ q^2 & A \end{pmatrix} \tag{21.29}$$

where **M** and **Γ** are Hermitian, and the equality $M_{11} - \mathrm{i}\Gamma_{11}/2 = M_{22} - \mathrm{i}\Gamma_{22}/2 = A$ follows from **CPT** invariance, which we shall assume. If **CP** is a good symmetry, then

$$
\begin{aligned}
\langle \bar{B}|\mathbf{H}|B\rangle &= \langle \bar{B}|(\mathbf{CP})^{-1}(\mathbf{CP})\mathbf{H}(\mathbf{CP})^{-1}\mathbf{CP}|B\rangle \\
&= \langle B|\mathbf{H}|\bar{B}\rangle
\end{aligned} \tag{21.30}
$$

so that p would equal q. Since **M** and **Γ** are both Hermitian, this would imply that M_{12} and Γ_{12} are both real; in the **CP** non-invariant world, this is not the case.

The eigenvalues of **H** are

$$\omega_{\mathrm{L}} \equiv m_{\mathrm{L}} - \mathrm{i}\Gamma_{\mathrm{L}}/2 = A + p\,q, \quad \omega_{\mathrm{H}} \equiv m_{\mathrm{H}} - \mathrm{i}\Gamma_{\mathrm{H}}/2 = A - p\,q, \tag{21.31}$$

and the corresponding eigenstates are

$$
\begin{aligned}
|B_{\mathrm{L}}\rangle &= (p\,|B\rangle + q|\bar{B}\rangle)/(|p|^2 + |q|^2)^{1/2} \\
|B_{\mathrm{H}}\rangle &= (p\,|B\rangle - q|\bar{B}\rangle)/(|p|^2 + |q|^2)^{1/2}.
\end{aligned} \tag{21.32}
$$

The states $|B_{\mathrm{L}}\rangle$, $|B_{\mathrm{H}}\rangle$ have definite masses $m_{\mathrm{H}}, m_{\mathrm{L}}$ and widths Γ_{L} and Γ_{H}. The widths $\Gamma_{\mathrm{L}}, \Gamma_{\mathrm{H}}$ are equal to a very good approximation for B and D mesons, because the Q-values of both are large; in the case of K-mesons (see section 21.3), one state decays predominantly to 2π and the other to 3π, with different Q-values, and the lifetimes are very different.

Suppose now that at time $t = 0$ the 'tag' shows that a B^0 has decayed. Then the partner is a $\bar{B}^0$ at $t = 0$, described by the superposition

$$|\bar{B}^0\rangle = -\frac{\sqrt{|p|^2 + |q|^2}}{2q}(|B_H\rangle - |B_L\rangle). \tag{21.33}$$

At a later time t in the $\bar{B}^0$ rest-frame, this state evolves to (problem 21.1)

$$|\bar{B}_t^0\rangle = g_+(t)|\bar{B}^0\rangle + (p/q)g_-(t)|B^0\rangle \tag{21.34}$$

where

$$g_+(t) = e^{-im_B t}e^{-\Gamma t/2}\cos(\Delta m_B t/2) \tag{21.35}$$
$$g_-(t) = ie^{-im_B t}e^{-\Gamma t/2}\sin(\Delta m_B t/2) \tag{21.36}$$

with $m_B = \frac{1}{2}(m_H + m_L)$ and $\Delta m_B = m_H - m_L$. Note, from (21.34), that the state which started as a $\bar{B}^0$ at $t = 0$ develops also a B^0 component at a later time. Similarly, if the tag shows that a $\bar{B}^0$ has decayed, the partner meson at $t = 0$ is a B^0, and its state evolves to

$$|B_t^0\rangle = (q/p)g_-(t)|\bar{B}^0\rangle + g_+(t)|B^0\rangle. \tag{21.37}$$

Consider first the semileptonic decays of B^0 and $\bar{B}^0$, where the only transitions that can occur are

$$B^0 \to \ell^+ \nu_\ell X, \quad \bar{B}^0 \to \ell^- \bar{\nu}_\ell X. \tag{21.38}$$

The state $|\bar{B}_t^0\rangle$ of (21.34), however, which was pure $\bar{B}^0$ at $t = 0$, will be able to decay to a positively charged lepton via the admixture of the $|B^0\rangle$ component; similarly negatively charged leptons may appear in the decay of $|B_t^0\rangle$. From (21.34) and (21.37) we obtain directly the amplitudes for these 'wrong sign' transitions:

$$\langle \ell^- \bar{\nu}_\ell X|\hat{\mathcal{H}}_{sl}|B_t^0\rangle = (q/p)g_-(t)\langle \ell^- \bar{\nu}_\ell X|\hat{\mathcal{H}}_{sl}|\bar{B}^0\rangle \tag{21.39}$$

and

$$\langle \ell^+ \nu_\ell X|\hat{\mathcal{H}}_{sl}|\bar{B}_t^0\rangle = (p/q)g_-(t)\langle \ell^+ \nu_\ell X|\hat{\mathcal{H}}_{sl}|B^0\rangle, \tag{21.40}$$

where $\hat{\mathcal{H}}_{sl}$ is the relevant semileptonic part of the complete weak current–current Hamiltonian. Hence the semileptonic asymmetry is

$$\mathcal{A}_{SL} = \frac{\Gamma(\bar{B}_t^0 \to \ell^+ \nu_\ell X) - \Gamma(B_t^0 \to \ell^- \bar{\nu}_\ell X)}{\Gamma(\bar{B}_t^0 \to \ell^+ \nu_\ell X) + \Gamma(B_t^0 \to \ell^- \bar{\nu}_\ell X)} = \frac{1 - |q/p|^4}{1 + |q/p|^4}, \tag{21.41}$$

independent of time. In (21.41) we have used the fact that $\langle \ell^- \bar{\nu}_\ell X|\hat{\mathcal{H}}_{sl}|\bar{B}^0\rangle = \langle \ell^+ \nu_\ell X|\hat{\mathcal{H}}_{sl}|B^0\rangle^*$. The upper bound on $\mathcal{A}_{SL}$ is of order 10^{-3} (Nakamura *et al.* 2010). At the present level of experimental precision, it is a very good approximation to take $|q/p| = 1$. Since $q/p = [(M_{12}^* - i\Gamma_{12}^*/2)/(M_{12} - i\Gamma_{12}/2)]^{1/2}$, it follows that in this approximation we can neglect Γ_{12}, and the phase of q/p is just minus the phase of M_{12}.

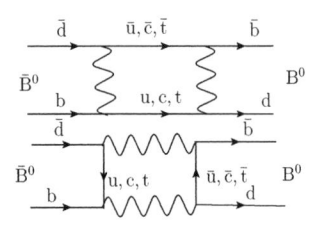

FIGURE 21.5
Box diagram contributions to B^0-$\bar{\mathrm{B}}^0$ mixing.

In the Standard Model, the B^0-$\bar{\mathrm{B}}^0$ mixing amplitude occurs via the box diagrams of figure 21.5. The box amplitude is approximately proportional to the product of the masses of the internal quarks, and in this case the t quark contribution dominates (the magnitudes of the CKM couplings are all comparable). The phase of M_{12} is then that of $(V_{\mathrm{td}}^* V_{\mathrm{tb}})^2$, which is the phase of $((1 - \rho - i\eta)^*)^2$ in the parametrization of (20.179), which in turn is equal to the angle 2β. Hence

$$(q/p) = \mathrm{e}^{-2i\beta}, \tag{21.42}$$

neglecting terms of order λ^4. Equation (21.42) will be important in what follows.

From (21.34) we can now read off that the probability that the state $|\bar{\mathrm{B}}_t^0\rangle$ (which – we remind the reader – is the partner of the state tagged as a B^0 at $t = 0$, and which is pure $\bar{\mathrm{B}}^0$ at $t = 0$) decays as a $\bar{\mathrm{B}}^0$ at $t \neq 0$, is $|g_+(t)|^2 = \exp(-\Gamma t) \cos^2 \Delta m_\mathrm{B}^2 t/2$. Similarly, the probability that this state decays as a B^0 at time t is $\exp(-\Gamma t) \sin^2 \Delta m_\mathrm{B} t/2$, taking $|(p/q)| = 1$. Hence the difference in these probabilities, normalized to their sum, is $\cos \Delta m_\mathrm{B} t$. Measurements of this *flavour asymmetry* yield the value of Δm_B, currently (Nakamura *et al.* 2010)

$$\Delta m_\mathrm{B} = 3.3337 \pm 0.033 \times 10^{-10}\ \mathrm{MeV}. \tag{21.43}$$

More generally, we define decay amplitudes to final states $|f\rangle$ by

$$A_f = \langle f|\hat{\mathcal{H}}_{\mathrm{wk}}|\mathrm{B}^0\rangle \quad , \quad \bar{A}_f = \langle f|\hat{\mathcal{H}}_{\mathrm{wk}}|\bar{\mathrm{B}}^0\rangle \tag{21.44}$$

$$A_{\bar{f}} = \langle \bar{f}|\hat{\mathcal{H}}_{\mathrm{wk}}|\mathrm{B}^0\rangle \quad , \quad \bar{A}_{\bar{f}} = \langle \bar{f}|\hat{\mathcal{H}}_{\mathrm{wk}}|\mathrm{B}^0\rangle, \tag{21.45}$$

where $\mathrm{CP}|f\rangle = |\bar{f}\rangle$ and $\hat{\mathcal{H}}_{\mathrm{wk}}$ is the weak interaction Hamiltonian responsible for the transition. We can now calculate the rates for $|\bar{\mathrm{B}}_t^0\rangle$ to go to $|f\rangle$, and for $|\mathrm{B}_t^0\rangle$ to go to $|f\rangle$; up to a common normalization factor, which we omit, these rates are (problem 21.2)

$$\Gamma(\bar{\mathrm{B}}_t^0 \to f) = \frac{1}{2}\mathrm{e}^{-\Gamma t}\{|\bar{A}_f|^2 + |(p/q)A_f|^2 + (|\bar{A}_f|^2 - |(p/q)A_f|^2)\cos \Delta m_\mathrm{B} t$$
$$+ 2\mathrm{Im}(\bar{A}_f \frac{q}{p} A_f^*)\sin \Delta m_\mathrm{B} t\}, \tag{21.46}$$

and

$$\Gamma(\mathrm{B}_t^0 \to f) = \frac{1}{2}\mathrm{e}^{-\Gamma t}\{|A_f|^2 + |(q/p)\bar{A}_f|^2 + (|A_f|^2 - |(q/p)\bar{A}_f|^2)\cos\Delta m_\mathrm{B}t$$

$$- 2\mathrm{Im}(\bar{A}_f\frac{q}{p}A_f^*)\sin\Delta m_\mathrm{B}t\}. \qquad (21.47)$$

The rates to $|\bar{f}\rangle$ are obtained by the substitutions $A_f \to A_{\bar{f}}, \bar{A}_f \to \bar{A}_{\bar{f}}$.

We can now derive the basic formulae for the time-dependent **CP** asymmetry of neutral B decays to a final state f common to B^0 and $\bar{\mathrm{B}}^0$ (problem 21.3):

$$\mathcal{A}_f = \frac{\Gamma(\bar{\mathrm{B}}_t^0 \to f) - \Gamma(\mathrm{B}_t^0 \to f)}{\Gamma(\bar{\mathrm{B}}_t^0 \to f) + \Gamma(\mathrm{B}_t^0 \to f)} = S_f \sin(\Delta m_\mathrm{B}\, t) - C_f \cos\Delta m_\mathrm{B}\, t) \quad (21.48)$$

where

$$S_f = \frac{2\mathrm{Im}\lambda_f}{1+|\lambda_f|^2}, \quad C_f = \frac{1-|\lambda_f|^2}{1+|\lambda_f|^2}, \quad \lambda_f = \frac{q}{p}\left(\frac{\bar{A}_f}{A_f}\right). \qquad (21.49)$$

21.2.2 Determination of the angles $\alpha(\phi_2)$ and $\beta(\phi_1)$ of the unitarity triangle

A very large number of measurements have been made, constraining the parameters of the CKM matrix, or equivalently the unitarity triangle of figure 20.10. We shall limit our discussion to those measurements which determine the angles $\alpha(\phi_2)$ and $\beta(\phi_1)$ of the triangle.

(i) The angle β (ϕ_1)

One of the cleanest examples is the decay

$$\mathrm{B}^0 \to J/\psi + \mathrm{K}_{\mathrm{S,L}}^0. \qquad (21.50)$$

The tree diagram is shown in figure 21.6(a), and the penguins in figure 21.6(b). The tree diagram contributes CKM factors $V_{\mathrm{cb}}^* V_{\mathrm{cs}} = A\lambda^2(1-\lambda^2/2)$. The $\bar{\mathrm{f}} = \bar{\mathrm{u}}$ penguin has factors $V_{\mathrm{ub}}^* V_{\mathrm{us}} = A\lambda^4(\rho - \mathrm{i}\eta)$ which is suppressed by two powers of λ; it also carries a loop factor $\sim \alpha_\mathrm{s}/\pi$, and it may therefore be safely neglected. The other two penguins have the same weak phase as the tree diagram. Hence to a good approximation we can write the amplitude as

$$A_{\psi\mathrm{K}} = (V_{\mathrm{cb}}^* V_{\mathrm{cs}})T_{\psi\mathrm{K}}. \qquad (21.51)$$

There is one subtlety: to get the two final states from B^0 and $\bar{\mathrm{B}}^0$ to interfere, we need K^0-$\bar{\mathrm{K}}^0$ mixing to produce the (very nearly) **CP** eigenstates K_S^0 (**CP** $= +1$) and K_L^0 (**CP** $= -1$). (We shall discuss the $\mathrm{K}^0 - \bar{\mathrm{K}}^0$ system briefly in section 21.3.) This introduces a factor $(q/p)_\mathrm{K} = (V_{\mathrm{cd}}^* V_{\mathrm{cs}}/V_{\mathrm{cd}}V_{\mathrm{cs}}^*)$, quite analogously to (21.42), but its effect on $\lambda_{\psi\mathrm{K}}$ is negligible. So, remembering

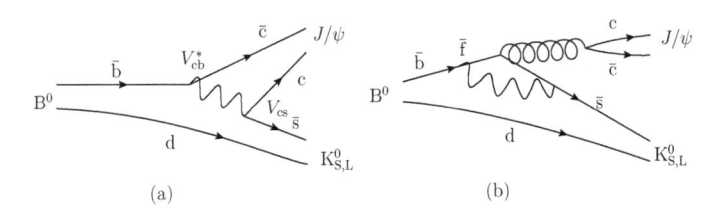

FIGURE 21.6
Tree (a) and penguin (b) contributions to $B^0 \to J/\psi + K^0_{S,L}$ via the quark transitions $\bar{b} \to \bar{c}c\bar{s}$.

that the relative orbital angular momentum of the two final state particles is $\ell = 1$, we have $\lambda_{\psi K_S} = -\exp(-2i\beta)$ and $S_f = \sin 2\beta$, while the $J/\psi K^0_L$ state has $\mathbf{CP}=+1$ and $S_f = -\sin 2\beta$. Hence $S_{\psi K}$ measures $-\eta_f \sin 2\beta$, where η_f is the $\mathbf{CP}$ eigenvalue of the $J/\psi K^0_{S,L}$ state: the sinusoidal oscillations in the asymmetry $\mathcal{A}_{\psi K}$ for the two modes S, L will have the same amplitude and opposite phase.

Both BaBar and Belle have reported increasingly precise measurements of $\mathcal{A}_{\psi K}$ in these modes. The early results (Abashian *et al.* 2001, Aubert *et al.* 2001) were the first direct measurements of one of the angles of the unitarity triangle, offering a test of the consistency of the CKM mechanism for $\mathbf{CP}$ violation. Later measurements have achieved accuracies of about $\pm 5\%$. The current world average for $\sin 2\beta$ is (see the review by Ceccucci *et al.* in Nakamura *et al.* 2010)

$$\sin 2\beta = 0.673 \pm 0.023. \tag{21.52}$$

Figure 21.7 shows the asymmetry (before corrections for experimental effects) for $\eta_f = -1$ and $\eta_f = +1$ candidates as measured by BaBar (Aubert *et al.* 2007a); Belle has reported similar results. We should note that a measurement of $\sin 2\beta$ still leaves ambiguities in β (for example, $\beta \to \pi/2 - \beta$), which can be resolved by other measurements (Ceccucci *et al.*, in Nakamura *et al.* 2010).

(ii) The angle $\alpha(\phi_2)$

The angle α is the phase between $V^*_{tb}V_{td}$ and $V^*_{ub}V_{ud}$. It can be measured in decays dominated by the quark transition $b \to u\,\bar{u}\,d$. Consider, for example, the decays $B^0 \to \pi^+\pi^-, \bar{B}^0 \to \pi^+\pi^-$. Figure 21.8 shows the tree graph (a) and penguin (b) contributions to $B^0 \to \pi^+\pi^-$. Exposing the weak phases as before, the amplitude is

$$\begin{aligned} A_{+-} &= V^*_{ub}V_{ud}(t + p_{\bar{u}} - p_{\bar{c}}) + V^*_{tb}V_{td}(p_{\bar{t}} - p_{\bar{c}}) \\ &\equiv V^*_{ub}V_{ud}T_{+-} + V^*_{tb}V_{td}P_{+-}. \end{aligned} \tag{21.53}$$

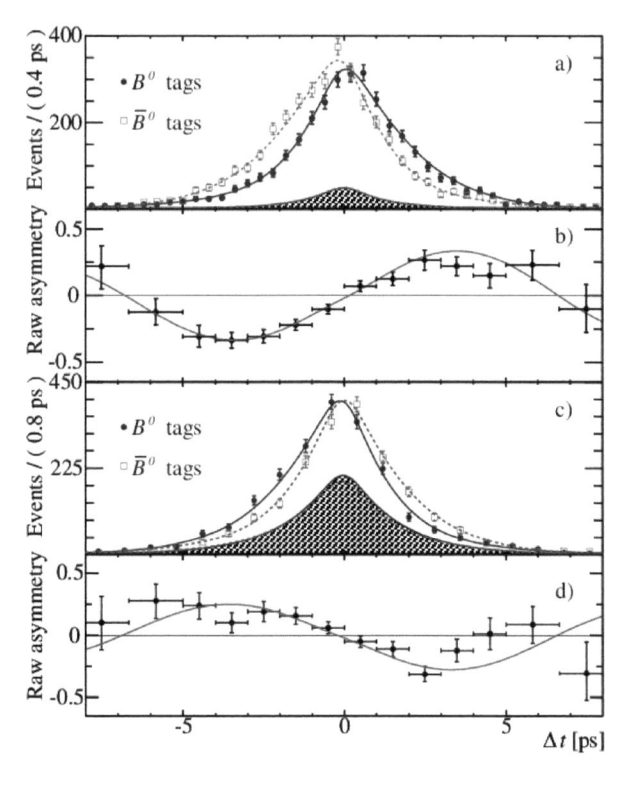

FIGURE 21.7

(a) Number of $\eta_f = -1$ candidates in the signal region with a B^0 tag (N_{B^0}) and with a $\bar{B}^0$ tag ($N_{\bar{B}^0}$), and (b) the measured asymmetry $(N_{B^0} - N_{\bar{B}^0})/(N_{B^0} + N_{\bar{B}^0})$, as functions of t; (c) and (d) are the corresponding distributions for the $\eta_f = +1$ candidates. Figure reprinted with permission from Aubert *et al.* (BaBar Collaboration) *Phys. Rev. Lett.* **99** 171803 (2007). Copyright 2007 by the American Physical Society. (See color plate IV.)

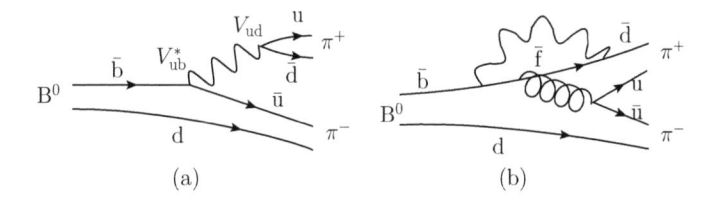

FIGURE 21.8

Tree graph (a) and penguin (b) contributions to $B^0 \rightarrow \pi^+\pi^-$, via quark transitions $\bar{b} \rightarrow \bar{d}u\bar{u}$.

Suppose first that the penguin contributions could be neglected. Then the asymmetry $\mathcal{A}_{\pi^+\pi^-}$ would measure

$$
\begin{aligned}
\mathrm{Im}\lambda_{\pi^+\pi^-} &= \mathrm{Im}\left(e^{-2i\beta}\frac{\bar{A}_{+-}}{A_{+-}}\right) = \mathrm{Im}\left(e^{-2i\beta}\frac{V_{ub}V_{ud}^*}{V_{ub}^*V_{ud}}\right) \\
&= \mathrm{Im}\,e^{-2i(\gamma+\beta)} = \sin 2\alpha
\end{aligned}
\tag{21.54}
$$

where α is defined as $\pi - \beta - \gamma$. Unfortunately, this simple result is spoiled by the penguin contributions, which there is no good reason to ignore. However, Gronau and London (1990) showed how an isospin analysis could disentangle the tree and penguin parts. The method involves the three amplitudes $A_{+-}, A_{00}(\mathrm{B}^0 \to \pi^0\pi^0)$, and $A_{+0}(\mathrm{B}^+ \to \pi^+\pi^0)$.

First of all, note that Bose statistics for the 2π states requires them to have only the symmetric isospin states $I = 0$ or 2, since the angular momentum is zero. Next, the effective non-leptonic weak Hamiltonian $\hat{\mathcal{H}}_{\mathrm{nl}}$ acting in the tree diagram transition contains both $\Delta I = 1/2$ and $\Delta I = 3/2$ pieces; combining with the initial $I = 1/2$ of the B meson, the first piece will lead only to the $I = 0$ final state, while the second contributes to both $I = 0$ and $I = 2$ final states. However, since the gluon in the penguin diagrams carries no isospin, these diagrams can only change the isospin by $\Delta I = 1/2$, which connects only to the $I = 0$ final state. The conclusion is that the $I = 2$ final state is free of penguins, and carries the pure tree phase.

This information can be exploited as follows (Gronau and London 1990). First, the action of $\hat{\mathcal{H}}_{\mathrm{nl}}$ on the B^0 state can be written as

$$
\hat{\mathcal{H}}_{\mathrm{nl}}|\tfrac{1}{2}\,-\tfrac{1}{2}\rangle = \frac{1}{\sqrt{2}}A_{3/2}|20\rangle + \frac{1}{\sqrt{2}}A_{1/2}|00\rangle
\tag{21.55}
$$

where as usual $|II_3\rangle$ is the state with isospin I and third component I_3. Expanding the states $\pi^+\pi^-, \pi^+\pi^0$ and $\pi^0\pi^0$ in terms of definite isospin states, one finds (problem 21.4)

$$
\begin{aligned}
A_{+-} &= \frac{1}{\sqrt{6}}A_{3/2} + \frac{1}{\sqrt{3}}A_{1/2} \\
A_{+0} &= \frac{\sqrt{3}}{2}A_{3/2} \\
A_{00} &= \frac{1}{\sqrt{3}}A_{3/2} - \frac{1}{\sqrt{6}}A_{1/2}
\end{aligned}
\tag{21.56}
$$

where A_{ij} is the amplitude $\langle \pi^i\pi^j|\hat{\mathcal{H}}_{\mathrm{nl}}|B^{i+j}\rangle$. The $\pi^+\pi^0$ state can have only $I = 2$, and arises solely from the tree diagram. Furthermore, the three complex amplitudes A_{+-}, A_{+0} and A_{00} are expressed in terms of only two reduced amplitudes $A_{3/2}$ and $A_{1/2}$, leading to one relation between them:

$$
\frac{1}{\sqrt{2}}A_{+-} + A_{00} = A_{+0},
\tag{21.57}
$$

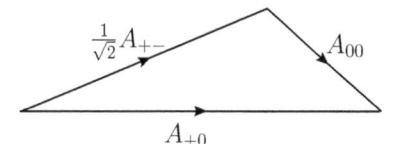

FIGURE 21.9
The triangle formed by the three amplitudes A_{ij} in equation (21.57).

which can be represented as a triangle in the complex plane, as shown in figure 21.9. There is a similar triangle for the charge conjugate processes

$$\frac{1}{\sqrt{2}}\bar{A}_{+-} + \bar{A}_{00} = \bar{A}_{+0}, \tag{21.58}$$

where the $\bar{A}$ amplitudes are obtained from the As by complex conjugating the CKM couplings, the strong phases remaining the same as usual.

Since A_{+0} is pure tree, its weak phase is well defined, namely that of $V_{ub}^*V_{ud}$, which is γ. It is convenient to define (Lipkin *et al.* 1991) $\tilde{A} = \exp(2i\gamma)\bar{A}$, so that $\tilde{A}_{+0} = A_{+0}$. Then the two triangles have a common base, A_{+0}. The failure of the two triangles to overlap exactly is a measure of the penguin contribution. In principle, by measuring the asymmetry coefficients $S_{\pi^+\pi^-}, C_{\pi^+\pi^-}$, the branching fractions of all three modes, and C_{00}, one can construct the triangles. But unfortunately the relative orientation of the triangles is not known, which leads to various possible solutions to α in the range $0 < \alpha < 2\pi$. In addition, the data on $\pi^0\pi^0$ (with a branching ratio of order 10^{-6}) has sizeable experimental errors, and only a relatively loose constraint on α can be obtained.

A much better constraint can be found from the **CP** asymmetries in $B \to \pi\rho$ decays (Snyder and Quinn 1993). The method is essentially a time-dependent version of the Dalitz plot analysis discussed in section 21.1. The available channels are

$$\begin{aligned}
B^0 &\to \{\rho^+\pi^-, \rho^-\pi^+, \rho^0\pi^0\} \to \pi^+\pi^-\pi^0 \\
\bar{B}^0 &\to \{\rho^-\pi^+, \rho^+\pi^-, \rho^0\pi^0\} \to \pi^+\pi^-\pi^0
\end{aligned} \tag{21.59}$$

where all result in the final state $\pi^+\pi^-\pi^0$ after the decay of the ρ mesons, and interferences following B^0-$\bar{B}^0$ mixing are possible.

Returning then to equations (21.46) and (21.47), the rate for the 3π decay following a B^0 tag at $t = 0$ is

$$\begin{aligned}
\Gamma(B_t^0 \to 3\pi) &= \frac{1}{4}\Gamma e^{-\Gamma t}\left[|A_{3\pi}|^2 + |\bar{A}_{3\pi}|^2 + (|\bar{A}_{3\pi}|^2 - |A_{3\pi}|^2)\cos\Delta m_B t \right. \\
&\quad \left. + 2\mathrm{Im}\left(\frac{q}{p}\bar{A}_{3\pi}A_{3\pi}^*\right)\sin\Delta m_B t\right],
\end{aligned} \tag{21.60}$$

and there is a similar formula, with appropriate changes, for the case of a $\bar{\mathrm{B}}^0$ tag at $t = 0$. We now write

$$A_{3\pi} = f_+(s_+)F^+ + f_-(s_-)F^- + f_0(s_0)F^0 \tag{21.61}$$

and similarly

$$\bar{A}_{3\pi} = f_+(s_+)\bar{F}^+ + f_-(s_-)\bar{F}^- + f_0(s_0)\bar{F}^0, \tag{21.62}$$

where $s_+ = (p_{\pi^+} + p_{\pi^0})^2$, $s_- = (p_{\pi^-} + p_{\pi^0})^2$, $s_0 = (p_{\pi^+} + p_{\pi^-})^2$, satisfying $s_+ + s_- + s_0 = m_{\mathrm{B}}^2 + 2m_{\pi^+}^2 + m_{\pi^0}^2$. $f_\kappa(s_\kappa)$ is the sum of three relativistic Breit-Wigner resonance amplitudes, together with appropriate angular momentum and angle factors, corresponding to the $\rho(770), \rho(1450)$ and $\rho(1700)$ resonances. F^κ is the amplitude for the quasi two-body mode $\mathrm{B}^0 \to \rho^\kappa \pi^{\bar{\kappa}}$. Here κ takes the values $+, -$ and 0, and correspondingly $\bar{\kappa} = -, +, 0$. The amplitudes F^κ are complex and include the strong and weak transition phases, from tree and penguin diagrams; they are, however, independent of the Dalitz plot variables.

The $\rho\pi$ states have the same decomposition into tree and penguin parts as discussed previously for the $\pi\pi$ states, namely

$$F^\kappa = e^{i\gamma}T^\kappa + e^{-i\beta}P^\kappa, \tag{21.63}$$

where the magnitudes of the weak couplings have been absorbed into T^κ and P^κ. We can rewrite (21.63) as

$$e^{i\beta}F^\kappa = -e^{-i\alpha}T^\kappa + P^\kappa \equiv A^\kappa, \tag{21.64}$$

and similarly

$$e^{i\beta}(q/p)\bar{F}^\kappa = -e^{i\alpha}T^{\bar{\kappa}} + P^{\bar{\kappa}} \equiv \bar{A}^\kappa. \tag{21.65}$$

Then (21.61) and (21.62) become

$$A_{3\pi} = \sum_\kappa f_\kappa(s_\kappa)A^\kappa \tag{21.66}$$

$$(q/p)\bar{A}_{3\pi} = \sum_\kappa f_\kappa(s_\kappa)\bar{A}^\kappa, \tag{21.67}$$

disregarding a common overall phase $e^{-i\beta}$. When (21.66) and (21.67) are inserted into (21.60), it is clear that one obtains many terms, for example

$$\mathrm{Re}(f_+f_-^*)\,\mathrm{Im}(\bar{A}^+A^{-*} + \bar{A}^-A^{+*}), \quad \mathrm{Im}(f_+f_-^*)\,\mathrm{Re}(\bar{A}^+A^{-*} - \bar{A}^-A^{+*}), \tag{21.68}$$

and so on, in which different resonances interfere on the Dalitz plot. The strong, and known, rapid phase variation in these interference regions, via factors such as $f_+f_-^*$, is a powerful tool for extracting the complex amplitudes $A^\kappa, \bar{A}^\kappa$, and hence via (21.64) and (21.65) the phase α. The quantities multiplying the interference terms $\mathrm{Re}(f_\kappa f_\sigma^*)$ and $\mathrm{Im}(f_\kappa f_\sigma^*)$ are the key degrees of

freedom which allow this analysis to determine the penguin contributions and the strong phases, and hence α. However, the resonance overlap regions cover a small fraction of the Dalitz plot, so that a substantial data sample (a few thousand events) is needed to constrain all the amplitude parameters.

An isospin analysis similar to that of the $\pi\pi$ states can be done for the $\rho\pi$ states, but now there is no reason to forbid the final state to have $I = 1$. Nevertheless, if charged B decays are also included, there are five physical amplitudes ($\rho^0 \to \pi^+\pi^-, \pi^-\pi^+, \pi^0\pi^0, \rho^+ \to \pi^+\pi^0, \rho^- \to \pi^-\pi^0$) which are expressible in terms of two pure tree ($\Delta I = 3/2$) transitions to $I = 1, 2$ final states. One of the pure tree amplitudes may be written (Gronau 1991) as the sum $A^+ + A^- + 2A^0$, and hence the ratio $(\bar{A}^+ + \bar{A}^- + 2\bar{A}^0)/(A^+ + A^- + 2A^0)$ has the phase 2α.

This approach has been followed by both BaBar and Belle, with the results

$$\text{BaBar (Aubert } et\ al.\ 2007b) \qquad \alpha = 87^{+45°}_{-13°} \qquad (21.69)$$

$$\text{Belle (Kusaka } et\ al.\ 2007) \qquad 68 < \alpha < 95°. \qquad (21.70)$$

These results are consistent with the values of β and γ given in (21.52), (21.25) and (21.26), given the definition $\alpha = \pi - \beta - \gamma$.

Of course, this is only one (at present not very tight) consistency check. But there are now very many independent measurements of the magnitudes of the CKM matrix elements, as well as the angles. We shall not describe these here, referring the reader to the regular updates by the Particle Data Group (currently Nakamura *et al.* 2010). We showed in figure 20.11 the 2010 plot of the contraints in the $\bar{\rho}, \bar{\eta}$ plane, presented by Ceccucci *et al.*. They concluded that the 95% CL regions all overlapped consistently around the global fit region, though the consistency of $|V^{ub}|$ and $\sin 2\beta$ was not very good. It would be premature to make too much of the minor reservation, though it may be noted that $\sin 2\beta$ could be sensitive to new physics via short-distance corrections to the box diagrams of figure 21.5, while $|V_{ub}|$ is obtained from a tree-level process, and is thus unlikely to be affected by new physics. Overall, the consistency represented in figure 20.11 must be counted as a major triumph of the Standard Model, in particular of the original analysis by Kobayashi and Maskawa (1973). It must be remembered, though, that many extensions of the Standard Model allow considerable room for new **CP**-violating effects, which could be revealed by increasingly precise determinations of the CKM parameters.

21.3 CP violation in neutral K-meson decays

Although the formalism is similar, the phenomenology of **CP** violation in neutral K-meson decays is very different from that in neutral B-meson decays. In the K case, **CP** violation is a very small effect, typically at the level of

parts per thousand or smaller; its observation by Cristenson *et al.* (1964) was a historic achievement. But the neutral K system is most simply (and traditionally) approached by starting with the assumption that **CP** is conserved.

We will define $CP|K^0\rangle = -|\bar{K}^0\rangle$; then the **CP** eigenstates are

$$|K_\pm\rangle = \frac{1}{\sqrt{2}}(|K^0\rangle \mp |\bar{K}^0\rangle) \tag{21.71}$$

The **CP** $= 1$ state can decay to two pions in an s-state, but not to three pions if (as we are assuming to start with) **CP** is a good symmetry; the situation is the opposite for the **CP** $= -1$ state. The Q-value for the three pion mode is very much smaller than for the two pion mode, with the result that the $|K_+\rangle$ state, decaying to two pions, has a much shorter lifetime than the $|K_-\rangle$ state: $\tau_{2\pi} \sim 0.9 \times 10^{-10}$s, $\tau_{3\pi} \sim 5 \times 10^{-8}$s. Due to **CP** violation, the actual eigenstates $|K_L\rangle$ and $|K_S\rangle$ of the effective Hamiltonian are slightly different from $|K_\pm\rangle$ (see (21.75) and (21.76)), with masses m_S and m_L, and widths Γ_S and Γ_L. At this point, however, we shall associate m_S and Γ_S with $|K_+\rangle$, and m_L and Γ_L with $|K_-\rangle$.

A K^0 is produced in strangeness-conserving reactions such as $K^+n \to K^0p$, and a $\bar{K}^0$ in $K^- + p \to \bar{K}^0 + n$, for example. However, the two states can mix following production, since (as usual) it is the Hamiltonian eigenstates which propagate in free space, and they are the superpositions $|K_\pm\rangle$, assuming **CP** is conserved. Hence, as time proceeds following production, a state produced as a K^0 at time $t = 0$ will evolve into the state

$$|K^0_t\rangle = \frac{1}{2}(e^{-\Gamma_L t/2 - im_L t} + e^{-\Gamma_S t/2 - im_S t})|K^0\rangle + (e^{-\Gamma_L t/2 - im_L t} - e^{-\Gamma_S t/2 - im_S t})|\bar{K}^0\rangle. \tag{21.72}$$

The probability that a $K^0(\bar{K}^0)$ will then be observed at time t following production (in the K-meson rest frame) is

$$P_{+(-)} = \frac{1}{4}[e^{-\Gamma_L t} + e^{-\Gamma_S t} + (-)2e^{-(\Gamma_L + \Gamma_S)t/2}\cos\Delta mt] \tag{21.73}$$

where $\Delta m = m_L - m_S$. This is the famous phenomenon of strangeness oscillations, predicted by Gell-Mann and Pais (1955). Experimentally, the strangeness of the state at time t is defined by the modes $K^0 \to \pi^-\ell^+\nu_\ell$ and $\bar{K}^0 \to \pi^+\ell^-\bar{\nu}_\ell$. The difference $P_+(t) - P_-(t)$ is measured, and although the oscillations are heavily damped by $\exp(-\Gamma_S t)$, the mass difference can be determined:

$$\Delta m = (3.483 \pm 0.006) \times 10^{-12} \text{ meV}. \tag{21.74}$$

However, this is not the whole story. Christenson *et al.* (1964) found that, after many τ_S lifetimes, some 2π events were observed, indicating that the surviving state K_L was capable of decaying to 2π after all (albeit very rarely). The same conclusion follows from the fact that $P_+(t) - P_-(t)$ does not go to zero at long times, as it should from (21.73). Accordingly, the true

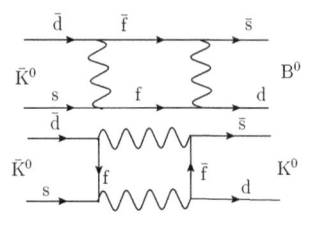

FIGURE 21.10
Box diagrams contributing to K^0-$\bar{K}^0$ mixing.

Hamiltonian eigenstates are not quite the **CP** eigenstates, but rather

$$|K_L\rangle = [(1 + \bar{\epsilon})|K^0\rangle + (1 - \bar{\epsilon})|\bar{K}^0\rangle]/\sqrt{2(1 + |\bar{\epsilon}|^2)} \qquad (21.75)$$

$$|K_S\rangle = [(1 + \bar{\epsilon})|K^0\rangle - (1 - \bar{\epsilon})|\bar{K}^0\rangle]/\sqrt{2(1 + |\bar{\epsilon}|^2)}. \qquad (21.76)$$

This is a traditional parametrization in K-physics, similar to that in (21.54) with $q/p = (1 - \bar{\epsilon})/(1 + \bar{\epsilon})$ (this is why we chose **CP** $|K^0\rangle = -|\bar{K}^0\rangle$). We now find that a state which starts at $t = 0$ as a K^0 evolves to

$$|K_t^0\rangle = g_+(t)|K^0\rangle + \frac{1 - \bar{\epsilon}}{1 + \bar{\epsilon}} g_-(t)|\bar{K}^0\rangle \qquad (21.77)$$

where

$$g_\pm(t) = e^{-\Gamma_L t/2} e^{-i m_L t}[1 \pm e^{-\Delta\Gamma t/2} e^{i\Delta m t}], \qquad (21.78)$$

with $\Delta\Gamma = \Gamma_S - \Gamma_L$, $\Delta m = m_L - m_S$, and we have omitted a normalization factor. Similarly, a state tagged as $\bar{K}^0$ at $t = 0$ evolves to

$$|\bar{K}_t^0\rangle = \frac{1 - \bar{\epsilon}}{1 + \bar{\epsilon}} g_-(t)|K^0\rangle + g_+(t)|\bar{K}^0\rangle. \qquad (21.79)$$

The K^0-$\bar{K}^0$ mixing amplitude arises in the Standard Model from the box graphs shown in figure 21.9 (cf figure 21.5). These contain factors of m_f^2, but the magnitude of the four CKM couplings to the t quark are of order λ^{10}, compared with λ^6 for the c quark, so that the c quark diagram dominates, with a CKM factor of $(V_{cs}V_{cd}^*)^2$, which is real to a good approximation. This means that Im$\bar{\epsilon}$ is very small. A comparison of the mass difference Δm predicted from figure 21.10 and the experimental value is complicated by uncertainties in the hadronic matrix element.

The traditional reactions in which **CP** violation is probed in K decays are the 2π modes, where one looks for the existence of $K_L \to 2\pi$. There is also the semileptonic asymmetry. Three common observables are defined by

$$\eta_{00} = \frac{\langle \pi^0 \pi^0 |\hat{\mathcal{H}}_{nl}|K_L\rangle}{\langle \pi^0 \pi^0 |\hat{\mathcal{H}}_{nl}|K_S\rangle}, \quad \eta_{+-} = \frac{\langle \pi^+ \pi^- |\hat{\mathcal{H}}_{nl}|K_L\rangle}{\langle \pi^+ \pi^- |\hat{\mathcal{H}}_{nl}|K_S\rangle} \qquad (21.80)$$

and

$$\delta_L = \frac{\Gamma(K_L \to \pi^- \ell^+ \nu_\ell) - \Gamma(K_L \to \pi^+ \ell^- \bar{\nu}_\ell)}{\Gamma(K_L \to \pi^- \ell^+ \nu_\ell) + \Gamma(K_L \to \pi^+ \ell^- \bar{\nu}_\ell)}. \tag{21.81}$$

The experimental numbers are (Nakamura *et al.* 2010)

$$|\eta_{00}| = (2.221 \pm 0.011) \times 10^{-3}, \quad |\eta_{+-}| = (2.232 \pm 0.011) \times 10^{-3} \tag{21.82}$$

$$\text{Arg } \eta_{00} \approx 43.5^\circ, \quad \text{Arg } \eta_\pm \approx 43.5^\circ \tag{21.83}$$

and

$$\delta_L = (3.32 \pm 0.06) \times 10^{-3}. \tag{21.84}$$

It is useful to describe the final 2π states in terms of their isospin, which then have a definite strong interaction phase. As noted in connection with the B decays, the allowed isospin states are only $I = 0$ and $I = 2$, and one has

$$A_\pm \equiv A_{K^0 \to \pi^+ \pi^-} = \sqrt{\frac{2}{3}} |A_0| e^{i(\delta_0 + \phi_0)} + \sqrt{\frac{1}{3}} |A_2| e^{i(\delta_2 + \phi_2)} \tag{21.85}$$

$$\bar{A}_\pm \equiv A_{\bar{K}^0 \to \pi^+ \pi^-} = -\sqrt{\frac{2}{3}} |A_0| e^{i(\delta_0 - \phi_0)} - \sqrt{\frac{1}{3}} |A_2| e^{i(\delta_2 - \phi_2)} \tag{21.86}$$

where the minus sign arises from our choice $\mathbf{CP}|K^0\rangle = -|\bar{K}^0\rangle$, and where δ_I and ϕ_I are the strong and weak phases, respectively, for the state with isospin I. Also,

$$A_{00} \equiv A_{K^0 \to \pi^0 \pi^0} = \sqrt{\frac{1}{3}} |A_0| e^{i(\delta_0 + \phi_0)} - \sqrt{\frac{2}{3}} |A_2| e^{i(\delta_2 + \phi_2)} \tag{21.87}$$

$$\bar{A}_{00} \equiv \bar{A}_{\bar{K}^0 \to \pi^0 \pi^0} = -\sqrt{\frac{1}{3}} |A_0| e^{i(\delta_0 - \phi_0)} + \sqrt{\frac{2}{3}} |A_2| e^{i(\delta_2 - \phi_2)}. \tag{21.88}$$

The significant fact experimentally is that $|A_2|/|A_0| \sim 1/22$, a manifestation of the '$\Delta I = 1/2$' rule in this case (i.e. $\Delta I = 3/2$ is suppressed; see, for example, Donoghue *et al.* 1992, section VIII-4). Inserting (21.85) and (21.86), (21.87) and (21.88), into (21.80) and retaining only first-order terms in $|A_2|/|A_0|$, and treating ϕ_0 and ϕ_2 as small, we find (problem 21.5)

$$\eta_{00} = \bar{\epsilon} + i\phi_0 - \sqrt{2} \frac{|A_2|}{|A_0|} i(\phi_2 - \phi_0) e^{i(\delta_2 - \delta_0)} \tag{21.89}$$

$$\eta_{+-} = \bar{\epsilon} + i\phi_0 + \frac{1}{\sqrt{2}} \frac{|A_2|}{|A_0|} i(\phi_2 - \phi_0) e^{i(\delta_2 - \delta_0)}. \tag{21.90}$$

These relations are usually written as

$$\eta_{00} = \epsilon - 2\epsilon', \quad \eta_{+-} = \epsilon + \epsilon', \tag{21.91}$$

where

$$\epsilon = \bar{\epsilon} + i\phi_0, \quad \epsilon' = i \frac{e^{i(\delta_2 - \delta_0)}}{\sqrt{2}} \frac{|A_2|}{|A_0|} (\phi_2 - \phi_0). \tag{21.92}$$

The merit of this manoeuvering is that the parameter ϵ' involves only the **CP** violation in the transition amplitude ('direct **CP** violation'), while ϵ involves both a transition phase and the mixing parameter $\bar{\epsilon}$.

What can experiment tell us about ϵ and ϵ'? Consider first δ_L. Assuming that $|A(K^0 \to \ell^+ \nu_\ell \pi^-)| = |A(\bar{K}^0 \to \ell^- \bar{\nu}_\ell \pi^+)|$ and that $A(K^0 \to \ell^- \bar{\nu}_\ell \pi^+) = A(\bar{K}^0 \to \ell^+ \nu_\ell \pi^-) = 0$, we find

$$\delta_L = 2\mathrm{Re}\,\bar{\epsilon}/(1 + |\bar{\epsilon}|^2) \approx 2\mathrm{Re}\,\epsilon, \qquad (21.93)$$

so that δ_L is sensitive to the same parameter as appears in the $K_L \to \pi\pi$ decays. An interesting observable is the ratio between the ratios of the decay rates to $\pi^+\pi^-$ and $\pi^0\pi^0$ of K_S and K_L. One finds

$$\frac{1}{6}\left(1 - \frac{|\eta_{00}|^2}{|\eta_{+-}|^2}\right) \approx \mathrm{Re}\left(\epsilon'/\epsilon\right), \qquad (21.94)$$

which from equation (21.82) is another small number, approximately equal to 1.64×10^{-3}. In the years before the B factories opened, ϵ' was the only window into **CP** violation in the transition amplitude. But all the branching ratios in (21.94) are of order 10^{-3}, and establishing a non-zero value of ϵ' was very difficult. The first claim for non-zero ϵ' was by the NA 31 experiment at CERN (Barr *et al.* 1993), a 3.5 standard deviation effect. But a contemporary experiment at Fermilab (Gibbons *et al.* 1993) found a result compatible with zero. The next generation of experiments produced agreement:

$$\mathrm{Re}\left(\epsilon'/\epsilon\right) = (2.07) \pm 0.28) \times 10^{-3} \text{ Alavi-Harati } et\ al.\ 2003\ (\mathrm{KTeV})$$
$$(21.95)$$

$$\mathrm{Re}\left(\epsilon'/\epsilon\right) = (1.47 \pm 0.22) \times 10^{-3} \text{ Batley } et\ al.\ 2002\ (\mathrm{NA\ 48}). \quad (21.96)$$

The current world average is $(1.65 \pm 0.26) \times 10^{-3}$. Fits to all the data also yield (Nakamura *et al.* 2010)

$$|\epsilon| = (2.228 \pm 0.011) \times 10^{-3}. \qquad (21.97)$$

The experimental value of δ_L gives us $\mathrm{Re}\,\epsilon \simeq 1.66 \times 10^{-3}$, and we can deduce that $\arg \epsilon \simeq \pi/4$. The phase of ϵ' is $\pi/2 + \delta_2 - \delta_0$ which happens also to be approximately $\pi/4$. It follows that ϵ'/ϵ is very nearly real.

Comparison of these small numbers with theoretical predictions is complicated by hadronic uncertainties, and it is beyond our scope to pursue that issue.

In closing this discussion of mesonic mixing and **CP** violation, we briefly discuss the charm sector. First, we note that D^0-$\bar{D}^0$ mixing has been observed (Aubert *et al.* 2007c, Staric *et al.* 2007, Aaltonen *et al.* 2008). **CP**-violating effects in charm decays have been generally expected to be very small. A rough estimate of the direct **CP**-violating asymmetries in D decays can be made following the method of section 21.1. Consider, for example, the decays

$D^0 \to K^+K^-$ and $\bar{D}^0 \to K^-K^+$. As in (21.5) and (21.10) , the amplitude for the first decay is

$$A(D^0 \to K^+K^-) = V_{cs}^* V_{us} T_{KK} + V_{cb}^* V_{ub} P_{KK} \qquad (21.98)$$
$$= T(1 + r_K \exp^{i(\delta_K - \gamma)}), \qquad (21.99)$$

where r_K is the relative magnitude of the penguin contribution, and δ_K is the relative strong phase. The amplitude for the **CP**-conjugate process is the same, with γ replaced by $-\gamma$. The penguin contribution is CKM-suppressed by a factor $V_{cb}^* V_{ub}/V_{cs}^* V_{us} \sim \lambda^4$, and there is also a loop factor, so that r_K would seem to be of order 10^{-4}. The asymmetry is then

$$\mathcal{A}_{KK}^D = \frac{|A(D^0 \to K^+K^-)|^2 - |A(\bar{D}^0 \to K^-K^+)|^2}{|A(D^0 \to K^+K^-)|^2 + |A(\bar{D}^0 \to K^-K^+)|^2} \qquad (21.100)$$
$$= 2r_K \sin\gamma \sin\delta_K, \qquad (21.101)$$

which is indeed very small. A similar argument predicts the asymmetry in the decays $D^0 \to \pi^+\pi^-$ and $\bar{D}^0 \to \pi^-\pi^+$ to be

$$\mathcal{A}_{\pi\pi}^D = -2r_K \sin\gamma \sin\delta_K. \qquad (21.102)$$

Recently, however, the LHCb collaboration has published a measurement of the difference between the time-integrated **CP** asymmetries in the KK and $\pi\pi$ decays, which to a very good approximation can be identified with the difference between the direct asymmetries (21.101) and (21.102). The LHCb result is (Aaij *et al.* 2012)

$$\mathcal{A}_{KK}^D - \mathcal{A}_{\pi\pi}^D = (-0.82 \pm 0.21 \pm 0.11)\%, \qquad (21.103)$$

which is substantially larger than the estimates (21.101) and (21.102).

It is possible that this 3.5 σ effect (the first evidence for **CP**-violation in the charm sector) indicates the presence of some new physics. However, it must be noted that the mass scale of the charm quark, $m_c \sim 1.3$ GeV, is not large enough to be safely in the perturbative QCD regime (as indicated by the parameter $\Lambda_{\overline{MS}}/m_c$), so that non-perturbative enhancements are possible. **CP**-violation in the charm sector promises to be an interesting area for experimental and theoretical exploration.

21.4   Neutrino mixing and oscillations

21.4.1   Neutrino mass and mixing

Experiments with solar, atmospheric, reactor and accelerator neutrinos have established the phenomenon of neutrino oscillations caused by non-zero neutrino masses, and mixing. We shall give an elementary introduction to this

topic, which is a highly active field of research in particle physics; there are analogies with the meson oscillations we have been considering.

It is fair to say that in the original Standard Model the neutrinos were taken to be massless, but there was no compelling theoretical reason for this, and the framework of the Standard Model can easily be extended to include massive neutrinos. However, one question immediately arises: are neutrinos Dirac or Majorana fermions? As explained in section 20.3, we do not yet know the answer, and it may be some time before we do. The way the mass terms enter the Lagrangian is, in fact, different in the two cases. We are familiar with the Dirac mass term

$$m\bar{\hat{\psi}}\hat{\psi} = m(\bar{\hat{\psi}}_{\mathrm{R}}\hat{\psi}_{\mathrm{L}} + \bar{\hat{\psi}}_{\mathrm{L}}\hat{\psi}_{\mathrm{R}}), \tag{21.104}$$

where $\hat{\psi}$ is a four-component Dirac field, and R and L refer to the chirality components. We learned in section 7.5.2 that a Majorana mass term can be written in the form

$$m\hat{\chi}_{\mathrm{L}}^{\mathrm{T}}\mathrm{i}\sigma_2\hat{\chi}_{\mathrm{L}} + \mathrm{h.c.} \tag{21.105}$$

where $\hat{\chi}_{\mathrm{L}}$ is a two-component field of L chirality. A similar expression could be written using a two-component R-chirality field. The difference in form between the Dirac and Majorana mass terms leads to a difference in the parametrization of neutrino mixing, as we shall see.

Suppose, first, that the neutrinos are Dirac particles, with both L and R chiralities (or equivalently either helicity) for a given mass. We remind the reader that this is not ruled out experimentally, since the non-observation of the 'wrong' helicity component may be accounted for by the appearance of a suppression factor (m/E), where m is a neutrino mass and E is an average neutrino energy (see section 20.2.2). We also assume that their interactions have the V-A structure indicated by the phenomenology of the previous chapter. Then only the L (R) chirality component of a neutrino (antineutrino) field feels the weak force; the R (L) component of a neutrino (antineutrino) field has no interactions of Standard Model type. But, just as in the quark case, it will in general be necessary to allow for the possibility that the L-components of the fields which have definite neutrino mass, call them $\hat{\nu}_{1\mathrm{L}}, \hat{\nu}_{2\mathrm{L}}, \hat{\nu}_{3\mathrm{L}}$, are not the same as the fields $\hat{\nu}_{e\mathrm{L}}, \hat{\nu}_{\mu\mathrm{L}}, \hat{\nu}_{\tau\mathrm{L}}$ which enter into the charged current V-A interaction. For Dirac neutrinos, we therefore write

$$\begin{pmatrix} \hat{\nu}_e \\ \hat{\nu}_\mu \\ \hat{\nu}_\tau \end{pmatrix}_{\mathrm{L}} = \begin{pmatrix} U_{e1} & U_{e2} & U_{e3} \\ U_{\mu1} & U_{\mu2} & U_{\mu3} \\ U_{\tau1} & U_{\tau2} & U_{\tau3} \end{pmatrix} \begin{pmatrix} \hat{\nu}_1 \\ \hat{\nu}_2 \\ \hat{\nu}_3 \end{pmatrix}_{\mathrm{L}} \equiv \mathbf{U} \begin{pmatrix} \hat{\nu}_1 \\ \hat{\nu}_2 \\ \hat{\nu}_3 \end{pmatrix}_{\mathrm{L}}, \tag{21.106}$$

where the unitary matrix $\mathbf{U}$ is the PMNS matrix, named after Pontecorvo (1957, 1958, 1967), and Maki, Nakagawa and Sakata (1962).

Now we showed in section 20.7.3 that the general 3×3 unitary matrix has three real (rotation angle) parameters, and 6 phase parameters, five of which we could get rid of by rephasing the quark fields by global U(1) transformations of the form $\hat{q}' = \exp(\mathrm{i}\theta)\hat{q}$. Such rephasing transformations are equally allowed

for the charged leptons, and also for Dirac neutrinos, since evidently the mass term (21.104) is invariant under a global U(1) transformation $\hat{\psi}' = \exp(i\theta)\hat{\psi}$. Hence the matrix **U** will, in this Dirac case, have a parametrization of the CKM form, with one **CP**-violating phase.

The mixing described by (21.106) implies that the individual lepton flavour numbers L_e, L_μ, L_τ are no longer conserved. However, since we are here taking the neutrinos to be Dirac particles, there will be a quantum number carried by ν_e, ν_μ and ν_τ which is conserved by the interactions. This could, for example, be the total lepton number $L_e + L_\mu + L_\tau$, assigning $L(\nu_\alpha) = 1$ for $\alpha = e, \mu, \tau$, which would follow from invariance under the global U(1) transformation $\hat{\ell}'_\alpha = \exp(i\delta)\hat{\ell}_\alpha, \hat{\nu}'_\alpha = \exp(i\delta)\hat{\nu}_\alpha$, where δ is independent of the flavour α.

This 'Dirac' option, though simple, may be thought uneconomical, however. As noted, the R components of neutrino fields have no interactions of Standard Model type. The charged leptons do have electromagnetic interactions, of course, as do the quarks, which also have strong interactions. But the neutral neutrinos only have weak interactions, which involve only their L-components. Why, then, enlarge the field content to include hypothetical $\hat{\nu}_R$ fields, which don't have any SM interactions? It seems more economical to make do with only the $\hat{\nu}_L$ fields. In this case, the Dirac mass term (21.104) is not possible, but a Majorana mass term (21.105) can still exist. Clearly, such a mass term is *not* invariant under U(1) global phase transformations, and it breaks lepton number conservation explicitly. As in the Dirac case, the chiral L component will include a 'wrong' (i.e. positive) helicity component with an amplitude proportional to m/E.

The fact that global phase changes on the neutrino fields are now no longer freely available, because that symmetry is lost if they are Majorana fields, has implications for the mixing matrix, call it $\mathbf{U}_M$, in this case. Since the three Majorana neutrino fields can no longer absorb phases, we have only the three phases from the charged leptons at our disposal, which leaves three phase parameters in $\mathbf{U}_M$, after rephasing. The PMNS matrix in the Majorana case therefore has two more irreducible phase parameters than the CKM matrix, and is conventionally parametrized as

$$\mathbf{U}_M = \mathbf{U}(\mathrm{CKM} - \mathrm{type}) \times \mathrm{diag.}(1, e^{i\alpha_{21}/2}, e^{i\alpha_{31}/2}). \qquad (21.107)$$

There are three **CP**-violating phases in the Majorana neutrino case.

The only information at present (2012) concerning the entries in **U** comes from neutrino oscillation experiments, which we shall discuss in the next sections. We shall see that the Majorana phases α_{21} and α_{31} cancel in the probabilities calculated for neutrino transitions, and no experiment so far is sensitive to **CP**-violating effects in the neutrino sector. We shall discuss how the values of the parameters θ_{12}, θ_{13} and θ_{23} can be inferred from the observed oscillations, and also the differences in the squared masses of the neutrinos. Anticipating these results, we state here that the two independent squared mass differences, $m_2^2 - m_1^2$ and $m_3^2 - m_1^2$, turn out to be very small indeed, and rather different from each other: namely approximately 7.6×10^{-5} eV^2 and

2.4×10^{-3} eV^2, respectively. The smaller value is associated with oscillations of solar or reactor neutrinos, and the larger with oscillations of atmospheric or accelerator neutrinos.

Data on the actual mass values are limited. There is a bound on the $\bar{\nu}_e$ mass from measurements of the electron spectrum near the end-point in tritium β-decay, which gives (Lobashev *et al.* 2003, Eitel *et al.* 2005)

$$m_{\bar{\nu}_e} < 2.3\text{eV} \quad 95\%\text{CL}. \tag{21.108}$$

A weaker limit on m_{ν_μ} comes from measurements of the muon spectrum in charged pion decay:

$$m_{\nu_\mu} < 0.19 \text{ MeV } 95\%\text{CL}. \tag{21.109}$$

The strongest upper bound comes from cosmology, assuming three neutrinos. The Cosmic Microwave Background data of the WMAP experiment, combined with supernovae data and data on galaxy clustering, can be used to obtain an upper limit on the sum of three neutrino masses (Spergel *et al.* 2007):

$$\sum_{i+1}^{3} m_{\nu_i} < 0.68 \text{ eV}, \quad 95\%\text{CL}. \tag{21.110}$$

Taking the squared mass differences as indicative of the actual mass scale, neutrino masses are evidently very much smaller than the masses of the other fermions in the Standard Model. We shall return to what this might tell us about the origin of neutrino mass in section 22.5, where we discuss how gauge-invariant masses are generated in the Standard Model.

Returning to the question of **CP** violation, we noted in section 4.2.3 that the **CP** violation present in the Standard Model was insufficient to account for the matter–antimatter asymmetry in the universe. However, we now see that it is possible to have **CP** violation in the lepton sector, in an extended Standard Model with massive neutrinos. Leptonic matter–antimatter asymmetries can be converted into baryon asymmetries in the very hot early universe by a non-perturbative process predicted by Standard Model dynamics – a process called leptogenesis (Fukugita and Yanagida 1986, Kuzmin, Rubakov and Shaposhnikov 1985). It has been argued that the Dirac and/or Majorana phases in the neutrino matrix **U** or $\mathbf{U}_M$ can provide the **CP** violation necessary in leptogenesis models for the generation of the observed baryon asymmetry of the universe (Pascoli *et al.* 2007a, 2007b). If such a proposal should prove to be the case, the reach of Pauli's 'desperate remedy' will have been vast indeed.

21.4.2 Neutrino oscillations: formulae

The existence of neutrino oscillations means that if a neutrino of a given flavour $\nu_\alpha(\alpha = \text{e}, \mu, \tau)$ with energy E is produced in a charged current weak interaction process, such as $\pi^+ \to \mu^+ \nu_\mu$, then at a sufficiently large distance L

from the ν_α source the probability $P(\nu_\alpha \to \nu_\beta; E, L)$ of detecting a neutrino of a different flavour ν_β is non-zero.[2] Such a flavour change will of course imply that the ν_α survival probability, $P(\nu_\alpha \to \nu_\alpha; E, L)$, is less than 1. We shall give a simplified version of the derivation of such probabilities, following the approach of the review by Nakamura and Petcov in section 13 of Nakamura *et al.* (2010). This review includes a large list of references to the time-dependent formalism; we mention here the contributions of Kayser (1981), Nauenberg (1999) and Cohen *et al.* (2009). We shall treat all the neutrinos as stable particles.

We consider the evolution of the state $|\nu_\alpha\rangle$ in the frame in which the detector which measures its flavour is at rest (the lab frame). As in the meson case, the states with simple space-time evolution in a vacuum are the mass eigenstates $|\nu_i\rangle$ ($i = 1, 2, 3$), a superposition of which is equal to $|\nu_\alpha\rangle$:

$$|\nu_\alpha\rangle = \sum_j U^*_{\alpha i}|\nu_i, p_i\rangle, \tag{21.111}$$

the complex conjugation arising from taking the dagger of the relation (21.106) for the field operators. Here **U** stands for either the Dirac or the Majorana matrix, and p_i is the 4-momentum of ν_i. Similarly,

$$|\bar{\nu}_\alpha\rangle = \sum_i U_{\alpha i}|\bar{\nu}_i, p_i\rangle. \tag{21.112}$$

We will consider highly relativistic neutrinos, as is the case for the experiments under discussion. We will assume that there are no degeneracies among the masses m_j. The states in the superpositions (21.111) and (21.112) will all have, in general, different energies and momenta E_i, p_i. We shall also treat the evolution as occurring in one spatial dimension, taking all the momenta to lie in the direction from the source to the detector. Note that the fractional deviation of E_i and p_i from the massless case $E = p$ is of order m^2/E^2 which will be extremely small, of order one part in 10^{16}, say.

Suppose now that the neutrinos of flavour ν_α started in the state (21.111) at time $t = 0$ in the detector frame are detected at time T after production, having travelled a distance L. Then the amplitude for finding a neutrino of flavour ν_β at (L, T) is

$$
\begin{aligned}
A(\nu_\alpha \to \nu_\beta; L, E) &= \sum_i U^*_{\alpha i}\, e^{-iE_iT + ip_iL} \langle \nu_\beta | \nu_i, p_i \rangle \\
&= \sum_i U^*_{\alpha i}\, U_{\beta i} e^{-iE_iT + ip_iL}.
\end{aligned}
\tag{21.113}
$$

We make two immediate comments on (21.113). First, the Majorana phases in (21.54) cancel in $A(\nu_\alpha \to \nu_\beta; L, E) = \delta_{\alpha\beta}$, since the same phase appears

---

[2]We shall not indicate the chirality explicitly from now on, it being assumed that we are referring to the L (R) component for neutrinos (antineutrinos).

in $U_{\alpha i}$ and $U_{\beta i}$. We conclude that oscillation experiments cannot distinguish Majorana from Dirac neutrinos. Second, if the neutrinos were massless, the phase factors in (21.113) would all be unity, and then $A(\nu_\alpha \to \nu_\beta; L, E) = \delta_{\alpha\beta}$, from the unitarity of the matrix $\mathbf{U}$, so there would be no flavour change.

Flavour oscillations come about via the interference in $|A(\nu_\alpha \to \nu_\beta; L, T)|^2$ between phase factors that are slightly different from one another, because of the different masses. A typical interference phase is then $\phi_{ij} = (E_i - E_j)T - (p_i - p_j)L$. Following the review by Nakamura and Petcov in Nakamura *et al.* (2010), we note that

$$\frac{m_i^2 - m_j^2}{p_i + p_j} = \frac{(E_i^2 - p_i^2) - (E_j^2 - p_j^2)}{p_i + p_j} = (E_i - E_j)\frac{(E_i + E_j)}{(p_i + p_j)} - (p_i - p_j) \quad (21.114)$$

so that

$$\phi_{ij} = (E_i - E_j)\left[T - \frac{E_i + E_j}{p_i + p_j}L\right] + \frac{m_i^2 - m_j^2}{p_i + p_j}L. \quad (21.115)$$

Bearing in mind that the energies differ from the momenta by terms of order m^2/E^2, we see that the first term in (21.115) can be dropped, and the interference phase is, to a very good approximation,

$$\phi_{ij} = \frac{m_i^2 - m_j^2}{2E} \equiv \frac{\Delta m_{ij}^2}{2E} \quad (21.116)$$

where E is the average energy, or momentum, of the neutrinos. We therefore obtain the probability

$$P(\nu_\alpha \to \nu_\beta; L, E) = \sum_i |U_{\alpha i}|^2 |U_{\beta i}|^2 \quad (21.117)$$

$$+ 2\sum_{i>j} |U_{\beta i}U_{\alpha i}^* U_{\alpha j}U_{\beta j}^*| \cos\left[\left(\frac{\Delta m_{ij}^2}{2E}\right)L - \phi_{\beta\alpha;ij}\right]$$

where

$$\phi_{\alpha\beta;ij} = \mathrm{Arg}\,(U_{\beta i}U_{\alpha i}^* U_{\alpha j}U_{\beta j}^*). \quad (21.118)$$

A more useful expression can be obtained by using the unitarity of $\mathbf{U}$ (problem 21.6):

$$P(\nu_\alpha \to \nu_\beta; L, E) = \delta_{\alpha\beta} - 4\sum_{i>j} \mathrm{Re}\,(U_{\beta i}U_{\alpha i}^* U_{\alpha j}U_{\beta j}^*) \sin^2\frac{\Delta m_{ij}^2 L}{4E}$$

$$+ 2\sum_{i>j} \mathrm{Im}\,(U_{\beta i}U_{\alpha i}^* U_{\alpha j}U_{\beta j}^*) \sin\frac{\Delta m_{ij}^2 L}{2E} \quad (21.119)$$

The expression for $P(\bar\nu_\alpha \to \bar\nu_\beta; L, T)$ is the same, except for a change in sign

of the last term in (21.119):

$$
P(\bar{\nu}_\alpha \to \bar{\nu}_\beta; L, E) = \delta_{\alpha\beta} - 4 \sum_{i>j} \text{Re}\,(U_{\beta i} U^*_{\alpha i} U_{\alpha j} U^*_{\beta j}) \sin^2 \frac{\Delta m^2_{ij} L}{4E}
$$

$$
- 2 \sum_{i>j} \text{Im}\,(U_{\beta i} U^*_{\alpha i} U_{\alpha j} U^*_{\beta j}) \sin \frac{\Delta m^2_{ij} L}{2E}. \quad (21.120)
$$

It follows from (21.119) and (21.120) that $P(\nu_\alpha \to \nu_\beta; L, E) = P(\bar{\nu}_\beta \to \bar{\nu}_\alpha; L, E)$, a consequence of **CPT** invariance. **CP** alone requires $P(\nu_\alpha \to \nu_\beta; L, E) = P(\bar{\nu}_\alpha \to \bar{\nu}_\beta; L, E)$. A measure of **CP** violation is provided by

$$
\mathcal{A}^{(\beta\alpha)}_{\mathbf{CP}} = P(\nu_\alpha \to \nu_\beta; L, E) - P(\bar{\nu}_\alpha \to \bar{\nu}_\beta; L, E)
$$

$$
= 4 \sum_{i>j} \text{Im}\,(U_{\beta i} U^*_{\alpha i} U_{\alpha j} U^*_{\beta j}) \sin \frac{\Delta m^2_{ij}}{2E} L. \quad (21.121)
$$

The reader will recognize the Jarlskog (1985) invariants in (21.121). In this 3×3 mixing situation, which is exactly analogous to quark mixing, all these invariants are equal up to a sign, and (21.121) becomes (Krastev and Petcov 1988)

$$
\mathcal{A}^{(\mu e)}_{\mathbf{CP}} = -\mathcal{A}^{(\tau e)}_{\mathbf{CP}} = \mathcal{A}^{(\tau\mu)}_{\mathbf{CP}}
$$

$$
= 4J_\nu \left[\sin\left(\frac{\Delta m^2_{32}}{2E} L\right) + \sin\left(\frac{\Delta m^2_{21}}{2E} L\right) + \sin\left(\frac{\Delta m^2_{13}}{2E} L\right) \right]
$$

$$
(21.122)
$$

where

$$
J_\nu = \text{Im}(U_{\mu 3} U^*_{e3} U_{e2} U^*_{\mu 2}). \quad (21.123)
$$

If any one mass-squared difference is zero, say Δm^2_{21}, then $\Delta m^2_{32} = -\Delta m^2_{13}$, and the right-hand side of (21.122) vanishes: we need all three mass-squared differences to be non-zero, in order to get **CP** violation.

In proceeding to discuss the experimental situation, it will be useful to define an 'oscillation length' $\lambda_{ij}(E)$ given by

$$
\lambda_{ij}(E) = 2E/\Delta m^2_{ij} \approx 0.4 \frac{(E/\text{GeV})}{(\Delta m^2_{ij}/\text{eV}^2)} \text{ km.} \quad (21.124)
$$

In practice, the three-state mixing formalism can often be simplified, making use of what is now known about the neutrino mass spectrum. One squared mass difference is considerably smaller than the other:

$$
|\Delta m^2_{21}| \sim 7.6 \times 10^{-5} \text{ eV}^2, \quad |\Delta m^2_{31}| \sim 2.4 \times 10^{-3} \text{eV}^2. \quad (21.125)
$$

Suppose now that $L/|\lambda_{31}(E)| \sim 1$, while $L/|\lambda_{21}(E)| \ll 1$. Then expression (21.119) reduces to (problem 21.7)

$$
\begin{aligned}
P(\nu_\alpha \to \nu_\beta; L, E) &\approx \delta_{\alpha\beta} - 4|U_{\alpha3}|^2[\delta_{\alpha\beta} - |U_{\beta3}|^2]\sin^2\frac{\Delta m_{31}^2}{4E}L \\
&= P(\bar\nu_\alpha \to \bar\nu_\beta; L, E).
\end{aligned}
\tag{21.126}
$$

In particular,

$$
P(\bar\nu_e \to \bar\nu_e; L, E) = 1 - 4|U_{e3}|^2(1 - |U_{e3}|^2)\sin^2\frac{\Delta m_{31}^2}{4E}L,
\tag{21.127}
$$

which can describe the survival probability of reactor $\bar\nu_e$s, for example.

Adopting a parametrization of the form (20.166), with rows labelled by e, μ and τ, and columns by 1, 2, and 3, $|U_{e3}|^2$ is $\sin^2\theta_{e3}$, which is found experimentally to be small (see the following section). It is often a good approximation to set $|U_{e3}|$ to zero, in which case $|U_{\mu3}|^2 = \sin^2\theta_{\mu3}$. Then (21.126) gives the ν_μ survival probability

$$
P(\nu_\mu \to \nu_\mu; L, E) = P(\bar\nu_\mu \to \bar\nu_\mu; L, E) \approx 1 - \sin^2 2\theta_{\mu3}\sin^2(L/2\lambda_{31}(E))
\tag{21.128}
$$

and the flavour-change probability

$$
P(\nu_\mu \to \nu_\tau; L, E) = P(\bar\nu_\mu \to \bar\nu_\tau; L, E) \approx \sin^2 2\theta_{\mu3}\sin^2(L/2\lambda_{31}(E)).
\tag{21.129}
$$

In this approximation, $P(\nu_\mu \to \nu_e) = P(\bar\nu_\mu \to \bar\nu_e) = 0$. Formulae (21.128) and (21.129) can be used to describe the dominant atmospheric ν_μ and $\bar\nu_\mu$ oscillations (see the following section), and the parameters $\theta_{\mu3}$ and Δm_{31}^2 (or Δm_{32}^2) are referred to as the atmospheric mixing angle and mass squared difference. The smaller mass squared difference Δm_{21}^2, and the angle θ_{e2}, are associated with solar ν_e oscillations.

The formulae (21.128) and (21.129) are, in fact, exactly what a simple 2-state mixing model would give. Suppose that the effective mixing matrix for the 2-state system has the form (see problem 1.6)

$$
\begin{pmatrix} -a\cos 2\theta & a\sin 2\theta \\ a\sin 2\theta & a\cos 2\theta \end{pmatrix},
\tag{21.130}
$$

where rows are labelled by e, μ and columns by 1, 3; then the survival probability is just

$$
1 - \sin^2 2\theta \sin^2(La),
\tag{21.131}
$$

where we have taken $L \approx T$ as before. We can therefore identify the mixing parameter as

$$
a = [2\lambda_{31}(E)]^{-1} = \frac{\Delta m_{31}^2}{4E}.
\tag{21.132}
$$

Note that the energies are here measured relative to a common average energy; if $|\ell\rangle$ is the lighter eigenstate and $|h\rangle$ the heavier, then

$$
\begin{aligned}
|\nu_e\rangle &= \cos\theta|\ell\rangle + \sin\theta|h\rangle \\
|\nu_\mu\rangle &= -\sin\theta|\ell\rangle + \cos\theta|h\rangle.
\end{aligned}
\tag{21.133}
$$

21.4.3   Neutrino oscillations: experimental results

Historically, the search for neutrino oscillations began when experiments by Davis *et al.* (1968) detected solar neutrinos (from ^{8}B decays) at a rate approximately one third of that predicted by the solar model calculations of Bahcall *et al.* (1968). Pontecorvo (1946) had proposed the experiment, in which the neutrinos are detected by the inverse β-decay process $\nu_e + ^{37}\text{Cl} \rightarrow e^- + ^{37}\text{Ar}$. The Davis experiment used 520 metric tons of liquid tetrachloroethylene (C_2Cl_4), buried 4850 feet underground in the Homestake gold mine, in South Dakota. Davis' findings provided the impetus to study solar neutrinos using Kamiokande, a 3000 ton imaging water Cerenkov detector situated about one kilometre underground in the Kamioka mine in Japan. Indeed, ^{8}B solar neutrinos were observed, and at a rate consistent with that of the Davis experiment (Hirata *et al.* 1989). Later results from the Homestake mine (Cleveland *et al.* 1998) reported a solar neutrino detection rate almost exactly one third of the updated calculations of Bahcall *et al.* (2001).

In a separate development, Kamiokande also reported (Hirata *et al.* 1988) an anomaly in the atmospheric neutrino flux. Atmospheric neutrinos are produced as decay products in hadronic showers which result from collisions of cosmic rays with nuclei in the upper atmosphere of the Earth. Production of electron and muon neutrinos is dominated by the decay chain $\pi^+ \rightarrow \mu^+ + \nu_\mu$, $\mu^+ \rightarrow e^+ + \bar{\nu}_\mu + \nu_e$ (and its charge-conjugate), which gives an expected value of about 2 for the ratio of $(\nu_\mu + \bar{\nu}_\mu)$ flux to $(\nu_e + \bar{\nu}_e)$ flux.[3] While the number of electron-like events was in good agreement with the Monte Carlo calculations based on atmospheric neutrino interactions in the detector, the number of muon-like events was about one half of the expected number, at the 4σ level.

This muon-like defect (and the lack of an electron-like defect) was later confirmed at the 9σ level by Super-Kamiokande (Fukuda *et al.* 1998). In this experiment, a marked dependence was observed on the zenith angle of the muon neutrinos. This angle is simply related to the distance travelled by the neutrinos from their point of production, which varies from about 20 km (from above the detector) to over 10,000 km (from below the detector). The Super-Kamiokande data was the first compelling evidence for neutrino oscillations. Interpreting their data in terms of a simple 2-state $\nu_\mu \leftrightarrow \nu_\tau$ model, as in (21.129), Fukuda *et al.* (1998) reported the values $\sin^2 2\theta_{\mu3} > 0.82$, and $5 \times 10^{-4} < \Delta m_{31}^2 < 6 \times 10^{-3}$ eV^2 at 90% CL.

We will postpone further discussion of the solar neutrino deficit for the moment, since it is complicated by interactions of the neutrinos with the Sun's matter (see the following subsection). We proceed to describe some of the main results which have come from the analysis of data from neutrinos produced in terrestrial accelerators and reactors.

---

[3]The detector could not measure the charge of the final state leptons, and therefore ν and $\bar{\nu}$ events could not be discriminated.

We begin with the CHOOZ experiment, which was the first experiment to limit the value of θ_{e3} (Apollonio *et al.* 1999, 2003). CHOOZ is the name of a nuclear power station situated near the French village of the same name. The experiment was designed to detect reactor $\bar{\nu}_e$s via the inverse β-decay reaction $\bar{\nu}_e + p \rightarrow e^+ + n$. The signature was a delayed coincidence between the prompt e^+ signal, and the signal from the neutron capture. The detector was located in an underground laboratory about 1 km from the neutrino source. It consisted of a central 5-ton target filled with 0.09 % Gd-doped liquid scintillator; Gd-doping was chosen to maximize the capture of the neutrons. The neutrino energy E was a few MeV, and L was 1 km. For these values $2\lambda_{21}(E)$ is greater than about 10 km, while $2\lambda_{31}(E)$ is about 0.3 km. The neglect of $\sin^2 L/2\lambda_{21}(E)$ is justified, and formula (21.127) can be used for the $\bar{\nu}_e$ survival probability. The experiment found no evidence for $\bar{\nu}_e$ disappearance, and reported the 90% CL upper limit of $\sin^2 2\theta_{e3} < 0.19$, for $|\Delta m_{31}^2| = 2 \times 10^{-3}$ eV^2. We shall for the moment set θ_{e3} to zero, and return to discuss its value at the end of the chapter.

The mass squared range $\Delta m^2 > 2 \times 10^{-3}$ eV^2 can be explored by accelerator-based long-baseline experiments, with typically $E \sim 1$ GeV and $L \sim$ several hundred kilometres. The K2K (KEK-to-Kamioka) experiment was the first accelerator-based experiment with a neutrino path length extending hundreds of kilometres. A horn-focused wide-band ν_μ beam with mean energy 1.3 GeV and path length 250 km was produced by 12 GeV protons from the KEK-PS and directed to the Super-Kamiokande detector. In this case, $L/2\lambda_{21}(E) \sim 10^{-2}$, which may be neglected. Then formulae (21.128) and (21.129) may be used, in the approximation $U_{e3} \approx 0$. The K2K data showed (Ahn *et al.* 2006) that $\sin^2 2\theta_{\mu3} \approx 1 (\theta_{\mu3} \approx \pi/4)$, and that $|\Delta m_{31}^2|$ had a value consistent with (21.125).

The first evidence for the appearance of ν_e in a ν_μ beam was obtained by the T2K collaboration (Abe *et al.* 2011). The ν_μ beam is produced using the high intensity proton accelerator at J-PARC, located in Tokai, Japan. The beam was directed 2.5° off-axis to the Super-Kamiokande detector at Kamioka, 295 km away. This configuration produces a narrow-band ν_μ beam, tuned at the first oscillation maximum $E_\nu = |\Delta m_{31}^2| L/2\pi \approx 0.6$ MeV, so as to reduce background from higher energy neutrino interactions. In the vacuum, the probability of the appearance of a ν_e in a ν_μ beam is given (in our customary effective 2-state mixing approximation) by (21.126) as

$$P(\nu_\mu \rightarrow \nu_e; L, E) = \sin^2 \theta_{\mu3} \sin^2 2\theta_{e3} \sin^2 \frac{\Delta m_{31}^2}{4E} L; \qquad (21.134)$$

$P(\bar{\nu}_\mu \rightarrow \bar{\nu}_e; L, E)$ is given by the same expression. Taking $|\Delta m_{31}^2| = 2.4 \times 10^{-3}$ eV^2 and $\sin^2 2\theta_{\mu3} = 1$, the number of expected ν_e events was 1.5 ± 0.3(syst.) for $\sin^2 2\theta_{e3} = 0$, and 5.5 ± 1.0 events if $\sin^2 \theta_{e3} = 0.1$. Six events were observed which passed all the ν_e selection criteria. As we will see in the following section, the value of $\sin^2 2\theta_{e3} = 0.1$ is entirely consistent with direct measurements of this quantity reported in 2012.

Another long baseline accelerator experiment is MINOS at Fermilab. Neutrinos are produced by the Neutrinos at the Main Injector facility (NuMI), using 120 GeV protons from the Fermilab main injector. The detector is a 5.4 kton iron-scintillator tracking calorimeter with a toroidal magnetic field, situated underground in the Soudan mine, 735 km from Fermilab. The neutrino energy spectrum from a wide-band beam is horn-focused to be enhanced in the 1-5 GeV range. The current MINOS results yield $|\Delta m^2_{31}| = (2.32^{+0.12}_{-0.08}) \times 10^{-3}$ eV^2, and $\sin^2 2\theta_{\mu3} > 0.90$ at 90 % CL (Adamson *et al.* 2011).

A second reactor experiment, KamLAND at Kamioka, was designed to be sensitive to the smaller squared mass difference Δm^2_{21}, and thus to θ_{e2}. The Kamioka Liquid scintillator AntiNeutrino Detector is at the site of the former Kamioka experiment. The detector is essentially one kiloton of highly purified liquid scintillator surrounded by photomultiplier tubes. $\bar{\nu}_e$s are detected as usual via the inverse β-decay reaction $\bar{\nu}_e + p \rightarrow e^+ + n$. KamLAND is surrounded by 55 nuclear power units, each an isotropic $\bar{\nu}_e$ source. The flux-weighted average path length is $L \sim 180$ km, and the energy E ranges from about 2 MeV to about 8 MeV. For $E = 3$ MeV, $2\lambda_{21}(E) \sim 30$ km, which allows for more than one oscillation. In this case (21.119) reduces to

$$P(\bar{\nu}_e \rightarrow \bar{\nu}_e; L, E) = 1 - 4|U_{e1}|^2 |U_{e2}|^2 \sin^2(L/2\lambda_{21}(E)) \qquad (21.135)$$

assuming $|U_{e3}| \approx 0$. In a parametrization of the form (20.166), this becomes

$$P(\bar{\nu}_e \rightarrow \bar{\nu}_e; L, E) = 1 - \sin^2 2\theta_{e2} \sin^2(L/2\lambda_{21}(E)), \qquad (21.136)$$

again a simple 2-state mixing result. Data shown in figure 21.11 (Abe *et al.* 2008) gives

$$|\Delta m^2_{21}| = 7.58^{+0.14+0.15}_{-0.13-0.15} \times 10^{-5} \text{ eV}^2 \qquad (21.137)$$

$$\tan^2 \theta_{e2} = 0.56^{+0.10+0.10}_{-0.70-0.06}. \qquad (21.138)$$

The KamLAND data showed for the first time the periodic behaviour of the $\bar{\nu}_e$ survival probability.

We now return to the solar neutrino problem, taking up the story after Davis' results. Some doubts remained as to whether the solar calculations could be absolutely relied upon, for example because of the extreme sensitivity to the core temperature ($\propto T^{18}$). One particular class of ν_e could, however, be reliably calculated, namely those associated with the initial reaction pp $\rightarrow$ ^{2}H$+e^+ +\nu_e$ of the pp cycle. Whereas the Davis experiments allowed detection of the higher energy ν_es (threshold 814 keV) from the B and Be stages of the cycle, the energy of the ν_es from the pp stage cuts off at around 400 keV. Detectors using the reaction $\nu_e + ^{71}$Ga $\rightarrow$ e$^- + ^{71}$Ge, which has a 233 keV energy threshold, were built (GALLEX, GNO and SAGE); their results (Altman *et al.* 2005, Abdurashitov *et al.* 2009) are in agreement, and again much smaller than the (updated) Bahcall *et al.* (2005) prediction.

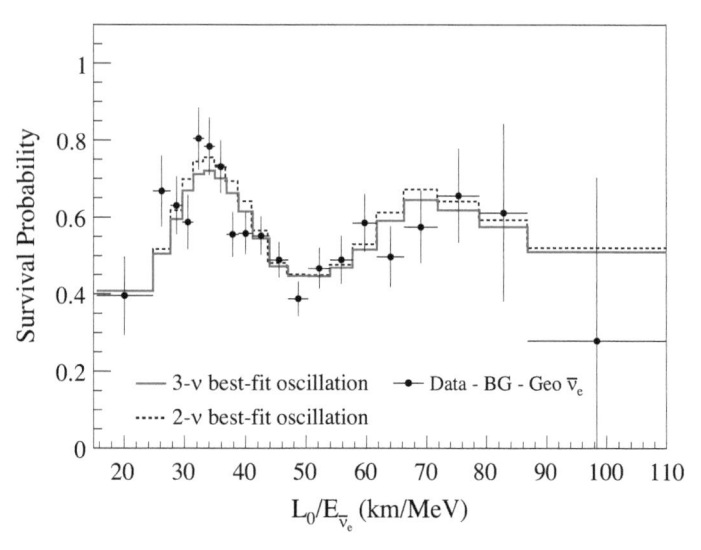

FIGURE 21.11

Ratio of the background and geo-neutrino subtracted $\bar{\nu}_e$ spectrum to the expectation for no-oscillation, as a function of L_0/E, where $L_0 = 180$ km. Figure reprinted with permission from S Abe *et al.* (KamLAND Collaboration) *Phys. Rev. Lett.* **100** 221803 (2008). Copyright 2008 by the American Physical Society.

In 1999, the Sudbury Neutrino Observatory (SNO) in Canada began observation. This experiment used 1 kiloton of ultra-pure heavy water (D_2O). It measured ^8B solar ν_es via both the CC reaction $\nu_e + d \rightarrow e^- + p + p$, and the NC reaction $\nu + d \rightarrow \nu + p + n$, as well as elastic $\nu\,e^-$ scattering. The CC reaction is sensitive only to ν_e, while the NC reaction is sensitive to all active neutrinos, as is $\nu\,e^-$ scattering. If the solar neutrino deficit were caused by neutrino oscillations, the solar neutrino fluxes measured by the CC and NC reactions would be significantly different. SNO found that, while the total neutrino flux was consistent with solar model expectations, the ratio of the ν_e flux to the total neutrino flux was about $1/3$ (Ahmad *et al.* 2001, 2002). This number can be understood in terms of the effect of dense matter on the propagation of the ν_es, as we now discuss.

21.4.4 Matter effects in neutrino oscillations

We have assumed in the foregoing that neutrinos propagate in vacuum between the source and the detector. Since neutrinos interact only weakly, it might seem that this is always an excellent approximation. But in the same way that light travelling through a transparent medium can have its refractive index changed, so can a neutrino. In particular, the refractive index can be

different for ν_e and ν_μ. The difference in refractive indices is determined by the difference in the real parts of the forward $\nu_e e^-$ and $\nu_\mu e^-$ elastic scattering amplitudes (Wolfenstein 1978). The essential point is that the scattering can be coherent, with the spins and momenta of the particles remaining unchanged. This means that the effect is going to be proportional to the density of electrons in the matter traversed, N_e. The scattering amplitude, in turn, is proportional to G_F, so that a figure of merit for the effect is given by the product $G_F N_e$. This has the dimensions of an energy, and can be interpreted as an addition to the effective 2-state mixing matrix of (21.130). Detailed analysis, which we omit, shows that the correct addition is actually $+\sqrt{2} G_F N_e$, so that (21.130) is modified to

$$\begin{pmatrix} -\frac{\Delta m^2}{4E} \cos 2\theta + \sqrt{2} G_F N_e & \frac{\Delta m^2}{4E} \sin 2\theta \\ \frac{\Delta m^2}{4E} \sin 2\theta & \frac{\Delta m^2}{4E} \cos 2\theta \end{pmatrix}, \tag{21.139}$$

where now $\Delta m^2 = m_2^2 - m_1^2$, and $\theta = \theta_{e2}$. Two-state mixing now gives (problem 21.8) a new mixing angle θ_m such that

$$\tan 2\theta_m = \frac{\tan 2\theta}{1 - N_e/N_{res}}, \quad N_{res} = \frac{\Delta m^2 \cos 2\theta}{2\sqrt{2} G_F E}, \tag{21.140}$$

and the mass eigenstates $|1\rangle_m, |2\rangle_m$ correspond to the eigenvalue difference

$$m_2 - m_1 = |\Delta m_{21}^2/2E| \left[\cos^2 2\theta (1 - N_e/N_{res})^2 + \sin^2 2\theta \right]^{1/2}. \tag{21.141}$$

We see that although the new term is certainly very small, being proportional to G_F, nevertheless since Δm^2 is very small also, a significant effect can occur. In particular, if it should happen that $N_e \approx N_{res}$ for some (θ, E), then θ_m will be 'maximal' ($\theta_m = \pi/4$), irrespective of the value of the original θ. This is called 'resonant mixing' (Mikheev and Smirnov 1985, 1986). It implies that the probability for a $\nu_e \to \nu_\mu$ flavour change could be greatly enhanced over the vacuum value, which is proportional to $\sin^2 2\theta_{e2}$. A point to note, also, is that the corresponding formulae for $\bar{\nu}_e$s are obtained by replacing N_e by $-N_e$; then, depending on the sign of $\Delta m^2 \cos 2\theta_{e2}$, resonant mixing can occur for one or the other of ν_e or $\bar{\nu}_e$ as they pass through matter, but not both. Similar considerations apply to the propagation of neutrinos through the earth, but we shall not pursue this here (see Nakamura and Petcov in Nakamura *et al.* 2010).

In the case of solar neutrinos, the effect of the above modifications is quite simple. For the highest energy neutrinos, $N_e \gg N_{res}$ at the centre of the sun, so that $\theta_m \sim \pi/2$ at production in the core, and the ν_e is in the heavier mass state $|2\rangle_m$. On the way to the surface of the Sun, N_e will decrease, and a point will be reached when $N_e = N_{res}$. Here the mass difference (21.141) reaches its minimum, and two limiting cases may be distinguished depending on the scale of the variation in the electron density, which has been assumed constant in (21.139)–(21.141). (i) If the density variation is slow enough that

at least one oscillation length fits into the resonant density region, then it can be shown that the state stays with state $|2\rangle_m$ ('adiabatic evolution') until it reaches the surface of the Sun, when $\theta_m \to \theta_{e2}$. The probability that the neutrino will survive to the earth is then (using (21.133)) $|\langle\nu_e|2\rangle_m|^2 = \sin^2\theta_{e2}$, which has a value of about 1/3. In the alternative limit, (ii), in which the oscillation length in matter is relatively large with respect to the scale of density variation, the state may 'jump' to the other mass state $|1\rangle_m$ ('extreme non-adiabatic evolution'), and then $|\langle\nu_e|1\rangle_m|^2 = \cos^2\theta_{e2}$. These are clearly extreme cases, and numerical work is required in the general case. However, the data from SNO and other water Cerenkov detectors are consistent with the first (adiabatic) alternative, and with the value $\sin^2\theta_{e2} \sim 1/3$. Note that the solar data imply that $(m_2^2 - m_1^2)\cos 2\theta_{e2} > 0$.

By contrast, for the lowest energy neutrinos we can take $\theta_m \approx \theta$, so that the neutrinos are produced in the state $\cos\theta_{e2}|1\rangle + \sin\theta_{e2}|2\rangle$, and propagate as in a vacuum, oscillating with maximum excursion $\sin^2 2\theta_{e2}$. The detectors average over many oscillations, giving a factor of 1/2, so that the survival probability for the low energy ν_es is $1 - \frac{1}{2}\sin^2 2\theta_{e2} \sim 5/9$. The Gallium experiments are sensitive to the lower energy neutrinos, and indeed record some 60–70% of the expected flux.

In summary, the solar neutrino data are consistent with the interpretation in terms of neutrino oscillations, as modified by the Wolfenstein-Mikheev-Smirnov (MSW) effect. A global solar + KamLAND analysis yields best fit values (Aharmim *et al.* 2010)

$$\theta_{e2} = 34.06^{+1.16}_{-0.84} \quad \Delta m^2_{21} = 7.59^{+0.20}_{-0.21} \times 10^{-5}~\text{eV}^2. \tag{21.142}$$

21.4.5 Further developments

Despite the remarkable experimental progress in the studies of neutrino oscillations over the last decade, there still remain some basic gaps in our knowledge. Perhaps the most fundamental is the Dirac/Majorana nature of massive neutrinos. The most feasible (but very difficult) test is neutrinoless double β-decay ($0\nu\beta\beta$-decay), already touched on in section 20.3. As noted there, the amplitude is proportional to an average Majorana mass parameter $\langle m\rangle$. Experiments place a lower bound on the half-life for the decay, which translates into an upper bound on $\langle m\rangle$. The most stringent lower bounds on the half-lives have been obtained with decays of ^{76}Ge (Klapdor-Kleingrothaus *et al.* 2001), ^{130}Te (Andreotti *et al.* 2011) and ^{100}Mo (Arnold *et al.* 2006). Lower bounds on the half-lives range from 10^{24} to 10^{25} years, with corresponding upper bounds on $\langle m\rangle$ of the order of 0.5 eV. It should, however, be noted that some participants of the Heidelberg-Moscow experiment claimed the observation of $0\nu\beta\beta$ decay of ^{76}Ge with a half-life of $2.23^{+0.44}_{-0.31} \times 10^{25}$ years, from which they deduced $\langle m\rangle = 0.32 \pm 0.03$ eV (Klapdor-Kleingrothaus *et al.* 2006). The GERDA experiment (Ur *et al.* 2011) should be able to check this claim after one year of running. Other experiments currently running, or planned, will

push the bound on half-lives up to 10^{26}–10^{27} years, and the upper bound on $\langle m \rangle$ down to magnitudes of the order of a few times 10^{-2} eV.

A second crucial question concerns the magnitude of **CP**-violation effects in neutrino oscillations. We recall from (20.172) that this vanishes if $\sin\theta_{e3} = 0$. As we saw earlier, CHOOZ set a 90% CL limit $\sin^2 2\theta_{e3} < 0.17$. A non-zero value of $\sin^2 2\theta_{e3}$ has now been observed by two groups, both $\bar{\nu}_e$ disappearance experiments: the Daya Bay collaboration (An *et al.* 2012) and the RENO collaboration (Ahn *et al.* 2012). Their reported results were

$$\sin^2 2\theta_{e3} = 0.092 \pm 0.016 \pm 0.005 \quad \text{(Daya Bay)} \qquad (21.143)$$
$$\sin^2 2\theta_{e3} = 0.113 \pm 0.013 \pm 0.019 \quad \text{(RENO)}, \qquad (21.144)$$

in a 3-neutrino framework. For this value of $\sin\theta_{e3}$, it should be possible to detect a **CP**-violating difference in the probabilities for $\nu_\mu \to \nu_e$ and $\bar{\nu}_\mu \to \bar{\nu}_e$, and it may be enough to sustain leptogenesis models.

The value of $\sin\theta_{e3}$ is also relevant to the determination of the sign of Δm_{31}^2; we shall mention just one possibility. We have seen that the MSW effect for solar neutrinos implies that $m_2 > m_1$ (using the fact that $\cos\theta_{e2} > 0$), but the mass spectrum (for 3-neutrino mixing) could be ordered as $m_1 < m_2 < m_3$ ('normal spectrum') or as $m_3 < m_1 < m_2$ ('inverted spectrum'). We have ignored the terrestrial MSW effect, but it can be significant in long-baseline accelerator-based experiments, and could be exploited to determine the sign of $m_3 - m_1$. In the vacuum, the probability of the appearance of a ν_e in a ν_μ beam is given by (21.134) (in our customary effective 2-state mixing approximation). As in the solar case, these probabilities will be modified by the MSW effect, which will enhance (suppress) the appearance probability for neutrinos (antineutrinos) in the case of the normal spectrum, and vice versa for the inverted spectrum. Clearly if θ_{e3} were too small, the effect would be very hard to see, but the value in (21.143) and (21.144) makes this a realistic experiment; it formed part of the physics motivation for the NOνA experiment at Fermilab (Ayres *et al.* 2005). NOνA is a long-baseline neutrino oscillation experiment now under construction, which aims to detect the appearance of ν_e and $\bar{\nu}_e$ in the NuMI muon neutrino beam. The beam from Fermilab is directed 14 mrad off-axis to a detector 810 kn away; the neutrino energy is narrowly peaked around 2.2 GeV. NOνA will also have sensitivity to leptonic **CP**-violation.

Problems

21.1 Verify equation (21.34).

21.2 Verify equations (21.46) and (21.47).

20.3 Verify equations (21.48) and (21.49).

21.4 Verify equations (21.56).

21.5 Verify equations (21.89) and (21.90).

21.6 Verify equation (21.119).

21.7 Verify equation (21.126).

21.8 Verify equations (21.140) and (21.141).

22

The Glashow–Salam–Weinberg Gauge Theory of Electroweak Interactions

---

22.1 Difficulties with the current–current and 'naive' IVB models

In chapter 20 we developed the 'V-A current–current' phenomenology of weak interactions. We saw that this gives a remarkably accurate account of a wide range of data – so much so, in fact, that one might well wonder why it should not be regarded as a fully-fledged theory. One good reason for wanting to do this would be in order to carry out calculations beyond the lowest order, which is essentially all we have used it for so far (with the significant exceptions of the GIM argument, and box diagrams in M-M̄ mixing). Such higher-order calculations are indeed required by the precision attained in modern high energy experiments. But the electroweak theory of Glashow, Salam and Weinberg, now recognized as one of the pillars of the Standard Model, was formulated long before such precision measurements existed, under the impetus of quite compelling theoretical arguments. These had to do, mainly, with certain in-principle difficulties associated with the current–current model, if viewed as a 'theory'. Since we now believe that the GSW theory is the correct description of electroweak interactions up to currently tested energies, further discussions of these old issues concerning the current–current model might seem irrelevant. However, these difficulties do raise several important points of principle. An understanding of them provides valuable motivation for the GSW theory – and some idea of what is 'at stake' in regard to experiments relating to the Higgs sector, which has only recently begun to be explored (see section 22.8.3).

Before reviewing the difficulties, however, it is worth emphasizing once again a more positive motivation for a gauge theory of weak interactions (Glashow 1961). This is the remarkable 'universality' structure noted in chapter 20, not only as between different types of lepton, but also (within the context of CKM mixing) between the quarks and the leptons. This recalls very strongly the 'universality' property of QED, and the generalization of this property in the non-Abelian theories of chapter 13. A gauge theory would provide a natural framework for such universal couplings.

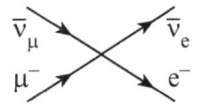

FIGURE 22.1
Current–current amplitude for $\bar{\nu}_\mu + \mu^- \to \bar{\nu}_e + e^-$.

22.1.1 Violations of unitarity

We have seen several examples, in chapter 20, in which cross sections were predicted to rise indefinitely as a function of the invariant variable s, which is the square of the total energy in the CM frame. We begin by showing why this is ultimately an unacceptable behaviour.

Consider the process (figure 22.1)

$$\bar{\nu}_\mu + \mu^- \to \bar{\nu}_e + e^- \tag{22.1}$$

in the current–current model, regarding it as fundamental interaction, treated to lowest order in perturbation theory. A similar process was discussed in chapter 20. Since the troubles we shall find occur at high energies, we can simplify the expressions by neglecting the lepton masses without altering the conclusions. In this limit the invariant amplitude is (problem 22.1), up to a numerical factor,

$$\mathcal{M} = G_F E^2 (1 + \cos\theta) \tag{22.2}$$

where E is the CM energy, and θ is the CM scattering angle of the e^- with respect to the direction of the incident μ^-. This leads to the following behaviour of the cross section (cf (20.83), remembering that $s = 4E^2$):

$$\sigma \sim G_F^2 E^2. \tag{22.3}$$

The dependence on E^2 is a consequence of the fact that G_F is not dimensionless, having the dimensions of $[M]^{-2}$. Its value is (Nakamura *et al.* 2010)

$$G_F = 1.16637(1) \times 10^{-5}~\text{GeV}^{-2}. \tag{22.4}$$

The cross section has dimensions of $[L]^2 = [M]^{-2}$, but must involve G_F^2 which has dimension $[M]^{-4}$. It must also be relativistically invariant. At energies well above lepton masses, the only invariant quantity available to restore the correct dimensions to σ is s, the square of the CM energy E, so that $\sigma \sim G_F E^2$.

Consider now a partial wave analysis of this process. For spinless particles the total cross section may be written as a sum of partial wave cross sections

$$\sigma = \frac{4\pi}{k^2} \sum_J (2J+1)|f_J|^2 \tag{22.5}$$

where f_J is the partial wave amplitude for angular momentum J and k is the CM momentum. It is a consequence of *unitarity*, or flux conservation (see, for example, Merzbacher 1998, chapter 13), that the partial wave amplitude may be written in terms of a phase shift δ_J:

$$f_J = e^{i\delta_J} \sin \delta_J \qquad (22.6)$$

so that

$$|f_J| \leq 1. \qquad (22.7)$$

Thus the cross section in each partial wave is bounded by

$$\sigma_J \leq 4\pi(2J+1)/k^2 \qquad (22.8)$$

which falls as the CM energy rises. By contrast, in (22.3) we have a cross section that rises with CM energy:

$$\sigma \sim E^2. \qquad (22.9)$$

Moreover, since the amplitude (equation (22.2)) only involves $(\cos\theta)^0$ and $(\cos\theta)^1$ contributions, it is clear that this rise in σ is associated with only a few partial waves, and is not due to more and more partial waves contributing to the sum in σ. Therefore, at some energy E, the unitarity bound will be violated by this lowest-order (Born approximation) expression for σ.

This is the essence of the 'unitarity disease' of the current–current model. To fill in all the details, however, involves a careful treatment of the appropriate partial wave analysis for the case when all particles carry spin. We shall avoid those details. Instead we argue, again on dimensional grounds, that the dimensionless partial wave amplitude f_J (note the $1/k^2$ factor in (22.5)) must be proportional to $G_F E^2$, which violates the bound (22.7) for CM energies

$$E \geq G_F^{-1/2} \sim 300\text{GeV}. \qquad (22.10)$$

At this point the reader may recall a very similar-sounding argument made in section 11.8, which led to the same estimate of the 'dangerous' energy scale (22.10). In that case, the discussion referred to a hypothetical '4-fermi' interaction without the V–A structure, and it was concerned with renormalization rather than unitarity. The gamma-matrix structure is irrelevant to these issues, which ultimately have to do with the dimensionality of the coupling constant, in both cases. In fact, as we shall see, unitarity and renormalizability are actually rather closely related.

Faced with this unitarity difficulty, we appeal to the most successful theory we have, and ask: what happens in QED? We consider an apparently quite similar process, namely $e^+e^- \to \mu^+\mu^-$ in lowest order (figure 22.2). In chapter 8 the total cross section for this process, neglecting lepton masses, was found to be (see problem 8.18 and equation (9.87))

$$\sigma = 4\pi\alpha^2/3E^2 \qquad (22.11)$$

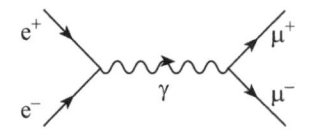

FIGURE 22.2
One-photon annihilation graph for $e^+e^- \to \mu^+\mu^-$.

which obediently falls with energy as required by unitarity. In this case the coupling constant α, analogous to G_F, is dimensionless, so that a factor E^2 is required in the denominator to give $\sigma \sim [L]^2$.

If we accept this clue from QED, we are led to search for a theory of weak interactions that involves a dimensionless coupling constant. Pressing the analogy with QED further will help us to see how one might arise. Fermi's current–current model was, as we said, motivated by the vector currents of QED. But in Fermi's case the currents interact directly with each other, whereas in QED they interact only indirectly via the mediation of the electromagnetic field. More formally, the Fermi current–current interaction has the 'four point' structure

$$'G_F(\bar{\hat{\psi}}\hat{\psi}) \cdot (\bar{\hat{\psi}}\hat{\psi})' \tag{22.12}$$

while QED has the 'three-point' (Yukawa) structure

$$'e\bar{\hat{\psi}}\hat{\psi}\hat{A}.' \tag{22.13}$$

Dimensional analysis easily shows, once again, that $[G_F] = M^{-2}$ while $[e] = M^0$. This strongly suggests that we should take Fermi's analogy further, and look for a weak interaction analogue of (22.13), having the form

$$'g\bar{\hat{\psi}}\hat{\psi}\hat{W}' \tag{22.14}$$

where $\hat{W}$ is a bosonic field. Dimensional analysis shows, of course, that $[g] = M^0$.

Since the weak currents are in fact vector-like, we must assume that the $\hat{W}$ fields are also vectors (spin-1) so as to make (22.14) Lorentz invariant. And because the weak interactions are plainly *not* long-range, like electromagnetic ones, the mass of the W quanta cannot be zero. So we are led to postulate the existence of a massive weak analogue of the photon, the 'intermediate vector boson' (IVB), and to suppose that weak interactions are mediated by the exchange of IVB's.

There is, of course, one further difference with electromagnetism, which is that the currents in β-decay, for example, carry charge (e.g. $\bar{\hat{\psi}}_e\gamma^\mu(1 - \gamma_5)\hat{\psi}_{\nu_e}$ creates negative charge or destroys positive charge). The 'companion'

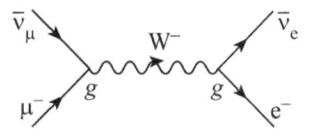

FIGURE 22.3
One-W^- annihilation graph for $\bar{\nu}_\mu + \mu^- \to \bar{\nu}_e + e^-$.

hadronic current carries the opposite charge (e.g. $\bar{\hat{\psi}}_p \gamma_\mu (1 - r\gamma_5)\hat{\psi}_n$ destroys negative charge or creates positive charge), so as to make the total effective interaction charge-conserving, as required. It follows that the $\hat{W}$ fields must then be charged, so that expressions of the form (22.14) are neutral. Because both charge-raising and charge-lowering currents exist, we need both W^+ and W^-. The reaction (22.1), for example, is then conceived as proceeding via the Feynman diagram shown in figure 22.3, quite analogous to figure 22.2.

Because we also have weak neutral currents, we need a neutral vector boson as well, Z^0. In addition to all these, there is the familiar massless neutral vector boson, the photon. Despite the fact that they are *not* massless, the $W^\pm$ and Z^0 can be understood as gauge quanta, thanks to the symmetry-breaking mechanism explained in section 19.6. For the moment, however, we are going to follow a more scenic route, and accept (as Glashow did in 1961) that we are dealing with ordinary 'unsophisticated' massive vector particles, charged and uncharged.

We now investigate whether the IVB model can do any better with unitarity than the current–current model. The analysis will bear a close similarity to the discussion of the renormalizability of the model in section 19.1, and we shall take up that issue again in section 22.1.2.

The unitarity-violating processes turn out to be those involving *external* W particles. Consider, for example, the process

$$\nu_\mu + \bar{\nu}_\mu \to W^+ + W^- \tag{22.15}$$

proceeding via the graph shown in figure 22.4. The fact that this is experimentally a somewhat esoteric reaction is irrelevant for the subsequent argument: the proposed theory, represented by the IVB modification of the four-fermion model, will necessarily generate the amplitude shown in figure 22.4, and since this amplitude violates unitarity, the theory is unacceptable. The amplitude for this process is proportional to

$$\mathcal{M}_{\lambda_1 \lambda_2} = g^2 \epsilon_\mu^{-*}(k_2, \lambda_2)\epsilon_\nu^{+*}(k_1, \lambda_1)\bar{v}(p_2)\gamma^\mu(1 - \gamma_5)$$
$$\times \frac{(\not{p}_1 - \not{k}_1 + m_\mu)}{(p_1 - k_1)^2 - m_\mu^2}\gamma^\nu(1 - \gamma_5)u(p_1) \tag{22.16}$$

where the $\epsilon^\pm$ are the polarization vectors of the W's: $\epsilon_\mu^{-*}(k_2, \lambda_2)$ is that

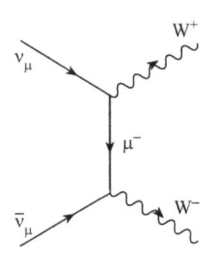

FIGURE 22.4

μ^--exchange graph for $\nu_\mu + \bar{\nu}_\mu \to W^+ + W^-$.

associated with the outgoing W^- with 4-momentum k_2 and polarization state λ_2, and similarly for ϵ_ν^{+*}.

To calculate the total cross section, we must form $|\mathcal{M}|^2$ and sum over the three states of polarization for each of the W's. To do this, we need the result

$$\sum_{\lambda=0,\pm 1} \epsilon_\mu(k,\lambda)\epsilon_\nu^*(k,\lambda) = -g_{\mu\nu} + k_\mu k_\nu/M_W^2 \qquad (22.17)$$

already given in (19.19). Our interest will as usual be in the high-energy behaviour of the cross section, in which regime it is clear that the $k_\mu k_\nu/M_W^2$ term in (22.17) will dominate the $g_{\mu\nu}$ term. It is therefore worth looking a little more closely at this term. From (19.17) and (19.18) we see that in a frame in which $k^\mu = (k^0, 0, 0, |\mathbf{k}|)$, the transverse polarization vectors $\epsilon^\mu(k, \lambda = \pm 1)$ involve no momentum dependence, which is in fact carried solely in the longitudinal polarization vector $\epsilon^\mu(k, \lambda = 0)$. We may write this as

$$\epsilon(k, \lambda = 0) = \frac{k^\mu}{M_W} + \frac{M_W}{(k^0 + |\mathbf{k}|)} \cdot (-1, \hat{\mathbf{k}}) \qquad (22.18)$$

which at high energy tends to k^μ/M_W. Thus it is clear that it is the longitudinal polarization states which are responsible for the $k^\mu k^\nu$ parts of the polarization sum (12.21), and which will dominate real production of W's at high energy.

Concentrating therefore on the production of longitudinal W's, we are led to examine the quantity

$$\frac{g^4}{M_W^4(p_1-k_1)^4}\text{Tr}[\slashed{k}_2(1-\gamma_5)(\slashed{p}_1-\slashed{k}_1)\,\slashed{k}_1\,\slashed{p}_1\,\slashed{k}_1(\slashed{p}_1-\slashed{k}_1)\,\slashed{k}_2\,\slashed{p}_2] \qquad (22.19)$$

where we have neglected m_μ, commuted the $(1-\gamma_5)$ factors through, and neglected neutrino masses, in forming $\sum_{\text{spins}}|\mathcal{M}_{00}|^2$. Retaining only the leading powers of energy, we find (see problem 22.2)

$$\sum_{\text{spins}} |\mathcal{M}_{00}|^2 \sim (g^4/M_W^4)(p_1 \cdot k_2)(p_2 \cdot k_2) = (g^4/M_W^4)E^4(1-\cos^2\theta) \qquad (22.20)$$

where E is the CM energy and θ the CM scattering angle. We see that the (unsquared) amplitude must behave essentially as $g^2 E^2 / M_W^2$, the quantity g^2 / M_W^2 effectively replacing G_F of the current–current model. The unitarity bound is violated for $E \geq M_W / g \sim 300$ GeV, taking $g \sim e$.

Other unitarity-violating processes can easily be invented, and we have to conclude that the IVB model is, in this respect, no more fitted to be called a theory than was the four-fermion model. In the case of the latter, we argued that the root of the disease lay in the fact that G_F was not dimensionless, yet somehow this was not a good enough cure after all: perhaps (it is indeed so) 'dimensionlessness' is necessary but not sufficient (see the following section). Why is this? Returning to $\mathcal{M}_{\lambda_1, \lambda_2}$ for $\nu \bar{\nu} \to W^+ W^-$ (equation (22.16)) and setting $\epsilon = k_\mu / M$ for the *longitudinal* polarization vectors, we see that we are involved with an effective amplitude

$$\frac{g^2}{M_W^2} \bar{v}(p_2) \; \not{k}_2 (1 - \gamma_5) \frac{\not{p}_1 - \not{k}_1}{(p_1 - k_1)^2} \; \not{k}_1 (1 - \gamma_5) u(p_1). \tag{22.21}$$

Using the Dirac equation $\not{p}_1 u(p_1) = 0$ and $p_1^2 = 0$, this can be reduced to

$$-\frac{g^2}{M_W^2} \bar{v}(p_2) \; \not{k}_2 (1 - \gamma_5) u(p_1). \tag{22.22}$$

We see that the longitudinal ϵ's have brought in the factors M_W^{-2}, which are 'compensated' by the factor $\not{k}_2$, and it is this latter factor which causes the rise with energy. The longitudinal polarization states have effectively reintroduced a dimensional coupling constant g/M_W.

What happens in QED? We learnt in section 7.3 that, for real photons, the longitudinal state of polarization is absent altogether. We might well suspect, therefore, that since it was the longitudinal W's that caused the 'bad' high-energy behaviour of the IVB model, the 'good' high-energy behaviour of QED might have its origin in the absence of such states for photons. And this circumstance can, in its turn, be traced (cf section 7.3.1) to the *gauge invariance* property of QED.

Indeed, in section 8.6.3 we saw that in the analogue of (22.17) for photons (this time involving only the two transverse polarization states), the right-hand side could be taken to be just $-g_{\mu\nu}$, *provided that* the Ward identity (8.166) held, a condition directly following from gauge invariance.

We have arrived here at an important theoretical indication that what we really need is a *gauge theory* of the weak interactions, in which the W's are gauge quanta. It must, however, be a peculiar kind of gauge theory, since normally gauge invariance requires the gauge field quanta to be massless. However, we have already seen how this 'peculiarity' can indeed arise, if the local symmetry is spontaneously broken (chapter 19). But before proceeding to implement that idea, in the GSW theory, we discuss one further disease (related to the unitarity one) possessed by both current–current and IVB models – that of non-renormalizability.

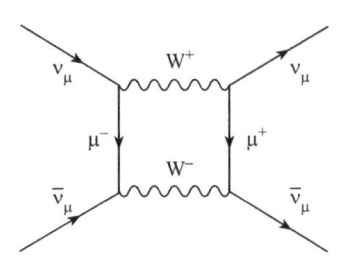

FIGURE 22.5
$O(g^4)$ contribution to $\nu_\mu \bar{\nu}_\mu \to \nu_\mu \bar{\nu}_\mu$.

22.1.2 The problem of non-renormalizability in weak interactions

The preceding line of argument about unitarity violations is open to the following objection. It is an argument conducted entirely within the framework of perturbation theory. What it shows, in fact, is simply that perturbation theory must fail, in theories of the type considered, at some sufficiently high energy. The essential reason is that the effective expansion parameter for perturbation theory is $EG_F^{1/2}$. Since $EG_F^{1/2}$ becomes large at high energy, arguments based on lowest-order perturbation theory are irrelevant. The objection is perfectly valid, and we shall take account of it by linking high-energy behaviour to the problem of renormalizability, rather than unitarity. We might, however, just note in passing that yet another way of stating the results of the previous two sections is to say that, for both the current–current and IVB theories, 'weak interactions become strong at energies of order 1 TeV'.

We gave an elementary introduction to renormalization in chapters 10 and 11 of volume 1. In particular, we discussed in some detail, in section 11.8, the difficulties that arise when one tries to do higher-order calculations in the case of a four-fermion interaction with the same form (apart from the V-A structure) as the current–current model. Its coupling constant, which we called G_F, also had dimension (mass)$^{-2}$. The 'non-renormalizable' problem was essentially that, as one approached the 'dangerous' energy scale (22.10), one needed to supply the values of an ever-increasing number of parameters from experiment, and the theory lost predictive power.

Does the IVB model fare any better? In this case, the coupling constant is dimensionless, just as in QED. 'Dimensionlessness' alone is not enough, it turns out: the IVB model is not renormalizable either. We gave an indication of why this is so in section 19.1, but we shall now be somewhat more specific, relating the discussion to the previous one about unitarity.

Consider, for example, the fourth-order processes shown in figure 22.5, for the IVB-mediated process $\nu_\mu \bar{\nu}_\mu \to \nu_\mu \bar{\nu}_\mu$. It seems plausible from the diagram that the amplitude must be formed by somehow 'sticking together' two copies

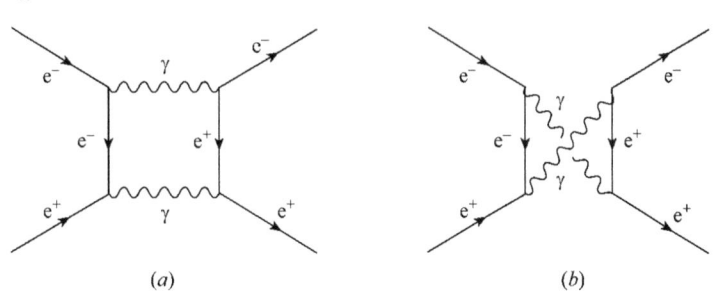

FIGURE 22.6
$O(e^4)$ contributions to $e^+e^- \to e^+e^-$.

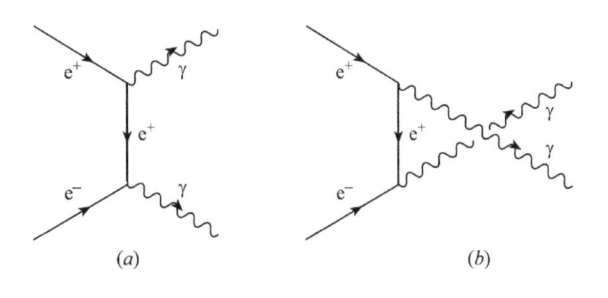

FIGURE 22.7
Lowest-order amplitudes for $e^+e^- \to \gamma\gamma$: (a) direct graph, (b) crossed graph.

of the tree graph shown in figure 22.4.[1] Now we saw that the high-energy behaviour of the amplitude $\nu\bar{\nu} \to W^+W^-$ (figure 22.4) grows as E^2, due to the k dependence of the longitudinal polarization vectors, and this turns out to produce, via figure 22.5, a non-renormalizable divergence, for the reason indicated in section 19.1 – namely, the 'bad' behaviour of the $k^\mu k^\nu / M_W^2$ factors in the W-propagators, at large k.

So it is plain that, once again, the blame lies with the longitudinal polarization states for the W's. Let us see how QED – a renormalizable theory – manages to avoid this problem. In this case, there are two box graphs, shown in figures 22.6. There are also two corresponding tree graphs, shown in figures 22.7(a) and (b). Consider, therefore mimicking for figures 22.7(a) and (b) the calculation we did for figure 22.4. We would obtain the leading high-energy behaviour by replacing the photon polarization vectors by the corresponding momenta, and it can be checked (problem 21.3) that when this replacement

---

[1]The reader may here usefully recall the discussion of unitarity for one-loop graphs in section 13.3.3.

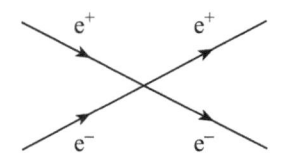

FIGURE 22.8

Four-point e^+e^- vertex.

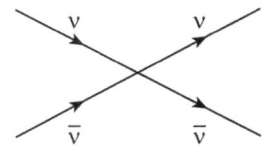

FIGURE 22.9

Four-point $\nu\bar{\nu}$ vertex.

is made for each photon the complete amplitude for the sum of figures 22.7(a) and (b) *vanishes*.

In physical terms, of course, this result was expected, since we knew in advance that it is always possible to choose polarization vectors for *real* photons such that they are purely transverse, so that no physical process can depend on a part of ϵ_μ proportional to k_μ. Nevertheless, the calculation is highly relevant to the question of renormalizing the graphs in figure 22.6. The photons in this process are not real external particles, but are instead virtual, internal ones. This has the consequence that we should in general include their longitudinal ($\epsilon_\mu \propto k_\mu$) states as well as the transverse ones (see section 13.3.3 for something similar in the case of unitarity for 1-loop diagrams). The calculation of problem 22.3 then suggests that these longitudinal states are harmless, provided that both contributions in figure 22.7 are included.

Indeed, the sum of these two box graphs for $e^+e^- \to e^+e^-$ is *not divergent*. If it were, an infinite counter term proportional to a four-point vertex $e^+e^- \to e^+e^-$ (figure 22.8) would have to be introduced, and the original QED theory, which of course lacks such a fundamental interaction, would not be renormalizable. This is exactly what *does* happen in the case of figure 22.5. The bad high-energy behaviour of $\nu\bar{\nu} \to W^+W^-$ translates into a divergence of figure 22.5 – and this time there is no 'crossed' amplitude to cancel it. This divergence entails the introduction of a new vertex, figure 22.9, not present in the original IVB theory. Thus the theory without this vertex is non-renormalizable – and if we include it, we are landed with a four-field pointlike vertex which is non-renormalizable, as in the Fermi (current–current) case.

Our presentation hitherto has emphasized the fact that, in QED, the bad high-energy behaviour is rendered harmless by a cancellation between contributions from figures 22.7(a) and (b) (or figures 22.6(a) and (b)). Thus one way to 'fix up' the IVB theory might be to hypothesize a new physical process, to be added to figure 22.4, in such a way that a cancellation occurred at high energies. The search for such high-energy cancellation mechanisms can indeed be pushed to a successful conclusion (Llewellyn Smith 1973), given sufficient ingenuity and, arguably, a little hindsight. However, we are in possession of a more powerful principle. In QED, we have already seen (section 8.6.2) that the vanishing of amplitudes when an ϵ_μ is replaced by the corresponding k_μ is due to *gauge invariance*: in other words, the potentially harmful longitudinal polarization states are in fact harmless in a gauge-invariant theory.

We have therefore arrived once more, after a somewhat more leisurely discussion than that of section 19.1, at the idea that we need a *gauge* theory of massive vector bosons, so that the offending $k^\mu k^\nu$ part of the propagator can be 'gauged away' as in the photon case. This is precisely what is provided by the 'spontaneously broken' gauge theory concept, as developed in chapter 19. There we saw that, taking the U(1) case for simplicity, the general expression for the gauge boson propagator in such a theory (in a 't Hooft gauge) is

$$\mathrm{i}\left[-g^{\mu\nu} + \frac{(1-\xi)k^\mu k^\nu}{k^2 - \xi M_\mathrm{W}^2}\right] \bigg/ (k^2 - M_\mathrm{W}^2 + \mathrm{i}\epsilon) \qquad (22.23)$$

where ξ is a gauge parameter. Our IVB propagator corresponds to the $\xi \to \infty$ limit, and with this choice of ξ all the troubles we have been discussing appear to be present. But for any finite ξ (for example $\xi = 1$) the high-energy behaviour of the propagator is actually $\sim 1/k^2$, the same as in the renormalizable QED case. This strongly suggests that such theories – in particular non-Abelian ones – are in fact renormalizable. 't Hooft's proof that they are ('t Hooft 1971b) triggered an explosion of theoretical work, as it became clear that, for the first time, it would be possible to make higher-order calculations for weak interaction processes using consistent renormalization procedures, of the kind that had worked so well for QED.

We now have all the pieces in place, and can proceed to introduce the GSW theory, based on the local gauge symmetry of SU(2) × U(1).

22.2 The SU(2) × U(1) electroweak gauge theory

22.2.1 Quantum number assignments; Higgs, W and Z masses

Given the preceding motivations for considering a gauge theory of weak interactions, the remaining question is this: what is the relevant symmetry

group of local phase transformations, i.e. the relevant *weak gauge group?* Several possibilities were suggested, but it is now very well established that the one originally proposed by Glashow (1961), subsequently treated as a spontaneously broken gauge symmetry by Weinberg (1967) and by Salam (1968), and later extended by other authors, produces a theory which is in remarkable agreement with currently known data. We shall not give a critical review of all the experimental evidence, but instead proceed directly to an outline of the GSW theory, introducing elements of the data at illustrative points.

An important clue to the symmetry group involved in the weak interactions is provided by considering the transitions induced by these interactions. This is somewhat analogous to discovering the multiplet structure of atomic levels and hence the representations of the rotation group, a prominent symmetry of the Schrödinger equation, by studying electromagnetic transitions. However, there is one very important difference between the 'weak multiplets' we shall be considering, and those associated with symmetries which are not spontaneously broken. We saw in chapter 12 how an unbroken non-Abelian symmetry leads to multiplets of states which are degenerate in mass, but in section 17.1 we learned that that result only holds provided the vacuum is left invariant under the symmetry transformation. When the symmetry is spontaneously broken, the vacuum is *not* invariant, and we must expect that the degenerate multiplet structure will then, in general, disappear completely. This is precisely the situation in the electroweak theory.

Nevertheless, as we shall see, essential consequences of the weak symmetry group – specifically, the relations it requires between otherwise unrelated masses and couplings – are accessible to experiment. Moreover, despite the fact that members of a multiplet of a global symmetry which is spontaneously broken will, in general, no longer have even approximately the same mass, the concept of a multiplet is still useful. This is because when the symmetry is made a *local* one, we shall find (in sections 22.2.2 and 22.2.3) that the associated gauge quanta still mediate interactions between members of a given symmetry multiplet, just as in the manifest local non-Abelian symmetry example of QCD. Now, the leptonic transitions associated with the weak charged currents are, as we saw in chapter 20, $\nu_e \leftrightarrow e, \nu_\mu \leftrightarrow \mu$ etc. This suggests that these pairs should be regarded as *doublets* under some group. Further we saw in section 20.7 how weak transitions involving charged quarks suggested a similar doublet structure for them also. The simplest possibility is therefore to suppose that, in both cases, a 'weak SU(2) group' is involved, called 'weak isospin'. We emphasize once more that this weak isospin is distinct from the hadronic isospin of chapter 12, which is part of $SU(3)_f$. We use the symbols t, t_3 for the quantum numbers of weak isospin, and make the specific assignments for the leptonic fields

$$t = \frac{1}{2}, \quad \begin{cases} t_3 = +1/2 \\ t_3 = -1/2 \end{cases} \quad \begin{pmatrix} \hat{\nu}'_e \\ \hat{e}^- \end{pmatrix}_L, \quad \begin{pmatrix} \hat{\nu}'_\mu \\ \hat{\mu}^- \end{pmatrix}_L, \quad \begin{pmatrix} \hat{\nu}'_\tau \\ \hat{\tau}^- \end{pmatrix}_L$$

$$(22.24)$$

where $\hat{e}_L = \frac{1}{2}(1 - \gamma_5)\hat{e}$ etc, and for the quark fields

$$t = \frac{1}{2}, \quad \begin{cases} t_3 = +1/2 \\ t_3 = -1/2 \end{cases} \quad \begin{pmatrix} \hat{u} \\ \hat{d'} \end{pmatrix}_L, \quad \begin{pmatrix} \hat{c} \\ \hat{s'} \end{pmatrix}_L, \quad \begin{pmatrix} \hat{t} \\ \hat{b'} \end{pmatrix}_L. \quad (22.25)$$

As discussed in section 20.2.2, the subscript 'L' refers to the fact that only the left-handed chiral components of the fields enter, in consequence of the V–A structure. For this reason, the weak isospin group is referred to as SU(2)$_L$, to show that the weak isospin assignments and corresponding transformation properties apply only to these left-handed parts. Notice that, as anticipated for a spontaneously broken symmetry, these doublets all involve pairs of particles which are not mass degenerate. In (22.24) and (22.25), the primes indicate that these fields are related to the (unprimed) fields of definite mass by the unitary matrices **U** (for neutrinos) and **V** (for quarks), as discussed in sections 21.4.1 and 20.7.3 respectively.

Making this SU(2)$_L$ into a local phase invariance (following the logic of chapter 13) will entail the introduction of three gauge fields, transforming as a $t = 1$ multiplet (a triplet) under the group. Because (as with the ordinary SU(2)$_f$ of hadronic isospin) the members of a weak isodoublet differ by one unit of charge, the two gauge fields associated with transitions between doublet members will have charge ± 1. The quanta of these fields will, of course, be the now familiar W$^\pm$ bosons mediating the charged current transitions, and associated with the weak isospin raising and lowering operators $t_\pm$. What about the third gauge boson of the triplet? This will be electrically neutral, and a very economical and appealing idea would be to associate this neutral vector particle with the photon, thereby *unifying* the weak and electromagnetic interactions. A model of this kind was originally suggested by Schwinger (1957). Of course, the W's must somehow acquire mass, while the photon remains massless. Schwinger arranged this by introducing appropriate couplings of the vector bosons to additional scalar and pseudoscalar fields. These couplings were arbitrary and no prediction of the W masses could be made. We now believe, following the arguments of the preceding section, that the W mass must arise via the spontaneous breakdown of a non-Abelian gauge symmetry, and as we saw in section 19.6, this *does* constrain the W mass.

Apart from the question of the W mass in Schwinger's model, we now know (see chapter 20) that there exist *neutral current* weak interactions, in addition to those of the charged currents. We must also include these in our emerging gauge theory, and an obvious suggestion is to have these currents mediated by the neutral member W^0 of the SU(2)$_L$ gauge field triplet. Such a scheme was indeed proposed by Bludman (1958), again pre-Higgs, so that W masses were put in 'by hand'. In this model, however, the neutral currents will have the same pure left-handed V–A structure as the charged currents: but, as we saw in chapter 20, the neutral currents are *not* pure V-A. Furthermore, the attractive feature of including the photon, and thus unifying weak and electromagnetic interactions, has been lost.

A key contribution was made by Glashow (1961); similar ideas were also advanced by Salam and Ward (1964). Glashow suggested enlarging the Schwinger–Bludman SU(2) schemes by inclusion of an additional U(1) gauge group, resulting in an 'SU(2)$_\mathrm{L}$ × U(1)' group structure. The new Abelian U(1) group is associated with a weak analogue of hypercharge – 'weak hypercharge' – just as SU(2)$_\mathrm{L}$ was associated with 'weak isospin'. Indeed, Glashow proposed that the Gell-Mann–Nishijima relation for charges should also hold for these weak analogues, giving

$$eQ = e(t_3 + y/2) \tag{22.26}$$

for the electric charge Q (in units of e) of the t_3 member of a weak isomultiplet, assigned a weak hypercharge y. Clearly, therefore, the lepton doublets, (ν'_e, e^-), etc, then have $y = -1$, while the quark doublets (u, d'), etc, have $y = +\frac{1}{3}$. Now, when *this* group is gauged, everything falls marvellously into place: the charged vector bosons appear as before, but there are now *two* neutral vector bosons, which between them will be responsible for the weak neutral current processes, and for electromagnetism. This is exactly the piece of mathematics we went through in section 19.6, which we now appropriate as an important part of the Standard Model.

For convenience, we reproduce here the main results of section 19.6. The Higgs field $\hat{\phi}$ is an SU(2) doublet

$$\hat{\phi} = \begin{pmatrix} \hat{\phi}^+ \\ \hat{\phi}^0 \end{pmatrix} \tag{22.27}$$

with an assumed vacuum expectation value (in unitary gauge) given by

$$\langle 0|\hat{\phi}|0\rangle = \begin{pmatrix} 0 \\ v/\sqrt{2} \end{pmatrix}. \tag{22.28}$$

Fluctuations about this value are parametrized in this gauge by

$$\hat{\phi} = \begin{pmatrix} 0 \\ \frac{1}{\sqrt{2}}(v + \hat{H}) \end{pmatrix} \tag{22.29}$$

where $\hat{H}$ is the (physical) Higgs field. The Lagrangian for the sector consisting of the gauge fields and the Higgs fields is

$$\mathcal{L}_{\mathrm{G\Phi}} = (\hat{D}_\mu\hat{\phi})^\dagger(\hat{D}^\mu\hat{\phi}) + \mu^2\hat{\phi}^\dagger\hat{\phi} - \frac{\lambda}{4}(\hat{\phi}^\dagger\hat{\phi})^2 - \frac{1}{4}\hat{\boldsymbol{F}}_{\mu\nu}\cdot\hat{\boldsymbol{F}}^{\mu\nu} - \frac{1}{4}\hat{G}_{\mu\nu}\hat{G}^{\mu\nu}, \tag{22.30}$$

where $\hat{\boldsymbol{F}}_{\mu\nu}$ is the SU(2) field strength tensor (19.80) for the gauge fields $\hat{\boldsymbol{W}}^\mu$ and $\hat{G}_{\mu\nu}$ is the U(1) field strength tensor (19.81) for the gauge field B^μ, and $\hat{D}^\mu\hat{\phi}$ is given by (19.79). After symmetry breaking (i.e. the insertion of (22.29)

in (22.30)) the quadratic parts of (22.30) can be written in unitary gauge as (see problem 19.9)

$$\hat{\mathcal{L}}_{G\Phi}^{\text{free}} = \frac{1}{2}\partial_\mu \hat{H} \partial^\mu \hat{H} - \mu^2 \hat{H}^2 \tag{22.31}$$

$$-\frac{1}{4}(\partial_\mu \hat{W}_{1\nu} - \partial_\nu \hat{W}_{1\mu})(\partial^\mu \hat{W}_1^\nu - \partial^\nu \hat{W}_1^\mu) + \frac{1}{8}g^2 v^2 \hat{W}_{1\mu}\hat{W}_1^\mu \tag{22.32}$$

$$-\frac{1}{4}(\partial_\mu \hat{W}_{2\nu} - \partial_\nu \hat{W}_{2\mu})(\partial^\mu \hat{W}_2^\nu - \partial^\nu \hat{W}_2^\mu) + \frac{1}{8}g^2 v^2 \hat{W}_{2\mu}\hat{W}_2^\mu \tag{22.33}$$

$$-\frac{1}{4}(\partial_\mu \hat{Z}_\nu - \partial_\nu \hat{Z}_\mu)(\partial^\mu \hat{Z}^\nu - \partial^\nu \hat{Z}^\mu) + \frac{v^2}{8}(g^2 + g'^2)\hat{Z}_\mu \hat{Z}^\mu \tag{22.34}$$

$$-\frac{1}{4}\hat{F}_{\mu\nu}\hat{F}^{\mu\nu} \tag{22.35}$$

where

$$\hat{Z}^\mu = \cos\theta_{\mathrm{W}} \hat{W}_3^\mu - \sin\theta_{\mathrm{W}} \hat{B}^\mu, \tag{22.36}$$

$$\hat{A}^\mu = \sin\theta_{\mathrm{W}} \hat{W}_3^\mu + \cos\theta_{\mathrm{W}} \hat{B}^\mu, \tag{22.37}$$

and

$$\hat{F}^{\mu\nu} = \partial^\mu A^\nu - \partial^\nu A^\mu, \tag{22.38}$$

with

$$\cos\theta_{\mathrm{W}} = g/(g^2 + g'^2)^{1/2}, \qquad \sin\theta_{\mathrm{W}} = g'/(g^2 + g'^2)^{1/2}. \tag{22.39}$$

Feynman rules for the vector boson propagators (in unitary gauge) and couplings, and for the Higgs couplings, can be read off from (22.30), and are given in appendix Q.

Equations (22.31)–(22.35) give the tree-level masses of the Higgs boson and the gauge bosons: (22.31) tells us that the mass of the Higgs boson is

$$m_{\mathrm{H}} = \sqrt{2}\mu = \sqrt{\lambda}\,v/\sqrt{2}, \tag{22.40}$$

where $v/\sqrt{2}$ is the (tree-level) Higgs vacuum value; (22.32) and (22.33) show that the charged W's have a mass

$$M_{\mathrm{W}} = gv/2 \tag{22.41}$$

where g is the SU(2)$_{\mathrm{L}}$ gauge coupling constant; (22.34) gives the mass of the Z^0 as

$$M_{\mathrm{Z}} = M_{\mathrm{W}}/\cos\theta_{\mathrm{W}} \tag{22.42}$$

and (22.35) shows that the A^μ field describes a massless particle (to be identified with the photon).

Still unaccounted for are the *right-handed* chiral components of the fermion fields. There is at present no evidence for any weak interactions coupling to the right-handed field components, and it is therefore natural – and a basic assumption of the electroweak theory – that all 'R' components are singlets

TABLE 22.1

Weak isospin and hypercharge assignments.

	t	t_3	y	Q
$\nu'_{eL},\ \nu'_{\mu L},\ \nu'_{\tau L}$	1/2	1/2	-1	0
$\nu'_{eR},\ \nu'_{\mu R},\ \nu'_{\tau R}$	0	0	0	0
$e_L,\ \mu_L,\ \tau_L$	1/2	-1/2	-1	-1
$e_R,\ \mu_R,\ \tau_R$	0	0	-2	-1
$u_L,\ c_L,\ t_L$	1/2	1/2	1/3	2/3
$u_R,\ c_R,\ t_R$	0	0	4/3	2/3
$d'_L,\ s'_L,\ b'_L$	1/2	-1/2	1/3	-1/3
$d'_R,\ s'_R,\ b'_R$	0	0	-2/3	-1/3
ϕ^+	1/2	1/2	1	1
ϕ^0	1/2	-1/2	1	0

under the weak isospin group. Crucially, however, the 'R' components do interact via the U(1) field $\hat{B}^\mu$; it is this that allows electromagnetism to emerge free of parity-violating γ_5 terms, as we shall see. With the help of the weak charge formula (equation (22.26)), we arrive at the assignments shown in table 22.1.

We have included 'R' components for the neutrinos in the table. It is, however, fair to say that in the original Standard Model the neutrinos were taken to be massless, with no neutrino mixing. We have seen in chapter 20 that it is for many purposes an excellent approximation to treat the neutrinos as massless, except when discussing neutrino oscillations. We shall mention their masses again in section 22.5.2, but for the moment we proceed in the 'massless neutrinos' approximation. In this case, there are *no* 'R' components for neutrinos, and no neutrino mixing.

We can now proceed to write down the *currents* of the electroweak theory. We will show that these dynamical symmetry currents are precisely the same as the phenomenological currents of the current–current model developed in chapter 20. The new feature here is that – as in the electromagnetic case – the currents interact with each other by the exchange of a gauge boson, rather than directly.

22.2.2 The leptonic currents (massless neutrinos): relation to current–current model

We write the $SU(2)_L \times U(1)$ covariant derivative, in terms of the fields $\hat{\boldsymbol{W}}^\mu$ and $\hat{B}^\mu$ of section 19.6, as

$$\hat{D}^\mu = \partial^\mu + ig\boldsymbol{\tau} \cdot \hat{\boldsymbol{W}}^\mu/2 + ig'y\hat{B}^\mu/2 \qquad \text{on 'L' SU(2) doublets} \qquad (22.43)$$

and as

$$\hat{D}^\mu = \partial^\mu + ig'y\hat{B}^\mu/2 \qquad \text{on 'R' SU(2) singlets.} \qquad (22.44)$$

The leptonic couplings to the gauge fields therefore arise from the 'gauge-covariantized' free leptonic Lagrangian:

$$\hat{\mathcal{L}}_{\text{lept}} = \sum_{f=e,\mu,\tau} \bar{\hat{l}}_{f\text{L}} i \hat{\slashed{D}} \hat{l}_{f\text{L}} + \sum_{f=e,\mu,\tau} \bar{\hat{l}}_{f\text{R}} i \hat{\slashed{D}} \hat{l}_{f\text{R}}, \tag{22.45}$$

where the $\hat{l}_{f\text{L}}$ are the left-handed doublets

$$\hat{l}_{f\text{L}} = \begin{pmatrix} \hat{\nu}_f \\ \hat{f}^- \end{pmatrix}_{\text{L}} \tag{22.46}$$

and $\hat{l}_{f\text{R}}$ are the singlets $\hat{l}_{e\text{R}} = \hat{e}_{\text{R}}$ etc.

Consider first the *charged leptonic currents*. The correct normalization for the charged fields is that $\hat{W}^\mu \equiv (\hat{W}_1^\mu - i\hat{W}_2^\mu)/\sqrt{2}$ destroys the W^+ or creates the W^- (cf (7.15)). The '$\boldsymbol{\tau} \cdot \boldsymbol{W}/2$' terms can be written as

$$\boldsymbol{\tau} \cdot \hat{\boldsymbol{W}}^\mu/2 = \frac{1}{\sqrt{2}} \left\{ \tau_+ \frac{(\hat{W}_1^\mu - i\hat{W}_2^\mu)}{\sqrt{2}} + \tau_- \frac{(\hat{W}_1^\mu + i\hat{W}_2^\mu)}{\sqrt{2}} \right\} + \frac{\tau_3}{2} \hat{W}_3^\mu, \tag{22.47}$$

where $\tau_\pm = (\tau_1 \pm i\tau_2)/2$ are the usual raising and lowering operators for the doublets. Thus the '$f=e$' contribution to the first term in (22.45) picks out the process $\text{e}^- \to \nu_e + \text{W}^-$ for example, with the result that the corresponding vertex is given by

$$-\frac{ig}{\sqrt{2}} \gamma^\mu \frac{(1 - \gamma_5)}{2}. \tag{22.48}$$

The 'universality' of the single coupling constant 'g' ensures that (22.48) is also the amplitude for the $\mu - \nu_\mu - \text{W}$ and $\tau - \nu_\tau - \text{W}$ vertices. Thus the amplitude for the $\nu_\mu + \text{e}^- \to \mu^- + \nu_e$ process considered in section 20.8 is

$$\left\{ -\frac{ig}{\sqrt{2}} \bar{u}(\mu)\gamma_\mu \frac{(1 - \gamma_5)}{2} u(\nu_\mu) \right\} \frac{i[-g^{\mu\nu} + k^\mu k^\nu/M_\text{W}^2]}{k^2 - M_\text{W}^2} \left\{ -i\frac{g}{\sqrt{2}} \bar{u}(\nu_e)\gamma_\nu \frac{(1 - \gamma_5)}{2} u(e) \right\} \tag{22.49}$$

corresponding to the Feynman graph of figure 22.10.

For $k^2 \ll M_\text{W}^2$ we can replace the W-propagator by the constant value $g^{\mu\nu}/M_\text{W}^2$, leading to the amplitude

$$-\frac{ig^2}{8M_\text{W}^2} \bar{u}(\mu)\gamma_\mu(1 - \gamma_5)u(\nu_\mu)\bar{u}(\nu_e)\gamma^\mu(1 - \gamma_5)u(e), \tag{22.50}$$

which may be compared with the form we used in the current–current theory, equation (20.50). This comparison gives

$$\frac{G_\text{F}}{\sqrt{2}} = \frac{g^2}{8M_\text{W}^2}. \tag{22.51}$$

This is an important equation, giving the precise version, in the GSW theory,

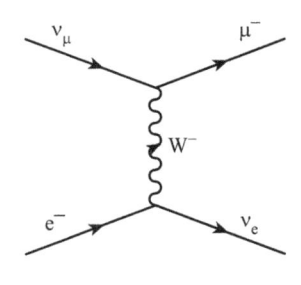

FIGURE 22.10
W-exchange process in $\nu_\mu + e^- \rightarrow \mu^- + \nu_e$.

of the qualitative relation $g^2/M_W^2 \sim G_F$ introduced following equation (22.20), and in volume 1, at equation (1.32).

Putting together (22.41) and (22.51) we can deduce

$$G_F/\sqrt{2} = 1/(2v^2) \tag{22.52}$$

so that from the known value (22.4) of G_F there follows the value of v:

$$v \simeq 246 \text{ GeV}. \tag{22.53}$$

Alternatively we may quote $v/\sqrt{2}$ (the vacuum value of the Higgs field):

$$v/\sqrt{2} \simeq 174 \text{ GeV}. \tag{22.54}$$

This parameter sets the scale of electroweak symmetry breaking, but as yet no theory is able to predict its value. It is related to the parameters λ, μ of (22.30) by $v/\sqrt{2} = \sqrt{2}\mu/\lambda^{1/2}$ (cf (17.98)).

In general, the charge-changing part of (22.45) can be written as

$$-\frac{g}{\sqrt{2}} \left\{ \bar{\hat{\nu}}_e \gamma^\mu \frac{(1-\gamma_5)}{2} \hat{e} + \bar{\hat{\nu}}_\mu \gamma^\mu \frac{(1-\gamma_5)}{2} \hat{\mu} + \bar{\hat{\nu}}_\tau \gamma^\mu \frac{(1-\gamma_5)}{2} \hat{\tau} \right\} \hat{W}_\mu$$

$$+\text{hermitian conjugate}, \tag{22.55}$$

where $\hat{W}^\mu = (\hat{W}_1^\mu - i\hat{W}_2^\mu)/\sqrt{2}$. (22.55) has the form

$$-\hat{j}_{CC}^\mu(\text{leptons})\hat{W}_\mu - \hat{j}_{CC}^{\mu\dagger}(\text{leptons})\hat{W}_\mu^\dagger \tag{22.56}$$

where the *leptonic weak charged current* $\hat{j}_{CC}^\mu$(leptons) is precisely that used in the current–current model (equation (20.38)), up to the usual factors of g's and $\sqrt{2}$'s. Thus the dynamical symmetry currents of the $SU(2)_L$ gauge theory are exactly the 'phenomenological' currents of the earlier current–current model. The Feynman rules for the lepton-W couplings (appendix Q) can be read off from (22.55).

Turning now to the *leptonic weak neutral current*, this will appear via the couplings to the Z^0, written as

$$-\hat{j}^\mu_{NC}(\text{leptons})\hat{Z}_\mu. \tag{22.57}$$

Referring to (22.36) for the linear combination of $\hat{W}^\mu_3$ and $\hat{B}^\mu$ which represents $\hat{Z}^\mu$, we find (problem 22.4)

$$\hat{j}^\mu_{NC}(\text{leptons}) = \frac{g}{\cos\theta_W}\sum_l \bar{\hat{\psi}}_l\gamma^\mu\left[t^l_3\left(\frac{1-\gamma_5}{2}\right) - \sin^2\theta_W Q_l\right]\hat{\psi}_l, \tag{22.58}$$

where the sum is over the six lepton fields $\nu_e, e^-, \nu_\mu, \dots \tau^-$. For the $Q = 0$ neutrinos with $t_3 = +\frac{1}{2}$,

$$\hat{j}^\mu_{NC}(\text{neutrinos}) = \frac{g}{2\cos\theta_W}\sum_l \bar{\hat{\nu}}_l\gamma^\mu\frac{(1-\gamma_5)}{2}\hat{\nu}_l, \tag{22.59}$$

where now $l = e, \mu, \tau$. For the other (negatively charged) leptons, we shall have both L and R couplings from (22.58), and we can write

$$\hat{j}^\mu_{NC}(\text{charged leptons}) = \frac{g}{\cos\theta_W}\sum_{l=e,\mu,\tau} \bar{\hat{l}}\gamma^\mu\left[c^l_L\left(\frac{1-\gamma_5}{2}\right) + c^l_R\left(\frac{1+\gamma_5}{2}\right)\right]\hat{l}, \tag{22.60}$$

where

$$c^l_L = t^l_3 - \sin^2\theta_W Q_l = -\frac{1}{2} + \sin^2\theta_W \tag{22.61}$$

$$c^l_R = -\sin^2\theta_W Q_l = \sin^2\theta_W. \tag{22.62}$$

As noted earlier, the Z^0 coupling is not pure 'V–A'. These relations (22.59)–(22.62) are exactly the ones given earlier, in (20.85)–(20.87); in particular, the couplings are independent of 'l' and hence exhibit lepton universality. The alternative notation

$$\hat{j}^\mu_{NC}(\text{charged leptons}) = \frac{g}{2\cos\theta_W}\sum_l \bar{\hat{l}}\gamma^\mu(g^l_V - g^l_A\gamma_5)\hat{l} \tag{22.63}$$

is often used, where

$$g^l_V = -\frac{1}{2} + 2\sin^2\theta_W \qquad g^l_A = -\frac{1}{2}, \text{independent of } l. \tag{22.64}$$

Note that the g^l_V vanishes for $\sin^2\theta_W = 0.25$. Again, the Feynman rules for lepton-Z couplings (appendix Q) are contained in (22.59) and (22.60).

As in the case of W-mediated charge-charging processes, Z^0-mediated processes reduce to the current–current form at low k^2. For example, the amplitude for $e^-\mu^- \to e^-\mu^-$ via Z^0 exchange (figure 22.11) reduces to

$$-\frac{ig^2}{4\cos^2\theta_W M^2_Z}\quad \bar{u}(e)\gamma_\mu[c^l_L(1-\gamma_5) + c^l_R(1+\gamma_5)]u(e)\bar{u}(\mu)\gamma^\mu$$
$$\times [c^l_L(1-\gamma_5) + c^l_R(1+\gamma_5)]u(\mu). \tag{22.65}$$

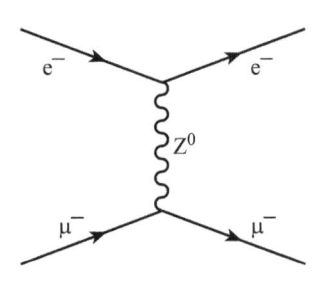

FIGURE 22.11
Z^0-exchange process in $e^- \mu^- \to e^- \mu^-$.

It is customary to define the parameter

$$\rho = M_W^2/(M_Z^2 \cos^2 \theta_W), \tag{22.66}$$

which is unity at tree-level, in the absence of loop corrections. The ratio of factors in front of the $\bar{u} \dots u$ expressions in (22.65) and (22.50) (i.e. 'neutral current process'/'charged current process') is then 2ρ.

We may also check the electromagnetic current in the theory, by looking for the piece that couples to $\hat{A}^\mu$. We find

$$\hat{\jmath}_{\text{emag}}^\mu = -g \sin \theta_W \sum_{l=e,\mu,\tau} \bar{\hat{l}} \gamma^\mu \hat{l} \tag{22.67}$$

which allows us to identify the electromagnetic charge e as

$$e = g \sin \theta_W \tag{22.68}$$

as already suggested in (19.97) of chapter 19. Note that all the γ_5's cancel from (22.67), as is of course required.

22.2.3   The quark currents

The charge-changing quark currents, which are coupled to the $W^\pm$ fields, have a form very similar to that of the charged leptonic currents, except that the $t_3 = -\frac{1}{2}$ components of the L-doublets have to be understood as the flavour-mixed (weakly interacting) states

$$\begin{pmatrix} \hat{d}' \\ \hat{s}' \\ \hat{b}' \end{pmatrix}_L = \begin{pmatrix} V_{\text{ud}} & V_{\text{us}} & V_{\text{ub}} \\ V_{\text{cd}} & V_{\text{cs}} & V_{\text{cb}} \\ V_{\text{td}} & V_{\text{ts}} & V_{\text{tb}} \end{pmatrix} \begin{pmatrix} \hat{d} \\ \hat{s} \\ \hat{b} \end{pmatrix}_L , \tag{22.69}$$

where $\hat{d}, \hat{s}$ and $\hat{b}$ are the strongly interacting fields with masses m_d, m_s and m_b, and the V-matrix is the CKM matrix used extensively in chapter 21. We

shall discuss this matrix further in section 22.5.2. Thus the *charge-changing weak quark current* is

$$\hat{j}^\mu_{CC}(\text{quarks}) = \frac{g}{\sqrt{2}} \left\{ \bar{\hat{u}}\gamma^\mu \frac{(1-\gamma_5)}{2}\hat{d}' + \bar{\hat{c}}\gamma^\mu \frac{(1-\gamma_5)}{2}\hat{s}' + \bar{\hat{t}}\gamma^\mu \frac{(1-\gamma_5)}{2}\hat{b}' \right\},$$

(22.70)

which generalizes (20.90) to three generations and supplies the factor $g/\sqrt{2}$, as for the leptons.

The neutral currents are diagonal in flavour if the matrix V is unitary (see also section 22.5.2). Thus $\hat{j}^\mu_{NC}(\text{quarks})$ will be given by the same expression as (20.103), except that now the sum will be over all six quark flavours. The *neutral weak quark current* is thus

$$\hat{j}^\mu_{NC}(\text{quarks}) = \frac{g}{\cos\theta_W} \sum_q \bar{\hat{q}}\gamma^\mu \left[c^q_L \frac{(1-\gamma_5)}{2} + c^q_R \frac{(1+\gamma_5)}{2} \right] \hat{q},$$

(22.71)

where

$$c^q_L = t^q_3 - \sin^2\theta_W Q_q$$

(22.72)

$$c^q_R = -\sin^2\theta_W Q_q.$$

(22.73)

These expressions are exactly as given in (20.103)–(20.105). As for the charged leptons, we can alternatively write (22.71) as

$$\hat{j}^\mu_{NC}(\text{quarks}) = \frac{g}{2\cos\theta_W} \sum_q \bar{\hat{q}}\gamma^\mu (g^q_V - g^q_A \gamma_5)\hat{q},$$

(22.74)

where

$$g^q_V = t^q_3 - 2\sin^2\theta_W Q_q$$

(22.75)

$$g^q_A = t^q_3.$$

(22.76)

Before proceeding to discuss some simple phenomenological consequences, we remind the reader of one important feature of the Standard Model currents in general. Reading (22.24) and (22.25) together 'vertically', the leptons and quarks are grouped in three *generations*, each with two leptons and two quarks. The theoretical motivation for such family grouping is that *anomalies* are cancelled within each complete generation, as discussed in section 18.4.

22.3 Simple (tree-level) predictions

The theory as so far developed has just 4 parameters: the gauge couplings g and g', and the parameters λ and μ of the Higgs potential. The previous two

subsections show that all the couplings to fermions can be written in terms of the known quantities G_F and e (or α), and one free parameter which may be taken to be $\sin\theta_W$. We noted in section 20.9 that, before the discovery of the W and Z particles, the then known neutrino data were consistent with a single value of θ_W given by $\sin^2\theta_W \simeq 0.23$. Using (22.51) and (22.68), it was then possible to predict the value of M_W:

$$M_W = \left(\frac{\pi\alpha}{\sqrt{2}G_F}\right)^{1/2} \frac{1}{\sin\theta_W} \simeq \frac{37.28}{\sin\theta_W}\text{GeV} \simeq 77.73 \text{ GeV}. \qquad (22.77)$$

Similarly, using (22.42) we predict

$$M_Z = M_W/\cos\theta_W \simeq 88.58 \text{ GeV}. \qquad (22.78)$$

These predictions of the theory (at lowest order) indicate the power of the underlying symmetry to tie together many apparently unrelated quantities, which are all determined in terms of only a few basic parameters. We now present a number of other simple tree-level predictions.

The width for $W^- \rightarrow e^- + \bar{\nu}_e$ can be calculated using the vertex (22.48), with the result (problem 22.5)

$$\Gamma(W^- \rightarrow e^-\bar{\nu}_e) = \frac{1}{12}\frac{g^2}{4\pi}M_W = \frac{G_F}{2^{1/2}}\frac{M_W^3}{6\pi} \simeq 205 \text{ MeV}, \qquad (22.79)$$

using (22.77). The widths to $\mu^-\bar{\nu}_\mu, \tau^-\bar{\nu}_\tau$ are the same. Neglecting CKM flavour mixing among the two energetically allowed quark channels $\bar{u}d$ and $\bar{c}s$, their widths would also be the same, apart from a factor of 3 for the different colour channels. The total W width for all these channels will therefore be about nine times the value in (22.79), i.e. 1.85 GeV, while the branching ratio for $W \rightarrow e\nu$ is

$$B(e\nu) = \Gamma(W \rightarrow e\nu)/\Gamma(\text{total}) \simeq 11\%. \qquad (22.80)$$

In making these estimates we have neglected all fermion masses.

The width for $Z^0 \rightarrow \nu\bar{\nu}$ can be found from (22.79) by replacing $g/2^{1/2}$ by $g/2\cos\theta_W$, and M_W by M_Z, giving

$$\Gamma(Z^0 \rightarrow \nu\bar{\nu}) = \frac{1}{24}\frac{g^2}{4\pi}\frac{M_Z}{\cos^2\theta_W} = \frac{G_F}{2^{1/2}}\frac{M_Z^3}{12\pi} \simeq 152 \text{ MeV}, \qquad (22.81)$$

using (22.78). Charged lepton pairs couple with both c_L^l and c_R^l terms, leading (with neglect of lepton masses) to

$$\Gamma(Z^0 \rightarrow l\bar{l}) = \left(\frac{|c_L^l|^2 + |c_R^l|^2}{6}\right)\frac{g^2}{4\pi}\frac{M_Z}{\cos^2\theta_W}. \qquad (22.82)$$

The values $c_L^\nu = \frac{1}{2}, c_R^\nu = 0$ in (22.82) reproduce (22.81). With $\sin^2\theta_W \simeq 0.23$, we find

$$\Gamma(Z^0 \rightarrow l\bar{l}) \simeq 76.5 \text{ MeV}. \qquad (22.83)$$

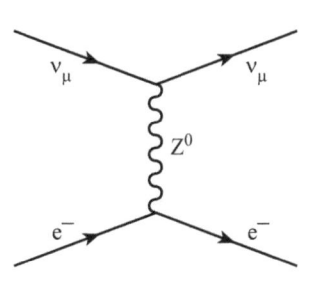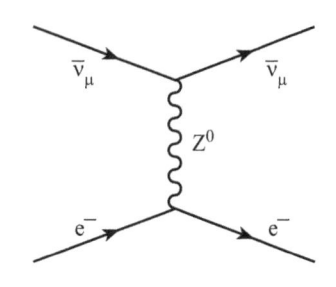

FIGURE 22.12
Neutrino-electron graphs involving Z^0 exchange.

Quark pairs couple as in (22.71), the GIM mechanism ensuring that all flavour-changing terms cancel. The total width to $u\bar{u}, d\bar{d}, c\bar{c}, s\bar{s}$ and $b\bar{b}$ channels (allowing 3 for colour and neglecting masses) is then 1538 MeV, producing an estimated total width of approximately 2.22 GeV. (QCD corrections will increase these estimates by a factor of order 1.1). The branching ratio to charged leptons is approximately 3.4%, to the three (invisible) neutrino channels 20.5%, and to hadrons (via hadronization of the $q\bar{q}$ channels) about 69.3%. In section 22.4.3 we shall see how a precise measurement of the total Z^0 width at LEP determined the number of light neutrinos to be 3.

Cross sections for neutrino–lepton scattering proceeding via Z^0 exchange can be calculated (for $k^2 \ll M_Z^2$) using the currents (22.59) and (22.60), and the method of section 20.5. Examples are

$$\nu_\mu e^- \to \nu_\mu e^- \tag{22.84}$$

and

$$\bar{\nu}_\mu e^- \to \bar{\nu}_\mu e^- \tag{22.85}$$

as shown in figure 22.12. Since the neutral current for the electron is not pure V–A, as was the charged current, we expect to see terms involving both $|c_L^l|^2$ and $|c_R^l|^2$, and possibly an interference term. The cross section for (22.84) is found to be ('t Hooft 1971c)

$$d\sigma/dy = (2G_F^2 E m_e/\pi)[|c_L^l|^2 + |c_R^l|^2(1-y)^2 - \frac{1}{2}(c_R^{l\,*} c_L^l + c_L^{l\,*} c_R^l)y m_e/E], \tag{22.86}$$

where E is the energy of the incident neutrino in the 'laboratory' system, and $y = (E-E')/E$ as before, where E' is the energy of the outgoing neutrino in the 'laboratory' system[2]. Equation (22.86) may be compared with the $\nu_\mu e^- \to \mu^- \nu_e$ (charged current) cross section of (20.84) by noting that $t = -2m_e E y$: the $|c_L^l|^2$ term agrees with the pure V–A result (20.84), while the $|c_R^l|^2$ term

---

[2] In the kinematics, lepton masses have been neglected wherever possible.

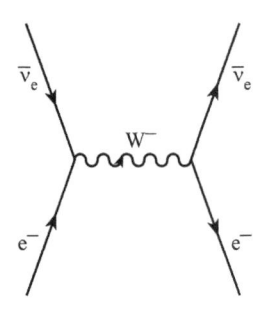

FIGURE 22.13
One-W annihilation graph in $\bar{\nu}_e e^- \to \bar{\nu}_e e^-$.

involves the same $(1 - y)^2$ factor discussed for $\nu \bar{q}$ scattering in section 20.7.2. The interference term is negligible for $E \gg m_e$. The cross section for the antineutrino process (22.85) is found from (22.86) by interchanging c_L^l and c_R^l.

A third neutrino–lepton process is experimentally available,

$$\bar{\nu}_e e^- \to \bar{\nu}_e e^-, \tag{22.87}$$

the cross section for which was measured by Reines, Gurr and Sobel (1976), using electron antineutrinos from an 1800-MW fission reactor at Savannah River. In this case there is a single W intermediate state graph, shown in figure 22.13, to consider as well as the Z^0 one; the latter is similar to the right-hand graph in figure 22.12, but with $\bar{\nu}_\mu$ replaced by $\bar{\nu}_e$. The cross section for (22.87) turns out to be given by an expression of the form (22.86), but with the replacements

$$c_L^l \to \frac{1}{2} + \sin^2 \theta_W, c_R^l \to \sin^2 \theta_W. \tag{22.88}$$

Reines, Gurr and Sobel reported the result $\sin^2 \theta_W = 0.29 \pm 0.05$.

We emphasize once more that all these cross sections are determined in terms of G_F, α and only one further parameter, $\sin^2 \theta_W$. As mentioned in section 20.9, experimental fits to these predictions are reviewed by Commins and Bucksbaum (1983), Renton (1990) and Winter (2000).

Particularly precise determinations of the Standard Model parameters were made at the $e^+ e^-$ colliders, LEP and SLC. Consider the reaction $e^+ e^- \to f \bar{f}$ where f is μ or τ, at energies where the lepton masses may be neglected in the final answers. In lowest order, the process is mediated by both γ-exchange and Z^0-exchange as shown in figure 22.14. Calculations of the cross section were made early on, by Budny (1973) for example. In modern notation, the differential cross section for the scattering of unpolarized e^- and e^+ is given by

$$\frac{d\sigma}{d\cos\theta} = \frac{\pi \alpha^2}{2s} [(1 + \cos^2 \theta) A + \cos\theta B] \tag{22.89}$$

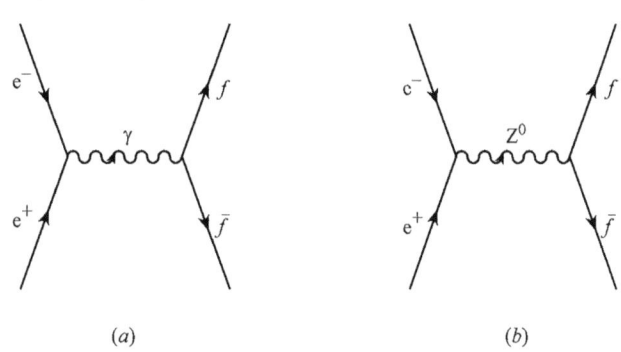

FIGURE 22.14
(a) One-γ and (b) one-W annihilation graphs in $e^+e^- \to f\bar{f}$.

where θ is the CM scattering angle of the final state lepton, $s = (p_{e^-} + p_{e^+})^2$, and

$$A = 1 + 2g_V^e g_V^f \mathrm{Re}\chi(s) + [(g_A^e)^2 + (g_V^e)^2][(g_A^f)^2 + (g_V^f)^2]|\chi(s)|^2 \quad (22.90)$$

$$B = 4g_A^e g_A^f \mathrm{Re}\chi(s) + 8g_A^e g_V^e g_A^f g_V^f |\chi(s)|^2 \quad (22.91)$$

$$\chi(s) = s/[4\sin^2\theta_W \cos^2\theta_W (s - M_Z^2 + i\Gamma_Z M_Z)]. \quad (22.92)$$

Notice that the term surviving when all the g's are set to zero, which is therefore the pure single photon contribution, is exactly as calculated in problem 8.18. The presence of the $\cos\theta$ term leads to the forward–backward asymmetry noted in that problem.

The forward–backward asymmetry A_{FB} may be defined as

$$A_{\mathrm{FB}} \equiv (N_F - N_B)/(N_F + N_B), \quad (22.93)$$

where N_F is the number scattered into the forward hemisphere $0 \leq \cos\theta \leq 1$, and N_B that into the backward hemisphere $-1 \leq \cos\theta \leq 0$. Integrating (22.89) one easily finds

$$A_{\mathrm{FB}} = 3B/8A. \quad (22.94)$$

For $\sin^2\theta_W = 0.25$ we noted after (22.64) that the g_V^l's vanish, so they are very small for $\sin^2\theta_W \simeq 0.23$. The effect is therefore controlled essentially by the first term in (22.91). At $\sqrt{s} = 29$ GeV, for example, the asymmetry is $A_{\mathrm{FB}} \simeq -0.063$.

This asymmetry was observed in experiments with PETRA at DESY and with PEP at SLAC (see figure 8.20(b)). These measurements, made at energies well below the Z^0 peak, were the first indication of the presence of Z^0 exchange in e^+e^- collisions.

However, QED alone produces a small positive A_{FB}, through interference between 1γ and 2γ annihilation processes (which have different charge conjugation parity), as well as between initial and final state bremsstrahlung corrections to figure 22.14(a). Indeed, *all* one-loop radiative effects must clearly be considered, in any comparison with modern high precision data.

At the CERN e^+e^- collider LEP, many such measurements were made 'on the Z peak', i.e. at $s = M_Z^2$ in the parametrization (22.92). In that case, $\mathrm{Re}\chi(s) = 0$, and (22.94) becomes (neglecting the photon contribution)

$$A_{\mathrm{FB}}(Z^0 \text{ peak}) = \frac{3g_A^e g_V^e g_A^f g_V^f}{\{[(g_A^e)^2 + g_V^e)^2][(g_A^f)^2 + (g_V^f)^2]\}}. \qquad (22.95)$$

Another important asymmetry observable is that involving the difference of the cross sections for left- and right-handed incident electrons:

$$A_{\mathrm{LR}} \equiv (\sigma_{\mathrm{L}} - \sigma_{\mathrm{R}})/(\sigma_{\mathrm{L}} + \sigma_{\mathrm{R}}), \qquad (22.96)$$

for which the tree-level prediction is

$$A_{\mathrm{LR}} = 2g_V^e g_A^e /[(g_V^e)^2 + (g_A^e)^2]. \qquad (22.97)$$

A similar combination of the g's for the final state leptons can be measured by forming the 'L–R F–B' asymmetry

$$A_{\mathrm{LR}}^{\mathrm{FB}} = [(\sigma_{\mathrm{LF}} - \sigma_{\mathrm{LB}}) - (\sigma_{\mathrm{RF}} - \sigma_{\mathrm{RB}})]/(\sigma_{\mathrm{R}} + \sigma_{\mathrm{L}}) \qquad (22.98)$$

for which the tree level prediction is

$$A_{\mathrm{LR}}^{\mathrm{FB}} = 2g_V^f g_A^f /[(g_V^f)^2 + (g_A^f)^2]. \qquad (22.99)$$

The quantity on the right-hand side of (22.99) is usually denoted by A_f:

$$A_f = 2g_V^f g_A^f /[(g_V^f)^2 + (g_A^f)^2]. \qquad (22.100)$$

The asymmetry A_{FB} is not, in fact, direct evidence for parity violation in $e^+e^- \to \mu^+\mu^-$, since we see from (22.90) and (22.91) that it is even under $g_A^l \to -g_A^l$, whereas a true parity-violating effect would involve terms odd (linear) in g_A^l. However, electroweak-induced parity violation effects in an apparently electromagnetic process were observed in a remarkable experiment by Prescott *et al.* (1978). Longitudinally polarized electrons were inelastically scattered from deuterium, and the flux of scattered electrons was measured for incident electrons of definite helicity. An asymmetry between the results, depending on the helicities, was observed – a clear signal for parity violation. This was the first demonstration of parity-violating effects in an 'electromagnetic' process; the corresponding value of $\sin^2\theta_{\mathrm{W}}$ was in agreement with that determined from ν data.

We now turn to some of the main experimental evidence, beginning with the discoveries of the $W^\pm$ and Z^0 1983.

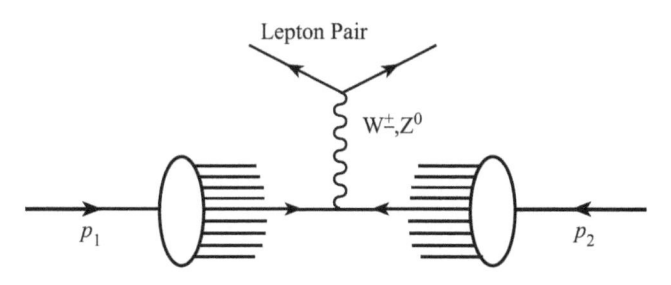

FIGURE 22.15
Parton model amplitude for W$^\pm$ or Z^0 production in p$\bar{\text{p}}$ collisions.

22.4 The discovery of the W$^\pm$ and Z^0 at the CERN p$\bar{\text{p}}$ collider

22.4.1 Production cross sections for W and Z in p$\bar{\text{p}}$ colliders

The possibility of producing the predicted W$^\pm$ and Z^0 particles was the principal motivation for transforming the CERN SPS into a p$\bar{\text{p}}$ collider using the stochastic cooling technique (Rubbia *et al.* 1977, Staff of the CERN $\bar{\text{p}}$p project 1981). Estimates of W and Z^0 production in p$\bar{\text{p}}$ collisions may be obtained (see, for example, Quigg 1977) from the parton model, in a way analogous to that used for the Drell–Yan process in section 9.4 with γ replaced by W or Z^0, as shown in figure 22.15 (cf figure 9.11), and for two-jet cross sections in section 14.3.2. As in (14.51), we denote by $\hat{s}$ the subprocess invariant

$$\hat{s} = (x_1 p_1 + x_2 p_2)^2 = x_1 x_2 s \qquad (22.101)$$

for massless partons. With $\hat{s}^{1/2} = M_W \sim 80$ GeV, and $s^{1/2} = 630$ GeV for the p$\bar{\text{p}}$ collider energy, we see that the x's are typically $\sim$0.13, so that the valence q's in the proton and $\bar{\text{q}}$'s in the antiproton will dominate (at $\sqrt{s} = 1.8$ TeV, appropriate to the Fermilab Tevatron, $x \simeq 0.04$ and the sea quarks contribute). The parton model cross section p$\bar{\text{p}} \to$ W$^\pm$+ anything is then (setting $V_{ud} = 1$ and all other $V_{ij} = 0$)

$$\sigma(\text{p}\bar{\text{p}} \to \text{W}^\pm + \text{X}) = \frac{1}{3} \int_0^1 \mathrm{d}x_1 \int_0^1 \mathrm{d}x_2 \hat{\sigma}(x_1, x_2) \left\{ \begin{array}{c} u(x_1)\bar{d}(x_2) + \bar{d}(x_1)u(x_2) \\ \bar{u}(x_1)d(x_2) + d(x_1)\bar{u}(x_2) \end{array} \right\}$$
$$(22.102)$$

where the $\frac{1}{3}$ is the same colour factor as in the Drell–Yan process, and the subprocess cross section $\hat{\sigma}$ for q$\bar{\text{q}} \to$ W$^\pm +$ X is (neglecting the W$^\pm$ width)

$$\begin{aligned} \hat{\sigma} &= 4\pi^2 \alpha (1/4 \sin^2 \theta_W) \delta(\hat{s} - M_W^2) & (22.103) \\ &= \pi 2^{1/2} G_F M_W^2 \delta(x_1 x_2 s - M_W^2). & (22.104) \end{aligned}$$

QCD corrections to (22.102) must as usual be included. Leading logarithms will make the distributions Q^2-dependent, and they should be evaluated at $Q^2 = M_W^2$. There will be further $(O(\alpha_s^2))$ corrections, which are often accounted for by a multiplicative factor 'K', which is of order 1.5–2 at these energies. $O(\alpha_s^2)$ calculations are presented in Hamberg *et al.* (1991) and by van der Neerven and Zijlstra (1992); see also Ellis *et al.* (1996) section 9.4. The total cross section for production of W$^+$ and W$^-$ at $\sqrt{s}$ =630 GeV is then of order 6.5 nb, while a similar calculation for the Z^0 gives about 2 nb. Multiplying these by the branching ratios gives

$$\sigma(\mathrm{p\bar{p}} \to \mathrm{W} + \mathrm{X} \to \mathrm{e}\nu\mathrm{X}) \quad \simeq \quad 0.7 \text{ nb} \qquad (22.105)$$

$$\sigma(\mathrm{p\bar{p}} \to \mathrm{Z}^0 + \mathrm{X} \to \mathrm{e^+e^-X}) \quad \simeq \quad 0.07 \text{ nb} \qquad (22.106)$$

at $\sqrt{s}$ =630 GeV.

The total cross section for p$\bar{\mathrm{p}}$ is about 70 mb at these energies: hence (22.105) represents $\sim 10^{-8}$ of the total cross section, and (22.106) is 10 times smaller. The rates could, of course, be increased by using the q$\bar{\mathrm{q}}$ modes of W and Z^0, which have bigger branching ratios. But the detection of these is very difficult, being very hard to distinguish from conventional two-jet events produced via the mechanism discussed in section 14.3.2, which has a cross section some 10^3 higher than (22.105). W and Z^0 would appear as slight shoulders on the edge of a very steeply falling invariant mass distribution, similar to that shown in figure 9.12, and the calorimetric jet energy resolution capable of resolving such an effect is hard to achieve. Thus despite the unfavourable branching ratios, the leptonic modes provide the better signatures, as discussed further in section 22.4.3.

22.4.2 Charge asymmetry in W$^\pm$ decay

At energies such that the simple valence quark picture of (22.102) is valid, the W$^+$ is created in the annihilation of a left-handed u quark from the proton and a right-handed $\bar{\mathrm{d}}$ quark from the $\bar{\mathrm{p}}$ (neglecting fermion masses). In the W$^+ \to \mathrm{e^+}\nu_\mathrm{e}$ decay, a right-handed e$^+$ and left-handed ν_e are emitted. Referring to figure 22.16, we see that angular momentum conservation allows e$^+$ production parallel to the direction of the antiproton, but forbids it parallel to the direction of the proton. Similarly, in W$^- \to \mathrm{e^-}\bar{\nu}_\mathrm{e}$, the e$^-$ is emitted preferentially parallel to the proton (these considerations are exactly similar to those mentioned in section 20.7.2 with reference to νq and $\bar{\nu}$q scattering). The actual distribution has the form $\sim (1 + \cos\theta_\mathrm{e}^*)^2$, where θ_e^* is the angle, in the rest frame of the W, between the e$^-$ and the p (for W$^- \to \mathrm{e^-}\bar{\nu}_\mathrm{e}$) or the e$^+$ and the $\bar{\mathrm{p}}$ (for W$^+ \to \mathrm{e^+}\nu_\mathrm{e}$).

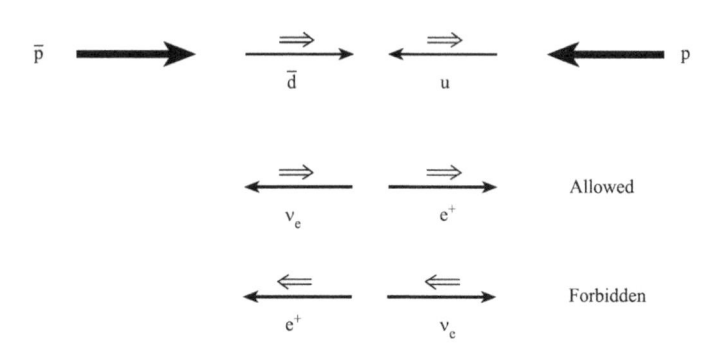

FIGURE 22.16
Preferred direction of leptons in W$^+$ decay.

22.4.3 Discovery of the W$^\pm$ and Z^0 at the p$\bar{\text{p}}$ collider, and their properties

As already indicated in section 22.4.1, the best signatures for W and Z production in p$\bar{\text{p}}$ collisions are provided by the leptonic modes

$$\text{p}\bar{\text{p}} \to \text{W}^\pm\text{X} \to \text{e}^\pm\nu\text{X} \qquad (22.107)$$
$$\text{p}\bar{\text{p}} \to \text{Z}^0\text{X} \to \text{e}^+\text{e}^-\text{X}. \qquad (22.108)$$

Reaction (22.107) has the larger cross section, by a factor of 10 (cf (22.105) and (22.106)), and was observed first (UA1, Arnison *et al.* 1983a; UA2, Banner *et al.* 1983). However, the kinematics of (22.108) is simpler and so the Z^0 discovery (UA1, Arnison *et al.* (1983b); UA2, Bagnaia *et al.* 1983) will be discussed first.

The signature for (22.108) is an isolated, and approximately back-to-back, e$^+$e$^-$ pair with invariant mass peaked around 90 GeV (cf (22.78)). Very clean events can be isolated by imposing a modest transverse energy cut – the e$^+$e$^-$ pairs required are coming from the decay of a massive relatively slowly moving Z^0. Figure 22.17 shows the transverse energy distribution of a candidate Z^0 event from the first UA2 sample. Figure 22.18 shows (Geer 1986) the invariant mass distribution for a later sample of 14 UA1 events in which both electrons have well measured energies, together with the Breit–Wigner resonance curve appropriate to $M_Z = 93$ GeV/c^2, with experimental mass resolution folded in. The UA1 result for the Z^0 mass was

$$M_Z = 93.0 \pm 1.4(\text{stat}) \pm 3.2(\text{syst.}) \ \text{GeV}. \qquad (22.109)$$

The corresponding UA2 result (DiLella 1986), based on 13 well measured pairs, was

$$M_Z = 92.5 \pm 1.3(\text{stat.}) \pm 1.5(\text{syst.}) \ \text{GeV}. \qquad (22.110)$$

In both cases the systematic error reflects the uncertainty in the absolute calibration of the calorimeter energy scale. Clearly the agreement with (22.78)

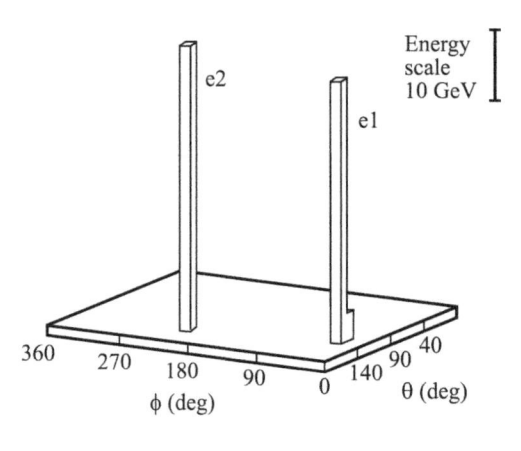

FIGURE 22.17
The cell transverse energy distribution for a $Z^0 \to e^+e^-$ event (UA2, Bagnaia
et al. 1983) in the θ and ϕ plane, where θ and ϕ are the polar and azimuth
angles relative to the beam axis.

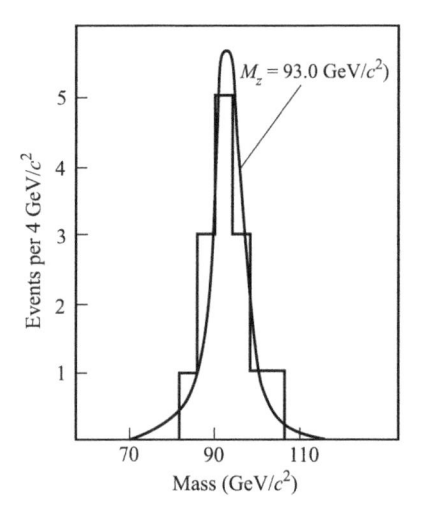

FIGURE 22.18
Invariant mass distribution for 14 well measured $Z^0 \to e^+e^-$ decays (UA1).
Figure reprinted with permission from S Geer in *High Energy Physics 1985,
Proc. Yale Theoretical Advanced Study Institute*, eds M J Bowick and F
Gursey; copyright 1986 World Scientific Publishing Company.

is good, but there is a suggestion that the tree-level prediction is on the low side. Indeed, loop corrections adjust (22.78) to a value $M_Z^{th} \simeq 91.19$ GeV, in excellent agreement with the current experimental value (Nakamura *et al.* 2010).

The total Z^0 width Γ_Z is an interesting quantity. If we assume that, for any fermion family additional to the three known ones, only the neutrinos are significantly less massive than $M_Z/2$, we have

$$\Gamma_Z \simeq (2.5 + 0.16\Delta N_\nu) \text{ GeV} \qquad (22.111)$$

from section 22.3, where ΔN_ν is the number of additional light neutrinos (i.e. beyond ν_e, ν_μ and ν_τ) which contribute to the width through the process $Z^0 \to \nu\bar{\nu}$. Thus (22.111) can be used as an important measure of the number of such neutrinos (i.e. generations) if Γ_Z can be determined accurately enough. The mass resolution of the $\bar{p}p$ experiments was of the same order as the total expected Z^0 width, so that (22.111) could not be used directly. The advent of LEP provided precision checks on (22.111); at the cost of departing from the historical development, we show data from DELPHI (Abreu *et al.* 1990, Abe 1991) in figure 22.19, which established $N_\nu = 3$.

We turn now to the $W^\pm$. In this case an invariant mass plot is impossible, since we are looking for the $e\nu$ ($\mu\nu$) mode, and cannot measure the ν's. However, it is clear that – as in the case of $Z^0 \to e^+e^-$ decay – slow moving massive W's will emit isolated electrons with high transverse energy. Further, such electrons should be produced in association with large *missing* transverse energy (corresponding to the ν's), which can be measured by calorimetry, and which should balance the transverse energy of the electrons. Thus electrons of high E_T accompanied by balancing high missing E_T (i.e. similar in magnitude to that of the e^- but opposite in azimuth) were the signatures used for the early event samples (UA1, Arnison *et al.* 1983a; UA2, Banner *et al.* 1983).

The determination of the mass of the W is not quite so straightforward as that of the Z, since we cannot construct directly an invariant mass plot for the $e\nu$ pair: only the missing transverse momentum (or energy) can be attributed to the ν, since some unidentified longitudinal momentum will always be lost down the beam pipe. In fact, the distribution of events in p_{eT}, the magnitude of the transverse momentum of the e^-, should show a pronounced peaking towards the maximum kinematically allowed value, which is $p_{eT} \approx \frac{1}{2}M_W$, as may be seen from the following argument. Consider the decay of a W at rest (figure 22.20). We have $|\boldsymbol{p}_e| = \frac{1}{2}M_W$ and $|\boldsymbol{p}_{eT}| = \frac{1}{2}M_W \sin\theta \equiv p_{eT}$. Thus the transverse momentum distribution is given by

$$\frac{d\sigma}{dp_{eT}} = \frac{d\sigma}{d\cos\theta}\left|\frac{d\cos\theta}{dp_{eT}}\right| = \frac{d\sigma}{d\cos\theta}\left(\frac{2p_{eT}}{M_W}\right)\left(\frac{1}{4}M_W^2 - p_{eT}^2\right)^{-1/2}, \qquad (22.112)$$

and the last (Jacobian) factor in (22.112) produces a strong peaking towards $p_{eT} = \frac{1}{2}M_W$. This peaking will be smeared by the width, and transverse motion, of the W. Early determinations of M_W used (22.112), but sensitivity

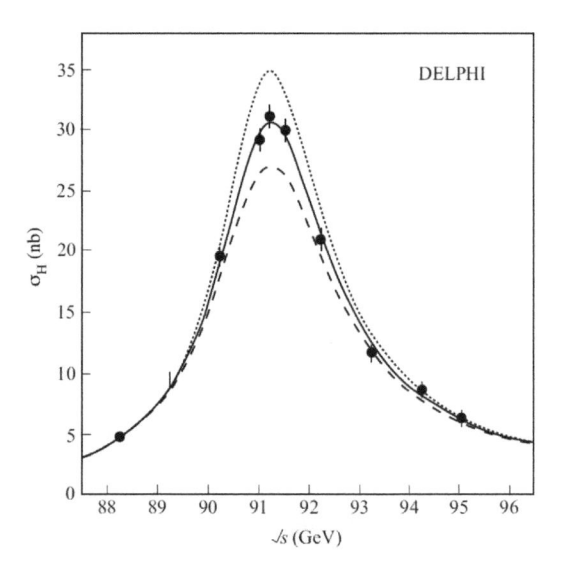

FIGURE 22.19

The cross-section for $e^+e^- \to$ hadrons around the Z^0 mass (DELPHI, 1990). The dotted, continuous and dashed lines are the predictions of the Standard Model assuming two, three and four massless neutrino species respectively. Figure reprinted with permission from K Abe in *Proc. 25th Int. Conf. on High Energy Physics* eds K K Phua and Y Yamaguchi; copyright 1991 World Scientific Publishing Company.

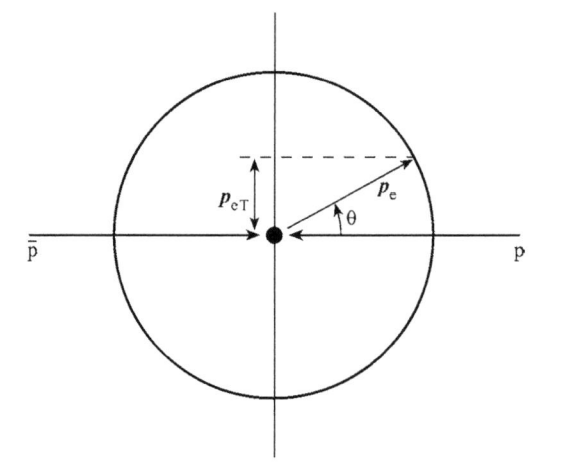

FIGURE 22.20

Kinematics of $W \to e\nu$ decay.

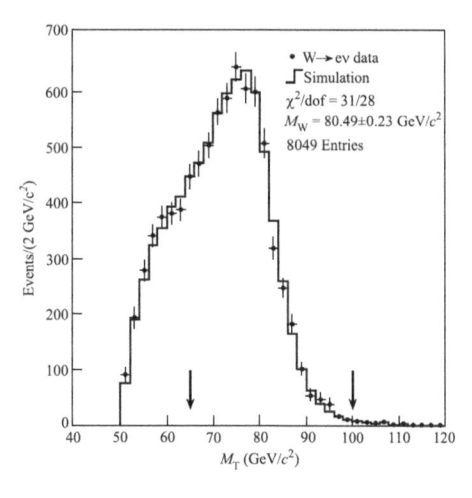

FIGURE 22.21

W $\rightarrow$ eν transverse mass distribution measured by the CDF collaboration. Figure reprinted with permission from F Abe *et al.* (CDF Collaboration) *Phys. Rev.* D **52** 4784 (1995). Copyright 1995 by the American Physical Society.

to the transverse momentum of the W can be much reduced (Barger *et al.* 1983) by considering instead the distribution in 'transverse mass', defined by

$$M_{\rm T}^2 = (E_{\rm eT} + E_{\nu \rm T})^2 - (\boldsymbol{p}_{\rm eT} + \boldsymbol{p}_{\nu \rm T})^2 \simeq 2p_{\rm eT}p_{\nu \rm T}(1 - \cos\phi), \qquad (22.113)$$

where ϕ is the azimuthal separation between $p_{\rm eT}$ and $p_{\nu \rm T}$. Here $E_{\nu \rm T}$ and $\boldsymbol{p}_{\rm T}$ are the neutrino transverse energy and momentum, measured from the missing transverse energy and momentum obtained from the global event reconstruction. This inclusion of additional measured quantities improves the precision as compared with the Jacobian peak method, using (22.112). A Monte Carlo simulation was used to generate $M_{\rm T}$ distributions for different values of $M_{\rm W}$, and the most probable value was found by a maximum likelihood fit. The quoted results were

$$\text{UA1 (Geer 1986):} \quad M_{\rm W} = 83.5 \pm^{1.1}_{1.0} \text{(stat.)} \pm 2.8\text{(syst.) GeV} \quad (22.114)$$
$$\text{UA2 (DiLella 1986):} \quad M_{\rm W} = 81.2 \pm 1.1\text{(stat.)} \pm 1.3\text{(syst.) GeV} \quad (22.115)$$

the systematic errors again reflecting uncertainty in the absolute energy scale of the calorimeters. The two experiments also quoted (Geer 1986, DiLella 1986)

$$\left.\begin{array}{ll} \text{UA1} & \Gamma_{\rm W} < 6.5 \text{ GeV} \\ \text{UA2} & \Gamma_{\rm W} < 7.0 \text{ GeV} \end{array}\right\} 90\% \text{ c.l.} \qquad (22.116)$$

Once again, the agreement between the experiments, and of both with (22.77), is good, the predictions again being on the low side. Loop corrections adjust

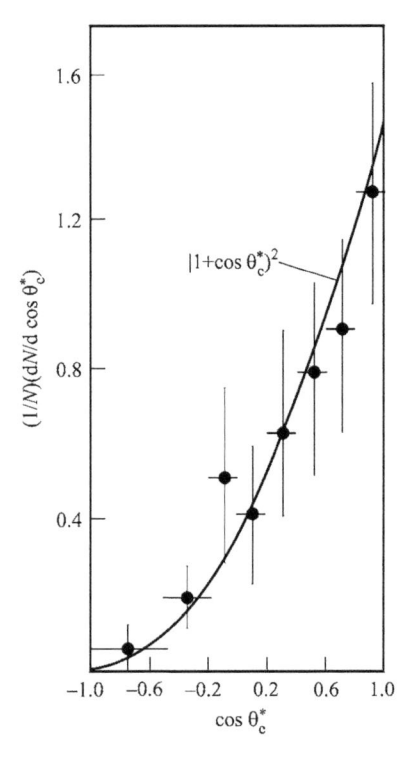

FIGURE 22.22

The W decay angular distribution of the emission angle θ_e^* of the positron (electron) with respect to the antiproton (proton) beam direction, in the rest frame of the W, for a total of 75 events; background subtracted and acceptance corrected (Arnison *et al.* 1986).

(22.77) to $M_W \simeq 80.38$ GeV (Nakamura *et al.* 2010). We show in figure 22.21 a later determination of M_W by the CDF collaboration (Abe *et al.* 1995a).

The W and Z mass values may be used together with (22.42) to obtain $\sin^2 \theta_W$ via

$$\sin^2 \theta_W = 1 - M_W^2/M_Z^2. \qquad (22.117)$$

The weighted average of UA(1) and UA(2) yielded

$$\sin^2 \theta_W = 0.212 \pm 0.022 \text{ (stat.)}. \qquad (22.118)$$

Radiative corrections have in general to be applied, but one renormalization scheme (see section 22.6) promotes (22.117) to a definition of the renormalized $\sin^2 \theta_W$ to all orders in perturbation theory. Using this scheme and quoted values of M_W, M_Z (Nakamura *et al.* 2010) one finds $\sin^2 \theta_W \simeq 0.223$.

Finally, figure 22.22 shows (Arnison *et al.* 1986) the angular distribution of the charged lepton in W $\rightarrow$ eν decay (see section 22.4.2); θ_e^* is the e$^+$(e$^-$) angle

in the W rest frame, measured with respect to a direction parallel (antiparallel) to the $\bar{\mathrm{p}}(\mathrm{p})$ beam. The expected form $(1 + \cos\theta_{\mathrm{e}}^*)^2$ is followed very closely.

In summary, we may say that the early discovery experiments provided remarkably convincing confirmation of the principal expectations of the GSW theory, as outlined in section 22.3.

We now consider some further aspects of the theory.

22.5 Fermion masses

22.5.1 One generation

The fact that the $SU(2)_L$ gauge group acts only on the L components of the fermion fields immediately appears to create a fundamental problem as far as the *masses* of these particles are concerned; we mentioned this briefly at the end of section 19.6. Let us recall first that the standard way to introduce the interactions of gauge fields with matter fields (e.g. fermions) is via the covariant derivative replacement

$$\partial^\mu \to D^\mu \equiv \partial^\mu + \mathrm{i}g\boldsymbol{\tau} \cdot \boldsymbol{W}^\mu/2 \tag{22.119}$$

for $SU(2)$ fields $\boldsymbol{W}^\mu$ acting on $t = 1/2$ doublets. Now it is a simple exercise (compare problem 18.3) to check that the ordinary 'kinetic' part of a free Dirac fermion does not mix the L and R components of the field:

$$\bar{\hat{\psi}} \, \slashed{\partial}\hat{\psi} = \bar{\hat{\psi}}_\mathrm{R} \, \slashed{\partial}\psi_\mathrm{R} + \bar{\hat{\psi}}_\mathrm{L} \, \slashed{\partial}\psi_\mathrm{L}. \tag{22.120}$$

Thus we can in principle contemplate 'gauging' the L and the R components differently. Of course, in the case of QCD (cf (18.39)) the replacement $\slashed{\partial} \to \slashed{D}$ was made equally in each term on the right-hand side of (22.120). But this was because QCD conserves parity, and must therefore treat L and R components the same. Weak interactions are parity violating, and the $SU(2)_L$ covariant derivative acts only in the *second* term of (22.120). On the other hand, a Dirac mass term has the form

$$-m(\bar{\hat{\psi}}_\mathrm{L}\hat{\psi}_\mathrm{R} + \bar{\hat{\psi}}_\mathrm{R}\hat{\psi}_\mathrm{L}) \tag{22.121}$$

(see equation (18.41) for example), and it precisely *couples* the L and R components. It is easy to see that if only $\hat{\psi}_\mathrm{L}$ is subject to a transformation, then (22.121) is not invariant. Thus mass terms for Dirac fermions will *explicitly* break $SU(2)_L$. The same is also true for Majorana fermions which might describe the neutrinos.

This kind of explicit breaking of the gauge symmetry cannot be tolerated, in the sense that it will lead, once again, to violations of unitarity, and then of

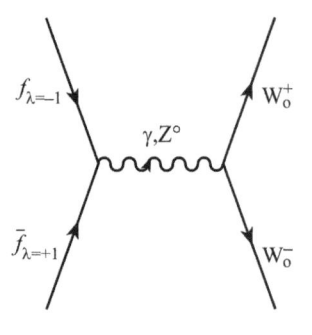

FIGURE 22.23
One-Z^0 and one-γ annihilation contribution to $f_{\lambda=-1}\bar{f}_{\lambda=1} \to W_0^+W_0^-$.

renormalizability. Consider, for example, a fermion–antifermion annihilation process of the form

$$f\bar{f} \to W_0^+W_0^-, \qquad (22.122)$$

where the subscript indicates the $\lambda = 0$ (longitudinal) polarization state of the $W^\pm$. We studied such a reaction in section 22.1.1 in the context of unitarity violations (in lowest-order perturbation theory) for the IVB model. Appelquist and Chanowitz (1987) considered first the case in which 'f' is a lepton with $t = \frac{1}{2}, t_3 = -\frac{1}{2}$ coupling to W's, Z^0 and γ with the usual $SU(2)_L \times U(1)$ couplings, but having an explicit (Dirac) mass m_f. They found that in the 'right' helicity channels for the leptons ($\lambda = +1$ for $\bar{f}, \lambda = -1$ for f) the bad high energy behaviour associated with a fermion-exchange diagram of the form of figure 22.4 was *cancelled* by that of the diagrams shown in figure 22.23. The sum of the amplitudes tends to a constant as s (or E^2) $\to \infty$. Such cancellations are a feature of gauge theories, as we indicated at the end of section 22.1.2, and represent one aspect of the renormalizability of the theory. But suppose, following Appelquist and Chanowitz (1987), we examine channels involving the 'wrong' helicity component, for example $\lambda = +1$ for the fermion f. Then it is found that the cancellation no longer occurs, and we shall ultimately have a 'non-renormalizable' problem on our hands, all over again.

An estimate of the energy at which this will happen can be made by recalling that the 'wrong' helicity state participates only by virtue of a factor (m_f/energy) (recall section 20.2.2), which here we can take to be $m_f/\sqrt{s}$. The typical bad high energy behaviour for an amplitude $\mathcal{M}$ was $\mathcal{M} \sim G_F s$, which we expect to be modified here to

$$\mathcal{M} \sim G_F s m_f/\sqrt{s} \sim G_F m_f \sqrt{s}. \qquad (22.123)$$

The estimate obtained by Appelquist and Chanowitz differs only by a factor of $\sqrt{2}$. Attending to all the factors in the partial wave expansion gives the result

that the unitarity bound will be saturated at $E = E_f$ (TeV) $\sim \pi/m_f$ (TeV). Thus for $m_t \sim 175$ GeV, $E_t \sim 18$ TeV. This would constitute a serious flaw in the theory, even though the breakdown occurs at energies beyond those currently reachable.

However, in a theory with spontaneous symmetry breaking, there is a way of giving fermion masses without introducing an explicit mass term in the Lagrangian. Consider the electron, for example, and let us hypothesize a 'Yukawa'–type coupling between the electron-type SU(2) doublet

$$\hat{l}_{\mathrm{eL}} = \begin{pmatrix} \hat{\nu}_{\mathrm{e}} \\ \hat{\mathrm{e}}^- \end{pmatrix}_{\mathrm{L}}, \tag{22.124}$$

the Higgs doublet $\hat{\phi}$, and the R-component of the electron field:

$$\hat{\mathcal{L}}^{\mathrm{e}}_{\mathrm{Yuk}} = -g_{\mathrm{e}}(\bar{\hat{l}}_{\mathrm{eL}}\hat{\phi}\hat{\mathrm{e}}_{\mathrm{R}} + \bar{\hat{\mathrm{e}}}_{\mathrm{R}}\hat{\phi}^{\dagger}\hat{l}_{\mathrm{eL}}). \tag{22.125}$$

In each term of (22.125), the two SU(2)$_{\mathrm{L}}$ doublets are 'dotted together' so as to form an SU(2)$_{\mathrm{L}}$ scalar, which multiplies the SU(2)$_{\mathrm{L}}$ scalar R-component. Thus (22.125) is SU(2)$_{\mathrm{L}}$-invariant, and the symmetry is preserved, at the Lagrangian level, by such a term. But now insert just the vacuum value (22.28) of $\hat{\phi}$ into (22.125): we find the result

$$\hat{\mathcal{L}}^{\mathrm{e}}_{\mathrm{Yuk}}(\mathrm{vac}) = -g_{\mathrm{e}}\frac{v}{\sqrt{2}}(\bar{\hat{\mathrm{e}}}_{\mathrm{L}}\hat{\mathrm{e}}_{\mathrm{R}} + \bar{\hat{\mathrm{e}}}_{\mathrm{R}}\hat{\mathrm{e}}_{\mathrm{L}}) \tag{22.126}$$

which is exactly a (Dirac) mass of the form (22.121), allowing us to make the identification

$$m_{\mathrm{e}} = g_{\mathrm{e}}v/\sqrt{2}. \tag{22.127}$$

When oscillations about the vacuum value are considered via the replacement (22.29), the term (22.125) will generate a coupling between the electron and the Higgs fields of the form

$$-g_{\mathrm{e}}\bar{\hat{\mathrm{e}}}\hat{\mathrm{e}}\hat{H}/\sqrt{2} = -(m_{\mathrm{e}}/v)\bar{\hat{\mathrm{e}}}\hat{\mathrm{e}}\hat{H} \tag{22.128}$$
$$= -(gm_{\mathrm{e}}/2M_{\mathrm{W}})\bar{\hat{\mathrm{e}}}\hat{\mathrm{e}}\hat{H}. \tag{22.129}$$

The presence of such a coupling, if present for the process $f\bar{f} \to \mathrm{W}^+_0\mathrm{W}^-_0$ considered earlier, will mean that, in addition to the f-exchange graph analogous to figure 22.4 and the annihilation graphs of figure 22.23, a further graph shown in figure 22.24, must be included. The presence of the fermion mass in the coupling to H suggests that this graph might be just what is required to cancel the 'bad' high energy behaviour found in (22.123) – and by this time the reader will not be surprised to be told that this is indeed the case.

At first sight it might seem that this stratagem will only work for the $t_3 = -\frac{1}{2}$ components of doublets, because of the form of $\langle 0|\hat{\phi}|0\rangle$. But we learned in section 12.1.3 that if a pair of states $\begin{pmatrix} u \\ d \end{pmatrix}$ forming an SU(2)

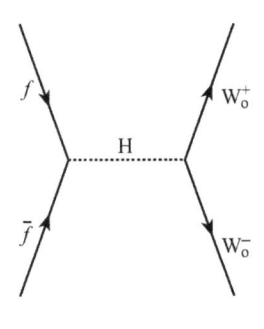

FIGURE 22.24
One-H annihilation graph.

doublet transform by

$$\left(\begin{array}{c} u \\ d \end{array} \right)' = e^{-i\boldsymbol{\alpha}\cdot\boldsymbol{\tau}/2} \left(\begin{array}{c} u \\ d \end{array} \right), \tag{22.130}$$

then the charge conjugate states $i\tau_2 \left(\begin{array}{c} u^* \\ d^* \end{array} \right)$ transform in exactly the same way. Thus if, in our case, $\hat{\phi}$ is the SU(2) doublet

$$\hat{\phi} = \left(\begin{array}{c} \frac{1}{\sqrt{2}}(\hat{\phi}_1 - i\hat{\phi}_2) \equiv \hat{\phi}^+ \\ \frac{1}{\sqrt{2}}(\hat{\phi}_3 - i\hat{\phi}_4) \equiv \hat{\phi}^0 \end{array} \right), \tag{22.131}$$

then the charge conjugate field

$$\hat{\phi}_{\mathbf{C}} \equiv i\tau_2\hat{\phi}^* = \left(\begin{array}{c} \frac{1}{\sqrt{2}}(\hat{\phi}_3 + i\hat{\phi}_4) \\ -\frac{1}{\sqrt{2}}(\hat{\phi}_1 + i\hat{\phi}_2) \end{array} \right) \equiv \left(\begin{array}{c} \hat{\bar{\phi}}^0 \\ -\hat{\phi}^- \end{array} \right) \tag{22.132}$$

is also an SU(2) doublet, transforming in just the same way as $\hat{\phi}$. ((22.131) and (22.132) may be thought of as analogous to the (K^+, K^0) and $(\bar{K}^0, K^-)$ isospin doublets in SU(3)$_f$). Note that the vacuum value (22.28) will now appear in the upper component of (22.132). With the help of $\hat{\phi}_{\mathbf{C}}$ we can write down another SU(2)-invariant coupling in the $\nu_e - e$ sector, namely

$$-g_{\nu_e}(\hat{\bar{l}}_{\mathrm{eL}}\hat{\phi}_{\mathbf{C}}\hat{\nu}_{\mathrm{eR}} + \hat{\bar{\nu}}_{\mathrm{eR}}\hat{\phi}_{\mathbf{C}}^\dagger \hat{l}_{\mathrm{eL}}), \tag{22.133}$$

assuming now the existence of the field $\hat{\nu}_{\mathrm{eR}}$. In the Higgs vacuum (22.28), (22.133) then yields

$$-(g_{\nu_e}v/\sqrt{2})(\hat{\bar{\nu}}_{\mathrm{eL}}\hat{\nu}_{\mathrm{eR}} + \hat{\bar{\nu}}_{\mathrm{eR}}\hat{\nu}_{\mathrm{eL}}) \tag{22.134}$$

which is precisely a (Dirac) mass for the neutrino, if we set $g_{\nu_e}v/\sqrt{2} = m_{\nu_e}$.

It is clearly possible to go on like this, and arrange for all the fermions, quarks as well as leptons, to acquire a mass by the same 'mechanism'. We will look more closely at the quarks in the next section. But one must admit to a certain uneasiness concerning the enormous difference in magnitudes represented by the couplings $g_{\nu_e}, \ldots g_e, \ldots g_t$. If $m_{\nu_e} < 1$ eV then $g_{\nu_e} < 10^{-11}$, while $g_t \sim 1$! Besides, whereas the use of the Higgs field 'mechanism' in the W–Z sector is quite economical, in the present case it seems rather unsatisfactory simply to postulate a different 'g' for each fermion–Higgs interaction. This does appear to indicate that we are dealing here with a 'phenomenological model', once more, rather than a 'theory'.

As far as the neutrinos are concerned, however, there is another possibility, already discussed in sections 7.5.2, 20.3 and 21.4.1, which is that they could be Majorana (not Dirac) fermions. In this case, rather than the four degrees of freedom (ν_{eL}, ν_{eR}, and their antiparticles) which exist for massive Dirac particles, only two possibilities exist for neutrinos, which we may take to be ν_{eL} and ν_{eR}. With these, it is certainly possible to construct a Dirac-type mass term of the form (22.134). But since, after all, the ν_{eR} component has been assigned zero quantum members both for SU(2)$_L$ W-interactions and for U(1) B-interactions (see table 22.1), we could consider economically dropping it altogether, making do with just the ν_{eL} component.

Suppose, then, that we keep only the field $\hat{\nu}_{eL}$. We need to form a mass term for it. The charge-conjugate field is defined by (see (7.151))

$$(\hat{\nu}_{eL})_C = i\gamma^2\gamma_0\bar{\hat{\nu}}_{eL}^T = i\gamma^2\hat{\nu}_L^{\dagger T}, \tag{22.135}$$

and we know that the charge-conjugate field transforms under Lorentz transformations in the same way as the original field. So we can use $(\hat{\nu}_{eL})_C$ to form a Lorentz invariant

$$\overline{(\hat{\nu}_{eL})_C}\, \nu_{eL} \tag{22.136}$$

which has mass dimension M^3. Hence we may write a mass term for $\hat{\nu}_{eL}$ in the form

$$-\frac{1}{2}m_M[\overline{(\hat{\nu}_{eL})_C}\,\hat{\nu}_{eL} + \bar{\hat{\nu}}_{eL}(\hat{\nu}_{eL})_C] \tag{22.137}$$

where the $\frac{1}{2}$ is conventional. Written out in more detail, we have

$$\overline{(\hat{\nu}_{eL})_C}\,\hat{\nu}_{eL} = \hat{\nu}_{eL}^T(-i\gamma^{2\dagger}\gamma_0)\hat{\nu}_{eL} = \hat{\nu}_{eL}^T i\gamma^2\gamma_0\hat{\nu}_{eL}, \tag{22.138}$$

in the representation (20.14). Now

$$i\gamma^2\gamma_0 = \begin{pmatrix} -i\sigma_2 & 0 \\ 0 & i\sigma_2 \end{pmatrix}. \tag{22.139}$$

But since $\hat{\nu}_{eL}$ is an L-chiral field, only its 2 lower components are present (cf (20.26)) and (22.138) is effectively

$$\overline{(\hat{\nu}_{eL})_C}\,\hat{\nu}_{eL} = \hat{\nu}_{eL}^T(i\sigma_2)\hat{\nu}_{eL}. \tag{22.140}$$

This is just the form of the mass term for a Majorana field, as we saw in equation (7.159). The two formalisms are equivalent.

As noted in section 21.4.1, the mass term (22.137) is not invariant under a global U(1) phase transformation

$$\hat{\nu}_{\text{eL}} \to e^{-i\alpha}\hat{\nu}_{\text{eL}} \tag{22.141}$$

which would correspond to lepton number (if accompanied by a similar transformation for the electron fields): the Majorana mass term violates lepton number conservation.

There is a further interesting aspect to (22.140) which is that, since two $\hat{\nu}_{\text{eL}}$ operators appear rather than a $\hat{\nu}_{\text{e}}$ and a $\hat{\nu}_{\text{e}}^{\dagger}$ (which would lead to L_{e} conservation), the (t, t_3) quantum numbers of the term are $(1,1)$. This means that we cannot form an SU(2)$_{\text{L}}$ invariant with it, using only the Standard Model Higgs $\hat{\phi}$, since the latter has $t = \frac{1}{2}$ and cannot combine with the $(1,1)$ operator to form a singlet. Thus we cannot make a 'tree-level' Majorana mass by the mechanism of Yukawa coupling to the Higgs field, followed by symmetry breaking.

However, we could generate suitable 'effective' operators via loop corrections, perhaps, much as we generated an effective operator representing an anomalous magnetic moment interaction in QED (cf section 11.7). But whatever it is, the operator would have to violate lepton number conservation, which is actually conserved by all the Standard Model interactions. Thus such an effective operator could not be generated in perturbation theory. It could arise, however, as a low energy limit of a theory defined at a higher mass scale, as the current–current model is the low energy limit of the GSW one. The typical form of such operator we need, in order to generate a term $\hat{\nu}_{\text{eL}}^{\text{T}}i\sigma_2\hat{\nu}_{\text{eL}}$, is

$$-\frac{g_{\text{eM}}}{M}(\hat{\bar{l}}_{\text{eL}}\hat{\phi}_{\text{C}})^{\text{T}}i\sigma_2(\hat{\phi}_{\text{C}}^{\dagger}\hat{l}_{\text{eL}}). \tag{22.142}$$

Note, most importantly, that the operator '$(l\phi)(\phi l)$' in (22.142) has mass dimension *five*, which is why we introduced the factor M^{-1} in the coupling; it is indeed a non-renormalizable effective interaction, just like the current–current one. We may interpret M as the mass scale at which 'new physics' enters, in the spirit of the discussion in section 11.7. Suppose, for the sake of argument, this was $M \sim 10^{16}$ GeV (a scale typical of Grand Unified Theories). After symmetry breaking, then, (22.142) will generate the required Majorana mass term, with

$$m_{\text{M}} \sim g_{\text{eM}}\frac{v^2}{M} \sim g_{\text{eM}}10^{-2} \text{ eV}. \tag{22.143}$$

Thus an effective coupling of 'natural' size $g_{\text{eM}} \sim 0.1$ emerges from this argument, if indeed the mass of the ν_{e} is of order 10^{-3}eV.

A more specific model can be constructed in which a relation of the form (22.143) can arise naturally. Suppose $\hat{\nu}_{\text{R}}$ is an R-type neutrino field which is an SU(2) $\times$ U(1) singlet, and which has a gauge-invariant Yukawa coupling

to the Higgs field, of the form (22.133). Then the Yukawa and the mass terms $\hat{\nu}_R$ are

$$\mathcal{L}_{Y,R} = -g_R(\bar{\hat{\ell}}_{eL}\hat{\phi}_C\hat{\nu}_R + \bar{\hat{\nu}}_R\hat{\phi}_C^\dagger\hat{\ell}_{eL}) - \frac{1}{2}m_R[\overline{(\hat{\nu}_R)_C}\,\hat{\nu}_R + \text{h.c.}]. \qquad (22.144)$$

Then, in the Higgs vacuum the first term in (22.144) becomes

$$-m_D(\bar{\hat{\nu}}_{eL}\hat{\nu}_R + \bar{\hat{\nu}}_R\hat{\nu}_{eL}) \qquad (22.145)$$

where $m_D = g_R v/\sqrt{2}$. The term (22.145) couples the fields $\hat{\nu}_R$ and $\hat{\nu}_{eL}$, so that we need to do a diagonalization to find the true mass eigenvalues and eigenstates. The combined mass terms from (22.144) and (22.145) can be written as

$$-\frac{1}{2}\overline{(\hat{N}_L)_C}\,\mathbf{M}\,\hat{N}_L + \text{h.c.} \qquad (22.146)$$

where

$$\hat{N}_L \equiv \begin{pmatrix} \hat{\nu}_{eL} \\ (\hat{\nu}_R)_C \end{pmatrix}, \quad \mathbf{M} = \begin{pmatrix} 0 & m_D \\ m_D & m_R \end{pmatrix}. \qquad (22.147)$$

CP invariance would imply that the parameters m_R and m_D are real, as we will assume, for simplicity.

Suppose now that $m_D \ll m_R$. Then the eigenvalues of $\mathbf{M}$ are approximately

$$m_1 \approx m_R, \quad m_2 \approx -m_D^2/m_R. \qquad (22.148)$$

The apparently troubling minus sign can be absorbed into the mixing parameters. Thus one eigenvalue is (by assumption) very large compared to m_D, and one is very much smaller. The vanishing of the first element in $\mathbf{M}$ ensures that the lepton number violating term (22.137) is characterized by a large mass scale m_R. It may be natural to assume that m_D is a 'typical' quark or lepton mass term, which would then imply that m_2 of (22.148) is very much lighter than that – as appears to be true for the neutrinos. This is the famous 'see-saw' mechanism of Minkowski (1977), Gell-Mann *et al.* (1979), Yanagida (1979) and Mohapatra and Senjanovic (1980, 1981). If in fact $m_R \sim 10^{16}$Gev, we recover an estimate for m_2 which is similar to that in (22.143). It is worth emphasizing that the Majorana nature of the massive neutrinos is an essential part of the see-saw mechanism.

These considerations are tending to take us 'beyond the Standard Model', so we shall not pursue them at any greater length. Instead, we must now generalize the discussion of fermion masses to the three-generation case.

22.5.2 Three-generation mixing

We introduce three doublets of left-handed quark fields

$$\hat{q}_{L1} = \begin{pmatrix} \hat{u}_{L1} \\ \hat{d}_{L1} \end{pmatrix}, \quad \hat{q}_{L2} = \begin{pmatrix} \hat{u}_{L2} \\ \hat{d}_{L2} \end{pmatrix}, \quad \hat{q}_{L3} = \begin{pmatrix} \hat{u}_{L3} \\ \hat{d}_{L3} \end{pmatrix} \qquad (22.149)$$

and the corresponding six singlets

$$\hat{u}_{R1}, \hat{d}_{R1}, \hat{u}_{R2}, \hat{d}_{R2}, \hat{u}_{R3}, \hat{d}_{R3}, \tag{22.150}$$

which transform in the now familiar way under $SU(2)_L \times U(1)$. The $\hat{u}$-fields correspond to the $t_3 = +\frac{1}{2}$ components of $SU(2)_L$, the $\hat{d}$ ones to the $t_3 = -\frac{1}{2}$ components, and to their 'R' partners. The labels 1, 2 and 3 refer to the family number; for example, with no mixing at all, $\hat{u}_{L1} = \hat{u}_L, \hat{d}_{L1} = \hat{d}_L$, etc. We have to consider what is the most general $SU(2)_L \times U(1)$–invariant interaction between the Higgs field (assuming we can still get by with only one) and these various fields. Apart from the symmetry, the only other theoretical requirement is renormalizability – for, after all, if we drop this we might as well abandon the whole motivation for the 'gauge' concept. This implies (as in the discussion of the Higgs potential $\hat{V}$) that we cannot have terms like $(\bar{\hat{\psi}}\hat{\psi}\hat{\phi})^2$ appearing – which would have a coupling with dimensions $(\text{mass})^{-4}$ and would be non-renormalizable. In fact the only renormalizable Yukawa coupling is of the form '$\bar{\hat{\psi}}\hat{\psi}\hat{\phi}$', which has a dimensionless coupling (as in the g_e and g_{ν_e} of (22.125) and (22.133)). However, there is no *a priori* requirement for it to be 'diagonal' in the weak interaction family index i. The allowed generalization of (22.125) and (22.133) is therefore an interaction of the form (summing on repeated indices)

$$\hat{\mathcal{L}}_{\psi\phi} = a_{ij}\bar{\hat{q}}_{Li}\hat{\phi}_C\hat{u}_{Rj} + b_{ij}\bar{\hat{q}}_{Li}\hat{\phi}\hat{d}_{Rj} + \text{h.c.} \tag{22.151}$$

where

$$\hat{q}_{Li} = \begin{pmatrix} \hat{u}_{Li} \\ \hat{d}_{Li} \end{pmatrix}, \tag{22.152}$$

and a sum on the family indices i and j (from 1 to 3) in (22.151) is assumed. After symmetry breaking, using the gauge (22.29), we find (problem 22.6)

$$\hat{\mathcal{L}}_{f\phi} = - \left(1 + \frac{\hat{H}}{v}\right)[\bar{\hat{u}}_{Li}m^u_{ij}\hat{u}_{Rj} + \bar{\hat{d}}_{Li}m^d_{ij}\hat{d}_{Rj} + \text{h.c.}], \tag{22.153}$$

where the 'mass matrices' are

$$m^u_{ij} = -\frac{v}{\sqrt{2}}a_{ij}, \qquad m^d_{ij} = -\frac{v}{\sqrt{2}}b_{ij}. \tag{22.154}$$

Although we have not indicated it, the m^u and m^d matrices could involve a 'γ_5' part as well as a '1' part in Dirac space. It can be shown (Weinberg 1973, Feinberg *et al.* 1959) that m^u and m^d can both be made Hermitean, γ_5-free, and diagonal by making four separate unitary transformations on the 'generation triplets'

$$\hat{u}_L = \begin{pmatrix} \hat{u}_{L1} \\ \hat{u}_{L2} \\ \hat{u}_{L3} \end{pmatrix}, \qquad \hat{d}_L = \begin{pmatrix} \hat{d}_{L1} \\ \hat{d}_{L2} \\ \hat{d}_{L3} \end{pmatrix}, \text{etc} \tag{22.155}$$

via

$$\hat{u}_{L\alpha} = (U_L^{(u)})_{\alpha i}\hat{u}_{Li}, \qquad \hat{u}_{R\alpha} = (U_R^{(u)})_{\alpha i}\hat{u}_{Ri} \qquad (22.156)$$

$$\hat{d}_{L\alpha} = (U_L^{(d)})_{\alpha i}\hat{d}_{Li}, \qquad \hat{d}_{R\alpha} = (U_R^{(d)})_{\alpha i}\hat{d}_{Ri}. \qquad (22.157)$$

In this notation, 'α' is the index of the 'mass diagonal' basis, and 'i' is that of the 'weak interaction' basis.[3] Then (22.153) becomes

$$\hat{\mathcal{L}}_{qH} = -\left(1 + \frac{\hat{H}}{v}\right)[m_u\bar{\hat{u}}\hat{u} + \ldots + m_b\bar{\hat{b}}\hat{b}]. \qquad (22.158)$$

Rather remarkably, we can still manage with only the one Higgs field. It couples to each fermion with a strength proportional to the mass of that fermion, divided by M_W.

Now consider the SU(2)$_L \times$U(1) gauge invariant interaction part of the Lagrangian. Written out in terms of the 'weak interaction' fields $\hat{u}_{L,Ri}$ and $\hat{d}_{L,Ri}$ (cf (22.43) and (22.44)), it is

$$\hat{\mathcal{L}}_{f,W,B} = i(\bar{\hat{u}}_{Lj}, \bar{\hat{d}}_{Lj})\gamma^\mu(\partial_\mu + ig\boldsymbol{\tau}\cdot\hat{\boldsymbol{W}}_\mu/2 + ig'y\hat{B}_\mu/2)\begin{pmatrix}\hat{u}_{Lj} \\ \hat{d}_{Lj}\end{pmatrix}$$

$$+ i\bar{\hat{u}}_{Rj}\gamma^\mu(\partial_\mu + ig'y\hat{B}_\mu/2)\hat{u}_{Rj} + i\bar{\hat{d}}_{Rj}\gamma^\mu(\partial_\mu + ig'y\hat{B}_\mu/2)\hat{d}_{Rj}$$

$$(22.159)$$

where a sum on j is understood. This now has to be rewritten in terms of the mass-eigenstate fields $\hat{u}_{L,R\alpha}$ and $\hat{d}_{L,R\alpha}$.

Problem 22.7 shows that the neutral current part of (22.159) is diagonal in the mass basis, provided the U matrices of (22.156) and (22.157) are unitary; that is, the neutral current interactions do not change the flavour of the physical (mass eigenstate) quarks. The charged current processes, however, involve the non–diagonal matrices τ_1 and τ_2 in (22.159), and this spoils the argument used in problem 22.7. Indeed, using (22.47) we find that the charged current piece is

$$\hat{\mathcal{L}}_{CC} = -\frac{g}{\sqrt{2}}(\bar{\hat{u}}_{Lj}, \bar{\hat{d}}_{Lj})\gamma_\mu\tau_+\hat{W}_\mu\begin{pmatrix}\hat{u}_{Lj} \\ \hat{d}_{Lj}\end{pmatrix} + \text{h.c.}$$

$$= -\frac{g}{\sqrt{2}}\bar{\hat{u}}_{Lj}\gamma^\mu\hat{d}_{Lj}\hat{W}_\mu + \text{h.c.}$$

$$= -\frac{g}{\sqrt{2}}\bar{\hat{u}}_{L\alpha}[(U_L^{(u)})_{\alpha j}(U_L^{(d)\dagger})_{j\beta}]\gamma^\mu\hat{d}_{L\beta}\hat{W}_\mu + \text{h.c.}, \qquad (22.160)$$

where the matrix

$$V_{\alpha\beta} \equiv [U_L^{(u)}U_L^{(d)\dagger}]_{\alpha\beta} \qquad (22.161)$$

is not diagonal, though it is unitary. This is the CKM matrix (Cabibbo

---

[3]So, for example, $\hat{u}_{L\alpha=t} \equiv \hat{t}_L$, $\hat{d}_{L\alpha=s} \equiv \hat{s}_L$, etc.

1963, Kobayashi and Maskawa 1973), originally introduced by Kobayashi and Maskawa in the context of their three-generation extension of the then-developing Standard Model, in order to provide room for **CP** violation within the SU(2) × U(1) gauge theory framework. The interaction (22.160) then has the form

$$-\frac{g}{\sqrt{2}}\hat{W}_\mu[\bar{\hat{u}}_L\gamma^\mu\hat{d}'_L + \bar{\hat{c}}_L\gamma^\mu\hat{s}'_L + \bar{\hat{t}}_L\gamma^\mu\hat{b}'_L] + \text{h.c.}, \qquad (22.162)$$

where

$$\begin{pmatrix} \hat{d}'_L \\ \hat{s}'_L \\ \hat{b}'_L \end{pmatrix} = \begin{pmatrix} V_{ud} & V_{us} & V_{ub} \\ V_{cd} & V_{cs} & V_{cb} \\ V_{td} & V_{ts} & V_{tb} \end{pmatrix} \begin{pmatrix} \hat{d}_L \\ \hat{s}_L \\ \hat{b}_L \end{pmatrix}, \qquad (22.163)$$

with the phenomenology described in the previous chapter.

An analysis similar to the above can be carried out in the leptonic sector. We would then have leptonic flavour mixing in charged current processes, via the leptonic analogue of the CKM matrix, namely the PMNS matrix (Pontecorvo 1957, 1958, 1967; Maki, Nakagawa and Sakata 1962); this is the matrix whose elements are probed in neutrino oscillations, as we saw in chapter 21.

22.6   Higher-order corrections

The Z^0 mass

$$M_Z = 91.1876 \pm 0.0021 \text{ GeV} \qquad (22.164)$$

has been determined from the Z-lineshape scan at LEP1 (Schael *et al.* 2006). The W mass is (Nakamura *et al.* 2010)

$$M_W = 80.399 \pm 0.023 \text{ GeV}. \qquad (22.165)$$

The asymmetry parameter A_e (see (22.100)) is (Abe *et al.* (2000))

$$A_e = 0.15138 \pm 0.00216 \qquad (22.166)$$

from measurements at SLD. These are just three examples from the table of 36 observables listed in the review of the electroweak model by Erler and Langacker in Nakamura *et al.* (2010). Such remarkable precision is a triumph of machine design and experimental art – and it is the reason why we need a renormalizable electroweak theory. The overall fit to the data, including higher-order corrections, is generally very good, as quoted by Erler and Langacker with $\chi^2/\text{d.o.f} = 43.0/44$. One of the few discrepancies is a 2.7σ deviation in the Z-pole forward-backward asymmetry $A_{\text{FB}}^{(0,b)}$ from LEP1; another is a 2.5σ deviation in the muon anomalous magnetic moment, $g_\mu - 2$. This strong numerical consistency lends impressive support to the belief that we

are indeed dealing with a *renormalizable spontaneously broken gauge theory*: renormalizable, because no extra parameters, not in the original Lagrangian, have had to be introduced; a gauge theory, because the fermion and gauge boson couplings obey the relations imposed by the local SU(2) × U(1) symmetry; and spontaneously broken because the same symmetry is not seen in the particle spectrum (consider the mass separation in the t-b doublet, for instance).

In fact, one can turn this around, in more than one way. First, one crucially important element in the theory – the Higgs boson – has a mass m_H which is largely unconstrained by theory (see section 22.8.2), and it is therefore a parameter in the fits. Some information about m_H can therefore be gained by seeing how the fits vary with m_H. Actually, we shall see in equation (22.181) that the dependence on m_H is only logarithmic – it acts rather like a cut-off, so the fits are not very sensitive to m_H. The 90 % central confidence range from all precision data is given by Erler and Langacker as 55 GeV$< m_H <$ 135 GeV. By contrast, some loop corrections are proportional to the square of the top mass (see (22.180)) and consequently very tight bounds could be placed on m_t via its *virtual* presence (i.e. in loops, for example as shown in figure 22.25) before its *real* presence was confirmed, as we shall discuss shortly and in section 22.7. Secondly, it is still entirely possible that very careful analysis of small discrepancies between precision data and electroweak predictions may indicate the presence of 'new physics'.

After all this (and earlier) emphasis on the renormalizability of the electroweak theory, and the introduction to one-loop calculations in QED at the end of volume 1, the reader perhaps has a right to expect, now, an exposition of loop corrections in the electroweak theory. But the fact is that this is a very complicated and technical story, requiring quite a bit more formal machinery, which would be outside the intended scope of this book (suitable references include Altarelli *et al.* 1989, especially the pedagogical account by Consoli *et al.* 1989; and the equally approachable lectures by Hollik 1991). Instead, we want to touch on just a few of the simpler and more important aspects of one-loop corrections, especially insofar as they have phenomenological implications.

As we have seen, we obtain cut-off independent results from loop corrections in a renormalizable theory by taking the values of certain parameters – those appearing in the original Lagrangian – from experiment, according to a well-defined procedure ('renormalization scheme'). In the electroweak case, the parameters in the Lagrangian are

$$\text{gauge couplings } g, g' \tag{22.167}$$

$$\text{Higgs potential parameters } \lambda, \mu^2 \tag{22.168}$$

$$\text{Higgs–fermion Yukawa couplings } g_f \tag{22.169}$$

$$\text{CKM angles } \theta_{12}, \theta_{13}, \theta_{23}; \text{ phase } \delta \tag{22.170}$$

$$\text{PMNS angles } \theta_{e2}, \theta_{e3}, \theta_{\mu3}, \text{ phase } \delta^\nu \ (+\ \alpha_{21}, \alpha_{31}?). \tag{22.171}$$

The fermion masses and mixings, and the Higgs mass, can be separated off, leaving g, g' and one combination of λ and μ^2 (for instance, the tree-level vacuum value v). These three parameters are usually replaced by the equivalent and more convenient set

$$\alpha \quad \text{(Bouchiendra \textit{et al.} 2011);} \tag{22.172}$$

$$G_{\rm F} \quad \text{(Marciano and Sirlin 1988, van Ritbergen and Stuart 1999),} \tag{22.173}$$

(see also Nir 1989, Pak and Czarnecki 2008, Chitwood $et\ al.$ 2007, and Barezyk $et\ al.$ 2008); and

$$M_{\rm Z} \quad \text{(Schael \textit{et al.} 2006).} \tag{22.174}$$

These are, of course, related to g, g' and v; for example, at tree-level

$$\alpha = g^2 g'^2/(g^2 + g'^2)4\pi, \quad M_{\rm Z} = \frac{1}{2} v \sqrt{g^2 + g'^2}, \quad G_{\rm F} = \frac{1}{\sqrt{2} v^2}, \tag{22.175}$$

but these relations become modified in higher order. The renormalized parameters will 'run' in the way described in chapters 15 and 16; the running of α, for example, has been observed directly, as noted in section 11.5.

After renormalization one can derive radiatively corrected values for physical quantities in terms of the set (22.172)–(22.174) (together with $m_{\rm H}$ and the fermion masses and mixings). But a renormalization scheme has to be specified, at any finite order (though in practice the differences are very small). One conceptually simple scheme is the 'on-shell' one (Sirlin 1980, 1984; Kennedy $et\ al.$ 1989; Kennedy and Lynn 1989; Bardin $et\ al.$ 1989; Hollik 1990; for reviews see Langacker 1995). In this scheme, the tree-level formula

$$\sin^2 \theta_{\rm W} = 1 - M_{\rm W}^2/M_{\rm Z}^2 \tag{22.176}$$

is promoted into a $definition$ of the renormalized $\sin^2 \theta_{\rm W}$ to all orders in perturbation theory, it being then denoted by $s_{\rm W}^2$:

$$s_{\rm W}^2 = 1 - M_{\rm W}^2/M_{\rm Z}^2 \approx 0.223. \tag{22.177}$$

The radiatively corrected value for $M_{\rm W}$ is then

$$M_{\rm W}^2 = \frac{(\pi \alpha/\sqrt{2} G_{\rm F})}{s_{\rm W}^2 (1 - \Delta r)} \tag{22.178}$$

where Δr includes the radiative corrections relating $\alpha, \alpha(M_{\rm Z}), G_{\rm F}, M_{\rm W}$ and $M_{\rm Z}$. Another scheme is the modified minimal subtraction ($\overline{\rm MS}$) scheme (appendix O) which introduces the quantity $\sin^2 \hat{\theta}_{\rm W}(\mu) \equiv \hat{g}'^2(\mu)/[\hat{g}'^2(\mu) + \hat{g}^2(\mu)]$ where the couplings $\hat{g}$ and $\hat{g}'$ are defined in the $\overline{\rm MS}$ scheme and μ is chosen to be $M_{\rm Z}$ for most electroweak processes. Attention is then focused on $\hat{s}_{\rm Z}^2 \equiv \sin^2 \hat{\theta}_{\rm W}(M_{\rm Z})$. This is the scheme used by Erler and Langacker in Nakamura $et\ al$ (2010).

We shall continue here with the scheme defined by (22.177). We cannot go into detail about all the contributions to Δr, but we do want to highlight two features of the result – which are surprising, important phenomenologically, and related to an interesting symmetry. It turns out (Consoli *et al.* 1989, Hollik 1991) that the leading terms in Δr have the form

$$\Delta r = \Delta r_0 - \frac{(1 - s_W^2)}{s_W^2}\Delta\rho + (\Delta r)_{\text{rem}}. \tag{22.179}$$

In (22.179), $\Delta r_0 = 1 - \alpha/\alpha(M_Z)$ is due to the running of α, and has the value $\Delta r_0 = 0.0664(2)$ (see section 11.5.3). $\Delta\rho$ is given by (Veltman 1977)

$$\Delta\rho = \frac{3G_F(m_t^2 - m_b^2)}{8\pi^2\sqrt{2}}, \tag{22.180}$$

while the 'remainder' $(\Delta r)_{\text{rem}}$ contains a significant term proportional to $\ln(m_t/m_Z)$, and a contribution from the Higgs boson which is (for $m_H \gg M_W$)

$$(\Delta r)_{\text{rem,H}} \approx \frac{\sqrt{2}G_F M_W^2}{16\pi^2}\frac{11}{3}\left[\ln\left(\frac{m_H^2}{M_W^2}\right) - \frac{5}{6}\right]. \tag{22.181}$$

As the notation suggests, $\Delta\rho$ is a leading contribution to the parameter ρ introduced in (22.66). As explained there, it measures the strength of neutral current processes relative to charged current ones. $\Delta\rho$ is then a radiative correction to ρ. It turns out that, to good approximation, electroweak radiative corrections in $e^+e^- \to Z^0 \to f\bar{f}$ can be included by replacing the fermionic couplings g_V^f and g_A^f (see (22.64), (22.75) and (22.76)) by

$$\bar{g}_V^f = \sqrt{\rho_f}(t_3^{(f)} - 2Q_f\kappa_f s_W^2) \tag{22.182}$$

and

$$\bar{g}_A^f = \sqrt{\rho_f}t_3^{(f)}, \tag{22.183}$$

together with corrections to the Z^0-propagator. The corrections have the form (in the on-shell scheme) $\rho_f \approx 1 + \Delta\rho$ (of equation (22.180)) and $\kappa_f \approx 1 + \frac{s_W^2}{(1-s_W^2)}\Delta\rho$, for $f \neq b, t$. For the b-quark there is an additional contribution coming from the presence of the virtual top quark in vertex corrections to $Z \to b\bar{b}$ (Akhundov *et al.* 1986, Beenakker and Hollik 1988).

The running of α in Δr_0 is expected, but (22.180) and (22.181) contain surprising features. As regards (22.180), it is associated with top-bottom quark loops in vacuum polarization amplitudes, of the kind discussed for $\bar{\Pi}_\gamma^{[2]}$ in section 11.5, but this time in weak boson propagators. In the QED case, referring to equation (11.39) for example, we saw that the contribution of heavy fermions '$(|q^2| \ll m_f^2)$' was suppressed, appearing as $O(|q^2|/m_f^2)$. In such a situation (which is the usual one) the heavy particles are said to 'decouple'. But the correction (22.180) is quite different, the fermion masses being in the

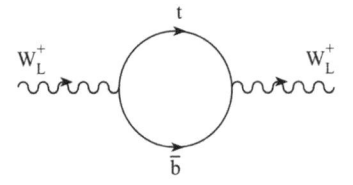

FIGURE 22.25

t - $\bar{\text{b}}$ vacuum polarization contribution.

numerator. Clearly, with a large value m_t, this can make a relatively big difference. This is why some precision measurements are surprisingly sensitive to the value of m_t, in the range near (as we now know) the physical value. Secondly, as regards the dependence on m_H, we might well have expected it to involve m_H^2 in the numerator if we considered the typical divergence of a scalar particle in a loop (we shall return to this after discussing (22.180)). Δr would then have been very sensitive to m_H, but in fact the sensitivity is only logarithmic.

We can understand the appearance of the fermion masses (squared) in the numerator of (22.180) as follows. The shift $\Delta\rho$ is associated with vector boson vacuum polarization contributions, for example the one shown in figure 22.25. Consider in particular the contribution from the longitudinal polarization components of the W's. As we have seen, these components are nothing but three of the four Higgs components which the $W^\pm$ and Z^0 'swallowed' to become massive. But the couplings of these 'swallowed' Higgs fields to fermions are determined by just the same Higgs-fermion Yukawa couplings as we introduced to generate the fermion masses via spontaneous symmetry breaking. Hence we expect the fermion loops to contribute (to these longitudinal W states) something of order $g_f^2/4\pi$ where g_f is the Yukawa coupling. Since $g_f \sim m_f/v$ (see (22.127)) we arrive at an estimate $\sim m_f^2/4\pi v^2 \sim G_F m_f^2/4\pi$ as in (22.180). An important message is that *particles which acquire their mass spontaneously do not 'decouple'.*

But we now have to explain why $\Delta\rho$ in (22.180) would vanish if $m_t^2 = m_b^2$, and why only $\ln m_H^2$ appears in (22.181). Both these facts are related to a symmetry of the assumed minimal Higgs sector which we have not yet discussed. Let us first consider the situation at tree level, where $\rho = 1$. It may be shown (Ross and Veltman 1975) that $\rho = 1$ is a natural consequence of having the symmetry broken by an $SU(2)_L$ doublet Higgs field (rather than a triplet, say) – or indeed by any number of doublets. The nearness of the measured ρ parameter to 1 is, in fact, good support for the hypothesis that there are only doublet Higgs fields. Problem 22.8 explores a simple model with a Higgs field in the triplet representation.

At tree level, it is simplest to think of ρ in connection with the mass ratio (22.66). To see the significance of this, let us go back to the Higgs-gauge field

Lagrangian $\hat{\mathcal{L}}_{G\Phi}$ of (22.30) which produced the gauge boson masses. With the doublet Higgs of the form (22.131), it is a striking fact that the Higgs potential only involves the highly symmetrical combination of fields

$$\hat{\phi}_1^2 + \hat{\phi}_2^2 + \hat{\phi}_3^2 + \hat{\phi}_4^2, \tag{22.184}$$

as does the vacuum condition (17.102). This suggests that there may be some extra symmetry in (22.30) which is special to the doublet structure. But of course, to be of any interest, this symmetry has to be present in the $(\hat{D}_\mu\hat{\phi})^\dagger(\hat{D}^\mu\hat{\phi})$ term as well.

The nature of this symmetry is best brought out by introducing a change of notation for Higgs doublet $\hat{\phi}^+$ and $\hat{\phi}^0$: instead of (22.131), we now write (cf (18.70))

$$\hat{\phi} = \begin{pmatrix} (\hat{\pi}_2 + i\hat{\pi}_1)/\sqrt{2} \\ (\hat{\sigma} - i\hat{\pi}_3)/\sqrt{2} \end{pmatrix} \tag{22.185}$$

while the $\hat{\phi}_{\text{C}}$ field of (22.132) becomes

$$\hat{\phi}_{\text{C}} = \begin{pmatrix} (\hat{\sigma} + i\hat{\pi}_3)/\sqrt{2} \\ -(\hat{\pi}_2 - i\hat{\pi}_1)/\sqrt{2} \end{pmatrix}. \tag{22.186}$$

We then find that these can be written as

$$\hat{\phi} = \frac{1}{\sqrt{2}}(\hat{\sigma} + i\boldsymbol{\tau} \cdot \hat{\boldsymbol{\pi}}) \begin{pmatrix} 0 \\ 1 \end{pmatrix}, \qquad \hat{\phi}_{\text{C}} = \frac{1}{\sqrt{2}}(\hat{\sigma} + i\boldsymbol{\tau} \cdot \hat{\boldsymbol{\pi}}) \begin{pmatrix} 1 \\ 0 \end{pmatrix}. \tag{22.187}$$

Consider now the covariant $SU(2)_L \times U(1)$ derivative acting on $\hat{\phi}$, as in (22.30), and suppose to begin with that $g' = 0$. Then

$$\begin{aligned}
\hat{D}_\mu\hat{\phi} &= \frac{1}{\sqrt{2}}(\partial_\mu + ig\boldsymbol{\tau} \cdot \hat{\boldsymbol{W}}_\mu/2)(\hat{\sigma} + i\boldsymbol{\tau} \cdot \hat{\boldsymbol{\pi}}) \begin{pmatrix} 0 \\ 1 \end{pmatrix} \\
&= \frac{1}{\sqrt{2}}\Big\{\partial_\mu\hat{\sigma} + i\boldsymbol{\tau} \cdot \partial_\mu\hat{\boldsymbol{\pi}} + i\frac{g}{2}\hat{\sigma}\boldsymbol{\tau} \cdot \hat{\boldsymbol{W}}_\mu \\
&\qquad - \frac{g}{2}[\hat{\boldsymbol{\pi}} \cdot \hat{\boldsymbol{W}}_\mu + i\boldsymbol{\tau} \cdot \hat{\boldsymbol{W}}_\mu \times \hat{\boldsymbol{\pi}}]\Big\} \begin{pmatrix} 0 \\ 1 \end{pmatrix} \tag{22.188}
\end{aligned}$$

using $\tau_i\tau_j = \delta_{ij} + i\epsilon_{ijk}\tau_k$. Now the vacuum choice (22.28) corresponds to $\hat{\sigma} = v, \hat{\boldsymbol{\pi}} = 0$, so that when we form $(\hat{D}_\mu\hat{\phi})^\dagger(\hat{D}^\mu\hat{\phi})$ from (22.188) we will get just

$$\frac{1}{2}(0, 1) \Big\{\frac{g^2}{4}v^2(\boldsymbol{\tau} \cdot \hat{\boldsymbol{W}}_\mu)(\boldsymbol{\tau} \cdot \hat{\boldsymbol{W}}^\mu)\Big\} \begin{pmatrix} 0 \\ 1 \end{pmatrix} = \frac{1}{2}M_W^2\hat{\boldsymbol{W}}_\mu \cdot \hat{\boldsymbol{W}}^\mu \tag{22.189}$$

with $M_W = gv/2$ as usual. The condition $g' = 0$ corresponds (cf (22.39)) to $\theta_W = 0$, and thus to $\hat{W}_{3\mu} = \hat{Z}_\mu$, and so (22.189) says that in the limit of $g' \to 0$, $M_W = M_Z$, as expected if $\cos\theta_W = 1$. It is clear from (22.188) that the three components $\hat{\boldsymbol{W}}_\mu$ are treated on a precisely equal footing by the

Higgs field (22.185), and indeed the notation suggests that $\hat{\boldsymbol{W}}_\mu$ and $\hat{\boldsymbol{\pi}}$ should perhaps be regarded as some kind of *new* triplets.

It is straightforward to calculate $(\hat{D}_\mu\hat{\phi})^\dagger(\hat{D}^\mu\hat{\phi})$ from (22.188); one finds (problem 22.9)

$$
\begin{aligned}
(D_\mu\hat{\phi})^\dagger D^\mu\hat{\phi} &= \frac{1}{2}(\partial_\mu\hat{\sigma})^2 + \frac{1}{2}(\partial_\mu\hat{\boldsymbol{\pi}})^2 - \frac{g}{2}\partial_\mu\hat{\sigma}\hat{\boldsymbol{\pi}}\cdot\hat{\boldsymbol{W}}^\mu \\
&+ \frac{g}{2}\hat{\sigma}\partial_\mu\hat{\boldsymbol{\pi}}\cdot\hat{\boldsymbol{W}}^\mu + \frac{g}{2}\partial_\mu\hat{\boldsymbol{\pi}}\cdot(\hat{\boldsymbol{\pi}}\times\hat{\boldsymbol{W}}^\mu) \\
&+ \frac{g^2}{8}\hat{\boldsymbol{W}}_\mu^2(\hat{\sigma}^2 + \hat{\boldsymbol{\pi}}^2).
\end{aligned}
\tag{22.190}
$$

This expression now reveals what the symmetry is: (22.190) is invariant under global SU(2) transformations under which $\hat{\boldsymbol{W}}_\mu$ and $\hat{\boldsymbol{\pi}}$ are vectors – that is

$$
\left.\begin{aligned}
\hat{\boldsymbol{W}}_\mu &\to \hat{\boldsymbol{W}}_\mu + \boldsymbol{\epsilon}\times\hat{\boldsymbol{W}}_\mu \\
\hat{\boldsymbol{\pi}} &\to \hat{\boldsymbol{\pi}} + \boldsymbol{\epsilon}\times\hat{\boldsymbol{\pi}} \\
\hat{\sigma} &\to \hat{\sigma}
\end{aligned}\right\}.
\tag{22.191}
$$

This is why, from the term $\hat{\boldsymbol{W}}_\mu^2\hat{\sigma}^2$, all three W fields have the same mass in this $g' \to 0$ limit.

If we now reinstate g', and use (22.36) and (22.37) to write $\hat{W}_{3\mu}$ and $\hat{B}_\mu$ in terms of the physical fields $\hat{Z}_\mu$ and $\hat{A}_\mu$ as in (19.96), (22.188) becomes

$$
\begin{aligned}
\frac{1}{\sqrt{2}}\Bigg\{ &\partial_\mu + ig\frac{\tau_1}{2}\hat{W}_{1\mu} + ig\frac{\tau_2}{2}\hat{W}_{2\mu} + ig\frac{\tau_3}{2}\frac{\hat{Z}_\mu}{\cos\theta_W} + ig\sin\theta_W\left(\frac{1+\tau_3}{2}\right)\hat{A}_\mu \\
&- \frac{ig}{\cos\theta_W}\sin^2\theta_W\left(\frac{1+\tau_3}{2}\right)\hat{Z}_\mu\Bigg\}(\hat{\sigma} + i\boldsymbol{\tau}\cdot\hat{\boldsymbol{\pi}})\begin{pmatrix}0\\1\end{pmatrix}.
\end{aligned}
\tag{22.192}
$$

We see from (22.192) that $g' \neq 0$ has two effects. First, there is a '$\boldsymbol{\tau}\cdot\hat{\boldsymbol{W}}$'– like term, as in (22.188), except that the '$\hat{W}_3$' part of it is now $\hat{Z}/\cos\theta_W$. In the vacuum $\hat{\sigma} = v, \hat{\boldsymbol{\pi}} = 0$ which simply means that the mass of the Z is $M_Z = M_W/\cos\theta_W$ i.e. $\rho = 1$; and this relation is preserved under 'rotations' of the form (22.191), since they do not mix $\hat{\boldsymbol{\pi}}$ and $\hat{\sigma}$. Hence this mass relation (and $\rho = 1$) is a consequence of the global SU(2) symmetry of the interactions and the vacuum under (22.191), and of the relations (22.36) and (22.37) which embody the requirement of a massless photon.

On the other hand, there are additional terms in (22.192) which single out the 'τ_3' component, and therefore break this global SU(2). These terms vanish as $g' \to 0$, and do not contribute at tree level, but we expect that they will cause $O(g'^2)$ corrections to $\rho = 1$ at the one loop level.

None of the above, however, yet involves the quark masses, and the question of why $m_t^2 - b_b^2$ appears in the numerator in (22.180). We can now answer this question. Consider a typical mass term, of the form discussed in section 22.5.2, for a quark doublet of the ith family

$$
\hat{\mathcal{L}}_m = -g_+(\bar{\hat{u}}_{Li}\bar{\hat{d}}_{Li})\hat{\phi}_C\hat{u}_{Ri} - g_-(\bar{\hat{u}}_{Li}\bar{\hat{d}}_{Li})\hat{\phi}\hat{d}_{Ri}.
\tag{22.193}
$$

Using (22.185) and (22.186), this can be written as

$$
\begin{aligned}
\hat{\mathcal{L}}_m &= \frac{-g_+}{\sqrt{2}}(\bar{\hat{u}}_{\mathrm{L}i}\bar{\hat{d}}_{\mathrm{L}i})(\hat{\sigma} + i\boldsymbol{\tau}\cdot\hat{\boldsymbol{\pi}})\begin{pmatrix}\hat{u}_{\mathrm{R}i}\\0\end{pmatrix} - \frac{g_-}{\sqrt{2}}(\bar{\hat{u}}_{\mathrm{L}i}\bar{\hat{d}}_{\mathrm{L}i})(\hat{\sigma}+i\boldsymbol{\tau}\cdot\hat{\boldsymbol{\pi}})\begin{pmatrix}0\\\hat{d}_{\mathrm{R}i}\end{pmatrix}\\
&= -\frac{(g_+ + g_-)}{2\sqrt{2}}(\bar{\hat{u}}_{\mathrm{L}i}\bar{\hat{d}}_{\mathrm{L}i})(\hat{\sigma}+i\boldsymbol{\tau}\cdot\hat{\boldsymbol{\pi}})\begin{pmatrix}\hat{u}_{\mathrm{R}i}\\\hat{d}_{\mathrm{R}i}\end{pmatrix}\\
&\quad - \frac{(g_+ - g_-)}{2\sqrt{2}}(\bar{\hat{u}}_{\mathrm{L}i}\bar{\hat{d}}_{\mathrm{L}i})(\hat{\sigma}+i\boldsymbol{\tau}\cdot\hat{\boldsymbol{\pi}})\tau_3\begin{pmatrix}\hat{u}_{\mathrm{R}i}\\\hat{d}_{\mathrm{R}i}\end{pmatrix}.
\end{aligned}
\tag{22.194}
$$

Consider now a simultaneous (infinitesimal) global SU(2) transformation on the two doublets $(\hat{u}_{\mathrm{L}i}, \hat{d}_{\mathrm{L}i})^{\mathrm{T}}$ and $(\hat{u}_{\mathrm{R}i}, \hat{d}_{\mathrm{R}i})^{\mathrm{T}}$:

$$
\begin{pmatrix}\hat{u}_{\mathrm{L}i}\\\hat{d}_{\mathrm{L}i}\end{pmatrix} \to (1 - i\boldsymbol{\epsilon}\cdot\boldsymbol{\tau}/2)\begin{pmatrix}\hat{u}_{\mathrm{L}i}\\\hat{d}_{\mathrm{L}i}\end{pmatrix}, \qquad \begin{pmatrix}\hat{u}_{\mathrm{R}i}\\\hat{d}_{\mathrm{R}i}\end{pmatrix} \to (1 - i\boldsymbol{\epsilon}\cdot\boldsymbol{\tau}/2)\begin{pmatrix}\hat{u}_{\mathrm{R}i}\\\hat{d}_{\mathrm{R}i}\end{pmatrix}.
\tag{22.195}
$$

Under (22.195), the first term of (22.194) becomes (to first order in $\boldsymbol{\epsilon}$)

$$
-\frac{(g_+ + g_-)}{2\sqrt{2}}(\bar{\hat{u}}_{\mathrm{L}i}\bar{\hat{d}}_{\mathrm{L}i})[\hat{\sigma} + i\boldsymbol{\tau}\cdot(\hat{\boldsymbol{\pi}} + \hat{\boldsymbol{\pi}}\times\boldsymbol{\epsilon})]\begin{pmatrix}\hat{u}_{\mathrm{R}i}\\\hat{d}_{\mathrm{R}i}\end{pmatrix}.
\tag{22.196}
$$

From (22.196) we see that if, at the same time as (22.195), we *also* make the transformation of $\boldsymbol{\pi}$ given in (22.191), then this first term in $\hat{\mathcal{L}}_m$ will be invariant under these combined transformations. The second term in (22.194), however, will not be invariant under (22.195), but only under transformations with $\epsilon_1 = \epsilon_2 = 0, \epsilon_3 \neq 0$. We conclude that the global SU(2) symmetry of (22.191), which was responsible for $\rho = 1$ at the tree level, can be extended also to the quark sector; but – because the $g_\pm$ in (22.193) are proportional to the masses of the quark doublet – this symmetry is explicitly broken by the quark mass difference. This is why a t–b̄ loop in a W vacuum polarization correction can produce the 'non-decoupled' contribution (22.180) to ρ, which grows as $m_{\mathrm{t}}^2 - m_{\mathrm{b}}^2$ and produces quite detectable shifts from the tree-level predictions, given the accuracy of the data.

Returning to (22.195), the transformation on the L-components is just the same as a standard SU(2)$_{\mathrm{L}}$ transformation, except that it is global; so the gauge interactions of the quarks obey this symmetry also. As far as the R-components are concerned, they are totally decoupled in the gauge dynamics, and we are free to make the transformation (22.195) if we wish. The resulting complete transformation, which does the same to both the L and R components, is a non-chiral one – in fact it is precisely an ordinary 'isospin' transformation of the type

$$
\begin{pmatrix}\hat{u}_i\\\hat{d}_i\end{pmatrix} \to (1 - i\boldsymbol{\epsilon}\cdot\boldsymbol{\tau}/2)\begin{pmatrix}\hat{u}_i\\\hat{d}_i\end{pmatrix}.
\tag{22.197}
$$

The reader will recognize that the mathematics here is exactly the same as that in section 18.3, involving the SU(2) of isospin in the σ-model. This

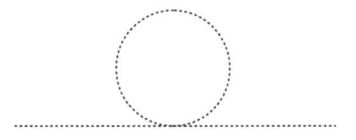

FIGURE 22.26
One-boson self-energy graph in $(\hat{\phi}^\dagger \hat{\phi})^2$.

analysis of the symmetry of the Higgs (or a more general symmetry breaking sector) was first given by Sikivie *et al.* (1980). The isospin-SU(2) is frequently called 'custodial SU(2)' since it 'protects' $\rho = 1$.

What about the *absence* of m_H^2 corrections? Here the position is rather more subtle. Without the Higgs particle H the theory is non-renormalizable, and hence one might expect to see some radiative correction becoming very large $(O(m_H^2))$ as one tried to 'banish' H from theory by sending $m_H \to \infty$ (m_H would be acting like a cut-off). The reason is that in such a $(\hat{\phi}^\dagger \hat{\phi})^2$ theory, the simplest loop we meet is that shown in figure 22.18, and it is easy to see by counting powers, as usual, that it diverges as the square of the cut-off. This loop contributes to the Higgs self-energy, and will be renormalized by taking the value of the coefficient of $\hat{\phi}^\dagger \hat{\phi}$ in (22.30) from experiment. We will return to this particular detail in section 22.8.1.

Even without a Higgs contribution however, it turns out that the electroweak theory is renormalizable at the one-loop level if the fermion masses are zero (Veltman 1968,1970). Thus one suspects that the large m_H^2 effects will not be so dramatic after all. In fact, calculation shows (Veltman 1977; Chanowitz *et al.* 1978, 1979) that one-loop radiative corrections to electroweak observables grow at most like $\ln m_H^2$ for large m_H. While there are finite corrections which are approximately $O(m_H^2)$ for $m_H^2 \ll M_{W,Z}^2$, for $m_H^2 \gg M_{W,Z}^2$ the $O(m_H^2)$ pieces cancel out from all observable quantities[4], leaving only $\ln m_H^2$ terms. This is just what we have in (22.181), and it means, unfortunately, that the sensitivity of the data to this important parameter of the Standard Model is only logarithmic. Fits to data typically give m_H in the region of 90 GeV at the minimum of the χ^2 curve, but the error (which is not simple to interpret) is of the order of 25 GeV.

At the two-loop level, the expected $O(m_H^4)$ behaviour becomes $O(m_H^2)$ instead (van der Bij and Veltman 1984, van der Bij 1984) – and of course appears (relative to the one-loop contributions) with an additional factor of $O(\alpha)$. This relative insensitivity of the radiative corrections to m_H, in the limit of large m_H, was discovered by Veltman (1977) and called a 'screening' phenomenon by him: for large m_H (which also means, as we have seen, large λ) we have an effectively strongly interacting theory whose principal effects are

---

[4]Apart from the $\hat{\phi}^\dagger \hat{\phi}$ coefficient! See section 22.8.1.

screened off from observables at lower energy. It was shown by Einhorn and Wudka (1989) that this screening is also a consequence of the (approximate) isospin-SU(2) symmetry we have just discussed in connection with (22.180). Phenomenologically, the upshot is that it was unfortunately very difficult to get an accurate handle on the value of m_H from fits to the precision data. With the top quark, the situation was very different.

22.7 The top quark

Having drawn attention to the relative sensitivity of radiative connections to loops containing virtual top quarks, it is worth devoting a little space to a 'backward glance' at the year immediately prior to the discovery of the t-quark (Abe *et al.* 1994a, b, 1995b, Abachi *et al.* 1995b) at the CDF and D0 detectors at FNAL's Tevatron, in p $-$ p̄ collisions at $E_{cm} = 1.8$ TeV.

The W and Z particles were, as we have seen, discovered in 1983 and at that time, and for some years subsequently, the data were not precise enough to be sensitive to virtual t-effects. In the late 1980's and early 1990's, LEP at CERN and SLC at Stanford began to produce new and highly accurate data which did allow increasingly precise predictions to be made for the top quark mass, m_t. Thus a kind of race began, between experimentalists searching for the real top, and theorists fitting ever more precise data to get tighter and tighter limits on m_t, from its virtual effects.

In fact, by the time of the actual experimental discovery of the top quark, the experimental error in m_t was just about the same as the theoretical one (and – of course – the central values were consistent). Thus, in their May 1994 review of the electroweak theory (contained in Montanet *et al.* 1994, p 1304ff) Erler and Langacker gave the result of a fit to all electroweak data as

$$m_t = 169 \pm^{16}_{18} \pm^{17}_{20} \text{ GeV}, \tag{22.198}$$

the central figure and first error being based on $m_H = 300$ GeV, the second (+) error assuming $m_H = 1000$ GeV and the second (−) error assuming $m_H = 60$ GeV.[5] At about the same time, Ellis *et al.* (1994) gave the extraordinarily precise value

$$m_t = 162 \pm 9 \text{ GeV} \tag{22.199}$$

without any assumption for m_H.

A month or so earlier, the CDF collaboration (Abe *et al.* 1994a,b) announced 12 events consistent with the hypothesis of production of a tt̄ pair, and on this hypothesis the mass was found to be

$$m_t = 174 \pm 10 \pm^{13}_{12} \text{ GeV}, \tag{22.200}$$

---

[5]The relatively small effect of large variations in m_H illustrates the lack of sensitivity to virtual Higgs effects, noted in the preceding section.

and this was followed by nine similar events from D0 (Abachi *et al.* 1995a). By February 1995 both groups had amassed more data and the discovery was announced (Abe *et al.* 1995b, Abachi *et al.* 1995b). The 2010 experimental value for m_t is 173.1±1.3 GeV (Nakamura *et al.* 2010) as compared to the value predicted by fits to the electroweak data of 173.2±1.3 GeV. This represents an extraordinary triumph for both theory and experiment. It is surely remarkable how the quantum fluctuations of a yet-to-be-detected new particle could pin down its mass so precisely. It seems hard to deny that Nature has indeed made use of the subtle intricacies of a spontaneously broken non-Abelian gauge theory.

One feature of the 'real' top events in particularly noteworthy. Unlike the mass of the other quarks, m_t is greater than M_W, and this means that it can decay to b + W via *real* W emission:

$$t \to W^+ + b. \tag{22.201}$$

In contrast, the b quark itself decays by the usual *virtual* W processes. Now we have seen that the virtual process is supressed by $\sim 1/M_W^2$ if the energy release (as in the case of b-decay) is well below M_W. But the real process (22.201) suffers no such suppression and proceeds very much faster. In fact (problem 22.10) the top quark lifetime from (22.201) is estimated to be $\sim 4 \times 10^{-25}$ s! This is quite similar to the lifetime of the W^+ itself, via $W^+ \to e^+ \nu_e$ for example. Consider now the production of a $t\bar{t}$ pair in the collision between two partons. As the t and $\bar{t}$ separate, the strong interactions which should eventually 'hadronize' them will not play a role until they are ~ 1 fm apart. But if they are travelling close to the speed of light, they can only travel some 10^{-16} m before decaying. Thus t's tend to decay before they experience the confining QCD interactions, a point we also made in section 1.2. Instead, the hadronization is associated with the b quark, which has a more typical weak lifetime ($\sim 1.5 \times 10^{-12}$ s). By the same token, this fast decay of the t quark means that there will be no detectable $t\bar{t}$ 'toponium', bound by QCD.

With the t quark safely real, the Higgs boson was the one remaining missing particle in the Standard Model complement, and its discovery was of the utmost importance. We end this book with a brief review of Higgs physics and the experiments leading to the probable discovery of this long-awaited particle in 2012.

22.8   The Higgs sector

It is worth noting that an essential feature of the type of theory which has been described in this note is the prediction of incomplete multiplets of scalar and vector bosons.

—P W Higgs (1964)

22.8.1 Introduction

The Lagrangian for an *unbroken* $SU(2)_L \times U(1)$ gauge theory of vector bosons and fermions is rather simple and elegant, all the interactions being determined by just two Lagrangian parameters g and g' in a 'universal' way. All the particles in this hypothetical world are, however, massless. In the real world, while the electroweak interactions are undoubtedly well described by the $SU(2)_L \times U(1)$ theory, neither the mediating gauge quanta (apart from the photon) nor the fermions are massless. They must acquire mass in some way that does not break the gauge symmetry of the Lagrangian, or else the renormalizability of the theory is destroyed, and its remarkable empirical success (at a level which includes loop corrections) would be some kind of freak accident. In chapter 19 we discussed how such a breaking of a gauge symmetry does happen, dynamically, in a superconductor. In that case 'electron pairing' was a crucial ingredient. In particle physics, while a lot of effort has gone into examining various analogous 'dynamical symmetry breaking' theories, none has yet emerged as both theoretically compelling and phenomenologically viable. However, a simple count of the number of degrees of freedom in a massive vector field, as opposed to a massless one, indicates that *some* additional fields must be present in order to give mass to the originally massless gauge bosons. And so, in the Standard Model, it is simply *assumed*, following the original ideas of Higgs and others (Higgs 1984, Englert and Brout 1964, Guralnik *et al.* 1964; Higgs 1966) that a suitable scalar ('Higgs') field exists, with a potential which causes the ground state (the vacuum) to break the symmetry spontaneously. Furthermore, rather than (as in BCS theory) obtaining the fermion mass gaps dynamically, they too are put in 'by hand' via Yukawa-like couplings to the Higgs field.

It has to be admitted that this part of the Standard Model appears to be the least satisfactory. Consider the Higgs couplings, which are listed in appendix Q, section Q.2.3. While the couplings of the Higgs field to the gauge fields are all determined by the gauge symmetry, the Higgs self-couplings (trilinear and quadrilinear) are not gauge interactions and are unrelated to anything else in the theory. Likewise, the Yukawa-like fermion couplings are not gauge interactions either, and they are both unconstrained and uncomfortably different in orders of magnitude. True, all these are renormalizable couplings – but this basically means that their values are not calculable and have all to be taken from experiment.

Such considerations may indicate that the 'Higgs Sector' of the Standard Model is on a somewhat different footing from the rest of it – a commonly held view, indeed. Perhaps it should be regarded as more a 'phenomenology' than a 'theory', much as the current–current model was. In this connection, we may mention a point which has long worried many theorists. In section 22.6 we noted that figure 22.26 gives a quadratically divergent ($O(\Lambda^2)$) and positive contribution to the $\hat{\phi}^\dagger \hat{\phi}$ term in the Lagrangian, at one loop order. This term would ordinarily, of course, be just the mass term of the scalar field. But in

the Higgs case, the matter is much more delicate. The whole phenomenology depends on the renormalized coefficient having a *negative* value, triggering the spontaneous breaking of the symmetry. This means that the $O(\Lambda^2)$ one-loop correction must be cancelled by the 'bare' mass term $\frac{1}{2}m_{\mathrm{H},0}^2\hat{\phi}^\dagger\hat{\phi}$ so as to achieve a negative coefficient of order $-v^2$. This cancellation between $m_{\mathrm{H},0}^2$ and Λ^2 will have to be very precise indeed if Λ – the scale of 'new physics' – is very high, as is commonly assumed (say 10^{16} GeV).

The reader may wonder why attention should *now* be drawn to this particular piece of renormalization: aren't all divergences handled this way? In a sense they are, but the fact is that this is the first case we have had in which we have to cancel a *quadratic* divergence. The other mass-corrections have all been logarithmic, for which there is nothing like such a dramatic 'fine-tuning' problem. There is a good reason for this in the case of the electron mass, which we remarked on in section 11.2. Chiral symmetry forces self-energy corrections for fermions to be proportional to their mass, and hence to contain only logarithms of the cut-off. Similarly, gauge invariance for the vector bosons prohibits any $O(\Lambda^2)$ connections in perturbation theory. But there is no symmetry, within the Standard Model, which 'protects' the coefficient of $\hat{\phi}^\dagger\hat{\phi}$ in this way. It is hard to understand what can be stopping it from being of order Λ^2, if we take the apparently reasonable point of view that the Standard Model will ultimately fail at some scale Λ where new physics enters. Thus the difficulty is: why is the empirical parameter v 'shielded' from the presumed high scale of new physics? This 'problem' is often referred to as the 'hierarchy problem', or the 'fine-tuning problem'. We stress again that we are dealing here with an absolutely crucial symmetry-breaking term, which one would really like to understand far better.

Of course, the problem would go away if the scale Λ were as low as, say a few TeV. As we shall see in the next section this happens to be, not accidentally, the same scale at which the Standard Model ceases to be a perturbatively calculable theory. Various possibilities have been suggested for the kind of physics that might enter at energies of a few TeV. For example, 'technicolour' models (Peskin 1997) regard the Higgs field as a composite of some new heavy fermions, rather like the BCS-pairing idea referred to earlier. A second possibility is supersymmetry (Aitchison 2007), in which there is a 'protective' symmetry operating, since scalar fields can be put alongside fermions in supermultiplets, and benefit from the protection enjoyed by the fermions. A third possibility is that of 'large' extra dimensions (Antoniadis 2002).

These undoubtedly fascinating ideas obviously take us well beyond our proper subject to which we must now return. Whatever may lie 'beyond' it, the Lagrangian of the Higgs sector of the Standard Model leads to many perfectly definite predictions which may be confronted with experiment, as we shall briefly discuss in section 22.8.3 (for a full account see Dawson *et al.* 1990, and for more compact ones see Ellis, Stirling and Webber 1996, chapter 11, and the review by Bernardi, Carena and Junk in Beringer *et al.* 2012). The

elucidation of the mechanism of gauge symmetry breaking is undoubtedly of the greatest importance to particle physics: quite apart from the $SU(2)_L \times U(1)$ theory, very many of the proposed theories which go 'beyond the Standard Model' face a similar 'mass problem', and generally appeal to some variant of the 'Higgs mechanism' to deal with it.

As Higgs noted in the final paragraph of his 2-page Letter (Higgs 1964), an essential feature of the spontaneous symmetry breaking mechanism, in a gauge theory, is the appearance of incomplete multiplets of both scalar and vector bosons. Let us just rehearse this once more, in the $SU(2) \times U(1)$ case. We started with 4 massless gauge fields, belonging to an $SU(2)$ triplet and a $U(1)$ singlet; and, in addition, 4 scalar fields of equal mass, in an $SU(2)$ doublet. After symmetry breaking, three massive vector bosons emerged, leaving the photon massless. In the scalar sector, three of the scalars became the longitudinal components of the three massive vector bosons, and one lone massive scalar field survived, all that remained of the original scalar doublet. Its mass is a free parameter of the theory, being given by $m_H = \sqrt{2}\mu = \sqrt{\lambda}v/\sqrt{2}$. The discovery – or otherwise – of this *Higgs boson* has therefore been a vital goal in particle physics for over forty years. Before turning to experiment, however, we want to mention some theoretical considerations concerning m_H by way of orientation.

22.8.2 Theoretical considerations concerning m_H

The coupling constant λ, which determines m_H given the known value of v, is unfortunately undetermined in the Standard Model. However, some quite strong theoretical arguments suggest that m_H cannot be arbitrarily large.

Like all coupling constants in a renormalizable theory, λ must 'run'. For the $(\hat{\phi}^\dagger \hat{\phi})^2$ interaction of (22.30), a one-loop calculation of the β-function leads to

$$\lambda(E) = \frac{\lambda(v)}{1 - \frac{3\lambda(v)}{8\pi^2} \ln(E/v)}. \tag{22.202}$$

Like QED, this theory is not asymptotically free: the coupling increases with the scale E. In fact, the theory becomes non-perturbative at the scale E^* such that

$$E^* \sim v \exp\left(\frac{8\pi^2}{3\lambda(v)}\right). \tag{22.203}$$

Note that this is exponentially sensitive to the 'low-energy' coupling constant $\lambda(v)$ – and that E^* decreases rapidly as $\lambda(v)$ increases. But (see (22.40)) m_H is essentially proportional to $\lambda^{1/2}(v)$. Hence as m_H increases, non-perturbative behaviour sets in increasingly early. Suppose we say that we should like perturbative behaviour to be maintained up to an energy scale Λ. Then we require

$$m_H < v \left[\frac{4\pi^2}{3\ln(\Lambda/v)}\right]^{1/2}. \tag{22.204}$$

For $\Lambda \sim 10^{16}$ GeV, this gives $m_{\rm H} < 160$ GeV. On the other hand, if the non-perturbative regime sets in at 1TeV, then the bound on $m_{\rm H}$ is weaker, $m_H < 750$ GeV.

This is an oversimplified argument for various reasons, though the essential point is correct. An important omission is the contribution of the top quark to the running of $\lambda(E)$. A more refined version (Hambye and Riesselmann 1997) concludes that for $m_{\rm H} < 180$ GeV the perturbative regime could extend all the way to the Planck mass, $\sim 10^{19}$ GeV.

There is another, independent, argument which suggests that $m_{\rm H}$ cannot be too large. We have previously considered violations of unitarity by the lowest-order diagrams for certain processes (see chapter 21 and section 22.6). As we saw, in a non-gauge theory with massive vector bosons, such violations are associated with the longitudinal polarization states of the bosons, which carry factors proportional to the 4-momentum k^μ (see (22.18)). In a gauge theory, strong cancellations in the high energy behaviour occur between different lowest-order diagrams. This behaviour is characteristic of gauge theories (Llewellyn Smith 1973, Cornwall *et al.* 1974), and is related to their renormalizability. One process of this sort which we did not yet consider, however, is that in which two longitudinally polarized W's scatter from each other. A considerable number of diagrams (7 in all) contribute to this process, in leading order : exchange of γ, Z and Higgs particles, together with the W–W self interaction. When all these are added up the high-energy behaviour of the total amplitude turns out to be proportional to λ, the Higgs coupling constant (see for example Ellis, Stirling and Webber 1996, chapter 8). This at first sight unexpected result can be understood as follows. The longitudinal components of the W's arise from the '$\partial^\mu \hat{\phi}$' parts in (22.30) (compare equation (19.48) in the U(1) case), which produce k^μ factors. Thus the scattering of longitudinal W's is effectively the scattering of the 3 Goldstone bosons in the complex Higgs doublet. These bosons have self interactions arising from the $\lambda(\hat{\phi}^\dagger \hat{\phi})^2$ Higgs potential, for which the Feynman amplitude is just proportional to λ. Now, although such a constant term obviously cannot violate unitarity as the energy increases (as happened in the other cases), it can do so if λ itself is too big – and since $\lambda \propto m_{\rm H}^2$, this puts a bound on $m_{\rm H}$. A constant amplitude is pure $J = 0$ and so, in order of magnitude, we expect unitarity to imply $\lambda < 1$. In terms of standard quantities,

$$\lambda = m_{\rm H}^2 G_{\rm F}/\sqrt{2}, \tag{22.205}$$

and so we expect

$$m_{\rm H} < G_{\rm F}^{-1/2} \sim 300 \text{ GeV}, \tag{22.206}$$

an energy scale we have seen several times before. A more refined analysis (Lee *et al.* 1977a,b) gives

$$m_{\rm H} < \left(\frac{8\sqrt{2}\pi}{3G_{\rm F}}\right)^{1/2} \approx 1\text{TeV}. \tag{22.207}$$

Like the preceding argument, this one does not say that m_H *must* be less than some fixed number. Rather, it says that if m_H gets bigger than a certain value, perturbation theory will fail, or 'new physics' will enter. It is, in fact, curiously reminiscent of the original situation with the four-fermion current–current interaction itself (compare (22.10) with (22.206)). Perhaps this is a clue that we may eventually need to replace the Higgs phenomenology. At all events, this line of reasoning seems to imply that the Higgs boson will either be found at a mass well below 1 TeV, or else some electroweak interactions will become effectively strong with new physical consequences. This 'no lose' situation provided powerful motivation for the construction of the LHC.

There is also an interesting *lower* bound on the Higgs mass, which is derived from the requirement of vacuum stability. If the Higgs mass is sufficiently lighter than the top quark mass, the top quark loop contribution to the running of the quartic coupling $\lambda(E)$ can cause the coupling to go negative at large energy scales (Cabibbo *et al.* 1979). This would imply that, at such scales, the effective scalar potential of the Standard Model would be unbounded below at large absolute values of the field, and there would no longer be a stable ground state (vacuum). This can be tolerated if the lifetime of the metastable vacuum is less that the age of the Universe (see Isidori *et al.* 2001, and references cited therein). A re-examination of the issue by Elias-Miro *et al.* (2012) showed that the Standard Model vacuum would become unstable at scales around the Planck mass, for $m_H < 130$ GeV. For $m_H \sim 125$ GeV, instability occurs at scales of order 10^{10} GeV, but the lifetime is greater than the age of the Universe. Of course, new physics may enter well before such a scale. It is nevertheless intriguing that a Higgs mass in this region may have implications for the physics of the early Universe.

We now consider some simple aspects of Higgs boson production and decay processes at collider energies, as predicted by the Standard Model, and conclude with the experiments leading to the probable Higgs boson discovery in 2012.

22.8.3 Higgs boson searches and the 2012 discovery

We begin by considering the main production and decay modes. The existing lower bound on m_H established at LEP (LEP 2003)

$$m_H \geq 114.4 \text{ GeV (95\% Confidence Level)} \qquad (22.208)$$

already excluded many possibilities in both production and decay. Subsequent searches were carried out at the hadron colliders. At both the Tevatron and the LHC, the dominant parton-level production mechanism is 'gluon fusion' via an intermediate top quark loop as shown in figure 22.27 (Georgi *et al.* 1978, Glashow *et al.* 1978, Stange *et al.* 1994a,b). The intermediate t quark dominates, because the Higgs couplings to fermions are proportional to the fermion mass. Since the gluon probability distribution rises rapidly at small x values, which are probed at larger collider energy $\sqrt{s}$, the cross section for

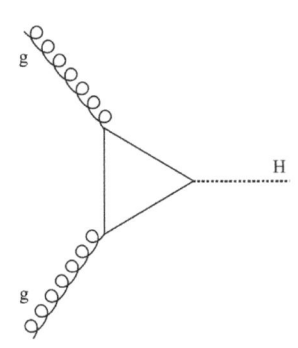

FIGURE 22.27
Higgs boson production process by 'gluon fusion'.

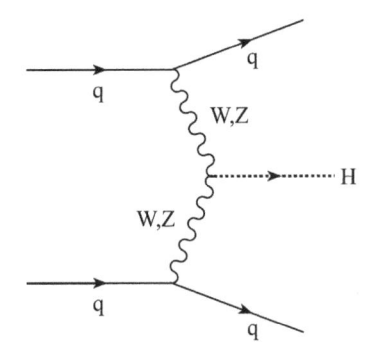

FIGURE 22.28
Higgs boson production process by 'vector boson fusion'.

this process (which is the same for pp and p$\bar{\text{p}}$ colliders) will rise with energy. At the Tevatron with $\sqrt{s} = 1.96$ TeV, the cross section ranges from about 1 pb for $m_H \simeq 100$ GeV to 0.2 pb for $m_H \simeq 200$ GeV. At an LHC energy of $\sqrt{s} = 7$ TeV, the cross section is about 25 pb for $m_H \simeq 100$ GeV and 0.1 pb for $m_H \simeq 700$ GeV, rising to about 70 pb and 1 pb respectively at $\sqrt{s} = 14$ TeV (Dittmaier *et al.* 2011). These numbers include QCD corrections, which increase the parton-level cross sections by a factor of about 2.

The next largest cross sections, some ten times smaller than the gluon fusion process, are for Higgs production via 'vector boson fusion' (qq' → qq'H, see figure 22.28) and for associated production of a Higgs boson with a vector boson (q$\bar{\text{q}}$ → WH, ZH, see figure 22.29).

These processes involve the trilinear Higgs couplings to the vector bosons, which are proportional to their masses (see appendix Q). At the LHC, the first of these cross sections is somewhat larger than the second for $m_H < 130$ GeV,

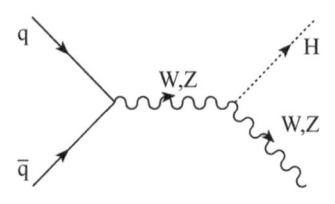

FIGURE 22.29
Higgs boson production in association with W or Z.

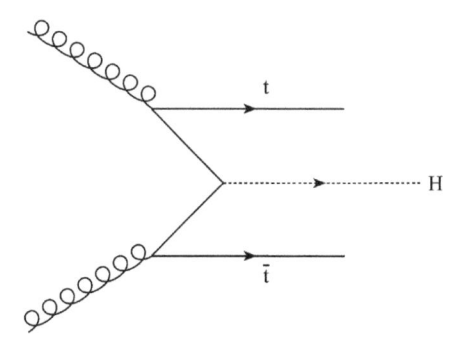

FIGURE 22.30
Higgs boson production in association with a t t̄ pair.

while the order is reversed at the Tevatron because the initial state is p$\bar{\text{p}}$. A fourth production possibility, at a significantly smaller rate, is 'associated production with top quarks' as shown in figure 22.30, for example. Figure 22.31 (taken from Ellis, Stirling and Webber 1996) shows the cross sections for the various production processes as a function of m_{H}, for pp collisions at $\sqrt{s} = 14$ TeV. Updated calculations (including QCD and electroweak corrections) are described in reports by Dittmaier *et al.* (2011, 2012), which present the results of a very large-scale theoretical effort.

The Higgs boson must be detected via its decays. For $m_{\text{H}} < 135$ GeV, decays to fermion–antifermion pairs dominate, of which b$\bar{\text{b}}$ has the largest branching ratio because of the larger value of m_{b}; the decay to $\tau^+\tau^-$ is roughly an order of magnitude smaller. The width of H $\to f\bar{f}$ is easily calculated to lowest order and is (problem 22.11)

$$\Gamma(\text{H} \to f\bar{f}) = \frac{CG_{\text{F}}m_f^2 m_{\text{H}}}{4\pi\sqrt{2}} \left(1 - \frac{4m_f^2}{m_{\text{H}}^2}\right)^{3/2}, \tag{22.209}$$

where the colour factor C is 3 for quarks and 1 for leptons. For such m_{H} values, $\Gamma(\text{H} \to f\bar{f})$ is less than 5 MeV, and the total decay width is less than

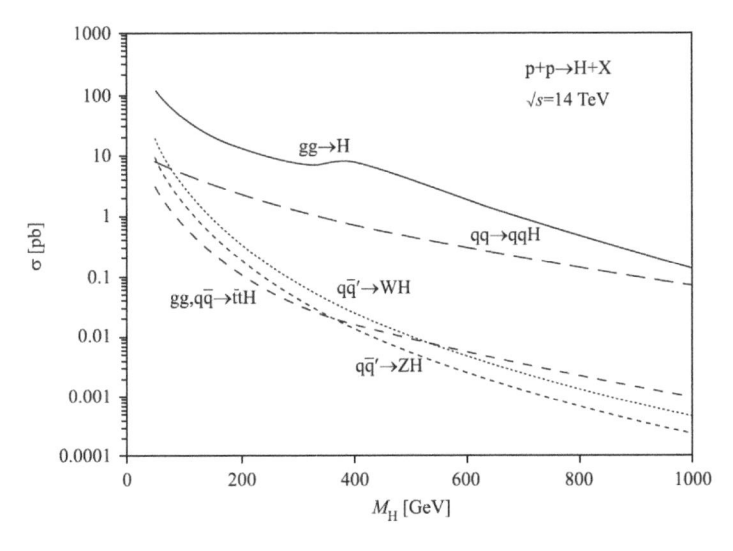

FIGURE 22.31
Higgs boson production cross sections in pp collisions at the LHC (figure from R K Ellis, W J Stirling and B R Webber *QCD and Collider Physics* 1996, courtesy Cambridge University Press).

10 MeV. QCD corrections are largely accounted for by replacing m_f^2 in the first factor on the right-hand side of (22.209), which arises from the Higgs-fermion Yukawa coupling, by the $\overline{\text{MS}}$ running mass value $\overline{m}_f^2(m_{\text{H}})$.

However, the large rate for the process gg $\rightarrow$ H $\rightarrow$ b$\bar{\text{b}}$ has to compete against a very large background from the inclusive production of pp (or p$\bar{\text{p}}$) $\rightarrow$ b$\bar{\text{b}}$+X via the strong interaction. The Higgs signal can be separated from such a background by using subleading decay modes such as H $\rightarrow$ $\gamma\gamma$. The Higgs boson's coupling to photons is induced by quark triangle loops (figure 22.32) or a W loop. In a similar way, the associated production modes W$^\pm$H, ZH, allow use of the leptonic W and Z decays to reject QCD backgrounds.

Decays to a pair of vector bosons are also important. The tree-level width for H $\rightarrow$ W$^+$W$^-$ is (problem 22.11)

$$\Gamma(\text{H} \rightarrow \text{W}^+\text{W}^-) = \frac{G_{\text{F}}m_{\text{H}}^3}{8\pi\sqrt{2}}\left(1 - \frac{4M_{\text{W}}^2}{m_{\text{H}}^2}\right)^{1/2}\left(1 - \frac{4M_{\text{W}}^2}{m_{\text{H}}^2} + 12\frac{M_{\text{W}}^4}{m_{\text{H}}^4}\right),$$

$$(22.210)$$

and the width for H $\rightarrow$ ZZ is the same with $M_{\text{W}} \rightarrow M_{\text{Z}}$ and a factor of $\frac{1}{2}$ to allow for the two identical bosons in the final state. These widths rise rapidly with m_{H}, reaching $\Gamma \sim 1$ GeV when $m_{\text{H}} \sim 200$ GeV. Even for values of m_{H} below the physical W$^+$W$^-$ and ZZ thresholds, H can still decay through modes mediated by virtual bosons, via the off-shell decays H $\rightarrow$ WW* and H $\rightarrow$ ZZ*.

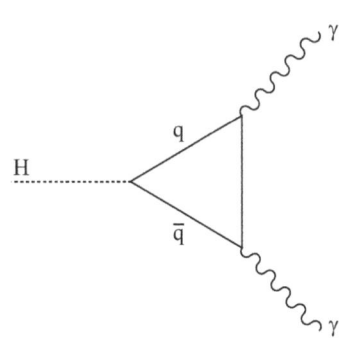

FIGURE 22.32
Higgs boson decay via quark triangle.

Figure 22.33, taken from Ellis, Stirling and Webber (1996), shows the complete set of phenomenologically relevant Higgs branching ratios for a Higgs boson with $m_H < 200$ GeV. Updated results for SM Higgs branching ratios are reported in Dittmaier *et al.* (2012).

We turn now to the experiments. The Tevatron p$\bar{p}$ collider at Fermilab operated at $\sqrt{s} = 1.96$ TeV until its shutdown in 2011. Higgs searches were conducted by two experiments, CDF and D0, which each collected approximately 10 fb^{-1} of data with the capability of seeing a Higgs signal in the mass range 90–185 GeV. The analyses searched for a Higgs boson produced through gluon fusion, in association with a vector boson, and through vector boson fusion. The decays H $\to$ b$\bar{\text{b}}$, H $\to$ W$^+$W$^-$, H $\to$ ZZ, H $\to$ $\tau^+\tau^-$ and H $\to$ $\gamma\gamma$ were all studied.

The LHC is a pp collider at CERN which started running in 2010. The two general purpose detectors ATLAS ('A Toroidal LHC ApparatuS') and CMS ('Compact Muon Solenoid') were designed to study physics at the TeV scale, and in particular to search for the Higgs boson. In 2011, the LHC delivered to ATLAS and CMS up to 5.1 fb^{-1} of integrated luminosity of pp collisions at $\sqrt{s} = 7$ TeV. In 2012 the CMS energy was increased to 8 TeV, and by July 2012 up to 5.9 fb^{-1} of further data was delivered. At the LHC, the main Higgs boson production processes are the same as at the Tevatron, but as mentioned above vector boson fusion is more important than production in association with W or Z, or with t$\bar{\text{t}}$. The LHC experiments are sensitive to Higgs bosons of much higher mass than the Tevatron experiments, ranging from the LEP bound (22.209) up to about 600 GeV. The same decay channels were studied as at the Tevatron.

By early 2012, the ATLAS and CMS experiments had excluded an m_H value in the interval 129 GeV to 539 GeV at the 95% CL, and the mass region 120–130 GeV was under intensive study, excesses of events having been

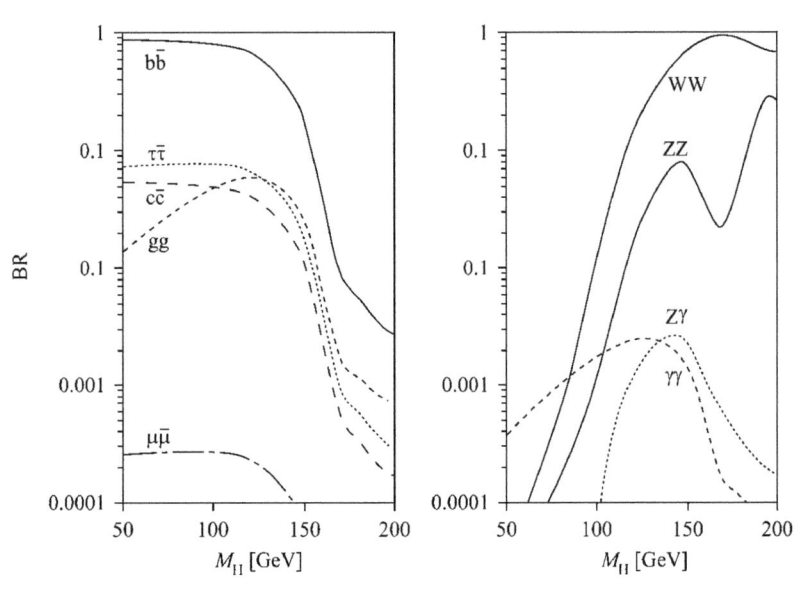

FIGURE 22.33
Branching ratios of the Higgs boson (figure from R K Ellis, W J Stirling and
B R Webber *QCD and Collider Physics* 1996, courtesy Cambridge University
Press).

reported by both experiments in the region 124–126 GeV (Aad *et al.* 2012a,
Chatrchyan *et al.* 2012a). Then, on July 4, 2012, the ATLAS and CMS
collaborations simultaneously announced the observation (at a significance
greater than 5σ) of a new boson with a mass in the range 125–126 GeV and
with properties compatible with those of a SM Higgs boson. These results
(updated) are reported in Aad *et al.* (2012b) and Chatrchyan *et al.* (2012b).
The crucial channels in the discovery were the decay modes H $\to \gamma\gamma$ and
H $\to$ ZZ* $\to$ 4 leptons, both of which provide a high-resolution invariant
mass for fully reconstructed candidates. The cover illustration for Volume 1
of this book (copyright CERN) shows a candidate $\gamma\gamma$ event recorded by CMS,
and that for volume 2 (copyright CERN) shows a candidate four muon event
recorded by ATLAS. The channel H $\to$ WW* $\to \ell\nu\ell\nu$ is equally sensitive but
has low resolution. The ATLAS result for the mass of the boson was (Aad *et
al.* 2012b)

$$126.0 \pm 0.4(\text{stat}) \pm 0.4(\text{syst.}) \text{ GeV} \qquad (22.211)$$

and the CMS result was (Chatrchyan *et al.* 2012b)

$$125.3 \pm 0.4(\text{stat}) \pm 0.5(\text{syst.}) \text{ GeV.} \qquad (22.212)$$

At about the same time, the CDF and D0 collaborations at the Tevatron reported the combined results of their searches for a SM Higgs boson produced in association with a W or a Z boson, and subsequently decaying to a b$\bar{\text{b}}$ pair. The data corresponded to an integrated luminosity of 9.7 fb^{-1}. An excess of events was observed in the mass range 120–135 GeV, at a significance of 3σ, which was interpreted as evidence for a new particle, consistent with the SM Higgs boson (Aaltonen *et al.* 2012). This provided the first strong indication for the decay of the new particle to a fermion–antifermion pair at a rate consistent with the SM prediction.

Is the particle discovered by the ATLAS and CMS collaborations the Higgs boson of the Standard Model? The decay to two photons implies that its spin cannot be unity (Landau 1948, Yang 1950), but spin-0 has not yet been established. Even so, this already implies that the particle is different from all the other SM particles. The decay modes $\gamma\gamma$, ZZ*, WW* have been observed by ATLAS and CMS, and b$\bar{\text{b}}$ by CDF/D0. The $\tau^+\tau^-$ mode has not yet been seen. A measure of the compatibility of the observed boson with the SM Higgs boson is provided by the best-fit value of the common signal strength parameter μ defined by

$$\mu = \sigma \cdot \text{BR}/(\sigma \cdot \text{BR})_{\text{SM}} \qquad (22.213)$$

where σ is the boson production cross section and BR is the branching ratio of the boson to the observed final state. 'SM' denotes the SM prediction, so that the value $\mu = 1$ is the SM hypothesis. ATLAS reported a best-fit μ-value of $\mu = 1.4 \pm 0.3$ for $m_\text{H} = 126$ GeV; the μ-values for the individual channels were all within one standard deviation (s.d.) of unity. CMS reported a best-fit value of $\mu = 0.87 \pm 0.23$ at $m_\text{H} = 125.5$ GeV, and again the individual values in the observed channels were within 1 s.d. of unity. The conclusion is that these results are consistent, within uncertainties, with the predictions for the SM Higgs boson.

We end this book with a discovery which opens a new era in particle physics, in which the electroweak symmetry-breaking (Higgs) sector will be rigorously tested. The aim will be to measure the couplings of the new boson to the other SM particles with increasing accuracy, so as to reveal possible deviations from the SM values. The level of precision required to provide clear pointers to physics beyond the SM may be very high (see for example Gupta *et al.* 2012). The LHC will continue running until early 2013, when it will be shut down for machine improvements needed to allow operation at $\sqrt{s} = 14$ TeV and higher luminosity; beyond that, the High Luminosity LHC is planned to begin data-taking in 2022. However, just as the discovery of the W and Z bosons at the CERN p$\bar{\text{p}}$ collider was followed by precision studies at the e$^+$e$^-$ colliders LEP and SLC, a lepton collider is likely to be needed on the next stage of this fundamental exploration.

Problems

22.1

(a) Using the representation for $\boldsymbol{\alpha}, \beta$ and γ_5 introduced in section 20.2.2 (equation (20.14)), massless particles are described by spinors of the form

$$u = E^{1/2} \begin{pmatrix} \phi_+ \\ \phi_- \end{pmatrix} \qquad (\text{normalized to } u^\dagger u = 2E)$$

where $\boldsymbol{\sigma} \cdot \hat{\boldsymbol{p}}\phi_\pm = \pm\phi_\pm, \hat{\boldsymbol{p}} = \boldsymbol{p}|\boldsymbol{p}|$. Find the explicit form of u for the case $\hat{\boldsymbol{p}} = (\sin\theta, 0, \cos\theta)$.

(b) Consider the process $\bar{\nu}_\mu + \mu^- \to \bar{\nu}_e + e^-$, discussed in section 22.1, in the limit in which all masses are neglected. The amplitude is proportional to

$$G_F \bar{v}(\bar{\nu}_\mu, R)\gamma_\mu(1 - \gamma_5)u(\mu^-, L)\bar{u}(e^-, L)\gamma^\mu(1 - \gamma_5)v(\bar{\nu}_e, R)$$

where we have explicitly indicated the appropriate helicities R or L (note that, as explained in section 20.2.2, $(1 - \gamma_5)/2$ is the projection operator for a right-handed antineutrino). In the CM frame, let the initial μ^- momentum be $(0, 0, E)$ and the final e^- momentum be $E(\sin\theta, 0, \cos\theta)$. Verify that the amplitude is proportional to $G_F E^2(1 + \cos\theta)$. (*Hint:* evaluate the 'easy' part $\bar{v}(\bar{\nu}_\mu)\gamma_\mu(1 - \gamma_5)u(\mu^-)$ first; this will show that the components $\mu = 0, z$ vanish, so that only the $\mu = x, y$ components of the dot product need to be calculated.)

22.2 Verify equation (22.20).

22.3 Check that when the polarization vector of each photon in figures 22.7(a) and (b) is replaced by the corresponding photon momentum, the sum of these two amplitudes vanishes.

22.4 By identifying the part of (22.45) which has the form (22.57), derive (22.58).

22.5 Using the vertex (22.48), verify (22.79).

22.6 Insert (22.29) into (22.151) to derive (22.153).

22.7 Verify that the neutral current part of (22.159) is diagonal in the 'mass' basis.

22.8 Suppose that the Higgs field is a triplet of $SU(2)_L$ rather than a doublet; and suppose that its vacuum value is

$$\langle 0|\hat{\phi}|0\rangle = \begin{pmatrix} 0 \\ 0 \\ f \end{pmatrix}$$

in the gauge in which it is real. The non-vanishing component has $t_3 = -1$, using

$$t_3 = \begin{pmatrix} 1 & 0 & 0 \\ 0 & 0 & 0 \\ 0 & 0 & -1 \end{pmatrix}$$

in the 'angular-momentum-like' basis. Since we want the charge of the vacuum to be zero, and we have $Q = t_3 + y/2$, we must assign $y(\hat{\phi}) = 2$. So the covariant derivative on $\hat{\phi}$ is

$$(\partial_\mu + igt \cdot \hat{W}_\mu + ig'\hat{B}_\mu)\hat{\phi},$$

where

$$t_1 = \begin{pmatrix} 0 & \frac{1}{\sqrt{2}} & 0 \\ \frac{1}{\sqrt{2}} & 0 & \frac{1}{\sqrt{2}} \\ 0 & \frac{1}{\sqrt{2}} & 0 \end{pmatrix}, \quad t_2 = \begin{pmatrix} 0 & \frac{-i}{\sqrt{2}} & 0 \\ \frac{i}{\sqrt{2}} & 0 & \frac{-i}{\sqrt{2}} \\ 0 & \frac{i}{\sqrt{2}} & 0 \end{pmatrix}$$

and t_3 is as above (it is easy to check that these three matrices do satisfy the required SU(2) commutation relations $[t_1, t_2] = it_3$). Show that the photon and Z fields are still given by (22.36) and (22.37), with the same $\sin\theta_W$ as in (22.39), but that now

$$M_Z = \sqrt{2}M_W/\cos\theta_W.$$

What is the value of the parameter ρ in this model?

22.9 Use (22.188) to verify (22.190).

22.10 Calculate the lifetime of the top quark to decay via $t \rightarrow W^+ + b$.

22.12 Using the Higgs couplings given in appendix Q, verify (22.209) and (22.210).

M

Group Theory

M.1 Definition and simple examples

A group $\mathcal{G}$ is a set of elements $(a, b, c, \ldots)$ with a law for combining any two elements a, b so as to form their ordered 'product' ab, such that the following four conditions hold:

(i)   For every $a, b \in \mathcal{G}$, the product $ab \in \mathcal{G}$ (the symbol '$\in$' means 'belongs to', or 'is a member of').

(ii) The law of combination is associative, i.e.

$$(ab)c = a(bc). \tag{M.1}$$

(iii) $\mathcal{G}$ contains a unique identity element, e, such that for all $a \in \mathcal{G}$,

$$ae = ea = a. \tag{M.2}$$

(iv) For all $a \in \mathcal{G}$, there is a unique inverse element, a^{-1}, such that

$$aa^{-1} = a^{-1}a = e. \tag{M.3}$$

Note that in general the law of combination is not commutative – i.e. $ab \neq ba$; if it is commutative, the group is *Abelian*; if not, it is *non-Abelian*. Any finite set of elements satisfying the conditions (i)–(iv) forms a finite group, the *order* of the group being equal to the number of elements in the set. If the set does not have a finite number of elements it is an infinite group.

As a simple example, the set of four numbers (1, i, –1, –i) form a finite Abelian group of order 4, with the law of combination being ordinary multiplication. The reader may check that each of (i)–(iv) is satisfied, with e taken to be the number 1, and the inverse being the algebraic reciprocal. A second group of order 4 is provided by the matrices

$$\begin{pmatrix} 1 & 0 \\ 0 & 1 \end{pmatrix}, \begin{pmatrix} 0 & 1 \\ -1 & 0 \end{pmatrix}, \begin{pmatrix} -1 & 0 \\ 0 & -1 \end{pmatrix}, \begin{pmatrix} 0 & -1 \\ 1 & 0 \end{pmatrix}, \tag{M.4}$$

with the combination law being matrix multiplication, 'e' being the first (unit) matrix, and the inverse being the usual matrix inverse. Although matrix

multiplication is not commutative in general, it happens to be so for these particular matrices. In fact, the way these four matrices multiply together is (as the reader can verify) exactly the same as the way the four numbers $(1, i, -1, -i)$ (in that order) do. Further, the correspondence between the elements of the two groups is 'one to one': that is, if we label the two sets of group elements by (e, a, b, c) and (e', a', b', c'), we have the correspondences $e \leftrightarrow e'$, $a \leftrightarrow a'$, $b \leftrightarrow b'$, $c \leftrightarrow c'$. Two groups with the same multiplication structure, and with a one-to-one correspondence between their elements, are said to be *isomorphic*. If they have the same multiplication structure but the correspondence is not one-to-one, they are *homomorphic*.

M.2   Lie groups

We are interested in *continuous groups* – that is, groups whose elements are labelled by a number of continuously variable real parameters $\alpha_1, \alpha_2, \ldots, \alpha_r$: $g(\alpha_1, \alpha_2, \ldots, \alpha_r) \equiv g(\boldsymbol{\alpha})$. In particular, we are concerned with various kinds of 'coordinate transformations' (not necessarily space-time ones, but including also 'internal' transformations such as those of SU(3)). For example, rotations in three dimensions form a group, whose elements are specified by three real parameters (e.g. two for defining the axis of the rotation, and one for the angle of rotation about that axis). Lorentz transformations also form a group, this time with six real parameters (three for 3-D rotations, three for pure velocity transformations). The matrices of SU(3) are specified by the values of eight real parameters. By convention, parametrizations are arranged in such a way that $g(\boldsymbol{0})$ is the identity element of the group. For a continuous group, condition (i) takes the form

$$g(\boldsymbol{\alpha})g(\boldsymbol{\beta}) = g(\boldsymbol{\gamma}(\boldsymbol{\alpha}, \boldsymbol{\beta})), \qquad (\text{M.5})$$

where the parameters $\boldsymbol{\gamma}$ are continuous functions of the parameters $\boldsymbol{\alpha}$ and $\boldsymbol{\beta}$. A more restrictive condition is that $\boldsymbol{\gamma}$ should be an *analytic* function of $\boldsymbol{\alpha}$ and $\boldsymbol{\beta}$; if this is the case, the group is a *Lie group*.

The analyticity condition implies that if we are given the form of the group elements in the neighbourhood of any one element, we can 'move out' from that neighbourhood to other nearby elements, using the mathematical procedure known as 'analytic continuation' (essentially, using a power series expansion); by repeating the process, we should be able to reach all group elements which are 'continuously connected' to the original element. The simplest group element to consider is the identity, which we shall now denote by I. Lie proved that the properties of the elements of a Lie group which can be reached continuously from the identity I are determined from elements lying in the neighbourhood of I.

M.3   Generators of Lie groups

Consider (following Lichtenberg 1970, chapter 5) a group of transformations defined by

$$x_i' = f_i(x_1, x_2, \ldots, x_N; \alpha_1, \alpha_2, \ldots, \alpha_r), \qquad (M.6)$$

where the x_i's $(i = 1, 2, \ldots, N)$ are the 'coordinates' on which the transformations act, and the α's are the (real) parameters of the transformations. By convention, $\boldsymbol{\alpha} = \mathbf{0}$ is the identity transformation, so

$$x_i = f_i(\boldsymbol{x}, \mathbf{0}). \qquad (M.7)$$

A transformation in the neighbourhood of the identity is then given by

$$\mathrm{d}x_i = \sum_{\nu=1}^{r} \frac{\partial f_i}{\partial \alpha_\nu} \mathrm{d}\alpha_\nu, \qquad (M.8)$$

where the $\{\mathrm{d}\alpha_\nu\}$ are infinitesimal parameters, and the partial derivative is understood to be evaluated at the point $(\boldsymbol{x}, \mathbf{0})$.

Consider now the change in a function $F(\boldsymbol{x})$ under the infinitesimal transformation (M.8). We have

$$
\begin{aligned}
F \to F + \mathrm{d}F &= F + \sum_{i=1}^{N} \frac{\partial F}{\partial x_i} \mathrm{d}x_i \\
&= F + \sum_{i=1}^{N} \left[\sum_{\nu=1}^{r} \frac{\partial f_i}{\partial \alpha_\nu} \mathrm{d}\alpha_\nu \right] \frac{\partial F}{\partial x_i} \\
&\equiv \left\{ 1 - \sum_{\nu=1}^{r} \mathrm{d}\alpha_\nu \mathrm{i}\hat{X}_\nu \right\} F, \qquad (M.9)
\end{aligned}
$$

where

$$\hat{X}_\nu \equiv \mathrm{i} \sum_{i=1}^{N} \frac{\partial f_i}{\partial \alpha_\nu} \frac{\partial}{\partial x_i} \qquad (M.10)$$

is a *generator of infinitesimal transformations*[1]. Note that in (M.10) ν runs from 1 to r, so there are as many generators as there are parameters labelling the group elements. Finite transformations are obtained by 'exponentiating' the quantity in braces in (M.9) (compare (12.30)):

$$\hat{U}(\boldsymbol{\alpha}) = \exp\{-\mathrm{i}\boldsymbol{\alpha} \cdot \hat{\boldsymbol{X}}\}, \qquad (M.11)$$

---

[1] Clearly there is lot of 'convention' (the sign, the i) in the definition of $\hat{X}_\nu$. It is chosen for convenient consistency with familiar generators, for example those of SO(3) (see section M.4.1).

where we have written $\sum_{\nu=1}^{r} \alpha_\nu \hat{X}_\nu = \boldsymbol{\alpha} \cdot \hat{\boldsymbol{X}}$.

An important theorem states that the commutator of any two generators of a Lie group is a linear combination of the generators:

$$[\hat{X}_\lambda, \hat{X}_\mu] = c^\nu_{\lambda\mu} \hat{X}_\nu, \tag{M.12}$$

where the constants $c^\nu_{\lambda\mu}$ are complex numbers called the *structure constants* of the group; a sum over ν from 1 to r is understood on the right-hand side. The commutation relations (M.12) are called the *algebra* of the group.

M.4   Examples

M.4.1   SO(3) and three-dimensional rotations

Rotations in three dimensions are defined by

$$\boldsymbol{x}' = R\boldsymbol{x}, \tag{M.13}$$

where R is a real 3×3 matrix such that the length of $\boldsymbol{x}$ is preserved, i.e. $\boldsymbol{x}'^T \boldsymbol{x}' = \boldsymbol{x}^T \boldsymbol{x}$. This implies that $R^T R = I$, so that R is an orthogonal matrix. It follows that

$$1 = \det(R^T R) = \det R^T \det R = (\det R)^2, \tag{M.14}$$

and so $\det R = \pm 1$. Those R's with $\det R = -1$ include a parity transformation ($\boldsymbol{x}' = -\boldsymbol{x}$), which is not continuously connected to the identity. Those with $\det R = 1$ are 'proper rotations', and they form the elements of the group SO(3): the *S*pecial *O*rthogonal group in *3* dimensions.

An R close to the identity matrix I can be written as $R = I + \delta R$ where

$$(I + \delta R)^T (I + \delta R) = I. \tag{M.15}$$

Expanding this out to first order in δR gives

$$\delta R^T = -\delta R, \tag{M.16}$$

so that δR is an antisymmetric 3×3 matrix (compare (12.19)). We may parametrize δR as

$$\delta R = \begin{pmatrix} 0 & \epsilon_3 & -\epsilon_2 \\ -\epsilon_3 & 0 & \epsilon_1 \\ \epsilon_2 & -\epsilon_1 & 0 \end{pmatrix}, \tag{M.17}$$

and an infinitesimal rotation is then given by

$$\boldsymbol{x}' = \boldsymbol{x} - \boldsymbol{\epsilon} \times \boldsymbol{x}, \tag{M.18}$$

(compare (12.64)), or

$$dx_1 = -\epsilon_2 x_3 + \epsilon_3 x_2, \quad dx_2 = -\epsilon_3 x_1 + \epsilon_1 x_3, \quad dx_3 = -\epsilon_1 x_2 + \epsilon_2 x_1. \quad \text{(M.19)}$$

Thus in (M.8), identifying $d\alpha_1 \equiv \epsilon_1$, $d\alpha_2 \equiv \epsilon_2$, $d\alpha_3 \equiv \epsilon_3$, we have

$$\frac{\partial f_1}{\partial \alpha_1} = 0, \quad \frac{\partial f_1}{\partial \alpha_2} = -x_3, \quad \frac{\partial f_1}{\partial \alpha_3} = x_2, \quad \text{etc.} \quad \text{(M.20)}$$

The generators (M.10) are then

$$\left.\begin{array}{rcl}
\hat{X}_1 &=& ix_3\frac{\partial}{\partial x_2} - ix_2\frac{\partial}{\partial x_3} \\
\hat{X}_2 &=& ix_1\frac{\partial}{\partial x_3} - ix_3\frac{\partial}{\partial x_1} \\
\hat{X}_3 &=& ix_2\frac{\partial}{\partial x_1} - ix_1\frac{\partial}{\partial x_2}
\end{array}\right\} \quad \text{(M.21)}$$

which are easily recognized as the quantum-mechanical angular momentum operators

$$\hat{\boldsymbol{X}} = \boldsymbol{x} \times -i\boldsymbol{\nabla}, \quad \text{(M.22)}$$

which satisfy the *SO(3) algebra*

$$[\hat{X}_i, \hat{X}_j] = i\epsilon_{ijk}\hat{X}_k. \quad \text{(M.23)}$$

The action of finite rotations, parametrized by $\boldsymbol{\alpha} = (\alpha_1, \alpha_2, \alpha_3)$, on functions F is given by

$$\hat{U}(\boldsymbol{\alpha}) = \exp\{-i\boldsymbol{\alpha} \cdot \hat{\boldsymbol{X}}\}. \quad \text{(M.24)}$$

The operators $\hat{U}(\boldsymbol{\alpha})$ form a group which is isomorphic to SO(3). The structure constants of SO(3) are $i\epsilon_{ijk}$, from (M.23).

M.4.2 SU(2)

We write the infinitesimal SU(2) transformation (acting on a general complex two-component column vector) as (cf (12.27))

$$\begin{pmatrix} q_1' \\ q_2' \end{pmatrix} = (1 + i\boldsymbol{\epsilon} \cdot \boldsymbol{\tau}/2) \begin{pmatrix} q_1 \\ q_2 \end{pmatrix}, \quad \text{(M.25)}$$

so that

$$\begin{array}{rcl}
dq_1 &=& \dfrac{i\epsilon_3}{2}q_1 + \left(\dfrac{i\epsilon_1}{2} + \dfrac{\epsilon_2}{2}\right)q_2 \\[3mm]
dq_2 &=& \dfrac{-i\epsilon_3}{2}q_2 + \left(\dfrac{i\epsilon_1}{2} - \dfrac{\epsilon_2}{2}\right)q_1.
\end{array} \quad \text{(M.26)}$$

Then (with $d\alpha_1 \equiv \epsilon_1$ etc.)

$$\frac{\partial f_1}{\partial \alpha_1} = \frac{iq_2}{2}, \quad \frac{\partial f_1}{\partial \alpha_2} = \frac{q_2}{2}, \quad \frac{\partial f_1}{\partial \alpha_3} = \frac{iq_1}{2}, \quad \text{(M.27)}$$

$$\frac{\partial f_2}{\partial \alpha_1} = \frac{iq_1}{2}, \quad \frac{\partial f_2}{\partial \alpha_2} = -\frac{q_2}{2}, \quad \frac{\partial f_2}{\partial \alpha_3} = -\frac{iq_2}{2}, \tag{M.28}$$

and (from (M.10))

$$\hat{X}_1' = -\frac{1}{2}\left\{ q_2 \frac{\partial}{\partial q_1} + q_1 \frac{\partial}{\partial q_2} \right\} \tag{M.29}$$

$$\hat{X}_2' = \frac{i}{2}\left\{ q_2 \frac{\partial}{\partial q_1} - q_1 \frac{\partial}{\partial q_2} \right\} \tag{M.30}$$

$$\hat{X}_3' = \frac{1}{2}\left\{ -q_1 \frac{\partial}{\partial q_1} + q_2 \frac{\partial}{\partial q_2} \right\}. \tag{M.31}$$

It is an interesting exercise to check that the commutation relations of the $\hat{X}_i'$'s are exactly the same as those of the $\hat{X}_i$'s in (M.23). The two groups are therefore said to have the same algebra, with the same structure constants, and they are in fact isomorphic in the vicinity of their respective identity elements. They are not the same for 'large' transformations, however, as we discuss in section M.7.

M.4.3   SO(4): The special orthogonal group in four dimensions

This is the group whose elements are 4×4 matrices S such that $S^T S = I$, where I is the 4×4 unit matrix, with the condition $\det S = +1$. The Euclidean (length)^2 $x_1^2 + x_2^2 + x_3^2 + x_4^2$ is left invariant under SO(4) transformations. Infinitesimal SO(4) transformations are characterized by the 4-D analogue of those for SO(3), namely by 4×4 real antisymmetric matrices δS, which have 6 real parameters. We choose to parametrize δS in such a way that the Euclidean 4-vector $(\boldsymbol{x}, x_4)$ is transformed to (cf (18.76) and (18.77))

$$\begin{aligned} \boldsymbol{x}' &= \boldsymbol{x} - \boldsymbol{\epsilon} \times \boldsymbol{x} - \boldsymbol{\eta} x_4, \\ x_4' &= x_4 + \boldsymbol{\eta} \cdot \boldsymbol{x}, \end{aligned} \tag{M.32}$$

where $\boldsymbol{x} = (x_1, x_2, x_3)$ and $\boldsymbol{\eta} = (\eta_1, \eta_2, \eta_3)$. Note that the first three components transform by (M.18) when $\boldsymbol{\eta} = 0$, so that SO(3) is a *subgroup* of SO(4). The six generators are (with $d\alpha_1 \equiv \epsilon_1$ etc.)

$$\hat{X}_1 = ix_3 \frac{\partial}{\partial x_2} - ix_2 \frac{\partial}{\partial, x_3}, \tag{M.33}$$

and similarly for $\hat{X}_2$ and $\hat{X}_3$ as in (M.21), together with (defining $d\alpha_4 = \eta_1$ etc.)

$$\hat{X}_4 = i\left(-x_4 \frac{\partial}{\partial x_1} + x_1 \frac{\partial}{\partial x_4} \right) \tag{M.34}$$

$$\hat{X}_5 = i\left(-x_4 \frac{\partial}{\partial x_2} + x_2 \frac{\partial}{\partial x_4} \right) \tag{M.35}$$

$$\hat{X}_6 = i\left(-x_4 \frac{\partial}{\partial x_3} + x_3 \frac{\partial}{\partial x_4} \right). \tag{M.36}$$

Relabelling these last three generators as $\hat{Y}_1 \equiv \hat{X}_4$, $\hat{Y}_2 \equiv \hat{X}_5$, $\hat{Y}_3 \equiv \hat{X}_6$, we find the following algebra:

$$[\hat{X}_i, \hat{X}_j] = i\epsilon_{ijk}\hat{X}_k \tag{M.37}$$

$$[\hat{X}_i, \hat{Y}_j] = i\epsilon_{ijk}\hat{Y}_k \tag{M.38}$$

$$[\hat{Y}_i, \hat{Y}_j] = i\epsilon_{ijk}\hat{X}_k, \tag{M.39}$$

together with

$$[\hat{X}_1, \hat{Y}_1] = [\hat{X}_2, \hat{Y}_2] = [\hat{X}_3, \hat{Y}_3] = 0. \tag{M.40}$$

(M.37) confirms that the three generators controlling infinitesimal transformations among the first three components $\boldsymbol{x}$ obey the angular momentum commutation relations. (M.37)–(M.40) constitute the algebra of SO(4).

This algebra may be simplified by introducing the linear combinations

$$\hat{M}_i = \frac{1}{2}(\hat{X}_i + \hat{Y}_i) \tag{M.41}$$

$$\hat{N}_i = \frac{1}{2}(\hat{X}_i - \hat{Y}_i), \tag{M.42}$$

which satisfy

$$[\hat{M}_i, \hat{M}_j] = i\epsilon_{ijk}\hat{M}_k \tag{M.43}$$

$$[\hat{N}_i, \hat{N}_j] = i\epsilon_{ijk}\hat{N}_k \tag{M.44}$$

$$[\hat{M}_i, \hat{N}_j] = 0. \tag{M.45}$$

From (M.43)–(M.45) we see that, in this form, the six generators have separated into two sets of three, each set obeying the algebra of SO(3) (or of SU(2)), and commuting with the other set. They therefore behave like two *independent* angular momentum operators. The algebra (M.43)–(M.45) is referred to as SU(2) × SU(2).

M.4.4   The Lorentz group

In this case the quadratic form left invariant by the transformation is the Minkowskian one $(x^0)^2 - \boldsymbol{x}^2$ (see appendix D of volume 1). We may think of infinitesimal Lorentz transformations as corresponding physically to ordinary infinitesimal 3-D rotations, together with infinitesimal pure velocity transformations ('boosts'). The basic 4-vector then transforms by

$$\left. \begin{array}{rl} x^{0\prime} &= x^0 - \boldsymbol{\eta} \cdot \boldsymbol{x} \\ \boldsymbol{x}' &= \boldsymbol{x} - \boldsymbol{\epsilon} \times \boldsymbol{x} - \boldsymbol{\eta}x^0 \end{array} \right\} \tag{M.46}$$

where $\boldsymbol{\eta}$ is now the infinitesimal velocity parameter (the reader may check that $(x^0)^2 - \boldsymbol{x}^2$ is indeed left invariant by (M.46), to first order in $\boldsymbol{\epsilon}$ and $\boldsymbol{\eta}$). The six generators are then $\hat{X}_1, \hat{X}_2, \hat{X}_3$ as in (M.21), together with

$$\hat{K}_1 = -i\left(x^1\frac{\partial}{\partial x^0} + x^0\frac{\partial}{\partial x^1}\right) \tag{M.47}$$

$$\hat{K}_2 = -\mathrm{i}\left(x^2\frac{\partial}{\partial x^0} + x^0\frac{\partial}{\partial x^2}\right) \tag{M.48}$$

$$\hat{K}_3 = -\mathrm{i}\left(x^3\frac{\partial}{\partial x^0} + x^0\frac{\partial}{\partial x^3}\right). \tag{M.49}$$

The corresponding algebra is

$$[\hat{X}_i, \hat{X}_j] = \mathrm{i}\epsilon_{ijk}\hat{X}_k \tag{M.50}$$

$$[\hat{X}_i, \hat{K}_j] = \mathrm{i}\epsilon_{ijk}\hat{K}_k \tag{M.51}$$

$$[\hat{K}_i, \hat{K}_j] = -\mathrm{i}\epsilon_{ijk}\hat{X}_k. \tag{M.52}$$

Note the minus sign on the right-hand side of (M.52) as compared with (M.39).

M.4.5   SU(3)

A general infinitesimal SU(3) transformation may be written as (cf (12.71) and (12.72))

$$\begin{pmatrix} q_1 \\ q_2 \\ q_3 \end{pmatrix}' = \left(1 + \mathrm{i}\frac{1}{2}\boldsymbol{\eta}\cdot\boldsymbol{\lambda}\right)\begin{pmatrix} q_1 \\ q_2 \\ q_3 \end{pmatrix}, \tag{M.53}$$

where there are now 8 of these $\boldsymbol{\eta}$'s, $\boldsymbol{\eta} = (\eta_1, \eta_2, \ldots, \eta_8)$, and the $\boldsymbol{\lambda}$-matrices are the Gell-Mann matrices

$$\lambda_1 = \begin{pmatrix} 0 & 1 & 0 \\ 1 & 0 & 0 \\ 0 & 0 & 0 \end{pmatrix}, \quad \lambda_2 = \begin{pmatrix} 0 & -\mathrm{i} & 0 \\ \mathrm{i} & 0 & 0 \\ 0 & 0 & 0 \end{pmatrix}, \quad \lambda_3 = \begin{pmatrix} 1 & 0 & 0 \\ 0 & -1 & 0 \\ 0 & 0 & 0 \end{pmatrix} \tag{M.54}$$

$$\lambda_4 = \begin{pmatrix} 0 & 0 & 1 \\ 0 & 0 & 0 \\ 1 & 0 & 0 \end{pmatrix}, \quad \lambda_5 = \begin{pmatrix} 0 & 0 & -\mathrm{i} \\ 0 & 0 & 0 \\ \mathrm{i} & 0 & 0 \end{pmatrix}, \quad \lambda_6 = \begin{pmatrix} 0 & 0 & 0 \\ 0 & 0 & 1 \\ 0 & 1 & 0 \end{pmatrix} \tag{M.55}$$

$$\lambda_7 = \begin{pmatrix} 0 & 0 & 0 \\ 0 & 0 & -\mathrm{i} \\ 0 & \mathrm{i} & 0 \end{pmatrix}, \quad \lambda_8 = \begin{pmatrix} \frac{1}{\sqrt{3}} & 0 & 0 \\ 0 & \frac{1}{\sqrt{3}} & 0 \\ 0 & 0 & -\frac{2}{\sqrt{3}} \end{pmatrix}. \tag{M.56}$$

In this parametrization the first three of the eight generators $\hat{G}_r$ ($r = 1, 2, \ldots, 8$) are the same as $\hat{X}'_1, \hat{X}'_2, \hat{X}'_3$ of (M.29)–(M.30). The others may be constructed as usual from (M.10); for example,

$$\hat{G}_5 = \frac{\mathrm{i}}{2}\left(q_3\frac{\partial}{\partial q_1} - q_1\frac{\partial}{\partial q_3}\right), \quad \hat{G}_7 = \frac{\mathrm{i}}{2}\left(q_3\frac{\partial}{\partial q_2} - q_2\frac{\partial}{\partial q_3}\right). \tag{M.57}$$

The SU(3) algebra is found to be

$$[\hat{G}_a, \hat{G}_b] = \mathrm{i}f_{abc}\hat{G}_c, \tag{M.58}$$

where a, b and c each run from 1 to 8. The structure constants are $\mathrm{i}f_{abc}$, and the non-vanishing $f's$ are as follows:

$$f_{123} = 1, \ f_{147} = 1/2, \ f_{156} = -1/2, \ f_{246} = 1/2, \ f_{257} = 1/2 \qquad \text{(M.59)}$$

$$f_{345} = 1/2, \ f_{367} = -1/2, \ f_{458} = \sqrt{3}/2, \ f_{678} = \sqrt{3}/2. \qquad \text{(M.60)}$$

Note that the f's are antisymmetric in all pairs of indices (Carruthers (1966) chapter 2).

M.5 Matrix representations of generators, and of Lie groups

We have shown how the generators $\hat{X}_1, \hat{X}_2, \ldots, \hat{X}_r$ of a Lie group can be constructed as differential operators, understood to be acting on functions of the 'coordinates' to which the transformations of the group refer. These generators satisfy certain commutation relations, the Lie algebra of the group. For any given Lie algebra, it is also possible to find sets of *matrices* $X_1, X_2, \ldots, X_r$ (without hats) which satisfy the same commutation relations as the $\hat{X}_\nu$'s – that is, they have the same algebra. Such matrices are said to form a (matrix) representation of the Lie algebra, or equivalently of the generators. The idea is familiar from the study of angular momentum in quantum mechanics (Schiff 1968, section 27), where the entire theory may be developed from the commutation relations (with $\hbar = 1$)

$$[\hat{J}_i, \hat{J}_j] = \mathrm{i}\epsilon_{ijk}\hat{J}_k \qquad \text{(M.61)}$$

for the angular momentum operators $\hat{J}_i$, together with the physical requirement that the $\hat{J}_i$'s (and the matrices representing them) must be Hermitian. In this case the matrices are of the form (in quantum-mechanical notation)

$$\left(J_i^{(J)}\right)_{M'_J M_J} \equiv \langle JM'_J|\hat{J}_i|JM_J\rangle, \qquad \text{(M.62)}$$

where $|JM_J\rangle$ is an eigenstate of $\hat{\mathbf{J}}^2$ and of $\hat{J}_3$ with eigenvalues $J(J+1)$ and M_J respectively. Since M_J and M'_J each run over the $2J+1$ values defined by $-J \leq M_J, \ M'_J \leq J$, the matrices $J_i^{(J)}$ are of dimension $(2J+1) \times (2J+1)$. Clearly, since the generators of SU(2) have the same algebra as (M.61), an identical matrix representation may be obtained for them; these matrices were denoted by $T_i^{(T)}$ in section 12.1.2. It is important to note that J (or T) can take an infinite sequence of values $J = 0, 1/2, 1, 3/2, \ldots$, corresponding physically to various 'spin' magnitudes. Thus there are infinitely many sets of three matrices $(J_1^{(J)}, J_2^{(J)}, J_3^{(J)})$ all with the same commutation relations as (M.61).

A similar method for obtaining matrix representations of Lie algebras may be followed in other cases. In physical terms, the problem amounts to finding a correct labelling of the base states, analogous to $|JM\rangle$. In the latter case, the quantum number J specifies each different representation. The reason it does so is because (as should be familiar) the corresponding operator $\hat{\boldsymbol{J}}^2$ commutes with every generator:

$$[\hat{\boldsymbol{J}}^2, \hat{J}_i] = 0. \tag{M.63}$$

Such an operator is called a *Casimir operator*, and by a lemma due to Schur (Hammermesh 1962, pages 100–101) it must be a multiple of the unit operator. The numerical value it has is different for each different representation, and may therefore be used to characterize a representation (namely as '$J = 0$', '$J = 1/2$', etc.).

In general, more than one such operator is needed to characterize a representation completely. For example, in SO(4), the two operators $\hat{\boldsymbol{M}}^2$ and $\hat{\boldsymbol{N}}^2$ commute with all the generators, and take values $M(M+1)$ and $N(N+1)$ respectively, where $M, N = 0, 1/2, 1, \ldots$. Thus the labelling of the matrix elements of the generators is the same as it would be for two independent particles, one of spin M and the other of spin N. For given M, N the matrices are of dimension $[(2M+1)+(2N+1)] \times [(2M+1)+(2N+1)]$. The number of Casimir operators required to characterize a representation is called the *rank* of the group (or the algebra). This is also equal to the number of independent mutually commuting generators (though this is by no means obvious). Thus SO(4) is a rank two group, with two commuting generators $\hat{M}_3$ and $\hat{N}_3$; so is SU(3), since $\hat{G}_3$ and $\hat{G}_8$ commute. Two Casimir operators are therefore required to characterize the representations of SU(3), which may be taken to be the 'quadratic' one

$$\hat{C}_2 \equiv \hat{G}_1^2 + \hat{G}_2^2 + \ldots + \hat{G}_8^2, \tag{M.64}$$

together with a 'cubic' one

$$\hat{C}_3 \equiv d_{abc} \hat{G}_a \hat{G}_b \hat{G}_c, \tag{M.65}$$

where the coefficients d_{abc} are defined by the relation

$$\{\lambda_a, \lambda_b\} = \frac{4}{3} \delta_{ab} I + 2 d_{abc} \lambda_c, \tag{M.66}$$

and are symmetric in all pairs of indices (they are tabulated in Carruthers 1966, table 2.1). In practice, for the few SU(3) representations that are actually required, it is more common to denote them (as we have in the text) by their dimensionality, which for the cases **1** (singlet), **3** (triplet), **3*** (antitriplet), **8** (octet) and **10** (decuplet) is in fact a unique labelling. The values of $\hat{C}_2$ in these representations are

$$\hat{C}_2(\mathbf{1}) = 0, \ \hat{C}_2(\mathbf{3}, \mathbf{3^*}) = 4/3, \ \hat{C}_2(\mathbf{8}) = 3, \ \hat{C}_2(\mathbf{10}) = 6. \tag{M.67}$$

Having characterized a given representation by the eigenvalues of the Casimir operator(s), a further labelling is then required to characterize the states within a given representation (the analogue of the eigenvalue of $\hat{J}_3$ for angular momentum). For SO(4) these further labels may be taken to be the eigenvalues of $\hat{M}_3$ and $\hat{N}_3$; for SU(3) they are the eigenvalues of $\hat{G}_3$ and $\hat{G}_8$ – i.e. those corresponding to the third component of isospin and hypercharge, in the flavour case (see figures 12.3 and 12.4).

In the case of groups whose elements are themselves matrices, such as SO(3), SO(4), SU(2), SU(3), and the Lorentz group, one particular representation of the generators may always be obtained by considering the general form of a matrix in the group which is infinitesimally close to the unit element. In a suitable parametrization, we may write such a matrix as

$$1 + i \sum_{\nu=1}^{r} \epsilon_\nu X_\nu^{(\mathcal{G})}, \tag{M.68}$$

where $(\epsilon_1, \epsilon_2, \ldots, \epsilon_r)$ are infinitesimal parameters, and $(X_1^{(\mathcal{G})}, X_2^{(\mathcal{G})}, \ldots, X_r^{(\mathcal{G})})$ are matrices representing the generators of the (matrix) group $\mathcal{G}$. This is exactly the same procedure we followed for SU(2) in section 12.1.1, where we found from (12.26) that the three $X_\nu^{(\mathrm{SU}(2))}$'s were just $\boldsymbol{\tau}/2$, satisfying the SU(2) algebra. Similarly, in section 12.2 we saw that the eight SU(3) $X_\nu^{(\mathrm{SU}(3))}$'s were just $\boldsymbol{\lambda}/2$, satisfying the SU(3) algebra. These particular two representations are called the *fundamental* representations of the SU(2) and SU(3) algebras, respectively; they are the representations of lowest dimensionality. For SO(3), the three $X_\nu^{(\mathrm{SO}(3))}$'s are (from (M.17))

$$X_1^{(\mathrm{SO}(3))} = \begin{pmatrix} 0 & 0 & 0 \\ 0 & 0 & -i \\ 0 & i & 0 \end{pmatrix}$$

$$X_2^{(\mathrm{SO}(3))} = \begin{pmatrix} 0 & 0 & i \\ 0 & 0 & 0 \\ -i & 0 & 0 \end{pmatrix}$$

$$X_3^{(\mathrm{SO}(3))} = \begin{pmatrix} 0 & -i & 0 \\ i & 0 & 0 \\ 0 & 0 & 0 \end{pmatrix} \tag{M.69}$$

which are the same as the 3×3 matrices $T_i^{(1)}$ of (12.48):

$$\left(T_i^{(1)} \right)_{jk} = -i\epsilon_{ijk}. \tag{M.70}$$

The matrices $\boldsymbol{\tau}_i/2$ and $T_i^{(1)}$ correspond to the values $J = 1/2$, $J = 1$, respectively, in angular momentum terms.

It is not a coincidence that the coefficients on the right-hand side of (M.70) are (minus) the SO(3) structure constants. One representation of a Lie algebra

is always provided by a set of matrices $\{X_\nu^{(R)}\}$ whose elements are defined by

$$\left(X_\lambda^{(R)}\right)_{\mu\nu} = -c_{\lambda\mu}^\nu, \tag{M.71}$$

where the c's are the structure constants of (M.12), and each of μ, ν, λ runs from 1 to r. Thus these matrices are of dimensionality $r \times r$, where r is the number of generators. That this prescription works is due to the fact that the generators satisfy the *Jacobi identity*

$$[\hat{X}_\lambda, [\hat{X}_\mu, \hat{X}_\nu]] + [\hat{X}_\mu, [\hat{X}_\nu, \hat{X}_\lambda]] + [\hat{X}_\nu, [\hat{X}_\lambda, \hat{X}_\mu]] = 0. \tag{M.72}$$

Using (M.12) to evaluate the commutators, and the fact that the generators are independent, we obtain

$$c_{\mu\nu}^\alpha c_{\lambda\alpha}^\beta + c_{\nu\lambda}^\alpha c_{\mu\alpha}^\beta + c_{\lambda\mu}^\alpha c_{\nu\alpha}^\beta = 0. \tag{M.73}$$

The reader may fill in the steps leading from here to the desired result:

$$\left(X_\lambda^{(R)}\right)_{\nu\alpha} \left(X_\mu^{(R)}\right)_{\alpha\beta} - \left(X_\mu^{(R)}\right)_{\nu\alpha} \left(X_\lambda^{(R)}\right)_{\alpha\beta} = c_{\lambda\mu}^\alpha \left(X_\alpha^{(R)}\right)_{\nu\beta}. \tag{M.74}$$

(M.74) is precisely the $(\nu\beta)$ matrix element of

$$[X_\lambda^{(R)}, X_\mu^{(R)}] = c_{\lambda\mu}^\alpha X_\alpha^{(R)}, \tag{M.75}$$

showing that the $X_\mu^{(R)}$'s satisfy the group algebra (M.12), as required. The representation in which the generators are represented by (minus) the structure constants, in the sense of (M.71), is called the *regular* or *adjoint* representation.

Having obtained any particular matrix representation $\boldsymbol{X}^{(P)}$ of the generators of a group $\mathcal{G}$, a corresponding *matrix representation of the group elements* can be obtained by exponentiation, via

$$D^{(P)}(\boldsymbol{\alpha}) = \exp\{i\boldsymbol{\alpha} \cdot \boldsymbol{X}^{(P)}\}, \tag{M.76}$$

where $\boldsymbol{\alpha} = (\alpha_1, \alpha_2, \ldots, \alpha_r)$ (see (12.31) and (12.49) for SU(2), and (12.74) and (12.81) for SU(3)). In the case of the groups whose elements are matrices, exponentiating the generators $\boldsymbol{X}^{(\mathcal{G})}$ just recreates the general matrices of the group, so we may call this the 'self-representation': the one in which the group elements are represented by themselves. In the more general case (M.76), the crucial property of the matrices $D^{(P)}(\boldsymbol{\alpha})$ is that they obey the same group combination law as the elements of the group $\mathcal{G}$ they are representing: that is, if the group elements obey

$$g(\boldsymbol{\alpha})g(\boldsymbol{\beta}) = g(\boldsymbol{\gamma}(\boldsymbol{\alpha}, \boldsymbol{\beta})), \tag{M.77}$$

then

$$D^{(P)}(\boldsymbol{\alpha})D^{(P)}(\boldsymbol{\beta}) = D^{(P)}(\boldsymbol{\gamma}(\boldsymbol{\alpha}, \boldsymbol{\beta})). \tag{M.78}$$

It is a rather remarkable fact that there are certain, say, 10×10 matrices which multiply together in exactly the same way as the rotation matrices of SO(3).

M.6 The Lorentz group

Consideration of matrix representations of the Lorentz group provides insight into the equations of relativistic quantum mechanics, for example the Dirac equation. Consider the infinitesimal Lorentz transformation (M.46). The 4×4 matrix corresponding to this may be written in the form

$$1 + i\boldsymbol{\epsilon} \cdot \boldsymbol{X}^{(\mathrm{LG})} - i\boldsymbol{\eta} \cdot \boldsymbol{K}^{(\mathrm{LG})}, \tag{M.79}$$

where

$$X_1^{(\mathrm{LG})} = \begin{pmatrix} 0 & 0 & 0 & 0 \\ 0 & 0 & 0 & 0 \\ 0 & 0 & 0 & -i \\ 0 & 0 & i & 0 \end{pmatrix} \quad \text{etc,} \tag{M.80}$$

(as in (M.69) but with an extra border of 0's), and

$$K_1^{(\mathrm{LG})} = \begin{pmatrix} 0 & -i & 0 & 0 \\ -i & 0 & 0 & 0 \\ 0 & 0 & 0 & 0 \\ 0 & 0 & 0 & 0 \end{pmatrix}$$

$$K_2^{(\mathrm{LG})} = \begin{pmatrix} 0 & 0 & -i & 0 \\ 0 & 0 & 0 & 0 \\ -i & 0 & 0 & 0 \\ 0 & 0 & 0 & 0 \end{pmatrix}$$

$$K_3^{(\mathrm{LG})} = \begin{pmatrix} 0 & 0 & 0 & -i \\ 0 & 0 & 0 & 0 \\ 0 & 0 & 0 & 0 \\ -i & 0 & 0 & 0 \end{pmatrix}. \tag{M.81}$$

In (M.80) and (M.81) the matrices are understood to be acting on the four-component vector

$$\begin{pmatrix} x^0 \\ x^1 \\ x^2 \\ x^3 \end{pmatrix}. \tag{M.82}$$

It is straightforward to check that the matrices $X_i^{(\mathrm{LG})}$ and $K_i^{(\mathrm{LG})}$ satisfy the algebra (M.50)–(M.52) as expected.

An important point to note is that the matrices $K_i^{(\mathrm{LG})}$, in contrast to $X_i^{(\mathrm{LG})}$ or $X_i^{(\mathrm{SO}(3))}$, and to the corresponding matrices of SU(2) and SU(3), are *not* Hermitian. A theorem states that only the generators of *compact* Lie groups can be represented by finite-dimensional Hermitian matrices. Here 'compact' means that the domain of variation of all the parameters is bounded (none exceeds a given positive number p in absolute magnitude) and closed

(the limit of every convergent sequence of points in the set also lies in the set). For the Lorentz group, the limiting velocity c is not included (the γ-factor goes to infinity), and so the group is *non-compact*.

In a general representation of the Lorentz group, the generators X_i, K_i will obey the algebra (M.50)–(M.52). Let us introduce the combinations

$$\boldsymbol{P} \equiv \frac{1}{2}(\boldsymbol{X} + \mathrm{i}\boldsymbol{K}) \tag{M.83}$$

$$\boldsymbol{Q} \equiv \frac{1}{2}(\boldsymbol{X} - \mathrm{i}\boldsymbol{K}). \tag{M.84}$$

Then the algebra becomes

$$[P_i, P_j] = \mathrm{i}\epsilon_{ijk}P_k \tag{M.85}$$

$$[Q_i, Q_j] = \mathrm{i}\epsilon_{ijk}Q_k \tag{M.86}$$

$$[P_i, Q_j] = 0, \tag{M.87}$$

which are apparently the same as (M.43)–(M.45). We can see from (M.81) that the matrices $\mathrm{i}\boldsymbol{K}^{(\mathrm{LG})}$ *are* Hermitian, and the same is in fact true in a general finite-dimensional representation. So we can appropriate standard angular momentum theory to set up the representations of the algebra of the $\boldsymbol{P}$'s and $\boldsymbol{Q}$'s – namely, they behave just like two independent (mutually commuting) angular momenta. The eigenvalues of $\boldsymbol{P}^2$ are of the form $P(P+1)$, for $P = 0, 1/2, \ldots$, and similarly for $\boldsymbol{Q}^2$; the eigenvalues of P_3 are M_P where $-P \leq M_P \leq P$, and similarly for Q_3.

Consider the particular case where the eigenvalue of $\boldsymbol{Q}^2$ is zero ($Q = 0$), and the value of P is $1/2$. The first condition implies that the $\boldsymbol{Q}$'s are identically zero, so that

$$\boldsymbol{X} = \mathrm{i}\boldsymbol{K} \tag{M.88}$$

in this representation, while the second condition tells us that

$$\boldsymbol{P} = \frac{1}{2}(\boldsymbol{X} + \mathrm{i}\boldsymbol{K}) = \frac{1}{2}\boldsymbol{\sigma}, \tag{M.89}$$

the familiar matrices for spin-$1/2$. We label this representation by the values of P ($1/2$) and Q (0) (these are the eigenvalues of the two Casimir operators). Then using (M.88) and (M.89) we find

$$\boldsymbol{X}^{(\frac{1}{2},0)} = \frac{1}{2}\boldsymbol{\sigma} \tag{M.90}$$

and

$$\boldsymbol{K}^{(\frac{1}{2},0)} = -\frac{\mathrm{i}}{2}\boldsymbol{\sigma}. \tag{M.91}$$

Now recall that the general infinitesimal Lorentz transformation has the form

$$1 + \mathrm{i}\boldsymbol{\epsilon} \cdot \boldsymbol{X} - \mathrm{i}\boldsymbol{\eta} \cdot \boldsymbol{K}. \tag{M.92}$$

In the present case this becomes

$$1 + i\boldsymbol{\epsilon} \cdot \boldsymbol{\sigma}/2 - \boldsymbol{\eta} \cdot \boldsymbol{\sigma}/2. \tag{M.93}$$

These matrices are of dimension 2×2, and act on two-component spinors, which therefore transform under an infinitesimal Lorentz transformation by (cf (4.19) and (4.42))

$$\phi' = (1 + i\boldsymbol{\epsilon} \cdot \boldsymbol{\sigma}/2 - \boldsymbol{\eta} \cdot \boldsymbol{\sigma}/2)\phi. \tag{M.94}$$

We say that ϕ 'transforms as the $(1/2, 0)$ representation of the Lorentz group'. The '$1 + i\boldsymbol{\epsilon} \cdot \boldsymbol{\sigma}/2$' part is the familiar (infinitesimal) rotation matrix for spinors, first met in section 4.4; it exponentiates to give $\exp(i\boldsymbol{\alpha} \cdot \boldsymbol{\sigma}/2)$ for finite rotations. The '$-\boldsymbol{\eta} \cdot \boldsymbol{\sigma}/2$' part shows how such a spinor transforms under a pure (infinitesimal) velocity transformation. The finite transformation law is

$$\phi' = \exp(-\boldsymbol{\vartheta} \cdot \boldsymbol{\sigma}/2)\phi \tag{M.95}$$

where the three real parameters $\boldsymbol{\vartheta} = (\vartheta_1, \vartheta_2, \vartheta_3)$ specify the direction and magnitude of the boost.

There is, however, a second two-dimensional representation, which is characterized by the labelling $P = 0, Q = 1/2$, which we denote by $(0, 1/2)$. In this case, the previous steps yield

$$\boldsymbol{X}^{(\frac{1}{2},0)} = \frac{1}{2}\boldsymbol{\sigma} \tag{M.96}$$

as before, but

$$\boldsymbol{K}^{(0,\frac{1}{2})} = \frac{i}{2}\boldsymbol{\sigma}. \tag{M.97}$$

So the corresponding two-component spinor χ transforms by (cf (4.19) and (4.42))

$$\chi' = (1 + i\boldsymbol{\epsilon} \cdot \boldsymbol{\sigma}/2 + \boldsymbol{\eta} \cdot \boldsymbol{\sigma}/2)\chi. \tag{M.98}$$

We see that ϕ and χ behave the same under rotations, but 'oppositely' under boosts.

These transformation laws are exactly what we used in section 4.1.2 when discussing the behaviour of the Dirac wavefunction ψ under Lorentz transformations, where ψ is put together from one ϕ and one χ via

$$\psi = \begin{pmatrix} \phi \\ \chi \end{pmatrix}, \tag{M.99}$$

and describes a *massive* spin-1/2 particle according to the equations

$$\begin{aligned} E\phi &= \boldsymbol{\sigma} \cdot \boldsymbol{p}\phi + m\chi \\ E\chi &= -\boldsymbol{\sigma} \cdot \boldsymbol{p}\chi + m\phi, \end{aligned} \tag{M.100}$$

consistent with the representation (3.40) of the Dirac matrices.

M.7 The relation between SU(2) and SO(3)

We have seen (sections M.4.1 and M.4.2) that the algebras of these two groups are identical. So the groups are isomorphic in the vicinity of their respective identity elements. Furthermore, matrix representations of one algebra automatically provide representations of the other. Since exponentiating these infinitesimal matrix transformations produces matrices representing group elements corresponding to finite transformations in both cases, it might appear that the groups are fully isomorphic. But actually they are not, as we shall now discuss.

We begin by re-considering the parameters used to characterize elements of SO(3) and SU(2). A general 3-D rotation is described by the SO(3) matrix $R(\hat{n}, \theta)$, where $\hat{n}$ is the axis of the rotation and θ is the angle of rotation. For example,

$$R(\hat{z}, \theta) = \begin{pmatrix} \cos\theta & \sin\theta & 0 \\ -\sin\theta & \cos\theta & 0 \\ 0 & 0 & 1 \end{pmatrix}. \qquad (M.101)$$

On the other hand, we can write the general SU(2) matrix V in the form

$$V = \begin{pmatrix} a & b \\ -b^* & a^* \end{pmatrix}, \qquad (M.102)$$

where $|a|^2 + |b|^2 = 1$ from the unit determinant condition. It therefore depends on three real parameters, the choice of which we are now going to examine in more detail than previously. In (12.32) we wrote V as $\exp(i\boldsymbol{\alpha} \cdot \boldsymbol{\tau}/2)$, which certainly involves three real parameters $\alpha_1, \alpha_2, \alpha_3$; and below (12.35) we proposed, further, to write $\boldsymbol{\alpha} = \hat{n}\theta$, where θ is an angle and $\hat{n}$ is a unit vector. Then, since (as the reader may verify)

$$\exp(i\theta\boldsymbol{\tau} \cdot \hat{n}/2) = \cos\theta/2 + i\boldsymbol{\tau} \cdot \hat{n}\sin\theta/2, \qquad (M.103)$$

it follows that this latter parametrization corresponds to writing, in (M.102),

$$a = \cos\theta/2 + in_z\sin\theta/2, \quad b = (n_y + in_x)\sin\theta/2, \qquad (M.104)$$

with $n_x^2 + n_y^2 + n_z^2 = 1$. Clearly the condition $|a|^2 + |b|^2 = 1$ is satisfied, and one can convince oneself that the full range of a and b is covered if $\theta/2$ lies between 0 and π (in particular, it is not necessary to extend the range of $\theta/2$ so as to include the interval π to 2π, since the corresponding region of a, b can be covered by changing the orientation of $\hat{n}$, which has not been constrained in any way). It follows that the parameters $\boldsymbol{\alpha}$ satisfy $\boldsymbol{\alpha}^2 \leq 4\pi^2$; that is, the space of the α's is the interior, and surface, of a sphere of radius 2π, as shown in figure M.1.

What about the parameter space of SO(3)? In this case, the same parameters $\hat{n}$ and θ specify a rotation, but now θ (rather than $\theta/2$) runs from 0 to π.

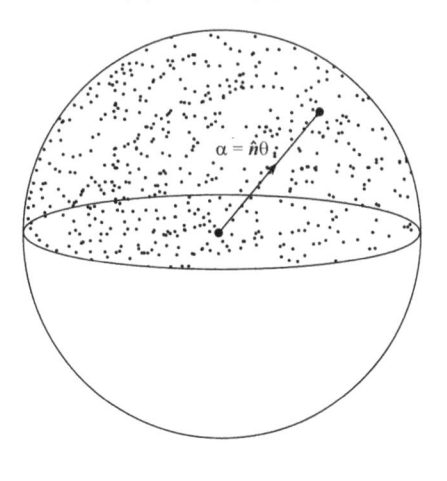

FIGURE M.1
The parameter spaces of SO(3) and SU(2): the whole sphere is the parameter space of SU(2), the upper (stippled) hemisphere that of SO(3).

However, we may allow the range of θ to extend to 2π, by taking advantage of the fact that

$$R(\hat{n}, \pi + \theta) = R(-\hat{n}, \theta). \tag{M.105}$$

Thus if we agree to limit $\hat{n}$ to directions in the upper hemisphere of figure M.1, for 3-D rotations, we can say that the whole sphere represents the parameter space of SU(2), but that of SO(3) is provided by the upper half only.

Now let us consider the correspondence – or *mapping* – between the matrices of SO(3) and SU(2): we want to see if it is one-to-one. The notation strongly suggests that the matrix $V(\hat{n}, \theta) \equiv \exp(i\theta\hat{n} \cdot \tau/2)$ of SU(2) corresponds to the matrix $R(\hat{n}, \theta)$ of SO(3), but the way it actually works has a subtlety.

We form the quantity $x \cdot \tau$, and assert that

$$x' \cdot \tau = V(\hat{n}, \theta) \, x \cdot \tau \, V^{\dagger}(\hat{n}, \theta), \tag{M.106}$$

where $x' = R(\hat{n}, \theta)x$. We can easily verify (M.106) for the special case $R(\hat{z}, \theta)$, using (M.101); the general case follows with more labour (but the general infinitesimal case should by now be a familiar manipulation). (M.106) establishes a precise mapping between the elements of SU(2) and those of SO(3), but it is not one-to-one (i.e. not an isomorphism), since plainly V can always be replaced by $-V$ and x' will be unchanged, and hence so will the associated SO(3) matrix $R(\hat{n}, \theta)$. It is therefore a homomorphism.

Next, we prove a little theorem to the effect that the identity element e of a group $\mathcal{G}$ must be represented by the unit matrix of the representation: $D(e) = I$. For, let $D(a), D(e)$ represent the elements a, e of $\mathcal{G}$. Then $D(ae) =$

$D(a)D(e)$ by the fundamental property (M.78) of representation matrices. On the other hand, $ae = a$ by the property of e. So we have $D(a) = D(a)D(e)$, and hence $D(e) = I$.

Now let us return to the correspondence between SU(2) and SO(3). $\boldsymbol{V}(\hat{\boldsymbol{n}}, \theta)$ corresponds to $R(\hat{\boldsymbol{n}}, \theta)$, but can an SU(2) matrix be said to provide a valid representation of SO(3)? Consider the case $\boldsymbol{V}(\hat{n} = \hat{z}, \theta = 2\pi)$. From (M.103) this is equal to

$$\begin{pmatrix} -1 & 0 \\ 0 & -1 \end{pmatrix}, \tag{M.107}$$

but the corresponding rotation matrix, from (M.101), is the identity matrix. Hence our theorem is violated, since (M.107) is plainly not the identity matrix of SU(2). Thus the SU(2) matrices can not be said to represent rotations, in the strict sense. Nevertheless, spin-1/2 particles certainly do exist, so Nature appears to make use of these 'not quite' representations! The SU(2) identity element is $\boldsymbol{V}(\hat{n} = \hat{z}, \theta = 4\pi)$, confirming that the rotational properties of a spinor are quite other than those of a classical object.

In fact, two and only two distinct elements of SU(2), namely

$$\begin{pmatrix} 1 & 0 \\ 0 & 1 \end{pmatrix} \quad \text{and} \quad \begin{pmatrix} -1 & 0 \\ 0 & -1 \end{pmatrix}, \tag{M.108}$$

correspond to the identity element of SO(3) in the correspondence (M.106) – just as, in general, $\boldsymbol{V}$ and $-\boldsymbol{V}$ correspond to the same SO(3) element $R(\hat{\boldsymbol{n}}, \theta)$, as we saw. The failure to be a true representation is localized simply to a sign: we may indeed say that, up to a sign, SU(2) matrices provide a representation of SO(3). If we 'factor out' this sign, the groups are isomorphic. A more mathematically precise way of saying this is given in Jones (1990, chapter 8).

N

Geometrical Aspects of Gauge Fields

N.1 Covariant derivatives and coordinate transformations

Let us go back to the U(1) case, equations (13.4)–(13.7). There, the introduction of the (gauge) covariant derivative D^μ produced an object, $D^\mu \psi(x)$, which transformed like $\psi(x)$ under local U(1) phase transformations, unlike the ordinary derivative $\partial^\mu \psi(x)$ which acquired an 'extra' piece when transformed. This followed from simple calculus, of course – but there is a slightly different way of thinking about it. The derivative involves not only $\psi(x)$ at the point x, but also ψ at the infinitesimally close, but different, point $x + \mathrm{d}x$; and the transformation law of $\psi(x)$ involves $\alpha(x)$, while that of $\psi(x + \mathrm{d}x)$ would involve the different function $\alpha(x + \mathrm{d}x)$. Thus we may perhaps expect something to 'go wrong' with the transformation law for the gradient.

To bring out the geometrical analogy we are seeking, let us write $\psi = \psi_\mathrm{R} + i\psi_\mathrm{I}$ and $\alpha(x) = q\chi(x)$ so that (13.3) becomes (cf (2.64))

$$
\begin{aligned}
\psi'_\mathrm{R}(x) &= \cos\alpha(x)\psi_\mathrm{R}(x) - \sin\alpha(x)\psi_\mathrm{I}(x) \\[6pt]
\psi'_\mathrm{I}(x) &= \sin\alpha(x)\psi_\mathrm{R}(x) + \cos\alpha(x)\psi_\mathrm{I}(x).
\end{aligned}
\tag{N.1}
$$

If we think of $\psi_\mathrm{R}(x)$ and $\psi_\mathrm{I}(x)$ as being the components of a 'vector' $\vec{\psi}(x)$ along the $\vec{e}_\mathrm{R}$ and $\vec{e}_\mathrm{I}$ axes, respectively, then (N.1) would represent the components of $\vec{\psi}(x)$ as referred to new axes $\vec{e}_\mathrm{R}'$ and $\vec{e}_\mathrm{I}'$, which have been rotated by $-\alpha(x)$ about an axis in the direction $\vec{e}_\mathrm{R} \times \vec{e}_\mathrm{I}$ (i.e. normal to the $\vec{e}_\mathrm{R}$–$\vec{e}_\mathrm{I}$ plane), as shown in figure N.1. Other such 'vectors' $\vec{\phi}_1(x), \vec{\phi}_2(x), \ldots$ (i.e. other wavefunctions for particles of the same charge q) *when evaluated at the same point x* will have 'components' transforming the same as (N.1) under the axis rotation $\vec{e}_\mathrm{R}, \vec{e}_\mathrm{I} \to \vec{e}_\mathrm{R}', \vec{e}_\mathrm{I}'$. But the components of the vector $\vec{\psi}(x + \mathrm{d}x)$ will behave differently. The transformation law (N.1) when written at $x + \mathrm{d}x$ will involve $\alpha(x + \mathrm{d}x)$, which (to first order in $\mathrm{d}x$) is $\alpha(x) + \partial_\mu \alpha(x)\mathrm{d}x^\mu$. Thus for $\psi'_\mathrm{R}(x + \mathrm{d}x)$ and $\psi'_\mathrm{I}(x + \mathrm{d}x)$ the rotation angle is $\alpha(x) + \partial_\mu \alpha(x)\mathrm{d}x^\mu$ rather than $\alpha(x)$. Now comes the key step in the analogy: we may think of the additional angle $\partial_\mu \alpha(x)\mathrm{d}x^\mu$ as coming about because, in going from x to $x + \mathrm{d}x$, the coordinate basis vectors $\vec{e}_\mathrm{R}$ and $\vec{e}_\mathrm{I}$ have been rotated through $+\partial_\mu \alpha(x)\mathrm{d}x^\mu$

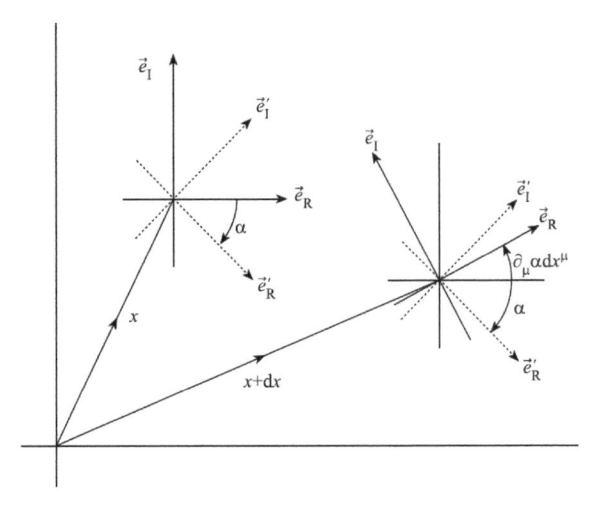

FIGURE N.1
Geometrical analogy for a U(1) gauge transformation.

(see figure N.2)! But that would mean that our 'naive' approach to rotations
of the derivative of $\vec{\psi}(x)$ amounts to using one set of axes at x, and another
at $x + dx$, which is likely to lead to 'trouble'. Consider now an elementary
example (from Schutz 1988, chapter 5) where just this kind of problem arises,
namely the use of polar coordinate basis vectors $\vec{e}_r$ and $\vec{e}_\theta$, which point in the
r and θ directions respectively. We have, as usual,

$$x = r \cos \theta, \quad y = r \sin \theta \tag{N.2}$$

and in a (real!) Cartesian basis $d\vec{r}$ is given by

$$d\vec{r} = dx \, \vec{i} + dy \, \vec{j}. \tag{N.3}$$

Using (N.2) in (N.3) we find

$$\begin{aligned}
d\vec{r} &= (dr \cos \theta - r \sin \theta \, d\theta)\vec{i} + (dr \sin \theta + r \cos \theta \, d\theta)\vec{j} \\
&= dr \, \vec{e}_r + d\theta \, \vec{e}_\theta \tag{N.4}
\end{aligned}$$

where

$$\vec{e}_r = \cos \theta \, \vec{i} + \sin \theta \, \vec{j}, \vec{e}_\theta = -r \sin \theta \, \vec{i} + r \cos \theta \, \vec{j}. \tag{N.5}$$

Plainly, $\vec{e}_r$ and $\vec{e}_\theta$ change direction (and even magnitude, for $\vec{e}_\theta$) as we move
about in the $x - y$ plane, as shown in figure N.2. So at each point (r, θ) we
have *different* axes $\vec{e}_r, \vec{e}_\theta$.

Now suppose that we wish to describe a vector field $\vec{V}$ in terms of $\vec{e}_r$ and
$\vec{e}_\theta$ via

$$\vec{V} = V^r \vec{e}_r + V^\theta \vec{e}_\theta \equiv V^\alpha \vec{e}_\alpha \quad (\text{sum on } \alpha = r, \theta), \tag{N.6}$$

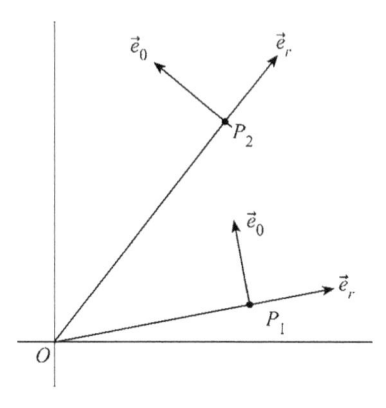

FIGURE N.2
Changes in the basis vectors $\vec{e}_r$ and $\vec{e}_\theta$ of polar coordinates.

and that we are also interested in the derivatives of $\vec{V}$, in this basis. Let us calculate $\frac{\partial \vec{V}}{\partial r}$, for example, by brute force:

$$\frac{\partial \vec{V}}{\partial r} = \frac{\partial V^r}{\partial r}\vec{e}_r + \frac{\partial V^\theta}{\partial r}\vec{e}_\theta + V^r\frac{\partial \vec{e}_r}{\partial r} + V^\theta\frac{\partial \vec{e}_\theta}{\partial r} \tag{N.7}$$

where we have included the derivatives of $\vec{e}_r$ and $\vec{e}_\theta$ to allow for the fact that *these vectors are not constant*. From (N.5) we easily find

$$\frac{\partial \vec{e}_r}{\partial r} = 0, \quad \frac{\partial \vec{e}_\theta}{\partial r} = -\sin\theta\,\vec{i} + \cos\theta\,\vec{j} = \frac{1}{r}\vec{e}_\theta, \tag{N.8}$$

which allows the last two terms in (N.7) to be evaluted. Similarly, we can calculate $\frac{\partial \vec{V}}{\partial \theta}$. In general, we may write these results as

$$\frac{\partial \vec{V}}{\partial q^\beta} = \frac{\partial V^\alpha}{\partial q^\beta}\vec{e}_\alpha + V^\alpha\frac{\partial \vec{e}_\alpha}{\partial q^\beta} \tag{N.9}$$

where $\beta = 1, 2$ with $q^1 = r, q^2 = \theta$, and $\alpha = r, \theta$.

In the present case, we were able to calculate $\partial\vec{e}_\alpha/\partial q^\beta$ explicitly from (N.5), as in (N.8). But whatever the nature of the coordinate system, $\partial\vec{e}_\alpha/\partial q^\beta$ is some vector and must be expressible as a linear combination of the basis vectors via an expression of the form

$$\frac{\partial \vec{e}_\alpha}{\partial q^\beta} = \Gamma^\gamma{}_{\alpha\beta}\vec{e}_\gamma \tag{N.10}$$

where the repeated index γ is summed over as usual ($\gamma = r, \theta$). Inserting (N.10) into (N.9) and interchanging the 'dummy' (i.e. summed over) indices

α and γ gives finally

$$\frac{\partial \vec{V}}{\partial q^\beta} = \left(\frac{\partial V^\alpha}{\partial q^\beta} + \Gamma^\alpha_{\gamma\beta} V^\gamma\right) \vec{e}_\alpha. \tag{N.11}$$

This is a very important result: it shows that, whereas the components of $\vec{V}$ in the basis $\vec{e}_\alpha$ are just V^α, the components of the derivative of $\vec{V}$ are not simply $\partial V^\alpha/\partial q^\beta$, but *contain an additional term*: the 'components of the derivative of a vector' are not just the 'derivatives of the components of the vector'.

Let us abbreviate $\partial/\partial q^\beta$ to ∂_β; then (N.11) tells us that in the $\vec{e}_\alpha$ basis, as used in (N.11), the components of the ∂_β derivative of $\vec{V}$ are

$$\partial_\beta V^\alpha + \Gamma^\alpha_{\gamma\beta} V^\gamma \equiv D_\beta V^\alpha. \tag{N.12}$$

The expression (N.12) is called the 'covariant derivative' of V^α within the context of the mathematics of general coordinate systems: it is denoted (as in (N.12)) by $D_\beta V^\alpha$ or, often, by $V^\alpha_{;\beta}$ (in the latter notation, $\partial_\beta V^\alpha$ is $V^\alpha_{,\beta}$). The most important property of $D_\beta V^\alpha$ is its transformation character under general coordinate transformations. Crucially, it transforms as a *tensor* T^α_β (see appendix D of volume 1) with the indicated 'one up, one down' indices; we shall not prove this here, referring instead to Schutz (1988), for example. This property is the reason for the name 'covariant derivative', meaning in this case essentially that it transforms the way its indices would have you believe it should. By contrast, and despite appearances, $\partial_\beta V^\alpha$ by itself does *not* transform as a 'T^α_β' tensor, and in a similar way $\Gamma^\alpha_{\gamma\beta}$ is *not* a '$T^\alpha_{\gamma\beta}$'-type tensor; only the combined object $D_\beta V^\alpha$ is a 'T^α_β'.

This circumstance is highly reminiscent of the situation we found in the case of gauge transformations. Consider the simplest case, that of U(1), for which $D_\mu \psi = \partial_\mu \psi + iqA_\mu \psi$. The quantity $D_\mu \psi$ transforms under a gauge transformation in the same way as ψ itself, but $\partial_\mu \psi$ does not. There is thus a close analogy between the 'good' transformation properties of $D_\beta V^\alpha$ and of $D_\mu \psi$. Further, the structure of $D_\mu \psi$ is very similar to that of $D_\beta V^\alpha$. There are two pieces, the first of which is the straightforward derivative, while the second involves a new field (Γ or A) and is also proportional to the original field. The 'i' of course is a big difference, showing that in the gauge symmetry case the transformations mix the real and imaginary parts of the wavefunction, rather than actual spatial components of a vector.

Indeed, the analogy is even closer in the non-Abelian – e.g. local SU(2) – case. As we have seen, $\partial^\mu \psi^{(\frac{1}{2})}$ does not transform as an SU(2) isospinor because of the extra piece involving $\partial^\mu \epsilon$; nor do the gauge fields $\boldsymbol{W}^\mu$ transform as pure $T = 1$ states, also because of a $\partial^\mu \epsilon$ term. But the gauge covariant combination $(\partial^\mu + ig\boldsymbol{\tau} \cdot \boldsymbol{W}^\mu/2)\psi^{(\frac{1}{2})}$ does transform as an isospinor under local SU(2) transformations, the two 'extra' $\partial^\mu \epsilon$ pieces cancelling each other out.

There is a useful way of thinking about the two contributions to $D_\beta V^\alpha$ (or $D_\mu \psi$). Let us multiply (N.12) by dq^β and sum over β so as to obtain

$$DV^\alpha \equiv \partial_\beta V^\alpha dq^\beta + \Gamma^\alpha_{\gamma\beta} V^\gamma dq^\beta. \tag{N.13}$$

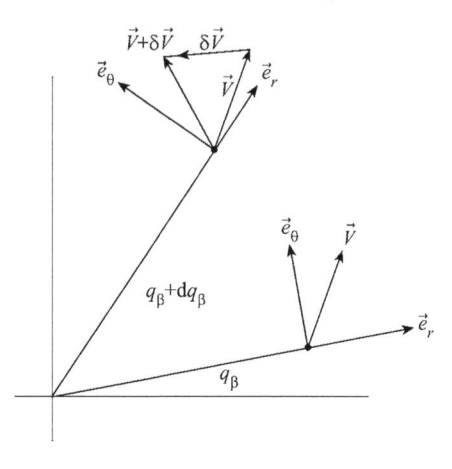

FIGURE N.3

Parallel transport of a vector $\vec{V}$ in a polar coordinate basis.

The first term on the right-hand side of (N.13) is $\frac{\partial V^{\alpha}}{\partial q^{\beta}}dq^{\beta}$ which is just the conventional differential dV^{α}, representing the change in V^{α} in moving from q^{β} to $q^{\beta}+dq^{\beta}$: $dV^{\alpha} = [V^{\alpha}(q^{\beta}+dq^{\beta}) - V^{\alpha}(q^{\beta})]$. Again, despite appearances, the quantities dV^{α} do not form the components of a vector, and the reason is that $V^{\alpha}(q^{\beta}+dq^{\beta})$ are components with respect to axes at $q^{\beta}+dq^{\beta}$, while $V^{\alpha}(q^{\beta})$ are components with respect to *different* axes at q^{β}. To form a 'good' differential DV^{α}, transforming as a vector, we must subtract quantities defined in the *same* coordinate system. This means that we need some way of 'carrying' $V^{\alpha}(q^{\beta})$ to $q^{\beta}+dq^{\beta}$, while keeping it somehow 'the same' as it was at q^{β}.

A reasonable definition of such a 'preserved' vector field is one that is unchanged in length, and has the same orientation relative to the axes at $q^{\beta}+dq^{\beta}$ as it had relative to the axes at q^{β} (see figure N.3). In other words, $\vec{V}$ is 'dragged around' with the changing coordinate frame, a process called *parallel transport*. Such a definition of 'no change' of course implies that change *has* occurred, in general, with respect to the *original* axes at q^{β}. Let us denote by δV^{α} the difference between the components of $\vec{V}$ after parallel transport to $q^{\beta}+dq^{\beta}$, and the components of $\vec{V}$ at q^{β} (see figure N.3). Then a reasonable definition of the 'good' differential of V^{α} would be $V^{\alpha}(q^{\beta}+dq^{\beta}) - (V^{\alpha}(q^{\beta}) + \delta V^{\alpha}) = dV^{\alpha} - \delta V^{\alpha}$. We interpret this as the covariant differential DV^{α} of (N.13), and accordingly, make the identification

$$\delta V^{\alpha} = -\Gamma^{\alpha}{}_{\gamma\beta}V^{\gamma}dq^{\beta}. \qquad (N.14)$$

On this interpretation, then, the coefficients $\Gamma^{\alpha}{}_{\gamma\beta}$ connect the components of a vector at one point with its components at a nearby point, after the vector

has been carried by 'parallel transport' from one point to the other; they are often called 'connection coefficients', or just 'the connection'.

In an analogous way we can write, in the U(1) gauge case,

$$
\begin{aligned}
D\psi \equiv D^{\mu}\psi \mathrm{d}x_{\mu} &= \partial^{\mu}\psi \mathrm{d}x_{\mu} + \mathrm{i}eA^{\mu}\psi \mathrm{d}x_{\mu} \\
&\equiv \mathrm{d}\psi - \delta\psi
\end{aligned}
\tag{N.15}
$$

with

$$
\delta\psi = -\mathrm{i}eA^{\mu}\psi \mathrm{d}x_{\mu}.
\tag{N.16}
$$

Equation (N.16) has a very similar structure to (N.14), suggesting that the electromagnetic potential A^{μ} might well be referred to as a 'gauge connection', as indeed it is in some quarters. Equations (N.15) and (N.16) generalize straightforwardly for $D\psi^{(\frac{1}{2})}$ and $\delta\psi^{(\frac{1}{2})}$.

We can relate (N.16) in a very satisfactory way to our original discussion of electromagnetism as a gauge theory in chapter 2, and in particular to (2.83). For transport restricted to the three spatial directions, (N.16) reduces to

$$
\delta\psi(\boldsymbol{x}) = \mathrm{i}e\boldsymbol{A} \cdot \mathrm{d}\boldsymbol{x}\psi(x).
\tag{N.17}
$$

However, the solution (2.83) gives

$$
\psi(\boldsymbol{x}) = \exp\left(\mathrm{i}e\int_{-\infty}^{\boldsymbol{x}} \boldsymbol{A} \cdot \mathrm{d}\boldsymbol{\ell}\right)\psi(\boldsymbol{A} = 0, \boldsymbol{x}),
\tag{N.18}
$$

replacing q by e. So

$$
\begin{aligned}
&\psi(\boldsymbol{x} + \mathrm{d}\boldsymbol{x}) \\
&= \exp\left(\mathrm{i}e\int_{-\infty}^{\boldsymbol{x}+\mathrm{d}\boldsymbol{x}} \boldsymbol{A} \cdot \mathrm{d}\boldsymbol{\ell}\right)\psi(\boldsymbol{A} = 0, \boldsymbol{x} + \mathrm{d}\boldsymbol{x}) \\
&= \exp\left(\mathrm{i}e\int_{\boldsymbol{x}}^{\boldsymbol{x}+\mathrm{d}\boldsymbol{x}} \boldsymbol{A} \cdot \mathrm{d}\boldsymbol{\ell}\right)\exp\left(\mathrm{i}e\int_{-\infty}^{\boldsymbol{x}} \boldsymbol{A} \cdot \mathrm{d}\boldsymbol{\ell}\right)\psi(\boldsymbol{A} = 0, \boldsymbol{x} + \mathrm{d}\boldsymbol{x}) \\
&\approx (1 + \mathrm{i}e\boldsymbol{A} \cdot \mathrm{d}\boldsymbol{x})\exp\left(\mathrm{i}e\int_{-\infty}^{\boldsymbol{x}} \boldsymbol{A} \cdot \mathrm{d}\boldsymbol{\ell}\right)[\psi(\boldsymbol{A} = 0, \boldsymbol{x}) + \boldsymbol{\nabla}\psi(\boldsymbol{A} = 0, \boldsymbol{x}) \cdot \mathrm{d}\boldsymbol{x}] \\
&\approx \psi(\boldsymbol{x}) + \mathrm{i}e\boldsymbol{A} \cdot \mathrm{d}\boldsymbol{x}\psi(\boldsymbol{x}) + \exp\left(\mathrm{i}e\int_{-\infty}^{\boldsymbol{x}} \boldsymbol{A} \cdot \mathrm{d}\boldsymbol{\ell}\right)\boldsymbol{\nabla}\psi(\boldsymbol{A} = 0, \boldsymbol{x}) \cdot \mathrm{d}\boldsymbol{x}, \quad \text{(N.19)}
\end{aligned}
$$

to first order in $\mathrm{d}\boldsymbol{x}$. On the right-hand side of (N.19) we see (i) the change $\delta\psi$ of (N.17), due to 'parallel transport' as prescribed by the gauge connection $\boldsymbol{A}$, and (ii) the change in ψ viewed as a function of $\boldsymbol{x}$, in the absence of $\boldsymbol{A}$. The solution (N.18) gives, in fact, the 'integrated' form of the small displacement law (N.19).

At this point the reader might object, going back to the $\vec{e}_r, \vec{e}_\theta$ example, that we had made a lot of fuss about nothing: after all, no one forced us

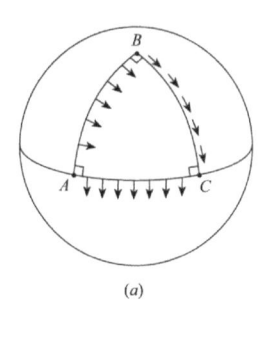

(a)

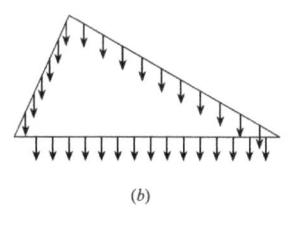

(b)

FIGURE N.4

Parallel transport (a) round a curved triangle on the surface of a sphere (b) round a triangle in a flat plane.

to use the $\vec{e}_r, \vec{e}_\theta$ basis, and if we had simply used the $\vec{i}, \vec{j}$ basis (which is constant throughout the plane) we would have had no such 'trouble'. This is a fair point, provided that we somehow knew that we are really doing physics in a 'flat' space, such as the Euclidean plane. But suppose instead that our two-dimensional space was the surface of a sphere. Then, an intuitively plausible definition of parallel transport is shown in figure N.4(a), in which transport is carried out around a closed path consisting of three great circle arcs $A \to B, B \to C, C \to A$, with the rule that at each stage the vector is drawn 'as parallel as possible' to the previous one. It is clear from the figure that the vector we end up with at A, after this circuit, is no longer parallel to the vector we started with; in fact, it has rotated by $\pi/2$ in this example, in which $\frac{1}{8}$th of the surface area of the unit sphere is enclosed by the triangle ABC. By contrast, the parallel transport of a vector round a flat triangle in the Euclidean plane leads to no such net change in the vector (figure N.4(b)).

It seems reasonable to suppose that the information about whether the space we are dealing with is 'flat' or 'curved' is contained in the connection $\Gamma^\alpha{}_{\gamma\beta}$. In a similar way, in the gauge case the analogy we have built up so far would lead us to expect that there are potentials A^μ which are somehow 'flat' ($E = B = 0$) and others which represent 'curvature' (non-zero E, B). This is what we discuss next.

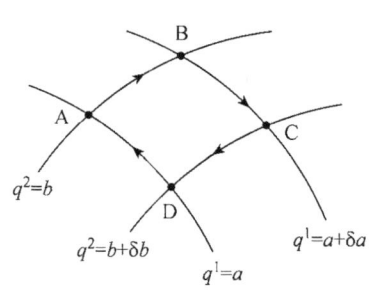

FIGURE N.5
Closed loop $ABCD$ in $q^1 - q^2$ space.

N.2   Geometrical curvature and the gauge field strength tensor

Consider a small closed loop in our (possibly curved) two-dimensional space – see figure N.5 – whose four sides are the coordinate lines $q^1 = a, q^1 = a + \delta a, q^2 = b, q^2 = b + \delta b$. We want to calculate the net change (if any) in δV^α as we parallel transport $\vec{V}$ around the loop. The change along $A \to B$ is

$$
\begin{aligned}
(\delta V^\alpha)_{AB} &= -\int_{q^2=b,q^1=a}^{q^2=b,q^1=a+\delta a} \Gamma^\alpha{}_{\gamma 1} V^\gamma dq^1 \\
&\approx -\delta a \Gamma^\alpha{}_{\gamma 1}(a,b) V^\gamma(a,b)
\end{aligned}
\tag{N.20}
$$

to first order in δa, while that along $C \to D$ is

$$
\begin{aligned}
(\delta V^\alpha)_{CD} &= -\int_{q^2=b+\delta b,q^1=a+\delta a}^{q^2=b+\delta b,q^1=a} \Gamma^\alpha{}_{\gamma 1} V^\gamma dq^1 \\
&= +\int_{q^2=b+\delta b,q^1=a}^{q^2=b+\delta b,q^1=a+\delta a} \Gamma^\alpha{}_{\gamma 1} V^\gamma dq^1. \\
&\approx \delta a \Gamma^\alpha{}_{\gamma 1}(a,b+\delta b) V^\gamma(a,b+\delta b).
\end{aligned}
\tag{N.21}
$$

Now

$$
\Gamma^\alpha{}_{\gamma 1}(a,b+\delta b) \approx \Gamma^\alpha{}_{\gamma 1}(a,b) + \delta b \frac{\partial \Gamma^\alpha{}_{\gamma 1}}{\partial q^2}
\tag{N.22}
$$

and, remembering that we are parallel-transporting $\vec{V}$,

$$
V^\gamma(a,b+\delta b) \approx V^\gamma(a,b) - \Gamma^\gamma{}_{\delta 2} V^\delta \delta b.
\tag{N.23}
$$

Combining (N.20) and (N.21) to lowest order, we find

$$
(\delta V^\alpha)_{AB} + (\delta V^\alpha)_{CD} \approx \delta a \delta b \left[\frac{\partial \Gamma^\alpha{}_{\gamma 1}}{\partial q^2} V^\gamma - \Gamma^\alpha{}_{\gamma 1} \Gamma^\gamma{}_{\delta 2} V^\delta \right]
\tag{N.24}
$$

or, interchanging dummy indices γ and δ in the last term,

$$(\delta V^\alpha)_{AB} + (\delta V^\alpha)_{CD} \approx \delta a \delta b \left[\frac{\partial \Gamma^\alpha{}_{\gamma 1}}{\partial q^2} - \Gamma^\alpha{}_{\delta 1} \Gamma^\delta{}_{\gamma 2} \right] V^\gamma. \tag{N.25}$$

Similarly,

$$(\delta V^\alpha)_{BC} + (\delta V^\alpha)_{DA} \approx \delta a \delta b \left[-\frac{\partial \Gamma^\alpha{}_{\gamma 2}}{\partial q^1} + \Gamma^\alpha{}_{\delta 2} \Gamma^\delta{}_{\gamma 1} \right] V^\gamma, \tag{N.26}$$

and so the net change around the whole small loop is

$$(\delta V^\alpha)_{ABCD} \approx \delta a \delta b \left[\frac{\partial \Gamma^\alpha{}_{\gamma 1}}{\partial q^2} - \frac{\partial \Gamma^\alpha{}_{\gamma 2}}{\partial q^1} + \Gamma^\alpha{}_{\delta 2} \Gamma^\delta{}_{\gamma 1} - \Gamma^\alpha{}_{\delta 1} \Gamma^\delta{}_{\gamma 2} \right] V^\gamma. \tag{N.27}$$

The indices '1' and '2' appear explicitly because the loop was chosen to go along these directions. In general, (N.27) would take the form

$$(\delta V^\alpha)_{loop} \approx \left[\frac{\partial \Gamma^\alpha{}_{\gamma \beta}}{\partial q^\sigma} - \frac{\partial \Gamma^\alpha{}_{\gamma \sigma}}{\partial q^\beta} + \Gamma^\alpha{}_{\delta \sigma} \Gamma^\delta{}_{\gamma \beta} - \Gamma^\alpha{}_{\delta \beta} \Gamma^\delta{}_{\gamma \sigma} \right] V^\gamma \mathrm{d}A^{\beta\sigma} \tag{N.28}$$

where $\mathrm{d}A^{\beta\sigma}$ is the area element. The quantity in brackets in (N.28) is the *Reimann curvature tensor* $R^\alpha{}_{\gamma\beta\sigma}$ (up to a sign, depending on conventions), which can clearly be calculated once the connection coefficients are known. A flat space is one for which all components $R^\alpha{}_{\gamma\beta\sigma} = 0$; the reader may verify that this is the case for our polar basis $\vec{e}_r, \vec{e}_\theta$ in the Euclidean plane. A non-zero value for any component of $R^\alpha{}_{\gamma\beta\sigma}$ means the space is curved.

We now follow exactly similar steps to calculate the net change in $\delta\psi$ as given by (N.16), around the small two-dimensional rectangle defined by the coordinate lines $x_1 = a, x_1 = a + \delta a, x_2 = b, x_2 = b + \delta b$, labelled as in figure N.5 but with q^1 replaced by x_1 and q^2 by x_2. Then

$$(\delta\psi)_{AB} = -ieA^1(a, b)\psi(a, b)\delta a \tag{N.29}$$

and

$$
\begin{aligned}
(\delta\psi)_{CD} &= +ieA^1(a, b + \delta b)\psi(a, b + \delta b)\delta a \\
&\approx ie\left(A^1(a, b) + \frac{\partial A^1}{\partial x_2}\delta b \right) [\psi(a, b) - ieA^2(a, b)\psi(a, b)\delta b]\delta a \\
&\approx ieA^1(a, b)\psi(a, b)\delta a \\
&\quad + ie\left[\frac{\partial A^1}{\partial x_2}\psi(a, b) - ieA^1(a, b)A^2(a, b)\psi(a, b) \right] \delta a \delta b. \tag{N.30}
\end{aligned}
$$

Combining (N.29) and (N.30) we find

$$(\delta\psi)_{AB} + (\delta\psi)_{CD} \approx \left[ie\frac{\partial A^1}{\partial x_2}\psi + e^2 A^1 A^2 \psi \right] \delta a \delta b. \tag{N.31}$$

Similarly,

$$(\delta\psi)_{BC} + (\delta\psi)_{DA} \approx \left[-\mathrm{i}e\frac{\partial A^2}{\partial x_1}\psi - e^2 A^1 A^2 \psi \right] \delta a \delta b, \qquad \text{(N.32)}$$

with the result that the net change around the loop is

$$(\delta\psi)_{ABCD} \approx \mathrm{i}e\left(\frac{\partial A^1}{\partial x_2} - \frac{\partial A^2}{\partial x_1} \right)\psi\delta a\delta b. \qquad \text{(N.33)}$$

For a general loop, (N.33) is replaced by

$$\begin{aligned}
(\delta\psi)_{loop} &= \mathrm{i}e\left(\frac{\partial A^\mu}{\partial x_\nu} - \frac{\partial A^\nu}{\partial x_\mu} \right)\psi\mathrm{d}x_\mu\mathrm{d}x_\nu \\
&= -\mathrm{i}eF^{\mu\nu}\psi\mathrm{d}x_\mu\mathrm{d}x_\nu \qquad \text{(N.34)}
\end{aligned}$$

where $F^{\mu\nu} = \partial^\mu A^\nu - \partial^\nu A^\mu$ is the familiar field strength tensor of QED.

The analogy we have been pursuing would therefore suggest that $F^{\mu\nu} = 0$ indicates 'no physical effect', while $F^{\mu\nu} \neq 0$ implies the presence of a physical effect. Indeed, when A^μ has the 'pure gauge' form $A^\mu = \partial^\mu\chi$ the associated $F^{\mu\nu}$ is zero; this is because such an A^μ can clearly be reduced to zero by a gauge transformation (and also, consistently, because $(\partial^\mu\partial^\nu - \partial^\nu\partial^\mu)\chi = 0$). If A^μ is not expressible as the 4-gradient of a scalar, then $F^{\mu\nu} \neq 0$ and an electromagnetic field is present, analogous to the spatial curvature revealed by $R^\alpha{}_{\gamma\beta\sigma} \neq 0$. Once again, there is a satisfying consistency between this 'geometrical' viewpoint and the discussion of the Aharonov-Bohm effect in Section 2.6. As in our remarks at the end of the previous section, and equations (N.17)–(N.19), equation (2.83) can be regarded as the integrated form of (N.34), for spatial loops. Transport round such a loop results in a non-trivial net phase change if non-zero $\mathbf{B}$ flux is enclosed, and this can be observed.

From this point of view there is undoubtedly a strong conceptual link between Einstein's theory of gravity and quantum gauge theories. In the former, matter (or energy) is regarded as the source of curvature of space-time, causing the space-time axes themselves to vary from point to point, and determining the trajectories of massive particles; in the latter, charge is the source of curvature in an 'internal' space (the complex ψ-plane, in the U(1) case), a curvature which we call an electromagnetic field, and which has observable physical effects.

The reader may consider repeating, for the local SU(2) case, the closed-loop transport calculation of (N.29)–(N.33). For this calculation, the place of the Abelian vector potential is taken by the matrix-valued non-Abelian potential $A^\mu = \boldsymbol{\tau}/2 \cdot \mathbf{A}^\mu$. It will lead to the expression for the non-Abelian field strength tensor as calculated in section 13.1.2.

O

Dimensional Regularization

After combining propagator denominators of the form $(p^2 - m^2 + i\epsilon)^{-1}$ by Feynman parameters (cf (10.40)), and shifting the origin of the loop momentum to complete the square (cf (10.42) and (11.16)), all one-loop Feynman integrals may be reduced to evaluating an integral of the form

$$I_d(\Delta, n) \equiv \int \frac{d^d k}{(2\pi)^d} \frac{1}{[k^2 - \Delta + i\epsilon]^n}, \tag{O.1}$$

or to a similar integral with factors of k (such as $k_\mu k_\nu$) in the numerator. We consider (O.1) first.

For our purposes, the case of physical interest is $d = 4$, and n is commonly 2 (e.g. in one-loop self-energies). Power-counting shows that (O.1) diverges as $k \to \infty$ for $d \geq 2n$. The idea behind *dimensional regularization* ('t Hooft and Veltman 1972) is to treat d as a variable parameter, taking values smaller than $2n$, so that (O.1) converges and can be evaluated explicitly as a function of d (and of course the other variables, including n).[1] Then the nature of the divergence as $d \to 4$ can be exposed (much as we did with the cut-off procedure in section 10.3), and dealt with by a suitable renormalization scheme. The crucial advantage of dimensional regularization is that it preserves gauge invariance, unlike the simple cut-off regularization we used in chapters 10 and 11.

We write

$$I_d = \frac{1}{(n-1)!} \left(\frac{\partial}{\partial \Delta}\right)^{n-1} \int \frac{d^d k}{(2\pi)^d} \frac{1}{[k^2 - \Delta + i\epsilon]}. \tag{O.2}$$

The d dimensions are understood as one time-like dimension k^0, and $d - 1$ spacelike dimensions. We begin by 'Euclideanizing' the integral, by setting $k^0 = ik^e$ with k^e real. Then the Minkowskian square k^2 becomes $-(k^e)^2 - \mathbf{k}^2 \equiv -k_E^2$, and $d^d k$ becomes $id^d k_E$, so that now

$$I_d = \frac{-i}{(n-1)!} \left(\frac{\partial}{\partial \Delta}\right)^{n-1} \int \frac{d^d k_E}{(2\pi)^d} \frac{1}{(k_E^2 + \Delta)}; \tag{O.3}$$

the 'iϵ' may be understood as included in Δ. The integral is evaluated by

---

[1] We concentrate here on ultraviolet divergences, but infrared ones (such as those met in section 14.4.2) can be dealt with too, by choosing d larger than $2n$.

introducing the following way of writing $(k_E^2 + \Delta)^{-1}$:

$$(k_E^2 + \Delta)^{-1} = \int_0^\infty d\beta e^{-\beta(k_E^2 + \Delta)}, \tag{O.4}$$

which leads to

$$I_d = \frac{1}{(n-1)!} \left(\frac{\partial}{\partial \Delta} \right)^{n-1} \int_0^\infty d\beta \int \frac{d^d k_E}{(2\pi)^d} e^{-\beta(k_E^2 + \Delta)}. \tag{O.5}$$

The interchange of the orders of the β and k_E integrations is permissible since I_d is convergent. The k_E integrals are, in fact, a series of Gaussians:

$$\int \frac{d^d k_E}{(2\pi)^d} e^{-\beta(k_E^2 + \Delta)} = e^{-\beta\Delta} \left\{ \prod_{j=1}^d \int \frac{dk_j}{(2\pi)} e^{-\beta k_j^2} \right\}$$

$$= \frac{e^{-\beta\Delta}}{(2\pi)^d} \left(\frac{\pi}{\beta} \right)^{d/2}. \tag{O.6}$$

Hence

$$I_d = \frac{-i}{(n-1)!} \frac{1}{(4\pi)^{d/2}} \left(\frac{\partial}{\partial \Delta} \right)^{n-1} \int d\beta e^{-\beta\Delta} \beta^{-d/2}$$

$$= \frac{-i}{(n-1)!} \frac{(-1)^{n-1}}{(4\pi)^{d/2}} \int d\beta e^{-\beta\Delta} \beta^{n-(d/2)-1}. \tag{O.7}$$

The last integral can be written in terms of Euler's integral for the *gamma function* $\Gamma(z)$ defined by (see, for example, Boas 1983, chapter 11)

$$\Gamma(z) = \int_0^\infty x^{z-1} e^{-x} dx. \tag{O.8}$$

Since $\Gamma(n) = (n-1)!$, it is convenient to write (O.8) entirely in terms of Γ functions as

$$I_d = i \frac{(-1)^n}{(4\pi)^{d/2}} \frac{\Gamma(n-d/2)}{\Gamma(n)} \Delta^{(d/2)-n}. \tag{O.9}$$

Equation (O.9) gives an explicit definition of I_d which can be used for any value of d, not necessarily an integer. As a function of z, $\Gamma(z)$ has isolated poles (see appendix F of volume 1) at $z = 0, -1, -2, \ldots$. The behaviour near $z = 0$ is given by

$$\Gamma(z) = \frac{1}{z} - \gamma + O(z), \tag{O.10}$$

where γ is the Euler–Mascheroni constant having the value $\gamma \approx 0.5772$. Using

$$z\Gamma(z) = \Gamma(z+1), \tag{O.11}$$

we find the behaviour near $z = -1$:

$$\Gamma(-1+z) = \frac{-1}{1-z}\Gamma(z)$$
$$= -[\frac{1}{z} + 1 - \gamma + O(z)]; \tag{O.12}$$

similarly

$$\Gamma(-2+z) = \frac{1}{2}[\frac{1}{z} + \frac{3}{2} - \gamma + O(z)]. \tag{O.13}$$

Consider now the case $n = 2$, for which $\Gamma(n - d/2)$ in (O.9) will have a pole at $d = 4$. Setting $d = 4 - \epsilon$, the divergent behaviour is given by

$$\Gamma(2 - d/2) = \frac{2}{\epsilon} - \gamma + O(\epsilon) \tag{O.14}$$

from (O.10). $I_d(\Delta, 2)$ is then given by

$$I_d(\Delta, 2) = \frac{i}{(4\pi)^{2-\epsilon/2}} \Delta^{-\epsilon/2} \left[\frac{2}{\epsilon} - \gamma + O(\epsilon)\right]. \tag{O.15}$$

When $\Delta^{-\epsilon/2}$ and $(4\pi)^{-2+\epsilon/2}$ are expanded in powers of ϵ, for small ϵ, the terms linear in ϵ will produce terms independent of ϵ when multiplied by the ϵ^{-1} in the bracket of (O.15). Using $x^\epsilon \approx 1 + \epsilon \ln x + O(\epsilon^2)$ we find

$$I_d(\Delta, 2) = \frac{i}{(4\pi)^2} \left[\frac{2}{\epsilon} - \gamma + \ln 4\pi - \ln \Delta + O(\epsilon)\right]. \tag{O.16}$$

Another source of ϵ-dependence arises from the fact (see problem 15.7) that a gauge coupling which is dimensionless in $d = 4$ dimensions will acquire mass dimension $\mu^{\epsilon/2}$ in $d = 4 - \epsilon$ dimensions (check this!). A vacuum polarization loop with two powers of the coupling will then contain a factor μ^ϵ. When expanded in powers of ϵ, this will convert the $\ln \Delta$ in (O.16) to $\ln(\Delta/\mu^2)$.

Renormalization schemes will subtract the explicit pole pieces (which diverge as $\epsilon \to 0$), but may also include in the subtraction certain finite terms as well. For example, in the 'minimal subtraction' (MS) scheme, one subtracts just the pole pieces; in the 'modified minimal subtraction' or $\overline{\text{MS}}$ ('emm-ess-bar') scheme (Bardeen *et al.* 1978) one subtracts the pole and the '$-\gamma + \ln 4\pi$' piece.

The change from one scheme 'A' to another 'B' must involve a finite renormalization of the form (Ellis *et al.* 1966, section 2.5)

$$\alpha_s^B = \alpha_s^A(1 + A_1\alpha_s^A + \ldots). \tag{O.17}$$

Note that this implies that the first two coefficients of the β function are unchanged under this transformation, so that they are scheme-independent. Subsequent coefficients are scheme-dependent, as is the QCD parameter Λ

introduced in section 15.3. From (15.54) the two corresponding values of Λ are related by

$$\ln\left(\frac{\Lambda_B}{\Lambda_A}\right) = \frac{1}{2}\int_{\alpha_s^A(|q^2|)}^{\alpha_s^B(|q^2|)} \frac{dx}{\beta_0 x^2(1+\dots)} \tag{O.18}$$

$$= \frac{A_1}{2\beta_0} \tag{O.19}$$

where we have taken $|q^2| \to \infty$ in (O.18) since the left-hand side is independent of $|q^2|$. Hence the relationship between the Λ's in different schemes is determined by the one-loop calculation which gives A_1 in (O.19). For example, changing from MS to $\overline{\text{MS}}$ gives (problem 15.8)

$$\Lambda_{\overline{\text{MS}}}^2 = \Lambda_{\text{MS}}^2 \exp(\ln 4\pi - \gamma), \tag{O.20}$$

as the reader may check.

Finally, consider the integral

$$I_d^{\mu\nu}(\Delta, n) \equiv \int \frac{d^d k}{(2\pi)^d} \frac{k^\mu k^\nu}{[k^2 - \Delta + i\epsilon]^n}. \tag{O.21}$$

From Lorentz covariance this must be proportional to the only second-rank tensor available, namely $g^{\mu\nu}$:

$$I_d^{\mu\nu} = A g^{\mu\nu}. \tag{O.22}$$

The constant 'A' can be determined by contracting both sides of (O.21) with $g_{\mu\nu}$, using $g^{\mu\nu} g_{\mu\nu} = d$ in d-dimensions. So

$$
\begin{aligned}
A &= \frac{1}{d}\int \frac{d^d k}{(2\pi)^d} \frac{k^2}{(k^2 - \Delta + i\epsilon)^n} \\
&= \frac{1}{d}\left\{\int \frac{d^d k}{(2\pi)^d} \frac{1}{(k^2 - \Delta + i\epsilon)^{n-1}} + \Delta\int \frac{d^d k}{(2\pi)^d} \frac{1}{(k^2 - \Delta + i\epsilon)^n}\right\} \\
&= \frac{i(-1)^n}{(4\pi)^{d/2}} \frac{\Delta^{(d/2)-n+1}}{d}\left\{\frac{-\Gamma(n-1-d/2)}{\Gamma(n-1)} + \frac{\Gamma(n-d/2)}{\Gamma(n)}\right\} \\
&= \frac{i(-1)^n}{(4\pi)^{d/2}} \frac{\Delta^{(d/2)-n+1}}{d} \frac{\Gamma(n-1-d/2)}{\Gamma(n)}\{-n + (n - d/2)\} \\
&= \frac{i(-1)^{n-1}\Delta^{(d/2)-n+1}}{(4\pi)^{d/2}} \frac{1}{2}\frac{\Gamma(n-1-d/2)}{\Gamma(n)}.
\end{aligned} \tag{O.23}
$$

Using these results, one can show straightforwardly that the gauge-non-invariant part of (11.18) – i.e. the piece in braces – vanishes. With the technique of dimensional regularization, starting from a gauge-invariant formulation of the theory the renormalization programme can be carried out while retaining manifest gauge invariance.

P

Grassmann Variables

In the path integral representation of quantum amplitudes (chapter 16) the fields are regarded as classical functions. Matrix elements of time-ordered products of bosonic operators could be satisfactorily represented (see the discussion following (16.79)). But something new is needed to represent, for example, the time-ordered product of two fermionic operators: there must be a sign difference between the two orderings, since the fermionic operators *anticommute*. Thus it seems that to represent amplitudes involving fermionic operators by path integrals we must think in terms of 'classical' anticommuting variables.

Fortunately, the necessary mathematics was developed by Grassmann in 1855, and applied to quantum amplitudes by Berezin (1966). Any two *Grassmann numbers* θ_1, θ_2 satisfy the fundamental relation

$$\theta_1\theta_2 + \theta_2\theta_1 = 0, \tag{P.1}$$

and of course

$$\theta_1^2 = \theta_2^2 = 0. \tag{P.2}$$

Grassmann numbers can be added and subtracted in the ordinary way, and muliplied by ordinary numbers. For our application, the essential thing we need to be able to do with Grassmann numbers is to integrate over them. It is natural to think that, as with ordinary numbers and functions, integration would be some kind of inverse of differentiation. So let us begin with differentiation.

We define

$$\frac{\partial(a\theta)}{\partial\theta} = a, \tag{P.3}$$

where a is any ordinary number, and

$$\frac{\partial}{\partial\theta_1}(\theta_1\theta_2) = \theta_2 \, ; \tag{P.4}$$

then necessarily

$$\frac{\partial}{\partial\theta_2}(\theta_1\theta_2) = -\theta_1. \tag{P.5}$$

Consider now a function of one such variable, $f(\theta)$. An expansion of f in powers of θ terminates after only two terms because of the property (P.2):

$$f(\theta) = a + b\theta. \tag{P.6}$$

So
$$\frac{\partial f(\theta)}{\partial \theta} = b, \tag{P.7}$$

but also
$$\frac{\partial^2 f}{\partial \theta^2} = 0 \tag{P.8}$$

for any such f. Hence the operator $\partial/\partial\theta$ has no inverse (think of the matrix analogue $A^2 = 0$: if A^{-1} existed, we could deduce $0 = A^{-1}(A^2) = (A^{-1}A)A = A$ for all A). Thus we must approach Grassmann integration other than via an inverse of differentiation.

We only need to consider integrals over the complete range of θ, of the form
$$\int d\theta f(\theta) = \int d\theta(a + b\theta). \tag{P.9}$$

Such an integral should be linear in f; thus it must be a linear function of a and b. One further property fixes its value: we require the result to be *invariant under translations of* θ *by* $\theta \to \theta + \eta$, where η is a Grassmann number. This property is crucial to manipulations made in the path integral formalism, for instance in 'completing the square' manipulations similar to those in section 16.3, but with Grassmann numbers. So we require
$$\int d\theta(a + b\theta) = \int d\theta([a + b\eta] + b\theta). \tag{P.10}$$

This has changed the constant (independent of θ) term, but left the linear term unchanged. The only linear function of a and b which behaves like this is a multiple of b, which is conventionally taken to be simply b. Thus we define
$$\int d\theta(a + b\theta) = b, \tag{P.11}$$

which means that integration is in some sense the same as differentiation!

When we integrate over products of different θ's, we need to specify a convention about the order in which the integrals are to be performed. We adopt the convention
$$\int d\theta_1 \int d\theta_2\, \theta_2\theta_1 = 1\,; \tag{P.12}$$

that is, the innermost integral is done first, then the next, and so on.

Since our application will be to Dirac fields, which are complex-valued, we need to introduce complex Grassmann numbers, which are built out of real and imaginary parts in the usual way (this would not be necessary for Majorana fermions). Thus we may define
$$\psi = \frac{1}{\sqrt{2}}(\theta_1 + i\theta_2), \quad \psi^* = \frac{1}{\sqrt{2}}(\theta_1 - i\theta_2), \tag{P.13}$$

and then
$$-i d\psi d\psi^* = d\theta_1 d\theta_2. \tag{P.14}$$

It is convenient to define complex conjugation to include reversing the order of quantities:

$$(\psi\chi)^* = \chi^*\psi^*. \tag{P.15}$$

Then (P.14) is consistent under complex conjugation.

We are now ready to evaluate some Gaussian integrals over Grassmann variables, which is essentially all we need in the path integral formalism. We begin with

$$
\begin{aligned}
\int\int \mathrm{d}\psi^* \mathrm{d}\psi\, e^{-b\psi^*\psi} &= \int\int \mathrm{d}\psi^* \mathrm{d}\psi (1 - b\psi^*\psi) \\
&= \int\int \mathrm{d}\psi^* \mathrm{d}\psi (1 + b\psi\psi^*) = b. \tag{P.16}
\end{aligned}
$$

Note that the analogous integral with ordinary variables is

$$\int\int \mathrm{d}x\mathrm{d}y\, e^{-b(x^2+y^2)/2} = 2\pi/b. \tag{P.17}$$

The important point here is that, in the Grassman case, b appears with a positive, rather than a negative, power. On the other hand, if we insert a factor $\psi\psi^*$ into the integrand in (P.16), we find that it becomes

$$\int\int \mathrm{d}\psi^* \mathrm{d}\psi\, \psi\psi^*(1 + b\psi\psi^*) = \int\int \mathrm{d}\psi^* \mathrm{d}\psi\, \psi\psi^* = 1, \tag{P.18}$$

and the insertion has effectively produced a factor b^{-1}. This effect of an insertion is the same in the 'ordinary variables' case:

$$\int\int \mathrm{d}x\mathrm{d}y(x^2 + y^2)/2\, e^{-b(x^2+y^2)/2} = 2\pi/b^2. \tag{P.19}$$

Now consider a Gaussian integral involving two different Grassmann variables:

$$\int \mathrm{d}\psi_1^* \mathrm{d}\psi_1 \mathrm{d}\psi_2^* \mathrm{d}\psi_2\, e^{-\psi^{*\mathrm{T}}M\psi}, \tag{P.20}$$

where

$$\psi = \begin{pmatrix} \psi_1 \\ \psi_2 \end{pmatrix}, \tag{P.21}$$

and M is a 2×2 matrix, whose entries are ordinary numbers. The only terms which survive the integration are those which, in the expansion of the exponential, contain each of ψ_1^*, ψ_1, ψ_2^* and ψ_2 exactly once. These are the terms

$$\frac{1}{2}\left[M_{11}M_{22}(\psi_1^*\psi_1\psi_2^*\psi_2 + \psi_2^*\psi_2\psi_1^*\psi_1) + M_{12}M_{21}(\psi_1^*\psi_2\psi_2^*\psi_1 + \psi_2^*\psi_1\psi_1^*\psi_2)\right]. \tag{P.22}$$

To integrate (P.22) conveniently, according to the convention (P.12), we need to re-order the terms into the form $\psi_2\psi_2^*\psi_1\psi_1^*$; this produces

$$(M_{11}M_{22} - M_{12}M_{21})(\psi_2\psi_2^*\psi_1\psi_1^*), \tag{P.23}$$

and the integral (P.20) is therefore just

$$\int\int d\psi_1^* d\psi d\psi_2^* d\psi_2 \, e^{-\psi^{*T}M\psi} = \det M. \tag{P.24}$$

The reader may show, or take on trust, the obvious generalization to N independent complex Grassmann variables ψ_1, ψ_2, ψ_3, ..., ψ_N. This result is sufficient to establish the assertion made in section 16.4 concerning the integral (16.90), when written in 'discretized' form.

We may contrast (P.24) with an analogous result for two ordinary complex numbers z_1, z_2. In this case we consider the integral

$$\int\int dz_1^* dz_1 dz_2^* dz_2 \, e^{-z^*Hz}, \tag{P.25}$$

where z is a two-component column matrix with elements z_1 and z_2. We take the matrix H to be Hermitian, with positive eigenvalues b_1 and b_2. Let H be diagonalized by the unitary transformation

$$\begin{pmatrix} z_1' \\ z_2' \end{pmatrix} = U \begin{pmatrix} z_1 \\ z_2 \end{pmatrix}, \tag{P.26}$$

with $UU^\dagger = I$. Then

$$dz_1' dz_2' = \det U \, dz_1 dz_2, \tag{P.27}$$

and so

$$dz_1' dz_1'^* dz_2' dz_2'^* = dz_1 dz_1^* dz_2 dz_2^*, \tag{P.28}$$

since $|\det U|^2 = 1$. The integral (P.25) then becomes

$$\int dz_1' dz_1'^* e^{-b_1 z_1'^* z_1'} \int dz_2' dz_2'^* e^{-b_2 z_2'^* z_2'}, \tag{P.29}$$

the integrals converging provided $b_1, b_2 > 0$. Next, setting $z_1 = (x_1 + iy_1)/\sqrt{2}$, $z_2 = (x_2 + iy_2)/\sqrt{2}$, (P.29) can be evaulated using (P.17), and the result is proportional to $(b_1 b_2)^{-1}$, which is the *inverse* of the determinant of the matrix H, when diagonalized. Thus – compare (P.16) and (P.17) – Gaussian integrals over complex Grassmann variables are proportional to the determinant of the matrix in the exponent, while those over ordinary complex variables are proportional to the inverse of the determinant.

Returning to integrals of the form (P.20), consider now a two-variable (both complex) analogue of (P.18):

$$\int d\psi_1^* d\psi_1 d\psi_2^* d\psi_2 \, \psi_1\psi_2^* \, e^{-\psi^{*T}M\psi}. \tag{P.30}$$

This time, only the term $\psi_1^* \psi_2$ in the expansion of the exponential will survive the integration, and the result is just $-M_{12}$. By exploring a similar integral (still with the term $\psi_1 \psi_2^*$) in the case of three complex Grassmann variables, the reader should be convinced that the general result is

$$\prod_i \int \mathrm{d}\psi_i^* \mathrm{d}\psi_i \, \psi_k \psi_l^* \, \mathrm{e}^{-\psi^{*\mathrm{T}} M \psi} = (M^{-1})_{kl} \det M. \qquad (\text{P.31})$$

With this result we can make plausible the fermionic analogue of (16.87), namely

$$\langle \Omega | T \left\{ \psi(x_1) \bar{\psi}(x_2) \right\} | \Omega \rangle = \frac{\int \mathcal{D}\bar{\psi}\mathcal{D}\psi \, \psi(x_1)\bar{\psi}(x_2) \exp[-\int \mathrm{d}^4 x_{\mathrm{E}} \bar{\psi}(\mathrm{i}\,\slashed{\partial} - m)\psi]}{\int \mathcal{D}\bar{\psi}\mathcal{D}\psi \exp[-\int \mathrm{d}^4 x_{\mathrm{E}} \bar{\psi}(\mathrm{i}\,\slashed{\partial} - m)\psi]};$$

$$(\text{P.32})$$

note that $\bar{\psi}$ and ψ^* are unitarily equivalent. The denominator of this expression is[1] $\det(\mathrm{i}\,\slashed{\partial} - m)$, while the numerator is this same determinant multiplied by the inverse of the operator $(\mathrm{i}\,\slashed{\partial} - m)$; but this is just $(\slashed{p} - m)^{-1}$ in momentum space, the familiar Dirac propagator.

---

[1] The reader may interpret this as a finite-dimensional determinant, after discretization.

Q

Feynman Rules for Tree Graphs in QCD and the Electroweak Theory

Q.1 QCD

Q.1.1 External particles

Quarks

The SU(3) colour degree of freedom is not written explicitly; the spinors have 3 (colour) × 4 (Dirac) components. For each fermion or antifermion line entering the graph include the spinor

$$u(p, s) \quad \text{or} \quad v(p, s) \tag{Q.1}$$

and for spin-$\frac{1}{2}$ particles leaving the graph the spinor

$$\bar{u}(p', s') \quad \text{or} \quad \bar{v}(p', s'), \tag{Q.2}$$

as for QED.

Gluons

Besides the spin-1 polarization vector, external gluons also have a 'colour polarization' vector $a^c (c = 1, 2, \ldots, 8)$ specifying the particular colour state involved. For each gluon line entering the graph include the factor

$$\epsilon_\mu(k, \lambda) \, a^c \tag{Q.3}$$

and for gluons leaving the graph the factor

$$\epsilon_\mu^*(k', \lambda') \, a^{c*}. \tag{Q.4}$$

Q.1.2 Propagators

Quark

$$\xrightarrow{\hspace{2cm}} = \frac{i}{\not{p} - m} = i \frac{\not{p} + m}{p^2 - m^2}. \tag{Q.5}$$

Gluon

$$\text{00000000} = \frac{i}{k^2}\left(-g^{\mu\nu} + (1-\xi)\frac{k^\mu k^\nu}{k^2}\right)\delta^{ab} \qquad (Q.6)$$

for a general ξ gauge. Calculations are usually performed in Lorentz or Feynman gauge with $\xi = 1$ and gluon propagator equal to

$$\text{00000000} = i\frac{(-g^{\mu\nu})\delta^{ab}}{k^2}. \qquad (Q.7)$$

Here a and b run over the 8 colour indices $1, 2, \ldots, 8$.

Q.1.3   Vertices

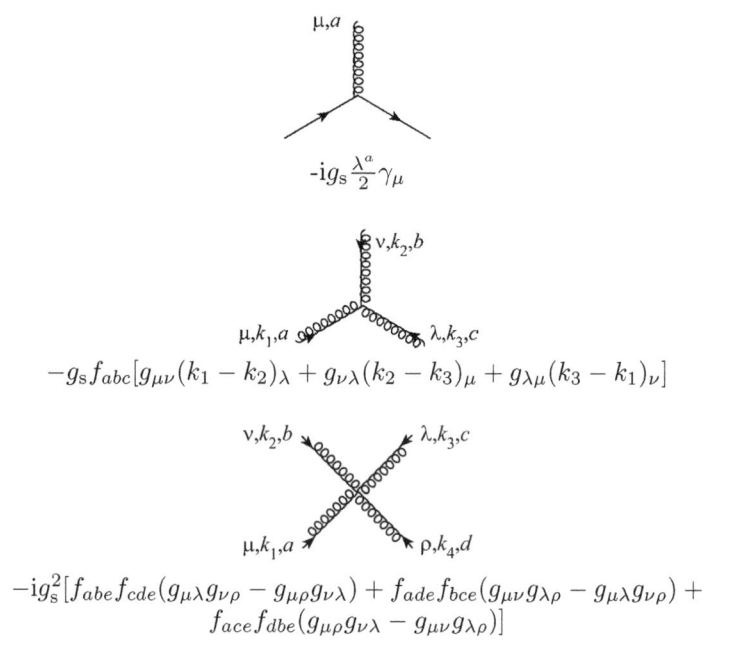

$$-ig_s\frac{\lambda^a}{2}\gamma_\mu$$

$$-g_s f_{abc}[g_{\mu\nu}(k_1 - k_2)_\lambda + g_{\nu\lambda}(k_2 - k_3)_\mu + g_{\lambda\mu}(k_3 - k_1)_\nu]$$

$$-ig_s^2[f_{abe}f_{cde}(g_{\mu\lambda}g_{\nu\rho} - g_{\mu\rho}g_{\nu\lambda}) + f_{ade}f_{bce}(g_{\mu\nu}g_{\lambda\rho} - g_{\mu\lambda}g_{\nu\rho}) + f_{ace}f_{dbe}(g_{\mu\rho}g_{\nu\lambda} - g_{\mu\nu}g_{\lambda\rho})]$$

It is important to remember that the rules given above are only adequate for tree diagram calculations in QCD (see section 13.3.3).

Q.2   The electroweak theory

For tree graph calculations, it is convenient to use the U gauge Feynman rules (sections 19.5 and 19.6) in which no unphysical particles appear. These U gauge rules are given below for the leptons $l = (e, \mu, \tau)$, $\nu_l = (\nu_e, \nu_\mu, \nu_\tau)$; for

the $t_3 = +1/2$ quarks denoted by f, where f = u, c, t; and for the $t_3 = -1/2$ CKM-mixed quarks denoted by f′ where f′ = d′, s′, b′.

Note that for simplicity we do not include neutrino flavour mixing.

Q.2.1 External particles

Leptons and quarks

For each fermion or antifermion line entering the graph include the spinor

$$u(p, s) \quad \text{or} \quad v(p, s) \tag{Q.8}$$

and for spin-$\frac{1}{2}$ particles leaving the graph the spinor

$$\bar{u}(p', s') \quad \text{or} \quad \bar{v}(p', s'). \tag{Q.9}$$

Vector bosons

For each vector boson line entering the graph include the factor

$$\epsilon_\mu(k, \lambda) \tag{Q.10}$$

and for vector bosons leaving the graph the factor

$$\epsilon_\mu^*(k', \lambda'). \tag{Q.11}$$

Q.2.2 Propagators

Leptons and quarks

$$\longrightarrow \quad = \frac{i}{\not{p} - m} = i\frac{\not{p} + m}{p^2 - m^2}. \tag{Q.12}$$

Vector bosons (U gauge)

$$\overset{W^\pm, Z^0}{\sim\!\sim\!\sim\!\sim\!\sim\!\sim} \quad = \frac{i}{k^2 - M_V^2}(-g_{\mu\nu} + k_\mu k_\nu / m_V^2) \tag{Q.13}$$

where 'V' stands for either 'W' (the W-boson) or 'Z' (the Z^0).

Higgs particle

$$\cdots\!\cdots\!\blacktriangleright\!\cdots\!\cdots \quad = \frac{i}{p^2 - m_H^2} \tag{Q.14}$$

Q.2.3 Vertices

Charged current weak interactions

Leptons

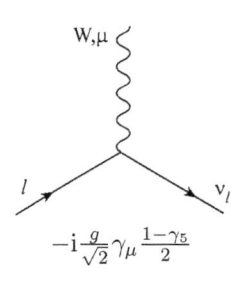

$$-\mathrm{i}\frac{g}{\sqrt{2}}\gamma_\mu\frac{1-\gamma_5}{2}$$

Quarks

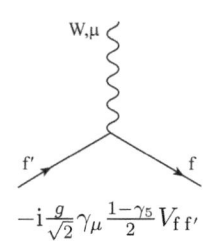

$$-\mathrm{i}\frac{g}{\sqrt{2}}\gamma_\mu\frac{1-\gamma_5}{2}V_{\mathrm{f\,f'}}$$

Neutral current weak interactions (no neutrino mixing)

Fermions

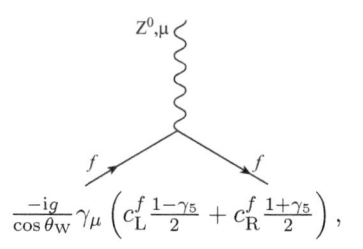

$$\frac{-\mathrm{i}g}{\cos\theta_{\mathrm{W}}}\gamma_\mu\left(c_{\mathrm{L}}^f\frac{1-\gamma_5}{2}+c_{\mathrm{R}}^f\frac{1+\gamma_5}{2}\right),$$

where

$$c_{\mathrm{L}}^f = t_3^f - \sin^2\theta_{\mathrm{W}}Q_f \qquad\qquad (\mathrm{Q}.15)$$

$$c_{\mathrm{R}}^f = -\sin^2\theta_{\mathrm{W}}Q_f, \qquad\qquad (\mathrm{Q}.16)$$

and f stands for any fermion.

Vector boson couplings

(i) Trilinear couplings:
γW^+W^- vertex

$$ie[g_{\nu\lambda}(k_1 - k_2)_\mu + g_{\lambda\mu}(k_2 - k_\gamma)_\nu + g_{\mu\nu}(k_\gamma - k_1)_\lambda]$$

$Z^0 W^+ W^-$ vertex

$$ig\cos\theta_W[g_{\nu\lambda}(k_1 - k_2)_\mu + g_{\lambda\mu}(k_2 - k_3)_\nu + g_{\mu\nu}(k_3 - k_1)_\lambda]$$

(ii) Quadrilinear couplings:

$$-ie^2(2g_{\alpha\beta}g_{\mu\nu} - g_{\alpha\mu}g_{\beta\nu} - g_{\alpha\nu}g_{\beta\mu})$$

$$-ieg\cos\theta_W(2g_{\alpha\beta}g_{\mu\nu} - g_{\alpha\mu}g_{\beta\nu} - g_{\alpha\nu}g_{\beta\mu})$$

$$-ig^2\cos^2\theta_W(2g_{\alpha\beta}g_{\mu\nu} - g_{\alpha\mu}g_{\beta\nu} - g_{\alpha\nu}g_{\beta\mu})$$

$$ig^2(2g_{\mu\alpha}g_{\nu\beta} - g_{\mu\beta}g_{\alpha\nu} - g_{\mu\nu}g_{\alpha\beta})$$

Higgs couplings

(i) Trilinear couplings
HW^+W^- vertex

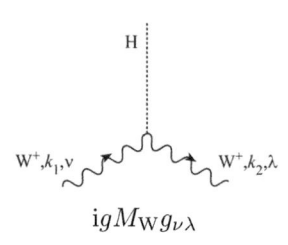

$$ig M_W g_{\nu\lambda}$$

HZ^0Z^0 vertex

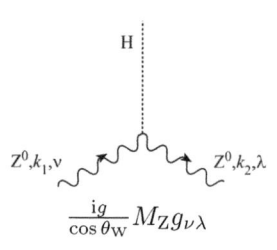

$$\frac{ig}{\cos\theta_W} M_Z g_{\nu\lambda}$$

Fermion Yukawa couplings (fermion mass m_f)

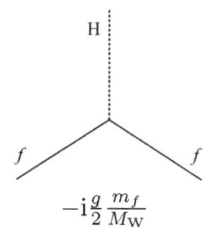

$$-i\frac{g}{2}\frac{m_f}{M_W}$$

Trilinear self-coupling

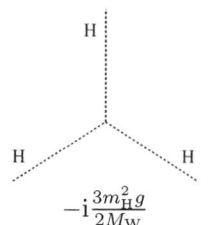

$$-i\frac{3m_H^2 g}{2M_W}$$

(ii) Quadrilinear couplings:
HHW^+W^- vertex

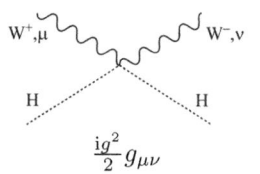

$$\frac{ig^2}{2}g_{\mu\nu}$$

HHZZ vertex

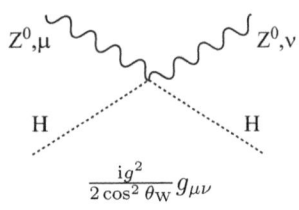

$$\frac{ig^2}{2\cos^2\theta_W}g_{\mu\nu}$$

Quadrilinear self-coupling

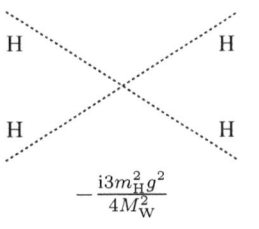

$$-\frac{i3m_H^2 g^2}{4M_W^2}$$

References

Aad G *et al.* 2012a (ATLAS Collaboration) *Phys. Lett.* B **710** 49
——2012b *Phys. Lett.* B **716** 1
Aaij R *et al.* 2012 (LHCb Collaboration) *Phys. Rev. Lett.* **108** 111602
Aaltonen T *et al.* 2008 (CDF Collaboration) *Phys. Rev. Lett.* **100** 121802
——2012 (CDF and D0 Collaborations) *Phys. Rev. Lett.* **109** 071804
Abachi S *et al.* 1995a (D0 Collaboration) *Phys. Rev. Lett.* **74** 2422
——1995b *Phys. Rev. Lett.* **74** 2632
Abashian A *et al.* 2001 (Belle Collaboration) *Phys. Rev. Lett.* **86** 2509
Abbiendi G *et al.* 2001 *Eur. Phys. J.* C **20** 601
Abdurashitov J N *et al.* 2009 *Phys. Rev.* C **80** 015807
Abe F *et al.* 1994a (CDF Collaboration) *Phys. Rev.* D **50** 2966
——1994b *Phys. Rev. Lett.* **73** 225
——1995a *Phys. Rev.* D **52** 4784
——1995b *Phys. Rev. Lett.* **74** 2626
Abe K 1991 *Proc. 25th Int. Conf. on High Energy Physics* eds K K Phua and Y
    Yamaguchi (Singapore: World Scientific) p 33
Abe K *et al.* 2000 *Phys. Rev. Lett.* **84** 5945
——2011 (T2K Collaboration) *Phys. Rev. Lett.* **107** 041801
Abe S *et al.* 2008 (KamLAND Collaboration) *Phys. Rev. Lett.* **100** 221803
Abramovicz H *et al.* 1982a *Z. Phys.* C **12** 289
——1982b *Z. Phys.* C **13** 199
——1983 *Z. Phys.* C **17** 283
Abreu P *et al.* 1990 *Phys. Lett.* B **242** 536
Adamson P *et al* 2011 (MINOS Collaboration) *Phys. Rev. Lett.* **106** 181801
Adler S L 1963 *Phys. Rev.* **143** 1144
——1965 *Phys. Rev. Lett.* **14** 1051
——1969 *Phys. Rev.* **177** 2426
——1970 *Lectures on Elementary Particles and Quantum Field Theory (Proceedings
    of the Brandeis Summer Institute)* vol 1, ed S Deser *et al.* (Boston, MA: MIT)
Adler S L and Bardeen W A 1969 *Phys. Rev.* **182** 1517
Aharmim B *et al.* 2010 (SNO Collaboration) *Phys. Rev.* C **81** 055504
Ahmad Q R *et al.* 2001 (SNO Collaboration) *Phys. Rev. Lett.* **87** 071301
——2002 *Phys. Rev. Lett.* **89** 011301
Ahn J K *et al.* 2012 (RENO Collaboration) *Phys. Rev. Lett.* **108** 191802
Ahn M H *et al.* 2006 (K2K Collaboration) *Phys. Rev.* D **74** 072003
Aitchison I J R 2007 *Supersymmetry in Particle Physics An Elementary Introduction*
    (Cambridge: Cambridge University Press)
Aitchison I J R *et al.* 1995 *Phys. Rev.* B **51** 6531
Akhundov A A *et al.* 1986 *Nucl. Phys.* B **276** 1
Akrawy M Z *et al.* 1990 (OPAL Collaboration) *Phys. Lett.* B **235** 389

Alavi-Harati A *et al.* 2003 (KTeV Collaboration) *Phys. Rev.* D **67** 012005; *ibid.* D **70** 079904 (erratum)

Ali A and Kramer G 2011 *Eur. Phys. J.* H **36** 245

Allaby J *et al.* 1988 *J. Phys. C: Solid State Phys.* **38** 403

Allasia D *et al.* 1984 *Phys. Lett.* B **135** 231

——1985 *Z. Phys.* C **28** 321

Allton C R *et al.* 1995 *Nucl. Phys.* B **437** 641

——2002 (UKQCD Collaboration) *Phys. Rev.* D **65** 054502

Alper B *et al.* 1973 *Phys. Lett.* B **44** 521

Altarelli G 1982 *Phys. Rep.* **81** 1

Altarelli G and Parisi G 1977 *Nucl. Phys.* B **126** 298

Altarelli G *et al.* 1978a *Nucl. Phys.* B **143** 521

——1978b *Nucl. Phys.* B **146** 544(E)

——1979 *Nucl. Phys.* B **157** 461

——1989 *Z. Phys. at LEP-1* CERN 89-08 (Geneva)

Altman M *et al.* 2005 *Phys. Lett.* B **616** 174

Amaudruz P *et al.* 1992 (NMC Collaboration) *Phys. Lett.* B **295** 159

An F P *et al.* 2012 (Daya Bay Collaboration) *Phys. Rev. Lett.* **108** 171803

Anderson P W 1963 *Phys. Rev.* **130** 439

Andreotti E *et al.* (CUORCINO Collaboration) 2011 *Astropart. Phys.* **34** 822

Antoniadis I 2002 *2001 European School of High Energy Physics* ed N Ellis and J March-Russell CERN 2002-002 (Geneva) pp 301ff

Apollonio M *et al.* 2003 (CHOOZ Collaboration) *Eur. Phys. J.* C **27** 331

Appel J A *et al.* 1986 *Z. Phys.* C **30** 341

Appelquist T and Chanowitz M S 1987 *Phys. Rev. Lett.* **59** 2405

Arnison G *et al.* 1983a *Phys. Lett.* B **122** 103

——1983b *Phys. Lett.* B **126** 398

——1984 *Phys. Lett.* B **136** 294

——1985 *Phys. Lett.* B **158** 494

——1986 *Phys. Lett.* B **166** 484

Arnold R *et al.* (NEMO Collaboration) 2006 *Nucl. Phys.* A **765** 483

Attwood D *et al.* 2001 *Phys. Rev.* D **63** 036005

Aubert B *et al.* 2001 (BaBar Collaboration) *Phys. Rev. Lett.* **86** 2515

——2004 *Phys. Rev. Lett.* **93** 131801

——2007a *Phys. Rev. Lett.* **99** 171803

——2007b *Phys. Rev.* D **76** 102004

——2007c *Phys. Rev. Lett.* **98** 211802

——2008 *Phys. Rev.* D **78** 034023

——2010 *Phys. Rev. Lett.* **105** 121801

Aubin C *et al.* 2004 *Phys. Rev.* D **70** 09505

Ayres D S (NOνA Collaboration) 1995 arXiv:hep-ex/0503053

Bagnaia P *et al.* 1983 *Phys. Lett.* B **129** 130

——1984 *Phys. Lett.* B **144** 283

Bahcall J N *et al.* 1968 *Phys. Rev. Lett.* **20** 1209

——2001 *Astrophys. J.* **555** 990

——2005 *ibid.* **621** L85

Baikov P A *et al.* 2008 *Phys. Rev. Lett.* **101** 012002

——2009 *Nucl. Phys. Proc. Suppl.* **189** 49

Bailin D 1982 *Weak Interactions* (Bristol: Adam Hilger)

Banks T *et al.* 1976 *Phys. Rev.* D **13** 1043
Banner M *et al.* 1982 *Phys. Lett.* B **118** 203
——1983 *Phys. Lett.* B **122** 476
Barber D P *et al.* 1979 *Phys. Rev. Lett.* **43** 830
Bardeen J, Cooper L N and Schrieffer J R 1957 *Phys. Rev.* **108** 1175
Bardeen W A, Fritzsch H and Gell-Mann M 1973 in *Scale and Conformal Symmetry in Hadron Physics* ed R Gatto (New York: Wiley) pp 139-151
Bardeen W A *et al.* 1978 *Phys. Rev.* D **18** 3998
Bardin D Yu *et al.* 1989 *Z. Phys.* C **44** 493
Barezyk A *et al.* 2008 (FAST Collaboration) *Phys. Lett.* B **663** 172
Barger V *et al.* 1983 *Z. Phys.* C **21** 99
Barr G D *et al.* 1993 (NA31 Collaboration) *Phys. Lett.* B **317** 233
Bartel *et al.* 1986 (JADE Collaboration) *Z. Phys.* C **33** 23
Batley J R *et al.* 2002 (NA48 Collaboration) *Phys. Lett.* B **544** 97
Beenakker W and Hollik W 1988 *Z. Phys.* C **40** 569
Belavin A A *et al.* 1975 *Phys. Lett.* B **59** 85
Bell J S and Jackiw R 1969 *Nuovo Cimento* A **60** 47
Benvenuti A C *et al.* 1989 (BCDMS Collaboration) *Phys. Lett.* B **223** 485
Berends F A *et al.* 1981 *Phys. Lett.* B **103** 124
Berezin F A 1966 *The Method of Second Quantisation* (New York: Academic)
Bergsma F *et al.* 1983 *Phys. Lett.* B **122** 465
Beringer J *et al.* 2012 (Partial Data Group) *Phys. Rev.* D **86** 010001
Berman S M, Bjorken J D and Kogut J B 1971 *Phys. Rev.* D **4** 3388
Bernard C W, Golterman M F and Shamir Y 2006 *Phys. Rev.* D **73** 114511
Bernreuther W and Wetzel W 1982 *Nucl. Phys.* B **197** 128
Bernstein J 1974 *Rev. Mod. Phys.* **46** 7
Bethke S 2009 *Eur. Phys. J.* C **64** 689
Bethke S *et al.* 1988 (JADE Collaboration) *Phys. Lett.* B **213** 235
Bettini A 2008 *Introduction to Elementary Particle Physics* (Cambridge: Cambridge University Press)
Bigi I I and Sanda A I 2000 *CP Violation* (Cambridge: Cambridge University Press)
Bijnens J *et al.* 1996 *Phys. Lett.* B **374** 2010
Binney J J *et al.* 1992 *The Modern Theory of Critical Phenomena* (Oxford: Clarendon)
Bjorken J D 1973 *Phys. Rev.* D**8** 4098
Bjorken J D and Glashow S L 1964 *Phys. Lett.* **11** 255
Blatt J M 1964 *Theory of Superconductivity* (New York: Academic)
Bloch F and Nordsieck A 1937 *Phys. Rev.* **52** 54
Bludman S A 1958 *Nuovo Cimento* **9** 443
Boas M L 1983 *Mathematical Methods in the Physical Sciences* (New York: Wiley)
Bogoliubov N N 1947 *J. Phys. USSR* **11** 23
——1958 *Nuovo Cimento* **7** 794
Bogoliubov N N *et al.* 1959 *A New Method in the Theory of Superconductivity* (New York: Consultants Bureau, Inc.)
Bouchiat C C *et al.* 1972 *Phys. Lett.* B **38** 519
Bouchiendra R *et al.* 2011 *Phys. Rev. Lett.* **106** 080801
Branco G C *et al.* 1999 *CP Violation* (Oxford: Oxford University Press)
Brandelik R *et al.* 1979 *Phys. Lett.* B **86** 243
Brodsky S J, Lepage G P and Mackenzie P B 1983 *Phys. Rev.* D **28** 228

Budny R 1975 *Phys. Lett.* B **55** 227

Buras A J *et al.* 1994 *Phys. Rev.* D **50** 3433

Büsser F W *et al.* 1972 *Proc. XVI Int. Conf. on High Energy Physics (Chicago, IL)* vol 3 (Batavia: FNAL)

——1973 *Phys. Lett.* B **46** 471

Cabibbo N 1963 *Phys. Rev. Lett.* **10** 531

Cabibbo N *et al.* 1979 *Nucl. Phys.* B **158** 295

Cacciari M *et al.* 2008 *JHEP* **0804** 063

Callan C G 1970 *Phys. Rev.* D **2** 1541

Callan C, Coleman S, Wess J, and Zumino B 1969 *Phys. Rev.* **177** 2247

Campbell J M *et al.* 2007 *Rept. on Prog. in Phys.* **70** 89

Carruthers P A 1966 *Introduction to Unitary Symmetry* (New York: Wiley)

Carter A B and Sanda A I 1980 *Phys. Rev. Lett.* **45** 952

——1981 *Phys. Rev.* D **23** 1567

Caswell W E 1974 *Phys. Rev. Lett.* **33** 244

Catani S *et al.* 1991 *Phys. Lett.* B **269** 432

——1993 *Nucl. Phys.* B **406** 187

Ceccucci A *et al.* 2010 in Nakamura K *et al.* 2010

Celmaster W and Gonsalves R J 1980 *Phys. Rev. Lett.* **44** 560

Chadwick J 1932 *Proc. R. Soc.* A **136** 692

Chanowitz M *et al.* 1978 *Phys. Lett.* B **78** 285

——1979 *Nucl. Phys.* B **153** 402

Chao Y *et al.* 2005 (Belle Collaboration) *Phys. Rev.* D **71** 031502

Charles J *et al.* 2005 (CKMfitter Group) *Eur. Phys. J.* C **41** 1

Chatrchyan S *et al.* 2012a (CMS Collaboration) *Phys. Lett.* B **710** 26

——2012b *Phys. Lett.* B **716** 30

Chau L L and Keung W Y 1984 *Phys. Rev. Lett.* **53** 1802

Chen M-S and Zerwas P 1975 *Phys. Rev.* D **12** 187

Cheng T-P and Li L-F 1984 *Gauge Theory of Elementary Particle Physics* (Oxford: Clarendon)

Chetyrkin K G *et al.* 1979 *Phys. Lett.* B **85** 277

——1997 *Phys. Rev. Lett.* **79** 2184

Chitwood D B *et al.* 2007 (MuLan Collaboration) *Phys. Rev. Lett.* **99** 032001

Christenson J H *et al* 1964 *Phys. Rev. Lett.* **13** 138

Cleveland B T *et al.* 1998 *Astrophys. J.* **496** 505

Cohen A G *et al.* 2009 *Phys. Lett.* B **678** 191

Colangelo G *et al.* 2001 *Nucl. Phys.* B **603** 125

Coleman S 1985 *Aspects of Symmetry* (Cambridge: Cambridge University Press)

——1966 *J. Math. Phys.* **7** 787

Coleman S and Gross D J 1973 *Phys. Rev. Lett.* 31 851

Coleman S, Wess J and Zumino B 1969 *Phys. Rev.* **177** 2239

Collins J C and Soper D E 1987 *Annu. Rev. Nucl. Part. Sci.* **37** 383

——1998 *Phys. Lett.* B **438** 184

Collins P D B and Martin A D 1984 *Hadron Interactions* (Bristol: Adam Hilger)

Combridge B L *et al.* 1977 *Phys. Lett.* B **70** 234

Combridge B L and Maxwell C J 1984 *Nucl. Phys.* B **239** 429

Commins E D and Bucksbaum P H 1983 *Weak Interactions of Quarks and Leptons* (Cambridge: Cambridge University Press)

Consoli M *et al.* 1989 Z. Phys. *at LEP-I* ed G Altarelli *et al.* CERN 89-08 (Geneva)

Cooper L N 1956 *Phys. Rev.* **104** 1189

Cornwall J M *et al* 1974 *Phys. Rev.* D 10 1145

Cowan C L *et al.* 1956 *Science* **124** 103

Czakon M 2005 *Nucl. Phys.* B **710** 485

Dalitz R H 1953 *Phil. Mag.* **44** 1068

——1965 *High Energy Physics* ed C de Witt and M Jacob (New York: Gordon and Breach)

Danby G *et al.* 1962 *Phys. Rev. Lett.* **9** 36

Davies C T H *et al.* 2008 (HPQCD Collaboration) *Phys. Rev.* D **78** 114507

Davies C T H *et al.* 2004 (HPQCD, UKQCD, MILC and Fermilab Collaborations) *Phys. Rev. Lett.* **92** 022001

Davis R 1955 *Phys. Rev.* **97** 766

——1964 *Phys. Rev. Lett.* **12** 303

Davis R *et al.* 1968 *Phys. Rev. Lett.* **20** 1205

Dawson S *et al.* 1990 *The Higgs Hunters Guide* (Reading, MA: Addison-Wesley)

de Groot J G H *et al.* 1979 *Z. Phys.* C **1** 143

DiLella L 1985 *Annu. Rev. Nucl. Part. Sci.* **35** 107

——1986 *Proc. Int. Europhysics Conf. on High Energy Physics, Bari, Italy, July 1985* eds L Nitti and G Preparata (Bari: Laterza) pp 761ff

Dine M and Sapirstein J 1979 *Phys. Rev. Lett.* **43** 668

Dirac P A M 1931 *Proc. R. Soc.* A **133** 60

Dittmaier S *et al.* 2011 (LHC Higgs Cross section Working Group Collaboration) *Handbook of LHC Higgs Cross sections: 1. Inclusive Observables* CERN-2011-002 (arXiv:1101.0593 [hep-ph])

——2012 *Handbook of LHC Higgs Cross Sections: 2. Differential Distributions* CERN-2012-002 (arXiv:1201.3084 [hep-ph])

Dokshitzer Yu L 1977 *Sov. Phys.JETP* **46** 641

Donoghue J F, Golowich E and Holstein B R 1992 *Dynamics of the Standard Model* (Cambridge: Cambridge University Press)

Duke D W and Owens J F 1984 *Phys. Rev.* D **30** 49

Dürr S *et al.* (Budapest-Marseille-Wuppertal Collaboration) *Science* **322** 1224

Eden R J, Landshoff P V, Olive D I and Polkinghorne J C 1966 *The Analytic S-Matrix* (Cambridge: Cambridge University Press)

Eichten E *et al.* 1980 *Phys. Rev.* D **21** 203

Einhorn M B and Wudka J 1989 *Phys. Rev.* D **39** 2758

Eitel K *et al.* 2005 *Nucl. Phys. (Proc. Suppl.)* B **143** 197

Elias-Miro J *et al.* 2012 *Phys. Lett.* B **709** 222

Ellis J *et al.* 1976 *Nucl. Phys.* B **111** 253

——1977 Erratum *ibid.* B **130** 516

——1994 *Phys. Lett.* B **333** 118

Ellis R K, Stirling W J and Webber B R 1996 *QCD and Collider Physics* (Cambridge: Cambridge University Press)

Ellis S D and Soper D E 1993 *Phys. Rev.* D **48** 3160

Ellis S D *et al.* 2008 *Prog. Part. Nucl. Phys.* **60** 484

Englert F and Brout R 1964 *Phys. Rev. Lett.* **13** 321

Enz C P 1992 *A Course on Many-Body Theory Applied to Solid-State Physics (World Scientific Lecture Notes in Physics 11)* (Singapore: World Scientific)
——2002 *No Time to be Brief* (Oxford: Oxford University Press)
Fabri E and Picasso L E 1966 *Phys. Rev. Lett.* **16** 408
Faddeev L D and Popov V N 1967 *Phys. Lett.* B **25** 29
Feinberg G *et al* 1959 *Phys. Rev. Lett.* **3** 527, especially footnote 9
Fermi E 1934a *Nuovo Cimento* **11** 1
——1934b *Z. Phys.* **88** 161
Feynman R P 1963 *Acta Phys. Polon.* **26** 697
——1977 in *Weak and Electromagnetic Interactions at High Energies* ed R Balian and C H Llewellyn Smith (Amsterdam: North-Holland) p 121
Feynman R P and Gell-Mann M 1958 *Phys. Rev.* **109** 193
Feynman R P and Hibbs A R 1965 *Quantum Mechanics and Path Intergrals* (New York: McGraw-Hill)
Fritzsch H and Gell-Mann M 1972 *Proc. XVI Int. Conf. on High Energy Physics, Batavia IL* eds J D Jackson and R G Roberts, pp 135-165
Fritzsch H, Gell-Mann M and Leutwyler H 1973 *Phys. Lett.* B **47** 365
Fukuda Y *et al.* 1998 *Phys. Rev. Lett.* **81** 1562
Fukugita M and Yanagida T 1986 *Phys. Lett.* B **174** 45
Gaillard M K and Lee B W 1974 *Phys. Rev.* D **10** 897
Gamow G and Teller E 1936 *Phys. Rev.* **49** 895
Gasser J and Leutwyler H 1982 *Phys. Rep.* **87** 77
——1984 *Ann. Phys.* **158** 142
——1985 *Nucl. Phys.* B **250** 465
Geer S 1986 *High Energy Physics 1985, Proc. Yale Theoretical Advanced Study Institute* eds Bowick M J and Gursey F (Singapore: World Scientific)
Gell-Mann M 1961 *California Institute of Technology Report* CTSL-20 (reprinted in Gell-Mann and Ne'eman 1964)
Gell-Mann M *et al.* 1979 *Supergravity* ed D Freedman and P van Nieuwenhuizen (Amsterdam: North-Holland) p 315
Gell-Mann M and Levy M 1960 *Nuovo Cimento* **16** 705
Gell-Mann M and Low F E 1954 *Phys. Rev.* **95** 1300
Gell-Mann M and Ne'eman 1964 *The Eightfold Way* (New York: Benjamin)
Gell-Mann M and Pais A 1955 *Phys. Rev.* **97** 1387
Georgi H *et al.* 1978 *Phys. Rev. Lett.* **40** 692
Georgi H and Politzer H D 1974 *Phys. Rev.* D **9** 416
Gibbons L K 1993 (E731 Collaboration) *Phys. Rev. Lett.* **70** 1203
Ginsparg P and Wilson K G 1982 *Phys. Rev.* D **25** 25
Ginzburg V I and Landau L D 1950 *Zh. Eksp. Teor. Fiz.* **20** 1064
Giri A *et al.* 2003 *Phys. Rev.* D **68** 054018
Glashow S L 1961 *Nucl. Phys.* **22** 579
Glashow S L *et al.* 1978 *Phys. Rev.* D **18** 1724
Glashow S L, Iliopoulos J and Maiani L 1970 *Phys. Rev.* D **2** 1285
Goldberger M L and Treiman S B 1958 *Phys. Rev.* **95** 1300
Goldhaber M *et al* 1958 *Phys. Rev.* **109** 1015
Goldstone J 1961 *Nuovo Cimento* **19** 154
Goldstone J, Salam A and Weinberg S 1962 *Phys. Rev.* **127** 965
Gorishnii S G and Larin S A 1986 *Phys. Lett.* **172** 109
Gorishnii S G *et al.* 1991 *Phys. Lett.* B **259** 144

Gorkov L P 1959 *Zh. Eksp. Teor. Fiz.* **36** 1918

Gottschalk T and Sivers D 1980 *Phys. Rev.* D **21** 102

Gray A *et al* 2005 (HPQCD and UKQCD Collaborations) *Phys. Rev.* D **72** 094507

Greenberg O W 1964 *Phys. Rev. Lett.* **13** 598

Gribov V N and Lipatov L N 1972 *Sov. J. Nucl. Phys.* **15** 438

Gronau M 1991 *Phys. Lett.* B **265** 389

Gronau M and London D 1990 *Phys. Rev. Lett.* **65** 3381

Gross D J and Llewellyn Smith C H 1969 *Nucl. Phys.* B **14** 337

Gross D J and Wilczek F 1973 *Phys. Rev. Lett.* **30** 1343

——1974 *Phys. Rev.* D **9** 980

Grossman Y *et al.* 2005 *Phys. Rev.* D **72** 031501

Gupta R S *et al.* 2012 *How well do we need to measure the Higgs boson couplings?*
    arXiv:1206:3560 [hep-ph]

Guralnik G S *et al.* 1964 *Phys. Rev. Lett.* **13** 585

——1968 *Advances in Particle Physics* vol 2, ed R Cool and R E Marshak (New
    York: Interscience) pp 567ff

Haag R 1958 *Phys. Rev.* **112** 669

Hagiwara K *et al.* 2002 *Phys. Rev.* D **66** 010001

Halzen F and Martin A D 1984 *Quarks and Leptons* (New York: Wiley)

Hamberg R *et al* 1991 *Nucl. Phys.* B **359** 343

Hambye T and Reisselmann K 1997 *Phys. Rev.* D **55** 7255

Hammermesh M 1962 *Group Theory and its Applications to Physical Problems*
    (Reading, MA: Addison-Wesley)

Han M Y and Nambu Y 1965 *Phys. Rev.* B **139** 1066

Harrison P F and Quinn H R 1998 *The BaBar physics book: Physics at an asym-
    metric B factory* SLAC-R-0504

Hasenfratz P *et al.* 1998 *Phys. Lett.* B **427** 125

Hasenfratz P and Niedermayer F 1994 *Nucl. Phys.* B **414** 785

Hasert F J *et al.* 1973 *Phys. Lett.* B **46** 138

Heisenberg W 1932 *Z. Phys.* **77** 1

Higgs P W 1964 *Phys. Rev. Lett.* **13** 508

——1966 *Phys. Rev.* **145** 1156

Hirata K S *et al.* 1989 *Phys. Rev. Lett.* **63** 16

Höcker A *et al.* 2001 *Eur. Phys. J.* C **21** 225

Hollik W 1990 *Fortsch. Phys.* **38** 165

——1991 *1989 CERN-JINR School of Physics* CERN 91-07 (Geneva) p 50ff

Hornbostel K, Lepage G P and Morningstar C 2003 *Phys. Rev.* D **67** 034023

Hosaka J *et al.* 2006 *Phys. Rev.* D **73** 112001

Hughes R J 1980 *Phys. Lett.* B **97** 246

——1981 *Nucl. Phys.* B **186** 376

Isgur N and Wise M B 1989 *Phys. Lett.* B **232** 113

——1990 *Phys. Lett.* B **237** 527

Isidori G *et al.* 2001 *Nucl. Phys.* B **609** 387

Jackiw R 1972 *Lectures in Current Algebra and its Applications* ed S B Treiman, R
    Jackiw and D J Gross (Princeton, NJ: Princeton University Press) pp 97–254

Jacob M and Landshoff P V 1978 *Phys. Rep.* C **48** 285

Jarlskog C 1985 *Phys. Rev. Lett.* **55** 1039

Jones D R T 1974 *Nucl. Phys.* B **75** 531

Jones H F 1990 *Groups, Representations and Physics* (Bristol: IOP Publishing)

Kabir P K 1968 *The CP Puzzle: Strange Decays of the Neutral Kaon* (London and New York: Academic Press)

Kadanoff L P 1977 *Rev. Mod. Phys.* **49** 267

Kaplan D B 1992 *Phys. Lett.* B **288** 342

Kayser B 1981 *Phys. Rev.* D **24** 110

Kennedy D C *et al.* 1989 *Nucl. Phys.* B **321** 83

Kennedy D C and Lynn B W 1989 *Nucl. Phys.* B **322** 1

Kibble T W B 1967 *Phys. Rev.* **155** 1554

Kim K J and Schilcher K 1978 *Phys. Rev.* D **17** 2800

Kinoshita T 1962 *J. Math. Phys.* **3** 650

Kittel C 1987 *Quantum Theory of Solids* second revised printing (New York: Wiley)

Klapdor-Kleingrothaus H V *et al.* (Heidelberg-Moscow Collaboration) 2001 *Eur. Phys. J.* A **12** 147

——2006 *Mod. Phys. Lett.* A **21** 1547

Klein O 1948 *Nature* **161** 897

Kluth S 2006 *Rept. on Prog. in Phys.* **69** 1771

Kobayashi M 2009 *Rev. Mod. Phys.* **81** 1019

Kobayashi M and Maskawa K 1973 *Prog. Theor. Phys.* **49** 652

Kogut J B and Susskind L 1975 *Phys. Rev.* D **11** 395

Kramer G and Lampe B 1987 *Z. Phys.* C **34** 497

Krastev P I and Petcov S T 1988 *Phys. Lett.* B **205** 84

Kugo T and Ojima I 1979 *Prog. Theor. Phys. Suppl.* **66** 1

Kunszt Z and Piétarinen E 1980 *Nucl. Phys.* B **164** 45

Kusaka A *et al.* 2007 (Belle Collaboration) *Phys. Rev. Lett.* **98** 221602

Kuzmin V A, Rubakov V A and Shaposhnikov M E 1985 *Phys. Lett.* B **155** 36

Landau L D 1948 *Dokl. Akad. Nauk. USSR* **60** 207

——1957 *Nucl. Phys.* **3** 127

Landau L D and Lifshitz E M 1980 *Statistical Mechanics* part 1, 3rd edn (Oxford: Pergamon)

Langacker P (ed) 1995 *Precision Tests of the Standard Electroweak Model* (Singapore: World Scientific)

Larin S A and Vermaseren J A M 1991 *Phys. Lett.* B **259** 345

——1993 *Phys. Lett.* B **303** 334

Lautrup B 1967 *Kon. Dan. Vid. Selsk. Mat.-Fys. Med.* **35** 1

Lee B W *et al.* 1977a *Phys. Rev. Lett.* **38** 883

——1977b *Phys. Rev.* D **16** 1519

Lee T D and Nauenberg M 1964 *Phys. Rev.* B **133** 1549

Lee T D, Rosenbluth R and Yang C N 1949 *Phys. Rev.* **75** 9905

Lee T D and Yang C N 1956 *Phys. Rev.* **104** 254

——1957 *Phys. Rev.* **105** 1671

——1962 *Phys. Rev.* **128** 885

LEP 2003 (The LEP Working Group for Higgs Searches, ALEPH, DELPHI, L3 and OPAL Collaborations) *Phys. Lett.* B **565** 61

Lepage G P and Mackenzie P B 1993 *Phys. Rev.* **48** 2250

Leutwyler H 1996 *Phys. Lett.* B **378** 313

Lichtenberg D B 1970 *Unitary Symmetry and Elementary Particles* (New York: Academic)

Lipkin H J *et al.* 1991 *Phys. Rev.* D **44** 1454

Llewellyn Smith C H 1973 *Phys. Lett.* B **46** 233

Lobashev V *et al.* 2003 *Nucl. Phys.* A **719** 153c
London F 1950 *Superfluids Vol I, Macroscopic theory of Superconductivity* (New York: Wiley)
Lüscher M 1981 *Nucl. Phys.* B **180** 317
——1986 *Commun. Math. Phys.* **105** 153
——1991a *Nucl. Phys.* B **354** 531
——1991b *Nucl. Phys.* B **364** 237
——1998 *Phys. Lett.* B **428** 342
Lüscher M and Weisz P 1985 *Phys. Lett.* B **158** 250
Lüscher M *et al.* 1980 *Nucl. Phys.* B **173** 365
Majorana E 1937 *Nuovo Cimento* **5** 171
Maki Z, Nakagawa M and Sakata S 1962 *Prog. Theor. Phys.* **28** 870
Mandelstam S 1976 *Phys. Rep.* C **23** 245
Mandl F 1992 *Quantum Mechanics* (New York: Wiley)
Marciano W J and Sirlin A 1988 *Phys. Rev. Lett.* **61** 1815
Marshak R E *et al* 1969 *Theory of Weak Interactions in Particle Physics* (New York: Wiley)
Martin A D *et al.* 1994 *Phys. Rev.* D **50** 6734
——2002 *Eur. Phys. J.* C **23** 73
Maskawa T 2009 *Rev. Mod. Phys.* **81** 1027
Merzbacher E 1998 *Quantum Mechanics* 3rd edn (New York: Wiley)
Mikheev S P and Smirnov A Y 1985 *Sov. J. Nucl. Phys.* **42** 913
——1986 *Nuovo Cimento* **9** C 17
Minkowski P 1977 *Phys. Lett.* B **67** 421
Mohapatra R N *et al.* 1968 *Phys. Rev. Lett.* **20** 1081
Mohapatra R N and Senjanovic G 1980 *Phys. Rev. Lett.* **44** 912
——1981 *Phys. Rev.* D **23** 165
Montanet L *et al.* 1994 *Phys. Rev.* D **50** 1173
Montvay I and Munster G 1994 *Quantum Fields on a Lattice* (Cambridge: Cambridge University Press)
Morningstar C and Peardon M J 2004 *Phys. Rev.* D **69** 054501
Muta T 2010 *Foundations of Quantum Chromodynamics* 3rd edtn (Singapore: World Scientific)
Nakamura K *et al.* 2010 (Particle Data Group) *J.Phys.* G **37** 075021
Nambu Y 1960 *Phys. Rev. Lett.* **4** 380
——1974 *Phys. Rev.* D **10** 4262
Nambu Y and Jona-Lasinio G 1961a *Phys. Rev.* **122** 345
——1961b *Phys. Rev.* **124** 246
Nambu Y and Lurie D 1962 *Phys. Rev.* **125** 1429
Nambu Y and Schrauner E 1962 *Phys. Rev.* **128** 862
Narayanan R and Neuberger H 1993a *Phys. Lett.* B **302** 62
——1993b *Phys. Rev. Lett.* **71** 3251
——1994 *Nucl. Phys.* B **412** 574
——1995 *Nucl. Phys.* B **443** 305
Nauenberg M 1999 *Phys. Lett.* B **447** 23
Ne'eman Y 1961 *Nucl. Phys.* **26** 222
Neuberger H 1998a *Phys. Lett.* B **417** 141
——1998b *Phys. Lett.* B **427** 353
Nielsen N K 1981 *Am. J. Phys.* **49** 1171

Nielsen H B and Ninomaya M 1981a *Nucl. Phys.* B **185** 20

——1981b *Nucl. Phys.* B **193** 173

——1981c *Nucl. Phys.* B **195** 541

Nir Y 1989 *Phys. Lett.* B **221** 184

Noaki J *et al.* 2008 *Phys. Rev. Lett.* **101** 202004

Noether E 1918 *Nachr. Ges. Wiss. Gottingen* 171

Oddone P 1989 *Ann. N.Y. Acad. Sci.* **578** 237

Okubo S 1962 *Prog. Theor. Phys.* **27** 949

Pais A 2000 *The Genius of Science* (Oxford: Oxford University Press)

Pak A and Czarnecki A 2008 *Phys. Rev. Lett.* **100** 241807

Parry W E 1973 *The Many Body Problem* (Oxford: Clarendon)

Pascoli S *et al.* 2007a *Phys. Rev.* D **75** 083511

——2007b *Nucl. Phys.* B **774** 1

Pauli W 1934 *Rapp. Septième Conseil Phys. Solvay, Brussels 1933* (Paris: Gautier-Villars), reprinted in Winter (2000) pp 7, 8

Peccei R D and Quinn H 1977a *Phys. Rev. Lett.* **38** 1440

——1977b *Phys. Rev.* D **16** 1791

Perkins D H 1975 in *Proc. Int. Symp. on Lepton and Photon Interactions at High Energies, Stanford, CA* p 571

Peskin M E 1997 in *1996 European School of High Energy Physics* ed N Ellis and M Neubert CERN 97-03 (Geneva) pp 49-142

Peskin M E and Schroeder D V 1995 *An Introduction to Quantum Field Theory* (Reading, MA: Addison-Wesley)

Politzer H D 1973 *Phys. Rev. Lett.* **30** 1346

Poluektov *et al.* 2010 (Belle Collaboration) *Phys. Rev.* D **81** 112002

Pontecorvo B 1946 *Chalk River Laboratory Report* PD-205

——1947 *Phys. Rev.* **72** 246

——1957 *Zh. Eksp. Theor. Phys.* **33** 549

——1958 *ibid.* **34** 247

——1967 *ibid.* **53** 1717 (Engl. transl. *Sov. Phys.JETP* **26** 984)

Prescott C Y *et al.* 1978 *Phys. Lett.* B **77** 347

Puppi G 1948 *Nuovo Cimento* **5** 505

Quigg C 1977 *Rev. Mod. Phys.* **49** 297

Rajaraman R 1982 *Solitons and Instantons* (Amsterdam: North-Holland)

Reines F and Cowan C 1956 *Nature* **178** 446

Reines F, Gurr H and Sobel H 1976 *Phys. Rev. Lett.* **37** 315

Renton P 1990 *Electroweak Interactions* (Cambridge: Cambridge University Press)

Richardson J L 1979 *Phys. Lett.* B **82** 272

Rodrigo G and Santamaria A 1993 *Phys. Lett.* B **313** 441

Ross D A and Veltman M 1975 *Nucl. Phys.* B **95** 135

Rubbia C *et al.* 1977 *Proc. Int. Neutrino Conf., Aachen, 1976* (Braunschweig: Vieweg) p 683

Ryder L H 1996 *Quantum Field Theory* 2nd edn (Cambridge: Cambridge University Press)

Sakurai J J 1958 *Nuovo Cimento* **7** 649

——1960 *Ann. Phys., NY* **11** 1

Salam A 1957 *Nuovo Cimento* **5** 299

——1968 *Elementary Particle Physics* ed N Svartholm (Stockholm: Almqvist and Wiksells)

Salam A and Ward J C 1964 *Phys. Lett.* **13** 168

Salam C P 2010 *Eur. Phys. J.* C **14** 47

Samuel M A and Surguladze L R 1991 *Phys. Rev. Lett.* **66** 560

Schael S *et al.* 2006 (ALEPH, DELPHI, L3, OPAL, SLD, LEP Electroweak Working Group, SLD Electroweak and Heavy Flavour Groups) *Phys. Reports* **427** 257

Schiff L I 1968 *Quantum Mechanics* 3rd edn (New York: McGraw-Hill)

Schrieffer J R 1964 *Theory of Superconductivity* (New York: Benjamin)

Schutz B F 1988 *A First Course in General Relativity* (Cambridge: Cambridge University Press)

Schwinger J 1957 *Ann. Phys., NY* **2** 407

——1962 *Phys. Rev.* **125** 397

Shaevitz M H *et al.* 1995 (CCFR Collaboration) *Nucl. Phys. B Proc. Suppl.* **38** 188

Sharpe S R 2006 *PoSLAT* 022 (hep-lat/0610094)

Shaw R 1995 The problem of particle types and other contributions to the theory of elementary particles *PhD Thesis* University of Cambridge

Sikivie P *et al.* 1980 *Nucl. Phys.* B **173** 189

Sirlin A 1980 *Phys. Rev.* D **22** 971

——1984 *Phys. Rev.* D **29** 89

Slavnov A A 1972 *Teor. Mat. Fiz.* **10** 153 (Engl. transl. *Theor. and Math. Phys.* **10** 99)

Snyder A E and Quinn H R 1993 *Phys. Rev.* D **48** 2139

Sommer R 1994 *Nucl. Phys.* B **411** 839

Spergel D *et al.* 2007 *Astrophys. J. Supp.* **170** 377

Staff of the CERN $\bar{\text{p}}$p project 1981 *Phys. Lett.* B **107** 306

Stange A *et al.* 1994a *Phys. Rev.* D **49** 1354

——1994b *Phys. Rev.* D **50** 4491

Staric M *et al.* 2007 (Belle Collaboration) *Phys. Rev. Lett.* **98** 211803

Steinberger J 1949 *Phys. Rev.* **76** 1180

Sterman G and Weinberg S 1977 *Phys. Rev. Lett.* **39** 1436

Stueckelberg E C G and Peterman A 1953 *Helv. Phys. Acta* **26** 499

Sudarshan E C G and Marshak R E 1958 *Phys. Rev.* **109** 1860

Susskind L 1977 *Phys. Rev.* D **16** 3031

——1979 *Phys. Rev.* D **19** 2619

Sutherland D G 1967 *Nucl. Phys.* B **2** 433

Symanzik K 1970 *Commun. Math. Phys.* **18** 227

——1983 *Nucl. Phys.* B **226** 187, 205

Tarasov O V *et al.* 1980 *Phys. Lett.* B **93** 429

Tavkhelidze A 1965 *Seminar on High Energy Physics and Elementary Particles* (Vienna: IAEA) p 763

Taylor J C 1971 *Nucl. Phys.* B **33** 436

——1976 *Gauge Theories of Weak Interactions* (Cambridge: Cambridge University Press)

't Hooft G 1971a *Nucl. Phys.* B **33** 173

——1971b *Nucl. Phys.* B **35** 167

——1971c *Phys. Lett.* B **37** 195

——1976a *Phys. Rev.* D **14** 3432

——1976b *High Energy Physics, Proc. European Physical Society Int. Conf.* ed A Zichichi (Bologna: Editrice Composition) p 1225

——1980 *Recent Developments in Gauge Theories, Cargese Summer Institute 1979* ed G 't Hooft *et al.* (New York: Plenum)

——1986 *Phys. Rep.* **142** 357

't Hooft G and Veltman M 1972 *Nucl. Phys.* B **44** 189 *Rev. Mod. Phys.* **21** 153

Tiomno J and Wheeler J A 1949 *Rev. Mod. Phys.* **21** 153

Ur A C *et al.* (GERDA Collaboration) 2011 *Nucl. Phys. Proc. Suppl.* **217** 38

Valatin J G 1958 *Nuovo Cimento* **7** 843

van der Bij J J 1984 *Nucl. Phys.* B **248** 141

van der Bij J J and Veltman M 1984 *Nucl. Phys.* B **231** 205

van der Neerven W L and Zijlstra E B 1992 *Nucl. Phys.* B **382** 11

van Ritbergen T and Stuart R G 1999 *Phys. Rev. Lett.* **82** 488

van Ritbergen *et al.* 1997 *Phys. Lett.* B **400** 379

Veltman M 1967 *Proc. R. Soc.* A **301** 107

——1968 *Nucl. Phys.* B **7** 637

——1970 *Nucl. Phys.* B **21** 288

——1977 *Acta Phys. Polon.* B **8** 475

von Weiszäcker C F 1934 *Z. Phys.* **88** 612

Wegner F 1972 *Phys. Rev.* B **5** 4529

Weinberg S 1966 *Phys. Rev. Lett.* **17** 616

——1967 *Phys. Rev. Lett.* **19** 1264

——1973 *Phys. Rev.* D **8** 605, especially footnote 8

——1975 *Phys. Rev.* D **11** 3583

——1978 *Phys. Rev. Lett.* **40** 223

——1979a *Physica* A **96** 327

——1979b *Phys. Rev.* D **19** 1277

——1996 *The Quantum Theory of Fields Vol II Modern Applications* (Cambridge: Cambridge University Press)

Weisberger W 1965 *Phys. Rev. Lett.* **14** 1047

Weisskopf V F and Wigner E P 1930a *Z. Phys.* **63** 54

——1930b *Z. Phys.* **65** 18

Wilczek F 1978 *Phys. Rev. Lett.* **40** 279

Williams E J 1934 *Phys. Rev.* **45** 729

Wilson K G 1969 *Phys. Rev.* **179** 1499

——1971a *Phys. Rev.* B **4** 3174

——1971b *Phys. Rev.* B **4** 3184

——1974 *Phys. Rev.* D **10** 2445

——1975 *New Phenomena in Subnuclear Physics, Proc. 1975 Int. School on Subnuclear Physics Ettore Majorana* ed A Zichichi (New York: Plenum)

Wilson K G and Kogut J 1974 *Phys. Rep.* **12C** 75

Winter K 2000 *Neutrino Physics* 2nd edn (Cambridge: Cambridge University Press)

Wolfenstein L 1978 *Phys. Rev.* D **17** 2369

——1983 *Phys. Rev. Lett.* **51** 1945

Wu C S *et al.* 1957 *Phys. Rev.* **105** 1413

Yanagida T 1979 *Proc. Workshop on Unified Theory and Baryon Number in the Universe* ed O Sawada and A Sugamoto (Tsukuba: KEK)

Yang C N 1950 *Phys. Rev.* **77** 242

Yang C N and Mills R L 1954 *Phys. Rev.* **96** 191

Yosida K 1958 *Phys. Rev.* **111** 1255

Index